The Days-Out Guide 2005

The AA Days Out Guide provides useful information about a large number of museums, art galleries, theme parks, national parks, visitor centres and stately homes across Britain and Ireland. Entries include contact details for each attraction, along with a short description and details of opening times, prices and special facilities. Each county has a list of events and festivals.

We hope that this guide will help you and your family get the most out of your time.

Happy Visiting!

Produced by AA Publishing © Automobile Association
Developments Limited 2004

A CIP catalogue record for this book is available from the
British Library

Directory generated by the AA Establishment Database,
Information Research, AA Hotel Services

Cover pictures: AA Picture Library

Advertisement Sales: advertisingsales@theAA.com

Lifestyle Guides: lifestyleguides@theAA.com

Typeset/Repro by Servis Filmsetting Ltd Manchester,
England.

Printed by Graficas Estella, S.A., Navarra, Spain

The contents of this book are believed correct at the time
of printing. Nevertheless, the Publisher cannot be held
responsible for any errors or omissions, or for changes in
the details given in this guide or for the consequences of
any reliance on the information provided in the same.
This does not affect your statutory rights. We have tried
to ensure accuracy in this guide but things do change and
we would be grateful if readers would advise us of any
inaccuracies they may encounter.

 This product includes mapping data
licensed from Ordnance Survey® with
the permission of the Controller of Her Majesty's
Stationery Office. © Crown copyright 2004.
All rights reserved. Licence number 399221.

This product includes mapping based upon
data licensed from Ordnance Survey of
Northern Ireland® reproduced by
permission of the Chief Executive, acting on behalf of the
Controller of Her Majesty's Stationery Office.
© Crown copyright 2004. Permit No 40069

Republic of Ireland mapping based on Ordnance Survey
Ireland Permit No. MP002104
© Ordnance Survey Ireland and Government of Ireland.

Maps prepared by the Cartography Department of The
Automobile Association. Maps © Automobile Association
Developments Limited 2004.

Published by AA Publishing, which is a trading name of
Automobile Association Developments Limited whose
registered office is Southwood East, Apollo Rise,
Farnborough, Hampshire, GU14 0JW.
Registered number 1878835.

ISBN 0749542241

A02155

Contents

The Directory

The directory is arranged in countries, counties, then in alphabetical location order within each county. Each county has an introductory panel that gives general information on selected events and festivals.

❶ Map References and Atlas
Map references for attractions are based on the National Grid, and can be used with the Atlas at the back of this book.

First comes the map page number, followed by the National Grid reference. To find the location, read the first figure horizontally and the second figure vertically within the lettered square.

❷ Directions may be given after the address of each attraction and where shown have been provided by the places of interest themselves.

❸ Telephone Numbers have the STD code shown before the telephone number. (If dialling Northern Ireland from England use the STD code, but for the Republic you need to prefix the number with 00353, and drop the first zero from the Irish area code).

Sample Entry

BEDFORD	Map 04 TL04 ──❶

BEDFORD MUSEUM
Castle Ln MK40 3XD   2 for 1 ──❹
❷── ➲ (close to town bridge and Embankment)
❸── ☎ 01234 353323   🖷 01234 273401
e-mail: bmuseum@bedford.gov.uk
Embark on a fascinating journey through the human and natural history of north Bedfordshire, pausing briefly to glimpse at wonders from more distant lands. The courtyard and galleries provide an excellent setting for the varied collections.
❺──**Times:** Open all year, Tue-Sat 11-5, Sun 2-5. (Closed Mon ex BH Mon afternoon, Good Fri & Xmas). **Fee:** ✱ £2.20 (ch, pen & con free). Fri ──❻
free for everyone. Annual ticket £8.80. **Facilities:** Ⓟ (50mtrs) ♨ ──❼
❽── ♿ (lift available on request, subject to staff availability) toilets for
disabled shop 🐾 (ex guide dogs) 🍴 ──❾

❹ 2-FOR-1
Voucher Scheme   2 for 1
This symbol indicates which attractions have chosen to participate in our 2-for-1 voucher scheme. Visitors using one of the vouchers from the front of this guide will be able to buy 2 tickets for the price of one, with certain restrictions that are detailed on the voucher itself. Some attractions also have individual restrictions, which are detailed in their entries.

❺ Opening Times quoted in the guide are inclusive - for instance, where you see Apr-Oct, that place will be open from the beginning of April to the end of October.

❻ Fees quoted for the majority of entries are current. If no price is quoted, you should check with the attraction concerned before you visit. Places which are open 'at all reasonable times' are usually free, and many places which do not charge admission at all may ask for a voluntary donation. Remember that prices can go up, and those provided to us by the attractions are provisional.

Free Entry   FREE
These attractions do not charge a fee for entry, although they may charge for use of audio equipment, for example. We have not included attractions that

expect a donation in this category.

7 Facilities
This section includes parking, dogs allowed, refreshments etc. See page 6 for a key to Symbols and Abbreviations used in this guide.

8 Visitors with Mobility Disabilities should look for the wheelchair symbol showing where all or most of the establishment is accessible to the wheelchair-bound visitor. We strongly recommend that you telephone in advance of your visit to check the exact details, particularly regarding access to toilets and refreshment facilities. Assistance dogs are usually accepted where the attractions show the 'No Dogs' symbol ✖ unless stated otherwise. For the hard of hearing induction loops are indicated by a symbol at the attraction itself.

9 Credit & Charge cards are taken by a number of attractions for admission charges. To indicate which

accept credit cards we have used this symbol at the end of the entry. ▰

Photography is restricted in some places and there are many where it is only allowed in specific areas. Visitors are advised to check with places of interest on the rules for taking photographs and the use of video cameras.

Special Events are held at many of these attractions, and although we have listed a few of the more important ones on the county introduction pages, we cannot hope to give details of them all, so please ring the places of interest for details of exhibitions, themed days, talks, guided walks and more.

Attractions with Italic headings These are entries that were unable to provide the relevant information in time for publication.

...and finally Opening times and admission prices can be subject to change. Please check with the attraction before making your journey.

Public Holidays

New Year's Day	1 January	Battle of the Boyne *(Orangemen's Day) (N.I. only)*	12 July
Bank Holiday *(Scotland only)*	2 January		
St Patrick's Day *(N.I. & R.O.I. only)*	17 March	Summer Bank Holiday *(Scotland & R.O.I. only)*	1 August
Good Friday	25 March	Summer Bank Holiday *(excluding R.O.I.)*	31 August
Easter Monday	28 March		
May Day Bank Holiday	2 May	Bank Holiday *(R.O.I. only)*	25 October
Spring Bank Holiday *(excluding R.O.I.)*	30 May	Christmas Day	25 December
June Bank Holiday *(R.O.I. only)*	6 June	Boxing Day *(St Stephen's Day in R.O.I.)*	26 December

Key to Symbols and Abbreviations

SYMBOLS

In order to give you as much information as possible in the space available, we have used the following symbols in the guide:

	ENGLISH	FRANÇAIS	DEUTSCH	ITALIANO	ESPAÑOL
☎	Telephone number	Numéro de téléphone	Telefonnummer	Numero telefonico	Número telefónico
🖹	Fax number				
♿	Suitable for visitors in wheelchairs	Les invalidens fauteuils roulants pourrant y accéder	Für Rollstuhltahrer zugänglich	Accessibile agli handicappeti	Acondicionado para visitantes en silla de reudas
🅿	Parking at Establishment	Stationnement à l'établissement	Parken an Ort und Stelle	Parcheggio in loco	Aparcamiento en el establecimiento
🅿	Parking nearby	Stationnement tout près	Parken in der Nähe	Parcheggio nelle	Aparcamiento cerca del
🍽	Refreshments	Rafraîchissements	Erfrischungen	vicinanze	Refrescos
✗	Restaurant	Restaurant	Restaurant	Snack-bar	Restaurante
🐕	No dogs	Chiens non permis	Hundeverbot	Ristorante	Se prohiben los perros
🚌	No coaches	Les groupes en cars pas admis	Keine Reisebusgesellschaften	Cani non accettati Non si accettano comitive in pullman	Non se admiten los grupos de viajeros en autobús
★	Admission prices relate to 2004. It should be noted that in some entries the opening dates and times may also have been supplied as 2004. Please check with the establshment before making your journey.				
✛	Cadw (Welsh Historic Monuments)	Cadw Monument ancien (Pays de Galles)	Cadw Historiches Gebaude (Walisland)	Cadw Monumento storico (Galles)	Cadw Monumento histórico (Gales)
✻	English Heritage	English Heritage	English Heritage	English Heritage	English Heritage
❦	National Trust	National Trust	National Trust	National Trust	National Trust
❧	National Trust for Scotland	National Trust en Ecosse	National Trust in Schottland	National Trust per la Scozia	The National Trust de Escocia
▮	Historic Scotland				

ABBREVIATIONS

In the same way, we have abbreviated certain pieces of information:

	ENGLISH	FRANÇAIS	DEUTSCH	ITALIAN	ESPAÑOL
BH	Bank Holidays	Jours fériés	Bankfeiertage	Festività nazionale	Días festivos (bancos y comercio)
PH	Public Holidays	Jours fériés	Feiertage	Festività nazionale	Días festivos
Etr	Easter	Pâques	Ostern	Pasqua	Semana Santa
ex	except	sauf	ausser	eccetto	excepto
Free	Admission free	Entrée gratuit	Freier eintritt	Ingresso gratuito	Entrada gratuita
£1	Admission £1	Entrée £1	Eintritt £1	Ingresso £1	Entrada £1
ch 50p	Children 50p	Enfants 50p	Kinder 50p	Bambini 50p	Niños 50p
ch 15 50p	Children under 15 50p	Enfants de moins de 15 ans 50p	Kinder unter 15 Jahren 50p	Bambini sotto i 15 anni 50p	Los niños de menores de 15 años 50p
Pen	Senior Citizens	Retraites	Rentner	Pensionati	Jubilados
Party	Special or reduced rates for parties booked in advance	Tarifs spéciaux ou réduits pour groupes réservés d'advance	Sondertarife oder Ermässigungen für im voraus bestellte Gesellschaften	Tariffe speciali o ridotte per comitive che prenotano in anticipo	Tarifas especiales o reducidas para los grupos de viajeros que reserven de anternano
Party 30+	Special or reduced rates for parties of 30 or more booked in advance	Tarifs spéciaux ou réduits pour groupes de 30 ou plus réservés d'advance	Sondertarife oder Ermässigungen für im voraus bestellte Gesellschaften von wenigstens 30 Personen	Tariffe speciali o ridotte per comitive di 30 o più persone che prenotano in anticipo	Tarifas especiales o reducidas para grupos de 30 viajeros, o más, que reserven de anternano

Eden Project, Cornwall

The People Behind the Places

By Julia Hynard

The Creators

There are some fascinating personalities behind some of our most popular and idiosyncratic tourist attractions. These are people who, down the centuries, have shown themselves capable of blue sky thinking and had the drive to make their dreams a reality.

Often it's hard to imagine where the creative impulse has sprung from. Take Tim Smit, for example, who came from the music business to restore **the Lost Gardens of Heligan (p42)**, an undertaking that inspired him to create the magnificent multi-domed **Eden Project (p43)** in a redundant Cornish clay pit. Smit overcame the odds stacked against the project, both elemental and financial, with the sheer force of his vision and the faith it inspired in those around him. This he calls 'the Tinkerbell theory' – if enough people believe in what you're doing it will happen.

Looking back to the 1790s, the Lincolnshire MP William Alexander Madocks seems an unlikely character to lay the foundation for the **Ffestiniog Railway (p360)** in North Wales. He had acquired land in the mountainous region and commissioned reclamation work from the shores of Traeth Mawr inland to Pont Aberglaslyn and on to the great embankment on the Cob, across the estuary. This led to the formation of the natural harbour – originally Port Madoc, now Porthmadog – which was to play a crucial role in the slate mining industry and the development of the Ffestiniog Railway, a narrow gauge steam railway running for 13.5 miles through the Snowdonia National Park, with some breathtaking views.

On the same coast, close to Porthmadog is another work of genius, the beautiful and bizarre Italianate village of **Portmeirion (p360)**, in a stunning setting on the

Dwyfor estuary, surrounded by woodland, sandy beaches and the Gwyllt sub-tropical gardens. This is the work of Sir Clough Williams-Ellis, a labour of love undertaken over a period of 50 years between 1925 and 1975. He was an architect and conservationist, passionate about the Welsh countryside, who set out to prove that buildings could complement rather than despoil a naturally beautiful landscape.

Madame Tussaud's (p153) is a unique and enduring attraction in the capital, founded by an extraordinary woman, born Marie Grosholz, in Strasbourg, 1761. Marie learnt how to model wax from her mother's employer, Dr Phillippe Curtius, in Paris. She must have been a gifted artist, as she was for a time employed as an art tutor in the royal court at Versailles. Following the Revolution she found herself working with Curtius again in Paris – moulding the heads of guillotine victims, some of whom she knew from the palace.

In 1795 Marie married François Tussaud, an engineer, but having inherited the Curtius collection of wax figures she headed for Britain, choosing the life of a show woman, exhibiting her models in town after town, surviving shipwreck in the Irish Sea and fire during the Bristol riots. All the time she added more and more models to the collection. In 1835 she established a permanent home for her waxworks in The Bazaar, Baker Street, London.

Madame Tussaud died in 1850, a very successful woman. The family business continued to thrive, and in 1885 her grandson, Joseph Randall, moved it to its present location in Marylebone Road, where it remains in the top ten of British tourist attractions, forever renewing itself with models of the most celebrated and vilified characters of our time.

From small beginnings popular attractions grow. Nowhere is this more apparent than in the **Fry Model Railway (p390)** collection, these days displayed in the lovely grounds surrounding Malahide Castle in Co Dublin. The '0' gauge model trains were handmade with exquisite care in the 1920s and 30s by Cyril Fry, a railway engineer and draughtsman, who began the collection in his attic. The working railway covers an area of 2,500 square feet, with Irish and international exhibits from the beginning

Ffestiniog Railway, North Wales

The Ashmolean

of railway history. The complex includes miniature trams, barges, Cork and Heuston Stations, O'Connel Bridge, the River Liffey and other landmarks from the city of Dublin, just eight miles away. Fry can hardly have imagined, in the early part of the 20th century, that his carefully crafted, home-made models would still be bringing such delight to families in the 21st century.

The Collectors

There's another intriguing breed behind some of our more edifying institutions and cultural attractions – the collectors. People of tenacity – even obsession – with passions ranging from the internal combustion engine to medieval art, who through history have formed the backbone of our great museums and galleries. Typical of these are Lord Montagu of Beaulieu who, in addition to being a historic house entrepreneur, founded the Montagu Motor Museum in 1952 at his own stately home in Hampshire. Twenty years later it became

the **National Motor Museum (p102)**, and the collection now numbers some 250 vehicles.

The first public museum in Britain was the **Ashmolean (p194)**, founded by Elias Ashmole (1617-1692), a barrister who expediently left London for Oxford during the Civil War and studied alchemy and astrology. He returned to London and set up a house which became a centre for intellectual thought and learning, and published his notable work on alchemy, Theatrum Chymicum Britannicum, in 1652. He subsequently moved into the Lambeth house of John Tradescant the Younger (1608-1662), the great horticulturalist, botanist and traveller, and gardener to the monarch – a role he took over from his father, John Tradescant the Elder (1577-1638). The house, known as The Ark, was stuffed full of treasures, exotica and rarities from the natural world, including plants, birds, fish, insects and minerals, along with other items of interest such as coins and medals. Tradescant bequeathed the collection to Ashmole, who by then had turned his interests to antiquity, publishing the History of the Order of the Garter, a book which was to make his reputation in the field – he became a Fellow of the Royal Society in 1661. In 1677 he presented the Tradescant collection, supplemented by books and materials of his own, to the University of Oxford, on the condition that they provided a building to house it. The university did him proud, with an impressive classical structure by architect C R Cockerell (also responsible for the Taylorian Institute next door).

The **Burrell Collection (p308)** in Glasgow is another priceless treasure trove of art and artefacts from all over the world; so extensive that only 3,000 of the 8,000 items can be displayed at any given time in the Burrell gallery. Sir William Burrell

(1861-1958) came from a shipping family, a business which had involved his father and grandfather before him. He and his brothers took over the running of the firm on their father's death, and as astute businessmen became very wealthy indeed. Burrell, interested in art from a young age, was instrumental in setting up the Glasgow International Art Exhibition in 1901. With the outbreak of World War I, the brothers sold off most of their modern fleet for a tidy profit. From this time on Burrell travelled widely and devoted himself to collecting art, including Egyptian, Greek and Roman artefacts; Persian and Indian rugs and furniture; Chinese ceramics, Japanese prints, European tapestries and stained glass; paintings by Rembrandt, Degas and Cezanne, and modern sculpture by Rodin and Epstein; reputedly spending around £20,000 a year.

In 1944 Burrell presented most of his collection to the City of Glasgow along with £250,000 with which to construct a building to house it. He posed quite a challenge to the city, as a condition of the gift the collection had to be placed in a rural setting away from the polluted atmosphere of the city, but not less than 16 miles from the centre. No suitable site had been identified by 1958 when Burrell died, but in 1966 Mrs Anne Maxwell Macdonald gave Pollock House and the 360-acre Pollock Estate to the city, which was agreed to be the perfect setting for the collection.

An architectural competition determined the final design for the gallery, which incorporated two 16th-century stone archways and some of the stained glass into its fabric, and the Burrell Collection finally opened in 1983.

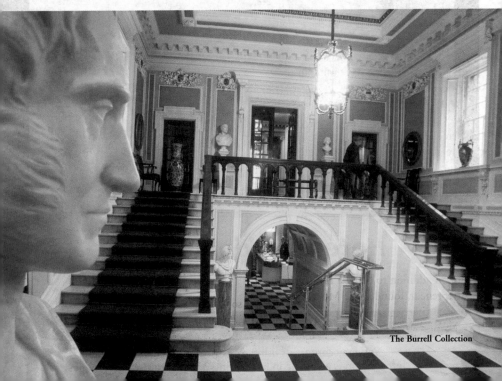

The Burrell Collection

Where do I look if I don't have time to book?

Booking a place to stay can be a time-consuming process. So why not search quickly and easily on-line for a place that best suits your needs.

Whatever your preference, we have the place for you. From a farm cottage to a city centre hotel - we have them all. Choose from around 8,000 quality rated hotels and B&Bs in Great Britain and Ireland.

Just **AA** sk.

Hotel Booking Service

www.theAA.com/hotels

ENGLAND

BEDFORDSHIRE

EVENTS & FESTIVALS

March
5th-12th Bedfordshire Festival of Music, Speech & Drama, various venues in Bedford

May
1st Ickwell May Festival, The Maypole, Ickwell Green
29th-30th Bedfordshire Classic Motor Show, Shuttleworth
30th Luton Carnival, Britain's multi-cultural showcase

June
tbc Bedford International Kite Festival

July
1st-3rd Popular Flying Association International Air Rally & Exhibition, Cranfield Airfield, Cranfield (provisional)

August
6th Proms in the Park, Bedford Park (provisional)

September
17th-18th Bedfordshire Steam & Country Fayre, Old Warden Park, near Biggleswade
28th-1st Oct Bedford Beer Festival, Bedford Corn Exchange

October
tbc National Apple Day at Bromham Mill, apples, cider, apple bobbing, farmers market and entertainment (provisional)

December
tbc Bedford Victorian Christmas Fayre, Bedford town centre

Above: Cottages in the village of Ickwell

AMPTHILL   Map 04 TL03

HOUGHTON HOUSE
➲ (1m NE off A421)   FREE
Now a ruin, the mansion was built for Mary Countess of Pembroke, the sister of Sir Philip Sidney. Inigo Jones is thought to have been involved in work on the house, which may have been the original 'House Beautiful' in Bunyan's *Pilgrim's Progress*.
Times: Open all reasonable times. **Facilities:** 🅿 & ♿

BEDFORD   Map 04 TL04

BEDFORD MUSEUM
Castle Ln MK40 3XD
➲ (close to town bridge and Embankment)
☎ 01234 353323   🖷 01234 273401   FREE
e-mail: bmuseum@bedford.gov.uk
Embark on a fascinating journey through the human and natural history of north Bedfordshire, pausing briefly to glimpse at wonders from more distant lands. Go back in time and visit the delightful rural room sets and the Old School Museum, where Blackbeard's Sword, 'Old Billy' the record breaking longest-living horse, and numerous other treasures and curiosities can be found. Housed in the former Higgins and Sons Brewery, Bedford Museum is situated within the gardens of what was once Bedford Castle, beside the Great Ouse embankment. The courtyard and galleries provide an excellent setting for the varied collections.
Times: Open all year, Tue-Sat 11-5, Sun 2-5. (Closed Mon ex BH Mon afternoon, Good Fri & Xmas). **Facilities:** 🅿 (50mtrs) 💷 & (lift available on request, subject to staff availability) toilets for disabled shop 🅇 (ex guide dogs) 🍴

CECIL HIGGINS ART GALLERY & MUSEUM
Castle Ln MK40 3RP
➲ (in town centre close to Embankment)
☎ 01234 211222   🖷 01234 327149
e-mail: chag@bedford.gov.uk
A recreated Victorian mansion, with the rooms arranged as though the house was still lived in. Includes a bedroom with furniture designed by Victorian architect William Burges, and the adjoining gallery has an outstanding collection of ceramics, glass and changing exhibition of prints, drawings and watercolours. Also includes the Thomas Lester lace collection.
Times: Open all year, Tue-Sat 11-5, Sun & BH Mon 2-5. (Closed Mon, Good Fri, 25-26 Dec & 1 Jan). **Fee:** £2.30 (ch & concessions free) includes entry to Bedford Museum. Free to all visitors Fri
Facilities: 🅿 (100yds) pay & display (free on Sun) 💷 & Wheelchair available toilets for disabled shop 🅇 (ex guide dogs) 🍴

LEIGHTON BUZZARD   Map 04 SP92

LEIGHTON BUZZARD RAILWAY
Pages Park Station, Billington Rd LU7 4TN
➲ (0.75m SE on A4146 signposted in and around Leighton Buzzard, near rdbt junct with A505)
☎ 01525 373888   🖷 01525 377814   2 for 1
e-mail: info@buzzrail.co.uk
The Leighton Buzzard Railway offers a 70 minute journey into the vanished world of the English light railway, with its sharp curves, steep gradients, level crossings and unique roadside running. Built in 1919 to serve the local sand

continued

industry, the railway has carried a steam passenger service, operated by volunteers, since 1968.
Times: Open Mar-Oct, Sun & BH wknds; Jul, Wed; Aug, Tue-Thu, Sat & BH wknds. **Fee:** ✱ Return ticket £5.50 (ch 2-15 £2.50, pen £4.50 & ch under 2 free). Party 10+. **Facilities:** 🅿 ▣ ♿ (platform & train access for wheelchairs) toilets for disabled shop 🍴

LUTON   Map 04 TL02

JOHN DONY FIELD CENTRE
Hancock Dr, Bushmead LU2 7SF
➲ (signposted from rdbt on A6, at Barnfield College on New Bedford Rd)
☎ 01582 486983
e-mail: donyj@luton.gov.uk   [FREE]
This is a purpose built study centre for exploring the landscapes, plants and animals of the Luton area. Featuring permanent displays on local archaeology, natural history and the management of the local nature reserve, it explains how ancient grasslands and hedgerows are conserved and follows 4000 years of history from Bronze Age to modern times.
Times: Open all year, Mon-Fri 9.30-4.45. Closed BHs.
Facilities: 🅿 ♿ toilets for disabled 🐕 (ex assist dogs)

LUTON MUSEUM & GALLERY
Wardown Park, Old Bedford Rd LU2 7HA
➲ (Follow brown signs from the town centre north.Turn off A6 towards Bedford)
☎ 01582 546722 & 546739   [FREE]
▣ 01582 546763
e-mail: museum.gallery@luton.gov.uk
A Victorian mansion, with displays illustrating the natural and cultural history, archaeology and industries of the area, including the development of Luton's hat industry, and the Bedfordshire and Hertfordshire Regimental Collections. New 'Luton Life' displays tell the story of the town and its residents over the past 200 years. Exhibitions and events throughout the year.
Times: Open all year, Tue-Sat 10-5, Sun 1-5 (Closed Xmas, 1 Jan & Mon ex BH Mons). **Facilities:** 🅿 ▣ ♿ (parking adjacent to entrance, lift to 1st floor) toilets for disabled shop 🐕 (ex guide dogs & hearing dogs)

STOCKWOOD CRAFT MUSEUM & GARDENS
Stockwood Country Park, Farley Hill LU1 4BH
➲ (signposted from M1 junct 10 and from Hitchin, Dunstable, Bedford and from Luton town centre)
☎ 01582 738714 & 546739   [FREE]
▣ 01582 546763
e-mail: museum.gallery@luton.gov.uk
The Museum is set in period gardens which incorporate the Ian Hamilton Finlay Sculpture Gardens. The Mossman collection of horse-drawn vehicles traces the history of transport from Roman times to the 1940s. Craft demonstrations are held at weekends in the summer. Please telephone for details of special events.
Times: Open all year; Mar-Oct, Tue-Sun 10-5; Nov-Mar, wknds 10-4. (closed Xmas & 1 Jan) **Facilities:** 🅿 ▣ ♿ (stair lift, parking, induction loop, automatic door) toilets for disabled shop 🐕 (ex guide & hearing dogs)

OLD WARDEN   Map 04 TL14

THE SHUTTLEWORTH COLLECTION
Old Warden Park SG18 9EA
➲ (2m W from rdbt on A1, Biggleswade by-pass)
☎ 01767 627288   ▣ 01767 626229
Housed in eight hangars on a classic grass aerodrome, 40 working historic aeroplanes span the progress of aviation with exhibits ranging from a 1909 Bleriot to a 1941 Spitfire. A garage of roadworthy motor vehicles explores the eras of the 1898 Panhard Levassor to the Railton sports car of 1937. The 19th-century coach house displays horse-drawn vehicles from 1880 to 1914.
Times: ✱ Open Apr-Oct 10-5 (last admission 4), Nov-Mar 10-4 (last admission 3). Closed Xmas-New Year. **Facilities:** 🅿 ▣ ✖ licensed ♿ toilets for disabled shop 🐕 (ex guide dogs) 🍴

SANDY   Map 04 TL14

RSPB NATURE RESERVE
The Lodge Shop SG19 2DL
➲ (1m E, on B1042 Potton road)
☎ 01767 680541   ▣ 01767 683508   [2 for 1]
e-mail: claire.wallace@rspb.org.uk
The headquarters of the Royal Society for the Protection of Birds. The house and buildings are not open to the public, but there are waymarked paths and formal gardens, and two species of woodpecker, nuthatches and woodland birds may be seen, as may muntjac deer. Another feature is the specialist wildlife garden created in conjunction with the Henry Doubleday Association.
Times: Open all year, Mon-Fri 9-5, Sat, Sun & BHs 10-5. (Closed 25-26 Dec). **Fee:** ✱ £3 (ch under 16 £1, concessions £1.50). Family ticket (2 ad & 2 ch) £6. **Facilities:** 🅿 ♿ (partial access) toilets for disabled shop 🐕 (ex in restricted areas) 🍴

SILSOE   Map 04 TL03

WREST PARK GARDENS
MK45 4HS
➲ (0.75m E off A6)
☎ 01525 860152
Audio tour through a century and a half of gardening styles as you explore the 90 acres of formal gardens that make up Wrest Park.
Times: Open Apr-Sep, Sat & Sun 10-6; Oct, Sat, Sun & BHs, 10-5.
Fee: ✱ £4.20 (ch £2.10, concessions £3.20, family £10.50). Prices & opening times relate to 2004, for further details phone or log onto www.english-heritage.org.uk/visits **Facilities:** 🅿 🐕 (ex on lead in certain areas) ⌗

WHIPSNADE   Map 04 TL01

WHIPSNADE WILD ANIMAL PARK
LU6 2LF
➲ (signposted from M1 junct 9 & 12)
☎ 01582 872171   ▣ 01582 872649
Set in 600 acres of countryside, Whipsnade is home to thousands of creatures, and is one of the largest wildlife conservation centres in Europe. Visitors can see tigers, elephants, penguins, giraffes, bears, chimps, hippos and more. The newest addition is the Chimpnasium, added in 2004. There are regular special events and keeper talks, so phone for details, and remember that by coming to

continued

Whipsnade you are helping to protect endangered species and conserve natural habitats.
Times: Open all year, daily. (Closed 25 Dec). Telephone 01582 872171 or check website **Fee:** ✱ £13.50 (ch 3-15 & concessions £9.35). Car entry £10 Family ticket (2 ad & 2 ch) £42.50 **Facilities:** 🅿 (charged) 🚐 ♿ (free entry for disabled cars) toilets for disabled shop ✕ ➡

WOBURN   Map 04 SP93

WOBURN ABBEY
MK17 9WA
☎ 01525 290666   📠 01525 290271
e-mail: enquiries@woburnabbey.co.uk
Standing in 3000 acres of parkland, this palatial 18th-century mansion was originally a Cistercian Abbey, and the Dukes of Bedford have lived here since 1547. The art collection includes works by Canaletto, Rembrandt, Van Dyck, and Gainsborough. 14 state apartments are on view, and the private apartments are shown when not in use. Special events are held during the year, including the De-Havilland Tiger Moth Fly-In and a garden show.
Times: ✱ Open Jan-23 Mar; Abbey Sat & Sun only 11-4, Deer park 10.30-3.45; 24 Mar-29 Sep; Abbey weekdays 11-4, Sun & BH 11-5; 5-27 Oct Sat & Sun only; Deer Park weekdays 10-4.30, Sun & BH 10-4.45.
Facilities: 🅿 (charged) 🚐 ✕ licensed ♿ (wheelchairs accommodated by prior arrangement) toilets for disabled shop ✕ ➡

WOBURN SAFARI PARK
Woburn Park MK17 9QN
➲ (Signposted from M1 junct 13)
☎ 01525 290407   📠 01525 290489
e-mail: info@woburnsafari.co.uk
Set in the 3000 acres of parkland belonging to Woburn Abbey, Woburn Safari Park has an extensive collection of many species. The safari road passes through an African plains area stocked with eland, zebra, hippo and rhino, then through well-keepered tiger and lion enclosures and on past bears and monkeys. Animal encounters, sea lion and parrot shows, and elephant displays, are all popular attractions. The large leisure complex also offers a boating lake, adventure playgrounds, railway train, walk-through aviary, squirrel monkey exhibit and 'the Australian Walkabout', with friendly wallabies. A new attraction is underwater viewing at Sealion Cove.
Times: ✱ Open daily, 10 Mar-27 Oct, 10-5. **Facilities:** 🅿 🚐 ✕ licensed ♿ toilets for disabled shop ✕ ➡

The Battle of Trafalgar.
2005 is the 200th anniversary of the sea battle between the British Royal Navy and the French and Spanish navies. 2005 will see a number of events celebrating this important British victory.

BERKSHIRE

EVENTS & FESTIVALS

February
8th Shrove Tuesday, Great Newbury Pancake Race

April
31st-2nd May Crafty Craft Race, Kennet & Avon Canal, fair and side shows in Victoria Park, Newbury

May
7th-20th Newbury International Spring Festival of music and the visual arts
tbc Royal Windsor Horse Show

June
14th-18th Royal Ascot, Ascot Race Course (provisional)
tbc Newbury International Orchid Show

July
1st-3rd Bracknell Festival
16th-17th Kennet Valley Kite Festival, Thatcham (provisional)
31st Cartier International Polo, Smiths Lawn, Windsor Great Park (provisional)
tbc De Beers Diamond Day, Ascot Race Course
tbc WOMAD World Music & Arts Festival, Rivermead, Reading

August
26th-28th Carling Reading Festival, Richfield Avenue, Reading (provisional)
tbc Cookham Regatta
tbc Shergar Cup (team competition), Ascot Race Course

September
17th-18th Newbury & Royal County of Berkshire Show, Newbury Showground
25th Windsor Half Marathon
tbc Ascot Festival of Racing (provisional)
tbc Windsor Festival

October
tbc Michaelmas Fair, Northcroft, Newbury

Above: Rowing boats by the River Thames

BRACKNELL — Map 04 SU86

THE LOOK OUT DISCOVERY CENTRE
Nine Mile Ride RG12 7QW
➲ (3m S of town centre. From M3 junct 3, take A322 to Bracknell and from M4 junct 10, take A329M to Bracknell. Follow brown tourist signs)   **2 for 1**
☎ 01344 354400 ▤ 01344 354422
e-mail: thelookout@bracknell-forest.gov.uk
A hands-on, interactive science and nature exhibition where budding scientists can spend many hours exploring and discovering over 70 fun filled exhibits within five themed zones, the topics covered are linked to the National Curriculum. Zones include Light and Colour, Forces and Movement and the Body and Perception. A new exciting zone, Woodland and Water, opens in summer 2004 with a vortex, stream, ant colony and many more interactive exhibits. Climb the 88 steps to the Look Out tower and look towards Bracknell and beyond or enjoy a nature walk in the surrounding 2,600 acres of Crown Estate woodland. Please note the tower is closed when wet.
Times: Open all year (Closed 24-26 Dec). **Fee:** £4.80 (ch & concessions £3.20). Family (2 adults + 2 ch or 1 adult + 3 ch) £12.80. **Facilities:** P ⬛ & lift to first floor toilets for disabled shop ✖ (ex in grounds) ◼

ETON — Map 04 SU97

DORNEY COURT
Dorney SL4 6QP
➲ (signposted from M4 junct 7, via B3026)
☎ 01628 604638 ▤ 01628 665772   **2 for 1**
e-mail: palmer@dorneycourt.co.uk
An enchanting brick and timber manor house (c1440) in a tranquil setting. With tall Tudor chimneys and a splendid great hall, it has been the home of the present family since 1510.
Times: Open BH Sun & Mon in May 1.30-4.30. Aug every afternoon ex Sat 1.30-4.30. **Fee:** ✱ £5.50 (ch £3.50, under 10's free). **Facilities:** P ⬛ & ramps toilets for disabled garden centre ✖ (ex guide dogs)

HAMPSTEAD NORREYS — Map 04 SU57

THE LIVING RAINFOREST
RG18 0TN
➲ (follow brown tourist signs from M4/A34)
☎ 01635 202444 ▤ 01635 202440
e-mail: enquiries@livingrainforest.org
By providing education and supporting research into the relationship between humanity and the rainforests, this wonderful attraction hopes to promote a more sustainable future. Visitors to the Living Rainforest will see plants and wildlife that are under threat in their natural habitat, and be encouraged to take part in a large variety of activities, workshops and exhibitions.
Times: ✱ Open daily 10-5.15. (Closed from 1pm 24 Dec & 25-26 Dec) **Facilities:** P ⬛ & toilets for disabled shop ✖ (ex guide dogs) ◼

LOWER BASILDON — Map 04 SU67

BASILDON PARK
RG8 9NR
➲ (7m NW of Reading on W side of A329 between Reading & Wallingford)
☎ 0118 984 3040 ▤ 0118 976 7370   **2 for 1**
e-mail: basildonpark@nationaltrust.org.uk
This 18th-century house, built of Bath stone, fell into decay in the 20th century, but has been beautifully restored by Lord and Lady Iliffe. The classical front has a splendid central portico and pavilions, and inside there are delicate plasterwork decorations on the walls and ceilings. The Octagon drawing room has fine pictures and furniture, and there is a small formal garden. The 2-for-1 voucher is only valid during normal visiting hours and cannot be used for any ticketed events.
Times: House open Apr-end Oct, Wed-Sun & BH Mon 1-5.30. Park & garden Apr-end Oct, Wed-Sun & BH Mon 12-5.30. **Fee:** House & grounds £5 (ch £2.50), family ticket £12.50; Grounds only £2.40 (ch £1.20), family ticket £5.70. **Facilities:** P ✖ licensed & (driven buggy, ltd access to main show rooms) toilets for disabled shop ✖ (ex on lead in grounds) ◼

BEALE PARK
Lower Basildon RG8 9NH
➲ (M4 junct 12, follow brown tourist signs to Pangbourne, A329 towards Oxford)
☎ 0118 984 5172 ▤ 0118 984 5171
e-mail: bealepark@bun.com
Beale Park is home to an extraordinary bird collection including peacocks, swans, parrots and owls. It also offers a steam railway, rare breeds of farm animals, a great pet corner, meerkats, wallabies, a deer park, two splash pools, a huge adventure playground, acres of gardens, sculptures, trails and environmental education in a traditional, family park, beside the Thames. There are summer riverboat trips and excellent lake and river fishing.
Times: ✱ Open Mar-Dec. **Facilities:** P ⬛ & (wheelchair available, parking) toilets for disabled shop ✖ (ex guide dogs)

NEWBURY — Map 04 SU46

WEST BERKSHIRE MUSEUM
The Wharf RG14 5AS
➲ (from London take M4 junct 13, then southbound on A34, follow signs for town centre)
☎ 01635 30511 ▤ 01635 38535   **FREE**
e-mail: heritage@westberks.gov.uk
Situated in two historic buildings in the centre of Newbury, the Cloth Hall built in 1627, and the Granary built in 1720. Apart from local history and archaeology, birds and fossils, the museum displays costume and other decorative art.
Times: Open all year: Apr-Sep, Mon-Fri (Wed during school hols only) 10-5, Sat 10-4.30. Oct-Mar, Mon-Sat (Wed during school hols only) 10-4. (Closed Sun & BHs). **Facilities:** P (15yds) & shop ✖ (ex guide dogs)

OLD WINDSOR — Map 04 SU97

RUNNYMEDE NEW

North Lodge, Windsor Rd SL4 2JL

➲ (From M25 junct 13. On the Thames, 2m W of Runnymede Bridge on S side of A308. 6m E of Windsor)

☎ 01784 432891   ▤ 01784 479007

e-mail: runnymede@nationaltrust.org.uk

Partly designated as a Site of Special Scientific Interest, Runnymede is an area of meadows, grassland, and woodland that sits alongside the Thames. Best known as the site where King John signed the Magna Carta in 1215, this momentous event was commemorated by the American Bar Association, who built a monument here in 1957. There is also a memorial to American President, JFK. Across the Thames at Ankerwycke, also owned by the NT, are the Fairhaven Lodges, designed by Edward Lutyens.

Times: Car parks; Oct-Mar 8.30-5, Apr-Sep 8.30-7 **Fee:** Car parks; 0-2hrs £1.50, 2-4hrs £2.50, all day £3.80 **Facilities:** ▯ (charged) ▱ ✗ ⅙ Braille guide, Audio tour toilets for disabled shop

READING — Map 04 SU77

MUSEUM OF ENGLISH RURAL LIFE

University of Reading, Whiteknights RG6 6AG

➲ (2m SE on A327)

☎ 0118 378 8660   ▤ 0118 975 1264

e-mail: merl@reading.ac.uk

This museum houses a national collection of agricultural, domestic and crafts exhibits, including wagons, tools and a wide range of other equipment used in the English countryside over the last 150 years. Special facilities such as videos and teaching packs are available for school parties. The museum also contains extensive documentary and photographic archives, which can be studied by appointment.

Times: ✱ Open all year, Tue-Sat, 10-1 & 2-4.30. (Closed BH's & Xmas-New Year). **Facilities:** ▯ ⅙ shop ✗

RISELEY — Map 04 SU76

WELLINGTON COUNTRY PARK

RG7 1SP

➲ (signposted off A33, between Reading & Basingstoke)

☎ 0118 932 6444   ▤ 0118 932 6445

e-mail: info@wellington-country-park.co.uk

350 acres of woodland and meadows, set around a lake in peaceful countryside. There is a collection of farm animals and a miniature railway. You can also fish and take a boat

continued

out on the 35-acre lake. Attractions also include crazy golf, an adventure playground and a sandpit.

Times: Open Mar-Oct, daily 10-5.30. **Fee:** ✱ £4.80 (ch 5-15 £2.50, under 5 free) **Facilities:** ▯ ▱ ⅙ (fishing platform & nature trail for disabled) toilets for disabled shop ▰

WINDSOR — Map 04 SU97

FROGMORE HOUSE

Home Park SL4 1NJ

➲ (entrance from B3021 between Datchet & Old Windsor)

☎ 020 7766 7305   ▤ 020 7930 9625

e-mail: windsorcastle@royalcollection.org.uk

Frogmore House, set in the private Home Park, is renowned for its beautiful landscaped garden and lake. Queen Victoria loved Frogmore so much that she broke with royal tradition and chose to build a mausoleum for herself and Prince Albert there. The house is no longer a royal residence but is frequently used by the Royal Family for entertaining. The former library is the setting for furniture and paintings from the Royal Yacht Britannia.

Times: ✱ Open 3 days May, 10-5.30 (last admission 4). Aug BH, 10-5.30 (last admission 4). Prebooked guided tours Aug-Sep.

Fee: Contact Ticket Sales and Information Office (020 7766 7305) for details of admission prices **Facilities:** ▯ shop ✗ ▰

HOUSEHOLD CAVALRY MUSEUM

Combermere Barracks, St Leonards Rd SL4 3DN

➲ (on St Leonards Rd opposite King Edward VII Hospital)

☎ 01753 755112   ▤ 01753 755161

One of the finest military museums in Britain, with comprehensive displays of the uniforms, weapons, horse furniture (tack, regalia, etc) and armour used by the Household Cavalry from 1600 to the present day.

Times: Open all year Mon-Fri (ex BH) 9-12.30 & 2-4.30. **Fee:** ✱ Free admission, however a donation would be appreciated.

Facilities: ⅙ shop ✗

LEGOLAND WINDSOR

Winkfield Rd SL4 4AY
➲ (on B3022 Windsor to Ascot road well signposted from M3 junct 3 & M4 junct 6)
☎ 08705 040404 01753 626111
🖹 01753 626113
e-mail: customer.services@legoland.co.uk

For a different and exciting day out, head for LEGOLAND® Windsor, where there's over 50 interactive and fun attractions, rides and shows to entertain families all day long.

Ride the brand new Jungle Coaster, drive a car, pan for gold, brave the Pirate Falls or explore Miniland made from millions of LEGO® bricks.

For further information or to book, call 08705 04 04 04 or visit www.legoland.co.uk

With over 50 interactive rides, live shows, building workshops, driving schools and attractions. Set in 150 acres of beautiful parkland, LEGOLAND Windsor is a different sort of family theme park. An atmospheric and unique experience for the whole family, a visit to LEGOLAND Windsor is more than a day out, it's a lifetime of memories.
Times: Open daily 20 Mar-Oct (Xmas shopping 4/5, 11/22 Dec)
Fee: ✱ Adult £21-£23 (ch under 3 free, ch 3-15 & pen £19-£20).
Tickets can be booked in advance by telephoning 08705 040404.
Facilities: 🅿 💺 ✗ licensed Ꮡ (signing staff, wheelchair hire, parking) toilets for disabled shop ✖ (ex guide dogs) ⊠
See advertisement on this page

ST GEORGE'S CHAPEL

SL4 1NJ
➲ (M4 junct 6 & M3 junct 3)
☎ 01753 865538 🖹 01753 620165
St George's Chapel, within the precincts of Windsor Castle, is one of the most beautiful ecclesiastical buildings in England. Founded by Edward IV in 1475, it is the burial place of ten monarchs, including Henry VIII and his favourite wife Jane Seymour. The Chapel is the spiritual home of the Order of the Garter, the oldest and most senior order of British Chivalry.
Times: ✱ Open Mar-Oct, 9.45-5.15 (last admission 4); Nov-Feb, 9.45-4.15 (last admission 3). May close at short notice 24-hr infoline 01753 831118. Closed Sun, worshippers very welcome.
Facilities: 🅿 400 yds ᏑᏑ shop ✖ (ex guide dogs)

SAVILL GARDEN (WINDSOR GREAT PARK)

Wick Ln, Englefield Green TW20 0UU
➲ (M25 junct 13, signposted off A30 between Egham & Virginia Water)
☎ 01753 847518 🖹 01753 847536 **2 for 1**
e-mail: savillgarden@crownestate.co.uk
The magnificent 35-acre garden lies within Windsor Great Park. It has spectacular woodland displays in spring,
continued

sweeping herbaceous borders in summer, fiery autumn colours and misty winter vistas. The garden's temperate house is a year-round delight.
Times: Open all year, daily 10-6 (10-4 Nov-Feb). (Closed 25-26 Dec).
Fee: Apr-May: £5.50 (ch 6-16 £2.50, pen £5); Jun-Oct: £4.50 (ch 6-16 £1.50, pen £4) Nov-Mar: £3.50 (ch £1.25, pen £3). Group rates available. Prices valid until 31 Mar 2005. **Facilities:** 🅿 💺 ✗ licensed ᏑᏑ (wheelchairs available) toilets for disabled shop garden centre ✖ (ex guide dogs) ⊠

WINDSOR CASTLE

SL4 1NJ
➲ (M4 junct 6 & M3 junct 3)
☎ 020 7766 7304 🖹 020 7930 9625
e-mail: windsorcastle@royalcollection.org.uk
Covering 13 acres, this is the official residence of HM The Queen and the largest inhabited castle in the world. Begun as a wooden fort by William the Conqueror, it has been added to by almost every monarch since. The Upper Ward includes the State Apartments, magnificently restored following the fire of 1992, and the Lower Ward where St George's Chapel is situated. The Doll's House designed for Queen Mary in the 1920s by Lutyens, is also on display.
Times: ✱ Open all year, daily except Good Friday & 25-26 Dec. Nov-Feb, 9.45-4.15 (last admission 3), Mar-Oct 9.45-5.15 (last admission 4). As Windsor Castle is a royal residence the opening arrangements may be subject to change at short notice. 24hr infoline 01753 831118.✱ **Fee:** £12 (ch 5-16 £6, under 5's free, pen & students £10) Family ticket £30 (2 adults & 2 ch) **Facilities:** 🅿 (400yds) ᏑᏑ (ramps) toilets for disabled shop ✖ (ex guide dogs) ⊠

BRISTOL

EVENTS & FESTIVALS

February
tbc Bristol Beer Festival

April
21st-24th Animated Encounters, Animation Festival, Watershed Media Centre

May
13th-15th Annual International Comic Festival, Empire & Commonwealth Museum

June
9th-13th Bristolive! International festival for amateur ensembles, various venues
12th Bristol Motor & Classic Car Show, The Downs
tbc Bristol Bike Fest, Ashton Court Estate, Long Ashton

July
2nd St Paul's Afrikan & Caribbean Carnival
16th-17th Ashton Court Festival, Ashton Court Estate, Long Ashton
30th-31st Bristol Harbour Festival
tbc Bristol Children's Festival, The Downs

August
11th-14th Bristol Balloon Fiesta, Ashton Court Estate, Long Ashton
24th-26th Bristol Flower Show, The Downs

September
3rd-4th International Kite Festival, Ashton Court Estate, Long Ashton

September/October
tbc Bristol Half Marathon

October
tbc Poetry Festival, various venues in Bristol

November
tbc Brief Encounters, Short Film Festival, Watershed, Bristol

Above: Clifton Suspension Bridge

BRISTOL   Map 03 ST57

AT-BRISTOL
Anchor Rd, Harbourside BS1 5DB
⊃ (from city centre, A4 to Anchor Rd. Located on left opposite Cathedral)
☎ 0845 345 1235 ▤ 0117 915 7200
e-mail: information@at-bristol.org.uk

For the interactive adventure of a lifetime head for At-Bristol's three attractions on the city's habourside. A clever fusion of sci-fi architecture and historic buildings are home to 'Wildwalk', a breathtaking journey through the plant and animal kingdoms; Explore, the UK's most exciting hands-on science centre; and the IMAX theatre, the largest cinema screen in the West of England.

Times: Open all year, term-time wkdays 10-5, wknds & school hols 10-6. Closed 25 Dec. **Fee:** Ticket for 3 attractions £16.50 (ch £11.45, concessions £13.45). Family ticket £52. **Facilities:** ⊡ (charged) ▆ ✗ licensed & (induction loop & mini com 0117 914 3475) toilets for disabled shop ✈ (ex guide dogs) ◀

BLAISE CASTLE HOUSE MUSEUM
Henbury Rd, Henbury BS10 7QS
⊃ (4m NW of city, off B4057)
☎ 0117 903 9818 ▤ 0117 959 3475   `FREE`
e-mail: general_museum@bristol-city.gov.uk

Built in the 18th century for a Quaker banker, this mansion is now Bristol's Museum of Social History. Nearby Blaise Hamlet is a picturesque estate village, designed by John Nash.

Times: Open all year, Sat-Wed, 10-5. **Facilities:** ⊡ & shop ✈ (ex guide dogs)

BRISTOL CITY MUSEUM & ART GALLERY
Queen's Rd, Clifton BS8 1RL
⊃ (follow signs to City Centre, then follow tourist board signs to City Museum & Art Gallery) `FREE`
☎ 0117 922 3571 ▤ 0117 922 2047
e-mail: general_museum@bristol-city.gov.uk

Regional and international collections representing ancient history, natural sciences, and fine and applied arts. Displays include dinosaurs, Bristol ceramics, silver, Chinese and Japanese ceramics. A full programme of Special Exhibitions take place throughout the year. Ring for details.

Times: Open all year, daily 10-5. (Closed 25-26 Dec). **Facilities:** ⊡ (NCP 400yds) ▆ & (lift) toilets for disabled shop ✈ (ex guide dogs)

BRISTOL INDUSTRIAL MUSEUM   `FREE`
Prince's Wharf, Prince St, City Docks BS1 4RN
⊃ (within walking distance of the city centre)
☎ 0117 925 1470 ▤ 0117 729 7318
e-mail: general_museum@bristol-city.gov.uk

The museum is housed in a converted dockside transit shed. Motor and horse-drawn vehicles from the Bristol area are shown, with locally built aircraft and aero-engines. Railway exhibits include the industrial locomotive *Henbury*. At weekends from April to October there are trips around the harbour in either the tug *John King* or the steam tug *Mayflower* or the fire boat *Pyronant*; or trips around the dockside on the Bristol Harbour Railway. On certain weekends visitors can watch the steam crane and electric crane at work.

Times: Open all year Sat-Wed 10-5 **Facilities:** ⊡ (charged) & toilets for disabled shop ✈ (ex guide dogs)

BRISTOL ZOO GARDENS

Clifton BS8 3HA

➲ (M5 junct 17, take A4018 then follow brown elephant signs. Also signed from city centre)

☎ 0117 973 8951 🖶 0117 973 6814

e-mail: information@bristolzoo.org.uk

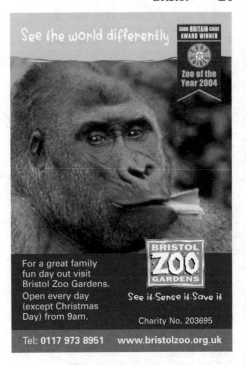

Enjoy a whole day filled with excitement and discovery at Bristol Zoo Gardens. From the smallest and rarest tortoise in the world to the largest ape, there are 300 exotic and endangered species to explore. The Zoo is dedicated to conservation and involved in international breeding programmes. In Zona Brazil, visitors can experience first hand the stunning and diverse species found in the threatened coastal rainforests of Brazil. A winding wooden walkway will lead you past stunning birds, dainty agouti, grazing tapirs, and the world's largest living rodent -the capybara. Award-winning Seal & Penguin Coasts enable visitors to come face to face with penguins and seals in their natural element - beneath the waves - through transparent underwater walkways. Other favourites include Bug World, Twilight World, and the Reptile House.

Times: Open all year, daily (ex 25 Dec) from 9. Closing times approx 5.30 (summer) 4.30 (winter). **Fee:** ✱ £9.50 (ch £6, concessions £8.50). Family ticket (2 ad & 2 ch) £28. **Facilities:** 🅿 (charged) 💷 ✗ licensed ♿ (wheelchairs/electric scooters for use in zoo grounds) toilets for disabled shop ✖ (kennels for service dogs) 🍴

See advertisement on this page

BRITISH EMPIRE & COMMONWEALTH MUSEUM

Station Approach, Temple Meads BS1 6QH

➲ (in city centre, near Temple Meads station)

☎ 0117 925 4980 🖶 0117 925 4983   **2 for 1**

e-mail: admin@empiremuseum.co.uk

Exploring the dramatic 500-year history of the rise and fall of the British Empire and the emergence of the modern Commonwealth, this internationally acclaimed museum uses video stations, interactive exhibits, and computer games, as well as more traditional techniques. Visitors have the opportunity to dress in period costume, learn Morse code or sample exotic spices. The museum is divided into three sections: Britain's first empire 1500-1790, the British Empire at its height 1790-1914, and Independence and Beyond, and is housed in a restored railway terminus built by Brunel. Regular events and activities. Phone for details.

Times: Open daily 10-5. (Closed 25-26 Dec) **Fee:** ✱ £6.50 (ch & pen £3.95 & students £5.50) **Facilities:** 🅿 (charged) 💷 ♿ toilets for disabled shop ✖ (ex guide dogs) 🍴

GEORGIAN HOUSE

7 Great George St, off Park St BS1 5RR

➲ (5 mins walk from Bristol City Centre)   **FREE**

☎ 0117 921 1362 🖶 0117 922 2047

e-mail: general_museum@bristol-city.gov.uk

A carefully preserved example of a late 18th-century merchant's town house, with many original features and furnished to illustrate life both above and below stairs. A bedroom is now open, featuring a four-poster bed plus a small display recounting Bristol's involvement in the slave trade.

Times: Open Sat-Wed, 10-5. **Facilities:** 🅿 (pay & display street parking) ✖ (ex guide dogs)

HORSEWORLD NEW

Staunton Manor Farm, Staunton Ln, Whitchurch BS14 0QJ

➲ (A37 Bristol to Wells Rd, follow brown signs from Maes Knoll traffic lights)

☎ 01275 540173 🖶 01275 540119

e-mail: visitor.centre@horseworld.org.uk

One of the largest horse rescue centres in Britain, set in Mendip-stone farm buildings on the edge of Bristol. Meet the friendly horses, ponies and donkeys. Enjoy the miniature farm, 'touch and groom' areas, pony rides, daily presentations, nature trail, educational displays, video theatre and adventure playground.

Times: Open 10-5 daily (Winter; closed Mon) **Fee:** ✱ £4.50 (ch & pen £3) **Facilities:** 🅿 💷 ✗ ♿ toilets for disabled shop 🍴

JOHN WESLEY'S CHAPEL (THE NEW ROOM)

36 The Horsefair, Broadmead BS1 3JE
➲ (M32 towards Broadmead. In the centre of
Broadmead Shopping Centre. Entrance opposite
Boots the Chemist)
☎ 0117 926 4740

The oldest Methodist chapel in the world, built in 1739 and
extended in 1748. Above the chapel are the preacher's
rooms where John Wesley, Charles Wesley and the early
Methodist preachers stayed.

Times: Open all year, Mon-Sat 10-4. **Fee:** Donation requested. £3 for
guided tour. **Facilities:** P (250yds) main entrance in pedestrian
precinct 🖼 ⅃ shop ✗ (ex guide dogs) ⬛

MARITIME HERITAGE CENTRE

Gas Ferry Rd BS1 6UN
➲ (M5 junct 18, follow brown signs 'Anchor')
☎ 0117 926 0680   📠 0117 925 5788
e-mail: commerical@ss-great-britain.com

Exploring 200 years of Bristol shipbuilding, with special
reference to Charles Hill & Son, and their predecessor, James
Hillhouse. At the Great Western Dock the museum forms
part of the *SS Great Britain* and John Cabot's *Matthew*
experience.

Times: Open all year, daily 10-5.30, 4.30 in winter. (Closed 24 & 25
Dec). **Facilities:** P (charged) 🖼 ⅃ toilets for disabled shop
✗ (ex guide dogs) ⬛

RED LODGE

Park Row BS1 5LJ
➲ (5 mins walk from Bristol City Centre)
☎ 0117 921 1360   📠 0117 922 2047   FREE
e-mail: general_museum@bristol-city.gov.uk

The house was built in 1590 and then altered in 1730. It has
fine oak panelling and carved stone chimney pieces and is
furnished in the style of both periods. The garden has now
been laid out in Elizabethan style.

Times: Open Sat-Wed 10-5. **Facilities:** P (NCP, adjacent)
✗ (ex guide dogs)

SS GREAT BRITAIN

Great Western Dock, Gas Ferry Rd BS1 6TY
➲ (off Cumberland Rd)
☎ 0117 926 0680   📠 0117 925 5788

Built and launched in Bristol in 1843, the *SS Great Britain*,
designed by Isambard Kingdom Brunel, was the first ocean-
going, propeller-driven, iron ship. After a life as a passenger
liner, troop transport and cargo carrier, she was abandoned
in the Falkland Islands in 1886. But in 1970 she was towed
back to Bristol and is now being conserved in the Great
Western Dock where she was built.

Times: ✱ Open all year daily 10-5.30, 4.30 in winter. (Closed 24 & 25
Dec). **Facilities:** P (charged) 🖼 ⅃ shop ✗ ⬛

An asterisk * indicates
that opening times and
prices are for 2004. Please
contact the attraction for
up-to-date information.

BUCKINGHAMSHIRE

EVENTS & FESTIVALS

February
8th Shrove Tuesday, Olney Pancake Day Race

May
2nd Marlow Spring Regatta, Higginson Park,
Marlow

June
5th Coombe Hill Run, Wendover
11th Marlow Town Regatta
12th Folk on the Green, Horsefair Green,
Stony Stratford (now part of
Milton Keynes)
26th Milton Keynes Carnival,
central Milton Keynes

July
2nd-9th Buckingham Festival

September
1st Bucks County Show, Weedon Park,
Aylesbury
11th Thames Valley Grand Prix Raft Race,
Higginson Park, Marlow
17th Marlow Carnival, Higginson Park,
Marlow

December
3rd Haddenham Festival, Haddenham Village,
between Thame & Aylesbury

*Above: Palladian Bridge in the
grounds of Stowe Mansion*

BEACONSFIELD Map 04 SU99

BEKONSCOT MODEL VILLAGE
Warwick Rd HP9 2PL
➲ (M40 junct 2, 4m M25 junct 16)
☎ 01494 672919 📠 01494 675284 `2 for 1`
e-mail: info@bekonscot.co.uk

A miniature world, depicting rural England in the 1930s. A Gauge 1 model railway meanders through six little villages, each with their own tiny population. Rides on the sit-on miniature railway take place weekends and school holidays. **Times:** Open mid Feb-Oct, 10-5. **Fee:** £5.30 (ch £3.20, concessions £4). **Facilities:** 🅿 💺 ⑤ (wheelchair loan) toilets for disabled shop 🐕 (ex guide dogs) 🍴

BLETCHLEY Map 04 SP93

BLETCHLEY PARK NEW
The Mansion, Bletchley Park MK3 6EB
➲ (Approach Bletchley from V7 Saxon St. At rdbt, southern end of Saxon St. go under railway bridge towards Buckingham & follow signs to Bletchley Park)
☎ 01908 640404 📠 01908 274381 `2 for 1`
e-mail: info@bletchleypark.org.uk
Known as 'Station X' during World War II, this was the home of the secret scientific team that worked to decipher German military messages sent using the Enigma code machine. Visitors can find out more about the Enigma machine; the 'bombes', computers used to crack the code; Alan Turing, one of the leading mathematicians of his day, who worked on the project; as well as see a number of other displays including the use of pigeons during the war, wartime vehicles, and a Churchill collection. **Times:** Open daily 9.30-5.30 (Tours at 11 & 2). Weekends open 10.30-5. Closed 25 & 26 Dec. **Fee:** £10 (ch & concessions £8) Family £25 under 8's free. **Facilities:** 🅿 (charged) 💺 ✕ licensed ⑤ shop 🍴

CHALFONT ST GILES Map 04 SU99

CHILTERN OPEN AIR MUSEUM
Newland Park, Gorelands Ln HP8 4AB
➲ (M25 junct 17, M40 junct 2. Follow brown signs)
☎ 01494 871117 📠 01494 872774
e-mail: coamuseum@netscape.net
Saved from demolition and moved brick by brick to Newland Park, this collection of old buildings includes barns, granaries and even a tin chapel. Step back in time and get a
continued

feel of the 1940s in a fully furnished Prefab, or experience 50AD at the Iron Age House. Demonstrations including brick making, rug making, black smithing and storytelling. Regular living history re-enactments.
Times: ✱ Open 31 Mar-Oct, daily 10-5. **Facilities:** 🅿 💺 ⑤ (Braille guide books & taped guides available, wheelchairs) toilets for disabled shop 🐕 (ex on lead) 🍴

MILTON'S COTTAGE
Dean Way HP8 4JH
➲ (0.5m W of A413. 3m N of M40 junct 2)
☎ 01494 872313
e-mail: info@miltonscottage.org
A timber-framed, 16th-century cottage, with a charming garden, the only surviving home in which John Milton lived and worked. He completed *Paradise Lost* and started *Paradise Regained* here. First editions of these works are among the many rare books and artefacts on display.
Times: Open Mar-Oct, Tue-Sun 10-1 & 2-6. Also open Spring & Summer BH. **Fee:** £3 (ch 15 £1). Party 20+ £2 each.
Facilities: 🅿 ✕ licensed ⑤ (special parking area closer to cottage) shop 🐕 (ex guide dogs)

CLIVEDEN Map 04 SU98

CLIVEDEN
SL6 0JA
➲ (2m N of Taplow, follow brown signs on A4)
☎ 01628 605069 📠 01628 669461
e-mail: cliveden@nationaltrust.org.uk
The 375 acres of garden and woodland overlook the River Thames, and include a magnificent parterre, topiary, lawns with box hedges, and water gardens. The palatial house, former home of the Astors, is now a hotel - The Great Hall and French Dining Room can be visited on certain afternoons. **Times:** Open Grounds 15 Mar-Oct daily 11-6, Nov-Dec daily 11-4 (Woodlands open all year). House Apr-Oct, Thu & Sun 3-5.30 by timed ticket. **Fee:** Grounds: £7.50 (ch £3.50). House: £1 extra (ch 50p extra). Family ticket £17.20. **Facilities:** 🅿 ✕ licensed ⑤ (powered vehicle & wheelchairs available, parking) toilets for disabled shop 🐕 (ex in woodland) 🌳 🍴

HIGH WYCOMBE Map 04 SU89

WYCOMBE LOCAL HISTORY & CHAIR MUSEUM
Castle Hill House, Priory Av HP13 6PX
➲ (signposted by brown tourism sign from A404 (Amersham Hill) N of High Wycombe town centre just past railway station)
☎ 01494 421895 📠 01494 421897 `FREE`
e-mail: museum@wycombe.gov.uk
Situated in an 18th-century house, set in attractive grounds. The displays explore the history of the Wycombe area, focusing on the chair-making industry, with interactive displays, and changing exhibitions.
Times: Open all year, Mon-Sat 10-5, Sun 2-5. Closed on BHs except special events - ring for details. **Facilities:** 🅿 💺 ⑤ (special parking & drop off point) toilets for disabled shop 🐕 (ex guide dogs) 🍴

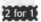

Directions are provided by the attractions.

HUGHENDEN   Map 04 SU89

HUGHENDEN MANOR
HP14 4LA
➲ (1.5m N of High Wycombe, on W side of A4128)
☎ 01494 755573   🖶 01494 474284   **2 for 1**
e-mail: hughenden@nationaltrust.org.uk

Benjamin Disraeli, later the Earl of Beaconsfield and twice Prime Minister, bought the house in 1847 and lived there until his death in 1881. It still has many of his books and other possessions. The gardens are a recreation of the colourful designs of Disraeli's wife, Mary-Anne. The 2-for-1 voucher is valid only during normal visiting hours, and cannot be used for any ticketed events.

Times: House open 5-27 Mar, Sat & Sun only. Apr-Oct, Wed-Sun & BH Mon 1-5. Last admission 4.30. Gardens same dates as house 12-5. Park open all year. Also open Good Friday. **Fee:** £5 (ch £2.50). Family ticket £12.50. Garden only £1.80 (ch 90p). Park free.

Facilities: 🅿 ✕ licensed ♿ (Braille leaflet, wheelchairs, ramp to house) toilets for disabled shop ✖ (guide dogs; in grounds) ❧

LONG CRENDON   Map 04 SP60

COURTHOUSE
HP18 9AN
➲ (2m N of Thame, via B4011 when entering village turn right into the High St. Courthouse on left at end of High St)
☎ 01296 381501   **2 for 1**
e-mail: nick.phillips@nationaltrust.org.uk

One of the finest examples of early timber framed building in the area. Probably built as a wool store in the early 1400s, but also used as a manorial courthouse until the late 19th century, this timber-framed building stands out, even in this picturesque village. Although the windows and doors have been altered and the chimney stack is Tudor, the magnificent timber roof is original.

Times: Open, Upper storey Apr-Sep, Wed 2-6, Sat, Sun & BH Mons 11-6. **Fee:** ✱ £1.10 **Facilities:** 🅿 (street) (not suitable for large vehicles) ✖ ❧

MIDDLE CLAYDON   Map 04 SP72

CLAYDON HOUSE
MK18 2EY
➲ (Off A413 in Padbury, follow National Trust signs. Entrance by north drive only)
☎ 01296 730349   🖶 01296 738511   **2 for 1**
e-mail: claydon@nationaltrust.org.uk

The rather sober exterior of this 18th-century house gives no clue to the extravagances that lie inside, in the form of fantastic rococo carvings. Ceilings, cornices, walls and overmantels are adorned with delicately carved fruits, birds, beasts and flowers by Luke Lightfoot. The Chinese room is particularly splendid. There is also a spectacular parquetry staircase. The 2-for-1 voucher is valid only during normal visiting hours, and cannot be used for any ticketed events.

Times: House open 27 Mar-24 Oct, Sat-Wed 1-5, 25-31 Oct 1-4.30 (Closed Thu & Fri). Grounds open 1-5. Last admission 4.30. Closed Good Fri. **Fee:** £5 (ch £2.50). Family ticket £12.50. Grounds £1.10 **Facilities:** 🅿 💷 ✕ licensed ♿ (Braille guide, photograph albums) toilets for disabled ✖ (ex guide dogs or in park) ❧

QUAINTON   Map 04 SP72

BUCKINGHAMSHIRE RAILWAY CENTRE
Quainton Rd Station HP22 4BY
➲ (Signposted off A41 Aylesbury-Bicester Road at Waddesdon, 7m NW of Aylesbury)
☎ 01296 655720   🖶 01296 655720
e-mail: bucksrailcentre@btopenworld.com

Housed in a former Grade II listed building, the Centre features an interesting and varied collection of about 20 locomotives with 40 carriages and wagons from places as far afield as South Africa, Egypt and America. Items date from the 1800s up to the 1960s. Visitors can take a ride on full-size and miniature steam trains, and stroll around the 20-acre site to see locomotives and rolling stock. The Centre runs locomotive driving courses for visitors. Regular 'Days out with Thomas' events take place throughout the year.

Times: Open with engines in steam Apr-Oct, Sun & BH Mon; Jun-Aug, Wed; 10.30-5.30. Dec Sat & Sun Santa's Magical Steamings-advanced booking recommended. Also open for static viewing Wed-Sun.

Fee: ✱ Steaming Days; £6 (ch & pen £4). Family ticket £18. BH wknds £7 (ch & pen £5). Family ticket £20. Static viewing £3 (ch & pen £2).

Facilities: 🅿 💷 ♿ (ramped bridge with wheelchair lift) toilets for disabled shop ▤

STOWE   Map 04 SP63

STOWE HOUSE
MK18 5EH
➲ (3m NW Buckingham)
☎ 01280 818282   🖶 01280 818186
e-mail: sses@stowe.co.uk

Set in the National Trust's landscaped gardens, Stowe is a splendid 18th-century mansion. The leading designers of the day were called in to lay out the gardens, and leading architects - Vanbrugh, Gibbs, Kent and Leoni - commissioned to decorate them with garden temples. The house is now a major public school.

Times: ✱ Open 14-16 Mar, 25-31 May, 4 Sep-19 Oct, 14-16 Nov, daily (ex Mon & Tue, but open May BH Mon) for guided tours only at 2pm; 3-27 Apr & 9 Jul-3 Sep, Wed-Sun 12-5 and daily tours at 2pm.

Facilities: 🅿 ♿ toilets for disabled shop ✖ (ex guide dogs)

STOWE LANDSCAPE GARDENS
MK18 5EH
➲ (3m NW of Buckingham via Stoke Ave, off A422)
☎ 01280 822850 🖹 01280 822437 `2 for 1`
e-mail: stowegarden@nationaltrust.org.uk
One of the finest Georgian landscape gardens, made up of valleys and vistas, narrow lakes and rivers with more than 30 temples and monuments designed by many of the leading architects of the 18th century. At the centre is Stowe House, and around all is Stowe Park. The creation of the Temple family, Stowe has been described as 'a work to wonder at' in its size, splendour and variety. Many of the garden buildings have been conserved, and thousands of new trees and shrubs have been planted in recent years. The 2-for-1 voucher is valid only during normal visiting hours, and cannot be used for any ticketed events.
Times: Open Mar-Oct (closed 29 May), Wed-Sun, 10-5.30, last admission 4; Nov-Feb, Sat-Sun, last admission 3. Open all BH Mons.
Fee: £5.80 (ch £2.90). Family ticket £14.50. **Facilities:** 🅿 ✗ licensed & (manual wheelchairs unsuitable, powered batricars available) toilets for disabled shop ✗ (on leads only) 🐾 🖼

WADDESDON
WADDESDON MANOR
Map 04 SP71
HP18 0JH
➲ (gates off A41, 6m NW of Aylesbury)
☎ 01296 653211, 653226 & 653203
🖹 01296 653212
e-mail: suzy.barron@nationaltrust.org.uk
Waddesdon was built by Baron Ferdinand de Rothschild between 1874 and 1879, in the style of a French château of the 16th century, and houses one of the finest collections of French 18th-century decorative arts in the world, which includes French furniture, Savonnerie carpets and Sèvres porcelain. There is also a fine collection of important portraits by Gainsborough and Reynolds along with works by Dutch and Flemish masters of the 17th century. The garden is renowned for its seasonal displays, colourful shrubs, mature trees and parterre. There is a rococo-style aviary housing many exotic birds, a rose and children's garden.
Times: Open, Grounds & Aviary only, 3 Mar-Oct, Wed-Sun & BH Mon 10-5. House 31 Mar-Oct, Wed-Sun & BH Mon 11-4. Entrance by timed ticket. **Fee:** Grounds & Aviary £4 (ch £2). House £7 (ch £6). Tickets bookable in advance at booking charge (tel 01296 653226). **Facilities:** 🅿 ✗ licensed & (wheelchairs, Braille guide, parking, scented plants) toilets for disabled shop ✗ (ex guide dogs) 🐾 🖼

> An asterisk * indicates that opening times and prices are for 2004. Please contact the attraction for up-to-date information.

WEST WYCOMBE
Map 04 SU89
THE HELL-FIRE CAVES
HP14 3AJ `2 for 1`
➲ (on A40 in West Wycombe)
☎ 01494 524411 (office) & 533739 (caves)
🖹 01494 471617
e-mail: mary@west-wycombe-estate.co.uk
The entrance to West Wycombe caves is halfway up the hill that dominates the village. On the summit stands the parish church and the mausoleum of the Dashwood family. The caves are not natural but were dug on the orders of Sir Francis Dashwood between 1748 and 1752. Sir Francis, the Chancellor of the Exchequer, was also the founder of the Hell Fire Club, whose members were reputed to have held outrageous and blasphemous parties in the caves, which extend approximately half a mile underground. The entrance, from a large forecourt, is a brick tunnel that leads into the caves, where tableaux and curiosities are exhibited.
Times: Open all year, Mar-Oct, daily 11-6; Nov-Feb, Sat & Sun 1-5.
Fee: £4 (ch, pen & students £3). Family ticket £12 (max 3 ch)
Facilities: 🅿 🖼 & toilets for disabled shop ✗ (ex guide dogs) 🖼

WEST WYCOMBE PARK
HP14 3AJ
➲ (S of A40, at W end of West Wycombe) `2 for 1`
☎ 01494 513569 🖹 01494 474284
Set in 300 acres of beautiful parkland, the house was rebuilt in the Palladian style, between 1745 and 1771, for Sir Francis Dashwood. Of particular note are the painted ceilings by Borgnis. The park was laid out in the 18th century and given an artificial lake and classical temples. The 2-for-1 voucher is valid only during normal visiting hours, and cannot be used for any ticketed events.
Times: Open, House & grounds Jun-Aug, Sun-Thu 2-6. Grounds only Apr-May, Sun-Thu 2-6 & Etr, May Day & Spring BH Sun & Mon 2-6. Last admission 5.15. Entry by timed tickets on wkdays. Parties must book in advance. **Fee:** House & grounds £5.40 (ch £2.70). Grounds only £2.80 (ch £1.40). **Facilities:** 🅿 & (partial access to ground floor & gardens) ✗ (ex on lead in car park) 🐾

WING
Map 04 SP82
ASCOTT
LU7 0PS
➲ (0.5m E of Wing, 3m SW of Leighton Buzzard on S side of A418)
☎ 01296 688242 🖹 01296 681904
e-mail: info@ascottestate.co.uk
A National Trust property since 1949, Ascott holds an exceptional collection of paintings, Chinese porcelain and English and French furniture. The 30-acre garden is a fine example of Victorian gardening and the grounds are stunning at any time of year.
Times: House & Gardens: mid Mar-Apr daily 2-6 (ex Mon), 3 May-28 Jul Tue-Thu 2-6, 2-31 Aug daily 2-6 (ex Mon). **Fee:** ✱ House & Garden £6.50 (ch £3.25). Gardens only: £4 (ch £2). National Trust members free ex 3 May & 23 Aug. **Facilities:** 🅿 & (w/chairs avail, assistance required, large print guide) toilets for disabled ✗ 🐾

CAMBRIDGESHIRE

EVENTS & FESTIVALS

January
5th-9th Whittlesea Straw Bear Festival
tbc Cambridge Winter Ale Festival
(provisional), venue tbc

March
19th-20th National Shire Horse Show, East of
England Showground, Peterborough
tbc Daffodil Weekend, Thriplow

May
2nd Stilton Cheese Rolling, Stilton
6th-8th East of England Garden Show, East of
England Showground, Alwalton
(provisional)
6th-8th St Neots Folk Festival, The Priory
Centre, St Neots
23rd-28th Cambridge Beer Festival, Jesus
Green, Cambridge

June
4th Strawberry Fair, free festival of music and
entertainment, Cambridge
17th-19th East of England Show, East of
England Showground, Peterborough
29th-3rd Jun Wisbech Rose Fair

July
8th-10th Ely Folk Weekend, Ely Outdoor
Sports Association, Downham Road
9th World Pea Shooting Championships &
Village Fair, Village Green, Witcham, Ely
(provisional)
28th-31st Charles Wells Cambridge Folk
Festival, Cherry Hinton Hall Grounds,
Cherry Hinton Road, Cambridge
tbc Cambridge Summer Music Festival,
various venues, mid July-mid August

August
23rd-28th Peterborough Beer Festival, biggest
locally organised real ale festival in the UK

October
9th The World Conker Championships,
Village Green, Ashton, Peterborough

Above: The Mathematical Bridge, Queen's College

CAMBRIDGE   **Map 05 TL45**

CAMBRIDGE & COUNTY FOLK MUSEUM
2/3 Castle St CB3 0AQ
➲ (Turn off A14 onto A3019, museum NW of
town)
☎ 01223 355159
e-mail: info@folkmuseum.org.uk
This timber-framed inn houses items covering the everyday
life of the people of Cambridgeshire from the 17th century to
the present day. There are also temporary exhibitions.
Special exhibitions and children's activity days take place
throughout the year. Please telephone for details.
Times: ✱ Open all year, Apr-Sep, Mon-Sat 10.30-5, Sun 2-5. Oct-Mar,
Tue-Sat 10.30-5, Sun 2-5. (Last admissions 30 mins before closing).
(Closed 1 Jan, Good Fri, 24-31 Dec). **Facilities:** P (300yds) (pay and
display on street parking) ૯ (Braille touch tables, tape guides & large
print guides) shop ✸ (ex guide dogs)

CAMBRIDGE UNIVERSITY BOTANIC GARDEN
Cory Lodge, Bateman St CB2 1JF
➲ (1m S of city centre)
☎ 01223 336265 🖹 01223 336278
e-mail: enquiries@botanic.cam.ac.uk
The Cambridge University Botanic Garden is a 40-acre oasis
of beautifully landscaped gardens and glasshouses close to
the heart of the historic city. Opened on its present site in
1846, the garden showcases a collection of some 8000 plant
species. This Grade II heritage landscape features the Rock
Garden, displaying alpine plants, the Winter and Autumn
Gardens, tropical rainforest and seasonal displays in the
Glasshouses, the historic Systematic Beds, the Scented
Garden, Herbaceous Beds and the finest collection of trees in
the east of England.
Times: Open all year daily 10-6 (summer), 10-5 (autumn & spring),
(10-4) winter. Glasshouses 10-3.45. (Closed 25 Dec-1 Jan). Entry by
Bateman St and Station Rd gates on wkdays & by Bateman St gate only
at wknds & BH. **Fee:** £3 (pen £2.50). **Facilities:** P (0.25km) (on
street parking pay & display) ⬛ ૯ (guiding service, manual &
motorised wheelchairs -prebooked) toilets for disabled shop (open
Mar-Oct) ✸ (ex guide dogs)

FITZWILLIAM MUSEUM
Trumpington St CB2 1RB
➲ (M11 junct 11, 12 or 13. Near city centre)   FREE
☎ 01223 332900 🖹 01223 332923
e-mail: fitzmuseum-enquiries@lists.cam.ac.uk
The Fitzwilliam is the art museum of the University of
Cambridge and one of the oldest public museums in Britain.
It contains magnificent collections spanning centuries and
civilisations including antiquities from Ancient Egypt, Greece
and Rome; sculpture, furniture, armour, ceramics;
manuscripts, coins and medals, paintings, drawings and
prints.
Times: Open all year Tue-Sat 10-5, Sun 12-5. (Closed Mon ex BH, &
24-26, 31 Dec & 1 Jan). **Facilities:** P (400yds) (2hr max, metered)
⬛ ૯ (induction loop) toilets for disabled shop ✸ (ex guide dogs)

LINTON ZOOLOGICAL GARDENS
See advert on opposite page, see full entry under LINTON.

SCOTT POLAR RESEARCH INSTITUTE MUSEUM
Lensfield Rd CB2 1ER
➲ (1km S of City Centre)
☎ 01223 336540 🖷 01223 336549 **FREE**
e-mail: rkh10@cam.ac.uk
An international centre for polar studies, including a museum featuring displays of Arctic and Antarctic expeditions, with special emphasis on those of Captain Scott. Other exhibits include Eskimo work and other arts of the polar regions, as well as displays on current scientific exploration. Public lectures run from October to December and February to April.
Times: Open all year, Tue-Sat 2.30-4. Closed some public & university hols. **Facilities:** 🅿 (400mtrs) ♿ shop ✖ (ex guide dogs)

UNIVERSITY MUSEUM OF ARCHAEOLOGY & ANTHROPOLOGY
Downing St CB2 3DZ
➲ (located opposite Crowne Plaza Hotel)
☎ 01223 333516 🖷 01223 333517 **FREE**
e-mail: cumaa@hermes.cam.ac.uk
The museum is part of the Faculty of Archaeology and Anthropology of the University of Cambridge. It was established in 1884 and is still housed in its 1916 building on the Downing Site in the city centre. It has three floors displaying renowned archaeological and anthropological collections from around the world.
Times: Open all year Tue-Sat 2-4.30. (Closed 1wk Etr & 1wk Xmas). Telephone for extended summer hours. **Facilities:** 🅿 (100yds) ♿ (lift available) shop ✖ (ex guide dogs)

DUXFORD   Map 05 TL44
IMPERIAL WAR MUSEUM DUXFORD
CB2 4QR
➲ (off M11 junct 10, on A505)
☎ 01223 835000 🖷 01223 837267
e-mail: duxford@iwm.org.uk
Duxford is one of the world's most spectacular aviation heritage complexes with a collection of nearly 200 aircraft, the American Air Museum and a fine collection of military vehicles plus special exhibitions including The Battle of Britain, Normandy Experience and Monty. The Museum holds four Air Shows throughout the summer plus other special events such as the Military Vehicle Show.
Times: ✱ Open all year, mid Mar-mid Oct daily 10-6; mid Oct-mid Mar daily 10-4. (Closed 24-26 Dec) **Facilities:** 🅿 🍽 ✖ licensed ♿ (wheelchair available-phone in advance) toilets for disabled shop ✖ (ex guide dogs) 🍴

ELY   Map 05 TL58
ELY CATHEDRAL
CB7 4DL
➲ (A10 or A142, 15m from Cambridge)
☎ 01353 667735 🖷 01353 665658
e-mail: receptionist@cathedral.ely.anglican.org
The Octagon Tower of Ely Cathedral can be seen for miles as it rises above the surrounding flat fenland. A monastery was founded on the site by St Etheldreda in 673, but the present cathedral church dates from 1083 and is a magnificent example of Romanesque architecture.
Times: Open daily, Summer 7-7, Winter 7.30-6 (5pm Sun). **Fee:** £4.80 (concessions £4.20). Ch free in family group. Group reductions (15+) **Facilities:** 🅿 (walking distance) 🍽 licensed ♿ (touch tour for blind/partially sighted) toilets for disabled shop ✖ (ex guide dogs)

See the wonderful combination of Beautiful Gardens and Wildlife from all over the world at LINTON ZOO
"Cambridgeshire's Wildlife Breeding Centre"

This famous wildlife breeding centre was opened in 1972 by the Simmons family and has been created out of their love, interest and concern for the World's Wildlife. The Zoo is continuously expanding as more of the world's threatened species are taken on board their land based 'Ark'. Emphasis is on conservation and education here whilst providing an enjoyable family day out! There is lots to interest everyone with a wealth of rare and exotic creatures to see including Tigers, Lemurs, African Lions, Snow Leopards, Lynx, Tapir, Binturongs, Zebra, Porcupines, Wallabies, Macaws, Eagle Owls, Toucans, Hornbills, Emus, Giant Tortoises, Snakes and many, many others.

Set in 16 acres of beautiful gardens with pleasant country surroundings.

Keeper talks and animal encounters usually during school holidays and at weekends. Please phone for details.

Free car and coach park, cafeteria (busy season only). Plenty of picnic areas, exciting children's play area and all other usual facilities.

Voted 'Best for Kids 2004' and 'Cambridgeshire's Family Attraction of the Year 2004'

OPEN ALL YEAR, every day (Closed 25/26 December only)

Tel. Cambridge 01223 891308 for further information, school information packs or party bookings.

www.lintonzoo.co.uk

Hadstock Road, Linton, Cambridgeshire. Situated along B1052 just off A1307, leave M11 at J9 from London

OLIVER CROMWELL'S HOUSE
29 St Mary's St CB7 4HF
➲ (follow brown tourist information signs from main roads. Adjacent to Saint Mary's Church.)
☎ 01353 662062 🖷 01353 668518 **2 for 1**
e-mail: tic@eastcambs.gov.uk
Cromwell inherited the house and local estates from a maternal uncle and moved here in 1636, along with his mother, sisters, wife and eight children. There are displays and period rooms dealing with Cromwell's life, the Civil War and domestic life in the 17th century, as well as the history of The Fens and the house itself, from its medieval origins to its role as an inn in the 19th century.
Times: Open all year: Apr-Oct, daily 10-5.30; Nov-Mar, Mon-Fri 11-4, Sat 10-5. Sun, 11.15-4. **Fee:** ✱ £3.75 (concessions £3.25). Family ticket £10. **Facilities:** 🅿 (100yds) ♿ shop ✖ (ex guide dogs) 🍴

THE STAINED GLASS MUSEUM
The Cathedral CB7 4DN
➲ (15m N of Cambridge via A10)
☎ 01353 660347 🖷 01353 665025 **2 for 1**
e-mail: curator@stainedglassmuseum.com
Situated in the cathedral, this museum is the only one of its kind in the country. Case exhibits show how stained-glass windows are designed and made, and there is an exhibition of approximately 100 panels dating from the 13th century to the present day, displayed at eye level in back-lit cases. The museum has recently reopened after a total refurbishment, with new loans from the Victoria & Albert Museum.
Times: Open daily, Mon-Fri 10.30-4.30, Sat & BH 10.30-5 & Sun 12-6. **Fee:** ✱ £3.50 (ch over 12, students & pen £2.50, ch under 12 free). Party 10+ £2.50 (concessions £2). **Facilities:** 🅿 400yds 🍽 ✖ licensed ♿ (Inter-active video visit) toilets for disabled shop ✖ (ex guide dogs) 🍴

HAMERTON — Map 04 TL17

HAMERTON ZOO PARK
PE28 5RE
➲ (off A1 junct 15, signed Sawtry)
☎ 01832 293362 📠 01832 293677
e-mail: office@hamertonzoopark.com
A wildlife breeding centre, dedicated to the practical conservation of endangered species including gibbons, marmosets, lemurs, wildcats, meerkats, sloths and many more. There is also a large and varied bird collection, with several species unique to Hamerton. Over 120 species in all. Other attractions include a children's play area, and new "creature contact" sessions.
Times: Open Summer daily 10.30-6; Winter daily 10.30-4. (Closed 25 Dec) **Facilities:** 🅿 💷 ♿ toilets for disabled shop ✕ 🍴

LINTON — Map 05 TL54

CHILFORD HALL VINEYARD
Chilford Hall, Balsham Rd CB1 6LE
➲ (signposted from A1307 and A11)
☎ 01223 892641 📠 01223 894056
e-mail: simonalper@chilfordhall.co.uk **2 for 1**
Taste and buy award-winning wines from the largest vineyard in Cambridgeshire. See the grapes growing in the 18-acre vineyard and take a winery tour to learn how English wine is made and appreciate the subtle difference between each of the Chilford quality wines. Telephone for details of special events.
Times: Open Mar-Oct , Fri-Sun & BH's **Fee:** Guided tours £6 (ch free). Party 15+. Includes wine to taste & tour of the vineyards.
Facilities: 🅿 💷 ♿ toilets for disabled shop 🍴

LINTON ZOOLOGICAL GARDENS
Hadstock Rd CB1 6NT
➲ (M11 junct 9/10, on B1052 off A1307 between Cambridge & Haverhill, signposted)
☎ 01223 891308 📠 01223 891308

Linton Zoo places emphasis on conservation and education where visitors can see a combination of beautiful gardens and a wealth of wildlife from all over the world. There are many rare and exotic creatures to see including tapirs, snow leopards, tigers, lions, Grevy's zebra, tamarin monkeys, lemurs, owls, parrots, giant tortoises, snakes, tarantula spiders and many others. The zoo is set in 16-acres of gardens with plenty of picnic areas, children's play area and bouncy castle.
Times: Open daily 29 May-19 Sep 10-6; 20 Sep-30 Oct 10-5; 31 Oct-18 Mar 10.30-4, last admission 1 hr before closing. Closed 25-26 Dec.
Fee: £6.50 (ch 2-13 £4.50) **Facilities:** 🅿 💷 ♿ toilets for disabled shop ✕ 🍴

See advertisement on page 27

LODE — Map 05 TL56

ANGLESEY ABBEY
CB5 9EJ
➲ (6m NE of Cambridge on B1102, signposted from A14)
☎ 01223 810080 📠 01223 810088
e-mail: angleseyabbey@ntrust.org.uk
A medieval undercroft has survived from the priory founded here in 1135, but the house dates mainly from 1600. Thomas Hobson of *Hobson's Choice* was one of the owners. A later owner was Lord Fairhaven, who amassed the huge collection of pictures, and laid out the beautiful gardens.
Times: Open House & Mill: 24 Mar-7 Nov, Wed-Sun & BH Mon's, 1-5. Gardens open 10.30-5.30 and also open in winter 10 Nov-20 Mar, daily, 10.30-4.30. Closed 24-28 Dec. **Fee:** House and garden £6.60. Garden only £4.10 (£3.40 in winter). Family & party discounts available.
Facilities: 🅿 💷 ✕ licensed ♿ (electric buggy, wheelchairs, large print & Braille guides) toilets for disabled shop garden centre ✕ (ex guide dogs) 🍴

PETERBOROUGH — Map 04 TL19

FLAG FEN BRONZE AGE CENTRE
The Droveway, Northey Rd PE6 7QJ
☎ 01733 313414 📠 01733 349957
e-mail: office@flagfen.freeserve.co.uk
Although visitors enter this site through a 21st-century roundhouse, the rest of their day will be spent in the Bronze Age, some 3,000 years ago. Flag Fen is one of Europe's most important Bronze Age sites, and contains reconstructions of Iron Age as well as Bronze Age roundhouses. There is also a museum of artefacts found on the site over the last 20 years, as well as a Preservation Hall that contains a 60ft mural depicting the fens in ancient times.
Times: ✱ Open daily 10-4 (last admission). Site closes 5pm. (Closed 24 Dec-2 Jan) **Facilities:** 🅿 💷 ♿ toilets for disabled shop ✕ (ex assistance dogs) 🍴

LONGTHORPE TOWER
Thorpe Rd, Longthorpe PE1 1HA
☎ 01733 268482
See the finest domestic wall paintings in northern Europe hidden in the tower for centuries until revealed by a World War II bomb.
Times: Open Apr-Oct, Sat-Sun & BH only 12-5. Pre-booked guided tours only. **Fee:** ✱ £2 (ch £1, concessions £1.50). Prices & opening times relate to 2004, for further details phone or log onto www.english-heritage.org.uk/visits **Facilities:** 🅿 ✕ ♿

PETERBOROUGH CATHEDRAL
PE1 1XS
➲ (access from A1 juncts with A605 or A47, follow signs)
☎ 01733 343342 📠 01733 552465
e-mail: a.watson@peterborough-cathedral.org.uk
With one of the most dramatic West fronts in the country, its three arches an extraordinary creation of medieval architecture, it would be easy for the interior to be an anticlimax, but it is not. The dramatic Romanesque interior is little altered since its completion 800 years ago. Particular highlights of a visit include the unique painted nave ceiling, the elaborate fan vaulting of the 'new' building, Saxon carvings from an earlier church and the burial place of two Queens. An exhibition in the North aisle tells the story of the
continued

cathedral. A range of tours can be booked in advance: please contact the Chapter office for details.
Times: Open all year, daily 9-5. Closed 25-26 Dec. **Fee:** Free - donations towards the cost of upkeep are requested but £3 charge for group tours (£2 for concessions). **Facilities:** P (300yds) (no parking within cathedral precincts) 🍺 ✗ licensed ♿ (touch & hearing centre, Braille guide, ramps) toilets for disabled shop ✈ (ex guide dogs or in grounds)

RAILWORLD NEW
Oundle Rd PE2 9NR
➲ (From A1(M) Peterborough, turn onto A1139 then off at junct 5 to city centre. At 1st rdbt, follow tourist signs for "Little Putter". Entrance for Railworld is off Oundle Rd at City end through car park)
☎ 01733 344240   `2 for 1`

An exhibition centre and museum dedicated to all things rail related. Attractions include model railways, hands on exhibits, a rail industry showcase, hovertrains, and local rail history gallery.
Times: Mar-Oct daily 11-4, Nov-Feb Mon-Fri 11-4 **Fee:** £4 (ch £2, concessions £3) Family £10 **Facilities:** P 🍺 ♿ Reasonable access toilets for disabled shop only ✈ (ex guide dogs)

RAMSEY   Map 04 TL28
RAMSEY ABBEY GATEHOUSE
Abbey School PE17 1DH
➲ (SE edge of Ramsey, where Chatteris Road joins B1096)
☎ 0870 609 5388   🖷 01263 734924

The ruins of this 15th-century gatehouse, together with the 13th-century Lady Chapel, are all that remain of the abbey. Half of the gatehouse was taken away after the Dissolution. Built in ornate late-Gothic style, it has panelled buttresses and friezes.
Times: ✱ Open Apr-Oct, daily 10-5. **Facilities:** ✈ 🥘

WANSFORD   Map 04 TL09
NENE VALLEY RAILWAY
Wansford Station, Stibbington PE8 6LR
➲ (A1 at Stibbington, W of Peterborough, 1m south of the A47 junct)
☎ 01780 784444   🖷 01780 784440
e-mail: nvrorg@aol.com

Visit Britain's International Steam Railway and see steam and diesel engines, carriages and wagons from Europe including the UK. All the sights and sounds of the golden age of steam come alive here. Travelling between Yarwell Junction, Wansford and Peterborough the 7.5 miles of track pass through the heart of the 500-acre Ferry Meadows Country Park. Nene Valley Railway is also the home of 'Thomas'- children's favourite engine.
Times: ✱ Train services operate on Sun from Jan; wknds from Apr-Oct; Wed from May, plus other mid-week services in summer.
Facilities: P 🍺 ♿ (disabled access to trains) toilets for disabled shop 🥘

WATERBEACH   Map 05 TL46
THE FARMLAND MUSEUM AND DENNY ABBEY
Ely Rd CB5 9PQ
➲ (on A10 between Cambridge and Ely)
☎ 01223 860988   🖷 01223 860988
e-mail: f.m.denny@tesco.net   `2 for 1`

Explore two areas of rural life at this fascinating museum.
continued

The Abbey tells the story of those who have lived there, including Benedictine monks, Franciscan nuns, and the mysterious Knights Templar. The farm museum features the craft workshops of a wheelwright, a basketmaker, and a blacksmith. There are also a 1940s farmworker's cottage and a village shop.
Times: Open daily Apr-Oct, noon-5pm **Fee:** ✱ £3.80 (concessions £2.90, ch £1.60) **Facilities:** P 🍺 ♿ toilets for disabled shop

WIMPOLE   Map 05 TL35
WIMPOLE HALL
SG8 0BW
➲ (M11 junct 12, 8m SW of Cambridge off A603)
☎ 01223 206000   🖷 01223 207838
e-mail: wimpolehall@nationaltrust.org.uk

Wimpole Hall is one of the grandest mansions in East Anglia, and has 360 acres of parkland devised and planted by no less than four celebrated landscape designers, Charles Bridgeman, 'Capability' Brown, Sanderson Miller and Humphrey Repton. The house dates back to 1640, but was altered into a large 18th-century mansion with a Georgian façade. The chapel has a trompe l'oeil ceiling.
Times: Open 20 Mar-Oct, Tue-Thu & Sat-Sun, BH Mon's & Good Fri, 1-5; Aug Tue-Sun, BH Mon's 11-5; Nov, Sun only 1-4. **Fee:** £6.40 (ch £3.20). **Facilities:** P 🍺 ✗ licensed ♿ (Braille guide, electric buggies, stairlift, wheelchairs) toilets for disabled shop ✈ (ex park only) 🥘 🍺

WIMPOLE HOME FARM
SG8 0BW
➲ (M11 junct 12 8m SW of Cambridge off A603)
☎ 01223 206000   🖷 01223 207838
e-mail: wimpolehall@nationaltrust.org.uk

When built in 1794, the Home Farm was one of the most advanced agricultural enterprises in the country. The Great Barn, now restored, holds a display of farm machinery and implements of the kind used at Wimpole over the past two centuries. On the farm there are rare breeds of domestic animals. Please ring for details of special events.
Times: Open 20 Mar-31 Oct, Tue-Thu & Sat-Sun, Good Fri & BH Mon's 10.30-5; Jul & Aug, Tue-Sun 10.30-5; Nov-Mar, Sat & Sun 11-4. (open everyday Cambridge Etr hols & Oct/Feb half terms) **Fee:** £5.10 (ch £3.20). NT members £2.70 (ch £1.70). **Facilities:** P 🍺 ✗ licensed ♿ (Braille guide, wheelchairs, electric buggies) toilets for disabled shop ✈ (ex guide dogs) 🥘 🍺

WISBECH   Map 09 TF40
PECKOVER HOUSE & GARDEN
North Brink PE13 1JR
➲ (Leave A47 & take town centre signs, then follow brown signs)
☎ 01945 583463   🖷 01945 583463
e-mail: peckover@nationaltrust.org.uk

Dating from 1722, Peckover House is a beautiful Georgian brick townhouse with a two-acre walled town garden, one of the finest such gardens in Britain and home to over 70 types of rose. The Victorian glasshouses include a fern house, and an orangery with 300-year-old trees that still bear fruit.
Times: Open, House, Garden & Tearoom Apr-Oct, wknds, Wed & BH Mons 12.30-5 (house also open Thu May-Aug). Garden open Apr-Oct, Mon-Tue & Thu 12.30-5. **Fee:** ✱ House & garden £4 (ch £1.50). Garden £2.50 on days when only garden is open.
Facilities: P (400yds) blue badge holders park directly outside 🍺 ✗ licensed ♿ (Batricar available on loan, Large print and Braille guides) toilets for disabled shop ✈ (ex guide dogs) 🥘 🍺

WOODHURST Map 05 TL37

THE RAPTOR FOUNDATION NEW
The Heath, St Ives Rd PE28 3BT
➲ (B1040 to Somersham, follow brown signs, 2m on left)
☎ 01487 741140 📄 01487 841140 **2 for 1**
e-mail: heleowl@aol.com

Permanent home to over 160 birds of which there are 40 different varieties. This is a unique opportunity to meet and learn about birds of prey. Depending on weather and time of year flying demonstrations are held, usually three times a day. There are nearly 60 birds in the flying team, so each display has a different set of birds.

Times: Open all year, daily 10-5. Closed 25-26 Dec & 1 Jan. **Fee:** £3 (ch £2, pen £2.50) **Facilities:** 🅿 💺 ✗ ♿ toilets for disabled shop ✗ 🍴

Above: Oliver Cromwell's House, Ely

The End of World War II.

2005 sees the 60th anniversary of both VE (Victory in Europe) and VJ (Victory over Japan) Days. Local celebrations are planned, as are a number of national events.

CHESHIRE

EVENTS & FESTIVALS

March
12th North of England Head of the River Race, Chester

April
24th The Cheshire Run, Historic Vehicle Road Run, Lymm

May
7th Knutsford Royal May Day
18th-21st Alderley Edge Music Festival, Festival Theatre and various venues
27th-30th Chester Folk Festival, Kelsall

June
17th-19th Folk & Boat Festival, Middlewich
21st-22nd Cheshire County Show, The Showground, Tabley, nr Knutsford
25th World Worm Charming Championship, Willaston Primary School, Willaston

July
16th-17th Halton Show, Spike Island, Halton
20th-24th Royal Horticultural Society Flower Show, Tatton Park, Knutsford
tbc Fringe Festival (drama, dance and music), various venues, Chester
tbc Summer Music Festival, Chester

August
21st Family Fun Day, West Park, Macclesfield
27th Poynton Show, east of A523 north of village centre
tbc Chester Regatta

September
10th-11th Yesteryear Steam Rally, Malpas
24th-25th Vintage Fair Organ & Steam Rally, Victoria Park, Widnes

October
1st-22nd Chester Literature Festival, various venues

November
tbc Festival of Trees, Chester

Above: Peak District National Park

BEESTON Map 07 SJ55

BEESTON CASTLE
Tarporley CW6 9TX
➲ (on minor road off A49 or A41)
☎ 01829 260464
Legend tells of a vast treasure hidden here by Richard II, but the real treasure at Beeston lies in its 4,000 years of history waiting to be discovered. Breathtaking views extend from the Pennines to the mountains of Wales.
Times: Open all year, Apr-Sep, daily 10-6; Oct-Mar, daily 10-4. (Closed 24-26 Dec & 1 Jan). **Facilities:** 🅿 shop ✈ (in certain areas) ✿

CAPESTHORNE Map 07 SJ87

CAPESTHORNE HALL
SK11 9JY
➲ (On A34 between Congleton and Wilmslow)
☎ 01625 861221 📠 01625 861619
e-mail: info@capesthorne.com
Capesthorne has been the home of the Bromley-Davenport family and their ancestors since Domesday times. The present house dates from 1719 and was designed by the Smiths of Warwick. It was subsequently altered by Edward Blore in 1837 and after a disastrous fire in 1861 the whole of the centre portion was rebuilt by Anthony Salvin. Capesthorne contains a great variety of sculptures, paintings and other items including a collection of American Colonial furnishings.
Times: Open Apr-Oct, Wed, Sun & BHs (Closed Xmas & New Year). Park & Garden 12-5.30, Hall 1.30-3.30. **Fee:** Park, Garden & Chapel £4 (ch £2). Park, Gardens, Chapel & Hall £6.50 (ch £3 & pen £5.50). Family ticket £12. Special deal on Wed £10 per car (up to 4 persons). **Facilities:** 🅿 🍽 ✕ licensed ♿ (ramp access to ground floor of hall & gardens) toilets for disabled ✈ (ex guide dogs & in gardens)

CHESTER Map 07 SJ46

CHESHIRE MILITARY MUSEUM
The Castle CH1 2DN
➲ (follow signs to Military Museum from town centre)
☎ 01244 327617 📠 01244 401700
This military museum boasts exhibits from the history of the Cheshire Regiment, Cheshire Yeomanry, 5th Royal Iniskilling Dragoon Guards, and 3rd Carabiniers. Display of the work of George Jones, Victorian battle artist, and an exhibition of life in barracks in the 1950s. Research available by written appointment and donation. There are special events throughtout the year, please phone for details.
Times: Open all year, daily 10-5 (last entry 4.30pm). (Closed 22 Dec-2 Jan). **Fee:** ✱ £2 (concessions £1). **Facilities:** 🅿 (400yds) ♿ all of museum accessible by wheelchairs toilets for disabled shop ✈ (ex guide dogs)

CHESTER CATHEDRAL
Saint Werburgh St CH1 2HU
➲ (opposite the town hall)
☎ 01244 324750 📠 01244 341110
e-mail: office@chestercathedral.org.uk
Founded as a Benedictine monastery in 1092 on the sites of earlier churches, in 1541 it became the cathedral of the newly created Diocese of Chester and is a good example of a medieval monastic complex. Restored in the 19th century, the building contains work by Gilbert Scott, Clayton, Pugin
continued

and Kempe. There are daily services and visitors are welcome to join in. A summer music festival is held in July.
Times: Mon-Sat, 10-7, Sun 12.30-6, Please telephone to check.
Fee: £4 (pen, student & groups 10+ £3, ch £1.50 5-16) £10 family ticket. **Facilities:** 🅿 (200yds) (multi-storey) 🍽 ✕ licensed ♿ (induction loop, tactile model, wide doors) toilets for disabled shop ✈ (ex guide dogs) 🎧

CHESTER VISITOR CENTRE
Vicars Ln CH1 1QX
➲ (opposite St Johns Church Roman Amphitheatre on Vicars Lane.)
☎ 01244 351609 📠 01244 403188 [FREE]
e-mail: tis@chestercc.gov.uk
Among the attractions at this large visitor information centre are guided walks of Chester; brass rubbing; candle-making; World of Names, which explores the history of family and first names; displays on the history of Chester; a café and a gift shop. Chester is the most complete walled city in Britain, and was originally settled by the Romans in the first century AD. The city also played its part in battles with the Vikings, the Norman invasion, and the Civil War.
Times: Open all year, Mon-Sat 10-5, Sun 10-4 **Facilities:** 🅿 (200mtrs) (short stay visitor parking) 🍽 ♿ (ramped access from Vicars Lane) toilets for disabled shop ✈ (ex guide dogs)

CHESTER ZOO
Upton-by-Chester CH2 1LH
➲ (2m N of city centre off A41 & M53 junct 10 southbound, junct 12 all other directions)
☎ 01244 380280 📠 01244 371273
e-mail: marketing@chesterzoo.co.uk

The largest zoological gardens in the UK, with more than 7000 animals of more than 500 species. Catch feeding time on Sealion Beach, visit Islands in Danger with the Komodo Dragons, feel the Spirit of the Jaguar, and the awesome Tsavo-the Black Rhino Experience. Take to the treetops in the Zoofari overhead railway. New in 2004: Bears of the Cloud Forest, miniature monkeys, Red River hogs and the Macaw forest zone.
Times: Open all year, daily from 10. Last admission varies with season from 5.30pm high summer to 3.30pm winter. (Closed 25 Dec).
Fee: £12 (£9.50 concessions). Family ticket £39.50 **Facilities:** 🅿 🍽 ✕ licensed ♿ (electric scooters, audio guide, induction loop, Braille) toilets for disabled shop ✈ (ex guide & sensory dogs) 🎧

DEVA ROMAN EXPERIENCE

Pierpoint Ln, (off Bridge St) CH1 1NL

☎ 01244 343407   📠 01244 347737

Stroll along reconstructed streets experiencing the sights, sounds and smells of Roman Chester. From the streets of Deva (the Roman name for Chester) you return to the present day on an extensive archeological 'dig', where you can discover the substantial Roman, Saxon and medieval remains beneath modern Chester.

Times: Open daily Feb-Nov 9-5, Dec-Jan 10-4 . (Closed 25-26 Dec). **Fee:** ✱ £4.25 (ch £2.50, under 5's free, pen & student £3.75). Family ticket £12. Party. **Facilities:** 🅿 (200yds) ♿ shop ✘ (ex guide dogs)

CHOLMONDELEY   Map 07 SJ55

CHOLMONDELEY CASTLE GARDENS

SY14 8AH

➲ (off A49 Tarporley to Whitchurch road)

☎ 01829 720383   📠 01829 720877

e-mail: pennypritchard@supanet.com

Dominated by a romantic Gothic Castle built in 1801 of local sandstone, the gardens are laid out with fine trees and water gardens, and have been replanted with rhododendrons, azaleas, cornus, and acer. There is also a rose and lavender garden, lakeside and woodland walks, and rare breeds of farm animals.

Times: ✱ Open Apr-Sep, Wed-Thu, Sun & BHs 11.30-5. **Facilities:** 🅿 💻 ♿ (disabled car park, part of garden accessible) toilets for disabled shop garden centre

DISLEY   Map 07 SJ98

LYME PARK

SK12 2NX

➲ (off A6, 6.5m SE of Stockport. 14m NW of Buxton. House & car park 1m from entrance)

☎ 01663 762023   📠 01663 765035

e-mail: lymepark@nationaltrust.org.uk

Home of the Legh family for 600 years and the largest house in Cheshire, Lyme Park featured as Pemberley in the BBC's production of *Pride and Prejudice*. It also featured in Granada's production of the *Forsyte Saga*. Parts of the original Elizabethan house remain, with 18th and 19th century additions. Set in extensive historic gardens with a lake and also a 1,400 acre park, home to red and fallow deer.

Times: Open daily Park: Apr-Oct, 8am-8.30pm; Nov-30 Mar, 8-6. Gardens: 29 Mar-30 Oct, Fri-Tue 11-5, Wed-Thu 1-5; 6 Nov-18 Dec, wknds 12-3. House: 29 Mar-30 Oct, Fri-Tue 1-5 (last admission 4.30),

continued

BH Mon's 11-5. Cage: Apr-Oct, 2nd & 4th wknd of each month 12-4. Paddock Cottage Apr-Oct, 1st & 3rd wknd of each month, 1-4. **Fee:** ✱ Park £3.80 per car (refundable on purchase of house & garden ticket). Garden £2.70 (ch £1.40), House only £4.20 (ch £2.10), House and Garden £5.80 (ch £2.90). Family ticket £12.50. NT members free, ch under 5 free. **Facilities:** 🅿 (charged) 💻 ✘ licensed ♿ (close parking, courtesy minibus from parking) toilets for disabled shop ✘ (ex park on lead) 🐾 ▬

ELLESMERE PORT   Map 07 SJ47

BLUE PLANET AQUARIUM

Cheshire Oaks CH65 9LF

➲ (off M53 junct 10 at Cheshire Oaks. Follow signs for aquarium).

☎ 0151 357 8804   📠 0151 356 7288

e-mail: info@blueplanetaquarium.co.uk

A voyage of discovery on the longest moving walkway in the world. Beneath the waters of the Carribean Reef, see giant rays and menacing sharks pass inches from your face and stroke some favourite fish in the special rock pools or pay a visit to the incredible world of poisonous frogs. Divers hand feed the fish and sharks throughout the day and they can answer questions via state of the art communication systems.

Times: ✱ Open all year, daily from 10. (Closed Xmas). Seasonal variations in closing times, please call to confirm. **Facilities:** 🅿 ✘ licensed ♿ (wheelchair hire, lifts) toilets for disabled shop ✘ (ex guide dogs) ▬

BOAT MUSEUM

South Pier Rd CH65 4FW

➲ (M53 junct 9)

☎ 0151 355 5017   📠 0151 355 4079   **2 for 1**

e-mail: bookings@thewaterwaystrust.org

Occupying a historic dock complex at the junction of the Shropshire Union and Manchester Ship Canals, this museum has the world's largest collection of floating canal craft, from a small weedcutter to a 300-ton coaster. Boat trips are also available. There are indoor exhibitions on canal life and local history, together with period worker's cottages, a blacksmith's forge and working engines.

Times: Open Summer daily 10-5. Winter daily (ex Thu & Fri) 11-4. (Closed 25 & 26 Dec). **Fee:** ✱ £5.50 (ch £3.70, pen & student £4.30). Family ticket £16.50, pen family ticket £14.50. **Facilities:** 🅿 💻 ♿ (tactile map for blind, wheelchairs) toilets for disabled shop ✘ (ex guide dogs) ▬

GAWSWORTH   Map 07 SJ86

GAWSWORTH HALL

SK11 9RN

➲ (2.5m S of Macclesfield on A536)

☎ 01260 223456   📠 01260 223469

e-mail: enquiries@gawsworthhall.com

This fine Tudor black-and-white manor house was the birthplace of Mary Fitton, thought by some to be the 'Dark Lady' of Shakespeare's sonnets. Pictures and armour can be seen in the house, which also has a tilting ground - now thought to be a rare example of an Elizabethan pleasure garden.

Times: Open daily, Etr-Sep. Flower Festival in Dec **Fee:** ✱ £5 (ch £2.50). Party 20+ £4.00 each. **Facilities:** 🅿 💻 ♿ (disabled parking in front of house) toilets for disabled shop ✘ (guide dogs in garden only) ▬

JODRELL BANK VISITOR CENTRE & ARBORETUM
Map 07 SJ77

SK11 9DL

➲ (M6 junct 18, A535 Holmes Chapel to Chelford road)

☎ 01477 571339 🖷 01477 571695

e-mail: visitorcentre@jb.man.ac.uk

`2 for 1`

At Jodrell Bank, a scientific and engineering wonder awaits you - the magnificent Lovell telescope, one of the largest radio telescopes in the world. A pathway leads you 180 degrees around the telescope as it towers above you surveying and exploring the Universe. Then, the visitor can wander along pathways amongst the trees of the extensive arboretum. The Centre is currently under a redevelopment, which will take 2-3 years to complete. The 2-for-1 voucher can only be used for the 3D theatre in the small Visitor Centre.

Times: Open daily Nov-mid Mar 10.30-3, wknds 11-4; mid Mar-end Oct 10.30-5.30 **Fee:** £3 per car, £1 for 3D Show.
Facilities: 🅿 (charged) 🍴♿ (wheelchair loan) toilets for disabled shop 🐕 (ex guide dogs) 🍴

KNUTSFORD
Map 07 SJ77

TABLEY HOUSE
WA16 0HB

➲ (leave M6 junct 19 onto A556 S towards Chester. Entrance for cars off A5033, 2m W of Knutsford)

☎ 01565 750151 🖷 01565 653230

e-mail: enquiries@tableyhouse.co.uk

This finest Palladian House in the North West, holds the first great collection of English pictures ever made, furniture by Chippendale, Gillow and Bullock, and fascinating Leicester family memorabilia. Friendly stewards are available to talk about the Leicester's 700 years at Tabley.

Times: ✱ Open Apr-end Oct, Thu-Sun & BHs, 2-5 (last entry 4.30).
Facilities: 🅿 🍴♿ (phone administrator in advance for help) toilets for disabled shop 🐕 (ex guide dogs)

TATTON PARK
WA16 6QN

➲ (5m from M6 junct 19, or M56 junct 7, Signposted on A556. 4m S of Altrincham. Entrance to Tatton Park on Ashley Road, 1.5m NE of junct A5034 with A50)

☎ 01625 534400 🖷 01625 534403

e-mail: tatton@cheshire.gov.uk

Tatton is one of England's most complete historic estates, with gardens and a 1000-acre country park. The centrepiece is the Georgian mansion, with gardens laid out by Humphry Repton and Sir Joseph Paxton. More recently, a Japanese garden with a Shinto temple was created. The Tudor Old Hall is the original manor house, where a guided tour is available. Special events most weekends include the RHS flower show and open air concerts.

Times: Open mid Mar-early Oct, Tue-Sun & BH 1-5; Gardens & parkland all year Tue-Sun & BH **Fee:** ✱ Mansion, £3 (ch £2), family £8, groups 12+ £2.40 (ch £1.60) Saver tickets available
Facilities: 🅿 (charged) 🍴✗ licensed ♿ (old hall & areas of farm not accessible, Braille guides) toilets for disabled shop garden centre 🐕 (ex in parkland) 🐾 🍴

MACCLESFIELD
Map 07 SJ97

HARE HILL
SK10 4QB

➲ (Between Alderley Edge and Macclesfield(B5087). Turn off onto Prestbury Road, continue 0.75m. Hare Hill entrance on left.)

☎ 01625 584412 🖷 01625 584412

The beautiful parkland at Hare Hill also features a pretty walled garden and pergola. There are woodland paths and ponds, and, in late spring, a brilliant display of rhododendrons and azaleas.

Times: Open Apr-9 May, Wed-Thu, Sat-Sun 10-5. Daily 10-30 May, 10-5. 2 Jun-30 Oct, Wed-Thur, Sat-Sun 10-5. (Last admission 1 hr before closing). **Fee:** ✱ £2.70 (ch £1.25). £1.50 per car (refundable on entry to garden). **Facilities:** 🅿 (charged) ♿ (wheelchair available, Braille guides) 🐕 (ex guide dogs) 🐾

MACCLESFIELD SILK MUSEUM
Heritage Centre, Roe St SK11 6UT

➲ (Turn off A523 & follow brown signs. Museum in town centre)

☎ 01625 613210 🖷 01625 617880

e-mail: silkmuseum@tiscali.co.uk

`2 for 1`

The story of silk in Macclesfield, told through a colourful audio-visual programme, exhibitions, textiles, garments, models and room settings. The Silk Museum is part of the Heritage centre, a restored Georgian Sunday school, which runs a full programme of musical and artistic events throughout the year.

Times: Open all year, Mon-Sat 11-5, Sun & BH Mon 12-5. (Closed 25-26 Dec, 1 Jan & Good Friday). Please ring for winter opening times.
Fee: ✱ £3.20 (concessions £2.20). Family ticket £9 Joint ticket with Paradise Mill £3.75 (concessions £2.75). Family ticket £10.80.
Facilities: 🅿 (50mtrs) 🍴✗ licensed ♿ (ramps, chairlift, audio guides, induction loop) toilets for disabled shop 🐕 (ex guide dogs) 🍴

This symbol indicates attractions which have chosen to participate in our 2-for-1 voucher scheme

`2-for-1`

continued

PARADISE MILL & SILK INDUSTRY MUSEUM
Park Ln SK11 6TJ
➲ (turn off A523 'The Silk Rd' & follow brown signs)
☎ 01625 612045   ▤ 01625 612048
e-mail: silkmuseum@tiscali.co.uk

A working silk mill until 1981, with restored jacquard hand looms in their original location. Knowledgeable guides, many of them former silk mill workers, illustrate the silk production process with the help of demonstrations from weavers. Exhibitions and room settings give an impression of working conditions at the mill during the 1930s. (2-for-1 Voucher applies to museum tour only.)
Times: Open all year, BH Mon & Mon-Sat from 11-5 (Closed Sundays, 25-26 Dec & 1 Jan, Good Fri). Ring for winter opening **Fee:** ✱ £3.75 (ch £2.75), family £10.80 **Facilities:** ℗ (100yds) ♿ (care needed on uneven floors) ✗ (ex guide dogs) ▦

MOULDSWORTH   Map 07 SJ57

MOULDSWORTH MOTOR MUSEUM
Smithy Ln CH3 8AR
➲ (6m E of Chester, off B5393, close to Delamere Forest & Oulton Park Racing Circuit, signposted. Or M56 junct 12 into Frodsham then B5393 into Mouldsworth, follow brown heritage signs in village)
☎ 01928 731781

Housed in an 1937 large Art Deco building close to Delamere Forest, this is a superb collection of over 60 motor cars, motorcycles and bicycles. There is also a massive collection of automobilia - old signs, pumps, tools, mascots and badges, as well as old motoring toys, Dinky cars and pedal cars all complemented by a motoring art gallery, that has posters and advertising material. School parties are encouraged for a guided tour and structured talk. Motoring clubs visit on Sundays. There is also a Harry Potter car for children to sit in.
Times: Open Feb-Nov (Sun only), Etr wknd, early May BH Mon, Spring BH Sun-Mon & Aug BH wknd; Sun, Feb-Nov; also Wed, Jul-Aug, noon-5. **Fee:** ✱ £3 (ch £1.50) **Facilities:** ℗ ♿ (hands on items) shop

NANTWICH   Map 07 SJ65

HACK GREEN SECRET NUCLEAR BUNKER NEW
French Ln, Hack Green CW5 8AP
➲ (From Nantwich take A530 towards Whitchurch, follow the brown signs)
☎ 01270 629219   ▤ 01270 629218
e-mail: coldwar@hackgreen.co.uk

One of the nations most secret defence sites. Declassified in 1993, this underground bunker would have been the centre of regional government had nuclear war broken out. Observe the preparations the government made for nuclear war and step into the lives of people who worked here. View the Minister of State's office, life support, communication centre, decontamination facilities, telephone exchange and much more.
Times: Open 20 Apr-30 Oct, daily 10.30-5.30; Nov, Jan, Feb wknds, 11-4. (closed Dec) **Fee:** £5.30 (ch £3.50, pen £5.50)
Facilities: ℗ ▦ ✗ ♿ (facilities for blind & hard of hearing) toilets for disabled shop ✗ guide dogs ▦

STAPELEY WATER GARDENS
London Rd, Stapeley CW5 7LH
➲ (off M6 junct 16, 1m S of Nantwich on A51)
☎ 01270 623868 & 628628
▤ 01270 624919
e-mail: info@stapeleywg.com

Stapeley Water Gardens consists of three main areas. The Palms Tropical Oasis is a glass pavilion which is home to Koi carp, Giant Amazon water-lilies, sharks, piranhas, parrots and exotic flowers. The two-acre Water Garden Centre houses the National Collection of water-lilies.
Times: Open Summer: Mon-Sat 9-6, BHs 10-6, Sun 10-4, Wed 9-8; Winter: Mon-Sat 9-5, BHs 10-5, Sun 10-4, (Wed 9-8 Angling dept only). The Palms Tropical Oasis open from 10am. **Fee:** The Palms Tropical Oasis £4.45 (ch £2.60, pen £3.95). Family ticket (2 ad & 2 ch) £12.10 (2 ad & 3 ch) £14.30. **Facilities:** ℗ ▦ ✗ licensed ♿ (free wheelchair loan service) toilets for disabled shop garden centre ✗ (ex guide dogs) ▦

NESTON   Map 07 SJ27

LIVERPOOL UNIVERSITY BOTANIC GARDENS (NESS GARDENS)
Ness Gardens CH64 4AY
➲ (off A540 near Ness-on-Wirral, follow signs)
☎ 0151 353 0123   ▤ 0151 353 1004
e-mail: nessgdns@liv.ac.uk

A long association with plant collectors ensures a wide range of plants, providing interest for academics, horticulturists and amateurs alike. There are tree and shrub collections, water and rock gardens, herbaceous borders and glasshouses. A regular programme of lectures, courses and special events take place throughout the year for which tickets must be obtained in advance.
Times: Open all year, Nov-Feb, daily 9.30-4; Mar-Oct, daily 9.30-5. (Closed 25 Dec). **Fee:** ✱ £4.70 (ch free admission when accompanied with an adult, concessions £4.30) **Facilities:** ℗ ▦ ♿ (wheelchair route, induction loop in lecture theatre) toilets for disabled shop garden centre ✗ (ex guide dogs) ▦

NETHER ALDERLEY   Map 07 SJ87

NETHER ALDERLEY MILL
Congleton Rd SK10 4TW
➲ (1.5m S of Alderley Edge on E side of A34)
☎ 01625 584412   ▤ 01625 587555
e-mail: netheralderleymill@nationaltrust.org.uk

Built in the 15th century, this water-mill is much larger inside than it looks. Inside there are tandem overshot water-wheels, original Elizabethan timber work, and Victorian *continued*

machinery which was restored to full working order in the 1960s after being derelict for 30 years. Wheat is ground regularly for demonstration purposes.
Times: Open Apr-Oct, Wed-Fri, Sun & BH Mon 1-5. Parties by arrangement. **Fee:** ✱ £2.20 (ch £1.10) **Facilities:** 🅿 ✖ ♨

NORTHWICH   Map 07 SJ67

ARLEY HALL & GARDENS
CW9 6NA
➲ (5m N of Northwich on B5075. 5m NW of Knutsford A556)
☎ 01565 777353 & 777284 🖷 01565 777465
e-mail: enquiries@arleyestate.zuunet.co.uk
Owned by the same family since medieval times, the present Arley Hall is a good example of the early Victorian Jacobean style and contains fine furniture, plasterwork, panelling and family portraits. The gardens include a walled garden, unique clipped Ilex avenue, herb garden, scented garden and a woodland garden with rhododendrons, azaleas and exotic trees. Special events throughout 2005, please phone for details.
Times: Open Etr-end Sep & wknds in Oct. **Facilities:** 🅿 💺
✖ licensed ♿ (ramps, parking by entrance) toilets for disabled shop garden centre ✖ (ex in gardens on lead) 🍴

SALT MUSEUM
162 London Rd CW9 8AB
➲ (on A533 0.5m S of town centre and 0.5m N of A556. Well signposted from A556)   **2 for 1**
☎ 01606 41331 🖷 01606 350420
e-mail: cheshiremuseums@cheshire.gov.uk
Britain's only Salt Museum tells the fascinating story of Cheshire's oldest industry. Models, reconstructions, original artefacts and audio-visual programmes throw new light on something we all take for granted.
Times: Open Tue-Fri 10-5, wknds 2-5 (Sun 12-5 in Aug). Open BH & Mons in Aug 10-5. **Fee:** £2.40 (ch £1.20, concessions £2) Family ticket (2 adults + 2 ch) £6 **Facilities:** 🅿 💺 ♿ (inductory video with induction loop facilities) toilets for disabled shop garden centre ✖ (ex guide dogs) 🍴

RUNCORN   Map 07 SJ58

NORTON PRIORY MUSEUM & GARDENS
Tudor Rd, Manor Park WA7 1SX
➲ (from M56 junct 11 in direction of Warrington, follow brown signs)
☎ 01928 569895 🖷 01928 589743   **2 for 1**
e-mail: info@nortonpriory.org

Thirty-eight acres of peaceful woodland gardens are the
continued

setting for the medieval priory remains, museum and Walled Garden. Displays tell the story of the transformation of the priory into a Tudor manor house and then into an elegant Georgian mansion. Please telephone for details of special events.
Times: Open all year, Apr-Oct, Mon-Fri 12-5; Sat, Sun & BHs 12-6; Nov-Mar daily 12-4. (Closed 24-26 Dec & 1 Jan). Walled Garden open Apr-Oct, daily 1.30-4.30 **Fee:** ✱ £4.25 (ch 5-16, students, UB40's & pen £2.95). Family ticket (2 adults & 3 ch) £10. **Facilities:** 🅿 💺 ♿ (wheelchairs, large print & audio guides, induction loop) toilets for disabled shop garden centre ✖ (guide dogs only wall garden)

SCHOLAR GREEN   Map 07 SJ85

LITTLE MORETON HALL
Newcastle Rd CW12 4SD
➲ (4m SW of Congleton, on E side of A34)
☎ 01260 272018
e-mail: littlemoretonhall@nationaltrust.org.uk
One of the best examples of half-timbered architecture in England. By 1580 the house was much as it is today, and the long gallery, chapel and the great hall are very impressive. The garden has a knot garden, orchard and herbaceous borders. Ring for details of special events.
Times: Open 20 Mar-Oct, Wed-Sun 11.30-5 or dusk if earlier; 6 Nov-19 Dec, wknds 11.30-4. BH Mon 11.30-5 **Fee:** ✱ £5 (ch £2.50) Family ticket £12, Groups £4.25, Special Openings £7.50
Facilities: 🅿 (charged) ✖ licensed ♿ (wheelchair, electric vehicle, Braille & large print guides) toilets for disabled shop ✖ (ex guide & assistance dogs) ♨ 🍴

STYAL   Map 07 SJ88

QUARRY BANK MILL & STYAL ESTATE
SK9 4LA
➲ (1.5m N of Wilmslow off B5166, 2.5m from M56 junct 5,10m S of Manchester. Heritage signs from A34 and M56)
☎ 01625 527468 🖷 01625 539267
e-mail: quarrybankmill@nationaltrust.org.uk
Quarry Bank Mill is a working water and steam powered cotton mill. Spinning and weaving from throughout the industrial revolution are demonstrated every day and items made from the cloth are sold in the shop. Quarry Bank Mill and its colony village is set in the beautiful Styal Estate beside the River Bollin. Lots of practical 'hands-on' activities plus a new children's playground and railway. The Apprentice House and its Victorian vegetable garden show how life was for the mill apprentices.
Times: Mill open all year, Apr-Sep daily 10.30-5.30 (last admission 4); Oct-19 Mar, daily 10.30-5 (closed Mon in term time). Last admission 3.30. Apprentice House & Garden, Tue-Fri from 11 (2-3.30 term time), Sat-Sun & Aug from 11. Closed Mon (ex school hols). **Fee:** ✱ Mill & Apprentice House £7.30 (ch £4.50). Family ticket £18. Mill only £5.20 (ch £3.50). Family ticket £15. Estate fee £2.50. **Facilities:** 🅿 (charged) 💺 ✖ licensed ♿ (wheelchairs, chairlift, ramps, Braille & large print guide) toilets for disabled shop ✖ (ex in park) ♨ 🍴

> If an attraction name appears in *italics*, details have not been confirmed for 2005.

WIDNES   Map 07 SJ58

CATALYST SCIENCE DISCOVERY CENTRE
Mersey Rd WA8 0DF
➲ (signed from M62 junct 7 and M56 junct 12)
☎ 0151 420 1121 🖷 0151 495 2030
e-mail: info@catalyst.org.uk

Discover a world where science and technology come alive, with over 100 interactive exhibits and hands-on displays which guarantee a fun-filled day out for all the family. Take a trip in an all-glass lift to the Observatory, 100 feet above the River Mersey. A range of special events is planned throughout the year. Please ring for details.

Times: ✱ Open all year, Tue-Fri daily & BH Mon 10-5, wknds 11-5. (Closed Mon ex BH's, 24-26 Dec & 1 Jan). **Facilities:** 🅿 💺 ♿ toilets for disabled shop ✖ (ex guide dogs) 🍴

Above: Mow Cop, Cheshire

Above: St German's Church, St German, Cornwall

CORNWALL & THE ISLES OF SCILLY

EVENTS & FESTIVALS

March
  26th-27th Falmouth Spring Flower Show, Princess Pavilion, Falmouth (provisional)

April
  29th-30th May Day Festival, St Ives
  30th Trevithick Day, Camborne

May
  1st Giant Bolster Festival, St Agnes, lantern procession with giant puppets and bonfire
  1st Padstow 'Obby 'Oss celebrations, Padstow
  6th-15th Daphne du Maurier Festival of Arts & Literature, Fowey
  7th Helston Flora Day (pre-Christian festival)
  14th-15th Re-enactment of the Battle of Stamford Hill, Bude (provisional)

June
  9th-11th Royal Cornwall Show, Wadebridge
  16th-26th Golowan Festival incorporating Mazey Eve (24th), Mazey Day (25th), Penzance
  18th-19th Murdoch Weekend, Redruth

July
  11th Stithians Show, Stithians Showground, Truro (provisional)
  tbs RNAS Culdrose Air Day

August
  5th-6th Falmouth Classics, regatta for traditional boats
  5th-7th Re-enactment of Arthurian Battle of Camlann, Tintagel (provisional)
  7th-13th Falmouth Week, sailing regatta with on shore entertainment
  15th-21st Fowey Royal Regatta
  17th-20th Tall Ships Festival, Falmouth
  25th-27th Dartmouth Regatta
  26th-29th Cornwall Folk Festival, Wadebridge
  27th-29th Morval Vintage Steam Rally, Bray Farm, Nomansland, Looe
  28th-3rd Sep Bude Jazz Festival (provisional)
  29th Newlyn Fish Festival (provisional)

September
  3rd Cornish Gorsedd, venue to be confirmed
  9th-11th Falmouth Festival of Literature & Arts
  10th-11th Lanlivery Vintage Rally & Country Fair

October
  13th-17th Falmouth Oyster Festival
  tbc Lowender Peran, Perranporth

December
  23rd Tom Bawcock's Eve, Mousehole
  tbc City of Lights Lantern Parade, Truro

Above: St Michael's Mount, Marazion

BODMIN   Map 02 SX06

MILITARY MUSEUM
The Keep PL31 1EG
➲ (on B3268, Lostwithiel Rd, beside steam railway station)
☎ 01208 72810 🖷 01208 72810   **2 for 1**
e-mail: dclimus@talk21.com
The history of a famous County Regiment with fascinating displays of uniforms, weapons, medals, badges and much more.
Times: Open all year Mon-Fri, Sun during Jul & Aug 9-5. (Closed Xmas). **Fee:** ✱ £2.50 (ch 50p). Parties 10+ £2 each.
Facilities: 🅿 ♿ shop

PENCARROW
Washaway PL30 3AG
➲ (4m NW of Bodmin, signposted off A389 & B3266)
☎ 01208 841369 🖷 01208 841722
e-mail: pencarrow@aol.com
Still a family home, this Georgian house has a superb collection of pictures, furniture and porcelain. The 50 acres of formal and woodland gardens include a Victorian rockery, a lake, 700 different rhododendrons and an acclaimed conifer collection. There is also a craft centre and a children's play area.
Times: Open House: 28 Mar-28 Oct, Sun-Thu 11-5 (last house tour 4pm). Gardens open daily Mar-28 Oct. **Facilities:** 🅿 💺 ♿ (2 wheelchairs for use, disabled parking at house) toilets for disabled shop 🗙 (ex in gardens)

CALSTOCK   Map 02 SX46

COTEHELE
St Dominick PL12 6TA
➲ (located between Tavistock and Callington. Turn off A390 at St. Anne's Chapel, signposted 2.5m S of junct)
☎ 01579 351346 & 352739 (info)
🖷 01579 351222
e-mail: cotehele@ntrust.org.uk
A 15th-century house that contains tapestries, embroideries, furniture and armour; and outside, a beautiful garden on different levels, including a formal Italian-style garden, medieval stewpond, dovecote, and an 18th-century tower with lovely views. There is a restored water mill in the valley below, and at the Victorian riverside quay an outstation of the National Maritime Museum.
Times: Open 19 Mar-30 Oct daily ex Fri (open Good Fri), 11-5 (11-4.30 Oct). Garden open all year, daily 10.30-dusk. **Fee:** ✱ House, Garden & Mill £7. Garden & Mill £4 (ch 1/2 price, under 5's & NT members free). Family ticket £16 for House, Garden and Mill, £9 for Garden and Mill only. Party £6 each. **Facilities:** 🅿 💺 ✗ licensed ♿ (garden limited access, Braille guide, audio loop, wheelchairs) toilets for disabled shop garden centre 🌺 🍴

CAMELFORD   Map 02 SX18

BRITISH CYCLING MUSEUM
The Old Station PL32 9TZ
➲ (1m N of Camelford on B3266 at junct with B3314)
☎ 01840 212811 🖷 01840 212811
This is the nation's foremost museum of cycling history from 1818 to the present day, with over 400 cycles; more than 1000 cycling medals, fobs and badges; an extensive library;
continued

displays of gas, candle, battery and oil lighting; and many ad posters and enamel signs.
Times: Open all year, Sun-Thu 10-5. **Fee:** ✱ £2.90 (ch 5-17 £1.70).
Facilities: 🅿 ♿ shop 🗙 (ex guide dogs)

CHYSAUSTER ANCIENT   Map 02 SW43
VILLAGE

CHYSAUSTER ANCIENT VILLAGE
TR20 8XA
➲ (2.5m NW of Gulval, off B3311)
☎ 07831 757934
This unique Celtic settlement includes probably the oldest known 'Village Street' in the country. Explore the remains of 2,000-year-old stone houses.
Times: Open Apr-Jun & Sep, daily 10-5; Jul-Aug, daily 10-6; Oct, daily 10-4. **Fee:** ✱ £2 (ch £1, concessions £1.50). Prices & opening times relate to 2004, for further details phone or log onto www.english-heritage.org.uk/visits **Facilities:** 🅿 🗙 ✿

DOBWALLS   Map 02 SX26

DOBWALLS FAMILY ADVENTURE PARK
PL14 6HB
➲ (turn off A38 in centre of Dobwalls and follow the brown signs for approx 0.5m)
☎ 01579 320325 & 321129   **2 for 1**
🖷 01579 321345
e-mail: dobwallsadventurepark@hotmail.com
Plenty to do here, with stretches of miniature American railroads to ride -there are steam and diesel locos, and visitors can take the Rio Grande ride through the forests or the Union Pacific route over the prairies. Also Adventureland - action-packed areas filled with both indoor and outdoor adventure play equipment.
Times: Open Etr to Oct, daily 10.30-5 (10-5.30 high season). Closed some days in Apr, May & Oct **Fee:** ✱ £8.95 (ch under 2 free, pen & disabled £5.50). Family tickets available from £17.50-£52.95. Groups 20+ £5.50 each. **Facilities:** 🅿 💺 ♿ (manual wheelchairs subject to availability) toilets for disabled shop 🍴

FALMOUTH   Map 02 SW83

NATIONAL MARITIME MUSEUM CORNWALL
Discovery Quay TR11 3QY
➲ (follow signs from A39 for park/float ride and museum)
☎ 01326 313388 🖷 01326 317878
e-mail: enquiries@nmmc.co.uk

This exciting award winning Museum has achieved wide
continued

national and international acclaim for its architecture, hands-on displays, world renowned boats and associated video footage, maritime heritage and interactive entertainment. With only one of three natural underwater viewing locations in the world, breathtaking views from the 29m high tower, and a new Olympic exhibition, the National Maritime Museum Cornwall is a great family day out. **Times:** Open daily 10-5 (Closed 25 & 26 Dec). **Fee:** £6.50 (pen, ch, students £4.30). Family ticket (2 adults + 3 ch) £17. **Facilities:** P (charged) ⬛ ✕ licensed ♿ (wheelchairs provided on arrival) toilets for disabled shop ✖ (ex guide dogs) ⬛

See advertisement on opposite page

PENDENNIS CASTLE
TR11 4LP
➲ (1m SE)
☎ 01326 316594 ▤ 01326 319911
Together with St Mawes Castle, Pendennis forms the end of a chain of castles built by Henry VIII along the south coast as protection from attack from France. Journey through 450 years of history and discover the castle's wartime secrets. **Times:** Open all year, Apr-Jun & Sep, daily 10-5; Jul-Aug, daily 10-6 (5 Sat); Oct-Mar, daily 10-4. (Closed 24-26 Dec & 1 Jan). Note: Apr-Oct, Sat access may be by guided tour only, closing at 4pm. Telephone to confirm. **Fee:** ✱ £4.50 (ch £2.30, concessions £3.40). Family £11.30. Prices & opening times relate to 2004, for further details phone or log onto www.english-heritage.org.uk/visits **Facilities:** P ⬛ ♿ shop ✖ (ex on lead in certain areas) ▦

FOWEY   Map 02 SX15
ST CATHERINE'S CASTLE
➲ (0.75m SW of Fowey along footpath off A3082)
A small sixteenth-century fort built by Henry VIII to defend Fowey Harbour. It has two storeys with gun ports at ground level. **Times:** Open all year, any reasonable time. **Facilities:** P (0.5m) ✖ (ex dogs on leads) ▦

GODOLPHIN CROSS   Map 02 SW63
GODOLPHIN HOUSE
TR13 9RE
➲ (situated on a minor road from Godolphin Cross to Townsend)
☎ 01736 763194 ▤ 01736 763194
e-mail: godo@euphony.net

A romantic Tudor and Stuart mansion, begun in 1475 and considerably extended over the centuries. The Godolphin family's taste is evident throughout the mansion, and of particular note are examples of 16th and 17th-century English oak furniture and Wootton's 1731 painting, *Godolphin Arabian*, one of the three Arab stallion ancestors of all British bloodstock. The gardens are Tudor, with some
continued

areas even earlier. Major repair programme on the mansion funded by English Heritage.
Times: ✱ National Trust Estate open all year. House open May-Sep, Thu & Fri 11-5 & Sun 2-5 (also Tue 11-5 in Jul & Aug). Open BH Mon 11-5. Phone for Etr opening details. **Facilities:** P ⬛ ✕ ♿ (telephone prior to visit, lift to first floor) toilets for disabled shop garden centre ✖ (ex guide dogs) ⬛

GOONHAVERN   Map 02 SW75
WORLD IN MINIATURE
Bodmin Rd TR4 9QE
➲ (turn off A30 at Boxheater junct onto B3285)
☎ 0870 458 4433 ▤ 01872 572829
e-mail: info@worldinminiature.co.uk
There are six major attractions for the price of one at this theme park. Visitors can stroll amongst famous landmarks such as the Taj Mahal and the Statue of Liberty, all in miniature scale, set in spectacular gardens. Then there is Tombstone, a wild-west town complete with saloon, bank, shops, livery stable and jail. The Adventure Dome is the original super cinema 180 direct from the USA, which shows two exciting films. The 12-acre gardens are beautifully landscaped with over 70,000 plants and shrubs. See Jurassic Adventure World, Super X Simulator and children's fairground rides.
Times: ✱ Open Etr-Oct, daily from 10am. **Facilities:** P ⬛ ♿ toilets for disabled shop garden centre ⬛

GORRAN   Map 02 SW94
CAERHAYS CASTLE GARDENS
PL26 6LY
➲ (off A390 onto B3287. Right at T-junct, left at next T-junct, next left and continue to Porthluney Beach car park)
☎ 01872 501144 & 501310 ▤ 01872 501870
e-mail: estateoffice@caerhays.co.uk
For centuries this magnolia filled garden was a deer park, and it was not until the late 19th century that John Charles Williams ("JCW") inherited Caerhays and not until the early 20th century that new and exotic plants were introduced here. Now the gardens are a blaze of plants from Chile, China, New Zealand, the Himalayas, and many other distant lands. Magnolias, Rhododendrons, Camellia, and Japonicas can all be seen on marked walks, and the house can be visited in small groups during the spring.
Times: Open 14 Feb-5 Jun, daily 10-5.30 (last admission 4.30). House open 14 Mar-May. **Fee:** £5.50 house or garden; £9.50 combined ticket **Facilities:** P ⬛ ♿ toilets for disabled garden centre ⬛

GWEEK   Map 02 SW72
NATIONAL SEAL SANCTUARY
TR12 6UG
➲ (pass RNAS Culdrose & take A3293 & then B3291 to Gweek, the sanctuary is signposted from village)
☎ 01326 221361 & 221874   [2 for 1]
▤ 01326 221210
e-mail: slcgweek@merlin-entertainments.com
Britain's largest seal rescue facility - offering a unique opportunity to learn more about these beautiful creatures. Every year it rescues, rehabilitates and releases around 30 sick or abandoned seal pups.
Times: Open all year, daily from 10am (Closed 25 Dec). **Fee:** Prices not confirmed for 2005 **Facilities:** P ⬛ ♿ toilets for disabled shop ⬛

HELSTON   Map 02 SW62

THE FLAMBARDS EXPERIENCE

Culdrose Manor TR13 0QA

➲ (0.5m SE of Helston on A3083, Lizard road)

☎ 01326 573404 📠 01326 573344   **2 for 1**

e-mail: info@flambards.co.uk

Three award-winning, all-weather attractions can be visited
on one site here. Flambards Victorian Village is a recreation
of streets, shops and houses from 1830-1910. Britain in the
Blitz is a life-size wartime street featuring shops, a pub and a
living room with Morrison shelter. The Science Centre is a
science playground that brings physics alive for the whole
family. Along with the Thunderbolt and Extreme Force, we
also offer the Hornet Rollercoaster, the Family Log Flume,
Go-Kart circuit, and rides and play areas for the very young.
The Wildlife Experience show features lizards, snakes, large
spiders and birds of prey.

Times: Winter opening: Nov-22 Mar, 11-4; closed Thu/Fri & 23
Dec-10 Jan. Open daily. 23 Mar-Oct **Fee:** ✱ £9.95 (ch 5-14 £8.45 over
55's £5.75). Family of 3 £27.31, of 4 £36, of 5 £44 of 6 £51.50
Facilities: 🅿 📖 ♿ (95% accessible, free loan of wheelchairs, route
guides) toilets for disabled shop garden centre ✖ (ex guide dogs) 🍴

GOONHILLY SATELLITE EARTH STATION
EXPERIENCE NEW

Goonhilly Downs TR12 6LQ

➲ (7m from Helston on the B3293 Helston to St
Keverne road)

☎ 0800 679593 📠 01326 221438

e-mail: goonhilly.visitorscentre@bt.com

Making a dramatic impression on the Lizard Peninsula
landscape, this is the largest earth station in the world, with
over 60 dishes. Opened in 1962 with only one dish,
Goonhilly now handles millions of e-mails, phone calls, and
TV broadcasts. In the fully interactive visitors centre, explore
the world of communications, experience tomorrow's
technology today, and see your own animated 3D virtual
head.

Times: Open all year, daily 10-6 (last entry 5pm). After 1 Nov please
call 0800 679593 for opening details. **Fee:** ✱ £5 (ch5-16 £3.50,
under 4's free; pen £4) **Facilities:** 🅿 📖 ✖ licensed ♿ toilets for
disabled shop ✖ (ex guide dogs) 🍴

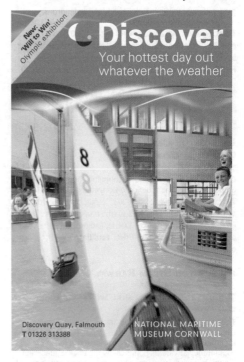
TREVARNO ESTATE GARDEN & MUSEUM OF
GARDENING

Trevarno Manor, Crowntown TR13 0RU

➲ (E of Crowntown. Leave Helston on the
Penzance road signed B3302)

☎ 01326 574274 📠 01326 574282

e-mail: enquiry@trevarnoestate.fsnet.co.uk

Victorian and Georgian gardens with the splendid fountain
garden conservatory, unique range of crafts and the National
Museum of Gardening. In the tranquil gardens and grounds,
follow the progress of restoration projects, visit craft areas
including handmade soap workshop, explore Britain's largest
and most comprehensive collection of antique tools,
implements, memorabilia and ephemera, creatively
displayed to illustrate how gardens and gardening influences
most peoples lives.

Times: ✱ Open daily 10.30-5 **Facilities:** 🅿 📖 ♿ limited access,
parking, disabled route toilets for disabled shop 🍴

LANHYDROCK   Map 02 SX06

LANHYDROCK

PL30 5AD

➲ (2.5m SE of Bodmin, signposted from A30, A38
& B3268)

☎ 01208 265950 📠 01208 265959

e-mail: lanhydrock@nationaltrust.org.uk

Part-Jacobean, part-Victorian building that gives a vivid
picture of life in Victorian times. The 'below stairs' sections
have a huge kitchen, larders, dairy, bakehouse, cellars, and
servants' quarters. The long gallery has a moulded ceiling
showing Old Testament scenes, and overlooks the formal
gardens with their clipped yews and bronze urns. The higher
continued

garden, famed for its magnolias and rhododendrons, climbs the hillside behind the house.
Times: Open Apr-Oct: House daily (ex Mon), 11-5.30 (11-5 in Oct), open BH Mon's. Gardens daily from mid Feb, (last admission half hour before closing). Winter: Gardens, Nov-Feb during daylight hours.
Fee: ✱ House & Grounds £7.50 (ch £3.75). Grounds £4.20 (ch £2.10). Family ticket £18.50 Party £6.50 each.(ch £3.25 each) **Facilities:** ℙ 🕭 ✕ licensed ♿ (lift, self drive buggy (pre-book), wheelchairs) toilets for disabled shop garden centre 🛪 (ex on lead in park) 🐾 🍴

LAUNCESTON   Map 02 SX38

LAUNCESTON CASTLE
Castle Lodge PL15 7DR
☎ 01566 772365
Commanding the town and surrounding countryside, this castle controlled the route onto Cornwall.
Times: Open Apr-Jun & Sep, daily 10-5; Jul-Aug, daily 10-6; Oct, daily 10-4. Closed Nov-Mar. **Fee:** ✱ £2.30 (ch £1.20, concessions £1.70). Prices & opening times relate to 2004, for further details phone or log onto www.english-heritage.org.uk/visits **Facilities:** ♿ (outer bailey only) shop 🛪 🎪

LAUNCESTON STEAM RAILWAY   [2 for 1]
St Thomas Rd PL15 8DA
➲ (turn off A30 Launceston, well signposted)
☎ 01566 775665
The Launceston Steam Railway links the historic town of Launceston with the hamlet of New Mills. Tickets are valid for unlimited travel on the day of issue and you can break your journey at various points along the track. Launceston Station houses railway workshops, a transport museum, gift shop and book shop.
Times: Open Good Fri for 8 days inclusive; Spring, BH Sun for 6 days; Jun, Sun-Wed; Jul-Sep, daily ex Sat; Oct half-term week. **Fee:** ✱ £6.50 (ch £4.25, pen £5). Family ticket £20 (2 adults & up to 4 ch). Dogs 50p.
Facilities: ℙ 🕭 ♿ shop

THE TAMAR OTTER SANCTUARY
North Petherwin PL15 8GW
➲ (5m NW off B3254 Bude road)
☎ 01566 785646   🖷 01986 892461
The Tamar Otter Sanctuary has a breeding programme for the British otter and has to date bred and released over 100 otters into the wild. Visitors to the sanctuary can see otters in large natural enclosures, as well as fallow and muntjac deer, waterfowl, and wallabies.
Times: Open Apr-Oct, daily 10.30-6 **Fee:** ✱ £6 (ch £3.50)
Facilities: ℙ 🕭 ♿ shop 🛪 (ex guide dogs)

LOOE   Map 02 SX25

MONKEY SANCTUARY
St Martins PL13 1NZ
➲ (signposted on B3253 at No Man's Land between East Looe & Hessenford)
☎ 01503 262532   🖷 01503 262532
e-mail: info@monkeysanctuary.org
Visitors can see a colony of Amazonian woolly monkeys in extensive indoor and outdoor territory. There are also conservation gardens, children's play area, activity room, a display room and vegetarian cafe. In addition a bat cave is on site where visitors can watch a colony of rare 'horseshoe' bats.
Times: Open Sun-Thu 11-4.30 from the Sun before Etr-end Sep. Also open Autumn Half Term. **Fee:** ✱ £5 (under 5's free, ch £3 & concession £4). Family ticket (2 ad + 2 ch) £15. **Facilities:** ℙ 🕭 ♿ toilets for disabled shop 🛪 🍴

MARAZION   Map 02 SW53

ST MICHAEL'S MOUNT
TR17 0HT
➲ (access is by Causeway on foot at low tide. 0.5m S of A394 at Marazion)
☎ 01736 710507 & 710265   🖷 01736 711544
e-mail: godolphin@manor-office.co.uk
Reached on foot by causeway at low tide, or by ferry at high tide in the summer only, St Michael's Mount rises dramatically from the sea, a medieval castle to which a magnificent east wing was added in the 1870s. It is home to Lord St Leven, whose ancestor John St Aubyn acquired it in the 17th century.
Times: ✱ Open 31 Mar-Oct, Mon-Fri 10.30-5.30. Last admission 4.45; Nov-Mar, telephone for details. The Castle and grounds are open most weekends during the summer season. Special charity open days, NT members are also asked to pay. Group bookings 01736 710507.
Facilities: ℙ (on mainland) 🕭 ✕ licensed (Braille guide) shop 🛪 (ex guide dogs) 🐾 🍴

MAWNAN SMITH   Map 02 SW72

GLENDURGAN
TR11 5JZ
➲ (4m SW of Falmouth. 0.5m SW of Mawnan Smith on road to Helford Passage)
☎ 01872 862090   🖷 01872 865808
e-mail: glendurgan@nationaltrust.org.uk
This delightful garden, set in a valley above the River Helford, was started by Alfred Fox in 1820. The informal landscape contains trees and shrubs from all over the world, including the Japanese loquat and tree ferns from New Zealand. There is a laurel maze, and a Giant's Stride which is popular with children. The house is not open.
Times: Open mid Feb-Oct, Tue-Sat & BH Mon. Last admission 4.30 (Closed Good Fri). **Fee:** ✱ £4.20 (ch £2.10). Family ticket £10.50
Facilities: ℙ 🕭 ♿ (Braille guide, limited access to gardens/ground floor) toilets for disabled shop garden centre 🛪 (ex guide dogs) 🐾 🍴

TREBAH GARDEN
TR11 5JZ
➲ (signposted at Treliever Cross rdbt at junct of A39/A394 & follow brown tourist signs)
☎ 01326 250448   🖷 01326 250781
e-mail: mail@trebah-garden.co.uk

A 25-acre wooded ravine garden, descending 200 feet from the 18th-century house down to a private cove on the Helford River. The cascading Water Garden has pools of

continued

giant koi and exotic water plants, winding through two acres of blue and white hydrangeas to the beach. There are glades of sub-tropical tree ferns and palms, as well as rhododendrons and many other trees and shrubs. The beach is open to visitors and there are children's trails and activities all year.

Times: Open daily 10.30-5 (last admission). **Fee:** Mar-Oct £5.50 (ch & disabled £3, pen £5, ch under 5 free); Nov-Feb 1/2 price
Facilities: 🅿 ⬛ ✕ licensed ⟐ (2 powered wheelchairs & wheelchair route) toilets for disabled shop garden centre ⬛

NEWQUAY   Map 02 SW86

BLUE REEF AQUARIUM
Towan Promenade TR7 1DU
➲ (from A30 follow signs to Newquay, follow Blue Reef Aquarium signs to car park in town centre)
☎ 01637 878134 🖷 01637 872578   **2 for 1**
e-mail: info@bluereefaquarium.co.uk
Take the ultimate undersea safari at the Blue Reef Aquarium. Discover Cornish marine life from native sharks and rays to the incredibly intelligent and playful octopus. From here journey through warmer waters to watch the magical seahorses, unusual shape shifting, jet-propelled cuttlefish and the vibrant, swaying tentacles of living sponges and anemones. Continue your safari through the underwater tunnel below a tropical sea. Here you will encounter the activities of a coral reef alive with shoals of brightly coloured fish and the graceful, black tip reef sharks which glide silently overhead. Daily talks and regular feeding demonstrations bring the experience to life.

Times: Open all year, daily 10-5. (Closed 25 Dec). Open until 6 during summer holidays. **Fee:** £5.95 (ch £3.95, pen & student £4.95). Family ticket £17.95 (2 ad & up to 3 ch) **Facilities:** 🅿 (5mins walk) (prior contact for disabled parking) ⬛ ⟐ (lifts, wheelchair, ramps) toilets for disabled shop ✕ (guide dogs & service dogs) ⬛

DAIRY LAND FARM WORLD
Summercourt TR8 5AA
➲ (Signposted from A30 at exit for Mitchell/Summercourt)
☎ 01872 510246 🖷 01872 510349   **2 for 1**
e-mail: info@dairylandfarmworld.co.uk
Visitors can watch while the cows are milked to music on a spectacular merry-go-round milking machine. The life of a Victorian farmer and his neighbours is explored in the Heritage Centre, and a Farm Nature Trail features informative displays along pleasant walks. Children will have fun getting to know the farm animals in the Farm Park. They will also enjoy the playground, assault course and indoor play areas.

Times: Open daily, late Mar-Oct 10.30-5. (Bull pen additional winter openings weekends & school hols, telephone for more information) **Fee:** £6.95 (ch £5.95, under 3s free, pen £4.95). Family Supersaver £22 (2 adults & up to 3 ch). Telephone for info about parties & groups. **Facilities:** 🅿 ⬛ ⟐ (wheelchairs for loan; disabled viewing gallery - milking) toilets for disabled shop ✕ ⬛

If an attraction name appears in *italics*, details have not been confirmed for 2005.

NEWQUAY ZOO
Trenance Gardens TR7 2LZ
➲ (off A3075 and follow signs to Zoo)
☎ 01637 873342 🖷 01637 851318
e-mail: info@newquayzoo.org.uk
There's always something new at Newquay Zoo. Explore the rainforest exhibit in the tropical house where you'll discover a world of exotic animals. Water cascades down the ancient temple walls to pools filled with tropical fish. Spot the iguanas, sloths and flying foxbats, and explore the mini-beasts room complete with Arrow Poison Frog enclosure. Among the sub-tropical lakeside gardens live hundreds of animals from around the world ranging from small monkeys to shy red pandas. Look out for meerkats on sentry duty, penguins splashing in their pool, or glimpse the endangered lemurs and fossa. The zoo gardens feature a Tarzan trail, children's play area, dragon maze, as well as picnic areas, snack bar and gift shop.

Times: Open Apr-Oct, daily 9.30-6; Nov-Mar 10-dusk. (Closed 25 Dec) **Fee:** ✱ £6.95 (ch 3+ £4.45, pen £5.45, ch under 3 free). Family ticket £19.95. Check website for more details **Facilities:** 🅿 (charged) ⬛ ✕ ⟐ (85% free wheelchairs, guided tours & sensory sculptures) toilets for disabled shop ✕ (ex guide dogs) ⬛

PADSTOW   Map 02 SW97

PRIDEAUX PLACE
PL28 8RP
➲ (off B3276 Padstow to Newquay road. Follow brown heritage signs)
☎ 01841 532411 🖷 01841 532945
e-mail: office@prideauxplace.fsnet.co.uk
Built by Sir Nicholas Prideaux in 1592, this impressive country house has been inhabited by his family for fourteen generations, and is still in use by them today. Visitors can see relics of the English Civil War, including a pardon from Charles II and a double-sided brooch of Cromwell and the King, as well as fascinating rooms filled with antique furniture, paintings and a 16th-century ceiling depicting the biblical story of Susannah. The house was used as a location for Trevor Nunn's film version of *Twelfth Night* and has been used in the making of many *Rosamunde Pilcher* films and television productions.

Times: Open 11-15 Apr; 16 May-7 Oct, Sun-Thu 1.30-4 (house tours). Grounds 12.30-5. Open all year to pre-booked groups (15+) **Fee:** ✱ House & grounds £6 (ch £2), Grounds only £2 (ch £1) **Facilities:** 🅿 ⬛ ⟐ shop ✕ (ex on leads in grounds) ⬛

PENDEEN   Map 02 SW33

GEEVOR TIN MINES NEW
TR19 7EW
➲ (Geevor is beside the B3306 Lands End to St Ives coast road. From Penzance take A3071 towards St Just, then the B3318 towards Pendeen. From St Ives follow B3306 to Pendeen)
☎ 01736 788662 🖷 01736 786059   **2 for 1**
e-mail: info@geevor.com
A preserved tin mine and museum provide an insight into the methods and equipment used in the industry that was once so important in the area. The Geevor Tin Mine only actually stopped operation in 1990. Guided tours let visitors see the tin treatment plant, and a video illustrates the techniques employed. The underground tour is well worth the trip.

Times: Open daily except Sat 9-5, closes at 4pm Nov-Mar. Closed 21-27 Dec & 1-2 Jan. **Fee:** ✱ £6.50 (ch & students £4, pen £6) Family £17.50 **Facilities:** 🅿 ⬛ ✕ ⟐ wheelchair, lift, ramps toilets for disabled shop (not underground) ⬛

PENTEWAN   Map 02 SX04

THE LOST GARDENS OF HELIGAN
PL26 6EN
➲ (signposted from A390 & B3273)
☎ 01726 845100 🖹 01726 845101
e-mail: info@heligan.com

Heligan, seat of the Tremayne family for more than 400 years, is one of the most mysterious estates in England. At the end of the 19th-century its thousand acres were at their zenith, but only a few years after the Great War, bramble and ivy were already drawing a green veil over this sleeping beauty. Today the garden offers 200 acres for exploration, which include productive gardens, pleasure grounds, sustainably-managed farmland, wetlands, and ancient woodlands.
Times: Open daily 10-6 (last admission 4.30pm): winter 10-dusk. Closed 24-25 Dec. **Fee:** ✸ £7.50. Please telephone to confirm concessions prices. **Facilities:** 🅿 💺 ✗ licensed ♿ (free loan of wheelchairs and trained access advisors) toilets for disabled shop garden centre 🐾 allowed Nov-Feb only ◀

PENZANCE   Map 02 SW43

TRENGWAINTON GARDEN
TR20 8RZ
➲ (2m NW Penzance, 0.5m W of Heamoor off Penzance - Morvah road (B3312), 0.5m off St Just road, A3071)
☎ 01736 363148 🖹 01736 367762
e-mail: trengwainton@nationaltrust.org.uk

Rhododendrons and magnolias grow in profusion at Trengwainton, along with many plants that are difficult to grow in Britain. The mild climate means that seed collected on expeditions to the Far East and southern hemisphere have flourished to produce a magnificent display in this 20th-century garden.
Times: Open 16 Feb-Oct, daily 10-5.30 (closed Fri-Sat) but open Good Fri 10-5.30 (Feb, Mar & Oct 10-5). Last admission 1 hr before closing.
Fee: ✸ £4.40. Family ticket £11. Party £3.80 each **Facilities:** 🅿 💺 ♿ (Braille guide, special route, 2 wheelchairs) toilets for disabled shop garden centre 🐾 ◀

POOL   Map 02 SW64

CORNISH MINES & ENGINES
TR14 7AW
➲ (2m W of Redruth on A3047, signposted from A30, Pool exit)
☎ 01209 315027 & 210900 🖹 01209 315027
e-mail: info@trevithicktrust.com

Impressive relics of the tin mining industry, these great beam engines were used for pumping water from 2000ft down and for lifting men and ore from the workings below ground. The mine at East Pool has been converted into the Cornwall Industrial Heritage Centre which includes audio visual theatre giving background to all aspects of Cornwall's industrial heritage.
Times: ✸ Open 31 Mar-2 Nov, daily (ex Sat) 11-5; Aug open daily 11-5. Nov-Mar by arrangement. **Facilities:** 🅿 ♿ (lift to all levels, parking by arrangement, Braille guide) toilets for disabled shop 🐾 (ex guide dogs) 🐾 ◀

PROBUS   Map 02 SW84

TREWITHEN GARDENS
Grampound Rd TR2 4DD
➲ (on A390 between Truro & St Austell) **2 for 1**
☎ 01726 883647 🖹 01726 882301
e-mail: gardens@trewithen-estate.demon.co.uk

The Hawkins family has lived in this charming, intimate country house since it was built in 1720. The internationally renowned landscaped garden covers some 30 acres and grows camellias, magnolias and rhododendrons as well as many rare trees and shrubs seldom seen elsewhere. The nurseries are open all year.
Times: Open Mar-Sep, Mon-Sat 10-4.30; daily Mar-May. **Fee:** ✸ £4.25 (pen £4) group 20+ £4 **Facilities:** 🅿 💺 ♿ toilets for disabled garden centre 🐾 (ex on lead) ◀

RESTORMEL   Map 02 SX16

RESTORMEL CASTLE
PL22 0BD
➲ (1.5m N of Lostwithiel off A390)
☎ 01208 872687

High on a moated mound, this splendid Norman stronghold offers spectacular views across the Cornish countryside.
Times: Open Apr-Jun & Sep, daily 10-6; Jul-Aug, daily 10-6; Oct, daily 10-4. **Fee:** ✸ £2.20 (ch £1.10, concessions £1.70). Prices & opening times relate to 2004, for further details phone or log onto www.english-heritage.org.uk/visits **Facilities:** 🅿 ♿ shop 🐾 (ex dogs on leads) ♨

ST AUSTELL   Map 02 SX05

CHARLESTOWN SHIPWRECK & HERITAGE CENTRE
Quay Rd, Charlestown PL25 3NJ
➲ (signposted off the A390 from St. Austell close to the Eden Project)
☎ 01726 69897 🖹 01726 69897
e-mail: admin@shipwreckcharlestown.com

Charlestown is a small and unspoilt village with a unique sea-lock, china-clay port, purpose built in the 18th century. The Shipwreck and Heritage Centre houses the largest display of shipwreck artefacts in the UK, along with local heritage and diving exhibits, and also a Titanic display.
Times: Open Mar-Oct, daily 10-5 (later in high season). Last admission 1 hour before closing. **Fee:** £4.95 (ch under 10 free if accompanied by paying adult, ch under 16 £2.50, concessions £3.45).
Facilities: 🅿 (charged) 💺 ✗ licensed ♿ (ramps in place) toilets for disabled shop ◀

THE CHINA CLAY MUSEUM - WHEAL MARTYN
Carthew PL26 8XG
➲ (2m N on B3274)
☎ 01726 850362 🖹 01726 850362
e-mail: info@wheal-martyn.com

This museum tells the story of Cornwall's most important present-day industry: china clay production. The open-air site includes a complete 19th-century clayworks, with huge granite-walled settling tanks, working water-wheels and a wooden slurry pump. There is a short audio-visual programme, nature trails and a children's adventure trail.
Times: ✸ Open Apr-Oct, 10-6 (last admission 5pm) phone for winter opening times. **Facilities:** 🅿 💺 ♿ shop ◀

EDEN PROJECT

Bodelva PL24 2SG

➲ (overlooking St Austell Bay signposted from A390/A30/A391)

☎ 01726 811911 ▤ 01726 811912

e-mail: information@edenproject.com

An unforgettable experience in a breathtaking location, the Eden Project is a gateway into the fascinating world of plants and human society. Space age technology meets the lost world in the biggest greenhouse ever built. Located in a 50 metre deep crater the size of 30 football pitches are two gigantic geodesic conservatories: the Humid Tropics Biome and the Warm Temperate Biome. This is a startling and unique day out.

Times: ✱ Open daily Mar-Oct 10-6 (last admission 5pm), Nov-Feb 10-4.30 (last admission 3pm). Closed 24-25 Dec. **Facilities:** 🅿 💻 ✗ licensed ♿ (wheelchairs, car shuttle to visitor centre/biomes) toilets for disabled shop garden centre 🗙 (ex guide dogs) ▰

ST IVES   Map 02 SW54

(Park your car at Lelant Station and take advantage of the park and ride service. The fee includes parking and journeys on the train between Lelant and St Ives during the day).

BARBARA HEPWORTH MUSEUM & SCULPTURE GARDEN

Barnoon Hill TR26 1AD

➲ (M5 to Exeter, A30 onto Penzance & St Ives, in town centre)

☎ 01736 796226 ▤ 01736 794480

e-mail: tatestives@tate.org.uk

Dame Barbara Hepworth lived here from 1949 until her death in 1975, and the house is now a museum displaying sculptures and drawings, photographs, documents and other memorabilia. Visitors can also visit her workshops, which house a selection of tools and some unfinished carvings. The garden contains a number of monumental sculptures, situated amongst semi-tropical plants.

Times: Open Mar-Oct, daily 10-5.30; Nov-Feb, Tue-Sun 10-4.30. **Fee:** ✱ £4.50. (concessions £2.25). **Facilities:** 🅿 (880yds) ♿ (accessible with assistance, please call) toilets for disabled shop 🗙 (guide dogs)

TATE ST IVES

Porthmeor Beach TR26 1TG

➲ (M5 to Exeter, then A30 onto Penzance & St Ives. Located on Porthmeor Beach)

☎ 01736 796226 ▤ 01736 794480

e-mail: tatestivesinfo@tate.org.uk

Tate St Ives offers a unique introduction to modern art, where many works can be seen in the surroundings and atmosphere, which inspired them. The gallery presents changing displays from the Tate Collection, focusing on the post-war modern movement St Ives is so famous for. Artists represented at the gallery include Alfred Wallis, Ben Nicholson, Barbara Hepworth, Naum Gabo, Peter Lanyon, Bryan Wynter, Roger Hilton, John Wells, Patrick Heron and Terry Frost. There is also a changing programme of temporary exhibitions by major contemporary artists.

Times: Open Mar-Oct, daily 10-5.30; Nov-Feb, Tue-Sun 10-4.30. **Fee:** ✱ £5.50 (concessions £2.50). **Facilities:** 🅿 (800yds) 💻 ✗ licensed ♿ (access ramp, lift, wheelchairs) toilets for disabled shop 🗙 (ex guide dogs) ▰

ST MARY'S (Isles of Scilly)   Map 02

ISLES OF SCILLY MUSEUM NEW

Church St, Hugh Town TR21 0LP

➲ (Located in the centre of Hugh Town)

☎ 01720 422337

e-mail: info@iosmuseum.org

A small, independent museum which seeks to safeguard and promote the islands' history and traditions, and reflect every aspect of island life. 2005 will see an exhibition of material from the HMS Colossus, a 72-gun frigate that sank close to the Scilly Isles in 1798.

Times: Etr-Sep, Mon-Sat 10-4.30. Oct-Etr, Mon-Sat 10-12 **Fee:** £2.50 (ch 50p sen & students £1.50) **Facilities:** 💻 ♿

ST MAWES   Map 02 SW83

ST MAWES CASTLE

TR2 3AA

➲ (on A3078)

☎ 01326 270526

Wonderful location alongside the pretty fishing village of St Mawes, this castle is Henry VIII's most picturesque fort.

Times: Open all year, Apr-Jun, daily 10-5; Jul-Aug, daily 10-6; Sep, daily 10-5 (Sat 4); Oct, daily 10-4; Nov-Mar, Fri-Mon 10-4. (Closed between 24-26 Dec & 1 Jan). **Fee:** ✱ £3.20 (ch £1.60, concessions £2.40). Prices & opening times relate to 2004, for further details phone or log onto www.english-heritage.org.uk/visits **Facilities:** 🅿 ♿ shop 🗙 (ex dogs on leads in grounds) ▦

SANCREED   Map 02 SW42

CARN EUNY ANCIENT VILLAGE

➲ (1.25m SW of Sancreed, off A30)

The remains of an Iron-Age settlement. Surviving features include the foundations of stone huts and an intriguing curved underground passage or 'fogou'.

Times: Open any reasonable time. **Facilities:** 🅿 (600mtrs) ▦

TINTAGEL   Map 02 SX08

TINTAGEL CASTLE

PL34 0HE

➲ (on Tintagel Head, 0.5m along uneven track from Tintagel, no vehicles)

☎ 01840 770328 ▤ 01840 770328

Overlooking the wild Cornish coast, Tintagel is one of the most spectacular spots in the country associated with King Arthur and Merlin. Recent excavations revealed Dark Age connections between Spain and Cornwall, alongside the discovery of 'Arthnou' stone suggesting that this was a royal place for the Dark Age rulers of Cornwall.

Times: Open all year, Apr-Sep, daily 10-6; Oct, daily 10-5; Nov-Mar, daily 10-4. (Closed 24-26 Dec & 1 Jan). **Fee:** ✱ £3.70 (ch £1.90, concessions £2.80). Prices & opening times relate to 2004, for further details phone or log onto www.english-heritage.org.uk/visits **Facilities:** 🅿 (in village) shop 🗙 (ex dogs on leads) ▦

Directions are provided by the attractions.

TORPOINT Map 02 SX45

ANTONY HOUSE
PL11 2QA
➲ (2m NW, off A374 from Trerulefoot rdbt, 2m from Torpoint Ferry)
☎ 01752 812191 ▤ 01752 815724
e-mail: philip.brunsdon@nationaltrust.org.uk
A fine, largely unaltered mansion, built in brick and Pentewan stone for Sir William Carew between 1711 and 1721. The stable block and outhouses remain from an earlier 17th-century building. The house contains contemporary furniture and family portraits. The grounds include a dovecote and the Bath Pond House.
Times: Open Apr-Oct, Tue-Thu & BH Mon 1.30-5.30 (last admission 4.45). Also open Sun in Jun-Sep. **Facilities:** 🅿 💺 ♿ (Braille guide, recommended route in garden) toilets for disabled shop ✈ (ex guide dogs) ⬧ ▦

MOUNT EDGCUMBE HOUSE & COUNTRY PARK
Cremyll PL10 1HZ
➲ (from Plymouth via Cremyll Foot Ferry, Torpoint ferry or Saltash Bridge. Via Liskeard to A374, B3247 follow brown heritage signs)
☎ 01752 822236 ▤ 01752 822199 `2 for 1`
e-mail: edgcumbe@plymouth.gov.uk
Covering some 800 acres, the country park surrounding Mount Edgcumbe contains a deer park, an amphitheatre, formal gardens, sculpture, the 18th-century Earl's Garden, and woodlands containing California redwoods. The coastal footpath runs along the shores of the Park from Cremyll to Whitsand Bay. Sir Richard Edgcumbe of Cotehele built Mount Edgcumbe between 1547 and 1553. It survived a direct hit by bombs in 1941, and was restored in the 1950s. It now contains antique paintings and furniture, 16th-century tapestries, and 18th-century porcelain. Events and exhibitions held each year.
Times: Open: House & Earl's Garden Apr-Sep, Sun-Thu & BH Mon's, 11-4.30. (Closed Fri & Sat). Country Park open all year. **Fee:** ✱ House & Earl's Garden £4.50 (ch 5-15 £2.25, concessions £3.50) Family ticket (2 ad & 2 ch or 1 ad & 3 ch) £10. Country Park free.
Facilities: 🅿 (charged) 💺 ✗ licensed ♿ toilets for disabled shop in the park ▦

TREDINNICK Map 02 SW97

CORNWALL'S CREALY GREAT ADVENTURE PARK
Trelow Farm PL27 7RA
➲ (signposted off A39)
☎ 01841 541215
e-mail: shirespark@tiscali.co.uk
Cornwall's best kept Park is once again even more fun this year with 'The Haunted Castle', full of demons, skeletons and ghosts. Enter the 'Dragon Kingdom', the Country's largest indoor adventure zone consisting of two floors of slides, climbs, ropes, balls and towers. Take a walk through the Enchanted Forest to Greengate Meadow and meet fully animated moles, Mr Badger and their woodland friends. New attractions include Thunder Falls, double log flume ride, plus Raging River Watercoaster and Viking Warrior Pirate Ship. Acres of outdoor adventure play with the highest aerial bridges and the longest, steepest slides in Cornwall. Plus train rides around the lakes and the majestic Shire Houses including new born foals with farmyard friends.
Times: Open Good Fri-end Oct, daily 10-5. **Facilities:** 🅿 💺 ✗ licensed ♿ (most areas are ramped) toilets for disabled shop

TRELISSICK GARDEN Map 02 SW83

TRELISSICK GARDEN
TR3 6QL
➲ (Trelissick is located 4m S of Truro on both sides of B3289, King Harry Ferry Road)
☎ 01872 862090 ▤ 01872 865808
e-mail: trelissick@nationaltrust.org.uk
Set amidst more than 500 acres of park and farmland, with panoramic views down the Carrick Roads to Falmouth and the sea. The garden is well known for its large collection of hydrangeas, camellias, rhododendrons and exotic and tender plants. The Cornish Apple Orchard contains the definitive collection of Cornish apple varieties and is particularly lovely in the spring. Two galleries on the property display Cornish Arts and Crafts.
Times: Open mid Feb-Oct, daily 10.30-5.30. Phone for winter opening hours. Park & woodland walks open all year. **Fee:** £4.80 (Family ticket £12). Party rate 15+ £4.10 each. Car park charge £2 (refundable on admission). **Facilities:** 🅿 (charged) 💺 ✗ licensed ♿ (audio guide, wheelchairs, batricar, induction loops) toilets for disabled shop garden centre ✈ ⬧ ▦

TRERICE Map 02 SW85

TRERICE
TR8 4PG
➲ (3m SE of Newquay off A3058 at Kestle Mill)
☎ 01637 875404 ▤ 01637 879300
e-mail: trerice@nationaltrust.org.uk
The Trerice you see today was built in 1571 by Sir John Arundell IV and, having suffered no major changes since then due to a succession of absentee landlords, it is still somehow caught in the spirit of its age. The plaster ceilings in the Great Hall and Great Chamber are of particular merit and the façade of the building is now thought to be the oldest such example of Dutch influenced architecture still extant in the country. The house contains many fine pieces of furniture and a large collection of clocks. A barn houses a fascinating display of lawnmowers. The garden is planted so as to provide colour and interest throughout the year and features an orchard containing many varieties of Cornish apple trees.
Times: Open 28 Mar-Oct, daily (ex Tue & Sat) 11-5.30 (11-5 Oct-Nov). Open daily from 19 Jul-12 Sep. **Fee:** ✱ House: £4.70. Family ticket (2 ad & 3 ch) £11.70. Party £3.90 each. **Facilities:** 🅿 ✗ licensed ♿ (Braille/large print guide, tape tour, wheelchair) toilets for disabled shop ✈ (car park only, ex guide dogs) ⬧ ▦

TRURO Map 02 SW84

ROYAL CORNWALL MUSEUM
River St TR1 2SJ
➲ (follow A390 towards town centre)
☎ 01872 272205 ▤ 01872 240514
e-mail: enquiry@
royal-cornwall-museum.freeserve.co.uk
Interesting displays on the history of the county, a world-famous collection of minerals, and paintings and drawings, including a number of Old Masters. Other galleries house displays of archaeology, Cornish history, and Egyptian artefacts. Recently completed galleries of Cornish wildlife, fashion and textiles.
Times: Open all year, Mon-Sat 10-5. Library closes 1-2. (Closed BHs). **Facilities:** 🅿 (200 yds) (disabled parking on street) 💺 ✗ licensed ♿ (lift, ramps to main entrances) toilets for disabled shop ✈ (ex guide dogs) ▦

WENDRON   Map 02 SW63

POLDARK MINE AND HERITAGE COMPLEX
TR13 0ER
➲ (3m from Helston on B3297 Redruth road, follow brown signs)
☎ 01326 573173 🖹 01326 563166
e-mail: info@poldark-mine.com

The centre of this attraction is the 18th century tin mine where visitors can join a guided tour of workings which retain much of their original character. The site's Museum explains the history of tin production in Cornwall from 1800BC through to the 19th century and the fascinating story of the Cornish overseas. In addition to the Museum, the audio-visual presentation gives more insight into Cornwall's mining heritage.

Times: Open Etr-1st wk Nov, 10-5.30 (last tour 4pm).
Facilities: 🅿 💺 ♿ (newly refurbished museum allowing disabled access) shop 🗪

ZENNOR   Map 02 SW43

WAYSIDE FOLK MUSEUM
TR26 3DA
➲ (4m W of St Ives, on B3306)
☎ 01736 796945   2 for 1

Founded in 1937, this museum covers every aspect of life in Zennor and surrounding district from 3000BC to the 1930s. Over 5000 items are displayed in 12 workshops and rooms covering wheelwrights, blacksmiths, agriculture, fishing, wrecks, mining, domestic and archaeological artefacts. A photographic exhibition entitled People of the Past tells the story of the village.

Times: Open Etr-end Oct, daily 10.30-5.30. **Fee:** ✱ £2.75 (ch £1.50, over 60's £2.50). Party rates 10+. **Facilities:** 🅿 (50yds) ♿ (not suitable for wheelchair users) shop 🐾 (ex guide dogs) 🗪

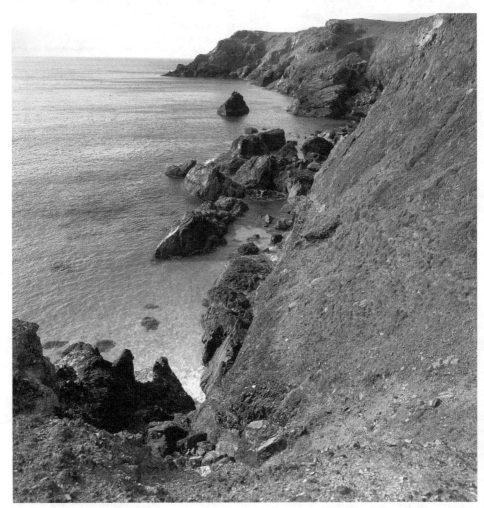

Above: Kynance Cliffs, near The Lizard

CUMBRIA

EVENTS & FESTIVALS

May
12th-15th Jennings Keswick Jazz Festival, various venues, Keswick
tbc Carlisle & Borders Spring Flower Show, Carlisle

June
2nd-8th Appleby Horse Fair, Roman Road, Appleby-in-Westmorland
3rd-4th Keswick Beer Festival, Davidson Park, Keswick
3rd-5th Holker Garden Festival, Holker Hall
3rd-5th La'al Cumbrian Beer Festival, Wasdale Head
25th-26th Whitehaven Maritime Festival, The Harbour

July
16th Cumberland County Show, Carlisle
24th Coniston County Fair, Coniston Hall
29th-31st Maryport Blues Festival, various venues
30th-31st The Cumbria Steam Gathering, Cark Airfield, Flookburgh

August
3rd Cartmel Show, Cartmel Park, Grange-Over-Sands
28th Grasmere Lakeland Sports & Show, Stock Lane, Grasmere, Ambleside

September
2nd-4th Wasdale Beer Festival, Wasdale Head (provisional)
8th Westmorland County Show, Lane Farm, Crooklands, Milnthorpe
9th Kendal Torchlight Procession
17th Egremont Crab Fair & Sports (including world renowned gurning competition)

November
12th-13th Kendal Mountain Film Festival, Highgate, Kendal
17th Biggest Liar in the World Competition, Santon Bridge (provisional)

Above: Ashness Bridge and Skiddaw mountain

ALSTON   Map 12 NY74

NENT VALLEY
Nenthead Mines Heritage Centre, Nenthead CA9 3PD
➲ (5m E of Alston, on A689)
☎ 01434 382726 📠 01434 382294
e-mail: administration.office@virgin.net
Set in 200 acres in the North Pennines, this hands-on heritage centre contains exhibitions and displays on geology, local wildlife, and social history. Visitors can operate three enormous water wheels, gaze down a 328ft deep brewery shaft, and take an underground trip through the Nenthead mines, last worked for lead in 1915.
Times: Open Etr-Oct, daily 10.30-5. Mine tours at 12, 1.30 & 3 daily
Fee: ✱ £4-£6.50 (pen £3.25-5.50, ch site free, mine £2). Family ticket £15.30 **Facilities:** 🅿 🍴 ♿ ramps & motorised scooter toilets for disabled shop ☕

SOUTH TYNEDALE RAILWAY
The Railway Station, Hexham Rd CA9 3JB
➲ (0.25m N, on A686)
☎ 01434 381696 & 382828
Running along the beautiful South Tyne valley, this narrow-gauge railway follows the route of the former Alston to Haltwhistle branch. At present the line runs between Alston and Kirkhaugh.
Times: Open Apr-Oct & Dec, wknds and BHs; 20 Jul-Aug, daily. Also open school holidays & some wknds in Dec. Please enquire for times of trains. **Fee:** ✱ Return £5 (ch 3-15 £2). Single £3 (ch 3-15 £1.50). All day £12.50 (ch 3-15 £5). **Facilities:** 🅿 🍴 ♿ (railway carriage for wheelchairs, pre-booking required) toilets for disabled shop

AMBLESIDE   Map 07 NY30

ARMITT MUSEUM
Rydal Rd LA22 9BL
➲ (On the main Kendal-Keswick A591 road, opposite Rydal Road car park in Ambleside. 2min stroll from town centre.)
☎ 015394 31212 📠 015394 31313
e-mail: info@armitt.com

A fascinating and entertaining place that celebrates over 2000 years of Lake District history, from the time of Ambleside's Roman occupation to the 20th century. Facts, artefacts, historic photographs and renowned works of art by not only the area's better known former inhabitants such as Beatrix Potter, Kurt Schwitters and John Ruskin, but also

continued

displays about the daily lives of its hard-working townspeople in past times.
Times: Open all year, daily 10-5 (last entrance 4.30). Closed 25-26 Dec. **Fee:** £2.50 (ch, students, pen £1.80) Family ticket £5.60.
Facilities: P (50yds) & (chairlift to upstairs library, parking at establishment) toilets for disabled shop ✘ (ex guide dogs) ◀

BARROW-IN-FURNESS   Map 07 SD26
THE DOCK MUSEUM NEW
North Rd LA14 2PW
➲ (A590 to Barrow-in-Furness. Follow brown tourist signs.)
☎ 01229 894444 ▤ 01229 811361   FREE
e-mail: dockmuseum@barrowbc.gov.uk
Explore this museum and relive the fascinating history of Barrow-in-Furness. Discover how the industrial revolution prompted the growth of the town from a small hamlet into a major industrial power through models, graphics and computer kiosks.
Times: Open mid Mar-Nov (Tue-Fri 10-5, Sat-Sun 11-5); Nov-Etr (Wed-Fri 10.30-4, Sat-Sun 11-4.30) **Facilities:** P ◀ & (Hearing loop, 2 w/chairs for loan) toilets for disabled shop ✘ (ex assist dogs) ◀

FURNESS ABBEY
LH13 0TJ
➲ (1.5m NE on unclass road)
☎ 01229 823420
Located in a peaceful valley, the majestic red sandstone remains of this beautiful abbey once housed a wealthy monastic order. View the fine stone carvings and visit the exhibition to find out more about the powerful religious community that was once based here.
Times: Open all year, Apr-Sep, daily 10-6; Oct-Mar, Thu-Mon 10-4. (Closed 24-26 Dec & 1Jan) **Fee:** ✱ £3 (ch £1.50, concessions £2.30). Prices & opening times relate to 2004, for further details phone or log onto www.english-heritage.org.uk/visits **Facilities:** P & shop ✘ (ex on lead in certain areas) ⌗

BASSENTHWAITE   Map 11 NY23
TROTTERS WORLD OF ANIMALS
Coalbeck Farm CA12 4RD
☎ 017687 76239 ▤ 017687 76598   2 for 1
e-mail: info@trottersworld.com
Home to hundreds of friendly creatures including lemurs, wallabies and other exotic animals along with reptiles and birds of prey and a family of gibbons which will keep families amused for hours. Informative, amusing demonstrations daily bring visitors closer to the animals. "Clown About" is an indoor play centre with soft play area and ballpools for toddlers upwards.
Times: Open all year, except 25 Dec & 1 Jan. Summer 10-5.30, Winter 11-4.30 **Fee:** £5.50 (ch £4.25, under 3yrs free) **Facilities:** P ◀ & toilets for disabled shop ✘ (ex guide dogs) ◀

BIRDOSWALD   Map 12 NY66
BIRDOSWALD ROMAN FORT
CA8 7DD
➲ (signposted off A69 between Brampton & Hexham)
☎ 016977 47602 ▤ 016977 47605
e-mail: birdoswald@dial.pipex.com
A visitor centre introduces you to Hadrian's Wall and the Roman Fort. This unique section of Hadrian's Wall overlooks
continued

the Irthing Gorge, and is the only point along the Wall where all the components of the Roman frontier system can be found together. Birdoswald isn't just about the Romans, though, it's also about border raids in the Middle Ages, and recent archaeological discoveries.
Times: Open Mar-Oct, 10-5.30. Winter season exterior only
Fee: ✱ English Heritage members half price. Prices & opening times relate to 2004, for further details phone or log onto www.english-heritage.org.uk/visits **Facilities:** P ◀ & (ramp outside, disabled parking, lift) toilets for disabled shop ◀

BORROWDALE   Map 11 NY21
HONISTER SLATE MINE NEW
Honister Pass CA12 5XN
➲ (From Keswick take B5289 through Borrowdale & Rosthwaite, follow road to top of pass. From Cockermouth take B5292 towards Keswick for 4m, turn right onto B5289 to Low Larton & Buttermere. Follow road to top of pass)
☎ 01768 777230 ▤ 01768 777958
e-mail: info@honister.com
The last working slate mine in Great Britain. Fully guided tours allow you to explore the caverns hacked out by Victorian miners. Learn the history of the famous Honister green slate, see local skills in action, and how to rive slates.
Times: Open Mon-Fri 9-5; Wknds 10-5 (closed 23 Dec-13 Jan)
Fee: Free entry to Visitor Centre. Tours £9.50 (ch £4.50) Family £26
Facilities: P ◀ ✘ licensed & toilets for disabled shop garden centre ◀

BOWNESS-ON-   Map 07 SD49
WINDERMERE
BLACKWELL THE ARTS & CRAFTS HOUSE
LA23 3JR
➲ (M6 junct 36. 1.5m S of Bowness on B5360, off A5074)
☎ 015394 46139 ▤ 015394 88486
e-mail: info@blackwell.org.uk
Blackwell was designed by architect M H Baillie Scott (1865-1945) and completed in 1900. Part of the late 19th-century Arts and Crafts Movement it houses changing exhibitions of high quality applied arts and crafts, as well as original design features including stained glass, stonework, carved oak panelling, and plasterwork.
Times: Open 19 Feb-Dec daily 10.30-5; (Nov-Dec, Feb-Mar 10-4). Closed 24-26 Dec. **Fee:** ✱ £4.75 (ch & students £2.50) Family ticket £13, groups £3.75 per person. Combined ticket with Abbot Hall £7.50.
Facilities: P ◀ & (lift to upper floor, photos for inaccessible rooms) toilets for disabled shop ✘ (ex guide dogs) ◀

BRAMPTON   Map 12 NY56
LANERCOST PRIORY
CA8 2HQ
➲ (2.5m NE)
☎ 01697 73030
Close to Hadrian's Wall are the atmospheric ruins of this Augustinian priory founded in the 12th-century.
Times: Open Apr-Sep, daily 10-6; Oct, Thu-Mon, 10-4. **Fee:** ✱ £2.50 (ch £1.30, concessions £1.90). Prices & opening times relate to 2004, for further details phone or log onto www.english-heritage.org.uk/visits
Facilities: P shop ✘ (ex dogs on leads) ⌗

BROUGH Map 12 NY71

BROUGH CASTLE

CA17 4EJ

➲ (8m SE of Appleby, S of A66)

☎ 0191 261 1585 [FREE]

Dating from Roman times the twelfth-century keep at this site replaced an earlier stronghold destroyed by the Scots in 1174. It was restored by Lady Anne Clifford in the seventeenth century. You can still see the outline of her kitchen gardens. **Times:** Open any reasonable time. **Facilities:** P ✖ (ex dogs on leads) ♯

BROUGHAM Map 12 NY52

BROUGHAM CASTLE

CA10 2AA

➲ (1.5m SE of Penrith on minor road off A66)

☎ 01768 862488

Explore the maze of stairs and passages in the ruins of this once glorious 11th-century castle on the banks of the River Eamont. Enjoy the lively exhibition where you'll see relics from the nearby Roman Fort.

Times: Open all year, Apr-Sep, daily 10-6; Oct, Thu-Mon, 10-4. **Fee:** ✱ £2.50 (ch £1.30, concessions £1.90). Prices & opening times relate to 2004, for further details phone or log onto www.english-heritage.org.uk/visits **Facilities:** P & (ex keep) shop ✖ (ex dogs on leads) ♯

CARLISLE Map 11 NY35

CARLISLE CASTLE

CA3 8UR

➲ (north side of city centre, close to station)

☎ 01228 591992 🖳 01228 514880

Discover a thrilling and bloody past and enjoy panoramic views over the city and hills of the Lake District and Southern Scotland. Uncover an exciting history through lively exhibitions, which tell of William Rufus, Mary Queen of Scots and Bonnie Prince Charlie.

Times: Open all year, Apr-Sep, daily 9.30-6; Oct-Mar, daily 10-4. (Closed 24-26 Dec & 1 Jan). **Fee:** ✱ £3.80 (ch £1.90, concessions £2.90). Prices & opening times relate to 2004, for further details phone or log onto www.english-heritage.org.uk/visits **Facilities:** P (400yds) & (parking for disabled at Castle) shop ✖ (ex on lead in certain areas) ♯

CARLISLE CATHEDRAL

Castle St CA3 8TZ

➲ (M6 junct 42,43 or 44, located in City Centre)

☎ 01228 535169 & 548151 🖳 01228 547049

e-mail: office@carlislecathedral.org.uk

The Cathedral, founded in 1122 as a Norman Priory for Augustinian canons has had services conducted for nearly 900 years. Items of special interest include the East Window, with its tracery containing some very fine fourteenth-century stained glass and the Brougham Triptych, a magnificent sixteenth-century carved Flemish altarpiece in St. Wilfrid's Chapel. There is an interesting fourteenth-century barrel vaulted painted ceiling in the Choir and in the north and south aisles medieval paintings depict the Life of St. Cuthbert and St. Anthony and the figures of the 12 Apostles.

Times: Open daily throughout the year, Mon-Sat 7.30-6.15, Sun 7.30-5, summer BHs 9.45-6.15, winter BHs, Xmas & New Year 9.45-4. **Fee:** Suggested donation of £2 per adult. **Facilities:** P (5 mins walk) (2 disabled spaces only) ✖ licensed & (parking, ramps, loop system, large print books, chairlifts) toilets for disabled shop ✖ (ex guide dogs)

GUILDHALL MUSEUM

Green Market CA3 8JE

➲ (town centre, opposite The Crown & Mitre Hotel)

☎ 01228 534781 🖳 01228 810249 [FREE]

e-mail: barbaral@carlisle-city.gov.uk

One of Carlisle's oldest buildings, c.1405 and Grade I listed. The Guildhall was once the meeting place of Carlisle's eight trade guilds, few of which still meet today. Experience the cabin-like atmosphere of the shoemaker's room and the 'modernised' butcher's room with its Victorian features. There are amazing objects such as the medieval town chest, dating from around 1400, two small silver balls (one dated 1599)- reputed to be the earliest surviving horse racing prizes in the country.

Times: Open Apr-Oct, 12-4.30 **Facilities:** P (500yds) (disc parking on street, 1 hr limit) ✖ (ex guide dogs)

TULLIE HOUSE MUSEUM & ART GALLERY

Castle St CA3 8TP

➲ (M6, junct 42, 43 or 44 follow signs to city centre. Car park located in Devonshire Walk)

☎ 01228 534781 🖳 01228 810249

e-mail: barbaral@carlisle.gov.uk

Dramatic audio-visual displays, striking recreations of long vanished scenes and imaginative hands-on displays. There is something for everyone, no matter what age - the stunning underground millennium gallery or Border River pathway linking to Carlisle Castle. This unique project combines the museum's own collections with the cutting edge of contemporary art. The new multi-media room features touch sensitive computer screens and a short film.

Times: Open: Nov-Mar, Mon-Sat 10-4, Sun 12-4; Apr-Jun & Sep-Oct, Mon-Sat 10-5, Sun 12-5. Jul-Aug, Mon-Sat 10-5, Sun 11-5. (Closed 25-26 Dec & 1 Jan). **Fee:** ✱ Ground floor (including Art Gallery & Old Tullie House) - Free. Upper floors & New Millenium Gallery - £5.20 (ch £2.60 concessions £3.60) Family ticket (2 adults 3 ch) £14.50 **Facilities:** P (5mins walk) (disabled parking on site by request) 🍵 ✖ licensed & (chair lift) toilets for disabled shop ✖ (ex guide dogs) 📷

COCKERMOUTH Map 11 NY13

JENNINGS BREWERY TOUR AND SHOP

The Castle Brewery CA13 9NE

➲ (A66 to Cockermouth, follow tourist signs to brewery)

☎ 0845 129 7190 🖳 0845 129 7186

e-mail: maskew@jenningsbrewery.co.uk

Jennings Brothers have been brewing traditional beers for 160 years and still use the methods used by the founder in 1828. Situated in the shadow of Cockermouth Castle, the water for the brewing process is still drawn from the well which supplied the Castle with pure water.

Times: Tours: Jan-Feb & Nov- Dec, Mon-Sat 2pm ; Mar-Jun & Sep-Oct, Mon-Sat, 11am & 2pm; Jul-Aug, daily, 11am & 2pm. **Fee:** ✱ £4.50 (ch 12-18 £1.50). **Facilities:** P Cooperage Bar accessible shop ✖ 📷

LAKELAND SHEEP & WOOL CENTRE

Egremont Rd CA13 0QX

➲ (M6 junct 40, W on A66 to rdbt at Cockermouth on A66/A586 junct)

☎ 01900 822673 🖳 01900 822673

e-mail: reception@sheep-woolcentre.co.uk

Come face to face with 19 different breeds of live sheep. Stage show with 'One Man and his Dog' demonstration and

continued

our Jersey cow. Shows four times daily, March-end Oct. All indoors. **Times:** Open all year, daily 9.30-5.30 (Closed 25 Dec & 4-18 Jan). **Fee:** £4 (ch £3) for sheep shows **Facilities:** P ⬤ ✖ licensed ♿ (hearing loop system) toilets for disabled shop ✖ (ex guide/hearing dogs) ◀

WORDSWORTH HOUSE
Main St CA13 9RX
➲ (W end of Main Street)
☎ 01900 824805   🖷 01900 824805
e-mail: wordsworthhouse@nationaltrust.org.uk
William Wordsworth was born here on 7th April 1770, and happy memories of the house had a great effect on his work. The house is imaginatively presented for the first time as the home of the Wordsworth family in the 1770s. It offers a lively and interactive visit with hands-on activities and costumed living history.
Times: Open 22 Jun-5 Nov, Mon-Sat 11-4.30 Shop open; 29 Mar-24 Dec Mon-Sat 10-5, 3-29 Jan Wed-Sat 10-4 **Fee:** ✱ £4.50 (ch £2.50). Family ticket £13. Groups(15+) £3.50 Ask for details of discount with Dove Cottage and Rydal Mount. **Facilities:** P (300yds) ♿ (Braille guide, touch list, computer) toilets for disabled shop ✖ (ex assist dogs) ❄ ◀

CONISTON   Map 07 SD39

BRANTWOOD
LA21 8AD
➲ (2.5m SE off B5285, unclass road. Regular ferry services from Coniston Pier)
☎ 015394 41396   🖷 015394 41263
e-mail: enquiries@brantwood.org.uk
Brantwood, home of John Ruskin, is a beautifully situated house with fine views across Coniston Water. Inside, there is a large collection of Ruskin paintings and memorabilia, and visitors can enjoy delightful nature walks through the Brantwood Estate.
Times: Open mid Mar-mid Nov, daily 11-5.30. Winter, Wed-Sun 11-4.30. (Closed 25-26 Dec). **Fee:** House & Estate £5.50 (ch £1, student £4). Family ticket £11.50. Estate only £3.75 **Facilities:** P ⬤ ✖ licensed ♿ (wheelchairs, photos of inaccessible areas, Braille guides) toilets for disabled shop ✖ (ex guide dogs & in grounds) ◀

RUSKIN MUSEUM
The Institute, Yewdale Rd LA21 8DU
➲ (In village centre opposite fire station, accessed from A593, A595 & B5285)
☎ 015394 41164   🖷 01539 441132   **2 for 1**
e-mail: vmj@ruskinmuseum.com
John Ruskin (1819-1900) was one of Britain's most versatile and important political thinkers and artists. The museum contains many of his watercolours, drawings, letters, sketchbooks and other relics. The geology, mines and quarries of the area, Arthur Ransome's 'Swallows and

continued

An asterisk * indicates that opening times and prices are for 2004. Please contact the attraction for up-to-date information.

Amazons' country, and Donald Campbell's Bluebird are also explored in the Museum.

Ruskin Museum

Times: Open all year, mid Mar-mid Nov, daily 10-5.30; Winter opening, mid Nov-mid Feb, 10.30-3.30, mid Feb-mid Mar, 10.30-4.30 **Fee:** £3.75 (ch £1.75). Family ticket £9. Ruskin passport gives exclusive discount for cruise on S.Y. Gondola. **Facilities:** P ♿ (audio guide, handling specimens) toilets for disabled shop ✖ (ex guide dogs) ◀

STEAM YACHT GONDOLA
Coniston Pier LA22 8AN
➲ (A593 to Coniston, follow signs near garage 'to boats' & S Y Gondola. Coniston Pier is at end of Lake Road.)
☎ 015394 41288   🖷 015394 41288
e-mail: gondola@nationaltrust.org.uk
Originally launched in 1859, the graceful Gondola worked on Coniston Water until 1936. Beautifully rebuilt, she came back into service in 1980, and visitors can once again enjoy her silent progress and old-fashioned comfort.
Times: Open Apr-Oct to scheduled daily timetable. Trips commence from 11 at Coniston Pier. Piers at Coniston & Brantwood.
Fee: ✱ Ticket prices on application. **Facilities:** P shop ❄ ◀

DALEMAIN   Map 12 NY42

DALEMAIN
CA11 0HB
➲ (M6 junct 40, between Penrith & Ullswater on A592)
☎ 017684 86450   🖷 017684 86223
e-mail: admin@dalemain.com
Originally a mediaeval pele tower, Dalemain was added to in Tudor times, and the imposing Georgian façade was completed in 1745. It has oak panelling, Chinese wallpaper, Tudor plasterwork and fine period furniture. The tower contains the Westmorland and Cumberland Yeomanry Museum, and there is a countryside collection in the 16th-century Great Barn. The gardens include a collection of old fashioned roses, and in early summer a magnificent display of blue Himalayan poppies.
Times: Open Gardens, Mediaeval Hall and agricultural & countryside collections: 28 Mar-21 Oct , Sun-Thu 10.30-5. House open 11-4.
Fee: ✱ House £5.50 (ch £3.50) Family ticket £14.50. Gardens £3.50. (ch free when accompanied). Party. **Facilities:** P ⬤ ✖ licensed ♿ (ramp access at entrance, electric scooter) toilets for disabled shop garden centre ✖ (ex guide dogs) ◀

DALTON-IN-FURNESS   Map 07 SD27

SOUTH LAKES WILD ANIMAL PARK
Crossgates LA15 8JR
➲ (M6 junct 36, A590 to Dalton-in-Furness, follow tourist signs)
☎ 01229 466086 ▤ 01229 461310
e-mail: office@wildanimalpark.co.uk
The North's leading zoo park is a unique safari on foot with many animals wandering free. Visitors can walk with kangaroos and emus in the bush, and watch parrots fly free in the trees. Hand feed (supervised at 2pm) families of nine different species of lemur, wonder at the amazing skills of gibbons, macaques and spider monkeys, and see the lions and tigers climb high into trees to catch their food. See both Amur and Sumatran tigers, and spectacled bears. An African plain is approximated by keeping four rhino, six giraffes and a family of baboons in the same field. Also see cheetah, red panda, and over 100 other species. This is an active conservation park with partnerships all over the world to save animals and their habitats.
Times: Open all year, daily 10-5 (last admission 4.15); Nov-Feb 10-4.30 (last admission 3.45). (Closed 25 Dec). **Fee:** ✱ £9.50 (ch, pen, wheelchair users & registered blind £6). Reduced prices Nov-Mar.
Facilities: 🅿 💷 ⅙ (wheelchair users may need help) toilets for disabled shop ✖ 🍴

EGREMONT   Map 11 NY01

FLORENCE MINE HERITAGE CENTRE NEW
Florence Mine CA22 2NR
➲ (On A595 Egremont by-pass. Turn off at Wilton/Haile, follow signs)
☎ 01946 825830 ▤ 01946 825830
e-mail: info@florencemine.co.uk
Based in the last deep working, iron ore mine in Western Europe, the centre offers a mining museum, geology and mineral room, a reconstructed drift (or tunnel) and a research facility. Underground tours are also available all year, including weekdays, by prior arrangement. Please phone the mine for details. Suitable footwear and old clothes are advised for underground tours.
Times: Open Apr-Oct, daily 10-4. Nov-Mar, wkdays only
Fee: ✱ Centre: £2 (ch £1); Mine Tour: £6.50 (ch £4.50)
Facilities: 🅿 💷 ⅙ hands-on display toilets for disabled shop ✖ (ex guide dogs)

GRASMERE   Map 11 NY30

DOVE COTTAGE & THE WORDSWORTH MUSEUM
LA22 9SH
➲ (S, off A591, immediately before Grasmere village)
☎ 015394 35544 ▤ 015394 35748
e-mail: enquiries@wordsworth.org.uk
Dove Cottage was the inspirational home of William Wordsworth for over eight years (1799-1808), and it was here that he wrote some of his best-known poetry. The cottage has been open to the public since 1891, and is kept in its original condition. The museum displays manuscripts, works of art and items that belonged to the poet.
Times: Open daily 9.30-5.30, last admission 5pm. (Closed early Jan-early Feb & 24-26 Dec). **Fee:** ✱ Admission charge, discount and concessions available. Reciprocal discount offer with Rydal Mount, Ambleside & Wordsworth House, Cockermouth. **Facilities:** 🅿 💷 ✖ licensed ⅙ (ramps, induction loop, virtual tour) toilets for disabled shop ✖ (ex guide dogs) 🍴

HARDKNOTT CASTLE ROMAN FORT   Map 07 NY20

HARDKNOTT CASTLE ROMAN FORT
➲ (9m NE of Ravenglass, at W end of Hardknott Pass)
One of the most dramatic Roman sites in Britain, with stunning views of the Lakeland falls. The fort built between AD120 and AD138, controlled the road from Ravenglass to Ambleside. The remains include the headquarters building and Commandant's house, with a bath house and parade ground outside the fort.
Times: Open any reasonable time. Access may be hazardous in winter.
Facilities: ✖ (ex dogs on leads) 🚐 🍴

HAWKSHEAD   Map 07 SD39

BEATRIX POTTER GALLERY
Main St LA22 0NS
➲ (Situated on the main street in the village centre)
☎ 015394 36355 ▤ 015394 36187
e-mail: beatrixpottergallery@nationaltrust.org.uk
An annually changing exhibition of Beatrix Potter's original illustrations from her children's storybooks, housed in the former office of her husband, solicitor William Heelis.
Times: Open 3 Apr-Oct & Good Fri Sat-Wed 10.30-4.30 (last admission 4). Admission is by timed ticket including NT members. **Fee:** ✱ £3 (ch £1.50) Family ticket £7.50 (2ad+3ch) **Facilities:** 🅿 (300mtrs) No parking in village centre (Braille guide) shop ✖ 🚐 🍴

HOLKER   Map 07 SD37

HOLKER HALL & GARDENS
Cark in Cartmel, Grange over Sands LA11 7PL
➲ (from M6 junct 36, follow A590, signposted)
☎ 015395 58328 ▤ 015395 58378
e-mail: publicopening@holker.co.uk
Dating from the 16th century, the new wing of the Hall was rebuilt in 1871, after a fire. It has a notable woodcarving and many fine pieces of furniture which mix happily with family photographs from the present day. There are magnificent gardens, both formal and woodland and the Lakeland Motor Museum, exhibitions, deer park and adventure playground are further attractions.
Times: Open 28 Mar-29 Oct, Sun-Fri 10-6. Hall open 10.30-4.45. (Closed Sat). **Fee:** ✱ Gardens & Grounds £4.50 (ch 6-15 £2.75) Family ticket £13.75. All 3 attractions £9.25 (ch £4.65) Family ticket £27.75. **Facilities:** 🅿 💷 ✖ licensed ⅙ (ramps, wheelchairs & scooters available for hire) toilets for disabled shop on lead, not in garden 🍴

KENDAL   Map 07 SD59

ABBOT HALL ART GALLERY
LA9 5AL
➲ (M6 junct 36, follow signs to Kendal. Located at south end of town centre beside parish church)
☎ 01539 722464 ▤ 01539 722494
e-mail: info@abbothall.org.uk
The ground floor rooms of this splendid house have been restored to their former glory, with original carvings and fine panelling. The walls are hung with paintings by Romney, Gardner, Turner and Ruskin. The gallery has notable temporary exhibitions and a fine permanent collection of 18th- and 19th-century watercolours of the Lake District, and

continued

20th-century British art, including works by Hepworth, Frink, Nicholson, Sutherland, Riley and Freud.
Times: Open 20 Jan-23 Dec, Mon-Sat 10.30-5 (Jan-Mar & Nov-Dec closes at 4pm). **Fee:** ✱ £3.75 (ch & students £2.75). Family ticket £11. Groups £3.75 per person. Abbot Hall/Blackwell combined group ticket £7.50. Exhibition & Collection £4.75 (ch & students £3.75). Family ticket £14 **Facilities:** ℙ ⏺ & (chair lifts in split level galleries, large print labels) toilets for disabled shop ✕ (ex guide dogs) ⬛

KENDAL MUSEUM
Station Rd LA9 6BT
➲ (opposite railway station)
☎ 01539 721374 ▤ 01539 737976
e-mail: info@kendalmuseum.org.uk
The archaeology and natural history of the Lakes is explored in this popular museum which also features a world wildlife exhibition and a display devoted to author Alfred Wainwright, who was honorary clerk to the museum.
Times: Open mid Feb-end Dec, Mon-Sat 10.30-5. Reduced hours Feb-Mar; Nov & Dec, 10.30-4. Closed Sun. **Fee:** ✱ £2.50 (ch, students free, seniors £2) **Facilities:** ℙ & toilets for disabled shop ✕ (ex guide dogs) ⬛

MUSEUM OF LAKELAND LIFE
Abbot Hall LA9 5AL
➲ (M6 junct 36, follow signs to Kendal. Located at south end of Kendal beside Abbot Hall Art Gallery)
☎ 01539 722464 ▤ 01539 722494
e-mail: info@lakelandmuseum.org.uk
The life and history of the Lake District is captured by the displays in this museum, housed in Abbot Hall's stable block. The working and social life of the area are well illustrated by a variety of exhibits including period rooms, a Victorian Cumbrian street scene and a farming display. Two of the rooms are devoted to the memory of Arthur Ransome.
Times: Open 20 Jan-23 Dec, Mon-Sat 10.30-5. (Closing at 4pm Jan, Feb, Mar, Nov, Dec) **Fee:** ✱ £3.50 (ch & students £2). Family ticket £9.50. Combined ticket with Abbot Hall & Lakeland Life (same day), £6.50. **Facilities:** ℙ ⏺ & (listening posts, large print labels) toilets for disabled shop ✕ (ex guide dogs) ⬛

KESWICK   Map 11 NY22
CUMBERLAND PENCIL MUSEUM
Southey Works, Greta Bridge CA12 5NG
➲ (M6 N onto A66 at Penrith. Left at 2nd Keswick exit, left at T-Junct, left over Greta Bridge)
☎ 017687 73626 ▤ 017687 74679
e-mail: museum@acco-uk.co.uk
Investigating the history and technology of an object most of us take utterly for granted, this interesting museum includes a replica of the Borrowdale mine where graphite was first discovered, the world's largest pencil, and displays on brass-rubbing and various artistic techniques that use pencils.
Times: ✱ Open daily 9.30-4 (hours may be extended during peak season). (Closed 25-26 Dec & 1 Jan) **Facilities:** ℙ & toilets for disabled shop ⬛

KESWICK MUSEUM & GALLERY
Fitz Park, Station Rd CA12 4NF
➲ (M6 junct 40, A66 to Keswick, follow tourist signs for Museum & Art Gallery when in Keswick)
☎ 017687 73263 ▤ 017687 80390
e-mail: keswick.museum@allerdale.gov.uk
Keswick's surprising past, from industrial mining centre to
continued

peaceful tourist town, is revealed in this fine example of a late Victorian museum. Set in the beautiful Fitz Park, the collections cover local and natural history, famous inhabitants and visitors, including the Lake Poets, and houses the work of many artists who have been captivated by the local landscape and history.
Times: ✱ Open Good Fri-Oct, 10-4. Tue-Thu, 10-7. **Facilities:** ℙ (on road outside) (2 hour limit) & (ramp at front entrance, with handrails) shop ✕ (ex guide & hearing dogs)

MIREHOUSE
CA12 4QE
➲ (3m N of Keswick on A591)
☎ 017687 72287 ▤ 017687 72287
e-mail: info@mirehouse.com
Visitors return to Mirehouse for many reasons: close links to Tennyson and Wordsworth, the spectacular setting of mountain and lake, the varied gardens, changing displays on the Poetry Walk, free children's nature notes, four woodland playgrounds, live classical piano music in the house, generous Cumbrian cooking in the tearoom, and a relaxed, friendly welcome.
Times: Open Apr-Oct. Grounds: daily 10.30-5.30 House: Wed, Sun, (also Fri in Aug) 2-last entry 4.30. Parties by arrangement.
Fee: ✱ House & grounds £4.60 (ch £2.30). Grounds only £2.20 (ch £1.10). Family ticket £13.80 (2 ad & 4 ch) **Facilities:** ℙ (charged) ⏺ & toilets for disabled ✕ (ex on leads & guide dogs)

LAKESIDE   Map 07 SD38
AQUARIUM OF THE LAKES
LA12 8AS
➲ (M6, junct 36, take A590 to Newby Bridge. Turn right over bridge, follow Hawkshead Road to Lakeside. Well signposted)
☎ 015395 30153 ▤ 015395 30152
e-mail: aquariumofthelakes@reallive.co.uk
Set on the southern shore of Lake Windermere at Lakeside, the award-winning Aquarium of the Lakes is the UK's largest collection of freshwater fish. Over 30 displays recreate the journey of a Lakeland river from mountaintop to the open sea. Naturally themed habitats are home to everything from diving ducks and mischievous otters to sharks and rays. An all-weather experience for all ages.
Times: Open all year, daily from 9am. Closed 25 Dec. **Fee:** ✱ £5.95 (ch £3.75, pen £4.95). Family ticket (2 adult & 2 ch £16.95, 2 adult & 3 ch £19.95, 2 adult & 4 ch £22.95). **Facilities:** ℙ (charged) ⏺ & (lift to first floor, wheelchairs) toilets for disabled shop ✕ (ex guide dogs) ⬛

LEVENS   Map 07 SD48
LEVENS HALL
LA8 0PD
➲ (M6 junct 36. 5m S of Kendal, on A6)
☎ 015395 60321 ▤ 015395 60669
e-mail: email@levenshall.fsnet.co.uk
An Elizabethan mansion, built onto a 13th-century pele tower, with fine plasterwork and panelling. The topiary garden, laid out in 1694, has been little changed.
Times: Open: House & gardens mid Apr-mid Oct, Sun-Thu. Gardens 10-5. House 12-5. Last admission 4.30. **Fee:** ✱ House & garden £7.50 (ch £3.70), garden only £5.80 (ch 2.60). **Facilities:** ℙ ⏺ & (ramps within garden) toilets for disabled shop garden centre ✕ (ex guide dogs) ⬛

NEAR SAWREY   Map 07 SD39
HILL TOP
LA22 0LF
➲ (2m S of Hawkshead. Behind The Tower Bank Arms)
☎ 015394 36269   🖷 015394 36811
e-mail: hilltop@nationaltrust.org.uk

This small 17th-century house is where Beatrix Potter wrote many of her famous children's stories. It remains as she left it, and in each room can be found something that appears in one of her books.
Times: Open 3 Apr-Oct, Sat-Wed 10.30-4.30, last admission 4pm. Garden only: 8 Apr-29 Oct, Thu-Fri 11-4. Shop 3 Apr-Oct, Sat-Wed 10.30-5; 8 Apr-29 Oct, Thu-Fri 11-4. **Fee:** ✱ £4.50 (ch £2) Family ticket £11(2ad + 3ch) **Facilities:** 🅿 (200 mtrs) (no parking for coaches) (Braille guide,handling items,accessibility by arrangement) shop ✈ (ex guide dogs) 🐾 🍴

PENRITH   Map 12 NY53
RHEGED - THE VILLAGE IN THE HILL
Redhills CA11 0DQ
➲ (M6 junct 40, on A66 towards Keswick)
☎ 01768 868000   🖷 01768 868002
e-mail: enquiries@rheged.com

Named after Cumbria's Celtic kingdom, this incredible attraction is the largest grass-covered building in Europe, and is designed to look like a Lakeland hill. Inside is a state-of-the-art Mega Systems cinema with a screen that measures 60 feet wide and 48 feet high. Among the films shown on this massive screen are Rheged-The Movie, a journey through the myths, legends and scenery of Cumbria; and Everest-The Movie, a breathtaking trip to the top of the world. Rheged also contains the permanent Helly Hansen National Mountaineering Exhibition.
Times: Open daily 10-5.30. (Closed 25 Dec) **Fee:** ✱ Each attraction £5.50 (ch £3.90 & pen £4.70). Family ticket £16 **Facilities:** 🅿 🍴 ✗ licensed ♿ toilets for disabled shop ✈ (ex guide dogs) 🍴

WETHERIGGS COUNTRY POTTERY
Clifton Dykes CA10 2DH
➲ (approx 2m off A6, S from Penrith, signposted)
☎ 01768 892733   `FREE`
🖷 01768 892733 ext 231
e-mail: info@wetheriggs-pottery.co.uk

The only steam-powered pottery in Britain, with 7.5 acres of things to do, including the Pots of Fun Studio, where you can
continued

throw or paint a pot, Designer-Makers at work, Café, Bistro, shops. Newt pond, play areas and pottery museum.
Times: Open daily, Winter 10-5, Summer 10-5.30 **Facilities:** 🅿 🍴 ✗ licensed ♿ toilets for disabled shop (ex guide dogs & dogs on lead) 🍴

RAVENGLASS   Map 06 SD09
RAVENGLASS & ESKDALE RAILWAY
CA18 1SW
➲ (close to A595, Barrow to Carlisle road)
☎ 01229 717171   🖷 01229 717011
e-mail: steam@ravenglass-railway.co.uk

From the Lake Disrict National Park's only coastal village of Ravenglass, small steam engines haul trains through 7 miles of outstanding, unspoilt beauty to the foot of England's highest mountains in Eskdale. Enjoy the freedom of open or cosy covered carriages. Children learn about steam with 'La'al Ratty', the Water-vole Stationmaster.
Times: Open: trains operate daily mid Mar-early Nov. Most winter wknds, plus daily in Feb Half term. **Fee:** ✱ Return fare £8.20 (ch 5-15 £4.10). 1 adult half price with 2+ fare paying children.
Facilities: 🅿 (charged) 🍴 ✗ ♿ (special coaches - prior notice advisable) toilets for disabled shop 🍴

RYDAL   Map 11 NY30
RYDAL MOUNT AND GARDENS
LA22 9LU
➲ (1.5m from Ambleside on A591 to Grasmere)
☎ 015394 33002   🖷 015394 31738
e-mail: rydalmount@aol.com

The family home of William Wordsworth from 1813 until his death in 1850. The house contains important family portraits, furniture, and many of the poet's personal possessions, together with first editions of his work. In a lovely setting overlooking Windermere and Rydal Water, the gardens were designed by Wordsworth himself. Evening visits for groups can be organised.
Times: Open Mar-Oct daily 9.30-5; Nov-Feb daily (ex Tue) 10-4 (Closed 8 Jan-1 Feb). **Fee:** £4.50 (ch £1.50, pen £3.50 & student £3.25). Garden only £2. Party 10+ (pre booked groups £3.25). Reciprocal discount ticket with Dove Cottage and Wordsworth House.
Facilities: 🅿 ♿ shop ✈ (ex guide dogs & garden) 🍴

SEDBERGH   Map 07 SD69
NATIONAL PARK CENTRE
72 Main St LA10 5AS
➲ (on Sedburgh main street at end of one way system)
☎ 015396 20125   🖷 015396 21732
e-mail: sedbergh@yorkshiredales.org.uk

At the north-western corner of the Yorkshire Dales National Park, Sedbergh is set below the Howgill Fells. The rich natural history of the area and the beautiful scenery created a need for this visitor centre; maps, walks, guides, local information and interpretative displays can be found here, and there is a full tourist information service.
Times: Open Apr-Oct, daily 10-4; Nov-Mar Fri-Sun.
Facilities: 🅿 (charged) ♿ (accessible with help Radar key scheme) shop

SHAP — Map 12 NY51

SHAP ABBEY
CA10 3NB
➲ (1.5m W of Shap on bank of River Lowther)
Dedicated to St Mary Magdalene, the abbey was founded by the Premonstratensian order in 1199, but most of the ruins are of 13th-century date. The most impressive feature is the 16th-century west tower of the church.
Times: ✱ Open any reasonable time. **Facilities:** 🅿 ♿ ✕ (ex dogs on leads)

SIZERGH — Map 07 SD48

SIZERGH CASTLE & GARDEN
LA8 8AE
➲ (3.5m S of Kendal, signed from A590)
☎ 015395 60070 ▤ 015395 60951
e-mail: sizergh@nationaltrust.org.uk
The castle has a 60-foot high tower, built in the 14th century, but most of the castle dates from the 15th to the 18th centuries. There are panelled rooms with fine carved overmantles and adze-hewn floors, and the gardens, laid out in the 18th century, contain the National Trust's largest limestone rock garden.
Times: Open Apr-Oct, Sun-Thu 1.30-5.30; Garden open Apr-Oct, from 12.30. (Last admission 5pm). **Fee:** ✱ House & Garden £5.50 (ch £2.70). Family ticket £13.70. Group rate £4.50 each. Garden only £3 (ch £1.50).
Facilities: 🅿 💷 ♿ (ramps, Braille guide, wheelchair, powered buggy) toilets for disabled shop ✕ (ex guide & hearing dogs) ✿ ▬

SKELTON — Map 12 NY43

HUTTON-IN-THE-FOREST
CA11 9TH
➲ (6m NW of Penrith on B5305 to Wigton, 2.5m from M6 junct 41)
☎ 017684 84449 ▤ 017684 84571
e-mail: info@hutton-in-the-forest.co.uk
A beautiful house, set in woods which were once part of the medieval forest of Inglewood. The house consists of a 14th-century pele tower with later additions, and contains a fine collection of furniture, portraits, tapestries and china, a 17th-century gallery and cupid staircase. The walled garden has a large collection of herbaceous plants, and there are 19th-century topiary terraces, a 17th-century dovecote and a woodland walk with impressive specimen trees.
Times: ✱ Open, House; 25 Mar-3 Apr & May-2 Oct Thu, Fri, Sun & BH 12.30-4. Gardens Daily ex Sat Good Fri-Oct 11-5 **Fee:** £5 (ch £2.50). Family ticket £13.50. Gardens £3 (ch free) **Facilities:** 🅿 💷 ♿ (electric wheelchair available) shop ✕ (ex in grounds on leads)

TEMPLE SOWERBY — Map 12 NY62

ACORN BANK GARDEN AND WATERMILL
CA10 1SP
➲ (6m E of Penrith on A66)
☎ 017683 61893 ▤ 017683 66824
e-mail: acornbank@nationaltrust.org.uk
A delightful garden of some two and a half acres, where an extensive collection of over 180 varieties of medicinal and culinary herbs is grown. Scented plants are grown in the small greenhouse, and a circular walk runs beside the Crowdundle Beck to the partially restored watermill. Please ring for details of special events.
Times: Open late Mar-Oct, daily (ex Tue) 10-5 (last admission 4.30).
Fee: ✱ £2.75 (ch £1.30). Family ticket £6.80. Party 15+ £2.
Facilities: 🅿 💷 ♿ (Braille guide, wheelchairs available) toilets for disabled shop ✕ (ex on lead on woodland walk) ✿ ▬

TROUTBECK — Map 07 NY40

TOWNEND
LA23 1LB
➲ (3m SE of Ambleside at S end of village)
☎ 015394 32628
e-mail: townend@nationaltrust.org.uk
The house is one of the finest examples of a 'statesman' (wealthy yeoman) farmer's house in Cumbria, built in 1626 for George Browne, whose descendents lived here until 1943. Inside is the original home-made carved furniture, with domestic utensils, letters and papers of the farm.
Times: Open Apr-Oct, Tue-Fri, Sun & BH Mon 1-5 or dusk if earlier. Last admission 4.30pm. **Fee:** ✱ £3.20 (ch £1.50). Family ticket £8.
Facilities: 🅿 ♿ (Braille guide) ✕ ✿

WHITEHAVEN — Map 11 NX91

THE BEACON NEW
West Strand CA28 7LY
➲ (A595, after Porton turn right onto New Rd. Follow one way system & tourist signs to the Beacon. From Barrow/Millom, A595, turn left at lights onto Inherman Terrace, left at next lights. At end turn right onto Swingpump Ln & to The Beacon)
☎ 0845 095 2131 ▤ 01946 598150
e-mail: thebeacon@copelandbc.gov.uk
Home to the town's museum collection, The Beacon traces the social, industrial and maritime heritage of the area using local characters, audio-visual displays and museum pieces. Enjoy panoramic views of the town and coast from the Met Office Weather Gallery.
Times: Open Tue-Sun, Etr-Oct 10-5.30, Nov-Mar 10-4.30. Open shool & BHs. Closed 25 Dec. **Fee:** ✱ £4.40 (ch £2.90, pen £3.60) Family £13.25. Art gallery free. **Facilities:** 🅿 (charged) 💷 ♿ (chair/stair lift, Braille signs) toilets for disabled shop ✕ ▬

THE RUM STORY NEW
27 Lowther St CA28 7DN
➲ (A595, follow town centre signs)
☎ 01946 592933 ▤ 01946 590595   **2 for 1**
e-mail: dutymanagers@rumstory.co.uk
Set in the original shop, courtyards, cellars and bonded warehouses of the Jefferson family, - the oldest rum trading family in the UK - this fascinating story takes the visitor back in time to the days of the rum trade, its links with the slave trade, sugar plantations, the Royal Navy, barrel-making and more.
Times: Open daily, Apr-Sep 10-5, Oct-Mar 10-4. Closed 25 Dec & 1 Jan.
Fee: ✱ £4.95 (ch £2.95, concessions £3.50) Family £13.60, Groups 15+ £3 **Facilities:** 🅿 (Various in area Disc zones up to 1hr) 💷 ✕ licensed ♿ (Wheelchairs, wide doors, lifts) toilets for disabled ▬

WINDERMERE — Map 07 SD49

LAKE DISTRICT VISITOR CENTRE AT BROCKHOLE
LA23 1LJ
➲ (on A591, between Windermere and Ambleside follow brown tourist signs)
☎ 015394 46601 ▤ 015394 45555
e-mail: infodesk@lake-district.gov.uk
Set in 32 acres of landscaped gardens and grounds, on the shore of Lake Windermere, this house became England's first National Park Visitor Centre in 1969. It offers exhibitions,

continued

audio-visual programmes, lake cruises, an adventure playground and an extensive events programme.
Times: Open Etr-Oct, daily 10-5. Grounds & gardens open all year.
Facilities: 🅿 (charged) 🍽 ✗ licensed ♿ (manual & electric wheelchairs, lifts, induction loops) toilets for disabled shop 🛍

WINDERMERE STEAMBOAT CENTRE
Rayrigg Rd LA23 1BN
➲ (0.5m N of Bowness-on-Windermere on A592)
☎ 015394 45565 📠 015394 48769   **2 for 1**
e-mail: steamboat@ecosse.net

A unique collection of Victorian and Edwardian steamboats and vintage motorboats, including the oldest steamboat in the world - the *S L Dolly* of 1850. Displays tell the social and commercial history of England's largest lake, and there are steamboat trips daily, weather permitting.
Times: Open 17 Mar-7 Nov daily, 10-5. Steamboat trips subject to availability & weather. **Fee:** £4.25 (ch £2.25). Family ticket £8.50, season ticket £15. **Facilities:** 🅿 🍽 ♿ toilets for disabled shop 🛍

Above: Grasmere Island

DERBYSHIRE

EVENTS & FESTIVALS

February
5th-6th Chesterfield Beer Festival, Winding Wheel, Chesterfield
8th Shrove Tuesday Winster Pancake Races, Main Street, Winster

March
29th Flagg Races, Flagg Moor

April
30th-2nd May Derbyshire Steam Fair, Hartington Moor Showground

May
14th-16th Chatsworth Horse Trials
28th Castleton Garland Ceremony

June
26th Derbyshire County Show, Showground, Elvaston

July
1st-3rd Dove Beer & Jazz Festival, Dove Holes, Buxton
8th-24th Buxton Festival, Buxton Opera House, Water Street, Buxton (provisional)
17th Ashbourne Highland Gathering (provisional)
26th Medieval Market, Chesterfield
tbc Derby Caribbean Carnival

August
3rd-4th Bakewell Show, Bakewell
29th Chesterfield Evening Fireworks

September
3rd-4th Chatsworth Country Fair
10th-11th Buxton Country Music Festival
10th-17th Chesterfield Well Dressing

October
13th Ilkeston Charter Fair, Ilkeston

November
6th Dovedale Dash, fun run at Thorpe Pastures, Thorpe

Above: Pilsbury Road in the Upper Dove Valley

BOLSOVER
Map 08 SK47

BOLSOVER CASTLE
Castle St S44 6PR
➲ (on A632)
☎ 01246 822844 📄 01246 241569

This award winning property has the air of a romantic storybook castle, with its turrets and battlements rising from a wooded hilltop. See the stunning Venus garden with its beautiful statuary and fountain. State of the art audio tours are available.

Times: Open all year, Apr & Sep-Oct, Thu-Mon 10-5; May-Jul, daily 10-6; Aug, daily 10-7; Nov-Mar, Thu-Mon 10-4. (Closed 24-26 Dec & 1 Jan). **Fee:** ✱ £6.50 (ch £3.30, concessions £4.90). Family £16.30. Prices & opening times relate to 2004, for further details phone or log onto www.english-heritage.org.uk/visits **Facilities:** 🅿 🖥 ♿ (keep not accessible) shop ✖ ⚏

BUXTON
Map 07 SK07

POOLE'S CAVERN (BUXTON COUNTRY PARK)
Green Ln SK17 9DH
➲ (1m from Buxton town centre, off A6 and A515)
☎ 01298 26978 📄 01298 73563
e-mail: info@poolescavern.co.uk

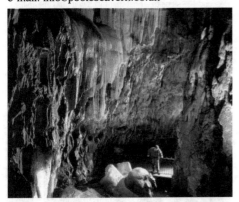

Limestone rock, water, and millions of years created this natural cavern containing thousands of crystal formations. A 45-minute guided tour leads the visitor through chambers used as a shelter by Bronze-Age cave dwellers, Roman metal workers and as a hideout by the infamous robber Poole. Attractions include the underground source of the River Wye, the 'Poached Egg Chamber', Mary, Queen of Scots' Pillar, the Grand Cascade and underground sculpture formations.

Times: ✱ Open Mar-Oct, daily 10-5. (Open in winter for groups only). **Facilities:** 🅿 ♿ toilets for disabled shop ✖ (ex guide dogs or in park) 🍴

See advertisement on this page

> We endeavour to be as accurate as possible, but changes to times and other information can occur after the guide has gone to press.

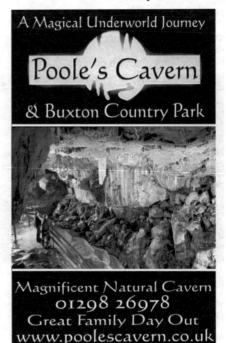

CALKE
Map 08 SK32

CALKE ABBEY
DE73 1LE
➲ (9m S of Derby, on A514)
☎ 01332 863822 📄 01332 865272
e-mail: calkeabbey@nationaltrust.org.uk

This fine baroque mansion dating from the early 18th century was built for Sir John Harpur. Among its treasures are an extensive natural history collection, a magnificent Chinese silk state bed, and a spectacular red and white drawing room. The house stands in extensive wooded parkland and also has walled flower gardens.

Times: ✱ Open 29 Mar-2 Nov, Sat-Wed & BH Mon; House & church 1-5.30 Gardens from 11am. Last admission 5pm. Park open all year until 9pm (dusk if earlier). House, church & garden closed Sat 16 Aug. **Facilities:** 🅿 ✖ licensed ♿ (Braille guide, hearing system, buggy/wheelchair available) toilets for disabled shop ✖ (ex guide dogs) ⚘

CASTLETON
Map 07 SK18

BLUE-JOHN CAVERN & MINE
Buxton Rd S33 8WP
➲ (follow brown "Blue-John Cavern" signs from Castleton)
☎ 01433 620638 & 620642 📄 01433 621586
e-mail: lesley@bluejohn.gemsoft.co.uk

A remarkable example of a water-worn cave, over a third of a mile long, with chambers 200ft high. It contains 8 of the 14 veins of Blue John stone, and has been the major source of this unique form of fluorspar for nearly 300 years.

Times: ✱ Open all year, daily 9.30-5 (or dusk). Guided tours of approx 1hr every 10 mins tour. **Facilities:** 🅿 🖥 (not suitable for disabled visitors) shop 🍴

PEAK CAVERN

S33 8WS
➲ (on A6187, in centre of Castleton)
☎ 01433 620285
e-mail: info@peakcavern.co.uk

One of the most spectacular natural limestone caves in the Peak District, with an electrically-lit underground walk of about half a mile. Ropes have been made for over 500 years in the 'Grand Entrance Hall', and traces of a row of cottages can be seen. Rope-making demonstrations are included on every tour.
Times: Open Etr-Oct, daily 10-5. Nov-Etr, wknds only 10-5
Facilities: 🅿 (charged) shop 🛍

PEVERIL CASTLE

Market Place S33 8WQ
➲ (on S side of Castleton)
☎ 01433 620613
The romantic ruins of this Norman fortress are situated high on a rocky crag and the views from the great square tower of the surrounding Peak District are breathtaking. Sir Walter Scott glamourised the castle in his novel, *Peveril of the Peak.*
Times: Open all year, Apr & Sep-Oct, daily 10-5; May-Jul, daily 10-6; Aug, daily 10-7; Nov-Mar, Thu-Mon 10-4. (Closed 24-26 Dec & 1 Jan).
Fee: ✱ £2.70 (ch £1.40, concessions £2). Family £6.80. Prices & opening times relate to 2004, for further details phone or log onto www.english-heritage.org.uk/visits **Facilities:** shop 🗙 (ex dogs on leads) 🏗

SPEEDWELL CAVERN

Winnats Pass S33 8WA
➲ (A625 becomes A6187 at Hathersage. 0.5m W of Castleton)
☎ 01433 620512 📠 01433 621888
e-mail: info@speedwellcavern.co.uk

Descend 105 steps to a boat that takes you on a one-mile underground exploration of the floodlit cavern.
Times: Open all year, Etr-Oct daily 9.30-5.30, Nov-Etr 10-5. (Closed 25 Dec). Phone to check Winter opening times due to weather.
Fee: ✱ £6 (ch £4). **Facilities:** 🅿 (charged) shop 🛍

TREAK CLIFF CAVERN

S33 8WP
➲ (0.75m W of Castleton on A6187)
☎ 01433 620571 📠 01433 620519
e-mail: treakcliff@bluejohnstone.com

An underground world of stalactites, stalagmites, flowstone, rock and cave formations, minerals and fossils. There are rich deposits of the rare and beautiful Blue John Stone, and the show caves include the Witch's Cave, Aladdin's Cave and Fairyland Grotto and some of the finest stalactites in the Peak District.
Times: Open all year, Mar-Oct, daily 10-last tour 4.20, Aug only, last tour 4.45; Nov-Feb daily 10-last tour at 3.20. All tours are guided & last about 40 mins. Enquire for last tour of day & possible closures.
Fee: ✱ £5.80 (ch 5-15 £3.20). Family ticket (2 ad & 2 ch) £16.
Facilities: 🅿 🖵 ♿ (establishment can only cater for walking disabled) shop 🛍

The End of World War II.

2005 sees the 60th anniversary of both VE (Victory in Europe) and VJ (Victory over Japan) Days. Local celebrations are planned, as are a number of national events.

CHATSWORTH — Map 08 SK27

CHATSWORTH
DE45 1PP
➲ (8m N of Matlock off B6012. 16m from M1 junct 29, signposted via Chesterfield, follow brown signs)
☎ 01246 582204   📠 01246 583536
e-mail: visit@chatsworth.org

Home of the Duke and Duchess of Devonshire, Chatsworth contains a massive private collection of fine and decorative arts. There is a splendid painted hall, and a great staircase leads to the chapel, decorated with statues and paintings. There are pictures, furniture and porcelain, and a trompe l'oeil painting of a violin on the music room door. The park was laid out by 'Capability' Brown, but is most famous as the work of Joseph Paxton, head gardener in the 19th century.
Times: Open 17 Mar-19 Dec, House & garden 11-5.30, Farmyard 10.30-5.30. **Fee:** ✱ House & Garden: £9 (ch £3.50, students & pen £7). Family ticket £21.50. Pre-booked group discounts available. Garden only: £5.50 (ch £2.50, students & pen £4). Family ticket £13.50. Farmyard & Adventure Playground: £4 (ch under 3 free, pen £3). Groups 5+ £3.50. Family pass to all attractions £35.
Facilities: 🅿 (charged) ⬛ ✕ licensed ♿ (3 electric wheelchairs available for garden) toilets for disabled shop garden centre ✈ (ex park & gardens on lead) 🖼

CRESWELL — Map 08 SK57

CRESWELL CRAGS MUSEUM AND EDUCATION CENTRE
Crags Rd, Welbeck S80 3LH
➲ (on the B6042, Crags Road, between A616 and A60, 1m E of Creswell village)
☎ 01909 720378   📠 01909 724726
e-mail: info@creswell-crags.org.uk

Creswell Crags, a picturesque limestone gorge with lakes and caves, is one of Britain's most important archaeological sites. The many caves on the site have yielded Ice Age remains, including bones of woolly mammoth, reindeer, hyena and bison, and the stone tools of Ice Age hunters from over 10,000 years ago. Visit the Museum and Education Centre to learn more about your Ice Age ancestors through an exhibition, touchscreen computers and video. Join a 'Virtually the Ice Age' cave tour, picnic in Crags Meadow, or try the new activity trail.
Times: Open all year, Feb-Oct, daily, 10.30-4.30; Nov-Jan, Sun only 10.30-4.30. **Fee:** ✱ Free. Cave & site tour £2.75 (ch £2, no under 5's). £1 parking donation requested. **Facilities:** 🅿 ♿ (mobility scooter, tour may be unsuitable due to steps) toilets for disabled shop 🖼

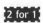
CRICH — Map 08 SK35

CRICH TRAMWAY VILLAGE
DE4 5DP
➲ (off B5035, 8m from M1 junct 28)
☎ 0870 758 7267   📠 01773 852326   **2 for 1**
e-mail: enquiry@tramway.co.uk

A mile-long scenic journey through a Period Street to open countryside with panoramic views. You can enjoy unlimited vintage tram rides, and the exhibition hall houses the largest collection of vintage electric trams in Britain. Ring for details of special events.
Times: Open Apr-Oct, daily 10-5.30 (6.30pm wknds Jun-Aug & BH wknds). Nov-Dec, wknds 10.30-4 **Fee:** ✱ £8 (ch 3-15 £4, pen £7). Family ticket (2 adults & 3 ch) £21. **Facilities:** 🅿 ⬛ ✕ licensed ♿ (Braille guidebooks, converted tram, talktype facility) toilets for disabled shop 🖼

CROMFORD — Map 08 SK25

ARKWRIGHT'S CROMFORD MILL
Mill Ln DE4 3RQ
➲ (off A6, 3m S of Matlock)
☎ 01629 824297   📠 01629 823256   **2 for 1**
e-mail: info@cromfordmill.co.uk

Sir Richard Arkwright established the world's first successful water-powered cotton spinning mill at Cromford in 1771. The Arkwright Society are involved in a major restoration to create a lasting monument to an extraordinary genius. Guided tours are available, and there is a programme of lectures and visits - ring for details. The Mill site is part of the Derwent Valley Mill World Heritage site.
Times: Open all year, daily 9-5 (Closed 25 Dec). **Fee:** Guided tour & exhibitions £2 (ch & pen £1.50). Mill site Free. **Facilities:** 🅿 ✕ ♿ ramps toilets for disabled shop 🖼

DENBY — Map 08 SK34

DENBY POTTERY VISITOR CENTRE
Derby Rd DE5 8NX
➲ (8m N of Derby off A38, on B6179, 2m S of Ripley)
☎ 01773 740799
📠 01773 740749   **FREE 2 for 1**
e-mail: visitor.centre@denby.co.uk

Situated around a cobbled courtyard with shops and a restaurant. Pottery tours are available daily including hands on activities such as paint-a-plate and make a clay souvenir. Extensive cookshop with free half hour demonstrations daily. There are lots of bargains on Denby seconds in the factory
continued

shop, hand-made blown glass from the Glass Studio, Dartington Crystal Shop, local artists gallery and hand painted Denby. (2-for-1 Voucher applies to factory tour only.)

Denby Pottery Visitor Centre

Times: Open all year. Factory tours, Mon-Thu 10.30 & 1. Craftroom tour, daily 11-3. Visitor Centre Mon-Sat 9.30-5, Sun 10-5. Closed 25-26 Dec. **Fee:** Free. Factory tour: £4.95 (ch £3.95); Craftroom tour: £3.50 (ch £2.50) **Facilities:** 🅿 💺 ✗ licensed ♿ (lift) toilets for disabled shop garden centre (outside only, ex guide dogs) 🍴

DERBY   Map 08 SK33

DERBY MUSEUM & ART GALLERY
The Strand DE1 1BS
➲ (follow directions to city centre)
☎ 01332 716659 ▤ 01332 716670
e-mail: david.fraser@derby.gov.uk   FREE

The museum has a wide range of displays, notably of Derby porcelain, and paintings by the local artist Joseph Wright (1734-97). Also antiquities, natural history and militaria, as well as many temporary exhibitions.
Times: Open all year, Mon 11-5, Tue-Sat 10-5, Sun & BHs 2-5. Closed Xmas & New Year, telephone for details. **Facilities:** 🅿 (50yds) ♿ (lift to all floors, portable mini-loop, large print labels) toilets for disabled shop ✗ (ex guide dogs)

INDUSTRIAL MUSEUM
The Silk Mill, Silk Mill Ln, off Full St DE1 3AR
➲ (From Derby inner ring road, head for Cathedral & Assembly Rooms car park. 5 mins walk from here)
☎ 01332 255308 ▤ 01332 716670
e-mail: david.fraser@derby.gov.uk   FREE

The museum is set in an early 18th-century silk mill and adjacent flour mill. Displays cover local mining, quarrying and industries, and include a major collection of Rolls Royce aero-engines from 1915 to the present. There is also a section covering the history of railway engineering in Derby.
Times: Open all year, Mon 11-5, Tue-Sat 10-5, Sun & BHs 2-5. (Closed Xmas & New Year, telephone for details). **Facilities:** 🅿 ♿ (lift to all floors) toilets for disabled shop ✗ (ex guide dogs)

PICKFORD'S HOUSE MUSEUM OF GEORGIAN LIFE & COSTUME
41 Friar Gate DE1 1DA
➲ (from A38 into Derby, follow signs to city centre)
☎ 01332 255363 ▤ 01332 255527   FREE
e-mail: ellen.malin@derby.gov.uk

The house was built in 1770 by the architect Joseph Pickford as a combined workplace and family home. It now shows domestic life at different periods, with Georgian reception rooms and service areas and a 1930s bathroom. Other galleries are devoted to temporary exhibitions. There is also a display on the growth of Georgian Derby, and on Pickford's contribution to Midlands architecture.
Times: Open all year, Mon 11-5, Tue-Sat 10-5, Sun & BHs 2-5. (Closed Xmas & New Year, telephone for details). **Facilities:** 🅿 ♿ (tape guides, video with sign language subtitles) shop ✗ (ex guide dogs)

ROYAL CROWN DERBY VISITOR CENTRE
194 Osmaston Rd DE23 8JZ
➲ (on A514, opposite Derby Royal Infirmary)
☎ 01332 712800 ▤ 01332 712899   2 for 1
e-mail: enquiries@
royal-crown-derby.co.uk

This museum traces the history of the company from 1750 to the present day, while the factory tour demonstrates the making of Royal Crown Derby in detail from clay through to the finished product. A demonstration studio gives you the opportunity to watch craftspeople at close quarters and try out a variety of different skills.
Times: Open all year, daily, Mon-Fri & Sat 9-5, Sun 10-4 (shop, Sun 10.30-5). **Fee:** ✱ Visitor centre £2.95 (concessions £2.75). Factory tour £4.95 (concessions £4.75). **Facilities:** 🅿 💺 ✗ licensed ♿ (ramps) toilets for disabled shop ✗ (ex guide dogs) 🍴

EYAM   Map 08 SK27

EYAM HALL
S32 5QW
➲ (Turn off A623 just after Calver Crossroads & village of Stoney Middleton. Turn left at the top of the hill. Eyam Hall in centre of village opposite the stocks).
☎ 01433 631976 ▤ 01433 631603   2 for 1
e-mail: nicola@eyamhall.com

An intimate 17th-century manor house in the heart of the famous "plague village". Home to the Wright family since 1671, the Hall offers a glimpse of domestic history through the eyes of one family, in portraits, furniture, tapestries, costumes and memorabilia. Converted farm buildings house the Eyam Hall Craft Centre. Please telephone for details of musical and theatrical events throughout the season.
Times: Open House: Jun-Aug, Wed-Thu, Sun & BH Mon 11-4. Craft Centre open all year Tue-Sun 11-5. **Fee:** House £4.75 (ch £3.50, pen £4.25). Family ticket £14.50. Craft centre free admission.
Facilities: 🅿 💺 ✗ licensed ♿ (disabled entrance via special gate, ramps) toilets for disabled shop ✗ (ex guide & dogs in grounds) 🍴

HADDON HALL   Map 08 SK26

HADDON HALL
DE45 1LA
➲ (1.5m S of Bakewell off A6)
☎ 01629 812855   📠 01629 814379
e-mail: info@haddonhall.co.uk

Originally held by the illegitimate son of William the
Conqueror, Haddon has been owned by the Manners family
since the 16th century. Little has been added since the reign
of Henry VIII, and, despite its time-worn steps, few medieval
houses have so successfully withstood the ravages of time.

Times: Open Apr-Sep, daily 10.30-4.30; Oct, Thu-Sun 10.30-4.
Fee: ✸ £7.25 (ch £3.75 & pen £6.25). Family ticket £19. Party 15+.
Facilities: 🅿 (charged) ✖ licensed ♿ (access is impossible for those
in wheelchairs) toilets for disabled shop 🐕 (ex guide dogs) 🏴

HARDWICK HALL   Map 08 SK46

HARDWICK HALL
Doe Lea S44 5QJ
➲ (2m S M1 junct 29)
☎ 01246 850430   📠 01246 854200
e-mail: hardwickhall@nationaltrust.org.uk

The romantic ruins of this impressive Elizabethan mansion
have spectacular views over the country park and New Hall.
An inclusive audio tour tells the story of 'Bess of Hardwick'.
Times: ✸ Open 29 Mar-26 Oct, Wed-Thu, Sat-Sun, BH Mon & Good
Fri, 12.30-5 (Oct 12.30-4). Last admission 30mins before closing.
Garden open 29 Mar-26 Oct daily ex Tue, 11-5.30.
Facilities: 🅿 ✖ licensed ♿ (large print & Braille guide, wheelchair
(pre-book)) toilets for disabled shop 🐕 (ex in park on leads) 🐾

ILKESTON   Map 08 SK44

AMERICAN ADVENTURE THEME PARK
DE7 5SX
➲ (off M1 junct 26, signposted, take A610 to A608
then A6007)
☎ 0845 330 2929   📠 01773 716140
e-mail: sales@americanadventure.co.uk

This is one of Britain's few fully themed parks, based on the
legend of a whole continent. The experiences here are
widely varied, from the Missile Rollercoaster in Spaceport
USA, to the wet and wild excitement of the Rocky Mountain
Rapids ride and the Nightmare Niagara log flume. Fort
Adventure is an action packed challenge and the driving
school is great for kids to find out if they've got what it takes
to be an advanced driver. There's also a Mississippi paddle
continued

steamer, a horse-show in Silver City, glamorous Lazy Lil's
Saloon Show Skycoaster, a 200ft free fall.
Times: ✸ Open 23 Mar-3 Nov, daily from 10. **Facilities:** 🅿 💺
✖ licensed ♿ (free wheelchair hire, must pre book, call 0845 330
2929) toilets for disabled shop 🐕 (ex guide dogs) 🏴

KEDLESTON HALL   Map 08 SK34

KEDLESTON HALL
DE22 5JH
➲ (5m NW of Derby)
☎ 01332 842191   📠 01332 841972
e-mail: kedleston@nationaltrust.org.uk

Kedleston has been the Derbyshire home of the Curzon
family for over eight centuries. The original house was
demolished at the end of the 17th century. In 1760 Robert
Adam built the south front and designed most of the interior
including the marble hall. There are pictures, furniture and
china displayed in the house together with an Indian
Museum containing the collection accumulated by Lord
Curzon, Viceroy of India.
Times: ✸ Open all year: House; 22 Mar-2 Nov, Sat-Wed 12-4.30. Last
admission 4pm. Garden; same as house but open 10-6. Park open
daily, Mar-Oct 10-6, Nov-Feb 10-4. **Facilities:** 🅿 ✖ licensed ♿ (Braille
guide, w/chair, self-drive vehicle) toilets for disabled shop 🐕 (ex in
park, must be on leads) 🐾

MATLOCK BATH   Map 08 SK25

THE HEIGHTS OF ABRAHAM CABLE CARS, CAVERNS & HILLTOP PARK
DE4 3PD
➲ (on A6, signposted from M1 junct 28 & A6.
Base station next to Matlock Bath railway station)
☎ 01629 582365   📠 01629 581128
e-mail: enquiries@h-of-a.co.uk

The visit begins with a spectacular cable car journey across
the Derwent Valley to the summit of the hill top country
park. The most famous aspects of the Heights of Abraham
are the two spectacular show caverns, which provide
exciting tours to the underground world within the hillside.
There's the 'miners tale', in the Great Rutland Cavern-Nestus
Mine and the 'story of the rock' at the Masson Cavern
Pavilion. There is also an Explorer's Challenge, woodland
walks and the Victoria Prospect Tower.
Times: ✸ Open daily 14-22 Feb & Etr-Oct 10-5; 28 Feb-26 Mar wknds
only (later in high season) for Autumn & Winter opening telephone for
details. **Fee: ✸** £8.50 (ch £5.50, senior £6.50)
Facilities: 🅿 (300mtrs) 💺 ✖ licensed ♿ (please ring for details)
toilets for disabled shop 🐕 (ex in grounds & cable car) 🏴

PEAK DISTRICT MINING MUSEUM
The Pavilion DE4 3NR
➲ (On A6 alongside River Derwent)
☎ 01629 583834
e-mail: mail@peakmines.co.uk

A large display explains the history of the Derbyshire lead industry from Roman times to the present day. The geology of the area, mining and smelting processes, the quarrying and the people who worked in the industry, are illustrated by a series of static and moving exhibits. The museum also features an early 19th-century water pressure pumping engine. There is a new recycling display in the Pump Room. **Times:** ✱ Open all year, daily 11-4 (later in summer season). Closed 25 Dec. **Facilities:** 🅿 (charged) 🍽 & (Chair lift to Mezzanine) shop ✖ (ex guide dogs)

TEMPLE MINE
Temple Rd DE4 3NR
➲ (off A6)
☎ 01629 583834
e-mail: mail@peakmines.co.uk

A typical Derbyshire mine which was worked from the early 1920s until the mid 1950s for fluorspar and associated minerals and shows examples of mining methods which give an insight into working conditions underground. **Times:** ✱ Open all year, Summer 10-5, Winter timed visits during afternoon. **Facilities:** 🅿 (100mtrs) ✖ (ex guide dogs)

MELBOURNE   Map 08 SK32
MELBOURNE HALL & GARDENS
DE73 1EN
➲ (9m S of Derby on A514, in Melbourne take turn by bus shelter in the Market Place, follow road to Church Sq)
☎ 01332 862502 📠 01332 862263
e-mail: gillweston@globalnet.co.uk

Sir John Coke (Charles I's Secretary of State) bought the lease of Melbourne Hall in 1628 and the house has been home to two Prime Ministers: Lord Melbourne and Lord Palmerston. The glorious formal gardens are among the finest in Britain. **Times:** Open, house daily throughout Aug only (ex first three Mons) 2-5 (last admission 4.15). Prebooked parties by appointment in Aug. Gardens Apr-Sep, Wed, Sat, Sun & BH Mon 1.30-5.30. Upstairs rooms available by appointment. **Fee:** House Tue-Sat (guided tour) £3.50 (ch £2, pen £3). Sun & BH Mon (no guided tour) £3 (ch £1.50, pen £2.50). House & Garden (Aug only) £5.50 (ch £3.50, pen £4.50). Garden only £3 (pen £2). Family £8. **Facilities:** 🅿 (200yds) no parking in visitor centre courtyard 🍽 & (ramp at garden entrance) shop ✖ (ex guide dogs)

MIDDLETON BY WIRKSWORTH   Map 08 SK25
MIDDLETON TOP ENGINE HOUSE
Middleton Top Visitor Centre DE4 4LS
➲ (Signed off A6 in Cromford then, 0.5m S from B5036 Cromford/Wirksworth road)
☎ 01629 823204 📠 01629 825336
e-mail: middletontop@derbyshire.gov.uk

A beam engine built in 1829 for the Cromford and High Peak Railway, and its octagonal engine house. The engine's job was to haul wagons up the Middleton Incline, and its last trip was in 1963 after 134 years' work. The visitor centre tells the story of this historic railway. **Times:** Open: Information Centre, daily, wknds only winter. Engine House Etr-Oct 1st wknd in month (engine in motion). **Fee:** Static Engine 70p (ch 40p). Working Engine £1.30 (ch 70p). **Facilities:** 🅿 (charged) & toilets for disabled shop 🍽

OLD WHITTINGTON   Map 08 SK37
REVOLUTION HOUSE
High St S41 9LA
➲ (3m N of Chesterfield town centre, on B6052 off A61, signposted)
☎ 01246 345727 📠 01246 345720   FREE
e-mail: museum@chesterfieldbc.gov.uk

Originally the Cock and Pynot alehouse, this 17th-century cottage was the scene of a meeting between local noblemen to plan their part in the Revolution of 1688. The house is now furnished in 17th-century style. A video relates the story of the Revolution and there is a small exhibition room. **Times:** Open Good Fri-Sep, daily 11-4 (ex Tue). Contact museum for Xmas opening hours. **Facilities:** 🅿 (100yds) & (signing available by prior arrangement) shop ✖ (ex guide dogs)

RIPLEY   Map 08 SK35
MIDLAND RAILWAY BUTTERLEY
Butterley Station DE5 3QZ
➲ (1m N of Ripley on B6179, signposted from A38)
☎ 01773 747674 & 749788   2 for 1
📠 01773 570721
e-mail: mrc@rapidial.co.uk

A regular steam-train passenger service runs here, to the centre where the aim is to depict every aspect of the golden days of the Midland Railway and its successors. Exhibits range from the steam locomotives of 1866 to an electric locomotive. There is also a large section of rolling stock spanning the last 100 years. **Times:** Open all year, wknds. May-Oct and most school hols. **Fee:** ✱ £8.95 (ch 5-16 £4.50, pen £7.95) children under 5 free. Party 15+. **Facilities:** 🅿 🍽 & (special accommodation on trains) toilets for disabled shop 🍽

ROWSLEY
Map 08 SK26

THE WIND IN THE WILLOWS
Peak Village DE4 2NP
➲ (at junct of A6 & B6012)
☎ 01629 733433 ▤ 01629 734850
e-mail: enquiries@windinthewillows.info

Based on the charming book written by Kenneth Grahame and illustrated by E H Shepard, this attraction brings to life the characters Mole, Ratty, Toad and Badger in an indoor recreation of the English countryside. Designed by the same team that created The World of Beatrix Potter.

Times: Open Apr-Sep, daily 10-5.30; Oct-Mar, daily 10-4.30. (Closed 25 Dec & 28-30 Jan). **Facilities:** 🅿 💺 ⚹ toilets for disabled shop ✻ (ex guide dogs) ▬

SUDBURY
Map 07 SK13

SUDBURY HALL
DE6 5HT
➲ (6m E of Uttoxeter)
☎ 01283 585305 ▤ 01283 585139
e-mail: sudburyhall@nationaltrust.org.uk

This country house was started in 1664 by Lord George Vernon. It has unusual diapered brickwork, a carved two-storey stone frontispiece, a cupola and tall chimneys. The interior features work by craftsmen including Edward Pierce and Grinling Gibbons. The Museum of Childhood contains a Victorian schoolroom, collections of toys, and displays.

Times: ✱ Open 2 Apr-2 Nov, Wed-Sun, BH Mon & Good Fri 1-5. Last admissions 30 mins before closing. Gardens open 11-6.
Facilities: 🅿 💺 ⚹ (w/chair available, large print/Braille guide & touch list) toilets for disabled shop ✻ (ex in grounds) ❧

WIRKSWORTH
Map 08 SK25

WIRKSWORTH HERITAGE CENTRE
Crown Yard DE4 4ET
➲ (on B5023 off A6 in centre of Wirksworth)
☎ 01629 825225 ▐2 for 1▌
e-mail: heritage@crownyard.fsnet.co.uk

The Centre has been created in an old silk and velvet mill. The three floors of the mill have interpretative displays of the town's past history as a prosperous lead-mining centre. Each floor offers many features of interest including a computer game called 'Rescue the injured lead-miner', a mock-up of a natural cavern, and a Quarryman's House. During the Spring Bank Holiday you can also see the famous Well Dressings. A new exhibition has opened, honouring the achievements of local girl, Ellen MacArthur, together with a gallery exhibiting and selling paintings, photographs, sculptures and ceramics by local artists.

Times: Open Mar-Etr & Nov, Wed-Sat, 11-4, Sun 1.30-4; Etr-Jun & Oct, Tue-Sat, 11-4, Sun 1.30-4; Jul-Sep, Tue-Sat 10-5, Sun 1.30-5. Also open BH Mon 10-5. Last admission 40 mins before closing. **Fee:** £3 (ch £1, pen £2). Party 20+ 10% discount **Facilities:** 🅿 (80yds) (pay & display) 💺 ✗ licensed shop ✻ (ex guide dogs)

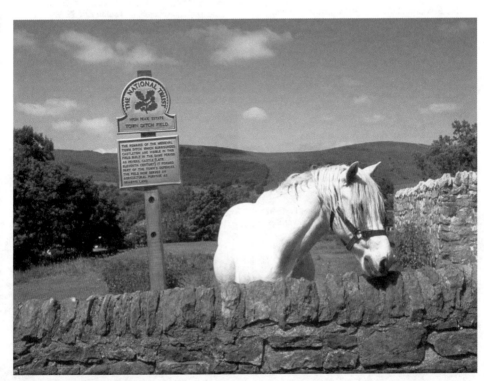

Above: A friendly pony near Castleton

DEVON

EVENTS & FESTIVALS

February
7th-19th Animated Exeter, films, workshops, exhibitions, events, various venues

March
4th-21st Vibraphonic, various venues in Exeter (jazz, soul, funk, blues, hip hop)

May
21st-22nd Devon County Show, Westpoint, Clyst St Mary
tbc Blackawton International Festival of Worm Charming, Normandy Arms, Blackawton
tbc Brixham Heritage Festival (music, dance, street theatre & fireworks)

July
tbc Exeter Summer Festival (music, entertainment, jazz, comedy & dance), various venues
tbc Okehampton Balloon Fiesta, Simmons Park, Okehampton

August
6th-7th Exeter Living History Weekend (re-enactment groups, combat displays, tournament ring)
11th Okehampton Agricultural Show
18th Chagford Agricultural Show
26th-28th West Country Balloon Fiesta, Tavistock College, Crowndale Road, Tavistock
29th-5th Aug Sidmouth International Festival (folk music, dance & song), various venues
tbc Dartmoor Folk Festival, South Zeal, Okehampton

September
8th Widecombe Fair, Old Field, Widecombe-in-the-Moor

November
tbc Plymouth American Thanksgiving Festival (various venues), Plymouth

Above: Plymouth Dome, Plymouth Hoe

ARLINGTON   Map 02 SS64

ARLINGTON COURT
EX31 4LP
➲ (7m NE of Barnstaple, on A39)
☎ 01271 850296 🖹 01271 851108
e-mail: arlingtoncourt@nationaltrust.org.uk

Arlington Court was built in 1822 and is situated in the thickly wooded Yeo Valley. The centrepiece is the Victorian mansion, surrounded by formal and informal gardens. Also open to visitors is the working stable yard, housing a collection of carriages and horse-drawn vehicles. The extensive parkland around the house is grazed by Jacob sheep and Red Devon cattle.
Times: Open 20 Mar-30 Oct, daily (ex Sat) 10.30-5. Last admission 4.30. Grounds open Nov-Mar during daylight hours. **Fee:** House & grounds £6.20 (ch £3), Family £15. Grounds only £4 (ch £2). Parties 15+ pre-booked 15% discount. **Facilities:** 🅿 🖳 ᛫ (wheelchairs, ramps at house, batricar, Braille guide) toilets for disabled shop ✈ (ex in grounds on lead) ⚙ ◧

BARNSTAPLE   Map 02 SS53

MARWOOD HILL GARDENS
Marwood EX31 4EB
➲ (signposted off A361 Barnstaple to Braunton road, follow brown tourist signs)
☎ 01271 342528

The 18-acre gardens with their three small lakes contain many rare trees and shrubs. There is a large bog garden and a walled garden, collections of clematis, camellias and eucalyptus. Alpine plants are also a feature, and there are plants for sale.
Times: Open daily (ex 25 Dec), dawn to dusk. **Fee:** £3 (ch under 12 free, if accompanied). **Facilities:** 🅿 🖳 ᛫ garden centre ✈ (ex dogs on lead) ◧

BEER   Map 03 SY28

PECORAMA PLEASURE GARDENS
Underleys EX12 3NA
➲ (from A3052 take B3174, Beer road, signed)
☎ 01297 21542 🖹 01297 20229

The gardens are high on a hillside, overlooking Beer. A miniature steam and diesel passenger line offers visitors a stunning view of Lyme Bay as it runs through the Pleasure Gardens. Attractions include an aviary, crazy golf, children's activity area and the Peco Millennium Garden. The main building houses an exhibition of railway modelling in various

continued

small gauges. There are souvenir and railway model shops, plus full catering facilities.

Times: Open Etr-Oct , Mon-Fri 10-5.30, Sat 10-1. Open Sun Etr & Whitsun-early Sep. **Fee:** ✱ £5.25 (ch 4-14 £3.50, pen £4.75, over 80 & under 4 free) **Facilities:** 🅿 💺 ✕ 🚻 (access with helper, wheelchair. Garden steep in places) toilets for disabled shop ✈ (ex guide dogs) ➥

BICTON   Map 03 SY08

BICTON PARK BOTANICAL GARDENS
East Budleigh EX9 7BJ
➲ (2m N of Budleigh Salterton on B3178, leave M5 at junct 30 & follow brown tourism signs)
☎ 01395 568465   📠 01395 568374
e-mail: info@bictongardens.co.uk

Unique Grade 1-listed 18th-century historic gardens with palm house, orangery, plant collections, extensive countryside museum, indoor and outdoor activity play areas, pinetum, arboretum, nature trail, woodland railway garden centre and restaurant. All this set in 63 acres of beautiful parkland that has been cherished for 300 years.

Times: Open Winter 10-5, Summer 10-6. (Closed 25 & 26 Dec)
Fee: ✱ £4.95 (ch & concessions £3.95). Family ticket £15.95.
Facilities: 🅿 💺 ✕ licensed 🚻 (adapted carriage on woodland railway, wheelchairs) toilets for disabled shop garden centre ➥

BLACKMOOR GATE   Map 03 SS64

EXMOOR ZOOLOGICAL PARK
South Stowford, Bratton Fleming EX31 4SG
➲ (off A399, follow brown tourist signs)
☎ 01598 763352   📠 01598 763352
e-mail: exmoorzoo@fsbdial.co.uk

Exmoor Zoo is both personal and friendly. Open since 1982 it is an ideal family venue, catering particularly for the younger generation. The zoo specialises in smaller animals, many endangered, such as the golden headed lion tamarins. Over 14 species of this type of primate are exhibited. Contact pens are provided throughout and children are encouraged to participate. Twice daily guided tours at feeding times along with handling sessions.

Times: ✱ Open daily, Apr-Oct 10-6; Nov-Mar 10-4. (Closed 21 Dec-1 Jan). **Facilities:** 🅿 💺 🚻 toilets for disabled shop ✈ (ex guide dogs) ➥

BUCKFASTLEIGH   Map 03 SX76

BUCKFAST ABBEY
TQ11 0EE
➲ (0.5m from A38, midway between Exeter and Plymouth. Turn off at 'Dart Bridge' junct and follow brown tourist signs)
☎ 01364 645500   📠 01364 643891
e-mail: enquiries@buckfast.org.uk

The Abbey, founded in 1018, was dissolved by Henry VIII in the 16th century. Restoration began in 1907, when four monks with little building experience began the work. The church was built on the old foundations, using local blue limestone and Ham Hill stone. The precinct contains several medieval monastic buildings, including the 14th-century guest hall which contains an exhibition of the history of the Abbey.

Times: Open all year daily. (Closed Good Fri, 24-26 Dec).
Facilities: 🅿 💺 🚻 (braile & audio information) toilets for disabled shop ✈ (ex guide dogs) ➥

BUCKFAST BUTTERFLY FARM & DARTMOOR OTTER SANCTUARY
TQ11 0DZ
➲ (off A38, at Dart Bridge junct, follow tourist signs)
☎ 01364 642916
e-mail: info@ottersandbutterflies.co.uk

Visitors can wander around a specially designed, undercover tropical garden, where free-flying butterflies and moths from around the world can be seen. The otter sanctuary has large enclosures with underwater viewing areas. Three types of otters can be seen including the native British otter along with Asian and North American otters.

Times: Open Good Fri-end Oct, daily 10-5.30 or dusk (if earlier).
Fee: ✱ £5.95 (ch £4.50, pen £5.50). Family ticket £16.95.
Facilities: 🅿 💺 🚻 (wheelchair ramps) shop ✈ (ex guide dogs) ➥

BUCKLAND ABBEY   Map 02 SX46

BUCKLAND ABBEY
PL20 6EY
➲ (off A386 0.25m S of Yelverton, signed)
☎ 01822 853607   📠 01822 855448
e-mail: bucklandabbey@nationaltrust.org.uk

Originally a prosperous 13th-century Cistercian Abbey, and then home of the Grenville family, Buckland Abbey was sold to Sir Francis Drake in 1581, who lived there until his death in 1596. Several restored buildings house a fascinating exhibition about the abbey's history. Among the exhibits is Drake's drum, which is said to give warning of danger to England. A recently created Elizabethan garden is also open.

Times: Open Apr-Oct, daily (ex Thu) 10.30-5.30. Nov-end Mar, Sat & Sun 2-5. Closed Xmas to mid-Feb. Last admissions 45mins before closing. **Fee:** ✱ Abbey & grounds £5.30. Grounds only £2.90. Party 15+ £4.40 each. **Facilities:** 🅿 ✕ licensed 🚻 (wheelchairs & motorised buggy available) toilets for disabled shop ✈ (ex guide dogs) ♨

CHITTLEHAMPTON   Map 03 SS62

COBBATON COMBAT COLLECTION
Cobbaton EX37 9RZ
➲ (signed from A361 & A377)
☎ 01769 540740   📠 01769 540141   **2 for 1**
e-mail: info@cobbatoncombat.co.uk

World War II British and Canadian military vehicles, war documents and military equipment can be seen in this private collection. There are over 50 vehicles including

continued

tanks, one a Gulf War Centurian, and a recently added Warsaw Pact section. There is also a section on 'Mum's War' and the Home Front. The Home Front section is now in a new purpose built building.
Times: Open Apr-Oct, daily (ex Sat) 10-5; Jul-Aug open daily. Winter open most wkdays, phone for details. **Fee:** ✱ £4.75 (ch £3.25, pen £4.25). **Facilities:** 🅿 💺 ⚒ (most areas accessible) toilets for disabled shop 🐾 (ex guide dogs, outside) 🍴

CHUDLEIGH Map 03 SX87

CANONTEIGN FALLS
EX6 7NT
➲ (off A38 at Chudleigh/Teign Valley junct onto B3193 and follow tourist signs for 3m)
☎ 01647 252434 🖬 01647 52617
e-mail: info@canonteignfalls.com
A magical combination of waterfalls, woodlands and lakes.
Times: Open all year, Mar-mid Nov, daily 10-5; Feb Half Term & Winter wknds. **Facilities:** 🅿 💺 ✗ licensed (grounds partly accessible) shop garden centre 🍴

CHURSTON FERRERS Map 03 SX95

GREENWAY GARDEN
TQ5 0ES
➲ (Turn off A3022 into Galmpton. Follow Manor Vale Road into village then follow brown signs for Greenway Garden and establishment signed)
☎ 01803 842382 🖬 01803 661900
e-mail: greenway@nationaltrust.org.uk
Greenway is a beautiful woodland garden set on the banks of the River Dart which time seems to have passed by. A garden held on the edge of wilderness, renowned for rare half-hardy trees and shrubs, underplanted by native wild flowers, Devon's best kept secret. The surrounding estate has many walks which give stunning views over the estuary. Travel by river to enjoy this peaceful haven. Greenway is not easily accessible, having some steep and slippery paths and all visitors are asked to wear walking shoes and to follow routes and directions according to their fitness on the day.
Times: Open 2 Mar-11 Oct, Wed-Sat. **Fee:** ✱ £3.90 (ch £1.95). **Facilities:** 🅿 💺 ⚒ (Part access to garden, Braille guide) toilets for disabled shop 🐾 (ex guide dogs & in Parkland) 🐾

CLOVELLY Map 02 SS32

THE MILKY WAY ADVENTURE PARK
EX39 5RY
➲ (on A39, 2m from Clovelly)
☎ 01237 431255 🖬 01237 431735
e-mail: info@themilkyway.co.uk
One of the West Country's leading attractions for the biggest rides and the best shows. Attractions include Clone Zone - Europe's first interactive adventure ride featuring a suspended roller coaster; Time Warp indoor adventure play area; daily displays from the North Devon Bird of Prey Centre; archery centre; golf driving nets; railway; pets corner and more. A new attraction 'Droid Destroyers' has been added which invites pilots to save the Earth from the Vega Asteroid.
Times: ✱ Open Etr-Oct, daily 10.30-6. Telephone for winter opening times. **Facilities:** 🅿 💺 ⚒ (ramps) toilets for disabled shop 🐾 (ex if dogs on leads) 🍴

CLYST ST MARY Map 03 SX99

CREALY ADVENTURE PARK
Sidmouth Rd EX5 1DR
➲ (leave M5 junct 30 onto A3052 Exeter to Sidmouth Road)
☎ 01395 233200 🖬 01395 233211
e-mail: fun@crealy.co.uk
Crealy Adventure Park is 15 years old in 2004, and celebrations will take place throughout the year. Among the exciting rides are Tidal Wave, Devon's first log flume which opened in 2003; El Pastil Loco Coaster; Queen Bess Pirate Ship; Techno Race Karts; Bumper Boats; Victorian Carousel, and huge indoor and outdoor playgrounds. The Animal Showtime is the showpiece of Crealy's Animal Realm, where you can ride, feed, milk, groom or cuddle the friendliest animals in Devon. Unearth the Farming Realm's original Great Farm Adventures, and discover the Summer Sunflower Maze.
Times: Open all year, Jan-mid Jul & 6 Sep-Dec, daily 10-5. (Closed winter term time Mon-Tue); mid Jul-5 Sep, daily 10-6.
Fee: ✱ £7.95-£8.95 (ch under 90cm free, pen £5.20-£6.20). Party 4+ £7.70-£8.70. **Facilities:** 🅿 💺 ✗ licensed ⚒ (Carers admitted free, rollercoaster has disabled facility) toilets for disabled shop 🍴

COMBE MARTIN Map 02 SS54

COMBE MARTIN WILDLIFE PARK & DINOSAUR PARK
EX34 0NG
➲ (M5 junct 27 then A361 towards Barnstaple and turn right onto A399)
☎ 01271 882486 🖬 01271 883869
e-mail: info@dinosaur-park.com

The land that time forgot. A subtropical paradise with hundreds of birds and animals and animatronic dinosaurs, so real they're alive! Fantastic sealion shows, falconry displays & animal handling sessions. Snow leopards, meerkats, timber wolves, apes & monkeys and lots more. A spectacular lightshow, Destination Mars, and Earthquake Canyon, the most unique train ride in the UK.
Times: Open 20 Mar-Oct, daily 10-4 (last admission 3pm).
Fee: ✱ £10 (ch 3-15 £6, ch under 3 free, pen £7). Family (2 adults & 2 ch) £29. **Facilities:** 🅿 💺 shop 🐾 (ex guide dogs) 🍴
See advertisement on opposite page

COMPTON   Map 03 SX86

COMPTON CASTLE
TQ3 1TA
➲ (off A381 Newton Abbot to Totnes road, 4m W of Torquay or 1.5m N of Maldon, off A380 (no coaches on this road))
☎ 01803 875740 ▤ 01803 875740
e-mail: greenway@nationaltrust.org.uk
Within an eight metre high curtain wall, which was built after there were French raids in the area, lies this impressive house built and extended during the 14th to 16th centuries. Compton has been the home of the Gilbert family for 600 years, and visitors can find out about their part in the exploration of the New World. The Great Kitchen still has its spiral staircase, bread ovens and knife-sharpening marks, and the withdrawing room has squints through which occupants could watch services in the chapel.
Times: Open Apr-late Oct, Mon, Wed & Thu 10-12.15 & 2-5.
Fee: ✲ Castle & garden £3.20 (ch £1.70) Party 15+ £2.60.
Facilities: 🅿 ✘ (ex guide dogs) ✖

CULLOMPTON   Map 03 ST00

DIGGERLAND NEW
Verbeer Manor EX15 2PE
➲ (M5 junct 27. E on A38 & at rdbt turn right onto A3181. Diggerland is 3m on left)
☎ 08700 344437 ▤ 0901 2010 300   **2 for 1**
e-mail: mail@diggerland
An adventure park with a difference, where kids of all ages can experience the thrills of driving real earth moving equipment. Choose from various types of diggers and dumpers ranging from 1 ton to 8 and a half tons. Supervised by an instructor complete the Dumper Truck Challenge or dig for buried treasure. New rides include JCB Robots, the Supertrack, Landrover Safari and Spin Dizzy. Even under 5's can join in, with mum or dad's help.
Times: Open 12 Feb-27 Nov, 12-5, wknds, BHs & school holidays.
Fee: £2.50 (pen £1.25, under 2's free). Additional charge to drive/ride machinery. **Facilities:** 🅿 💺 ♿ shop ✘ (ex guide dogs) ⬛

DARTMOUTH   Map 03 SX85

BAYARD'S COVE FORT
TQ6 9AT
➲ (in Dartmouth on riverfront)
Built by the townspeople to protect the harbour, the remains of the circular stronghold still stand at the southern end of the harbour.
Times: Open at all reasonable times. **Facilities:** ✘ ⚏

DARTMOUTH CASTLE
Castle Rd TQ6 0JN
➲ (1m SE off B3205, narrow approach road)
☎ 01803 833588 ▤ 01803 834445
Built at the water's edge in a superb scenic setting, the castle's military history spans well over 500 years.
Times: Open all year, Apr-Jun & Sep, daily 10-5; Jul-Aug, daily 10-6; Oct, daily 10-4; Nov-Mar, Sat-Sun 10-4 (Closed 24-26 Dec & 1 Jan).
Fee: ✲ £3.50 (ch £1.80, concessions £2.60). Prices & opening times relate to 2004, for further details phone or log onto www.english-heritage.org.uk/visits **Facilities:** 🅿 (charged) shop ✘ ⚏

WOODLANDS LEISURE PARK
Blackawton TQ9 7DQ
➲ (W, off A3122)
☎ 01803 712598 ▤ 01803 712680
e-mail: fun@woodlandspark.com

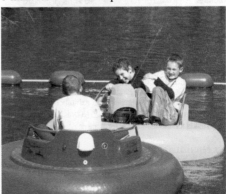

All weather fun with an outstanding range of indoor and outdoor attractions. Experience the biggest indoor venture centre in the UK. Enjoy 60 acres of outdoor attractions for all the family including three watercoasters, a 500mtr toboggan run, Arctic Gliders, Mystic Maze and 15 massive play zones. There is an indoor falconry centre with flying displays, and a wide selection of animals and birds. The Master Blaster is a game for the whole family. Blast, propel & vortex thousands of balls around the alien planet. The new rock'n'roll tugboat is a ride that's definitely different.
Times: Open 26 Mar-5 Nov daily, also wknds & school holidays.
Fee: ✲ £8.25. Family ticket £31.20 (2 ad & 2 ch). **Facilities:** 🅿 💺 ♿ (ramps) toilets for disabled shop ✘ (ex guide dogs) ⬛

DREWSTEIGNTON   Map 03 SX79

CASTLE DROGO
EX6 6PB
➲ (5m S of A30 Exeter-Okehampton. Coaches
turn off A382 at Sandy Park)
☎ 01647 433306   📠 01647 433186
e-mail: castledrogo@nationaltrust.org.uk
India tea baron Julius Drewe's dream house. This granite
castle, built between 1910 and 1930, is one of the most
remarkable works of Sir Edward Lutyens, and combines the
grandeur of a medieval castle with the comfort of the 20th
century. A great country house with terraced formal garden,
woodland spring garden, huge circular croquet lawn and
colourful herbaceous borders. Standing at more than 900ft
overlooking the wooded gorge of the River Teign with
stunning views of Dartmoor, and delightful walks.
Times: Castle open 20 Mar-7 Nov, daily (ex Tue) 11-5. Garden open all
year, daily 10.30-5.30 (or dusk if earlier). **Fee:** ✱ Castle £6.20. Garden
& grounds only £3.15. Ch half price, under 5's free. Family ticket £15.
Facilities: 🅿 💷 ♿ (Braille & large print guide, touch list) toilets for
disabled shop garden centre ✖ (ex guide/hearing dogs) 🐾 🍴

EXETER   Map 03 SX99

GUILDHALL
High St EX4 3EB
➲ (city centre)
☎ 01392 665500   FREE
e-mail: guildhall@exeter.gov.uk
This is one of the oldest municipal buildings still in use. It
was built in 1330 and then altered in 1446, and the arches
and façade were added in 1592-5. The roof timbers rest on
bosses of bears holding staves, and there are portraits of
Exeter dignitaries, guild crests, civic silver and regalia.
Times: Open when there are no mayoral functions. Times are posted
outside weekly. Special opening by arrangement.
Facilities: 🅿 (200yds) ♿ toilets for disabled ✖ (ex guide dogs)

ROYAL ALBERT MEMORIAL MUSEUM NEW
Queen St EX4 3RX city centre
☎ 01392 265858   📠 01392 421252   FREE
Situated in the heart of Exeter and home to 16 galleries of
displays and a lively programme of events and exhibitions.
Travel in time from pre-history to the present day and take a
voyage of discovery from Exeter all around the world. Also
home to the city's largest gallery and exhibition space.
Times: Open Mon-Sat 10-5. **Facilities:** 🅿 (200yds) 💷 ♿ (parking,
ramp) toilets for disabled shop ✖ (ex guide dogs)

ST NICHOLAS' PRIORY
The Mint, off Fore St EX4 3AT
➲ (Follow signs for city centre)
☎ 01392 665858   📠 01392 421252
e-mail: ramm@exeter.gov.uk
The Benedictine priory was founded in 1087. This building
was the guest wing and features a Norman undercroft, a
Tudor room, a 15th-century kitchen and a grand guest hall
with a fine arch-braced timber ceiling. Some fine plaster
decoration can be seen, and there are displays of furniture
and wood carving.
Times: Access by guide tours only, daily at 2, 2.30, 3, 3.30.
Fee: ✱ 50p per person **Facilities:** 🅿 (200yds) shop
✖ (ex guide dogs)

EXMOUTH   Map 03 SY08

THE WORLD OF COUNTRY LIFE
Sandy Bay EX8 5BU
➲ (M5 junct 30, take A376 to Exmouth. Follow
signs to Sandy Bay)
☎ 01395 274533   📠 01392 273457
All-weather family attraction including owl displays, and a
safari train that rides through a forty acre deer park. Kids will
enjoy the friendly farm animals, pets centre and animal
nursery. There are also a Victorian street, working models
and thousands of exhibits from a bygone age, including
steam and vintage vehicles.
Times: ✱ Open Etr-Oct, daily 10-5. **Facilities:** 🅿 💷 ✖ ♿ (all parts
accessible ex 'safari train') toilets for disabled shop
✖ (ex guide dogs) 🍴

GREAT TORRINGTON   Map 02 SS41

DARTINGTON CRYSTAL
EX38 7AN
➲ (Turn off A386 in centre of Great Torrington
down School Lane (opposite church). Dartington
Crystal is 200mtrs on left)
☎ 01805 626242   📠 01805 626263   [2 for 1]
e-mail: sfrench@dartington.co.uk
Dartington Crystal has won many international design
awards in recognition of its excellence. The factory tour
allows visitors to watch the glassware being crafted, from
the safety of elevated viewing galleries. All age groups are
encouraged to have fun in the glass activity area and to
discover the fascinating story of glass and the history of
Dartington in the Visitor Centre.
Times: Open all year. Visitor centre, Factory tour, Pavilion Cafe and
Shops Mon-Fri 9-5 (last tour 3.15), Sat 10-5, Sun 10-4 (tours closed
wknds). For Xmas, New Year and BH opening please telephone for
details. **Fee:** ✱ £4.50 (ch under 16 free, pen £3.50). Max 5 ch with
every full paying adult. **Facilities:** 🅿 💷 ✖ licensed ♿ toilets for
disabled shop ✖ (ex guide dogs) 🍴

RHS GARDEN ROSEMOOR
EX38 8PH
➲ (1m SE of town on A3124)
☎ 01805 624067   📠 01805 624717   [2 for 1]
e-mail: rosemooradmin@rhs.org.uk
RHS Garden Rosemoor is situated in the beautiful Torridge
Valley, set within extensive woodlands. Rich in variety, the
Formal Garden includes 200 varieties of roses, and there is a
herb garden, potager, cottage garden, winter garden, alpine
terrace and extensive herbaceous borders.
Times: Open: Gardens all year; Apr-Sep 10-6, Oct-Mar 10-5 (closed 25
Dec); Visitor Centre as for Gardens but closed 24-26 Dec. **Fee:** ✱ £5
(ch 6-16 £1; under 6 free). Party 10+ £4 **Facilities:** 🅿 💷 ✖ licensed
♿ (Herb garden for disabled) toilets for disabled shop garden centre
✖ (ex guide dogs) 🍴

HONITON   Map 03 ST10

ALLHALLOWS MUSEUM
High St EX14 1PG
➲ (next to parish church of St Paul in the High
Street)
☎ 01404 44966 & 42996
e-mail: info@honitonmuseum.co.uk
The museum, housed in a chapel dating back to around
1200, has a wonderful display of Honiton lace, and there are
continued

lace demonstrations from June to August. The town's history is also illustrated.

Times: Open Mon before Etr-Sep, Mon-Fri 9.30-4.30 & Sat 9.30-1. Oct, Mon-Fri 9.30-3.30, Sat 9.30-12.30. **Fee:** £2 (pen £1.50, accompanied ch free). **Facilities:** P (400yds) & (stair lift between floors, wheelchair available) shop ✗ (ex guide dogs)

ILFRACOMBE   Map 02 SS54

ILFRACOMBE MUSEUM
Runnymede Gardens, Wilder Rd EX34 8AF
➲ (Situated next to the Landmark Theatre & TIC on seafront)
☎ 01271 863541
e-mail: ilfracombe@devonmuseums.net   `2 for 1`

Ilfracombe was an important trading port from the 14th to the 16th centuries and during the Napoleonic Wars became a popular resort. The history, archaeology, geology, natural history and maritime traditions of the area are illustrated here, along with Victoriana, costumes, photographs and china.

Times: Open all year, Apr-Oct, daily 10-5; Nov-Mar, Mon-Fri 10-1. **Fee:** ✱ £1.50 (ch 50p, concessions £1). Booked disabled school groups free. **Facilities:** P (10yds) & (ramp to front door, wide aisles) shop ✗ (ex guide dogs)

WATERMOUTH CASTLE & FAMILY THEME PARK
EX34 9SL
➲ (3m NE off A399, midway between Ilfracombe & Combe Martin)
☎ 01271 863879   ▤ 01271 865864
e-mail: enquiries@watermouthcastle.com

A popular family attraction including mechanical music demonstrations, musical water show, dungeon labyrinths, Victorian displays, bygone pier machines, animated fairy tale scenes, tube slide, mini golf, children's carousel, swingboats, aeroplane ride, water fountains, river ride, gardens and a maze.

Times: Open Apr-end Oct, closed Sat. (Also closed some Mon & Fri off season). Ring for further details. **Fee:** ✱ £9 (ch 3-13 £7.50 & pen £6.50) **Facilities:** P ▣ & (special wheelchair route) toilets for disabled shop ✗ (ex guide dogs) ▬

KILLERTON HOUSE &   Map 03 SS90
GARDEN

KILLERTON HOUSE & GARDEN
EX5 3LE
➲ (off B3181 Exeter to Culhampton road)
☎ 01392 881345   ▤ 01392 883112   `2 for 1`

Elegant 18th-century house set in an 18-acre garden with sloping lawns and herbaceous borders. A majestic avenue of beech trees runs up the hillside, past an arboretum of rhododendrons and conifers. The garden has an ice house and rustic summer house where the family's pet bear was once kept. Inside the house are displays from the Killerton Dress Collection, and a Victorian kitchen.

Times: Open: House, daily (ex Tue), Mar & Oct, Wed-Sun, Aug daily 11-5. Gardens open all year, daily from 10.30. **Fee:** ✱ House & grounds £5.80. Grounds only £4.20 **Facilities:** P ▣ ✗ licensed & (wheelchairs & motorised buggy available) toilets for disabled shop garden centre ✗ (ex in park & guide dogs) ♨

KINGSBRIDGE   Map 03 SX74

COOKWORTHY MUSEUM OF RURAL LIFE
The Old Grammar School, 108 Fore St TQ7 1AW
➲ (A38 onto A384, then A381 to Kingsbridge, museum at the top of the town)
☎ 01548 853235
e-mail: wcookworthy@talk21.com

The 17th-century schoolrooms of this former grammar school are now the setting for another kind of education. Reconstructed room-sets of a Victorian kitchen, an Edwardian pharmacy, a costume room and extensive collection of local historical items are gathered to illustrate South Devon life. A walled garden and farm gallery are also features of this museum, founded to commemorate William Cookworthy, 'father' of the English china clay industry. The Local Heritage Resource Centre with public access databases, microfilm of local newspapers since 1855 and Devon record service point are available to visitors. Please ring for details of special events.

Times: Open all year, 21 Mar-Sep, Mon-Sat 10.30-5; Oct 10.30-4. Nov-Mar groups by arrangement. Local Heritage Resource Centre open all year, Mon-Thu 10-12 & Wed also 2-4, other times by appointment. **Fee:** ✱ £2 (ch 90p, pen £1.50). Family ticket £5 (2 ad & 4 ch). Party rates available. **Facilities:** P (100mtrs) (max 3hrs) & (Braille labels on selected exhibits) toilets for disabled shop ✗ (ex guide dogs)

KINGSWEAR   Map 03 SX85

COLETON FISHACRE HOUSE & GARDEN
Brownstone Rd TQ6 0EQ
➲ (3m from Kingswear. Take Ferry Road and turn off at Toll House, follow brown tourist signs)
☎ 01803 752466   ▤ 01803 753017
e-mail: coletonfishacre@nationaltrust.org.uk

The house, set in a stream-fed valley on a beautiful stretch of south Devon coastline, was designed in the 1920s for Rupert and Lady D'Oyly Carte (of Gilbert & Sullivan fame) reflecting the Arts & Crafts tradition, but with refreshingly modern interiors. A luxuriant garden was created around it, and has year-round interest with a wide variety of rare and exotic plants.

Times: Garden open 1-30 Mar, Sat & Sun only 11-5; 31 Mar-Oct, Wed-Sun & BH Mon 10.30-5.30. House open 31 Mar-Oct, Wed-Sun & BH Mon 11-4.30. **Fee:** ✱ House & garden £5.25 (ch £2.60). Family ticket £13. Party £4.50 (ch £2.25). Garden only £4.10 (ch £2). **Facilities:** P ▣ & (wheelchairs available, Braille guides) toilets for disabled shop garden centre ✗ (ex guide dogs) ♨ ▬

KNIGHTSHAYES COURT   Map 03 SS91

KNIGHTSHAYES COURT
EX16 7RQ
➲ (M5 junct 27, 2m N of Tiverton off A396)
☎ 01884 254665 & 257381   ▤ 01884 243050
e-mail: knightshayes@nationaltrust.org.uk

This fine Victorian mansion, a rare example of William Burges' work, offers much of interest to all ages. The garden is one of the most beautiful in Devon, with formal terraces, amusing topiary, a pool garden and woodland walks.

Times: House & garden open 27 Mar-Oct, daily (House closed Fri) 11-5.30. **Facilities:** P ▣ ✗ licensed & (wheelchairs available, lift, Braille & audio guide) toilets for disabled shop garden centre ✗ (ex guide dogs in house) ♨

LYDFORD
LYDFORD CASTLE AND SAXON TOWN

EX20 4BH

⮕ (in Lydford off A386)

Map 02 SX58

Standing above the gorge of the River Lyd, this tower, dating back to the twelfth century, was notorious as a prison. The earthworks of the original Norman fort lie to the south.

Times: Open all reasonable times. **Facilities:** 🅿 ✈ (ex dogs on leads) 🐾

LYDFORD GORGE

EX20 4BH

⮕ (off A386, between Okehampton & Tavistock)

☎ 01822 820320 & 820441 ▯ 01822 822000

e-mail: lydfordgorge@nationaltrust.org.uk

The spectacular gorge has been formed by the River Lyd, which has cut into the rock and caused swirling boulders to scoop out potholes in the stream bed. This has created some dramatic features, notably the Devil's Cauldron close to Lydford Bridge. At the end of the gorge is the 90ft-high White Lady Waterfall.

Times: Open Apr-Sep, daily 10-5.30; Oct, daily 10-4. (Nov-Mar, waterfall entrance only, daily 10.30-3). **Fee:** ✱ £4 (ch 5-16 £2, under 5 free) Party £3.40 (ch £1.70). **Facilities:** 🅿 ▣ (easy access path above gorge, audio tapes) shop 🐾

MORWELLHAM
MORWELLHAM QUAY

PL19 8JL

⮕ (4m W of Tavistock, off A390. Midway between Gunnislake & Tavisock. Signed)

Map 02 SX47

☎ 01822 832766 & 833808 ▯ 01822 833808

e-mail: enquiries@morwellham-quay.co.uk

Morwellham was the greatest copper port in Queen Victoria's empire. Once the mines were exhausted the port area disintegrated into wasteland, until 1970 when a charitable trust was set up for its restoration. Visitors can ride by electric tramway underground into a copper mine, last worked in 1869. The staff wear Victorian costume and visitors can try on replica costumes in the Limeburner's Cottage.

Times: Open all year (ex Xmas wk) 10-6 (4.30 Nov-Etr). Last admission 3.30 (2.30 Nov-Etr). **Fee:** ✱ £8.90 (ch 5-16 £6, pen & students £7.80). **Facilities:** 🅿 ▣ ✖ licensed ♿ (smooth paths, but difficult areas in Victorian village) toilets for disabled shop 🍴

NEWTON ABBOT
BRADLEY MANOR

TQ12 6BN

⮕ (SW of Newton Abbot on A381 Totnes road. 1m from town centre)

Map 03 SX87

☎ 01626 354513

e-mail: greenway@nationaltrust.org

A National Trust property of 70 acres, the 15th-century house and chapel are surrounded by woodland. The River Lemon and a millstream flow through the estate.

Times: Open Apr-Sep, Tue-Thu, 2-5; Oct by appointment **Fee:** ✱ £3 (ch £1.50) **Facilities:** 🅿 ♿ ✈ 🚻 🐾

HEDGEHOG HOSPITAL AT PRICKLY BALL FARM

Denbury Rd, East Ogwell TQ12 6BZ

⮕ (1.5m from Newton Abbot on A381 towards Totnes, follow brown heritage signs)

☎ 01626 362319 & 330685 ▯ 01626 330685

e-mail: hedgehog@hedgehog.org.uk

See, touch and learn about this wild animal. In mid-season see baby hogs bottle feeding. Find out how to encourage hedgehogs into your garden and how they are put back into the wild. Talks on hedgehogs throughout the day, short basic video information about hedgehogs available.

Times: Open wk before Etr-end Oct, 10.30-5. Last admission 1hr before closing. **Facilities:** 🅿 ▣ ♿ (large print menu, use of wheelchair, Braille menu) toilets for disabled shop garden centre ✈ (ex guide dogs) 🍴

TUCKERS MALTINGS

Teign Rd TQ12 4AA

⮕ (follow brown tourist signs from Newton Abbot railway station)

☎ 01626 334734 ▯ 01626 330153

e-mail: info@tuckersmaltings.com

The only working Malthouse in England open to the public, producing malt from barley for over 30 West Country breweries. Learn all about the process of malting - and taste the end product at the in-house brewery. Guided tours last an hour.

Times: Open Good Fri-end Oct, Mon-Sat (Closed Sun ex in Jul & Aug). Speciality bottled beer shop open throughout the year. Phone to check winter opening. **Fee:** ✱ £5.25 (ch 5-15 £3.25, 16-17 £3.95, pen £4.75). Family ticket £14.95. **Facilities:** 🅿 (100yds) (pay & display car park) ♿ toilets for disabled shop 🍴

OKEHAMPTON
MUSEUM OF DARTMOOR LIFE

3 West St EX20 1HQ

⮕ (follow brown signs off all major roads into Okehampton. Museum on main road next to White Hart Hotel)

Map 02 SX59

☎ 01837 52295 ▯ 01837 659330

e-mail: dartmoormuseum@eclipse.co.uk

Housed on three floors in an early 19th century mill, the museum tells the story of how people have lived, worked and played on and around Dartmoor through the centuries. It shows how the moorland has shaped their lives just as their work has shaped the moorland. In the Cranmere Gallery, temporary exhibitions feature local history, art and crafts.

Times: ✱ Open Etr-Oct, Mon-Sat 10-5 (also Sun, Jun-Sep). Winter opening times, telephone for details. **Facilities:** 🅿 ▣ shop

OKEHAMPTON CASTLE

Castle Lodge EX20 1JB

⮕ (1m SW of town centre)

☎ 01837 52844

Once the largest castle in Devon set amongst the stunning Dartmoor foothills. A free audio tour brings this romantic ruin to life.

Times: Open Apr-Jun & Sep, daily 10-5; Jul-Aug, daily 10-6. Closed Oct-Mar. **Fee:** ✱ £2.80 (ch £1.40, concessions £2.10). Prices & opening times relate to 2004, for further details phone or log onto www.english-heritage.org.uk/visits **Facilities:** 🅿 shop ✈ (ex dogs on leads) 🎋

OTTERTON   Map 03 SY08
OTTERTON MILL CENTRE
EX9 7HG
➲ (on the B3178 between Budleigh Salterton and Newton Poppleford)
☎ 01392 568521   FREE
e-mail: escape@ottertonmill.com

Set beside the River Otter in one of Devon's loveliest valleys, Otterton Mill is a centuries-old working watermill, a famous bakery and shop full of local produce, a restaurant, and a gallery of arts and crafts from local artists.
Times: Open every day from 10. **Facilities:** 🅿 ✗ licensed ♿ (free entry to ground floor) shop ▰

PAIGNTON   Map 03 SX86
PAIGNTON & DARTMOUTH STEAM RAILWAY
Queens Park Station, Torbay Rd TQ4 6AF
➲ (from Paignton follow brown tourist signs)
☎ 01803 555872   ▤ 01803 664313
e-mail: pdsr@talk21.com

Steam trains run for seven miles from Paignton to Kingswear on the former Great Western line, stopping at Goodrington Sands, Churston, and Kingswear, connecting with the ferry crossing to Dartmouth. Combined river excursions available. Ring for details of special events.
Times: Open Jun-Sep, daily 9-5.30 & selected days Oct & Apr-May.
Fee: ✱ Paignton to Kingswear £7 (ch £5, pen £6.50). Family £22. Paignton to Dartmouth (including ferry) £8.50 (ch £5.80, pen £8). Family £26. **Facilities:** 🅿 (5mins walk) 🍽 ♿ (wheelchair ramp for boarding train) toilets for disabled shop ▰

PAIGNTON ZOO ENVIRONMENTAL PARK
Totnes Rd TQ4 7EU
➲ (1m from Paignton town centre on A3022 Totnes road)
☎ 01803 697500   ▤ 01803 523457
e-mail: info@paigntonzoo.org.uk

Paignton is one of Britain's biggest zoos, set in a beautiful and secluded woodland valley, where new enclosures are spacious and naturalistic. A tour will take you through some of the world's threatened habitats - Forest, Savannah, Wetland and Desert, with hundreds of species, many of them endangered and part of conservation breeding programmes.
continued

There are regular keeper talks, a children's play area, and special events include an annual Easter Egg Safari.
Times: Open all year, daily 10-6 (5pm in winter). Last admission 5pm (4pm in winter). (Closed 25 Dec). **Fee:** ✱ £8.50 (ch 3-15 £6.20, students £7). Family ticket £26.70 **Facilities:** 🅿 🍽 ✗ licensed ♿ (some steep hills, wheelchair loan-booking essential) toilets for disabled shop 🐾 (ex guide dogs) ▰
See advertisement on this page

PLYMOUTH   Map 02 SX45
CITY MUSEUM & ART GALLERY
Drake Circus PL4 8AJ
➲ (turn off A38 onto A374, follow signs to city centre, museum on NW of city centre, opposite university)
☎ 01752 304774   ▤ 01752 304775
e-mail: museum@plymouth.gov.uk

The City Museum and Art Gallery is home to a Fine and Decorative Art Collection of paintings, prints and Reynolds family portraits, silver and Plymouth China, and the Cottonian Collection of drawings, sculpture and books. There is a lively programme of art exhibitions, as well as archaeology, local and natural history displays, and the Discovery Centre with a 'hands-on' section for children.
Times: ✱ Open all year, Tue-Fri 10-5.30, Sat 10-5, BH Mon 10-5. (Closed Good Fri & 25-26 Dec). **Facilities:** 🅿 (200yds) ♿ (wheelchair available) toilets for disabled shop 🐾 (ex guide dogs)

THE GREEN HOUSE VISITOR CENTRE NEW
The Ride PL9 7JA
➲ (Located 2 miles E of Plymouth City Centre on the A379 Kingsbridge road. Follow signs for Chelson Meadow)
☎ 01752 482392
e-mail: nowaste@the greenhouseplymouth.org.uk
The UK's first leisure-based, sustainable waste, education exhibition. A responsible attitude to waste is promoted via informal, yet informative, interactive exhibitions. These include a giant energy-generating hamster wheel; underground caves where the whole family can learn about waste separation and the machinery used to do it, helped along by Colin the Can and Betty the Bottle; waste disposal challenges, and more.
Times: Tue-Sat 10-5. Last entry at 4pm **Fee:** ✱ £3, under 5's free. Groups 4+ £2.50 **Facilities:** 🅿 ◪ ⭑ toilets for disabled shop ✖ (ex guide dogs)

MERCHANT'S HOUSE MUSEUM
33 St Andrews St PL1 2AX
➲ (Turn off A38 onto A374, follow signs to city centre, house located behind St Andrew's Church).
☎ 01752 304774   ▤ 01752 304775
e-mail: plymouth.museum@plymouth.gov.uk
The largest and finest 16th-century house surviving in Plymouth. Inside visitors can discover various aspects of Plymouth's past, including a reconstructed Victorian pharmacy, life during World War II, and a Victorian schoolroom which is available for group bookings.
Times: ✱ Open Apr-Sep, Tue-Fri 10-5.30, Sat 10-5, BH Mon 10-5 during summer (closed 1-2). **Facilities:** 🅿 (400yds) ⭑ shop ✖

PLYMOUTH DOME
The Hoe PL1 2NZ
☎ 01752 603300 & 600608 (recorded message)   ▤ 01752 256361
This high-tech visitor centre lets you explore the sounds and smells of an Elizabethan street, walk the gun-deck of a galleon, dodge the press gang, stroll with film stars on an ocean liner, and witness the devastation of the Blitz. Examine satellite weather pictures as they arrive from space, keep up to date with shipping movements and monitor the busy harbour on radar. An excellent introduction to Plymouth and a colourful interpretation of the past. Ring for details of special events.
Times: Open Apr-Oct, daily 10-5; Nov-Mar, Tue-Sat 10-4 **Fee:** ✱ £4.75 (ch £3.25 ch under 5 free, pen & students £3.75). Family (2 ad+2 ch) £13. **Facilities:** 🅿 (200yds) ◪ ⭑ (audio descriptions, induction loop, wheelchairs available) toilets for disabled shop ✖ (ex guide dogs) ▦

ROYAL CITADEL
PL1 2PD
➲ (at the end of Plymouth Hoe)
☎ 01752 775841
e-mail: plymouthbbg@hotmail.com
A dramatic 17th-century fortress built to defend the coastline from the Dutch. It is still in use today.
Times: Open May-Sep, daily. Access by guided tour only. **Fee:** ✱ £3 (EH Members £2.75). Prices & opening times relate to 2004, for further details phone or log onto www.english-heritage.org.uk/visits
Facilities: ✖ ▥

PLYMPTON   Map 02 SX55

SALTRAM
PL7 1UH
➲ (3.5m E of Plymouth, between A38 & A379. Take Plympton turn at Marsh Mill rdbt, turn right at 4th traffic lights to Cot Hill. At t-junct right into Merafield Rd, Saltram 0.25m on right)
☎ 01752 333500 & 01752 333503
▤ 01752 336474
e-mail: saltram@nationaltrust.org.uk
This magnificent George II house still has its original contents. The collection of paintings was begun at the suggestion of Reynolds and includes many of his portraits. The saloon and dining room were designed by Robert Adam and have superb decorative plasterwork and period furniture.
Times: ✱ Open House: late Mar-late Oct, Sat-Thu 12-4.30. Garden open all year, Mar-Nov 10.30-5.30, Nov-Feb 11-4. **Facilities:** 🅿 ◪ ✖ licensed ⭑ (wheelchairs available, lift, Braille & audio guides) toilets for disabled shop ✖ (ex in park on leads) ▦ ▦

POWDERHAM   Map 03 SX98

POWDERHAM CASTLE
EX6 8JQ
➲ (signposted off A379 Exeter/Dawlish road)
☎ 01626 890243   ▤ 01626 890729
e-mail: castle@powderham.co.uk
Built between 1390 and 1420, this ancestral home of the Earls of Devon was damaged in the Civil War. The house was restored and altered in later times and is set in beautiful rose gardens with views over the deer park to the Exe Estuary. Ring for details of special events.
Times: Open Etr-end Oct, 10-5.30 (last admission 5pm). Closed Sat.
Facilities: 🅿 ◪ ✖ licensed ⭑ (ramps) toilets for disabled shop garden centre ▦

SALCOMBE   Map 03 SX73

OVERBECKS MUSEUM & GARDEN
Sharpitor TQ8 8LW
➲ (1.5m SW of Salcombe, signed from Malborough & Salcombe, narrow approach road)
☎ 01548 842893   ▤ 01548 845020
e-mail: dovrcx@smtp.ntrust.org.uk
The garden is on the most southerly tip of Devon, and allows many exotic plants to flourish. The Edwardian house displays toys, dolls and a natural history collection, and there is a secret room for children where they can search for 'Fred' the friendly ghost.
Times: Open Apr-Jul Sun-Fri 11-5.30; Aug daily 11-5.30; Sep Sun-Fri 11-5.30; Oct Sun-Thu 11-5. Gardens open all year, 10-6 (or sunset if earlier). **Fee:** ✱ Museum & gardens £4.60 (ch £2.30). Gardens only £3.40 (ch £1.70). Family ticket £11.50. **Facilities:** 🅿 ◪ ⭑ (ramp from garden, Braille guide) shop ✖ (ex guide dogs) ▦ ▦ ▦

SOUTH MOLTON   Map 03 SS72

QUINCE HONEY FARM
EX36 3AZ
➲ (3.5m W of A361, on N edge of South Molton)
☎ 01769 572401   ▤ 01769 574704   **2 for 1**
e-mail: info@quincehoney.co.uk
Follow the story of honey and beeswax from flower to table. The exhibition allows you to see the world of bees close up in complete safety; hives open at the press of a button

continued

revealing the honeybees' secret life. After viewing the bees at work, sample the fruits of their labour in the café or shop.
Times: Open daily, Apr-Sep 9-6; Oct 9-5; Shop only Nov-Etr 9-5. (Closed 25 Dec-4 Jan). **Fee:** ✱ £3.50 (ch 5-16 £2, pen £2.80)
Facilities: 🅿 🍴 ♿ toilets for disabled shop ✖ (ex guide dogs) 🍴

STICKLEPATH   Map 03 SX69

FINCH FOUNDRY
EX20 2NW
➲ (Turn off A30 at Okehampton junct, follow brown signs to Finch Foundry. Located in main street of village. Approx 4m from Okehampton).
☎ 01837 840046   🖷 01837 840046
Finch Foundry was, in the 19th century, a water-powered factory for making sickles, scythes, shovels and other hand tools. Although no longer in production, three waterwheels can still be seen driving huge hammers, shears, grindstone and other machinery, with daily working demonstrations. These demonstrations explain the key role the foundry played in the local community.
Times: Open Apr-Nov, daily ex Tue, 11-5.30. **Facilities:** 🅿 🍴 ♿ (access to shop/tea room, view main foundry via shop) shop ✖ 🍴

TAVISTOCK

See **Morwellham**

TIVERTON   Map 03 SS91

TIVERTON CASTLE
EX16 6RP
➲ (M5 junct 27, then 7m on A361 towards Tiverton to rdbt where Castle is signposted)
☎ 01884 253200 & 255200   `2 for 1`
🖷 01884 254200
e-mail: **tiverton.castle@ukf.net**
The original castle, built in 1106 by order of Henry I, was rebuilt late 13th-14th centuries. It resisted General Fairfax during the Civil War but fell to him when a lucky shot hit the drawbridge chain. Now a private house, the gardens are lovely and there's a fine Civil War armoury.
Times: Open Etr Sun-end Oct, Sun,Thu & BH Mon's only 2.30-5.30. Last admission 5pm **Fee:** £4 (ch 7-16 £2, under 7 free). Disabled half price if accessing ground floor only. **Facilities:** 🅿 ♿ toilets for disabled shop ✖ (ex guide dogs)

TIVERTON MUSEUM OF MID DEVON LIFE
Beck's Square EX16 6PJ
➲ (in centre of town next to Beck's Square car park)
☎ 01884 256295   `2 for 1`
e-mail: **curator@tivertonmusuem.org.uk**
This large and comprehensive museum now with 15 galleries, re-opened after extensive rebuilding and redisplayed throughout. It is housed in a 19th-century school and the exhibits include a Heathcote Lace Gallery featuring items from the local lace-making industry. There is also an agricultural section with a collection of farm wagons and implements. Other large exhibits include two waterwheels and a railway locomotive with many GWR items.
Times: Open Feb-mid Dec, Mon-Fri 10.30-4.30, Sat 10-1. **Fee:** £3.50 (ch £1, pen £2.50) **Facilities:** 🅿 (100yds) ♿ (lift, induction loop) toilets for disabled shop ✖ (ex guide dogs)

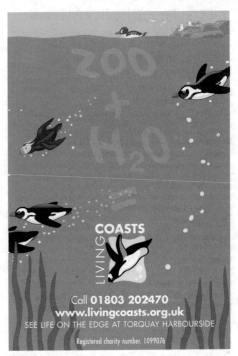

Call **01803 202470**
www.livingcoasts.org.uk
SEE LIFE ON THE EDGE AT TORQUAY HARBOURSIDE
Registered charity number. 1099076

TORQUAY   Map 03 SX96

BABBACOMBE MODEL VILLAGE
Hampton Av, Babbacombe TQ1 3LA
➲ (follow brown tourist signs from outskirts of town)
☎ 01803 328669 & 315315   🖷 01803 315173
e-mail: **ss@babbacombemodelvillage.co.uk**
Set in four acres of beautifully maintained, miniature landscaped garden, the village contains over 400 models and 1200ft of model railway. City Lights, an evening illuminations feature, depicts Piccadilly Circus in miniature. At the end of your visit, enjoy a new facility that offers breathtaking views over the model village. There are also free trips on an open-top bus. Computer presentation area; undercover display area; vintage model railway layout; and the new Aquaviva, an evening water, light and sound spectacular.
Times: Apr-May, 10-5.30; Jun-Aug, 10am-10.30pm; Sep, 10-9.30; Oct, 10-5; Nov-Feb 10-4.30. Closed 25 Dec. **Fee:** ✱ £6.40 (ch £3.95, pen £5.40). Family ticket £18.50. **Facilities:** 🅿 (charged) 🍴 ✖ ♿ (push button audio information) toilets for disabled shop garden centre 🍴

'BYGONES'
Fore St, St Marychurch TQ1 4PR
➲ (follow tourist signs into Torquay and St Marychurch)
☎ 01803 326108   🖷 01803 326108
Step back in time in this life-size Victorian exhibition street of over 20 shops including a forge, pub and period display rooms, housed in a former cinema. Exhibits include a large model railway layout, illuminated fantasyland, railwayana and military exhibits including a walk-through World War I trench. At Christmas the street is turned into a winter wonderland. A new set piece features Babbacombe's John
continued

Lee ('the man they couldn't hang') in his cell. There is something here for all the family.

Times: ✱ Open all year, Summer 10-9.30, (Fri-Sun 10-6); Spring & Autumn 10-6; Winter 10-4, wknds & school hols 10-5. (Last entry 1hr before closing). **Facilities:** 🅿 (50yds) 🖭 (ramp) shop ✱ (ex guide dogs)

KENTS CAVERN

Cavern House, 91 Ilsham Rd, Wellswood TQ1 2JF
➲ (1.25m NE off B3199, follow brown tourist signs. 1m from Torquay Harbour)
☎ 01803 215136 🖹 01803 211034
e-mail: caves@kents-cavern.co.uk

Probably the most important Palaeolithic site in Britain and recognised as one of the most significant archaeological areas. This is not only a world of spectacular natural beauty, but also a priceless record of past times, where a multitude of secrets of mankind, animals and nature have become trapped and preserved over the last 500,000 years. 170 years after the first excavations and with over 80,000 remains already unearthed, modern research is still discovering new clues to our past.

Times: Open daily (ex 25 Dec). Oct-Mar 10-last tour 4pm; Apr-Jun & Sep 10-last tour 4.30pm; Jul-Aug 9.30-last tour 5pm. Evenings: Jul-Aug (Mon-Thu) 6-9.30. **Fee:** ✱ Daytime: £6 (ch 4-15 £3.80) Family £17.60. Ghost evening tour: £6.30 (ch £3.90) Family £18.40. **Facilities:** 🅿 🖭 ✗ licensed ♿ toilets for disabled shop ✱ (ex guide dogs) 🍴

LIVING COASTS

Beacon Quay TQ1 2BG
➲ (once in Torquay follow A379 and brown tourist signs)
☎ 01803 202470 🖹 01803 202471
e-mail: info@livingcoasts.org.uk

Living Coasts is an unusual and ambitious attraction that allows visitors to take a trip around the coastlines of the world without leaving Torquay. Specially designed environments are home to fur seals, puffins, penguins, ducks, rats, and waders among others. All the animals can

continued

be seen above and below the water, whilst the huge meshed aviary allows the birds to fly free over your head. Visitors can obtain special joint tickets which will allow them to visit nearby Paignton Zoo.

Times: Open daily from 10. (Closed 25 Dec) **Fee:** ✱ £5.70 (ch over 3 £4, pen £4.40). Family ticket (2 adults, 2 ch) £17.50 **Facilities:** 🅿 🖭 ✗ licensed ♿ (wheelchair hire) toilets for disabled shop ✱ (ex assist dogs) 🍴

See advertisement on page 71

TOTNES   Map 03 SX86

GUILDHALL

Rampart Walk, off High St TQ9 5QH
➲ (behind St Mary's Church on the main street)
☎ 01803 862147 🖹 01803 864275
e-mail: totnestowncouncil@btinternet.com

Originally the refectory, kitchens, brewery and bakery for the Benedictine Priory of Totnes (1088-1536), the building was established as the Guildhall in 1553 during the reign of Edward VI. A magistrates' court and a prison opened in 1624, and the council chamber is still used today.

Times: Open Apr-Sep, Mon-Wed 10-3; Other times by appointment. **Fee:** ✱ £1 (ch 25p). **Facilities:** 🅿 (50yds)

TOTNES CASTLE

TQ9 5NU
➲ (on hill overlooking town)
☎ 01803 864406

One of the best surviving examples of a Norman motte and bailey castle with spectacular views. The once great ditch that surrounded the keep is today filled with the cottages and gardens of the town.

Times: Open Apr-Jun & Sep, daily 10-5; Jul-Aug, daily 10-6; Oct, daily 10-4. **Fee:** ✱ £2 (ch £1, concessions £1.50). Prices & opening times relate to 2004, for further details phone or log onto www.english-heritage.org.uk/visits. **Facilities:** 🅿 (70yds) (payment required) shop ✱ (ex dogs on leads) ✚

TOTNES MUSEUM

70 Fore St TQ9 5RU
➲ (from bottom of Totnes Town, turn into Fore St by Royal Seven Stars Hotel. The museum on left of main street, just before East Gate Arch Clock Tower)
☎ 01803 863821
e-mail: totnesmuseum@btconnect.com `2 for 1`

An Elizabethan merchant's house, dating from 1575, said to have been built for Sir Walter Kelland, a wealthy merchant. The building houses archaeological and social history collection and room dedicated to Charles Babbage, inventor of the first computer. Study centre archives located at the rear of the museum.

Times: Open 15 Mar-29 Oct, Mon-Fri 10.30-5 (last entry 4.30) **Fee:** ✱ £1.50 (ch 5-16 50p, students & pen £1). **Facilities:** 🅿 (440yds) (restricted parking on main street) ♿ (personal guided tours available) shop

UFFCULME
Map 03 ST01

COLDHARBOUR MILL WORKING WOOL MUSEUM
Coldharbour Mill EX15 3EE
➲ (2m from M5 junct 27, off B3181. Follow signs to Willand, then brown signs to Working Wool Museum)
☎ 01884 840960 📄 01884 840858
e-mail: info@coldharbourmill.org.uk

The Picturesque Coldharbour Mill is set in idyllic Devon countryside. It has been producing textiles since 1799 and is now a working museum, still making knitting wools and fabrics on period machinery. The Fox Gallery exhibits a variety of temporary exhibitions including textiles, photography, mixed media and craft. With machine demonstrations, a water wheel and steam engines, Coldharbour Mill is a wonderful and very different family day out.

Times: Open Mar-Oct, daily 10.30-5. Shop & Restaurant open all year.
Fee: ✱ £5.75 (ch 5-16 £2.75, pen £5.25). Family ticket £16.
Facilities: 🅿 💺 ✕ licensed ♿ (helpful guides & lift, indoor restaurant not accessible) toilets for disabled shop ✈ (ex guide dogs or in grounds) 🖭

YELVERTON
Map 02 SX56

YELVERTON PAPERWEIGHT CENTRE
4 Buckland Ter, Leg O'Mutton Corner PL20 6AD
➲ (at Yelverton off A386, Plymouth to Tavistock road)
☎ 01822 854250 📄 01822 854250 [FREE]
e-mail: paperweightcentre@btinternet.com

This unusual centre is the home of the Broughton Collection - a glittering permanent collection of glass paperweights of all sizes and designs. The centre also has an extensive range of modern glass paperweights for sale. Prices range from a few pounds to over £1000. There is also a series of oil and watercolour paintings by talented local artists.

Times: Open Apr-Oct, daily 10.30-5; 10-24 Dec, daily; Nov & Jan-Mar wknds only or by appointment. **Facilities:** 🅿 (100yds) ♿ (ramp on request) shop 🖭

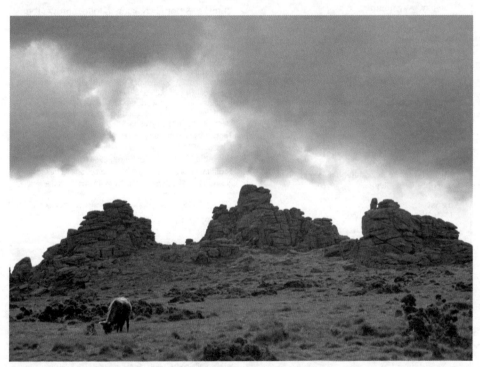

Above: Hound Tor, Dartmoor

DORSET

EVENTS & FESTIVALS

January
1st Annual Bath Race, Poole Quay, Poole

May
tbc Old Harbour Oyster Festival, Brewers Quay, Weymouth
tbc Trawler Race & Water Carnival, Weymouth Old Harbour, Weymouth
tbc Weymouth International Beach Kite Festival, Weymouth Beach

June
10th-12th Wimborne Folk Festival, town centre, Wimborne
18th Dorchester Carnival (provisional)
tbc Bournemouth Live Music Festival

July
1st-3rd Lyme Regis Jazz Festival
17th Tolpuddle Martyrs Memorial Rally & Festival, Tolpuddle
23rd-31st Lyme Regis Lifeboat Week, The Cobb, Lyme Regis

August
17th Weymouth Carnival, Weymouth Seafront
27th-29th Swan Fair, Abbotsbury Swannery, Abbotsbury
31st-4th Sep Great Dorset Steam Fair, South Down Farm, Tarrant Hinton
tbc Bournemouth Regatta

September
tbc Dorchester Show, Cokers Frome Showground, Dorchester

November
tbc Weymouth Guy Fawkes, The Beach

Above: Gold Hill, Shaftesbury

ABBOTSBURY   Map 03 SY58

ABBOTSBURY SWANNERY
New Barn Rd DT3 4JG
➲ (turn off A35 at Winterborne Steepleton near Dorchester. Abbotsbury on B3157 coastal road, between Weymouth and Bridport)
☎ 01305 871858   📠 01305 871092
e-mail: info@abbotsbury-tourism.co.uk

Abbotsbury is the breeding ground of the only managed colonial herd of mute swans. The swans can be seen safely at close quarters, and the site is also home or stopping point for many wild birds. The highlight of the year is the cygnet season, end of May to the end of June, when there may be over 100 nests on site. Visitors can often take pictures of cygnets emerging from eggs at close quarters. There is an audio-visual show, as well as mass feeding at noon & 4pm daily, and an ugly duckling trail.

Times: ✱ Open 24 Mar-2 Nov, daily 10-6, last admission 5.
Facilities: 🅿 💷 ✗ licensed ♿ (free wheelchair loan, herb garden for blind) toilets for disabled shop ✇ ➡

ATHELHAMPTON   Map 03 SY79

ATHELHAMPTON HOUSE & GARDENS
DT2 7LG
➲ (off A35 Northbrook junct, follow brown tourist signs towards Puddletown, at traffic lights turn left, Athelhampton is approx 1m on left)
☎ 01305 848363   📠 01305 848135
e-mail: pcooke@athelhampton.co.uk

Athelhampton, one of the finest 15th-century houses in England, contains magnificently furnished rooms including The Great Hall of 1485 and the library. The glorious Grade I gardens contain the world-famous topiary pyramids, fountains, and collections of tulips, magnolias, roses, clematis and lilies in season.

Times: Open Mar-Oct, daily 10.30-5. Also Sun in winter (ex Xmas). (Closed Fri & Sat). **Fee:** ✱ House & Garden £7.75 (ch free, pen £7, student & disabled £5.50). Garden only £5.50 (ch free).
Facilities: 🅿 💷 ✗ licensed ♿ (2 motorised scooter for use in grounds) toilets for disabled shop ✇ (ex assistance dogs) ➡

BEAMINSTER   Map 03 ST40

MAPPERTON
DT8 3NR
➲ (2m SE off A356 & B3163)
☎ 01308 862645   📠 01308 863348
e-mail: office@mapperton.com

Several acres of terraced valley gardens with specimen trees and shrubs, and formal borders surround a manor house that dates back to the 16th century. There are also fountains, grottoes, stone sculpture fishponds and an orangery, and the garden offers good views and walks. The Mapperton Courtyard Fair is held annually in August with craft demonstrations, stalls, house tours and local displays.

Times: Open Gardens: Mar-Oct, daily 2-6. House open 27 Jun-5 Aug, weekday afternoons 2-4.30. **Fee:** Gardens £4 (ch 5-18 £2, under 5 free). House £2.50. Guided tours £3.50. **Facilities:** 🅿 💷 ♿ (ramp from parking area to garden) toilets for disabled shop ✇ (ex guide dogs)

BLANDFORD FORUM   Map 03 ST80

ROYAL SIGNALS MUSEUM

Blandford Camp DT11 8RH

➲ (signposted off the B3082 Blandford/Wimborne road & A354 Salisbury road. Follow brown signs for the Royal Signals Museum.)

☎ 01258 482248   🖳 01258 482084   **2 for 1**

e-mail: info@royalsignalsmuseum.com

The Royal Signals Museum depicts the history of military communications, science and technology from the Crimea to current day. As well as displays on all major conflicts involving British forces, there are the stories of the ATS, the Long Range Desert Group, Air Support, Airborne, Para and SAS Signals. For children there are trails and interactive exhibits.

Times: Open Mon-Fri 10-5, Mar-Oct Sat-Sun 10-4. Closed 10 days over Xmas & New Year **Fee:** £5 (ch £3, pen £4). Family £13

Facilities: 🅿 🖳 ♿ (ramps & lifts) toilets for disabled shop ✈ (ex guide dogs) 🍴

BOURNEMOUTH   Map 04 SZ09

OCEANARIUM

Pier Approach, West Beach BH2 5AA

➲ (from A338 Wessex Way, follow the Oceanarium tourist signs)

☎ 01202 311993   🖳 01202 311990

e-mail: oceanarium@reallive.co.uk

Explore the secrets of the ocean in an adventure that will take you to some of the world's most amazing waters. The Oceanarium Bournemouth brings you face to face with a vast array of creatures from piranhas and clownfish to tiny freshwater turtles. Take a walk through our amazing underwater tunnel to get even closer to sharks, sea turtles, stingrays and eels.

Times: Open all year, daily from 10am. (Closed 25 Dec).
Fee: ✱ Telephone for admission charges. **Facilities:** 🅿 (100mtrs) 🖳 ♿ (wheelchair for hire) toilets for disabled shop ✈ (ex guide dogs) 🍴

BOVINGTON CAMP   Map 03 SY88

CLOUDS HILL

BH20 7NQ

➲ (1m N of Bovington Camp & Tank Museum)

☎ 01929 405616

T E Lawrence ('Lawrence of Arabia') bought this cottage in 1925 when he was a private in the Tank Corps at Bovington. He would escape here to play records and entertain friends to feasts of baked beans and China tea. The furniture and contents were Lawrence's own and a new display tells the story of Lawrence's life.

Times: Open Apr-Oct, Thu-Sun. 12-5 **Fee:** ✱ £3.10.
Facilities: 🅿 (Braille guide) shop ✈ 🚍 🍴

THE TANK MUSEUM

BH20 6JG

➲ (off A352 or A35, follow brown tank signs from Bere Regis & Wool)

☎ 01929 405096   🖳 01929 405360   **2 for 1**

e-mail: info@tankmuseum.co.uk

The Tank Museum houses the world's finest international collection of Armoured Fighting Vehicles. Tanks in Action displays are held every Thursday at noon during July-September and every Tuesday from end July to August Bank Holiday. Armoured vehicle rides are available throughout the

continued

summer, and various special events take place - please telephone for details.

Times: Open all year, daily 10-5 (Closed from 23-28 Dec). **Fee:** £8 (ch £6, pen £7.50). Family saver £23 (2 adult & 2 ch); £22 (1 adult & 3 ch). Group rates available. **Facilities:** 🅿 🖳 ✗ licensed ♿ (wheelchairs available, Braille & audio tours) toilets for disabled shop ✈ (ex guide dogs) 🍴

BROWNSEA ISLAND   Map 03 SZ08

BROWNSEA ISLAND

BH15 7EE

➲ (located in Poole Harbour)

☎ 01202 707744   🖳 01202 701635   **2 for 1**

This is a 250-acre nature reserve partly managed by the Dorset Trust for Nature Conservation. The island is most famous as the site of the first scout camp, held by Lord Baden-Powell in 1907. Scouts and Guides are still the only people allowed to stay here overnight. It is a haven for red squirrels and seabirds.

Times: Open 12 Mar-22 Jul, 10-5 all week 23 Jul-2 Sep, 10-6 all week 3-30 Sep 10-5 all week 1-30 Oct, 10-4 all week **Fee:** £4.20 (ch £2). Family ticket £10.40. Party. **Facilities:** 🖳 ✗ ♿ (Braille/Audio guide, 2 selfdrive vehicles - booking advised) toilets for disabled shop ✈ 🍴

CANFORD CLIFFS   Map 04 SZ08

COMPTON ACRES GARDENS

Canford Cliffs Rd BH13 7ES

➲ (on B3065, follow brown tourist signs)

☎ 01202 700778   🖳 01202 707537

e-mail: sales@comptonacres.co.uk

The ten acres of Compton Acres incorporate Japanese and Italian gardens, rock and water gardens, and heather gardens. There are fine views over Poole Harbour and the Purbeck Hills. The beautiful wooded valley is an amazing place to explore the wide range of plants.

Times: Open Apr-Nov 9-5.30, Dec-Mar 9-4 (last entry 1hr before close). Closed 25 & 26 Dec **Fee:** ✱ £5.95 (ch £3.95, pen £5.45). Party 15+ £5.45 (ch £3.95, pen £4.95) **Facilities:** 🅿 🖳 ✗ licensed ♿ (level paths and ramps into shops and cafe) toilets for disabled shop garden centre ✈ (ex guide & hearing dogs) 🍴

CHRISTCHURCH   Map 04 SZ19

CHRISTCHURCH CASTLE & NORMAN HOUSE

➲ (near Christchurch Priory)

Set on the river bank, the ruins of this Norman keep and constable's house date back to the twelfth century.

Times: Open any reasonable time. **Facilities:** ✈ (ex dogs on leads) ⛝

RED HOUSE MUSEUM & GARDENS

Quay Rd BH23 1BU

➲ (follow brown tourist signs from Christchurch, Red House is on the corner of Quay Rd)

☎ 01202 482860   🖳 01202 481924   **2 for 1**

A museum with plenty of variety, featuring local history, archaeology, and natural history, displayed in a beautiful Georgian house. There's an excellent costume collection, some Arthur Romney-Green furniture and gardens with a woodland walk and herb garden. Regularly changing

continued

temporary exhibitions include contemporary art and crafts, plus historical displays.

Times: Open all year, Tue-Sat 10-5 Sun 2-5 Oct-Dec, 11-4.15 (Closed: Mon ex BH, Good Fri, & 25-26 Dec & Jan-mid Feb). Last admission 4.30pm. **Fee:** £1.80 (concessions 90p). Family ticket £3.50.

Facilities: P (200yds) 🚌 ♿ (hearing aid and loop in reception only) toilets for disabled shop ✖ (ex guide & hearing dogs)

CORFE CASTLE   Map 03 SY98

CORFE CASTLE
BH20 5EZ

➜ (follow A351 from Wareham to Swanage. Corfe Castle approx 5m along this road)

☎ 01929 481294 📠 01929 477067

e-mail: corfecastle@nationaltrust.org.uk   **2 for 1**

Built in Norman times, the castle was added to by King John. It was defended during the Civil War by Lady Bankes, who surrendered after a stout resistance. Parliament ordered the demolition of the castle, and today it is one of the most impressive ruins in England. Ring for details of special events.

Times: Shop & Castle open daily, Mar 10-5; Apr-end Sep 10-6; Oct 10-5; Nov-Feb 10-4. Last admission 30 mins before closing (Closed 25-26 Dec). Tearoom open daily Mar 10-5, Apr-Sep 10-5.30, Oct 10-5, Nov-Feb 10-4. **Fee:** ✱ £4.70 (ch £2.30). Family ticket (2 ad & 3 ch) £11.50 or (1 ad & 3 ch) £6.90. National Trust members free.

Facilities: P 🚌 ✖ licensed (Braille/Large print guide & menu) shop ♿ 🍴

CORFE CASTLE MUSEUM
West St BH20 5HE

➜ (to side of church on left of West St upon leaving village square)

☎ 01929 480974 📠 01929 480974   **FREE**

e-mail: kenwollaston@tesco.net

The tiny, rectangular building was partly rebuilt in brick after a fire in 1780, and is the smallest town hall building in England. It has old village relics, and dinosaur footprints 130 million years old. A council chamber on the first floor is reached by a staircase at one end. The Ancient Order of Marblers meets here each Shrove Tuesday.

Times: Open all year, Apr-Oct, daily 9.30-6; Nov-Mar, wknds and Xmas holidays 10-5. **Facilities:** P (200yds) ♿ ✖

DORCHESTER   Map 03 SY69

DINOSAUR MUSEUM
Icen Way DT1 1EW

➜ (off A35 into Dorchester, museum in town centre just off High East Street)

☎ 01305 269880 📠 01305 268885

e-mail: info@thedinosaurmuseum.com

Britain's award-winning museum devoted to dinosaurs has an appealing mixture of fossils, skeletons, life-size reconstructions and interactive displays such as the 'feelies'. There are audio-visual presentations and computer displays providing an all-round family attraction with new displays each year.

Times: Open all year, daily 9.30-5.30 (10-4.30 Nov-Mar). (Closed 24-26 Dec). **Fee:** ✱ £6 (ch £4.50, pen & student £5.25, under 4's free). Family ticket £18.50 **Facilities:** P (50yds) ♿ (Many low level displays) shop 🍴

DORSET COUNTY MUSEUM
High West St DT1 1XA

➜ (turn off A354 signposted Dorchester, attraction on right half way up main street)

☎ 01305 262735 📠 01305 257180

e-mail: dorsetcountymuseum@dor-mus.demon.co.uk

Displays cover prehistoric and Roman times, including sites such as Maiden Castle, and there's a gallery on Dorset writers with sections on the poet William Barnes, Thomas Hardy (with a reconstruction of his study), and 20th-century writers. Also geology, local wildlife and social history are explored in the museum.

Times: Open all year, Mon-Sat, 10-5. Also open Sun during May-Oct. (Closed 24-26 Dec & Good Friday). **Facilities:** P (600yds) (nearby parking is charged) ♿ (Free entry for disabled visitors, ramp, audio commentary) shop ✖ (ex guide dogs) 🍴

DORSET TEDDY BEAR MUSEUM
Antelope Walk, Cornhill DT1 1BE

➜ (turn off A35 and museum in town centre near Tourist Information Centre)

☎ 01305 263200 📠 01305 268885

e-mail: info@teddybearmuseum.co.uk

A visit to the museum begins with the home of Edward Bear and his extended family of human-sized teddy bears. Then, in a more traditional museum setting, view hundreds of teddy bears from throughout the last century in atmospheric and evocative displays.

Times: Open daily, Mon-Sat 9.30-5, Sun 10-4.30. (Closed 25-26 Dec). **Fee:** ✱ £3.50(ch £2.50, under 4's free). Family £10.50 **Facilities:** P (500mtrs) shop ✖ (ex guide dogs) 🍴

HARDY'S COTTAGE
Higher Bockhampton DT2 8QJ

➜ (3m NE of Dorchester, 0.5m S of A35. Turn off A35 at Kingston Maurward rdbt towards Stinsford and Bockhampton. Left onto Bockhampton Ln, signed to Hardy's Cottage)

☎ 01305 262366

The small cob and thatch cottage where novelist and poet Thomas Hardy was born in 1840 and from where he would walk 6 miles to school in Dorchester every day. It was built by his great-grandfather and is little altered since. The interior has been furnished by the Trust. It was here that he wrote his early novels 'Under the Greenwood Tree' and 'Far from the Madding Crowds'. It has a charming cottage garden.

Times: Open 18 Mar-Oct **Fee:** £3 **Facilities:** P (10 min walk) (no coach parking) ♿ (parking by arrangement, large print/Braille guide) ✖ ♿

MAIDEN CASTLE
DT1 9PR

➜ (2m S of Dorchester, access off A354, N of bypass)

The Iron Age fort ranks among the finest in Britain. It covers 47 acres, and has daunting earthworks, with a complicated defensive system around the entrances. One of its main purposes may well have been to protect grain from marauding bands. The first single-rampart fort dates from around 700BC, and by 100BC the earthworks covered the whole plateau. It was finally overrun by Roman troops in AD43.

Times: Open any reasonable time. **Facilities:** P ✖ (ex dogs on leads) ♿

THE MILITARY MUSEUM OF DEVON & DORSET
The Keep, Bridport Rd DT1 1RN
➲ (situated near the top of High West St leading out of town towards Bridport)
☎ 01305 264066   📠 01305 250373
e-mail: keep.museum@talk21.com

Three hundred years of military history, with displays on the Devon Regiment, Dorset Regiment, Dorset Militia and Volunteers, the Queen's Own Dorset Yeomanry, and Devonshire and Dorset Regiment (from 1958). The Museum uses modern technology, interactive and creative displays to tell the stories of the Infantry, Cavalry and Artillerymen.
Times: Open Apr-Sep, Mon-Sat 9-5; Oct-Mar, Tue-Sat 9-5; (also Jul & Aug, Sun 10-4). Closed Xmas & New Year. **Fee:** £3 (ch, student & pen £2). Family ticket £9 **Facilities:** 🅿 ♿ (lift availble to 3 floors) toilets for disabled shop 🐕 (ex guide dogs) 🍴

TUTANKHAMUN EXHIBITION
High West St DT1 1UW
➲ (off A35 into Dorchester town centre)
☎ 01305 269571   📠 01305 268885
e-mail: info@tutankhamun-exhibition.co.uk

The exhibition recreates the excitement of one of the world's greatest discoveries of ancient treasure. A reconstruction of the tomb and recreations of its treasures are displayed. The superbly preserved mummified body of the boy king can be seen, wonderfully recreated in every detail. Facsimiles of some of the most famous treasures, including the golden funerary mask and the harpooner can be seen in the final gallery.
Times: Open all year daily, Apr-Oct, 9.30-5.30; Nov-Mar wkdays 9.30-5, wknds 10-4.30. (Closed 24-26 Dec). **Fee:** £6 (ch £4.50, pen & student £5.25, under 5's free). Family ticket £18.50
Facilities: 🅿 (200yds) ♿ shop 🐕 (ex guide dogs) 🍴

MINTERNE MAGNA   Map 03 ST60
MINTERNE GARDENS
DT2 7AU
➲ (2m N of Cerne Abbas on A352 Dorchester-Sherborne road)
☎ 01300 341370

Wander through 20 acres of wild woodland, where magnolias, rhododendrons, eucryphias, hydrangeas, water plants and water lillies provide a new vista at each turn. This was the home of the Churchill and Digby families for 350 years, and contains small lakes and cascades landscaped in the 18th century.
Times: Open Mar-10 Nov, daily 10-7. **Fee:** £3 (accompanied ch free). **Facilities:** 🅿

POOLE   Map 03 SZ09
WATERFRONT MUSEUM
4 High St BH15 1BW
➲ (off Poole Quay)
☎ 01202 262600   📠 01202 262622   `FREE`
e-mail: museums@poole.gov.uk

The museum tells the story of Poole's seafaring past. Learn of the Roman occupation and see material raised from the Studland Bay wreck. Scaplen's Court, just a few yards from the museum, is a beautifully restored domestic building dating from the medieval period. Although it is only open to the public in August, Scaplen's Court is not to be missed, with a Victorian school room, a kitchen and scullery.
Times: Museum: open Apr-Oct, Mon-Sat 10-5, Sun noon-5; Nov-Mar, Mon-Sat 10-3, Sun noon-3. Scaplen's Court: Aug, Mon-Sat 10-5, Sun noon-5. **Facilities:** 🅿 (250mtrs) ♿ (Scaplen's Court not accessible) toilets for disabled 🐕 (ex guide dogs) 🍴

PORTLAND   Map 03 SY67
PORTLAND CASTLE
Castleton DT5 1AZ
➲ (overlooking Portland harbour)
☎ 01305 820539   📠 01305 860853

Visit one of Henry VIII's finest coastal forts in use right up to the Second World War. Home to the Wrens and scene of the US troops' embarkation for the D-Day invasion in 1944. Explore the Captain's House and Gardens.
Times: Open, Apr-June & Sep, daily 10-5; Jul-Aug, daily 10-6; Oct, daily 10-4. Closed Nov-Mar. **Fee:** £3.50 (ch £1.80, concessions £2.60). Prices & opening times relate to 2004, for further details phone or log onto www.english-heritage.org.uk/visits **Facilities:** 🅿 🍴 ♿ shop 🐕 ♨

PORTLAND MUSEUM
217 Wakeham DT5 1HS
➲ (A354, through Fortuneswell to Portland Heights Hotel, then English Heritage signs)
☎ 01305 821804   📠 01305 761654   `2 for 1`
e-mail: tourism@weymouth.gov.uk

Avice's cottage in Thomas Hardy's book *The Well-Beloved*, this building is now a museum of local and historical interest, with varied displays. Regular temporary exhibitions are held. The adjoining Marie Stopes cottage houses the shop and a display of maritime history.
Times: Open Good Fiday-Oct, Fri-Tue (ex school holidays open daily), 10.30-5 (Closed 1-1.30 daily). **Fee:** £2 (concessions free)
Facilities: 🅿 (50yds) (coach parking on roadside) ♿ shop

SHAFTESBURY   Map 03 ST82
SHAFTESBURY ABBEY MUSEUM & GARDEN
Park Walk SP7 8JR
➲ (follow signs to Shaftesbury town centre. Shaftesbury Abbey is signed from opposite Wharf's Restaurant)
☎ 01747 852910   📠 01747 852910
e-mail: user@shaftesburyabbey.fsnet.co.uk

The Abbey at Shaftesbury was part of a nunnery founded by King Alfred in 888. It became one of the wealthiest in the country but was destroyed during the Dissolution in 1539. The excavated ruins show the foundations of the abbey church. The story is told through the use of carved stone and medieval floor tiles and illustrations from ancient manuscripts.
Times: Open Apr-Oct, daily, 10-5. **Fee:** £2 (ch 60p, concessions £1.50). **Facilities:** 🅿 (250yds) 2hr restriction on nearest car park ♿ (large print guides & audio tour) toilets for disabled shop (only on leads)

SHERBORNE   Map 03 ST61

SHERBORNE CASTLE
New Rd DT9 5NR
➲ (off A30/A352, 0.5m SE of Sherborne)
☎ 01935 813182 🖹 01935 816727
e-mail: enquiries@sherbornecastle.com
Built by Sir Walter Raleigh in 1594, Sherborne Castle has
been the home of the Digby family since 1617. Prince
William of Orange was entertained here in 1688, and George
III visited in 1789. Splendid collections of art, furniture and
porcelain are on show in the Castle. Lancelot 'Capability'
Brown created the lake in 1753 and beautiful gardens and
grounds surround it.
Times: Open 22 Mar-Oct, Tue-Thu, Sat-Sun & BH Mon 11-4.30. Castle
opens from 2.30 on Sat. Last admission 4.30. **Fee:** ✱ £7 (pen £6.50).
Gardens only £3.50. ch under 15 free (max 4 ch per adult). Party 15+
pen £6.50 **Facilities:** 🅿 💷 ⛺ (Braille guide book) toilets for
disabled shop 🍴

SHERBORNE MUSEUM
Abbey Gate House, Church Ln DT9 3BP
➲ (From the bottom of Cheap St (main shopping
street), walk through Church Ln towards the
Abbey, museum on left)
☎ 01935 812252
e-mail: admin@shermus.fsnet.co.uk
The museum features a model of Sherborne's original
Norman castle, as well as a fine Victorian doll's house and
other domestic and agricultural bygones. There are also
items of local geological, natural history and archaeological
interest, including Roman material.
Times: ✱ Open Apr-Oct, Tue-Sat 10.30-4.30, Sun 2.30-4.30; BH Mon
2.30-4.30 **Facilities:** 🅿 (200yds) ⛺ toilets for disabled shop
🐕 (ex guide dogs)

SHERBORNE OLD CASTLE
Castleton D19 3SA
➲ (0.5m E off B3145)
☎ 01935 812730 🖹 01935 812730
The ruins of this early 12th-century castle are a testament to
the 16 days Oliver Cromwell's army took capture of it during
the Civil War.
Times: Open Apr-Jun & Sep, Tue-Thu & Sat-Sun 10-5; Jul-Aug, Tue-Thu
& Sat-Sun 10-6; Oct, Tue-Thu & Sat-Sun 10-4. Open BH Mons. Closed
Nov-Mar. **Fee:** ✱ £2.30 (ch £1.20, concessions £1.70). Joint ticket with
Castle Grounds £5. Prices & opening times relate to 2004, for further
details phone or log onto www.english-heritage.org.uk/visits
Facilities: 🅿 ⛺ shop 🐕 ⚑

SWANAGE   Map 03 SZ07

SWANAGE RAILWAY
Station House BH19 1HB
➲ (signed from A351)
☎ 01929 425800 🖹 01929 426680
e-mail: general@swanrail.freeserve.co.uk
The railway from Swanage to Wareham was closed in 1972,
and in 1976 the Swanage Railway took possession and have
gradually restored the line, which now runs for 6 miles,
passing the ruins of Corfe Castle. Ring for details of special
events.
Times: ✱ Open every weekend throughout the year, daily Apr-Oct.
Facilities: 🅿 💷 ✗ licensed ⛺ (special disabled persons coach)
toilets for disabled shop (shop at Swanage Station) 🍴

TOLPUDDLE   Map 03 SY79

TOLPUDDLE MARTYRS MUSEUM
DT2 7EH
➲ (off A35 from Dorchester, Tolpuddle is
signposted at Troytown turn off. Continue on old
A35, Museum has brown heritage signpost giving
clear directions)
☎ 01305 848237 🖹 01305 848237   🅵🆁🅴🅴
e-mail: jpickering@tuc.org.uk

One dawn, in the bitter February of 1834, six Tolpuddle farm
labourers were arrested after forming a trade union. A
frightened squire's trumped up charge triggered one of the
most celebrated stories in the history of human rights. That
dawn arrest created the Tolpuddle Martyrs, who were
punished with transportation as convicts to Australia. Packed
with illustrative displays, this new state-of-the-art,
interactive exhibition tells the Tolpuddle Martyrs story. Every
summer the weekend of the third Sunday in July, the
museum holds the Tolpuddle Martyrs Festival. The weekend
combines celebration with tradition offering traditional and
contemporary music as well as many other attractions.
Times: Open all year, Apr-Oct, Tue-Sat 10-5.30, Sun 11-5.30; Nov-Mar,
Tue-Sat 10-4, Sun 11-4. Open BH Mon. (Closed 20 Dec-2 Jan).
Facilities: 🅿 (outside museum) ⛺ (interactive computers at
wheelchair height & parking) toilets for disabled shop
🐕 (ex guide dogs)

WEST LULWORTH   Map 03 SY88

LULWORTH CASTLE
BH20 5QS
➲ (from Wareham, W on A352 for 1m, left onto
B3070 to E Lulworth, follow tourist signs)
☎ 01929 400352 🖹 01929 400563
e-mail: estate.office@lulworth.com
Glimpse life below stairs in the restored kitchen, and enjoy
beautiful views from the top of the tower of this historic
castle set in beautiful parkland. The 18th-century chapel is
the first Catholic chapel built in England after the
Reformation. Children will enjoy the animal farm, play area,
indoor activity room and pitch and putt.
Times: ✱ Open Castle: Summer 10.30-6; Winter 10.30-4. Lulworth
Castle House open Wed 28 May-30 Jul, 2-5. **Facilities:** 🅿 💷
⛺ (limited in castle due to grade one listing) toilets for disabled
shop 🍴

WEYMOUTH — Map 03 SY67

DEEP SEA ADVENTURE & SHARKY'S PLAY & PARTY

9 Custom House Quay, Old Harbour DT4 8BG
⮑ (follow signs on A35 to Weymouth. Follow signs for the Old Harbour North, Deep Sea Adventure & Sharkys Play Zone, which is located on the Old Harbour between pavillion and town bridge)
☎ 0871 222 5760 ▤ 0871 222 5760   **2 for 1**
e-mail: enquiries@deepsea-adventure.co.uk

A fascinating attraction telling the story of underwater exploration and marine exploits. Discover the history of Weymouth's Old Harbour, compelling tales of shipwreck survival, explore the Black Hole and search for Ollie the Oyster. Also a unique display telling the gripping tale of the *Titanic* disaster. Sharky's Play Area is four floors of fun-packed adventure. Separate toddler area for the under fives. New for 2004 is the 'Paint your own Pottery' studio.
Times: Open all year, daily 9.30-7 (high season 9.30-8). (Closed 25 & 26 Dec & 1 Jan). **Fee:** ✱ Sharky's Play Zone: Adults free (ch £3.30). Deep Sea Adventure: £3.75 (ch 5-15 £2.75, pen & student £3.25). Combined ticket for both attractions, ch £4.75. **Facilities:** ℙ (100yds) ✘ licensed � (lift & sign language for deaf) toilets for disabled shop ✖ (ex guide dogs) ▦

RSPB NATURE RESERVE RADIPOLE LAKE

The Swannery Car Park DT4 7TZ
⮑ (Follow signs to town centre. From A354, turn left, and left again into Swannery car park. From A553, turn right at clock tower, and right at 1st rdbt. Nature Reserve is close to seafront & railway station)
☎ 01305 778313 ▤ 01305 778313

Covering 222 acres, the Reserve offers firm paths, hide and a visitor centre. Several types of warblers, mute swans, gadwalls, teals and great crested grebes may be seen, and the visitor centre has viewing windows overlooking the lake. Phone for details of special events.
Times: Open daily 9-5 **Fee:** Prices not confirmed for 2005
Facilities: ℙ (charged) ⅆ toilets for disabled shop ▦

SEA LIFE PARK

Lodmoor Country Park DT4 7SX
⮑ (on A353)
☎ 01305 788255 ▤ 01305 760165
e-mail: simongrove@merlinentertainments.biz

Set in the beautiful Lodmoor Country Park. Marvel at the mysteries of the deep and discover amazing sea creatures from around our own shores in spectacular marine displays.
Times: ✱ Open all year, daily from 10am. (Closed 25 Dec).
Facilities: ℙ (charged) ▦ ✘ ⅆ toilets for disabled shop ✖ (ex guide dogs) ▦

WIMBORNE — Map 03 SZ09

KINGSTON LACY HOUSE, GARDEN & PARK

BH21 4EA   **2 for 1**
⮑ (1.5m W of Wimborne, B3082)
☎ 01202 883402 (Mon-Fri) & 842913 (wknds)
▤ 01202 882402
e-mail: kingstonlacy@nationaltrust.org.uk

Kingston Lacy House was the home of the Bankes family for over 300 years. The original house is 17th century, but in the 1830s was given a stone façade. The Italian marble staircase,

Venetian ceiling, treasures from Spain and an Egyptian obelisk were also added. There are outstanding pictures by Titian, Rubens, Velasquez, Reynolds and Van Dyck. No photography is allowed in the house.
Times: House 20 Mar-Oct, 11-5, Wed-Sun. Garden & Park, 10.30-6, all week 5 Nov-19 Dec, 10.30 4, Fri-Sun 5 Feb-20 Mar, 10.30-4, Sat-Sun. **Fee:** ✱ House, Garden & Park £7.20 (ch £3.60) family £19. Park & Gardens only £3.60 (ch £1.80) family £9.50. **Facilities:** ℙ ▦ ✘ licensed ⅆ 4 manual wheelchairs, Braille guides, parking toilets for disabled shop ✖ (ex on leads in park & wood) ▩

KNOLL GARDENS & NURSERY

Stapehill Rd, Hampreston BH21 7ND
⮑ (3m E between Wimborne and Ferndown off A31, at Canford Bottom rdbt, into B3073 signed Ham Lane)
☎ 01202 873931 ▤ 01202 870842
e-mail: enquiries@knollgardens.co.uk

Over 6000 plant species from all over the world thrive here, within a six-acre site. There are water gardens with waterfalls, pools and a stream, herbaceous borders, and many other features. There is also a 'Dragon' formal garden and a Mediterranean-style gravel garden. The nursery offers a wide range of plants; best known for its range of Ornamental Grasses and 'plants for the modern lifestyle'.
Times: Open all year, Wed-Sun, 10-5 (or dusk if earlier).
Facilities: ℙ ▦ ⅆ (wheelchairs available) toilets for disabled garden centre ✖ (ex guide dogs) ▦

PRIEST'S HOUSE MUSEUM AND GARDEN

23-27 High St BH21 1HR
☎ 01202 882533 ▤ 01202 882533
e-mail: priestshouse@eastdorset.gov.uk

An award-winning local history museum, set in an historic house with a Victorian kitchen where regular cooking demonstrations are held (4th Saturday in the month, 2pm-5pm). There are nine other rooms to see, along with regular special exhibitions, a new costume and textile gallery and a beautiful 300ft-long walled garden.
Times: ✱ Open Apr-Oct, Mon-Sat, 10-4.30. Also every Sun Jul-Aug & BH wknds 2-5. **Facilities:** ℙ (200yds) ▦ ⅆ (hands on archaeology gallery, audio tapes) shop ✖ (ex guide dogs)

STAPEHILL ABBEY

Wimborne Rd West BH21 2EB
⮑ (2.5m E off A31 at Canford Bottom rdbt)   **2 for 1**
☎ 01202 861686 ▤ 01202 894589

This early 19th-century abbey, home for nearly 200 years to Cistercian nuns, is now a busy working crafts centre with many attractions under cover. There are award-winning landscaped gardens, parkland and picnic spots, and the Power to the Land exhibition. Telephone for details of special events.
Times: Open Etr-Sep, daily 10-5; Oct-Etr Wed-Sun 10-4. (Closed 22 Dec-Feb). **Fee:** ✱ £7.50 (ch 4-16 £4.50, students & pen £7). Family ticket (2 ad & 2 ch) £19.50. **Facilities:** ℙ ▦ ⅆ toilets for disabled shop garden centre ✖ (ex guide dogs) ▦

continued

WOOL   Map 03 SY88

MONKEY WORLD
Longthorns BH20 6HH
➲ (1m N of Wool on Bere Regis Rd)
☎ 01929 462537 & 0800 456600
🖹 01929 405414
e-mail: apes@monkeyworld.org

Set up in order to rescue monkeys and apes from abuse and illegal smuggling, Monkey World houses over 100 primates in 60 acres of Dorset woodland. There are 45 chimps, the largest grouping outside Africa, as well as orang-utans, gibbons, woolly monkeys, lemurs, macaques and marmosets. Those wishing to help the centre continue in its quest to rescue primates from lives of misery may like to take part in the adoption scheme which includes free admission to the park for one year.
Times: Open daily 10-5 (Jul-Aug 10-6). Last admission 1 hour before closing **Facilities:** 🅿 🍽 ✕ ♿ toilets for disabled shop ✕ (ex guide dogs) 🍴

COUNTY DURHAM

EVENTS & FESTIVALS

April
30th-2nd May Teesdale Thrash, concerts, ceilidhs, music and morris dancing in Bernard Castle

June
11th-12th Durham Regatta, River Wear, Durham (provisional)
tbc Weardale Steam Transport Festival, Bondisle Field, Stanhope

July
2nd-3rd Summer Festival, Durham city centre
9th Durham Miners Gala, colourful miners' banners paraded through the city of Durham (provisional)
9th-10th Chester-le-Street Traction Engine Rally, South Burn Grange
tbc Durham County Show, Lambton Park, nr Chester-le-Street

August
27th-28th Weardale Agricultural Show, Showfield, St John's Chapel (provisional)
28th-29th Durham Light Infantry Vehicle Rally, DLI Museum and Durham Art Gallery (provisional)
tbc Billingham International Folklore Festival, Billingham, Stockton-on-Tees

September
3rd-4th Wolsingham & Wear Valley Agricultural Show, Wolsingham (provisional)
10th-11th Stanhope Agricultural Show & Country Fair, Stanhope (provisional)

December
3rd-4th Victorian Christmas Festival, Durham city centre (provisional)

Above: Durham Cathedral

BARNARD CASTLE — Map 12 NZ01

BARNARD CASTLE
DL12 9AT
☎ 01833 638212
Imposing remains of one of England's largest medieval castles perched high on a rugged escarpment above the banks of the River Tees.
Times: Open all year, Apr-Sep, daily 10-6; Oct, daily, 10-4; Nov-Mar, Thur-Mon 10-4. (Closed 24-26 Dec & 1 Jan). **Fee:** ✱ £3 (ch £1.50, concessions £2.30). Prices & opening times relate to 2004, for further details phone or log onto www.english-heritage.org.uk/visits
Facilities: ♿ shop ✗ (ex dogs on leads) ✿

THE BOWES MUSEUM
DL12 8NP
➲ (located in Barnard Castle, just of the A66. 12m from the A1 at Scotch Corner)
☎ 01833 690606 🖷 01833 637163
e-mail: info@bowesmuseum.org.uk

Enjoy a great family day out at the Bowes Museum, as you immerse yourself in the atmosphere of this magnificent French-style château, and explore the extravagant life stories of founders John and Joséphine Bowes. The museum contains an outstanding collection of fine and decorative art, including the world-famous Silver Swan. Activities for all the family, dining, shopping, and beautiful parkland.
Times: Open daily 11-5. (closed 25-26 Dec & 1 Jan) **Fee:** £6 (concessions £5, U16 free). **Facilities:** 🅿 💻 ♿ (lift, ramped entrance, reserved parking) toilets for disabled shop (grounds only, ex guide dogs) 🍴

EGGLESTONE ABBEY
DL12 8QN
➲ (1m S of Barnard Castle on minor road off B6277)
The scant, but charming remains of a small medieval monastery. The picturesque ruins of Egglestone are located above a bend in the River Tees. A large part of the church can be seen, as can remnants of monastic buildings.
Times: Open any reasonable time. **Facilities:** 🅿 ♿ ✗ (ex dogs on leads) ✿

BEAMISH — Map 12 NZ25

BEAMISH, THE NORTH OF ENGLAND OPEN-AIR MUSEUM
DH9 0RG
➲ (off A693 & A6076 signposted off A1(M) junct 63. In County Durham midway between Durham City and Newcastle-upon-Tyne)
☎ 0191 370 4000 🖷 0191 370 4001
e-mail: museum@beamish.org.uk

Set in 200 acres of countryside, award winning Beamish recreates life in the early 1800s and 1900s. Costumed staff welcome visitors to a 1913 town street, colliery village, farm and railway station; a display of how people lived and worked. Ride on early electric tramcars, take a ride on a replica of an 1825 steam railway and visit Pockerley Manor where a yeoman farmer and his family would have lived.
Times: Open 3 Apr-Oct, daily 10-5; Nov-18 Mar 10-4 (ex Mon & Fri). Closed 13 Dec-3 Jan, last admission 3pm. **Fee:** ✱ Summer £14 (ch £7, over 60's £11)(group 20+ £9, £5 & £8). Winter £5 (ch & over 60's £5). NB a winter visit is centered on the town and tramway only, other areas are closed. **Facilities:** 🅿 💻 ♿ (not ideal for wheelchairs, free entry essential helpers) toilets for disabled shop 🍴

BISHOP AUCKLAND — Map 08 NZ22

AUCKLAND CASTLE
DL14 7NR
➲ (from A1(M), exit at junct 61 and join A688 signposted to Bishop Auckland, follow signs to Bishop Auckland Market Place and then Brown Tourist sign for Auckland Castle)
☎ 01388 601627 🖷 01388 609323
e-mail: auckland.castle@zetnet.co.uk
Serving as the principal county residence of the Prince Bishops since the 12th century, Auckland Castle is the home of the Bishop of Durham. Built on a promontory overlooking the River Wear and the Roman Fort of Binchester, the Castle has been added to and adapted over the centuries. St Peter's Chapel houses many of the treasures of past Bishops.
Times: ✱ Open Etr Mon-Sep, Sun-Mon 2-5. Aug also Wed (Closed 13 Jun, 1 & 26 Sep). **Fee:** £4 (ch 12 free, concessions £3)
Facilities: 🅿 💻 ♿ (chair walker available by prior arrangement) toilets for disabled shop ✗ (ex guide dogs) 🍴

BOWES   Map 12 NY91

Bowes Castle
DL12 9LD
➲ (in Bowes village, just off A66)
Massive ruins of Henry II's tower keep, three storeys high,
set within the earthworks of a Roman fort and overlooking
the valley of the River Greta.
Times: Open any reasonable time. **Facilities:** ⅋ ✕ (ex
dogs on leads) 🚌 ♯

The Otter Trust's North Pennines Reserve
Vale House Farm DL12 9RH
➲ (S side of A66 Scotch Corner to Penrith Rd, 2m
W of Bowes)
☎ 01833 628339 ▯ 01986 892461
Set in 230 acres of upland farmland, the Otter Trust reserve
isn't just about otters, although there is an ongoing release
programme that aims to protect the otter from extinction.
Visitors can also see red and fallow deer, mouflon sheep,
and a wide range of birds including curlew, oystercatchers,
snipe, and black grouse. The visitor centre contains exhibits
on some of the animals as well as local history, and
overlooks the charming River Greta.
Times: Open Apr-Oct, daily 10.30-6 **Fee:** ✱ £5 (ch £3)
Facilities: ▯ 🍴 ⅋ toilets for disabled shop ✕ (ex guide dogs)

COWSHILL   Map 12 NY84

Killhope The North of England Lead Mining Lead Mining Museum
DL13 1AR
➲ (beside A689 midway between Stanhope &
Alston)
☎ 01388 537505 ▯ 01388 537617   `2 for 1`
e-mail: killhope@durham.gov.uk
Equipped with hard hats and lamps, you can explore the
working conditions of lead miners. The lead mine and 19th-
century crushing mill have been restored to look as they
would have done in the 1870s, and the 34ft water wheel has
been restored to working order. There is also a visitor centre
and mineral exhibition, a woodland walk, children's play
area and a red squirrel and bird hide.
Times: Open 19-20 & 25 Mar-Oct, daily 10.30-5 (BH's & summer
school hols open until 5.30); Open Dec 3-4 & 10-11 **Fee:** Mine & Site:
£6 (ch £3, concessions £5.50) family £17. Site: £4.50 (ch £1.70,
concessions £4) family £11 **Facilities:** ▯ 🍴 ⅋ (electric scooter,
sympathetic hearing scheme) toilets for disabled shop 🍴

DARLINGTON   Map 08 NZ21

Darlington Railway Centre & Museum
North Rd Station DL3 6ST
➲ (0.75m N, off A167)
☎ 01325 460532 ▯ 01325 287746
e-mail: museum@darlington.gov.uk
Housed in the carefully restored North Road Station, this
museum's prize exhibit is *Locomotion*, which pulled the first
passenger train on the Stockton to Darlington railway and
was built by Robert Stephenson & Co in 1825. Several other
steam locomotives are also shown, together with models
and other exhibits relating to the Stockton and Darlington
and the North Eastern Railway companies. Recently arrived
at the museum for a two year period is an A2 Pacific
No60532 'Blue Peter'. Refreshments are available.
Times: Open daily 10-5 (closed 25-26 Dec & 1 Jan). **Fee:** ✱ £2.50
(ch £1.50, pen £1.50). **Facilities:** ▯ ⅋ toilets for disabled shop
✕ (ex guide dogs) 🍴

DURHAM   Map 12 NZ24

Durham Cathedral
DH1 3EH
➲ (A1(M) to Durham, turn off at A690 into city,
follow signs to car parks).
☎ 0191 386 4266 ▯ 0191 386 4267
e-mail: enquiries@durhamcathedral.co.uk
Founded in 1093 as a shrine to St Cuthbert, the cathedral is a
remarkable example of Norman architecture, set in an
impressive position high above the River Wear. A full
programme of concerts throughout the year. St Cuthbert's
Day Procession (phone for details).
Times: ✱ Open all year, daily 9.30-6.15; 21 Jun-8 Sep 9.30-8. (Sun
12.30-5). Cathedral is closed to visitors during evening recitals &
concerts. **Facilities:** ▯ (in city centre) ✕ licensed ⅋ (Braille guide,
touch/hearing centre, stairclimber) toilets for disabled shop
✕ (ex guide dogs)

Durham Light Infantry Museum & Durham Art Gallery
Aykley Heads DH1 5TU
➲ (0.5m NW, turn right off A691)
☎ 0191 384 2214 ▯ 0191 386 1770
e-mail: dli@durham.gov.uk
The history of the Regiment is told in displays of artefacts,
medals, uniforms and vehicles. The Art Gallery has a
continuous programme of temporary exhibitions, and holds
regular lectures and concerts.
Times: Open all year, Apr-Oct, daily 10-5; Nov-Mar, daily 10-4 (closed
25 Dec). **Facilities:** ▯ 🍴 ⅋ (wheelchair available, lift, ramps) toilets
for disabled shop ✕ (ex guide dogs) 🍴

Finchale Priory
Brasside, Newton Hall DH1 5SH
➲ (3m NE)
☎ 0191 386 3828
Dating from the 13th-century, these beautiful priory ruins are
in a wooded setting besides the River Wear.
Times: Open Apr-Sep, Sat, Sun & Bank Hols, 10-6. **Fee:** ✱ £2 (ch £1,
concessions £1.50). Prices & opening times relate to 2004, for further
details phone or log onto www.english-heritage.org.uk/visits
Facilities: ▯ (charged) 🍴 shop ✕ (ex dogs on lead) ♯

Oriental Museum
University of Durham, Elvet Hill DH1 3TH
➲ (signposted from A167 & A177)
☎ 0191 334 5694 ▯ 0191 334 5694
e-mail: oriental.museum@durham.ac.uk
The Marvels of China gallery opened in 2000 and introduces
the visitor to contemporary China, its history and decorative
arts. Other displays cover the Islamic World, Buddhism,
Chinese archaeology, the story of writing, a Javanese
Gamelan Orchestra and an Egyptian Gallery containing
everything from mummies to magic amulets.
Times: Open Mon-Fri 10-5, wknds 12-5. (Closed Xmas-New Year).
Fee: £1.50 (concessions 75p). Family ticket £3.50. **Facilities:** ▯ 🍴
⅋ (lifts to all floors) toilets for disabled shop ✕ 🍴

HARTLEPOOL   Map 08 NZ53
HMS TRINCOMALEE
Jackson Dock TS24 0SQ
➲ (From A19 take A689 or A179, follow signs for Hartlepool Historic Quay)
☎ 01429 223193 ▤ 01429 864385
e-mail: office@hms-trincomalee.co.uk
HMS Trincomalee, is the oldest ship afloat in the UK and the last of the commissioned frigates of the Nelson era. Now fully restored in an award-winning maritime heritage project. Come aboard for a unique experience of navy life two centuries ago. Excellence in England Silver Award 2004.
Times: Open all year, Summer: 10-5, Winter: 10.30-4. Closed Xmas & New Year. **Fee:** ✱ £4.25 (ch, students, disabled, pen & unemployed £3.25. Family ticket (2 adults & 3 ch) £11.75. Group tickets available. **Facilities:** ▣ ♿ (3 out of the 4 decks are accessible by lift) shop ✖ (ex guide dogs) ◼

MUSEUM OF HARTLEPOOL
Jackson Dock, Maritime Av TS24 0XZ
➲ (Historic Quay & Museum towards the Marina)
☎ 01429 860077 ▤ 01429 523477
This museum tells the story of Hartlepool from prehistory to the present day and includes many original artefacts, models, computer interactives and hands-on exhibits. See how iron and steel ships were built and climb aboard the Humber ferry Wingfield Castle, a paddle steamer built in Hartlepool in 1934.
Times: ✱ Open all year, daily (closed 25-26 Dec & 1 Jan). **Facilities:** ▣ ◼ ♿ toilets for disabled shop ✖ (ex guide dogs)

LANGLEY PARK   Map 12 NZ24
DIGGERLAND NEW
DH7 9TT
➲ (A1(M) junct 62. Head W following signs to Consett. After 6m turn left at rdbt, signed Langley Park, then right into Riverside Ind Est)
☎ 08700 344437 ▤ 09012 010300   `2 for 1`
e-mail: mail@diggerland.com
An adventure park with a difference, where kids of all ages can experience the thrills of driving real earth moving equipment. Choose from various types of diggers and dumpers ranging from 1 ton to 8 and a half tons. Supervised by an instructor complete the Dumper Truck Challenge or dig for buried treasure. New rides include JCB Robots, the Supertrack, Landrover Safari and Spin Dizzy. Even under 5's can join in, with mum or dad's help.
Times: Open 12 Feb-27 Nov, 10-5 wknds BH's & school holidays **Fee:** £2.50 (sen £1.25, under 2's free). Additional charge to drive/ride machinery **Facilities:** ▣ ◼ ♿ toilets for disabled shop ✖ (ex guide dogs) ◼

SHILDON   Map 08 NZ22
LOCOMOTION: THE NATIONAL RAILWAY MUSEUM AT SHILDON
DL4 1PQ
➲ (From junct 68 of A1(M) take A68 & A6072 to Shildon. Locomotion is 0.25m SE of Shildon Town Centre)
☎ 01388 777999 ▤ 01388 777999   `FREE`
e-mail: gill@hamer-loco.fsnet.co.uk
Timothy Hackwood (1786-1850) was an important figure in the development of steam travel. He constructed Puffing Billy for William Hedley, ran Stephenson's Newcastle Works, and
continued

also became the first superintendent of the Stockton & Darlington Railway. The museum and house detail Hackwood's life and the steam transport revolution, as well as displaying working models and locomotives from various periods. New attraction 'Locomotion' opens late 2004, containing sixty vehicles from the national collection in York. Steam train rides are available throughout the year.
Times: Open: 3 Nov-18 Mar, Wed-Sun 10-4 (closed 13 Dec-5 Jan) 19 Mar-30 Oct daily 10-5 **Facilities:** ▣ ◼ ♿ bus available to transport guests. Please contact toilets for disabled shop ✖ (ex guide dogs)

STAINDROP   Map 12 NZ12
RABY CASTLE
DL2 3AH
➲ (on A688, Barnard Castle to Bishop Auckland road, 1m N of Staindrop. Travelling S, A1(M) J58 onto A68, turning left onto A688 to Barnard Castle, Castle on right. Travelling N A1(M) J60. W on A688 to West Auckland & Barnard Castle)
☎ 01833 660202 ▤ 01833 660169
e-mail: admin@rabycastle.com
This dramatic 14th-century castle, built by the Nevills has been home to Lord Barnard's family since 1626. It has an impressive gateway, nine towers, a vast hall and an octagonal Victorian drawing room that has re-emerged as one of the most striking interiors from the 19th century. Rooms contain fine furniture, impressive artworks and elaborate architecture. In the grounds are a deer park, large walled gardens, coach and carriage collections, a woodland adventure playground, a picnic area and gift shop.
Times: Open May & Sep, Wed & Sun only. Jun-Aug, Sun-Fri. Castle open 1-5. Park & gardens 11-5.30, (last admission 4.30pm). Open BH wknds **Fee:** Castle, Park & Gardens £9 (ch £4 & pen £8). Family ticket £25 (2 adults & 3 ch). Park & Gardens £4 (ch £2.50 & pen £3.50). Group rates available **Facilities:** ▣ ◼ ♿ (most of ground floor accessible) toilets for disabled shop ✖ (ex guide dogs & on lead) ◼

TANFIELD   Map 12 NZ15
TANFIELD RAILWAY
Old Marley Hill NE16 5ET
➲ (on A6076 1m S of Sunniside)
☎ 0191 388 7545 ▤ 0191 387 4784
e-mail: tanfield@ingsoc.demon.co.uk
A 3-mile working steam railway and the oldest existing railway in the world. The Causey Arch, the first large railway bridge of its era, is the centrepiece of a deep wooded valley, with picturesque walks. You can ride in carriages that first saw use in Victorian times, and visit Marley Hill shed, the home of 35 engines; inside the shed you can see the stationary steam engine at work driving some of the vintage machine tools. The blacksmith is also often at work forging new parts for the restoration work. Special events are held throughout the year, please telephone for details.
Times: ✱ Open all year, summer daily 10-5; winter daily 10-4. Trains: Sun & Summer BH's wknds; also Thu & Sat mid Jul-Aug. Santa's Specials Sat & Sun in Dec (booking essential). Mince pie specials Boxing Day. **Facilities:** ▣ ◼ ♿ (all trains carry ramps for wheelchair access) toilets for disabled shop

ESSEX

EVENTS & FESTIVALS

January
2nd Maldon Mud Race (500 competitors
racing 400 metres on the river bed at low
tide)

May
15th Essex Young Farmers Show, Essex County
Showground, Great Leighs
29th-30th Southend Air Show, Europe's largest
free show (provisional)
23rd Tour de Tendring Cycle Ride,
Tendring area
30th Redoubt Fete, Redoubt Fort, Harwich

June
4th-5th Thaxted Morris Ring Meet, various
venues, annual meeting of morris men

July
1st-10th Harwich Festival, various venues
9th Tendring Hundred Show, Lawford House
Park, Manningtree (agricultural show)
tbc Classic Car Rally London-Southend
tbc RNLI Sea Festival, Harwich

August
13th-21st Clacton Carnival (provisional)
25th-29th Clacton Jazz Festival (provisional)
tbc Clacton Air Show, Clacton Seafront
tbc Southend Jazz Festival (various venues)

September
10th-11th Colchester Festival, street festival
with carnival, dance, parade, comedy,
samba and the Great Tent (provisional)
tbc Walton Folk Festival

Above: Tilbury Fort

AUDLEY END   Map 05 TL53
AUDLEY END HOUSE & GARDENS
CB11 4JF
➲ (1m W of Saffron Walden on B1383)
☎ 01799 522399   🖪 01799 521276
One of the most significant Jacobean houses in England with
31 opulent rooms on view. Set in 'Capability' Brown
landscaped park, with walled Victorian kitchen garden.
Times: House; Mar, Thur-Mon, 10-4 (Tours Only); Apr-Sep, Wed-Mon,
12-5; Oct, Thu-Mon, 10-4 (Tours only); Garden: Mar Thu-Mon, 10-5;
Apr-Sep, Wed-Mon, 10-6; Oct, Thu-Mon, 10-5 **Fee:** ✱ House &
Gardens: £8.50 (ch £4.30, concessions £6.40, family £21.30). Grounds
only £4.50 (ch £2.30, concessions £3.40, family £11.30). Prices &
opening times relate to 2004, for further details phone or log onto
www.english-heritage.org.uk/visits **Facilities:** 🅿 (charged) 💭
& shop ✕ (ex on leads) ✿

BRENTWOOD   Map 05 TQ69
KELVEDON HATCH SECRET NUCLEAR
BUNKER NEW
CM14 5TL
➲ (on A128 Brentwood to Chipping Ongar road)
☎ 01277 364883   🖪 01277 362260
e-mail: bunker@jasper.demon.co.uk
Witness the three phases of the bunker's life. From its role
with the RAF where the overall tactical controller would
react to a nuclear attack from Britain's enemies, through to
its role as Regional Government HQ. When there could have
been up too 600 personnel, possibly including the Prime
Minister, organising the survival of the civilian population in
the aftermath of nuclear war. See for yourself the equipment
and rooms needed to support the plotting of nuclear fall out
patterns.
Times: Mar-Oct, wkdays 10-4 wknds 10-5; Nov-Feb, Thu-Sun 10-4.
Fee: £5 (ch£3). Family ticket (2adults+2ch) £12 **Facilities:** 🅿 💭
✕ licensed shop 📧

CASTLE HEDINGHAM   Map 05 TL73
COLNE VALLEY RAILWAY & MUSEUM
Castle Hedingham Station CO9 3DZ
➲ (4m NW of Halstead on A1017)
☎ 01787 461174
Many former Colne Valley and Halstead railway buildings
have been rebuilt here. Stock includes seven steam
locomotives plus 80 other engines, carriages and wagons.
Visitors can dine in style in restored Pullman carriages while
travelling along the line. Please telephone for a free
timetable and details of the many special events.
Times: Open all year, daily 10-dusk. Steam days, rides from 12-4.
(Closed 23 Dec-1 Feb). Steam days every Sun and BH from Mothering
Sunday to end Oct, Wed of school summer holidays & special events.
Railway Farm Park open May-Sep. Phone 01787 461174 for timetable
information or visit website. **Fee:** Steam days: £6 (ch £3, pen £5)
Family ticket £18. Diesel days £5 (ch £2.50); Family ticket £15.
Facilities: 🅿 💭 ✕ licensed & (ramps for wheelchairs to get onto
carriages) shop ✕ (ex guide dogs) 📧

> Directions are provided
> by the attractions.

HEDINGHAM CASTLE

CO9 3DJ

➲ (on B1508, 1m off A1017
Colchester/Cambridge. Follow brown heritage
signs to Hedingham Castle)

☎ 01787 460261 🖹 01787 461473
e-mail: hedinghamcastle@aspects.net

2 for 1

This impressive Norman castle was built in 1140. It was
besieged by King John, and visited by Henry VII, Henry VIII
and Elizabeth I, and was home to the de Veres, Earls of
Oxford, for over 500 years. During the summer months
Hedingham's colourful heritage comes to life with a full
programme of special events. There are medieval jousts and
sieges with authentic living history displays and
encampments. Please telephone for details.
Times: Open Etr-Oct, Thu, Fri & Sun, 11-4. **Fee:** £4 (ch £3,
concessions £3.50). Family ticket £14. **Facilities:** 🅿 🖭 shop
✹ (ex in grounds) ➰

CHELMSFORD   Map 05 TL70

RHS GARDEN HYDE HALL

Rettendon CM3 8ET

➲ (from M25 junct 28 (signed A12) or 29 (signed
A127). SE of Chelmsford signed from A130. Exit
Rettendon Turnpike, N through Rettendon Village,
follow brown tourist signs)

☎ 01245 400256 🖹 01245 402100
e-mail: hydehall@rhs.org.uk

Calling itself "A garden of inspirational beauty", RHS Garden
Hyde Hall is a great day out for flower-lovers, and includes
highlights such as the Dry Garden, a modern rose garden
designed by Robin Williams, colour themed herbaceous
borders, a farmhouse garden, and the NCCPG National
Collection™ of Viburnum. New areas include The Queen
Mother's Garden and a Wildlife Garden.
Times: Open Jan-Sep, daily 10-6; Oct onwards 10-5.
Facilities: 🅿 ✗ licensed 🚻 (ramps and easy access to visitor centre)
toilets for disabled shop garden centre ✹ (ex guide dogs) ➰

COGGESHALL   Map 05 TL82

PAYCOCKE'S

West St CO6 1NS

➲ (Signposted from A120, on S side of West
Street)

☎ 01376 561305

This timber-framed house is a fine example of a medieval
merchant's home. It was completed in about 1505 and has
interesting carvings on the outside timbers, including the
continued

Paycocke trade sign. Inside there are further elaborate
carvings and linenfold panelling. Behind the house is a pretty
garden.
Times: Open 27 Mar-9 Oct Tue, Thu, Sun & BH Mon 2-5.30.
Fee: ✱ £2.30, joint ticket with Coggeshall Grange Barn £3.40.
Facilities: 🅿 (400yds) 🚻 ✹ (ex guide dogs) ⚘

COLCHESTER   Map 05 TL92

BETH CHATTO GARDENS

Elmstead Market CO7 7DB

➲ (5m E of Colchester on A133)

☎ 01206 822007 🖹 01206 825933
e-mail: info@bethchatto.fsnet.co.uk

Begun almost 40 years ago, when Beth Chatto and her late
husband began working on acres of wasteland. Now an area
of landscaped gardens with many unusual plants grown in a
variety of conditions.
Times: Open all year, Mar-Oct, Mon-Sat 9-5; Nov-Feb, Mon-Fri 9-4.
(Closed Sun). **Fee:** ✱ £3.50, from May 2005 £4 (accompanied
ch under 14 free) **Facilities:** 🅿 🖭 🚻 (parts of garden may be
awkward, parking, large print guide) toilets for disabled garden centre
✹ (ex guide dogs) ➰

COLCHESTER CASTLE MUSEUM

Castle Park, High St CO1 1TJ

➲ (at E end of High St)

☎ 01206 282939 🖹 01206 282925

2 for 1

The largest Norman castle keep in Europe - built over the
remains of the magnificent Roman Temple of Claudius which
was destroyed by Boudicca in AD60. Colchester was the first
capital of Roman Britain, and the archaeological collections
are among the finest in the country. Please telephone for
details of a range of events held throughout the year.
Times: Open all year, Mon-Sat 10-5, Sun 11-5. Closed Xmas/New Year
Fee: ✱ £4.50 (ch u5's free, ch & concessions £2.90).
Facilities: 🅿 (town centre) 🚻 (all parts accessible except vaults/roof
tour) toilets for disabled shop ✹ (ex guide dogs) ➰

COLCHESTER ZOO

Stanway, Maldon Rd CO3 0SL

➲ (turn off A12 onto A1124 and follow elephant
signs)

☎ 01206 331292 🖹 01206 331392
e-mail: enquiries@colchester-zoo.co.uk

One of England's finest zoos, Colchester Zoo has over 200
types of animals. Visitors can meet the elephants, handle a
snake, and see parrots, seals, penguins and birds of prey all
appearing in informative daily displays. New enclosures
include Spirit of Africa, Elephant Kingdom, Penguin Shores,
the Wilds of Asia for orangutans, and Chimp World. There is
also an undercover soft play complex, road train, four
adventure play areas, eating places and gift shops, all set in
40 acres of gardens. The new PlayaPatagonia Sealion
experience features a 24m under water tunnel.
Times: Open all year, daily from 9.30. Last admission 5.30 (1hr before
dusk out of season). Closed 25 Dec. **Fee:** ✱ £11.99 (ch 3-14 £6.99,
disabled £4.99, pen £ 8.99). **Facilities:** 🅿 🖭 ✗ licensed 🚻 (easy
route developed, but zoo has hills) toilets for disabled shop garden
centre ✹ ➰

HADLEIGH
Map 05 TQ88

HADLEIGH CASTLE
⮑ (0.75m S of A13)
☎ 01760 755161
FREE

The subject of several of Constable's paintings, the castle has fine views of the Thames estuary. It is defended by ditches on three sides, and the north-east and south-east towers are still impressive.

Times: Open any reasonable time. **Facilities:** (limited access due to hilly surroundings) ✖ (ex dogs on leads) ✪

HARWICH
Map 05 TM23

HARWICH REDOUBT FORT
CO12 3TE
⮑ (behind 29 Main Rd)
☎ 01255 503429   ▤ 01255 503429
2 for 1
e-mail: theharwichsociety@quista.net

The 180ft-diameter circular fort was built in 1808 in case of invasion by Napoleon. It has a dry moat and 8ft-thick walls, with 18 rooms for stores, ammunition and quarters for 300 men. The Redoubt is being restored by the Harwich Society, and contains three small museums. Ten guns can be seen on the battlements.

Times: Open May-Aug, daily 10-4.30; Sep-Apr, Sun only 10-4. **Fee:** £1 (accompanied ch free). **Facilities:** ⓟ (200yds) shop

HEDINGHAM
See **Castle Hedingham**

LAYER MARNEY
Map 05 TL91

LAYER MARNEY TOWER
CO5 9US
⮑ (off B1022 Colchester to Maldon road, signposted)
☎ 01206 330784   ▤ 01206 330884
e-mail: info@layermarneytower.co.uk

The tallest Tudor gatehouse in the country, intended to be the entrance to a courtyard which would have rivalled Hampton Court Palace. The death of Henry, 1st Lord Marney in 1523, and of his son in 1525, meant that the building work ceased before completion. The beautiful parish church lies within the grounds and a wildlife walk offers the chance to see a range of livestock.

Times: Open Apr-Sep, Mon-Thu 12-5, Sun 12-5 & BHs 11-5. **Fee:** ✱ £3.50 (ch £2). Family ticket £10. Guided tour £4.75. Party 20+. **Facilities:** ⓟ 🍽 ✖ licensed ⅊ (ramps in garden and farm) toilets for disabled shop ✖ (ex guide dogs & dogs on lead) 🍴

MISTLEY
Map 05 TM13

MISTLEY TOWERS
CO11 1NJ
⮑ (on B1352, 1.5m E of A137 at Lawford)
☎ 01206 393884
FREE

All that remains of the grand hall and church, designed by Robert Adam, are the lodges built in 1782 for the hall, and two square towers, topped with drums and domes which came from an earlier church.

Times: Open all reasonable time. Key available from Mistley Quay Workshops & Teashop. **Facilities:** ⅊ ✪

NEWPORT
Map 05 TL53

MOLE HALL WILDLIFE PARK
Widdington CB11 3SS
⮑ (M11 junct 8. Situated between Stansted & Saffron Walden, off B1383)
☎ 01799 540400 & 541359   ▤ 01799 542408
e-mail: enquiries@molehall.co.uk

The Park covers 20 acres and has been lovingly developed by the Johnstone family for over 40 years. The wide variety of animals range from South American Lama Guanaco to Red squirrels, Leopard-like Serval Cat and the Formosan Sika Deer, which is extinct in the wild. Mole Hall is also home to 2 species of otter, being the first regular breeders in the UK of the North American Otter. Other residents include chimpanzees, capuchins, lemurs and much more. In the tropical butterfly pavilion, see butterflies on the wing and free flying small birds. Tarantulas, snakes, leaf-eating ants, pools of aquatic life, small monkeys, tortoises and lovebirds.

Times: ✱ Open all year, daily 10.30-6 (or dusk). (Closed 25 Dec). Butterfly House open mid Mar-Oct. **Facilities:** ⓟ 🍽 ⅊ (Difficult in wet weather for wheelchairs) toilets for disabled shop garden centre ✖ (ex guide dogs) 🍴

SAFFRON WALDEN
Map 05 TL53

SAFFRON WALDEN MUSEUM
Museum St CB10 1JL
⮑ (Close to M11, take B184/B1052 & follow signs to Saffron Walden)
☎ 01799 510333   ▤ 01799 510334
2 for 1
e-mail: museum@uttesford.gov.uk

Opened in 1835, this friendly, family-size museum lies near the castle ruins in the centre of town. Its collections include local history and archaeology, natural history, ceramics, glass, costume, furniture, toys, an ancient Egyptian room, a natural history gallery, Discovery Centre and important ethnography collections. This museum has won the Museum of the Year award for being the best museum of social history and awards for disabled access. There is a regular programme of special exhibitions, events and family holiday activities.

Times: Open all year, Mar-Oct, Mon-Sat 10-5, Sun & BHs 2-5; Nov-Feb, Mon-Sat, 10-4.30, Sun & BHs 2-4.30. (Closed 24 & 25 Dec). **Fee:** £1 (concessions 50p, ch 18 & under free) **Facilities:** ⓟ ⅊ (ramps, wheelchairs available, stairlifts, hearing loop) toilets for disabled shop ✖ (ex guide & hearing dogs)

SOUTHEND-ON-SEA
Map 05 TQ88

SOUTHEND MUSEUM, PLANETARIUM & DISCOVERY CENTRE
Victoria Av SS2 6ES
⮑ (take A127 or A13 towards town centre. Museum is adjacent to Southend Victoria Railway Station)
☎ 01702 434449   ▤ 01702 349806
e-mail: southendmuseum@hotmail.com

A fine Edwardian building housing displays of archaeology, natural history and local history, telling the story of man in the south-east Essex area. Also the only planetarium in the South East outside London. Ring for details of special events.

Times: Open Central Museum: Tue-Sat 10-5 (Closed Sun-Mon & BH); Planetarium: Wed-Sat, shows at 11, 2 & 4. **Fee:** Central Museum free. Planetarium £2.40 (ch & pen £1.70). Family tickets £7.50 Party rates on request. **Facilities:** ⓟ (50mtrs) (disabled only behind museum) ⅊ (planetarium not accessible, disabled access to centre) shop ✖ (ex guide dogs)

SOUTHEND PIER MUSEUM
Western Esplanade SS1 2EL
➲ (A127 follow signs to seafront and pier. The Pier museum is at the shore end of the pier, access from the shore train station.)
☎ 01702 611214 & 614553

Southend Pier is one and a third miles long and was built in 1830. This living museum portrays the history of the pier, its railway, its disasters, and the people who have lived and worked there. Exhibits include ex-pier rolling stock, a reconstructed signal box with working levers, and antique slot machines.
Times: Open May-Oct. Tue, Wed, Sat, Sun & BH's 11-5 (during school hols 5.30) **Fee:** ✱ £1(accompanied ch under 12 free)
Facilities: P (50yds) ♿ (Access to museum through fire door at Adventure Island) shop ✘ (ex guide dogs)

STANSTED   Map 05 TL52
HOUSE ON THE HILL MUSEUM ADVENTURE
CM24 8SP
➲ (off B1383 in the centre of Stansted Mountfitchet)
☎ 01279 813567   🖷 01279 816391
e-mail: mountfitchetcastle1066@btinternet.com

A large, privately-owned toy museum, housed on two floors covering 7,000 sq. ft. A huge variety of toys, books and games from the late Victorian period up to the 1970s. There is a space display, Teddy Bears' picnic, Action Man, Sindy, Barbie, military displays and much more. Additional displays of film, theatre and television memorabilia are on show, plus end of the pier slot machines.
Times: Open daily, 10-5; (closed for a few days over the Xmas period & Mon in Jan & Feb) **Fee:** ✱ £3.80 (ch under 14's £3, pen £3.50). Party 15+. **Facilities:** P (charged) shop ✘ (ex guide dogs) 🖦

MOUNTFITCHET CASTLE & NORMAN VILLAGE
CM24 8SP
➲ (off B1383, in centre of village. 5 min from M11 junct 8)
☎ 01279 813237   🖷 01279 816391
e-mail: mountfitchetcastle1066@btinternet.com

Norman motte and bailey castle and village reconstructed as it was in Norman England of 1066, on its original historic site. A vivid illustration of village life in Domesday England, complete with houses, church, seige tower, seige weapons, and many types of animals roaming freely. Animated wax figures in all the buildings give historical information to visitors.
Times: Open daily, 13 Mar-13 Nov, 10-5. **Fee:** ✱ £6 (ch under 2 free, ch 2-14 £5, pen £5.50). **Facilities:** P (charged) 🖦♿ (laser commentaries) toilets for disabled shop ✘ (ex guide dogs) 🖦

Britain's best-selling B&B guide featuring over 4,000 great places to stay.

The B&B Guide 2005

Just **AA** sk.

www.theAA.com

TILBURY   Map 05 TQ67
TILBURY FORT
No 2 Office Block, The Fort RM18 7NR
➲ (0.5 mile E off A126)
☎ 01375 858489

View the finest example of 17th-century military engineering, a spectacular sight on the River Thames. View the World War I and II gun emplacements and even fire a real anti-aircraft gun.
Times: Open all year, Apr-Sep, daily 10-6; Oct, daily 10-5; Nov-Mar, Thu-Mon 10-4. **Fee:** ✱ £3.20 (ch £1.60, concessions £2.40). Prices & opening times relate to 2004, for further details phone or log onto www.english-heritage.org.uk/visits **Facilities:** ♿ shop ✘ (ex on lead in certain areas) ▥

WALTHAM ABBEY   Map 05 TL30
LEE VALLEY PARK FARMS
Stubbins Hall Ln, Crooked Mile EN9 2EG
➲ (M25 junct 26, follow to Waltham Abbey. 2m from Waltham Abbey on B914)
☎ 01992 892781 & 892291   `2 for 1`
🖷 01992 892291
e-mail: hayeshill@leevalleypark.com

Set in the heart of Lee Valley Country Park, Hayes Hill Farm offers young and old the chance to view many types of farm animals. Meet a variety of rare breeds in the traditional-style farmyard. In the pet centre, see many creatures from meerkats to chipmunks. During summer, there are tractor and trailor rides to Holyfield Hall, a 700-acre working dairy and arable farm.
Times: Open all year, Mon-Fri 10-4.30, wknds & BH 10-5.30. **Fee:** £4 (ch 3+ £3, concessions £3.50). Family (2ad + 3ch) £16
Facilities: P 🖦♿ (graded concrete paths, signed routes) toilets for disabled shop 🖦

ROYAL GUNPOWDER MILLS NEW
Beaulieu Dr EN9 1JY
➲ (Leave M25 Jct 26. Follow signs for A121 to Waltham Abbey at rdbt, Entrance is in Beaulieu Drive)
☎ 01992 707370   🖷 01992 707372
e-mail: info@royalgunpowdermills.com

Set in 175 acres of parkland, this amazing scientific complex has 21 buildings of historical importance. Before it closed in 1991 this was the site of major scientific research and development, including work on Congreve's Rocket in the early 19th century, up to more recent work on ejector seats and fuel for rocket motors. Explosives were made in many of the buildings on the site which are connected by five miles of navigational canals.
Times: 30 Apr-25 Sep, 11-5, last entry at 3.30. Weekends and B/H's only **Fee:** £5.50 (ch £3, concessions £4.70, under 5's free) Family £17
Facilities: P 🖦♿ ramps, lift, tactile with audio tour toilets for disabled shop ✘ (ex guide dogs) 🖦

WALTHAM ABBEY GATEHOUSE, BRIDGE & ENTRANCE TO CLOISTERS
➲ (in Waltham Abbey off A112)   `FREE`
☎ 01992 702200

Beside the great Norman church at Waltham are the slight remains of the abbey buildings - bridge, gatehouse and part of the north cloister. The bridge is named after King Harold, founder of the abbey.
Times: Open any reasonable time. **Facilities:** ♿ (sensory trail guide) ✘ (ex dogs on leads) ▥

GLOUCESTERSHIRE

EVENTS & FESTIVALS

February
11th-13th Cheltenham Folk Festival
March
15th-18th National Hunt Festival (Gold Cup Week), Prestbury Park, Cheltenham
April
28th-2nd May Cheltenham International Jazz Festival
May
2nd Cheese Roll, A46 nr Brockworth
4th-15th Cheltenham Competitive Festival, a showcase of local talent (provisional)
5th-8th Badminton Horse Trials (provisional)
13th-15th The Spring Gardening Show, Three Counties Showground, Malvern
June
3rd Robert Dover's Cotswold Olimpick Games, Dover's Hill, Chipping Coopers Hill
9th-12th Cheltenham Festival of Science
17th-19th Three Counties Show, Three Counties Showground, Malvern
July
1st-17th Cheltenham Fringe Festival
1st-17th Cheltenham International Festival of Music
9th-10th The Cotswold Show & Country Fair, Cirencester Park, Cirencester
9th-10th Tewkesbury Medieval Festival
10th-16th Longborough Festival Opera, Longborough Festival Opera House
16th-17th Royal International Air Tattoo, RAF Fairford, Gloucestershire
16th-17th Tewkesbury Water Festival
23rd-24th International Kite Festival, Tewkesbury (provisional)
tbc Gloucester Festival
tbc Musica Deo Sacra, Tewkesbury Abbey,
August
tbc Gloucester International Blues Festival
tbc Twyning to Tewkesbury Raft Race
September
24th-25th The Malvern Autumn Garden & Country Show, Three Counties Showground
October
tbc Cheltenham Festival of Literature
tbc Tewkesbury Mop Fair (street fair)

Above: The rooftops of Chipping Campden

ALDSWORTH   Map 04 SP11

LODGE PARK & SHERBORNE ESTATE NEW
GL54 3PP
➲ (approach from A40 only between Northleach & Burford rdbts)
☎ 01451 844130 & 844257 ▯ 01451 844131
e-mail: lodgepark@ntrust.org.uk
Situated on the picturesque Sherborne Estate in the Cotswolds, Lodge Park was created in 1634 by John 'Crump' Dutton. Inspired by his passion for gambling and banqueting it is a unique survival of what would have been called a grandstand, with its deer course and park.
Times: Open Grandstand: mid Mar-30 Oct, Mon, Fri & Sun 11-4, Sat 11-3; Estate: daily all year. **Fee:** ✱ Grandstand: £4.50 (ch £2.50). Family £11. Estate: free. **Facilities:** 🅿 (charged) ♿ (Braille guide, manual wheelchair) toilets for disabled ♨

BERKELEY   Map 03 ST69

BERKELEY CASTLE
GL13 9BQ
➲ (just off A38 midway between Bristol & Gloucester. From M5 take junct 14 or 15)
☎ 01453 810332 ▯ 01453 512995
e-mail: info@berkeley.castle.com

Berkeley Castle is the amazing fortress home of the Berkeley family, who have lived in the building since the Keep was completed in 1153. The castle is still intact, from dungeon to elegant drawing rooms, and reflects nearly a thousand years of English history: a king's murder, the American Colonies, London's Berkeley Square. Rose-clad terraces surround this most romantic castle.
Times: Open Apr-2 Oct, Tue-Sat & BH Mon 11-4, Sun 2-5; Oct, Sun only 2-5. **Fee:** ✱ Castle & Gardens & Butterfly House: £7(ch 5-15 £4, pen £5.50). Family ticket (2 adult & 2 ch) £18.50. **Facilities:** 🅿 ▱ ♿ Special tours can be arranged shop ✖ (ex guide dogs) ◀

JENNER MUSEUM
Church Ln, High St GL13 9BN
➲ (follow tourist signs from A38 to town centre, turn left into High Street & left again into Church Lane)
☎ 01453 810631 ▯ 01453 811690   **2 for 1**
e-mail: manager@jennermuseum.com
This beautiful Georgian house was the home of Edward Jenner, the discoverer of vaccination against smallpox. The house and the garden, with its Temple of Vaccinia, are much as they were in Jenner's day. The displays record Jenner's life
continued

as an 18th-century country doctor, his work on vaccination and his interest in natural history.
Times: Open Apr-Sep, Tue-Sat 12.30-5.30, Sun 1-5.30. Oct, Sun 1-5.30. (Closed Mon, ex BH Mon 12.30-5.30). **Fee:** ✱ £3.50 (ch £2, students & pen £2.80). Family ticket £9. Party 20+. **Facilities:** 🅿 ⅊ toilets for disabled shop ✖ (ex guide dogs)

BOURTON-ON-THE-HILL Map 04 SP13

BOURTON HOUSE GARDEN NEW
GL56 9AE
➲ (1.75m W of Moreton-in-Marsh on A44)
☎ 01386 700754 🖶 01386 701081
e-mail: cd@bourtonhouse.com
Since 1983 a dedicated team has been working to restore this 18th-century house and its large gardens. The result is an impressive landscape full of hedges, water features, paths and plants.
Times: 25 May-Aug, Wed-Fri, Sep-28 Oct Thu-Fri, 10-5 **Fee:** £5, children free **Facilities:** 🅿 ⅊ ⅊ garden is 70% accessible shop garden centre ✖

BOURTON-ON-THE-WATER Map 04 SP12

BIRDLAND
Rissington Rd GL54 2BN
➲ (on A429)
☎ 01451 820480 🖶 01451 822398
e-mail: sb.birdland@virgin.net
Birdland is a natural setting of woodland, river and gardens, which is inhabited by over 500 birds; flamingos, pelicans, penguins, cranes, storks, cassowary and waterfowl can be seen on various aspects of the water habitat. Over 50 aviaries of parrots, falcons, pheasants, hornbills, touracos, pigeons, ibis and many more. Tropical, Toucan and Desert Houses are home to the more delicate species.
Times: Open all year, Apr-Oct, daily 10-6; Nov-Mar, daily 10-4. Last admission 1hr before closing. (Closed 25 Dec). **Fee:** ✱ £4.85 (ch 4-14 £2.85, pen £3.85). Family ticket (2 ad & 2 ch) £14. Party 10+.
Facilities: 🅿 (adjacent) ⅊ ⅊ toilets for disabled shop (ex dogs on lead) ▤

MODEL VILLAGE
Old New Inn GL54 2AF
☎ 01451 820467 🖶 01451 810236
e-mail: reception@theoldnewinn.co.uk
The model is built of Cotswold stone to a scale of one-ninth, and is a perfect replica of the village. It includes a miniature River Windrush, a working model waterwheel, churches and shops, with tiny trees, shrubs and alpine plants.
Times: Open all year 9-5.45 (summer), 10-dusk (winter). (Closed 25 Dec). **Facilities:** 🅿 (500yds) ⅊ ✖ licensed shop ✖ (ex guide dogs) ▤

CHEDWORTH Map 04 SP01

CHEDWORTH ROMAN VILLA
Yanworth GL54 3LJ
➲ (3m NW of Fossebridge on A429)
☎ 01242 890256 🖶 01242 890544
e-mail: chedworth@smtp.ntrust.org.uk
The remains of a Romano-British villa, excavated 1864-66 'Britains oldest county house'. Set in a beautiful wooded combe, there are fine 4th-century mosaics, two bath houses, and a temple with spring. The museum houses the smaller

continued

finds and there is a 9-minute video programme. Telephone for further details of special events.
Times: Open 8 Feb-26 Mar, daily (ex Mon) 11-4; 27 Mar-24 Oct, daily (ex Mon) 10-5; 26 Oct-14 Nov, daily (ex Mon) 11-4. Closed Mon (ex BH Mon's). **Fee:** ✱ £4.10 (ch £2). Family ticket £10.20.
Facilities: 🅿 ⅊ (audio tour, induction loop, Braille guide) toilets for disabled shop ✖ ⅊ ▤

CHELTENHAM Map 03 SO92

CHELTENHAM ART GALLERY & MUSEUM
Clarence St GL50 3JT
➲ (close to town centre and bus station, 2 min walk from the promenade.)
☎ 01242 237431 🖶 01242 262334
e-mail: artgallery@cheltenham.gov.uk
The museum has an outstanding collection relating to the Arts and Crafts Movement, including fine furniture and exquisite metalwork. The Art Gallery contains Dutch and British paintings from the 17th century to the present day. The Oriental Gallery features pottery, costumes and treasures from the Ming Dynasty to the reign of the last Chinese Emperor. There is also a display about Edward Wilson who journeyed with Captain Scott in 1911-12, together with the history of Britain's most complete Regency town and archaeological treasures from the neighbouring Cotswolds. Special exhibitions are held throughout the year.
Times: Open all year, Mon-Sat 10-5.20. First Thu in month, 11-5.20 (Closed BH's). **Fee:** Free, donations welcome. **Facilities:** 🅿 (500 metres) disabled parking on site ⅊ ⅊ (handling tables; speech reinforcement system) toilets for disabled shop ✖ (ex guide dogs) ▤

HOLST BIRTHPLACE MUSEUM
4 Clarence Rd GL52 2AY
➲ (opposite gateway of Pittville Park. 10 min walk from town centre)
☎ 01242 524846 🖶 01242 580182
e-mail: holstmuseum@btconnect.com

Gustav Holst, composer of *The Planets* was born at this Regency house in 1874. The museum contains unique displays on Holst's life, including his original piano. The rooms of the house have been carefully restored, each area evoking a different period in the history of the house from Regency to Edwardian times.
Times: Open Tue-Sat 10-4 (Closed Mon & Dec-Jan, ex pre-booked groups) **Fee:** ✱ £2.50 (ch & concessions £2). Family ticket (2 ad & 3 ch) £7. **Facilities:** 🅿 (250yds) (large print & Braille guide, special hands-on tours) shop ✖ (ex guide dogs)

CIRENCESTER Map 04 SP00

CORINIUM MUSEUM
Park St GL7 2BX
➲ (in town centre)
☎ 01285 655611
e-mail: museums@cotswold.gov.uk

Discover the treasures of the Cotswolds at the new Corinium Museum. Two years and over £5 million in the making, it has been transformed into a must-see attraction. Featuring archaeological and historical material from Cirencester and the Cotswolds, from prehistoric times to the 19th century. The museum is known for its Roman mosaic sculpture and other material from one of Britain's largest Roman towns. New on display are Anglo-Saxon treasures from Lechlade bringing to life this little known period. The museum also houses Medieval, Tudor, Civil War and 18th-19th century displays.

Times: Mon-Sat 10-5, Sun 2-5 (closed 1 Jan, 25-26 Dec)
Fee: ✱ £3.50 (ch £2, students £2, pen £2.50). Family ticket £8.
Facilities: 🅿 (2mins walk) 💷 ✗ ♿ toilets for disabled shop ✗ 📼

CLEARWELL Map 03 SO50

CLEARWELL CAVES ANCIENT IRON MINES
GL16 8JR
➲ (1.5m S of Coleford town centre, off B4228 follow brown tourism signs)
☎ 01594 832535 📠 01594 833362
e-mail: jw@clearwellcaves.com

These impressive natural caves have also been mined since the earliest times for paint pigment and iron ore. Today visitors explore nine large caverns with displays of local mining and geology. Colour room where ochre pigments are still produced and blacksmith shop.

Times: Open Mar-Oct daily 10-5. Jan-Feb Sat-Sun 10-5. Christmas Fantasy 1-24 Dec, daily 10-5. **Fee:** ✱ £4 (ch £2.50, concessions £3.50) Family ticket £11. **Facilities:** 🅿 💷 ♿ (hands-on exhibits, Braille guide book, contact in advance) toilets for disabled shop ✗ (ex guide & hearing dogs) 📼

CRANHAM Map 03 SO81

PRINKNASH ABBEY AND POTTERY
GL4 8EX
➲ (on A46 between Cheltenham & Stroud)
☎ 01452 812066 📠 01452 812529   FREE
e-mail: shop@prinknash135.fsnet.co.uk

Set in a large park, the old priory building is a 12th to 16th-century house, used by Benedictine monks and guests of Gloucester Abbey until 1539. It became an abbey for Benedictine monks from Caldey in 1928. Rich beds of clay were discovered when foundations were being dug for the new abbey building, and so the pottery was established, employing local craftspeople.

Times: Open all year. Abbey Church: daily 5am-8pm. Shop & tearoom 9-5.30. (Closed Good Fri, 25 & 26 Dec). **Facilities:** 🅿 💷 ♿ Radar approved toilets for disabled shop

PRINKNASH BIRD & DEER PARK
GL4 8EU
➲ (M5 junct 11a, A417 Cirencester. Take 1st exit signposted A46 Stroud. Follow brown tourist signs)
☎ 01452 812727 📠 01452 812727

Nine acres of parkland and lakes make a beautiful home for black swans, geese and other water birds. There are also exotic birds such as white and Indian blue peacocks and crown cranes, as well as tame fallow deer and pygmy goats.
continued

The Golden Wood is stocked with ornamental pheasants, and leads to the reputedly haunted monks' fishpond, which contains trout. An 80-year old, free-standing, 16ft tall Wendy House in the style of a Tudor house has recently been erected near the picnic area.

Times: Open all year, daily 10-5 (4pm in winter). (Closed 26 Dec & Good Fri). **Fee:** ✱ £4 (ch £2.50, pen £3.50). Party 10+ £3.50 (ch £2, pen £3). **Facilities:** 🅿 💷 shop ✗

DEERHURST Map 03 SO82

ODDA'S CHAPEL
➲ (off B4213 near River Severn at Abbots Court SW of parish church)

This rare Saxon chapel was built by Earl Odda and dedicated in 1056. When it was discovered, it had been incorporated into a farmhouse. It has now been carefully restored.

Times: Open Apr-Oct, daily 10-6; Nov-Mar, daily 10-4. Closed 24-26 Dec & 1 Jan. **Facilities:** 🅿 (charged) ✗

DYRHAM Map 03 ST77

DYRHAM PARK
SN14 8ER
➲ (8m N of Bath, 2m from M4 junct 18)
☎ 0117 937 2501
e-mail: wfijew@smtp.ntrust.org.uk

Dyrham Park is a splendid Baroque Country house, with interiors that have hardly altered since the late 17th century. It has contemporary Dutch-style furnishings, Dutch pictures and blue-and-white Delft ware. Around the house is an ancient park with fallow deer, where Dyrham derives its name. In the beautiful gardens, famous for the tulip festival in April, is a medieval Church.

Times: House 18 Mar-30 Oct, 12-4.45, Fri-Tue. Garden 18 Mar-30 Oct, 11-5, Fri-Tue. Park all year, 11-5, all week. Shop 18 Mar-30 Oct, 11-5, Fri-Tue. Tea room, 18 Mar-30 Oct, 11-5, Fri-Tue. **Fee:** House £8.80 (ch £4.35, family £21.75). Ground only £3.40 (ch £1.70, family £7.75). Park only £2.25 (ch £1.40). **Facilities:** 🅿 💷 ✗ licensed ♿ (Braille/audio guides, stairclimber, free bus from car park) toilets for disabled shop ✗ (ex in dog walk area) 🐾

GLOUCESTER Map 03 SO81

GLOUCESTER CITY MUSEUM & ART GALLERY
Brunswick Rd GL1 1HP
➲ (centre of Gloucester)
☎ 01452 396131 📠 01452 410898   FREE
e-mail: city.museum@gloucester.gov.uk

An impressive range of Roman artefacts including the Rufus Sita tombstone; the amazing Iron Age Birdlip Mirror; one of
continued

the earliest backgammon sets in the world; dinosaur fossils; and paintings by famous artists such as Turner and Gainsborough. There is something for everyone, full-sized dinosaurs; wildlife from the City and the Gloucestershire countryside; beautiful antique furniture, glass, ceramics and silver; hands-on displays, computer quizzes and activity workstations throughout the galleries. There is an exciting range of temporary exhibitions from contemporary art and textiles to dinosaurs and local history; children's holiday activities and regular special events.

Times: Open all year, Tue-Sat 10-5. **Facilities:** P (500yds) & toilets for disabled shop ✖ (ex guide dogs) ◼

GLOUCESTER FOLK MUSEUM

99-103 Westgate St GL1 2PG
➲ (accessed by A40 and A48 from the W, A38 and M5 from the N, A40 & B4073 from the E and A4173 & A38 from the S)
☎ 01452 396467 ▤ 01452 330495 FREE
e-mail: folk.museum@gloucester.gov.uk

Three floors of splendid Tudor and Jacobean timber-framed buildings dating from the 16th and 17th centuries along with new buildings housing the Dairy, Ironmonger's shop and Wheelwright and Carpenter workshops. Local history, domestic life, crafts, trades and industries from 1500 to the present, including Toys and Childhood gallery with hands-on toys and a puppet theatre, the Siege of Gloucester, a Victorian Class Room, Victorian Kitchen and laundry equipment. A wide range of exhibitions, hands-on activities, events, demonstrations and role play sessions are held throughout the year. There is an attractive cottage garden and courtyard for events, often with live animals, and outside games.

Times: Tue-Sat, 10-5 (For ten weeks only during half terms and holidays) **Facilities:** P (500yds) & (hands-on displays, virtual tour of Protal gallery) shop ✖ (ex guide dogs) ◼

We endeavour to be as accurate as possible, but changes to times and other information can occur after the guide has gone to press.

THE NATIONAL WATERWAYS MUSEUM

Llanthony Warehouse, The Docks GL1 2EH
➲ (follow signs for historic docks off M5 and A40 and also within the city, situated to the south of the city centre)
☎ 01452 318200 ▤ 01452 318202
e-mail: bookingsnwm@thewaterwaystrust.org

Based in Gloucester Docks, this museum takes up three floors of a seven-storey Victorian warehouse, and documents the 200-year history of Britain's water-based transport. The emphasis is on hands-on experience, including working models and engines, interactive displays, actual craft, computer interactions and the national collection of inland waterways. Boat trips are also available between Easter and October.

Times: Open all year, daily 10-5. Last admissions 4pm (Closed 25 Dec). **Facilities:** P (charged) ▣ & (wheelchair, lifts, limited access to floating exhibits) toilets for disabled shop ✖ (ex guide dogs) ◼

NATURE IN ART

Wallsworth Hall, Tewkesbury Rd, Twigworth GL2 9PA
➲ (0.5 mile off main A38 between Gloucester and Tenkesbury, 2 miles N of Gloucester. Follow brown tourist signs from village)
☎ 01452 731422 0845 4500233
▤ 01452 730937
e-mail: ninart@globalnet.co.uk

Nature is the theme at this museum and art gallery, and there are many outstanding exhibits including sculpture, tapestries and ceramics. There is a 'artist in residence' programme for ten months of the year, and events include regular monthly talks, film showings and a full programme of temporary exhibitions and art courses. Work from over 60 countries spanning 1500 years is included in the collection, which has been specially commended twice in the National Heritage Museum of the Year Awards. From Picasso to David Shepherd, Flemish masters to ethnic art, contemporary sculpture to Japanese prints - there is something for everyone.

Times: Open all year, Tue-Sun & BH's 10-5. (Closed 24-26 Dec). **Fee:** £3.60 (ch, pen & students £3.0, ch under 8 free). Family ticket £11. Party 15+. **Facilities:** P ▣ ✖ licensed & (lift & ramps at entrance) toilets for disabled shop ✖ (ex guide dogs)

GUITING POWER   Map 04 SP02

COTSWOLD FARM PARK

GL54 5UG

➲ (signposted off B4077 from M5 Junct 9)

☎ 01451 850307   🖷 01451 850423

e-mail: info@cotswoldfarmpark.co.uk

2 for 1

At the Cotswold Farm Park there are nearly 50 breeding herds and flocks of the rarest British breeds of sheep, cattle, pigs, goats, horses, and poultry. Lots of activities for children including rabbits and guinea pigs to cuddle, lambs and calves to bottle feed, tractor and trailer riders, battery powered tractors and safe rustic-themed play areas indoors and outdoors. Lambing occurs in early May, followed by shearing and then milking demonstrations later in the season.

Times: Open 20 Mar-12 Sep, daily 10.30-5 (then open wknds only until end Oct & Autumn half term 10.30-4). **Fee:** ✱ £4.95 (ch £3.50, pen £4.65). Family ticket £15.50 **Facilities:** 🅿 🍽 ♿ (ramps, wheelchair to let) toilets for disabled shop ✖ (ex guide dogs) 🎐

HAILES   Map 04 SP02

HAILES ABBEY

GL54 5PB

➲ (2m NE of Winchcombe off B4632)

☎ 01242 602398

Explore the atmospheric ruins of this great medieval pilgrimage abbey, in the midst of the Cotswolds. Built in the 13th-century Hailes become famous when presented with a phial that was said to contain the blood of Christ.

Times: Open Apr-Jun & Sep, daily 10-5; Jul-Aug, daily 10-6; Oct, daily 10-4. **Fee:** ✱ £3.20 (ch £1.60, concessions £2.40). Prices & opening times relate to 2004, for further details phone or log onto www.english-heritage.org.uk/visits **Facilities:** 🅿 ♿ shop ✖ (ex dogs on leads) 🎏 🐾

Are there any excellent Days Out that we've missed? Use the Readers' Report form at the back of the book to tell us about them.

LYDNEY   Map 03 SO60

DEAN FOREST RAILWAY

Norchard Railway Centre, New Mills, Forest Rd GL15 4ET

➲ (At Lydney, turn off the Gloucester to Chepstow (A48) road and follow brown tourist signs to Norchard Railway Centre, on B4234 Lydney-Parkend road)

☎ 01594 843423 (info) & 845840

🖷 01594 845840

e-mail: commercial@deanforestrailway.co.uk

Just north of Lydney lies the headquarters of the Dean Forest Railway where a number of steam locomotives, plus lots of coaches, wagons and railway equipment are on show and guided tours are available by prior arrangement. Standard gauge passenger service on steam haulage runs from Norchard to Lydney Junction and back to Norchard, the diesel train runs from Lydney Junction to Tufts and back to Lydney Junction.

Times: Open Apr-Oct, Sun; June-Sep, Wed, Sat, Sun; Aug, Thu; Dec wknds (Santa Specials) **Fee:** ✱ £6.50 (under 5's free, ch £4.50, pen £5.50) **Facilities:** 🅿 🍽 ✖ licensed ♿ (specially adapted coach for wheelchairs, phone for details) toilets for disabled shop 🎐

MICKLETON   Map 04 SP14

HIDCOTE MANOR GARDEN

Chipping Campden GL55 6LR

➲ (1m E of B4632, near the village of Mickleton)

☎ 01386 438333   🖷 01386 438817

e-mail: hidcote@nationaltrust.org.uk

One of the most delightful arts and crafts gardens in England, created by the horticulturist Major Laurence Johnston and comprising a series of small gardens within the whole, separated by walls and hedges of different species. It is famous for its rare shrubs and trees, outstanding herbaceous borders and unusual worldwide plant species.

Times: Garden: 19 Mar-2 Oct, 10.30-6, Sat-Wed, 3-30 Oct 10.30-5 Sat-Wed   Shop: 19 Mar-30 Oct, 10.30-5, Sat-Wed, 4 Nov-18 Dec, 12-4, Fri-Sun   Restaurant: 9 Mar-30 Oct, 10.30-5, Sat-Wed, 5 Nov-18 Dec, 12-4, Sat-Sun   Tea Bar & Plant centre: 19 Mar-2 Oct, 10.30-5, Sat-Wed **Fee:** £6.60 (ch £3.30) family £16. **Facilities:** 🅿 🍽 ✖ licensed ♿ (partial access, limited due to stone paths, wheelchair available) toilets for disabled shop garden centre ✖ (ex guide dogs) 🐾

KIFTSGATE COURT GARDEN

Mickleton GL55 6LN

➲ (0.5m S off A46, adjacent Hidcote NT garden)

☎ 01386 438777 📠 01386 438777

e-mail: kiftsgte@aol.com

Kiftsgate Garden is spectacularly set on the edge of the Cotswold Escarpment, with views over the Vale of Evesham. It contains many rare plants collected by three generations of women gardeners, including the largest rose in England, the R. Filipes Kiftsgate.

Times: Open Apr-May & Aug-Sep; Wed, Thu, Sun & BH Mon 2-6. Jun-Jul Mon, Wed, Thu, Sat & Sun 12-6. **Fee:** ✱ £5 (ch £1.50). **Facilities:** 🅿 🍴 garden centre ✖ (ex guide dogs)

MORETON-IN-MARSH   Map 04 SP23

BATSFORD ARBORETUM

Admissions Centre, Batsford Park GL56 9QB

➲ (1.5m NW, off A44 from Moreton-in-Marsh)

☎ 01386 701441   `2 for 1`

📠 01386 701829

e-mail: batsarb@batsfound.freeserve.co.uk

Batsford Arboretum has one of the largest private collections of trees in Great Britain and wonderful views across the Vale of Evenlode. Visitors can stroll amongst the spring flowers that cascade down the hillside, and see many rare and unusual trees. There is an impressive display of colour during autumn, and peace and tranquillity are ever present. View the Buddha and cave and try and negotiate the waterfall without getting too wet. Sheer Cotswold magic.

Times: Open Feb-mid Nov, daily 10-5; mid Nov-Jan, wknds only 10-4. **Fee:** £5 (ch 4-15 £1, concessions £4). Party 12+. **Facilities:** 🅿 🍴 ♿ (some steep, slippery paths, wheelchair available) toilets for disabled shop garden centre Specialises in ferns & trees 🍴

COTSWOLD FALCONRY CENTRE

Batsford Park GL56 9QB

➲ (1m W of Moreton-in-Marsh on A44)

☎ 01386 701043   `2 for 1`

e-mail: geoffdalton@yahoo.co.uk

Conveniently located by the Batsford Park Arboretum, the Cotswold Falconry gives daily demonstrations in the art of falconry. The emphasis here is on breeding and conservation, and eagles, hawks, owls and falcons can be seen.

Times: Open mid Feb-mid Nov, 10.30-5.30. (Last admission 5pm). **Fee:** £5 (ch 4-15 £2.50, concession £4). Joint ticket with Batsford Arboretum £8.50 (ch 4-15 £3, concession £8). **Facilities:** 🅿 ♿ (no steps, wide doorways) toilets for disabled shop garden centre ✖ (ex on leads in arboretum) 🍴

SEZINCOTE

GL56 9AW

➲ (1.5m out of Moreton-in-Marsh on A44, Evesham road)

☎ 01386 700444

The Indian-style house at Sezincote was the inspiration for Brighton Pavilion; its charming water garden adds to its exotic aura and features trees of unusual size.

Times: Open: House, May-Jul & Sep, Thu & Fri 2.30-6. Garden only, all year (ex Dec) Thu, Fri & BH Mon 2-6 or dusk if earlier. **Fee:** House & garden £5.50 Garden only £4 (ch £1 under 5 free). Children not allowed in the House. Groups by appointment only. **Facilities:** 🅿 ♿ toilets for disabled ✖ (ex guide dogs)

NEWENT   Map 03 SO72

THE NATIONAL BIRDS OF PREY CENTRE

GL18 1JJ

➲ (follow A40, right onto B4219 towards Newent. Follow brown tourist signs from Newent town)

☎ 0870 9901992 📠 01531 821389

e-mail: katherine@nbpc.co.uk

Trained birds can be seen at close quarters in the Hawk Walk and the Owl Courtyard and there are also breeding aviaries, a gift shop, bookshop, picnic areas, coffee shop and children's play area. Birds are flown three times daily in summer and winter, giving an exciting and educational display. There are over 80 aviaries on view with 40 species.

Times: Open Feb-Oct, daily 10.30-5.30. **Fee:** ✱ £6.75 (ch £4, pen £5.75). Family ticket £18.50 (2+2). **Facilities:** 🅿 🍴 ♿ (special tours available, pre-booking required) toilets for disabled shop ✖ 🍴

See advertisement on this page

THE SHAMBLES
Church St GL18 1PP
➲ (close to town centre near church)
☎ 01531 822144

Cobbled streets, alleyways, cottages and houses set in over an acre with display shops and trades, even a tin chapel and cottage garden all helping to recreate the feel and atmosphere of a small Victorian town.
Times: Open mid Mar-end Oct, Tue-Sun & BHs 10-5 (or dusk); Nov-Dec wknds only. **Fee:** ✱ £4.25 (ch £2.65, pen £3.65).
Facilities: Ⓟ (100yds) 🍽 & toilets for disabled shop ◼

NORTHLEACH   Map 04 SP11
KEITH HARDING'S WORLD OF MECHANICAL MUSIC
The Oak House, High St GL54 3ET
➲ (at crossroads of A40 & A429)
☎ 01451 860181 🖷 01451 861133   **2 for 1**
e-mail: keith@mechanicalmusic.co.uk

A fascinating collection of antique clocks, musical boxes, automata and mechanical musical instruments, restored and maintained in the world-famous workshops, displayed in a period setting, and played during regular tours. There is an exhibition of coin operated instruments which visitors can play.
Times: Open all year, daily 10-6. Last tour 5pm. Closed 25-26 Dec.
Fee: ✱ £5 (ch £2.50, pen & students £4). Discounts for families & groups. **Facilities:** Ⓟ & Safety rails, non-slip floor toilets for disabled shop 🐕 (ex guide dogs) ◼

OWLPEN   Map 03 ST79
OWLPEN MANOR
GL11 5BZ
➲ (3m E of Dursley, signposted at village green in Uley off B4066)
☎ 01453 860261 🖷 01453 860819
e-mail: sales@owlpen.com

A romantic Tudor manor house, with unique 17th-century painted cloth wallhangings, furniture, pictures and textiles. The house is set in formal terraced gardens, and is part of a picturesque Cotswold manorial group including a Jacobean Court House, a Victorian church and medieval tithe barn.
Times: Open Apr-Sep, Tue-Sun & BH Mon, 2-5. **Fee:** £4.80 (ch £2). Coaches by appointment **Facilities:** Ⓟ 🍽 ✗ licensed 🐕 ◼

PAINSWICK   Map 03 SO80
PAINSWICK ROCOCO GARDEN
GL6 6TH
➲ (on B4073 0.5m NW of Painswick)
☎ 01452 813204 🖷 01452 814888
e-mail: info@rococogarden.co.uk

This beautiful Rococo garden (a compromise between formality and informality) is the only one of its period to survive complete. There are ponds, woodland walks, a maze, kitchen garden and herbacious borders, all set in a Cotswold valley famous for snowdrops in the early spring. Ring for details of special events.
Times: Open 10 Jan-Oct, daily 11-5. **Fee:** £4 (ch £2, pen £3.50).
Facilities: Ⓟ 🍽 ✗ licensed shop garden centre ◼

SLIMBRIDGE   Map 03 SO70
WWT SLIMBRIDGE
GL2 7BT
➲ (off A38, signed from M5 junct 13 & 14)
☎ 01453 891900 🖷 01453 890827   **2 for 1**
e-mail: slimbridge@wwt.org.uk

Slimbridge is home to the world's largest collection of exotic wildfowl - and the only place in Europe where all six types of flamingo can be seen. Up to 8,000 wild birds winter on the 800-acre reserve of flat fields, marsh and mudflats on the River Severn. Facilities include a Tropical House, Discovery Centre, shop and restaurant.
Times: Open all year, daily from 9.30-5 (winter 4pm). (Closed 25 Dec). **Fee:** ✱ £6.75 (ch £4, pen £5.50). Family ticket £17.50.
Facilities: Ⓟ 🍽 ✗ licensed & (wheelchair loan, tapes for blind, hearing pads & loops) toilets for disabled shop 🐕 (ex guide & hearing dogs) ◼

SNOWSHILL   Map 04 SP03
SNOWSHILL MANOR
WR12 7JU
➲ (3m SW of Broadway, off A44)
☎ 01386 852410 🖷 01386 842822   **2 for 1**
e-mail: snowshillmanor@nationaltrust.org.uk

Arts and crafts garden designed by its owner Charles Paget Wade in collaboration with M.H. Baillie Scott, as a series of outdoor rooms to compliment his traditional Cotswold manor house filled with his unique collection of craftsmanship including musical instruments, clocks, toys, bicycles and Japanese armour. This was the first National Trust garden to be managed following organic principles. It is a lively mix of cottage flowers, bright colours and delightful scents with stunning views across Cotswold countryside. The house is closed to the public during 2004, please contact for details, however Architectural tours will be available.
Times: House: 25 Mar-2 May, 12-5, Thu-Sun, 4 May-30 Oct, 12-5, Wed-Sun. Garden: 25 Mar-2 May, 11-5.30, Thu-Sun, 4 May-30 Oct, 11-5.30, Wed-Sun. Shop: As garden, also 5 Nov-11Dec, 12-4, Sat & Sun. Restaurant: As shop **Fee:** House & Garden: £7 (ch £3.50), Family £17.80 Garden, Restaurant & shop: £4, ch£2, family £10
Facilities: Ⓟ ✗ licensed & (Braille guides, audio tapes) 2 manual wheelchairs toilets for disabled shop 🐕 (ex guide dogs) 😾 ◼

SOUDLEY   Map 03 SO61
DEAN HERITAGE CENTRE
Camp Mill GL14 2UB
➲ (on B4227, in Forest of Dean)
☎ 01594 822170   ▤ 01594 823711   **2 for 1**
e-mail: deanmuse@btinternet.com

The Centre tells the story of this unique area, and its people, from pre-historic times to present day. Displays include a reconstructed cottage, a working beam engine from Lightmore Colliery, charcoal burners camp and art gallery. There are also nature trails with animals. There is an adventure playground that includes a maze and swing bridge. Library and research facilities are available by appointment.
Times: Open all year, daily, British Winter 10-4, British Summer 10-5.30. (Closed 24-26 Dec & 1 Jan) **Fee:** £4.50 (ch £2.50, pen & concessions £3.50). Family ticket £13. Under 5's free.
Facilities: 🅿 💺 ♿ (lift, ramps, help from establishment staff) toilets for disabled shop ✖ (ex guide dogs) ◧

TETBURY   Map 03 ST89
CHAVENAGE HOUSE
GL8 8XP
➲ (2m NW of Tetbury signposted off B4014. 7m SE of Stroud, signposted off A46)
☎ 01666 502329 & 01453 832700   **2 for 1**
▤ 01453 836778
e-mail: info@chavenage.com

Built in 1576, this unspoilt Elizabethan house contains stained glass from the 16th-century and earlier with some good furniture and tapestries. The owner during the Civil War was a Parliamentarian, and the house contains Cromwellian relics. In more recent years, the house has been the location for *Grace and Favour, Poirot, The House of Elliot, Berkeley Square, Casualty* and *Cider with Rosie*. Tours of the house are enlivened by ghost stories.
Times: Open May-Sep, Thu, Sun & BHs 2-5. Also Etr Sun & Mon. Other days by appointment only. **Fee:** ✱ £5 (ch £2.50).
Facilities: 🅿 ♿ ✖ (ex guide dogs)

ULEY   Map 03 ST79
ULEY LONG BARROW (HETTY PEGLER'S TUMP)
➲ (3.5m NE of Dursley on B4066)

This 180ft Neolithic long barrow is popularly known as Hetty Pegler's Tump. The mound, surrounded by a wall, is about 85ft wide. It contains a stone central passage, and three burial chambers.
Times: Open any reasonable time. **Facilities:** ⊞

WESTBURY ON SEVERN   Map 03 SO71
WESTBURY COURT GARDEN
GL14 1PD
➲ (9m SW of Gloucester on A48)
☎ 01452 760461
e-mail: westbury@smtp.ntrust.org.uk

This formal water garden with canals and yew hedges was laid out between 1696 and 1705. It is the earliest of its kind remaining in England and was restored in 1971 and planted with species dated pre-1700, including apple, pear and plum trees.
Times: Open Mar-Oct daily (ex Mon/Tue) but open BH Mon's. 10-5 Other months by appointment. **Fee:** ✱ £3.50 (ch £1.70).
Facilities: 🅿 ♿ (Braille guide, w/chair available) toilets for disabled shop ✖ (ex guide dogs) ◈

WESTONBIRT   Map 03 ST88
WESTONBIRT ARBORETUM
GL8 8QS
➲ (3m S Tetbury on A433)
☎ 01666 880220   ▤ 01666 880559

Begun in 1829, this arboretum contains one of the finest and most important collections of trees and shrubs in the world. There are 18,000 specimens, planted from 1829 to the present day, covering 600 acres of landscaped Cotswold countryside. Magnificent displays of Rhododendrons, Azaleas, Magnolias and wild flowers, and ablaze with colour in the autumn from the national collection of Japanese Maples.
Times: Open all year, daily 10-8 or sunset. Visitor centre & shop all year. (Closed Xmas & New Year) **Fee:** ✱ Jun-Nov £7.50 (pen £6.50) Family ticket £15. Nov-Mar £5 (pen £4) Family ticket £11. Apr-Jun £6 (pen £5) Family ticket £12 **Facilities:** 🅿 💺 ✖ licensed ♿ (electric & manual wheelchair for loan, telephone to book) toilets for disabled shop garden centre ◧

WINCHCOMBE   Map 04 SP02
SUDELEY CASTLE & GARDENS
GL54 5JD
➲ (B4632 to Winchcombe, Castle is signposted from town)
☎ 01242 602308   ▤ 01242 602959
e-mail: marketing@sudeley.org.uk

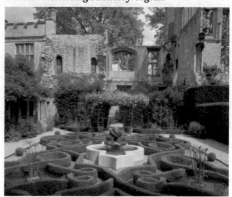

Sudeley Castle was home to Katherine Parr, who is buried in the Chapel. Henry VIII, Anne Boleyn, Lady Jane Grey and Elizabeth I all stayed or visited here; and it was the headquarters of Prince Rupert during the Civil War. The Queen's Garden is famous for its rose collection, there are exhibitions and a children's adventure playground.
Times: Open daily Mar-Oct, Grounds, Gardens, exhibition, shop & plant centre 10.30-5.30. 29 Mar-2 Nov, Castle apartments, Church & restaurant 11-5. **Fee:** ✱ Castle & Gardens £6.85-£7.85 (ch 5-15 £3.85-£4.85 & concessions £5.85-£6.85). Gardens only £5.50-£6.50 (ch £2.75-£3.75 & concessions £4.50-£5.50). Family ticket (2 ad & 2 ch) £18.50-£22. Party 20+ £5.85 (ch £3.85, concessions £4.85).
Facilities: 🅿 ✖ licensed ♿ (limited access to gardens only, parking) toilets for disabled shop garden centre ✖ (by request on arrival) ◧

GREATER MANCHESTER

EVENTS & FESTIVALS

February
9th Chinese New Year Celebrations, parade from Town Hall to Chinatown

May
tbc Streets Ahead, street festival, Manchester

June
11th-12th Greater Manchester Youth Games, Robin Park Stadium, Wigan (provisional)

July
2nd Unity Festival, Chorlton Park, Manchester, celebrating diversity
23rd-24th Chadkirk Festival, Stockport, music and entertainment (provisional)
23rd-31st Manchester Jazz Festival, various venues including outdoors (provisional)
tbc Lord Mayor's Parade, Manchester, cavalcade of floats, bands and walking parties in the city centre
tbc Manchester Mega Mela, Platt Fields Park, Rusholme, Manchester, celebration of Asian Culture

August
13th Bramhall Horticultural Show
tbc Caribbean Carnival, Alexandra Park, Manchester
tbc Manchester Pride, city centre

September
tbc Fashion Manchester, celebration of fashion and lifestyle

Above: Bramhall Hall, Stockport

ALTRINCHAM   Map 07 SJ78
DUNHAM MASSEY
WA14 4SJ
⮕ (3m SW of Altrincham (off A56), off M6 junct 19 or off M56 junct 7, then follow brown signs)
☎ 0161 941 1025   📠 0161 929 7508
e-mail: dunhammassey@nationaltrust.org.uk
A fine 18th-century house, garden and park, home of the Earls of Stamford until 1976. The house contains fine furniture and silverware, and some thirty rooms, including the library, billiard room, fully-equipped kitchen, butler's pantry and laundry. The garden is on an ancient site with waterside plantings, mixed borders and fine lawns. There is also a 300 acre deer park. Telephone for details of special events.
Times: Open: Park, restaurant & shop open all year. House open 27 Mar-3 Nov, 12-5 (11 Sun & BH Mon, closes at 4 during late Oct). Garden, 11-5.30 (closes 4.30 in late Oct). Last entry to house 30mins before closing time. **Fee:** ✱ House & Garden £6 (ch £3). House only £4 (ch £2). Garden only £4 (ch £2). Family ticket £15. Park only, £3.50 per car. £1 per motorbike **Facilities:** 🅿 (charged) ✖ licensed ♿ (loan of batricar/wheelchairs, lift, Braille guide, parking) toilets for disabled shop ✖ (ex on lead in Park) ♨ ▰

ASHTON-UNDER-LYNE   Map 07 SJ99
CENTRAL ART GALLERY
Central Library Building, Old St OL6 7SG
☎ 0161 342 2650   📠 0161 342 2650   FREE
e-mail: central.artgallery@tameside.gov.uk
Set in a fine Victorian Gothic building, the Central Art Gallery has three areas, each of which offers a varied programme of temporary exhibitions. A range of tastes and styles are covered, with group and solo shows of work by artists from the region including paintings, sculpture, installation and textiles.
Times: Open all year, Tue, Wed & Fri 10-12.30 & 1-5; Thu 1-7.30 & Sat 9-12.30 & 1-4. **Facilities:** 🅿 100mtrs Pay and Display ♿ Induction loop toilets for disabled shop ✖ (ex guide dogs)

MUSEUM OF THE MANCHESTER REGIMENT
The Town Hall, Market Place OL6 6DL
⮕ (in town centre, on market square, follow signs for museum)
☎ 0161 342 3078 & 0161 342 3710   FREE
📠 0161 343 2869
e-mail: portland.basin@tameside.gov.uk
The social and regimental history of the Manchesters is explored at this museum, tracing the story back to its origins in the 18th century. The Manchesters fought in both World Wars, the Boer War, and the Crimea.
Times: Open all year, Mon-Sat, 10-4. (Closed Sun).
Facilities: 🅿 (50yds) (pay & display) ♿ toilets for disabled shop ✖ (ex guide dogs)

An asterisk * indicates that opening times and prices are for 2004. Please contact the attraction for up-to-date information.

PORTLAND BASIN MUSEUM
Portland Place OL7 0QA
➲ (M60 junct 23 into Ashton town centre. Follow Park Parade dual carriageway to rdbt, go right around & back onto dual carriageway. At 2nd turning, turn left. Museum is near Cross Hill street & car park)
☎ 0161 343 2878 🖷 0161 343 2869 FREE
e-mail: portland.basin@tameside.gov.uk
Exploring the social and industrial history of Tameside, this museum is part of the recently rebuilt Ashton Canal Warehouse, built in 1834. Visitors can walk around a 1920s street, dress up in old hats and gloves, steer a virtual canal boat, and see the original canal powered waterwheel that once drove the warehouse machinery. Portland Basin Museum also features changing exhibitions and event programme- so there's always something new to see!
Times: Open all year, Tue-Sun 10-5. (Closed Mon, ex BHs)
Facilities: 🅿 🔊 ♿ (Wheelchair, lift, loop system) toilets for disabled shop 🐕 (ex guide dogs) 📻

BRAMHALL   Map 07 SJ88
BRAMALL HALL & PARK
SK7 3NX
➲ (from A6 turn right at Blossoms public house through Davenport village then turn right - signposted)
☎ 0161 485 3708 🖷 0161 486 6959
e-mail: bramall.hall@stockport.gov.uk
This large timber-framed hall dates from the 14th century, and is one of the finest black-and-white houses in the North West. It has rare 16th-century wall paintings and period furniture, and was the home of the Davenport family for 500 years. Much of the house is open to the public and available for hire. Open air concerts and plays are a feature in summer.
Times: Open all year, Good Fri-Sep, Mon-Sat 1-5, Sun & BHs 11-5; Oct-New Year's Day Tue-Sat 1-4, Sun & BH's 11-4; 2 Jan-Good Fri Sat & Sun 12-4. Closed 25-26 Dec. **Facilities:** 🅿 (charged) 🔊 ♿ (access for wheelchair users) toilets for disabled shop 🐕 (ex guide dogs) 📻

MANCHESTER   Map 07 SJ89
GALLERY OF COSTUME
Platt Hall, Rusholme M14 5LL
➲ (situated in Platt Fields Park, Rusholme, access from Wilmslow Rd. 2m S of city centre)
☎ 0161 224 5217 🖷 0161 256 3278 FREE
e-mail: a.jarvis@notes.manchester.gov.uk
With one of the most comprehensive costume collections in Great Britain, this gallery makes captivating viewing. Housed in a fine Georgian mansion, the displays focus on the changing styles of everyday fashion and accessories over the last 400 years. Contemporary fashion is also illustrated. Because of the vast amount of material in the collection, no one period is permanently illustrated.
Times: Open to public on last Sat of month. Mon-Fri by appointment, please ring; 0161 224 5217 **Facilities:** 🅿 ♿ shop 🐕 (ex guide dogs)

IMPERIAL WAR MUSEUM NORTH
The Quays, Trafford Wharf Rd, Trafford Park M17 1TZ
➲ (Leave the M60 at Jct 9, join Parkway (A5081) towards Trafford Park. At 1st island take 3rd exit onto Village Way. At next island take 2nd exit onto Warren Bruce Road. Turn right at T-Jct onto Trafford Wharf Road. Alternatively, leave M602, Jct 2 and follow signs)
☎ 0161 836 4000 🖷 0161 836 4012 FREE
e-mail: info@iwmnorth.org.uk

This recently-opened war museum is built to resemble three shards of a shattered globe, representing conflict on land, sea, and in the air. Inside are thousands of exhibits, interactive sessions, performances, and recreations that explore the way that 20th century conflict has shaped our lives.
Times: Mar-Oct 10-6, Nov-Feb 10-5 Daily. (Closed 24-26 Dec)
Facilities: 🅿 (charged) 🔊 licensed ♿ lifts, parking, manual wheelchairs toilets for disabled shop 🐕 (ex guide dogs) 📻

MANCHESTER ART GALLERY
Mosley St/Princess St M2 3JL
☎ 0161 234 1456 🖷 0161 236 7369
e-mail: cityart@mcrl.poptel.org.uk
The Mosley Street Galleries have permanent displays of European art, ceramics and silver, displayed with furniture in an elaborate decorative scheme. There's a superb collection of Victorian art, including some major Pre-Raphaelite paintings. Decorative and applied arts, including porcelain, furniture and sculpture can also be seen.
Times: ✱ Gallery now reopened after expansion scheme. Unfortunately at the time of going to print we have not received confirmation of new details.

MANCHESTER MUSEUM
The University, Oxford Rd M13 9PL
➲ (S of city centre on B5117)
☎ 0161 275 2634 🖷 0161 275 2676
e-mail: anna.j.davey@man.ac.uk
After a major refurbishment the Manchester Museum has leading research facilities and collections in archaeology, botany, Egyptology, ethnology, mineralogy, numismatics, and zoology, among others. There are large galleries devoted to most of these departments, but the Egyptology collection is particularly impressive, and includes mummies excavated by Sir William Flinders Petrie.
Times: ✱ Open all year, Mon-Sat 10-5, Sun & BHs 11-4.
Facilities: 🅿 (350mtrs) ♿ (Provision for disabled telephone in advance) shop 🐕 (ex guide dogs) 📻

MANCHESTER UNITED MUSEUM & TOUR CENTRE

Sir Matt Busby Way, Old Trafford M16 0RA
➲ (2m from city centre, off A56)
☎ 0870 442 1994   ▤ 0161 868 8861   **2 for 1**
e-mail: tours@manutd.co.uk

This museum was opened in 1986 and is the first purpose-built British football museum. It covers the history of Manchester United in words, pictures, sound and vision, from its inception in 1878 to the present day.
Times: Open daily 9.30-5 (open until 1/2hr before kick off on match days). (Closed some days over Xmas & New Year) **Fee:** ✱ Stadium tour & Museum: £9 (ch & pen £6) Family ticket £25. Museum only: £5.50 (ch & pen £3.75) Family ticket £15.50. **Facilities:** ▣ ▭ ✗ licensed ♿ (wheelchair, audio visual scripts, part of tour not accessible) toilets for disabled shop ✖ (ex dogs only) ▰

THE MUSEUM OF SCIENCE AND INDUSTRY IN MANCHESTER

Liverpool Rd, Castlefield M3 4FP
➲ (follow brown tourist signs from city centre)
☎ 0161 832 2244 & 0161 832 1830
▤ 0161 833 1471
e-mail: marketing@msim.org.uk
This museum is housed in the buildings of the world's oldest passenger railway station. Colourful galleries packed full of fascinating facts and amazing artefacts bring the past to life. Walk away from your own shadow in Xperiment! The mind bending science centre, see wheels of industry turning in the Power Hall, and the planes that made flying history in the Air and Space Hall. A programme of changing exhibitions.
Times: Open all year, daily 10-5. Last admission 4.30. (Closed 24-26 Dec). **Facilities:** ▣ (charged) ▭ ✗ licensed ♿ (lifts, wheelchair loan service) toilets for disabled shop ✖ (ex guide dogs) ▰

MUSEUM OF TRANSPORT

Boyle St, Cheetham M8 8UW
➲ (museum adjacent to Queens Rd bus depot, and is 1.25m N of City Centre)
☎ 0161 205 2122   ▤ 0161 205 2122
e-mail: Gmts.enquire@btinternet.com

This museum is a must-see for fans of public transport! Among the many interesting exhibits are more than 80 beautifully restored buses and coaches from the region - the biggest collection in the UK. Displays of old photographs, tickets and other memorabilia complement the vehicles, some of which date back to 1890. Please telephone for details of special events.
Times: ✱ Open all year, Wed, Sat, Sun & BH 10-5 ex Xmas.
Facilities: ▣ ▭ ♿ toilets for disabled shop ▰
See advertisement on opposite page

URBIS

Cathedral Gardens M4 3BG
➲ (next to Victoria Railway Station)
☎ 0161 907 9099   ▤ 0161 605 8201   **FREE**
e-mail: info@urbis.org.uk
Urbis explores the dynamic culture of the modern city of Manchester. The top three floors of interactive exhibits explore cities around the world from Tokyo to Paris, revealing how different cities work, how they change and how they affect others.
Times: Open all year daily 10-6 **Facilities:** ▣ (200yds) ▭ ✗ licensed ♿ toilets for disabled shop ✖ (ex guide dogs) ▰

THE WHITWORTH ART GALLERY

The University of Manchester, Oxford Rd M15 6ER
➲ (follow brown tourist signs, on Oxford road on B5117 to S of Manchester City Centre. The Gallery is in Whitworth Park, opposite Manchester Royal Infirmary)
☎ 0161 275 7450   **FREE**
▤ 0161 275 7451
e-mail: whitworth@man.ac.uk
The gallery houses an impressive range of modern and historic drawings, prints, paintings and sculpture, as well as the largest collection of textiles and wallpapers outside London and an internationally famous collection of British watercolours. The gallery hosts an innovative programme of touring exhibitions. A selection of tour lectures, workshops and concerts complement the exhibition programme.
Times: Open Mon-Sat 10-5, Sun 2-5. (Closed Good Fri & Xmas-New Year). **Facilities:** ▣ ▭ ♿ (wheelchair available, induction loop, Braille lift buttons) toilets for disabled shop ✖ (ex guide dogs)

PRESTWICH — Map 07 SD80

HEATON HALL

Heaton Park M25 2SW

☎ 0161 773 1231 or 0161 234 1456

▤ 0161 236 2880

Designed by James Wyatt for Sir Thomas Egerton in 1772, the house has magnificent period interiors decorated with fine plasterwork, paintings and furniture. Other attractions include a unique circular room with Pompeian-style paintings, and the original Samuel Green organ still in working order.

Times: ✱ Open Etr-end Oct, but phone for time details on 0161-234 1456. **Facilities:** ℗ (charged) ♿ (occasional 'touch tours'. Phone for details) toilets for disabled shop ✖ (ex guide dogs)

SALFORD — Map 07 SJ89

THE LOWRY

Pier Eight, Salford Quays M50 3AZ

➲ (from M60 take junct 12 for M602. Salford Quays is 0.25m from J3 of the M602, follow brown Lowry signs)

☎ 0870 787 5774 ▤ 0161 876 2001   FREE

e-mail: info@thelowry.com

The Lowry is an award-winning building housing galleries, shops, cafés and a restaurant, plus two theatres showing everything from West End plays and musicals, comedians, ballet and live bands. With regular family activity too, you can make a whole day of your visit.

Times: Open daily from 10am. Galleries, Sun-Fri from 11, Sat from 10 (Closed 25 Dec). **Facilities:** ℗ (charged) � ✖ licensed ♿ Sennheiser System toilets for disabled shop ✖ (ex guide dogs) ▤

SALFORD MUSEUM & ART GALLERY

Peel Park, Crescent M5 4WU

➲ (from N leave M60 junct 13, A666. From S follow signs from end of M602. Museum on A6)

☎ 0161 736 2649 ▤ 0161 745 9490 FREE

e-mail: salford.museum@salford.gov.uk

The museum features a reconstruction of a 19th-20th century northern street with original shop fronts. Upstairs in the galleries there are temporary exhibitions and a gallery displaying paintings, sculptures and ceramics. Recent additions include is the lifetimes gallery, featuring audio, IT zones, temporary exhibitions, a spectacular Pilkington's display and lots of hands-on activities and dressing up areas

Times: Open all year Mon-Fri 10-4.45, Sat & Sun 1-5. (Closed Good Fri, Etr Sat, 25 & 26 Dec, 1 Jan). **Facilities:** ℗ ▤ ♿ (Braille & large print labels & visitor packs, hearing loop) toilets for disabled shop ✖ (guide dogs) ▤

STALYBRIDGE — Map 07 SJ99

ASTLEY CHEETHAM ART GALLERY

Trinity St GK15 2BN

☎ 0161 338 6767 FREE

e-mail: astley.cheetham@tameside.gov.uk

Built as a gift to the town in 1901 by mill owner John Frederick Cheetham, this one-time lecture hall has been an art gallery since 1932 when Cheetham left his collection to the town. Among the works are Italian paintings from the Renaissance, British masters such as Cox and Burne-Jones, and more recent gifts such as works by Turner and local artist Harry Rutherford. The gallery hosts a programme of temporary exhibitions of the collection and regional artists, and a variety of workshops are run for families throughout the year.

Times: Open all year, Mon-Wed & Fri 10-12.30, 1-5; Sat 9-12.30, 1-4.

Facilities: ℗ 2hrs on street parking. Induction loop shop ✖ (ex guide dogs)

STOCKPORT   Map 07 SJ89

HAT WORKS MUSEUM

Wellington Mill, Wellington Rd South SK3 0EU

➲ (Leave M60 at J1, follow signs for town centre. Continue to bus station. Hatworks is opposite Stockport bus station)

☎ 0161 355 7770/6   📠 0161 480 8735   **2 for 1**

e-mail: hatworks@stockport.gov.uk

Hat Works is the UK's only museum of the hatting industry, hats and headwear, offering an insight into a once flourishing industry. See how hats are made with a unique working collection of Victorian millinery machinery and take a tour with expert guides who will give visitors an insight into the Hatter's World. Browse an extensive collection of hats before relaxing in the Level 2 café.

Times: Open daily Mon-Fri 10-5, Sat & Sun 1-5. (Closed 25-26 Dec & 1 Jan). **Fee:** £3.95 (ch £2.50, concessions £2.50, under 5's free). Family ticket £11 **Facilities:** P Limited pay & display parking 🅿 & toilets for disabled shop ✖ (ex guide dogs) 🍽

UPPERMILL   Map 07 SD90

SADDLEWORTH MUSEUM & ART GALLERY

High St OL3 6HS

➲ (From M62 E exit at junct 22 or from M62 W exit at junct 21. On A670)

☎ 01457 874093   📠 01457 870336

e-mail: museum-curator@saddleworth.net

Based in an old mill building next to the Huddersfield canal, the museum explores the history of the Saddleworth area. Wool weaving is the traditional industry, displayed in the 18th-century Weaver's Cottage and the Victoria Mill Gallery. The textile machinery is run regularly by arrangement. The Art Gallery has regular exhibitions.

Times: Open all year, Nov-late Mar, daily 1-4; late Mar-Oct, Mon-Sat 10-5, Sun 12-5. (Closed 24-25 Dec & 31 Dec-1 Jan).

Facilities: P & (stairlift, ramps, Braille & large print guides, wheelchair) toilets for disabled shop ✖ (ex guide dogs)

WIGAN   Map 07 SD50

WIGAN PIER

Trencherfield Mill WN3 4EF

➲ (follow brown tourist signs from M6 junct 25-27/M61 junct 6-8)

☎ 01942 323666   📠 01942 701927   **2 for 1**

e-mail: wiganpier@wlct.org

Wigan Pier is a journey never to be forgotten. Part museum, part theatre, Wigan Pier is a mixture of entertainment and education. Step back in time at 'The Way We Were' heritage centre, visit the world's largest original mill steam engine, or enjoy trips along the Leeds-Liverpool canal, walks in the grounds, or events from a regular programme.

Times: Open all year, Mon-Thu 10-5; Sat & Sun 11-5. (Closed every Fri ex Good Fri, 25-26 Dec, 1 Jan). **Fee:** ✱ £8.50 (concessions £6.25). Site ticket £23.50 (2 ad & 2 concessions). **Facilities:** P 🅿 ✖ licensed & (Braille guide, audio tape, large text leaflet, minicom) toilets for disabled shop ✖ (ex guide dogs) 🍽

HAMPSHIRE

EVENTS & FESTIVALS

February

14th-19th Children's Festival, The Tower, Romsey Road, Winchester

April

30th-2nd Heavy Horse Show, Castle Field and Southsea Common

June

28th Trafalgar 200 Fleet Review, Spithead/Southsea Seafront

29th Trafalgar 200 Drumhead Ceremony

30th-3rd Jul Hat Fair, Winchester, the oldest street theatre fair in England

30th-3rd Jul IFOS/Trafalgar 200, Naval Base Heritage Area

tbc Power in the Park, pop concert, Southampton Common

July

1st-3rd Southampton Festival, The Common, Southampton

8th-17th Winchester Festival (multi-arts festival)

22nd-24th Netley Marsh Steam Engine Rally, Netley Marsh, Southampton

tbc New Forest Show

August

5th-7th Portsmouth & Southsea Show, Southsea Common

27th-29th Kite Festival, Southsea Common

September

10th Romsey Show, Broadlands Park, Romsey

16th-25th Southampton International Boat Show, Mayflower Park, Southampton

October

9th Great South Run, 10-mile international event, Southsea Seafront

21st Trafalgar Night, HMS Victory, Portsdown

November

2nd Bonfire Night Firework Spectacular, King George V Playing Field, Cosham

24th-27th A Festival of Christmas, Naval Base Heritage Area, Portsmouth

tbc Winchester Grand Firework Display

Above: Winchester Cathedral

ALDERSHOT Map 04 SU85

AIRBORNE FORCES MUSEUM

Browning Barracks, Queens Av GU11 2BU
➲ (from M3 take A325 to Aldershot then take next left)
☎ 01252 349619 ▤ 01252 349203
e-mail: airborneforcesmuseum@
army.mod.uk.net

The museum traces the history of the Parachute Regiment and British Airborne Forces since 1940. Using weapons, equipment, dioramas and briefing models it depicts the story of airborne actions such as the early raids, D-Day, Arnhem, the Rhine Crossing, and post-war campaigns such as Suez, the Falklands and Kosovo.
Times: Open all year, Mon-Fri 10-4.30 (last admission 3.45), Sat-Sun & BH 10-4. (Closed Xmas). **Fee:** ✱ £3 (ch, pen & former members of the Regiment £1, under 5s free) **Facilities:** ▣ & (wheelchair ramps) shop ✖ (ex guide dogs)

ALDERSHOT MILITARY MUSEUM

Evelyn Woods Rd, Queens Av GU11 2LG
➲ (A331 exit for 'Aldershot Military Town (North)', attraction near to North Camp)
☎ 01252 314598 ▤ 01252 342942   **2 for 1**
e-mail: musmim@hants.gov.uk

Follow the development of the 'Home of the British army' and the 'Birthplace of British aviation' through brand new displays. Also discover the fascinating local history of Aldershot and Farnborough including British first powered flight.
Times: Open Mar-Oct, daily 10-5; Nov-Feb, daily 10-5. **Fee:** ✱ £2 (ch & unemployed £1, pen £1.50) **Facilities:** ▣ & shop ✖ (ex guide dogs)

AMPFIELD Map 04 SU42

THE SIR HAROLD HILLIER GARDENS & ARBORETUM

Jermyns Ln SO51 0QA
➲ (3m NE of Romsey, signposted off A3090 & B3057)
☎ 01794 368787 ▤ 01794 368027

Established in 1953, this 180-acre public garden comprises the greatest collection of hardy trees and shrubs in the world. A garden for all seasons with stunning range of seasonal colour and interest and featuring eleven national plant collections. Champion trees, the Gurkha Memorial Garden and the largest Winter Garden in Europe.
Times: ✱ Open all year, Apr-Oct wkdays 10.30-6, wknds & BHs 9.30-6. Nov-Mar daily 10.30-5 or dusk if earlier (closed Xmas).
Facilities: ▣ ✖ licensed & (all ability path) toilets for disabled garden centre ✖ (ex guide dogs)

ANDOVER Map 04 SU34

FINKLEY DOWN FARM PARK

SP11 6NF
➲ (signposted from A303 & A343, 1.5m N of A303 and 2m E of Andover)
☎ 01264 352195 ▤ 01264 363172
e-mail: admin@finkleydownfarm.co.uk

This fun family farm park is jam packed with things to do. You can join in with feeding time, groom a pony, cuddle a rabbit, or collect duck eggs. Lots of activities are scheduled throughout the day, or kids can just let off steam in the playground or on the trampolines. From chipmunks to
continued

chinchillas, pygmy goats to peacocks, and lambs to llamas, Finkley Down Farm has something for everyone!
Times: Open mid Mar-Oct, daily 10-6. Last admission 5pm.
Fee: ✱ £4.75 (ch £3.75, pen £4.25). Family ticket £16 (2 ad & 2ch).
Facilities: ▣ ▣ & toilets for disabled shop ✖ (ex guide dogs) ◥

ASHURST Map 04 SU31

LONGDOWN DAIRY FARM

Longdown SO40 7EH
➲ (off A35 between Lyndhurst & Southampton)
☎ 023 8029 3326 ▤ 023 8029 3376
e-mail: enquiries@longdownfarm.co.uk

Fun for all the family with a variety of hands-on activities every day, including small animal handling and pony grooming. Indoor and outdoor play areas, with trampolines and ball pools. Land Rover driving for adults, pedal tractors for children. Tearoom, picnic area and excellent gift shop.
Times: Open Feb-Dec, daily 10-5. **Fee:** ✱ £5 (ch 3-14 & pen £4.25). Saver ticket £17.50 (2 ad & 2 ch). **Facilities:** ▣ ▣ & concrete path for wheelchairs toilets for disabled shop ✖ (kennels provided) ◥

AVINGTON Map 04 SU53

AVINGTON PARK NEW

SO21 1DD
➲ (Off the B3047 at Itchen Abbey between Winchester and Alresford. 4 miles from both on River Itchen)
☎ 01962 779260
e-mail: enquiries@avingtonpark.co.uk

Avington is a charming hamlet in the Itchen Valley, and Avington Park is its great house, a 17th-century Palladian mansion built largely of red brick. Standing in wooded parkland with a lake, with interior paintings and gildings, and two very unusual 19th-century wrought iron conservatories.
Times: Open May-Sep, Sun, BH & Mon 2.30-5.30. **Fee:** £4
Facilities: ▣ ▣ & toilets for disabled (on leads)

BASINGSTOKE Map 04 SU65

MILESTONES - HAMPSHIRE'S LIVING HISTORY MUSEUM

Basingstoke Leisure Park, Churchill Way West RG21 6YR
➲ (M3 junct 6, take ringway road (West) and follow brown signs for Leisure Park)
☎ 01256 477766 ▤ 01256 477784   **2 for 1**
e-mail: jane.holmes@hants.gov.uk

Milestones brings Hampshire's recent past to life through stunning period street scenes and exciting interactive areas,
continued

all under one roof. Nationally important collections of transport, technology and everyday life are presented in an entertaining way. Staff in period costumes, mannequins and sounds all bring the streets to life.
Times: Open Tue-Fri & BHs 10-5, Sat-Sun 11-5 (Closed 25-26 Dec & 1 Jan). **Fee:** £6.50 (ch £3.50, concessions £5.75). Family ticket (2ad & 2ch) £16.50. Group discounts 15+. (may be subject to change)
Facilities: 🅿 💷 🚻 ♿ (induction loops, subtitles screens, scooters, wheelchairs) toilets for disabled shop ✗ (ex guide dogs) 🍴

BEAULIEU Map 04 SU30

BEAULIEU : NATIONAL MOTOR MUSEUM
SO42 7ZN
➲ (M27 junct 2, A326, B3054, then follow tourist signs)
☎ 01590 612345 📠 01590 612624
e-mail: info@beaulieu.co.uk
Set in the heart of William the Conqueror's New Forest, on the banks of the Beaulieu River, stands this 16th-century house. It has become most famous as the home of the National Motor Museum. The site also contains the picturesque abbey building ruins, which have an exhibition on life in the middle ages, and various family treasures and memorabilia. In 2004 the Abbey celebrated the 800th anniversary since its founding with a special audio visual presentation.
Times: Open all year - Palace House & Gardens, National Motor Museum, Beaulieu Abbey & Exhibition of Monastic Life, May-Sep 10-6; Oct-Apr 10-5. (Closed 25 Dec). **Fee:** ✱ £15 (ch 5-12 £7.50, 12-17 £8.50, pen £13.50). Family ticket £42. **Facilities:** 🅿 💷 ♿ (ramp access, lift to upper level, induction loop) toilets for disabled shop 🍴

BISHOP'S WALTHAM Map 04 SU51

BISHOP'S WALTHAM PALACE
SO32 1DH
➲ (on A333)
☎ 01489 892460
Discover the medieval seat of the Bishops of Winchester. Enjoy the wonderful moated grounds and an exhibition about the powerful Winchester Bishops.
Times: May-Sep, Sun-Fri (closed Sat) 10-5 **Fee:** ✱ £2.50 (ch £1.30, concessions £1.90). Prices & opening times relate to 2004, for further details phone or log onto www.english-heritage.org.uk/visits
Facilities: 🅿 ♿ shop ✗ (ex on lead in certain areas) 🎫

BOLDRE Map 04 SZ39

SPINNERS GARDEN AND NURSERY
School Ln SO41 5QE
➲ (off A337, between Brockenhurst & Lymington)
☎ 01590 673347
The garden has been entirely created by the owners since 1960. It has azaleas, rhododendrons, camellias, magnolias and Japanese Maples interspersed with a huge range of woodland and bog plants. National collection of Trilliums is also present. The nursery is well known for its rare trees, shrubs and plants.
Times: Open mid Apr-mid Sep, daily 10-5. Other times on application. Mid Sep-mid Apr Nursery and part of garden open, free entry.
Fee: Prices not confirmed for 2005 **Facilities:** 🅿 help provided where possible garden centre ✗ (ex guide dogs)

BREAMORE Map 04 SU11

BREAMORE HOUSE & COUNTRYSIDE
SP6 2DF
➲ (turn off A338, between Salisbury & Fordingbridge and follow signs for 1m)
☎ 01725 512468 📠 01725 512858
e-mail: breamore@ukonline.co.uk   `2 for 1`
The handsome manor house was completed in around 1583 and has a fine collection of paintings, china and tapestries. The museum has good examples of steam engines, and uses reconstructed workshops and other displays to show how people lived and worked a century or so ago. There is also a children's playground.
Times: Open Apr, Tue, Sun & Etr, May-Jul & Sep, Tue-Thu & Sat, Sun & all BH, Aug, daily 2-5.30 (Countryside Museum 1pm). **Fee:** £6 (ch £4). Party £5 each. **Facilities:** 🅿 💷 ♿ (ramps, parking, recorded message & book about 2nd floor) toilets for disabled shop ✗ (ex guide dogs)

BUCKLER'S HARD Map 04 SU40

BUCKLER'S HARD VILLAGE & MARITIME MUSEUM
SO42 7XB
➲ (M27 junct 2, A326, B3054 then follow tourist signs to Beaulieu & Bucklers Hard)
☎ 01590 616203 📠 01590 612624
e-mail: info@bucklershard.co.uk
An enticing port of call, the historic and picturesque shipbuilding village of Buckler's Hard is where ships from Nelson's fleet were built. After setting a course for the Bucklers Hard Story and authentically reconstructed 18th century Historic Cottages savour the sight and sounds of the countryside on a ramble along the Riverside Walk or enjoy a cruise on the Beaulieu River on 'Swiftsure' during the summer months.
Times: Open all year, Etr-Sep 10.30-5, winter 11-4. (Closed 25 Dec). **Fee:** ✱ £5.25 (ch £3.75, pen £4.75). Family £16 **Facilities:** 🅿 💷 ✗ licensed ♿ toilets for disabled shop 🍴

BURGHCLERE Map 04 SU46

SANDHAM MEMORIAL CHAPEL
RG20 9JT
➲ (4m S Newbury, 0.5m E of A34. Follow signs to Highclere/Burghclere, then brown signs to Sandham Memorial Chapel)
☎ 01635 278394 📠 01635 278394
e-mail: sandham@nationaltrust.org.uk
This red brick chapel was built in the 1920s for the artist Stanley Spencer to fill with murals inspired by his experiences in WWI. Influenced by Giotto's Arena Chapel in Padua, Spencer took 5 years to complete what is arguably his finest achievement. The chapel is set amongst lawns and orchards with views over Watership Down.
Times: Open Apr-Oct, Wed-Sun, 11-5 & BH Mon. Nov & Mar, Sat & Sun 11-4. Dec-Feb by appointment only. **Fee:** £3 (ch £1.50). **Facilities:** 🅿 (20yds) ♿ (Braille guide, large print guide, ramps) ✗ (ex on leads in garden) 🐾

CHAWTON — Map 04 SU73

JANE AUSTEN'S HOUSE

GU34 1SD

➲ (1m SW of Alton, in centre of village)

☎ 01420 83262 ▤ 01420 83262

e-mail: enquiries@jane-austens-house-museum.org.uk

Jane Austen lived and wrote here from 1809 to 1817. Restored to look as it would have done in the early 1800s, with items such as the author's donkey cart and writing table to be seen.

Times: ✱ Open daily Mar-Nov; Dec-Feb wknds only. Also open 27 Dec-1 Jan & Feb half term. **Fee:** £4.50 (ch 8-18 £1, senior & students £3.50. Parties 15+ £3.50) **Facilities:** ℙ (300yds) ♿ (wheelchair ramp) toilets for disabled shop ✖ (ex guide dogs & service dogs) ⬛

See advertisement on this page

EXBURY — Map 04 SU40

EXBURY GARDENS & RAILWAY

Exbury Estate Office SO45 1AZ

➲ (from M27 W junct 2, 3m from Beaulieu, off B3054)

☎ 023 8089 1203 ▤ 023 8089 9940

A 200-acre landscaped woodland garden on the east bank of the Beaulieu River, with one of the finest collections of rhododendrons, azaleas, camellias and magnolias in the world - as well as many rare and beautiful shrubs and trees. A labyrinth of tracks and paths enable you to explore the beautiful gardens and walks. Year round interest is ensured in various parts of the gardens and a steam railway has several features.

Times: Open 28 Feb-31 Oct, daily 10-5.30; Santa Steam Specials 11,12,18-21 Dec **Fee:** ✱ £4-£6 (ch under 5s free, ch 5-15 £1-£1.50, pen £3.50-£5.50, £5 Tue-Thu). Railway £2-£2.50. **Facilities:** ℙ ✖ licensed ♿ (free wheelchair loans & access maps, buggy tours £3) toilets for disabled shop garden centre ⬛

FAREHAM — Map 04 SU50

ROYAL ARMOURIES FORT NELSON

Downend Rd PO17 6AN

➲ (from M27 junct 11, follow brown tourist signs for Royal Armouries)

☎ 01329 233734 ▤ 01329 822092 **FREE**

e-mail: fnenquiries@armouries.org.uk

Superbly restored 19 acre Victorian fort overlooking Portsmouth Harbour, with spectacular views. Built in the 1860s to deter a threatened French invasion there are secret

continued

tunnels, underground chambers and grass ramparts to explore. Home to the Royal Armouries' collection of artillery, part of the National Museum of Arms and Armour, with over 350 pieces from the Romans to the infamous Iraqi supergun.

Times: Open all year, daily. Closed 25-26 Dec. **Facilities:** ℙ 🍴 ♿ (access & audio guide, ramps, induction loop, wheelchair) toilets for disabled shop ✖ (ex guide & hearing dogs) ⬛

GOSPORT — Map 04 SZ69

EXPLOSION! MUSEUM OF NAVAL FIREPOWER

Priddy's Hard PO12 4LE

➲ (A32 and follow signs)

☎ 023 9250 5600 ▤ 023 9250 5605 **2 for 1**

e-mail: info@explosion.org.uk

Explosion! The Museum of Naval Firepower set in the green Heritage Area of Priddy's Hard in Gosport on the shores of Portsmouth Harbour, telling the story of naval firepower from the days of gunpowder to modern missiles. Come face to face with the atom bomb, the Exocet missile and the Gatling Gun and take a trip into the fascinating story of the men and woman who supplied the Royal Navy. Walk around the buildings that were a state secret for 200 years and discover the Grand Magazine, an amazing vault once packed full with gunpowder, now a stunning multimedia film show.

Times: Open all year, Apr-Oct & all school hols, daily 10-5.30; Nov-Mar, Thu, Sat/Sun 10-4.30. (Closed 24-26 Dec) **Fee:** ✱ £5 (ch £3.50, pen £4.50). Family ticket £15 **Facilities:** ℙ 🍴 ♿ toilets for disabled shop ✖ (ex guide dogs) ⬛

ROYAL NAVY SUBMARINE MUSEUM & HMS ALLIANCE

Haslar Jetty Rd PO12 2AS

➲ (M27 junct 11, follow signs for Submarine Museum)

☎ 023 9252 9217 & 9251 0354

🗐 023 9251 1349

e-mail: rnsubs@rnsubmus.co.uk

The great attraction of this museum is the chance to see inside a submarine, and there are guided tours of *HMS Alliance*, as well as displays exploring the development of submarines. Two periscopes from *HMS Conqueror* can be seen in the reconstruction of a nuclear submarine control room, giving panoramic views of Portsmouth Harbour. A new gallery shows the development of submarine weapons from the tiny torpedo to the huge polaris nuclear missile. The Navy's first submarine is back on display in a new gallery and exhibition space.

Times: ✱ Open all year, Apr-Oct 10-5.30; Nov-Mar 10-4.30. (Closed 24 Dec-1 Jan). Allow 3 hrs for visit. Last tour 1 hour before closing.
Facilities: 🅿 💺 ♿ (information in Braille, lift to upper gallery) toilets for disabled shop ✸ (ex guide dogs) 🖼

HARTLEY WINTNEY   Map 04 SU75

WEST GREEN HOUSE GARDENS

West Green RG27 8JB

➲ (off A30, at Phoenix Green take sign to West Green, along Thackhams Lane. House last left)

☎ 01252 844611   🗐 01252 844611

The gardens are now considered to be one of the top 50 gardens in England and were the subject of a BBC television programme. Today the Queen Anne house is surrounded by four walled gardens, lakes, follies, the green theatre, nymphaeum, mixed border and potager. The owner is a noted garden writer and lecturer.

Times: Open May-Aug, Wed-Sun 11-4.30. **Fee:** £5 (ch under 7 free, 7-16 half price). **Facilities:** 🅿 ✕ ♿ (most areas accessible) shop garden centre ✸ (ex guide dogs)

HAVANT   Map 04 SU70

STAUNTON COUNTRY PARK

Middle Park Way PO9 5HB

➲ (off B2149, between Havant & Horndean)

☎ 023 9245 3405   🗐 023 9249 8156

e-mail: amanda.fallbrown@hants.gov.uk

This colourful Victorian Park offers a wonderful range of attractions for all age groups. Meet and feed the friendly animals at the Ornamental Farm where there is a broad range of animals from llama and shirehorses to pigs and pigmy goats. Explore the Victorian tropical glasshouses with exotic flowers from around the world, including the giant Amazonian waterlily (summer months only). 1000 acres of parkland. With hidden follies to explore and an ornamental lake available for angling.

Times: Open 10-5 (4pm winter). **Fee:** £4.50 (ch £3.30, pen £4).
Facilities: 🅿 💺 ✕ ♿ (wheelchair for visitors, most areas accessible) toilets for disabled shop ✸ (dogs in parkland only) 🖼

Directions are provided by the attractions.

HIGHCLERE   Map 04 SU45

HIGHCLERE CASTLE & GARDENS

RG20 9RN

➲ (4.5m S of Newbury, off A34)

☎ 01635 253210   🗐 01635 255315

e-mail: theoffice@highclerecastle.co.uk

This splendid early Victorian mansion stands in beautiful parkland. It has sumptuous interiors and numerous Old Master pictures. Also shown are early finds by the 5th Earl of Carnarvon, one of the discoverers of Tutankhamun's tomb.

Times: ✱ Open Jul-Aug (may occasionally be subject to closure during this period), Tue-Fri & Sun 11-5 (last admission 4pm); Sat 11-3.30 (last admission 2.30pm). Also open BH 25-26 May & 25 Aug). Closed 5 Jul.
Facilities: 🅿 💺 ✕ licensed ♿ (wheelchair available) toilets for disabled shop ✸ (ex guide dogs) 🖼

HINTON AMPNER   Map 04 SU62

HINTON AMPNER GARDEN

SO24 0LA

➲ (off A272, 1m W of Bramdean)

☎ 01962 771305   🗐 01962 793101   `2 for 1`

e-mail: hintonampner@nationaltrust.org.uk

A masterpiece of design by Ralph Dutton, 8th and last Lord Sherborne, the 12 acre garden unites a formal layout with varied and informal plantings in pastel shades. There are magnificent vistas over 80 acres of parkland and rolling Hampshire countryside. The house, which is tenanted, contains Ralph Dutton's fine collection of Regency furniture, Italian paintings and hardstone items.

Times: Open Garden: Apr-Sep, Sat-Wed 12-5. House: Apr-Sep, Tue & Wed 1.30-5 (also Aug, Sat & Sun 1.30-5). **Fee:** House and Garden £6 (ch £3) Garden only £5, (ch £2.50) **Facilities:** 🅿 💺 ♿ (Braille guides, special parking, map for wheelchair users) toilets for disabled ✸ (ex guide dogs) 🐌

HURST CASTLE   Map 04 SZ38

HURST CASTLE

SO4 0FF

➲ (on Pebble Spit S of Keyhaven)

☎ 01590 642344

Built by Henry VIII, Hurst Castle was the pride of Tudor England's coastal defences. Crouched menacingly on a shingle spit, the castle has a fascinating history, including involvement in the smuggling trade in the 17th and 18th centuries.

Times: Open Apr-Oct, daily 10.30-5. **Fee:** ✱ £3 (ch £1.80, concessions £2.70). Prices & opening times relate to 2004, for further details phone or log onto www.english-heritage.org.uk/visits **Facilities:** 💺 ✸ (ex on lead in certain areas) ⌗

LIPHOOK   Map 04 SU83

BOHUNT MANOR

GU30 7DL

➲ (on old A3 opposite junct)

☎ 01428 727936   🗐 01428 727936

e-mail: eddie@bohuntmanor.freeserve.co.uk

Bohunt includes woodland gardens with a lakeside walk, a water garden, roses, tulips and herbaceous borders, and a collection of ornamental ducks, white swans, and geese. Several unusual trees and shrubs include a handkerchief tree and a Judas tree. The property has been given to the Worldwide Fund for Nature.

Times: ✱ Open all year, daily 10-5. **Facilities:** 🅿 ♿ garden centre ✸ (ex guide dogs)

HOLLYCOMBE STEAM COLLECTION

Iron Hill, Midhurst Rd GU30 7LP
➲ (1m SE Liphook on Midhurst road, follow brown tourist signs)
☎ 01428 724900 ▪ 01428 723682
e-mail: info@hollycombe.co.uk

A comprehensive collection of working steam-power, including a large Edwardian fairground, three railways, one with spectacular views of the South Downs, traction engine hauled rides, steam agricultural machinery, pets corner, sawmill and even a paddle steamer engine.
Times: Open Etr-9 Oct, Sun & BHs; 1-29 Aug, daily 12-5 **Fee:** ✱ £8.50 (ch 3-15 & pen £7). **Facilities:** 🅿 💺 ♿ toilets for disabled shop ➡

LYMINGTON   Map 04 SZ39

BRAXTON GARDENS

Braxton Courtyard, Lymore Ln SO41 0TX
➲ (leave A337 at Everton onto B3058 then turn left into Lymore Ln, Braxton Courtyard on left)
☎ 01590 642008
Beautiful gardens set around attractive Victorian farm buildings. A courtyard with raised lily pool leads into a walled garden, which overflows with aromatic plants during the summer. A converted barn is available for private hire.
Times: ✱ Open daily 10-5. Shorter opening hours in winter, please telephone for details. **Facilities:** 🅿 💺 ♿ shop garden centre ✈ (ex guide dogs) ➡

LYNDHURST   Map 04 SU30

NEW FOREST MUSEUM & VISITOR CENTRE

Main Car Park, High St SO43 7NY
➲ (leave M27 at Cadnam & follow A337 to Lyndhurst. Museum signposted)
☎ 023 8028 3444 ▪ 023 8028 4236
e-mail: office@newforestmuseum.org.uk
The story of the New Forest - history, traditions, character and wildlife, told through an audio-visual show and exhibition displays. With life-size models of Forest characters, and the famous New Forest embroidery.
Times: Open daily, from 10am. Closed 25 & 26 Dec.
Facilities: 🅿 ♿ toilets for disabled shop ➡

MARWELL   Map 04 SU52

MARWELL ZOOLOGICAL PARK

Colden Common SO21 1JH
➲ (M3 junct 11 or M27 junct 5. Zoo located on B2177, follow brown tourist signs)
☎ 01962 777407 ▪ 01962 777511
e-mail: marwell@marwell.org.uk
Marwell has over 200 species of rare and wonderful animals including tigers, snow leopards, rhino, meerkats, hippo and zebra. Highlights include The World of Lemurs, Encounter Village with unusual domesticated animals, Tropical World with its rainforest environment, Into Africa for giraffes and monkeys, Penguin World and Desert Carnivores. Recent additions include an exciting new leopard enclosure. Marwell is dedicated to saving endangered species and every visit helps conservation work. With road and rail trains, holiday activities, restaurant, gift shops and adventure playgrounds Marwell provides fun and interest for all ages.
Times: Open all year, daily (ex 25 Dec), 10-6 (in summer), 10-4 (in winter). Last admission 90 min before closing. **Fee:** ✱ £11.50 (ch £8, pen £9.50). Family ticket (2 ad & 2 ch) £37.50. **Facilities:** 🅿 💺 ✕ ♿ (wheelchairs & tours for visually impaired/disabled groups) toilets for disabled shop ✈ ➡

MIDDLE WALLOP   Map 04 SU23

MUSEUM OF ARMY FLYING & EXPLORERS WORLD

SO20 8DY
➲ (on A343, between Andover & Salisbury)
☎ 01980 674421 ▪ 01264 781694   **2 for 1**
e-mail: enquiries@flying-museum.org.uk
One of the country's finest historical collections of military kites, gliders, aeroplanes and helicopters. Imaginative dioramas and displays trace the development of Army flying from before the First World War to more recent conflicts in Ireland, the Falklands and the Gulf. Sit at the controls of a real Scout helicopter and test your skills on the helicopter flight simulator, plus children's science and education centre.
Times: Open all year, daily 10-4.30. Closed week prior to Xmas. Evening visits by special arrangement. **Fee:** ✱ £5 (ch £3.50, pen & student £4) Family £15. Party 10+. **Facilities:** 🅿 💺 ✕ licensed ♿ (lifts to upper levels) toilets for disabled shop ➡

MINSTEAD   Map 04 SU21

FURZEY GARDENS

SO43 7GL
➲ (1m S of junct A31/M3 Cadnam off A31 or A337 near Lyndhurst)
☎ 023 8081 2464 & 8081 2297   **2 for 1**
▪ 023 8081 2297
e-mail: info@furzey-gardens.org
A large thatched gallery is the venue for refreshments and displays of local arts and crafts, and the eight acres of peaceful glades which surround it include winter and summer heathers, rare flowering trees and shrubs and a mass of spring bulbs. There is a 16th-century cottage, lake, and the nursery, run by the Minstead Training Project for Young People with Learning Disabilities, sells a wide range of produce.
Times: Gardens open daily 10-5 (or dusk if earlier). (Closed Xmas). Gallery Open: Mar-Oct, 10-5. **Fee:** ✱ Mar-Oct: £3.50 (ch £1.50, pen £2.80) Family £9. Nov-Feb: £1.50 (ch 50p, pen £1) Family £3. Party 10+. **Facilities:** 🅿 💺 ♿ (garden access for wheelchair visitors with assistance) toilets for disabled shop garden centre ✈ (ex guide dogs)

MOTTISFONT — Map 04 SU32

MOTTISFONT ABBEY GARDEN

SO51 0LP

➲ (4.5m NW Romsey, 1m W of A3057)

☎ 01794 340757 🖷 01794 341492 **2 for 1**

e-mail: mottisfontabbey@nationaltrust.org.uk

In a picturesque setting by the River Test, Mottisfont Abbey is an 18th-century house adapted from a 12th-century priory. The north front shows its medieval church origins quite clearly, and the garden has splendid old trees and a walled garden planted with the national collection of old-fashioned roses. The estate includes Mottisfont village and surrounding farmland and woods.

Times: Open Garden Only 5 Feb-20 Mar 11-4. Garden & House: 21 Mar-1 Jun, Sat-Wed 11-6; 5-27 Jun daily from 11-6 (garden to 8.30); 28 Jun-31 Aug, Sat-Thu 11-6; 1 Sep-31 Oct, Sat-Wed 11-6. Last admission to grounds 1hr before closing. **Fee:** £7 (ch £3.50) Family ticket £17.50 **Facilities:** 🅿 🗪 ✗ licensed ♿ (Braille guide, wheelchair available, driven buggy) toilets for disabled shop closed 5 Feb-20 Mar garden centre ✕ (ex guide dogs) ❄ 🖼

NETLEY — Map 04 SU40

NETLEY ABBEY

SO31 5FB

➲ (4m SE of Southampton, facing Southampton Water)

☎ 02392 581059 **FREE**

A romantic ruin, set among green lawns and trees, this 13th-century Cistercian abbey was founded by Peter des Roches, tutor to Henry III. Nearby is the 19th-century Gothic Netley Castle.

Times: Open any reasonable time. **Facilities:** 🅿 ♿ ✕ ⛫

NEW ALRESFORD — Map 04 SU53

WATERCRESS LINE

The Railway Station SO24 9JG

➲ (stations at Alton & Alresford signposted off A31, follow brown tourist signs)

☎ 01962 733810 🖷 01962 735448 **2 for 1**

e-mail: info@watercressline.co.uk

The Watercress Line runs through ten miles of rolling scenic countryside between Alton and Alresford. All four stations are 'dressed' in period style, and there's a locomotive yard and picnic area at Ropley.

Times: Open May-Sep Tue-Thu & wknds; Jan-Apr & Oct wknds only. **Fee:** ✱ Unlimited travel for the day, £10 (ch £5, pen £9). Family ticket £25. **Facilities:** 🅿 (charged) 🗪 ✗ licensed ♿ (ramp access to trains) toilets for disabled shop (at Alresford, Alton & Ropley stations) charge for dogs 🖼

See advertisement on opposite page

NEW MILTON — Map 04 SZ29

SAMMY MILLER MOTORCYCLE MUSEUM

Bashley Cross Rd BH25 5SZ

➲ (signposted off A35, 15m W of Southampton, 10m E of Bournemouth, N of New Milton Town Centre)

☎ 01425 620777 🖷 01425 619696

e-mail: info@sammymiller.co.uk

The museum houses over 300 rare & classic bikes & with machines dating back to 1900, some are the only surviving examples of their type. The Racing collection features World Record breaking bikes & their history, including the first bike to lap a Grand Prix Course at over 100 miles per hour. Special events include marquee days.

Times: Open daily 10-4.30. (closed 2 Jan-1 Feb for refurbishment) **Fee:** £4.50 (ch £2). **Facilities:** 🅿 🗪 ✗ licensed ♿ (special rates for disabled people) toilets for disabled shop ✕ (ex guide dogs) 🖼

OLD BASING — Map 04 SU65

BASING HOUSE

Redbridge Ln RG24 7HB

➲ (signed from Basingstoke Ring Road)

☎ 01256 467294 🖷 01256 326283 **2 for 1**

The largest house of Tudor England, almost entirely destroyed by Parliament during a two-year siege ending in 1645. Built on the site of a Norman castle in 1530, the ruins include a 300ft long tunnel. There is a re-creation of a

continued

garden of 1600 and exhibitions showing the history of the house. A fine 16th-century barn stands nearby.
Times: Open Apr-Sep, Wed-Sun & BH 2-6. **Fee:** ✱ £2 (ch & pen £1). Registered disabled free. **Facilities:** 🅿 ♿ (disabled parking by prior arrangement) toilets for disabled shop

OWER   Map 04 SU31
PAULTONS PARK
SO51 6AL
➲ (exit M27 junct 2, near junct A31 & A36)
☎ 023 8081 4442 🗎 023 8081 3025
e-mail: info@paultons.co.uk

Paultons Park offers a great day out for all the family with over 50 different attractions. Many fun activities include two new drop rides, roller coaster, bumper boats, 6-lane astroglide, teacup ride, log flume, pirate ship swingboat, dragon roundabout, and wave-runner coaster. Attractions for younger children include Kid's Kingdom, Tiny Tots Town, Rabbit Ride, the Magic Forest where nursery rhymes come to life, Wonderful World of Wind in the Willows and the Ladybird ride. In beautiful parkland setting with extensive 'Capability' Brown gardens landscaped with ponds and aviaries for exotic birds; lake and hedge maze. There is also the Romany Experience Museum with unique collection of gypsy wagons and the Village Life Museum. Something for everyone.
Times: Open mid Mar-Oct, daily 10-6; Nov & Dec, wknds only until Xmas. **Fee:** ✱ £13.50 (ch under 14). Children under 1m tall enter for free. Range of Family Supersavers. **Facilities:** 🅿 🍽 ✗ licensed ♿ (pre-booked wheelchair hire, some rides unsuitable) toilets for disabled shop ✖ (ex guide dogs) ◄

PORTCHESTER   Map 04 SU60
PORTCHESTER CASTLE
Castle St PO16 9QW
➲ (off A27)
☎ 01705 378291

Discover 2,000 years of history from its Roman beginnings to the years of medieval splendour. Stand where Henry V rallied his troops before setting out to the battle of Agincourt in 1415.
Times: Open all year, Apr-Sep, daily 10-6; Oct-Mar, daily 10-4. (Closed 24-26 Dec & 1 Jan). **Fee:** ✱ £3.50 (ch £1.80, concessions £2.60). Prices & opening times relate to 2004, for further details phone or log onto www.english-heritage.org.uk/visits **Facilities:** 🅿 ♿ shop ✖ (ex on lead in certain areas) ✿

PORTSMOUTH   Map 04 SU60
BLUE REEF AQUARIUM
Clarence Esplanade PO5 3PB
➲ (On approach to city follow brown tourist signs to the seafront or Aquarium. Located on Southsea seafront between the D-Day Museum and The Hoverport)
☎ 023 9287 5222 🗎 023 9229 4443   **2 for 1**
e-mail: portsmouth@bluereefaquarium.co.uk

Spectacular underwater walkthrough tunnels offer amazing sights of exotic coral reefs - home to sharks and shimmering shoals of brightly-coloured fish. Mediterranean and tropical waters are recreated in giant ocean tanks, home to a stunning array of undersea life including seahorses, puffer fish, coral, piranhas, and incredible crustaceans. Visit the website for current special events.
Times: Open daily from 10am. Closing times vary with season, please telephone for details. **Fee:** ✱ £5.95 (pen £4.95, ch 3-16 £3.95)
Facilities: 🅿 under 50m 🍽 ♿ all on 1 level toilets for disabled shop ✖ (ex assist dogs) ◄

CHARLES DICKENS' BIRTHPLACE MUSEUM
393 Old Commercial Rd PO1 4QL
➲ (accessible from M27, 1st left at 1st rdbt)
☎ 023 9282 7261 🗎 023 9287 5276
e-mail: Christopher.Spendlove@portsmouthcc.gov.uk

A small terraced house built in 1805 which became the birthplace and early home of the famous novelist, born in 1812. On display are items pertaining to Dickens' work, portraits of the Dickens' family, and the couch on which he died. Dickens readings are given in the exhibition room on the first Sunday of each month at 3pm.
Times: Open Apr-Sep, daily 10-5.30; Oct, daily 10-5. (Last admission 5pm). **Fee:** ✱ £2.50 (ch & student £1.50, accompanied ch 13 free, pen £1.80). Family ticket £6.50. **Facilities:** 🅿 (150mtrs) shop ✖ (ex guide & helper dogs) ◄

CITY MUSEUM & RECORDS OFFICE
Museum Rd PO1 2LJ
➲ (M27/M275 into Portsmouth, follow museum symbol signs)
☎ 023 9282 7261 🗎 023 9287 5276   **FREE**
e-mail: Christopher.Spendlove@portsmouthcc.gov.uk

Dedicated to local history, fine and decorative art, 'The Story of Portsmouth' displays room settings showing life here from the 17th century to the 1950s. The 'Portsmouth at Play' exhibition features leisure pursuits from the Victorian period to the 1970s. The museum has a fine and decorative art gallery, plus a temporary exhibition gallery with regular changing exhibitions. The Record Office contains the official records of the City of Portsmouth from the 14th century.
Times: Open all year, Apr-Oct daily 10-5.30; Nov-Mar daily 10-5. Closed 24-26 Dec and Record Office closed on public holidays.
Facilities: 🅿 🍽 ♿ (induction loops, lift & wheelchairs available, parking) toilets for disabled shop ✖ (ex guide & helper dogs)

D-Day Museum & Overlord Embroidery
Clarence Esplanade PO5 3NT
⮕ (M27/M275 into Portsmouth follow D Day
Museum & seafront signposts)
☎ 023 9282 7261 ▤ 023 9287 5276
e-mail: Christopher.Spendlove@
portsmouthcc.gov.uk

Portsmouth's D-Day Museum tells the dramatic story of the Allied landings in Normandy in 1944. Centrepiece is the magnificent 'Overlord Embroidery', 34 individual panels and 83 metres in length. Experience the world's largest ever seaborne invasion, and step back in time to scenes of wartime Britain. Military equipment, vehicles, landing craft and personal memories complete this special story.
Times: Open all year, Apr-Oct daily 10-5.30. Nov-Mar, 10-5. **Fee:** ✱ £5 (ch £3, pen £3.75). Family ticket £13. **Facilities:** ▣ (charged) ▆ ♿ (induction loops,sound aids,wheelchairs available) toilets for disabled shop ✖ (ex guide & helper dogs) ◀

Eastney Beam Engine House
Henderson Rd, Eastney PO4 9JF
⮕ (accessible from A3(M), A27 & A2030, turn left at Bransbury Park traffic lights)
☎ 023 9282 7261 ▤ 023 9287 5276   `FREE`
e-mail: christopher.spendlove@
portsmouthcc.gov.uk
The main attraction here is a magnificent pair of James Watt Beam Engines still housed in their original High-Victorian engine house opened in 1887. One of these engines is in steam when the museum is open. A variety of other pumping engines, many in running order are also on display.
Times: Open last wknd of month, 1-5 (last admission 30 minutes before closing). (Closed Aug & Dec). **Facilities:** ▣ (300mtrs) ✖ (ex guide & helper dogs)

Natural History Museum & Butterfly House
Cumberland House, Eastern Pde PO4 9RF
⮕ (Can be reached via A3(M), A27 or A2030, follow signs to seafront)
☎ 023 9282 7261 ▤ 023 9282 5276
e-mail: Christopher.Spendlove@
portsmouthcc.gov.uk
Focusing on the natural history and geology of the area, with wildlife dioramas including a riverbank scene with fresh

continued

water aquarium. During the summer British and European butterflies fly free in the Butterfly House.
Times: Open all year daily, Apr-Oct 10-5.30; Nov-Mar 10-5. **Fee:** ✱ Nov-Mar, £2 (ch £1.20, accompanied child under 13 free, pen £1.50). Apr-Oct, £2.50 (ch £1.50, accompanied ch under 13 free & pen £1.80). Family ticket £6.50. **Facilities:** ▣ (200mtrs) shop ✖ (ex guide & helper dogs) ◀

Portsmouth Historic Dockyard
HM Naval Base PO1 3LJ
⮕ (follow brown historic ships sign from M27/M275)
☎ 023 9287 0999 ▤ 023 9229 5252
e-mail: enquiries@historicdockyard.co.uk
Portsmouth Historic Dockyard is home to the world's greatest historic ships: *Mary Rose*, *HMS Victory*, *HMS Warrior* and the Royal Naval Museum. Action Stations is an attraction demonstrating life aboard a modern naval frigate. Many special events held throughout the year. Telephone for details.
Times: Open all year, Apr-Oct, daily 10-5.30; Nov-Mar, daily 10-5. (Closed 25 Dec). **Fee:** All inclusive ticket: £15.50 (ch & pen £12.50, under 5's free) family £45 **Facilities:** ▣ (charged) ▆ ✖ ♿ wheelchairs, facilities for visually & hearing impaired toilets for disabled shop ✖ ex guide dogs ◀

The Royal Marines Museum
Southsea PO4 9PX
⮕ (signposted from seafront)
☎ 023 9281 9385 ▤ 023 9283 8420   `2 for 1`
e-mail: info@royalmarinesmuseum.co.uk
Telling the story of the 330-year history of the Marines through dramatic displays, exciting films and videos, state of the art interactives and there's even a live snake and scorpion. Also a world famous medal collection, portraits and silverware.
Times: Open all year, Jun-Aug, daily 10-5; Sep-May, daily 10-4.30. (Closed 24-26 Dec). **Facilities:** ▣ ▆ ♿ (wheelchairs, hearing loops, special tours-prior notice) toilets for disabled shop ✖ (ex guide dogs or in grounds) ◀

Southsea Castle
Clarence Esplanade PO5 3PA
⮕ (accessible from M27, A27, A3M, A2030, follow castle signposts)
☎ 023 9282 7261 ▤ 023 9287 5276
e-mail: Christopher.Spendlove@
portsmouthcc.gov.uk
Part of Henry VIII's national coastal defences, this fort was built in 1544. In the 'Time Tunnel' experience, the ghost of the castle's first master gunner guides you through the dramatic scenes from the castle's eventful history. Audio-visual presentation, underground passages, Tudor military history displays, artillery, and panoramic views of the Solent and Isle of Wight.
Times: Open all year, Apr-Sep, daily 10-5.30; Oct-Mar, daily 10-5. **Fee:** ✱ £2.50 (ch & students £1.50, ch accompanied under 13 free, pen £1.80). Family ticket £6.50. **Facilities:** ▣ ♿ (wheelchair available) shop ✖ (ex guide & helper dogs) ◀

SPITBANK FORT

P O Box 129 PO12 2XY

⮌ (Ferries depart from HM Naval Base Portsmouth, Portsmouth Hard, Gosport Ferry Pontoon, by the side of Portsmouth Harbour Railway Stn and Gunwarf Quays shopping centre)

☎ 02392 504207 ▤ 02392 504207

e-mail: enquiries@spitbankfort.co.uk

Built in the 1860s as part of the coastal defences against the French, this massive granite and iron fortress stands a mile out to sea, with magnificent views across the Solent. The interior is a maze of passages connecting over 50 rooms on two levels.

Times: Open Etr-Sep, Wed-Sun. (Weather permitting). **Fee:** ✱ £6.50 (ch £5) includes ferry charge. Boat ride takes approx 20 mins, visitors should allow 2hr to view. Pub nights: (Wed/Thu) £16 (ch £10). Parties: (Fri/Sat) £25 (adult only). Sun Lunch: £16 (ch £10) **Facilities:** 🅿 ▬ ✖ licensed many steps ✖ ex guide dogs ▬

RINGWOOD   Map 04 SU10

MOORS VALLEY COUNTRY PARK

Horton Rd, Ashley Heath BH24 2ET

⮌ (1.5m from Ashley Heath rdbt on A31 near Three Legged Cross)

☎ 01425 470721 ▤ 01425 471656

e-mail: moorsvalley@eastdorsetdc.gov.uk

Fifteen hundred acres of forest, woodland, heathland, lakes, river and meadows provide a home for a wide variety of plants and animals, and there's a Visitor Centre, Adventure Playground, picnic area, Moors Valley Railway, Tree Top Trail and the 'Go Ape'- high ropes course (book on 0870 444 5562). Cycle hire is also available.

Times: Open all year (ex 25 Dec), 8-dusk. Visitor centre open 9.30-4.30 (later in summer). **Fee:** ✱ No admission charge but parking up to £5 per day. **Facilities:** 🅿 (charged) ▬ ✖ licensed ᴕ (visitor centre & park mostly accessible, wheelchairs) toilets for disabled shop (on lead) ▬

ROCKBOURNE   Map 04 SU11

ROCKBOURNE ROMAN VILLA

SP6 3PG

⮌ (from Salisbury exit A338 at Fordingbridge, take B3078 westwards through Sandleheath & follow signs. Or turn off A354 Salisbury to Blandford road, W of Coombe Bissett.)

☎ 01725 518541

Discovered in 1942, the site features the remains of a 40-room Roman villa and is the largest in the area. Displays include mosaics and a very rare hypocaust system. The museum displays the many artefacts found on the site during excavations. Roman re-enactments are performed - please ring for details.

Times: Open Apr-Sep, daily 10.30-6. Last admission 5.30pm. **Facilities:** 🅿 ▬ ᴕ (ramps in & out of museum) toilets for disabled shop ✖ (ex guide/hearing dogs)

ROMSEY   Map 04 SU32

BROADLANDS

SO51 9ZD

⮌ (main entrance on A3090 Romsey by-pass)

☎ 01794 505010 ▤ 01794 518605

e-mail: admin@broadlands.net

Famous as the home of the late Lord Mountbatten, Broadlands is now home to his grandson Lord Romsey. An *continued* *continued*

elegant Palladian mansion in a beautiful landscaped setting on the banks of the River Test, Broadlands was also the country residence of Lord Palmerston, the great Victorian statesman.

Times: Open weekdays,30 Jun-2 Sep, 1-5.30. Last admission 4pm. **Fee:** ✱ £7 (ch 12-16 £4, concessions £6). Party 15+. **Facilities:** 🅿 ᴕ toilets for disabled ✖ (ex guide dogs)

ROWLAND'S CASTLE   Map 04 SU71

STANSTED PARK NEW

PO9 6DX

⮌ (Follow brown heritage signs "Stansted House" from A3)

☎ 01705 412265 ▤ 01705 413773

e-mail: enquiry@stanstedpark.co.uk

This neo-Wren house is surrounded by a beautiful forest, through which runs the longest avenue of beech trees in the south of England. Attached to the house are an ancient chapel, walled gardens, a theatre museum and a botanical tree garden. The interior of the chapel was described by John Keats in his poem 'Eve of St Mark'. There is a garden shop, which sells plants and organically grown produce. Cricket matches are played in front of the house on most Sundays throughout the season.

Times: Open Etr Sun-end Sep. Sun & Mon 1-5, Jul & Aug Sun-Wed **Fee:** ✱ £5.50 (ch £3.50, sen £4.50) Family £14.50 (2ad+2ch) **Facilities:** 🅿 ✖ licensed ᴕ toilets for disabled garden centre ✖ (ex guide dogs)

SELBORNE   Map 04 SU73

GILBERT WHITE'S HOUSE & THE OATES MUSEUM

High St GU34 3JH

⮌ (on village High St)

☎ 01420 511275 ▤ 01420 511040

Charming 18th-century house, home of famous naturalist, the Rev. Gilbert White, author of *The Natural History and Antiquities of Selborne*. An attractive garden, shop and tea parlour serving 18th-century fare can also be found. Special events include an unusual plants fair and jazz evening in June, Gilbert White day in July and mulled wine day in December.

Times: Open daily Jan-24 Dec, 11-5. **Fee:** ✱ £5 (ch £3, concessions £4.50). **Facilities:** 🅿 ▬ ✖ ᴕ toilets for disabled shop ✖ (ex guide dogs) ▬

SHERBORNE ST JOHN   Map 04 SU65

THE VYNE
RG24 9HL
➲ (4m N of Basingstoke, off A340, signposted
from A33, A339 & A340)
☎ 01256 883858 📠 01256 881720   **2 for 1**
e-mail: thevyne@nationaltrust.org.uk

Built in the early 16th-century for Lord Sandy's, Henry VIII's
Lord Chamberlain, the house acquired a classical portico in
the mid 17th-century (the first of its kind in England) and
contains a fascinating Tudor chapel with renaissance glass, a
palladian staircase and a wealth of old panelling and fine
furniture. The attractive grounds feature herbaceous borders
and a wild garden, with lawns, lakes and woodland walks.
The 2-for-1 voucher is not valid for special events such as
classical concerts in the grounds.
Times: Open House & Gardens 20 Mar-Oct daily ex Thu & Fri 1-5,
wknds 11-5. Gardens also open wknds in Feb & Mar, 11-5. (gardens
11-5 Mon-Wed) **Fee:** House & Grounds £7 (ch £3.50). Family £17.50,
Grounds & Gardens only £4 (ch £2). NT members free.
Facilities: 🅿 💺 ✗ licensed ♿ (Braille guides & touch tours) toilets
for disabled shop 🐕 (ex guide & hearing dogs) ♨ 🛥

SILCHESTER   Map 04 SU66

CALLEVA MUSEUM
Bramley Rd RG7 2LU
➲ (between Basingstoke & Reading. Reached
from A340, follow brown tourist signs)
Little remains of the Roman town of Calleva Atrebatum except
the 1.5 miles of city wall, still an impressive sight, and the
ampitheatre. This small museum shows what life may have
been like in a Roman town, while the main artefacts from the
site can be seen in the Silchester Gallery at Reading Museum.
Times: Open daily 9.30am-sunset. Closed 25 Dec. **Facilities:** 🅿 ♿

SOUTHAMPTON   Map 04 SU41

MUSEUM OF ARCHAEOLOGY
God's House Tower, Winkle St SO14 2NY
➲ (near the waterfront close to Queen's Park and
the Town Quay)
☎ 023 8063 5904 & 8083 2768   **FREE**
📠 023 8033 9601
e-mail: historic.sites@southampton.gov.uk
The museum housed in an early fortified building, dating
from the 1400s and taking its name from the nearby
medieval hospital. Exhibits on the Roman, Saxon and
medieval towns of Southampton are displayed.
Times: Open Nov-Mar: Tue-Fri 10-4; Sat 10-12 & 1-4; Sun 1-4. Apr-Oct:
Tue-Fri 10-12 & 1-5; Sat 10-12 & 1-4; Sun 2-5. Also open BH Mon.
Facilities: 🅿 (400 yds) (designated areas only, parking charges)
♿ shop 🐕 (ex guide dogs)

SOUTHAMPTON CITY ART GALLERY
Civic Centre, Commercial Rd SO14 7LP
➲ (situated on the Watts Park side of the Civic
Centre, a short walk from the station, on
Commercial Rd)
☎ 023 8083 2277 📠 023 8083 2153
e-mail: art.gallery@southampton.gov.uk
The largest gallery in the south of England, with the finest
collection of contemporary art in the country outside
London. Varied displays of landscapes, portrait paintings or
recent British art are always available, as well as a special
display, selected by members of the public.
Times: Open all year, Tue-Sat 10-5, Sun 1-4. (Closed 25-27 & 31 Dec).
Facilities: 🅿 (50yds) (nearby street parking is 1hr only) 💺
✗ licensed ♿ (free BSL signed tours by arrangement, 'touch tour')
toilets for disabled shop 🐕 (ex guide dogs)

SOUTHAMPTON MARITIME MUSEUM
The Wool House, Town Quay SO14 2AR
➲ (on the waterfront, near to the Town Quay)
☎ 023 8022 3941 & 8063 5904   **FREE**
📠 023 8033 9601
e-mail: historic.sites@southampton.gov.uk
The Wool House was built in the 14th century as a
warehouse for wool, and now houses a maritime museum,
with models and displays telling the history of the Victorian
and modern port of Southampton. There are exhibitions of
the *Titanic*, *The Queen Mary* and an interactive area for
children.
Times: Open Nov-Mar: Tue-Fri 10-4; Sat 10-1 & 2-4; Sun 1-4. Apr-Oct:
Tue-Fri 10-1 & 2-5; Sat 10-1 & 2-4; Sun 2-5. Also open BH Mon.
Facilities: 🅿 (400yds) (metered parking adjacent) ♿ hearing loop on
Titanic presentation shop 🐕 (ex guide dogs)

STRATFIELD SAYE   Map 04 SU66

STRATFIELD SAYE HOUSE
RG7 2BZ
➲ (off A33 between Reading & Basingstoke)
☎ 01256 882882 📠 01256 881466
Stratfield Saye House was bought for the 1st Duke of
Wellington as his country house. The family still live here.
The house contains the personal possessions, collections of
painting and furniture of the great Duke. The Duke's
magnificent funeral carriage is on display in the grounds.
Times: ✱ Open 7 Jul-3 Aug, daily. **Facilities:** 🅿 💺 ♿ toilets for
disabled shop 🐕 (ex in grounds)

TITCHFIELD — Map 04 SU50

TITCHFIELD ABBEY
Place House Studio, Mill Ln PO15 5RA
➲ (0.5m N off Titchfield, off A27) **FREE**
☎ 01329 842133
Also known as 'Place House', in Tudor times this was the
seat of the Earl of Southampton, built on the site of the
abbey founded in 1232. He incorporated the gatehouse and
the nave of the church into his house.
Times: Open Apr-Sep, daily 10-6; Oct, daily 10-5; Nov-Mar, daily 10-4.
Closed 25 Dec. **Facilities:** 🅿 ♿ ✈ (ex dogs on leads)

WEYHILL — Map 04 SU34

THE HAWK CONSERVANCY AND COUNTRY PARK
SP11 8DY
➲ (3m W of Andover, signposted from A303)
☎ 01264 772252   📠 01264 773772
e-mail: info@hawk-conservancy.org
This is the largest centre in the south for birds of prey from
all over the world including eagles, hawks, falcons, owls,
vultures and kites. Exciting birds of prey demonstrations are
held daily at noon, 2pm, and 3.30pm, including the 'Valley of
the Eagles' at 2pm. Different birds are flown at these times
and visitors may have the opportunity to hold a bird and
adults can fly a Harris hawk.
Times: Open Feb half term-Oct half term, daily from 10.30-5.30 (last
admission 4pm). **Fee:** ✱ £7.25 (ch £4.65, pen & student £6.70).
Family ticket £23. **Facilities:** 🅿 ♨ ♿ (wheelchair area in flying
grounds, viewing areas in hides) toilets for disabled shop ✈ 🍴

WHITCHURCH — Map 04 SU44

WHITCHURCH SILK MILL
28 Winchester St RG28 7AL
➲ (halfway between Winchester & Newbury
signposted clearly on the A34. Located in centre
of the town)
☎ 01256 892065   📠 01256 893882
e-mail: silkmill@btinternet.com
The mill is idyllically located on the river Test. Whitchurch
Silk Mill is the oldest surviving textile mill in Southern
England. Fine silks and ribbons are still woven for interiors
and fashion. See the 19th century waterwheel pounding and
learn about winding, warping and weaving. There is a
programme of exhibitions, workshops and children's
activities.
Times: Open Tue-Sun & BH Mon 10.30-5 (last admission 4.15). Closed
24 Dec-1 Jan. **Facilities:** 🅿 ♨ ♿ (disabled parking adjacent site)
toilets for disabled shop ✈ (ex guide dogs) 🍴

WINCHESTER — Map 04 SU42

GURKHA MUSEUM
Peninsula Barracks, Romsey Rd SO23 8TS
➲ (M3 junct 9 to Winchester, follow round traffic
circuit into High St 1st left after Westgate)
☎ 01962 842832   📠 01962 877597
e-mail: curator@thegurkhamuseum.co.uk
This museum tells the fascinating story of the Gurkha's
involvement with the British Army. Travel from Nepal to the
North-West Frontier and beyond, with the help of life-sized
dioramas, interactive exhibits and sound displays.
Times: Open all year, BH Mon, Tue-Sat 10-5, Sun 12-4. Telephone for
Xmas opening times. (Closed 25-26 Dec, 1 Jan and Tue following
BH Mon) **Fee:** ✱ £1.50 (pen 75p). Party 15+ 75p each.
Facilities: 🅿 ♿ (lift & chair lift) toilets for disabled shop
✈ (ex guide dogs)

HOSPITAL OF ST CROSS
St Cross SO23 9SD
➲ (on B3335, 0.5miles from M3 Jct11)
☎ 01962 851375   📠 01962 878221 **2 for 1**
e-mail: visitors@stcrosshospital.co.uk
A beautiful group of Grade I listed medieval and Tudor
buildings, in a tranquil setting by the water meadows, St.
Cross is home to 25 elderly brothers. In keeping with
tradition, they wear gowns and trencher hats and act as
visitor guides. The hospital is world-famous for its ancient
and unique tradition of the Wayfarers Dole - a beaker of beer
and a morsel of bread is given by the porter to all visitors
who request it. Visitors can admire the medieval and Tudor
architecture, explore the medieval hall, the Georgian kitchen
and the Tudor cloister as well as the walled garden with
many plants of American origin.
Times: Apr-Oct, 9.30-5; Nov-Mar 10.30-3.30. **Fee:** ✱ £2.50 (ch 50p,
senior citizens £2). **Facilities:** 🅿 ♨ ♿ toilets for disabled shop
✈ (ex guide dogs) 🍴

INTECH - HAMPSHIRE TECHNOLOGY CENTRE & TECHNOLOGY CENTRE
Telegraph Way, Morn Hill SO21 1HX
➲ (M3 junct 10 onto A31 then B3404 Alresford
road)
☎ 01962 863791   📠 01962 868524
e-mail: htct@intech-uk.com
This purpose-built 3500 square metre building houses 100
interactive exhibits, which demonstrate the science and
technology of the world around us in an engaging and
exciting way. The philosophy is most definitely 'hands-on',
and the motto of the centre is 'Doing is Believing'. Exhibits
deal with things like viscosity, tornados, and Newton's Cradle
among others.
Times: Open daily 10-4. (Closed Xmas & 1 Jan) **Fee:** ✱ £5.95
(pen £3.75, ch £4.30) **Facilities:** 🅿 ♨ ♿ toilets for disabled shop
✈ ex guide dogs

THE KING'S ROYAL HUSSARS REGIMENTAL MUSEUM
Peninsula Barracks, Romsey Rd SO23 8TS
➲ (exit M3 junct 9/10 follow signs for city centre,
then hospital A&E red signs to Romsey road.
Vehicle access is from Romsey road.
A3090/B3040 at centre of city before heading
uphill towards Royal Hampshire Hospital)
☎ 01962 828539 & 828541 **FREE**
📠 01962 828538
e-mail: beresford@krhmuseum.freeserve.co.uk
The Royal Hussars were formed by the amalgamation of two
regiments raised at the time of the Jacobite Rebellion in
1715, the 10th Royal Hussars and the 11th Hussars. This
museum tells their story.
Times: Open 5 Jan-18 Dec, Tue-Fri 10-4, wknds, BH's & half term Mon,
12-4. Closed daily between 12.45-1.15. (closed 1 Nov 2005-Spring 2006
for refurbishment) **Facilities:** 🅿 ♿ (lift to first floor) toilets for
disabled shop ✈ (ex guide dogs)

> **Directions are provided by the attractions.**

ROYAL HAMPSHIRE REGIMENT MUSEUM & MEMORIAL GARDEN

Serle's House, Southgate St SO23 9EG

➲ (Museum near city centre, 150mtrs from traffic lights in High St)

☎ 01962 863658   FREE

e-mail: mail@royalhampshireregiment.org.uk

Regimental Museum of the Royal Hampshire Regiment 1702-1992, set in an 18th-century house by the regiment's Memorial Garden. The museum tells the history of the regiment, its regulars, militia, volunteers and Territorials.
Times: Normally open all year (ex 2 wks Xmas & New Year), Mon-Fri 11-3.30; Apr-Oct wknds & BH 12-4. **Facilities:** Ⓟ (800mtrs) ♿ shop ✈ (ex guide dogs)

THE GREAT HALL

Castle Av SO23 8PJ

➲ (Great Hall situated at top of High St. Pedestrians only- turn left into Castle Ave nearest public car park is Tower St. Park & Ride recommended)

☎ 01962 846476   ▤ 01962 841326

The only surviving part of Winchester Castle, once home to the Domesday Book, this 13th-century hall was the centre of court and government life. Built between 1222-1235 during the reign of Henry III, it is one of the largest and finest five bay halls in England to have survived to the present day. The Round Table based on the Arthurian Legend and built between 1230-1280 hangs in the hall. Queen Eleanor's Garden, a re-creation of a late 13th century ornamental garden, was opened in 1986 by the Queen Mother.
Times: ✱ Open all year, Mar-Oct daily 10-5; Nov-Feb, daily 10-5, wknds 10-4. (Closed 25-26 Dec). **Facilities:** Ⓟ (200yds) ♿ toilets for disabled shop ✈ (ex guide/hearing dogs) ▦

WINCHESTER CATHEDRAL

SO23 9LS

➲ (in city centre - follow city heritage signs)

☎ 01962 857200 & 866854   FREE

▤ 01962 857201

e-mail: cathedral.office@
winchester-cathedral.org.uk

The longest medieval church in Europe, founded in 1079 on a site where Christian worship had already been offered for over 400 years. Among its treasures are the 12th-century illuminated Winchester Bible, the font, medieval wall paintings and Triforium Gallery Museum.
Times: Open all year, daily 8.30-5.30. Subject to services and special events. **Facilities:** Ⓟ (500mtrs) ▆ ✗ licensed ♿ (chair lift to east end of Cathedral, touch & hearing model) toilets for disabled shop ✈ (ex guide dogs) ▦

WINCHESTER CITY MILL

Bridge St SO23 8EJ

➲ (by the city bridge between King Alfred's statue & Chesil St)

☎ 01962 870057

▤ 01962 870057

e-mail: winchestercitymill@nationaltrust.org.uk

Built over the fastflowing River Itchen in 1744, the mill has a delightful small island garden and an impressive millrace. The 2-for-1 is not valid for ticketed events.
Times: Mill & Shop open, 21 Apr-27 Jun: Wed-Sun 11-5. 28 Jun-5 Sep: daily 11-5. 8 Sep-31 Oct: Wed-Sun 11-5. 1 Nov-23 Dec: daily 11-4 (weather permitting). Open BH Mon & daily during BH wk. **Fee:** £3 (ch £1.50) Family £7.50, Group £2.50 each **Facilities:** Ⓟ (200 yds) shop ✈ ex guide dogs ♨ ▦

WINCHESTER COLLEGE

College St SO23 9NA

➲ (in Winchester City Centre S of Cathedral Close, beyond Kingsgate arch. Limited vehicle access along College St)

☎ 01962 621209   ▤ 01962 621166

e-mail: enterprises@wincoll.ac.uk

Founded in 1382, Winchester College is believed to be the oldest continuously running school in England. The College has greatly expanded over the years but the original buildings remain intact. Visitors can follow in the footsteps of John Keats, and see the College's many historic buildings, including a schoolhouse thought to have been designed by Christopher Wren. Also the 14th century gothic chapel with one of the earliest examples of a Fan vaulted roof constructed from wood rather than stone, the original scholars dining room and the cloister containing memorials to former members of the college including one to Mallory the Mountaineer.
Times: Open all year (ex 24 Dec-1 Jan). Guided tours available Mon, Wed, Fri & Sat; 10.45, 12, 2.15 & 3.30. Tue & Thu 10.45 & 12. Sun 2.15 & 3.30. Groups of 10+ at times to suit by arrangement only. **Fee:** Prices not confirmed for 2005 **Facilities:** Ⓟ (250yds) (Street parking max stay 1hr) ♿ (access ramps) toilets for disabled shop ✈ (ex guide dogs) ▦

Above: Butterflies at Hambledon Hill

HEREFORDSHIRE

EVENTS & FESTIVALS

May
1st-2nd Blossom Time Weekend,
Putley, nr Ledbury
3rd-5th Hereford May Fair (provisional)

June
3rd-12th Leominster Festival, mixed arts,
various venues
24th-26th Music Festival, Dore Abbey,
Abbeydore

July
1st-10th Ledbury Poetry Festival

August
12th-21st Ross-on-Wye International Festival

September
tbc Bromyard Folk Festival

October
1st-29th Exposure, the Hereford Photography
Festival, various venues
tbc Big Apple Weekend, Much Marcle, nr
Ledbury

Above: Butterflies at Symond's Yat

ASHTON
Map 03 SO56

BERRINGTON HALL
Berrington HR6 0DW
➲ (3m N of Leominster, on A49)
☎ 01568 615721 ▤ 01568 613263 **2 for 1**
e-mail: berrington@nationaltrust.org.uk

An elegant neo-classical house of the late 18th century,
designed by Henry Holland and set in a park landscape by
'Capability' Brown. There is a restored bedroom suite, a
nursery, a Victorian laundry and a tiled Georgian dairy.
Times: Open 6 Mar-Oct, Sat-Wed & Good Fri 1-4.30. Last admission
30mins before closing. Garden open 12-5 (4.30pm in Oct). Park walk
open Jul-29 Oct, 12-5 **Fee:** £4.80 (ch £2.40) Family ticket £12. Garden
only £3.40. Joint ticket with Croft Castle £6 **Facilities:** ⊞ ✕ licensed
& (by arrangement, wheelchairs/batricar, steps to entrance toilets for
disabled shop ✖ (ex guide dogs) ✖ ▰

BROCKHAMPTON
Map 03 SO65

BROCKHAMPTON ESTATE
WR6 5TB
➲ (2m E of Bromyard on A44)
☎ 01885 482077 & 488099 ▤ 01885 482151
e-mail: brockhampton@nationaltrust.org.uk
Lower Brockhampton on the Brockhampton Estate near
Bromyard is a late 14th-century moated manor house, with
an attractive half-timbered 15th-century gatehouse, a rare
example of this type of structure, and the ruins of a 12th-
century chapel. It is part of a larger National Trust property
covering over 1700 acres of Herefordshire countryside with
various walks including a Sculpture Trail.
Times: Open Mar-Oct daily (ex Mon/Tue) but open BH Mon's Apr-Oct
12-5 (12-4 in Oct). Woodland walks open to dusk throughout the year.
Fee: ✱ Lower Brockhampton £3.50 (ch £1.75) Family £8.50
Facilities: ⊞ ▰ & (special parking, ramps, Braille guide) toilets for
disabled shop on leads, not immediate garden ✖ ▰

CROFT　　　　　　　　　　Map 03 SO46
CROFT CASTLE
HR6 9PW
➲ (off B4362)
☎ 01568 780246　◨ 01568 780462　`2 for 1`
e-mail: croft@nationaltrust.org.uk

Home of the Croft family since Domesday (with a break of 170 years from 1750); walls and towers date from the 14th and 15th centuries; the interior is mainly 18th century. There is a splendid avenue of 350-year-old Spanish chestnuts, and an Iron Age Fort (Croft Ambrey) may be reached by footpath. **Times:** Park open all year, daily. Gardens & Tea Room open 29 Mar-Jun, Wed-Sun 12-5; Jul-Aug, Tue-Sun 12-5; Sep, Wed-Sun 12-5; Oct-2 Nov, Sat-Sun 12-5. Castle open 18 Apr-Jun & Sep, Wed-Sun 1-5; Jul-Aug, Tue-Sun 1-5; Oct-2 Nov, Sat-Sun 1-5. **Fee:** ✱ Garden only £3 (ch £1.50). Castle & Garden £4.20 (ch £2.10). Family ticket £10.50. Joint ticket with Berrington Castle £5.50. Car park £2.20.
Facilities: ◪ (charged) ◪ ⴟ (parking available, Braille guide) toilets for disabled ✚ (ex guide dogs & in park) ⵙ

GOODRICH　　　　　　　　Map 03 SO51
GOODRICH CASTLE
HR9 6HY
➲ (5m S of Ross-on-Wye, off A40)
☎ 01600 890538

A magnificent red sandstone fortress rising out of a rocky outcrop above the Wye Valley. Climb the huge towers for exhilarating views and explore a maze of small rooms and passageways. Hear about the doomed civil war lovers on our audio tour.
Times: Open all year, Mar, daily, 10-5; Apr-May, daily, 10-5; Jun-Aug, daily, 10-6; Sep-Oct, daily, 10-5; Nov-Feb, Thu-Mon, 10-4. (Closed 24-26 Dec & 1 Jan) **Fee:** ✱ £4 (ch £2, concessions £3, family £10). Prices & opening times relate to 2004, for further details phone or log onto www.english-heritage.org.uk/visits **Facilities:** ◪ shop ✚ ▨

HEREFORD　　　　　　　　Map 03 SO53
CIDER MUSEUM & KING OFFA DISTILLERY
21 Ryelands St HR4 0LW
➲ (off A438 Hereford to Brecon road)
☎ 01432 354207　◨ 01432 371641　`2 for 1`
e-mail: info@cidermuseum.fsnet.co.uk

Explore the fascinating history of cider making - old cidermaking equipment, the cooper's workshop and Vat house with hydraulic presses and bottling machinery. An annual International cider competition is held and cidermaking festival weekends take place.
Times: Open all year, Apr-Oct, daily 10-5.30; Nov-Dec, daily 11-3. Jan-Mar, Tue-Sun 11-3. Pre-booked groups at anytime.
Fee: ✱ £2.80 (concessions £2.30). Party 15+, 50p reduction per person. **Facilities:** ◪ ◪ ⴟ (audiotapes, large print guide sheets) toilets for disabled shop ✚ (ex guide dogs)

HEREFORD CATHEDRAL
HR1 2NG
➲ (A49 signed from city inner ring roads)
☎ 01432 374200　◨ 01432 374220
e-mail: office@herefordcathedral.co.uk

The first bishop was appointed to the See of Hereford in 676AD. The cathedral is mainly Norman with a 13th-century Lady Chapel. Hereford's two outstanding treasures are exhibited together in the museum building at the West front. The Mappa Mundi - drawn in 1289, and the famous Chained Library - containing over 1400 chained books and 227 manuscripts dating from the 8th century.
Times: ✱ Cathedral open daily for visitors 9.30-5; Mappa Mundi & Chained Library Exhibition Summer: Mon-Sat 10-4.15, Sun 11-3.15. Winter: Mon-Sat 11-3.15 (closed Sun). **Facilities:** ◪ (0.25m) ◪ ⴟ (touch facility for blind, Braille & large print info) toilets for disabled shop ✚ (ex guide dogs) ▨

OLD HOUSE
High Town HR1 2AA
➲ (located in the centre of the High Town)
☎ 01432 260694

The Old House is a fine Jacobean building dating from around 1621, and was once in a row of similar houses. Its rooms are furnished in 17th-century style and give visitors the chance to learn what life was like in Cromwell's time.
Times: ✱ Open all year, 10-5. Apr-Sep, Tue-Sat 10-5, Sun & BH Mon 10-4. **Facilities:** ◪ ⴟ shop (very small) ✚ (ex guide dogs)

KINGTON　　　　　　　　Map 03 SO25
HERGEST CROFT GARDENS
HR5 3EG
➲ (turn off A44 W of Kington and follow signs)
☎ 01544 230160　◨ 01544 232031　`2 for 1`
e-mail: gardens@hergest.co.uk

From spring bulbs to autumn colour, this is a garden for all seasons. A fine collection of trees and shrubs surrounds the Edwardian house. There's an old fashioned kitchen garden with spring and summer borders, and Park Wood, a hidden valley with splendid rhododendrons.
Times: Open weekends in Mar, 25 Mar-30 Oct, 12.30-5.30; May-Jun noon-6. **Fee:** ✱ £4.50 (ch under 16 free). Party 20+ £4
Facilities: ◪ ◪ ⴟ (portable ramp & wheelchair available) toilets for disabled shop garden centre ✚ (ex dogs on lead) ▨

An asterisk * indicates that opening times and prices are for 2004. Please contact the attraction for up-to-date information.

The Battle of Trafalgar.
2005 is the 200th anniversary of the sea battle between the British Royal Navy and the French and Spanish navies. 2005 will see a number of events celebrating this important British victory.

LEDBURY — Map 03 SO73

EASTNOR CASTLE
Eastnor HR8 1RL
➲ (the castle is 2.5m E of Ledbury on the A438 Tewkesbury road)
☎ 01531 633160 🖷 01531 631776
e-mail: eastnorcastle@eastnorcastle.com

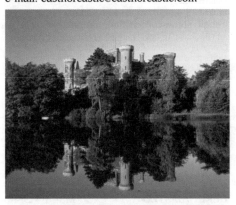

A magnificent Georgian castle in a lovely setting, with a deer park, arboretum and lake. Inside are tapestries, fine art and continued

armour, and the Italianate and Gothic interiors have been beautifully restored. There's an adventure playground, nature trails and lakeside walks.
Times: Open 11 Apr-3 Oct, Sun & BH Mon; Jul & Aug, Sun-Fri 11-5.
Facilities: 🅿 💺 ♿ (please telephone for access & facilities details) shop 🛍

SWAINSHILL — Map 03 SO44

THE WEIR GARDENS
HR4 7QF
➲ (5m W of Hereford, on A438)
☎ 01981 590509
e-mail: theweir@nationaltrust.org.uk

2 for 1

A delightful riverside garden, which is at its best in spring when there are lovely displays of naturalised bulbs set in woodland and grassland walks. Cliff garden walks can be taken here, with fine views of the River Wye and the Black Mountains. The tranquil garden, planted largely with trees and shrubs, stretches over 10 acres.
Times: Open mid Jan-Feb wknds only, 11-4. Mar daily 11-6. Apr-Sep, Wed-Sun & BH's, 11-6. Oct, Wed-Sun, 11-4. (Closed Nov-mid Jan)
Fee: ✱ £3.50 (ch £1.75) Family £8. **Facilities:** 🅿 ♿ Access limited 🐕 on lead in car park 🚐 ♨

Above: Eastner deer park

HERTFORDSHIRE

EVENTS & FESTIVALS

April
18th-23rd Hertford Theatre Week

May
7th-22nd Baldock Festival, a variety of events in the community
21st-22nd Herts Garden Show, Knebworth House (provisional)
28th-29th Herts County Show, Herts County Showground, Redbourn

June
19th Rock in the Park, Fairlands Valley Park, Stevenage (provisional)
tbc Hertford Carnival
Waltham Abbey Festival Week, community festival

July
2nd-17th Hitchin Festival, various events and venues
2nd-31st Ware Festival, including carnival
7th-16th International Organ festival, St Albans Cathedral and various venues
tbc Rhythms of the World, largest free world music festival in UK in the streets of Hitchin
tbc St Albans Carnival

August
28th-29th Knebworth Classic Motor Show, Knebworth

September
10th Hoddesdon Carnival
28th-1st Oct St Albans Beer Festival (provisional)

December
10th-11th Hitchin Christmas Tree Festival, Holy Saviour Church

Above: Poppies in the grounds of Knebworth House

AYOT ST LAWRENCE — Map 04 TL11

SHAW'S CORNER
AL6 9BX
➲ (A1(M) junct 4 or M1 junct 10. Follow B653 signed Wheathampstead & follow National Trust signs to Shaw's Corner located in village of Ayot St Lawrence)
☎ 01438 820307   ▤ 01438 820307
e-mail: shawscorner@nationaltrust.org.uk

An Edwardian Arts and Crafts influenced house, the home of George Bernard Shaw from 1906 until his death in 1950. The rooms remain much as he left them, with many literary and personal effects evoking the individuality and genius of this great dramatist. The kitchen and outbuildings are evocative of early 20th-century domestic life. Shaw's writing hut is hidden at the bottom of the garden, which has richly planted borders and views over the Hertfordshire countryside. A selection of plants as well as a small collection of George Bernard Shaw plays are available to buy.

Times: Open 20 Mar-Oct, Wed-Sun (also open BH Mons), 12-5.30 (gardens), 1-5 (house). **Fee:** ✱ £3.80 (ch £1.90). Family ticket £9.50.
Facilities: ▣ ♿ (Braille/large print guides, scented plants, items to touch) ✖ (ex on lead in car park) ❧ ▬

BERKHAMSTED — Map 04 SP90

ASHRIDGE ESTATE VISITOR CENTRE NEW
Moneybury Hill, Ringshall HP4 1LX
➲ (Between Northchurch & Ringshall, just off the B4056)
☎ 01442 851227 & 755557   ▤ 01442 850000
e-mail: ashridge@nationaltrust.org.uk

Miles of paths through woodland and open country with spring bluebells, ancient trees, fungi and breath-taking views. Discover more about the wildlife in the visitor centre next to the Bridgewater monument, with an interactive exhibition room. A wide range of activities and events for all the family take place through out the year.

Times: Estate open all year. Visitor Centre; 27 Mar-12 Dec, Mon-Fri 1-5, Sat & Sun 12-5 (or dusk if earlier) Tea Room; 27 Mar-12 Dec, Tue- Sun, 12-5. Bridgewater Monument; 27 Mar-Oct, Sat, Sun, BH Mon 1-5 (last entry 5) **Fee:** ✱ Visitor centre free, Monument £1.20 (ch60p)
Facilities: ▣ ▣ ♿ toilets for disabled shop

BERKHAMSTED CASTLE
HP4 1HF
➲ (by Berkhamsted station)

Roads and a railway have cut into the castle site, but its huge banks and ditches remain impressive. The original motte-and-bailey was built after the Norman Conquest, and there is a later stone keep, owned by the Black Prince, eldest son of King Edward III, where King John of France was imprisoned.

Times: Open all year, daily, summer 10-6; winter 10-4. (Closed 25 Dec & 1 Jan). **Facilities:** ✖ (ex dogs on leads) ⬡

HATFIELD — Map 04 TL20

HATFIELD HOUSE, PARK AND GARDENS
AL9 5NQ
➲ (2m from junct 4 A1(M) on A1000, 7m from M25 junct 23. House is opposite Hatfield railway station)
☎ 01707 287010   ▤ 01707 287033
e-mail: visitors@hatfield-house.co.uk

The house, built by Robert Cecil in 1611, is the home of the Marquess of Salisbury and is full of exquisite tapestries,

continued

furniture and famous paintings. The 42 acres of gardens include formal, knot, scented and wilderness areas, which reflects their Jacobean history. Includes the national collection of model soldiers and children's play area. The Old Tudor Place, close by the house, is the childhood home of Elizabeth I and where she held her first Council of State when she became Queen in 1558.

Hatfield House, Park and Gardens

Times: Open Etr Sat-Sep. House: Sat-Wed 12-4, guided tours only on Mons, ex BH. Park & gardens: Sat-Wed 11-5.30. **Fee:** House Park & Gardens: £8 (ch £4). Park only £2 (ch £1). Park & gardens: £4.50 (ch 3.50). Mon (Garden Connoisseurs' Day); Park & gardens: £6.50. House Tour, £5 **Facilities:** 🅿 ✕ licensed & (lift to 1st floor, wheelchairs) toilets for disabled shop 🔳

KNEBWORTH   Map 04 TL22

KNEBWORTH HOUSE, GARDENS & COUNTRY PARK
SG3 6PY
➲ (direct access from A1(M) junct 7 Stevenage South)
☎ 01438 812661   🖷 01438 811908
e-mail: info@knebworthhouse.com

Home of the Lytton family since 1490, the original Tudor Manor was transformed in 1843 by the spectacular high Gothic decoration of Victorian novelist Sir Edward Bulwer
continued

Knebworth
HOUSE, GARDENS & PARK

Home of the Lytton family for over 500 years, where Elizabeth I visited, Dickens acted and Churchill painted. Extensive Gardens, Dinosaur Trail, Maze, Indian Raj Display Adventure Playground, Miniature Railway, Gift Shop and Garden Terrace Tea Room, set in 250 acres of deer park.

For full details of opening times, entrance fees and the full programme of exciting events in the Park, From Easter till Sept, please visit www.knebworthhouse.com or telephone for details.

For further information, please contact:

The Estate Office, Knebworth Park, Nr Stevenage, Herts SG3 6PY
Tel: 01438 812661   Fax: 01438 811908
email: info@knebworthhouse.com   website: www.knebworthhouse.com
Immediate access off the A1(M), via our own slip road at Junction 7, 15 miles from M25 (J23).

Lytton. The formal gardens, laid out by Edwin Lutyens in 1908, include a Gertrude Jekyll herb garden, a maze, recently restored walled garden and the dinosaur trail in the wilderness garden. The 250-acre park includes a miniature railway, an adventure playground and a deer park.

Times: Open daily 26 Mar-10 Apr, 28 May-5 Jun & Jul- Aug. Wknds & BH's 19-20 Mar, 16 Apr-22 May, 11-26 Jun & 3-25 Sep. Park, Playground & Gardens 11-5.30; House & Exhibition noon-5 (last admission 4.15). **Fee:** Please contact for details, or visit website. **Facilities:** 🅿 🚻 & (transport to door, wheelchair, Carers free entry.) toilets for disabled shop (2 shops) garden centre ✖ (ex guide dogs & in park) 🔳

See advertisement on this page

LETCHWORTH   Map 04 TL23

MUSEUM & ART GALLERY
Broadway SG6 3PF
➲ (Museum is situated next door to the Public Library, in the Town Centre, near the Broadway Cinema)
☎ 01462 685647   🖷 01462 481879   **FREE**
e-mail: letchworth.museum@north-herts.gov.uk

Opened in 1914 to house the collections of the Letchworth Naturalists' Society, this friendly town-centre museum has exhibits on local wildlife, geology, arts and crafts, and archaeology. There is also a museum shop and a regular programme of art exhibitions and workshops.
Times: Open all year Mon-Tue, Thu-Sat (Closed BHs), 10-5.
Facilities: 🅿 (100yds) & (special provisions on request) shop ✖ (ex guide dogs)

LONDON COLNEY — Map 04 TL10
DE HAVILLAND AIRCRAFT HERITAGE CENTRE
Salisbury Hall AL2 1EX
➲ (signposted from junct 22 of M25. Follow signs for 'Mosquito Aircraft Museum' onto B556).
☎ 01727 822051 & 826400
▤ 01727 826400

The oldest aircraft museum in Britain, opened in 1959 to preserve and display the de Havilland Mosquito prototype on the site of its conception. A working museum with displays of 20 de Havilland aircraft and sections together with a comprehensive collection of de Havilland engines and memorabilia. Selective cockpits are open to enter. Education storyboard 'maze style' now open.
Times: Open first Sun Mar-last Sun Oct, Sun & BH's 10.30-5.30, Tue, Thu & Sat 2-5.30. **Fee:** £5 (ch under 5 free, ch & pen £3) Family ticket £13 (2 adults & 2 ch) **Facilities:** 🅿 🖵 ♿ (wheelchairs available) toilets for disabled shop (not accessible for wheelchairs) ◀

ST ALBANS — Map 04 TL10
CLOCK TOWER
Market Place AL3 3DR
➲ (City centre, junct of High St (A1081) & Market Place)
☎ 01727 819340 ▤ 01727 837472
e-mail: museum@stalbans.gov.uk
This early 15th-century curfew tower, which faces the High Street, provides fine views over the city (especially of the abbey) and the surrounding countryside. This is one of the only two medieval curfew towers in the country. It has a bell, older than the tower itself, which strikes on the hour.
Times: Open Good Fri-mid Sep, Sat, Sun & BH 10.30-5. **Fee:** 30p (ch 5-11 15p, accompanied ch under 5 free) **Facilities:** 🅿 (400yds) shop ✗

GARDENS OF THE ROSE (ROYAL NATIONAL ROSE SOCIETY)
Chiswell Green Ln AL2 3NR
➲ (2m S off B4630 Watford Rd in Chiswell Green Ln)
☎ 01727 850461 ▤ 01727 850360
e-mail: mail@rnrs.org.uk
The gardens of the Royal National Rose Society, which include the International Trial Ground for new roses. The gardens contain over 30,000 plants in 1,650 different varieties. These include old-fashioned roses, modern roses and the roses of the future. The National Miniature Rose Show takes place during July.
Times: ✱ Open 31 May-late Sep, Mon-Sat 10-5 (Sun & BH Mon 10-6).
Facilities: 🅿 🖵 ♿ (ramps where necessary) toilets for disabled shop garden centre ✗ (ex guide dogs) ◀

GORHAMBURY
AL3 6AH
➲ (entry via lodge gates on A414)
☎ 01727 855000 ▤ 01727 843675
This house was built by Sir Robert Taylor between 1774 and 1784 to house an extensive picture collection of 17th-century portraits of the Grimston and Bacon families and their contemporaries. Also of note is the 16th-century enamelled glass collection and an early English pile carpet.
Times: Open May-Sep, Thu 2-5. **Fee:** £6 (ch £3, pen £4).
Facilities: 🅿 ✗

MUSEUM OF ST ALBANS
Hatfield Rd AL1 3RR
➲ (city centre on A1057 Hatfield road)
☎ 01727 819340 ▤ 01727 837472
e-mail: museum@stalbans.gov.uk
Exhibits include the Salaman collection of craft tools, and reconstructed workshops. The history of St Albans is traced from the departure of the Romans up to the present day. There is a special exhibition gallery with a surprising variety of exhibitions and a wildlife garden with picnic area.
Times: Open all year, daily 10-5, Sun 2-5. (Closed 25 & 26 Dec).
Facilities: 🅿 ♿ toilets for disabled shop ✗ (ex guide dogs) ◀

ROMAN THEATRE OF VERULAMIUM
St Michaels AL3 6AH
➲ (Gorhambury Drive off Bluehouse Hill A4147)
☎ 01727 835035 ▤ 01727 843675
The theatre was discovered in 1847 and excavated in 1935. It is unique in England. First constructed around AD160, it is semicircular in shape, 180ft across and could hold over 2000 spectators.
Times: Open all year, daily 10-5 (4 in winter). Closed 25-26 Dec. 1 Jan by appointment only. **Fee:** ✱ £1.50 (ch 50p, students & pen £1, ch under 5yrs & disabled free) **Facilities:** 🅿 ♿ (limited access to viewing path) shop

St Albans Cathedral

Sumpter Yard AL1 1BY

➲ (M25 junct 22a, in the centre of St Albans)

☎ 01727 860780 📠 01727 850944

e-mail: admin@stalbanscathedal.org.uk

An imposing Norman abbey church built on the site of the execution of St Alban, Britain's first martyr (c250AD). The cathedral is constructed from recycled Roman brick taken from nearby Verulamium.

Times: Open daily, 9-5.45, closed 25 Dec (pm) **Fee:** Admission free. Suggested donation £2.50 per adult. **Facilities:** P (200mtrs) ♨ ♿ (touch & hearing centre, Braille guides) toilets for disabled shop

Verulamium Museum

St Michaels AL3 4SW

➲ (follow signs for St Albans, museum signposted)

☎ 01727 751810 📠 01727 859919 **2 for 1**

e-mail: a.coles@stalbans.gov.uk

Verulamium was one of the largest and most important Roman towns in Britain - by the lst century AD it was declared a 'municipium', giving its inhabitants the rights of Roman citizenship, the only British city granted this honour. A mosaic and underfloor heating system can be seen, and the museum has wall paintings, jewellery, pottery and other domestic items. On the second weekend of every month legionaries occupy the galleries and describe the tactics and equipment of the Roman Imperial Army and the life of a legionary.

Times: Open all year wkdys 10-5.30, Sun 2-5.30. (Closed 25-26 Dec). **Fee:** £3.30 (ch, pen & students £2). Family ticket £8. Subject to change. **Facilities:** P (charged) ♿ (ramp access to main entrance) toilets for disabled shop ✖ (ex guide dogs) ◼

Above: Statue at Knebworth House

TRING Map 04 SP91

The Walter Rothschild Zoological Museum

Akeman St HP23 6AP

➲ (signposted from A41)

☎ 020 7942 6171 📠 020 7942 6150 **FREE**

e-mail: tring-enquiries@nhm.ac.uk

An unusual museum, founded in the 1890s by Lionel Walter, 2nd Baron Rothschild, scientist, eccentric and natural history enthusiast. Now part of the Natural History Museum, it houses more than 4000 specimens from whales to fleas, and humming birds to tigers.

Times: Open all year, Mon-Sat 10-5, Sun 2-5. (Closed 24-26 Dec). **Facilities:** P ♨ ♿ (ramps to shop & cafe, disabled parking space) toilets for disabled shop ✖ (ex guide dogs)

WARE Map 05 TL31

Scott's Grotto

Scott's Rd SG12 9JQ

➲ (off A119)

☎ 01920 464131 📠 0870 120 6902 **FREE**

e-mail: jg@ware-herts.org.uk

Scott's Grotto, built in the 1760s by the Quaker poet John Scott, has been described by English Heritage as 'one of the finest in England'. Recently restored by the Ware Society, it consists of underground passages and chambers decorated with flints, shells, minerals and stones, and extends 67ft into the side of the hill. Please wear flat shoes and bring a torch.

Times: Open Apr-Sep, Sat & BH Mon 2-4.30. Other times by appointment only. **Facilities:** P (on street) ✖ ♿

The End of World War II.

2005 sees the 60th anniversary of both VE (Victory in Europe) and VJ (Victory over Japan) Days. Local celebrations are planned, as are a number of national events.

KENT

EVENTS & FESTIVALS

May
28th-30th Kent Garden Show, Kent County
    Showground (provisional)
28th-30th Sellindge Steam Festival, Ashford
tbc Tonbridge Carnival

June
16th-25th Broadstairs Dickens Festival
18th Canterbury Carnival

July
9th-11th Son et Lumiere, Canterbury
    Cathedral precincts
24th-30th Deal Regatta Week
28th Deal Carnival
tbc Dover Carnival
tbc Kent Beer Festival, Merton Farm,
    Canterbury
tbc Kent County Show, Maidstone
tbc Whitstable Regatta, Whitstable

August
5th-12th Broadstairs Folk Week
6th-7th Dover Regatta, Dover
    Promenade/Harbour
6th-14th Herne Bay Festival
7th Broadstairs & St Peters Carnival
24th-29th Sandwich Festival, a variety of
    events around Sandwich
29th Sedan Chair Race, The Pantiles,
    Tunbridge Wells
tbc Whitstable Oyster Festival

September
tbc Deal Maritime Folk Festival,
    various venues
tbc Sandwich Carnival

October
8th-22nd Canterbury Festival, classical
    concerts, theatre, dance, opera, jazz, blues,
    folk, children's events, exhibitions and
    walks

Above: Front lawn of Aylesford Priory

AYLESFORD   Map 05 TQ75

AYLESFORD PRIORY
The Friars ME20 7BX
⮎ (M20 junct 6 onto A229, M2 junct 3 onto A229,
signposted)
☎ 01622 717272   ▤ 01622 715575
e-mail: friarsevents@hotmail.com

Built in the 13th and 14th centuries, the Priory has been
restored and is now a house of prayer, guesthouse,
conference centre and a place of pilgrimage and retreat. It
has fine cloisters, and displays sculpture and ceramics by
modern artists.
Times: Open all year, daily 9-dusk. Gift & book shop May-Sep, 10-5;
Oct-Apr, 10-4 (Sun 11am). Guided tours of the priory by arrangement.
Facilities: 🅿 💷 ♿ (wheelchairs available, ramps) toilets for disabled
shop ✈ (ex guide & hearing dogs)

BEKESBOURNE   Map 05 TR15

HOWLETTS WILD ANIMAL PARK
CT4 5EL
⮎ (off A2, 3m S of Canterbury, follow brown
tourist signs)
☎ 01303 264647   ▤ 01303 264944
e-mail: info@howletts.net

Set in 90 acres of parkland, Howletts is home to some of the
world's most rare and endangered animals. Howletts boasts
the UK's largest group of African elephants, Indian and
Siberian tigers, many small cats and rare monkeys and the
world's largest group of Western Lowland gorillas. Glass
fronted tiger enclosures, children's adventure playground
and the new Jurassic Mine with ice and gem cave are not to
be missed.
Times: ✱ Open all year, daily 10-6 during summer (last admission
4.30), 10-dusk during winter (last admission 3). Closed 25 Dec.
Facilities: 🅿 💷 ✗ ♿ toilets for disabled shop
✈ (ex guide dogs) 🍴

BELTRING   Map 05 TQ64

HOP FARM & COUNTRY PARK
TN12 6PY
⮎ (on A228 at Paddock Wood)
☎ 01622 872068   ▤ 01622 872630
e-mail: enquiry@thehopfarm.co.uk

The Hop Farm is a popular South East family visitor attraction
and event location. Set among the largest collection of
Victorian Oast houses attractions include museums and
exhibitions, indoor and outdoor play areas, animal farm and
continued

shire horses, and restaurant and gift shop. Special events throughout the year include craft shows, motor shows, food and drink festivals and themed holiday weeks.
Times: Open from 10am (Closed 24-26 Dec, 23 May & 20 June)
Fee: ✹ £7.50 (ch 4-15 £6.50). Family ticket £27 (2 ad & 2 ch).
Facilities: 🅿 💺 ✗ licensed ♿ toilets for disabled shop ⬛

BIDDENDEN — Map 05 TQ83

BIDDENDEN VINEYARDS & CIDER WORKS
Little Whatmans, Gribble Bridge Ln TN27 8DF
➲ (0.5m S off A262, 0.5m from Biddenden Village. Bear right at Woolpack Corner)
☎ 01580 291726 🖷 01580 291933
e-mail: info@biddendenvineyards.co.uk
The present vineyard was established in 1969 and now covers 22 acres. Visitors are welcome to stroll around the vineyard and to taste wines, ciders and apple juice available at the shop.
Times: Open all year, Shop: Mon-Fri 10-5, Sat 10-5, Sun & BH 11-5. Closed noon 24 Dec-2 Jan & Sun in Jan & Feb. **Fee:** Non-guided groups and individuals free. Pre-booked guided tours (minimum 15 adults) £3.70 (ch 10-18 £1.35, ch under 10 free). **Facilities:** 🅿 💺 ♿ shop ⬛

BIRCHINGTON — Map 05 TR36

POWELL-COTTON MUSEUM, QUEX HOUSE & GARDENS
Quex Park CT7 0BH
➲ (W of Margate on A28. Drive in to Birchington and turn right into Park Lane before rdbt in centre of town. The entrance to Quex Park 600 yds on left)
☎ 01843 842168 🖷 01843 846661
e-mail: powell-cotton.museum@virgin.net
Major Powell-Cotton spent much of his life on the study of African animals and many different cultures. This museum, founded in 1895, is his legacy, consisting of animal dioramas, photographs, extensive notes, and artefacts from around the world. Also on display in Quex House, the family home, are collections of Eastern and Asian furniture, Kashmir walnut wall carvings, Chinese silk embroidery, and English period furniture.
Times: Open Apr-Oct Tue-Thu, Sun & BH 11-5, Quex House 2-4.30. Nov & Mar Sun 11-4, Quex House closed. (Closed Dec-Feb).
Fee: ✹ Summer £5 (ch & pen £4, under 5's free), Family ticket (2 adults & 3 children) £14. Winter £4 (ch & pen £3), Family ticket (2 adults & 3 children) £10. Garden only £1.50 (ch & pen £1).
Facilities: 🅿 💺 ✗ licensed ♿ (two wheelchairs available) toilets for disabled shop ✖ (ex assistance dogs) ⬛

BOROUGH GREEN — Map 05 TQ65

GREAT COMP GARDEN
TN15 8QS
➲ (2m E off B2016)
☎ 01732 882669 886154   2 for 1
e-mail: greatcompgarden@aol.com
A beautiful seven-acre garden created since 1957 by Mr and Mrs R Cameron for low maintenance and year-round interest. There is a plantsmans' collection of trees, shrubs, heathers and herbaceous plants in a setting of fine lawns and grass paths. The 17th-century house is not open. Chamber music, classical concerts and other events are organised by the Great Comp Society, details from the Secretary, Great Comp Society at the above address.
Times: Open Apr-Oct, daily 11-5.30. **Fee:** ✹ £4 (ch £1). Annual ticket £12 (pen £8). **Facilities:** 🅿 💺 ✗ ♿ (wheelchair for hire) toilets for disabled garden centre ✖ (ex guide dogs)

BRASTED — Map 05 TQ45

EMMETTS GARDEN
Ide Hill TN14 6AY
➲ (1m S of A25, Sundridge-Ide Hill road)
☎ 01732 750367 🖷 01732 750490
e-mail: emmetts@nationaltrust.org.uk
Emmetts is a charming hillside shrub garden, with bluebells, azaleas and rhododendrons in spring and fine autumn colours. It has magnificent views over Bough Beech Reservoir and the Weald.
Times: Open 20 Mar-27 Jun, Wed-Sun & BH 11-5 (last admission 4.15); 30 Jun-Oct Wed, Sat & Sun **Fee:** ✹ £4 (ch £1). Family ticket £9. Group 15+ £3.50 **Facilities:** 🅿 💺 ♿ (wheelchairs, buggy service, Braille/large print guide) toilets for disabled shop ✖

BROADSTAIRS — Map 05 TR36

BLEAK HOUSE DICKENS MARITIME & SMUGGLING
Fort Rd CT10 1EY
➲ (off Eastern Esplanade, near Viking Bay)
☎ 01843 862224
The house was a favourite seaside residence of Charles Dickens, and he wrote all of *David Copperfield* and other works here, and drafted the idea for *Bleak House*. There are also exhibitions of relics salvaged from the Goodwin Sands and Kent's only smuggling museum.
Times: ✹ Open mid Feb-mid Dec, daily; Jan-mid Feb wknds only.10-6
Facilities: 🅿 (100 yds) ♿ (provisions made for blind) shop

DICKENS HOUSE MUSEUM
2 Victoria Pde CT10 1QS
➲ (on the seafront)
☎ 01843 863453 🖷 01843 863453
e-mail: aleeault@aol.com
The house was immortalised by Charles Dickens in *David Copperfield* as the home of the hero's aunt, Betsy Trotwood, whom Dickens based on owner Miss Mary Pearson Strong. Dickens' letters and possessions are shown, with local and Dickensian prints, costumes and general Victoriana.
Times: Open Etr-Oct, daily 2-5, also Sat-Sun mid Jun-Aug 10.30-5.
Facilities: 🅿 (400yds) (pay & display) shop ✖ (ex guide dogs)

CANTERBURY — Map 05 TR15

CANTERBURY ROMAN MUSEUM
Butchery Ln, Longmarket CT1 2RA
➲ (in the centre close to the cathedral and city centre car parks)
☎ 01227 785575 🖷 01227 455047
e-mail: museums@canterbury.gov.uk
Step below today's Canterbury to discover an exciting part of the Roman town including the real remains of a house with fine mosaics. Experience everyday life in the reconstructed market place and see exquisite silver and glass. Try your skills on the touch screen computer, and in the hands-on area with actual finds. Use the computer animation of Roman Canterbury to join the search for the lost temple.
Times: Open all year, Mon-Sat 10-5 & Sun (Jun-Oct) 1.30-5. Last admission 4pm. (Closed Good Fri & Xmas period). **Fee:** ✹ £2.80 (ch 5-18, disabled, pen & students £1.75). Family ticket £7.20
Facilities: 🅿 walking ♿ (lift) toilets for disabled shop
✖ (ex guide dogs)

THE CANTERBURY TALES

St. Margaret's St CT1 2TG

➲ (In heart of city centre, follow finger sign-posting)

☎ 01227 479227 🖷 01227 765584 **2 for 1**

e-mail: info@canterburytales.org.uk

Step back in time to experience the sights sounds and smells of the Middle Ages in this reconstruction of 14th Century England. Travel from the Tabard Inn, in London, to St. Thomas Becket's Shrine in Canterbury with Chaucer's colourful pilgrims. Their tales of chivalry, romance and intrigue are vividly brought to life for you along your journey.
Times: Open all year, Mar-Jun 10-5, Jul-Aug 9.30-5, Sep-Oct 10-4 & Nov-Feb 10-4.30. Closed 25 Dec **Fee:** ✱ £6.95 (ch £5.25, pen £5.75, student £5.95) Family ticket (2 ad & 2 ch) £22.50
Facilities: P (200mtrs) 🍺 & (notice required for wheelchairs) toilets for disabled shop ✹ (ex guide dogs) 🍴

CANTERBURY WEST GATE MUSEUM

St. Peter's St CT1 2RA

➲ (at the end of the main street beside the river, the entrance is under the main arch)

☎ 01227 789576 🖷 01227 455047

e-mail: museums@canterbury.gov.uk

The last of the city's fortified gatehouses sits astride the London road with the river as a moat. Rebuilt in around 1380 by Archbishop Sudbury, it was used as a prison for many years. The battlements give a splendid panoramic view of the city and are a good vantage point for photographs. Arms and armour can be seen in the guardroom, and there are cells in the towers. Brass rubbings can be made and children can try on replica armour.
Times: Open all year (ex Good Fri & Xmas period), Mon-Sat; 11-12.30 & 1.30-3.30. Last admission 15 mins before closure. **Fee:** ✱ £1.10 (ch, disabled, pen, students & UB40 70p). Family ticket £2.60.
Facilities: P (100yds) shop ✹ (ex guide dogs)

DRUIDSTONE PARK & ART PARK

Honey Hill, Blean CT2 9JR

➲ (3m NW on A290 from Canterbury) **2 for 1**

☎ 01227 765168 🖷 01227 768860

Idyllic garden setting for a range of sculptures. Enchanted woodland walks where dwells the sleeping dragon. See the mystical Oak circle with the old man of the oaks. Children's farmyard, play areas, gift shop & cafeteria.
Times: Open Etr-Nov, daily, 10-5.30. **Fee:** £4.80 (ch £3.50 & pen £4). Family ticket £14.50 **Facilities:** P 🍺 & toilets for disabled shop ✹ (ex guide dogs) 🍴

MUSEUM OF CANTERBURY

Stour St CT1 2RA

➲ (in the Medieval Poor Priests' Hospital, just off St Margaret's St or High St)

☎ 01227 475202 🖷 01227 455047

e-mail: museums@canterbury.gov.uk

Discover the story of Canterbury in new interactive displays for all the family. See the city's treasures including the famous Canterbury Cross. Try the fun activities in the Medieval Discovery Gallery, find out about the mysteries surrounding Christopher Marlowe's life and death and spot friend or foe planes in the WW2 Blitz gallery. Meet favourite children's TV character Bagpuss and friends and enjoy the Rupert Bear Museum - full of adventure and surprises.
Times: Open all year, Mon-Sat 10.30-5 & Sun (Jun-Sep) 1.30-5 (last admission 4pm). (Closed Good Fri & Xmas period). **Fee:** ✱ £3.10 (concessions £2.10). Family ticket £8.20 (2 Adults + 3 ch)
Facilities: P walking & toilets for disabled shop ✹ (ex guide dogs)

ROYAL MUSEUM & ART GALLERY WITH BUFFS MUSEUM

High St CT1 2RA

➲ (in the Beaney Institute (1st floor) in the High St)

☎ 01227 452747 🖷 01227 455047 **FREE**

e-mail: museums@canterbury.gov.uk

A splendid Victorian building, houses decorative arts and the city's picture collections- including a gallery for T.S. Cooper, England finest cattle painter. The art gallery is the major space in the area for the visual arts with a varied exhibition programme. Here too is the Buffs Museum, which tells the story of one of England's oldest infantry regiments and its worldwide service.
Times: Open all year, Mon-Sat 10-5. (Closed Good Fri and Xmas period). Last admission 4.45 **Facilities:** P (500mtrs) shop ✹ (ex guide dogs)

ST AUGUSTINE'S ABBEY

CT1 1TF

➲ (off A28)

☎ 01227 767345

Part of the Canterbury World Heritage site, this is considered by many as the birthplace of Christianity in England. Visit the fascinating museum and take the free interactive audio tour.
Times: Open all year, Apr-Sep, daily 10-6; Oct-Mar, Wed-Sun & BH Mons 10-4. (Closed 24-26 Dec & 1 Jan). **Fee:** ✱ £3.50 (ch £1.80, concessions £2.60). Prices & opening times relate to 2004, for further details phone or log onto www.english-heritage.org.uk/visits
Facilities: P & shop ✹ (ex dogs on leads) 🎫

CHARTWELL   Map 05 TQ45

CHARTWELL

TN16 1PS

➲ (Turn off A25 onto B2026 at Westerham, Chartwell 2m S of village)

☎ 01732 866368 (info line) & 868381

🖷 01732 868193

e-mail: chartwell@nationaltrust.org.uk

The former home of Sir Winston Churchill is filled with reminders of the great statesman, from his hats and uniforms to gifts presented by Stalin, Roosevelt, de Gaulle and many other State leaders. There are portraits of

continued

Churchill and other works by notable artists, and also many paintings by Churchill himself.
Times: Open 20 Mar-7 Nov, house, garden & studio, Wed-Sun 11-5. Open BH Mon's & Tue in Jul/Aug. Last admission 4.15pm (5.30pm BH) **Fee:** ✱ House, Garden & studio £7 (ch £3.50). Gardens and studio only £3.50 (ch £1.65). Family ticket £17.50. **Facilities:** 🅿 ✕ licensed ♿ (2 steps to lift, parking, guides, sensory facilities) toilets for disabled shop (garden/grounds only on lead) 🐾 🍴

CHATHAM   Map 05 TQ76

FORT AMHERST
Dock Rd ME4 4UB
➲ (adjacent to the A231 dock road, 0.5m from Chatham Dockyard)
☎ 01634 847747   🖹 01634 830612
e-mail: amherstman2@hotmail.com
A fine Georgian fortress set in over 15 acres of attractive parkland. A fascinating collection of caves, tunnels, gun-batteries and barracks gives visitors an insight into the life of the Napoleonic soldier. Please telephone for details of special events, including historic re-enactments.
Times: ✱ Open daily Nov-Mar Sat/Sun 10-3.30. Apr-Oct daily 10-4 **Facilities:** 🅿 💷 ♿ (wheelchair provided, road access up to fort) toilets for disabled shop ✕ (ex guide dogs) 🍴

THE HISTORIC DOCKYARD CHATHAM
ME4 4TZ
➲ (from M20 & M2 junct 3, follow signs for Chatham on A229. Then take A230 and A231, following brown tourist signs. Brown anchor signs lead to visitors entrance)
☎ 01634 823800   🖹 01634 823801   **2 for 1**
e-mail: info@chdt.org.uk
The Historic Dockyard celebrates over 400 years of naval history in one 80-acre site. Exhibits include Battle Ships with WWII destroyer *HMS Cavalier* and the spy sub *Ocelot*. Lifeboat with a display of 15 full size boats, archive film and artefacts; and Wooden Walls which looks at the life of a carpenter's apprentice in the 18th century. The naval architecture is spectacular.
Times: Open mid Feb-early Nov, daily 10-6. Last entry 4pm.
Fee: ✱ £10 (ch 5-15 £6.50, concession £7.50). Family ticket (2 ad & 2 ch) £26.50, additional child £3.25 **Facilities:** 🅿 💷 ✕ licensed ♿ (wheelchair available, Braille guides, virtual tours) toilets for disabled shop 🍴

CHIDDINGSTONE   Map 05 TQ54

CHIDDINGSTONE CASTLE
TN8 7AD
➲ (off B2027, at Bough Beech)
☎ 01892 870347
The 'castle' is a 17th-century house, almost completely rebuilt in the castle style c1800 by William Atkinson. It contains Stewart and Jacobite paintings and other relics, Egyptian and Oriental antiquities, and a fine collection of Japanese lacquer and swords. The interior has recently been refurbished with extra rooms open to visitors.
Times: ✱ Open Apr-May, Oct, Easter & Public Holidays, Jun-Sep, Wed-Fri & Sun. Weekdays 2-5.30; Sun & BH 11.30-5.30.
Facilities: 🅿 💷 ♿ shop ✕ (ex guide dogs on lead)

DEAL   Map 05 TR35

DEAL CASTLE
Victoria Rd CT14 7BA
➲ (SW of Deal town centre)
☎ 01304 372762
Discover the history of this formidable fortress as you explore the long, dark passages that once linked a garrison of 119 guns.
Times: Open Apr-Sep, daily 10-6 **Fee:** ✱ £3.50 (ch £1.80, concessions £2.60). Prices & opening times relate to 2004, for further details phone or log onto www.english-heritage.org.uk/visits **Facilities:** ♿ (parking available) shop ✕ ▥

WALMER CASTLE
Kingsdown Rd CT14 7LJ
➲ (1m S on coast, off A258)
☎ 01304 364288
Originally built by Henry VIII as a formidable and austere fortress, the castle has since been transformed into an elegant stately home, formerly used by HM The Queen Mother. Many of her rooms are open to view, but the special highlight is the magnificent gardens.
Times: Open Mar, daily 10-4; Apr-Sep, daily 10-6; Oct, Wed-Sun 10-4. Closed when Lord Warden in residence. **Fee:** ✱ £5.80 (ch £2.90, concessions £4.40). Prices & opening times relate to 2004, for further details phone or log onto www.english-heritage.org.uk/visits **Facilities:** 🅿 💷 ♿ (parking available) shop ✕ ▥

DOVER   Map 05 TR34

CRABBLE CORN MILL
Lower Rd, River CT17 0UY
➲ (M20 into Dover towards Eastern Docks onto A2. Take road as far as Whitfield rdbt. At rdbt 2nd turning down Whitfield Hill towards North Dover. At bottom of hill left. At traffic lights right into River Crabble, under railway bridge and 1st right, Mill 500mtrs on left)
☎ 01304 823292   🖹 01304 823292
e-mail: miller@ccmt.org.co.uk
Visit this beautifully restored working Kentish water mill dating from 1812. Regular demonstrations of waterwheel working and making stoneground wholemeal flour from Kentish organic wheat. Flour for sale, also home-baked produce in café. Exhibition space displays work of local artists and craftspeople.
Times: Open all year, Mar-Sep, daily 11-5; Winter, Sun only (except by appointment). Open all year for groups by arrangement. Closed Xmas & Jan. **Facilities:** 🅿 💷 ♿ shop ✕ (ex guide dogs)

DOVER CASTLE & SECRET WARTIME TUNNELS
CT16 1HU
☎ 01304 211067   🖹 01304 214739
Various exhibitions demonstrate how Dover Castle has served as a vital strategic centre for the Iron Age onwards. In May 1940 the tunnels under the castle became the nerve centre for 'Operation Dynamo' - the evacuation of Dunkirk. These wartime secrets are now revealed for all to see.
Times: Open all year, Apr-Jun & Sep, daily 10-6; Jul-Aug, daily 9.30-6.30; Oct, daily 10-5; Nov-Jan, Thu-Mon 10-4; Feb-Mar, daily 10-4; Closed 24-26 Dec & 1 Jan. **Fee:** ✱ £8.50 (ch £4.30, concessions £6.40). Family £21.30 (2 adults+2 children). Prices & opening times relate to 2004, for further details phone or log onto www.english-heritage.org.uk/visits **Facilities:** 🅿 ✕ ♿ shop ✕ (ex on lead in certain areas) ▥

ROMAN PAINTED HOUSE
New St CT17 9AJ
➲ (follow A20 to York St bypass, located in town centre)
☎ 01304 203279
Visit five rooms of a Roman hotel built 1800 years ago, famous for its unique, well-preserved Bacchic frescos. The Roman underfloor heating system and part of a late-Roman defensive wall are also on view. There are extensive displays on Roman Dover, and special events are held throughout the year.
Times: Open Apr-Sep, Tue-Sun 10-5, also BH Mon & Mon Jul & Aug.
Fee: ✱ £2 (ch & pen 80p) **Facilities:** 🅿 ↯ (touch table, glass panels on gallery for wheelchairs) shop ✱

DYMCHURCH   Map 05 TR12
DYMCHURCH MARTELLO TOWER
High St CT16 1HU
➲ (access from High St not seafront)
☎ 01304 211067
This artillery tower formed part of a chain of strongholds intended to resist invasion by Napoleon.
Times: Telephone for opening details. Pre-booked guided tours only.
Facilities: ✱ ▯

EDENBRIDGE
See **Hever**

EYNSFORD   Map 05 TQ56
EAGLE HEIGHTS NEW
Lullingstone Ln DA4 0JB
➲ (M25 junct 3/A20 towards West Kingsdown. After 2 rdbts turn right onto A225. Follow brown signs for Eagle Heights.)
☎ 01322 866466   🖅 01322 861024
e-mail: office@eagleheights.co.uk
Kents Bird of Prey Centre has four primary objectives - conservation, education, recreation and sanctuary. Eagle Heights educates and inspires visitors through demonstrating as near natural behaviour as possible with live exhibits - including a bald eagle and a griffon vulture. Flying displays take place twice daily and daily owl and reptile indoor demonstrations are also available.
Times: Mar-Oct, daily 10.30-5; Nov-Feb Sat-Sun only 11-4
Fee: ✱ £6.60 (ch£5.60, concessions £4.60) **Facilities:** 🅿 ▱
↯ toilets for disabled shop ✱ ➡

EYNSFORD CASTLE
➲ (in Eynsford, off A225)
One of the first stone castles to be built by the Normans. The moat and remains of the curtain wall and hall can still be seen.
Times: Open all year, Apr-Sep, daily 10-6; Oct-Feb, daily 10-4. Opening times relate to 2004, for further details phone or log onto www.english-heritage.org.uk/visits. **Facilities:** 🅿 ↯ ▯

LULLINGSTONE CASTLE
DA4 0JA
➲ (1m SW of Eynsford via A225 & Lullingstone Roman Villa)
☎ 01322 862114   🖅 01322 862115
The house was altered extensively in Queen Anne's time, and has fine state rooms and beautiful grounds. The 15th-century gate tower was one of the first gatehouses in England to be made entirely of bricks, and there is a church with family monuments. Please telephone for details of special events.
Times: Open, House May-Aug, Sat, Sun & BH 2-6. Parties by arrangement. **Fee:** ✱ House & Gardens £5 (ch £2 & pen £4) family £10. **Facilities:** 🅿 ↯ shop ✱

LULLINGSTONE ROMAN VILLA
Lullingstone Ln DA4 0JA
➲ (0.5m SW off A225)
☎ 01322 863467
One of the most exciting finds with wonderful mosaic floors, wall paintings and skeletal remains. Audio tours offer a fascinating insight into the life of a well-to-do Roman family.
Times: Open all year, Apr-Sep, daily 10-6; Oct-Nov, daily 10-4; Dec-Jan, Wed-Sun 10-4; Feb-Mar, daily 10-4. (Closed 24-26 Dec & 1 Jan).
Fee: ✱ £3.50 (ch £1.80, concessions £2.60). Prices & opening times relate to 2004, for further details phone or log onto www.english-heritage.org.uk/visits **Facilities:** 🅿 ✱ ▯

FAVERSHAM   Map 05 TR06
FLEUR DE LIS HERITAGE CENTRE
10-13 Preston St ME13 8NS
➲ (3 minutes drive from M2 junct 6)
☎ 01795 534542
e-mail: faversham@btinternet.com   **2 for 1**
Recently expanded and updated, and housed in 16th-century premises, the Centre features colourful displays and room settings that vividly evoke the 2000 year history of Faversham. Special features include the 'Gunpowder Experience' and a working old-style village telephone exchange, one of only two remaining in Britain. In July, during the Faversham Open House Scheme, over 20 historic properties in the town are opened to the public.
Times: Open all year, Mon-Sat, 10-4; Sun 10-1. **Fee:** £2 (ch & pen £1)
Facilities: 🅿 (200yds) ↯ toilets for disabled shop ➡

GILLINGHAM   Map 05 TQ76
ROYAL ENGINEERS MUSEUM
Prince Arthur Rd ME4 4UG
➲ (follow brown signs from Gillingham & Chatham town centres)
☎ 01634 822839   🖅 01634 822371   **2 for 1**
e-mail: mail@re-museum.co.uk
The museum covers the diverse and sometimes surprising work of the Royal Engineers. Learn about the first military divers, photographers, aviators and surveyors; see memorabilia relating to General Gordon and Field Marshal Lord Kitchener, Wellington's battle map from Waterloo and a Harrier jump-jet. The superb medal displays include 26 Victoria Crosses.
Times: Open all year, Tue-Fri 9-5, Sat-Sun & BH Mon 11.30-5. (Closed Good Fri, Xmas week & 1 Jan). **Fee:** ✱ £5.50 (ch, pen & UB40s £2.75). **Facilities:** 🅿 ↯ (help available if required, chair lift to upper level) toilets for disabled shop ✱ (ex guide dogs) ➡

GOUDHURST Map 05 TQ73

FINCHCOCKS

TN17 1HH

➲ (off A262)

☎ **01580 211702** 🖹 **01580 211007**

e-mail: katrina@finchcocks.co.uk

This fine early Georgian house stands in a spacious park with a beautiful garden, and contains an outstanding collection of keyboard instruments from the 17th century onwards. They have been restored to playing condition, and there are musical tours on all open days and private visits. Visually handicapped visitors may touch the instruments as well as hear them.

Times: Open Etr-Sep, Sun & BH Mon 2-6; Aug, Wed, Thu & Sun only 2-6. Private groups on other days by appointment Apr-Oct.

Facilities: 🅿 💻 ✕ licensed ♿ (wheelchair available) toilets for disabled shop garden centre 🐕 (ex guide dogs)

GROOMBRIDGE PLACE Map 05 TQ53

GROOMBRIDGE PLACE GARDENS & ENCHANTED FOREST

TN3 9QG

➲ (turn off A264 onto B2110 0.5m from Langton Green. Follow signs to Groombridge. Entrance at bottom of Groombridge Hill in Groombridge village)

☎ **01892 861444 (office) & 863999 (info line)**

🖹 **01892 863996**

e-mail: office@groombridge.co.uk

These award winning gardens, set in 200 acres, feature magnificent walled gardens and herbaceous borders, rose gardens, secret gardens, drunken topiary and much more, against the romantic backdrop of a 17th century moated manor. In the ancient woodland of the 'Enchanted Forest' there's mystery, innovation and excitement for all ages.

continued

Groombridge Place Gardens & Enchanted Forest

Times: ✱ Open 21 Mar-5 Nov, daily 9.30-6. **Fee:** £8.50 (ch 3-12 £7, pen £7.20). Family ticket (2 ad & 2 ch) £29.50. Groups 20+ available on request. **Facilities:** 🅿 💻 ♿ (ramps, canal boat) toilets for disabled shop 🐕 (ex guide/hearing dogs) 🍴

See advertisement on this page

HAWKINGE Map 05 TR23

KENT BATTLE OF BRITAIN MUSEUM

Aerodrome Rd CT18 7AG

➲ (off A260, 1m along Aerodrome road)

☎ **01303 893140**

e-mail: kentbattleofbritainmuseum@btinternet.com

Once a Battle of Britain Station, today it houses the largest collection of relics and related memorabilia of British and

continued

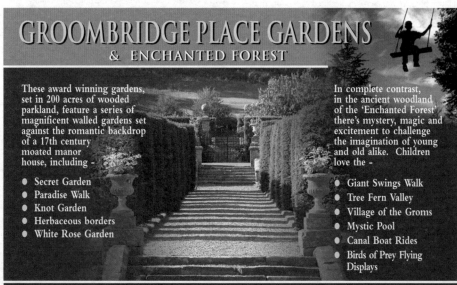

German aircraft involved in the fighting. Also shown full-size replicas of the Hurricane, Spitfire and Me109 used in Battle of Britain films. The year 2000 was the 60th anniversary of the Battle of Britain and a new memorial has been dedicated. Artefacts on show, recovered from over 600 battle of Britain aircraft all form a lasting memorial to all those involved in the conflict.

Times: ✱ Open Etr-Sep, daily 10-5; Oct, daily 11-4. Last admission 1 hour before closing. **Facilities:** 🅿 💭 ⑤ shop ✖ (ex guide dogs)

HEVER   Map 05 TQ44

HEVER CASTLE & GARDENS
TN8 7NG
➲ (M25 junct 5 or 6, 3m SE of Edenbridge, off B2026)
☎ 01732 865224 📠 01732 866796
e-mail: mail@hevercastle.co.uk

This enchanting, double-moated, 13th-century castle was the childhood home of Anne Boleyn. Restored by the American millionaire William Waldorf Astor at the beginning of the 20th century, it shows superb Edwardian craftsmanship. Astor also transformed the grounds, creating topiary, a yew maze, 35 acre lake and Italian gardens filled with antique sculptures. There is also a 100 metre herbaceous border, 'splashing' water maze' on the Sixteen Acre Island, as well as a woodland walk known as Sunday Walk. Adventure play area with new Henry VIII's Tower Maze.

Times: Open Mar-Nov, daily. Castle 12-6, Gardens 11-6. Last admission 5pm. (Closes 4pm Mar & Nov). **Fee:** ✱ Castle & Gardens £8.80 (ch 5-14 £4.80, pen £7.40). Family ticket £22.40. Gardens only £7 (ch 5-14 £4.60, pen £6). Family ticket £18.60. Party 15+.
Facilities: 🅿 💭 ✖ licensed ⑤ (wheelchairs available, book in advance) toilets for disabled shop garden centre ◀

HYTHE   Map 05 TR13

ROMNEY, HYTHE & DYMCHURCH RAILWAY
TN28 8PL
➲ (off M20 junct 11, off A259 signed New Romney)
☎ 01797 362353 & 363256 📠 01797 363591
e-mail: rhdr@romneyrail.fsnet.co.uk

The world's smallest public railway has its headquarters here. The concept of two enthusiasts coincided with Southern Railway's plans for expansion, and so the thirteen-and-a-half mile stretch of 15 inch gauge railway came into

continued

being, running from Hythe through New Romney and Dymchurch to Dungeness Lighthouse.

Romney, Hythe & Dymchurch Railway

Times: Open daily Etr-Sep, also wknds in Mar & Oct. For times apply to: The Manager, RH & DR., New Romney, Kent.
Facilities: 🅿 (charged) 💭 ⑤ (stairlift to Toy & Model Museum) toilets for disabled shop (Dymchurch & Dungeness high season only) ◀

IGHTHAM   Map 05 TQ55

IGHTHAM MOTE
TN15 0NT
➲ (2.5m S off A227, 6m E of Sevenoaks)
☎ 01732 810378 & 811145 (info line)
📠 01732 811029
e-mail: igthammote@nationaltrust.org.uk

This moated manor house, nestling in a sunken valley, dates from 1330. The main features of the house span many centuries and include the Great Hall, old chapel and crypt, Tudor chapel with painted ceiling, drawing room with Jacobean fireplace, frieze and 18th century handpainted Chinese wallpaper and the billiards room. There is an extensive garden as well as interesting walks in the surrounding woodland.

Times: Open Apr-Nov, daily ex Tue & Sat, 10-5.30. Open Good Fri. Last admission 5pm. **Fee:** ✱ £6.50 (ch £3). Family ticket £16.50.
Facilities: 🅿 💭 ✖ licensed ⑤ (wheelchairs, special parking ask at office, virtual tour) toilets for disabled shop ✖ (ex hearing guide dogs) ⚐

LAMBERHURST   Map 05 TQ63

BAYHAM ABBEY
TN3 8DE
➲ (off B2169, 2m W in East Sussex)
☎ 01892 890381

Explore the romantic ruins of this 13th-century abbey built by French monks in an 18th-century landscaped setting.
Times: Open Apr-Sep, daily 10-5. Closed Oct-Mar. **Fee:** ✱ £3 (ch £1.50, concessions £2.30). Prices & opening times relate to 2004, for further details phone or log onto www.english-heritage.org.uk/visits
Facilities: 🅿 ⑤ ⚏

SCOTNEY CASTLE GARDEN
TN3 8JN
➲ (1m S, of Lamberhurst on A21)
☎ 01892 891081   ▤ 01892 890110
e-mail: scotneycastle@nationaltrust.org.uk

The beautiful gardens at Scotney were planned in the 19th century around the remains of the old, moated Scotney Castle. There is something to see at every time of year, with spring flowers followed by rhododendrons, azaleas and a mass of roses, and then superb autumn colours. Estate walks all year through 770 acres of woodlands and meadows, walker's guide available.

Times: Garden: Apr-end Oct. Old Castle: May-mid Sep, Wed-Sun, 11-6 or sunset if earlier. BH Mon 11-6. (Closed Good Fri). Last admission 1hr before closing. **Fee:** Telephone for details.
Facilities: 🅿 ♿ (wheelchair hire, Braille/large print guidebook, audio tape) toilets for disabled shop garden centre small plant stand ✻ (ex guide & hearing dogs) 🦮 🍴

LYDD   Map 05 TR02
RSPB NATURE RESERVE
Boulderwall Farm, Dungeness Rd TN29 9PN
➲ (off Lydd to Dungeness road, 1m SE of Lydd, follow tourist signs)
☎ 01797 320588   ▤ 01797 321962   `2 for 1`
e-mail: dungeness@rspb.org.uk

This coastal reserve comprises 2106 acres of shingle beach and flooded pits. An excellent place to watch breeding terns, gulls and other water birds. Wheatears, great crested and little grebes also nest here, and outside the breeding season there are large flocks of teals, shovelers, and goldeneyes, goosanders, smews and both Slavonian and red-necked grebes.

Times: Visitor Centre open all year, daily 10-5 (10-4 Nov-Feb). Reserve open all year, daily 9am-9pm (or sunset if earlier). (Closed 25-26 Dec). **Fee:** £3 (ch £1, concessions £2). **Facilities:** 🅿 ♿ (access by car to some hides) toilets for disabled shop ✻ (ex guide dogs) 🍴

LYMPNE   Map 05 TR13
PORT LYMPNE WILD ANIMAL PARK, MANSION & GARDEN
CT21 4PD
➲ (off M20 junct 11, follow brown tourist signs. Also follow brown tourist signs from A20 between Ashford and Folkestone)
☎ 01303 264647   ▤ 01303 264944
e-mail: info@howletts.net

A 400-acre wild animal park that houses hundreds of rare
continued

animals: Indian elephants, rhinos, wolves, bison, snow leopards, Siberian and Indian tigers, gorillas and monkeys. The mansion designed by Sir Herbert Baker is surrounded by 15 acres of spectacular gardens. Inside, the most notable features include the restored Rex Whistler Tent Room, Moroccan Patio and hexagonal library where the Treaty of Paris was signed after World War I. Visit the Spencer Roberts Mural room and the Martin Jordan animal mural room.

Times: ✱ Open all year, daily 10-6 (closes at dusk in summer), last admission 4.30pm summer, 3pm winter. (Closed 25 Dec).
Facilities: 🅿 🍴 ✗ licensed ♿ (very limited access for disabled, special route available) toilets for disabled shop garden centre (in season) ✻ 🍴

See advertisement on this page

MAIDSTONE   Map 05 TQ75
LEEDS CASTLE
ME17 1PL
➲ (7m E of Maidstone at junct 8 of M20/A20, clearly signposted)
☎ 01622 765400   ▤ 01622 735616
e-mail: enquiries@leeds-castle.co.uk

Set on two islands in the centre of a lake, Leeds Castle has been called the 'loveliest castle in the world', and was home to six medieval Queens of England, as well as being Henry VIII's Royal Palace. Among the treasures inside are many paintings, tapestries and furnishings. Attractions in the grounds include formal gardens, exotic aviary, dog collar museum, vineyard, woodland walks, toddlers play area, yew
continued

maze with secret underground grotto and daily falconry displays from April to September.

Leeds Castle

Times: Open daily, Mar-Oct 10-5 (Castle 11-5.30). Nov-Mar 10-3 (Castle 10-3). Closed 26 Jun; 3 Jul; 5 Nov; 25 Dec **Fee:** ✱ Mar-Oct, Castle, Park & Gardens, £12.50 (ch 4-15 £9, students & pen £11); Family ticket (2ad & 3ch) £39. Nov-Feb, Castle Park & gardens £10.50 (ch £7, students & pen £9). Family ticket £33 **Facilities:** 🅿 ⭕ ✖ licensed ♿ (Braille information, induction loops & wheelchair, lift) toilets for disabled shop garden centre 🐕 (ex guide dogs) 🍴

MAIDSTONE MUSEUM & BENTLIF ART GALLERY

Saint Faith's St ME14 1LH
➲ (close to County Hall & Maidstone E train stn)
☎ 01622 602838 🖩 01622 685022 FREE
e-mail: **alexgurr@maidstone.gov.uk**

Set in an Elizabethan manor house which has been much extended over the years, this museum houses an outstanding collection of fine and applied arts, including watercolours, furniture, ceramics, and a collection of Japanese art and artefacts. The museum of the Queen's Own Royal West Kent Regiment is also housed here. Please apply for details of temporary exhibitions, workshops etc.
Times: Open all year, Mon-Sat 10-5.15, Sun & BH Mon 11-4. (Closed 25-26 Dec). **Facilities:** 🅿 (150 mtrs) ⭕ ♿ shop 🐕 (ex guide dogs) 🍴

MUSEUM OF KENT LIFE

Lock Ln, Sandling ME14 3AU
➲ (from M20 junct 6 onto A229 Maidstone road, follow signs for Aylesford)
☎ 01622 763936 🖩 01622 662024
e-mail: **enquiries@museum-kentlife.co.uk**
Kent's award-winning open air museum is home to an outstanding collection of historic buildings which house exhibitions on life in Kent over the last 100 years. An early 20th-century village hall and reconstruction of cottages from the 17th & 20th-centuries are more recent buildings to be viewed.
Times: ✱ Open Feb-1 Nov, daily 10-5.30, in winter open every wknd 10-3. **Facilities:** 🅿 ⭕ ✖ licensed ♿ (wheelchairs available, ramps, transport available) toilets for disabled shop 🍴

TYRWHITT DRAKE MUSEUM OF CARRIAGES

The Archbishop's Stables, Mill St ME15 6YE
➲ (close to River Medway & Archbishops Palace, just off A229 in town centre)
☎ 01622 602838 🖩 01622 685022 FREE
e-mail: **museuminfo@maidstone.gov.uk**

The museum is home to a unique collection of horse-drawn vehicles and transport curiosities. More than 60 vehicles are on display, from grand carriages and ornate sleighs to antique sedan chairs and Victorian cabs, there is even an original ice-cream cart.
Times: Open Jul-mid Sep, 10.30-4.30 **Facilities:** 🅿 (50 yds) ♿ shop 🐕 (ex guide dogs)

MINSTER-IN-THANET   Map 05 TR36

MINSTER ABBEY

CT12 4HF
➲ (turn off A253 at Minster rdbt. Down the hill through the village. Turn left at St. Mary's Church).
☎ 01843 821254
One of the first nunneries in England was built on this site in the 7th century. Rebuilt in later centuries, it is still home to a religious community, run by Benedictine nuns. The ruins of the old abbey and the cloisters are open to the public. One wing dates back to 1027, and there is a 12th century carving of Christ.
Times: ✱ Open all year, May-Sep, Mon-Fri 11-12 & 2.30-4, Sat 11-12; Oct-Apr, Mon-Sat 11-12. **Facilities:** 🅿 ♿ toilets for disabled shop (ex guide dogs)

PENSHURST   Map 05 TQ54

PENSHURST PLACE & GARDENS

TN11 8DG

➲ (from M25 junct 5 take A21 Hastings road then exit at Hildenborough, then follow signs)

☎ 01892 870307   ▤ 01892 870866

e-mail: enquiries@penshurstplace.com

Built between 1340 and 1345, the original house is perfectly preserved. Enlarged by successive owners during the 15th, 16th and 17th centuries, the great variety of architectural styles creates a dramatic backdrop for the extensive collections of English, French and Italian furniture, tapestries and paintings. The chestnut-beamed Baron's Hall is the oldest and finest in the country, and the house is set in magnificent formal gardens. There is a toy museum, venture playground, woodland trail and 10 acres of walled formal gardens.

Times: Open: wknds from 5 Mar, daily from 19 Mar-30 Oct. Grounds open 10.30-6. House open noon-5.30 (4pm on Sat) **Fee:** ✱ House & Grounds £7(ch 5-16 £5, pen & students £6.50). Family £20. Grounds only £5.50 (ch 5-16 £4.50, pen & students £5) Family £17. Party 20+. Garden season ticket £35. **Facilities:** ▣ ✗ licensed ዸ (ramp into Barons Hall, Braille & large print guides) toilets for disabled shop ✖ (ex guide dogs) ▰

RAMSGATE   Map 05 TR36

MARITIME MUSEUM

Clock House, Pier Yard, Royal Harbour CT11 8LS

➲ (follow Harbour signs)

☎ 01843 587765 & 570622   `2 for 1`

▤ 01843 582359

e-mail: museum@ekmt.fsnet.co.uk

The Maritime Museum Ramsgate is housed in the early 19th-century Clock House, and contains four galleries depicting various aspects of the maritime heritage of the East Kent area. The adjacent restored dry dock and floating exhibits from the museum's historic ship collection include the steam tug *Cervia* and the Dunkirk little ship motor yacht *Sundowner*.

Times: Open Etr-Sep, Tue-Sun 10-5. Oct-Etr Thu-Sun 10-4.30.

Fee: ✱ Combined ticket for museum £1.50. (ch & pen 75p). Family £4.

Facilities: ▣ (charged) ዸ (restricted) shop ✖

RECULVER   Map 05 TR26

RECULVER TOWERS & ROMAN FORT

CT6 6SU

➲ (3m E of Herne Bay)

☎ 01227 740676   `FREE`

An imposing 12th-century landmark: twin towers and the walls of a Roman fort.

Times: Open any reasonable time. **Facilities:** ▣ ዸ (long slope from carpark to fort) ⚏

RICHBOROUGH   Map 05 TR36

RICHBOROUGH CASTLE

CT13 9JW

➲ (1.5m N of Sandwich off A257)

☎ 01304 612013

Explore the site of the first Roman landing in Britain and visit the museum with its collection of artefacts uncovered on site. See the remains of the huge triumphal arch, once 25 metres high.

Times: Open Apr-Sep, daily 10-6. **Fee:** ✱ £3.50 (ch £1.80, concessions £2.60). Prices & opening times relate to 2004, for further details phone or log onto www.english-heritage.org.uk/visits

Facilities: ▣ ዸ shop ⚏

ROCHESTER   Map 05 TQ76

GUILDHALL MUSEUM

High St ME1 1PY

➲ (follow signs from A2 to Rochester city centre, museum is at N end of High St)

☎ 01634 848717   ▤ 01634 832919   `FREE`

e-mail: guildhall.museum@medway.gov.uk

Housed in two adjacent buildings, one dating from 1687 and the other from 1909. The collections are arranged chronologically from Prehistory to the Victorian and Edwardian periods. They cover local history and archaeology, fine and decorative art. There is a gallery devoted to the prison hulks of the River Medway. The museum stages a regular programme of temporary exhibitions.

Times: Open all year, daily 10-4.30. Last admissions 4 (Closed Xmas & New Year). **Facilities:** ▣ (250 yds) ዸ shop ✖ (ex guide & hearing dogs)

ROCHESTER CASTLE

ME1 1SX

➲ (by Rochester Bridge, A2, junct 1 M2, junct 2 M25)

☎ 01634 402276

Built on the Roman City Wall, this Norman bishop's castle was a vital royal stronghold.

Times: Open all year, Apr-Sep, daily 10-6; Oct-Mar, daily 10-4. (Closed 24-26 Dec & 1 Jan). **Fee:** ✱ £4 (ch & concessions £3). Family £11. Prices & opening times relate to 2004, for further details phone or log onto www.english-heritage.org.uk/visits **Facilities:** shop ✖ ⚏

ROLVENDEN   Map 05 TQ83

C M BOOTH COLLECTION OF HISTORIC VEHICLES

Falstaff Antiques, 63 High St TN17 4LP
➲ (on A28, 3 miles from Tenterden)
☎ 01580 241234
e-mail: info@morganmuseum.co.uk   2 for 1

Not just vehicles, but various other items of interest connected with transport. There is a unique collection of three-wheel Morgan cars, dating from 1913, and the only known Humber tri-car of 1904, as well as a 1929 Morris van, a 1936 Bampton caravan, motorcycles and bicycles. There is also a toy and model car display.
Times: Open all year, Mon-Sat 10-5.30. (Closed 25-26 Dec). **Fee:** £2 (ch £1) **Facilities:** P (roadside) shop 🛒

SEVENOAKS   Map 05 TQ55

KNOLE

TN15 0RP
➲ (S end of Sevenoaks, E of A225)
☎ 01732 462100 & 450608 (info line)
📄 01732 465528
e-mail: knole@nationaltrust.org.uk

In the 15th century Thomas Bourchier, Archbishop of Canterbury, transformed Knole from a simple medieval manor house into a palace. A century later Henry VIII extended it to even grander proportions. In the middle of the 16th century Elizabeth I gave it to Thomas Sackville and the Sackvilles kept the house for ten generations.
Times: Open mid Mar-early Nov, Wed-Sun & BH, 11-4. **Fee:** ✱ £6 (ch £3). Deer Park free to pedestrians. Family ticket £15. Parking £2.50 per car. **Facilities:** P (charged) 🍴 & Audio loop/Braille guide, virtual tour toilets for disabled shop ✖ (ex guide dogs + in park) 🐾🛒

SISSINGHURST   Map 05 TQ73

SISSINGHURST CASTLE GARDEN

TN17 2AB
➲ (1m E of Sissinghurst village on A262)
☎ 01580 710700 📄 01580 710702
e-mail: sissinghurst@nationaltrust.org.uk

Made in the ruins of a large Elizabethan house and set in unspoilt countryside, Sissinghurst Castle Garden is one of the most celebrated gardens created by Vita Sackville-West and her husband Sir Harold Nicolson. Phone for details of special events.
Times: Open: Gardens 19 Mar-30 Oct, Mon, Tue & Fri 11-6.30, Sat, Sun & BH's 10-6.30 (last admission 5.30) closed Wed & Thu. Peace & Tranquillity after 3 **Fee:** ✱ £7 (ch £3.50) family £17.50 National Trust Members free **Facilities:** P ✖ licensed & (Admission restricted to 2 wheelchairs at any one time) toilets for disabled shop ✖ (ex guide dogs) 🐾🛒

> Are there any excellent Days Out that we've missed? Use the Readers' Report form at the back of the book to tell us about them.

SITTINGBOURNE   Map 05 TQ96

DOLPHIN SAILING BARGE MUSEUM

Crown Quay Ln ME10 3SN
➲ (N on A2, signed)
☎ 01795 421549 & 424132   2 for 1

The museum presents the history of the Thames spritsail sailing barge, many of which were built along the banks of Milton Creek. Tools of the trade, photographs and associated artefacts can be seen at the barge yard along with the sailing barge Cambria. Privately owned barges are repaired - there's a forge, shipwright's shop and sail loft. There are many fine models.
Times: Open Etr-Oct, Sun & BHs 11-5. May only, Sat 1-4. Other times by arrangement. **Fee:** ✱ £1.50 (concession £1).
Facilities: P & toilets for disabled shop

SMALLHYTHE   Map 05 TQ83

SMALLHYTHE PLACE

TN30 7NG
➲ (2m S of Tenterden, on E side of the Rye Road on B2082)
☎ 01580 762334 📄 01580 762334
e-mail: smallhytheplace.ntrust.org.uk

Once a Tudor harbour master's house, this half-timbered, 16th-century building was Dame Ellen Terry's last home, and is now a museum of Ellen Terry memorabilia. The barn is situated at the rear of the house and is open most days to view.
Times: Open 27 Mar-3 Nov, Sat-Wed 11-5, also Good Fri. Last admission 30 mins before closing. **Fee:** ✱ £3.75 (ch £1.80). Family ticket £9.30. **Facilities:** P & (album of descriptions & photos of upstairs, Braille guide) ✖ (ex guide dogs) 🐾

STROOD   Map 05 TQ76

DIGGERLAND NEW

Medway Valley Leisure Park ME2 2NU
➲ (M2 junct 2, follow A228 towards Rochester. At rdbt turn right. Diggerland on right)
☎ 08700 344437 📄 09012 010300
e-mail: mail@diggerland.com   2 for 1

An adventure park with a difference. Experience the thrills of driving real earth moving equipment. Choose from various types of diggers and dumpers ranging from 1 ton to 8.5 tons. Complete the Dumper Truck Challenge or dig for buried treasure supervised by an instructor. New rides include JCB Robots, the Supertrack, Landrover Safari and Spin Dizzy.
Times: 10-5 wknds, BH's & school hols **Fee:** £2.50 for all over 2yrs (pen £1.25) Additional charges to ride/drive real machinery
Facilities: P 🍴 & toilets for disabled shop ✖ guide dogs 🛒

SWINGFIELD MINNIS   Map 05 TR24

THE BUTTERFLY CENTRE

McFarlanes Garden Centre CT15 7HX
➲ (on A260 by junction with Elham-Lydden road)
☎ 01303 844244

A tropical greenhouse garden with scores of colourful free-flying butterflies from all over the world among exotic plants such as bougainvillea, oleander and banana. The temperate section houses British butterflies, with many favourite species and some rarer varieties.
Times: ✱ Open Apr-1 Oct, daily 10-5. Closed Easter Sunday.
Facilities: P 🍴 & shop garden centre ✖ (ex guide dogs) 🛒

TUNBRIDGE WELLS (ROYAL) Map 05 TQ53

TUNBRIDGE WELLS MUSEUM AND ART GALLERY

Civic Centre, Mount Pleasant TN1 1JN
➲ (adjacent to Town Hall, off A264)
☎ 01892 554171 & 526121   FREE
🖷 01892 534227

The museum displays local history, along with Tunbridge ware, archaeology, toys and dolls, and domestic and agricultural bygones. The art gallery has regularly changing art and craft exhibitions and touring displays from British and European museums.
Times: Open all year, daily 9.30-5. Sun 10-4 (Closed BHs & Etr Sat).
Facilities: 🅿 (200 yds) ⅋ parking adjacent to building shop ✕ (ex guide dogs)

UPNOR   Map 05 TQ77

UPNOR CASTLE

ME2 4XG
➲ (on unclass road off A228)
☎ 01634 718742 & 338110

16th-century gun fort built to protect Elizabeth I's warships. It saw action in 1667, when the Dutch navy sailed up the Medway to attack the dockyard at Chatham.
Times: Open Apr-Sep, daily 10-6; Oct, daily 10-4. **Fee:** ✱ Telephone for details of admission fees. **Facilities:** 🅿 ⅋ ✕ (ex on leads in certain areas) ✿

WESTERHAM   Map 05 TQ45

QUEBEC HOUSE

TN16 1TD
➲ (at E end of village on N side of A25 facing junct with B2026 Edenbridge Road.)
☎ 01892 890651   🖷 01892 890110
e-mail: chartwell@nationaltrust.org.uk

Westerham was the birthplace of General Wolfe, who spent his childhood in this multi-gabled, square brick house, now renamed Quebec House. The house probably dates from the 16th century and was extended and altered in the 17th century. It contains a Wolfe museum and an exhibition on Wolfe and the Quebec campaign.
Times: Open Apr-Oct, Tue & Sun only 2-5.30 (last admission 5.00pm). Parties by written arrangement. **Fee:** ✱ £3.00 (ch £1.50). Family ticket £7.50. Booked groups £2.50 **Facilities:** 🅿 (150m) ⅋ (tactile items) toilets for disabled ✕ (ex guide dogs) ✿

SQUERRYES COURT MANOR HOUSE & GARDENS

TN16 1SJ
➲ (0.5m W of town centre, signposted off A25)
☎ 01959 562345 & 563118   🖷 01959 565949
e-mail: squerryes.court@squerryes.co.uk

This beautiful manor house, built in 1681, has been the home of the Wardes since 1731. It contains a fine collection of pictures, furniture, porcelain and tapestries. The lovely garden was landscaped in the 18th century and has a lake, restored formal garden, and woodland walks.
Times: ✱ Open Apr-Sep, Wed, Sat, Sun & BH Mon's. Garden open 12-5.30, House 1.30-5.30 (last entry 5pm) **Facilities:** 🅿 ⏝ ⅋ (telephone in advance, part of grounds accessible) toilets for disabled shop ✕ (ex on leads in grounds)

WEST MALLING   Map 05 TQ65

ST LEONARD'S TOWER

ME19 6PE
➲ (on unclass road W of A228)
☎ 01732 870872   FREE

Early example of a Norman tower keep, built c.1080 by Gundulf, Bishop of Rochester. The tower stands almost to its original height and takes its name from a chapel dedicated to St Leonard that once stood nearby.
Times: Open any reasonable time for exterior viewing. Contact West Malling Parish Council for interior viewing - 01732 870872.
Facilities: ⅋ ✕ (ex dogs on leads) ✿

YALDING   Map 05 TQ75

YALDING ORGANIC GARDENS NEW

Benover Rd ME18 6EX
➲ (On B2162, 0.5m S of Yalding.)
☎ 01622 814650   🖷 01622 814650
e-mail: enquiry@hdra.org.uk

Fourteen gardens tell the history of gardening in an imaginatively landscaped setting. Travel through representations of ancient woodlands, medieval physic, knot and paradise gardens and a 19th-century artisan's plot, borders inspired by Gertrude Jekyll's ideas before reaching a 1950s 'Dig for Victory' allotment. The remainder of the garden is devoted to the vision of the 'organic' future of horticulture - including one of Britains largest pergolas, constructed of discarded hop poles.
Times: Apr & Oct wknds only; May-Sep Wed-Sun & BH's 10-5
Fee: ✱ £3.50 (ch free, concessions £3) **Facilities:** 🅿 ⏝ ⅋ shop garden centre ✕ (ex guide dogs)

LANCASHIRE

EVENTS & FESTIVALS

January
22nd-23rd Pigeon Racing: British Homing World Show of the Year, Winter Gardens & Opera House, Blackpool

March
25th-28th Burnley National Blues Festival, various venues
25th-28th Easter Maritime Festival, Lancaster

June
3rd-5th Clitheroe Great Days Festival, music to suit all tastes
19th Blackpool Marathon
24th-26th Chorley Folk Festival

July
15th-17th Saddleworth Folk Festival, Uppermill, Oldham
19th-21st New Alternative festival, Blackpool (punk, goth, ska etc)
19th-22nd Wasted, punk festival, Morecambe, various venues
tbc Glasson Festival, Glasson Docks, folk and traditional

August
29th Lancaster Georgian Festival & National Sedan Chair Carrying Championships
tbc Great British R&B Festival, Colne

September
1st-3rd Fylde 2005 (folk festival), Fleetwood
16th-19th Jazz Festival Lancaster (provisional)

November
tbc Fireworks Spectacular over historic Lancaster and Beacon Lighting
tbc Jacobite Day, Lancaster

December
tbc Annual Lancaster Festival of Christmas Trees

Above: Donkeys on Blackpool Beach

BLACKPOOL   Map 07 SD33

BLACKPOOL ZOO PARK
East Park Dr FY3 8PP
⮑ (M55 junct 4, follow brown tourist signs)
☎ 01253 830830   🖷 01253 830800
e-mail: info@blackpoolzoo.freeserve.co.uk
This modern zoo, built in 1972, houses over 1500 animals within its 32 acres of landscaped gardens. There is a miniature railway, lots of close encounters and animals in action, a children's play area, animal feeding times and keeper talks throughout the day.
Times: Open all year daily, summer 10-6; winter 10-5 or dusk. (Closed 25 Dec). **Fee:** ✱ £8.50 (ch £6.50). Family (2 ad & 2 ch) £26, (2 ad & 3 ch) £31. Concessions for seniors, disabled people, carers and groups are available. **Facilities:** 🅿 ⬛ ✕ licensed ♿ (wheelchair loan, Braille factsheets, sensory experiences) toilets for disabled shop ✖ 🍴

CHARNOCK RICHARD   Map 07 SD51

CAMELOT THEME PARK
PR7 5LP
⮑ (from M6 junct 27/28, or M61 junct 8 follow brown tourism signs)
☎ 01257 453044   🖷 01257 452320   **2 for 1**
e-mail: kingarthur@camelotthemepark.co.uk

Join Merlin, King Arthur and the Knights of the Round Table at the magical kingdom of Camelot. Explore five magic lands filled with thrilling rides, spectacular shows, and many more attractions. From white-knuckle thrills on The Whirlwind spinning rollercoaster, to wet-knuckle thrills on Pendragon's Plunge, there's something for everyone.
Times: Open Etr-Oct. Telephone for further details. **Fee:** ✱ £15 (ch over 1mtr £12, under 1mtr free, pen & disabled £11)
Facilities: 🅿 ⬛ ♿ (disabled car parking) toilets for disabled shop ✖ (ex guide dogs) 🍴

CHORLEY   Map 07 SD51

ASTLEY HALL MUSEUM & ART GALLERY
Astley Park PR7 1NP
⮑ (2m W of Chorley off A581 Southport road)
☎ 01257 515555   🖷 01257 515556   **FREE**
e-mail: astleyhall@lineone.net
A charming Tudor/Stuart building set in beautiful parkland, this lovely Hall retains a comfortable 'lived-in' atmosphere. There are pictures and pottery to see, as well as fine furniture and rare plasterwork ceilings.
Times: Open Apr-Sep, Sat-Sun 12-5; By appointment only during the week **Facilities:** 🅿 ♿ (video of upper floors, print/Braille guide, CD audio guide) shop ✖ (ex guide dogs) 🍴

CLITHEROE　　　　　　Map 07 SD74

CLITHEROE CASTLE MUSEUM

Castle Gate, Castle St BB7 1BA

➲ (follow Clitheroe signs from A59 Preston-Skipton by-pass. Museum located in castle grounds near town centre).

☎ 01200 424635

e-mail: museum@ribblevalley.gov.uk

`2 for 1`

The museum has a good collection of carboniferous fossils, and items of local interest. Displays include local history and the industrial archaeology of the Ribble Valley, while special features include the restored Hacking ferry boat believed to be the inspiration for "Buckleberry Ferry" featured in JRR Tolkien's *Fellowship of the Ring*, printer's and clogger's shops and Edwardian kitchen. The area is renowned for its early 17th-century witches, and the museum has a small display on witchcraft.

Times: Open 11-4.30; late Feb-Etr, Sat-Wed; Etr-Oct, daily inc BH; Nov, Dec & Feb, wknds & school half terms. (Closed Jan) **Fee:** ✱ £1.70 (ch 25p, pen 85p). Family ticket £3.65 **Facilities:** P (500yds) (disabled only parking at establishment) ⬤ & shop ✳ (ex guide dogs)

LANCASTER　　　　　　Map 07 SD46

CITY MUSEUM (ALSO 15 CASTLE HILL)

Market Sq LA1 1HT

➲ (In city centre just off A6)

☎ 01524 64637　🖷 01524 841692

e-mail: paul.thompson@mus.lancscc.gov.uk

The fine Georgian town hall is the setting for the museum, which explores the history and archaeology of the city from prehistoric and Roman times onwards. Also housed here is the museum of the King's Own Royal Lancaster Regiment. The Cottage Museum, furnished in the style of an artisan's house of around 1820, faces Lancaster Castle.

Times: ✱ Open all year, Mon-Sat 10-5, (Closed 25 Dec-1 Jan). 15 Castle Hill, Etr-Sep, daily 2-5. **Facilities:** P (5 mins walk) & (ramp to entrance/ground floor, 2 stairlifts) shop ✳ (ex guide dogs)

LANCASTER MARITIME MUSEUM

St George's Quay LA1 1RB

➲ (close to M6, junct 33 & 34. From A6 follow signs to Lancaster town centre)

☎ 01524 64637　🖷 01524 841692

e-mail: paul.thompson@mus.lancscc.gov.uk

Graceful Ionic columns adorn the front of the Custom House, built in 1764. Inside, the histories of the 18th-century transatlantic maritime trade of Lancaster, the Lancaster Canal and the fishing industry of Morecambe Bay are well illustrated.

Times: ✱ Open all year, daily, Etr-Oct 11am-5pm; Nov-Etr 12.30-4pm.

Facilities: P ⬤ & (ramped access, lift to all floors, ground floor entry) toilets for disabled shop ✳ (ex guide dogs)

SHIRE HALL

Lancaster Castle, Castle Pde LA1 1YJ

➲ (follow brown tourist signs from M6 junct 33/34)

☎ 01524 64998　🖷 01524 847914

e-mail: christine.goodier@mus.lancscc.gov.uk

Founded on the site of three Roman forts, Lancaster Castle dominates Castle Hill, above the River Lune. The Norman keep was built in about 1170 and King John added a curtain wall and Hadrian's Tower. The Shire Hall, noted for its Gothic revival design, contains a splendid display of heraldry. The Crown Court was notorious as having handed out the greatest number of death sentences of any court in the land.

Times: Open daily ex Xmas/New Year 10.30 (1st tour)-4 (last tour). Court sittings permitting - it is advisable to telephone before visiting. **Fee:** ✱ £4 (ch, pen & students £2.50). Family ticket £11.

Facilities: P (100mtrs) (voucher system) & shop ✳ (ex guide dogs) ◼

LEIGHTON HALL　　　　　Map 07 SD47

LEIGHTON HALL

LA5 9ST

➲ (off M6 at junct 35 onto A6 & follow signs)

☎ 01524 734474　🖷 01524 720357

e-mail: info@leightonhall.co.uk

`2 for 1`

Early Gillow furniture is displayed among other treasures in the fine interior of this neo-Gothic mansion. Outside a large collection of birds of prey can be seen, and flying displays are given each afternoon. There are also fine gardens, a maze and a woodland walk.

Times: Open May-Sep, Sun, Tue-Fri & BH Mon from 2pm. For Aug only open from 12.30. (Last admission 4.30pm). **Fee:** ✱ £5 (ch 5-16 £3.50, pen & student £4.50). Family ticket £15. **Facilities:** P ⬤ & toilets for disabled shop garden centre ✳ (ex guide dogs & in park)

LEYLAND　　　　　　Map 07 SD52

BRITISH COMMERCIAL VEHICLE MUSEUM

King St PR5 1LE

➲ (0.75m from M6, junct 28 in town centre)

☎ 01772 451011　🖷 01772 623404

A unique line-up of historic commercial vehicles and buses spanning a century of truck and bus building. There are more than 50 exhibits on permanent display.

Times: Open Apr-Sep, Sun, Tue-Thu & BH Mons (Oct open Sun only).

Fee: £4 (ch & pen £2). Family ticket (2 ad & 3 ch) £10.

Facilities: P ⬤ & (ramps to decked viewing area) toilets for disabled shop ✳ (ex guide dogs)

MARTIN MERE   Map 07 SD41
WWT MARTIN MERE
L40 0TA

⮑ (signposted from M61, M58 &M6, 6m from Ormskirk, off A59)

☎ 01704 895181   🖷 01704 892343   **2 for 1**

e-mail: info@martinmere.co.uk

One of Britain's most important wetland sites, where you can get really close to a variety of ducks, geese and swans from all over the world as well as two flocks of flamingos. Thousands of wildfowl, including pink-footed geese, Bewick's and Whooper swans, winter here. Other features include a children's adventure playground, exhibition gallery, craft area and an educational centre. The Annual North West Bird Fair takes place during November and wild swans by floodlight from 1st November to 31st January.

Times: Open all year, daily 9.30-5.30 (5 in winter). (Closed 25 Dec). **Fee:** £5.75 (ch £3.75, concession £4.75). Family ticket £15. £1 off each for group members **Facilities:** 🅿 💭 ⑆ (wheelchair loan, Braille trail, heated hide, audio tours) toilets for disabled shop
🐾 (ex guide dogs) 🍴

PADIHAM   Map 07 SD73
GAWTHORPE HALL
BB12 8UA

⮑ (off A671)

☎ 01282 771004   🖷 01282 770178

e-mail: rpmgaw@smtp.ntrust.org.uk

An early 17th-century manor house, built around Britain's most southerly pele tower, restored in 1850. A collection of portraits from the National Portrait Gallery and the Kay Shuttleworth Collections of costume, embroidery and lace are on show in the expanded exhibition areas.

Times: Open Apr-2 Nov, Garden: daily 10-6. Hall: Tue-Thu, Sat & Sun 1-5. Also open BH Mons & Good Fri. (Last admission 4.30). **Fee:** ✱ House: £3 (ch & con £1.50). Garden free. **Facilities:** 🅿 💭 ⑆ level entrance to shop, photo album toilets for disabled shop 🐾 (ex in grounds) 🐕

PRESTON   Map 07 SD52
HARRIS MUSEUM & ART GALLERY
Market Square PR1 2PP

⮑ (exit M6 at junct 31, follow signs for Preston city centre, park at bus stn car park)

☎ 01772 258248   🖷 01772 886764   **FREE**

e-mail: harris.museum@preston.gov.uk

An impressive grade 1 listed Greek Revival building containing extensive collections of fine and decorative art including a gallery of Clothes and Fashion. The Story of Preston covers the city's history and the lively exhibition programmes of contemporary art and social history are accompanied by events and activities throughout the year.

Times: Open all year, Mon-Sat 10-5, Sun 11-4. (Closed BHs). **Facilities:** 🅿 (5 mins walk) (blue badge disabled parking only) 💭 ⑆ (Wheelchair available. Chair lift to mezzanine galleries) toilets for disabled shop 🐾 (ex guide/assistance dogs) 🍴

THE NATIONAL FOOTBALL MUSEUM
Sir Tom Finney Way, Deepdale PR1 6RY

⮑ (2m from M6 juncts 31, 31A or 32. Follow brown tourist signs in Preston)

☎ 01772 908442   🖷 01772 908433   **FREE**

e-mail: enquiries@nationalfootballmuseum.com

What location could be more fitting for a National Football Museum than Deepdale Stadium, the home of Preston North End, first winners of the professional football league in 1888-9? This fascinating trip through football past and present includes the FIFA Museum Collection, a fine display of memorabilia and artefacts; interactive displays that allow visitors to commentate on matches, and take virtual trips to every League ground in the country; and an art gallery dedicated to the Beautiful Game.

Times: Open Tue-Sat 10-5, Sun 11-5. (Closed Mon ex BHs). Contact for opening times on match days. **Facilities:** 🅿 💭 ⑆ (Lifts, multi-sensory exhibitions) toilets for disabled shop
🐾 (ex guide dogs) 🍴

ROSSENDALE   Map 07 SD72
WHITAKER PARK & ROSSENDALE MUSEUM
Whitaker Park, Haslingden Rd, Rawtenstall BB4 6RE

⮑ (off A681, 0.25m W of Rawtenstall centre)

☎ 01706 244682   **FREE**

🖷 01706 250037

e-mail: rossendalemuseum@btconnect.com

Former mill owner's house, built in 1840 and set in the delightful Whitaker Park. Displays include fine and decorative arts, a Victorian drawing room, natural history, costume, local and social history and regular temporary exhibitions.

Times: Closed for refurbishment until mid-Feb 2005. From then open Sun/Wed/Thu 1-4.30, phone to verify **Facilities:** 🅿 ⑆ (large print, audio guides, induction loop, lift) toilets for disabled shop
🐾 (ex guide dogs)

RUFFORD   Map 07 SD41
RUFFORD OLD HALL
L40 1SG

⮑ (From M6 junct 27 take A59, follow signs to Rufford. E of A59 in Village of Rufford 7m North of Ormskirk)

☎ 01704 821254   🖷 01704 82323

e-mail: ruffordoldhall@nationaltrust.org.uk

There is a story that William Shakespeare performed here for the owner Sir Thomas Hesketh in the magnificent Great Hall. Built in 1530, Rufford remained in the Hesketh family for over 400 years. The Carolean Wing, altered in 1821, features fine collections of 16th and 17th century oak furniture, arms, armour and tapestries.

Times: Open 3 Apr-27 Oct, Sat-Wed. Hall 1-5 (last admission 4.30pm). Garden, restaurant & shop 11-5. **Fee:** ✱ House and garden: £4.50 (ch £2). Family ticket £11. Groups £2.75 each (ch £1). Garden only £2.50 (ch £1). No groups Sun and BH Mon. **Facilities:** 🅿 ✕ licensed ⑆ (Braille guide, wheelchairs, large print guide) toilets for disabled shop 🐕

SAMLESBURY   Map 07 SD53

SAMLESBURY HALL
Preston New Rd PR5 OUP
➲ (M6 junct 31/A677 for 3m, as indicated by brown tourist signs)
☎ 01254 812010 & 812229   `2 for 1`
🖷 01254 812174
e-mail: samlesburyhall@btconnect.co.uk

A well restored half-timbered manor house, built during the 14th and 15th centuries, and set in 5 acres of beautiful grounds. Sales of antiques and collector's items, craft shows and temporary exhibitions are held all year round. Live theatre productions and seasonal events throughout the year.
Times: Open all year, daily, 11-4.30. Closed 25-26 Dec and on Sat for weddings **Fee:** ✻ £3 (ch 4-16 £1). **Facilities:** 🅿 💺 ✗ licensed ♿ toilets for disabled garden centre ✗ (ex guide dogs) 🖶

SILVERDALE   Map 07 SD47

RSPB NATURE RESERVE
Myers Farm LA5 0SW
➲ (M6 junct 35, head west on A501(M) for 0.5m to end. Turn right and head N on A6. Follow brown tourist signs)
☎ 01524 701601   🖷 01524 701601   `2 for 1`
e-mail: leighton.moss@rspb.org.uk
A large reed swamp with meres with willow and alder scrub in a valley with woodland on its limestone slopes. The reserve covers 321 acres, and is home to the North West's largest concentration of bitterns, together with bearded tits, reed, sedge and grasshopper warblers, shovelers, pochards, tufted ducks and marsh harriers. Black terns and ospreys regularly pass through in spring and greenshanks and various sandpipers in the autumn. Wintering wildfowl include large flocks of mallards, teals, wigeons, and shovelers.
Times: Reserve: open daily 9am-Dusk (or sunset if earlier). Visitor Centre daily 9.30-5. Feb-Oct 9.30-4.30 Nov-Jan. Closed 25 Dec.
Fee: ✻ £4.50 (ch £1, concessions £3) Family £9. RSPB members Free
Facilities: 🅿 💺 ✗ ♿ (Stairlift available to tea room) toilets for disabled shop ✗ (ex guide dogs) 🖶

WATERSLACK FARM, CAFE & GARDEN CENTRE
Ford Lane, LA5 OUH
➲ (M6 junct 35, follow A6 towards Milnthorpe. Turn off A6 at Nineteen Acre Lane & follow signs for Leighton Moss Nature Reserve. Pass Reserve, turn right at T-junct & follow signs)
☎ 01524 701255   🖷 01524 701255
e-mail: welcome@waterslack.com

With a beautiful plant section, unique Vesage arts and crafts collection, freshly made foods and stunning surroundings, Waterslack offers everything for your perfect day out. Come and see the sheep, geese, chickens, ducks and many other animals or enjoy a walk through one of the nature reserves around Waterslack.
Times: Open Apr-Sep Mon, Wed, Fri & Sat 9.30-6, Tue & Thu 9-5, Sun 10-5; Oct-Mar Mon-Sat 9.30-5, Sun 10.30-5 **Fee:** Free admission
Facilities: 🅿 💺 ♿ Disabled access ground floor and grounds only 🖶

TURTON BOTTOMS   Map 07 SD71

TURTON TOWER
BL7 OHG
➲ (on B6391, off A666 or A676)
☎ 01204 852203   🖷 01204 853759
e-mail: turton.tower@mus.lanscc.gov.uk
A historic house incorporating a 15th-century tower house and Elizabethan half-timbered buildings, and displaying a major collection of carved wood furniture. During the 19th century, the house became associated with the Gothic revival and later typified the idealism of the Arts and Crafts movement. The gardens are being restored in late-Victorian style. The exhibition gallery houses three exhibitions per season, usually consisting of one high profile, one by regional artists and finally a touring show from elsewhere in the country.
Times: ✻ Open May-Sep, Mon-Thu 11-5, wknds 1-5; Mar-Oct, Mon-Wed 1-5, wknds 1-4; Apr Sat-Wed 1-5; Nov & Feb, Sun 1-4. Other times by prior arrangement. **Facilities:** 🅿 💺 ♿ toilets for disabled shop ✗ (ex in grounds) 🖶

WHALLEY   Map 07 SD73

WHALLEY ABBEY
BB7 9SS

➲ (Just off A59 4m S of Clitheroe).
☎ 01254 828400   🖶 01254 828401
e-mail: office@whalleysbbey.org

The ruins of a 14th-century Cistercian abbey, set in the delightful gardens of the Blackburn Diocesan Retreat and Conference House, a 17th-century manor house with gardens reaching down to the River Calder. The remains include two gateways, a chapter house and the abbot's lodgings and kitchen.

Times: Open from 5 Jan daily 10-5 (closed around Xmas/New Year)
Fee: £2 (ch 50p, pen £1.25) Family (2 ad + children) £4.50
Facilities: 🅿 💺 ✗ licensed & (chair lifts, ramps) toilets for disabled shop ✕ (ex guide dogs)

Above: The Ashton Memorial, William Park

LEICESTERSHIRE

EVENTS & FESTIVALS

February
11th-20th Comedy Festival, Leicester

May
1st-2nd Leicestershire County Show, Dishley Grange, Loughborough
21st-11th Jun Leicester Early Music Festival

June
17th-26th International Music Festival, Leicester
tbc Leicester Pride, events, city centre parade and park site festival

July
9th Belgrave Mela, Abbey Park, Leicester

August
5th-7th Leicestershire Country Music Festival, Sapcote Playing Fields (provisional)
tbc Abbey Park Music Festival, Leicester
tbc Caribbean Carnival, Victoria Park, Leicester
tbc Castle Park Festival, Leicester
tbc City of Leicester Horticultural Show

September
Riverside Festival, Bede Park, boat trips, live music, stalls and events

October
tbc Dashera, Hindu festival
tbc Navrati, Asian religious festival

November
tbc Abbey Park Bonfire & Fireworks Display
tbc Diwali Celebrations, Leicester

Above: Hose

ASHBY-DE-LA-ZOUCH   Map 08 SK31

ASHBY-DE-LA-ZOUCH CASTLE
South St LE65 1BR
☎ 01530 413343
Impressive ruins of a late medieval castle. The magnificent 24 metre Hastings Tower offers panoramic views of the surrounding countryside. Ashby was used for the famous jousting scene in Sir Walter Scott's classic romance *Ivanhoe*.
Times: Open Apr-Jun & Sep-Oct, Thu-Mon 10-5; Jul-Aug, daily 10-6; Nov-Mar, Thu-Mon 10-4. (Closed 24-26 Dec & 1 Jan). **Fee:** ✱ £3.20 (ch £1.60, concessions £2.40). Prices & opening times relate to 2004, for further details phone or log onto www.english-heritage.org.uk/visits
Facilities: 🅿 & shop ⌗

BELVOIR   Map 08 SK83

BELVOIR CASTLE
NG32 1PD
➲ (between A52 & A607, follow the brown heritage signs from A1, A52, A607 & A46)
☎ 01476 871002 📠 01476 871018
e-mail: info@belvoircastle.com
Although Belvoir Castle has been the home of the Dukes of Rutland for many centuries, the turrets, battlements, towers and pinnacles of the house are a 19th-century fantasy. Amongst the many treasures to be seen inside are paintings by Murillo, Holbein and other famous artists. Also here is the museum of the Queens Royal Lancers. Lovingly restored gardens are also open to visitors. Special events planned every weekend throughout the season, phone for details.
Times: Open 16-20 Feb; Apr-Sep, daily (closed Mon & Thu); Mar & Oct Sun only. **Fee:** ✱ £9 (ch £7 pen £8). **Facilities:** 🅿 🍽 ✗ licensed & (permitted to be driven/drive right up to castle entrance) toilets for disabled shop ✖ (ex guide dogs) ◀

CASTLE DONINGTON   Map 08 SK42

DONINGTON GRAND PRIX COLLECTION
Donington Park DE74 2RP
➲ (2m from M1 junct 23a/24 and M42/A42 close to Nottingham Derby and Leicester)
☎ 01332 811027 📠 01332 812829
e-mail: enquiries@doningtoncollection.co.uk
From the turn of the twentieth century to the new millennium, it's all here. The largest collection of McLaren racing cars on public display. The world's only complete collection of the famous Racing Green Vanwalls, every William F1 car from 1983 to 1999, a superb BRM display, more rare four wheel drive racing cars than you'll see anywhere else, Ferraris driven by Asvar; and Ickx, Senna's winning McLaren from the 1993 European Grand Prix at Donington, Stirling Moss's Lotus which defeated the might of the works Ferraris at Monaco in 1961, Jim Clark's beautiful Lotus 25, Ronnie Peterson's Unique six wheel Tyrell, together with several other examples of his famous marque-including Jacky Stewart's Tyrell 001, they're all here, and many, many more.
Times: ✱ Open daily 10-5 (last admission 4pm). Open later on race days. (Closed over Xmas period - telephone to confirm opening times over this period). **Facilities:** 🅿 🍽 ✗ licensed & shop ✖ (ex guide dogs) ◀

COALVILLE   Map 08 SK41

SNIBSTON DISCOVERY PARK
Ashby Rd LE67 3LN
➲ (4.5m from M1 junct 22/2m or from A42/M42 junct 13 on A511 on the West side of Coalville)
☎ 01530 278444 📠 01530 813301   **2 for 1**
e-mail: snibston@leics.gov.uk
At Leicestershire's all-weather science and industry museum, visitors can try over 50 hands-on experiments, or explore our rich heritage in the Transport, Extractive, Engineering and Textile and Fashion Galleries. Ex-miners give tours of Snibston's colliery buildings, and kids can let off steam in the outdoor science and water playgrounds.
Times: Open daily, 10-5 (Closed 1 week in Jan & Christmas period).
Fee: ✱ £5.70 (ch £3.60, concessions £3.90). Family ticket £17.50. Party.
Facilities: 🅿 🍽 & (Braille labels, touch tables, parking available) toilets for disabled shop ✖ (ex guide dogs) ◀

DONINGTON-LE-HEATH   Map 05 SK41

DONINGTON-LE-HEATH MANOR HOUSE
Manor Rd LE67 2FW
➲ (S of Coalville)
☎ 01530 831259 📠 01530 831259   **FREE**
e-mail: museum@leics.gov.uk
This is a rare example of a medieval manor house, tracing its history back to about 1280. It has now been restored as a period house, with fine oak furnishings. The surrounding grounds include period gardens, and the adjoining stone barn houses a restaurant.
Times: Open Apr-Sep, 11-5; Oct, Nov & Mar 11-3. Dec-Feb wknds only
Facilities: 🅿 🍽 ✗ & toilets for disabled shop ✖ (ex guide dogs)

LEICESTER   Map 04 SK50

ABBEY PUMPING STATION
Corporation Rd, Abbey Ln LE4 5PX
➲ (off A6, 1m N from city centre)
☎ 0116 299 5111 📠 0116 299 5125
Built as a sewage pumping station in 1891, this fascinating museum features some of the largest steam beam engines in the country, and an exhibition on the history and technology of toilets, water and hygiene. There are also a steam shovel and a passenger carrying a narrow gauge railway.
Times: Open Apr-Sep, Mon-Sat 10-5, Sun 1-5; Oct-Mar, Mon-Sat 10-4, Sun 1-4 (Closed 24-26 & 31 Dec-1 Jan). **Facilities:** 🅿 & (loan of wheelchairs, wheelchair lift) toilets for disabled shop ✖ (ex guide dogs) ◀

BELGRAVE HALL & GARDENS
Church Rd, off Thurcaston Rd, Belgrave LE4 5PE
➲ (off Belgrave/Loughborough road, 1m from city centre)
☎ 0116 266 6590 📠 0116 261 3063
A delightful three-storey Queen Anne house dating from 1709 with beautiful period and botanic gardens. Authentic room settings contrast Georgian elegance with Victorian cosiness and include the kitchen, drawing room, music room and nursery.
Times: Open all year, Apr-Sep, Mon-Sat 10-5, Sun 1-5; Oct-Mar, Mon-Sat 10-4, Sun 1-4. Closed 24-26 Dec & 31 Dec-1 Jan.
Facilities: 🅿 & (loan of wheelchair) toilets for disabled shop ✖ (ex guide dogs)

THE GUILDHALL

Guildhall Ln LE1 5FQ
➲ (Next to Leicester Cathedral)
☎ 0116 253 2569 🖹 0116 253 9626

A preserved medieval building dating back to the 14th century, the Guildhall is the city's oldest building still in use. Over the centuries it has served as the Hall of the Guild of Corpus Christi, the Civic Centre and Town Hall, a judicial centre for court sessions and home to Leicester's first police force. The Guildhall now houses one of the oldest libraries in the country, as well as hosting events, activities and performances.

Times: Open all year: Apr-Sep, Mon-Sat 10-5, Sun 1-5; Oct-Mar, Mon-Sat 10-4, Sun 1-4. (Closed 24-26 Dec & 1 Jan)
Facilities: 🅿 (100yds) 💻 & wheelchair loan, induction loop, voice minicom toilets for disabled shop 🐕 (ex guide dogs) 🍴

JEWRY WALL MUSEUM & SITE

St Nicholas Circle LE1 4LB
➲ (opposite The Holiday Inn)
☎ 0116 225 4971 🖹 0116 225 4966

Behind the massive fragment of the Roman Jewry wall and a Roman Baths site of the 2nd century AD is the Museum of Leicestershire Archaeology, which covers finds from the earliest times to the Middle Ages.

Times: Open Apr-Sep, Mon-Sat 10-5, Sun 1-5; Oct-Mar, Mon-Sat 10-4, Sun 1-4 (Closed 24-26 Dec & 31 Dec-1 Jan). **Facilities:** 🅿 (300yds) (limited on-street parking) & toilets for disabled shop 🐕 (ex guide dogs)

LEICESTERSHIRE MUSEUM & ART GALLERY

53 New Walk LE1 7EA
➲ (situated on New Walk. Access by car from A6 onto Waterloo Way at Railway Stn. Right into Regent Rd, right onto West St, right onto Princess Rd which leads to car park)
☎ 0116 225 4900 🖹 0116 225 4927

This major regional venue houses local and national collections. There's an internationally famous collection of German Expressionism and other displays include the Rutland Dinosaur and the Egyptian Gallery. An Extensive Natural History collection augmented by art from the renaissance to contemporary.

Times: Open all year, Apr-Sep, Mon-Sat 10-5, Sun 1-5. Oct-Mar, Mon-Sat 10-4, Sun 1-4. (Closed 24-26 Dec & 31 Dec-1 Jan).
Facilities: 🅿 💻 & (wheelchairs for loan, minicom, induction loop) toilets for disabled shop 🐕 (ex guide dogs) 🍴

NATIONAL SPACE CENTRE

Exploration Dr LE4 5NS
➲ (off A6, 2m N of Leicester city centre midway between Leicester's central & outer ring roads. Brown signs will direct you from the M1 (junct 21,21a and 22) & all arterial routes around Leicester)
☎ 0116 261 0261 🖹 0116 258 2100
e-mail: info@spacecentre.co.uk

Offering five themed galleries, cutting-edge audio-visual technology and glimpses into genuine space research, the National Space Centre is a unique experience. Learn about the planets, astronaut life, weather forecasting, space-stations and satellites. Visit the Space Theatre and the

continued

Newsdesk, and take a look at the scientists and astronomers doing genuine research in the Space Science Research Unit.
Times: During school term: Tue-Fri, 10-5 (last entry 3.30pm) Sat & Sun 10-6 (last entry 4.30pm) closed Mon. During school holidays: Mon 12-6 (last entry 4.30pm) Tue-Sun 10-6 (last entry 4.30pm). Open all Bank Hols 10-6 (Last entry 6.30pm) **Fee:** £8.95 (ch 4-16yrs, concessions & students £6.95). Family of four £28.00 & family of five £34.00
Facilities: 🅿 💻 ✕ licensed & toilets for disabled shop 🐕 (ex guide dogs) 🍴

NEWARKE HOUSES

The Newarke LE2 7BY
➲ (opposite De Montfort University)
☎ 0116 225 4980 🖹 0116 225 4982

This museum follows Leicestershire's social history from the 15th century to the present, showing everyday life and social change throughout the county. Clocks, toys, domestic objects, greetings cards and Asian arts are among the many collections. A reconstructed street scene gives a glimpse of Victorian life and the fascinating story of Daniel Lambert, the famous 52-stone gaoler of the 18th century, is also told.

Times: Open Apr-Sep, Mon-Sat 10-5, Sun 1-5; Oct-Mar, Mon-Sat 10-4, Sun 1-4 (Closed 24-26 Dec & 31 Dec-1 Jan). **Facilities:** 🅿 (200yds) & (car parking can be arranged) shop 🐕 (ex guide dogs)

THE RECORD OFFICE FOR LEICESTERSHIRE & RUTLAND

Long St, Wigston Magna LE18 2AH
➲ (Old A50, S of Leicester City)
☎ 0116 257 1080 🖹 0116 257 1120 〔FREE〕
e-mail: museums@leics.gov.uk

Housed in a converted 19th-century school in Wigston, the Record Office holds photographs, electoral registers and archive film, files of local newspapers, history tapes and sound recordings, all of which can be studied.

Times: Open all year, Mon, Tue & Thu 9.15-5, Wed 9.15-7.30, Fri 9.15-4.45, Sat 9.15-12.15. (Closed Sun & BH wknds Sat-Tue).
Facilities: 🅿 & toilets for disabled 🐕 (ex guide dogs) 🚌

UNIVERSITY OF LEICESTER HAROLD MARTIN BOTANIC GARDEN

Beaumont Hall, Stoughton Dr South, Oadby LE2 2NA
➲ (3m SE A6, entrance at 'The Knoll', Glebe Rd, Oadby)
☎ 0116 271 7725 〔FREE〕

The grounds of four houses, now used as student residences and not open to the public, make up this 16-acre garden. A great variety of plants in different settings provide a delightful place to walk, including rock, water and sunken gardens, trees, borders, heathers and glasshouses.

Times: Open Mon-Fri 10-4 (ex 25-26 Dec & 1 Jan), Sat & Sun 10-4 (from 3rd weekend in Mar to 2nd weekend in Nov inclusive).
Facilities: 🅿 (adjacent) & toilets for disabled 🐕 (ex guide dogs)

Are there any excellent Days Out that we've missed? Use the Readers' Report form at the back of the book to tell us about them.

LOUGHBOROUGH   Map 08 SK51

GREAT CENTRAL RAILWAY
Great Central Rd LE11 1RW
➲ (signposted from A6)
☎ 01509 230726   ◾ 01509 239791
e-mail: booking_office@gcrailway.co.uk

This private steam railway runs over eight miles from
Loughborough Central to Leicester North, with all trains
calling at Quorn & Woodhouse and Rothley. The locomotive
depot and museum are at Loughborough Central. A buffet
car runs on most trains.
Times: Open all year Sat, Sun & BH Mon & daily during June, July, Aug
and school holidays **Fee:** ✱ Runabout (all day unlimited travel) £11
(ch & pen £7.50). Family ticket £27.50 **Facilities:** 🅿 🖵 ✗ licensed
♿ (disabled coach available on most trains, check beforehand) toilets
for disabled shop ◼

MARKET BOSWORTH   Map 04 SK40

THE BATTLEFIELD LINE
Shackerstone Station, Shackerstone, Nuneaton CV13
6NW
➲ (from A444/A447 take B585 to Market
Bosworth and follow signs for
Congerstone/Shackerstone. Follow brown tourist
signs from M42 Junct 11).
☎ 01827 880754   ◾ 01827 881050
Together with a regular railway service (mainly steam) from
Shackerstone to Shenton, there is an extensive railway
museum featuring a collection of rolling stock and many
other relics from the age of steam
Times: ✱ Open all year, Passenger steam train service operates
Apr-Oct, Sat, Sun & BH Mon. Heritage Railcar Wed Jul-Aug
Facilities: 🅿 🖵 ✗ ♿ toilets for disabled shop ◼

BOSWORTH BATTLEFIELD VISITOR CENTRE & COUNTRY PARK
Ambion Hill, Sutton Cheney CV13 0AD
➲ (follow brown tourist signs from A447, A444 &
A5)
☎ 01455 290429   ◾ 01455 292841
e-mail: bosworth@leics.gov.uk
The Battle of Bosworth Field was fought in 1485 between the
armies of Richard III and the future Henry VII. The visitor
centre offers a comprehensive interpretation of the battle,
with exhibitions, models and a film theatre. Special medieval
attractions are held in the summer months.
Times: Open Country Park and Battle Trails all year. Visitor Centre open
Apr-Oct, daily, 11-5; Nov-Dec, Sun 11-4; Mar, wknds 11-5. Parties all
year by arrangement. **Facilities:** 🅿 (charged) 🖵 ♿ (wheelchair &
electric scooter hire, tactile exhibits) toilets for disabled shop ◼

MOIRA   Map 08 SK31

CONKERS
Millennium Av, Rawdon Rd DE12 6GA
➲ (located on B5003 in Moira, signposted from
A444 and M42)
☎ 01283 216633   ◾ 01283 210321
e-mail: info@visitconkers.com
Conkers, located at the heart of the National Forest, is a
unique mix of indoor and outdoor hands on experiences.
Indoors at the Discovery Centre there are 4 discovery zones
designed for children and adults of all ages where you can
get really close to the forest and experience its life and
energy - for example see the world through the eyes of a
spider or crawl through a living leaf. At Waterside, a new
indoor play centre for children and the Gallery Restaurant
have just opened. Visitors can travel between the centres on
a miniature railway. Outdoors there are 23 different activities
including nature trails, an assault course, playgrounds and
mazes. In addition, new in 2004, Tree Top Tremor & feature
Timber Ramp.
Times: Open daily, summer 10-6, winter 10-5. (Closed 25 Dec).
Fee: £5.95 (ch 3-15yrs £3.95, concessions £4.95). Family ticket (2 ad &
2 ch) £17.50 **Facilities:** 🅿 🖵 ✗ licensed ♿ (multi access walks &
trails accessible to wheelchairs) toilets for disabled shop garden centre
🐕 (ex guide dogs) ◼

SWINFORD   Map 04 SP57

STANFORD HALL
LE17 6DH
➲ (7.5m NE of Rugby, 1.5m from Swinford. 2m
from the M1, M6, A14 junct)
☎ 01788 860250   ◾ 01788 860870
e-mail: enquiries@stanfordhall.co.uk
A beautiful William and Mary house, built in 1697 by Sir
Roger Cave, ancestor of the present owner. The house
contains antique furniture, paintings (including the Stuart
Collection) and family costumes. Special events include car
and motorcycle owners' club rallies.
Times: Open Etr Sun-end Sep, Sun & BH Mon 1.30-5; grounds open
noon on BH & earlier on Event Days. Open any day or evening during
season for pre-booked parties of 20+. **Fee:** ✱ House & Grounds £5
(ch £2); Grounds only £3 (ch £1); Motorcycle Museum £1 (ch 35p).
Party 20+ £4.75 each. **Facilities:** 🅿 🖵 ♿ (please contact for details)
toilets for disabled shop 🐕 (ex guide dogs & in park)

TWYCROSS   Map 04 SK30

TWYCROSS ZOO PARK

CV9 3PX

➲ (On A444 Burton to Nuneaton road, directly off M42 Junct 11)

☎ 01827 880250 ▤ 01827 880700

Set in 50 acres of parkland, the zoo is home to around 1000 animals, most of which are endangered species. Twycross is the only zoo in Britain to house Bonobos - humans' 'closest living relative'. There are also various other animals such as lions, elephants and giraffes, and a pets' corner for younger children. Other attractions include a Penguin Pool with underwater viewing and a Children's Adventure Playground.

Times: Open all year, daily 10-6 (4pm in winter). (Closed 25 Dec).
Fee: ✱ Please telephone for prices. **Facilities:** ℙ (charged) ▆ ♿ toilets for disabled shop ✘ (ex guide dogs) ◆

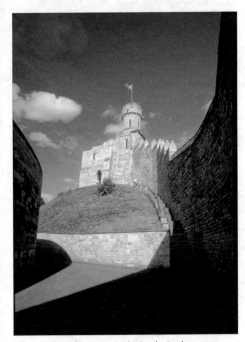

Above: William the Conqueror's Lincoln Castle

LINCOLNSHIRE

EVENTS & FESTIVALS

January
23rd The Great Australian Breakfast (celebrating Australia Day), Lawn Visitor Centre, Lincoln

April
3rd Lincoln 10km Run (provisional)
30th Spalding Flower Parade & Springfields Country Fair

May
8th Lincoln Grand Prix Cycle Race
27th-30th Folk Festival, Cleethorpes

June
8th-12th Newark on Water Festival (provisional)
22nd-23rd Lincolnshire Show, Lincolnshire Showground, Grange-de-Lings, Lincoln
tbc Royal Air Force Waddington International Air Show, RAF Waddington

July
2nd Riverside Festival, Stamford Meadows, Stamford
30th-31st Heckington Show, Estate Showground, Heckington (provisional)
tbc Lincoln Water Carnival, Brayford Pool

August
20th-21st Lincolnshire Steam & Vintage Rally, Lincolnshire Showground, Grange-de-Lings, Lincoln

November
tbc Bonfire night celebrations, Cleethorpes

December
tbc Lincoln Christmas Market, Up-Hill, Lincoln

Above: Lincoln Cathedral

BELTON Map 08 SK93

BELTON HOUSE PARK & GARDENS

NG32 2LS

➔ (3m NE Grantham on A607)

☎ 01476 566116 🖷 01476 579071

e-mail: belton@nationaltrust.org.uk

The ground floor of the house has a succession of state rooms, with the Marble Hall as its centrepiece. Splendid furnishings and decorations throughout the house include tapestries and hangings, family portraits, porcelain and fine furniture.

Times: Open 23 Mar-30 Oct, Wed-Sun. House open 12.30-5 (last admission 4.30). Garden & Park open 11-5.30. Garden open 4 Nov-18 Dec, Fri-Sun 12-4. **Fee:** House & garden £6.80 (ch £3.40) Family £16. **Facilities:** 🅿 ✖ licensed ♿ (Braille guide, hearing scheme, audio guide) toilets for disabled shop 🐾 (ex in grounds) ❦

CLEETHORPES Map 08 TA30

PLEASURE ISLAND FAMILY THEME PARK

Kings Rd DN35 0PL

➔ (Follow signs to Pleasure Island from A180)

☎ 01472 211511 🖷 01472 211087

e-mail: pleasureisland@btinternet.com

Pleasure Island is packed with over seventy rides and attractions. Hold on tight as the colossal wheel of steel rockets you into the sky at a G-force of 2.5, then hurtles you around 360 degrees, sending riders into orbit and giving the sensation of complete weightlessness. It's not just grown ups and thrill seekers who are catered for at Pleasure Island. For youngsters there's hours of fun in Tinkaboo Town, an indoor themed area full of rides and attractions.

Times: ✳ Open 6 Apr-7 Sep, daily from 10. Plus wknds during Sep-Oct & daily during half term (25 Oct-2 Nov). **Facilities:** 🅿 💺 ✖ licensed ♿ toilets for disabled shop 🍴

CONINGSBY Map 08 TF25

BATTLE OF BRITAIN MEMORIAL FLIGHT VISITOR CENTRE

LN4 4SY

➔ (on A153)

☎ 01526 344041 🖷 01526 342330 **2 for 1**

e-mail: bbmf@lincolnshire.gov.uk

View the aircraft of the Battle of Britain Memorial Flight, comprising the only flying Lancaster in Europe, five Spitfires, two Hurricanes, a Dakota and two Chipmunks. Because of operational commitments, specific aircraft may not be available. Ring for information before planning a visit.

Times: Open all year, Mon-Fri, conducted tours 10-3.30. (Closed 2 wks Xmas). (Phone prior to visiting to check security situation) **Fee:** £3.70 (con £2.20) Family £9.60 **Facilities:** 🅿 💺 ♿ (electric wheelchairs not allowed in hangar) toilets for disabled shop 🐾 (ex guide dogs) 🍴

EPWORTH Map 08 SE70

OLD RECTORY

1 Rectory St DN9 1HX

➔ (on A161, 3m S of M180 junct 2)

☎ 01427 872268

e-mail: curator@epwortholdrectory.org.uk

John and Charles Wesley were brought up in this handsome rectory, built in 1709. Maintained by the World Methodist Council as 'The Home of the Wesleys', the house displays items which belonged to John and Charles Wesley and their

continued

parents Samuel and Susanna. The house is a registered museum.

Times: ✳ Open daily Mar-Oct, Mon-Sat 10-12 & 2-4, Sun 2-4 (only in Mar, Apr & Oct) May-Sep Mon-Sat 10-4.30. Sun 2-4.30. Other times by prior arrangement. **Facilities:** 🅿 💺 ✖ ♿ shop 🐾 (ex guide dogs) 🍴

GAINSBOROUGH Map 08 SK88

GAINSBOROUGH OLD HALL

Parnell St DN21 2NB

➔ (turn off A1 onto A57 to Gainsborough. Follow brown heritage signs in city centre. Old Hall is adjacent to town centre.)

☎ 01427 612669 🖷 01427 612779

e-mail: gainsborougholdhall@lincolnshire.gov.uk

A complete medieval manor house dating back to 1460-80 and containing a remarkable Great Hall and original kitchen with a variety of room settings. Richard III, Henry VIII, the Mayflower Pilgrims and John Wesley all visited the Old Hall.

Times: Open all year, Mon-Sat 10-5; Etr-Oct, Sun 1-4.30. (Closed 24-26 & 31 Dec & 1 Jan). **Fee:** £3.20 (concession £2.40). Family ticket (2 ad & 3 ch) £8.80. Prices & opening times relate to 2004, for further details phone or log onto www.english-heritage.org.uk/visits **Facilities:** 🅿 (100yds) (unrestricted parking 100yds from Hall) 💺 ♿ (audio tour, induction loop, wheelchair for visitors use) shop 🐾 (ex guide dogs)

GRIMSBY Map 08 TA20

NATIONAL FISHING HERITAGE CENTRE

Alexandra Dock DN31 1UZ

➔ (follow signs off M180)

☎ 01472 323345 🖷 01472 323555

Sign on as a crew member for a journey of discovery, and experience the harsh reality of life on board a deep sea trawler built inside the Centre. Through interactive games and displays, your challenge is to navigate the icy waters of the Arctic in search of the catch.

Times: ✳ Open Apr-Sep, Mon-Thu 10-4, Sat-Sun 11-5 (10.30-5.30 Jul-Sep). **Facilities:** 🅿 💺 ♿ (easy access route) toilets for disabled shop 🐾 (ex guide dogs) 🍴

GRIMSTHORPE Map 08 TF02

GRIMSTHORPE CASTLE

PE10 0NB

➔ (on A151, 8m E of Colsterworth rbt on A1)

☎ 01778 591205 🖷 01778 591259 **2 for 1**

e-mail: ray@grimsthorpe.co.uk

Seat of the Willoughby de Eresby family since 1516, the castle has a medieval tower and a Tudor quadrangular house with a Baroque north front by Vanbrugh. There are eight state rooms and two picture galleries, and an important collection of furniture, pictures and tapestries.

Times: Open early Apr-late Sep, Sun, Thu & BH Mon. Daily in Aug ex Fri & Sat. Park & Gardens 11-6, Castle 1-5 (last admission 4.30). **Fee:** ✳ Park & Gardens £3 (ch £2, concessions £2.50). Combined ticket £7 with castle (ch £3.50, concessions £6). **Facilities:** 🅿 💺 ✖ licensed ♿ toilets for disabled shop 🍴

LINCOLN   Map 08 SK97

LINCOLN CASTLE
Castle Hill LN1 3AA
➲ Lincoln Castle is situated just off the A46
Lincoln Ring Road in the heart of the historic city
of Lincoln
☎ 01522 511068 🖷 01522 512150
e-mail: lincoln_castle@lincolnshire.gov.uk

Situated in the centre of Lincoln, the Castle, built in 1068 by
William the Conqueror, dominates the Bailgate area
alongside the great Cathedral. In addition to its many
medieval features, Lincoln Castle has strong 19th-century
connections and the unique Victorian prison chapel is
perhaps the most awe-inspiring. The beautiful surroundings
are ideal for historical adventures, picnics and special events
that include jousting, Roman re-enactments, and Vintage
vehicle rallies. The Castle is the home of the Magna Carta
and there is an exhibition interpreting and displaying this
important document.
Times: Open - Summer: Mon-Sat 9.30-5.30, Sun 11-5.30. Winter:
Mon-Sat 9.30-4.30, Sun 11-4.30. (Closed 24-26 & 31 Dec & 1 Jan).
Fee: ✱ £3.60 (ch £1) Family ticket (2 adults & 3 children) £9.30
Facilities: 🅿 (100yds) 🍽 �鯨 (hearing loop, audio visual tour) toilets
for disabled shop ✖ (ex guide dogs) ◀
See advertisement on opposite page

MUSEUM OF LINCOLNSHIRE LIFE
Burton Rd LN1 3LY
➲ (100mtr walk from Lincoln Castle)
☎ 01522 528448 🖷 01522 521264
e-mail: lincolnshirelife.museum@
lincolnshire.gov.uk
A large and varied social history museum, where two
centuries of Lincolnshire life are illustrated by enthralling
displays of domestic implements, industrial machinery,
agricultural tools and a collection of horse-drawn vehicles.
The exciting and interactive Royal Lincolnshire Regiment
Museum contains videos, an audio tour, and touch screen
computers.
Times: Open all year, May-Sep, daily 10-5.30; Oct-Apr, Mon-Sat
10-5.30, Sun 2-5.30. Closed Sun Oct-Apr **Fee:** ✱ £2.05 (concessions
£1.25). Family (2ad+3ch) £5.35. **Facilities:** 🅿 🍽 ⅙ (wheelchair
available, parking space) toilets for disabled shop ✖

USHER GALLERY
Lindum Rd LN2 1NN
➲ (in city centre, signed)
☎ 01522 527980 🖷 01522 560165   `FREE`
e-mail: usher.gallery@lincolnshire.gov.uk
Built as the result of a bequest by Lincoln jeweller James
Ward Usher, the Gallery houses his magnificent collection of
watches, porcelain and miniatures, as well as topographical
works, watercolours by Peter de Wint, Tennyson
memorabilia and coins. The gallery has a popular and
changing display of contemporary visual arts and crafts.
There is a lively lecture programme and children's activity
diary.
Times: Open all year, Tue-Sat 10-5 (last entry 4.30), Sun 1-5. (last
entry 4.30) from 1 Jun daily 10-5. (Closed 24-26 Dec & 1 Jan). Open
BHs. **Facilities:** 🅿 🍽 ⅙ (large print guides, induction loop, parking)
toilets for disabled shop ✖ (ex guide dogs) ◀

SCUNTHORPE   Map 08 SE81

NORMANBY HALL COUNTRY PARK
Normanby DN15 9HU
➲ (4m N of Scunthorpe off B1430
☎ 01724 720588 🖷 01724 721248
e-mail: normanbyhall@northlincs.gov.uk
A whole host of activities and attractions are offered in the
300 acres of grounds that surround Normanby Hall, including
riding, nature trails and a farming museum. Inside the
Regency mansion the fine rooms are decorated and
furnished in period style. Fully restored and working
Victorian kitchen garden. There is also a Victorian walled
garden with a new nursery selling a wide range of Victorian
and other unusual plants.
Times: Open, Park all year, daily 9am-dusk. Walled garden: daily
10.30-5 (4pm winter). Hall & Farming Museum: Apr-Sep daily 1-5.
Fee: ✱ Apr-Sep £4 (ch £2, concessions £3.60). Family ticket £12.
Season ticket (resident) £12 (non resident) £16, Oct-Mar £2.20 per car.
Facilities: 🅿 (charged) 🍽 ✖ licensed ⅙ (audio tour, sensory bed in
garden, wheelchair/scooter) toilets for disabled shop garden centre
✖ (ex guide dogs & park on lead) ◀

SKEGNESS   Map 09 TF56

CHURCH FARM MUSEUM
Church Rd South PE25 2HF
➲ (follow brown museum signs on entering
Skegness)
☎ 01754 766658 🖷 01754 898243   `FREE`
e-mail: churchfarmmuseum@
lincolnshire.gov.uk
A farmhouse and outbuildings, restored to show the way of
life on a Lincolnshire farm at the end of the 19th century,
with farm implements and machinery plus household
equipment on display. Temporary exhibitions are held in the
barn with special events throughout the season. A timber
framed mud & stud cottage is restored on site.
Times: Open Apr-Oct, daily 10-5 **Facilities:** 🅿 🍽 ⅙ (wheelchair
available, grounds accessible with care) toilets for disabled shop
✖ (ex guide dogs)

SKEGNESS NATURELAND SEAL SANCTUARY
North Pde PE25 1DB
➲ (N end of seafront)
☎ 01754 764345 🖷 01754 764345
e-mail: natureland@fsbdial.co.uk
Natureland houses seals, penguins, tropical birds, aquarium,
reptiles, pets' corner etc. Also free-flight tropical butterflies
continued

(May-Oct). Natureland is well known for its rescue of abandoned seal pups, and has successfully reared and returned to the wild a large number of them. The hospital unit incorporates a public viewing area, and a large seascape seal pool (with underwater viewing).

Times: Open all year, daily at 10am. Closing times vary according to season. (Closed 25-26 Dec & 1 Jan). **Fee:** ✱ £4.95 (ch under 3 free, ch £3.25, pen £3.95). Family ticket £14.70. **Facilities:** P (100yds) ⬤ & (low windows on seal pools) toilets for disabled shop 🛒

SPALDING   Map 08 TF22

BUTTERFLY & WILDLIFE PARK
Long Sutton PE12 9LE   `2 for 1`
➲ (off A17 at Long Sutton)
☎ 01406 363833 & 363209 📠 01406 363182
e-mail: butterflypark@hotmail.com

The Park contains one of Britain's largest walk-through tropical houses, in which hundreds of butterflies and birds from all over the world fly freely. Outside are 15 acres of butterfly and bee gardens, wildflower meadows, nature trail, farm animals, a pets' corner and a large adventure playground. At The Lincolnshire Birds of Prey Centre, there are daily birds of prey displays. See an ant room where visitors can observe leaf-cutting ants in their natural working habitat, and Reptile Land, home to crocodiles and snakes.

Times: Open 20 Mar-end Oct, daily 10-5. (Sep & Oct 10-4).
Fee: ✱ £5.50 (ch 3-16 £3.80, pen £4.80). Family ticket £17-£20. Party rates on application. **Facilities:** P ✗ licensed & (wheelchairs available) toilets for disabled shop 🐕 (ex guide dogs) 🛒

STAMFORD   Map 04 TF00

BURGHLEY HOUSE
PE9 3JY
➲ (1.5m off A1 at Stamford)
☎ 01780 752451 📠 01780 480125
e-mail: burghley@burghley.co.uk

This great Elizabethan palace, built by William Cecil, has all the hallmarks of that ostentatious period. The vast house is three storeys high and the roof is a riot of pinnacles, cupolas and paired chimneys in classic Tudor style. However, the interior was restyled in the 17th century, and the state rooms are now Baroque, with silver fireplaces, elaborate plasterwork and painted ceilings. These were painted by Antonio Verrio, whose Heaven Room is quite awe-inspiring.

Times: Open end Mar-Oct, daily. Please telephone for details.
Fee: ✱ £7.80 (ch 5-11 £3.50, pen £6.90) Family £19.50
Facilities: P ⬤ ✗ licensed & (chairlift access, some mobility required) toilets for disabled shop 🐕 (ex guide dogs) 🛒

STAMFORD MUSEUM
Broad St PE9 1PJ
➲ (from A1 follow town centre signs from any Stamford exit)   `FREE`
☎ 01780 766317 📠 01780 480363
e-mail: stamford_museum@lincolnshire.gov.uk

Displays illustrate the history of this fine stone town and include Stamford Ware pottery, the visit of Daniel Lambert and the Town's more recent industrial past. The new Stamford Tapestry depicts the history of the town in wool.

Times: Open all year, Apr-Sep, Mon-Sat 10-5, Sun 1-4; Oct-Mar Mon-Sat 10-5. (Closed 24-26 & 31 Dec & 1 Jan).
Facilities: P (200yds) (on street parking is limited waiting) & (audio loop at reception, Braille leaflets) shop 🐕 (ex guide dogs)

Lincoln Castle

TATTERSHALL   Map 08 TF25

TATTERSHALL CASTLE
LN4 4LR
➲ (S of A153, 15m NE of Sleaford)
☎ 01526 342543
e-mail: tattershallcastle@nationaltrust.org.uk

This large fortified house was built in 1440 by Ralph Cromwell, Treasurer of England, and has a keep 100ft high. Restored in 1911-14, it contains four great chambers with large Gothic fireplaces, tapestries and brick vaulting. Spectacular views from battlements and museum room in guardhouse.

Times: Open 5 Mar-11 Dec, Mar, Sat & Sun 12-4, Apr-Oct, Sat-Wed 11-5.30 (Oct 4pm); 5 Nov-11 Dec, Sat & Sun 12-4. **Fee:** £3.70 (ch £1.90). Family £9.30. **Facilities:** P & (Braille guide) toilets for disabled shop 🐕 (ex guide dogs) 🐾

THORNTON   Map 08 TA11

THORNTON ABBEY AND GATEHOUSE
DN39 6TU
➲ (7m SE of Humber Bridge, on a road E of A1077)

This abbey, founded in 1139 for a community of Augustinian cannons, was reconstructed from the 1260s as its prestige and riches grew. The remains of a beautiful octagonal chapter-house are notably fine. Most impressive is the fourteenth-century gatehouse, recognised as one of the grandest in England.

Times: Open Abbey Grounds: Apr-Sep, 10-6. Gatehouse: Apr-Sep, 1st & 3rd Sun of month, 12-6; Oct-Mar, 3rd Sun of month 12-4. Opening times relate to 2004, for further details phone or log onto www.english-heritage.org.uk/visits **Facilities:** P & (mostly accessible apart from gatehouse) ♿

WOOLSTHORPE   Map 08 SK92

WOOLSTHORPE MANOR
23 Newton Way NG33 5NR
➲ (7m S of Grantham, 1m W of A1)
☎ 01476 860338 ▤ 01476 860338
e-mail: **woolsthorpemanor@**
nationaltrust.org.uk

A fine stone-built, 17th-century farmhouse which was the
birthplace of the scientist and philosopher Sir Isaac Newton.
He also lived at the house from 1665-67 during the Plague.
An early edition of his Principia Mathematica (1687) is in the
house. Science Discovery Centre and exhibition.

Times: Open Apr-Sep, Wed-Sun 1-5; Oct, Sat & Sun, 1-5, BH Mon
Fee: £4.20 (ch £2.10). Family ticket £10.50 **Facilities:** ▣ (Braille &
large print guide, wheelchair available) ✈ (ex guide dogs) ♨

Above: The London Eye, South Bank

The End of World War II.
2005 sees the 60th anniversary of both VE (Victory in Europe) and VJ (Victory over Japan) Days. Local celebrations are planned, as are a number of national events.

LONDON

EVENTS & FESTIVALS

January
1st New Year's Day Parade, Parliament Square,
SW1, to Berkeley Square
February
tbc Chinese New Year Celebrations, Gerrard
Street and Leicester Square
March
19th Head of the River Race, River Thames,
Mortlake to Putney (provisional)
27th Oxford & Cambridge Boat Race
April
17th London Marathon
May
24th-27th Chelsea Flower Show, Royal
Chelsea Hospital
June
4th-5th Biggin Hill International Air Fair,
Biggin Hill Airfield (provisional)
11th Trooping the Colour for the Queen's
Birthday, Horse Guards Parade
12th London to Brighton Classic Car Run
tbc Beating Retreat by the Household Division
Massed Bands, Horse Guards Parade
July
4th-9th Hampton Court Palace Flower Show,
Hampton Court Palace, East Molesey
August
28th-29th Notting Hill Carnival
September
5th-6th City of London Flower Show,
Guildhall, Gresham Street
17th-18th Mayor's Thames Festival,
Southbank between London Eye
& Oxo Tower
October
2nd Pearly Harvest Festival,
St Martin in the Fields
23rd Trafalgar Day Parade,
Trafalgar Square (provisional)
November
6th London to Brighton Veteran Car Run,
Hyde Park
12th Lord Mayor's Show, City of London
13th Remembrance Day Service & Parade,
Cenotaph, Whitehall
December
tbc Christmas Tree, Trafalgar Square

Above: Tower Bridge

W1

APSLEY HOUSE, THE WELLINGTON MUSEUM

Hyde Park Corner WIJ 7NT

⮌ (Underground - Hyde Park Corner, exit 1 overlooking rdbt)

☎ 020 7499 5676 ▯ 020 7493 6576

Number One, London, is the popular name for one of the Capital's finest private residences, 19th-century home of the first Duke of Wellington. Built in the 1770s, its rich interiors have been returned to their former glory, and house the Duke's magnificent collection of paintings, silver, porcelain, sculpture and furniture.
Times: Open Apr-Oct, Tue-Sun 10-5. Nov-Mar, Tue-Sun 10-4. (Closed Mon ex BH Mon, 24-26 Dec & 1 Jan). **Fee:** ✱ £4.50 (ch £2.30, concessions £3). Joint ticket to House & Wellington Arch: £6 (ch £3, consessions £4.20). Family £15 (2 adults+ 2 children). Prices & opening times relate to 2004, for further details phone or log onto www.english-heritage.org.uk/visits **Facilities:** P (NCP 10mins walk) ⅙ (lift) shop ✕ (ex guide dogs) ▰

EC2

BANK OF ENGLAND MUSEUM

Threadneedle St EC2R 8AH

⮌ (museum housed in Bank of London, entrance in Bartholomew Lane)

☎ 020 7601 5545 ▯ 020 7601 5808   FREE
e-mail: museum@bankofengland.co.uk

The museum tells the story of the Bank of England from its foundation in 1694 to its role in today's economy. Interactive programmes with graphics and video help explain its many and varied roles. Popular exhibits include a unique collection of banknotes and a genuine gold bar, which may be handled.
Times: Open all year, Mon-Fri 10-5. (Closed wknds & BHs). Open on the day of the Lord Major's Show. **Facilities:** P (10 mins walk) ⅙ (special need presentation, advance notice helpful) toilets for disabled shop

SE1

BANKSIDE GALLERY

48 Hopton St SE1 9JH

⮌ (E of Blackfriars Bridge, South Bank of the Thames, adjacent to Tate Modern and the Millennium Bridge)

☎ 020 7928 7521 ▯ 020 7928 2820   FREE
e-mail: info@banksidegallery.com

Bankside Gallery is the home of the Royal Watercolour Society (RWS) and the Royal Society of Painter-Printmakers (RE). A series of regularly changing exhibitions throughout the year displays the work of both societies.
Times: Opening dates vary according to exhibitions programme - Mon-Fri 10-5, Sat & Sun 11-5 **Facilities:** P ⅙ shop ✕ ▰

SW1

BANQUETING HOUSE AT WHITEHALL PALACE

Whitehall SW1A 2ER

⮌ (Underground - Westminster, Charing Cross or Embankment)

☎ 020 7930 4179 ▯ 020 7930 8268
e-mail: valerie.jarvis@hrp.org.uk

Designed by Inigo Jones, this is the only surviving building of the vast Whitehall Palace, destroyed by fire 300 years ago. The Palace has seen many significant royal events, including the execution of Charles I in 1649. The Banqueting House's Rubens ceiling paintings are stunning examples of the larger
continued

works of the Flemish Master and its classical Palladian style set the fashion for much of London's later architecture.
Times: ✱ Open all year, Mon-Sat 10-5. (Closed Good Fri, 24 Dec-1 Jan & BH's). Liable to close at short notice for Government functions.
Facilities: P (5 mins) (no parking in Whitehall) ⅙ toilets for disabled shop ✕ (ex guide/hearing dogs) ▰

SE1

BRITISH AIRWAYS LONDON EYE

Riverside Building, County Hall, Westminster Bridge Rd SE1 7PB

⮌ (Underground - Waterloo/Westminster)

☎ 0870 500 0600 ▯ 0870 990 8882
e-mail: customer.services@ba-londoneye.com

British Airways London Eye is one of the most inspiring and visually dramatic additions to the London skyline. At 135m/443ft high, it is the world's tallest observation wheel, allowing you to see one of the world's most exciting cities from a completely new perspective. The London Eye takes you on a gradual, 30 minute, 360 degree rotation, revealing parts of the city, which are simply not visible from the ground. For Londoners and visitors alike, it is the best way to see London and its many celebrated landmarks. The London Eye provides the perfect location for private parties and entertaining and offers a wide variety of in flight hospitality packages, like champagne and canapés, which are available to enjoy from the privacy of a private capsule.
Times: Open May, Mon-Thu 9.30-8, Fri-Sun 9.30-9, (24-31 May last flight 10pm); June, Mon-Thu 9.30am-9pm, Fri-Sun 9.30am-10pm; July-Aug daily 9.30am-10pm; Sep, Mon-Thu 9.30-8, Fri-Sun 9.30-9, (1-7 Sep last flight 10pm); Oct-Dec, daily 9.30-8. (Closed 25 Dec)
Fee: ✱ £11.50 (ch under 5 free, ch £5.75, disabled visitors £9, pen £9). Fast track entry £25. **Facilities:** P (500yds) ▰⅙ (Braille guidebooks, wheelchair hire, carer ticket) toilets for disabled shop ✕ (ex guide & hearing dogs) ▰

W12

BBC TELEVISION CENTRE TOURS

BBC Television Centre, Wood Ln W12 7RJ

⮌ (Underground - Central Line/White City)

☎ 0870 603 0304 ▯ 020 8576 7466
e-mail: bbctours@bbc.co.uk

Take a look behind the scenes at the world's most famous TV centre. As the BBC TV Centre is a working building, no guarantees can be made as to what visitors will see, although dressing rooms, the News Centre, the Weather Centre, and various studios are all possible. The uncertain nature of the visit means that no two are the same, and that only pre-booked guided tours are available.
Times: Open Mon-Sat. Tours at 10, 10.20, 1.15, 1.30, 3.30 & 3.45. (Closed 24 Dec-2 Jan). All tours must be pre-booked. **Fee:** ✱ £7.95 (concessions £6.95, student £5.95). Family ticket £21.95
Facilities: P ⅙ (wheelchair & sign language available) toilets for disabled shop ✕ (ex guide/hearing dogs) ▰

WC1

BRITISH MUSEUM

Great Russell St WC1B 3DG

⮌ (Underground - Russell Sq, Tottenham Court Rd, Holborn)

☎ 020 7323 8000 ▯ 020 7323 8616   FREE
e-mail: information@thebritishmuseum.ac.uk

Behind its imposing Neo-Classical façade the British Museum displays the rich and varied treasures which make it one of the great museums of the world. Founded in 1753, displays
continued

cover the works of humanity from pre-historic to modern times. The galleries are the responsibility of eight departments, which include Egyptian, Greek and Roman, Japanese, Prehistory and Europe, Prints and Drawings, and Ethnography. Among the treasures to be seen are the Egyptian mummies, the sculptures from the Parthenon, the Anglo-Saxon treasure from the Sutton Hoo ship burial and the Vindolanda Tablets from Hadrian's Wall. There is a regular programme of gallery talks, guided tours and lectures, and young visitors can enjoy special children's trails.
Times: Open all year, Gallery: Mon-Sat 10-5.30 & Thu-Fri 10-8.30. Great Court: Sun-Wed 9-6, Thu-Sat 9am-11pm. (Closed Good Fri, 24-26 Dec & 1 Jan). **Facilities:** P (5 mins walk) ⬛ ✕ licensed ⴺ (parking by arrangement) toilets for disabled shop ✈ (ex guide/companion dogs)

SW1
BUCKINGHAM PALACE
Buckingham Palace Rd SW1 1AA
➲ (Underground - Victoria, Green Park, St James' Park)
☎ 020 7766 7300 🖷 020 7930 9625
e-mail: buckinghampalace@
royalcollection.org.uk
Buckingham Palace has been the official London residence of Britain's sovereigns since 1837. Today it serves as both the home and office of Her Majesty the Queen. Its nineteen State Rooms, which open for eight weeks a year, form the heart of the working palace and more than 50,000 people visit each year as guests at State, ceremonial and official occasions and garden parties. After visiting the State Rooms, visitors can enjoy a walk along the south side of the garden, which offers superb views of the west front of the Palace and the 19th century lake.
Times: ✱ Open Aug-Sep 9.30-4.30 last admission 4.15. Entry by timed-ticket **Fee:** ✱ £12.95 (ch 17 £6.50, pen & students £11). Family ticket (2ad+3ch) £32.50. Tickets bought in advance £1 booking fee. **Facilities:** P (200yds) (very limited, driving not recommended) ⴺ (ex gardens, pre-booking essential) toilets for disabled shop ✈ (ex guide dogs) 🖃

SW1
CABINET WAR ROOMS
Clive Steps, King Charles St SW1A 2AQ
➲ (Underground - Westminster (exit 6) or St James Park)
☎ 020 7930 6961 🖷 020 7839 5897
e-mail: cwr@iwm.org.uk
The underground emergency accommodation used to protect the Prime Minister, Winston Churchill, his War Cabinet and the Chiefs of Staff during WWII provides a fascinating insight into those tense days and nights. Among the 30 rooms are the Cabinet Room, the Map Room (where information about operations on all fronts was collected) and the Prime Minister's room, all carefully preserved since the end of the war. In 2003 a further 9 secret historic rooms, including Churchill's kitchen, dining room and Mrs Churchill's bedroom, were revealed to the public for the first time. These rooms provide an insight into the domestic side of Britain's wartime Prime Minister, they were intended to provide a sheltered space where the people he valued most could eat, sleep and work in safety, while the bombs rained down outside. New for February 2005 will be the opening of The Churchill Museum.
Times: Open all year, daily 9.30-6. (10-6 Oct-Mar) last admission 5.15 (Closed 24-26 Dec). **Fee:** ✱ £7.50 (ch under 16 free, students & pen £6). Party 10+ £6 (students & pen £5.50) **Facilities:** P (2 mins walk) Meter parking ⬛ ⴺ (education service, object handling session, induction loop) toilets for disabled shop ✈ (ex guide dogs) 🖃

SW3
CARLYLE'S HOUSE
24 Cheyne Row SW3 5HL
➲ (Underground - Sloane Square. Off Cheyne Walk between Battersea & Albert Bridges).
☎ 020 7352 7087 🖷 020 7352 5108
e-mail: carlyleshouse@nationaltrust.org.uk
'The Sage of Chelsea' - distinguished essayist and writer of historical works, Thomas Carlyle - lived here from 1834 until his death in 1881. Such literary notables as Tennyson, Thackeray, Browning, George Eliot and Dickens were frequent visitors. The 2-for-1 voucher is valid only during normal visiting hours, and cannot be used for any ticketed events.
Times: Open Apr-Oct, Wed-Fri 2-5. Sat-Sun & BH Mons 11-5. Last admission 4.30. (Closed Mon-Tue). **Fee:** £4 (ch 5-16, £2). **Facilities:** P (street metered) Residents parking Mon-Fri & Sat ✈ (ex guide & hearing dogs) 🚐 ♨

WC1
THE CHARLES DICKENS MUSEUM
48 Doughty St WC1N 2LX
➲ (Underground - Russell Square or Chancery Lane)
☎ 020 7405 2127 🖷 020 7831 5175
e-mail: info@dickensmuseum.com

Charles Dickens lived in Doughty Street in his twenties and it was here he worked on his first full-length novel, *The Pickwick Papers*, and later *Oliver Twist* and *Nicholas Nickleby*. Pages of the original manuscripts are on display, together with valuable first editions, his marriage licence and many other personal mementoes.
Times: Open all year, Mon-Sat 10-5, Sun 11-5. **Fee:** ✱ £5 (ch under 16 £3, concessions £4). Family ticket £14. **Facilities:** P (in street) (metered, 2 hrs max) ⴺ shop ✈ 🖃

SW3
CHELSEA PHYSIC GARDEN
66 Royal Hospital Rd,
➲ (entrance in Swan Walk) SW3 4HS
(Underground - Sloane Square)
☎ 020 7352 5646 🖷 020 7376 3910
e-mail: maureen.cpgarden@demon.co.uk
Begun in 1673 for the study of plants used by the Society of Apothecaries, this garden is one of Europe's oldest botanic gardens and is the only one to retain the title 'Physic' after the old name for the healing arts. The garden is still used for

continued

botanical and medicinal research, and offers displays of many fascinating plants in lovely surroundings.
Times: Open Apr-Oct, Wed 12-5, Sun 2-6. Additional opening during Chelsea Flower Show week, late May & Chelsea Festival week late Jun. Groups at other times by appointment. **Fee:** ✱ £5 (ch 5-15, students with proof & UB40 £3, ch under 5 free). **Facilities:** P (0.5m) (west end of Battersea Park) 🅿 & (disabled parking, wheelchair access) toilets for disabled shop 🦮 (ex guide dogs)

W4
CHISWICK HOUSE
Burlington Ln, Chiswick W4 2RD
➲ (Underground - Gunnersbury)
☎ 020 8995 0508 ▤ 020 8742 3104
Discover the story of this celebrated Palladian villa, a fine example of 18th-century English architecture with lavish interiors and classical landscaping.
Times: Open Apr-Oct, Wed-Sun & BHs 10-5 (closes 2pm Sat). Closed Nov-Mar but pre-booked are available, please telephone for details. **Fee:** ✱ £3.70 (ch £1.90, concessions £2.80). Prices & opening times relate to 2004, for further details phone or log onto www.english-heritage.org.uk/visits **Facilities:** P 🅿 & (telephone in advance for wheelchair facilities) shop ♯

WC2
COURTAULD GALLERY
Somerset House, Strand WC2R 0RN
➲ (Underground - Temple, Embankment, & Covent Garden)
☎ 020 7848 2526 ▤ 020 7848 2589
e-mail: galleryinfo@courtauld.ac.uk
The Galleries contain the superb collection of paintings begun by Samuel Courtauld in the 1920s and 1930s and presented to the University of London in memory of his wife. This is the most important collection of Impressionist and post-Impressionist works in Britain and includes major works by Cezanne, Renoir, Degas, van Gogh, Monet, Manet, Seurat and others. A programme of temporary exhibitions regularly includes works from the prints and drawings collection, while the long-term loan or early 20th-century paintings have added to the depth and range of the displays. Contact the gallery for current exhibition schedule.
Times: Open daily 10-6. Last admission 5.15. **Fee:** £5 (concessions £4). **Facilities:** P (NCP Drury Lane) 🅿 & (parking by arrangement only, call 020 7836 8686, lift) toilets for disabled shop 🦮 (ex guide dogs) 🍴

SE10
CUTTY SARK CLIPPER SHIP
King William Walk, Greenwich SE10 9HT
➲ (situated in dry dock beside Greenwich Pier)
☎ 020 8858 2698 ▤ 020 8858 6976
e-mail: info@cuttysark.org.uk
The fastest tea clipper ever, built in 1869, she once sailed 363 miles in a single day. Preserved in dry dock since 1957, her graceful lines dominate the riverside at Greenwich. Exhibitions and a video presentation the story of the ship, and restoration work can be seen.
Times: Open all year, daily 10-4.30 (Closed 24-27 Dec). **Fee:** ✱ £4.25(concessions £3.25, ch £2.95). Family ticket £10.50. **Facilities:** P (50mtrs) & shop 🦮 (ex guide dogs) 🍴

SE1
DALI UNIVERSE
County Hall Gallery, Riverside Building, South Bank SE1 7PB Waterloo Station
➲ (Follow signs to South Bank and County Hall attractions. We are located next to the London Eye. Westminster Underground - Cross Westminster Bridge and County Hall is on your left)
☎ 0870 744 7485 ▤ 020 7620 3120
e-mail: info@countyhallgallery.com

Set in County Hall Gallery, the Dali Universe is host to the worlds largest exhibit of surreal and anthropomorphic sculpture by Salvador Dali, including the *Profile of Time* and *Alice in Wonderland*. The exhibition also features a multiplicity of gold ornaments and works in crystal, an unrivalled collection of rare graphics and surreal furniture - including the Mae West Lips Sofa - and the monumental *Spellbound* canvas commissioned for the 1945 Hitchcock film of the same name.
Times: 10-6.30 (last entry 5.30pm) Open every day except 25 Dec. Check the website for late summer openings. **Fee:** ✱ £8.50-£9 (ch: 4-7yrs, £3.50; 8-16yrs, £5.50, concessions £7-£7.50) **Facilities:** P (5 mins) & (elevator, ramp access) toilets for disabled shop 🦮 🍴

SE1
DESIGN MUSEUM
Shad Thames SE1 2YD
➲ (Turn off Tooley St onto Shad Thames. Underground - London Bridge or Tower Hill)
☎ 0870 909 9009 ▤ 0870 909 1909 `2 for 1`
e-mail: info@designmuseum.org
The Design Museum is the first museum in the world to be dedicated to 20th and 21st century design. Since opening in 1989, it has become one of London's most inspiring attractions and has won international acclaim for its ground-breaking exhibition and education programmes. As one of the leading museums of design, fashion and architecture, the Design Museum has a changing programme of exhibitions, combining compelling insights into design history with innovative contemporary design.
Times: Open all year, daily 10-5.45 (last entry 5.15). Late opening on Fri, during summer months only 9pm (last entry 8.30pm). Closed 25 Dec only. **Fee:** £6 (concessions £4) Family ticket £16. **Facilities:** P (3 mins) (Gainsford St car park is chargeable) 🅿 ✗ licensed & (ramped entrance, wheelchair & lift) toilets for disabled shop 🦮 (ex guide dogs) 🍴

EC4
DR JOHNSON'S HOUSE
17 Gough Square EC4A 3DE
⮑ (Underground - Temple, Blackfriars, Chancery Lane)
☎ 020 7353 3745 📄 020 7353 3745
e-mail: curator@drjohnsonshouse.org
The celebrated literary figure, Dr Samuel Johnson, lived here between 1748 and 1759. He wrote his English Dictionary here, and a facsimile third edition is on display at the house. The dictionary took nine and a half years to complete and contained 40,000 words. Johnson then undertook the formidable task of editing the complete works of Shakespeare. The house is a handsome example of early 18th-century architecture, and includes a collection of prints, letters and other Johnson memorabilia.
Times: Open all year, May-Sep, daily 11-5.30; Oct-Apr 11-5. (Closed Sun, BH's, Good Fri & 24 Dec). **Facilities:** P (500yds) (limited meters) (Large print info sheets, handrails, seating) shop ✖ (ex guide dogs)

SE21
DULWICH PICTURE GALLERY
Gallery Rd, Dulwich SE21 7AD
⮑ (off South Circular A205 follow signs to Dulwich village)
☎ 020 8693 5254 📄 020 8299 8700   **2 for 1**
e-mail: info@dulwichpicturegallery.org.uk
This is the oldest public picture gallery in England, housing a magnificent collection of Old Masters, including works by Poussin, Claude, Rubens, Murillo, Van Dyck, Rembrandt, Watteau and Gainsborough. The gallery was designed by Sir John Soane in 1811. The collection, the building and the critically acclaimed loan exhibitions make the gallery a must see for art lovers.
Times: Open all year, Tue-Fri 10-5, wknds & BH Mon 11-5. (Closed Mon). **Fee:** ✱ £4 (pen £3, students, UB40, disabled & ch free). **Facilities:** P ✖ licensed ♿ (wheelchairs available, hearing loop) toilets for disabled shop ✖ (garden only, ex guide dogs) ▰

SE9
ELTHAM PALACE HOUSE & GARDENS
Court Yard SE9 5QE
☎ 020 8294 2548
Stephen and Virginia Courtauld's stunning country house shows the glamour and allure of 1930's Art Deco style and is a feast of luxurious design ideas. The house incorporates the medieval Great Hall and stunning moated gardens.
Times: Open Apr-Oct, Wed-Fri, Sun & BH's 10-5; Oct, Nov-23 Dec & 2 Feb-Mar, Wed-Fri & Sun 10-4. **Fee:** ✱ House & Gardens: £7 (ch £3.50, concessions £5.30). Gardens only: £4.30 (ch £2.30, concessions £3.40). Family £17.50. Prices & opening times relate to 2004, for further details phone or log onto www.english-heritage.org.uk/visits
Facilities: P ♿ shop ✖ ▰ ▦

SE1
THE FASHION & TEXTILE MUSEUM
83 Bermondsey St SE1 3XF
☎ 020 7403 0222 📄 020 7407 8664
e-mail: info@ftmlondon.org
Set on the South Bank, and opened in 2002, the FTM is the first exhibition space in London to dedicate itself to the global fashion industry. The Museum will hold two or three major exhibitions a year, manage an education and outreach
continued

programme, and host an extensive digital fashion and textile archive.
Times: ✱ Open Tue-Sun 11-5.45 (last admission 5.15pm)
Facilities: P ♿ toilets for disabled shop ✖ ▰

NW3
FENTON HOUSE
Windmill Hill NW3 6RT
⮑ (Underground - Hampstead, right out of station. Cross Heath St, up Holly Hill. Take right fork at top of hill into Hampstead Grove. Entrance on left of Hampstead Grove)
☎ 020 7435 3471 📄 020 7435 3471   **2 for 1**
e-mail: fentonhouse@nationaltrust.org.uk
A William and Mary merchants house built about 1686 and set in a walled garden, Fenton House is now owned by the National Trust. It contains outstanding displays of Oriental and European porcelain, 17th century needlework pictures and Georgian furniture as well as the Benton Fletcher collection of early keyboard instruments.
Times: Open Mar, Sat & Sun 2-5; Apr-Oct, Sat-Sun & BH Mon 11-5pm, Wed-Fri 2-5pm. Last admission 4.30pm. **Fee:** £4.80 (ch £2.40). Family ticket £12. Group 15+ £4. **Facilities:** ♿ (photographs of areas which are not accessible) ✖ ▨

SE18
FIREPOWER
Royal Arsenal, Woolwich SE18 6ST
⮑ (A205, right at Woolwich ferry onto A206, Firepower is signposted from there).
☎ 020 8855 7755 📄 020 8855 7100
e-mail: info@firepower.org.uk
Firepower is the Royal Artillery Museum in the historic Royal Arsenal. It spans 2000 years of artillery and shows how it developed from Roman catapult to guided missile to self-propelled gun. Put science into action with touchscreen displays and be awed by the big guns.
Times: ✱ Open Wed-Sun & BHs 11-5.30. Phone for winter opening times. **Facilities:** P (charged) ♿ (wheelchairs available) toilets for disabled shop ✖ (ex guide dogs) ▰

SE1
FLORENCE NIGHTINGALE MUSEUM
Gassiot House, 2 Lambeth Palace Rd SE1 7EW
⮑ (Underground - Westminster, Waterloo. On the site of St Thomas' Hospital)
☎ 020 7620 0374 📄 020 7928 1760
e-mail: info@florence-nightingale.co.uk
Florence Nightingale needs no introduction, but this museum shows clearly that she was more than 'The Lady with the Lamp'. Beautifully designed, the museum creates a personal setting in which a large collection of Florence's personal items including childhood souvenirs, her dress, furniture from her houses and honours awarded to her in old age are displayed. There is a small military history collection of souvenirs from the Crimean War, including military medals and a military nursing uniform.
Times: Open all year, Mon-Fri 10-5; wknds & BHs 11.30-4.30. Last admission 1hr before closing. (Closed Good Fri, Etr Sun & 24 Dec-2 Jan). **Facilities:** P (20mtrs) (hospital parking limited and charged) ♿ toilets for disabled shop ✖ (ex guide dogs) ▰

N7
FREIGHTLINERS CITY FARM NEW
Sheringham Rd, Islington N7 8PF
➲ (off Liverpool Rd)
☎ 020 7609 0467 🖥 020 7609 9934 FREE
e-mail: robert@freightlinersfarm.org.uk
A city farm bringing rural life into an urban setting. A variety of animals can be seen at the farm, including cows, pigs, goats, sheep and poultry. Some interesting building projects are taking place at the farm, including a strawbale building, solar dome, an outside bread oven and a continental beehive.
Times: Winter: 10-4. Summer: 10-4.45 **Facilities:** 🅿 (charged) 🍽 ♿ toilets for disabled shop garden centre ✖ (ex guide dogs) 📷

NW3
FREUD MUSEUM
20 Maresfield Gardens, Hampstead NW3 5SX
➲ (Underground - Finchley Road)
☎ 020 7435 2002 & 7435 5167
🖥 020 7431 5452
e-mail: freud@gn.apc.org
In 1938, Sigmund Freud left Vienna as a refugee from the Nazi occupation and chose exile in England, transferring his entire domestic and working environment to this house. He worked here until his death a year later. His extraordinary collection of Egyptian, Greek, Roman and Oriental antiquities, his working library and papers, and his fine furniture including the famous desk and couch are all here.
Times: Open all year, Wed-Sun 12-5 (Closed BHs, telephone for Xmas Holiday times). **Facilities:** 🅿 ♿ (personal tours can be arranged if booked in advance) shop ✖ (ex guide dogs) 📷

E2
GEFFRYE MUSEUM
136 Kingsland Rd, Shoreditch E2 8EA
➲ (establishment at the Southern end of Kingsland Rd A10 in Shoreditch, between Cremer Street and Pearson Street.)
☎ 020 7739 9893 🖥 020 7729 5647 FREE
e-mail: info@geffrye-museum.org.uk
The only museum in the UK to specialise in the domestic interiors and furniture of the urban middle classes. Displays span the 400 years from 1600 to the present day, forming a sequence of period rooms which capture the nature of English interior style. The museum is set in elegant, 18th-century buildings, surrounded by delightful gardens including an award-winning walled herb garden and a series of historical gardens which highlight changes in urban middle-class gardens from the 17th to 20th centuries. One of the museum's historic almshouses has recently been fully restored to its original condition and is open on selected days (ring for details).
Times: Open all year, Tue-Sat 10-5, Sun & BH Mons 12-5 (Closed Mon, Good Fri, 24-26 Dec & New Year). **Facilities:** 🅿 (150yds) (meter parking) Very restricted ✖ licensed ♿ (ramps, lift, wheelchair available) toilets for disabled shop ✖ (ex guide dogs)

WC2
GILBERT COLLECTION
Somerset House, Strand WC2R 1LA
➲ (Underground - Temple, Covent Garden)
☎ 020 7420 9400 🖥 020 7420 9440
e-mail: info@gilbert-collection.org.uk
An outstanding collection of decorative arts and an important bequest to the nation. The Gilbert Collection is the
continued

gift of Sir Arthur Gilbert and is on permanent display at Somerset House. The museum includes European silver, gold snuff boxes and Italian mosaics, the displays also include furniture, clocks and portrait miniatures. Temporary exhibitions run throughout the year.
Times: Open daily 10-6, last admission 5.15. **Facilities:** 🅿 (400mtrs) 🍽 ✖ licensed ♿ (lifts, hearing loop, wheelchair hire, disabled parking) toilets for disabled shop ✖ (ex guide dogs) 📷

SE1
GOLDEN HINDE EDUCATIONAL MUSEUM
St Mary Overie Dock, Cathedral St SE1 9DE
➲ (On the Thames path between Southwark Cathedral and the new Globe Theatre)
☎ 020 7403 0123 🖥 020 7407 5908
e-mail: info@goldenhinde.co.uk
A full size replica of Sir Francis Drake's famous 16th century galleon. Just like the original, this *Golden Hinde* has circumnavigated the globe. You can explore the five decks, and replica furnishings add to the atmosphere. Special events include Living History re-enactments. There are holiday workshops for children and the ship is also available for private hire.
Times: ✻ Open all year, 9.30-5.30. Visitors are advised to check opening times as they may vary due to closures for functions.
Facilities: 🅿 (on street parking) 🍽 shop ✖ (ex guide dogs) 📷

EC2
THE GUILDHALL
Gresham St EC2V 5AE
➲ (Underground - Bank, St Paul's)
☎ 020 7606 3030 🖥 020 7260 1119 FREE
e-mail: pro@corpoflondon.gov.uk
The Court of Common Council (presided over by the Lord Mayor) administers the City of London and meets in the Guildhall. Dating from 1411, the building was badly damaged in the Great Fire and again in the Blitz. The great hall, traditionally used for the Lord Mayor's Banquet and other important civic functions, is impressively decorated with the banners and shields of the livery companies, of which there are more than 90. The Clock Museum, which has a collection of 700 exhibits, charts the history of 500 years of time-keeping.
Times: Open all year, May-Sep, daily 10-5; Oct-Apr, Mon-Sat 10-5. (Closed Xmas, New Year, Good Fri, Etr Mon & infrequently for Civic occasions). Please contact 020 7606 3030 ext 1463 before visit to be certain of access. **Facilities:** ♿ Lift for east and west crypts toilets for disabled shop ✖

W1
HANDEL HOUSE MUSEUM
25 Brook St W1K 4HB
➲ (off Park Lane into Brook Gate, then Upper Brook Street. Pass Claridge's Hotel on right. The entrance is Lancashire Court)
☎ 020 7495 1685 🖥 020 7495 1759
e-mail: mail@handelhouse.org
Home to George Frideric Handel from 1723 until his death in 1759, the Handel House Museum celebrates Handel's career and times. It was here that Handel composed, *Messiah*, *Zadok the Priest* and *Fireworks Music*. Over 200 years later, live music, educational projects and public events still bring the address to life.
Times: ✻ Open Tue, Wed & Sat 10-6, Thu 10-8, Sun 12-6. (Closed BH Mon 25-26 Dec & 1 Jan) **Facilities:** 🅿 ♿ toilets for disabled shop ✖ (ex guide dogs) 📷

N6
HIGHGATE CEMETERY
Swains Ln N6 6PJ

➲ (Underground - Archway, see directions posted at exit)

☎ 020 8340 1834

Highgate Cemetery is the most impressive of a series of large, formally arranged and landscaped cemeteries which were established around the perimeter of London in the mid-19th century. There's a wealth of fine sculpture and architecture amongst the tombstones, monuments and mausoleums as well as the graves of such notables as the Rossetti family, George Eliot, Michael Faraday and Karl Marx. It is also a Grade II listed park.

Times: Open all year. Eastern Cemetery: daily 10 (11 wknds)-5 (4 in winter). Western Cemetery by guided tour only: Sat & Sun 11-4 (3 in winter); midweek tours at 2pm, advisable to book. (Closed 25-26 Dec & during funerals). **Fee:** ✱ East cemetery £2. Tour of West cemetery £3 (ch 8-16 £1, no ch under 8 on tours). Donations encouraged to assist restoration. Camera permits for private use £1 on each side (no video or flash). **Facilities:** ✖ (guide dogs)

SE1
HMS BELFAST
Morgans Ln, Tooley St SE1 2JH

➲ (Underground - London Bridge/Tower Hill/Monument. Rail: London Bridge)

☎ 020 7940 6300　▤ 020 7403 0719

e-mail: hmsbelfast@iwm.org.uk

Europe's last surviving big gun armoured warship from the Second World War, *HMS Belfast* was launched in 1938 and served in the North Atlantic and Arctic with the Home Fleet. She led the Allied naval bombardment of German positions on D-Day, and was saved for the nation in 1971. A tour of the ship will take you from the Captain's Bridge through nine decks to the massive Boiler and Engine Rooms. You can visit the cramped Messdecks, Officers' Cabins, Galley, Sick Bay, Dentist and Laundry.

Times: Open all year, daily. Mar-Oct 10-6, last admission 5.15; Nov-Feb 10-5, last admission 4.15. (Closed 24-26 Dec). **Fee:** ✱ £7 (ch under 16 free, concessions £4.50). Party £5.50 per person. **Facilities:** ▣ ♿ (wheelchair lift for access on board) toilets for disabled shop ✖ (ex guide dogs) ▭

W4
HOGARTH HOUSE
Hogarth Ln, Great West Rd W4 2QN

➲ (50yds W of Hogarth rdbt on Great West Road A4).

☎ 020 8994 6757　▤ 0845 456 2880　　FREE

This 18th-century house was the country home of artist William Hogarth (1697-1764) during the last 15 years of his life. The house contains displays on the artist's life, and many of his satirical engravings. The gardens contain Hogarth's famous mulberry tree.

Times: Open Apr-Oct, Tue-Fri 1-5, Sat-Sun 1-6; Nov-Mar, Tue-Fri 1-4, Sat-Sun 1-5. (Closed Mon (ex BHs), Jan, 25-26 Dec, Good Fri). **Facilities:** ▣ (25 & 50yds) (spaces marked in Axis Centre car park) ♿ toilets for disabled shop ✖ (ex guide dogs)

SE23
THE HORNIMAN MUSEUM & GARDENS
London Rd, Forest Hill SE23 3PQ

➲ (situated on A205)

☎ 020 8699 2339 (rec info) 020 8699 1872

▤ 020 8291 5506

e-mail: marketing@horniman.ac.uko.uk

Founder Frederick Horniman, a tea merchant, gave the museum to the people of London in 1901. The collection covers Natural History - including Vanishing Birds; African Worlds; and The Music Room, which is currently undergoing redevelopment. There are 16 acres of gardens, and the museum hosts a variety of workshops and activities.

Times: ✱ Open all year, Mon-Sat 10.30-5.30, Sun 2-5.30 (Closed 24-26 Dec). Gardens close at sunset. **Facilities:** ▣ (opposite museum) ▭ ♿ (chair lift to parts of upper floor) toilets for disabled shop ✖ (ex guide dogs or in gardens)

SW1
HOUSES OF PARLIAMENT
Westminster SW1A 0AA

➲ (Underground - Westminster)

☎ 020 7219 4272　▤ 020 7219 5839

The Houses of Parliament occupy the Palace of Westminster, a royal palace for nearly 1000 years. Visitors will see the Queen's Robing Room, the Royal Gallery, the Chambers of both the House of Lords and House of Commons, the voting lobbies, historic Westminster Hall (c.1097) where Charles I and Guy Fawkes were put on trial, plus other areas normally hidden from public view.

Times: Open 24 Jul-4 Sep, Mon, Tue, Fri & Sat, 9.15-4.30, Wed & Thu, 1.15-4.30; 18 Sep-2 Oct, Mon, Fri & Sat, 9.15-4.30, Tue, Wed & Thu 1.15-4.30. Times are for 1st and last tours of the day. **Fee:** ✱ £7 (ch 5-16 £5, concessions £5) Family ticket £22. Foreign language tours £7.50-£9. Group rates on application. **Facilities:** ▣ (50mtrs) (limited parking, metered) ▭ ♿ (touch & sound model for visually impaired) toilets for disabled shop ✖ (ex guide dogs) ▭▭ ▭

SE1
IMPERIAL WAR MUSEUM
Lambeth Rd SE1 6HZ

➲ (Underground - Lambeth North, Elephant & Castle or Waterloo)

☎ 020 7416 5000　▤ 020 7416 5374

e-mail: mail@iwm.org.uk

Founded in 1917, this museum illustrates and records all aspects of the two World Wars and other military operations involving Britain and the Commonwealth since 1914. There are always special exhibitions and the programme of events includes film shows and lectures. The museum has a wealth of military reference material, although some reference departments are open to the public by appointment only.

Times: ✱ Open all year, daily 10-6. (Closed 24-26 Dec). **Facilities:** ▣ (on street 100mtrs) (metered Mon-Fri) ▭ ✖ licensed ♿ (parking & wheelchair hire book in advance, study room) toilets for disabled shop ✖ (ex guide dogs) ▭

N3
THE JEWISH MUSEUM
The Sternberg Centre, 80 East End Rd, Finchley N3 2SY
➲ (Underground - Finchley Central, 10 mins walk
via Station Rd & Manor View)
☎ 020 8349 1143 ▤ 020 8343 2162
e-mail: enquiries@jewishmuseum.org.uk
The Jewish Museum traces the story of Jewish immigration
and settlement in London, including a reconstruction of an
East End tailoring workshop. It also has a Holocaust
Education Gallery with an exhibition on Leon Greenman -
British Citizen and Auschwitz survivor. There is a regular
programme of changing exhibitions and events.
Times: Open all year, Sun 10.30-4.30, Mon-Thu 10.30-5. Closed Jewish
festivals, public holidays & 24 Dec-4 Jan. Also closed Sun in Aug & BH
wknds. **Fee:** ✸ £2 (concessions £1, ch free) **Facilities:** P (50mtrs)
(on street parking) 🚾 & toilets for disabled shop ✖

NW1
THE JEWISH MUSEUM
Raymond Burton House, 129-131 Albert St, Camden
Town NW1 7NB
➲ (Underground - Camden Town, 3 mins walk
from station)
☎ 020 7284 1997 ▤ 020 7267 9008 2 for 1
e-mail: marketing@jmus.org.uk

Attractive galleries illustrating Jewish history and religious
life in Britain and beyond. One of the world's finest
collections of Jewish ceremonial art. There are constantly-
changing temporary exhibitions, events and workshops.
Times: Open Mon-Thu, 10-4, Sun 10 5. Closed Jewish Festivals &
public holidays. **Fee:** ✸ £3.50 (ch, students, disabled & UB40 £1.50,
pen £2.50) Family ticket £8. **Facilities:** P (outside museum) (pay &
display parking) & (induction loop in lecture room linked to
audio-visual unit) toilets for disabled shop ✖ (ex guide dogs) 🝖

NW3
KEATS HOUSE
Keats Grove, Hampstead NW3 2RR
➲ (Underground - Hampstead, about 15mins walk
from station)
☎ 020 7435 2062 ▤ 020 7431 9293
e-mail: keatshouse@corpoflondon.gov.uk
The poet John Keats lived in this house from 1818-1820 and
wrote some of his most famous poems, including *Ode to a
Nightingale* here. His fiancée, Fanny Brawne, lived next door,
and they often walked together on nearby Hampstead Heath.
continued

The house contains many of his personal items including
inkstand, engagement ring, paintings, jewellery and
manuscripts.
Times: ✸ Open 23 Apr-10 Dec, Tue-Sat 12-5. Tue-Sat between 10-12
guided tours, schools & visits by appointment take place. Wed between
5-8 a programme of tours & lectures are available. Sun & BHs 12-5.
Facilities: P (500yds) (residents parking in operation) & shop
✖ (ex guide dogs)

W8
KENSINGTON PALACE STATE APARTMENTS & ROYAL CEREMONIAL DRESS COLLECTION
Kensington Gardens W8 4PX
➲ (Underground - High Street Kensington or
Notting Hill Gate)
☎ 0870 751 5170 ▤ 020 7376 0198
Highlights of a visit to Kensington include the recently
restored Kings Apartments with a fine collection of Old
Masters; Tintoretto and Van Dyke amongst them. The Royal
Ceremonial Dress Collection includes a selection of HM The
Queen's dresses, representations of tailor's and dressmaker's
workshops, and a display of dresses belonging to Diana,
Princess of Wales.
Times: ✸ Open Mar-Oct 10-6, last admission 5; Nov-end Feb 10-5, last
admission 4. (Closed 24-26 Dec). **Facilities:** P (500yds) 🚾
& (cafeteria has wheelchair access ramp) toilets for disabled shop
✖ (ex guide dogs) 🍴

NW3
KENWOOD HOUSE
Hampstead Ln NW3 7JR
➲ (Underground - Hampstead)
☎ 020 8348 1286 ▤ 020 7973 3891 FREE
In splendid grounds beside Hampstead Heath, this
outstanding neo-classical house contains one of the most
important collections of paintings ever given to the nation.
Works by Rembrandt, Vermeer, Turner, Gainsborough and
Reynolds are all set against a backdrop of sumptuous rooms.
Scenes from *Notting Hill* and *Mansfield Park* were both filmed
here.
Times: Open all year, Apr-Oct, daily 10-5; Nov-Mar, daily 10-4 (park
stays open later, see notices). On Wed & Fri house opens at 10.30.
(Closed 24-26 Dec & 1 Jan). **Facilities:** P 🚾 ✖ licensed & toilets
for disabled shop ⊞

W14
LEIGHTON HOUSE MUSEUM & ART GALLERY
12 Holland Park Rd W14 8LZ
➲ (Underground - High Street Kensington.
Museum is N of Kensington High Street, off
Melbury Rd.)
☎ 020 7602 3316
e-mail: museums@rbkc.gov.uk
An opulent and exotic example of high Victorian taste,
Leighton House was built for the President of the Royal
Academy, Frederic Lord Leighton. The main body of the
house was built in 1866 but the fabulous Arab Hall, an
arresting 'Arabian Nights' creation, was not completed until
13 years later.
Times: Open all year, daily 11-5. (Closed Tue). **Fee:** ✸ £3
(concessions £1). Joint tours of Leighton House Museum & Linley
Sambourne House £10. **Facilities:** P (100mtrs) (metered) shop
✖ 🍴

W8
Linley Sambourne House
18 Stafford Ter W8 7BH
➲ (Underground - High Street Kensington)
☎ 020 7602 3316 ext 305 🖷 020 7371 2467
e-mail: **museums@rbkc.gov.uk**

The home of Linley Sambourne (1844-1910), chief political cartoonist at *Punch* magazine, has had its magnificent artistic interior preserved, almost unchanged, since the late 19th century. Also displayed are many of Sambourne's own drawings and photographs. Tours are lead by costumed actors with scripts developed from the Sambourne family archive.
Times: all access by guided tour. 5 Mar-11 Dec. Sat/Sun tours 10am, 11.15am, 1pm, 2.15pm, 3.30pm. Weekdays book in advance
Fee: ✱ £6 (ch £1, concessions £4) **Facilities:** P 2 min walk (metered parking) shop ✖ ➡

SE1
London Aquarium
County Hall, Riverside Building, Westminster Bridge Rd SE1 7PB
➲ (Underground-Waterloo & Westminster. On south bank next to Westminster Bridge, nr Big Ben & London Eye)
☎ 020 7967 8000 🖷 020 7967 8029
e-mail: **info@londonaquarium.co.uk**

The London Aquarium is one of Europe's largest displays of global aquatic life with over 350 species in over 50 displays, ranging from the mystical seahorse to the deadly stonefish. The huge Pacific display is home to a variety of jacks, stingrays and eight sharks. Come and witness the spectacular Atlantic feed where our team of divers hand feed rays and native British sharks. The rainforest feed incorporates a frenzied piranha attack with the amazing marksmanship of the archerfish. There is also a range of education tours and literature to enhance any visit.
Times: ✱ Open all year, daily 10-6. Last admission 1hr before closing. Closed 25 Dec. late opening over summer months see website for details **Facilities:** P (300mtrs) 🅿 ⓰ (wheelchairs available) toilets for disabled shop ✖ (ex guide & hearing dogs) ➡

N1
The London Canal Museum
12/13 New Wharf Rd N1 9RT
➲ (Underground - Kings Cross. Follow York Way along East side of King's Cross Stn, turn right at Wharfdale Rd, then left into New Wharf Rd).
☎ 020 7713 0836 🖷 020 7689 6679
e-mail: **info@canalmuseum.org.uk**

The museum covers the development of London's canals (particularly Regent's Canal), canal vessels and trade, and the way of life of the canal people. Housed in a former ice warehouse and stables, it also illustrates horse transport and the unusual trade of importing ice from Norway; there are two large ice wells under the floor. Facilities include temporary moorings, so you can arrive by boat if you want. There are regular special exhibitions.
Times: Open all year, Tue-Sun & BH Mon 10-4.30 (last admission 3.45). Closed 24-26 & 31 Dec. **Fee:** £3 (ch £1.50, students, pen & UB40s £2, under 8's free). Groups 10+ **Facilities:** P (0.25m) (parking Mon-Fri before 6.30pm, Sat 1.30) ⓰ (large print guides, induction loop, Braille signs) toilets for disabled shop ✖ (ex guide dogs) ➡

SE1
London Dungeon
28-34 Tooley St SE1 2SZ
➲ (Next to London Bridge Station)
☎ 020 7403 7221 🖷 020 7378 1529
e-mail: **londondungeon@
merlin-entertainments.com**

Blood and guts, torture and terror, in re-enactments of some of the most gruesome events in British history. Brave the Great Fire of London, sail down the Thames towards Traitor's Gate, or visit Executioners corner. You can also meet some especially Wicked Women. Step back to 1665 to dodge the rats inhabiting London's newest feature, 'The Great Plague'.
Times: ✱ Open all year, daily, Apr-Sep 10-5.30; Oct-Mar 10.30-5. Late night opening in the Summer. Telephone for exact times.
Facilities: P (NCP 200yds) 🅿 ⓰ toilets for disabled shop ✖ (ex guide dogs) ➡

WC2
London's Transport Museum
The Piazza, Covent Garden WC2E 7BB
➲ (Underground - Covent Garden, Leicester Sq or Holburn)
☎ 020 7379 6344 & 020 7565 7299
🖷 020 7565 7250
e-mail: **resourced@ltmuseum.co.uk**

Covent Garden's original Victorian flower market is home to this excellent museum which explores the colourful story of London and its famous transport system from 1800 to the present day. There are buses, trams, tube trains, and posters, as well as touch-screen displays, videos, working models and tube simulators to bring the story to life.
Times: ✱ Open all year, daily 10-6, Fri 11-6. Last admission 5.15pm. (Closed 24-26 Dec). **Facilities:** P (5 mins walk) (parking meters) 🅿 ⓰ (lift & ramps, touch & sign tours) toilets for disabled shop ✖ (ex guide dogs) ➡

SW13
London Wetland Centre
Queen Elizabeth Walk SW13 9WT
➲ (underground - Hammersmith).
☎ 020 8409 4400 🖷 020 8409 4401
e-mail: **info@wetlandcentre.org.uk**

An inspiring wetland landscape that stretches over 105 acres, almost in the heart of London, in Barnes SW13. 30 wild wetland habitats have been created from reservoir lagoon to ponds, lakes and reedbeds and all are home to a wealth of wildlife.
Times: Winter 9.30-4, Summer 9.30-5. **Fee:** £6.75 (ch £4 & pen £5.50). Family ticket £17.50. Groups 10+. Car park £2 charge on Sun & BH's per vehicle. **Facilities:** P (charged) 🅿 ✖ licensed ⓰ (ramps, lifts) toilets for disabled shop ✖ (ex guide dogs)

NW1
London Zoo
Regents Park NW1 4RY
➲ (Underground - Camden Town or Regents Park)
☎ 020 7449 6235 🖷 020 7586 5743
e-mail: **marketing@zsl.org**

London Zoo is home to over 12,000 animals, insects, reptiles and fish. First opened in 1828, the Zoo can claim the world's first aquarium, insect and reptile house. There's lots to do, plenty to see and so much to learn. Visit the cheeky, the deadly and the wild. Meet the world's largest lizards in the
continued

new Komodo dragon exhibit. Get closer to your favourite animals, learn about them at the keeper talks and watch them show off their skills at special events. By visiting London Zoo, visitors help protect endangered species, conserve natural habitats and bring learning to life for all ages.
Times: Open all year, daily from 10am. (Closed 25 Dec). **Fee:** ✱ £13 (ch 3-15 £9.75, concessions £11). Family £41. **Facilities:** 🅿 (charged) 💺 ✗ licensed & (wheelchairs & booster scooter available) toilets for disabled shop ✗ 🎦

NW8
LORD'S TOUR & M.C.C. MUSEUM
Lord's Ground NW8 8QN
⮑ (Underground - St John's Wood)
☎ 020 7616 8595 & 7616 8596
🖨 020 7266 3825

2 for 1

e-mail: tours@mcc.org.uk
Established in 1787, Lord's is the home of the MCC and cricket. Guided tours take you behind the scenes, and highlights include the Long Room and the MCC Museum, where the Ashes and a large collection of paintings and memorabilia are displayed. The Museum is open on match days for spectators. (2-for-1 Voucher applies to public guided tours only, not match day admission to museum)
Times: Open all year, Oct-Mar tours at 12 & 2pm. Apr-Sep 10am, 12 & 2pm (restrictions on some match days). Telephone for details & bookings. **Fee:** Guided tour £7 (ch £4.50, students & pen £5.50). Family ticket (2 ad & 2 ch) £20. Party 25+. Museum only £2.50 (concessions £1) plus ground admission (match days only).
Facilities: 🅿 ✗ licensed & (by arrangement) toilets for disabled shop ✗ (ex guide dogs) 🎦

NW1
MADAME TUSSAUD'S & THE LONDON PLANETARIUM
Marylebone Rd NW1 5LR
⮑ (Underground - Baker Street)
☎ 020 7935 6861 🖨 020 7465 0862
e-mail: csc@madame-tussauds.com
Madame Tussaud's world-famous waxwork collection was founded in Paris in 1770. It moved to England in 1802 and found a permanent home in London's Marylebone Road in 1884. The 21st century has brought new innovations and new levels of interactivity. Listen to Kylie Minogue whisper in your ear, become an A-list celeb in the 'Blush' nightclub, and take your chances in a high security prison populated by dangerous serial killers. Madame Tussaud's has recently been combined with the equally memorable London Planetarium, where visitors can now interact with characters from Disney's *Treasure Planet*.
Times: ✱ Open all year 10-5.30 (9.30am wknds, 9am summer).
Facilities: 🅿 (200mtrs) ✗ licensed & (All parts accessible except Spirit of London ride) toilets for disabled shop ✗ (ex guide dogs) 🎦

SW1
MALL GALLERIES
The Mall SW1Y 5BD
⮑ (Underground - Charing Cross, situated on the Mall, near Trafalgar Square and Admiralty Arch)
☎ 020 7930 6844 🖨 020 7839 7830
e-mail: info@mallgalleries.com

2 for 1

The venue for the annual open exhibitions of nine national art societies. There is also a wide range of individual and group shows. The galleries display work which is both traditional and contemporary by a large number of

prominent international artists. A variety of subjects are displayed in a number of mediums, including oil, watercolour, drawings and sculpture. Phone for details of special events.
Times: Open all year, daily 10-5. Closed between exhibitions and at Christmas. Some late night opening, please phone for details
Fee: £2.50 depending on exhibition (ch & pen £1). Groups 10+ £1 each **Facilities:** 🅿 (50 yds) (no parking at the Mall) 💺 & (chairlift to galleries) toilets for disabled ✗ (ex guide dogs) 🎦

EC4
MIDDLE TEMPLE HALL
The Temple EC4Y 9AT
⮑ (Underground - Temple, Blackfriars. Turn left at the embankment & left into Middle Temple Lane. Hall half way up on left)
☎ 020 7427 4800 🖨 020 7427 4801
e-mail: library@middletemple.org.uk
Between Fleet Street and the Thames are the Middle and Inner Temples, separate Inns of Court, so named after the Knights Templar who occupied the site from about 1160. Middle Temple Hall is a fine example of Tudor architecture and was completed in about 1570. The hall has a double hammerbeam roof and beautiful stained glass. The 29ft-long high table was made from a single oak tree from Windsor Forest. Sir Francis Drake was a visitor to and friend of the Middle Temple, and a table made from timbers from the *Golden Hind* - the ship in which he sailed around the world - is shown.
Times: ✱ Open all year, Mon-Fri 10-12 & 3-4 (Closed BH & legal vacations). **Facilities:** & ✗ 🚌

EC3
THE MONUMENT
Monument St EC3R 8AH
⮑ (Underground - Monument)
☎ 020 7626 2717 🖨 020 7403 4477
Designed by Wren and Hooke and erected in 1671-7, the Monument commemorates the Great Fire of 1666 which is reputed to have started in nearby Pudding Lane. The fire destroyed nearly 90 churches and about 13,000 houses. This fluted Doric column stands 202ft high (Pudding Lane is exactly 202ft from its base) and you can climb the 311 steps to a platform at the summit, and receive a certificate as proof of your athletic abilities.
Times: ✱ Open Mon-Sun, 10-6. Last admission 5.40pm.
Facilities: ✗

E2
MUSEUM OF CHILDHOOD AT BETHNAL GREEN
Cambridge Heath Rd E2 9PA
⮑ (Underground - Bethnal Green)
☎ 020 8980 2415 🖨 020 8983 5225
e-mail: bgmc@vam.ac.uk

FREE

The Museum of Childhood houses a multitude of childhood delights. Toys, dolls and dolls' houses, model soldiers, puppets, games, model theatres, children's costume and nursery antiques are all included in its well planned displays. Art activities and soft play every weekend throughout the school holidays. Permanent under 5's play area and games zone with board games and giant snakes & ladders.
Times: Open all year, Mon-Thu & Sat-Sun 10-5.50 (Closed Fri, 24-26 Dec & 1 Jan). **Facilities:** 🅿 (Metered parking) 💺 & (disabled parking by arrangement) toilets for disabled shop ✗

continued

SE1
MUSEUM OF GARDEN HISTORY
Lambeth Palace Rd SE1 7LB
➲ (Underground - Waterloo/Lambeth North, next to Lambeth Palace opposite Houses of Parliament)
☎ 020 7401 8865   📱 020 7401 8869   FREE
e-mail: info@museumgardenhistory.org

Situated in the restored church of St. Mary-At-Lambeth, adjacent to Lambeth Palace, the Museum of Garden History provides an insight into the history and development of gardens and gardening in the UK. It houses a fine public display of tools and artefacts. In addition, there is a replica 17th-century knot garden filled with flowers and shrubs of the period, created around the tombs of the famous plant hunters, the John Tradescants, father and son, and Captain William Bligh of the 'Bounty'.
Times: Daily, 10.30-5. **Facilities:** 🅿 (100yds) (metered) 🍽 ♿ toilets for disabled shop 🐕 (ex guide dogs)

EC2
MUSEUM OF LONDON
150 London Wall EC2Y 5HN
➲ (Underground - St Paul's, Barbican)
☎ 020 7600 3699   📱 020 7600 1058
e-mail: info@museumoflondon.org.uk

Dedicated to the story of London and its people, the Museum of London exists to inspire a passion for London in all who visit it. As well as the permanent collection, the Museum has a varied exhibition programme with three major temporary exhibitions and six topical displays each year. There are also smaller exhibitions in the newly-developed foyer gallery. A wide programme of lectures and activities are provided.
Times: ✱ Open all year, Mon-Sat 10-5.50, Sun 12-5.50 (closed 24-26 Dec & 1 Jan). **Facilities:** 🅿 🍽 ♿ (wheelchairs available, lifts & induction loops, parking) toilets for disabled shop 🐕 (ex guide dogs) 🍴

EC1
MUSEUM OF THE ORDER OF ST JOHN
St John's Gate, St John's Ln, Clerkenwell EC1M 4DA
➲ (Underground - Farringdon, Barbican)
☎ 020 7324 4070   📱 020 7336 0587

One of the most obscure and fascinating museums in London, St John's Gate displays treasures that once belonged to the Knights Hospitaller, the crusading knights who are now better known as first aiders. Maltese silver, Italian furniture, paintings, coins and pharmacy jars are among the objects on view. Guided tours are available.
Times: Open all year, Mon-Sat 10-5, Sat 10-4 (Closed Etr, Xmas wk & BH wknds). Guided tours 11 & 2.30 Tue, Fri & Sat. **Fee:** ✱ Museum free. For tours of St John's Gate & Grand Priory Church a donation of £4 (pen £3). **Facilities:** 🅿 (meters/NCP 300yds) ♿ toilets for disabled shop 🐕 (ex guide dogs)

WC2
MUSEUMS OF THE ROYAL COLLEGE OF SURGEONS
35-43 Lincoln's Inn Fields WC2A 3PE
➲ (Underground - Holborn)
☎ 020 7869 6560   📱 020 7869 6564   FREE
e-mail: museums@rcseng.ac.uk

The newly-refurbished Hunterian Museum houses the anatomical and pathological specimens collected by John Hunter FRS (1728-1793), a renowned surgeon and teacher of anatomy. The museum also contains the Science of Surgery Gallery which provides an insight into the development of surgical practice from the 18th century to the present day.
continued

The Collection Study Centre holds the museum's reserve collection and provides a dedicated space for learning, exploration and study.
Times: Due to reopen in Feb 2005, Mon-Fri 10-5
Facilities: 🅿 (15mtrs) (pay & display 8.30-6.30pm) ♿ (prior notice required, external lift) shop 🐕 (ex guide dogs)

SW3
NATIONAL ARMY MUSEUM
Royal Hospital Rd, Chelsea SW3 4HT
➲ (Underground - Sloane Square)
☎ 020 7730 0717   📱 020 7823 6573
e-mail: info@national-army-museum.ac.uk

The museum offers a unique insight into the lives of Britain's soldiers, with displays including weapons, paintings, equipment, models, medals, and uniforms.
Times: ✱ Open all year, daily 10-5.30. (Closed Good Fri, May Day, 24-26 Dec & 1 Jan). **Facilities:** 🅿 🍽 ♿ (wheelchair lift to access lower ground floor) toilets for disabled shop 🐕 (ex guide dogs)

WC2
NATIONAL GALLERY
Trafalgar Square WC2N 5DN
➲ (Underground - Charing Cross, Leicester Square, Embankment & Piccadilly Circus. Rail: Charing Cross. Located on N side of Trafalgar Sq)
☎ 020 7747 2885   📱 020 7747 2423   FREE
e-mail: information@ng-london.org.uk

All the great periods of Western European painting from 1260-1900 are represented here. The Gallery's particular treasures include Velázquez's *Toilet of Venus*, Leonardo da Vinci's Cartoon (*The Virgin and Child with Saints Anne and John the Baptist*), Rembrandt's *Belshazzar's Feast*, Van Gogh's *Sunflowers*, and Titian's *Bacchus and Ariadne*. The British paintings include Gainsborough's *Mr and Mrs Andrews* and Constable's *Haywain*. Free guided tours everyday.
Times: Open all year, daily 10-6, (Wed until 9pm). Special major charging exhibitions open normal gallery times. Closed 24-26 Dec & 1 Jan. **Facilities:** 🅿 (100yds) 🍽 ✕ licensed ♿ (wheelchair, induction loop, lift, deaf/blind visitor tours) toilets for disabled shop 🐕 (ex guide & hearing dogs) 🍴

SE10
NATIONAL MARITIME MUSEUM
Romney Rd SE10 9NF
➲ (central Greenwich)
☎ 020 8312 6565   📱 020 8312 6632   FREE

Britain's seafaring history displayed in an impressive modern museum. Themes include exploration and discovery, Nelson, trade and empire, passenger shipping and luxury liners, maritime London, costume, art and the sea, and the future of the sea. There are interactive displays for children.
Times: Open all year, daily 10-5. (Closed Xmas/New Year)
Facilities: 🅿 (50 yds) (parking in Greenwich limited) 🍽 ✕ licensed ♿ (wheelchairs, advisory service for hearing/sight impaired) toilets for disabled shop 🐕 (guide dogs) 🍴

WC2
NATIONAL PORTRAIT GALLERY
St Martin's Place WC2H 0HE
➲ (Underground - Charing Cross, Leicester Square. Buses to Trafalgar Square)
☎ 020 7306 0055   📱 020 7306 0056   FREE

The National Portrait Gallery is home to the largest collection of portraiture in the world featuring famous British men and
continued

woman who have created history from the Middle Ages until the present day. Over 1000 portraits are on display across three floors form Henry VIII and Florence Nightingale to The Beatles and The Queen. And, if you want to rest those weary feet, visit the fabulous Portrait Restaurant on the top floor with roof-top views across London.

Times: Open all year, Mon-Wed & Sat-Sun 10-6, Thu-Fri 10-9. (Closed Good Fri, 24-26 Dec & 1 Jan). Gallery closure commences 10mins prior to stated time. **Facilities:** P (200yds) ♨ ✗ licensed ও (stair climber, touch tours, audio guide, large print captions) toilets for disabled shop ✶ (ex guide dogs) ▰

SW7
THE NATURAL HISTORY MUSEUM
Cromwell Rd SW7 5BD
➲ (Underground - South Kensington)
☎ 020 7942 5000 ▤ 020 7942 5075
e-mail: marketing@nhm.ac.uk   `FREE`

This vast and elaborate Romanesque-style building, with its terracotta facing showing relief mouldings of animals, birds and fishes, covers an area of four acres. Holding over 70 million specimens from all over the globe, from dinosaurs to diamonds and earthquakes to ants, the museum provides a journey into Earth's past, present and future. Discover more about the work of the museum in the Darwin Centre, where you can go behind the scenes and talk to some of the scientists.

Times: Mon-Sat 10-5.50, Sun 11-5.50 (last admission 5.30). Closed 24-26 Dec. **Facilities:** P (180yds) (limited parking, use public transport) ♨ ✗ licensed ও (top floor/one gallery not accessible, wheelchair hire) toilets for disabled shop ✶ (ex guide dogs) ▰

SE10
OLD ROYAL NAVAL COLLEGE
2 Cutty Sark Gardens, Greenwich SE10 9LW
➲ (In centre of Greenwich, off the one way system, (college approach), located on the Thames next to the Cutty Sark and Greenwich Pier)
☎ 020 8269 4791 ▤ 020 8269 4757   `FREE`
e-mail: info@greenwichfoundation.org.uk

The grade one listed Old Royal Naval College buildings are now in the care of the Greenwich Foundation. They occupy the site of the Tudor palace where Henry VIII and Elizabeth I were born. The former Greenwich Hospital buildings incorporate the magnificent Painted Hall by Thornhill and a Chapel by James Stuart. Also open to the public are the beautiful grounds of the estate, and a visitor centre featuring an exhibition on the World Heritage Site of maritime Greenwich and the history of the site.

Times: Open all year (Painted Hall, Chapel and Visitor Centre), daily 10-5 (last admission 4.15). Chapel closed until 12.30 on Sundays.
Facilities: P (200mtrs) (all local streets, yellow line roads) ♨ ✗ licensed ও (parking, wheelchair, staircrawler, access, all with notice) toilets for disabled shop ✶ (ex guide dogs) ▰

WC1
PETRIE MUSEUM OF EGYPTIAN ARCHAEOLOGY
Malet Place, Univerity College London WC1E 6BT
➲ (on 1st floor of the D M S Watson building, in Malet Place, off Torrington Place)
☎ 020 7679 2884 ▤ 020 7679 2886
e-mail: petrie.museum@ucl.ac.uk

One of the largest and most inspiring collections of Egyptian archaeology anywhere in the world. The displays illustrate life in the Nile Valley from prehistory, through the era of the

Pharoahs to Roman and Islamic times. Especially noted for its collection of the personal items that illustrate life and death in Ancient Egypt, including the world's earliest surviving dress (c 2800BC).

Times: ✳ Open all year, Tue-Fri 1-5, Sat 10-1. Closed for 1 wk at Xmas/Etr. **Facilities:** ♨ ✗ ও toilets for disabled shop ✶ (ex guide dogs)

W1
POLLOCK'S TOY MUSEUM
1 Scala St W1T 2HL
➲ (Underground - Goodge Street)
☎ 020 7636 3452
e-mail: info@pollocksmuseum.co.uk

Teddy bears, wax and china dolls, dolls' houses, board games, toy theatres, tin toys, mechanical and optical toys, folk toys and nursery furniture, are among the attractions to be seen in this appealing museum. Items from all over the world and from all periods are displayed in two small, interconnecting houses with winding staircases and charming little rooms. Toy theatre performances available for groups.

Times: ✳ Open all year, Mon-Sat 10-5. (Closed BHs, Sun & Xmas).
Facilities: P (100yds) (Central London restrictions) ও shop ▰

SW1
THE QUEEN'S GALLERY
Buckingham Palace, Buckingham Palace Rd SW1A 1AA
➲ (Underground - Victoria, Green Park & St. James' Park)
☎ 020 7766 7301 ▤ 020 7930 9625
e-mail: buckinghampalace@royalcollection.org.uk

The Gallery hosts changing exhibitions of works of art from the Royal Collection. The collection has largely been formed since the restoration of the Monarchy in 1660 and includes paintings, drawings and watercolours, furniture, ceramics, clocks, silver, sculpture, jewellery, books, manuscripts, prints and maps, arms and armour, fans, and textiles. Works of art from the Royal Collection are also on display at the principal royal residences. Exhibitions in 2005 include: Enchanting the Eye: Dutch Paintings of the Golden Age (11 February to 30 October 2005).

Times: Open all year, daily, 10-5.30. Last admission 4.30. (Closed Good Fri, 25 & 26 Dec and between exhibitions) Entry by timed ticket.
Fee: (Free, except special exhibitions) **Fee:** ✳ £7.50 (ch 5 free, ch 17 £4, pen £6) Family ticket (2ad+2ch) £19 **Facilities:** P (200yds) ও toilets for disabled shop ✶ (ex guide dogs) ▰

SE10
THE QUEENS HOUSE
Romney Rd, Greenwich SE10 9NF
➲ (central Greenwich)
☎ 020 8312 6565 ▤ 020 8312 6632

The first Palladian-style villa in England, designed by Inigo Jones for Anne of Denmark and completed for Queen Henrietta Maria, wife of Charles I. Restoration means that the house can be seen as it appeared when new, with bright silks and furnishings. The Great Hall, the State Rooms and a Loggia overlooking Greenwich Park are notable features.

Times: Please telephone for opening times **Fee:** Free, except special exhibitions **Facilities:** P (50 yds) ✗ licensed ও (Blind kit/stairclimber/wheelchairs) toilets for disabled shop ✶ ▰

continued

W1
ROYAL ACADEMY OF ARTS
Burlington House, Piccadilly W1J 0BD
➲ (Underground - Piccadilly Circus, head towards Green Park)
☎ 020 7300 8000   📄 020 7300 5886

Known principally for its exhibitions, the Royal Academy of Arts was founded in 1768 and is Britain's oldest Fine Arts institution. Two of its founding principles were to provide a free school and to mount 'an annual exhibition open to all artists of distinguished merit', now known as the Summer Exhibition. Both continue today. The Royal Academy's most prized possession, Michelangelo's Tondo, 'The Virgin and Child with the Infant St John', one of only four marble sculptures by the artist outside Italy, is on permanent display in the Sackler Wing. The recently opened John Madejski Fine Rooms are a suit of six rooms displaying the highlights from the RA collection. Many exhibitions planned for 2005.
Times: Open daily 10-6. (Closed 25 Dec & Good Fri) late night opening Fri 10am-10pm. **Fee:** £7-£9 (ch, students, pen & group visitors reduced price). Prices vary for each exhibition **Facilities:** 🅿 400yds (disabled parking call in advance) 🍽 ✖ licensed ᴕ Large-print guides/labels, sign language toilets for disabled shop ✈ (ex guide dogs) 📼

NW9
ROYAL AIR FORCE MUSEUM
Grahame Park Way, Hendon NW9 5LL
➲ (within easy reach of the A5, A41, M1 and North Circular A406 roads. Tube on Northern Line to Colindale. Rail to Mill Hill Broadway station. Bus route 303 passes the door)
☎ 020 8205 2266   FREE 2 for 1
📄 020 8358 4981
e-mail: groups@rafmuseum.org
Take off to the Royal Air Force Museum and soar through the history of aviation from the earliest balloon flights to the latest Eurofighter. New for 2004 is the dramatic 'Milestones of Flight' hall, with an exciting display of suspended aircraft and touch screen technology. Visitors can experience the bi-plane era in the beautifully restored Grahame-White factory, or have some hands-on fun in the expanded Aeronauts Interactive centre. All this plus a huge collection of aircraft, simulator rides, uniforms, light and sound show, and much more. (2-for-1 Voucher applies to simulator ride in Historic Hangers only)
Times: Open daily 10-6. Last admission 5.30. Closed 24-26 Dec & 1 Jan **Facilities:** 🅿 🍽 ✖ licensed ᴕ (lifts, ramps & wheelchairs available) toilets for disabled shop ✈ (ex guide dogs) 📼

SW3
ROYAL HOSPITAL CHELSEA
Royal Hospital Rd SW3 4SR
➲ (near Sloane Square, off A3216 & A3031)
☎ 020 7881 5204   📄 020 7881 5463   FREE
e-mail: info@chelsea-pensioners.org.uk
Founded in 1682 by Charles II as a retreat for army veterans who had become unfit for duty, through injury or long service. The Royal Hospital Chelsea was built on the site of a theological college founded by James I in 1610. The buildings were designed and built by Sir Christopher Wren, and then added to by Robert Adam and Sir John Soane. The hospital houses some 350 'In-Pensioners', some of whom do voluntary work as tour guides, clerical assistants and ground staff. Visitors can stroll around the grounds, gain admission to the Chapel, Great Hall and visit the Museum.
Times: Open Mon-Sat 10-12 & 2-4, Sun 2-4. (Museum closed Oct-Mar)
Facilities: 🅿 Limited ᴕ toilets for disabled shop

SW1
THE ROYAL MEWS
Buckingham Palace, Buckingham Palace Rd SW1W 0QH
➲ (Underground - Victoria, Green Park, St. James Park)
☎ 020 7766 7302   📄 020 7930 9625
e-mail: buckinghampalace@
royalcollection.org.uk
Designed by John Nash and completed in 1825, the Royal Mews houses the State Coaches, horse drawn carriages and motor cars used for coronations, state visits, royal weddings and the State Opening of Parliament. These include the Gold State Coach, made in 1762, with panels painted by the Florentine artist Cipriani. As one of the finest working stables in existence, the Royal Mews provides a unique opportunity for you to see a working department of the Royal Household.
Times: ✸ Open Mar-Oct, 11-4 (daily Aug-Sep 10-5). (Last admission 3.15; Aug-Sep 4.15 Closed Fri). **Fee:** £5.50 (ch under 5 free, ch 5-16 £3, pen & students £4.50) Family ticket (2ad+3ch) £14
Facilities: 🅿 (200yds) ᴕ (telephone for access information) toilets for disabled shop ✈ (ex guide dogs) 📼

SE10
ROYAL OBSERVATORY GREENWICH
Greenwich Park, Greenwich SE10 9NF
➲ (off A2, Greenwich Park)
☎ 020 8312 6565   📄 020 8312 6632   FREE
Charles II founded the Royal Observatory in 1675 'for perfecting navigation and astronomy'. It stands at zero meridian longitude and is the original home of Greenwich Mean Time. It houses an extensive collection of historic timekeeping, astronomical and navigational instruments. Planetarium shows throughout the year. Events are planned for the school holidays.
Times: Open all year, daily 10-5 (Closed 24-26 Dec & 1 Jan)
Facilities: 🅿 (charged) ᴕ toilets for disabled shop ✈ 📼

EC4
ST PAUL'S CATHEDRAL
St Pauls Courtyard EC4M 8AD
☎ 020 7246 8348   📄 020 7248 3104
e-mail: chapterhouse@stpaulscathedral.org.uk
Completed in 1710, Sir Christopher Wren's architectural masterpiece is the cathedral church of the Bishop of London, and arose, like so much of this area of London, from the ashes of the Great Fire of London in 1666. Among the worthies buried here are Nelson and the Duke of Wellington, while Holman Hunt's masterpiece, *Light of the World* hangs in
continued

the nave. Impressive views of London can be seen from the Golden Gallery.

Times: Cathedral, Crypt, Ambulatory, Open Mon-Sat 8.30. Galleries 9.30. Last admission 4pm Cathedral may close for special services. **Fee:** ✱ £7 (ch £3, concessions £6) Family £17 (2 ad + 2 ch). Groups 10+ £6.50 (ch £2.50, concessions £5.50) **Facilities:** Ⓟ 400mtrs Meter parking in area ⏩ ✗ licensed ♿ toilets for disabled shop ✈ (ex guide dogs) 🍴

SW7
SCIENCE MUSEUM
Exhibition Rd, South Kensington SW7 2DD
⮑ (Underground - South Kensington, Signposted from tube stn)
☎ 020 7942 4000   🖷 020 7942 4421
e-mail: sciencemuseum@nmsi.ac.uk

Ideal for children and adults too, the displays feature many working models with knobs to press, handles to turn and buttons to push to various different effects: exhibits are set in motion, light up, rotate and make noises. The collections cover science, technology, engineering and industry through the ages; there are galleries dealing with printing, chemistry, nuclear physics, navigation, photography, electricity, communications and medicine. The new Wellcome Wing includes an IMAX cinema, 6 new galleries and a restaurant.
Times: ✱ Open all year, daily 10-6. (Closed 24-26 Dec).
Facilities: ⏩ ✗ licensed ♿ (personal 2hr tour of museum) toilets for disabled shop ✈ (ex guide dogs) 🍴

W2
SERPENTINE GALLERY
Kensington Gardens W2 3XA
⮑ (Underground - Knightsbridge, Lancaster Gate, South Kensington. Bus- 9, 10, 12, 52, 94)
☎ 020 7402 6075   🖷 020 7402 4103   FREE
e-mail: varind@serpentinegallery.org

The Serpentine Gallery, named after the lake in Hyde Park, is situated in the heart of Kensington Gardens in a 1934 tea pavilion, and was founded in 1970 by the Arts Council of Great Britain. Today the Gallery attracts over 400,000 visitors a year and is one the best places in London for modern and contemporary art and architecture.
Times: Open daily 10-6. **Facilities:** Ⓟ (charged) ♿ toilets for disabled shop Bookshop ✈ (ex guide dogs) 🍴

SE1
SHAKESPEARE'S GLOBE EXHIBITION AND THEATRE TOUR
21 New Globe Walk, Bankside SE1 9DT
⮑ (Underground - London Bridge, walk along Bankside. Mansion House, walk across Southwark Bridge. St Pauls, walk across Millennium Bridge)
☎ 020 7902 1500   🖷 020 7902 1515
e-mail: info@shakespearesglobe.com

Guides help to bring England's theatrical heritage to life at the 'unparalleled and astonishing' recreation of this famous theatre. Discover what an Elizabethan audience would have been like, find out about the rivalry between the Bankside theatres, the bear baiting and the stews, hear about the penny stinkards and find out what a bodger is.
Times: Open all year, May-Sep, daily 9-12 (12-5 Rose Theatre tour); Oct-Apr 10-5. **Fee:** ✱ Oct-Apr £8 (ch £5.50, pen & students £6.50). May-Sep £8.50 (ch £6, pen & students £7) Group rates available.
Facilities: Ⓟ (0.5m) (very limited on-street parking) ⏩ ✗ licensed ♿ (parking spaces, 'touch tours' available by appointment) toilets for disabled shop ✈ (ex guide & hearing dogs) 🍴

WC2
SIR JOHN SOANE'S MUSEUM
13 Lincoln's Inn Fields WC2A 3BP
⮑ (Underground - Holborn)
☎ 020 7405 2107   🖷 020 7831 3957   FREE
e-mail: jnrock@sloane.org.uk

Sir John Soane was responsible for some of the most splendid architecture in London, and his house, built in 1812, contains his collections of antiquities, sculpture, paintings, drawings and books. Amongst his treasures are the *Rake's Progess* and *Election* series of paintings by Hogarth.
Times: Open all year, Tue-Sat 10-5. Also first Tue of month 6-9pm. (Closed BH). Lecture tour Sat 2.30 (limited no of tickets sold from 2pm) **Facilities:** Ⓟ (200yds) (metered parking) ♿ (wheelchair available, phone for details of accessibility) shop ✈ (ex guide dogs) 🍴

SE5
SOUTH LONDON GALLERY
65 Peckham Rd SE5 8UH
⮑ (from Vauxhall take A202 to Camberwell Green. SLG is halfway between Camberwell Green and Peckham).
☎ 020 7703 6120 & 7703 9799-info
🖷 020 7252 4730   FREE
e-mail: mail@southlondongallery.org

The gallery presents a programme of up to eight exhibitions a year of cutting-edge contemporary art, and has established itself as South East London's premier venue for contemporary visual arts. The Gallery also aims to bring contemporary art of the highest standards to audiences in South London and to assist in the regeneration of the area by attracting audiences from across Britain and abroad.
Times: Tue-Sun 12-6 & Thu 12-8.30 . Closed Mon
Facilities: Ⓟ on-street parking ♿ (disabled access, induction loop) toilets for disabled ✈ (ex guide dogs)

SE1
SOUTHWARK CATHEDRAL
London Bridge SE1 9DA
⮑ (Adjacent to London Bridge (Rd & Station), off Borough High St)
☎ 020 7367 6700   🖷 020 7367 6730
e-mail: cathedral@dswark.org.uk

Originally an Augustinian priory, this is London's oldest gothic church building, and has been a place of worship for more than 1,000 years. It became a cathedral for the Diocese of Southwark in 1905, and has links with Chaucer, Dickens and Shakespeare. John Gower and Shakespeare's brother Edmund are buried here. John Harvard of US university fame was baptised here in 1607, and there is a chapel to his memory. Visitors can view part of a Roman road, 14th-century cloister work, and kilns used for Southwark delftware in the 17th/18th centuries.
Times: Open daily: Cathedral 9-6. (No tourism permitted on Good Fri & 25 Dec) **Fee:** Free, suggested donation £4. Mandatory charge for groups, which should pre-book on 020 7367 6730
Facilities: Ⓟ 10min walk ✗ licensed ♿ toilets for disabled shop ✈ (ex service dogs)

E9

SUTTON HOUSE

2 & 4 Homerton High St E9 6JQ

➲ (10 minute walk from Hackney Central train station)

☎ 020 8986 2264 🖷 020 8525 9051 **2 for 1**

e-mail: suttonhouse@nationaltrust.org.uk

In London's East End, the building is a rare example of a Tudor red-brick house. Built in 1535 by Sir Ralph Sadleir, Principal Secretary of State for Henry VIII, the house has 18th-century alterations and later additions. The 2-for-1 voucher is valid only during normal visiting hours, and cannot be used for any ticketed events.

Times: Open 21 Jan-18 Dec, Fri & Sat 1-5; Sun & BH Mon 11.30-5. Closed Good Fri **Fee:** £2.50.(ch 50p) Family ticket £5.50.

Facilities: P (on street parking) (meters) 🖳 ৬ (induction loop, Braille/large print guide) toilets for disabled shop ✖ (ex guide dogs) 🐾

SW1

TATE BRITAIN

Millbank SW1P 4RG

➲ (Underground - Pimlico)

☎ 020 7887 8000 & rec info 020 7887 8008

e-mail: information@tate.org.uk

Tate Britain is the national gallery of British art from 1500 to the present day, from Tudors to the Turner Prize. Tate holds the greatest collection of British art in the world, including works by Blake, Constable, Epstein, Gainsborough, Gilbert and George, Hatoum, Hirst, Hockney, Hodgkin, Hogarth, Moore, Rossetti, Sickert, Spencer, Stubbs and Turner. The gallery is the world centre for the understanding and enjoyment of British art. The opening of the Tate Centenary provides Tate Britain with ten new and five refurbished galleries used for special exhibitions and the permanent collection.

Times: Open daily 10-5.50. (Closed 24-26 Dec). **Fee:** Free. Donations welcomed. Prices vary for special exhibitions. **Facilities:** P (100mtrs) (1hr stay) 🖳 ✕ licensed ৬ (wheelchairs on request, parking by prior arrangement) toilets for disabled shop ✖ (ex guide & hearing dogs) 🖃

SE1

TATE MODERN

Bankside SE1 9TG

➲ (Underground - Southwark, Blackfriars)

☎ 020 7887 8008 (info) & 020 7887 8888

🖷 020 7401 5052

e-mail: information@tate.org.uk

Tate Modern, on the bank of the River Thames, is the world's most popular art museum. Presenting a permanent collection of modern and contemporary art and hosting special exhibitions.

Times: Open all year, Sun-Thu 10-6, Fri & Sat 10am-10pm. (Closed 24-26 Dec). **Facilities:** P (very limited) 🖳 ✕ licensed ৬ (parking & wheelchairs available call 020 7887 8888) toilets for disabled shop ✖ (ex guide dogs) 🖃

> If an attraction name appears in *italics*, details have not been confirmed for 2005.

SE18

THAMES BARRIER INFORMATION & LEARNING CENTRE

1 Unity Way SE18 5NJ

➲ (Turn off A102(M) onto A206, turn onto Eastmoor St and follow signs)

☎ 020 8305 4188 🖷 020 8855 2146 **2 for 1**

e-mail: learningcentre@ environment-agency.gov.uk

Spanning a third of a mile, the Thames Barrier is the world's largest movable flood barrier. The visitors' centre and exhibition on the South Bank explains the flood threat and the construction of this £535 million project, now valued at £1 billion. Each month a test closure of all ten gates, lasting over 2 hours, is carried out and the annual full day closure of all ten gates takes place in the autumn.

Times: Open 31 Mar-29 Sep, 10.30-4.30. 30 Sep-30 Mar 11-3.30. Closed 25 Dec-3 Jan **Fee:** £1 (ch 50p, pen 75p). Car park £1. Coach park £10 **Facilities:** P (charged) 🖳 ৬ (lift from river pier approach) toilets for disabled shop ✖ (ex guide dogs) 🖃

WC2

THEATRE MUSEUM

Russell St, Covent Gardent WC2E 7PR

➲ (Underground - Covent Garden, Leicester Sq)

☎ 020 7943 4700 🖷 020 7943 4777 **FREE**

e-mail: tmenquiries@vam.ac.uk

Major developments, events and personalities from the performing arts, including stage models, costumes, prints, drawings, posters, puppets, props and a variety of other theatre memorabilia. There are guided tours, demonstrations on the art of stage make-up, and you can dress up in costumes from National Theatre companies. Groups are advised to book in advance. Theatre and walking tours 2pm Saturdays.

Times: Open all year, Tue-Sun 10-6. (closed 24-26 Dec & 1 Jan) **Facilities:** P (meters, NCP 250yds) ৬ Braille guides, audio tours toilets for disabled shop ✖ (ex guide dogs) 🖃

SE1

THE TOWER BRIDGE EXHIBITION

Tower Bridge Rd SE1 2UP

➲ (Underground - Tower Hill or London Bridge)

☎ 020 7940 3985 🖷 020 7357 7935

e-mail: enquiries@towerbridge.org.uk

One of the capital's most famous landmarks, its glass-covered walkways stand 142ft above the Thames, affording panoramic views of the river. Much of the original machinery for working the bridge can be seen in the engine rooms. The Tower Bridge Exhibition uses state-of-the-art effects to present the story of the bridge in a dramatic and exciting fashion.

Times: ✱ Open all year, 9.30-6 (last ticket sold 5pm). (Closed 1 Jan & 24-25 Dec). **Facilities:** P (100yds) ৬ toilets for disabled shop ✖ 🖃

EC3

TOWER OF LONDON

Tower Hill EC3N 4AB

➲ (Underground - Tower Hill)

☎ 0870 756 6060

Perhaps the most famous castle in the world, the Tower of London has played a central part in British history. The White Tower, built by William the Conqueror as a show of strength to the people of London, remains one of the most outstanding examples of Norman military architecture in Europe. For hundreds of years the Tower was used, among

continued

other things, as the State Prison. It was here that Henry VIII had two of his wives executed, here that Lady Jane Grey died and here that Sir Walter Raleigh was imprisoned. The Yeoman Warders, or 'Beefeaters' play an important role in the protection of the Tower - home of the Crown Jewels - and are informative and entertaining. Look out for the ravens, whose continued residence is said to ensure that the Kingdom does not fall. The Crowns and Diamonds exhibition features a number of crowns never displayed to the public before and more than 12,000 rough and polished diamonds. Also open to the public are the Royal Armouries, which received their first recorded visitor as long ago as 1489. The displays include an extensive range of arms and armour dating from the Norman ages, a collection of Spanish arms and the Line of Kings.

Times: ✱ Open all year, Mar-Oct, Mon-Sat 9-6, Sun 10-6 (last admission 5pm); Nov-Feb, Tue-Sat 9-5, Sun 10-5 (last admission 4pm). (Closed 24-26 Dec & 1 Jan). **Facilities:** P (100yds) (NCP Lower Thames St) ⬛ ✗ licensed ♿ (access guide can be obtained in advance call 020 7488 5694) toilets for disabled shop ✈ (ex guide dogs) 🖚

NW3
2 WILLOW ROAD NEW
2 Willow Rd, Hampstead NW3 1TH
➲ (Best accessed on foot as parking very limited. Hampstead tube (Northern Line), along high street, left Flask Walk, Right at end into Willow Rd. From Hampstead Heath Stn (North London Line), turn right Willow Rd 5 mins away)
☎ 020 7435 6166   📄 020 7435 6166   **2 for 1**
e-mail: 2willowroad@nationaltrust.org.uk
Discover the 1939 home built by the architect Ernö Goldfinger for himself and his family. On display is his modern art collection including works by Henry Moore, Brigit Riley, Max Ernst and Marcel Duchamp as well as an extensive collection of original furniture designed by the architect.

Times: Mar & Nov, Sat only (open Good Fri). Apr-end Oct, Thu, Fri & Sat: guided tours 12,1 & 2; Free flow 3-5 **Fee:** £4.60 (ch £2.30) Joint admission £6.60. **Facilities:** P (100mtrs very limited, car park closes often) video tour of house in cinema ✈

SW7
VICTORIA AND ALBERT MUSEUM
Cromwell Rd, South Kensington SW7 2RL
➲ (Underground - South Kensington, Museum situated on A4, Buses C1,14,74,414 stop outside the Cromwell Road entrance)
☎ 020 7942 2000   FREE
e-mail: vanda@vam.ac.uk
The world's finest museum of art and design, with collections spanning 3000 years, and comprising sculpture, furniture, fashion and textiles, paintings, silver, glass, ceramics, jewellery, books, prints, and photographs from Britain and all over the world. Highlights include the national collection of paintings by John Constable, the Dress Court showing fashion from 1500 to the present day, a superb Asian collection, the Jewellery Gallery including the Russian Crown Jewels, and the 20th Century Gallery, devoted to contemporary art and design. The stunning British Galleries 1500-1900 tell the story of British design from the Tudor age to the Victorian era.

Times: Open all year, Mon-Sun 10-5.45. (Closed 24-26 Dec). Wed & last Fri of month open late, 10-10. **Facilities:** P (500yds) (limited, charged parking) ⬛ ✗ licensed ♿ (Facilities available. Call for details 020 7942 2211) toilets for disabled shop ✈ (ex guide dogs) 🖚

SE1
VINOPOLIS, CITY OF WINE
1 Bank End SE1 9BU
➲ (Underground-London Bridge. Borough High Street West exit, right into Stoney St, then left into Park St & follow road round to Vinopolis main entrance)
☎ 0870 241 4040   📄 020 7940 8302
e-mail: sales@vinopolis.co.uk
Vinopolis is London's premiere wine attraction, situated on a 2.5 acre site on the vibrant South Bank. It offers an imaginative, interactive tour around the world of wine as well as great tastings. The setting is delightful, with Victorian vaulted ceilings and intricate, almost rustic red brickwork. The 2-for-1 voucher is not valid on Saturdays.

Times: Open all year, Mon, Fri & Sat 12-9, Tue-Thu & Sun 12-6, (last admission 2 hrs before closing). Please call for opening hours in Dec and BH's. **Fee:** Mon, Fri-Sun, £12.50, (ch u16 free, seniors (60+) £11.50), Tue-Thu £11, (ch u16 free, seniors (60+) £10). **Facilities:** P (5-10 min walk) (NCP parking) ⬛ ✗ licensed ♿ (lifts & ramps) toilets for disabled shop ✈ (ex guide dogs) 🖚

W1
WALLACE COLLECTION
Hertford House, Manchester Square W1U 3BN
➲ (Underground - Bond Street, Baker Street, Oxford Circus)
☎ 020 7563 9500   📄 020 7224 2155
e-mail: enquiries@wallacecollection.org
An elegant 18th-century town house is an appropriate gallery for this outstanding collection of art. Founded by the 1st Marquis of Hertford, it was bequeathed to the nation in 1897 and came on public display three years later. As well as an unrivalled representation of 18th-century French art with paintings by Boucher, Watteau and Fragonard, Hertford House is the home of Frans Hals' *Laughing Cavalier* and of paintings by Gainsborough, Rubens, Delacroix and Titian. It also houses the largest collection of arms and armour outside the Tower of London.

Times: Open all year, Mon-Sat 10-5, Sun 12-5. (Closed Good Fri, May BH, 24-26 Dec & 1 Jan). **Fee:** Prices not confirmed for 2005 **Facilities:** P (NCP & meters) (meters are free on Sun) ⬛ ✗ licensed ♿ (lift, ramp, wheelchair available upon request) toilets for disabled shop ✈ guide dogs only 🖚

SE3
THE WERNHER COLLECTION AT RANGER'S HOUSE
Chesterfield Walk, Blackheath SE10 8QY
☎ 020 8853 0035   📄 020 8853 0090
Handsome 18th-century house with lovely views over London, Greenwich Park, Blackheath and the Thames. View the 'Wernher Collection' of self-made millionaire Julius Wernher, who made his fortune in the diamond mines of South Africa.

Times: Open Jun-Aug, Wed-Sun & BHs 10-5; Sep-May pre-booked tours only. Closed 22 Dec-2 Mar. **Fee:** ✱ £5 (ch £2.50, concessions £3.80). Prices & opening times relate to 2004, for further details phone or log onto www.english-heritage.org.uk/visits **Facilities:** P ♿ toilets for disabled shop ✈ (in certain areas) ♯

EC1
WESLEY'S CHAPEL, HOUSE & MUSEUM OF METHODISM
49 City Rd EC1Y 1AU
➲ (Underground - Old Street - exit number 4)
☎ 020 7253 2262 🖷 020 7608 3825
e-mail: museum@wesleychapel.org.uk [FREE]

Wesley's Chapel has been the Mother Church of World Methodism since its construction in 1778. The crypt houses a museum which traces the development of Methodism from the 18th century to the present day. Wesley's house - built by him in 1779 - was his home when not touring and preaching. Special events are held on May 24th (the anniversary of Wesley's conversion), and November 1st (the anniversary of the Chapel's opening).
Times: Open all year, Mon-Sat, 10-4, Sun 12-2 (Closed Thu 12.45-1.30. Xmas & New Year, BHs, except Good Fri). **Facilities:** P 5min (NCP at Finsbury Square) ♿ (lift to the crypt of the chapel) toilets for disabled shop ✸ (ex guide dogs) ⬛

SW1
WESTMINSTER ABBEY
Broad Sanctuary SW1P 3PA
➲ (Underground - Westminster, St James's Park. Next to Parliament Square and opposite the Houses of Parliament)
☎ 020 7222 5152 7654 4900
🖷 020 7233 2072
e-mail: info@westminster-abbey.org

Westminster Abbey was originally a Benedictine monastery. In the 11th century, it was re-founded by St. Edward the Confessor. The great Romanesque abbey Edward built next to his royal palace became his burial place shortly after it was completed. Over the centuries that followed, many more kings and queens have been buried, and many great figures commemorated, in the abbey. The abbey has been the setting for nearly every coronation since that of William the Conqueror in 1066, and for numerous other royal occasions. The present building, begun by Henry III in 1245, is one of the most visited churches in the world.
Times: Abbey: Mon-Fri 9.30-3.45, Sat 9-1.45. Wed late night opening 6-7pm. Last admission 60 mins before closing. Cloister: daily 8-6. No tourist visiting on Sundays, however visitors are welcome at services. The Abbey may at short notice be closed for special services & other events. **Fee:** ✱ £7.50 (ch 11-15 £5, under 11's free, pen & students £4). Family ticket (2 ad & 2 ch) £15. **Facilities:** ⬛ ♿ (areas accessible induction loop) shop ✸ (ex guide dogs) ⬛

SW1
WESTMINSTER CATHEDRAL
Victoria St SW1P 1QW
➲ (300 yds from Victoria Station)
☎ 020 7798 9055 🖷 020 7798 9090
e-mail: barrypalmer@rcdow.org.uk [FREE]

Westminster Cathedral is a fascinating example of Victorian architecture. Designed in the Early Christian Byzantine style by John Francis Bentley, its strongly oriental appearance makes it very distinctive. The foundation stone was laid in 1895 but the interior decorations are not fully completed. The Campanile Bell Tower is 273ft high and has a four-sided viewing gallery with magnificent views over London. The lift is open daily 9am-5pm Mar-Nov but shut Mon-Wed from Dec-Feb.
Times: Open all year, daily 7-7. **Facilities:** P (0.25m) (2hr metered parking) ⬛ ♿ (all parts accessible except side chapels) shop ✸ (ex guide dogs)

SW1
WESTMINSTER HALL
Houses of Parliament, Westminster SW1A 0AA
➲ (Underground - Westminster Tube)
☎ 020 7219 4272

The great Westminster Hall, where Charles I was tried in 1649, has survived virtually intact since it was remodelled at the end of the 14th century. It escaped the fire in 1834 which destroyed much of the medieval Palace of Westminster, and the magnificent hammerbeam roof is the earliest surviving example of its kind.
Times: Summer opening; 24 Jul-4 Sep, 18 Sep-2 Oct. At other times by application to MP. (UK constituents only) **Fee:** ✱ £7 (concessions £5, tours in English), (£9 foreign language tours, £7 concessions). Tours via MP free. **Facilities:** P limited 50yds ⬛ ♿ toilets for disabled shop ✸ (ex guide dogs) ⬛

E17
WILLIAM MORRIS GALLERY
Lloyd Park, Forest Rd E17 4PP
➲ (Underground-Blackhorse Rd, take bus no. 123 along Forest Rd, get off at the Lloyd Park stop)
☎ 020 8527 3782
🖷 020 8527 7070 [FREE]

Victorian artist, craftsman, poet and free thinker William Morris lived here from 1848 to 1856, and the gallery houses displays illustrating his life and work. Exhibits include fabrics, stained glass, wallpaper and furniture, as well as Pre-Raphaelite paintings, ceramics and a collection of pictures by Frank Brangwyn, who worked briefly for Morris.
Times: Open all year, Tue-Sat and 1st Sun in each month 10-1 & 2-5. (Closed Mon & BH's). Telephone for Xmas/New Year opening times.
Facilities: P ♿ shop ✸ (ex guide dogs) ⬛

SW19
WIMBLEDON LAWN TENNIS MUSEUM
Centre Court, Church Rd SW19 5AE
➲ (Underground - Southfields, 15mins walk)
☎ 020 8946 6131 🖷 020 8944 6497
e-mail: museum@aeltc.com

Pictures, displays and memorabilia trace the development of the game over the last century. See the world famous Championship's trophies, as well as film and video footage of great players in action from the 1920s to the present day. There is also the chance to go for a behind-the-scenes guided tour of Centre Court, No. 1 Court, and the press interview room.
Times: ✱ Open daily all year, 10.30-5. (Closed middle Sun of Championships, Mon immediately following the Championships, 24-26 Dec & 1 Jan). **Facilities:** P ⬛ ✕ licensed ♿ (lift, stairlift to cafe) toilets for disabled shop ✸ (ex guide dogs) ⬛

SE1
WINSTON CHURCHILL'S BRITAIN AT WAR EXPERIENCE
64/66 Tooley St SE1 2TF
➲ (Mid way down Tooley St, between London Bridge & Tower Bridge. 2min walk from London Bridge Stn).
☎ 020 7403 3171 📠 020 7403 5104
e-mail: britainatwar@dial.pipex.com

A realistic adventure back to the home front to experience life in war-torn Britain during World War II. Take the lift to the underground, where many spent sleepless nights. Explore evacuation, rationing, air-raids, the blackout and endure the sights, sounds and smells in the dramatic blitz area.
Times: Open all year, Apr-Sep 10-5.30pm; Oct-Mar 10-4.30. (Closed 24-26 Dec) **Fee:** ✱ £8.50 (ch 5-16 £4.50, student & pen £5.50). Family ticket (2 ad+2 ch) £18. **Facilities:** 🅿 (100mtrs) ♿ (wheelchair for loan) toilets for disabled shop (small) 🐕 (ex guide dogs) ▄
See advertisement on this page

Above: Covent Garden café society

BARNET   Map 04 TQ29

MUSEUM OF DOMESTIC DESIGN & ARCHITECTURE
Middlesex University, Cat Hill EN4 8HT
➲ (From M25, junct 24 signposted A111 Cockfosters to Cat Hill rdbt, straight over onto Chase side. Entrance 1st right opposite the Chicken Shed Theatre on Cat Hill Campus)
☎ 020 8411 5244 ▤ 020 8411 6639   FREE
e-mail: moda@mdx.ac.uk

MoDA is a museum of the history of the home. It holds one of the world's most comprehensive collections of decorative design for the period 1870 to 1960, and is a rich source of information on how people decorated and lived in their homes. MoDA has two galleries, a lecture theatre for study days, a seminar room with practical workshops for both adults and children, and a study room which gives visitors access to the collections.
Times: Open Tue-Sat 10-5, Sun 2-5. (Closed Mon, Etr, Xmas & New Year). Facilities: P & induction loop fitted in lecture theatre toilets for disabled shop ✖ (ex guide dogs)

BEXLEY   Map 05 TQ47

HALL PLACE
Bourne Rd DA5 1PQ
➲ (near junct of A2 & A233)
☎ 01322 526574 ▤ 01322 522921   FREE

Hall Place is an attractive Grade I listed mansion of chequered flint and brick, with wonderful gardens. There is topiary in the form of the 'Queen's Beasts'; rose, rock, peat and water gardens; and a herb garden with a fascinating range of plants (labelled in Braille) for medicine and cooking. There is also a conservatory, a local studies centre and museum. Please telephone for details of the programme of temporary exhibitions, lectures and concerts in the museum and Great Hall.
Times: Open all year, House: Mon-Sat 10-5, Sun & BHs 11-5 (Apr-Oct); Tue-Sat 10-4.15 (Nov-Mar). Gardens: Mon-Fri 7.30-dusk, Sat & Sun 9-dusk. Facilities: P ▣ ✖ licensed & toilets for disabled shop garden centre (award winning Greenflag) ✖ (ex guide/hearing dogs)

BRENTFORD   Map 04 TQ17

KEW BRIDGE STEAM MUSEUM
Green Dragon Ln TW8 0EN
➲ (Underground - Kew Gardens, District line then 391 bus. Museum 100yds from N side of Kew Bridge. From M4 junct 2 follow A4 to Chiswick rdbt, take A315 to Kew Bridge, Green Dragon Ln 1st right after lights)
☎ 020 8568 4757 ▤ 020 8569 9978   2 for 1
e-mail: info@kbsm.org

This Victorian pumping station has steam engines and six beam engines, of which five are working and one is the largest in the world. A diesel house and waterwheel can also be seen along with London's only steam narrow-gauge railway, which operates every Sunday (Mar-Nov). The Water for Life Gallery tells the story of London's water supply from Pre-Roman times. The newest exhibit is a water pump, once powered by horses.
Times: Open all year, daily 11-5. Engines in steam, wknds & BHs. (Closed Good Fri, Xmas wk & New Year) Fee: ✱ Weekdays £4, wknds £5.20 (reductions for pen, students & ch). Facilities: P ▣ & (partially sighted tours, wheelchairs, large print guide) toilets for disabled shop ◀

MUSICAL MUSEUM
368 High St TW8 0BD
➲ (Underground - Gunnersbury, nr Kew Bridge)
☎ 020 8560 8108

This museum will take you back to a bygone age to hear and see a marvellous working collection of automatic musical instruments from small music boxes to a mighty Wurlitzer theatre organ. Working demonstrations.
Times: Open Apr-Oct, Sat & Sun 2-5. Fee: ✱ £3.20 (ch & pen £2.50). Family ticket £10. Facilities: P (200 yds) & shop ✖ (guide dogs)

CHESSINGTON   Map 04 TQ16

CHESSINGTON WORLD OF ADVENTURES
Leatherhead Rd KT9 2NE
➲ (M25 junct 9/10, on A243)
☎ 0870 444 7777 ▤ 01372 725050

Feel the fantasy of Hocus Pocus Hall - the magical 4-D experience home to a wacky wizard and mischievous goblins and where magical mayhem is literally brought to life in front of your eyes! Plus don't miss the fang-tastic Vampire, quick fire challenge of Tomb Blaster or fun-filled Dennis's Madhouse in Beanoland. Take a safari trip down Trail of the Kings then journey into Toytown with Toadie's Crazy Cars, Berry Bouncers and Tiny Truckers. Or, for the more daring, face a power of the mighty Samurai, or find Rameses waiting to seek his Revenge. There's so much to feed the imagination and excite the senses!
Times: ✱ Open 10 Apr-2 Nov (excluding some off peak days) either 10-5, 10-6 or 10-7 (telephone for details). Open until 7.30 during Halloween Hocus Pocus. Facilities: P ▣ ✖ licensed & (some rides not accessible, disabled guide available) toilets for disabled shop ✖ (ex guide dogs & hearing dogs) ◀

CHISLEHURST   Map 05 TQ47

CHISLEHURST CAVES
Old Hill BR7 5NB
➲ (off A222 near Chislehurst railway stn. Turn into station approach, then right & right again into Caveside Close)
☎ 020 8467 3264 ▤ 020 8295 0407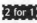
e-mail: enquiries@chislehurstcaves.co.uk

Miles of mystery and history beneath your feet. Grab a lantern and get ready for an amazing adventure! Visit the caves and your whole family can travel back in time as you explore the maze of passageways dug through the chalk deep beneath Chislehurst. Accompanied by an experienced guide on a 45 minute tour you'll see the tunnels made famous as a shelter during the Second World War, visit the cave's church, druid altar, the haunted pool and much more!
Times: Open all year, Wed-Sun, 10-4. Daily during local school hols (incl half terms). Closed Xmas. Fee: £4 (ch & pen £2).
Facilities: P ▣ ✖ licensed shop ✖ (ex guide dogs) ◀

DOWNE   Map 05 TQ46

DOWN HOUSE - HOME OF CHARLES DARWIN
BR6 7JT
➲ (Off A233, signposted)
☎ 01689 859119

Charles Darwin, perhaps the most influential scientist of the 19th-century, lived at Down House for over 40 years. He wrote the revolutionary book, *On the Origin of Species* here.
continued

Explore the exhibition on the first floor and visit the ground floor study, which was the centre of his life.
Times: Open Apr-Sep, Wed-Sun & BHs 10-6; Oct, Wed-Sun 10-5; Nov-18 Dec & 3 Feb-Mar, Wed-Sun 10-4. **Fee:** ✱ £6.30 (ch £3.20, concessions £4.70). Family £15.80. Prices & opening times relate to 2004, for further details phone or log onto www.english-heritage.org.uk/visits **Facilities:** 🅿 & shop ✖

ESHER Map 04 TQ16
CLAREMONT LANDSCAPE GARDEN
Portsmouth Rd KT10 9JG
➲ (E of A307)
☎ 01372 467806 📠 01372 464394
e-mail: claremont@nationaltrust.org.uk
Laid out by Vanbrugh and Bridgeman before 1720, extended and naturalised by Kent, this is the earliest surviving example of an English landscaped garden. Its 50 acres include a lake with an island pavilion, a grotto and a turf amphitheatre. Telephone 0870 090 0379 for details of events.
Times: Open all year Apr-Oct daily, Mon-Fri 10-6, Sat-Sun & BH Mon 10-7, Nov-Mar daily (ex Mon) 10-5 or sunset if earlier. (Closed all day 19-22 & 26 Jul, closed 2pm 23-24 Jul). Closed 25 Dec & 1 Jan. House not National Trust. **Fee:** ✱ £4 (ch £2). Family ticket £10
Facilities: 🅿 💻 & (wheelchairs available, Braille guide) toilets for disabled shop ✖ (ex on leads, Nov-Mar only) 🐾 🍴

HAM Map 04 TQ17
HAM HOUSE
TW10 7RS
➲ (W of A307, between Kingston & Richmond)
☎ 020 8940 1950 📠 020 8332 6903
e-mail: hamhouse@nationaltrust.org.uk
Ham House is a fine example of 17th-century fashion and power. Built in 1610, the house was enlarged in the 1670s when it was at the heart of Restoration court life and intrigue. It was then occupied by the same family until 1948. The formal garden is significant for its survival in an area known as the cradle of the English Landscape Movement. The outbuildings include an orangery, an ice house, a still house, and a dairy.
Times: Open Gardens: all year, Sat-Wed 11-6 or dusk if earlier. (Closed 25-26 Dec & 1 Jan). House: 3 Apr-Oct, Sat-Wed 1-5. Last admission 4.30. **Fee:** House £7.50 (ch £3.75). Family ticket £18.75. Garden only £3.50 (ch £1.75). Family ticket £8.75. **Facilities:** 🅿 (400yds) 💻 & (Braille guide, wheelchairs, stairclimber, lift, parking) toilets for disabled shop ✖ (ex guide/hearing dogs) 🐾 🍴

HAMPTON COURT Map 04 TQ16
HAMPTON COURT PALACE
KT8 9AU
➲ (on A308, close to A3, M3 & M25 exits. Train from Waterloo - Hampton Court, 2mins walk from station)
☎ 0870 752 7777 & 8781 9501
📠 020 8781 9669
With over 500 years of royal history Hampton Court Palace has something to offer everyone, from the magnificent State Apartments to the domestic reality of the Tudor Kitchens. Costumed guides and audio tours bring the palace to life and provide an insight into how life in the palace would have been in the time of Henry VIII and William III.
Times: Open mid Mar-mid Oct, daily, 9.30-6 (10.15-6 on Mon); mid Oct-mid Mar, daily, 9.30-4.30 (10.15-4.30 on Mon).
Facilities: 🅿 (charged) 💻 ✖ licensed & (lifts, buggies for gardens, wheelchairs, wardens to assist) toilets for disabled shop (4 shops on site) ✖ (ex guide/hearing dogs) 🍴

ISLEWORTH Map 04 TQ17
SYON HOUSE
TW8 8JF
➲ (A310 Twickenham road into Park Rd)
☎ 020 8560 0882 020 8560 0883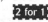
📠 020 8568 0936
e-mail: info@syonpark.co.uk
Set in 200 acres of parkland, Syon House is the London home of the Duke of Northumberland, whose family have lived here since the late 16th century. During the second half of the 18th century the first Duke of Northumberland engaged Robert Adam to remodel the interior and 'Capability' Brown to landscape the grounds. Adam was also responsible for the furniture and decorations, and the result is particularly spectacular in the superbly coloured Ante-Room and Long Gallery.
Times: Open 24 Mar-Oct, Wed-Thu, Sun & BH 11-5 (last ticket 4.15pm). **Fee:** ✱ Combined ticket for house and gardens £7.25 (ch & concessions £5.95). Family ticket £16. **Facilities:** 🅿 💻 & stairclimber available toilets for disabled shop garden centre ✖ 🍴

SYON PARK
TW8 8JF
➲ (A310 Twickenham road into Park Rd)
☎ 020 8560 0882 📠 020 8568 0936 2 for 1
e-mail: info@syonpark.co.uk
Contained within the 40 acres that make up Syon Park Gardens is one of the inspirations for the Crystal Palace at the Great Exhibition of 1851: a vast crescent of metal and glass, the first construction of its kind in the world and known as the Great Conservatory. Although the horticultural reputation of Syon Park goes back to the 16th century, its beauty today is thanks to the master of landscape design, 'Capability' Brown.
Times: Open all year, daily 10.30-5.30 or dusk if earlier. (Closed 25 & 26 Dec). **Fee:** ✱ £3.50 (concessions £2.50). Combined ticket for house & gardens £7.25 (ch & concessions £5.95). Family ticket £9. **Facilities:** 🅿 💻 & stair lift for show house toilets for disabled shop garden centre ✖ (ex guide dogs) 🍴

KEW Map 04 TQ17
KEW GARDENS (ROYAL BOTANIC GARDENS)
TW9 3AB
➲ (Underground - Kew Gdns)
☎ 020 8332 5655 📠 020 8332 5197
e-mail: info@kew.org
Kew Gardens is a paradise throughout the seasons. Lose yourself in the magnificent conservatories and discover plants from the world's deserts, mountains and oceans. Wide-open spaces, stunning vistas, listed buildings and wildlife contribute to the Garden's unique atmosphere. As well as being famous for its beautiful gardens, Kew is world renowned for its contribution to botanical and horticultural science.
Times: Open all year, Gardens daily 9.30-between 4 & 7.30pm (seasonal, visit website or phone to verify)(Closed 25 Dec & 1 Jan) **Fee:** ✱ £8.50 (concessions £6.50, ch under 17 free). **Facilities:** 🅿 (charged) 💻 ✖ licensed & (16 seat bus tour: enquiries ring 020 8332 5643) toilets for disabled shop ✖ (ex guide dogs) 🍴

KEW PALACE
Royal Botanic Gardens TW9 3AB
➲ (Underground - Kew Bridge)
☎ 020 8781 9540

A favourite country residence during the reign of the first three Hanoverian Kings, Kew was the site of several royal houses. A fairly modest red-brick building, built in the Dutch style with gables, Kew Palace was built in 1631 and used for nearly a century until 1818 when Queen Charlotte died. Family paintings and personal relics, furniture and tapestries are on display, and a charming 17th-century garden has been recreated.

Times: Closed for major repairs. Please telephone 020 8332 5655 or visit www.hrp.org.uk for further details.

THE NATIONAL ARCHIVES
Ruskin Av TW9 4DU
➲ (Underground - Kew Gardens)
☎ 020 8392 5202 & 020 8487 9202
▤ 020 8487 9202
e-mail: events@pro.gov.uk

The National Archives houses one of the finest, most complete archives in Europe, comprising the records of the central government and law courts from the Norman Conquest to the present century. It is a mine of information and some of the most interesting material including Domesday Book.

Times: ✱ Open Mon, Wed & Fri, 9-4.45; Tue, 10-7; Thu, 9-7 (closed 1st wk in Dec, Sun & public holiday wknds). **Facilities:** ▣ ▣
& (hearing loops & large print text in museum) toilets for disabled shop ✖ (ex guide dogs)

QUEEN CHARLOTTE'S COTTAGE
Royal Botanic Gardens TW9 3AB
➲ (Underground - Kew Bridge)
☎ 020 8332 5189

Typical of the fashionable rustic style popular with the gentry in the 18th century, the cottage was built for George III and Queen Charlotte as a home for their menagerie of exotic pets, as well as a picnic spot and summer house.

Times: ✱ Open weekends only between May & Sep. **Facilities:** shop ✖

MORDEN   Map 05 TQ26

MORDEN HALL PARK
Morden Hall Rd SM4 5JD
➲ (M25 junct 10, take A3. From A3 take A298 (Bushey Rd), turn right at 2nd lights into Martin Way. Morden Hall signposted, follow one-way system, turn right into Aberconway Rd. Then right at lights into Morden Hall Rd. Car park 1st left)
☎ 020 8545 6850   ▤ 020 8687 0094   FREE
e-mail: mordenhallpark@nationaltrust.org.uk

A green oasis in the heart of South West London. A former deer park, with a network of waterways including meadow, wetland and woodland habitats. Also discover the picturesque rose garden with over 2000 roses, fragrant from May to September.

Times: Open daily, 8-6. Closed 25-26 Dec & 1 Jan **Facilities:** ▣ ▣
& wheelchair, Braille guides, large handled cutlery. toilets for disabled shop garden centre

OSTERLEY   Map 04 TQ17

OSTERLEY PARK HOUSE
TW7 4RB Signposted from A4.
➲ (Underground - Osterley)
☎ 020 8232 5050   ▤ 020 8232 5080   2 for 1
e-mail: osterley@nationaltrust.org.uk

This Elizabethan mansion has been transformed into an 18th-century villa, its elegant interior decoration designed in neo-classical style by Robert Adam. The State Apartments include a Gobelin tapestry ante-room and a dressing-room decorated in the Etruscan style.

Times: Open all year: Park & pleasure grounds, daily 9-7.30 or sunset if earlier. House: Mar Sat & Sun 1-4.30, Apr-Oct, Wed-Sun 1-4.30, BH Sun & Mon 1-4.30. Last admission 4.30. (Closed Good Fri & 25-26 Dec).
Fee: £4.90. (ch £2.40) Family ticket £12.20. **Facilities:** ▣ (charged)
▣ & Braille guide, wheelchairs, electric carts, stair climber toilets for disabled shop ✖ (ex on lead in park) ♨

If an attraction name appears in *italics*, details have not been confirmed for 2005.

We endeavour to be as accurate as possible, but changes to times and other information can occur after the guide has gone to press.

The National Trust
For over a hundred years, the NT has been acquiring and protecting threatened coastline, countryside and buildings. To find about more about this organisation, its sites, and policies, click on their website:
www.nationaltrust.org.uk

This symbol indicates attractions **2-for-1** which have chosen to participate in our 2-for-1 voucher scheme

TWICKENHAM   Map 04 TQ17

MARBLE HILL HOUSE
Richmond Rd TW1 2NL

☎ **020 8892 5115** 🖹 **020 8607 9976**

A magnificent Thames-side Palladian villa built for Henrietta Howard, mistress of King George II, set in 66 acres of riverside parklands.

Times: Open Apr-Oct, Sat 10-2, Sun & BHs 10-5. (Closed Nov-Mar but pre-booked groups by arrangement). **Fee:** ✱ £3.50 (ch £2, concessions £3). Prices & opening times realte to 2004, for further details phone or log onto www.english-heritage.org.uk/visits
Facilities: 🅿 🖳 ✗ licensed ♿ toilets for disabled shop
🐾 (ex on lead in certain areas) ⧓

MUSEUM OF RUGBY & TWICKENHAM STADIUM TOURS
Rugby Football Union, Rugby Rd TW1 1DZ
⮕ (take M3 into London, then onto A316 following signs to museum)

☎ **020 8892 8877** 🖹 **020 8892 2817**   2 for 1
e-mail: **museum@rfu.com**

Located beneath the East Stand of the Twickenham Stadium, home of the England team and headquarters of the Rugby Football Union, the museum uses interactive displays, period set pieces and video footage to bring the history of the game

continued

to life. The tour includes a visit to the England dressing room, and magnificent views of the stadium from the top of the north stand. After that why not spend time in the Scrummery or Rugby Store.

Times: Open, Tue-Sat 10-5 (last admission 4.30pm), Sun 11-5 (last admission 4.30pm). (Closed post Twickenham match days, Etr Sun, 24-26 Dec & 1 Jan). **Fee:** ✱ Museum Tour: £8 (concessions £5).
Facilities: 🅿 🖳 ✗ licensed ♿ toilets for disabled shop
🐾 (ex guide dogs) 🍴

ORLEANS HOUSE GALLERY
Riverside TW1 3DJ
⮕ (From Twickenham drive along Richmond road (A305), Orleans Rd is on right just past Orleans Park School)

☎ **020 8892 0221** 🖹 **020 8744 0501**
e-mail: **m.denovellis@richmond.gov.uk**

Stroll beside the Thames and through the woodland gardens of Orleans House, where you will find stunning 18th century interior design and an excellent public art gallery. Visitors of all ages can try out their own artistic talents in pre-booked workshops, and wide-ranging temporary exhibitions are held throughout the year - please telephone for details.

Times: ✱ Open Oct-Mar, Tue-Sat 1-4.30, Sun & BH 2-4.30; Apr-Sep Tue-Sat 1-5.30, Sun & BH 2-5.30. **Facilities:** 🅿 ♿ (handling objects & large print labels for some exhibitions) toilets for disabled shop
🐾 (ex guide dogs)

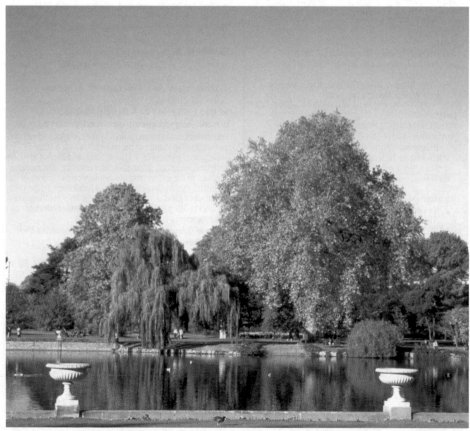

Above: Royal Botanical Gardens, Kew

MERSEYSIDE

EVENTS & FESTIVALS

February
tbc Chinese New Year celebrations, in and around Chinatown, Liverpool

April
7th-9th Grand National Festival, Aintree Racecourse, Liverpool

May
15th Liverpool Women's 10k Run, Liverpool City Centre

June
10th-12th Mersey International Shanty Festival, Albert Dock, Pier Head and Birkenhead
tbc The Mersey River Festival, River Mersey and Albert Dock, Liverpool

July
3rd Liverpool-Chester-Liverpool Bike Ride
9th-10th Wirral Show, Promenade, New Brighton, Wirral (provisional)
29th-31st St Helens Show, Sherdley Park, St Helens
tbc Merseyside International Street Festival

August
29th Creamfields Festival, Old Liverpool Airfield, Speke Boulevard
27th-29th International Beatles Week & Convention, various venues in Liverpool city centre (provisional)
tbc Southport Flower Show, Victoria Park, Rotten Row, Southport

September
tbc Liverpool Corporate Cup Run, 5km course in the city centre
tbc The Southport Airshow, The Promenade, Southport

Above: Anglican Cathedral, Liverpool

BIRKENHEAD   Map 07 SJ38

BIRKENHEAD PRIORY
Priory St CH41 5JH
☎ 0151 666 1249

Founded in 1150, the Priory provided accommodation for the Prior and 16 Benedictine monks. Most of the buildings were neglected after the Dissolution, but not all are ruined. An interpretive centre traces the history and development of the site. St Mary's, the first parish church of Birkenhead, was opened in 1821 adjacent to the Priory: only the tower now stands.
Times: ✱ Open all year, Sat & Sun 1-5 (in summer), 12-4 (in winter) & Tue-Sun 1-5 (school holidays), 12-4 (Oct & Feb half term). Telephone to confirm. **Facilities:** 🅿 ♿ toilets for disabled shop ✈ (ex guide dogs)

HISTORIC WARSHIPS
East Float, Dock Rd CH41 1DJ
➲ (end of M53 all docks turn off follow tourist signs. From Liverpool Wallasey tunnel 1st exit after toll & follow brown heritage signs)
☎ 0151 650 1573 🖷 0151 650 1473
e-mail: manager@warships.freeserve.co.uk
HMS Onyx served in the Falklands and is the only submarine afloat in the UK that visitors can explore. *HMS Plymouth*, an anti-submarine frigate also served in the Falklands. The U534 is the only WWII German U-Boat to be raised from the sea bed. Pre-booking required, adults only admitted to U-Boat.
Times: ✱ Open all year, Sep-Mar daily 10-4, Apr-Aug daily 10-5. (Closed 24-26 Dec, only open wknds for the first 6 wks of the year). **Facilities:** 🅿 🖳 ♿ museum only, access to HMS Plymouth, multimedia tour of U534 shop ✈ (ex guide dogs) 🍴

WILLIAMSON ART GALLERY & MUSEUM
Slatey Rd CH43 4UE
☎ 0151 652 4177 🖷 0151 670 0253
e-mail: wag@museum-service.freeserve.co.uk
English watercolours and works by the Liverpool school are an outstanding feature of the gallery. There is a large collection of pictures by P Wilson Steer, and also on view are sculpture, ceramics, glass, silver and furniture. The museum is linked to the gallery, and has displays on the history of the town and its port. Birkenhead was a hamlet before the 19th century, but grew large and rich through ship-building and the docks. Also on view are the Baxter Motor Collection, cars and motorbikes in a period garage setting.
Times: ✱ Open all year, Tue-Sun & BHs 1-5, (Closed Xmas & Good Fri). **Facilities:** 🅿 ♿ toilets for disabled shop ✈

LIVERPOOL   Map 07 SJ39

THE BEATLES STORY
Britannia Pavilion, Albert Dock L3 4AD
➲ (Follow signs to the Albert Dock. Located outside Britannia Pavilion, next to Premier Lodge Hotel)
☎ 0151 709 1963 🖷 0151 708 0039
e-mail: info@beatlesstory.com
Relive the story of the four lads from Liverpool who took the world by storm and changed the face of popular music for ever.
Times: Open all year (except Xmas & Boxing Day) 10-6 (last admission 5pm) **Fee:** £8.45 (ch 5-16yrs £4.95 & concessions £5.75). Family ticket (2ad & 3ch) £23 **Facilities:** 🅿 ♿ shop ✈ (ex guide dogs) 🍴

CENTRAL LIBRARY

William Brown St L3 8EW

➲ (Adjacent to St. George's Hall, which is opposite Lime St. Station. Central Library is located betwen the museum and the art gallery)

☎ 0151 233 5858 🖷 0151 233 5824

e-mail: refham.central.library@liverpool.gov.uk

The Picton, Hornby and Brown buildings, situated in the Victorian grandeur of William Brown Street, house Liverpool's collection of over one million books, forming one of Britain's largest and oldest public libraries. The Liverpool Record Office is one of the country's largest and most significant County Record offices.

Times: ✱ Open all year, Mon-Thu 9-7.30, Fri 9-5, Sat 10-4 & Sun 12-4. Closed BHs. **Facilities:** P (50 yds) (pay & display parking only) ⅅ (lift, text magnification, reading machine) toilets for disabled ✘ (ex guide dogs)

CONSERVATION CENTRE

White Chapel L1 6HZ

➲ (Follow brown tourist signs to Whitechapel)

☎ 0151 478 4999 🖷 0151 478 4990 FREE

Award winning centre, the only one of its kind, gives the public an insight into the world of museum and gallery conservation.

Times: Mon-Sat 10-5, Sun 12-5, Closed 23-26 Dec & 1 Jan **Facilities:** P (charged) ⬛ ⅅ toilets for disabled shop ✘ ex guide dogs 🔊

THE GRAND NATIONAL EXPERIENCE

Aintree Racecourse, Ormskirk Rd L9 5AS

➲ (Aintree Racecourse is located on the A59 (Liverpool to Preston Road) and is clearly signposted)

☎ 0151 522 2921 🖷 0151 522 2920

e-mail: aintree@rht.net

A fascinating look at Britain's most famous horserace, the Grand National. Visitors can sit in the jockey's weighing-in chair, walk around the dressing rooms, watch video presentations, and view a gallery of paintings and photography depicting the race.

Times: Open 23 May-14 Oct **Fee:** ✱ £7 (concessions £4) **Facilities:** P ✘ licensed ⅅ toilets for disabled shop ✘ (ex guide dogs) 🔊

HM CUSTOMS & EXCISE NATIONAL MUSEUM

Merseyside Maritime Museum, Albert Dock L3 4AQ

➲ (Albert Dock - follow Brown signs)

☎ 0151 478 4499 🖷 0151 478 4590 FREE

Enter the exciting world of smuggle busting where everyday items reveal their hidden secrets. Find a fake, rummage for hidden goods and spot a suspect traveller. Look into the illustrious history of HM Customs & Excise, it's the longest battle in history and it's still going on today!

Times: Open daily 10-5. (Closed 23-26 Dec & 1 Jan) **Facilities:** P ⬛ ✘ licensed ⅅ (restricted wheelchair access, no access to basement) toilets for disabled shop ✘ (ex guide dogs) 🔊

LIVERPOOL CATHEDRAL

St James' Mount L1 7AZ

➲ (M6 junct 21a - W along M62 to Liverpool - follow City Centre signs 'Cathedrals'. St James' Mount is off upper Duke St in south side of City Centre, adjacent to 'Chinatown')

☎ 0151 709 6271 🖷 0151 702 7292

e-mail: lew.eccleshall@
liverpoolcathedral.org.uk

Although it appears at first sight to be as old as any other monumental cathedral in Britain, Liverpool Cathedral is in fact a 20th century structure, that was only completed in 1978. Its foundation stone was laid in 1904, and through two World Wars the building continued. It is the largest Anglican Cathedral in Europe, and has the largest pipe organ and the heaviest ringing peal of bells in the world.

Times: Open daily 8-6 **Fee:** ✱ Free. £3 donation per person recommended. Tower £3.25 (concessions £1.50) **Facilities:** P (charged) ⬛ ✘ ⅅ toilets for disabled shop ✘ (ex guide dogs)

LIVERPOOL FOOTBALL CLUB VISITORS CENTRE TOUR

Anfield Rd L4 0TH

☎ 0151 260 6677 🖷 0151 264 0149   2 for 1

e-mail: Museum1@liverpoolfc.tv

Touch the famous "This is Anfield" sign as you walk down the tunnel to the sound of the crowd at the LFC museum and tour centre. Celebrate all things Liverpool, past and present. Bright displays and videos chart the history of England's most successful football club and more recent glories are recalled, as the 2001 "Treble" is on display, as well as the "Fab Four" European cups.

Times: Open all year: Museum daily 10-5 last admission 4pm. (Closed 25-26 Dec). Match days 9am until last admission - 1hr before kick off. Museum & Tour - tours are run subject to daily demand. Advance booking is essential to avoid disappointment. **Fee:** Museum only, £5 (ch under 6 & pen £3) Family £13. Museum & Tour £9.00 (ch under 16 & pen £5.50) Family £23. Special deals for schools & groups. **Facilities:** P ⬛ ✘ licensed ⅅ (lifts, ramps to all areas for wheelchairs) toilets for disabled shop ✘ (ex guide dogs) 🔊

LIVERPOOL MUSEUM

William Brown St L3 8EN

➲ (in city centre next to St George's Hall and Lime St, follow brown signs)

☎ 0151 478 4393   `FREE`

e-mail: themuseum@liverpoolmuseums.org.uk

One of Britain's most interesting museums, the Liverpool Museum has diverse collections ranging from the Amazonian rain forests to the mysteries of outer space. Special attractions include the award-winning hands-on Natural History Centre and the Planetarium. The museum is currently undergoing extensive building improvements and refurbishment, and many new features are due in 2005. Please note that during construction work some galleries may be closed.

Times: Open Mon-Sat 10-5, Sun noon-5. (Closed 23-26 Dec & 1 Jan)

Facilities: 🅿 💺 ♿ toilets for disabled shop ✕ (ex guide dogs) ◀

MERSEYSIDE MARITIME MUSEUM

Albert Dock L3 4AQ

➲ (The Albert Dock is situated near Liverpool's historic waterfront. Entry into the dock is from the Strand).

☎ 0151 478 4499 ▤ 0151 478 4590   `FREE`

Set in the heart of Liverpool's magnificent waterfront, the Merseyside Maritime Museum offers a unique insight into the history of the great port of Liverpool, its ships and its people.

Times: Open daily 10-5 (Closed 23-26 Dec & 1 Jan).

Facilities: 🅿 ✕ licensed ♿ (lifts, wheelchairs, ramps, ex pilot boat & basement) toilets for disabled shop ✕ (ex guide dogs) ◀

METROPOLITAN CATHEDRAL OF CHRIST THE KING

Mount Pleasant L3 5TQ

➲ (5 mins walk from either Liverpool Lime Street or Liverpool Central Railway Station. 'Smart' buses stop outside. Cathedral is well signposted from Liverpool City Centre)

☎ 0151 709 9222 ▤ 0151 708 7274

e-mail: met.cathedral@boltblue.com

A modern Roman Catholic cathedral which provides a focal point on the Liverpool skyline. The imposing structure of curving concrete ribs and stained glass was designed by Sir Frederick Gibberd and consecrated in 1967. Monumental crypt of brick and granite by Sir Edwin Lutyens 1933.

Times: Open daily 8-6 (Sun 5pm in winter). **Fee:** Free admission, although donations welcome. **Facilities:** 🅿 (charged) 💺 ♿ (lift, loop system, no access to Crypt) toilets for disabled shop ✕ (ex guide dogs) ◀

MUSEUM OF LIVERPOOL LIFE

Pier Head L3 4AA

➲ (follow signs for Albert Dock, museum is on Pier Head side)

☎ 0151 478 4080 ▤ 0151 478 4090   `FREE`

e-mail: liverpoollife@liverpoolmuseums.org.uk

The Museum of Liverpool Life celebrates the contribution of the people of Liverpool to national life. Recently expanded to include three new galleries, City Lives exploring the richness of Liverpool's cultural diversity, The River Room featuring life around the river Mersey and City Soldiers about the King's Regiment. Other galleries include Mersey Culture from

continued

Brookside to the Grand National, Making a Living and Demanding a Voice.

Times: Open daily 10am - 5pm (closed from 2pm on 24 Dec and all day 25, 26 Dec & 1 Jan) **Facilities:** 🅿 (charged) ♿ (wheelchairs, audio handsets, subtitles on video terminals) toilets for disabled shop ✕ (ex guide/hearing dogs) ◀

NATIONAL WILDFLOWER CENTRE

Court Hey Park L16 3NA

➲ (M62 junct 5, take A5080 to rdbt. Exit into Roby Rd, entrance 0.5m on left)

☎ 0151 738 1913 ▤ 0151 737 1820   `2 for 1`

e-mail: info@nwc.org.uk

Set in a public park on the outskirts of Liverpool, the National Wildflower Centre promotes the creation of wildflower habitats around the country and provides educational materials, wildflower seeds and interactive facilities. The Centre has demonstration areas, children's activities, a working nursery, compost display and rooftop walk. The centre has a comprehensive programme of events through the summer.

Times: Open Apr-Sep, daily 10-5. **Fee:** ✱ £3 (ch 5-16, pen, students & unemployed £1.50). Family ticket (2 adults & 2 ch) £7.50. Season tickets & group discount tickets available. **Facilities:** 🅿 💺 ♿ Electric buggy & wheelchair available for use. toilets for disabled shop garden centre ✕ (ex guide dogs & in park) ◀

SUDLEY HOUSE

Mossley Hill Rd L18 8BX

➲ (near Aigburth Station and Mossley Hill Station)

☎ 0151 724 3245   `FREE`

e-mail: sudley@liverpoolmuseums.org.uk

The former family home of the Liverpool merchant George Holt in the Liverpool suburb of Mossley Hill. Works on show are drawn mainly from his collection of British paintings including Landseer, Turner, Gainsborough, Reynolds and Romney as well as major pre-Raphaelite painters. Many of the original Victorian features of the building survive, including tiles, ceramics, stained glass and wallpaper.

Times: Open Mon-Sat 10-5, Sun noon-5. (Closed 23-26 Dec & 1 Jan).

Facilities: 🅿 💺 ♿ ✕ (ex guide dogs)

TATE LIVERPOOL
Albert Dock L3 4BB
➲ (within walking distance of Liverpool Lime
Street train station)
☎ 0151 702 7400 & 0151 702 7402
▤ 0151 702 7401
e-mail: liverpoolinfo@tate.org.uk
A converted Victorian warehouse with stunning views across
the River Mersey, Tate Liverpool displays the best of the
National Collection of 20th-Century Art. A changing
programme of exhibitions draws on works from public and
private collections across the world.
Times: ✱ Open Tue-Sun, 10-5.30. (Closed Mon ex BH Mon, 25-26
Dec, 1 Jan & Good Fri). Facilities: P ▟ & (wheelchairs available,
leaflets in Braille, hearing loop) toilets for disabled shop ✖ ▰

WALKER ART GALLERY
William Brown St L3 8EL
➲ (follow brown and white signs)
☎ 0151 478 4199 ▤ 0151 478 4390 FREE
For over 120 years, visitors have been surprised, charmed &
moved by The Walker's world-famous collection including
masterpieces by Rembrandt, Poussin, Rubens & Murillo.
Newly refurbished galleries will display an exciting and
varied programme of must see exhibitions.
Times: Open Mon-Sat 10-5, Sun 12-5 (closed 23-26 Dec & 1 Jan)
Facilities: P (charged) ▟ ✖ & (prior notice appreciated,
wheelchair on request) toilets for disabled shop ✖ (ex guide dogs)

PORT SUNLIGHT   Map 07 SJ38
LADY LEVER ART GALLERY
CH62 5EQ
➲ (Follow brown heritage signs)
☎ 0151 478 4136 ▤ 0151 478 4140 FREE
e-mail: ladyleverartgallery@nmgm.org
The Lady Lever Art Gallery houses many world famous
works of art, including Pre-Raphaelite masterpieces by
Millais, Burne-Jones and Rossetti. Dramatic landscapes by
the great British painters, Turner & Constable are also
displayed alongside portraits by Gainsborough, Romney &
Reynolds.
Times: Open all year, Mon-Sat 10-5, Sun 12-5. (Closed 23-26 Dec &
1 Jan) Facilities: P (charged) ▟ & (prior notice appreciated,
wheelchair on request) toilets for disabled ✖ (ex guide dogs)

PRESCOT   Map 07 SJ49
KNOWSLEY SAFARI PARK
L34 4AN
➲ (M62 junct 6 onto M57 junct 2. Follow 'safari
park' signs)
☎ 0151 430 9009 ▤ 0151 426 3677
e-mail: safari.park@knowsley.com
A five-mile drive through the reserves enables visitors to see
lions, tigers, elephants, rhinos, monkeys and many other
animals in spacious, natural surroundings. Also a children's
amusement park, reptile house, pets' corner plus sealion
shows. Other attractions include an amusement park and a
miniature railway.
Times: Open all year, Mar-Oct, daily 10-4. Winter Nov-Feb, 11-3.
Fee: £9 (ch & pen £6). Facilities: P ▟ & toilets for disabled shop
✖ (kennels provided) ▰

PRESCOT MUSEUM
34 Church St L34 3LA
➲ (situated on corner of High St (A57) & Church
St. Follow the brown heritage signs)
☎ 0151 430 7787 ▤ 0151 430 7219
e-mail: prescot.museum.dlcs@knowsley.gov.uk
Permanent exhibitions reflecting the local history of the area,
including the important clock and watch making heritage.
There is a programme of special exhibitions, events and
holiday activities, telephone for details.
Times: Open all year, Tue-Sat 10-5 (closed 1-2), Sun 2-5 (closed BHs)
Facilities: P (100 yds) & (ramp to ground floor) shop
✖ (ex guide dogs)

ST HELENS   Map 07 SJ59
WORLD OF GLASS
Chalon Way East WA10 1BT
➲ (5mins from M62 junct 7)
☎ 08700 114466 ▤ 01744 616966
e-mail: info@worldofglass.com

Ideal for all the family, this fascinating attraction is in the
heart of St Helens, a town shaped by glass-making. Features
include the world's first continuous glass-making furnace,
and two museum galleries that show glass in the ancient
world and Victorian life in St Helens. There is also a Mirror
Maze where Wizard Filligrano works, a newly refurbished
café and a gift shop.
Times: Open Tue-Sun & BH, 10-5. Closed 25-26 Dec & 1 Jan.
Fee: £5.30 (ch £3.80, seniors £3.80) Family & group discounts.
Facilities: P ▟ & toilets for disabled shop ✖ (ex guide dogs) ▰

SOUTHPORT   Map 07 SD31
ATKINSON ART GALLERY
Lord St PR8 1DH
➲ (located in centre of Lord St, next to the Town
Hall)
☎ 01704 533133 ext 2110   FREE
▤ 0151 934 2110
e-mail: atkinson.gallery@leisure.sefton.gov.uk
The gallery specialises in 19th-and 20th-century oil
paintings, watercolours, drawings and prints, as well as
20th-century sculpture. Temporary exhibitions are shown
regularly at the art gallery.
Times: Open all year, Mon-Wed & Fri 10-5, Thu & Sat 10-1. (Closed
25-26 Dec & 1 Jan). Facilities: P (next street) (pay & display)
✖ licensed & shop ✖ (ex guide dogs)

THE BRITISH LAWNMOWER MUSEUM

106-114 Shakespeare St PR8 5AJ

➲ (From M6, M58 or M57 follow signs towards town centre, then brown heritage signs to museum)

☎ 01704 501336 📄 01704 500564 **2 for 1**

e-mail: info@lawnmowerworld.com

This award-winning museum houses a private collection of over 200 rare exhibits of garden machinery of special interest dating from 1799. There is also the largest collection of vintage toy lawnmowers and games in the world. See the lawnmowers of the rich and famous as well as machines made by Rolls Royce, Royal Enfield, Hawker Sidley and many more. A tribute to the garden machine industry over the last 200 years.

Times: Open daily, 9-5.30, ex Sun & BH Mon. **Fee:** £1 (ch 50p). Guided tour £4. **Facilities:** 🅿 shop 🍴 🍺

PLEASURELAND

Marine Dr PR8 1RX

➲ (signed from Southport Town Centre)

☎ 0870 220 0204 📄 01704 537936 **2 for 1**

e-mail: mail@pleasurelandltd.freeserve.co.uk

Pleasureland is home to over 100 rides and attractions, including the awesome TRAUMAtizer suspended rollercoaster. Go all Jurassic on the new Lost Dinosaurs of the Sahara - a mysterious boat ride to prehistoric times.

Times: Open Mar-Nov opening times vary please call for information. **Fee:** ✱ £17 all day (juniors £12). Entry for 4 (adults and/or children) £60. **Facilities:** 🅿 (charged) 🍺 🍴 licensed ♿ (access on some rides) toilets for disabled shop 🍴 (ex guide dogs) 🍺

SPEKE Map 07 SJ48

SPEKE HALL

The Walk L24 1XD

➲ (on N bank of Mersey, 1m off A561 on W side of Liverpool Airport. Follow airport signs from M62 exit 6, A5300; M56 exit 12, follow brown signs)

☎ 0151 427 7231 📄 0151 427 9860

e-mail: spekehall@nationaltrust.org.uk

A remarkable timber-framed manor house set in tranquil gardens and grounds. The house has a Tudor Great Hall, Stuart plasterwork, and William Morris wallpapers. Outside are varied grounds, including a rose garden, bluebell woods and woodland walks. Also, a live interpretation by costumed guides.

Times: House open: 20 Mar-Oct, Wed-Sun (open BH Mon) 1-5.30; 6 Nov-5 Dec, Sat & Sun 1-4.30. Garden open daily (ex Mon & closed 24-26 & 31 Dec, 1 Jan & Good Fri). 11-5.30 or dusk. **Fee:** ✱ Hall & Gardens: £6 (ch £3.50). Gardens only: £3 (ch £1.50). Family ticket £17. Gardens Family ticket £9. Reduced rate when arriving by public transport, cycle or on foot. **Facilities:** 🅿 (charged) 🍺 🍴 ♿ (Wheelchairs, Electric car, Braille guide) toilets for disabled shop 🐕 🍺

Above: The New Bedford River, Welney, Norfolk

NORFOLK

EVENTS & FESTIVALS

May
1st King's Lynn May Garland Procession,
town centre, King's Lynn
4th-14th Norfolk & Norwich Festival (music
and the arts)

June
11th Deepdale Jazz Festival, Marsh Barn,
Burnham Deepdale (provisional)
29th-30th Royal Norfolk Show, Royal Norfolk
Showground

July
2nd-3rd Morris & Folk Festival, Sheringham
6th-10th Lord Mayor's Celebrations, Norwich
16th-17th Weeting Steam Rally, Weeting
30th-31st Aug Worstead Village Festival
31st Sandringham Flower Show (provisional)
tbc Norwich Music Festival

August
7th-13th Mundesley Festival
29th Aylsham Agricultural Show

September
10th-11th Great Yarmouth Maritime Festival,
South Quay, Great Yarmouth

December
27th-29th Great Yarmouth Christmas Fayre
tbc Norwegian Christmas Fayre, Market Place,
Great Yarmouth

Above: Windmill at Cley-next-the-Sea

BACONSTHORPE   Map 09 TG13

BACONSTHORPE CASTLE
NR25 6LN

➲ (0.75m N of Baconsthorpe off unclass road, 3m
E of Holt)

☎ 01799 322399   `FREE`

The remains of a fifteenth-century castle, built by Sir John
Heydon during the Wars of the Roses. The exact date when
the building was started is not known, since Sir John did not
apply for the statutory royal licence necessary to construct a
fortified house. In the 1560s, Sir John's grandson added the
outer gatehouse, which was inhabited until the 1920s, when
one of the turrets fell down. The remains of red brick and
knapped flint are reflected in the lake, which partly embraces
the castle as a moat.

Times: Open all year, any reasonable time. **Facilities:** 🅿 ✕ (ex
dogs on leads) ♯

BANHAM   Map 05 TM08

BANHAM ZOO
The Grove NR16 2HE

➲ (on B1113, signed off A11 and A140. Follow
brown tourist signs)

☎ 01953 887771 & 887773 🖹 01953 887445
e-mail: info@banhamzoo.co.uk

Set in 35 acres of magnificent parkland, see hundreds of
animals ranging from big cats to birds of prey and siamangs
to shire horses. Tiger Territory is a purpose-built enclosure
for Siberian tigers, including a rock pool and woodland
setting. See also Lemur Island and Tamarin and Marmoset
Islands. The Heritage Farm Stables & Falconry displays
Norfolk's rural heritage with majestic shire horses and birds
of prey. Other attractions include Children's Farmyard Barn
and Adventure Play Area.

Times: Open all year, daily from 10am. Last admission 1 hour before
closing. (Closed 25 & 26 Dec) **Fee:** Please phone Zoo for details
Facilities: 🅿 🍽 ✕ licensed & (3 wheelchairs for hire, special
parking) toilets for disabled shop ✕ ▄

BLICKLING   Map 09 TG12

BLICKLING HALL
NR11 6NF

➲ (on B1354, 1.5m NW of Aylsham, signposted off
A140 Norwich to Cromer road)

☎ 01263 738030 🖹 01263 731660
e-mail: blickling@nationaltrust.org.uk

Flanked by dark yew hedges and topped by pinnacles, the
warm red brick front of Blickling is a memorable sight. The
grounds include woodland and a lake, a formal parterre, and
a dry moat filled with roses, camellias and other plants.

Times: ✱ Hall open 31 Mar-28 Oct, Wed-Sun & BH, 1-4.30 (1-3.30
Oct). Also open Tue in Aug. Garden, shop & restaurant same days as
hall 10.15-5.15. **Facilities:** 🅿 🍽 ✕ licensed & (wheelchairs &
batricars, Braille guide, lift, parking) toilets for disabled shop garden
centre ✕ (ex guide dogs) ♨ ▄

BRESSINGHAM   Map 05 TM08

BRESSINGHAM STEAM MUSEUM & GARDENS
IP22 2AB
➲ (on A1066 2.5m W of Diss. Between Thetford & Diss)
☎ 01379 686900 & 687386   **2 for 1**
🖨 01379 686907
e-mail: info@bressingham.co.uk

Alan Bloom is an internationally recognised nurseryman and a steam enthusiast, and has combined his interests to great effect at Bressingham. There are three miniature steam-hauled trains, including a 15in gauge running through two and a half miles of the wooded Waveney Valley. The Dell Garden has 5000 species of perennials and alpines; Foggy Bottom has wide vistas, pathways, trees, shrubs, conifers and winter colour (restricted opening). A steam roundabout is another attraction, and the Norfolk fire museum is housed here. Various events are held, including Friends of Thomas the Tank Engine, please telephone for details.
Times: Open: Steam Museum, Dad's Army collection, Foggy Bottom & Dell Garden Apr-Sep, daily 10.30-5.30 (10.30-4.30 Mar & Oct). Last admission 1 hour before closing time. **Fee:** ✱ £7-£10 (ch 3-16 £5-£8, pen £6-£8). Family £21-£30. Season tickets available.
Facilities: ▣ 💺 ✕ licensed & (wheelchairs can be taken onto Nursery & Waveney lines) toilets for disabled shop garden centre ✖ (ex guide dogs) ◥

BURGH CASTLE   Map 05 TG40

BERNEY ARMS WINDMILL
NR30 1SB
☎ 01493 700605

One of the largest and best-preserved Victorian windmills in Norfolk, with seven floors to explore. Built to grind cement, its superb machinery is still fully operational.
Times: Open Apr-Sep, pre-booked groups only. **Fee:** ✱ £2 (ch £1, concessions £1.50). Prices & opening times relate to 2004, for further details phone or log onto www.english-heritage.org.uk/visits
Facilities: shop ✖ (ex dogs on leads) ✿

BURGH CASTLE
NR31 9PZ
➲ (at far W end of Breydon Water on unclass road, 3m W of Great Yarmouth)

Burgh Castle was built in the third century AD by the Romans, as one of a chain of forts along the Saxon Shore - the coast where Saxon invaders landed. Sections of the massive walls still stand.
Times: Open any reasonable time. **Facilities:** ✖ (ex dogs on leads) ✿

CAISTER-ON-SEA   Map 09 TG51

CAISTER ROMAN SITE
➲ (3m N of Great Yarmouth)

The name Caister has Roman origins, and this was in fact a Roman naval base. The remains include the south gateway, a town wall built of flint with brick courses and part of what may have been a seamen's hostel.
Times: Open any reasonable time. **Facilities:** ✖ (ex dogs on leads) ✿

CASTLE ACRE   Map 09 TF81

CASTLE ACRE PRIORY AND CASTLE
Stocks Green PE32 2XD
☎ 01760 755394   🖨 01760 755594

Britain's best-preserved Cluniac priory with walled herb garden where visitors can find out about the medieval uses of herbs. Nearby Castle Acre Castle is also well worth a visit.
Times: Open all year Apr-Sep, daily 10-6; Oct-Mar, Wed-Sun 10-4. (Closed 24-26 Dec & 1 Jan). **Fee:** ✱ Castle; Free entry; Priory; £4.20 (ch £2.10, concessions £3.20, family £10.50). Prices & opening times relate to 2004, for further details phone or log onto www.english-heritage.org.uk/visits **Facilities:** ▣ & shop ✖ (ex dogs on leads) ✿

CASTLE RISING   Map 09 TF62

CASTLE RISING CASTLE
PE31 6AH
➲ (off A149)
☎ 01553 631330

A fine twelfth-century domestic keep, set amid huge defensive earthworks, once the palace and home to Isabella, the 'She Wolf' of France, dowager Queen of England. The keep walls stand to their original height.
Times: Open all year, Apr-Nov, daily 10-6; Oct, daily 10-dusk; Nov-Mar, Wed-Sun 10-4. (Closed 24-26 Dec). **Fee:** ✱ £3.75 (ch £2.10, concessions £3, family £11). Prices & opening times relate to 2004, for further details phone or log onto www.english-heritage.org.uk/visits
Facilities: ▣ & (exterior only) toilets for disabled shop ✖ (ex dogs on leads) ✿

CROMER   Map 09 TG24

HENRY BLOGG MUSEUM
No 2 Boathouse, The Promenade NR27 9HE
➲ (located at the bottom of East Gangway)
☎ 01263 511294   🖨 01263 513018
e-mail: rfmuirhead@csma-netlink.co.uk

A lifeboat has been stationed at the Cromer since 1804, and the museum in No 2 boat house at the bottom of The Gangway covers local lifeboat history and the RNLI in general. The main exhibit is the WWII Watson Class lifeboat *H F Bailey*, the boat Henry Blogg coxed. In ten years he helped to save over 500 lives.
Times: ✱ Open Etr-Oct, daily 10-4. Or by appointment with the Curator. **Facilities:** ▣ (pay & display in town) & shop

NORTH NORFOLK RAILWAY
See advert on opposite page, see full entry under SHERINGHAM.

ERPINGHAM   Map 09 TG13

WOLTERTON PARK
NR11 7LY
➲ (signposted from A140 Norwich to Cromer)
☎ 01263 584175   **2 for 1**
🖨 01263 761214

Covering some 800 hectares this estate contains managed conservation areas, 18th-century landscaped gardens, and Wolterton Hall, built in the 1720s. Special events include gardening demonstrations, concerts, plays, opera, craft fairs, guided walks and history lectures.
Times: Open: Park daily; Hall, late Apr-end Oct, Fri 2-5 (last entry 4). **Fee:** ✱ Hall £5. Car park £2 (free for hall visitors) (ch £1, concessions £1.50). Prices & opening times relate to 2004, for further details phone

continued

or log onto www.english-heritage.org.uk/visits **Facilities:** 🅿 (charged) & partly accessible toilets for disabled shop ✖ (ex on lead & guide dogs) 🛥

FAKENHAM   Map 09 TF93

See also **Thursford Green**

PENSTHORPE WATERFOWL PARK & NATURE RESERVE

Pensthorpe NR21 0LN

➲ (just outside Fakenham on the A1067 to Norwich)

☎ 01328 851465 📠 01328 855905

e-mail: info@pensthorpe.com

Covering 500 acres of beautiful Wensum Valley countryside, with five lakes which are home to one of the largest collections of waterfowl and waders in Europe. Spacious walk-through enclosures and a network of hardsurfaced pathways ensures close contact with birds at the water's edge.

Times: Open Jan-Mar: daily 10-4. Apr-Dec: 10-5 **Fee:** £6 (ch £3, pen £5) **Facilities:** 🅿 🍴 & (network of hard surfaced pathways ensures access) toilets for disabled shop ✖ (ex guide dogs) 🛥

FELBRIGG   Map 09 TG23

FELBRIGG HALL

NR11 8PR

➲ (off B1436 betweeen A148 Cromer to Kings Lynn & A140 Cromer to Norwich)

☎ 01263 837444 📠 01263 837032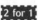

e-mail: felbrigg@nationaltrust.org.uk

Felbrigg is a 17th-century house built on the site of an existing medieval hall. It contains a superb collection of 18th-century furniture and pictures and an outstanding library. A 550-acre wood shelters the house from the North Sea and contains waymarked walks and a working dovecot.

Times: Open house and garden: late Mar-early Nov, Sat-Wed, house 1-5, garden 11-5. Park walks available daily dawn-dusk. **Fee:** ✱ House & garden £6.30 (ch £3). Garden only £2.60 (ch £1) **Facilities:** 🅿 🍴 ✗ licensed & (electric wheelchair for garden, Braille guide) toilets for disabled shop 🐾 🛥

FILBY   Map 09 TG41

THRIGBY HALL WILDLIFE GARDENS

NR29 3DR

➲ (on unclass road off A1064, between Acle & Caister on Sea)

☎ 01493 369477 📠 01493 368256

e-mail: mail@thrigbyhall.co.uk

The 250-year-old park of Thrigby Hall is now the home of animals and birds from Asia, and the lake has ornamental wildfowl. There are tropical bird houses, a unique blue willow pattern garden and tree walk and a summer house as old as the park. The enormous jungled swamp hall has special features such as underwater viewing of large crocodiles.

Times: Open all year, daily from 10. **Fee:** ✱ £6.90 (ch 4-14 £4.90, pen £5.90). **Facilities:** 🅿 🍴 & (wheelchairs available, ramps, parking) toilets for disabled shop ✖ (ex guide dogs) 🛥

Directions are provided
by the attractions.

GREAT BIRCHAM   Map 09 TF73

BIRCHAM WINDMILL   2 for 1

PE31 6SJ

➲ (0.5m W off unclassified Snettisham road).

☎ 01485 578393

e-mail: birchamwindmill@btinternet.com

This windmill is one of the last remaining in Norfolk. Sails turn on windy days, and the adjacent tea room serves home-made cakes, light lunches and cream teas. There is also a bakery shop and cycle hire.

Times: Open Etr-Sep, 10-5. **Fee:** Prices not confirmed for 2005 **Facilities:** 🅿 🍴 & toilets for disabled shop

GREAT YARMOUTH   Map 05 TG50

ELIZABETHAN HOUSE MUSEUM

4 South Quay NR30 2QH

➲ (from A12 & A47 follow town centre signs, then Historic South Quay signs, leading onto South Quay)

☎ 01493 855746 📠 01493 745459

e-mail: yarmouth.museums@norfolk.gov.uk

Experience the lives of families who lived in this splendid quayside house from Tudor to Victorian times. Decide for yourself if the death of Charles I was plotted in the Conspiracy Room. Dress the family in Tudor costumes. Discover Victorian life, upstairs and downstairs, and what it was like to work in the kitchen and scullery. Children can play in the toy room, while parents relax in the small but delightful walled garden.

Times: Open 5 Apr-Oct, Mon-Fri 10-5; Sat & Sun 1.15-5. **Fee:** ✱ £2.70 (ch £1.50, concessions £2.30). Adult in a family group £2.20 **Facilities:** 🅿 (250yds) & shop ✖ (ex guide dogs)

MERRIVALE MODEL VILLAGE
Wellington Pier Gardens, Marine Pde NR30 3JG
➲ (Marine parade seafront. Next to Wellington Pier)
☎ 01493 842097   `2 for 1`

Set in more than an acre of attractive landscaped gardens, this comprehensive miniature village is built on a scale of 1:12, and features streams, a lake and waterfalls. Among the models are a working fairground, a stone quarry, houses, shops, and a garden railway. There are even illuminations at dusk! The new Penny Arcade gives you the chance to play old amusements.
Times: Open 3 Apr-28 May, 10-5. 29 May-12 Sep, 10-9. 13 Sep-Oct, 10-5 **Fee:** ✱ £3 (ch 3-16, pen £2.50). **Facilities:** P (opposite) ☕ ♿ toilets for disabled shop

ROW 111 HOUSES/OLD MERCHANT'S HOUSE AND GREYFRIARS CLOISTERS
South Quay NR30 2RQ
➲ (follow signs to dock and south quay)
☎ 01493 857900

Visit these 17th-century houses unique to Great Yarmouth, and the remains of a Franciscan friary with rare early wall paintings. Guided tours explain how the rich and poor lived in these properties over various time periods.
Times: Open Apr-Oct, daily 10-5. Guided tours depart from Row 11 House at 10, 12, 2 & 5. All tours include Old Merchant's House and Greyfriar's Cloisters. **Facilities:** shop ✈ ♯

TOLHOUSE MUSEUM
Tolhouse St NR30 2SH
➲ (from A12 & A47 follow signs to Town Centre, then signs to South Quay. Museum attached to Central Library)
☎ 01493 858900 📠 01493 745459
e-mail: yarmouth.museums@norfolk.gov.uk

Visit one of the oldest prisons in the country and explore Great Yarmouth's story of crime and punishment. With the free audio guide you can hear the gaoler and his prisoners describe their experiences. Discover the fate of thieves, smugglers, witches, pirates and murderers at a time when punishment included transportation or execution. Other exhibits detail the history of this 12th-century former merchant's house that went on to become one of the town's most important civic buildings.
Times: Open 5 Apr-Oct, Mon-Fri 10-5; Sat & Sun 1.15-5. **Fee:** ✱ £2.70 (ch £1.50, concessions £2.30). Adult in family group £2.20
Facilities: P (500yds) lift to ground & 2nd floor, notice preferable shop ✈ (ex guide dogs)

GRESSENHALL   Map 09 TF91

ROOTS OF NORFOLK
Beech House NR20 4DR
➲ (on the B1146 3m NW of Dereham, follow the brown signs from the A47 or Dereham Town Centre)
☎ 01362 860563 📠 01362 860385
e-mail: gressenhall.museum@norfolk.gov.uk

Set among 50 acres of beautiful Norfolk countryside, this museum looks at the folkways, history and traditions of the area. Visit a workhouse and hear stories of the people who lived there. Explore traditional cottages and village shops. Take a free cart ride round the farm and get up close with rare breed animals. Relax in the tranquil gardens, or let off

continued

steam in the adventure playground. Extra family activities during school holidays.
Times: Open 19 & 20 Feb, 11-4. 27 Feb-13 Mar: Sun 11-4. 20 Mar-30 Oct: daily 10-5. 6-27 Nov: Sun 11-4. **Fee:** ✱ £5.70 (ch £4.40, concessions £5, under 4's free). **Facilities:** P ☕ ♿ (sound guide, wheelchair loan, induction loops) toilets for disabled shop ✈ 🔊

GRIMES GRAVES   Map 05 TL88

GRIMES GRAVES
IP26 5DE
➲ (7m NW of Thetford off A134)
☎ 01842 810656

These unique and remarkable Neolithic flint mines are the earliest major industrial site in Europe.
Times: Open Mar; Thu-Mon, 10-5; Apr-Sep, daily 10-6; Oct, Thu-Mon 10-5; (Closed Nov-Feb) **Fee:** ✱ £2.60 (ch £1.30, concessions £2, family £6.50). Prices & opening times relate to 2004, for further details phone or log onto www.english-heritage.org.uk/visits
Facilities: P ♿ (exhibition area, grounds only; access track rough) shop ♯

HEACHAM   Map 09 TF63

NORFOLK LAVENDER
Caley Mill PE31 7JE
➲ (follow signs on A149 & A148. Car park entrance on B1454, 100yds E of junct with A149)
☎ 01485 570384 📠 01485 571176   `2 for 1`
e-mail: admin@norfolk-lavender.co.uk

This is the largest lavender-growing and distilling operation in Britain. Different coloured lavenders are grown in strips and harvested in July and August. There are also herb gardens and a fragrant Plant Centre, and guided tours of the distillery and gardens. The 2-for-1 voucher is valid for garden tours, available from May to September.
Times: Open all year, daily, Apr-Oct 10-5; Nov-Mar 10-4. (Closed 25-26 Dec & 1 Jan). **Fee:** ✱ Admission to grounds free. Guided tours £2.25 (May-Sep). Trip to Lavender Field £4.50, mid Jun-mid Aug.
Facilities: P ☕ ✗ licensed ♿ (wheelchairs for loan) toilets for disabled shop garden centre 🔊

HOLKHAM   Map 09 TF84

HOLKHAM HALL & BYGONES MUSEUM
NR23 1AB
➲ (off A149, 2m W of Wells-next-the-Sea)
☎ 01328 710227 📠 01328 711707
e-mail: l.herrieven@holkham.co.uk

This classic Palladian mansion was built between 1734 and 1764 by Thomas Coke, 1st Earl of Leicester, and is home to his descendants. It has a magnificent alabaster entrance hall and the sumptuous state rooms house Roman statuary, fine furniture and paintings by Rubens, Van Dyck, Gainsborough and others. The Bygones Museum, housed in the stable block, has over 5,000 items of domestic and agricultural display - from gramophones to fire engines.
Times: Open May-Sep, Thu-Mon 1-5; Etr, May & Summer BHs also open Sat-Mon 11.30-5. **Fee:** Prices not confirmed for 2005
Facilities: P ☕ ♿ (wheelchair ramps at all entrances) toilets for disabled shop garden centre ✈ (ex guide dogs) 🔊

HORSEY   Map 09 TG42
HORSEY WINDPUMP
NR29 4EF
⮑ (15m N of Great Yarmouth, on the B1159 4m
NE of Martham)
☎ 01493 393904

Set in a remote part of the Norfolk Broads, the windpump
mill was built 200 years ago to drain the area, and then
rebuilt in 1912 by Dan England, a noted Norfolk millwright. It
has been restored since being struck by lightning in 1943,
and overlooks Horsey Mere and marshes, noted for their
wild birds and insects, as a site of International Importance
for Nature Conservation.

Times: ✱ Open 10.30-4.30, last admission 4pm; Mar, Sat-Sun only;
Apr-Jun, Wed-Sun; Jul-Aug, daily; Sep-Oct, Wed-Sun; Open bank
holidays. **Facilities:** 🅿 (charged) 🍺 ♿ (parking, ramps to ground
floor) toilets for disabled shop 🐕 (ex guide dogs) 🦌

HORSHAM ST FAITH   Map 09 TG21
CITY OF NORWICH AVIATION MUSEUM
Old Norwich Rd NR10 3JF
⮑ (follow brown tourist signs from A140 Norwich
to Cromer Road)
☎ 01603 893080   🖷 01603 893080   **2 for 1**
e-mail: norwichairmuseum@hotmail.com

A massive Avro Vulcan bomber, veteran of the Falklands
War, dominates the collection of military and civilian aircraft
at this museum. There are several displays relating to the
aeronautical history of Norfolk, including some on the role
played by Norfolk-based RAF and USAAF planes during
World War II, and a section dedicated to the operations of
RAF Bomber Command's 100 group.

Times: Open all year, Apr-Oct Tue-Sat, 10-5. Sun & BH Mons 12-5
(Mons during school hols). Nov-Mar, Wed & Sat 10-4. Sun 12-4.
Fee: ✱ £2.80 (ch & concessions £1.50, pen £2.30) Family ticket £8.
Facilities: 🅿 🍺 ♿ (assistance available) shop
🐕 (ex guide dogs) 🍴

HOUGHTON   Map 09 TF72
HOUGHTON HALL
PE31 6UE
⮑ (1.25m off A148. 13m E of King's Lynn & 10m
W of Fakenham on A148)
☎ 01485 528569   🖷 01485 528167   **2 for 1**
e-mail: administrator@houghtonhall.com

Houghton Hall built in the 1720s by Sir Robert Walpole,
Britain's first Prime Minister, is one of the grandest surviving
Palladian Houses in England. Now owned by the 7th
Marquess of Cholmondeley. The spectacular 5-acre walled
garden, restored by Lord Cholmondeley, has been divided
into areas for fruit and vegetables, spacious herbaceous
borders, and formal rose gardens with over 150 varieties. A
collection of Model Soldiers contains over 20,000 models
laid out in various battle formations.

Times: Open Etr-Sep, Wed, Thu, Sun & BHs. House open 2-5.30,
grounds, museum, tea shop 1-5.30. **Fee:** ✱ £6.50 (ch 5-16 £3,
ch under 5 free). Excluding house £4 (ch 5-16 £2). **Facilities:** 🅿 🍺
🍴 licensed ♿ lift, motorised buggies toilets for disabled shop 🐕 (ex
guide dogs)

HUNSTANTON   Map 09 TF64
SEA LIFE AQUARIUM & MARINE SANCTUARY
Southern Promenade PE36 5BH
☎ 01485 533576   🖷 01485 533531

With over 30 fascinating displays of marine life, this
fascinating aquarium offers close encounters with starfish,
sharks, octopus, eels and many other underwater wonders.
Feeding demonstrations, talks and special presentations.
Latest addition: Otters.

Times: ✱ Open all year, daily from 10. (Closed 25 Dec)
Facilities: 🅿 (charged) 🍺 ✗ ♿ toilets for disabled shop
🐕 (ex guide dogs) 🍴

KING'S LYNN   Map 09 TF62
AFRICAN VIOLET CENTRE
Terrington St Clement PE34 4PL
⮑ (situated beside A17 5m from Kings Lynn and
3m from A47/A17 junct)
☎ 01553 828374   🖷 01553 828376   **FREE**
e-mail: info@africanvioletcentre.ltd.uk

A warm and friendly welcome awaits you at the African
Violet Centre. As a major plant specialist the centre offers a
wide variety of plants for any enthusiast. Best known for
their vast selection and display of African violets. The
African Violet Centre is a winner of many Chelsea Gold
Medals.

Times: ✱ Open daily Mon-Sat 9-5, Sun 10-5. (Closed Xmas & New
Year). **Facilities:** 🅿 🍺 ♿ (ramps & wide doors) toilets for disabled
shop garden centre 🐕 (ex guide dogs) 🍴

KING'S LYNN ARTS CENTRE
27-29 King St PE30 1HA
⮑ (located just off Tuesday Market Place in King
Street, next to Globe Hotel)
☎ 01553 764864   🖷 01553 762141   **FREE**
e-mail: entertainment_admin@
west-norfolk.gov.uk

Although it has been used for many purposes, the theatrical
associations of this 15th-century Guildhall are strongest:
Shakespeare himself is said to have performed here. A year
round programme of film, performing and visual arts takes
place. Contact box office for details.

Times: Open Mon-Fri, 10-2. Closed show days, Sun, BHs, Good Fri &
24 Dec-1st Mon in Jan. **Facilities:** 🅿 (50yds) (pay & display) 🍺
✗ licensed ♿ (hearing loop, ramp) 🐕 🦌

TOWN HOUSE MUSEUM
46 Queen St PE30 5DQ
⮑ (in town centre close to historic South Quay)
☎ 01553 773450
e-mail: lynn.museum@norfolk.gov.uk

A charming museum set in a 19th-century town house.
Explore everyday life in King's Lynn through the ages in a
series of carefully re-constructed rooms, from medieval
times to the 1950s. Enjoy collections of historic toys and
costumes, and take the air in the delightful garden. Dotted
around the displays are colourful games and activities that
will keep the children amused.

Times: Open May-Sep, Mon-Sat 10-5; Sun 2-5. Oct-Apr, Mon-Sat 10-4.
Fee: ✱ £1.80 (ch 90p, concessions £1.40). **Facilities:** 🅿 (100yds)
♿ shop 🐕 🍴

LENWADE   Map 09 TG01

DINOSAUR ADVENTURE PARK

Weston Park NR9 5JW

➲ (9m from Norwich. Follow Weston Park signs
from A47 or A1067)

☎ 01603 876310   🖷 01603 876315

e-mail: info@dinosaurpark.co.uk

Children will have great fun coming face to face with lots of
friendly farm animals (real), and giant dinosaurs (thankfully
not real). Alongside the animals there are adventure play
areas, a fossil workshop, raptor racers, Jurassic putt, a
Victorian walled garden, and the Neanderthal walk.

Times: ✱ Open Etr-8 Sep & Oct half term, daily; 9 Sep-20 Oct, Fri, Sat
& Sun. **Facilities:** 🅿 ⏻ ᵫ toilets for disabled shop
✖ (ex guide dogs) 🞃

LITTLE WALSINGHAM   Map 09 TF93

WALSINGHAM ABBEY GROUNDS & SHIREHALL MUSEUM

NR22 6BP

➲ (Follow B1105 from Fakenham. Entrance to
museum through tourist info centre in village)

☎ 01328 820510 & 820259   🖷 01328 820098

e-mail: walsingham.museum@farmline.com

In the grounds of the Abbey are the ruins of the original
Augustinian priory built in the 1100s. The priory was built
over the shrine of Our Lady of Walsingham which had been
established in 1061. Shirehall Museum consists of an original
Georgian Courthouse, displays on the history of Walsingham
and local artefacts. The museum is situated in 20 acres of
tranquil and picturesque gardens with access to woodland
and river walks across the historic parkland.

Times: Open Feb daily 10-4. 19 Mar-30 Oct, daily 10-4.30; Nov-Dec,
wknds only 10-4; **Fee:** ✱ £3 (concessions £1.50)
Facilities: 🅿 (100yds) ᵫ toilets for disabled shop garden centre 🞃

NORTH CREAKE   Map 09 TF83

CREAKE ABBEY

NR21 9LF

➲ (off B1355)

The ruins of the church of an Augustinian almshouse, later
converted to an abbey.

Times: Open any reasonable time. **Facilities:** ✖ (ex dogs on leads)
▦

NORWICH   Map 05 TG20

AIR DEFENCE RADAR MUSEUM

RAF Neatishead, Norwich, NR12 8YB

➲ (follow brown signs from A1062 at Horning)

☎ 01692 633309   🖷 01692 633214   **2 for 1**

e-mail: curator@radarmuseum.co.uk

This multi-award winning Museum, housed in the original
1942 Radar Operations building, features the Battle of Britain
Room, 1942 Ground Controlled Interception Room, Radar
Engineering, Military Communications Systems, Cold War

continued

Operations Room, Royal Observer Corps, Space Defence,
Bloodhound Missiles and Original Mobile Radar Vehicles.

Air Defence Radar Museum

Times: Open year round 2nd Sat each month; Apr-Oct Tue & Thu &
BH Mons 10-5 **Fee:** £4 (ch £3, under 13 free, concessions £3.50)
Facilities: Parking, Café disabled symbol (ground floor and grounds
only accessible, video tour for inaccessible areas) Gift shop, ✖ (ex
guide dogs)

BRIDEWELL MUSEUM

Bridewell Alley NR2 1AQ

➲ (in town centre)

☎ 01603 629127   🖷 01603 765651

e-mail: museums@norfolk.gov.uk

Built in the late 14th century, this flint-faced merchant's
house was used as a prison from 1583 to 1828. It now
houses displays illustrating the trades and industries of
Norwich during the past 200 years, including a large
collection of locally made boots and shoes. There are also a
reconstructed 1930s pharmacy, pawnbrokers shop and a
blacksmith's smithy.

Times: Open Apr-29 Oct, Tue-Fri 10-4.30; Sat 10-5. School hols,
Mon-Sat 10-5. **Fee:** £2.20 (ch £1.30, concessions £1.80) Family ticket
£5. **Facilities:** 🅿 5 min walk shop ✖ (ex guide dogs)

NORWICH CASTLE MUSEUM

Castle Meadow NR1 3JU

➲ (located in city centre)

☎ 01603 493625   🖷 01603 493623

e-mail: museums@norfolk.gov.uk

The Castle keep was built in the 12th century, and the
museum houses displays of art, archaeology, natural history,
Lowestoft porcelain, Norwich silver, a large collection of
paintings (with special emphasis on the Norwich School of
Painters) and British ceramic teapots. There are also guided
tours of the dungeons and battlements. A programme of
exhibitions, children's events, gallery and evening talks takes
place throughout the year. Please ring for details.

Times: Open all year, Mon-Fri 10-4.30, Sat 10-5, Sun 1-5; School
holidays, Mon-Sat 10-6, Sun 1-5. (Closed 24-27 Dec & 1 Jan). **Fee:** All
zones £5.25 (ch 4-16 £3.70, conc £4.50). Castle & History Zone £3.50
(ch £2.50, concessions £2.95). Art & Exhibitions Zone £3 (ch £2.10,
concessions £2.55) **Facilities:** 🅿 (200mtrs) ⏻ ᵫ (lift to first floor,
special parking by prior arrangement) toilets for disabled shop
✖ (ex guide dogs)

NORWICH CATHEDRAL

The Close NR1 4DH

➲ (A47, A11 to city centre, inner ring road to Barrack St rdbt, take road towards city centre to Tombland)

☎ 01603 218321   ▤ 01603 766032

e-mail: vis-profficer@cathedral.org.uk

The splendour and tranquillity of Norwich Cathedral have attracted visitors and pilgrims for nearly 1000 years. Norwich has the second highest spire, and the largest monastic cloister in England, and the 1,000 carved medieval roof bosses are amazing. The building remains a place of quiet reflection and prayer as well as for participation in daily worship or the rich pageantry of the Church's festivals.

Times: Open daily, 7.30-7 (6pm mid Sep-mid May). **Fee:** ✱ Donations welcomed £3 (ch £1). Guided tours £3 (ch £1). **Facilities:** P (440yds) ✗ licensed ৬ (lift, touch & hearing centre, audio-induction loop) toilets for disabled shop

ROYAL NORFOLK REGIMENTAL MUSEUM

Shirehall, Market Av NR1 3JQ

➲ (adjacent to Norwich Castle Museum)

☎ 01603 493649   ▤ 01603 493623

e-mail: regimental.museum@norfolk.gov.uk

Museum displays deal with the social as well as military history of the county regiment from 1685, including the daily life of a soldier. Audio-visual displays and graphics complement the collection and there's a programme of temporary exhibitions.

Times: Open all year, Tue-Fri 10-4.30; Sat 10-5. School Hols Mon-Sat 10-5 (Closed Xmas period & 1 Jan). **Fee:** ✱ £2.20 (ch £1.30, concessions £1.80). Family £5 **Facilities:** P (400yds) ৬ (stair lift available, ring for details) shop ✗ (ex guide dogs)

OXBOROUGH   Map 05 TF70

OXBURGH HALL

PE33 9PS

➲ (7m SW of Swaffham. Signposted from A134 at Stoke ferry & Swaffham).   **2 for 1**

☎ 01366 328258   ▤ 01366 328066

e-mail: oxburghhall@nationaltrust.org.uk

The outstanding feature of this 15th-century moated building is the 80ft high Tudor gatehouse which has remained unaltered throughout the centuries. Henry VII lodged in the King's Room in 1487. A parterre garden of French design stands outside the moat. Rare needlework by Mary Queen of Scots and Bess of Hardwick is on display. A particular attraction is a genuine 17th century priests hole, which is accessible to members of the public.

Times: Open House: 22 Mar-2 Nov, daily (ex Thu & Fri) 1-5, BH Mon 11-5, last admission 4.30. Garden: 1-16 Mar, wknds, 11-4; 23 Mar-3 Nov daily (ex Thu & Fri) 11-5.30; Aug daily 11-5.30. **Fee:** ✱ House & Gdns £5.75 (ch £2.90), Family ticket £15. Gdns only £2.90 (ch £1.45). Party 15+ £4.65. **Facilities:** P ◾ ✗ licensed ৬ (Braille guide, wheelchairs available, touch tour) toilets for disabled shop ✗ (ex guide dogs) ⛺ ◾

REEDHAM   Map 05 TG40

PETTITTS ANIMAL ADVENTURE PARK

NR13 3UA

➲ (off A47 at Acle)

☎ 01493 700094 & 701403   ▤ 01493 700933

Three parks in one, aimed at the younger child. Rides include a railway and roller coaster; the adventure play area has a golf course, ball pond and tearoom; and entertainment is provided by clowns, puppets and live musicians. Among the animals that can be seen are small horses, wallabies, birds of prey, goats, chickens and ducks.

Times: Open daily 27 Mar-Oct, 10-5/5.30. **Fee:** ✱ £7.75 (ch 3-15 £7.25, pen/disabled £5.85, under 3's free). **Facilities:** P ◾ ৬ (ramps to all areas) toilets for disabled shop ✗ ◾

ST OLAVES   Map 05 TM49

ST OLAVE'S PRIORY

➲ (5.5m SW of Great Yarmouth on A143)

Remains of an Augustinian priory founded nearly 200 years after the death in 1030 of the patron saint of Norway, after whom it was named.

Times: Open any reasonable time. **Facilities:** ✗ (ex on lead in certain areas) ♯

SANDRINGHAM   Map 09 TF62

SANDRINGHAM HOUSE, GROUNDS, MUSEUM & COUNTRY

PE35 6EN

➲ (off A148)

☎ 01553 772675 & 612908   ▤ 01485 541571

e-mail: visits@sandringhamestate.co.uk

The private country retreat of Her Majesty The Queen, this neo-Jacobean house was built in 1870 for King Edward VII. The main rooms used by the Royal Family when in residence are all open to the public. Sixty acres of glorious grounds surround the House and offer beauty and colour throughout the season. Sandringham Museum contains fascinating displays of Royal memorabilia.

Times: Open Etr Sat-mid Jul & early Aug-Oct. House open 11-4.45, Museum 11-5 & Grounds 10.30-5. **Fee:** ✱ House, Museum & Grounds: £6.50 (ch £4, pen £5). Family ticket £17. **Facilities:** P ◾ ✗ licensed ৬ (wheelchair loan, free transport in grounds, Braille guide) toilets for disabled shop garden centre ✗ (ex guide dogs) ◾

SAXTHORPE   Map 09 TG13

MANNINGTON GARDENS & COUNTRYSIDE

Mannington Hall NR11 7BB

➲ (signposted from Corpusty/Saxthorpe on B1149 Norwich-Holt road. Follow brown signs)   **2 for 1**

☎ 01263 584175   ▤ 01263 761214

The moated manor house, built in 1460 and still a family home, forms a centre-piece for the pretty gardens which surround it. Visitors can take in the Heritage rose garden, lakes, a scented garden, a ruined church, and horse graves.

Times: Open: Gardens Jun-Aug, Wed-Fri 11-5; also Sun noon-5; 30 Apr-1 Oct. Walks open every day from 9am. Hall open by prior appointment only. **Fee:** ✱ Garden £3 (accompanied ch 16 free, students & pen £2.50). Walks free (car park for walkers £2). **Facilities:** P ◾ ৬ (boardwalk across meadow, wheelchair entrance) toilets for disabled shop ✗ (ex guide dogs) ◾

SHERINGHAM   Map 09 TG14
NORTH NORFOLK RAILWAY
Sheringham Station NR26 8RA
➲ (from A148 take A1082. Next to large car park by rdbt in town centre).
☎ 01263 820800 ▤ 01263 820801
e-mail: enquiries@nnrailway.com

A steam railway with trains operating on most days (Apr-Sep), with extra days as the season progresses and a daily service in the summer. At Weybourne Station there is a collection of steam locomotives and rolling stock, some of which are undergoing or awaiting restoration. There is also a museum of railway memorabilia.
Times: Open mid Feb-Oct; daily steam trains; Dec & Jan, Santa specials. Telephone for details **Fee:** ✱ £8 (ch under 4 free, ch 4-15 £4.50, pen £7). Family ticket £23 (free brochure while stocks last).
Facilities: ▣ ▣ ♿ (ramps to trains, carriage converted for wheelchair access) toilets for disabled shop ▰

See advertisement on page 173

SOUTH WALSHAM   Map 09 TG31
FAIRHAVEN WOODLAND & WATER GARDEN
School Rd NR13 6DZ
➲ (follow brown heritage signs from A47 onto B1140 to South Walsham. Drive through village towards Gt Yarmouth. Turn left into School Road, 100yds past South Walsham Hall) **2 for 1**
☎ 01603 270449 ▤ 01603 270449
e-mail: fairhavengardens@norfolkbroads.com
These delightful woodland and water gardens offer a combination of cultivated and wild flowers. In spring there are masses of primroses and bluebells, with azaleas and rhododendrons in several areas. Candelabra primulas and some unusual plants grow near the waterways, and in summer the wild flowers provide a habitat for butterflies, bees and dragonflies. Summer flowers include Day Lillies, Ligularia, Hostas, Hydrangeas and flowering shrubs, including Viburnum Mariesii (Wedding Cake Viburnum),
continued

Cornus Kousa Chinensis (large white bracts like flowers) and Cornus Florida Rubra (large pink bracts like flowers)

Fairhaven Woodland & Water Garden
Times: Open daily 10-5, extended opening until 9pm Wed & Thu, May-Aug. (Closed 25 Dec). **Fee:** £4 (ch £1.50, under 5 free, pen & concessions £3.50). Single membership tickets £15. Family membership ticket £35. Dog membership £2.50. Wildlife Sanctuary £1.50.
Facilities: ▣ ▣ ♿ (ramp, grab rail) toilets for disabled shop garden centre ▰

THETFORD   Map 05 TL88
ANCIENT HOUSE MUSEUM
White Hart St IP24 1AA
➲ (in town centre)
☎ 01842 752599
e-mail: ancient.house.museum@norfolk.gov.uk
An early Tudor timber-framed house with beautifully carved beamed ceilings, it now houses an exhibition on Thetford and Breckland life. This has been traced back to very early times, and there are examples from local Neolithic settlements. Brass rubbing facilities are available and there is a small period garden recreated in the rear courtyard.
Times: Open all year, Mon-Sat, 10-5 (Closed Mon 12.30-1); Jun-Aug also Sun 2-5. (Closed Good Fri, Xmas period & New Year's Day).
Facilities: ▣ (20yds) shop garden centre ✖

THETFORD PRIORY
➲ (on W side of Thetford near station)
A glimpse of medieval religious life before the dissolution of the monasteries. The Priory of Our Lady of Thetford belonged to the Order of Cluny, and was founded in 1103 by Roger Bigod, an old soldier and friend of William the Conqueror.
Times: Open all year, any reasonable time. **Facilities:** ✖ (ex dogs on leads) ⚑

THETFORD WARREN LODGE
➲ (2m W of Thetford, off B1107)
The remains of a two-storey hunting lodge, built in the 15th-century of flint with stone dressings.
Times: Open any reasonable time. Currently closed for repair, contact regional office on 01233 582700 before visiting. **Facilities:** ✖ (ex dogs on leads) ⚑

THURSFORD GREEN   Map 09 TF93
THURSFORD COLLECTION
NR21 0AS
➲ (1m off A148. Halfway between Fakenham and Holt)
☎ 01328 878477   🖷 01328 878415
e-mail: admin@thursfordcollection.co.uk

This exciting collection specialises in organs, with a Wurlitzer cinema organ, fairground organs, barrel organs and street organs among its treasures. There are live musical shows every day. The collection also includes showmen's engines, ploughing engines and farm machinery. There is a children's play area and a breathtaking 'Venetian gondola' switchback ride.

Times: Open Good Fri-last Sun in Sep, daily, 12-5. Closed Sat.
Fee: £5.50 (ch under 4 free, ch 4-14 £3, students £4.75 pen £5.20). Party 15+ £4.75 each. **Facilities:** 🅿 💺 ✗ licensed 🚻 toilets for disabled shop (five different giftshops) 💢 (ex guide dogs) ⬛

TITCHWELL   Map 09 TF74
RSPB NATURE RESERVE
PE31 8BB
➲ (6m E of Hunstanton on A149, signposted entrance)
☎ 01485 210779   🖷 01485 210779   **FREE**
e-mail: titchwell@rspb.org.uk

A firm path takes you to three hides and on to the beach where a platform overlooking the sea is suitable for wheelchairs. A colony of avocets nest on the enclosed marsh with gadwalls, tufted ducks, shovelers and black-headed gulls. During the season many migrants visit the marsh including wigeon, black-tailed godwits, curlews, and sandpipers.

Times: Open at all times. Visitor Centre daily 9.30-5 (4pm Nov-Mar).
Facilities: 🅿 (charged) 💺 🚻 (ramps to hides, wheelchair bays in hides) toilets for disabled shop ⬛

WEETING   Map 05 TL78
WEETING CASTLE
IP27 0RQ
➲ (2m N of Brandon off B1106)
This ruined 11th-century fortified manor house stands in a moated enclosure. There are interesting but slight remains of a three-storey cross-wing.
Times: Open any reasonable time. **Facilities:** 💢 (ex dogs on leads) ⛫

WELLS-NEXT-THE-SEA   Map 09 TF94
WELLS & WALSINGHAM LIGHT RAILWAY
NR23 1QB
➲ (A149 Cromer road)
☎ 01328 711630
The railway covers the four miles between Wells and Walsingham, and is the longest ten and a quarter inch gauge track in the world. The line passes through some very attractive countryside, particularly noted for its wild flowers and butterflies. This is the home of the unique Garratt Steam Locomotive specially built for this line.
Times: Open daily Good Fri-end Oct. **Fee:** ✱ £6.50 return (ch £5 return). **Facilities:** 🅿 💺 🚻 shop

WELNEY   Map 05 TL59
WWT WELNEY
Hundred Foot Bank PE14 9TN
➲ (off A1101, N of Ely)
☎ 01353 860711   🖷 01353 860711
e-mail: welney@wwt.org.uk

This important wetland site on the beautiful Ouse Washes is famed for the breathtaking spectacle of wild ducks, geese and swans which spend the winter here. Impressive observation facilities, including hides, towers and an observatory, offer outstanding views of the huge numbers of wildfowl which include Bewicks and whooper swans, wigeon, teal and shoveler. Floodlit evening swan feeds take place between November and February. There are two hides for wheelchair users.

Times: Open all year, daily 10-5. (Closed 25 Dec). **Fee:** ✱ £3.90 (ch £2.30, pen £3.20). Family ticket £10.50. **Facilities:** 🅿 💺 🚻 toilets for disabled shop 💢 (ex guide/hearing dogs) ⬛

WEST RUNTON   Map 09 TG14
NORFOLK SHIRE HORSE CENTRE
West Runton Stables NR27 9QH
➲ (off A149 in village of West Ranton half-way between Cromer & Sheringham, follow brown signs)
☎ 01263 837339   🖷 01263 837132
e-mail: bakewell@norfolkshirehorse.fsnet.co.uk

The Shire Horse Centre has a collection of draught horses and some breeds of mountain and moorland ponies. There are also exhibits of horse-drawn machinery, waggons and carts, and harnessing and working demonstrations are given twice every day. Other attractions include a children's farm, a photographic display of draught horses past and present, talks and a video show. There is a riding school on the premises as well.

Times: Open 4 Apr-29 Oct, Sun-Fri; also Sats BHs. Last admission 3.45pm **Fee:** ✱ £5.50 (ch £3.50, pen £4.50). **Facilities:** 🅿 💺 🚻 concrete yards all ramped toilets for disabled shop 💢 (ex on lead) ⬛

WEYBOURNE   Map 09 TG14
THE MUCKLEBURGH COLLECTION
Weybourne Military Camp NR25 7EG
➲ (on A149, coast road, 3m W of Sheringham)
☎ 01263 588210 & 588608   **2 for 1**
🖷 01263 588425
e-mail: info@muckleburgh.co.uk

The largest privately-owned military collection of its kind in the country, which incorporates the Museum of the Suffolk and Norfolk Yeomanry. Exhibits include restored and working tanks, armoured cars, trucks and artillery of WWII, and equipment and weapons from the Falklands and the Gulf War. Live tank demonstrations are run daily (except Sat) during school holidays.

Times: check website or phone for details **Fee:** £5.50 (ch £3 & pen £4.50). Family ticket £13.50. **Facilities:** 🅿 💺 ✗ 🚻 (ramped access, wheelchairs available) toilets for disabled shop 💢 (ex guide, kennels provided) ⬛

NORTHAMPTONSHIRE

EVENTS & FESTIVALS

May
20th-30th Moulton Village Festival (Sat main day of event)
28th-30th British Waterways Annual Boat Show, Crick (provisional)

June
tbc Northampton Music & Arts Festival

July
2nd-3rd Hollowell Steam & Heavy Horse Show, Hollowell nr Northampton
tbc Northampton Town Show, Abington Park, Northampton

August
tbc Northampton Hot Air Balloon Festival, Northampton Racecourse, Northampton

October
8th World Conker Championship, Village Green, Ashton, near Oundle

Top: St Mary Church & All Saints by River Nene
Above: Dallington Heath

ALTHORP   Map 04 SP66

ALTHORP
NN7 4HQ
➲ (from South, exit M1 junct 16, follow signs towards Northampton until directed by brown signs. From North, exit M1 junct 18, follow signs towards Northampton until directed by brown signs)
☎ 01604 770107 0870 167 9000
🖷 01604 770042
e-mail: mail@althorp.com

Althorp House has been the home of the Spencer family since 1508. The house was built in the 16th century, but has been changed since, most notably by Henry Holland in the 18th century. Recently restored by the present Earl, the house is carefully maintained and in immaculate condition. The award-winning exhibition 'Diana, A Celebration' is located in six rooms and depicts the life and work of Diana, Princess of Wales. There is in addition, a room which depicts the work of the Diana, Princess of Wales Memorial Fund.
Times: Open Jul-Sep, daily 11-5. (Closed 31 Aug) **Fee:** £11.50 (ch £5.50 & pen £9.50). Family ticket £28.50. Tickets discounted if pre-booked. (not confirmed) **Facilities:** 🅿 🅿 � (disabled parking, wheelchairs, audio tour, shuttle) toilets for disabled shop ✖ (ex guide dogs) ◀

CANONS ASHBY   Map 04 SP55

CANONS ASHBY HOUSE
NN11 3SD
➲ (easy access from either M40, junct 11 or M1, junct 16)
☎ 01327 861900 🖷 01327 861909
e-mail: canonashby@nationaltrust.org.uk

Home of the Dryden family since the 16th century, this is an exceptional small manor house, with Elizabethan wall paintings and Jacobean plasterwork. It has restored gardens, a small park and a church - part of the original 13th-century Augustinian priory.
Times: ✱ Open 23 Mar-2 Nov, Sat-Wed & BH Mon 1-5.30 (12-4.30 Oct & Nov) or dusk if earlier. Gardens, shop, tearoom open 5 Nov-18 Dec, wknds 12-4 Closed Good Fri. **Fee:** House & gardens £5.80 (ch £2.90). Family £14.50. Gardens only £2 (ch £1) Family £5 **Facilities:** 🅿 🅿 ⅰ (Braille/large print guide, taped guide, w/lchair available) toilets for disabled shop 🐾

DEENE   Map 04 SP99

DEENE PARK
NN17 3EW
➲ (0.5m off A43, between Kettering & Stamford)
☎ 01780 450278 & 450223 🖷 01780 450282
e-mail: admin@deenepark.com

A mainly 16th-century house of great architectural importance, and home of the Brudenell family since 1514 (including the 7th Earl of Cardigan who led the Charge of the Light Brigade). There's a large lake and park, and extensive gardens with old-fashioned roses, rare trees and shrubs. Phone for details of garden openings and any other special events.
Times: Open 2-5 BHs (Sun & Mon) Etr, May, Spring & Aug; Jun-Aug, Sun. Party 20+ by prior arrangement with House Keeper.
Fee: ✱ House & Gardens: £6 (ch 10-14 £2.50, concessions £5.50). Gardens only: £3.50 (ch £1.50). Children under 10 free admission with accompanying adult. **Facilities:** 🅿 🅿 ⅰ (ramps to cafeteria and gardens) toilets for disabled shop ✖ (ex guide dogs)

KIRBY HALL
NN17 5EN
➲ (on unclass road off A43, 4m NE of Corby)
☎ 01536 203230

An outstanding Elizabethan mansion with unusually strict symmetry and amazing Renaissance detail. The beautiful formal gardens gained a reputation in the 17th-century as being the finest in England.
Times: Open all year, Apr-Jun & Sep-Oct, Thu-Mon 10-5; Jul-Aug, daily 10-6; Nov-Mar, Thu-Mon 10-4. (Closed 24-26 Dec & 1 Jan). **Fee:** ✱ £4 (ch £2, concessions £3). Prices & opening times relate to 2004, for further details phone or log onto www.english-heritage.org.uk/visits
Facilities: 🅿 ♿ shop ⌗

KETTERING　　　　　Map 04 SP87
ALFRED EAST GALLERY
Sheep St NN16 OAN
➲ (A43/A6, located in town centre)
☎ 01536 534274　🖷 01536 534370
e-mail: museum@kettering.gov.uk

The Gallery has a permanent exhibition space showing work by Sir Alfred East, Thomas Cooper Gotch and other local artists, as well as selections from the Gallery's contemporary collection, including Sir Howard Hodgkin and John Bevan. Two further display spaces are dedicated to monthly changing sales exhibitions of art, craft and photography.
Times: ✱ Open all year, Mon-Sat 9.30-5 (closed BHs)
Facilities: 🅿 (300yds) ♿ shop ✖ (ex guide dogs)

LYVEDEN NEW BIELD　　　Map 04 SP98
LYVEDEN NEW BIELD
PE8 5AT
➲ (4m SW Oundle via A427)
☎ 01832 205358
e-mail: lyvedennewbield@nationaltrust.org.uk

An incomplete Elizabethan garden house and moated garden. Building began in 1595 by Sir Thomas Tresham, to symbolise his Catholic faith, and Lyveden remains virtually unaltered since work stopped when he died in 1605. The house has fascinating Elizabethan detail and in the grounds is one of the oldest garden layouts in Britain.
Times: ✱ House, Elizabethan Water Garden & Visitor Information Room open 31 Mar-31 Oct Wed-Sun 10.30-5, 5-27 Nov & 4 Feb-27 Mar Sat & Sun 10.30-4. **Fee:** £3.50 (ch free). **Facilities:** 🅿 (0.5 m along track) 🐾

NASSINGTON　　　　Map 04 TL09
PREBENDAL MANOR HOUSE
PE8 6QG
➲ (turn off A605 Warmington rdbt and follow brown heritage signs, the manor is opposite the church)
☎ 01780 782575
e-mail: info@prebendal-manor.co.uk

Dating from the early 13th-century, this is the oldest manor in Northamptonshire. There's a 15th-century dovecote and tithe barn museum, and the largest re-created medieval garden in Europe, boasting fishponds, herbers, arbours, turf seats, trellised herbers, medieval vegetable garden and vineyard. The gardens and the manor have been featured in BBC2's *Royal Gardeners* and Channel 4's *Time Team* respectively. Special events every month throughout the summer.
Times: Open Etr Mon-Sep, Wed & Sun & BH Mon 1-5.30.
Fee: ✱ House & garden £4.50 (ch £2). Garden only £4.
Facilities: 🅿 📺 ♿ (ramps, video of park) shop ✖ (ex guide dogs)

NORTHAMPTON　　　　Map 04 SP76
NORTHAMPTON MUSEUM & ART GALLERY
Guildhall Rd NN1 1DP
➲ (situated in the town centre, opposite the Demgate Theatre in Guildhall Road)
☎ 01604 838111　🖷 01604 838720　FREE
e-mail: museums@northampton.gov.uk

Reflecting Northampton's proud standing as Britain's boot and shoe capital, the museum houses a collection of boots and shoes in two new galleries. 'Life and Sole' focuses on the industrial, commercial and health aspects of footwear and includes interactives and an audio-visual display. 'Followers of Fashion' looks at shoe fashion and design. There are galleries and displays with changing programmes. Workshops for children during school holidays.
Times: Open all year, Mon-Sat 10-5, Sun 2-5. **Facilities:** 🅿 (200 yds) ♿ (wheelchairs available, large print catalogues) toilets for disabled shop ✖ (ex guide/assistance dogs) 🍴

ROCKINGHAM　　　　Map 04 SP89
ROCKINGHAM CASTLE
LE16 8TH
➲ (2m N of Corby, off A6003)
☎ 01536 770240　🖷 01536 771692　2 for 1
e-mail: a.norman@rockinghamcastle.com

Set on a hill overlooking five counties, the castle was built by William the Conqueror. The site of the original keep is now a rose garden, but the outline of the curtain wall remains as do the foundations of the Norman hall, and the twin towers of the gatehouse. A royal residence for 450 years, the castle was granted to Edward Watson in the 16th century, and the Watson family have lived there ever since.
Times: Open Apr-Sep, Sun & BHs. Jun-Aug, Sun, BHs Mon & Tue, Grounds noon, Castle 1 **Fee:** ✱ £7 (ch £4.50 & pen £6). Family ticket £18.50. **Facilities:** 🅿 📺 ♿ (Ramps, audio tour, parking adjacent to Castle) toilets for disabled shop 🍴

RUSHTON　　　　　Map 04 SP88
TRIANGULAR LODGE
NN14 1RP
☎ 01536 710761

A delightful Elizabethan folly designed to symbolise the Holy Trinity, with its three sides, three floors, trefoil windows and three triangular gables on each side.
Times: Open Apr-Sep, daily 10-6; Oct, daily 10-5. **Facilities:** 🅿 shop ⌗

STOKE BRUERNE　　　Map 04 SP74
CANAL MUSEUM
NN12 7SE
➲ (A508, 4m S of junct 15 of M1. 5m from Towcester A43/A5 junct)
☎ 01604 862229　🖷 01604 864199
e-mail: canal.museum@thewaterwaystrust.co.uk

Housed on three floors of an old cornmill, the colourful collection vividly portrays the many aspects of inland waterways from their origins to the present day, complementing the flight of locks and long canal tunnel outside.
Times: Open Etr-Oct daily, 10-5; Nov-Etr Tue-Sun, 10-4. Closed 25-26 Dec. Last admission 30 mins before closing time.
Facilities: 🅿 (charged) ♿ toilets for disabled shop ✖ (ex guide dogs) 🍴

SULGRAVE
Map 04 SP54

SULGRAVE MANOR
Manor Rd OX17 2SD
➲ (off B4525 Banbury to Northampton road. 6m from M40 junct 11, 15m From M1 junct 15a)
☎ 01295 760205 ▤ 01295 768056
e-mail: sulgrave-manor@talk21.com

`2 for 1`

Home to George Washington's ancestors until 1656 when his great grandfather, John, emigrated to Virginia. Inside the house there are many relics of George Washington. Though much of the house is a 20th-century restoration, original parts include the porch (with a carving of the original American flag), a screens passage, the great hall and the great Chamber.

Times: Open Apr-Oct 2-5.30. Closed Mon & Fri ex BH's. Other times by appointment **Fee:** £5.75 (ch £2.50). Party 20+. £5 (ch £2.50) Special event days £7.50 (ch £3.50). Family ticket £20.

Facilities: ▣ ⬛ ᕫ toilets for disabled shop ✖ (ex guide dogs) ▭

NORTHUMBERLAND

EVENTS & FESTIVALS

April
1st-3rd Morpeth Northumbrian Gathering, Morpeth Town Hall

May
1st Riding the Bounds, Berwick-upon-Tweed (traditional horseback ride)
30th Northumberland County Show, Tynedale Park, Corbridge

June
11th-12th Annual Steam & Vintage Rally, Tynedale Rugby Club, Corbridge
26th-3rd Jul Alnwick Medieval Fair
tbc Ovingham Goose Fair, Ovingham Village Green

July
2nd-3rd Amble Sea Fair, Amble
31st Alnwick Castle Tournament, Alnwick
tbc Rothbury Traditional Music Festival, Rothbury

August
6th Powburn Show & Sheepdog Trials
6th-12th Alnwick International Music Festival (provisional)
13th Slaley Show, Townhead Field, Slaley
tbc Military Tattoo, Barracks, Berwick-upon-Tweed

September
3rd Alnwick District Horticultural Show

November
5th Northumbrian Gathering

Above: Bamburgh Castle

ALNWICK   Map 12 NU11

ALNWICK CASTLE
NE66 1NQ
➲ (off A1 on outskirts of town, follow signs for
The Alnwick Garden & Castle)
☎ 01665 510777 🖷 01665 510876
e-mail: enquiries@alnwickcastle.com

Alnwick Castle is the main seat of the Duke of
Northumberland whose family have lived here since 1309.
The stern, medieval exterior belies the treasure house within,
furnished in Renaissance style, with paintings by Titian, Van
Dyck and Canaletto, and an exquisite collection of Meissen
china. The Regiment Museum of Royal Northumberland
Fusiliers is housed in the Abbot's Tower of the Castle.
Recently refurbished towers include museums of local
archaeology and the Percy Tenantry volunteers.
Times: ✶ Open 28 Mar-25 Oct, daily 11-5 (last admission 4.15).
Facilities: 🅿 💺 ♿ (Castle lift for those able to walk a little) toilets
for disabled shop ✖ (ex guide dogs) 🍽

BAMBURGH   Map 12 NU13

BAMBURGH CASTLE
NE69 7DF
➲ (A1 Belford by-pass, E on B1342 to Bamburgh)
☎ 01668 214515 & 214208 🖷 01668 214060
e-mail: bamburghcastle@aol.com

Rising dramatically from a rocky outcrop, Bamburgh Castle is
a huge, square Norman castle. Last restored in the 19th
century, it has an impressive hall and an armoury with a
large collection of armour from the Tower of London. Guide
services are available.
Times: ✶ Open 15 Mar-Oct, daily 11-5 (last admission 4.30pm). Other
times by prior arrangement. **Facilities:** 🅿 (charged) 💺 ♿ shop
✖ (ex guide dogs)

GRACE DARLING MUSEUM
Radcliffe Rd NE69 7AE
➲ (follow A1, turn off at Bamburgh & follow
signposts to Northumbria Coastal route, museum
on right)
☎ 01668 214465 🖷 01668 214465

Pictures, documents and other reminders of the heroine are
on display, including the boat in which Grace Darling and
her father, keeper of Longstone Lighthouse, Farne Islands,
rescued nine survivors from the wrecked SS *Forfarshire* in
1838.
Times: ✶ Open Etr-Oct, daily 10-5 (Sun 12-5). **Facilities:** 🅿 (400yds)
♿ (ramps) shop ✖ (ex guide dogs)

BARDON MILL   Map 12 NY76

VINDOLANDA (CHESTERHOLM)
Vindolanda Trust NE47 7JN
➲ (signposted from A69 or B6318)
☎ 01434 344277 🖷 01434 344060
e-mail: info@vindolanda.com

Vindolanda was a Roman fort and frontier town. It was
started well before Hadrian's Wall, and became a base for
500 soldiers. The civilian settlement lay just west of the fort
and has been excavated. The excellent museum in the
country house of Chesterholm nearby has displays and
reconstructions. There are also formal gardens and an open-
continued

air museum with Roman Temple, shop, house and
Northumbrian croft.
Times: Open Feb-Mar, daily 10-5. Apr-Sep 10-6, Oct & Nov 10-5.
Fee: ✶ £4.50 (ch £2.90, student & pen £3.80, free admission for
disabled). Saver ticket for joint admission to sister site - The Roman
Army Museum £6.50 (ch £4.30, pen £5.50) Party. **Facilities:** 🅿 💺
♿ (please contact for further info) toilets for disabled shop
✖ (ex guide dogs) 🍽

BELSAY   Map 12 NZ07

BELSAY HALL, CASTLE AND GARDENS
NE20 0DX
➲ (on A696)
☎ 01661 881636 🖷 01661 881043

Beautiful neo-classical hall, built from its own quarries with
a spectacular garden deservedly listed Grade 1 in the
Register of Gardens. It is slightly unclear who built the
'Grecian-style hall', however it was designed by Sir Charles
in 1807, in Greek Revival style. The magnificent 30 acres of
grounds contain the ruins of a 14th-century castle.
Times: Open all year, Apr-Sep, daily 10-6; Oct, daily 10-4; Nov-Mar,
Thurs-Mon 10-4. (Closed 24-26 Dec & 1 Jan). **Fee:** ✶ £5 (ch £2.50,
concessions £3.80). Prices & opening times relate to 2004, for further
details phone or log onto www.english-heritage.org.uk/visits
Facilities: 🅿 💺 ♿ toilets for disabled shop ♻

BERWICK-UPON-TWEED   Map 12 NT95

BERWICK-UPON-TWEED BARRACKS
TD15 1DF
➲ (on the Parade, off Church St, Berwick town
centre)
☎ 01289 304493

Take an informative journey into our military past at the
famous border town's barracks.
Times: Open all year, Apr-Sep, daily 10-6 (Oct daily 10-4); Nov-Mar,
Thurs-Mon 10-4. (Closed between 24-26 Dec & 1 Jan and during Tattoo
events). **Fee:** ✶ £3 (ch £1.50, concessions £2.30). Prices & opening
times relate to 2004, for further details phone or log onto
www.english-heritage.org.uk/visits **Facilities:** 🅿 (town centre) shop ♻

PAXTON HOUSE
TD15 1SZ
➲ (3m from A1 Berwick-upon-Tweed bypass on
B6461 Kelso road)
☎ 01289 386291 🖷 01289 386660
e-mail: info@paxtonhouse.com

Built in 1758 for the Laird of Wedderburn, the house is a fine
example of neo-Palladian architecture. Much of the house is
furnished by Chippendale and there is a large picture gallery.
The house is set in 80 acres beside the River Tweed, and the
grounds include an adventure playground.
Times: ✶ Open daily from Apr-Oct, House & gallery 11-5 (last tour of
house 4.15pm). Grounds 10-sunset. **Facilities:** 🅿 💺 ✖ licensed
♿ (lifts to main areas of house, parking close to reception) toilets for
disabled shop 🍽

CAMBO — Map 12 NZ08

WALLINGTON HOUSE WALLED GARDEN & GROUNDS

NE61 4AR

➲ (6m NW of Belsay)

☎ 01670 773600   📠 01670 774420

e-mail: nwaplr@smtp.ntrust.org.uk

The house is set in a great moorland estate of over 12,000 acres. It features delicate plasterwork, Capability Brown gardens and William Bell Scott murals. In the 19th century Ruskin and other writers and artists came here as guests. Special events include open air concerts and theatre productions.

Times: Open: House Apr-Sep, daily (ex Tue) 1-5.30, Oct daily (ex Tue) 1-4.30. Last admission half hour before closing. Walled garden Apr-Oct, daily 10-7 or dusk; Nov-Mar, 10-4 or dusk if earlier. Grounds open all year. **Facilities:** 🅿 💻 ✗ ♿ (Vessa Ventura scooter, Braille guide) toilets for disabled shop garden centre ⚌ 🖛

CARRAWBROUGH — Map 12 NY87

TEMPLE OF MITHRAS (HADRIAN'S WALL)

➲ (3.75m W of Chollerford on B6318)

This fascinating Mithraic temple was uncovered by a farmer in 1949. Its three altars to the war god, Mithras date from the third century AD, and are now in the Museum of Antiquities in Newcastle, but there are copies on site.

Times: Open any reasonable time. **Facilities:** 🅿 ▦

CHILLINGHAM — Map 12 NU02

CHILLINGHAM CASTLE

NE66 5NJ

➲ (signposted from A1 & A697)

☎ 01668 215359   📠 01668 215463   `2 for 1`

e-mail: enquiries@chillingham.castle.com

This remarkable castle with its alarming dungeons and torture chamber is now undergoing restoration. Romantic grounds laid out by Sir Jeffry Wyatville command views over the Cheviots and include topiary gardens and woodland walks. Weddings, private functions and meals can be arranged, and fishing is available. Please ring for details of special events.

Times: Open Etr wknd & May-Sep, Sun-Fri (Last admission 4.30pm). Other times ring by prior arrangement. Castle 1-5, grounds & tearoom 12-5. **Fee:** ✱ £6(ch £3, pen £5.50). Party 10+ £5.30 **Facilities:** 🅿 💻 ♿ shop ✈ ex guide dogs 🖛

CHILLINGHAM WILD CATTLE PARK

NE66 5NP

➲ (off B6348, follow brown tourist signs off A1 and A697)

☎ 01668 215250   📠 01668 215250   `2 for 1`

The park, a registered charity, at Chillingham boasts an extraordinary survival: a herd of wild white cattle descended from animals trapped in the park when the wall was built in the 13th century; they are the sole surviving pure-bred examples of their breed in the world. Binoculars are recommended for a close view. Visitors are accompanied into the park by the Warden.

Times: Open Apr-Oct, daily 10-12 & 2-5, Sun 2-5. (Closed Tue). **Fee:** £4 (ch £1.50 & pen £3). **Facilities:** 🅿 ✈

CORBRIDGE — Map 12 NY96

CORBRIDGE ROMAN SITE AND MUSEUM

NE45 5NT

➲ (0.5m NW of Corbridge on minor road - signposted)

☎ 01434 632349

Originally a fort, which evolved into a prosperous town during the Roman era. An excellent starting point to explore Hadrian's Wall. The museum houses a fascinating collection of finds.

Times: Open all year, Apr-Sep, daily 10-6; Oct, daily 10-4; Nov-Mar, Sat-Sun 10-4. (Closed 24-26 Dec & 1 Jan). **Fee:** ✱ £3.50 (ch £1.80, concessions £2.60). Prices & opening times relate to 2004, for further details phone or log onto www.english-heritage.org.uk/visits **Facilities:** 🅿 ♿ toilets for disabled ▦

EMBLETON — Map 12 NU22

DUNSTANBURGH CASTLE

Craster NE66 2RD

➲ (1.5m E on footpaths from Craster or Embleton)

☎ 01665 576231

An easy 12 mile coastal walk leads to the eerie skeleton of this wonderful 14th century castle situated on a basalt crag more than 30 metres high with breathtaking views. The castle was built by Thomas Earl of Lancaster, nephew to King Edward II.

Times: Open all year, Apr-Sep, daily 10-6; Oct, daily 10-4; Nov-Mar, Thur-Mon 10-4. **Fee:** ✱ £2.50 (ch £1.30, concessions £1.90). Free to NT members. Prices & opening times relate to 2004, for further details phone or log onto www.english-heritage.org.uk/visits **Facilities:** 🅿 (charged) ▦

GREENHEAD — Map 12 NY66

ROMAN ARMY MUSEUM NEW

Carvoran CA8 7JB

➲ (follow brown tourist signs from A69 or B6318)

☎ 016977 47485

e-mail: info@vindolanda.com

Situated alongside the Walltown Grags Section of Hadrian's Wall, the museum is a great introduction to the Roman Army. Find out about Roman weapons, training, pay, off-duty activities and much more. See if you can be persuaded to join up by watching the recruitment film, or view the Eagle's Eye film and soar with the eagle over Hadrian's Wall.

Times: Feb-Mar, Oct-Nov (10am-5pm), Apr-Sept (10am-6pm) **Fee:** ✱ £3.50(ch £2.20, concessions £3, family £10) **Facilities:** 🅿 💻 ♿ toilets for disabled shop ✈ (ex guide dogs) 🖛

HOLY ISLAND (LINDISFARNE) — Map 12 NU14

LINDISFARNE CASTLE

TD15 2SH

➲ (8m S Berwick from A1 on Holy Island)

☎ 01289 389244   📠 01289 389349

The 16th-century castle was restored by Sir Edwin Lutyens in 1903 for the owner of *Country Life* magazine. The austere outside walls belie the Edwardian comfort within, and there is a little garden designed by Gertrude Jekyll.

Times: ✱ Open Apr-Oct, daily (closed Fri ex Good Fri) as Lindisfarne is a tidal island, the Castle will open 4.5 hrs which will always include 12-3 and then either earlier opening or later closing as the tide allows. **Facilities:** 🅿 (1m in village) ✈ ⚌

LINDISFARNE PRIORY

TD15 2RX

➲ (Can only be reached at low tide across a causeway. Tide tables posted at each end of the causeway)

☎ 01289 389200

One of the holiest Anglo-Saxon sites in England, renowned for the original burial place of St Cuthbert whose corpse was discovered 11 years after his burial and found to be mysteriously undecayed. An award-winning museum.
Times: Open all year, Apr-Sep, daily 10-6; Oct, daily 10-4; Nov-Jan, Sat & Sun 10-4; Feb-Mar, daily, 10-4 (Closed 24-26 Dec & 1 Jan).
Fee: ✱ £3.50 (ch £1.80, concessions £2.60). Prices & opening times relate to 2004, for further details phone or log onto www.english-heritage.org.uk/visits **Facilities:** shop ✿

HOUSESTEADS   Map 12 NY76

HOUSESTEADS ROMAN FORT

Haydon Bridge NE47 6NN

➲ (2.5m NE of Bardon Mill on B6318)

☎ 01434 344363

The jewel in the crown of Hadrian's Wall and the most complete Roman fort in Britain. These superb remains offer a fascinating glimpse into the past glories of one of the world's greatest empires.
Times: Open all year, Apr-Sep, daily 10-6; Oct-Mar, daily 10-4. (Closed 24-26 Dec & 1 Jan). **Fee:** ✱ £3.50 (ch £1.80, concessions £2.60, family £8.80). Prices & opening times relate to 2004, for further details phone or log onto www.english-heritage.org.uk/visits **Facilities:** P (0.25m from fort) (charge payable) (disabled parking) shop ✿

LONGFRAMLINGTON   Map 12 NU10

BRINKBURN PRIORY

NE65 8AF

➲ (off B6344)

☎ 01665 570628

This late 12th-century church is a fine example of early gothic architecture set in beautiful riverside surroundings. Look out for some unusual modern sculptures.
Times: Open Apr-Sep, daily, 10-6. **Fee:** ✱ £2 (ch £1, concessions £1.50). Prices & opening times relate to 2004, for further details phone or log onto www.english-heritage.org.uk/visits **Facilities:** P shop ✿

MORPETH   Map 12 NZ28

MORPETH CHANTRY BAGPIPE MUSEUM

Bridge St NE61 1PJ

➲ (off A1)

☎ 01670 500717   FREE

e-mail: amoore@castlemorpeth.gov.uk

This unusual museum specialises in the history and development of Northumbrian small pipes and their music. They are set in the context of bagpipes from around the world, from India to Inverness.
Times: Open all year, Mon-Sat, 10-5, open Sun in Aug & Dec. (Closed 25-26 Dec, 1 Jan & Etr Mon). **Facilities:** P (100 metres) & (induction loop, not suitable for wheelchairs) shop ◀

NORHAM   Map 12 NT94

NORHAM CASTLE

TD15 2JY

☎ 01289 382329

A mighty border fortress built in 1160, was one of the strongest of the border castles. Take an audio tour conjuring up four centuries of sieges and war with the Scots.
Times: Open Apr-Sep, Sat, Sun & Bank Hols, 10-6. **Fee:** ✱ £2.50 (ch £1.30, concessions £1.90). Prices & opening times relate to 2004, for further details phone or log onto www.english-heritage.org.uk/visits.
Facilities: P & ✈ ✿

PRUDHOE   Map 12 NZ06

PRUDHOE CASTLE

NE42 6NA

➲ (on minor road off A695)

☎ 01661 833459

Explore the romantic remains of this 13th-century fortress perched on a steep wooded spur rising above the Tyne and set in lovely grounds.
Times: Open Apr-Sep, daily 10-6. **Fee:** ✱ £3 (ch £1.50, concessions £2.30). Prices & opening times relate to 2004, for further details phone or log onto www.english-heritage.org.uk/visits **Facilities:** P shop ✿

ROTHBURY   Map 12 NU00

CRAGSIDE

NE65 7PX

➲ (1m NW of Morpeth on A697, turn left onto B6341, entrance 1m N of Rothbury).

☎ 01669 620333 & 620150   📠 01669 620066

e-mail: ncrvmx@smtp.ntrust.org.uk

This Victorian mansion was the first building in the world to be lit by hydro-electricity. In the 1880s the house had hot and cold running water, central heating, telephones and a passenger lift. There is a vast forest garden to explore containing one of Europe's largest rock gardens, formal gardens, lakes and an adventure play area.
Times: ✱ Open, Estate & Gardens: 23 Mar-4 Nov, Tue-Sun & BH Mons 10.30-7 last admission 5;. House: 23 Mar-Sep 1-5.30. Oct-3 Nov 1-4. Last admission 1hr before closing. **Facilities:** P ✗ licensed & (ltd access, Braille guide, wheelchair path, lift) toilets for disabled shop ✕

WALWICK   Map 12 NY97

CHESTERS ROMAN FORT & MUSEUM

Chollerford NE46 4EP

➲ (0.5m W of Chollerford on B6318)

☎ 01434 681379

The best-preserved Roman cavalry fort in Britain. The museum holds displays of carved stones, altars and sculptures from all along Hadrian's Wall.
Times: Open all year, Apr-Sep, daily 9.30-6; Oct-Mar, daily 10-4. (Closed 24-26 Dec & 1 Jan) **Fee:** ✱ £3.50 (ch £1.80, concessions £2.60) Prices & opening times relate to 2004, for further details phone or log onto www.english-heritage.org.uk/visits **Facilities:** P 🅿 & (wheelchair access limited) shop ✿

WARKWORTH — Map 12 NU20

WARKWORTH CASTLE & HERMITAGE

NE66 OUJ

☎ 01665 711423

The magnificent eight-towered keep of Warkworth Castle stands on a hill high above the River Coquet, dominating all around it. A complex stronghold, it was home to the Percy family, which at times wielded more power in the North than the King himself.

Times: Open all year. Castle; Apr-Sep, daily 10-6; Oct, daily 10-4; Nov-Mar, Sat-Mon 10-4. Hermitage; Apr-Sep, Wed, Sun & Bank Hols (24-26 Dec & 1 Jan). **Fee:** ✱ Castle; £3 (ch £1.50, concessions £2.30). Hermitage; £2 (ch £1, concessions £1.50). Prices & opening times relate to 2004, for further details phone or log onto www.english-heritage.org.uk/visits **Facilities:** 🅿 ♿ (limited access) shop ✖ (ex on lead in certain areas) ⌗

Above: The Cheviots

This symbol **2-for-1** indicates attractions which have chosen to participate in our 2-for-1 voucher scheme

We endeavour to be as accurate as possible, but changes to times and other information can occur after the guide has gone to press.

NOTTINGHAMSHIRE

EVENTS & FESTIVALS

March
17th St Patrick's Day Parade, Nottingham

May
14th-15th Newark & Nottingham County Show, Newark & Nottingham Showground, Winthorpe

June
tbc Newark on Water Festival

July
3rd Mansfield Fun Run
7th-10th Americana International Festival, Newark Showground, Winthorpe, Newark
tbc Newark Festival, Riverside Park, Newark
tbc Nottingham Mela, Asian festival with music, dance and children's activities

August
1st-7th Annual Robin Hood Festival, Sherwood Forest Country Park & Visitor Centre, Edwinstowe
6th-7th Riverside Festival, Victoria Embankment, Nottingham (world and roots music, street theatre, children's entertainers)
13th-14th Caribbean Carnival, Forest Recreation Ground, Nottingham (and parade through city)

September
25th Robin Hood Marathon, Nottingham (from Victoria Embankment)

October
5th-8th Goose Fair, Forest Recreation Ground, Nottingham (Europe's largest travelling fair)

November
22nd-23rd Robin Hood Pageant, Nottingham Castle

Above: Wollaton Hall

EASTWOOD
Map 08 SK44

D H LAWRENCE HERITAGE
Durban House Heritage Centre, Mansfield Rd NG16 3DZ
➲ (M1 J26, then take A610, follow brown tourist signs from this road. From M1 J27 take A608 through Brinsley towards Eastwood)
☎ 01773 717353 📠 01773 713509
e-mail: durban@broxbcl.demon.co.uk

2 for 1

D H Lawrence Heritage brings to life the world of the famous novelist, poet and artist David Herbert Lawrence, best known as the writer of *Lady Chatterly's Lover*, *Women in Love* and *The Rainbow*. Discover how his home town of Eastwood, near Nottingham, shaped his creative and often controversial works. The site includes the museum and heritage centre, an art gallery, two gift shops, and a teashop. The 2-for-1 voucher is only valid for weekends and Bank Holidays.
Times: Open all year, Apr-Oct, daily 10-5; Nov-Mar, daily 10-4. Closed 24 Dec-2 Jan. **Fee:** Free Mon-Fri. Single site £2 (concessions £1.20). Both sites £3.50 (concessions £1.80). Family Ticket (2ad & 2ch) Joint Site £8; Single Site £5.80 **Facilities:** 🅿 💺 ✕ licensed ♿ (lift to exhibition, wheelchair available) toilets for disabled shop ✖ (ex guide dogs) 🍴

EDWINSTOWE
Map 08 SK66

SHERWOOD FOREST COUNTRY PARK & VISITOR CENTRE
NG21 9HN
➲ (on B6034 N of Edwinstowe between A6075 and A616)
☎ 01623 823202 & 824490
📠 01623 823202
e-mail: sherwood.forest@nottscc.gov.uk

FREE

At the heart of the Robin Hood legend is Sherwood Forest. Today it is a country park and visitor centre with 450 acres of ancient oaks and shimmering silver birches. Waymarked pathways guide you through the forest. A year round programme of events includes the spectacular Robin Hood Festival.
Times: Country Park: open daily dawn to dusk. Visitor Centre: open daily 10-5 (4.30pm Nov-Mar) **Facilities:** 🅿 (charged) ✕ ♿ wheelchair loan toilets for disabled shop 🍴
See advertisement on this page

FARNSFIELD
Map 08 SK65

WHITE POST FARM CENTRE
NG22 8HL
➲ (12m N of Nottingham on A614)
☎ 01623 882977 & 882026 📠 01623 883499
e-mail: tim@whitepostfarmcentre.co.uk

This award-winning working farm gives an introduction to a variety of modern farming methods. It explains how farms work, with exhibits such as llamas, deer, pigs, cows, snails, quails, snakes and fish. There's a lot to see indoors, including the incubator room, mousetown and a reptile house. There is also a large indoor play area including a sledge run, trampoline and a large bouncy slide.
Times: Open daily from 10am **Fee:** ✱ £6.75 (ch 3-16 £6, under 3's free) **Facilities:** 🅿 💺 ♿ (free hire wheelchairs, book if more than 6) toilets for disabled shop ✖ (ex guide dogs) 🍴

NEWARK-ON-TRENT   Map 08 SK75

MILLGATE MUSEUM
48 Millgate NG24 4TS
➲ (easy access from A1 & A46)
☎ 01636 655730 📠 01636 655735
e-mail: museums@nsdc.info
    FREE

Fascinating exhibitions - recreated streets, shops and houses in period settings. The museum displays illustrate the working and domestic life of local people, from Victorian times to 1950. The mezzanine gallery, home to a number of temporary exhibitions showing the work of local artists, designers and photographers.
Times: Open all year, Mon-Fri 10-5, Sat & Sun & BH 1-5. Last admission 4.30. **Facilities:** P (250yds) ⬤ & toilets for disabled shop ✈ (ex aid dogs)

NEWARK AIR MUSEUM
The Airfield, Winthorpe NG24 2NY
➲ (easy access from A1, A46, A17 & Newark relief road, follow tourism signs)
☎ 01636 707170 📠 01636 707170
    2 for 1
e-mail: newarkair@onetel.com

A diverse collection of transport, training and reconnaissance aircraft, jet fighters, bombers and helicopters, now numbering more than sixty. An Undercover Aircraft Display Hall and an Engine Hall make the museum an all-weather attraction. Everything is displayed around a WWII airfield.
Times: Open all year, Mar-Sep daily 10-5; Oct-Feb, daily 10-4. (Closed 24-26 Dec & 1 Jan). Other times by appointment. **Fee:** £4.75 (ch £3, pen £4). Family ticket £13.50. Party 10+. **Facilities:** P ⬤ & toilets for disabled shop 🎁

VINA COOKE MUSEUM OF DOLLS & BYGONE CHILDHOOD
The Old Rectory, Cromwell NG23 6JE
➲ (5m N of Newark off A1)
☎ 01636 821364

All kinds of childhood memorabilia are displayed in this 17th-century house: prams, toys, dolls' houses, costumes and a large collection of Victorian and Edwardian dolls including Vina Cooke hand-made character dolls.
Times: ✱ Open Apr-Sep, Sat-Thu 10.30-12 & 2-5. Oct-Mar, opening times vary. **Facilities:** P & shop

NEWSTEAD   Map 09 SK55

NEWSTEAD ABBEY
Newstead Abbey Park NG15 8NA
➲ (off A60, between Nottingham & Mansfield, at Ravenshead)
☎ 01623 455900 📠 01623 455904

This beautiful house is best known as the home of poet Lord Byron. Visitors can see Byron's own rooms, mementoes of the poet and other splendidly decorated rooms. The grounds of over 300 acres include waterfalls, ponds, water gardens and Japanese gardens. Special events include outdoor theatre and opera, Christmas events and Ghost Tours.
Times: Open: Grounds all year, daily 9-dusk (ex last Fri in Nov & 25 Dec); House Apr-Sep, daily 12-5. Last admission 4pm. **Fee:** ✱ House & Grounds £5 (ch £1.50, concessions £2.50) Family ticket £12. Grounds only £2.50 (ch & concessions £1.50) Family ticket £7. Subject to change.
Facilities: P ⬤ & (audio tour & wheelchair for loan Apr-Sep) toilets for disabled shop (open Apr-Sep) ✈ (ex guide dogs) 🎁

NOTTINGHAM   Map 08 SK53

THE CAVES OF NOTTINGHAM
Upper Level, Broadmarsh Shopping Centre NG1 7LS
➲ (within Broadmarsh Shopping Centre, on the first floor)
☎ 0115 924 1424 📠 0115 924 1430
e-mail: info@cavesofnottingham.co.uk

A unique 750-year-old cave system situated beneath a modern day shopping centre. A digital audio tour guides you through the only remaining underground medieval tannery in England, beer cellars, an air raid shelter and the remains of Drury Hill, one of the oldest streets in Nottingham.
Times: ✱ Open daily 10-5, Sun 11-5 (last admission 4.15pm, Sun 4pm). (Closed 24-26 Dec, 1 Jan & Etr Sun). **Facilities:** P (charged) & (non-accessible to wheelchairs, induction loop, textual guide) shop ✈ (ex guide dogs) 🎁

GALLERIES OF JUSTICE
The Shire Hall, High Pavement, Lace Market NG1 1HN
➲ (follow signs to City Centre, brown heritage signs to Lace Market & Galleries of Justice)
☎ 0115 952 0555 📠 0115 993 9828
e-mail: info@galleriesofjustice.org.uk

The Galleries of Justice are located on the site of an original Court and County Gaol. Visitors can take an authentic tour through three centuries of Crime and Punishment and witness a trial re-created in the authentic Victorian courtroom before being 'sent down' to the original cells and medieval caves. In the genuine Edwardian police station, an interactive forensic science display allows visitors to 'crack the case'. A series of innovative and stimulating temporary exhibitions run throughout the year. Special activities for all the family run in school holidays.
Times: ✱ Open all year, Tue-Sun & BH Mons 10-5 (also open Mon in school hols). Last admission one hour before closing. Contact for Xmas opening times. **Facilities:** P (5 mins walk) ⬤ & (Braille control lifts, induction loop, large print lables) toilets for disabled shop ✈ (ex guide dogs) 🎁

GREEN'S WINDMILL **NEW**
Windmill Ln, Sneinton NG2 4QB
➲ (Off B686, 500yds from Ice Centre.)
☎ 0115 915 6878 📠 0115 915 6875
e-mail: info@greensmill.org.uk
    FREE

Restored to working order, take a look around the mill and see how grain is turned into flour by harnessing the power of the wind. Find out about the "mathematician miller" George Green and his theories, and test your mind with hands on puzzles and experiments. There's also a guinea pig piggery.
Times: Open all year Wed-Sun, 10-4, also BHs. (Phone for Xmas & New Year closing). **Facilities:** P & toilets for disabled shop ✈ 🎁

THE LACE CENTRE
Severns Building, Castle Rd NG1 6AA
➲ (follow signs for the Castle, situated opposite the Robin Hood statue)
    FREE
☎ 0115 941 3539 📠 0115 941 3539

Exquisite Nottingham lace fills this small 14th-century building to capacity, with panels also hanging from the beamed ceiling. There are weekly demonstrations of lace-making on Thursday afternoons from Easter to October. Telephone for details.
Times: Open Jan-Mar, daily 10-4; Apr-Nov, 10-5. Every Sun 11am-4pm. (Closed Xmas & New Year) **Facilities:** P (100yds) (metered street parking) shop 🎁

THE LACE MARKET CENTRE
3-5 High Pavement, The Lace Market NG1 1HF
➲ (Follow signs for Lace Market. Parking in the city centre)
☎ 0115 988 1849 ▤ 0115 950 5166
e-mail: info@nottinghamlace.org

'Nottingham Lace and its People' is a free exhibition that includes a photographic story, hand-lace and machine-lace demonstrations. The Lace Market Trail, which takes about an hour, guides you to all the points of interest around this historical part of the city.

Times: Open Mon-Sat, 10-5: Sun 10.30-4 (Closed Xmas).
Facilities: P (100yds) ♿ (counters at lower level, lift, audio & written tour) shop ✻ (ex guide dogs) ▰

THE MUSEUM OF NOTTINGHAM LIFE
Brewhouse Yard, Castle Boulevard NG7 1FB
➲ (follow signs to Nottingham City Centre)
☎ 0115 915 3600 & 0115 915 3640
▤ 0115 915 3601

Nestled in the rock below Nottingham Castle and housed in a row of 17th-century cottages, the museum presents a realistic glimpse of life in Nottingham over the last 300 years. Discover the caves behind the museum and peer through 1920s shop windows.

Times: Open daily, 10-4.30. Last admission 4pm **Fee:** ✱ Free Mon-Fri but donations appreciated. Wknds & BHs £1.50 (con 80p). Family ticket £3.80. **Facilities:** P (100yds) ♿ (call 0115 915 3700 for info on access) toilets for disabled shop ✻ (ex guide dogs)

NOTTINGHAM CASTLE
NG1 6EL
☎ 0115 915 3700 ▤ 0115 915 3653

This 17th-century building is both museum and art gallery, with major temporary exhibitions, by historical and contemporary artists, as well as the permanent collections. There is a 'Story of Nottingham' exhibition and a gallery designed especially to entertain young children. Guided tours of the underground passages take place on most days.

Times: ✱ Open all year, daily 10-5. Grounds 8-dusk. (Closed 25 & 26 Dec). **Facilities:** P (400yds) ▰ ♿ (parking at castle, for more info call 0115 915 3700) toilets for disabled shop ✻ (ex guide dogs)

NOTTINGHAM INDUSTRIAL MUSEUM
Courtyard Buildings, Wollaton Park NG8 2AE
➲ (4m from Nottingham City Centre off A6514)
☎ 0115 915 3900 ▤ 0115 915 3941
e-mail: carol@ncmg.demon.co.uk

Nottingham's industrial history is on display in this 18th-century stable block. Lace, hosiery, pharmaceuticals (Nottingham was the home of the founder of Boots the Chemists), tobacco and much else are among the exhibits. There is a beam engine and other steam engines, regularly in steam.

Times: Open Daily 11-5 **Fee:** ✱ Mon-Fri free. Sat, Sun & BHs £1.50 (ch, concession 80p) Family £3.80 **Facilities:** P (charged) ▰ ♿ (hand & powered wheelchairs available) toilets for disabled shop ✻ (ex guide dogs)

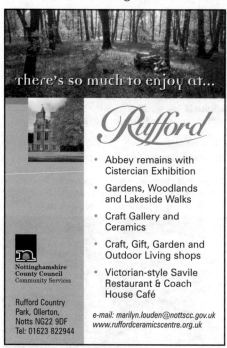

there's so much to enjoy at...

Rufford

- Abbey remains with Cistercian Exhibition
- Gardens, Woodlands and Lakeside Walks
- Craft Gallery and Ceramics
- Craft, Gift, Garden and Outdoor Living shops
- Victorian-style Savile Restaurant & Coach House Café

Nottinghamshire
County Council
Community Services

Rufford Country
Park, Ollerton,
Notts NG22 9DF
Tel: 01623 822944

e-mail: marilyn.louden@nottscc.gov.uk
www.ruffordceramicscentre.org.uk

TALES OF ROBIN HOOD
30-38 Maid Marian Way NG1 6GF
➲ (in Nottingham city centre, follow brown & white signs. Situated minutes from Nottingham Castle)
☎ 0115 948 3284 ▤ 0115 950 1536
e-mail: robinhoodcentre@mail.com

Special effects and adventure cars transport the visitor back to medieval Nottingham and Sherwood Forest, legendary home of Robin Hood. There is commentary in seven languages via portable CD players. Medieval banquets and other events take place throughout the year.

Times: Open all year, daily 10-5.30. Last admission 4pm. (Closed 25-26 Dec). **Fee:** £6.95 (ch £4.95, pen & students £5.95) Family ticket from £21.50. **Facilities:** P (NCP 200 yds) ▰ ♿ (specially adapted 'car', lift) toilets for disabled shop ✻ (ex guide dogs) ▰

WOLLATON HALL & PARK
Wollaton NG8 2AE
➲ (M1 junct 25 signed from A52, A609, A6154, A60 and city centre)
☎ 0115 915 3900 ▤ 0115 915 3932
e-mail: info@wollatonhall.org.uk

Built in the late 16th century, and extended in the 19th, Wollaton Hall and Park holds Nottingham's Natural History Museum, Nottingham's Industrial Museum, the Wollaton Park Visitor Centre, and the Yard Gallery, which has changing exhibitions exploring art and the environment. The Hall itself is set in 500 acres of deer park, with herds of red and fallow deer roaming wild. There are also formal gardens, a lake, nature trails, adventure playgrounds, a sensory garden and a water garden. The many events

continued

throughout the year include pop concerts, opera, and twilight bat walks.

Times: Open Hall, visitor centre, shop, yard gallery daily, Oct-Mar 11-4, Apr-Sep 11-5. Industrial Museum open Apr-Sept, daily 11-5. Park & grounds weekdays 8am-dusk, weekends 9am-dusk. **Fee:** ✱ Free weekdays. Ticket for either Hall or Museum £1.50 (ch & concessions 80p), family ticket £3.80. Ticket for Hall & Museum £2 (concessions £1) family ticket £5. Charge made at wknds & BH's only.

Facilities: 🅿 (charged) ⬛ & (call 0115 915 3700 for info on access) toilets for disabled shop ✕ (ex guide dogs) ◢

OLLERTON Map 08 SK66

RUFFORD ABBEY AND COUNTRY PARK
NG22 9DF
➲ (2m S of Ollerton, adjacent to A614)
☎ 01623 822944 📠 01623 824840
e-mail: marilyn.louden@nottscc.gov.uk

At the heart of the wooded country park stand the remains of a 12th-century Cistercian Abbey, housing an exhibition on the life of a Cistercian Monk at Rufford. Many species of wildlife can be seen on the lake, and there are lovely formal gardens, with sculptures and Britain's first centre for studio ceramics.

Times: Open all year 10.30-5.30 (craft centre closes 4pm Jan & Feb). For further details of opening times telephone establishment.

Facilities: 🅿 (charged) ⬛ ✕ licensed & (lift to craft centre gallery, free parking,wheelchair loan) toilets for disabled shop garden centre ✕ (ex guide dogs) ◢

See advertisement on page 189

SOUTHWELL Map 08 SK65

THE WORKHOUSE
Upton Rd NG25 0PT
☎ 01636 817250 📠 01636 817251
e-mail: theworkhouse@nationaltrust.org.uk

Enter this 19th-century brick institution and discover the thought-provoking story of the 'welfare' system of the New Poor Law. The least altered workhouse in existence today, it survives from hundreds that once covered the country. Explore the segregated stairs and rooms, use the audio guide, based on archive records, to bring the 19th-century inhabitants to life in the empty rooms, then try the interactive displays exploring poverty through the years and across the country.

Times: Open 28 Mar-Oct, Thu-Mon noon-5 (Aug 11-5). Last admission 1hr before closing. Wk beginning 26 May, daily & wk beginning 27 Oct, daily (ex Wed) **Fee:** £4.60 (ch £2.30) Family £11.50.

Facilities: 🅿 & toilets for disabled ✕ (ex guide dogs) ✤

SUTTON-CUM-LOUND Map 08 SK68

WETLANDS WATERFOWL RESERVE & EXOTIC BIRD PARK
Off Loundlow Rd DN22 8SB
➲ (Signposted on A638)
☎ 01777 818099

The Reserve is a 32-acre site for both wild and exotic waterfowl. Visitors can see a collection of birds of prey, parrots, geese, ducks, and wigeon among others. There are also many small mammals and farm and wild animals, including llamas, wallabies, emus, monkeys, red squirrels, deer and goats.

Times: ✱ Open all year, daily 10-5.30 (or dusk - whichever is earlier). (Closed 25 Dec). **Facilities:** 🅿 ⬛ & (wheelchair available) shop ✕ (ex guide dogs)

WORKSOP Map 08 SK57

CLUMBER PARK
The Estate Office, Clumber Park S80 3AZ
➲ (4.5m SE of Worksop, signposted from A1).
☎ 01909 476592 📠 01909 500721
e-mail: clumberpark@nationaltrust.org.uk

An impressive, landscaped park, laid out by 'Capability' Brown. An outstanding feature is the lake running through the park, a haven for wildfowl, covering an area of 80 acres. The park is a mixture of woodland, open grass and heathland.

Times: Park open all year during daylight hours. **Fee:** Pedestrians free. Vehicle entry charge per car £4, car trailer/caravan, minibus £5.20.

Facilities: 🅿 (charged) ⬛ ✕ licensed & (powered self-drive vehicle available if booked) toilets for disabled shop garden centre ✤

The End of World War II.

2005 sees the 60th anniversary of both VE (Victory in Europe) and VJ (Victory over Japan) Days. Local celebrations are planned, as are a number of national events.

OXFORDSHIRE

EVENTS & FESTIVALS

March
tbc Poohsticks World Championships,
Little Wittenham

May
1st 6am Choir singing from Magdalen Tower,
Magdalen College, Oxford
30th Lord Mayor's Parade, Oxford
tbc Oxford Annual Balloon Fiesta,
Cutterslowe Park

June
22nd Encaenia, Oxford University graduation
event with gowned procession
through the city
30th-4th Jul Henley Royal Regatta,
Henley-on-Thames

July
6th-10th Henley Festival, various venues
18th-22nd Swan Upping, River Thames,
Sunbury-Abingdon (provisional)

September
5th-6th St Giles Fair, Oxford
10th Henley Show
15th Thame & Oxfordshire County Show
25th The Great British Cheese Festival,
Blenheim Palace

October
2nd Ploughing Match, Bishopsland Farm,
Dunsden, nr Reading
tbc Banbury Folk & Good Music Day

Above: Green fields of Watlington

BANBURY   Map 04 SP44

BANBURY MUSEUM
Spiceball Park Rd OX16 2PQ
➲ (M40 junct 11 straight across at first rdbt into
Hennef Way, left at next rdbt into Concord Ave,
right at next rdbt & left at next rdbt, Castle Quay
Shopping Centre & Museum on right)
☎ 01295 259855 📠 01295 269469   `FREE`
e-mail: banburymuseum@cherwell-dc.gov.uk
Come and visit Banbury's stunning new museum! It is
situated in an attractive canal-side location in the centre of
Banbury. Exciting modern displays tell of Banbury's origins
and historic past. The Civil War; the plush manufacturing
industry; the Victorian market town; costume from the 17th
century to the present day; Tooley's Boatyard and the Oxford
Canal, are just some of the subjects illustrated in the new
museum.
Times: Open all year, Mon-Sat, 10-5, Sun 10.30-4.30.
Facilities: P (500yds) 🍽 ✗ licensed ♿ toilets for disabled shop
✗ (ex guide dogs) ▥

BROUGHTON   Map 04 SP43

BROUGHTON CASTLE
OX15 5EB
➲ (2m W of Banbury Cross on B4035 Shipston-on-
Stour in Broughton village, turn off B4035 by Saye
& Sele Arms)
☎ 01295 276070 📠 01295 276070   `2 for 1`
e-mail: admin@broughtoncastle.demon.co.uk

Built by Sir John de Broughton, then owned by William of
Wykeham, and later by the first Lord Saye and Sele, the
castle is an early 14th-and mid 16th-century house with a
moat and gatehouse. Period furniture, paintings and Civil
War relics are displayed. There are fine borders in the walled
garden, and against the castle walls.
Times: Open Etr Sun & Mon, May-15 Sep, Wed, Sun & BH Mon, 2-5
(also open Thu in Jul & Aug). **Fee:** ✱ £5.50 (ch 5-15 £2.50, pen &
students £4.50). Family ticket £13.50 (2 ad & up to 3 ch). Garden
£2.50. Group rates **Facilities:** P 🍽 ♿ toilets for disabled shop

BURFORD
Map 04 SP21

COTSWOLD WILDLIFE PARK
OX18 4JW
➲ (on A361 2m S of A40 at Burford)
☎ 01993 823006 ▤ 01993 823807

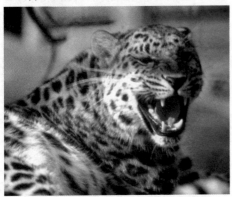

This 160-acre landscaped zoological park, surrounds a listed Gothic-style manor house. There is a varied collection of animals from all over the world, many of which are endangered species such as Asiatic Lions, Leopards, White Rhinos and Red Pandas. There's an adventure playground, a children's farmyard, and train rides during the summer. The park has also become one of the Cotswold's leading attractions for garden enthusiasts, with its exotic summer displays and varied plantings offering interest all year.
Times: Open all year, daily (ex 25 Dec) from 10, last admission 4.30 Mar-Sep, 3 Oct-Feb **Fee:** ✱ £8 (ch & pen £5.50). Party rate £6.50 (ch £4 pen £5). **Facilities:** 🅿 ⬛ ✗ licensed ♿ (parking, free hire of wheelchairs) toilets for disabled shop ▤

See advertisement on opposite page

BUSCOT
Map 04 SU29

BUSCOT PARK
SN7 8BU
➲ (on A417 between Faringdon & Lechdale)
☎ 01367 240786 ▤ 01367 241794
e-mail: estbuscot@aol.com

An 18th-century Palladian house with park and water garden. Home of the Faringdon collection of paintings and furniture. The park is landscaped with extensive water

continued

gardens designed by Harold Peto with parkland walks and a walled garden boasting seasonal herbaceous borders.
Times: Grounds only open Good Fri-Sep, Mon & Tue 2-6. House & Grounds open Good Fri -Sep, Wed-Fri 2-6 also open BHs, 26&27 Mar, 9&10, 23&24 & 30 Apr, 1, 14&15, 28&29 May, 11&12, 25&26 Jun, 9&10, 23&24 Jul, 13&14, 27&28 Aug, 10&11, 24&25 Sep, Last entry 5.30pm
Fee: House & Grounds £6.50 ch £3.25; Grounds only £4.50 (ch £2.25).
Facilities: 🅿 ⬛ ♿ (2 motorised mobility vehicles-must pre-book) toilets for disabled ✗ ♨ ▤

CHASTLETON
Map 04 SP22

CHASTLETON HOUSE NEW
GL56 0SU
➲ (6m from Stow-on-the-Wold.)
☎ 01608 674355 ▤ 01608 674355
e-mail: chastleton@nationaltrust.org.uk
One of England's finest and most complete Jacobean houses, Chastleton House is filled with a mixture of rare and everyday objects, furniture and textiles maintaining the atmosphere of this 400-year-old home. The gardens have a typical Elizabethan and Jacobean layout with a ring of topiary. The National Trust has focussed on conserving rather than restoring the house.
Times: Apr-Sep, Wed-Sat 1-5pm, Oct Wed-Sat, 1-4pm **Fee:** £6 (ch £3, family £15) **Facilities:** 🅿 ♿ toilets for disabled ✗ ♨

DEDDINGTON
Map 04 SP43

DEDDINGTON CASTLE
OX5 4TE
➲ (S of B4031 on E side of Deddington)
The large earthworks of the outer and inner baileys can be seen; the remains of 12th-century castle buildings have been excavated, but they are not now visible.
Times: Open any reasonable time. ✿

DIDCOT
Map 04 SU58

DIDCOT RAILWAY CENTRE
OX11 7NJ
➲ (on A4130 at Didcot Parkway Station)
☎ 01235 817200 ▤ 01235 510621 [2 for 1]
e-mail: didrlyc@globalnet.co.uk
Based around the original GWR engine shed, the Centre is home to the biggest collection anywhere of Great Western Railway steam locomotives, carriages and wagons. A typical GWR station has been re-created and a section of Brunel's original broad gauge track relaid.
Times: Open all year, Sat & Sun. 25 Mar-17 Apr, 30 Apr-25 Sep. Steamdays Sat & Sun 23 Apr-2 Oct, Wed 13 Jul-31 Aug. 10-4 steamdays & wknds Mar-Oct, 10-5 **Fee:** ✱ £4-£8 depending on event (ch £3-£7.50, over 60's £3.50-£6.50). **Facilities:** 🅿 (100yds) ⬛ ♿ (advance notice recommended, some awkward steps) toilets for disabled shop ▤

GREAT COXWELL
Map 04 SU29

GREAT COXWELL BARN
➲ (2m SW of Faringdon between A420 & B4019)
☎ 01793 762209
e-mail: greatcoxwellbarn@nationaltrust.org.uk
William Morris said that the barn was 'as noble as a cathedral'. It is a 13th-century stone-built tithe barn, 152ft long and 44ft wide, with a beautifully crafted framework of timbers supporting the lofty stone roof. The barn was built for the Cistercians.
Times: Open all reasonable times. For details please contact Estate Office. **Fee:** 50p **Facilities:** 🅿 ♨

HENLEY-ON-THAMES   Map 04 SU78

Greys Court
Rotherfield Greys RG9 4PG

➲ (M4 junct 8 or 9, take A404 (M) to Henley-on-Thames. From Nettlebed mini rdbt on A4130 take B481. Property is signposted 3m on left. Can also be accessed from Henley town centre by following signs to Peppard/Greys for 3m)

☎ 01491 628529

e-mail: greyscourt@nationaltrust.org.uk

A picturesque house, originating from the 14th century but with later additions. There is a beautiful courtyard and the surviving tower which dates from 1347. The outbuildings include a Tudor wheelhouse - one supplying water to the house, walled gardens and an ornamental vegetable garden.

Times: Open: House: part of ground floor only, Apr-24 Sep Wed-Fri & BH Mons 2-5 (closed Good Fri). Garden: Mar-Oct 2-5.30 (Mar & Oct Wed only), Apr-Sep, Tue-Sat **Fee:** House & Garden £5.20 ch £2.60. Family ticket £12.50. Garden only £3.70 ch £1.80 Family ticket £9.20. **Facilities:** 🅿 💷 ⛐ (ground floor & gardens partly accessible) shop (bookshop) ⚘

River & Rowing Museum
Mill Meadows RG9 1BF

➲ (off A4130, signposted to Mill Meadows)

☎ 01491 415600   🖷 01491 415601

e-mail: museum@rrm.co.uk

THE WIND IN THE WILLOWS™
at the River & Rowing Museum

The award-winning River and Rowing Museum is the only museum in the world with galleries dedicated to rowing and the 'Quest for Speed', from the Greek Trireme to modern Olympic rowing boats; the River Thames from source to sea with its rich history and varied wildlife. See the boats that won gold in Sydney and the riverside town of Henley featuring the Royal Regatta. Now for 2004/05 the permanent *Wind in the Willows* exhibition.

Times: Open Summer: May-Aug 10-5.30. Winter: Sep-Apr 10-5. (museum closed 24-25 & 31 Dec & 1 Jan). **Fee:** ✱ £6 (concessions £4 & pens £5). Family ticket from £18. Party 10+. **Facilities:** 🅿 💷 ✗ licensed ⛐ Lift access to upstairs galleries, ramps at entrance toilets for disabled shop ✖ (ex guide dogs) 🎏

LONG WITTENHAM   Map 04 SU59

Pendon Museum
OX14 4QD

➲ (follow brown signs from A4130 Didcot-Wallingford or A415 Abingdon-Wallingford road)

☎ 01865 407365

This charming exhibition shows highly detailed and historically accurate model railway and village scenes transporting the visitor back into 1930s country landscapes. Skilled modellers can often be seen at work on the exhibits.

Times: ✱ Open Sat & Sun 2-5, BH wknds 11-5 also Wed in Jul, Aug & Oct half term. (Closed Dec). **Facilities:** 🅿 💷 ⛐ (phone in advance, special seating with handrails) toilets for disabled shop ✖ (ex guide dogs) 🎏

MAPLEDURHAM   Map 04 SU67

Mapledurham House
RG4 7TR

➲ (off A4074, follow brown heritage signs from Reading)

☎ 0118 972 3350   🖷 0118 972 4016

e-mail: mtrust1997@aol.com

The small community at Mapledurham includes the house, a watermill and a church. The fine Elizabethan mansion, surrounded by quiet parkland that runs down to the River Thames, was built by the Blount family in the 16th century. The estate has literary connections with the poet Alexander Pope, with Galsworthy's *Forsyte Saga* and Kenneth Graham's *Wind in the Willows*, and was a location for the film *The Eagle has Landed*.

Times: Open Etr-Sep, Sat, Sun & BHs 2-5.30. Picnic area 2-5.30. Last admission 5pm. Group visits midweek by arrangement. **Fee:** ✱ Combined house, watermill & grounds £6 (ch £3). House & grounds £4 (ch £2). Watermill & grounds £3 (ch £1.50). **Facilities:** 🅿 💷 ⛐ shop ✖ (ex park area) 🎏

MAPLEDURHAM WATERMILL

RG4 7TR

➲ (off A4074, follow brown heritage signs from Reading)

☎ 0118 972 3350 🖶 0118 972 4016

e-mail: mtrust1997@aol.com

Close to Mapledurham House stands the last working corn and grist mill on the Thames, still using traditional wooden machinery and producing flour for local bakers and shops. The watermill's products can be purchased in the shop. When Mapledurham House is open the mill can be reached by river launch.

Times: Open Etr-Sep, Sat, Sun & BHs 2-5.30. Picnic area 2-5.30. Last admission 5. Groups midweek by arrangement. **Fee:** ✱ Watermill & grounds £3 (ch £1.50) **Facilities:** 🅿 🍽 ⚹ shop ⚹ (ex in country park) 🖀

MINSTER LOVELL   Map 04 SP31

MINSTER LOVELL HALL & DOVECOT

OX8 5RN

➲ (adjacent to Minster Lovell church, 3m W of Witney off A40)

Home of the ill-fated Lovell family, the ruins of the 15th-century house are steeped in history and legend. One of the main features of the estate is the medieval dovecote.

Times: Open any reasonable time. ⚌

NORTH LEIGH   Map 04 SP31

NORTH LEIGH ROMAN VILLA

OX8 6QB

➲ (2m N of North Leigh)

This is the remains of a large and well-build Roman courtyard villa. The most important feature is an almost complete mosaic tile floor, which is intricately patterned in reds and browns.

Times: Open, grounds all year. Viewing window for mosaic tile floor. Pedestrian access only from the main road - 600 yds. **Facilities:** 🅿 ⚌

OXFORD   Map 04 SP50

ASHMOLEAN MUSEUM OF ART & ARCHAEOLOGY

Beaumont St OX1 2PH

➲ (city centre, opposite The Randolph Hotel)

☎ 01865 278000 🖶 01865 278018

The oldest museum in the country, opened in 1683, the Ashmolean contains Oxford University's priceless collections. Many important historical art pieces and artefacts are on display, including work from Ancient Greece through to the twentieth century.

Times: Open all year, Tue-Sat 10-5, Sun & BH Mons 2-5. (Closed Etr & during St.Giles Fair in early Sep, Xmas & 1 Jan). **Fee:** ✱ Free. Guided tours by arrangement. **Facilities:** 🅿 (100-200mtrs) (pay & display) 🍽 ✕ licensed ⚹ (entry ramp from Beaumont St. Tel. before visit) toilets for disabled shop ⚹ 🖀

HARCOURT ARBORETUM

Nuneham Courtenay OX44 9PX

➲ (400 yds S of Nuneham Courtenay on A4074)

☎ 01865 343501 🖶 01865 341828

e-mail: piers.newth@botanic-garden.ox.ac.uk

The gardens consist of 75 acres of mixed woodland, meadow, pond, rhododendron walks and fine specimen trees.

Times: Apr-Nov, daily 10-5, Dec-Mar, Mon-Fri 10-4.30. Closed 22 Dec-4 Jan. **Fee:** ✱ £2 pay & display for car park or £5 for 1yr season ticket. **Facilities:** 🅿 (charged) ⚹ ⚹ (ex guide dogs)

MUSEUM OF OXFORD

St Aldate's OX1 1DZ

☎ 01865 252555 🖶 01865 252254

e-mail: museum@oxford.gov.uk

Permanent displays depict the archaeology and history of the city through the ages. There are temporary exhibitions, facilities for school parties and groups, and an audio tour.

Times: Open all year, Tue-Fri 10-4, Sat 10-5 & Sun 12-4. (Closed 25-26 Dec, Good Fri) **Fee:** £2 (ch under 17 50p & concessions £1.50). Family ticket £5 **Facilities:** shop ⚹ (ex guide dogs) 🖀

MUSEUM OF THE HISTORY OF SCIENCE

Old Ashmolean Building, Broad St OX1 3AZ

➲ (Next to Sheldonian Theatre in city centre, on Bond Street)

☎ 01865 277280 🖶 01865 277288

e-mail: museum@mhs.ox.ac.uk

The first purpose built museum in Britain, containing the world's finest collection of early scientific instruments used in astronomy, navigation, surveying, physics and chemistry.

Times: ✱ Open Tue-Sat 12-4, Sun 2-5 (closed Xmas wk).

Facilities: 🅿 (300mtrs) (limited street parking, meters) ⚹ (lift) toilets for disabled shop ⚹ (ex guide dogs) 🖀

THE OXFORD STORY

6 Broad St OX1 3AJ

➲ (Park and ride car parks provide a quick and frequent bus service into the city centre. By car follow signs for City Centre. Follow finger post signs to the attraction)

☎ 01865 728822 🖶 01865 791716

e-mail: info@oxfordstory.co.uk

The Oxford Story offers the very best introduction to the city's world famous University. Climb aboard our indoor 'dark' ride to travel through the university's 900 years of

continued

history. In our interactive exhibition, 'innovate' you can quiz experts from Oxford University on modern day issues, from heart disease to climate change.

Times: Open Jan-Jun & Sep-Dec, Mon-Sat 10-4.30 & Sun 11-4.30. Jul & Aug daily 9.30-5. Closed 25 Dec. **Fee:** ✱ £6.95 (ch £5.25, pen £5.75 & students £5.95), Family ticket (2 ad & 2 ch) £22.50

Facilities: P (300mtrs) ♿ (advisable to phone in advance) toilets for disabled shop ✕ (ex guide dogs) 🍴

OXFORD UNIVERSITY MUSEUM OF NATURAL HISTORY

Parks Rd OX1 3PW

➲ (opposite Keble College)

☎ 01865 272950 🖷 01865 272970

e-mail: info@oum.ox.ac.uk

Built between 1855 and 1860, this museum of "the natural sciences" was intended to satisfy a growing interest in biology, botany, archaeology, zoology, entomology and so on. The museum reflects Oxford University's position as a 19th-century centre of learning, with displays of early dinosaur discoveries, Darwinian evolution and Elias Ashmole's collection of preserved animals. Although visitors to the Pitt-Rivers Museum must pass through the University Museum, the two should not be confused.

Times: Open daily 12-5. Times vary at Xmas & Etr.

Facilities: P (200mtrs) (meter parking) ♿ toilets for disabled shop ✕

PITT RIVERS MUSEUM

South Parks Rd OX1 3PP

➲ (10 min walk from Oxford city centre)

☎ 01865 270927 🖷 01865 270943

e-mail: prm@prm.ox.ac.uk

The museum is one of the city's most popular attractions, it is part of the University of Oxford and was founded in 1884. The collections held at the museum are internationally acclaimed, and contain many objects from different cultures of the world and from various periods, all grouped by type, or purpose.

Times: Open Mon-Sat 12-4.30 & Sun 2-4.30. (Closed Xmas & Etr, open BH's) **Facilities:** ♿ (audio guide, wheelchair trail and map to ground floor) toilets for disabled shop ✕ (ex guide dogs)

ST EDMUND HALL

College of Oxford University OX1 4AR

➲ (Queen's Lane Oxford at the end of the High St).

☎ 01865 279000 🖷 01865 279090

e-mail: bursary@seh.ox.ac.uk

This is the only surviving medieval academic hall and has a Norman crypt, 17th-century dining hall, chapel and quadrangle. Other buildings are of the 18th and 20th centuries.

Times: Open all year. (Closed 24 Dec-4 Jan, 9-18 Apr & 28-31 Aug). **Facilities:** 🅿 ♿ toilets for disabled ✕ (ex guide dogs)

> An asterisk * indicates that opening times and prices are for 2004. Please contact the attraction for up-to-date information.

UNIVERSITY OF OXFORD BOTANIC GARDEN

Rose Ln OX1 4AZ

➲ (E end of High St on banks of river Cherwell)

☎ 01865 286690 🖷 01865 286693

e-mail: postmaster@botanic-garden.ox.ac.uk

Founded in 1621, this botanic garden is the oldest in the country. There is a collection of over 8000 species of plants from all over the world.

Times: Open all year daily: 9-4.30 Jan, Feb, Nov & Dec last admission 4.15. 9-5 Mar, Apr & Oct last admission 4.15. 9-6 May-Sep last admission 5.15. 9-8 Thu in Jun, Jul & Aug last admission 7.15. (Closed Good Fri & 25 Dec). **Fee:** £2.50 (ch free in full time education accompanied by an adult family member/guardian, UB40 & disabled/carers, pen & students £2) **Facilities:** P (0.5m) park and ride system ♿ toilets for disabled ✕ (ex guide dogs)

ROUSHAM   Map 04 SP42

ROUSHAM HOUSE

OX25 4QX

➲ (1m E of A4260. 0.5m S of B4030)

☎ 01869 347110 🖷 01869 347110

This attractive mansion was built by Sir Robert Dormer in 1635. During the Civil War it was a Royalist garrison. The house contains over 150 portraits and other pictures, and also much fine contemporary furniture. The gardens are a masterpiece by William Kent, and are his only work to survive unspoiled.

Times: Open all year, garden only, daily 10-4.30. House, Apr-Sep, Wed, Sun & BH Mon 2-4.30 (last entry). **Fee:** ✱ House £3, Garden £3. Groups by arrangement. No children under 15.

Facilities: 🅿 ♿ ✕ (ex guide dogs)

RYCOTE   Map 04 SP60

RYCOTE CHAPEL

OX9 2PE

➲ (off B4013)

This small private chapel was founded in 1449 by Richard Quatremayne. It has its original font, and a particularly fine 17th-century interior. The chapel was visited by both Elizabeth I and Charles I.

Times: Open Apr-Sep, Fri-Sun 2-6. May close at short notice for services or functions. **Fee:** ✱ £3 (ch £1, concessions £2). Prices & opening times relate to 2004, for further details phone or log onto www.english-heritage.org.uk/visits **Facilities:** 🅿 ♿ (if assisted) shop ✕ ✿

STONOR   Map 04 SU78

STONOR HOUSE & PARK

RG9 6HF

➲ (M40 junct 6, through Wattington, towards Nettlebed. At top of hill, left along B480 towards Henley. Stonor approx 3m further on left just before Stonor village)

☎ 01491 638587 🖷 01491 639348

e-mail: jweaver@stonor.com

The house dates back to 1190 but features a Tudor façade. It has a medieval Catholic chapel which is still in use today, and shows some of the earliest domestic architecture in Oxfordshire. Its treasures include rare furniture, paintings, sculptures and tapestries from Britain, Europe and America. The house is set in beautiful gardens commanding views of the surrounding deer park.

Times: Open Apr-Sep, Sun 2-5.30; Jul, Aug, & Sep also Wed 2-5.30; BH Mons. Parties by appointment Tue-Thu, Apr-Sep. **Fee:** ✱ £6 (ch 14 accompanied free). Gardens only £3.50. Private guided tours £7 each. **Facilities:** 🅿 🅿 shop ✕ (ex in grounds on lead)

UFFINGTON   Map 04 SU38

UFFINGTON CASTLE, WHITE HORSE & DRAGON HILL

➲ (S of B4507)

☎ 01793 762209   **FREE**

The 'castle' is an Iron Age fort on the ancient Ridgeway Path. It covers about eight acres and has only one gateway. On the hill below the fort is the White Horse, a 375ft prehistoric figure carved in the chalky hillside and thought to be about 3000 years old.

Times: Open all year. **Facilities:** 🅿 Disabled car park 🚻

WATERPERRY   Map 04 SP60

WATERPERRY GARDENS

OX33 1JZ 2.5m from A40, turn off at Wheatley, M40 J8 from London, M40 J8a from Birmingham

☎ 01844 339226 & 339254   🖷 01844 339883

e-mail: office@waterperrygardens.fsnet.co.uk

The manor of Waterperry is mentioned in the Domesday Book. The present house (not open) was rebuilt by Sir John Curson in 1713. The peaceful gardens and nurseries which surround the house were the home of a celebrated horticultural school between 1932 and 1971, and have fine herbaceous borders, a rock garden, riverside walk, shrub borders, lawns and trees. Please phone for details of special events.

Times: Open all year, Gardens (ex Xmas & New Year & during "Art in Action" 15-18 Jul). Apr-Oct 9-5.30, Nov-Mar 9-5 daily. **Fee:** £4 (ch 10-16 £2.50, ch under 10 free, pen £3.50). Nov-Mar £2 Party 20+ £3.25. **Facilities:** 🅿 💺 ✗ licensed ♿ (grounds mostly accessible) toilets for disabled shop garden centre ✖ (ex guide dogs) 🛍

WITNEY   Map 04 SP31

COGGES MANOR FARM MUSEUM

Church Ln, Cogges OX28 3LA

➲ (0.5m SE off A4022)

☎ 01993 772602   🖷 01993 703056

e-mail: info@cogges.org

The museum includes the Manor, dairy and walled garden, and has breeds of animals typical of the Victorian period. The first floor of the manor contains period rooms. Special events take place through the season.

Times: Open Apr-Oct, Tue-Fri & BH Mon 10.30-5.30, Sat & Sun 12-5.30. Early closing Oct. (Closed Good Fri). **Fee:** ✱ £4.40 (ch £2.30, pen, students & UB40 £2.85). Family ticket £12.90 (2 ad & 2 ch).

Facilities: 🅿 💺 ♿ (wheelchair available,commentary/history file for 1st floor) toilets for disabled shop 🛍

WOODSTOCK   Map 04 SP41

BLENHEIM PALACE

OX20 1PX

➲ (M40 junct 9, follow signs to Blenheim, on A44 8m N of Oxford)

☎ 08700 602080   🖷 01993 810570   **2 for 1**

e-mail: admin@blenheimpalace.com

Home of the 11th Duke of Marlborough and birthplace of Sir Winston Churchill, Blenheim Palace is an English Baroque masterpiece. Fine furniture, sculpture, paintings and tapestries are set in magnificent gilded staterooms that overlook sweeping lawns and formal gardens. 'Capability' Brown landscaped the 2100-acre grounds, which are open to visitors for pleasant walks and beautiful views.

Times: Palace & Gardens 12 Feb-11 Dec (ex Mon & Tue) daily 10.30-5.30 (last admission 4.45pm). Park daily all year (ex 25 Dec) 9-4.45 **Fee:** ✱ Palace, Park & Gardens £11-12.50 (ch £5.50-£7, concession £8.50-£10). Park & Gardens £6-£7.50 (ch £2-£3.50, concession £4-£5.50) **Facilities:** 🅿 💺 ✗ licensed ♿ (ramps, disabled parking, buggies, wheelchairs) toilets for disabled shop 🛍

OXFORDSHIRE MUSEUM

Fletcher's House OX20 1SN

➲ (A44 Evesham-Oxford, follow signs for Blenheim Palace. Museum opposite church)

☎ 01993 811456   🖷 01993 813239   **FREE**

e-mail: oxon.museum@oxfordshire.go.uk

Situated in the heart of the historic town of Woodstock, the award-winning redevelopment of Fletcher's House provides a home for the new county museum. Set in attractive gardens, the new museum celebrates Oxfordshire in all its diversity and features collections of local history, art, archaeology, landscape and wildlife as well as a gallery exploring the Country's innovative industries from nuclear power to nanotechnology. Interactive exhibits offer new learning experiences for visitors of all ages. The museum's purpose built Garden Gallery houses a variety of touring exhibitions of regional and national interest.

Times: Open all year, Tue-Sat 10-5. Last admission 4.30. (Closed Good Fri, 25-26 Dec & 1 Jan). Galleries are closed on Mon (but open BH Mon's, 2-5). **Facilities:** 🅿 (outside entrance) Free parking 💺 ✗ licensed ♿ (chair lifts to all galleries) toilets for disabled ✖ (ex guide dogs)

The Battle of Trafalgar.

2005 is the 200th anniversary of the sea battle between the British Royal Navy and the French and Spanish navies. 2005 will see a number of events celebrating this important British victory.

RUTLAND

EVENTS & FESTIVALS

July
tbc Whissendine Feast Week, various venues and events

August
18th-19th Stapleford Steam, Stapleford Miniature Railway, Stapleford Park
19th-21st British Birdwatching Fair, Egleton Nature Reserve, Rutland Water
28th-29th Stapleford Miniature Railway Open Weekend, Stapleford Park

Above: Rutland Water

LYDDINGTON   Map 04 SP89

LYDDINGTON BEDE HOUSE
Blue Coat Ln LE15 9LZ
☎ 01572 822438

Once a prominent medieval palace later converted into an almshouse for the poor. Its history is bought to life in an evocative audio tour.

Times: Open Apr-Sep, daily 10-6; Oct, daily 10-5). **Facilities:** ❧ ✖ ♯

OAKHAM   Map 04 SK80

OAKHAM CASTLE
Catmos St LE15 6HW
➲ (off Market Place)
☎ 01572 758440   🖷 01572 758445   `FREE`
e-mail: museum@rutland.gov.uk

An exceptionally fine Norman Great Hall of a 12th-century fortified manor house. Earthworks, walls and remains of an earlier motte can be seen along with medieval sculptures and unique presentation horseshoes forfeited by peers of the realm and royalty to the Lord of the Manor. Licensed for Civil Marriages. Please enquire for details of the Oakham Festival.

Times: Open all year, Mon-Sat 10.30-5 (closed 1-1.30), Sun 2-4. Closed Good Fri & Xmas. **Facilities:** Ⓟ (400yds) (disabled parking only by notification) ❧ shop ✖ (ex guide dogs)

RUTLAND COUNTY MUSEUM
Catmos St LE15 6HW
➲ (on A6003, S of town centre)
☎ 01572 758440   🖷 01572 758445   `FREE`
e-mail: museum@rutland.gov.uk

Rutland County Museum has displays of farming equipment, machinery and wagons, rural tradesmen's tools, domestic collections and local archaeology, all housed in a splendid late 18th-century cavalry riding school. The new 'Welcome to Rutland' gallery houses a guide to the history of Rutland and includes a shop and study area.

Times: Open all year, Mon-Sat 10.30-5, Sun 2-4. Closed Good Fri & Xmas. **Facilities:** Ⓟ (adjacent) (pay & display, free on Sun) ❧ (induction loop in meeting room) toilets for disabled shop ✖ (ex guide dogs)

Above: Rutland Water

SHROPSHIRE

EVENTS & FESTIVALS

May
1st-2nd British Falconry & Raptor Fair,
Chetwynd Park, Newport, nr Telford

June
12th Royal Air Force Show, Royal Air Force
Museum, Cosford
18th Shrewsbury Carnival & Show,
Quarry Park
25th-26th Shropshire & West Midlands Show,
Showground, Berwick Road, Shrewsbury
tbc Ludlow Festival in the ruins
of Ludlow Castle

July
15th-17th Festival at the Edge (storytelling),
Stokes Barn, Much Wenlock
16th-17th Wem Sweet Pea Festival, New Town
Hall, High Street, Wem

August
12th-13th Shrewsbury Flower Show
26th-28th Bridgnorth Folk Festival
28th-29th County of Salop Steam Rally,
Onslow Park, Shrewsbury
28th-29th Shropshire Game Fair, Chetwynd
Park, Newport, Telford

September
3rd-4th Shrewsbury Real Ale Festival
(provisional)
17th-18th The Midland Game & Country
Sports Fair, Weston Park, Weston-under-
Lizard, Nr Shifnel

Above: Longmynd at Church Stretton

ACTON BURNELL   Map 07 SJ50

ACTON BURNELL CASTLE
SY5 7PE
➲ (located in Acton Burnell on unclass road 8m S
of Shrewsbury)
The warm red sandstone shell of a fortified thirteenth-
century manor house. The site of the first parliament at
which the commons were fully represented.
Times: Open at all reasonable times. **Facilities:** & ✿

ATCHAM   Map 07 SJ50

ATTINGHAM PARK
SY4 4TP
➲ (4m SE of Shrewsbury on B4380)
☎ 01743 708123 ▤ 01743 708155
e-mail: attingham@nationaltrust.org.uk
Attingham Park is centred on one of Britain's finest regency
mansions, set in a landscaped deer park. Close by one can
meet the animals at one of Britain's only organic open farms.
Times: House open mid Mar-end Oct, Fri-Tue 12-5, (last admission
4pm). BH Mon 11-5. Deer Park & Grounds daily Mar-Oct, 9am-8pm;
Nov-Feb 9am-5pm. **Fee:** ✱ House & Grounds £5.50 (ch £2.75) Family
ticket £12.75. Grounds only £2.70 (ch £1.35) Family £6.75
Facilities: ▣ 🖃 & (2 electric self drive buggies, 1 staff driven
8-seater toilets for disabled shop (ex guide & hearing dogs) ❧

BENTHALL   Map 07 SJ60

BENTHALL HALL
TF12 5RX
➲ (on B4375)
☎ 01952 882159
e-mail: benthall@ntrust.org.uk
The main part of the house was built around 1585. A wing at
the back, which has been altered at various times, dates
originally from about 1520. It is an attractive sandstone
building with mullioned windows, fine oak panelling and a
splendid carved staircase.
Times: Open Apr-Sep, Tue, Wed, BH Mon & Sun before BH Mon's;
Jul-Sep open every Sun. House 2-5.30, Garden 1.30-5.30.
Fee: ✱ House £3.60 (ch £1.80). Garden only £2.30.
Facilities: ▣ & (Braille sheets) toilets for disabled ✈ (ex guide dogs)
❧ ➥

BOSCOBEL   Map 07 SJ80

BOSCOBEL HOUSE AND THE ROYAL OAK
Brewood ST19 9AR
➲ (on unclass road between A41 and A5)
☎ 01902 850244 ▤ 01902 850295
This fully restored and refurbished lodge and famous Royal
Oak tree is where King Charles II sought refuge from
Cromwell's troops in 1651. The house was built around 1632.
Times: Open Apr-May, Thu-Mon, 10-5; Jun-Aug, daily, 10-6; Sep-Oct,
Thu-Mon, 10-5 **Fee:** ✱ £4.40 (ch £2.20, concessions £3.30, family
£11). Grounds only; £1.50 (ch 80p, concessions £1). Prices & opening
times relate to 2004, for further details phone or log onto
www.english-heritage.org.uk/visits **Facilities:** ▣ 🖃 shop ✈ ✿

WHITELADIES PRIORY
➲ (1m SW of Boscobel House, off an unclass road
between A41 and A5)
Only the ruins are left of this Augustinian nunnery, which
dates from 1158 and was destroyed in the Civil War. After

continued

the Battle of Worcester Charles II hid here and in the nearby woods before going on to Boscobel House.
Times: Open any reasonable time. **Facilities:** ✝ (ex dogs on leads) ✿

BUILDWAS   Map 07 SJ60
BUILDWAS ABBEY
Iron Bridge TF8 7BW
➲ (on S bank of River Severn on B4378)
☎ 01952 433274
Set beside the River Severn, against a backdrop of wooded grounds, are the extensive remains of this Cistercian abbey founded in 1135.
Times: Open Apr-May, Thu-Mon, 10-5; Jun-Aug, daily, 10-6; Sep, Thu-Mon, 10-5. **Fee:** ✱ £2.50 (ch £1.30, concessions £1.90). Prices & opening times relate to 2004, for further details phone or log onto www.english-heritage.org.uk/visits **Facilities:** 🅿 & shop ✝ ✿

BURFORD   Map 03 SO56
BURFORD HOUSE GARDENS
WR15 8HQ
➲ (off A456, 1m W of Tenbury Wells, 8m from Ludlow)
☎ 01584 810777 🖨 01584 810673
e-mail: info@burford.co.uk
Burford Garden Company's store at Burford House Gardens has been designed to inspire and delight all garden lovers. Together with everything imaginable for the English garden, Burford House Gardens specialise in Clematis, the Queen of climbers, which in popularity, is second only to the Rose in Britain. Hundreds of varieties are for sale, many of which were bred and are grown on site in the Treasure's Clematis Nursery.
Times: ✱ Open all year 9-6 or dusk if earlier. **Fee:** ✱ £3.95 (ch £1).
Facilities: 🅿 💷 ✗ licensed & (ramp into gardens, sloping paths) toilets for disabled shop garden centre ✝ (ex in Plant Centre) 🍴

COSFORD   Map 07 SJ70
ROYAL AIR FORCE MUSEUM
TF11 8UP
➲ (on A41, 1m S of M54 junct 3)
☎ 01902 376200 🖨 01902 376211
e-mail: cosford@rafmuseum.org
This is one of the largest aviation collections in the UK. Exhibits include the Victor and Vulcan bombers, the Hastings, York and British Airways airliners, the Belfast freighter and the last airworthy Britannia. The research and development collection includes the notable TSR2, Fairey Delta, Bristol 188 and many more important aircraft.
Times: Open all year daily, 10-6 (last admission 4). Closed 24-26 Dec & 1 Jan **Facilities:** 🅿 ✗ licensed & (free loan of 3 manual wheelchairs) toilets for disabled shop ✝ (ex guide dogs)

CRAVEN ARMS   Map 07 SO48
SECRET HILLS, THE SHROPSHIRE HILLS DISCOVERY CENTRE
School Rd SY7 9RS
➲ (on A49, on southern edge of Craven Arms)
☎ 01588 676000 🖨 01588 676030   2 for 1
e-mail: jill.jarrett@shropshire-cc.gov.uk
This new attraction explores the history, nature and geography of the Shropshire Hills, through a series of interactive displays and simulations. These include Landscape of Contrasts, Ancient Landscape, a simulated Balloon Flight, and Land of Inspiration. The Centre has 23

continued

acres of meadow lands sloping down to the River Onny for all visitors to explore. There is a network of cycle routes and walks and during the summer a shuttle bus service operates from the centre, at weekends, which allows visitors to explore the local landscape, hills, villages and market towns. The Centre also houses the Secret Hills Gallery which features changing displays of craft and artworks that celebrate Shropshire's creative industry. There is also a shop, restaurant and visitors information centre.

Secret Hills, the Shropshire Hills Discovery Centre

Times: Open all year, daily from 10. Last admission 3.30 (Nov-Mar), 4.30 (Apr-Oct). **Fee:** ✱ £4.25 (ch £2.75 & pen £3.75, ch under 5 free). Family ticket £12.20. Groups 20+ £3.75 each, ch £2.50 each.
Facilities: 🅿 💷 ✗ licensed & (wheelchair available) toilets for disabled shop ✝ (ex guide dogs) 🍴

HAUGHMOND ABBEY   Map 07 SJ51
HAUGHMOND ABBEY
Upton Magna SY4 4RW
➲ (off B5062)
☎ 01743 709661
Absorb these extensive 12th-century Augustinian abbey ruins, and visit the small museum.
Times: Open Apr-May, Thu-Mon, 10-5; Jun-Aug, daily, 10-6; Sep, Thu-Mon, 10-5. **Fee:** ✱ £2.50 (ch £1.30, concessions £1.90). Prices & opening times relate to 2004, for further details phone or log onto www.english-heritage.org.uk/visits **Facilities:** 🅿 & (limited access for wheelchair users) shop ✿

HODNET   Map 07 SJ62
HODNET HALL GARDENS
TF9 3NN
➲ (M6 junct 12/15 or M54 junct 3. Hodnet is on the A442, Telford-Whitchurch road and A53 Shrewsbury-Market Drayton road).
☎ 01630 685786 🖨 01630 685853
e-mail: marlene@heber-percy.freeserve.co.uk
Over sixty acres of brilliantly coloured flowers, magnificent forest trees, sweeping lawns, and a chain of ornamental pools which run along the cultivated garden valley to provide a habitat for waterfowl and other wildlife. Big game trophies adorn the 17th-century tearooms, and plants are usually for sale in the kitchen gardens. The House, rebuilt in Victorian-Elizabethan style, is not open.
Times: Open Apr-Sep, Tue-Sun & BH Mon 12-5. Oct, Sun only 12-5 **Fee:** ✱ £3.75 (ch £1.75, pen £3.25). Party £3.25 **Facilities:** 🅿 💷 & (2 wheelchairs available) toilets for disabled shop garden centre

IRONBRIDGE   Map 07 SJ60

IRONBRIDGE GORGE MUSEUMS
Coach Rd TF8 7DQ
➲ (M54 junct 4, signposted)
☎ 01952 433522 & 0800 590258
▤ 01952 432204
e-mail: info@ironbridge.org.uk
Ironbridge is the site of the world's first iron bridge, it was cast and built here in 1779, to span a narrow gorge over the River Severn. Now Ironbridge is the site of a remarkable series of museums relating the story of the bridge, recreating life in Victorian times and featuring ceramics and social history displays.
Times: ✱ Open all year, 10-5. Some small sites closed Nov-Mar. Telephone or write for exact winter details. **Facilities:** ▯ ▱
✗ licensed ♿ (wheelchairs, potters wheel, Braille guide, hearing loop) toilets for disabled shop ✖ (ex Blists Hill & guide dogs) ▥

LILLESHALL   Map 07 SJ71

LILLESHALL ABBEY
TF10 9HW
➲ (off A518 on unclass road)   **FREE**
☎ 0121 625 6820
In the beautiful grounds of Lilleshall Hall, ruined Lilleshall Abbey was founded shortly before the middle of the 12th century and from the high west front visitors can look down the entire 228ft length of the abbey church.
Times: Open any reasonable time. ✿

LUDLOW   Map 07 SO57

LUDLOW CASTLE
Castle Square SY8 1AY
➲ (A49, turn off into Ludlow Town centre).
☎ 01584 873355
Ludlow Castle dates from about 1086. In 1473, Edward IV sent the Prince of Wales and his brother - later to become the Princes in the Tower - to live here, and Ludlow Castle became a seat of government. John Milton's *Comus* was first performed at Ludlow Castle in 1634; now contemporary performances of Shakespeare's plays, together with concerts, are put on in the castle grounds during the Ludlow Festival (end June-early July).
Times: Open all year, Jan Sat-Sun 10-4; Feb-Mar daily 10-4; Apr-Jul daily 10-5; Aug daily 10-7; Sep daily 10-5; Oct-Dec daily 10-4 (last admission 30 minutes before closing). (Closed 25 Dec) **Fee:** £4 (ch under 6 free, ch £2, pen £3.50). Family ticket £11.
Facilities: ▯ (100yds) ♿ toilets for disabled shop ▥

LYDBURY NORTH   Map 07 SO38

WALCOT HALL
SY7 8AZ
➲ (3m E of Bishops Castle, on B4385, beside the Powis Arms)
☎ 01568 610693   ▤ 01568 610693
e-mail: lesley@walcothall.com
Re-designed by Sir William Chambers for Lord Clive of India in 1763. The Georgian House possesses a free-standing and recently restored ballroom, stableyard with matching clock towers and extensive walled garden. There is an Arboretum, noted for its rhododendrons and azaleas, specimen trees, pools and a lake. The ballroom is available for hire and the Hall holds a licence for civil weddings.
Times: ✱ Open 25 & 26 May. Arboretum & gardens open Apr-Oct .
Facilities: ▯ ♿ (lift to 1st floor)

MORETON CORBET   Map 07 SJ52

MORETON CORBET CASTLE
➲ (off B5063, in Moreton Corbet)
Inherited by the Corbets in 1235, who are thought to have remodelled the great keep, this castle may already have been standing for over 100 years. It was remodelled in the 16th century and then partially demolished to make way for a great Elizabethan mansion House. Although damaged in the civil war, the castle and mansion stand today as one of the most picturesque ruins of the Shropshire Marches.
Times: Open all reasonable times. **Facilities:** ▯ ♿ ✿

MUCH WENLOCK   Map 07 SO69

MUCH WENLOCK PRIORY
TA3 6HS
☎ 01952 727466
Experience the ruins of this large Cluniac priory and the atmospheric remains of the 13th-century church and Norman chapter house. The audio tour offers a fascinating insight into its history. Impressive topiary figures guard the priory ruins.
Times: Open all year, Mar-May, Thu-Mon, 10-5; Jun-Aug, daily, 10-6; Sep-Oct, Thu-Mon, 10-5; Nov-Feb, Fri-Sun, 10-4. (Closed 24-26 Dec & 1 Jan). **Fee:** ✱ £3 (ch £1.50, concessions £2.30). Prices & opening times relate to 2004, for further details phone or log onto www.english-heritage.org.uk/visits **Facilities:** ▯ ✿

OSWESTRY   Map 07 SJ22

OLD OSWESTRY HILL FORT
➲ (1m N of Oswestry, off an unclass road off A483)
An impressive Iron Age hill-fort of 68 acres, defended by a series of five ramparts, with an elaborate western entrance and unusual earthwork cisterns.
Times: Open any reasonable time. ✿

QUATT   Map 07 SO78

DUDMASTON
WV15 6QN
➲ (4m SE of Bridgnorth on A442)
☎ 01746 780866   ▤ 01746 780744
e-mail: sue.pope@nationaltrust.org.uk
The 17th-century flower paintings which belonged to Francis Darby of Coalbrookdale are exhibited in this house of the same period, with modern works, botanical art and fine furniture. The house stands in an extensive parkland garden and there are dingle and lakeside walks.
Times: Open Apr-Sep, Tue, Wed & Sun & BH Mons, 2-5.30. Garden noon-6. Closed Good Fri. **Fee:** ✱ House & Garden £4.50. Garden only £3.20. Family ticket £10.50. Parties 15+ £3.50 **Facilities:** ▯ ▱ ♿ (Braille guides, taped tours) toilets for disabled shop ✖ (ex in grounds & guide dogs) ▦ ▥

Are there any excellent Days Out that we've missed? Use the Readers' Report form at the back of the book to tell us about them.

SHREWSBURY — Map 07 SJ41

SHREWSBURY CASTLE AND SHROPSHIRE REGIMENTAL MUSEUM

The Castle, Castle St SY1 2AT

➲ (located in town centre, adjacent to railway station)

☎ 01743 358516 🖹 01743 354811

e-mail: shropsrm@zoom.co.uk

The museum of The King's Shropshire Light Infantry and The Shropshire Yeomanry is housed in the main surviving building of Shrewsbury Castle which once dominated the town. The grounds contain the medieval 'motte' and the romantic 'Laura's Tower'.

Times: ✱ Open Tue-Sat 10-4.30, also Sun from Etr-1 Oct & BH Mon. Closed Dec & Jan. Telephone for winter opening times. Castle grounds open Mon-Sat & Sun as above, 9-5 **Facilities:** Ⓟ (3 mins NCP) (on street parking by voucher only) Ⓔ (please ask staff for assistance) toilets for disabled shop ✖ (ex guide dogs)

STOKESAY — Map 07 SO48

STOKESAY CASTLE

SY7 9AH

➲ (1m S of Craven Arms off A49)

☎ 01588 672544

Most perfectly preserved 13th-century fortified manor house. See its superb timber-framed Jacobean gatehouse and stroll through the impressive great hall. Delightful cottage gardens.

Times: Open all year, Mar-May, Thu-Mon, 10-5; Jun-Aug, daily, 10-6; Sep-Oct, Thu-Mon, 10-5; Nov-Feb, Fri-Sun, 10-4. (Closed 24-26 Dec & 1 Jan). **Fee:** ✱ £4.50 (ch £2.30, concessions £3.40, family £11.30). Prices & opening times relate to 2004, for further details phone or log onto www.english-heritage.org.uk/visits **Facilities:** Ⓟ Ⓔ (tape tour for visually handicapped, ramp for wheelchairs) toilets for disabled ✖

TELFORD — Map 07 SJ60

HOO FARM ANIMAL KINGDOM

Preston-on-the-Weald Moors TF6 6DJ

➲ (M54 junct 6, follow brown tourist signs)

☎ 01952 677917 🖹 01952 677944

e-mail: info@hoofarm.com

Hoo Farm is a real children's paradise where there is always something happening. A clean, friendly farm that appeals to all ages and offers close contact with a wide variety of animals from fluffy yellow chicks and baby lambs to foxes, llamas, deer and ostriches. A daily programme of events encourages audience participation in the form of bottle feeding lambs, pig feeding and collecting the freshly laid eggs. New for this year is ferret racing! The Craft Area offers the chance to try your hand at candle dipping, glass or pottery painting or even throwing a pot on the potters wheel. There are Junior Quad Bikes and a Rifle Range, Pony Rides, powered mini tractors as well as indoor and outdoor play areas and a new games room.

Times: ✱ Open 23 Mar-8 Sep, daily 10-6 (last admission 5). 10 Sep-22 Nov, Tue-Sun 10-5 (last admission 4. Closed Mon ex Halloween). 23 Nov-24 Dec daily 10-5 (closes at 1pm 24 Dec). (Closed 25 Dec-mid Mar). **Facilities:** Ⓟ ⬛ Ⓔ toilets for disabled shop ✖ (ex guide dogs) ◀

WESTON-UNDER-REDCASTLE — Map 07 SJ52

HAWKSTONE HISTORIC PARK & FOLLIES

SY4 5UY

➲ (3m from Hodnet off A53, follow the brown heritage signs)

☎ 01939 200611 🖹 01939 200311

e-mail: info@hawkstone.co.uk

Created in the 18th century by the Hill family, Hawkstone was once one of the greatest historic parklands in history. After almost one hundred years of neglect it has now been restored and designated a Grade 1 historic park. Visitors can once again experience the magical world of intricate pathways, arches and bridges, towering cliffs and follies, and an awesome grotto. The Grand Valley and woodlands have centuries-old oaks, wild rhododendrons and lofty monkey puzzles. The park covers nearly 100 acres of hilly terrain and visitors are advised to wear sensible shoes and clothing and to bring a torch. Allow 3-4 hours for the tour, which is well signposted and a route map is provided in the admission price. Attractions include 'Hear King Arthur' and meeting the Duke of Wellington in the White Tower to discuss the Battle of Waterloo.

Times: ✱ Open Sat & Sun Jan-Mar; Wed-Sun, Apr-May & Sep-Oct; Jun-Aug, daily. Closed Nov & Dec. Open from 10. **Facilities:** Ⓟ ⬛ ✖ licensed Ⓔ (no access to follies due to terrain access Valley only) toilets for disabled shop ◀

WROXETER — Map 07 SJ50

WROXETER ROMAN CITY

SY5 6PH

➲ (5m E of Shrewsbury, 1m S of A5)

☎ 01743 761330

Discover what urban life was like 2,000 years ago in the forth largest city in Roman Britain. See the remains of the impressive 2nd-century municipal baths and view the excavated treasures in the museum.

Times: Open all year, Mar-May, daily, 10-5; Jun-Aug, daily, 10-6; Sep-Oct, daily, 10-5; Nov-Feb, daily, 10-4. (Closed 24-26 Dec & 1 Jan) **Fee:** ✱ £4 (ch £2, concessions £3, family £10). Prices & opening times relate to 2004, for further details phone or log onto www.english-heritage.org.uk/visits **Facilities:** Ⓟ Ⓔ shop ⌗

SOMERSET

EVENTS & FESTIVALS

February
26th-6th Mar Bath Literature Festival (provisional)

April
30th-2nd May Bath Annual Spring Flower Show, Royal Victoria Park

May
20th-5th Jun Bath International Music Festival (various venues)
27th-12th June Bath Fringe Festival (various venues)

June
1st-4th The Royal Bath & West Show, Royal Bath & West Showground, Shepton Mallet
24th-26th Glastonbury Festival, Worthy Farm, Pilton, Glastonbury (provisional)

July
9th-10th Glastonbury Pilgrimage, Glastonbury Abbey

August
3rd-4th Taunton Flower Show, Vivary Park, Taunton
tbc Glastonbury Children's Festival

October
15th Taunton Carnival

November
tbc Bridgwater Guy Fawkes Carnival, Bridgwater
tbc Glastonbury Chilkwell Guy Fawkes Carnival

Above: Heather growing on Exmoor

AXBRIDGE — Map 03 ST45

KING JOHN'S HUNTING LODGE — FREE
The Square BS26 2AP
➲ (on corner of Axbridge High St, in the Square)
☎ 01934 732012

Nothing to do with King John or with hunting, this jettied and timber-framed house was built around 1500. It gives a good indication of the wealth of the merchants of that time and is now a museum of local history, with old photographs, paintings and items such as the town stocks and constables' staves.

Times: Open Apr-Sep, daily 1-4. **Facilities:** ♿ shop ✸ ♨

BARRINGTON — Map 03 ST31

BARRINGTON COURT GARDEN
TA19 0NQ
➲ (5m NE of Ilminster on B3168)
☎ 01460 241938   🖷 01460 241938 — 2 for 1

The house is a Tudor Manor, the interior of which is now let out to Stuart Interiors as showrooms with antique furniture for sale. The gardens were created in the 1920s, with the help (through the post) of Gertrude Jekyll. They are laid out in 'rooms' and there is a large walled kitchen garden supplying fresh fruit and vegetables to the restaurant.

Times: Open Mar Thu-Sun 11-4.30; Apr-Sep daily (ex Wed) 11-5.30; Oct Thu-Sun 11-4.30. **Fee:** ✱ £5.50 (ch £2.50). Family £13.50. Groups £4.80 **Facilities:** 🅿 🍽 licensed ♿ (batricars available, Braille guides, wheelchairs) toilets for disabled shop garden centre ✸ (except guide dogs) ♨

BATH — Map 03 ST76

AMERICAN MUSEUM
Claverton Manor BA2 7BD
➲ (2.5m SE)
☎ 01225 460503   🖷 01225 469160
e-mail: info@americanmuseum.org

Claverton Manor is just two miles south east of Bath, in a beautiful setting above the River Avon. The house was built in 1820 by Sir Jeffrey Wyatville, and is now a museum of American decorative arts. The gardens are well worth seeing, and include an American arboretum and a replica of George Washington's garden at Mount Vernon. The Folk Art Gallery and the New Gallery are among the many exhibits in the grounds along with seasonal exhibitions.

Times: Open 14 Mar-30 Oct, Tue-Sun 2-5. Gardens 12-6. Open Mon in Aug & BHs. **Fee:** £6.50 (ch £3.50, pen £5.50). **Facilities:** 🅿 🍽 ♿ toilets for disabled shop 🍴

BATH ABBEY
BA1 1LT
➲ (centre of Bath, next to Pump Rooms)
☎ 01225 422462 & 446300   🖷 01225 429990
e-mail: office@bathabbey.org

The 15th-century abbey church was built on the site of the Saxon abbey where King Edgar was crowned in 973. The church is Perpendicular style with Norman arches and superb fan-vaulting. The famous West Front carvings represent the founder-bishop's dream of angels ascending and descending from heaven.

Times: Open all year, Etr-Oct, Mon-Sat 9-6; Nov-Etr 9-4.30. Sun all year 1-2.30 & 4.30-5.30. **Fee:** ✱ Visitors invited to donate £2.50 each. **Facilities:** 🅿 (5 mins) (limited street parking) ♿ (level access throughout) toilets for disabled shop ✸ (ex guide & hearing dogs)

BATH POSTAL MUSEUM
8 Broad St BA1 5LJ
➲ (M4 junct 18. Follow A46 to Bath, on entering city fork left at mini rdbt. After all traffic lights into Walcot St. Podium car park facing)
☎ 01225 460333 📠 01225 460333
e-mail: info@bathpostalmuseum.org

Discover how 18th-century Bath influenced and developed the Postal System, including the story of the Penny Post. The first letter sent with a stamp was sent from this very building. Visitors can explore the history of written communication from Egyptian clay tablets, thousands of years ago, to the first Airmail flight from Bath to London in 1912. See the Victorian Post Office and watch three continuous video films including the in-house production entitled 'History of Writing'. Visit the children's activity room, tearoom and shop.
Times: ✱ Open all year, Mon-Sat 11-4.30. Last admission Mar-Oct 4.30; Oct-Mar 4 (Closed Sun, 25-26 Dec & 1 Jan).
Facilities: P (150yds) (no on street parking) 💷 ﻉ (films and computer games for hearing impaired) toilets for disabled shop ✖ (ex guide dogs)

THE BUILDING OF BATH MUSEUM
Countess of Huntingdons Chapel, The Vineyards, The Paragon BA1 5NA
➲ (M4 junct 18 down A46 towards Bath city centre. Take A4, 2nd exit at mini rdbt. Along road on right)
☎ 01225 333895 📠 01225 445473
e-mail: cathryn@bathmuseum.co.uk
This new museum relates the fascinating story of how Georgian Bath was created. 17th century Bath was a medieval market town but in the space of 100 years it was transformed into one of the most beautiful and glamorous cities in Europe. The exhibition depicts elegant society life in "Beau" Nash's spa resort and explains how the houses were constructed. After a visit, the street scene outside seems like an extension of the exhibition. Ring for details of special events such as concerts and lectures.
Times: ✱ Open 15 Feb-1 Dec, Tue-Sun & BHs 10.30-5.
Facilities: P (500mtrs) ﻉ shop ✖ (ex guide dogs) 🚩

HOLBURNE MUSEUM OF ART
Great Pulteney St BA2 4DB
➲ (M4 junct 18 to A4 and follow brown signs)
☎ 01225 466669 📠 01225 333121 ┃2 for 1┃
e-mail: holburne@bath.ac.uk
This jewel in Bath's crown was once the Georgian Sydney Hotel, whose glittering society Jane Austen watched from her house opposite. It displays the treasures collected by Sir William Holbourne: superb English and continental silver, porcelain, maiolica, glass and Renaissance bronzes. Since Sir William's time the collection has been greatly expanded and now includes landscapes by Guardi and Turner, and portraits by Stubbs, Ramsay, Raeburn, Zoffany and Bath's own artists Gainsborough, Hoare, and the Barkers of Bath.
Times: Open mid Feb-mid Dec, Tue-Sat 10-5, Sun 2.30-5.30. (Closed Mon ex group bookings by appointment). **Fee:** ✱ £4 (ch £1.50, pen £3.50, concessions available). Group rates available. **Facilities:** P 💷 ﻉ (lift to 1st floor) shop ✖ (ex guide dogs) 🚩

THE JANE AUSTEN CENTRE NEW
40 Gay St, Queen Square BA1 2NT
➲ (In the heart of Bath by Queen Square)
☎ 01225 443000 📠 01225 443018 ┃2 for 1┃
e-mail: info@janeausten.co.uk
Celebrating Bath's most famous resident, the centre offers a snapshot of life during Regency times and explores how living in this city affected Jane Austen's life and writing. Every September, Bath holds a Jane Austen festival.
Times: Open all year, daily 10-5.30 (Closed 24 & 25 Dec, 1 Jan)
Fee: £4.65 (ch £2.50, pen & student £3.95) **Facilities:** P (50mtrs) ﻉ shop ✖ (ex guide dogs) 🚩

MUSEUM OF BATH AT WORK
Julian Rd BA1 2RH
➲ (from city centre, off Lansdown Rd into Julian Rd. Museum is next to church on right)
☎ 01225 318348 📠 01225 318348 ┃2 for 1┃
e-mail: mobaw@hotmail.com
Two thousand years of Bath's commercial and industrial development are explored with exhibits on 'The Story of Bath Stone', a Bath cabinet makers workshop, a 1914 Horstmann car and a reconstruction of J B Bowllers' engineering and mineral water business. A computer info point is available.
Times: Open all year, Etr-1 Nov, daily 10-5; Nov-Etr, wknds 10.30-5. (Closed 25-26 Dec). **Fee:** ✱ £3.50 (ch, pen & students £2.50). Family ticket £10. **Facilities:** P (0.25m) 💷 ﻉ shop ✖ (ex guide dogs)

The Battle of Trafalgar.
2005 is the 200th anniversary of the sea battle between the British Royal Navy and the French and Spanish navies. 2005 will see a number of events celebrating this important British victory.

MUSEUM OF COSTUME

Bennett St BA1 2QH

➲ (M4 junct 18, follow A46 into Bath. Museum near city centre)

☎ 01225 477785 📠 01225 477743

e-mail: costume_bookings@bathnes.gov.uk

The Museum of Costume is one of the finest collections of fashionable dress in the world, covering the period from the late 16th-century to the present day. It is housed in Bath's famous 18th-century Assembly Rooms designed by John Wood the Younger in 1771. Entrance to the Assembly Rooms is free.

Times: Open all year, daily 10-4.30 (Closed 25 & 26 Dec). **Fee:** ✱ £6 (ch £4). Family ticket £16.50. Combined ticket with Roman Baths, £12 (ch £7). **Facilities:** P (5 mins walk) (park & ride recommended) 💷 ⓓ (audio guides available) toilets for disabled shop ✈ (ex guide dogs) 🍴

NO 1 ROYAL CRESCENT

BA1 2LR

➲ (1st house in Royal Crescent situated above Victoria Avenue & Victoria Park, Charlotte St car park)

☎ 01225 428126 📠 01225 481850

e-mail: no1@bptrust.demon.co.uk

Bath is very much a Georgian city, but most of its houses have naturally altered over the years to suit changing tastes and lifestyles. Built in 1768 by John Wood the Elder, No 1 Royal Crescent has been restored to look as it would have done some 200 years ago. Visitors can see a grand townhouse of the late 18th-century with authentic furniture, paintings and carpets. On the ground floor are the study and dining room and on the first floor a lady's bedroom and drawing room. In the basement a period kitchen and museum shop.

Times: Open 12 Feb-29 Oct, 10.30-5; 30 Oct-27 Nov, 10.30-4. Open BH Mon. Open wknds 3-4, 10-11 Dec (Closed Good Fri). Last admission 30 mins before closing. **Fee:** £4 (concessions £3.50). Family ticket £12. Party 10+ £3 each. Schools £2.50 each

Facilities: P (5 mins walk) (street parking with card £1 per hour) ⓓ (large print handouts, handling items, limited access) shop ✈ (ex guide dogs)

PRIOR PARK LANDSCAPE GARDEN NEW

Ralph Allen Dr BA2 5AH City centre

☎ 01225 833422

This beautiful and intimate 18th century landscape garden was created by local entrepreneur, Ralph Allen, with the help
continued

of Alexander Pope and 'Capability' Brown. With views of Bath, the garden holds many interesting features including a Palladian bridge and three lakes.

Times: Open: Feb-29 Nov, Wed-Mon 11-5.30; 3 Dec-Jan, Fri-Sun 11-dusk. (BH's 11-5.30) **Fee:** £4 (ch £2) **Facilities:** P park & ride ⓓ (Braille, large print guides, designated parking) toilets for disabled

ROMAN BATHS & PUMP ROOM

Abbey Church Yard BA1 1LZ

➲ (M4 junct 18, A46 into city centre)

☎ 01225 477785 📠 01225 477743

e-mail: romanbaths_bookings@bathnes.gov.uk

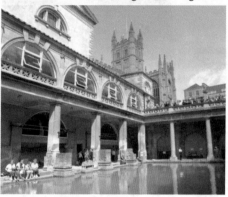

The remains of the Roman baths and temple give a vivid impression of life nearly 2000 years ago. Built next to Britain's only hot spring, the baths served the sick, and the pilgrims visiting the adjacent Temple of Sulis Minerva. Above the Temple Courtyard, the Pump Room became a popular meeting place in the 18th century. The site still flows with natural hot water and no visit is complete without a taste of the famous hot spa water.

Times: Open all year, Mar-Jun & Sep-Oct, daily 9-5; Jul & Aug daily 9am-10pm; Jan-Feb & Nov-Dec, daily 9.30-4.30. (Closed 25 & 26 Dec). Last exit 1hr after closing. **Fee:** ✱ £9 (ch £5). Family ticket £24. Combined ticket with Museum of Costume £12 (ch £7). Disabled visitors free admission to ground floor areas. **Facilities:** P (5 mins walk) (park & ride recommended) ✗ licensed ⓓ (sign language & audio tours) toilets for disabled shop ✈ (ex guide dogs) 🍴

SALLY LUNN'S REFRESHMENT HOUSE & MUSEUM

4 North Pde Passage BA1 1NX

➲ (Centre of Bath, follow signs, next to Bath Abbey)

☎ 01225 461634 📠 01225 447090

e-mail: david@sallylunns.co.uk

This Tudor building is Bath's oldest house and was a popular 17th-century meeting place. The traditional 'Sally Lunn' is similar to a brioche, and it is popularly believed to carry the name of its first maker who came to Bath in 1680. The bun is still served in the restaurant, and the original oven, Georgian cooking range and a collection of baking utensils are displayed in the museum.

Times: Open all year, Museum - Mon-Fri 10-6, Sat 10-5, Sun 11-5. (Closed 25-26 Dec & 1 Jan). **Fee:** ✱ 30p (concessions free). **Facilities:** P (2-3 min walk) (cards required for street parking) 💷 ✗ licensed ⓓ (Braille menu for the blind) shop ✈ (ex guide dogs) 🍴

CASTLE CARY   Map 03 ST63

Hadspen Garden & Nursery

Hadspen House BA7 7NG

➲ (2m SE off A371)

☎ 01749 813707   🖷 01749 813707   **2 for 1**

e-mail: pope@hadspengarden.co.uk

Situated within a 17th-century curved wall, this five acre garden has borders planted with roses and herbaceous plants, many of which have been developed here. Plants grown in the garden are available in the adjoining nursery.
Times: Open 4 Mar-26 Sep, Thu-Sun & BHs 10-5. **Fee:** ✳ £4 (ch 50p). Free admission for wheelchair users. **Facilities:** 🅿 ✖ ♿ garden centre ✖ (ex guide dogs) 🍴

CHARD   Map 03 ST30

Forde Abbey

TA20 4LU

➲ (5m SE of Chard, signposted from A30 and A358)

☎ 01460 221290   🖷 01460 220296

e-mail: forde.abbey@virgin.net

As one of the top gardens in England, Forde Abbey has much to offer keen gardeners. The 30 acres include a colourful bog garden, a walled kitchen garden, cascades, ponds, Ionic temple, rockery, herbaceous borders and much more. The privately owned magnificent 12th century house contains outstanding Mortlake tapestries, spectacularly decorated plaster ceilings and fine furniture and paintings.
Times: Gardens, open all year, daily 10-4.30. House Apr-Oct, Tue-Fri, Sun & BH 12-4. **Fee:** Gardens £5.50 (under 15's free, pen £5). House & Gardens £7.50 (ch free, pen £7). **Facilities:** 🅿 ▦ ✖ licensed ♿ (wheelchair and batricar available) toilets for disabled shop garden centre ✖ 🍴

CLEVEDON   Map 03 ST47

Clevedon Court

Tickenham Rd BS21 6QU

➲ (off B3130 1.5m E of Clevedon)

☎ 01275 872257

Clevedon Court is a remarkably complete manor house of around 1320. Additions have been made in each century, so it has a pleasing variety of styles, with an 18th-century, terraced garden.
Times: Open 27 Mar-29 Sep, Wed-Thu, Sun & BH Mon 2-5. Car park & Gardens will open at 1pm. **Fee:** £5 (ch £2.50). Party 20+ by arrangement. **Facilities:** 🅿 ♿ (access via steps, Braille/large print guide) ✖ 🌿

CRICKET ST THOMAS   Map 03 ST30

The Wildlife Park at Cricket St Thomas

TA20 4DB

➲ (3m E of Chard on A30, follow brown heritage signs. Clearly signposted from M5 junct 25)

☎ 01460 30111   🖷 01460 30817

e-mail: teresa.white2@bourne-leisure.co.uk

The Wildlife Park offers you the chance to see more than 60 species of animals at close quarters. Visitors can learn about what is being done to save endangered species, take a walk through the Lemur Wood, ride on the Safari Train or visit the Children's Farm. During peak season, park mascot Larry the Lemur stars in his own show.
Times: Open all year, daily 10-dusk, last admission 4pm in summer. (Closed 25 Dec). **Facilities:** 🅿 ▦ ✖ licensed ♿ (some steep slopes) toilets for disabled shop ✖ (ex guide dogs) 🍴

DUNSTER   Map 03 SS94

Dunster Castle

TA24 6SL

➲ (3m SE of Minehead, approach from A39. Approx 2m from Dunster Stn)

☎ 01643 821314   🖷 01643 823000

e-mail: wdugen@smtp.ntrust.org.uk

The castle's picturesque appearance is largely due to 19th-century work, but older features can also be seen, the superb 17th-century oak staircase for example. Sub-tropical plants flourish in the 28-acre park and the terraced gardens are noted for exotica such as a giant lemon tree, yuccas, mimosa and palms. The National collection of Strawberry Trees.
Times: Castle: 20 Mar-23 Oct, Sat-Wed 11-5; 24-31 Oct, Sat-Wed 11-4. Garden & Park: Jan-19 Mar & 24 Oct-Dec, daily 11-4; 20 Mar-23 Oct, daily 10-5. Shop: 20 Mar-23 Oct, daily 10-5; 24 Oct-1 Jan & 31 Jan-17 Mar, daily 11-4. **Fee:** ✳ Castle, Garden & Park £6.80 (ch under 16 £3.40). Family ticket £16.80. Garden & Park only £3.70 (ch under 16 £1.60). Family ticket £9. **Facilities:** 🅿 ♿ (Braille & audio guides, large print guides & Batricar) toilets for disabled shop ✖ (ex in park only) 🌿

EAST LAMBROOK   Map 03 ST41

East Lambrook Manor Garden

TA13 5HH

➲ (signed off A303, at South Petherton rdbt)

☎ 01460 240328   🖷 01460 242344   **2 for 1**

e-mail: enquiries@eastlambrook.com

It was the late Margery Fish who created the concept of 'cottage gardening' in the 1940s. Her wonderful Grade I listed gardens are known to garden lovers throughout the world. The gardens now house the National Collection of Geraniums, a specialist plant nursery, a tea shop and art gallery.
Times: Open Feb-Oct, daily 10-5. **Fee:** ✳ £3.95 (ch £1 & pen £3.50). Group rate available. **Facilities:** 🅿 ▦ ♿ (gardens partly accessible) shop garden centre ✖ (ex guide dogs) 🍴

FARLEIGH HUNGERFORD   Map 03 ST85

Farleigh Hungerford Castle

BA2 7RS

➲ (3.5m W of Trowbridge on A366)

☎ 01225 754026

Set in a picturesque valley, this castle hides many secrets and a sinister past. An audio tour reveals all.
Times: Open all year, Apr-Jun & Sep, daily 10-5; Jul-Aug, daily 10-6; Oct-Mar, Sat-Sun 10-4. (Closed 24-26 Dec & 1 Jan). **Fee:** ✳ £2.80 (ch £1.40, concessions £2.10). Prices & opening times relate to 2004, for further details phone or log onto www.english-heritage.org.uk/visits **Facilities:** 🅿 ♿ shop ✖ ⛺

GLASTONBURY   Map 03 ST43

FLEET AIR ARM MUSEUM
See advert on opposite page, see full entry under YEOVILTON.

GLASTONBURY ABBEY
Abbey Gatehouse, Magdalene St BA6 9EL
➲ (Located on A361 between Frome & Taunton. M5 junct 23 then take A39 to Glastonbury)
☎ 01458 832267   🖷 01458 832267
e-mail: info@glastonburyabbey.com

Few places in Britain are as rich in myth and legend as Glastonbury. Tradition maintains that the impressive ruins mark the birth place of Christianity in Britain. Joseph of Arimathea is said to have founded a chapel here in AD61, planting his staff in the ground where it flowered both at Christmas and Easter. Later, it is said, King Arthur and Guinevere were buried here, and the abbey has been a place of pilgrimage since the Middle Ages. The present abbey ruins date mostly from the 12th and 13th centuries, fell into decay after the Dissolution. The display area contains artefacts and a model of the Abbey as it might have been in 1539. During the summer months meet Brother Thomas, who will tell you how the monks used to live. Two wildlife areas add some seasonal colour.
Times: Open all year, daily, Jun-Aug 9-6; Sep-May 9.30-6 or dusk, whichever is the earliest. Dec-Feb open at 10am. (Closed 25 Dec).
Fee: £4 (ch 5-15 £1.50, pen & students £3.50). Family ticket £10 (2ad+2ch) **Facilities:** 🅿 (charged) 💻 ♿ (no access in Lady Chapel,audio tape,deaf loop,wheelchairs) toilets for disabled shop ◼

KINGSDON   Map 03 ST52

LYTES CARY MANOR
TA11 7HU
➲ (off A303, signposted from Padimore rdbt at junction of A303 & A37, take A372)
☎ 01458 224471   🖷 01458 224471   **2 for 1**
Fine medieval manor house and delightful 14th-century chapel, surrounded by gardens with an enchanting mixture of formality and simplicity. Much of the present house was built in the 16th century although the oldest part, the chapel, dates from 1343. The Great Hall was a 15th-century addition. Unfortunately the gardens did not survive, but the present formal gardens are being restocked with plants that were commonly grown at the time of building, according to the 'Lytes Cary Herbal'-a manuscript still on display within the property. High yew topiary hedges enclose large borders and hidden paths.
Times: Open Apr-Oct, Sun, Mon, Wed & Fri 11-5. **Fee:** ✱ £5 (ch £2). Garden only £3, ch £1. **Facilities:** 🅿 ♿ (Braille guide, scented plants) toilets for disabled ✖ (ex guide dogs) ♨

MONTACUTE   Map 03 ST41

MONTACUTE HOUSE
TA15 6XP
➲ (off A3088)
☎ 01935 823289   🖷 01935 826921   **2 for 1**
e-mail: wmogen@smtp.ntrust.org.uk
Set amidst formal gardens, Montacute House was built by Sir Edward Phelips. He was a successful lawyer, and became Speaker of the House of Commons in 1604. Inside there are decorated ceilings, ornate fireplaces, heraldic glass and fine wood panelling. The Long Gallery displays a permanent collection of Tudor and Jacobean portraits from the National Portrait Gallery in London. Montacute has been used as the setting for successful films such as *Sense and Sensibility*.
Times: House: 19 Mar-Oct, Wed-Mon 11-5. Garden: Jan-18 Mar & 3 Nov-Dec Wed-Sun 11-4; 19 Mar-Oct, Wed-Mon 11-6. Shop: 3-18 Mar & 3 Nov-19 Dec, Wed-Sun 11-4; 19 Mar-Oct, Wed-Mon 11-5.30. Restaurant: 5-14 Mar & 5 Nov-19 Dec, Fri-Sun 11-4; 19 Mar-Oct, Wed-Sun 11-5.30. **Fee:** ✱ House, Garden & Park £6.90 (ch £3.40). Family ticket £16. Garden & Park only £3.70 (ch £1.70), 3 Nov-Mar 2005, £2, ch £1. **Facilities:** 🅿 💻 ✖ licensed ♿ (Braille guide 3 manual wheelchairs) toilets for disabled shop garden centre ✖ (ex in park) ♨

MUCHELNEY   Map 03 ST42

MUCHELNEY ABBEY
TA10 0DQ
☎ 01458 250664   🖷 01458 253842
The monastery was first established at Muchelney by Ine, a 7th-century king of Wessex. It did not survive the Viking invasions, but the abbey was re-founded about AD950 and lasted for nearly six centuries. The present remains date largely from the 12th-century. The best preserved feature of the site today is the Abbot's lodging, which had only just been completed in 1539 when the abbey was surrendered to Henry VIII.
Times: Open Apr-Jun & Sep, daily 10-5; Jul-Aug, daily 10-6; Oct, daily 10-4. **Fee:** ✱ £2.50 (ch £1.30, concessions £1.90). Prices & opening times relate to 2004, for further details phone or log onto www.english-heritage.org.uk/visits **Facilities:** 🅿 ♿ shop ✖ ✿

NETHER STOWEY   Map 03 ST13

COLERIDGE COTTAGE
35 Lime St TA5 1NQ
➲ (At W end of Nether Stowey, on S Side of A39, 8m W of Bridgwater)
☎ 01278 732662
It was in this small cottage that Coleridge was most inspired as a poet and here that he wrote *The Rime of the Ancient Mariner*, part of *Christabel*, *Frost at Midnight* and "Kubla Khan". The Coleridge family moved to Nether Stowey in 1797 and became friendly with the Wordsworths who lived nearby.
Times: Open Apr-Sep, Tue-Thu & Sun 2-5. **Fee:** ✱ £3.20 (ch £1.60). **Facilities:** 🅿 500yds ♿ (Steps to entrance,Braille & large print guides) ✖ ♨

> If an attraction name appears in *italics*, details have not been confirmed for 2005.

NUNNEY   Map 03 ST74

NUNNEY CASTLE
➲ (3.5m SW of Frome, off A361)
Built in 1373, and supposedly modelled on France's Bastille, this crenellated manor house has one of the deepest moats in England. It was ruined by Parliamentarian forces in the Civil War.
Times: Open any reasonable time. **Facilities:** ☒ ✿

SPARKFORD   Map 03 ST62

HAYNES MOTOR MUSEUM
BA22 7LH
➲ (from A303 follow A359 road towards Castle Cary, the museum is clearly signposted)
☎ 01963 440804 ▤ 01963 441004
e-mail: info@haynesmotormuseum.co.uk
Spectacular collection of historic cars, motorcycles and motoring memorabilia. Vehicles range from a 1903 Oldsmobile to sports cars of the 50s and 60s and modern day classics. Also at the Museum is a 70 seat video cinema, the Hall of Motorsports, a millennium hall and a picnic area and children's adventure playground.
Times: Open all year, Mar-Oct, daily 9.30-5.30; Nov-Feb, 10-4.30. (Closed 24-26 Dec & 1 Jan). **Fee:** ✱ Adult £6.50 (ch £3.50, concessions £5). Family £8.50 (1 ad & 1 ch), £19 (2 ad & 3 ch). **Facilities:** ▣ ✗ licensed ☒ (ramps & loan wheelchairs available) toilets for disabled shop ✈ (ex guide dogs & in grounds) ▰

STOKE ST GREGORY   Map 03 ST32

WILLOW & WETLANDS VISITOR CENTRE
Meare Green Court TA3 6HY
➲ (between North Curry & Stoke St Gregory, signed from A361 & A378)
☎ 01823 490249 ▤ 01823 490814   `2 for 1`
e-mail: phcoate@globalnet.co.uk
The centre is owned and run by Somerset Basketmakers and willow growers P H Coate & Son. The environmental exhibition gives a fascinating insight into the Somerset Levels and Moors. Guided tours are available.
Times: Open all year, Mon-Fri 9-5 (guided tours 10-4), Sat (no tours) 9-5. Closed Sun. **Fee:** ✱ Admission free, tour charge: £3.50 (ch £1.75, pen £3). Family ticket £8. Credit cards accepted if total admission price exceeds £10. **Facilities:** ▣ ▰ ☒ (some areas of gardens accessible) toilets for disabled shop ▰

STOKE-SUB-HAMDON   Map 03 ST41

STOKE-SUB-HAMDON PRIORY
North St TA4 6QP
➲ (between A303 & A3088)   `FREE`
☎ 01985 843600
A complex of buildings, begun in the 14th century for the priests of the Chantry Chapel of St Nicholas (now destroyed).
Times: Open 27 Mar-Oct, daily 10-6 or dusk if earlier.
Facilities: ▣ (5mtrs) ☒ (Braille guides/large print guides) ▭ (on road parking only) ✿

Directions are provided
by the attractions.

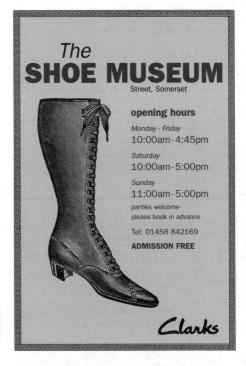

STREET   Map 03 ST43

THE SHOE MUSEUM
C & J Clark Ltd, High St BA16 0YA

➲ (M5 Junct 23, take A39 to Street, follow signs for Clarks Village)

☎ 01458 842169   🖨 01458 442226   FREE

The museum is in the oldest part of the shoe factory set up by Cyrus and James Clark in 1825. It contains shoes from Roman times to the present, buckles, engravings, fashion plates, machinery, hand tools and advertising material.
Times: Open all year, Mon-Fri 10-4.45, Sat 10-1.30 & 2-5, Sun 11-1.30 & 2-5. (Closed 10 days over Xmas) **Facilities:** 🅿 & (access weekdays only) shop ✖ (ex guide dogs)

See advertisement on page 207

TAUNTON   Map 03 ST22

HESTERCOMBE GARDENS
Cheddon Fitzpaine TA2 8LG

➲ (3m N of Taunton near Cheddon Fitzpaine. Signposted from all main roads)

☎ 01823 413923   🖨 01823 413747

e-mail: info@hestercombegardens.com

There are three period gardens to enjoy at Hestercombe: the 40-acre Georgian pleasure grounds with woodland walks, temples, Witch House and Great Cascade; the Victorian terrace and newly established Victorian shrubbery; and the Edwardian gardens, where the work of Gertrude Jekyll and architect Edwin Lutyens are shown off to full effect.
Times: Open daily, 10-6 (last admission 5). **Fee:** ✱ £5.20 (ch 5-15 £1.30, pen £4.90). Family ticket £11.50 **Facilities:** 🅿 💺 ✖ licensed & (gardens partially accessible) toilets for disabled shop garden centre (open Apr-Oct) 🍴

TINTINHULL   Map 03 ST41

TINTINHULL HOUSE GARDEN
BA22 9PZ

➲ (0.5m S off A303. Follow signs to Tintinhull village, garden is well signposted from village)

☎ 01935 822545   🖨 01935 826357

e-mail: floyd.summerhayes@nationaltrust.org.uk

An attractive, mainly 17th-century farmhouse with a Queen Anne façade, it stands in two acres of beautiful formal gardens. The gardens were largely created by Mrs Reiss, who gave the property to the National Trust in 1953.
Times: Open 24 Mar-Sep, Wed-Sun & BH Mons 12-6. Tea room: as garden, 12-5.30 **Fee:** ✱ £4.20 (ch £2.10). **Facilities:** 🅿 💺 ✖ (ex guide dogs) 🐾

WASHFORD   Map 03 ST04

CLEEVE ABBEY
TA23 0PS

➲ (0.25m S of A39)

☎ 01984 640377

This 13th-century monastic site features some of the finest cloister buildings in England; medieval wall paintings, a mosaic tiled floor and an interesting exhibition.
Times: Open Apr-Jun & Sep, daily 10-5; Jul-Aug, daily 10-6; Oct, daily 10-4 (Closed Nov-Mar) **Fee:** ✱ £3.20 (ch £1.60, concessions £2.40). Prices & opening times relate to 2004, for further details phone or log onto www.english-heritage.org.uk/visits **Facilities:** 🅿 & shop ♯

TROPIQUARIA ANIMAL AND ADVENTURE PARK
TA23 0QB

➲ (on A39, between Williton and Minehead)

☎ 01984 640688   🖨 01984 641105

e-mail: office@tropiquaria.co.uk

Housed in a 1930s BBC transmitting station, the main hall has been converted into an indoor jungle with a 15-foot waterfall, tropical plants and free-flying birds. (Snakes, lizards, iguanas, spiders, toads and terrapins are caged!) Downstairs is the submarine crypt with local and tropical marine life. Other features include landscaped gardens, the Shadowstring Puppet Theatre, and 'Wireless in the West' museum. Also two new full size pirate adventure ships are moored on the front lawn accessible to pirates of all ages!.The park has an indoor playcastle for adventure and fun whatever the weather.
Times: ✱ Open Apr-Sep, daily 10-6 (last entry 4.30); Oct daily 11-5 (last entry 4); Nov-Mar wknds 11-4 (last entry 3). **Facilities:** 🅿 💺 & (ramp to pirate galleon & indoor castle) toilets for disabled shop ✖ (ex guide dogs) 🍴

WELLS   Map 03 ST54

THE BISHOP'S PALACE
Henderson Rooms BA5 2PD

➲ (next to cathedral off the Market Sq)

☎ 01749 678691   🖨 01749 678691

Close to the cathedral is the moated bishop's palace. The early part of the palace, the bishop's chapel and the ruins of the banqueting hall date from the 13th century and the undercroft remains virtually unchanged from this time. There are several state rooms and a long gallery which houses portraits of former Bishops. Events include a Living History re-enactment.
Times: ✱ Open Apr-Oct, Tue-Fri & BHs; daily in Aug 10.30-5, Sun 1-5. Gates close at exactly 6pm. **Facilities:** 🅿 (100yds) 💺 ✖ licensed & (free use of electric wheelchair) shop

WESTON-SUPER-MARE   Map 03 ST36

THE HELICOPTER MUSEUM
The Heliport, Locking Moor Rd BS24 8PP
➲ (outskirts of town on A371, nr M5 junct 21)
☎ 01934 635227 📠 01934 645230
e-mail: office@helimuseum.fsnet.co.uk

The world's largest rotary-wing collection and the only helicopter museum in Britain. More than 70 helicopters and autogyros are on display - including examples from France, Germany, Poland, Russia and the United States, from 1935 to the present day - with displays of models, engines and other components explaining the history and development of the rotocraft. Special events include 'Open Cockpit Days', when visitors can learn more about how the helicopter works.
Times: Open all year, Nov-Mar Wed-Sun 10-4.30. Apr-Oct 10-5.30. (closed 24-26 Dec & 1 Jan) Open daily during Etr & Summer school hols 10-6.30. **Fee:** ✱ £4.95 (ch under 5 free, ch 5-16 £2.95, pen £3.95). Family ticket (2ad+2ch) £13, (2ad+3ch) £15. Party 12+.
Facilities: 🅿 💻 ♿ (large print and Braille information sheet) toilets for disabled shop 🛒

NORTH SOMERSET MUSEUM
Burlington St BS23 1PR
☎ 01934 621028 📠 01934 612526
e-mail: museum.service@n-somerset.gov.uk

This museum, housed in the former workshops of the Edwardian Gaslight Company, has displays on the seaside holiday, an old chemist's shop, a dairy and Victorian pavement mosaics. Adjoining the museum is Clara's Cottage, a Westonian home of the 1900s with period kitchen, parlour, bedroom and back yard. One of the rooms has an additional display of Peggy Nisbet dolls. Other displays include wildlife gallery, Mendip minerals, mining and local archaeology, costume, ceramics and cameras.
Times: Open all year: Mon-Sat 10-4.30, (Closed 25-26 Dec & 1 Jan).
Fee: £3.50 (ch free when accompanied by an adult, pen £2.50)
Facilities: 🅿 (800yds) (some disabled parking outside museum) 💻 ♿ toilets for disabled shop 🐕 (ex guide dogs) 🛒

WOOKEY HOLE   Map 03 ST54

WOOKEY HOLE CAVES & PAPERMILL
BA5 1BB
➲ (M5 junct 22 follow signs via A38 & A371, from Bristol & Bath A39 to Wells then 2m to Wookey Hole)
☎ 01749 672243 📠 01749 677749 **2 for 1**
e-mail: witch@wookey.co.uk

Some of Europe's most spectacular caves, legendary haunts of the Witch of Wookey. Much more to see and do whatever the weather: authentic Victorian Pier attractions, Britain's last surviving handmade paper mill, and spectacular light and sound show.
Times: Open all year, Nov-Mar, daily 10.30-5.30 (last admission 4pm); Apr-Oct, daily 10-7 (last admission 5pm) **Fee:** ✱ £8.80 (ch 4-14, concessions £5.50, under 4's free). **Facilities:** 🅿 🗙 licensed ♿ (papermill only accessible) toilets for disabled shop 🐕 (ex guide dogs) 🛒

YEOVILTON   Map 03 ST52

FLEET AIR ARM MUSEUM
Royal Naval Air Station BA22 8HT
➲ (on B3151, just off A303)
☎ 01935 840565 📠 01935 842630
e-mail: info@fleetairarm.com

The Fleet Air Arm Museum is a national museum in a rural setting with an area the size of a football pitch under cover. It is the only British museum sited next to an operational military airfield. From the viewing galleries you may see some of the Royal Navy's aircraft flying. The museum shows over 40 aircraft within the many exhibitions throughout the four large halls. 'Leading edge' tells the story of aircraft from the early biplane to Concorde and the Sea Harrier. Innovative touch screen displays shows how aircraft fly and tell the stories of the aircraft and the men who flew them.
Times: Open all year, daily (ex 24-26 Dec) 10-5.30 (4.30 Nov-Mar).
Facilities: 🅿 💻 🗙 licensed ♿ (wheelchairs available) toilets for disabled shop 🐕 (ex guide dogs) 🛒

See advertisement on page 207

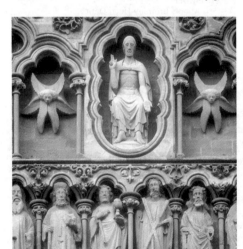

Above: Wells Cathedral

STAFFORDSHIRE

EVENTS & FESTIVALS

January
22nd Manchester Dog Show, Staffordshire
   Show Ground
tbc Winter Beer & Wine Festival, Lichfield

June
1st-2nd Staffordshire County Show,
   County Showground
17th-19th Lichfield Folk Festival,
   (various venues)

July
tbc FUSE, the Event in a Tent,
   Beacon Park, Lichfield
tbc Lichfield International Arts Festival,
   (various venues)
tbc Lichfield Real Ale, Jazz & Blues Festival
tbc Stafford Festival, Stafford

September
5th Abbots Bromley Horn Dance,
   throughout village
10th-11th The Early National
   Chrysanthemum Show, Staffordshire
   County Showground (provisional)

November
4th-5th The Late National Chrysanthemum
   Show, Staffordshire County Showground
   (provisional)

Above: Peak District National Park

ALTON   Map 07 SK04

ALTON TOWERS
ST10 4DB
➲ (Travelling North M1 junct 23a or M6 junct 15)
☎ 08705 204060   📠 01538 704097
e-mail: info@alton-towers.com

Alton Towers is a fantastic day out for all the family. With
world first rides and attractions as well as some beautiful
gardens, this is more than just a theme park. New for 2004 -
Spinball Whizzer, a spinner coaster, as well as The Flume, in
which visitors now travel in red bath tubs, rather than rustic
logs.

Times: Open 12 Mar-30 Oct **Fee:** ✱ From £20 (ch fr £17)
Facilities: 🅿 (charged) 💭 ✗ licensed & (disabled guest guide
books) toilets for disabled shop ✖ (ex guide dogs) ☎

BIDDULPH   Map 07 SJ85

BIDDULPH GRANGE GARDEN
Grange Rd ST8 7SD
➲ (Access from A527 (Tunstall-Congleton Road).
Entrance on Grange Road 0.5m N of Biddulph)
☎ 01782 517999   📠 01782 510624
e-mail: biddulphgrange@nationaltrust.org.uk

This exciting and rare survival of a high Victorian garden has
undergone extensive restoration. Conceived by James
Bateman, the fifteen acres are divided into a number of
smaller gardens which were designed to house specimens
from his extensive plant collection.

Times: Open mid Mar-Oct, Wed-Fri 12-5.30. Sat-Sun & BH Mon
11-5.30 (last admission 5.30 or dusk if earlier); early Nov-mid Dec,
Sat-Sun 12-4 or dusk. **Fee:** ✱ £4.80 (ch £2.40) Mar-Oct. Family ticket
£12. £2 (ch £1) Nov-Dec. Family ticket £5. **Facilities:** 🅿 💭 & (not
suitable for people with mobility problems) shop ✖ (ex guide dogs &
hearing dogs) 🐾 ☎

BURTON-UPON-TRENT   Map 08 SK22

THE BASS MUSEUM
PO Box 220, Horninglow St DE14 1YQ
➲ (off A38 at Burton-on-Trent, well signposted
through town)
☎ 0845 600 0598   📠 01283 513613   **2 for 1**
e-mail: enquiries@coorsvisitorcentre.com

The Coors Visitor Centre houses The Museum of Brewing
and offers a unique blend of historic galleries and living
heritage, including shire horse stables, authentic cooperage,
vintage vehicle collection and working stationary steam
engine. England's oldest micro-brewery is also based here,
built in 1920 with vessels dating back to 1830. It is here that
the Museum Brewing Company produces and packages for
Coors Brewers. End the day appropriately in the bar, or visit
the restaurant or beer and gift shop.

Times: Open all year, daily 10-5. Last admission 4. (Closed 25-26 Dec
& 1 Jan). **Fee:** £5.50 (ch over 6yrs £3, pen £4). Family ticket £16.50 (2
ad+3 ch); admission includes complimentary drink. **Facilities:** 🅿 💭
✗ licensed & (lift) toilets for disabled shop ✖ (ex guide dogs) ☎

CHEDDLETON Map 07 SJ95
CHEDDLETON FLINT MILL
Beside Caldon Canal, Leek Rd ST13 7HL
➲ (3m S of Leek on A520)
☎ 01782 502907 **FREE**

Twin water-wheels on the River Churnet drive flint-grinding pans in the two mills. Museum collection of machinery used in the preparation of materials for the ceramic industry. This includes a 100 HP Robey horizontal steam engine, model Newcomen beam engine, edge-runner mill, and the narrow boat Vienna, moored on the Caldon Canal. Display panels explain the processes of winning and treating clays, stone and flint for the pottery industry.
Times: Open all year, Sat & Sun 2-5, Mon-Fri 10-5 (by arrangement). Phone to check **Facilities:** 🅿 ⚿ toilets for disabled

CHURNET VALLEY RAILWAY
The Station ST13 7EE
➲ (3m S from Leek, 3m N from Cellarhead along the A520)
☎ 01538 360522 📠 01538 361848 **2 for 1**
e-mail: mgt@cheddcvr.freeserve.co.uk
The Churnet Valley Railway runs through the hidden countryside between Cheddleton, with its grade II Victorian station, and Froghall, with the newly built station and Canal Wharf. The journey incorporates Consall, which has a sleepy rural station and nature reserve, and Leekbrook with one of the longest tunnels on a preserved railway. 2-for-1 voucher is not valid on Special Event days.
Times: Open every Sun, Mar-mid Oct; Wed & Sat, Jun-Aug; Diesel trains every Tue & Thu in Aug & all BH's. **Fee:** ✱ Return ticket £7 (ch £4, pen £6). **Facilities:** 🅿 ⚿ (ramps) toilets for disabled shop 🍴

HALFPENNY GREEN Map 07 SO89
HALFPENNY GREEN VINEYARDS
DY7 5EP
➲ (0.5m off B4176 Dudley to Telford road)
☎ 01384 221122 📠 01384 221101
e-mail: enquiries@
halfpenny-green-vineyards.co.uk
Using German, French and hybrid varieties that can prosper even in the poorest British summer, this vineyard offers "The complete English wine experience." This includes a self-guided vineyard trail as well as guided tours, wine-tasting, a craft centre and a visitor centre. Visitors can purchase wines
continued

with personalised labels for special occasions. Coarse fishing is also available.
Times: Open all year, daily 10.30-5. **Facilities:** 🅿 ⚿ ✗ licensed ⚿ toilets for disabled shop 🍴 (ex guide dogs) 🍴

HIMLEY Map 07 SO89
HIMLEY HALL & PARK
DY3 4DF
➲ (off A449, on B4176)
☎ 01384 817817 📠 01384 817818
e-mail: himley.hall@dudley.gov.uk
The extensive parkland offers a range of attractions, including a nine-hole golf course and coarse fishing. The hall is open to the public when exhibitions are taking place. Permanent orienteering course, a charge is made for the maps. Guided tours at the hall available by prior arrangement. The Hall is available for private hire. There are also a large variety of outdoor events and concerts.
Times: Open Hall: early Apr-mid Sep, 2-5. (Closed Mon ex BH). Park open all year. **Fee:** ✱ Free admission except for special events **Facilities:** 🅿 (charged) ⚿ ⚿ toilets for disabled 🍴 (ex guide dogs & in park)

LEEK Map 07 SJ95
BLACKBROOK ZOOLOGICAL PARK NEW
Winkhill ST13 7QR off the A523
➲ (Leek to Ashbourne Rd)
☎ 01538 308293 📠 01538 308293
e-mail: enquiries@
blackbrookzoologicalpark.co.uk
Set in the Staffordshire Moorlands, Blackbrook Zoological Park has a large and varied collection of some of the most rare and endangered species to be found in the world. Included is the largest collection of wildfowl in the British Isles, as well as a number of aviaries containing exotic birds like cranes, flamingos and vultures. There are also plenty of mammals, including lemurs, tapir, and marmots. Other areas include the children's farm with donkeys, goats and rabbits, an aquarium, a tropical area, and a new exhibit focusing on Sulcata Tortoises. Blackbrook is heavily involved in many conservation breeding programs.
Times: Open daily 10.30-5.30; Winter 10.30-dusk **Fee:** ✱ £6.50 (ch £4, pen £5.50) **Facilities:** 🅿 ⚿ ⚿ (fully accessible) toilets for disabled shop 🍴 🍴

LICHFIELD Map 07 SK10
ERASMUS DARWIN HOUSE
Beacon St WS13 7AD
➲ (signposted to Lichfield Cathedral. Access by foot through cathedral close, at West End)
☎ 01543 306260 📠 01543 306261 **2 for 1**
e-mail: erasmus.d@virgin.net
The House is dedicated to Erasmus Darwin, the grandfather of Charles Darwin, and a talented doctor, inventor, philosopher, poet and founder member of the Lunar Society. A resident of Lichfield for more than 20 years, the displays are contained within his beautiful 18th-century home, and recreate the story of Erasmus' life, ideas and inventions, through period rooms, audio visual and interactive displays.
Times: Open Apr-Sep: Tue-Sun noon-5, Oct-Mar: Sat & Sun noon-5. Last admission 4.15. **Fee:** ✱ £2.50 (concessions £2). Family ticket (2ad & 2ch) £6. **Facilities:** 🅿 (200mtrs) ⚿ (audio tour) toilets for disabled shop 🍴 (ex guide dogs)

LICHFIELD CATHEDRAL

WS13 7LD

➲ (signposted from all major roads and within city A38, A5, A461 & A51)

☎ 01543 306240 & 306100   🖹 01543 306109

e-mail: enquiries@lichfield-cathedral.org

The Cathedral's three spires, known as the Ladies of the Vale, dominate the landscape. The first cathedral here was founded in AD700 to house the shrine of St Chad. The present building, with its elaborate carvings, has been much restored since it was attacked during the Civil War. Among its treasures are an 8th-century illuminated manuscript, the St Chad Gospels and a collection of modern silver. Many musical events take place here.

Times: Open daily 7.45-6.30. **Fee:** Suggested donation of £4 for each adult visitor. **Facilities:** P (200mtrs) (no parking ex disabled in close) 🍽 ✗ licensed ৬ (touch & hearing centre for blind) toilets for disabled shop ✖ (ex guide/hearing dogs)

LICHFIELD HERITAGE CENTRE

Market Square WS13 6LG

➲ (situated on Market Sq in city centre, easily accessible from A38, A5 and A51)

☎ 01543 256611   🖹 01543 414749

e-mail: info@lichfieldheritage.org.uk

A colourful new exhibition, 'The Lichfield Story' gives a vivid account of Lichfield's rich and varied history over 2000 years. It is the home to the Staffordshire Millennium Embroideries which are displayed within their own gallery. In addition, the Exhibition houses fine examples of City, Diocesan and Regimental silver, ancient Charters and archives. Two audio visual presentations, a Family Trail and for younger children a Mouse Hole Trail provide interest and fun for all the family as they tour the Exhibition.

Times: ✱ Open all year, daily 10-5, Sun 10.30-5. Last admission 4. (Closed Xmas & New Year) **Facilities:** P (200yds) 🍽 ৬ (lift to first floor) toilets for disabled shop ✖ (ex guide dogs) 🍽

SAMUEL JOHNSON BIRTHPLACE MUSEUM

Breadmarket St WS13 6LG

➲ (located in city centre market place)

☎ 01543 264972   🖹 01543 414779

e-mail: sjmuseum@lichfield.gov.uk

Dr Samuel Johnson, author of the famous English dictionary of 1755, lexicographer, poet, critic, biographer & personality. One of England's greatest writers, Dr Johnson was born in this house in 1709. The birthplace now houses a museum dedicated to his extraordinary life, work and personality. Five floors of exhibits featuring period room settings, introductory video and personal items owned by Johnson, his family and his famous friends.

Times: Open daily Apr-Sep 10.30-4.30; Oct-Mar 12-4.30. Last admission 4. **Fee:** £2.50 (ch 5-6yrs £1, concessions, students & unwaged £2). Family ticket £6 (2ad + 4ch) **Facilities:** P (500yds) ৬ (large print text literature, induction loop system) shop ✖ (ex guide dogs)

> If an attraction name appears in *italics*, details have not been confirmed for 2005.

SHUGBOROUGH   Map 07 SJ92

SHUGBOROUGH ESTATE

ST17 0XB

➲ (6m E of Stafford off A513, signposted from M6 junct 13)

☎ 01889 881388   🖹 01889 881323

e-mail: shugborough.promotions@staffordshire.gov.uk

Set on the edge of Cannock Chase, Shugborough is the magnificent 900-acre seat of the Earls of Lichfield. The 18th-century mansion house contains fine collections of ceramics, silver, paintings and French furniture. Part of the house is still lived in by the Lichfield family. Visitors can enjoy the Grade I listed historic garden and a unique collection of neo-classical monuments. Other attractions include the museum and the original servants' quarters, the laundry, kitchens, brewhouse and coachhouses which have all been restored and are fully operational. Shugborough Park Farm is a Georgian farmstead with an agricultural museum, working corn mill and rare breeds centre.

Times: Open 27 Mar-26 Sep, daily (ex Mon, but open BH Mon) 11-5. Sun only during Oct. Site open all year to pre-booked parties. **Facilities:** P (charged) 🍽 ✗ licensed ৬ (step climber for wheelchairs, 2 Batricars) toilets for disabled shop ✖ (ex guide dogs & in parkland) 🌲 🍽

STAFFORD   Map 07 SJ92

SHIRE HALL GALLERY

Market Square ST16 2LD

➲ (M6 junct 13, follow signs to Stafford town centre & gallery is signed from there).

☎ 01785 278345   🖹 02785 278327

e-mail: shirehallgallery@staffordshire.gov.uk

A fine gallery housed in the 18th-century Shire Hall - one of Staffordshire's most magnificent buildings. It holds exhibitions of contemporary arts, contains historic courtrooms and a Crafts Council selected craft shop.

Times: ✱ Open all year Mon-Sat, 9.30-5. Gallery closes for exhibition changes and at BHs, please call for further details. **Facilities:** P (5 mins walk) ✗ ৬ toilets for disabled shop ✖ (ex guide dogs) 🍽

STOKE-ON-TRENT   Map 07 SJ84

CERAMICA

Market Place, Burslem ST6 3DS

➲ (exit M6 junct 15/16 take A500 leave at A4527 (signposted Tunstall). After 0.5m right onto B5051 for Burslem. Ceramica is in Old Town Hall in centre of town.)

☎ 01782 832001   🖹 01782 823300   **2 for 1**

e-mail: info@ceramicauk.com

A unique experience for all the family, Ceramica is housed in the Old Town Hall in the centre of Burslem, Mother Town of the Potteries. Explore the hands-on activities in Bizarreland, and learn how clay is transformed into china. Dig into history with the time team and take a magic carpet ride over the town. Discover the past, present and future of ceramics with the interactive displays in the Pavillions. Explore the Memory Bank and read the local news on Ceramica TV.

Times: Open Mon-Sat 9.30-5, Sun 10.30-4.30. For Xmas opening please telephone. **Fee:** ✱ £3.75, (concessions £2.50, under 4's free). Family ticket (2ad+2ch) £10. Group of 12 £2.50 per person. **Facilities:** P (charged) ৬ (ramps, lift to all floors, tactile displays) toilets for disabled shop ✖ (ex guide dogs) 🍽

GLADSTONE WORKING POTTERY MUSEUM

Uttoxeter Rd, Longton ST3 1PQ

➲ (M6 junct 15, follow A500 to A50 then follow brown heritage signs. From M1 follow A50 westbound then follow brown signs)

☎ 01782 319232 📠 01782 598640

e-mail: gladstone@stoke.gov.uk

Located at the heart of the Potteries, Gladstone Pottery Museum is the last remaining Victorian Pottery industry. Whilst touring the original factory building discover what it was like for the men, women and children to live and work in a potbank during the era of the coal firing bottle ovens. In original workshops working potters can be found demonstrating traditional pottery skills. There are also lots of opportunities for you to have a go at pottery making, throw your own pot on the potters wheel, make china flowers and decorate pottery items to take home. Also explore Flushed with Pride, dedicated to the story of the development of the toilet, and The Tile Gallery, a fine collection which traces the development of decorative tiles.

Times: Open all year, daily 10-5 (last admission 4pm). Limited opening Xmas & New Year. **Fee:** £4.95 (ch £3.50, students & pen £3.95). Family ticket £14 (2ad & 3ch 4-16yrs). Passport ticket available annual admission to Gladstone Pottery Museum £7.50 (concessions £6.50), Family £16. **Facilities:** 🅿 💷 ✗ licensed ♿ (Electric buggy available to loan) toilets for disabled shop ✖ (ex guide dogs) 📧

ROYAL DOULTON VISITOR CENTRE

Nile St, Burslem ST6 2AJ

➲ (M6 junct 15 from S or 16 from N. Join A500 leaving at exit for Tunstall A527, follow tourist signs)

☎ 01782 292434 📠 01782 292424

e-mail: visitor@royal-doulton.com

The centre has extensive displays of both current products and out of production pieces together with ranges from the museum tracing the history of Royal Doulton. Live demonstrations showing the skill and craftsmanship in the creation and hand painting of figurines. Behind the scenes look at the working factory weekdays only, prior booking advised.

Times: ✱ Open all year, Mon-Sat 9.30-5, Sun 10.30-4.30. Factory tours by advance booking Mon-Fri 10.30-2 (1.30 Fri). (Closed Xmas week). No tours during factory holidays. **Facilities:** 🅿 💷 ♿ toilets for disabled shop ✖ (ex guide dogs) 📧

SPODE

Church St ST4 1BX

➲ (M6 junct 15/A500 to Stoke. Ignore city centre signs. Turn left at Stoke rdbt, follow brown tourist signs)

☎ 01782 744011 📠 01782 744012

e-mail: visitorcentre@spode.co.uk

Spode is the oldest English pottery company still on its original site. Here Josiah Spode first perfected the formula for fine bone china. The Spode site houses a restaurant, factory shops, concession outlets, and a visitors centre with exhibits on the history and heritage of the ceramics industry. Fully guided factory tours are available, pre-booking essential.

Times: ✱ Visitor Centre, Museum, Factory Shops, concessions & licensed restaurant, Mon-Sat 9-5, Sun 10-4. Factory Tours by prior appointment weekdays only, not available during factory closures-please ring for details. **Facilities:** 🅿 (charged) ✗ licensed ♿ (ramps) toilets for disabled shop ✖ (ex guide dogs) 📧

THE POTTERIES MUSEUM & ART GALLERY

Bethesda St, Hanley ST1 3DW

➲ (M6 junct 15/16 take A500 to Stoke-on-Trent. Follow signs for city centre (Hanley), Cultural Quarter & The Potteries Museum)

☎ 01782 232323 📠 01782 232500

e-mail: museums@stoke.gov.uk

The history of the Potteries under one roof, including a dazzling display of the world's finest collection of Staffordshire ceramics. Other displays introduce natural, local and archaeological history from in and around The Potteries, and a Mark 16 Spitfire commemorating its locally born designer - Reginald Mitchell.

Times: Open Mar-Oct, Mon-Sat 10-5, Sun 2-5; Nov-Feb, Mon-Sat 10-4, Sun 1-4; (Closed 25 Dec-1 Jan) **Facilities:** 🅿 (charged) 💷 ♿ (lift, induction loop, 2 wheelchairs available) toilets for disabled shop ✖ (ex guide/helping dogs) 📧

WEDGWOOD VISITOR CENTRE

Barlaston ST12 9ES

➲ (follow tourist signs southwards on the A34, from M6 junct 15, or northwards on A34, from M6 junct 14).

☎ 01782 282986 📠 01782 374083

e-mail: bookings@wedgwood.com

The Wedgwood Visitor Centre is situated at the home of the internationally renowned ceramic company. A variety of self-guided factory tours are available 7 days a week, together with a film theatre, two exhibition areas, demonstration/hands-on area, restaurants and shopping.

Times: Open all year, Mon-Fri 9-5, Sat & Sun 10-5; (Closed 24 Dec-2 Jan) **Fee:** £7.75-£9.49 (concessions £5.75-£7.49). Family ticket £25.99-£32.99 **Facilities:** 🅿 ✗ licensed ♿ (fully wheelchair accessible) toilets for disabled shop ✖ (ex guide dogs) 📧

TAMWORTH   Map 07 SK20

DRAYTON MANOR THEME PARK & ZOO

B78 3TW

➲ (M42 junct 9, follow brown tourist board signs on A409. Exit T2 of the M6 toll)

☎ 01827 287979 📠 01827 288916

e-mail: info@draytonmanor.co.uk

A popular family theme park with over 100 brilliant rides and attractions set in 280 acres of parkland and lakes. Drayton Manor features world-class rides like 'Apocalypse'- the world's first stand-up tower drop, 'Stormforce 10' - the best water ride in the country and 'Shockwave' - Europe's only stand-up rollercoaster. Fantastic family thrills in 'Excalibur - a Dragon's Tale' and 'Private Adventure' - plus a host of children's rides, zoo, museum, shops and attractions.

Times: Park open end Mar-Oct. Rides from 10.30-5 or 6. Zoo open all year. **Fee:** ✱ Please telephone for details. **Facilities:** 🅿 💷 ✗ licensed ♿ (ramps or lifts to most rides, some rides limited access) toilets for disabled shop garden centre ✖ (ex in park) 📧

An asterisk * indicates that opening times and prices are for 2004. Please contact the attraction for up-to-date information.

TAMWORTH CASTLE

The Holloway, Ladybank B79 7NA

➲ (from M42 junct 10 & M6 junct 12, access via A5)

☎ **01827 709629 & 709626**   `2 for 1`

🖷 **01827 709630**

e-mail: **heritage@tamworth.gov.uk**

The dramatic Norman motte and bailey castle was once the home of England's Royal Champions and today is (reputedly) haunted by two lady ghosts. Quizzes, dressing-up, brass rubbing and a 'feelie' box make it a great family destination.
Times: Open mid Feb-Oct: Tue-Sun noon- 5.15, last admission 4.30. Nov-mid Feb: Thu-Sun 12-5.15, last admission 4.30. **Fee:** £4.75 (ch £2.75 & pen £3.75). Family £13. Prices subject to change.
Facilities: 🅿 (100yds & 400yds) ☕ ♿ (one wheelchair for use inside the castle) shop ✖ (ex guide dogs & hearing dogs) 🍴

WALL   Map 07 SK10

WALL ROMAN SITE

Watling St WS14 0AW

➲ (off A5)

☎ **01543 480768**

Explore the haunting remains of a 2,000 year old wayside staging post situated along Watling Street, the famous Kent to North Wales Roman road.
Times: Open Apr-May, daily, 10-5; Jun-Aug, daily, 10-6; Sep-Oct, daily, 10-5. **Fee:** ✱ £2.60 (ch £1.30, concessions £2). National Trust members free. Prices & opening times relate to 2004, for further details phone or log onto www.english-heritage.org.uk/visits
Facilities: 🅿 shop ♿ ♨

WESTON PARK   Map 07 SJ81

WESTON PARK

TF11 8LE

➲ (on A5 at Weston-under-Lizard, 30min from central Birmingham 3m off M54 junct 3 and 8m off M6 junct 12).

☎ **01952 852100** 🖷 **01952 850430**

e-mail: **enquiries@weston-park.com**

Built in 1671, this fine mansion stands in elegant gardens and a vast park designed by 'Capability' Brown. Three lakes,
continued

a miniature railway, and a woodland adventure playground are to be found in the grounds, and in the house itself there is a magnificent collection of pictures, furniture and tapestries. There is also an animal centre and Deer Park.
Times: Open wknds from 19 Apr-Jul, then daily until 7 Sep.
Facilities: 🅿 ☕ ✖ licensed ♿ (disabled route, access to restaurant & shop) toilets for disabled shop 🍴

WHITTINGTON   Map 07 SK10

STAFFORDSHIRE REGIMENT MUSEUM

Whittington Barracks WS14 9PY

➲ (on A51 between Lichfield/Tamworth)   `2 for 1`

☎ **01543 434390** 🖷 **01543 434391**

e-mail: **museum@rhqstaffords.fsnet.co.uk**

Located next to Whittington Barracks, the museum tells the story of the soldiers of the Staffordshire Regiment and its predecessors. Exhibits include vehicles, uniforms, weapons, medals and memorabilia relating to three hundred years of regimental history, including distinguished service in the First and Second World Wars and the Gulf War. Visitors can experience a World War I trench system with sound effects and a World War II Anderson shelter.
Times: Open all year, Tue-Fri 10-4.30 (last admission 4); also Apr-Oct wknds and BH 12.30-4.30. (Closed Xmas-New Year). Parties at other times by arrangement. **Fee:** ✱ £2 (concessions £1.50) Family ticket £5. Regimental Association Members & serving soldiers free.
Facilities: 🅿 ♿ (ramps, lowered kerbs, graded access to attraction) toilets for disabled shop ✖ (outside only ex guide dogs)

WILLOUGHBRIDGE   Map 07 SJ74

THE DOROTHY CLIVE GARDEN

TF9 4EU

➲ (on A51 between Nantwich & Stone)

☎ **01630 647237** 🖷 **01630 647902**

This 200-year-old gravel quarry has been converted into a delightful woodland garden. The quarry is at the top of a small hill and the garden has fine views of the countryside and adjoining counties. There is a variety of rare trees and shrubs. The garden provides colour and interest throughout the seasons from spring to glowing autumn tints.
Times: ✱ Open Apr-Oct, daily 10-5.30. **Facilities:** 🅿 ☕ ♿ (wheelchairs for use, special route) toilets for disabled

Above: Thor's Cave

SUFFOLK

EVENTS & FESTIVALS

March
25th-27th Easter Festival, Snape Maltings
Concert Hall, Snape

April
tbc East Anglian Beer Festival, Corn Exchange,
Bury St Edmunds

May
8th South Suffolk Show, Point-to-Point
Course, Ampton Park, Ingham
21st Hadleigh Show, Holbecks Park, Hadleigh
tbc Bury St Edmunds Festival, arts festival,
(various venues)
tbc Sagitta Guineas Festival, Newmarket
Racecourse, Newmarket

June
1st-2nd Suffolk Show, Suffolk Showground,
Bucklesham Road, Ipswich
10th-26th Aldeburgh Festival of Music & the
Arts, Snape Maltings Concert Hall, and
surrounding venues and churches

June/July
tbc East Coast Regatta, Lowestoft

July
3rd Ipswich Music Day
16th-18th Southwold Festival of the Sea
30th-29th Aug Snape Proms, Snape Maltings
Concert Hall, Snape

August
6th Lowestoft Sunrise Coast Carnival
(provisional)
tbc Lowestoft Seafront Air Festival

October
14th-16th Britten Festival, Snape Maltings
Concert Hall, Snape
29th Historic Lowestoft Firework Display
(provisional)

Above: Beach huts at Southwold

BUNGAY Map 05 TM38

OTTER TRUST
Earsham NR35 2AF
➲ (off A143, 1m W of Bungay)
☎ 01986 893470 ▤ 01986 892461

The Otter Trust's main aim is to breed this endangered
species in captivity in sufficient numbers so that it can re-
introduce young otters into the wild wherever suitable
habitat remains. This re-introduction programme has been
running since 1983. The Otter Trust covers 23 acres on the
banks of the River Waveney. As well as otter pens, there are
three lakes with a large collection of European waterfowl.
Times: ✱ Open Apr (or Good Fri if earlier)-Oct, daily 10.30-6.
Facilities: ▣ 💺 ♿ toilets for disabled shop ✖ (ex guide dogs)

BURY ST EDMUNDS Map 05 TL86

MANOR HOUSE MUSEUM
Honey Hill IP33 1RT
➲ (edge of town centre, follow signs to Police
Station, opposite is museum car park)
☎ 01284 757076 ▤ 01284 747231 **2 for 1**
e-mail: stedmundsbury@burybo.stedbc.gov.uk

The Georgian mansion specialises in costumes, textiles,
horology and fine and decorative art from the 17th to the
20th centuries. There is a temporary exhibition gallery as
well as workshops in textiles and horology - new features
are feely pictures and boxes.
Times: Open all year Wed-Sun, 11-4. (Closed Good Fri, 25-26 Dec &
1 Jan). Other times by arrangement. **Fee:** ✱ £2.50 (ch & concessions
£2). (free to Borough residents) **Facilities:** ▣ (charged) 💺 ✖
♿ (Special tours can be arranged for disabled groups) toilets for
disabled shop ✖ (ex guide dogs) 🍴

MOYSE'S HALL MUSEUM
Cornhill IP33 1DX
➲ (take Bury central exit from A14, follow signs
for town centre, museum situated in town centre)
☎ 01284 706183 ▤ 01284 765373 **2 for 1**
e-mail: maggie.goodger@
stedsbc/gov.uk

Moyse's Hall is a 12th-century Norman house built of flint
and stone which now serves as a local history museum, and
among the fascinating exhibits are memorabilia of the
notorious William Corder "Murder in the Red Barn".
Times: Open all year, Mon-Fri 10.30-4.30, Sat & Sun 11-4. (Closed
25-26 Dec, 1 Jan & Good Fri) **Fee:** £2.50 (ch & concessions £2). Free
for residents of St Edmondsbury. **Facilities:** ▣ (200yds) ♿ (stairlift,
lift, hearing loop, Braille pictures) toilets for disabled shop
✖ (ex guide dogs) 🍴

CAVENDISH Map 05 TL84

THE SUE RYDER CARE VISITOR CENTRE
PO Box 5736 CO10 8RN
➲ (on A1092 Long Melford to Clare road)
☎ 01787 282591 ▤ 01787 282991

The museum was conceived by Sue Ryder as a tribute to
those whose suffering and courage during the World War II
brought the charity into being. On site is a chapel open daily
for private prayer, beautiful and peaceful gardens
overlooking the lake, gift and care shop and a coffee shop.
Times: Open all year, daily 10-5. (Closed 24-27 Dec).
Facilities: ▣ 💺 ♿ toilets for disabled shop ✖ (access to gardens
only)

EASTON Map 05 TM25

EASTON FARM PARK
IP13 0EQ
➲ (signed from A12 at Wickam Market, and from A1120)
☎ 01728 746475 📠 01728 747861
e-mail: easton@eastonfarmpark.co.uk
Award winning Farm Park on the banks of the River Deben. There are lots of breeds of farm animals, including Suffolk Punch horses, ponies, pigs, lambs, calves, goats, rabbits, guinea pigs & poultry. Chicks hatching and egg collecting daily. Free pat-a-pet & pony rides every day.
Times: ✱ Open Mar-end Sep, daily 10.30-6. Also open Feb & Oct half term hols. **Facilities:** 🅿 🚐 & (special parking) toilets for disabled shop 🍴

EUSTON Map 05 TL87

EUSTON HALL
IP24 2QP
➲ (on A1088, 3m S of Thetford)
☎ 01842 766366 📠 01842 766764
e-mail: lcampbell@euston-estate.co.uk
Home of the Duke and Duchess of Grafton, this 18th-century house is notable for its fine collection of pictures, by Stubbs, Lely, Van Dyck and other Masters. The grounds were laid out by John Evelyn, William Kent and 'Capability' Brown, and include a 17th-century church in the style of Wren and a river walk to the newly restored watermill.
Times: Open 17 Jun-16 Sep, Thu only. Also open Sun 27 Jun, 18 Jul & 5 Sep, 2.30-5. **Fee:** ✱ £4 (ch 5-16 £2, students & pen £3). Parties 12+ £3 each. Ground only £2. **Facilities:** 🅿 🚐 & toilets for disabled shop ✗ (ex guide dogs)

FLIXTON Map 05 TM38

NORFOLK & SUFFOLK AVIATION MUSEUM
Buckeroo Way, The Street NR35 1NZ
➲ (off A143, take B1062, 2m W of Bungay)
☎ 01986 896644
e-mail: nsam.flixton@virgin.net
FREE
Situated in the Waveney Valley, the museum has over 40 historic aircraft. There is also a Bloodhound surface-to-air missile, the 446th Bomb Group Museum, RAF Bomber Command Museum, the Royal Observer Corps Museum, RAF Air-Sea Rescue and Coastal Command and a souvenir shop. Among the displays are Decoy Sites and Wartime Deception, Fallen Eagles - Wartime Luftwaffe Crashes and an ex-Ipswich airport hangar made by Norwich company Boulton and Paul Ltd.
Times: Open Apr-Oct, Sun-Thu 10-5 (last admission 4); Nov-Mar Tue, Wed & Sun 10-4 (last admission 3) (Closed late Dec-early Jan).
Facilities: 🅿 🚐 & (helper advised, ramps/paths to all buildings) toilets for disabled shop ✗ (ex guide dogs)

This symbol indicates attractions **2-for-1** which have chosen to participate in our 2-for-1 voucher scheme

---

FRAMLINGHAM Map 05 TM26

FRAMLINGHAM CASTLE
IP8 9BT
➲ (on B1116)
☎ 01728 724189
Walk the 12th-century battlements that encircle the castle site with their impressive thirteen towers. Exceptional views over the countryside and a very popular audio tour.
Times: Open all year, Apr-Sep, daily 10-6; Oct, daily 10-5; Nov-Mar, daily 10-4. (Closed 24-26 Dec & 1 Jan). **Fee:** ✱ £4.20 (ch £2.10, concessions £3.20). Prices & opening times relate to 2004, for further details phone or log onto www.english-heritage.org.uk/visits
Facilities: 🅿 & shop ♿

HORRINGER Map 05 TL86

ICKWORTH HOUSE, PARK & GARDENS
The Rotunda IP29 5QE
➲ (2.5m S of Bury St Edmunds in the village of Horringer on the A143)
☎ 01284 735270 📠 01284 735175
e-mail: ickworth@ntrust.org.uk
The eccentric Earl of Bristol created this equally eccentric house, begun in 1795, to display his collection of European art. The Georgian Silver Collection is considered the finest in private hands. 'Capability' Brown designed the parkland, and also featured are a deer enclosure, waymarked walks and an adventure playground.
Times: Open: House 19 Mar-Oct, Mon, Tue, Fri, wknds & BH Mons 1-5 (4.30 in Oct) last admission 4.30; Garden open daily 19 Mar-Oct 10-5. Last admission 4.30. Nov-22 Dec wkdays 10-4; Park daily 7-7.
Fee: ✱ House, Garden & Park £6.40 (National Trust members & ch under 5 free, ch £2.90) Garden & park £2.95 (ch 85p). Discount for pre-booked parties. **Facilities:** 🅿 ✗ licensed & (Braille guide batricars, stairlift to shop & restaurant) toilets for disabled shop garden centre ✗ (ex guide dogs & in park) ♨

IPSWICH Map 05 TM14

CHRISTCHURCH MANSION
Soane St IP4 2BE
➲ (South side of Christchurch Park)
☎ 01473 253246 & 213761 📠 01473 210328
e-mail: mansion@ipswich.gov.uk
The house was built in 1548 on the site of an Augustinian priory. Set in a beautiful park, it displays period rooms and an art gallery which has changing exhibitions. The Suffolk Artists' Gallery has a collection of paintings by Constable and Gainsborough.
Times: ✱ Open all year, Tue-Sat 10-5 (dusk in winter), Sun 2.30-4.30 (dusk in winter). (Closed Good Fri, 24-26 Dec & 1-2 Jan). Open BH Mon. **Facilities:** 🅿 & (tape guide for partially sighted) shop ✗

IPSWICH MUSEUM
High St IP1 3QH
➲ (Follow tourist signs to Crown St car park. Museum 3 mins walk from here)
☎ 01473 433550 📠 01473 433558
e-mail: museum.service@ipswich.gov.uk
The Museum has sections on Victorian Natural History, Suffolk wildlife, Suffolk geology, Roman Suffolk, Anglo-Saxon Ipswich and Peoples of the World. There is also one of the best bird collections in the country.
Times: ✱ Open all year, Tue-Sat 10-5. (Closed Sun, BH's, 24-26 Dec & 1 Jan). **Facilities:** 🅿 (3 min walk) & (lift) toilets for disabled shop ✗ (ex guide dogs)

LAVENHAM   Map 05 TL94

LAVENHAM GUILDHALL
Market Place CO10 9QZ

➲ (Lavenham Market Place. A1141 & B1071)

☎ 01787 247646   🖷 01787 246345

e-mail: jane.gosling@nationaltrust.org.uk

The Guildhall of Corpus Christi is one of the finest timber framed buildings in Britain. It was built around 1530 by the prosperous Corpus Christi Guild, for religious rather than commercial reasons. The hall now houses a local history museum telling the story of Lavenham's 15th- and 16th-century cloth-trade riches. Visitors can also see the walled garden with its 19th-century lock-up and mortuary.

Times: Open Mar & Nov, Sat & Sun 11-4; Apr, Wed-Sun 11-5; May-Oct daily 11-5. (Closed Good Fri but open BH Mon) **Fee:** £3.25 (accompanied ch free). Parties £2.75 each. School parties by arrangement 60p per ch. **Facilities:** 🅿 (adjacent) 🍽 ♿ (photo album of upstairs floors) shop garden centre ✗ (ex guide dogs) 🐾

LEISTON   Map 05 TM46

LEISTON ABBEY
IP16 4TB

➲ (N of Leiston, off B1069)

☎ 01728 831354   🖷 01728 832500   FREE

e-mail: mo@leistonabbey.fsnet.co.uk

For hundreds of years this 14th-century abbey was used as a farm and its church became a barn. A Georgian house, now used as a school for young musicians, was built into its fabric and remains of the choir, the church transepts and parts of the cloisters still stand.

Times: Open any reasonable time. **Facilities:** 🅿 ♿

LONG SHOP STEAM MUSEUM
Main St IP16 4ES

➲ (Turn off A12, follow B1119 from Saxmundham to Leiston. Museum is in the middle of town)

☎ 01728 832189   🖷 01728 832189

e-mail: longshop@care4free.net

Discover the Magic of Steam through a visit to the world famous traction engine manufacturers. Trace the history of the factory and Richard Garrett engineering. See the traction engines and road rollers in the very place that they were built. Soak up the atmosphere of the Long Shop, built in 1852 as one of the first production line engineering halls in the world. An award-winning museum with five exhibition halls full of items from the glorious age of steam and covering 200 years of local, social and industrial history.

Times: Open Apr-Oct, Mon-Sat 10-5, Sun 11-5.
Facilities: 🅿 ♿ (wheelchair available) toilets for disabled shop ✗ (ex guide dogs)

LINDSEY   Map 05 TL94

LINDSEY CHAPEL
Rose Green

➲ (on unclass road 0.5m E of Rose Green)

Built mainly in the 13th century, this small thatched, flint-and-stone chapel incorporates some earlier work.

Times: Open all year, daily 10-4. **Facilities:** ♿ ✗ ⚑

LONG MELFORD   Map 05 TL84

KENTWELL HALL
CO10 9BA

➲ (signposted off A134, between Bury St Edmunds & Sudbury)

☎ 01787 310207   🖷 01787 379318

e-mail: info@kentwell.co.uk

Kentwell Hall is a moated red brick Tudor manor with gardens, woodland walks and a rare breeds farm. The house and grounds are open to the public at certain times of the year, and recreations of Tudor and 1940s life take place at weekends. Ring for details.

Times: Open: Gardens & Farm Sun during Mar, Apr-Jun. House, Gardens & Farm 14 Jul-early Sep daily; Oct, Sun only. Also open BH wknds & school hols. Historical recreations on selected wknds throughout year. **Facilities:** 🅿 🍽 ♿ (wheelchair ramp & 2 wheelchairs for loan) toilets for disabled shop ✗ (ex guide dogs) 🚩

MELFORD HALL
CO10 9AA

➲ (off A134, 3m N of Sudbury, next to village green)

☎ 01787 880286   🖷 01787 880286

e-mail: kathy.lintin@nationaltrust.org.uk

Queen Elizabeth I was a guest at this turreted, brick-built Tudor house in 1578. It features an 18th-century drawing room, a Regency library and a Victorian bedroom. There is also a large collection of Chinese porcelain, and a display on Beatrix Potter, who was related to the owners and often stayed here. The garden has a Tudor pavilion, which may have been built as a banqueting house.

Times: ✱ Open Etr wknd & Etr Mon; Apr & Oct wknds only; May-Sep, Wed-Sun (open BH Mon) 2-5.30. **Facilities:** 🅿 ♿ (stairlift, ramp, Braille & large print guides) toilets for disabled ✗ (ex guide dogs & dogs in park) 🐾

LOWESTOFT   Map 05 TM59

EAST ANGLIA TRANSPORT MUSEUM
Chapel Rd, Carlton Colville NR33 8BL

➲ (3m SW of Lowestoft, follow brown signs from A12, A146 & B1384)

☎ 01502 518459   🖷 01502 584658

e-mail: enquiries@eatm.org.uk

A particular attraction of this museum is the reconstructed 1930s street scene which is used as a setting for working vehicles: visitors can ride by tram, trolley bus and narrow gauge railway. Other motor, steam and electrical vehicles are exhibited. There is also a woodland picnic area served by trams.

Times: Open Good Fri & Etr Sat 2-4, Etr Sun-Etr Mon 11-5. May-Sep, Sun & BH's 11-5; Wed & Sat 2-5 (last entry 1 hour before closing).
Fee: £5 (ch 5-15 & pen £3.50). Price includes rides. Party rates available. **Facilities:** 🅿 🍽 ♿ toilets for disabled shop 🚩

MARITIME MUSEUM
Sparrow Nest Gardens, Whapload Rd NR32 1XG

➲ (on A12, 100mtrs N of Lowestoft Lighthouse, turn right down Ravine)

☎ 01502 561963   2 for 1

Models of ancient and modern fishing and commercial boats, fishing gear and shipwrights' tools are among the exhibits. Exhibition of the evolution of lifeboats, a replica of the aft cabin of a steam drifter. There is also an art gallery.

Times: Open Good Fri, Sat, Sun & Mon (25-28 Mar); 30 Apr-9 Oct, daily 10-5. **Fee:** 75p (ch & students 25p, pen 50p).
Facilities: 🅿 ♿ (hear for all) shop ✗ (ex guide & small dogs)

NEW PLEASUREWOOD HILLS
Leisure Way, Corton NR32 5DZ
➲ (off A12 at Lowestoft)
☎ 01502 586000 (admin) & 508200 (info)
🖳 01502 567393
e-mail: info@pleasurewoodhills.co.uk
There are over 40 rides, shows and attractions at New Pleasurewood Hills, set in 50 acres of beautiful parkland. Old favourites such as the Tidal Wave Watercoaster and the Fairytale Fantasy Ride combine with more recent attractions such as Formula K Raceway Go-Karts, the new 100ft Drop Tower, the Crazy Coaster and the Double Decker Carousel.
Times: ✱ Open Apr-Oct & Xmas. Telephone for details.
Facilities: 🅿 💺 ✗ licensed ♿ (all shows accessible, most ride operators able to assist) toilets for disabled shop
✖ (ex guide dogs) ◼

NEWMARKET   Map 05 TL66
NATIONAL HORSERACING MUSEUM AND TOURS
99 High St CB8 8JL
➲ (located in centre of High St).
☎ 01638 667333 🖳 01638 665600
This friendly award-winning museum tells the story of the people and horses involved in racing in Britain. Have a go on the horse simulator in the hands-on gallery and chat to retired jockeys and trainers about their experiences. Special mini bus tours visit the gallops, a stable and yard and horses' swimming pool.
Times: ✱ Open 15 Apr-3 Nov, Tue-Sun (also BH Mons & Mons in Jul & Aug) 11-5. 10am opening on race days. **Facilities:** 🅿 (300yds) (coach drop off in front of museum) 💺 ✗ licensed ♿ (ramps) toilets for disabled shop ✖ (ex guide dogs) ◼

ORFORD   Map 05 TM45
ORFORD CASTLE
IP12 2ND
➲ (on B1084)
☎ 01394 450472
A great keep of Henry II with three huge towers and commanding views over Orford Ness. Climb the spiral staircase leading to a maze of rooms and passageways.
Times: Open all year, Apr-Sep, daily 10-6; Oct-Mar, Thu-Mon, 10-4.
Fee: ✱ £4 (ch £2, concessions £3, family £10). Prices & opening times relate to 2004, for further details phone or log onto www.english-heritage.org.uk/visits **Facilities:** 🅿 shop ✖ ⊞

SAXTEAD GREEN   Map 05 TM26
SAXTEAD GREEN POST MILL
The Mill House IP13 9QQ
➲ (2.5m NW of Framlingham on A1120)
☎ 01728 685789
A post mill since 1287, Saxtead Green Post Mill is still in working order. Climb the wooden stairs to the various floors full of fascinating mill machinery. An audio tour explains the workings of the mill.
Times: Open Apr-Sep, Mon-Sat 10-6; **Fee:** ✱ £2.60 (ch £1.30, concessions £2). Prices & opening times relate to 2004, for further details phone or log onto www.english-heritage.org.uk/visits
Facilities: ♿ (exterior only) shop ✖ ⊞

STOWMARKET   Map 05 TM05
MUSEUM OF EAST ANGLIAN LIFE
IP14 1DL
➲ (located in centre of Stowmarket opposite ASDA Supermarket & is signposted from A14 & B1115)
☎ 01449 612229 🖳 01449 672307
e-mail: meal@meal.fsnet.co.uk
This 70-acre, all-weather museum is set in an attractive river-valley site. There are reconstructed buildings, including a water mill, a smithy and also a wind pump, and the Boby Building houses craft workshops. There are displays on Victorian domestic life, gypsies, farming and industry. These include working steam traction engines, the only surviving pair of Burrell ploughing engines of 1879, and a working Suffolk Punch horse. New: William Bone Building illustrating the history of ransomes of Ipswich.
Times: ✱ Open Apr-Oct. **Facilities:** 🅿 (adjacent) 💺
♿ (wheelchairs available, special vehicle facilities) toilets for disabled shop ◼

SUDBURY   Map 05 TL84
GAINSBOROUGH'S HOUSE
46 Gainsborough St CO10 2EU
➲ (Situated in the centre of Sudbury. Follow pedestrian signs from the town centre car parks or from the train stn)
☎ 01787 372958 🖳 01787 376991
e-mail: mail@gainsborough.org
The birthplace of Thomas Gainsborough RA (1727-88). The Georgian-fronted town house, with an attractive walled garden, displays more of the artist's work than any other gallery, together with 18th-century furniture and memorabilia. There's a varied programme of exhibitions throughout the year including fine art, craft, photography, printmaking and sculpture.
Times: Open all year, House: Mon-Sat 10-5, BH Sun & BH Mons 2-5. (Closed on other Suns, Good Fri & Xmas-New Year). **Fee:** ✱ £3.50 (ch, students & disabled £1.50, pen £2.80). Party rates available.
Facilities: 🅿 (300yds) (no parking in Gainsborough Street) 💺
♿ toilets for disabled shop ✖ (ex guide dogs) ◼

SUFFOLK WILDLIFE PARK   Map 05 TM58
SUFFOLK WILDLIFE PARK
Kessingland NR33 7TF
➲ (25min S of Gt. Yarmouth, just S of Lowestoft off the A12)
☎ 01502 740291 🖳 01502 741104
e-mail: info@suffolkwildlifepark.co.uk
Enjoy the atmosphere and excitement of your very own African Adventure at Suffolk Wildlife Park. Spend the whole day exploring 100 acres of dramatic coastal parkland, filled with animals from the African continent and around the world. Guide your expedition to giraffe, lion, buffalo, hyena and many more exciting animals. Capture the true splendour and atmosphere of the park by going walkabout amongst the large open paddocks or join the children's favourite - the Safari Roadtrain with its live commentary of fascinating animal facts.
Times: Open all year, daily from 10am. (Closed 25-26 Dec).
Fee: ✱ Please call park reception for full admission prices
Facilities: 🅿 💺 ✗ ♿ (wheelchairs available for hire) toilets for disabled shop ✖ ◼

WESTLETON   Map 05 TM46

RSPB NATURE RESERVE MINSMERE
IP17 3BY

➲ (signposted from A12 at Yoxford & Blythburgh
and from Westleton Village)

☎ 01728 648281 📠 01728 648770

e-mail: minsmere@rspb.org.uk

Set on the beautiful Suffolk coast, Minsmere offers an
enjoyable day out for all. Nature trails take you through a
variety of habitats to the excellent birdwatching hides.
Spring, is a time for birdsong, including nightingales and
booming bitterns. In summer, you can watch breeding
avocets and marsh harriers. Autumn is excellent for
migrants, and in winter, hundreds of wildfowl visit the
reserve. Look out for otters and red deer. The visitor centre
has a well-stocked shop and licensed tearoom, and you can
find out more about the reserve. There is a programme of
events throughout the year, including several for children
and families. Self-guided activity booklets for families.

Times: Open daily (ex closed Tue) 9-9 (or dusk if earlier). Visitor
centre open 9-5 (Nov-Jan 9-4). (Closed 25-26 Dec). **Fee:** £5 (ch £1.50,
concessions £3). Family ticket £10. RSPB members free

Facilities: 🅿 🍽 ♿ (batricar available for loan, booking advised)
toilets for disabled shop ✖ (ex guide dogs) 🍴

WEST STOW   Map 05 TL87

WEST STOW ANGLO SAXON VILLAGE
West Stow Country Park, Icklingham Rd IP28 6HG

➲ (off A1101, follow brown heritage signs located
7m North West of Bury St Edmunds)

☎ 01284 728718 📠 01284 728277

e-mail: weststow@stedsbc.gov.uk   `2 for 1`

The village is a reconstruction of a pagan Anglo-Saxon
settlement dated 420-650 AD. Seven buildings have been
reconstructed on the site of the excavated settlement. There
is a Visitors' Centre and a children's play area. A new Anglo-
Saxon Centre houses the original objects found on the site.
The village is located in the West Stow Country Park. The
park is 125 acres with river, lake, woodland and heath and
has many trails and paths.

Times: Open all year, daily 10-5. Last entry 4pm (3.30 in Winter)
Fee: ✱ £5 (ch £4). Family ticket £15. (prices subject to changes for
special events) **Facilities:** 🅿 🍽 ♿ (ramps) toilets for disabled shop
✖ (ex guide dogs) 🍴

WOODBRIDGE   Map 05 TM24

SUTTON HOO NEW
IP12 3DJ

➲ (off B1083 Woodbridge to Bawdsey Rd. Follow
signs from A12 avoiding Woodbridge itself)

☎ 01394 389700

e-mail: suttonhoo@nationaltrust.org.uk

Discovered in 1939 by an amateur archaeologist, this is the
site of one of the most important archaeological finds in
Britain's history: the complete 7th-century ship burial of an
Anglo-Saxon king, which had been missed by grave-robbers
for 1300 years. Sutton Hoo Displays reveal how Anglo-Saxon
nobles lived, went to war and found a new kingdom in East
Anglia. The centre-piece is a full sized replica of an Anglo-
Saxon warrior king's burial chamber.

Times: Open Mar-end Sep, daily 10-5; Oct, Wed-Sun 10-5; Nov-Feb,
Fri-Sun 10-4 **Fee:** ✱ £4 or free to NT members

Facilities: 🅿 ✖ licensed ♿ (ramps, no stairs to main areas) toilets for
disabled shop ✖ (ex outdoors on lead) 🍴

WOODBRIDGE TIDE MILL
Tide Mill Way IP12

➲ (follow signs for Woodbridge off A12, 7m E of
Ipswich - Tide Mill is on riverside)

☎ 01728 746959 📠 01728 748226

e-mail: wtm@redpoll.co.uk

The machinery of this 18th-century mill has been completely
restored. There are photographs and working models on
display. Situated on a busy quayside, the unique building
looks over towards the historic site of the Sutton Hoo Ship
Burial. Every effort is made to run the machinery for a while
whenever the mill is open and the tides are favourable.

Times: Open Etr, then daily May-Sep; Apr, Oct wknds only, 11-5.
Fee: ✱ £1.50 (concessions £1, accompanied ch free).
Facilities: 🅿 (400yds) (no parking or turning in Tide Mill Way)
♿ shop ✖ (ex guide dogs)

Above: The Scrape at Minsmere

SURREY

EVENTS & FESTIVALS

March
4th-20th Guildford International Music Festival, various venues

May
30th Surrey County Show, Stoke Park, Guildford

June
7th-9th Wisley Flower Show, Royal Horticultural Society Garden, Wisley (provisional)
25th-31st Jul Guildford Summer Festival (various events throughout the month)

July
15th-17th Guilfest, live music festival (provisional)

August
7th Cranleigh Show, Showground, Cranleigh
23rd-25th Wisley Flower Show, Royal Horticultural Society Garden, Wisley

September
24th Surbiton Festival, various events and street festival
25th Country Fair & Ploughing Match, Losely Park, Guildford

October
16th-29th Guildford Book Festival, various venues in the town centre

Above: Gibbet Hill, Hindhead Common

ASH VALE　　　　　　　Map 04 SU85

ARMY MEDICAL SERVICES MUSEUM
Keogh Barracks GU12 5RQ
➲ (M3 junct 4 on A331 to Mytchett then follow tourist signs)
☎ 01252 868612　🗎 01252 868832　**FREE**
e-mail: museum@keogh72.freeserve.co.uk
The museum traces the history of Army medicine, nursing, dentistry, and veterinary science from 1660 until the present day. Medical equipment and ambulances complement displays including uniforms and medals.
Times: Open all year, Mon-Fri 10-3.30. (Closed Xmas, New Year & BH). Wknds & BH by appointment only. **Facilities:** 🅿 ⅙ (hand rails, wide doors) toilets for disabled shop ✖ (ex guide dogs)

CHERTSEY　　　　　　　Map 04 TQ06

THORPE PARK
Staines Rd KT16 8PN
➲ (M25 junct 11 or 13 and follow signs via A320 to Thorpe Park)
☎ 0870 444 4466　🗎 01932 566367
Home to one of the world's most intense, disorientating, exhilarating rollercoasters - Nemesis Inferno - the legendary feet-free, suspended coaster with volcanic theming and effects, plus the wrenching Quantum. Back for a second sense-ational season, Colossus, the world's first 10-looping rollercoaster will continue to demonstrate the mighty power of Ten. Experience the trio of "must ride" thrill sensations - explosive Detonator, awesome Vortex and spinning Zodiac. Plus Tidal Wave, one of Europe's highest water drop rides, the white water thrills of Ribena Rumba Rapids, X:/No Way Out, Loggers Leap, Pirates-4D, Neptune's Beach, Thorpe farm and lots more besides.
Times: ✱ Open from 5 Apr-2 Nov (ex some off-peak days) 9/10-5/6 (times vary), 7.30pm from 25 Jul-7 Sep, until 8pm on fireworks night & from noon-11 on Fri nights. **Facilities:** 🅿 ⬛ ✖ licensed ⅙ (some rides not accessible, wheelchair hire available) toilets for disabled shop ✖ (ex guide dogs) 🍴

EAST CLANDON　　　　　Map 04 TQ05

HATCHLANDS PARK
GU4 7RT
➲ (E off Guildford, off A246)
☎ 01483 222482　🗎 01483 223176
e-mail: hatchlands@nationaltrust.org.uk
Built in the 1750s for Admiral Boscawen, hero of the battle of Louisburg and set in a beautiful 430 acre Repton Park offering a variety of park and woodlands walks, Hatchlands boasts the earliest known decorative works by Robert Adam. Hatchlands is home to the Cobbe collection, the world's largest group of keyboard instruments associated with famous composers. There is also a small garden by Gertrude Jekyll, flowering from late May to early July and a beautiful bluebell wood in May.
Times: House & Gardens: Apr-Oct, Tue-Thu & Sun, 2-5.30 (also open BH & Fri in Aug). Park Walks open Apr-Oct, daily, 11-6. **Fee:** ✱ £6. (ch £3). Park walks: £2.50 (ch £1.25) Family ticket £15. Combined ticket with Clandon Park £9 (ch £4.50). Family £22.50
Facilities: 🅿 ✖ licensed ⅙ (wheelchair available & special parking) toilets for disabled shop ✖ (ex guide dogs) 🐾 🍴

FARNHAM   Map 04 SU84

BIRDWORLD & UNDERWATERWORLD
Holt Pound GU10 4LD
➲ (3m S of Farnham on A325)
☎ 01420 22140 ▤ 01420 23715
e-mail: bookings@birdworld.co.uk

Birdworld is the largest bird collection in the country and
includes toucans, pelicans, flamingoes, ostriches and many
others. Underwater World is a tropical aquarium with
brilliant lighting that shows off collections of marine and
freshwater fish, as well as the swampy depths of the alligator
exhibit. Visitors can also visit some beautiful gardens, the
Jenny Wren farm and the Heron Theatre.
Times: Open daily, 10-6 (summer), 10-4.30 (winter).
Facilities: ▣ ▣ ⅁ (wheelchairs available) toilets for disabled shop
garden centre ✕ (ex guide dogs) ◗

FARNHAM CASTLE KEEP
Castle Hill GU6 0AG
➲ (0.5m N on A287)
☎ 01252 713393
A motte and bailey castle, once one of the seats of the
bishop of Winchester, has been in continuous occupation
since the 12th-century.
Times: Open Apr-Sep, Sat, Sun & BH Mon 10-5. **Fee:** ✱ £2.50
(ch £1.30, concessions £1.90). Prices & opening times relate to 2004,
for further details phone or log onto www.english-heritage.org.uk/visits
Facilities: ▣ shop ⌗

GODSTONE   Map 05 TQ35

GODSTONE FARM
RH9 8LX
➲ (M25 junct 6, south of village, signposted)
☎ 01883 742546 ▤ 01883 740380
e-mail: havefun@godstonefarm.co.uk
An ideal day out for children, Godstone Farm has lots of
friendly animals, big sand pits and play areas. The Indoor
Play Barn costs 80p extra on rainy days.
Times: Open Mar-Oct, 10-6 (last admission 5); Nov-Feb 10-5 (last
admission 4). Closed 25 & 26 Dec. **Fee:** ✱ Contact for admission
prices. **Facilities:** ▣ ▣ ⅁ toilets for disabled shop
✕ (ex guide dogs) ◗

GREAT BOOKHAM   Map 04 TQ15

POLESDEN LACEY
RH5 6BD
➲ (2m S off A246 from village of Bookham)
☎ 01372 452048 ▤ 01372 452023
e-mail: polesdenlacey@nationaltrust.org.uk
King George VI and Queen Elizabeth (the Queen Mother)
spent part of their honeymoon here, and photographs of
other notable guests can be seen. The house is handsomely
furnished and full of charm, and it is set in spacious grounds.
There is also a summer festival, where concerts and plays
are performed. Please phone 01372 452048 for details of
special events.
Times: Open all year. Grounds, Garden & Landscape walks: daily 11-6.
House: 23 Mar-6 Nov, Wed-Sun 11-5. Also BH Mon 11-5 (last
admission 30mins before closing) **Fee:** Ground, Garden & Landscape
walks: £5 (Family ticket £12.50); House: £3 extra (Family £7.50 extra).
Ch under 17 half price, ch under 5 free. Party 15+ **Facilities:** ▣ ▣
✗ licensed ⅁ (Braille guide & disabled parking by arrangement) toilets
for disabled shop garden centre ✖

GUILDFORD   Map 04 SU94

DAPDUNE WHARF
Wharf Rd GU1 4RR
➲ (off Woodbridge Rd to rear of Surrey County
Cricket Ground)
☎ 01483 561389 ▤ 01483 531667
e-mail: riverwey@nationaltrust.org.uk
The visitor centre at Dapdune Wharf is the centrepiece of
one of the National Trust's most unusual properties, the
River Wey Navigations. A series of interactive exhibits and
displays allow you to discover the fascinating story of
Surrey's secret waterway, one of the first British rivers to be
made navigable. See where huge Wey barges were built and
climb aboard Reliance, one of the last surviving barges.
Children's trails and special events run throughout the
season.
Times: Open Apr-Oct, Thu-Mon 11-5. River trips Thu-Mon 11-5
(conditions permitting) **Fee:** ✱ £2.50 (ch £1.50). Family ticket £6.50.
National Trust Members Free **Facilities:** ▣ ▣ ⅁ (Braille guide)
toilets for disabled shop ✖

GUILDFORD HOUSE GALLERY
155 High St GU1 3AJ
➲ (N side of High St, opposite Sainsbury's)
☎ 01483 444740 ▤ 01483 444742   FREE
e-mail: guildfordhouse@guildford.gov.uk
An impressive building in its own right, Guildford House
dates from 1660 and has been Guildford's art gallery since
1959. A changing selection from the Borough's Art Collection
is on display, including pastel portraits by John Russell,
topographical paintings and contemporary craftwork, as well
as temporary exhibitions.
Times: Open Tue-Sat 10-4.45. (Closed Good Fri & Xmas)
Facilities: ▣ (100yds) ▣ ✕ ⅁ shop ✕ (ex guide dogs) ◗

LOSELEY PARK

GU3 1HS

➔ (2m SW of Guildford, off A3 onto B3000)

☎ 01483 304440 & 505501

▤ 01483 302036   **2 for 1**

e-mail: enquiries@loseley-park.com

Magnificent Elizabethan mansion, home of the More-Molyneux family for over 450 years. Set in magnificent parkland scenery. Based on a Gertude Jekyll design. The walled garden contains five gardens each with its own theme and character. These include the award-wining Rose Garden, Vine Walk, Fruit, Flower Garden & the Serene White Fountain Garden.

Times: Grounds and Walled Garden: 2 May-29 Sep, Wed-Sun & BH 11-5. House: Jun-29 Aug, Wed-Sun & BH 1-5 **Fee:** ✱ House & Gardens £6 (ch £3, ch under 5 free, concessions £5). Gardens only £3 (ch £1.50, concessions £2.50). Party. Garden summer ticket £15, admits ticket holder & guest from May-Sep. **Facilities:** ▣ ▆ ✗ licensed ⅍ (wheelchair available, parking outside shop) toilets for disabled shop garden centre ✖ (ex guide dogs)

HASCOMBE   Map 04 SU94

WINKWORTH ARBORETUM

Hascombe Rd GU8 4AD

➔ (2m NW on B2130, follow brown tourist signs from Godalming)

☎ 01483 208477   ▤ 01483 208252

e-mail: winkwortharboretum@
nationaltrust.org.uk

This lovely woodland covers a hillside of nearly 100 acres, with fine views over the North Downs. The best times to visit are April and May, for the azaleas, bluebells and other flowers, and October for the autumn colours. A delightful Victorian boathouse is open Apr-Oct with fine views over Rowes Flashe lake, although access may be limited owing to dam restoration work during 2004. With many rare trees and shrubs in group plantings for spring and autumn colour effect.

Times: Open all year, daily during daylight hours. (Could close when weather is bad) **Fee:** ✱ £4 (ch £2). Family ticket £10, additional family member £1.75. **Facilities:** ▣ ▆ ⅍ (suggested route, free entry for helpers) toilets for disabled shop ✖ ▆

OUTWOOD   Map 04 TQ34

OUTWOOD WINDMILL

Outwood Common RH1 5PW

➔ (M25 junct 6, take A25 through Godstone towards Redhill, after 1m turn S off A25 at Bletchingly, between The Prince Albert & the White Hart. Mill is 3m on left)

☎ 01342 843458 & 843644   ▤ 01342 843458

e-mail: info@outwoodwindmill.co.uk

This award-winning example of a post-mill dates from 1665 and is the oldest working windmill in England and one of the best preserved in existence. Standing 400ft above sea level, it is surrounded by common land and National Trust property. Ducks and geese wander freely in the grounds.

Times: Open Etr Sun-3rd Sun in Oct, Sun & BH Mons only 2-6. Other times for parties only by arrangement. **Fee:** ✱ £2 (ch £1). **Facilities:** ▣ (10yds) ⅍ toilets for disabled shop

PAINSHILL PARK   Map 04 TQ06

PAINSHILL PARK

KT11 1JE

➔ (W of Cobham on A245)

☎ 01932 868113   ▤ 01932 868001

e-mail: info@painshill.co.uk

Painshill Park, created by the Hon. Charles Hamilton between 1738 and 1773, was a pleasure ground for fashionable society. His vision influenced the future of England's countryside, culture and gardening. Staged around a huge serpentine lake, surprises come at every turn - a Gothic Temple, Chinese Bridge, Ruined Abbey, Grotto, Turkish Tent, Gothic Tower, spectacular waterwheel, 18th century planting and a working vineyard.

Times: Open Mar-Oct, Tue-Sun & BH, 10.30-6. (last entry 4.30). Nov-Feb, Wed-Sun, & BH 11-4 (gates close 3). Closed 25 Dec.

Fee: ✱ £6 (ch 5-16 £3.50, concessions £5.25). Pre-booked adult groups 10+ £5. Please telephone 01932 868113 for 2005 prices **Facilities:** ▣ ▆ ✗ licensed ⅍ (wheelchairs & buggies available - pre-booked) toilets for disabled shop ✖ (ex guide dogs) ▆

REIGATE   Map 04 TQ24

REIGATE PRIORY MUSEUM

Bell St RH2 7RL

➔ (next to Bell Street car park)   **FREE**

☎ 01737 222550

The Priory Museum is housed in Reigate Priory which was originally founded before 1200, this Grade I listed building was converted to a mansion in Tudor times. Notable features include the magnificent Holbein fireplace, 17th century oak staircase and murals. The small museum has changing exhibitions on a wide range of subjects, designed to appeal to both adults and children. The collection includes domestic bygones, local history and costume.

Times: Open Etr-early Dec, Wed & Sat, 2-4.30 in term time. **Facilities:** ▣ (50yds) ⅍ (hands on facilities) shop ✖

TILFORD   Map 04 SU84

RURAL LIFE CENTRE
Reeds Rd GU10 2DL
➲ (off A287, 3m S of Farnham, signposted)
☎ 01252 795571 🖹 01252 795571   **2 for 1**
e-mail: rural.life@lineone.net

The museum covers village life from 1750 to 1960. It is set in over ten acres of garden and woodland and incorporates purpose-built and reconstructed buildings, including a chapel. Displays show village crafts and trades, such as wheelwrighting, thatching, ploughing and gardening. The historic village playground provides entertainment for children and there is an arboretum featuring over 100 trees from around the world.

Times: Open late Mar–early Oct, Wed-Sun & BH 10-5; Winter Wed & Sun only 11-4 **Fee:** £5 (ch £3 & pen £4). Family ticket £14 (2 ad & 2 ch). **Facilities:** 🅿 💺 ✗ licensed ♿ (3 wheelchairs for use) toilets for disabled shop ➡

WEST CLANDON   Map 04 TQ05

CLANDON PARK
GU4 7RQ
➲ (E of Guildford on A247)
☎ 01483 222482 🖹 01483 223479
e-mail: clandonpark@nationaltrust.org.uk

A grand Palladian mansion built c.1730 by the Venetian architect Giacomo Leoni, and notable for its magnificent marble hall. The house is filled with the superb Gubbay collection of 18th century furniture, porcelain, textiles and carpets. The attractive gardens contain a parterre, grotto, sunken Dutch garden and a Maori meetinghouse.

Times: House and garden open Apr-Oct, Tue-Thu & Sun 11-5 (also BH's) **Fee:** ✱ House & Garden £6 (ch £3). Family ticket £15. Combined ticket with Hatchlands Park £9, (ch £4.50). Family £22.50 **Facilities:** 🅿 ✗ licensed ♿ (wheelchairs, Braille guide & disabled parking) toilets for disabled shop ➡ (ex guide dogs) 🐾 ➡

WEYBRIDGE   Map 04 TQ06

BROOKLANDS MUSEUM
Brooklands Rd KT13 0QN
➲ (M25 junct 10/11, museum off B374)
☎ 01932 857381 🖹 01932 855465
e-mail: info@brooklandsmuseum.com

Brooklands racing circuit was the birthplace of British motorsport and aviation. From 1907 to 1987 it was a world-renowned centre of engineering excellence. The Museum features old banked track and the 1-in-4 Test Hill. Many of the original buildings have been restored including the Clubhouse, the Shell and BP Petrol Pagodas, and the Malcolm Campbell Sheds in the Motoring Village. Many motorcycles, cars and aircraft are on display. Ring for details of special events.

Times: ✱ Open Tue-Sun & BHs 10-5 (4pm in winter). **Facilities:** 🅿 💺 ♿ toilets for disabled shop ✗ (ex guide dogs) ➡

WISLEY   Map 04 TQ05

RHS GARDEN WISLEY
GU23 6QB
➲ (on A3, close to M25 junct 10)
☎ 01483 224234 🖹 01483 211750

Covering over 240 acres, Wisley is the flagship of the Royal Horticultural Society demonstrating the very best in gardening practices. The gardens have a wide variety of trees, shrubs and plants, many of which are unusual in Britain. Whatever the season the garden serves as a working encyclopedia for gardeners of all levels.

Times: Open all year, Mon-Fri 10-6 (4.30 Nov-Feb), Sat-Sun, 9-6 (4.30 Nov-Feb). (Closed 25 Dec). **Fee:** ✱ £7 (ch 6-16 £2) group bookings 10+ £5.50 (ch £1.60) **Facilities:** 🅿 💺 ✗ licensed ♿ (free wheelchairs, electric buggies, wheelchair route) toilets for disabled shop garden centre ✗ (ex guide dogs) ➡

Above: Deer in Richmond Park

EAST SUSSEX

EVENTS & FESTIVALS

May
1st-2nd Battle Medieval Fair, Abbey Green, High Street, Battle
7th-29th Brighton International Festival, various venues (England's largest mixed arts festival)
19th-28th Aug Glyndebourne Festival Opera, Glyndebourne, Glynde, Lewis

June
12th London to Brighton Bike Race
12th London to Brighton Classic Car Run

July
6th-9th Hastings Beer & Music Festival, The Tennis Lawns, Alexandra Park, Dordrecht Way, Hastings
tbc The Siege of Rye, medieval longbow tournament

August
13th Pride in Brighton & Hove, parade, Preston Park (provisional)
tbc Rye Medieval Festival

September
3rd-18th Rye Festival (provisional)

October
8th-16th Hastings Week (various venues)
15th Hastings Borough Bonfire Celebrations (provisional)

November
6th London to Brighton Veteran Car Run, Hyde Park

December
21st Burning of the Clocks Parade with lanterns and fireworks, Brighton seafront

Above: Brighton Pier

ALFRISTON   Map 05 TQ50

ALFRISTON CLERGY HOUSE
The Tye BN26 5TL
➲ (4m NE of Seaford, E of B2108, next to church)
☎ 01323 870001   🖷 01323 871318
e-mail: alfriston@nationaltrust.org.uk

This 14th-century thatched Wealden 'hall house' was the first building to be acquired by the National Trust in 1896. It has an unusual chalk and sour milk floor, and its pretty cottage garden is in an idyllic setting beside Alfriston's parish church, with views across the meandering River Cockmere.

Times: Open 6-21 Mar Sat-Sun 11-4, Apr-Oct Sat-Mon, daily (ex Tue & Fri), 10-5. 3 Nov-19 Dec, Wed-Sun 11-4. **Fee:** ✱ £3 (ch £1.50) Family ticket £7.50 **Facilities:** P (0.25m) & (Braille/large print guides) shop 🐕 (ex guide dogs) 🍴 ▬

DRUSILLAS PARK
BN26 5QS
➲ (off A27 near Alfriston between Brighton & Eastbourne)
☎ 01323 874100   🖷 01323 874101
e-mail: info@drusillas.co.uk

Situated amidst the stunning scenery of the Cuckmere Valley at Alfriston, Drusillas is widely recognised as the Best Small Zoo in England. There are over 100 animal species in naturalistic environments, including meerkats, bats, penguins, monkeys, reptiles and creepy crawlies. The large adventure play area is paradise for anyone who needs to let off steam. There are also beautiful gardens, Panning for Gold, a Wacky Workshop, Jungle Adventure Golf, Explorers Lagoon, Mokomo's Jungle Rock, Vertical Limit, Penguin Plunge, a train that goes through the llama paddock and the Discovery Centre. New for 2005, Alfriston Adventure, a vast indoor play area.

Times: Open all year, daily 10-6 (winter 10-5). (Closed 24-26 Dec). **Fee:** ✱ Family super saver tickets: Family of 3 £27.45, family of 4 £36.45, family of 5 £44.95 **Facilities:** P ▬ ✕ licensed & (rear train carriage & sensory trails) toilets for disabled shop 🐕 (ex guide dogs) ▬

BATTLE — Map 05 TQ71

BATTLE MUSEUM OF LOCAL HISTORY
The Almonry, High St TN33 0EA
➲ (A21 towards Hastings. Turn right onto A2001 on entering Battle at rdbt, cross & park on Market Sq. Museum on High St adjacent to Market Sq, N end of town)
☎ 01424 775955 ▤ 01424 772827
e-mail: enquiries@battlemuseum.org.uk **2 for 1**

The focal point of this museum is the only battle-axe head yet from the Battle of Hastings and a reproduction of the Bayeux Tapestry. There are also local history exhibits. There is a special exhibition displaying the wealth of finds at the Beauport Park Roman Bath House excavated just outside Battle. The museum holds two or three temporary exhibitions each year.
Times: Open Apr-Oct, daily 10.30-4.30 (Sun 2-5). **Fee:** £1 (ch 20p, ch accompanied free). **Facilities:** Ⓟ (20yds) ঙ (single storey building) toilets for disabled shop ✖ (ex guide dogs)

BUCKLEYS YESTERDAY'S WORLD
89-90 High St TN33 0AQ
➲ (A21 onto A2100 towards Battle, opposite Battle Abbey)
☎ 01424 775378 & 774269 **2 for 1**
▤ 01424 775174
e-mail: info@yesterdaysworld.co.uk

A fun day out for all the family, as the past is brought to life. Walk down the cobbled streets of yesteryear and meet the colourful characters in over 30 shop and room settings including a 1930s grocer's and a Victorian kitchen. The exhibition contains many rarities from the 1850s onwards, including some of Queen Victoria's personal effects and letters written by the present queen. The museum is housed in beautiful gardens with children's play village, miniature golf and summer tea rooms.
Times: Open all year, Winter, daily 10-5; Summer, daily 10-6. (Closed 25-26 Dec). **Fee:** ✱ £4.99 (ch £3.75, pen & students £4.75). Family ticket £16.75. Discount for special needs visitors & groups of 15+.
Facilities: Ⓟ (100yds) (£2 per day) ▱ ঙ (limited access for wheelchairs) toilets for disabled shop ◼

1066 BATTLE OF HASTINGS ABBEY & BATTLEFIELD
TN33 0AD
➲ (A21 onto A2100)
☎ 01424 773792 ▤ 01424 775059

Explore the site of the Battle of Hastings where on 14th October 1066, one of the most famous events in English history took place. Free interactive wand tour of the battlefield and atmospheric abbey ruins.
Times: Open all year, Apr-Sep, daily 10-6 (Oct 10-5); Nov-Mar, daily 10-4. (Closed 24-26 Dec & 1 Jan). **Fee:** ✱ £5 (ch £2.50, concessions £3.80). Family £12.50. Prices & opening times relate to 2004, for further details phone or log onto www.english-heritage.org.uk/visits
Facilities: Ⓟ (charged) ঙ shop ✖ (ex in certain areas) ⌗

BODIAM — Map 05 TQ72

BODIAM CASTLE
TN32 5UA
➲ (2m E of A21 Hurst Green)
☎ 01580 830436 ▤ 01580 830398
e-mail: bodiamcastle@nationaltrust.org.uk

With its tall round drum towers at each corner, Bodiam is something of a fairytale castle. It was built in 1386 by Sir Edward Dalnygrigge, for comfort and defence. The walls measure some 6ft 6in thick, and the great gatehouse was defended by gun loops and three portcullises.
Times: Open 16 Feb-Oct, daily 10-6 or dusk if earlier; Nov-15 Feb, Sat & Sun 10-4 or dusk. Last admission 1 hour before closing.
Fee: ✱ £4.20 (ch £2.10). Family ticket £10.50. Group 15+ £3.60, (ch £1.80). Car £2, Coach £5. **Facilities:** Ⓟ (charged) ▱ ঙ (Braille/large print guides, special parking on request) toilets for disabled shop ✖ (ex in grounds on a lead) ❧ ◼

BRIGHTON — Map 04 TQ30

BOOTH MUSEUM OF NATURAL HISTORY
194 Dyke Rd BN1 5AA
➲ (from A27 Brighton by pass, 1.5m NW of town centre, opposite Dyke Rd Park)
☎ 01273 292777 ▤ 01273 292778 **FREE**
e-mail: boothmus@pavilion.co.uk

The museum was built in 1874 to house the bird collection of Edward Thomas Booth (1840-1890). His collection is still on display, but the museum has expanded considerably since Booth's day and now includes thousands of butterfly and insect specimens, geology galleries with fossils, rocks and local dinosaur bones, a magnificent collection of animal skeletons, largely collected by the Brighton solicitor F W Lucas (1842-1932), and an interactive discovery gallery.
Times: Open all year, Mon-Sat (ex Thu) 10-5, Sun 2-5. (Closed Good Fri, Xmas & 1 Jan). **Facilities:** Ⓟ (road opposite) (4 hr limit) ঙ shop ✖ (ex guide dogs)

BRIGHTON MUSEUM & ART GALLERY
Royal Pavilion Gardens BN1 1EE
➲ (A23/M23 from London, in City centre near seafront. New entrance in the Royal Pavilion Gardens)
☎ 01273 290900 ▤ 01273 292841 **FREE**

A £10 million redevelopment has transformed Brighton museum into a State-of-the-art visitor attraction. Dynamic and innovative new galleries, including fashion, 20th century design and world art, featuring exciting interactive displays

continued

appealing to all ages. The museum also benefits from a spacious new entrance located in the Royal Pavilion gardens and full disabled access.
Times: Open all year, Tue 10-7, Wed-Sat 10-5 & Sun 2-5. (closed Mon ex BHs). **Facilities:** P (5 mins walk) (Church St NCP & on street) ▣ & (lift, tactile exhibits, induction loops, ramps, automatic door) toilets for disabled shop ✘ (ex guide dogs)

PRESTON MANOR
Preston Drove BN1 6SD
➲ (off A23, 2m N of Brighton)
☎ 01273 292770 ▤ 01273 292771
e-mail: visitor.services@brighton-hove.gov.uk
This charming Edwardian manor house is beautifully furnished with notable collections of silver, furniture and paintings and presents a unique opportunity to see an Edwardian home both 'upstairs' and 'downstairs'. The servants' quarters can also be seen, featuring kitchen, butler's pantry and boot hall. The house is set in beautiful gardens, which include a pet cemetery and the 13th-century parish church of St Peter. The newly restored walled garden enables disabled people to explore the garden for the first time.
Times: ✱ Open all year, Tue-Sat 10-5, Sun 2-5, Mon 1-5 (BH Mons 10-5). (Closed Good Fri & 25-26 Dec). **Facilities:** P & (access to ground floor with prior notice) shop ✘ (ex guide dogs)

ROYAL PAVILION
BN1 1EE
➲ (M23/A23 from London, situated in city centre near seafront. 15 min walk from train station)
☎ 01273 290900 ▤ 01273 292871 【2 for 1】
e-mail: visitor.services@brighton-hove.gov.uk
Acclaimed as one of the most exotically beautiful buildings in the British Isles, the Royal Pavilion was the magnificent seaside residence of George IV. The breathtaking Regency palace is decorated in Chinese style, with a romanticised Indian exterior, and surrounded by restored Regency gardens.
Times: Open all year, Apr-Sep, daily 9.30-5.45 (last admission 5); Oct-Mar, daily 10-5.15 (last admission 4.30). **Fee:** ✱ £5.95 (ch £3.50, concessions £4.20) Family ticket £9.20-£15. Groups 20+ £4.95 each. Family ticket (2ad & 4ch) £15.40, (1ad & 4ch) £9.45.
Facilities: P (5 mins walk) (NCP & on Church St) ▣ & (tours for the disabled by arrangement, wheelchairs) toilets for disabled shop ✘ (ex guide dogs) ▦

SEA LIFE CENTRE
Marine Pde BN2 1TB
➲ (Situated next to Brighton Pier between Marine Parade and Madeira Drive)
☎ 01273 604234 ▤ 01273 681840
e-mail: slcbrighton@merlinentertainments.biz
Experience amazing marine displays, set in the world's oldest functioning aquarium. Take a look at over 100 species in their natural habitat, including seahorses, sharks and rays. Over forty exhibits include Adventures at 20,000 Leagues complete with NASA-designed walkthrough observation tunnel. Features also include a Captain Pugwash quiz trail, a soft play area, a cafe and a giftshop.
Times: ✱ Open all year, daily (ex 25 Dec), 10-6. Last admission 5. (Open later on wknds in summer & school holidays)
Facilities: P (200yds) (pay & display) ▣ & toilets for disabled shop ✘ (ex guide dogs) ▦

BATEMAN'S
TN19 7DS
➲ (0.5m SW off A265)
☎ 01435 882302 ▤ 01435 882811
e-mail: batemans@nationaltrust.org.uk

Rudyard Kipling lived for over 34 years in this 17th-century manor house and it remains much the same as it was during his lifetime. His 1928 Rolls Royce Phantom is on display, and the watermill at the bottom of the garden grinds wheat into flour on Saturday afternoons.
Times: Open Apr-1 Nov, Sat-Wed 11-5.30, also open Good Fri, (last admission 4.30). House closes at 5. **Fee:** ✱ £5.20 (ch £2.60). Family ticket £13. Party 15+. **Facilities:** P ▣ ✘ licensed & (Braille guide,touch test,computerised tour of upper floors) toilets for disabled shop ✘ (ex guide/hearing dogs) ▦ ▦

"HOW WE LIVED THEN" MUSEUM OF SHOPS & SOCIAL HISTORY
20 Cornfield Ter BN21 4NS
➲ (just off seafront, between town centre & theatres, signposted)
☎ 01323 737143
e-mail: howwelivedthen@btconnect.com
Over the last 40 years, Jan and Graham Upton have collected over 100,000 items which are now displayed on four floors of authentic old shops and room-settings, transporting visitors back to their grandparents' era. Other displays, such as seaside souvenirs, wartime rationing and Royal mementoes, help to capture 100 years of social history.
Times: Open all year daily, 10-5.30 (last entry 5). Winter times subject to change, telephone establishment. **Fee:** £4 (ch 5-15 £3, under 5's free, pen £3.50). Party 10+. **Facilities:** P (outside) & (no charge for disabled) shop

WISH TOWER PUPPET MUSEUM
Martello Tower No 73, King Edward Pde BN21 4BU
➲ (on seafront, W of pier)
☎ 01323 417776 ▤ 01323 644440
e-mail: puppet.workshop@virgin.net
This museum hosts a unique display of puppets from all over the world. From early shadow puppets of Asia, through over 300 years of Punch and Judy in England to television and film puppets of today. Puppet shows sometimes take place during the summer.
Times: ✱ Open May-mid Jul & Sep, wknds 11-5; mid Jul-Aug, daily 11-5. **Facilities:** P (100mtrs) shop ✘ ▦

FIRLE   Map 05 TQ40
FIRLE PLACE
BN8 6LP
➲ (off A27, Eastbourne to Brighton road)
☎ 01273 858307   🖷 01273 858188
e-mail: firleestate@aol.com

Home of the Gage family for over 500 years, the house has a Tudor core but was remodelled in the 18th century. Its treasures include important European and English Old Master paintings, fine English and French furniture, and porcelain, including notable examples from Sèvres and English factories. There are family monuments and brasses in the church at West Firle.

Times: ✱ Open 12 May-Sep, Sun, Wed, Thu & BHs 1.45-4.15.
Facilities: 🅿 ✖ licensed ♿ toilets for disabled shop ✖ (ex in garden)

FOREST ROW   Map 05 TQ43
ASHDOWN FOREST LLAMA PARK NEW
Wych Cross RH18 5JN
➲ (on A22 between Uckfield & East Grinstead, 250mtrs S of junct with A275)
☎ 01825 712040   🖷 01825 713698
e-mail: info@llamapark.co.uk

One of the leading llama breeding centres in the country. Walk around three 18th-century barns and a new visitor centre to discover over 100 llamas and alpacas. Llamas and alpacas were first domesticated in South America more than 5,000 years ago, and visitors can learn all about their contribution to these societies at the museum. Visitors can also walk with llamas in the grounds, but these walks do need to be booked and paid for in advance. Contact the park for more details.

Times: Open daily 10-5 (closed 25 & 26 Dec) **Fee:** ✱ £4 (ch, pen & concessions £3.50) **Facilities:** 🅿 💷 ♿ (ramps, wheelchairs provided for free) toilets for disabled shop 🍴

GLYNDE   Map 05 TQ40
GLYNDE PLACE
BN8 6SX
➲ (off A27 between Lewes & Eastbourne)
☎ 01273 858224   🖷 01273 858224
e-mail: hampden@glyndeplace.co.uk

A lovely Elizabethan manor with 18th-century additions, in a beautiful downland setting. Glynde Place is the family home of Viscount and Viscountess Hampden whose forebears built the house in 1569 using a mixture of flint and stone. Portraits, furniture, silver, embroidery and books testify to 400 years of family life.

Times: Open Jun-Sep, Wed, Sun & Aug BH 2-4.45. **Facilities:** 🅿 💷 shop ✖ (guide dogs)

HAILSHAM   Map 05 TQ50
MICHELHAM PRIORY
Upper Dicker BN27 3QS
➲ (off A22 & A27, 2m W of Hailsham, 8m NW of Eastbourne, signposted from A27 & A22)
☎ 01323 844224   🖷 01323 844030
e-mail: adminmich@sussexpast.co.uk

Set on a moated island surrounded by glorious gardens, Michelham Priory is one of the most beautiful historic houses in Sussex. Founded in 1229 for Augustinian canons, the Priory is approached through a 14th-century gatehouse spanning the longest water-filled medieval moat in the country. Most of the original priory was demolished during the Dissolution, but the remains were incorporated into a
continued

Tudor farm that became a country house. Outside, the gardens are enhanced by a working watermill, physic garden, smithy, rope museum and the dramatic Elizabethan Great Barn.

Times: ✱ Open Mar-Oct, Tue-Sun (daily in Aug & BH Mons). Mar & Oct 10.30-4, Apr-Jul & Sep 10.30-5, Aug 10.30-5.30. **Facilities:** 🅿 💷 ✖ licensed ♿ (pre-booked wheelchairs, Braille guide & tactile tours) toilets for disabled shop ✖ (ex guide dogs) 🍴

HALLAND   Map 05 TQ51
BENTLEY WILDFOWL & MOTOR MUSEUM
BN8 5AF
➲ (7m NE of Lewes, signposted off A22, A26 & B2192)
☎ 01825 840573   🖷 01825 841322
e-mail: barrysutherland@pavilion.co.uk

Hundreds of swans, geese and ducks from all over the world can be seen on lakes and ponds along with flamingoes and peacocks. There is a fine array of Veteran, Edwardian and Vintage vehicles, and the house has splendid antiques and wildfowl paintings. The gardens specialise in old fashioned roses. Other attractions include woodland walks, a nature trail, Education Centre, adventure playground and a miniature train.

Times: ✱ Open 17 Mar-Oct, daily 10.30-4.30. House open from noon, Apr-Nov, Feb & part of Mar, wknds only. Estate closed Dec & Jan. House closed all winter. **Facilities:** 🅿 💷 ♿ (wheelchairs available) toilets for disabled shop ✖ (ex guide dogs) 🍴

HASTINGS   Map 05 TQ80
OLD TOWN HALL MUSEUM OF LOCAL HISTORY
Old Town Hall, High St TN34 3EW
➲ (off A259 coast road into High St in Hastings old town. Signposted)
☎ 01424 781166   🖷 01424 781165   `FREE`
e-mail: oldtownmuseum@hastings.gov.uk

Situated in the heart of Hastings Old Town, the museum was originally a Georgian Town Hall built in 1823. Refurbished displays tell the story of Hastings Old Town as a walk back in time, with features including a Cinque Ports ship, and interactive displays.

Times: Open Apr-Sep, daily 10-5; Oct-Mar, daily 11-4.
Facilities: 🅿 (150yds) (parking meters in operation) ♿ (lift, evac chair, low-level displays, audio tour) toilets for disabled shop ✖ (ex guide dogs)

SMUGGLERS ADVENTURE
St Clements Caves, West Hill TN34 3HY
➲ (follow brown and cream signs along A259 coast road through Hastings. Use seafront carpark and then take West cliff railway or follow signed footpath)
☎ 01424 422964   🖷 01424 721483
e-mail: smugglers@discoverhastings.co.uk

A Smuggler's Adventure is a themed experience housed in a labyrinth of caverns and passages deep below the West Hill. Visitors first tour a comprehensive exhibition and museum, followed by a video theatre, before embarking on the Adventure Walk - a trip through several acres of caves with life-size tableaux, push-button automated models and dramatic scenic effects depicting life in the days of 18th-century smuggling.

Times: Open all year daily, Etr-Sep 10-5.30; Oct-Etr 11-4.30. (Closed 24-26 Dec). **Fee:** ✱ £5.95 (ch £3.95, concessions £4.95). Family ticket £16.50. **Facilities:** 🅿 (500yds) (parking meters on some streets) shop ✖ (ex guide dogs) 🍴

1066 STORY IN HASTINGS CASTLE
Castle Hill Rd, West Hill TN34 3RG
➲ (close to A259 seafront, 2m from B2093)
☎ 01424 781111 & 781112 (info line)
🖷 01424 781186
e-mail: bookings@discoverhastings.co.uk

The ruins of the Norman castle stand on the cliffs, close to the site of William the Conqueror's first motte-and-bailey castle in England. It was excavated in 1825 and 1968, and old dungeons were discovered in 1894. An unusual approach to the castle can be made via the West Hill Cliff Railway.
Times: Open daily, Oct-26 Mar 11-3.30, 27 Mar-Sep 10-5 (Closed 24-26 Dec). **Fee:** ✱ £3.40 (ch £2.25, pen & students £2.75, disabled free). Family ticket £10. (fee entitles visitor to third off Caves & Underwater World) **Facilities:** P (seafront) (time restrictions, pay & display) ♿ (concrete slope, some uneven ground) shop ✖ (ex guide dogs)

HERSTMONCEUX   Map 05 TQ61

THE OBSERVATORY SCIENCE CENTRE
BN27 1RN
➲ (2m E of village on Boreham Street to Pevensey Road)
☎ 01323 832731   🖷 01323 832741
e-mail: info@the-observatory.org

From the 1950s to the 1980s this was part of the Royal Greenwich Observatory, and was used by astronomers to observe and chart movements in the night sky. Visitors can learn about not only astronomy, but also other areas of science in a series of interactive and engaging displays. There are also exhibitions, a discovery park, and a collection of unusual giant exhibits.
Times: Open Apr-Sep daily 10-6; Mar & Oct 10-5; Nov-Feb 10-4; (wknds only in Jan & Dec starting 10 Jan & finishing 12 Dec) **Fee:** ✱ £5.80 (ch 4-15 £4.20). Family ticket (2 ad & 3 ch or 1ad & 4 ch) £17.50 **Facilities:** P 🍴 ♿ (ramps+ disabled entrance) toilets for disabled shop ✖ (ex guide dogs) 🖼

THE TRUGGERY
Coopers Croft BN27 1QL
➲ (from A22 at Hailsham, Boship rdbt, take A271 towards Bexhill for 4m)
☎ 01323 832314   🖷 01323 832314
e-mail: sarah@truggery.fsnet.co.uk

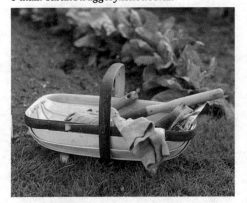

The art of Sussex trug making can be seen through all the work processes including preparing timber, use of the draw knife and assembly of trug.
Times: Open Mon-Fri 10-5, Sat 10-1. Closed Sun. Jan-Apr opening times may vary. **Facilities:** P ♿ shop 🚻 🖼

HOVE   Map 04 TQ20

BRITISH ENGINEERIUM-MUSEUM OF STEAM & MECHANICAL ANTIQUITIES
off Nevill Rd BN3 7QA
➲ (signposted off A27 from Worthing & Eastbourne)
☎ 01273 559583   🖷 01273 566403
e-mail: info@britishengineerium.com

This restored Victorian water pumping station has an original working beam engine of 1876, and a French Corliss horizontal engine which won first prize at the Paris International Exhibition of 1889. There are also traction engines, fire engines, and many other full-size and model engines. Also an exhibition of craftsmen's tools and domestic appliances. Boilers are fired up and in steam on special days.
Times: ✱ Open all year, daily 10-4. In steam first Sun in month & Sun & Mon of BH's. Telephone for details of days closed prior to Xmas. **Facilities:** P ♿ shop ✖ (ex guide dogs)

LEWES   Map 05 TQ41

ANNE OF CLEVES HOUSE
52 Southover High St BN7 1JA
➲ (S of town centre off A27/A26/A275)
☎ 01273 474610   🖷 01273 486990
e-mail: anne@sussexpast.co.uk

Henry VIII gave this beautiful timber-framed house to Anne of Cleves, his fourth wife, as part of her divorce settlement. Today there are collections of early English furniture, Sussex pottery and stone from Lewes Priory, plus a local social history exhibition. The Wealden Iron Gallery tells the story of the industrial past of Sussex and contains a large collection of iron artefacts.
Times: ✱ Open Jan-Feb & Nov-Dec, Tue-Sat 10-5; Mar-Oct, Tue-Sat 10-5, Sun, Mon & BH's 11-5. Closed 24-26 Dec. **Facilities:** P (25yds) (on street-2hr restriction) ♿ shop ✖ (ex guide dogs) 🖼

LEWES CASTLE & BARBICAN HOUSE MUSEUM
169 High St BN7 1YE
➲ (N of High St off A27/A26/A275)
☎ 01273 486290   🖷 01273 486990
e-mail: castle@sussexpast.co.uk

High above the medieval streets stands Lewes Castle, begun soon after the Norman Conquest by William de Warenne as his stronghold in Sussex and added to over the next 300 years, culminating in the magnificent Barbican. Thomas Read Kemp and his family owned and updated the ruins during Georgian times. Barbican House is next to the castle, and now houses a museum covering the area from pre-history to the late medieval period. Visitors can climb to the top of the castle, from where they are rewarded with stunning views. A 'sound and light' show in the museum below tells the story of the town of Lewes through the ages.
Times: ✱ Open daily, Tue-Sat 10-5.30, Sun & Mon 11-5.30. Last admission 30 mins before closing. Closed Mon in Jan & Xmas. **Facilities:** P (on street parking) shop ✖ (ex guide dogs) 🖼

> An asterisk * indicates that opening times and prices are for 2004. Please contact the attraction for up-to-date information.

NEWHAVEN Map 05 TQ40

PARADISE PARK & GARDENS

Avis Rd BN9 0DH

➲ (signposted off A26 & A259)

☎ 01273 512123 ▤ 01273 616005 **2 for 1**

e-mail: enquiries@paradisepark.co.uk

A perfect day out for plant lovers whatever the season. Discover the unusual garden designs with waterfalls, fountains and lakes, including the Caribbean garden and the tranquil Oriental garden. The Conservatory Gardens complex contains a large variety of the world's flora divided into several zones. There's also a Sussex history trail and Planet Earth with moving dinosaurs and interactive displays, plus rides and amusements for children.

Times: Open all year, daily 9-6 (Closed 25-26 Dec). **Fee:** ✱ £5.99 (ch £4.99). Family ticket £19.99 (2 ad & 3 ch). **Facilities:** ▣ ⬛ ✖ licensed � (all areas level or ramped) toilets for disabled shop garden centre ✖ (ex guide dogs) ◼

NORTHIAM Map 05 TQ82

GREAT DIXTER

TN31 6PH

➲ (off A28, signposted)

☎ 01797 252878 ▤ 01797 252879

e-mail: office@greatdixter.co.uk

Birthplace and home of Christopher Lloyd, gardening writer, Great Dixter was built in 1460 and boasts one of the largest timber-framed buildings in the country. Lutyens was employed to restore both the house and gardens in 1910. The gardens are now a combination of meadows, ponds, topiary and notably the Long Border and Exotic Garden.

Times: Open 29 Mar-26 Oct, Tue-Sun & BH Mon, 2-5.30 (last admission 5); Gardens only open from 11 on Sun & Mon BH wknds only. **Fee:** House & Gardens £6.50 (ch £2). Gardens only £5 (ch £1.50). Party 25+. **Facilities:** ▣ ⅹ (one wheelchair available free of charge) toilets for disabled shop garden centre ✖ (ex guide dogs) ◼

PEVENSEY Map 05 TQ60

PEVENSEY CASTLE

BN24 5LE

➲ (off A259)

☎ 01323 762604

William the Conqueror landed here in 1066 and established his first stronghold. Discover the history of the Norman castle and the remains of an unusual keep through the free audio tour.

Times: Open all year, Apr-Sep, daily 10-6; Oct-Mar, Sat-Sun & BH Mons 10-4 (Closed 24-26 Dec & 1 Jan). **Fee:** ✱ £3.50 (ch £1.80, concessions £2.60). Prices & opening times relate to 2004, for further details phone or log onto www.english-heritage.org.uk/visits **Facilities:** ▣ (charged) ⬛ ⅹ shop ⬛

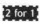

This symbol indicates attractions which have chosen to participate in our 2-for-1 voucher scheme

RYE Map 05 TQ92

LAMB HOUSE

West St TN31 7ES

➲ (facing W end of Church)

☎ 01732 453401 ▤ 01732 452023

This 18th-century house was the home of novelist Henry James from 1898 until his death in 1916, and was later occupied by the writer, E F Benson. Some of James' personal posessions can be seen. There is also a charming walled garden.

Times: Open 27 Mar-30 Oct, Wed & Sat 2-6, (last admission 5.30). **Fee:** ✱ £2.75 (ch £1.30). Family ticket £6.90. Groups £2.35 per person **Facilities:** ▣ (200mtrs) ⅹ (scented plants & herbs, some steps to house) ✖ (ex guide dogs) ◼

RYE CASTLE MUSEUM

3 East St TN31 7JY

➲ (In town centre, on A259)

☎ 01797 226728 **2 for 1**

Part of the museum is housed in a stone tower built as a fortification in 1249. The museum's collection of ironwork, medieval pots and smuggling items are on display here, while the East Street site contains the rest of the collection, including pottery made in Rye, fashions, an eighteenth-century fire engine, toys, cinque port regalia, a special exhibition on Rye in WWII, descriptions of the changes to the harbour and shipbuilding in Rye and businesses & leisure in Rye during the 19th & 20th centuries. The museum tells the story of Rye's long and illustrious history.

Times: Open all year Nov-Mar wknds only 10.30-3; Apr-Oct Thu-Mon 10.30-5. (last entry 4.30). Closed between 1-2. **Fee:** Entrance to both sites: £2.90 (ch under 7 free, ch 7-16 £1.50, concessions £2). Family ticket £5.90. Single entry only: £1.90 (ch under 7 free, ch 7-16 £1, concessions £1.50). Family ticket £4.50. Party 8+. **Facilities:** ▣ (30yds) (street 1hr) (long stay 10mins away) ⅹ (only East Street accessible) toilets for disabled shop ✖ (ex guide dogs)

SHEFFIELD PARK Map 05 TQ42

SHEFFIELD PARK GARDEN

TN22 3QX

➲ (Midway between East Grinstead & Lewes, 5m NW of Uckfield, on E side of A275 between A272 & A22)

☎ 01825 790231 ▤ 01825 791264

e-mail: sheffieldpark@nationaltrust.org.uk

Sheffield Park was originally landscaped by 'Capability' Brown, in about 1775 to create a beautiful park with four lakes and cascades. Further extensive planting was done at the beginning of the 20th century, to give emphasis to autumn colour among the trees. In May and June masses of azaleas and rhododendrons bloom and later there are magnificent waterlilies on the lakes. Autumn brings stunning colours from the many rare trees and shrubs. Special events throughout the season.

Times: Open Jan-Feb, Sat-Sun 10.30-4; Mar-Oct, Tue-Sun (open BH Mons) 10.30-6; Nov-Dec, Tue-Sun 10.30-4 (Last admission 1 hour before closing or dusk if earlier). **Fee:** ✱ £5.20 (ch £2.60, under 5's free). Family ticket £13. NT members free. **Facilities:** ▣ ⬛ ⅹ (powered self drive cars & wheelchairs available) toilets for disabled shop ✖ (ex guide/hearing dogs) ◼ ◼

SHEFFIELD PARK STATION Map 05 TQ42

BLUEBELL RAILWAY
Sheffield Park Station TN22 3QL
➲ (4.5m E of Haywards Heath, off A275)
☎ 01825 720800 & 722370 📠 01825 720804
e-mail: info@bluebell-railway.co.uk
A volunteer-run heritage steam railway with nine miles of track running through pretty Sussex countryside. Please note that there is no parking at Kingscote Station. If you wish to board the train here, catch the bus (service 473) which connects Kingscote and East Grinstead.
Times: Open all year, Sat & Sun, daily May-Sep & during school holidays. Santa Specials run Dec. For timetable and information regarding trains contact above. **Fee:** ✱ 3rd class return fare £9 (ch £4.50). Family ticket £25. Admission to Sheffield Park Station only £1.60 (ch 80p). Other tickets available on request. **Facilities:** 🅿 🍺 ✗ licensed ♿ (special carriage for wheelchairs & carers with lift) toilets for disabled shop 🍴

TICEHURST   Map 05 TQ63

PASHLEY MANOR GARDENS
TN5 7HE
➲ (on B2099 between A21 and Ticehurst village, brown tourist signposted)
☎ 01580 200888 📠 01580 200102
e-mail: info@pashleymanorgardens.com
Once belonging to the family of Anne Boleyn, Pashley Manor has a beautiful traditional English garden that has been open to the public since 1992. Visitors can wander among fine old trees, fountains, springs and large ponds, all surrounded by romantic landscaping and imaginative plantings. Statues and sculptures by Europe's leading sculptors are on display both in the gardens and in the Great Hall. A series of craft and plant fairs take place throughout the year.
Times: Open 6 Apr-Sep, Tue-Thu, Sat & BH Mon 11-5; Garden only Oct, Mon-Fri 10-4. **Fee:** ✱ £6 (pen £5.50) **Facilities:** 🅿 ✗ licensed ♿ toilets for disabled shop ✈ (ex guide dogs) 🍴

Above: Beachy Head

WEST SUSSEX

EVENTS & FESTIVALS

March
25th British & World Marbles Championships, Greyhound pub, Radford Road, Crawley

May
1st-2nd Spring Garden & Leisure Show, Showground, Ardingly, Haywards Heath
25th-26th Corpus Christi Carpet of Flowers & Floral Festival, Cathedral of Our Lady & St Philip Howard, Arundel
30th Spring Carnival, Southgate Playing Field, Southgate Avenue, Crawley

June
9th-11th South of England Show, Showground, Ardingly, Haywards Heath
18th-19th Parham Steam Rally, Parham House, Pulborough
25th-26th Crawley Folk Festival, The Hawth, Hawth Avenue, Crawley

July
2nd Pop in the Park, Tilgate Park, Crawley
3rd Prom in the Park, Tilgate Park, Crawley
15th-31st Petworth Festival, various venues
30th-31st Crawley International Mela
tbc Chichester Festivities, various venues

August
13-14th Crawley Circus Festival, Crawley
tbc Arundel Festival
tbc Bognor Birdman, attempts at self-powered flight, esplanade & seafront, Bognor Regis
tbc Littlehampton Regatta, River Arun, Arun Parade and Oyster Pond, Littlehampton

September
10th Findon Great Sheep Fair, Findon

October
1st-2nd South of England Autumn Show, Showground, Ardingly, Haywards Heath

December
3rd-4th Festive Food & Drink Fayre, South of England Showground, Haywards Heath

Above: Clayton on the South Downs Way

AMBERLEY   Map 04 TQ01
AMBERLEY WORKING MUSEUM
BN18 9LT

➲ (on B2139, between Arundel and Storrington, adjacent to Amberley railway station)

☎ 01798 831370   ▤ 01798 831831

e-mail: office@amberleymuseum.co.uk

36 acre open-air museum dedicated to the industrial heritage of the south east of England. Traditional craftspeople on site (including a blacksmith and potter), working narrow-gauge railway and vintage bus collection, Connected Earth telecommunications display, Seeboard Electricity Hall, stationary engines, print workshop, woodturners, wheelwrights, nature trails, restaurant, shop and much more.

Times: ✱ Open 12 Mar-2 Nov, Wed-Sun & BH Mon 10-5.30 (last admission 4.30). Also open daily during school holidays.
Facilities: 🅿 🖳 ♿ (wheelchairs available for loan & large print guides) toilets for disabled shop ➡

ARDINGLY   Map 05 TQ32
WAKEHURST PLACE & MILLENNIUM SEED BANK
RH17 6TN

➲ (M23 junct 10. 1.5m NW of Ardingly, on B2028)

☎ 01444 894066   ▤ 01444 894069

e-mail: wakehurst@kew.org

Woodland and lakes linked by a pretty watercourse make this large garden a beautiful place to walk, and it also has an amazing variety of interesting trees and shrubs, a winter garden, and a rock walk. It is administered and maintained by the Royal Botanic Gardens, Kew.

Times: Open all year (except 24 & 25 Dec) Nov-Jan 10-4, Feb & Oct 10-5, Mar 10-6, Apr-Sep 10-7. Last admission 30 mins before close. Mansion restaurant, shop & exhibition closes 1hr before garden & car park. **Fee:** £8 (concessions £7.50) **Facilities:** 🅿 🖳 ✗ licensed ♿ (wheelchair available) toilets for disabled shop garden centre ➡ (ex guide dogs) ➡

ARUNDEL   Map 04 TQ00
ARUNDEL CASTLE
BN18 9AB

➲ (on A27 between Chichester & Worthing)

☎ 01903 883136   ▤ 01903 884581

e-mail: info@arundelcastle.org

Set high on a hill in West Sussex, this magnificent castle and stately home, seat of the Dukes of Norfolk for nearly 1000 years, commands stunning views across the river Arun and out to sea. Climb to the keep and battlements; marvel at a fine collection of 16th-century furniture; portraits by Van Dyke, Gainsborough, Canaletto and others; tapestries and the personal possessions of Mary, Queen of Scots; wander in the grounds and renovated Victorian flower and vegetable gardens.

Times: Open 25 Mar-Oct, Sun-Fri 11-5, Castle open 12-5. Last admission 4. (Closed Sat) **Fee:** ✱ £9 (ch 5-16 £5.50, pen £7). Family ticket £24.50. Party 20+. **Facilities:** 🅿 🖳 ♿ toilets for disabled shop ➡ (ex guide dogs) ➡

WWT ARUNDEL
Mill Rd BN18 9PB

➲ (signposted from A27 & A29)

☎ 01903 883355   ▤ 01903 884834

e-mail: arundel@wwt.org.uk

More than a thousand ducks, geese and swans from all over the world can be found here, many of which are so friendly that they will eat from your hand. The wild reserve attracts a variety of birds and includes a reedbed habitat considered so vital to the wetland wildlife it shelters that it has been designated a Site of Special Scientific Interest. Visitors can walk right through this reedbed on a specially designed boardwalk. There is a packed programme of events and activities throughout the year.

Times: Open all year, daily. Summer 9.30-5; Winter 9.30-4.30. Last admission Summer 5; Winter 4. (Closed 25 Dec). **Fee:** ✱ £5.75 (ch £3.50, pen £4.50). Family ticket £14.50. **Facilities:** 🅿 🖳 ✗ licensed ♿ (level paths, free wheelchair loan) toilets for disabled shop ➡ (ex guide/hearing dogs) ➡

ASHINGTON   Map 04 TQ11
HOLLY GATE CACTUS GARDEN
Billingshurst Rd RH20 3BB

➲ (off A24, towards Ashington then B2133 towards Billingshurst for 0.5m)

☎ 01903 892930   2 for 1

e-mail: info@hollygatecactus.co.uk

A mecca for the cactus enthusiast, with more than 30,000 succulent and cactus plants, including many rare types. They come from both arid and tropical parts of the world, and are housed in over 10,000 sq ft of greenhouses.

Times: Open all year, daily 9-5. (Closed 25-26 Dec). **Fee:** £2 (ch & pen £1.50). Family ticket £6. Party 20+ 25p deduction.
Facilities: 🅿 ♿ shop garden centre ➡ (ex guide dogs) ➡

BIGNOR   Map 04 SU91
BIGNOR ROMAN VILLA & MUSEUM
RH20 1PH

➲ (6m S of Pulborough and 6m N of Arundel on A29, signposted. 8m S of Petworth on A285, sign posted)

☎ 01798 869259   ▤ 01798 869259

e-mail: bignorromanvilla@care4free.net

Rediscovered in 1811, this Roman house was built on a grand scale. It is one of the largest known, and has spectacular mosaics. The heating system can also be seen, and various finds from excavations are on show. The longest mosaic in Britain (82ft) is on display here in its original position.

Times: Open Mar-Apr, Tue-Sun & BH 10-5; May daily 10-5; Jun-Sep daily 10-6; Oct daily 10-5 **Fee:** ✱ £4 (ch 5-15 £1.70, pen £2.85). Party 10+. Guided tours by arrangement. **Facilities:** 🅿 🖳 ♿ (Most areas accessible) shop ➡ (ex guide dogs) ➡

BRAMBER   Map 04 TQ11
BRAMBER CASTLE
BN4 3FB

➲ (on W side of village off A283)

The remains of a Norman motte and bailey castle. The gatehouse, still standing almost to its original height, and walls are still visible.

Times: Open any reasonable time. **Facilities:** 🅿 🐾

CHICHESTER   Map 04 SU80

CHICHESTER CATHEDRAL
West St PO19 1PX
➲ (in city centre)
☎ 01243 782595 📠 01243 812499
e-mail: visitors@chichestercathedral.org.uk
The beauty of the 900-year-old cathedral, site of the shrine of St Richard, is enhanced by many art treasures, ancient and modern.
Times: ✱ Open end Mar-end Sep daily 7.15-7; end Sep-end Mar 7.15-6. **Facilities:** 🅿 (within city walls) 🍴✗♿ (touch & hearing centre, loop system) toilets for disabled shop ✖ (ex guide dogs)

MECHANICAL MUSIC & DOLL COLLECTION
Church Rd, Portfield PO19 4HN
➲ (1m E of Chichester, signposted off A27)
☎ 01243 372646 📠 01243 370299
A unique opportunity to see and hear barrel organs, polyphons, musical boxes, fair organs etc - all fully restored and playing. A magical musical tour to fascinate and entertain all ages. The doll collection contains fine examples of Victorian china and wax dolls, and felt and velvet dolls of the 1920s.
Times: Open Jun-Sep, Wed 1-4; Group bookings anytime in the year by prior arrangement. **Fee:** ✱ £2.50 (ch £1.25).
Facilities: 🅿♿ shop ✖ (ex guide dogs)

PALLANT HOUSE GALLERY
9 North Pallant PO19 1TJ
➲ (from city centre (the Cross) take East St turning right at Superdrug. Gallery at end of North Pallant on left)
☎ 01243 774557 📠 01243 536038
e-mail: info@pallant.org.uk
A Queen Anne townhouse and a modern building have been combined to house a fine collection of 20th century British art. The permanent collection includes pieces by: Auerbach, Blake, Bomberg, Caulfield, Freud, Hamilton, Hitchens, Lege, Moore, Nash, Nicholson, Piper, Richards, Severini, Sickert and Sutherland. Telephone for details of temporary exhibitions.
Times: Closed until Spring 2005 for refurbishment **Facilities:** 🅿 (100 yds) 🍴✗ licensed ♿ toilets for disabled shop ✖ (ex guide dogs) 🛒

EAST GRINSTEAD   Map 05 TQ33

STANDEN
RH19 4NE
➲ (2m S of East Grinstead, signposted from B2110)
☎ 01342 323029 📠 01342 316424
e-mail: standen@nationaltrust.org.uk
Standen is a showpiece of the 19th-century Arts and Crafts Movement. It was designed by Philip Webb for the Beale family, and is decorated throughout with William Morris wallpapers and fabrics. The interior has been carefully preserved. Webb also designed some of the furniture and details. There is a beautiful hillside garden. Telephone for details of special events.
Times: House open Apr-Nov, Wed-Sun & BH 11-5. Garden open same dates as house 11-6 & Nov-mid Dec, Fri-Sun 11-3. Last entry to house 4.30 **Fee:** ✱ House & garden £6. Garden only £3.20. (ch half price). Family ticket £15. Joint ticket which includes same day entry to Nymans garden £10, available Wed-Fri. **Facilities:** 🅿✗ licensed ♿ (Braille guide & touch list & large print guide) toilets for disabled shop ✖ (ex guide dogs & on wood walk) 🐾🛒

FISHBOURNE   Map 04 SU80

FISHBOURNE ROMAN PALACE
Salthill Rd PO19 3QR
➲ (off A27 onto A259 into Fishbourne. Turn right into Salthill Rd & right into Roman Way)
☎ 01243 785859 📠 01243 539266
e-mail: adminfish@sussexpast.co.uk
This is the largest known Roman residence in Britain. It was occupied from the 1st to the 3rd centuries AD, and has mosaic floors and painted walls. 25 of these mosaic floors can still be seen in varying states of completeness, including others rescued from elsewhere in the area. Outside, part of the garden has been replanted to its original 1st-century plan. The museum displays a collection of finds from the excavations and tells the story of the site's discovery. An audio-visual presentation helps bring the site back to life, as it would have been many centuries ago.
Times: ✱ Open all year, daily Feb-15 Dec. Feb, Nov-Dec 10-4; Mar-Jul & Sep-Oct 10-5; Aug 10-6. Winter wknds 10-4. **Facilities:** 🅿🍴 ♿ (self guiding tapes & tactile objects for the blind) toilets for disabled shop garden centre ✖ (ex guide dogs) 🛒

FONTWELL   Map 04 SU90

DENMANS GARDEN
Denmans Ln BN18 0SU
➲ (5m E of Chichester off A27 W between Chichester and Arundel, adjacent to Fontwell racecourse)
☎ 01243 542808 📠 01243 544064 **2 for 1**
e-mail: denmans@denmans-garden.co.uk
A unique 20th-century garden artistically planted with an emphasis on colour, shape and texture. Plants within the garden are allowed to self-seed and ramble. The garden makes much use of gravel throughout, including a gravel 'stream'. A remarkable collection of plants, including glass areas for tender plants, a walled garden and plenty of quiet sitting areas.
Times: Open all year daily 9-5 (ex 24-31 Dec & 3 Jan) **Fee:** £3.50 (ch £1.95, ch under 4 free, pen £3). Party 15+ £2.80 each.
Facilities: 🅿🍴♿ shop garden centre ✖ (ex guide dogs) 🛒

GOODWOOD   Map 04 SU81

GOODWOOD HOUSE
PO18 0PX
➲ (3m NE of Chichester)
☎ 01243 755000 📠 01243 755005
e-mail: curator@goodwood.co.uk
Ancestral home of the Dukes of Richmond for 300 years. Following refurbishment the State Apartments have taken on new life, including the restored tapestry drawing room. Goodwood was the country home of the scandalous and glamorous Lennox sisters, immortalised in the BBC TV production of *Aristocrats*. Unrivalled as an English ancestral collection, the paintings include works by Van Dyck, Reynolds, Stubbs and Canaletto.
Times: ✱ Open 30 Mar-6 Oct, Sun & Mon; 3-28 Aug, Sun-Thu 1-5. (Closed 13 Apr, 22 Jun, 6, 7, 13 & 14 Jul & 7 Sep). **Facilities:** 🅿🍴 ♿ (ramp at front of house, disabled parking area) toilets for disabled shop ✖ 🛒

HANDCROSS   Map 04 TQ22

NYMANS GARDEN
RH17 6EB
➲ (on B2114)
☎ 01444 400321 & 400777   🖷 01444 400253
e-mail: nymans@nationaltrust.org.uk

Nymans is one of the great gardens of the Sussex Weald. It has a fascinating and exotic plant collection, with romantic ruins and woodland walks. There are great opportunities to enjoy Nymans and the surrounding estate in any season. **Times:** Open Garden: 23 Feb-30 Oct, Wed-Sun & BH. Nov-Mar, wknds 11-4 (restricted access due to ground conditions). House open end Mar-30 Oct, 11-5. (Closed 25-26 Dec & 1-2 Jan). **Fee:** ✱ £6.50 (ch £3.25). Family ticket £16.25, joint ticket which includes same day entry to Standen £10. **Facilities:** 🅿 💷 ㊓ (wheelchair route, wheelchair available, Braille guide) toilets for disabled shop ✖ (ex guide dogs & hearing dogs) 🍴🍽

HAYWARDS HEATH   Map 05 TQ32

BORDE HILL GARDEN
Balcombe Rd RH16 1XP
➲ (0.5m N of Haywards Heath on Balcombe Road, 3m from A23)
☎ 01444 450326   🖷 01444 440427
e-mail: info@bordehill.co.uk

Open daily, this beautiful Grade II heritage garden is a collection of rare trees and shrubs from around the world, and appeals to visitors of all ages. Spring is heralded by magnificent magnolias, rhododendron and azaleas, blending into summer with fragrant roses and herbaceous plants, developing into rich autumn borders before winter's icy splendour. Formal garden rooms, such as the Rose and Italian Garden, combine with informal areas like the Azalea Ring, Garden of Allah, and Round Dell. **Times:** Open all year, daily 10-6 or dusk if earlier. **Fee:** ✱ £6 (ch £3.50). Party 20+ £5 (ch £3) each. **Facilities:** 🅿 💷 ✖ licensed ㊓ (wheelchairs available, audio/Braille guides) toilets for disabled shop garden centre 🍽

HIGHDOWN   Map 04 SU91

HIGHDOWN NEW
Highdown Gardens BN12 6PE
➲ (N off A259 between Worthing & Littlehampton. Access is off dual carriageway, when coming from E proceed to rdbt)
☎ 01903 501054   🖷 01903 218757   FREE
e-mail: chris.beardsley@worthing.gov.uk

Set on downland countryside this unique garden overlooks the sea, and has been deemed a National collection due to the unique assortment of rare plants and trees. The garden was the achievement of Sir Frederick and Lady Stern, who worked for fifty years to prove that plants could grow on chalk. Many of the original plants were collected in China and the Himalayas. **Times:** Open all year: Apr-Sep, Mon-Fri 10-6. Winter: Mon-Fri, Oct-Nov & Feb-Mar, 10-4.30; Dec-Jan, 10-4. **Facilities:** 🅿 ㊓ toilets for disabled ✖ (ex guide dogs)

LITTLEHAMPTON   Map 04 TQ00

LOOK & SEA! VISITOR CENTRE
63-65 Surrey St BN17 5AW
➲ (on harbour front 10 mins walk from Littlehampton Station)
☎ 01903 718984   🖷 01903 718036   2 for 1
e-mail: info@lookandsea.co.uk

An interactive museum exploring the history and geography of Littlehampton and the surrounding area. Inside the modern waterfront building you can meet the 500,000 year old Boxgrove Man, become a ship's captain in an interactive computer game, and enjoy spectacular panoramic views of the Sussex coast from the circular glass tower. **Times:** Open all year, daily 9-5 **Fee:** ✱ £2.95 (ch £2.50, pen & student £2.50). **Facilities:** 🅿 💷 ✖ ㊓ toilets for disabled shop ✖ (ex guide dogs) 🍽

LOWER BEEDING   Map 04 TQ22

LEONARDSLEE LAKES & GARDENS
RH13 6PP
➲ (4m SW from Handcross, at junct of B2110 & A281)
☎ 01403 891212   🖷 01403 891305
e-mail: gardens@leonardslee.com

This Grade I listed garden is set in a peaceful valley with walks around seven beautiful lakes. It is a paradise in spring, with banks of rhododendrons and azaleas along paths lined with bluebells. Wallabies live in parts of the valley, deer in the parks and wildfowl on the lakes. Enjoy the Rock Garden, the fascinating Bonsai, the new 'Behind the Doll's House' exhibition and the collection of Victorian Motorcars (1889-1900). **Times:** Open Apr-Oct, daily 9.30-6 **Fee:** Apr & Jun-Oct £6, May (Mon-Fri) £8, (wknds & BH) £9 (ch £4 anytime). **Facilities:** 🅿 💷 ✖ licensed ㊓ (No wheelchair access) shop garden centre ✖ 🍽

This symbol indicates attractions **2-for-1** which have chosen to participate in our 2-for-1 voucher scheme

PETWORTH Map 04 SU92

PETWORTH HOUSE & PARK

GU28 0AE

➲ (in town centre, A272/283)

☎ 01798 342207 & 343929 📄 01798 342963

e-mail: petworth@ntrust.org.uk

Petworth house is an impressive 17th-century mansion set in a 700 acre Deer Park, landscaped by 'Capability' Brown, and immortalised in Turner's paintings. At Petworth you will find the National Trust's finest art collection including work by Van Dyck, Titian, and Turner as well as sculpture ceramics and fine furniture. Fascinating servants' quarters show the domestic side of life of this great estate.

Times: Open 27 Mar-Oct (closed Thu & Fri) 11-5.30, last entry 5
Fee: ✱ £7 (ch £4). Family ticket £18. Party 15+ £6 NT members free Pleasure Ground £1.50 (ch free). **Facilities:** 🅿 💷 ✗ licensed ♿ (wheelchairs available, Braille guide) toilets for disabled shop ✘ (ex guide/hearing dogs) 🦮 🖼

PULBOROUGH Map 04 TQ01

PARHAM HOUSE & GARDENS

Parham Park RH20 4HS

➲ (midway between A29 & A24, off A283 between Pulborough & Storrington)

☎ 01903 744888 & 742021 📄 01903 746557

e-mail: enquiries@parhamsussex.co.uk

Surrounded by a deer park, fine gardens and 18th-century Pleasure Grounds in a beautiful downland setting, this Elizabethan family home contains an important collection of paintings, furniture, carpets and rare needlework. A brick and turf maze has been created in the grounds - designed with children in mind, it is called 'Veronica's Maze'.

Times: ✱ Open Etr Sun-Sep, Wed, Thu, Sun & BH (also open Tue & Fri in Aug). Gardens open 12-6; House 2-6 (last entry 5). Guided tours on Wed & Thu mornings & Tue & Fri afternoons by special arrangement. **Facilities:** 🅿 💷 ♿ (wheelchairs, ramps, recorded tour tape, parking) toilets for disabled shop garden centre ✘ (ex guide dogs & in grounds) 🖼

RSPB PULBOROUGH BROOKS NATURE RESERVE

Uppertons Barn Visitor Centre, Wiggonholt RH20 2EL

➲ (signposted on A283, 2m SE of Pulborough & 2m NW of Storrington)

☎ 01798 875851

e-mail: pulborough.brooks@rspb.org.uk

Set in the scenic Arun Valley and easily reached via the visitor centre at Wiggonholt, this is an excellent reserve for year-round family visits. A nature trail winds through hedgerow-lined lanes to viewing hides overlooking water-meadows. Breeding summer birds include nightingales and warblers, ducks and wading birds, and nightjars and hobbies on nearby heathland. Unusual wading birds and hedgerow birds regularly pass through on spring and autumn migration.

Times: Open daily, Reserve: 9-9, (or sunset if earlier). Visitor centre: 10-5. Reserve closed 25 Dec, Visitor Centre closed 25-26 Dec.
Fee: £3.50 (ch £1, concessions £2.50). Family ticket £7.
Facilities: 🅿 💷 ♿ (free hire electric buggy for use on nature trail) toilets for disabled shop ✘ (ex guide dogs) 🖼

SINGLETON Map 04 SU81

WEALD & DOWNLAND OPEN AIR MUSEUM

PO18 0EU

➲ (6m N of Chichester on A286)

☎ 01243 811348 📄 01243 811475

e-mail: office@wealddown.co.uk

A showcase of English architectural heritage, where historic buildings have been rescued from destruction and rebuilt in a parkland setting. Vividly demonstrating the evolution of building techniques and use of local materials, these fascinating buildings bring to life the homes, farms and rural industries of the south east of the past 500 years.

Times: Open all year, Mar-Oct, daily 10.30-6 (last admission 5); Nov-Feb, Sat & Sun 10.30-4, also 26 Dec-1 Jan daily & Feb half term, 10.30-4. **Fee:** £7.50 (ch £4, over 60's £6.50). Family ticket (2 adults & 3 ch) £20. Party. **Facilities:** 🅿 💷 ♿ (separate entrance and ramps available for some buildings) toilets for disabled shop 🖼

SOUTH HARTING   Map 04 SU71
UPPARK
GU31 5QR
➲ (A3 take A272, B2146 to South Harting, follow signs to Uppark)
☎ 01730 825415 & 825857   📠 01730 825873
e-mail: uppark@nationaltrust.org.uk

A late 17th-century house set high on the South Downs with magnificent sweeping views to the sea. An extensive exhibition tells the dramatic story of the 1989 fire and subsequent restoration of the house and its collections. The elegant Georgian interior houses a famous Grand Tour collection that includes paintings, furniture and ceramics. An 18th-century dolls' house with original features is one of the more impressive items. The servants' quarters appear as they did in Victorian days, when H G Wells' mother was housekeeper, while the garden is restored in the early 19th-century 'Picturesque' style.

Times: Open 24 Mar-28 Oct, Sun-Thu. House 1-5. Car park, woodland walk, garden & Exhibition 11-5. Last admission to house 4.15. Timed tickets will be in operation on BH Sun & Mon & Sun in Aug. (House open 12-5 on Sun in Aug and 11-5 on BH Mons). **Fee:** ✱ House, garden & exhibition £5.50. Family ticket £13.75. **Facilities:** 🅿 💷 ✗ licensed ♿ (ramps, lift to basement, chair lift in exhibition) toilets for disabled shop 🐕 (ex woodland walk & car park) 🎎 ☕

An asterisk * indicates that opening times and prices are for 2004. Please contact the attraction for up-to-date information.

TANGMERE   Map 04 SU90
TANGMERE MILITARY AVIATION MUSEUM TRUST
PO20 2ES
➲ (off A27, 3m E of Chichester on the Arundel side)
☎ 01243 775223   📠 01243 789490
e-mail: admin@tangmere-museum.org.uk

Based at an airfield that played an important role during the World Wars, this museum spans 80 years of military aviation. There are photographs, documents, aircraft and aircraft parts on display along with a Hurricane replica, Spitfire replica and cockpit simulator. A hangar houses a Supermarine Swift and the record-breaking aircraft Meteor and Hunter. Aircraft outside include Lockheed T33, English Electric Lightning. Gloster Meteor and Westland Whirlwind helicopter.

Times: Open Mar-Oct, daily 10-5.30; Feb & Nov, daily 10-4.30. **Fee:** £5 (ch £1.50 & pen £4) Family £11 (2 ad & 2 ch). **Facilities:** 🅿 💷 ♿ (wheelchairs available) toilets for disabled shop 🐕 (ex guide dogs)

WEST DEAN   Map 04 SU81
WEST DEAN GARDENS
Estate Office PO18 0QZ
➲ (on A286, 6m N of Chichester)
☎ 01243 818210 & 811301   📠 01243 811342
e-mail: gardens@westdean.org.uk

Award winning historic garden of 35 acres in a tranquil downland setting. Noted for its 300ft long Harold Peto pergola, mixed and herbaceous borders, rustic summerhouses and specimen trees. Walled kitchen garden with magnificent collection of 16 Victorian glasshouses and frames. The visitors' centre provides a high level of facilities with a beautiful prospect of the River Lavant and West Dean Park.

Times: Open Mar, Apr & Oct, daily 11-5; May-Sep 10.30-5. Last ticket 4.30pm. **Fee:** ✱ £5.50 (ch £2, over 60's £5). Party+ £5.
Facilities: 🅿 ✗ licensed ♿ (reserved parking, 2 wheelchairs available) toilets for disabled shop 🐕 (ex guide dogs) ☕

Above: A sheep under a tree on the South Downs

TYNE & WEAR

EVENTS & FESTIVALS

April
tbc Gateshead Spring Flower Show, Gateshead
Central Nursery (provisional)

July
15th-17th Whitby Bay International Jazz
Festival
30th-31st Sunderland International Air Show,
Promenade, Seaburn, Sunderland
(provisional)
tbc Gateshead Summer Flower Show,
Gateshead Central Nursery
tbc Sunderland International Festival, kites,
music and dance, Stephenson, Washington

August
28th-29th Newcastle Mela, free Asian festival,
Exhibition Park, Newcastle-upon-Tyne
tbc North of England Motorshow, Gosforth
Park Racecourse, Newcastle

September/October
tbc Great North Run, Newcastle-upon-Tyne to
South Shields
tbc Junior Great North Run, Gateshead
International Stadium, Gateshead

October
tbc Houghton Feast, traditional local event
with various activities and events

November
tbc Newcastle Comedy Festival (various
venues), Newcastle-upon-Tyne

Above: The Angel of the North, Gateshead

GATESHEAD   Map 12 NZ26

BALTIC CENTRE FOR CONTEMPORARY ART
South Shore Rd NE8 3BA
➲ (Follow signs for Quayside, Millenium Bridge.
15 mins walk from Gateshead Metro & Newcastle
Central Station.)
☎ 0191 478 1810 & 0191 440 4944   `FREE`
▯ 0191 478 1922
e-mail: info@balticmill.com

Once a 1950s grain warehouse, part of the old Baltic Flour
Mills, the Baltic Centre for Contemporary Art is an
international centre presenting a dynamic and ambitious
programme of complementary exhibitions and events. It
comprises of five art spaces, cinema, auditorium, library and
archive, eating and drinking areas and a shop. Check
website for current events information.
Times: Please see website for details (www.balticmill.com)
Facilities: ▯ (charged) ▣ ✗ licensed ら (Wheelchairs/scooters,
Braille/large-print guides) toilets for disabled shop ✖ (ex guide dogs &
hearing dogs)

JARROW   Map 12 NZ36

BEDES WORLD & ST PAUL'S CHURCH
Church Bank NE32 3DY
➲ (off A185 near south end of Tyne tunnel)
☎ 0191 489 2106 ▯ 0191 428 2361   `2 for 1`
e-mail: visitor.info@bedesworld.co.uk

The Venerable Bede lived over 1300 years ago and was one
of early Britain's greatest scholars, author of the *Historia
Ecclesiastica Gentis Anglorum* - the definitive history of the
early medieval period. As well as exhibits detailing Bede's
monastic life and work, the museum re-creates an Anglo-
Saxon farm and incorporates the ruins of the medieval
monastery.
Times: Open all year, Apr-Oct, Mon-Sat 10-5.30, Sun noon-5.30;
Nov-Mar, Mon-Sat 10-4.30 & Sun 12-4.30; Xmas-New Year opening
times vary. Church open Mon-Sat 10-4 & Sun 2.30-4, unless service
being held. **Fee:** ✳ £4.50 (ch & concessions £3). Family ticket £10.
Concession Family ticket £7. Party rates 15+. **Facilities:** ▯ ▣
✗ licensed ら (wheelchair & elec. wheelchair on request, disabled
parking) toilets for disabled shop ✖ (ex guide dogs) ◼

NEWCASTLE UPON TYNE   Map 12 NZ26

HANCOCK MUSEUM
Barras Bridge NE2 4PT
➲ (Follow exit signs for city centre A167 off the A1)
☎ 0191 222 7418 ▯ 0191 261 7537   `2 for 1`
e-mail: hancock@twmuseums.org.uk

Newcastle's premier Natural History museum unravels the
natural world, through sensational galleries and close
encounters with resident reptiles and insects. For more than
one hundred years the Hancock Museum has provided
visitors with a glimpse of the animal kingdom and the
powerful and often destructive forces of nature. From the
Dinosaurs to live animals, the Hancock is home to creatures
past and present and the odd Egyptian mummy or two.
Times: Open all year, Mon-Sat, 10-5, Sun 2-5. Closed 25-26 Dec &
1 Jan. **Fee:** Prices vary with special exhibitions. Phone for details
Facilities: ▯ ▣ ら (stair lift, audio & Braille guide, sign language)
toilets for disabled shop ✖ (ex guide dogs) ◼

LIFE SCIENCE CENTRE
Times Square NE1 4EP
➲ (A1M, A69, A184, A1058 & A167, follow signs to the Life Science Centre or Central station)
☎ 0191 243 8223 & 0191 243 8210
🖺 0191 243 8201
e-mail: bookings@lifesciencecentre.co.uk
The Life Science Centre is an interactive, action-packed day out that takes the visitor to the beginning of life and back again. From single-celled organisms to dinosaurs, from 4 billion years ago to today, this is a fascinating attraction that deals with perhaps the most fundamental subject of all: Life Itself.
Times: ✱ Open Mon-Sat 10-6, Sun 11-6 . Closed 25 Dec & 1 Jan. (Last entry subject to seasonal demand). **Facilities:** 🅿 (charged) 💻 ✗ licensed ♿ (ramps, wheelchairs, induction loops) toilets for disabled shop 🏠 (ex guide dogs) 📼

MUSEUM OF ANTIQUITIES
The University NE1 7RU
➲ (Positioned on main campus of Newcastle University between The Haymarket and Queen Victoria Road)
☎ 0191 222 7849 🖺 0191 222 8561   FREE
e-mail: m.o.antiquities@ncl.ac.uk
Artefacts from north east England from prehistoric times to AD 1600 are on display here. The principal museum for Hadrian's Wall, this collection includes models of the wall, life-size Roman soldiers and a recently refurbished reconstruction of the Temple of Mithras.
Times: Open all year, daily (ex Sun), 10-5 (Closed Good Fri, 24-26 Dec & 1 Jan). **Facilities:** 🅿 (400yds) ♿ (Large print guide) shop 🏠 (ex guide dogs) 📼

ROWLANDS GILL   Map 12 NZ15
GIBSIDE
NE16 6BG
➲ (turn off A1 western Bypass following brown tourist signs from Gibside & Gibside Chapel, 3m W of Metro Centre & 6m SW of Gateshead, on B6314)
☎ 01207 542255
e-mail: tony.walton@ntrust.org.uk
The important early 18th-century landscaped park contains a chapel - an outstanding example of Palladian architecture, built to a design by James Paine as the mausoleum for members of the Bowes family. It stands at one end of the Great Walk of Turkey oaks, looking towards the column of British Liberty.
Times: ✱ Open: Grounds all year (ex Mon), 10-4.30. Open BH Mon (Mar-Oct 10-5, Nov-Feb 10-3.30). Chapel: Apr-Oct as grounds 11-5, otherwise by prior arrangment. **Facilities:** 🅿 💻 ♿ (Braille guide, wheelchairs & wheelchair carrier) toilets for disabled shop 🐾 📼

SOUTH SHIELDS   Map 12 NZ36
ARBEIA ROMAN FORT & MUSEUM
Baring St NE33 2BB
➲ (5 mins walk from South Shields Town Centre)
☎ 0191 456 1369 & 454 4093
🖺 0191 427 6862
In South Shields town are the extensive remains of Arbeia, a Roman fort in use from the 2nd to 4th century. It was the supply base for the Roman army's campaign against Scotland. On site there are full size reconstructions of a fort gateway, a barrack block and part of the commanding
continued

officer's house. Archaeological evacuations are in progress throughout the summer.
Times: ✱ Open all year, Etr-Sep, Mon-Sat 10.30-5.30, Sun 1-5; Oct-Etr, Mon-Sat 10-4. Closed 25-26 Dec, 1 Jan & Good Fri.
Facilities: 🅿 ♿ (Minicom system) toilets for disabled shop 📼

SUNDERLAND   Map 12 NZ35
MUSEUM & WINTER GARDENS
Burdon Rd SR1 1PP
➲ (situated in Sunderland City Centre)
☎ 0191 553 2323 🖺 0191 553 7828
e-mail: sunderland.museum@
tyne-wear-museums.org.uk
This award-winning attraction re-opened in 2001. The wide-ranging displays, with many hands-on exhibits, cover the archaeology and geology of Sunderland, the coal mines and shipyards of the area and the spectacular glass and pottery made on Wearside. Other galleries show the changes in the lifestyles of Sunderland women over the past century, works by LS Lowry and wildlife from all corners of the globe. The Winter Gardens are a horticultural wonderland where the exotic plants from around the world can be seen growing to their full natural height in a spectacular glass and steel rotunda.
Times: ✱ Open all year, Mon 10-4, Tue-Sat 10-5, Sun 2-5.
Facilities: 🅿 (150 yds) ✗ licensed ♿ (lifts to all floors, induction loops) toilets for disabled shop 🏠 (ex guide dogs) 📼

NATIONAL GLASS CENTRE
Liberty Way SR6 0GL
➲ (A19 onto A1231, signposted from all major roads)
☎ 0191 515 5555 🖺 0191 515 5556   2 for 1
e-mail: info@nationalglasscentre.com
Housed in a striking modern building, the National Glass Centre celebrates the unique material and explains its history. Visitors can see the changing exhibitions of glass art, featuring pieces by leading artists. There is also the opportunity to witness the glass-making process and learn more about the substance and how it impacts on our lives. The brave can even walk on the glass roof 30 feet above the riverside.
Times: Open daily 10-5 (last admission to glass tour 4). Closed 25 Dec & 1 Jan. **Fee:** £5 (concessions £3). Family ticket £12.
Facilities: 🅿 ✗ licensed ♿ (lifts, ramps, parking facilites) toilets for disabled shop 🏠 (ex guide dogs) 📼

TYNEMOUTH   Map 12 NZ36
BLUE REEF AQUARIUM
Grand Pde NE30 4JF
➲ (Follow the A19, taking the A1058 (coast road), signposted to Tynemouth. Situated on seafront)
☎ 0191 258 1031 🖺 0191 257 2116   2 for 1
e-mail: tynemouth@
bluereefaquarium.co.uk
From its position overlooking one of the North East's prettiest beaches, Blue Reef is home to a dazzling variety of creatures including seahorses, puffer fish, octopi, and even the deadly piranha. Visitors can walk through an underwater tunnel in a 250,000 litre tropical ocean tank. This offers close encounters with all manner of undersea wonders like sharks and stingrays.
Times: Open daily from 10am. (Closed 25 Dec) **Fee:** ✱ £4.95 (pen & student £4.25, ch £3.25). Family ticket (2 adults + 3 ch) £14.95
Facilities: 🅿 (charged) 💻 ♿ toilets for disabled shop 🏠 (ex guide dogs) 📼

TYNEMOUTH PRIORY AND CASTLE
NE30 4BZ
➲ (near North Pier)
☎ 0191 257 1090

Discover a rich and varied history as you explore the priory, castle and underground chambers beneath a World War I gun battery.

Times: Open all year, Apr-Sep, daily 10-6; Oct, daily 10-4; Nov-Mar, Thu-Mon 10-4. Gun Battery: Apr-Sep, Sat, Sun & Bank Hols, 10-6. (Closed 24-26 Dec & 1 Jan). **Fee:** ✱ £3 (ch £1.50, concessions £2.30, family £7.50). Prices & opening times relate to 2004, for further details phone or log onto www.english-heritage.org.uk/visits
Facilities: ♿ (wheelchair access to priory) shop ⚑

WALLSEND   Map 12 NZ26
SEGEDUNUM ROMAN FORT, BATHS & MUSEUM
Buddle St NE28 6HR
➲ (A187 from Tyne Tunnel, signposted)
☎ 0191 236 9347   ▤ 0191 295 5858   **2 for 1**
e-mail: segedunum@twmuseums.org.uk

Hadrian's Wall was built by the Roman Emperor, Hadrian in 122AD, Segedunum was built as part of the Wall, serving as a garrison for 600 soldiers until the collapse of Roman rule around 410AD. This major historical venture shows what life would have been like then, using artefacts, audio-visuals, reconstructed buildings and a 34m high viewing tower.
Times: Open all year, 9 Apr-Aug 9.30-5.30, Sep-Oct 10-5, Nov-Apr 10-3.30 **Fee:** ✱ £3.50 (ch, pen & concessions £1.95). Family ticket £9
Facilities: 🅿 🖥 ♿ (lifts) toilets for disabled shop
🐕 (ex guide dogs) ◀

WASHINGTON   Map 12 NZ35
WASHINGTON OLD HALL
The Avenue, Washington Village NE38 7LE
➲ (from A1 and A19 follow signs to Washington, then District 4. The Avenue, next to Holy Trinity Church)
☎ 0191 416 6879   ▤ 0191 4192065
e-mail: nwohal@smtp.ntrust.org.uk

The home of George Washington's ancestors from 1183 to 1613, the Old Hall was originally an early medieval manor, but was rebuilt in the 17th century. The house has been restored and filled with period furniture. Exhibitions include stepping back in time and enjoying the peace and quiet in the beautifully-planted Knot Parterre gardens, The Jacobean
continued

Great Hall, Kitchen, Panelled room and the Liberty Room celebrating American Independence and the life of George Washington.
Times: ✱ Open Apr-Oct, Sun-Wed & Good Fri 11-5. Last admission 4.30. **Facilities:** 🅿 🖥 ♿ (Braille guide, sensory scented gardens, handrails, ramps) toilets for disabled shop 🐕 (ex guide dogs) ◀

WWT WASHINGTON
District 15 NE38 8LE
➲ (signposted off A195, A1231 & A182)
☎ 0191 416 5454   ▤ 0191 416 5801   **2 for 1**
e-mail: washington@wwt.org.uk

In a parkland setting, on the north bank of the River Wear, WWT Washington is the home of a wonderful collection of exotic wildfowl from all over the world. There is also a heronry where visitors can watch a colony of wild Grey Herons on CCTV. The 100-acre site includes an area for wintering wildfowl which can be observed from hides, and a flock of Chilean Flamingos. Other features include a discovery centre, waterfowl nursery, picture windows and a viewing gallery from which to observe the birds.
Times: Open all year, daily 9.30-5 (summer) or 9.30-4 (winter). Closed 25 Dec. **Fee:** ✱ £5.75 (ch £3.75, concessions £4.75). Family £15.
Facilities: 🅿 🖥 ✕ licensed ♿ (lowered windows in certain hides, wheelchairs to hire free) toilets for disabled shop 🐕 (ex guide/hearing dogs) ◀

WHITBURN   Map 12 NZ46
SOUTER LIGHTHOUSE
Coast Rd SR6 7NH
➲ (On A183 coast road, 2m S of South Shields, 3m N of Sunderland)
☎ 0191 529 3161 & 01670 773966
▤ 0191 529 0902
e-mail: nslhse@smtp.ntrust.org.uk

When it opened in 1871, Souter was the most advanced lighthouse in the world. Painted red and white and standing at 150ft high, it is a dramatic building and hands-on displays and volunteers help bring it to life. The Engine and Battery Rooms are all in working order and are included in the guided tour, along with the light tower and museum cottage.
Times: ✱ Open Apr-Oct daily ex Fri, (open Good Fri), 11-5. Last admission 4.30. Please contact for opening at other times.
Facilities: 🅿 ✕ ♿ (Braille guide, induction loops, tactile exhibits) toilets for disabled shop 🐕 (ex guide dogs) ◀ ◀

Above: Marsden Rock

WARWICKSHIRE

EVENTS & FESTIVALS

April
23rd Shakespeare Birthday Celebrations,
Stratford-Upon-Avon
29th-8th May Leamington Festival

June
30th-10th Jul Warwick Festival
(various venues)

July
3rd-6th The Royal Show, National Agricultural
Centre, Stoneleigh Park
22nd-24th Warwick Folk Festival
(various venues)

August
20th-21st Warwickshire & West Midlands
Game Fair, Ragley Hall, Alcester
(provisional)
27th-29th Town & Country Festival, NAC
Stoneleigh

October
14th-23rd Stratford-Upon-Avon Music Festival

Top : Warwick Castle
Above: Fields near Long Compton

ALCESTER   Map 04 SP05
RAGLEY HALL
B49 5NJ
➲ (8m SW of Stratford upon Avon, off A46/A435,
follow brown tourist signs)
☎ 01789 762090 🖹 01789 764791
e-mail: info@ragleyhall.com
Built in 1680, Ragley is the family home of the Marquess and
Marchioness of Hertford and houses a superb collection of
18th century paintings, porcelain and furniture. Set in 27
acres of gardens and 400 acres of parkland, The House
contains a stunning mural by Graham Rust "The Temptation"
and England's finest Baroque plasterwork dated 1750. Ticket
includes the house, Terrace Tea Rooms overlooking the rose
garden, gift shop, adventure playground, unique 3D maze,
lakeside picnic area, woodland walk and stables containing
equestrian memorabilia. Location for BBC production of
Scarlet Pimpernel.
Times: ✱ Open mid Apr-end Sep, Thu-Sun & BH Mon. Park & Garden
open daily, mid Jul-end Aug. **Facilities:** 🅿 💷 ♿ (lift to first floor)
toilets for disabled shop

BADDESLEY CLINTON   Map 04 SP27
BADDESLEY CLINTON HALL
B93 0DQ
➲ (0.75m W off A4141, 7.5m NW of Warwick)
☎ 01564 783294 🖹 01564 782706   `2 for 1`
e-mail: baddesleyclinton@
nationaltrust.org.uk
A romantically-sited medieval moated house, dating from
the 14th century, that has changed very little since 1634.
With family portraits, priest holes, chapel, garden, ponds,
nature trail and lake walk.
Times: Open Garden, Restaurant & Shop: 3 Mar-30 Apr & Oct-7 Nov,
Wed-Sun 12-5; May-Sep, Wed-Sun 12-5.30; 10 Nov-12 Dec, Wed-Sun
12-4.30. House: 3 Mar-30 Apr & Oct-7 Nov, Wed-Sun 1.30-5; May-Sep,
Wed-Sun 1.30-5.30. **Fee:** ✱ Garden only £3.10 (ch £1.55). House &
Garden £6.20 (ch £3.10). Family ticket £15.50. Joint ticket with
Packwood House £9 (ch £4.50). Family ticket £22.50. Joint ticket for
gardens only £4.50 (ch £2.25). National Trust members and children
under 5 free. **Facilities:** 🅿 ✗ licensed ♿ (wheelchairs for hire, Braille
guides, tactile route) toilets for disabled shop 🐕 (ex guide dogs)
🥢 🍴

CHARLECOTE   Map 04 SP25
CHARLECOTE PARK   `2 for 1`
CV35 9ER
➲ (5m E of Stratford, 1m W of Wellesbourne on
B4086)
☎ 01789 470277 Events 07788 658495
🖹 01789 470544
e-mail: charlecote.park@nationaltrust.org.uk
Queen Elizabeth I and William Shakespeare knew Charlecote
Park well. Follow in their footsteps at this impressive
Warwickshire house and ancient deer park. Special events
held every week, from outdoor picnic concerts to family
events, outdoor theatre and specialist tours. Call for event
details.
Times: Open 6 Mar-2 Nov, Fri-Tue (Fri-Wed Jul & Aug); Grounds
10.30-5.30, (Park until 6), House noon-5. Open wkends Nov & Dec
Fee: ✱ House & Grounds; £6.40 (ch £3.20), Family £26, Groups £5.40.
Grounds Only; £3 (ch £1.50). NT members free. **Facilities:** 🅿 💷
✗ licensed ♿ (Braille guides & hearing scheme available) toilets for
disabled shop 🐕 🥢

COUGHTON   Map 04 SP06

COUGHTON COURT

B49 5JA

➲ (2m N of Alcester on E side of A435)

☎ 01789 762435 & 400702   📠 01789 765544

During the Civil War this formerly moated and mainly Elizabethan house was attacked by both Parliamentary and Royalist forces. There are exhibitions on the Gunpowder Plot and Children's Clothes. Outdoor concert with fireworks in July.

Times: Open Apr-Jun, Wed-Sun; Jul-Aug, Tue-Sun; Sep, Wed-Sun; Oct wknds only. Also open BH Mons. (Closed 21 Jun). **Fee:** ✱ £7.95 (ch £3.95). Family ticket £23-£26.50. Garden only £5.10 (ch £2.50). Family ticket £15-£17.25. **Facilities:** 🅿 (charged) ✗ licensed ♿ (Braille guide, wheelchair available) toilets for disabled shop ✗ (ex guide dogs) 🐾🍽

FARNBOROUGH   Map 04 SP44

FARNBOROUGH HALL

OX17 1DU

➲ (6m N of Banbury, 0.5m W of A423)

☎ 01295 690002

A classical mid 18th-century stone house with notable plasterwork; the entrance hall, staircase and two principal rooms are shown. The grounds contain charming 18th-century temples, a 3/4-mile terrace walk and an obelisk.

Times: House, grounds & terrace walk open Apr-Sep, Wed & Sat, 5 & 6 May 2-6. Terrace walk Thu & Fri by appointment only, 2-6. Last admission 5.30pm. (Closed Good Fri) **Fee:** ✱ House, Garden & Terrace walk £3.60 (ch £1.80), Family £9. Terrace walk £1.80. Terrace walk only (Thu & Fri) £1. **Facilities:** 🅿 ♿ ✗ (ex guide dogs) 🐾

GAYDON   Map 04 SP35

HERITAGE MOTOR CENTRE

Banbury Rd CV35 0BJ

➲ (M40 junct 12 and take B4100. Heritage motor centre is signposted from this junct)

☎ 01926 641188   📠 01926 641555

e-mail: enquiries@heritage-motor-centre.co.uk

Home to the largest collection of historic British cars anywhere in the world, the Heritage Motor Centre is set in 65 acres of grounds. Attractions at the Centre include the Time Road, a fascinating journey through Britain's motoring and social history, the motoring cinema, and the 'Get Behind the Wheel' zone, where visitors get the chance to sit in a variety
continued

of cars from the collection. Outside, there are go-kart tracks and a children's electric roadway.

Times: Open daily 10-5. (Closed 24-26 Dec). **Fee:** ✱ £8 (ch 5-16 £6, under 5 free, & pen £7). Family ticket £25. Additional charges apply to outdoor activities **Facilities:** 🅿 💻 ♿ (lift to all floors, limited number of manual wheelchairs) toilets for disabled shop ✗ (ex guide/hearing dogs) 🍽

KENILWORTH   Map 04 SP27

KENILWORTH CASTLE

CV8 1NE

☎ 01926 852078   📠 01926 851514

Explore the largest and most extensive castle ruin in England, with a past rich in famous names and events in history. Its massive red sandstone towers, keep and wall glow brightly in the sunlight. Discover the history of Kenilworth through the interactive model in Leicester's Barn.

Times: Open all year, Mar, daily, 10-5; Apr-May, daily, 10-5; Jun-Aug, daily, 10-6; Sep-Oct, daily, 10-5; Nov-Feb, daily, 10-4. (closed 24-26 Dec & 1 Jan) **Fee:** ✱ £4.80 (ch £2.40, concessions £3.60, family, £12). Prices & opening times relate to 2004, for further details phone or log onto www.english-heritage.org.uk/visits **Facilities:** 🅿 💻 ♿ shop ⊞

STONELEIGH ABBEY

CV8 2LF

➲ (Entrance to the abbey is off the B4115 close to junct of A46 and A452)

☎ 01926 858535 & 858585   📠 01926 850724

e-mail: enquire@stoneleighabbey.org

Stoneleigh Abbey is one of the finest country house estates in the Midlands and has seen the subject of considerable restoration work. The abbey, founded in the reign of Henry ll, is now managed by a charitable trust. Visitors will experience a wealth of architectural styles spanning more than 800 years. The magnificent state rooms and chapel, the medieval Gatehouse and the Regency stables are some of the major areas to be admired. Set in 690 acres of parkland.

Times: Open Good Fri-Oct, Tue-Thu, Sun & BHs for guided tours at 11, 1 & 3pm. Grounds open 10-5. **Facilities:** 🅿 💻 ♿ (West Wing, Ground Level and grounds) toilets for disabled shop ✗ (ex guide dogs)

MIDDLETON   Map 07 SP19

ASH END HOUSE CHILDRENS FARM

Middleton Ln, Middleton B78 2BL

➲ (signposted from A4091)

☎ 0121 329 3240   📠 0121 329 3240

e-mail: contact@thechildrensfarm.co.uk

Ideal for young children, this is a small family-owned farm with many friendly animals to feed and stroke, including some rare breeds. Cafe, shop, gift shop, play areas, picnic barns and lots of undercover activities.

Times: Open daily 10-5 or dusk in winter. (Closed 25 Dec-1 Jan and weekdays in Jan). **Fee:** £3.90 (ch £4.90 includes animal feed, pony ride, farm badge & all activities). **Facilities:** 🅿 💻 ♿ toilets for disabled shop ✗ (ex guide dogs) 🍽

MIDDLETON HALL
B78 2AE
➲ (M42 junct 9, on A4091 midway between Belfry & Drayton Manor, follow brown heritage signs)
☎ 01827 283095   ▯ 01827 285717
e-mail: middletonhall@btconnect.com

Once the home of two great 17th-century naturalists, Francis Willughby and John Ray, the Hall shows several architectural styles, from c1300 to a Georgian west wing. The grounds include a nature reserve, lake, meadow, orchard and woodland, all Sites of Special Scientific Interest.
Times: ✱ Open Apr-13 Oct, Sun 2-5, BH 11-5. **Facilities:** ▯ ▭ & (wheelchair available) toilets for disabled shop

NUNEATON   Map 04 SP39
ARBURY HALL
CV10 7PT
➲ (2m SW of Nuneaton, off B4102 Meriden road)
☎ 024 7638 2804   ▯ 024 7664 1147
e-mail: brenda.newell@arburyhall.net

The 16th-century Elizabethan house, Gothicised in the 18th century, has been the home of the Newdegate family for over 450 years. It is the finest complete example of Gothic revival architecture in existence, and contains pictures, furniture, and beautiful plasterwork ceilings. The 17th-century stable block, with a central doorway by Wren, houses the tearooms and lovely gardens with lakes and wooded walks.
Times: Open Etr-Sep 2-5.30 (last admission 5pm). Hall & gardens: Sun & Mon of BH wknds only. For other opening days & times, contact the Administrator. **Fee:** ✱ £6.50 (ch £4) gardens only £4.50 (ch £3)
Facilities: ▯ ▭ & shop ✖ (ex guide dogs & in grounds)

PACKWOOD HOUSE   Map 07 SP17
PACKWOOD HOUSE
B94 6AT
➲ (on unclass road off A34)
☎ 01564 782024   ▯ 01564 787920   [2 for 1]
e-mail: packwood@nationaltrust.org.uk

Dating from the 16th century, Packwood House has been extended and much changed over the years. An important collection of tapestries and textiles is displayed. Equally important are the stunning gardens with renowned herbaceous borders, attracting many visitors, and the almost surreal topiary garden based on the Sermon on the Mount.
Times: Open Gardens: 3 Mar-7 Nov Wed-Sun, BH Mon, Good Fri. Mar/Oct/Nov 11-4.30. May-Sep 11-5.30; House Mar-Nov 12-4.30
Fee: ✱ House & Garden £5.60 (ch £2.80). Family ticket £14. Garden only £2.80 (ch £1.40). Joint ticket with other establishments available.
Facilities: ▯ & (w/chairs available, tactile tour, Braille guide) toilets for disabled shop ✖ (ex guide dogs) ✤ ▭

RUGBY   Map 04 SP57
THE JAMES GILBERT RUGBY FOOTBALL MUSEUM
5 Saint Matthew's St CV21 3BY
➲ (on A428 opposite Rugby School)
☎ 01788 567777   ▯ 01788 537400   [FREE]
e-mail: service@webb-ellis.co.uk

An intriguing collection of Rugby football memorabilia is housed in the shop in which rugby balls have been made since 1842. Visitors can watch a craftsman at work, hand-stitching the footballs. Situated near to Rugby School and its famous playing field.
Times: Open all year, Mon-Sat 9-5. Phone for holiday opening times.
Facilities: ▯ (500yds) & shop ✖ (ex guide dogs)

RYTON-ON-DUNSMORE   Map 04 SP37
RYTON ORGANIC GARDENS
CV8 3LG
➲ (5m SE of Coventry signposted off A45, on the road to the village of Wolston)
☎ 024 7630 3517   ▯ 024 7663 9229   [2 for 1]
e-mail: enquiry@hdra.org.uk

Ten acres of glorious gardens show how you can grow flowers, fruit and vegetables nature's way without added chemicals. More than thirty individual gardens to look at and enjoy, plus 'The Vegetable Kingdom' - learn all about vegetables, their history, varieties, and how they help to keep us healthy, in a fully interactive visitor centre. Ryton Organic Gardens is the home of HDRA, the organic organisation. Special events, tours, restaurant and coffee shop.
Times: Open daily 9-5. (Closed Xmas). **Fee:** ✱ £4.50 (ch £2, concessions £4). **Facilities:** ▯ ▭ ✖ licensed & (wheelchairs available & scooter) toilets for disabled shop garden centre ✖ (ex guide dogs) ▭

SHOTTERY   Map 04 SP15
ANNE HATHAWAY'S COTTAGE
Cottage Ln CV37 9HH
➲ (House in Shottery Village, 1m from Stratford)
☎ 01789 292100   ▯ 01789 296083
e-mail: info@shakespeare.org.uk

Before her marriage to William Shakespeare, Anne Hathaway lived in this substantial 12-roomed thatched Tudor farmhouse with her prosperous yeoman family. The house now shows many aspects of domestic life in 16th-century England, and has a lovely traditional cottage garden, Shakespeare tree and sculpture gardens, maze, gardening history exhibition and romantic willow cabin.
Times: Open Nov-Mar, daily 10-4; Apr-May & Oct-Nov, Mon-Sat 9.30-5, Sun 10-5; Jun-Aug, Mon-Sat 9-5, Sun 9.30-5. **Fee:** ✱ £5.20 (ch £2, concessions £4). Family ticket £12. All five Shakespeare Houses £13 (ch £6.50, concessions £12) Family ticket £29. **Facilities:** ▯ ▭ & (Access room with virtual reality tours of the cottage) toilets for disabled shop ✖ (ex assist dogs) ▭

STRATFORD-UPON-AVON   Map 04 SP25

HALL'S CROFT

Old Town CV37 6EP
➲ (Located in the centre of Stratford upon Avon)
☎ 01789 292107   🖹 01789 296083
e-mail: info@shakespeare.org.uk

A Tudor house with outstanding furniture and paintings where Shakespeare's daughter Susanna and her husband, Dr John Hall, lived before moving to New Place on the dramatist's death. There is an exhibition on Tudor medicine, and fine walled gardens can also be seen.

Times: Open Nov-Mar, daily 11-4; Apr-May and Sep-Oct, daily 11-5; Jun-Aug, Mon-Sat 9.30-5, Sun 10-5. **Fee:** ✱ £3.50 (ch £1.70, concessions £3) Family ticket £9. All five Shakespeare Houses £13 (ch £6.50, concessions £12) Family ticket £29. Three in Town Shakespeare Houses £10 (ch £5, concessions £8) Family ticket £20.

Facilities: 🅿 💺 ♿ toilets for disabled shop 🐕 (ex assist dogs) 🍴

NEW PLACE / NASH'S HOUSE

Chapel St CV37 6EP
➲ (Located in the centre of Stratford upon Avon)
☎ 01789 292325   🖹 01789 292083
e-mail: info@shakespeare.org.uk

The elegant home of Shakespeare's granddaughter, Elizabeth Hall's first husband Thomas Nash. The adjacent site of New Place, where Shakespeare retired and subsequently died in 1616, is now preserved as a picturesque garden space with an attractive Elizabethan knot garden.

Times: Open Nov-Mar, daily 11-4; Apr-May & Sep-Oct, daily 11-5; Jun-Aug, Mon-Sat 9.30-5, Sun 10-5.30. **Fee:** ✱ £3.50 (ch £1.70, concessions £3) Family ticket £9. All five Shakespeare Houses £13 (ch £6.50, concessions £12) Family ticket £29. All three Town Shakespeare Houses £10 (ch £5, concessions £8) Family ticket £20.

Facilities: 🅿 (250yds) ♿ toilets for disabled 🐕 (ex assist dogs) 🍴

ROYAL SHAKESPEARE COMPANY COLLECTION

Royal Shakespeare Theatre, Waterside CV37 6BB
➲ (M40 junct 14 take A46 S. At 1st rdbt take 1st exit (A439). Parking in town centre, follow RSC signposted)
☎ 01789 262870   🖹 01789 262870
e-mail: info@rsc.org.uk

The RSC gallery opened in 1881, and was part of the first Shakespeare Memorial Theatre. In 1926 fire destroyed the theatre leaving only a semi circular wall and the gallery. The exhibition space now displays costumes from past RSC productions, paintings and other Theatre Memorabilia.

Times: ✱ Open all year, Mon-Fri 1.30-6.30, Sat 10.30-6.30 & Sun 11.30-4.30. (Closed 24 & 25 Dec). Theatre tours usually Mon-Fri (ex matinee days), 1.30 & 5.30, Sun 12, 1, 2 & 3. **Facilities:** 🅿 (charged) 💺 ✗ ♿ (services for hearing impaired,Braille books/reading room) toilets for disabled shop 🐕 (ex guide dogs)

SHAKESPEARE'S BIRTHPLACE

Henley St CV37 6QW
➲ (In town centre)
☎ 01789 204016   🖹 01789 292083
e-mail: info@shakespeare.org.uk

Shakespeare was born in the half-timbered house in 1564. It is now presented as it may have been when he was a boy. The ticket price includes entrance to an exhibition of the author's life, including a first edition of his complete works.

Times: Open Nov-Mar, Mon-Sat 10-4, Sun 10.30-4; Apr-May & Sep-Oct, Mon-Sat 10-5, Sun 10.30-5; Jun-Aug, Mon-Sat 9-5, Sun 9.30-5.
Fee: ✱ £6.70 (ch £2.60, concessions £5.50) Family ticket £15. All five Shakespeare Houses £13 (ch £6.50, concessions £12) Family ticket £29. All three Town Shakespeare Houses £10 (ch £5, concessions £8) Family ticket £20. **Facilities:** 🅿 ♿ (Computer based virtual reality tour of upper floor) toilets for disabled shop 🐕 (ex assist dogs) 🍴

See advertisement on opposite page

STRATFORD BUTTERFLY FARM

Tramway Walk, Swan's Nest Ln CV37 7LS
➲ (south bank of River Avon opposite RSC)
☎ 01789 299288   🖹 01789 415878
e-mail: sales@butterflyfarm.co.uk

Europe's largest live Butterfly and Insect Exhibit. Hundreds of the world's most spectacular and colourful butterflies, in the unique setting of a lush tropical landscape, with splashing waterfalls and fish-filled pools. See also the strange and fascinating Insect City, a bustling metropolis of ants, bees, stick insects, beetles and other remarkable insects. See the dangerous and deadly in Arachnoland!

Times: Open daily 10-6 (winter 10-dusk). Closed 25 Dec.
Fee: ✱ £4.45 (ch £3.45, pen & students £3.95). Family £12.95
Facilities: 🅿 (opposite entrance) (site parking orange badge holders only) ♿ toilets for disabled shop 🐕 🍴

The Teddy Bear Museum
19 Greenhill St CV37 6LF
➲ (M40 junct 15 follow signs to Stratford Town Centre)
☎ 01789 293160
e-mail: info@thetheddybearmuseum.com

Collection of some of the oldest and rarest teddy bears in the world, displayed in a house once owned by Henry VIII. Lots of modern teddy bear stars too, including the original Fozzie Bear, Paddington Bear from the earliest television series, Mr Bean's bear, and many more.
Times: Open all year, daily 9.30-5.30 (ex Jan & Feb 10-4.30) Closed 25-26 Dec. **Fee:** £2.95 (ch £1.95, concessions £2.45). Family ticket £9.50 (2+3 or 1+4) **Facilities:** P (30yds & 200yds) (access to ground floor shop only) shop ✖ (ex guide dogs)

UPTON HOUSE   Map 04 SP34
Upton House
OX15 6HT
➲ (M40 junct 12, on A422, 7m NW of Banbury, 12m SE of Stratford)
☎ 01295 670266 ▤ 01295 670266
e-mail: uptonhouse@nationaltrust.org.uk

The house, built of mellow local stone, dates from 1695, but its outstanding collections are the chief attraction. They include paintings by English and Continental Old Masters, Brussels tapestries, Sèvres porcelain, Chelsea figures, 18th-century furniture, and a collection of original artwork used to advertise Shell oil during the 1920s and 30s. Viscount Bearsted, the donor of Upton, was chairman of Shell at one time.
Times: Open 6-28 Mar & 6 Nov-19 Dec, Sat & Sun 12-4. 3 Apr-Oct, Sat-Wed House 1-5, Garden 12-5, Sat & Sun 11-5 **Fee:** ✱ £6.50 (ch £3.50) Family £16. Garden only £3.50 (ch £2, under 5's free) Party 15+ **Facilities:** P ◗ ৬ (Braille guide, parking nr house, buggy for lower garden) toilets for disabled shop ✖ (ex guide dogs)

WARWICK   Map 04 SP26
Warwick Castle
CV34 4QU
➲ (2m from M40 exit 15)
☎ 0870 442 2000 ▤ 0870 442 2394
e-mail: customer.information@warwick-castle.com

From the days of William the Conqueror to the reign of Queen Victoria, Warwick Castle has provided a backdrop for many turbulent times. Attractions include the gloomy Dungeon and Torture Chamber, the grand State Rooms, the

continued

Great Hall, and a reconstruction of the Royal Weekend Party of 1898, where "Daisy", Countess of Warwick held sway. **Times:** Open all year, daily 10-6 (5pm Nov-Mar, 7pm Aug wknds). Closed 25 Dec. **Fee:** ✱ £11.50-£14.50 (ch 4-16 £7.25-£8.75, pen £8.20-£10.50, student £8.75-£10.75). Family ticket (2 ad & 2 ch) £33-£39. Wheelchair bound visitors free. Group discounts are available. **Facilities:** 🅿 (charged) 🍽 ✗ licensed ♿ (free parking, wheelchair hire, advance notice needed) toilets for disabled shop ✘ (ex assistance dogs) ⬛

WARWICKSHIRE YEOMANRY MUSEUM

The Court House Vaults, Jury St CV34 4EW
➲ (situated on the corner of Jury Street & Castle Street, 2m E of M40 junct 15)
☎ 01926 492212 🖷 01926 494837
The vaults of the courthouse display militaria from the county Yeomanry, dating from 1794 to 1945. It includes regimental silver, paintings, uniforms and weapons. A small room in the cellars now houses the HUJ Gun project, a field gun captured by the Yeomanry in 1917.
Times: ✱ Open Good Fri-Sep, Fri-Sun & BHs 10-1 & 2-4. Other times by prior arrangement. **Facilities:** 🅿 (300yds) (2hr max in nearby streets) shop ✘

WILMCOTE   Map 04 SP15

MARY ARDEN'S HOUSE AND THE SHAKESPEARE COUNTRYSIDE MUSEUM

Station Rd CV37 9UN
➲ (3m NW off A34)
☎ 01789 293455 🖷 01789 292083
e-mail: info@shakespeare.org.uk
This picturesque, half-timbered Tudor house was the childhood home of Shakespeare's mother, Mary Arden. The site also includes Palmers Farm - a working farm with rare breed farm animals, including Gloucester Old Spot Pigs, Cotswold Sheep and Longhorn cattle. Falconry displays take place and there is a childrens' adventure playground.
Times: Open Nov-Mar, Mon-Sat 10-4, Sun 10.30-4; Apr-May & Sep-Oct, Mon-Sat 10-5, Sun 10.30-5; Jun-Aug, Mon-Sat 9.30-5, Sun 10-5.
Fee: ✱ £5.70 (ch £2.50, concessions £5) Family ticket £13.50. All five Shakespeare Houses £13 (ch £6.50, concessions £12) Family ticket £29.
Facilities: 🅿 🍽 ♿ toilets for disabled shop ✘ (ex assist dogs) ⬛

Above: Little Compton

WEST MIDLANDS

Above: Dudley Castle

EVENTS & FESTIVALS

February
tbc Chinese New Year Celebrations, Birmingham

March
10th-13th Crufts Dog Show, National Exhibition Centre, Birmingham
17th St Patrick's Day Pageant, Coventry

June
15th-19th BBC Gardeners' World Live, NEC, Birmingham
tbc Coventry Classic Car Run, War Memorial Park, Coventry
tbc Godiva Festival, free festival with three stages, War Memorial Park, Coventry

July
1st City of Wolverhampton Show (provisional)
23rd-24th Wolvestock Music Festival, Hickman Park, Bilston (provisional)
29th-30th Lord Mayor's Show, Birmingham, weekend of free family entertainment
tbc Birmingham International Jazz Festival, 70 venues citywide

August
tbc Coventry Jazz Festival

September
10th-11th Birmingham Artsfest, UK's largest free arts festival, city centre

November
tbc Coombe Fireworks, Coventry
tbc Firework Display, West Park, Wolverhampton

BIRMINGHAM   Map 07 SP08

ASTON HALL
Trinity Rd, Aston B6 6JD
➲ (M6 junct 6 follow A38(M) Aston Expressway towards city centre. Leave at Aston Waterlinks and follow brown signs to Aston Hall)
☎ 0121 327 0062 📠 0121 327 7162 ▐FREE▌
e-mail: bmag-enquiries@birmingham.gov.uk
Built by Sir Thomas Holte, Aston Hall is a fine Jacobean mansion complete with a panelled Long Gallery, balustraded staircase and magnificent plaster friezes and ceilings. King Charles I spent a night here during the Civil War and the house was damaged by Parliamentary troops. It was also leased to James Watt Junior, the son of the great industrial pioneer.
Times: Open Etr-Oct, Tue-Sun 11.30-4. Closed Mon ex BHs.
Facilities: 🅿 ♿ ⚹ (ground floor only partially accessible) shop ✖ (ex guide dogs)

BIRMINGHAM BOTANICAL GARDENS & GLASSHOUSES
Westbourne Rd, Edgbaston B15 3TR
➲ (2m W of city centre, follow signs for Edgbaston, then brown heritage signs)
☎ 0121 454 1860 📠 0121 454 7835
e-mail: admin@
birminghambotanicalgardens.org.uk

Originally opened in 1832, the gardens include the Tropical House, which has a 24ft-wide lily pool and lush vegetation. The Mediterranean house features a wide variety of citrus fruits and the Arid House has a desert scene with its giant agaves and opuntias. Outside, a tour of the gardens includes rhododendrons and azalea borders and a collection of over 200 trees. Young children's discovery garden and a sculpture trail.
Times: Open daily all year, wkdays 9-7 or dusk, Sun 10-7 or dusk whichever is earlier. (Closed 25 Dec). **Fee:** ✱ £5.70 (concessions £3.30); £6 summer Sun & BHs. Family £16 (£17 summer & BH's) Groups 10+ £4.70 (concessions £3) **Facilities:** 🅿 ♿ ✖ licensed ⚹ (3 wheelchairs, 2 electric scooters & Braille guides) toilets for disabled shop garden centre ✖ (ex guide dogs) ▱
See advertisement on this page

THE BIRMINGHAM BOTANICAL GARDENS & GLASSHOUSES
Garden of the World
Open in 1832, the Gardens are a 15 acre "Oasis of Delight" with over 200 trees and the finest collection of plants in the Midlands. Tropical, Mediterranean and Arid glasshouses. National Bonsai Collection.
Children's Playground, Children's Discovery Garden, exotic birds, art gallery and Sculpture Trail. Gift shop. Plant sales. Restaurant. Bands play summer Sunday afternoons and Bank Holidays. Open Daily.

Westbourne Road, Edgbaston, Birmingham
West Midlands B15 3TR
Tel: 0121 454 1860 Fax: 0121 454 7835
Group bookings by prior appointment
Email: admin@birminghambotanicalgardens.org.uk
Internet: www.birminghambotanicalgardens.org.uk

BIRMINGHAM MUSEUM & ART GALLERY
Chamberlain Sq B3 3DH
☎ 0121 303 2834 📠 0121 303 1394 ▐FREE▌
e-mail: bmag-enquiries@birmingham.gov.uk
One of the world's best collections of Pre-Raphaelite paintings can be seen here, including important works by Burne-Jones, a native of Birmingham. Also on display are fine silver, ceramics and glass. The archaeology section has prehistoric Egyptian, Greek and Roman antiquities, and also objects from the Near East, Mexico and Peru.
Times: Open all year, Mon-Thu & Sat 10-5, Fri 10.30-5 and Sun 12.30-5. **Facilities:** 🅿 ♿ ✖ licensed ⚹ (lift) toilets for disabled shop ✖ ▱

BLAKESLEY HALL
Blakesley Rd, Yardley B25 8RN
➲ (A4040 onto Blakesley Rd, Blakesley Hall 100yds on right)
☎ 0121 783 2193 📠 0121 235 1343 ▐FREE▌
Blakesley Hall is a fine Yeoman farmers residence, built by Richard Smalbroke in 1590. It has a half-timbered exterior and a Stuart interior, with a wonderful herb garden. The visitor centre has a varied exhibition programme, tea room and gift shop. Regular weekend events take place throughout the summer holidays.
Times: Open Apr-Oct, Tue-Sun, BHs (11.30-4) **Facilities:** 🅿 ♿ shop ✖

MUSEUM OF THE JEWELLERY QUARTER
75-79 Vyse St, Hockley B18 6HA
➲ (off A41 into Vyse St, museum on left hand side after 1st side street).
☎ 0121 554 3598 🖷 0121 554 9700   FREE
e-mail: bmag-enquiries@birmingham.gov.uk

The Museum tells the story of jewellery making in Birmingham from its origins in the Middle Ages right through to the present day. Discover the skill of the jeweller's craft and enjoy a unique tour of an original jewellery factory frozen in time. For over eighty years the family firm of Smith and Pepper produced jewellery from the factory. This perfectly preserved 'time capsule' workshop has changed little since the beginning of the century. The Jewellery Quarter is still very much at the forefront of jewellery manufacture in Britain and the Museum showcases the work of the city's most exciting new designers.

Times: Open Etr-Oct, Tue-Sun 11.30-4. (Closed Mon ex BH Mon)
Facilities: P (limited 2hr stay/pay & display) 🍽 & (tours for hearing/visually impaired booked in advance) toilets for disabled shop ✈ (ex guide dogs) 🍴

RSPB SANDWELL VALLEY NATURE RESERVE
20 Tanhouse Av, Great Barr B43 5AG
➲ (off B4167 Hamstead Road into Tanhouse Avenue)
☎ 0121 357 7395 🖷 0121 358 3013

Opened in 1983 on the site of an old colliery, Sandwell Valley is home to hundreds of bird, animal and insect species in five different habitats. Summer is the best time to see the yellow wagtail or reed warblers, while wintertime attracts goosanders, snipe, and redshanks. There are guided walks and bug hunts for the kids in summer, and a shop and visitor centre all year round.

Times: Open Tue-Fri 9-5, Sat & Sun 10-5, closes at dusk in winter. (Closed Mon, 24 Dec-2 Jan) **Facilities:** P & toilets for disabled shop

SAREHOLE MILL
Cole Bank Rd, Hall Green B13 0BD
➲ (M42 junct 4. Take A34 towards Birmingham. After 5m turn left on B4146 Sarehole Mill on left)
☎ 0121 777 6612 🖷 0121 303 2891   FREE

Home to Birmingham's only working watermill; Sarehole Mill was built in the 1760s. Used for both flour production and metal rolling up to the last century, the Mill can still be seen in action during the summer months. Restored with financial backing from JRR Tolkien, who grew up in the area and cites Sarehole as an influence for writing *The Hobbit* and *Lord of the Rings*.

Times: Open Etr-Oct, Tue-Sun 11.30-4. (Closed Mon, ex BH Mons)
Facilities: P ✈ (ex guide dogs)

SELLY MANOR MUSEUM
Maple Rd, Bournville B30 2AE
➲ (off A38)
☎ 0121 472 0199 🖷 0121 471 4101
e-mail: gillianellis@bvt.org.uk

These two timber-framed manor houses date from the 13th and early 14th centuries, and have been re-erected in the 'garden suburb' of Bournville. There is a herb garden and events are held all year.

Times: Open mid Jan-mid Dec, Tue-Fri 10-5 (Apr-Sep & BH, Sat-Sun 2-5). **Fee:** ✱ £2 (ch 50p, concessions £1.50). Family ticket £4.50.
Facilities: P & toilets for disabled shop

SOHO HOUSE
Soho Av, Handsworth B18 5LB
➲ (from city centre follow A41 to Soho Rd, follow brown heritage signs to Soho Av)
☎ 0121 554 9122 🖷 0121 554 5929   FREE
e-mail: bmag-enquiries@birmingham.gov.uk

Soho House was the elegant home of industrial pioneer Matthew Boulton between 1766 and 1809. Here, he met with some of the most important thinkers and scientists of his day. The house has been carefully restored and contains many of Boulton's possessions including furniture, clocks, silverware and the original dining table where the Lunar Society met.

Times: Open Etr-Oct, Tue-Sun 11.30-4. (Closed Mon ex BH Mons)
Facilities: P 🍽 & (induction loop) toilets for disabled shop ✈ (ex guide dogs) 🍴

THINKTANK AT MILLENNIUM POINT
Millennium Point, Curzon St B4 7XG
☎ 0121 202 2222 🖷 0121 202 2280
e-mail: findout@thinktank.ac

Thinktank is the Birmingham Museum of Science and Discovery, and has four floors with ten themed galleries that are packed with interactive exhibits that explore everything from locomotives and aircraft to intestines and spit glands! The special LEGO lab offers kids the chance to programme their own LEGO robots and find out how LEGO itself evolved.

Times: ✱ Open daily 10-5 (last entry 4). (Closed 24-26 Dec)
Facilities: P (charged) 🍽 & toilets for disabled shop ✈ (ex guide dogs) 🍴

BOURNVILLE   Map 07 SP08

CADBURY WORLD
Linden Rd B30 2LD
➲ (1m S of A38 Bristol Rd, on A4040 Ring Rd)
☎ 0121 451 4159 🖷 0121 451 1366
e-mail: cadbury.world@csplc.com

Lots of recent changes have meant Cadbury World now has much more to see, do and taste. There is the chance to get involved in the chocolate making process, and to find out how the chocolate is used to make famous confectionery. Visitors can learn about the early struggles and triumphs of the Cadbury business, and follow the history of Cadbury television advertising. Besides all this, visitors can relax on the gentle Cadabra ride, and be a big kid in CadburyLand, the Fantasy Factory, and on the Cocoa Road.

Times: ✱ Contact information line 0121 451 4180 for opening times.
Facilities: P 🍽 ✕ & (adapted ride & lift to 2nd floor, subtitles) toilets for disabled shop ✈ (ex guide dogs) 🍴

CASTLE BROMWICH   Map 07 SP18

CASTLE BROMWICH HALL GARDENS NEW
Chester Rd B36 9BT
➲ (M6 junct 5, follow brown tourist signs)
☎ 0121 749 4100 🖷 0121 749 4100
e-mail: admin@cbhgt.colebridge.net

This recently-restored 17th-century formal garden illustrates a period of history in an unusual and fascinating way. Although the garden is an accurate reconstruction of the garden as it was around 1680-1740, there is an addition: the holly maze, which was created in the 19th century, based on 17th-century plans.

Times: Open: Apr-Oct, Wed-Fri 12-4; Sat, Sun & BH Mon 1-5
Fee: £3.50 (ch £1.50, pen £2.50) **Facilities:** P 🍽 & (wheelchairs available for free) toilets for disabled shop garden centre

COVENTRY   Map 04 SP37

COVENTRY CATHEDRAL & VISITOR CENTRE
7 Priory Row CV1 5ES
➲ (signposted on all approaches to the city)
☎ 024 7622 7597   🖹 024 7663 1448
e-mail: information@coventrycathedral.org
Coventry's old cathedral was bombed during an air raid of November 1940 which devastated the city. The remains have been carefully preserved. The new cathedral was designed by Sir Basil Spence and consecrated in May 1962. It contains outstanding modern works of art, including a huge tapestry designed by Graham Sutherland, the west screen (a wall of glass engraved by John Hutton with saints and angels), bronzes by Epstein, and the great baptistry window by John Piper.
Times: Open all year, daily, Etr-Oct 8.30-6, Oct-Etr 8.30-5.30.
Facilities: 🅿 (250yds) 🍽 ♿ (lift, touch and hearing centre, paved wheelchair access) toilets for disabled shop 🐕 (ex guide dogs)

COVENTRY TRANSPORT MUSEUM
Hales St CV1 1PN
➲ (just off junct 1, Coventry ring road, Tower Street in City Centre)
☎ 024 7683 2425   🖹 024 7683 2465
e-mail: museum@mbrt.co.uk
Coventry is the traditional home of the motor industry. The Coventry Transport Museum displays the largest collection of British cars, buses, cycles and motorcycles in the world. Visitors can learn about motoring's early days in 'landmarques', how Royalty travelled, and see Thrust 2 and Thrust SSC, the world land speed record cars.
Times: Open all year, daily 10-5. (Closed 24-26 Dec).
Facilities: 🅿 (adjacent) (pay & display) 🍽 ♿ (audio tour, tactile floor & models, wheelchairs for hire) toilets for disabled shop 🐕 (ex guide dogs) 🍴

HERBERT ART GALLERY & MUSEUM
Jordan Well CV1 5QP
➲ (located in city centre near Cathedral)
☎ 024 7683 2381 & 7683 2565
🖹 024 7683 2410
e-mail: artsandheritage@coventry.gov.uk
'Godiva City', tells Coventry's story over 1,000 years, through interactive exhibits, objects, pictures and words. Changing displays of art, craft, social and industrial history. It is Coventry's premier museum hosting a range of exhibitions and events.
Times: Open all year, Mon-Sat 10-5.30, Sun 12-5. (Closed 24-26, 31 Dec & 1 Jan) **Facilities:** 🅿 (500yds) 🍽 ♿ (disabled parking, automatic doors, tactile/audio displays) toilets for disabled shop 🐕 (ex guide/assistance dogs)

JAGUAR DAIMLER HERITAGE CENTRE
Browns Ln, Allesley CV5 9DR
➲ (on A45, follow signs for Browns Lane Plant)
☎ 024 7620 3322   🖹 024 7620 2835   `FREE`
e-mail: jagtrust@jaguar.com
Established in 1983, the Jaguar-Daimler Heritage Trust maintains a unique collection of motor vehicles and artefacts manufactured by Jaguar Cars Ltd, and the many other renowned marques associated with the company.
Times: Open Mon-Thu 9-4, Fri 9-3 & last Sun of month 10-4.
Facilities: 🅿 🍽 ♿ toilets for disabled shop 🐕 (ex guide dogs)

LUNT ROMAN FORT
Coventry Rd, Baginton CV8 3AJ
➲ (S side of city, off Stonebridge highway, A45)
☎ 024 7683 2381 & 7683 2565
🖹 024 7683 2410
e-mail: artsandheritage@coventry.co.uk
The turf and timber Roman fort from around the end of the 1st century has been faithfully reconstructed. An Interpretation Centre is housed in the granary.
Times: Open 27 Mar-Oct, Sat-Sun & BH Mons 10-5; mid Jul-end Aug, Thu-Tue 10-5; Spring BH wk, Thu-Tue 10-5. **Facilities:** 🅿 ♿ (ramp to Granary Interpretation Centre) toilets for disabled shop 🐕 (ex guide/assistance dogs)

PRIORY VISITOR CENTRE
Priory Row CV1 5EX
➲ (in city centre near Cathedral)
☎ 024 7683 2381   🖹 024 7683 2410
e-mail: artsandheritage@coventry.gov.uk
Earl Leofric and his wife Lady Godiva founded a monastery in Coventry in the 11th century. This priory disappeared somewhere beneath the cathedral that was built on the site, until this cathedral was in turn demolished by Henry VIII in the 16th century. Soon after that most of the buildings on the site had been reduced to ground level, leaving modern archaeologists to discover the outlines of history. This visitor centre displays finds from the site as well as telling the story of Coventry's first cathedral.
Times: Open Mon-Sat 10-5.30, Sun noon-4 **Facilities:** 🅿 (500yds) ♿ toilets for disabled shop 🐕 (ex guide/assistance dogs)

ST MARY'S GUILDHALL
Bayley Ln CV1 5QP
➲ (in city centre near ruined Cathedral)
☎ 024 7683 2381   🖹 024 7683 2410
e-mail: artsandheritage@coventry.gov.uk
This impressive medieval Guildhall has stood in the heart of Coventry for over 650 years, and has played its part in the history of the area. It served as Henry VI's court during the War of the Roses, was a prison to Mary Queen of Scots, and was used as a setting by George Eliot in her novel *Adam Bede*. The Great Hall contains a Tournai tapestry commissioned for the visit of Henry VII and Queen Elizabeth in 1500.
Times: Open Etr Sun-Sep, Sun-Thu 10-4 **Facilities:** 🅿 (600yds) ♿ shop 🐕 (ex guide/assistance dogs)

The Battle of Trafalgar.
2005 is the 200th anniversary of the sea battle between the British Royal Navy and the French and Spanish navies. 2005 will see a number of events celebrating this important British victory.

DUDLEY Map 07 SO99

BLACK COUNTRY LIVING MUSEUM

Tipton Rd DY1 4SQ

➲ (on A4037, nr Showcase cinema)

☎ 0121 557 9643 & 0121 520 8054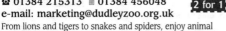

📠 0121 557 4242

e-mail: info@bclm.co.uk

On the 26-acre site is a recreated canal-side village, with shops, houses and workplaces. Meet the costumed guides and find out what life was like around 1900. Ride on a tramcar, take a trip down the underground mine, venture into the limestone caverns or visit the olde tyme fairground (additional charge). There are also demonstrations of chainmaking, glass engraving and sweet-making. Watch a silent movie in the Limelight cinema, taste fish and chips cooked on a 1930s range, and finish your visit with a glass of real ale in the Bottle and Glass Inn.

Times: Open all year, Mar-Oct daily 10-5; Nov-Feb, Wed-Sun 10-4. (Telephone for Xmas closing) **Fee:** ✱ £9.95 (ch 5-18 £5.75, pen £8.75). Family ticket (2 ad+3 ch) £28. **Facilities:** 🅿 (charged) ⬛
✖ licensed & (ramps available) toilets for disabled shop
✖ (ex guide dogs) 🍴

DUDLEY ZOOLOGICAL GARDENS

2 The Broadway DY1 4QB

➲ (M5 junct 2 towards Wolverhampton/Dudley. Signposted)

☎ 01384 215313 📠 01384 456048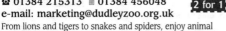

e-mail: marketing@dudleyzoo.org.uk

From lions and tigers to snakes and spiders, enjoy animal encounters and feeds. Get closer to some furry, and some not so furry creatures, and have fun on the fair rides, land train, and the adventure playground. Step back in time and see history come to life in the castle.

Times: Open all year, Etr-mid Sep, daily 10-4; mid Sep-Etr, daily 10-3. (Closed 25 Dec). **Fee:** ✱ £8.50 (ch 4-15 £5.25, concessions £5.75). Family ticket £28.50 (2ad+3ch) **Facilities:** 🅿 (charged) ⬛
✖ licensed & (land train from gates-castle, wheelchair hire) toilets for disabled shop ✖ (ex guide dogs) 🍴

MUSEUM & ART GALLERY

St James's Rd DY1 1HU

➲ (M5 northbound, exit at junct 2. Take A4123 signposted to Dudley)

☎ 01384 815575 📠 01384 815576

e-mail: museum.pls@mbc.dudley.gov.uk

The museum houses the Brooke Robinson collection of 17th, 18th and 19th century European painting, furniture, ceramics and enamels. A fine geological gallery, 'The Time Trail' has spectacular displays of fossils from the local Wenlock limestone and coal measures.

Times: ✱ Open all year, Mon-Sat 10-4. (Closed BHs).
Facilities: 🅿 (25mtrs) & (Braille & large print text. Tactile objects) shop ✖ (ex guide dogs)

KINGSWINFORD Map 07 SO88

BROADFIELD HOUSE GLASS MUSEUM NEW

Compton Dr DY6 9NS

➲ (Off A491 Stourbridge to Wolverhampton road, just S of Kingswinford Village Centre)

☎ 01384 812745 FREE

e-mail: glass.museum@dudley.gov.uk

This magnificent collection of 19th-and 20th-century glass focuses on the cut, etched, engraved and coloured glass

continued

made in nearby Stourbridge during the last century. Highlights include cameo glass by Alphonse Lechevrel and George Woodall, and rock crystal engraving by William Fritsche. Also on display are the Michael Parkington collection of 18th-, 19th-and 20th-century British glass, the Hulbert of Dudley collection, and the Notley/Lerpiniere collection of Carnival Glass.

Times: Open all year, Tue-Sun 12-4, BHs 12-4. Please phone for Xmas/Etr openings **Facilities:** 🅿 & toilets for disabled shop ✖ (ex guide dogs) 🍴

SOLIHULL Map 07 SP17

NATIONAL MOTORCYCLE MUSEUM

Coventry Rd, Bickenhill B92 0EJ

➲ (near junct 6, of M42, off A45 near NEC)

☎ 01675 443311 📠 0121 711 3153

Five exhibition halls showing British motorcycles built during the Golden Age of motorcycling. Spanning 90 years, the immaculately restored machines are the products of around 150 different factories. Over 700 machines are on show, most are owned by the museum, while others are from collections or private owners. Restoration work is carried out by enthusiasts, and new motorcycles are acquired from all over the world.

Times: Open all year, daily 10-6. (Closed 24-26 Dec). **Fee:** ✱ £5.95 (ch 12 & pen £4.75). Party 20+ £4.95 **Facilities:** 🅿 ✖ licensed & toilets for disabled shop ✖ (ex guide dogs) 🍴

STOURBRIDGE Map 07 SO88

THE FALCONRY CENTRE

Hurrans Garden Centre, Kidderminster Rd South, Hagley DY9 0JB

➲ (off A456)

☎ 01562 700014 📠 01562 700014

The centre houses some 70 birds of prey including owls, hawks and falcons and is also a rehabilitation centre for sick and injured birds of prey. Spectacular flying displays are put on daily from midday. There are picnic areas, special fun days and training courses available.

Times: Open all year, daily 10-5 & Sun 11-5. (Closed 25, 26 Dec & Etr Sun). **Facilities:** 🅿 ⬛ & toilets for disabled shop garden centre ✖ (ex guide dogs) 🍴

WALSALL Map 07 SP09

NEW ART GALLERY WALSALL

Gallery Square WS2 8LG

➲ (signed from all major routes into Walsall town centre, including M6 junct 7, 9, 10 - just a few minutes drive away)

☎ 01922 654400 📠 01922 654401 FREE

e-mail: info@artatwalsall.org.uk

Opened in 2000, this exciting new art gallery has at its core the Garman Ryan Collection, and a Children's Discovery Gallery that offers access to the very best in contemporary art in the only interactive art gallery designed especially for young people. Exhibits in 2005 include Jim Bird, Hew Locke, and Conrad Shawcross.

Times: Open all year Tue-Sat 10-5, Sun noon-5. (Closed Mon ex BH Mons). **Facilities:** 🅿 ⬛ ✖ & (lift access to facilties, induction loop, large print) toilets for disabled shop ✖ (ex guide dogs)

WALSALL LEATHER MUSEUM

Littleton St West WS2 8EQ

➲ (On Walsall ring-road A4148 on North side of town)

☎ 01922 721153 ▤ 01922 725827

FREE

e-mail: leathermuseum@walsall.gov.uk

Award winning working museum in the saddlery and leathergoods 'capital' of Britain. Watch skilled craftsmen and women at work in this restored Victorian leather factory. Displays tell the story of Walsall's leatherworkers past and present. Large shop stocks range of Walsall made leathergoods, many at bargain prices. Saddle Room Cafe serves delicious home-cooked cakes and light lunches. Groups very welcome, guided tours available.

Times: Open all year, Tue-Sat 10-5 (Nov-Mar 4pm), Sun noon-5 (Nov-Mar 4pm). Open BH Mon. (Closed 24-26 Dec, 1 Jan, Good Fri, Etr Sun & May Day). **Facilities:** P (10mtrs) 🖵 ♿ (staff with sign language skills,tactile activities,parking) toilets for disabled shop ✖ (ex guide dogs) ▬

WOLVERHAMPTON   Map 07 SO99

BANTOCK HOUSE AND PARK NEW

Finchfield Rd WV3 0DD

➲ (follow signs for Wolverhampton. Bantock House is 1m out of city & is well signposted from the ring road)

☎ 01902 552195 ▤ 01902 552196

FREE

e-mail: bantockhouse@dial.pipex.com

A rare survival of a Georgian farmhouse that was extended in the early 19th century to double its size. The current interior represents the Edwardian era, when the décor was radically altered. The ground floor is set out as the family home, while upstairs visitors can discover Wolverhampton's history. The gardens have been restored to their Edwardian designs and include a rose garden, Dutch garden and woodland pond.

Times: Open early Apr-end Oct, 11-5 (closed Mon). Nov-end Mar, 12-4 (closed Mon) **Facilities:** P 🖵 ♿ (wheelchair, induction loop, Braille guide) toilets for disabled shop

MOSELEY OLD HALL

Fordhouses WV10 7HY

➲ (4m N of Wolverhampton, off A460 and A449)

☎ 01902 552195 ▤ 01902 782808

2 for 1

e-mail: moseleyoldhall@nationaltrust.org.uk

Charles II sheltered in Moseley Old Hall after the Battle of Worcester in 1651. There are numerous pictures and other reminders of the king. The house itself is an Elizabethan timber-framed building which was encased in brick in the 19th century. The small garden has a nut walk, period herbs and plants, and a formal knot garden. For details of special events please send a 9" x 4" envelope.

Times: Open 20 Mar-Oct, Sat, Sun & Wed 1-5; 7 Nov-19 Dec, Sun 1-4.

Fee: ✱ £4.60 (ch £2.30). Family ticket £11.50. **Facilities:** P 🖵 ♿ (Braille & large print, 1 wheelchair, thick handled cutlery) toilets for disabled shop ❀ ▬

WIGHTWICK MANOR

WV6 8EE

➲ (3m W, beside Mermaid Inn off A454 Bridgnorth)

☎ 01902 761400 ▤ 01902 764663

2 for 1

e-mail: wightwickmanor@nationaltrust.org.uk

This house was begun in 1887 and is one of the finest examples of 19th-century decorative style. All aspects of William Morris's talents are shown in the house - wallpapers, textiles, carpets, tiles, embroidery and even books. The garden reflects late Victorian and Edwardian design.

Times: Open Mar-23 Dec, Thu, Sat & BH Sun & Mon 1.30-5. Last admission 4.30. Garden & servant tours throughout the year, please phone for details. **Fee:** ✱ £6 (accompanied ch & students £3). Gardens only £3 (ch free in garden) **Facilities:** P 🖵 ♿ (car parking call 01902 761400 for details) shop ❀

Above: Timber-frame cottages in Halesown

ISLE OF WIGHT

EVENTS & FESTIVALS

March
25th-27th Easter Challenge yacht racing –
start of the yachting season

May
tbc Schneider Trophy Air Races,
Bembridge Airport

June
3rd-5th Old Gaffers Festival, Yarmouth,
festival of gaff-rigged vessels, entertainment
and stalls
18th Round the Island Yacht Race
tbc Isle of Wight Festival, Seaclose Park,
Newport

July
9th-23rd Admiral's Cup, Cowes
23rd-24th Isle of Wight County Show,
Showground, Northwood, nr Newport
30th-5th Aug Cowes Week, international
yachting regatta, music and street theatre
tbc Annual Regatta, Royal Solent Yacht Club,
Yarmouth

August
27th-30th The Island Steam Show,
Havenstreet
tbc Cowes Powerboat Festival
tbc Isle of Wight Garlic Festival, Newchurch

September
tbc Medina Fun Festival, River Medina, at
Cowes, East Cowes and Newport

Above: Chalk cliffs as seen from Headon Warren

ALUM BAY   Map 04 SZ38

THE NEEDLES OLD BATTERY
West High Down PO30 0JH
➲ (at Needles Headland, W of Freshwater Bay and
Alum Bay, B3322)
☎ 01983 754772   🖹 01983 756978
e-mail: jean.pitt@nationaltrust.org.uk

The threat of a French invasion prompted the construction in
1862 of this spectacularly sited fort, which still retains its
original gun barrels. The laboratory, searchlight position-
finding cells have all been restored and a 65m tunnel leads
to stunning views of the Hampshire and Dorset coastline.
The 2-for-1 voucher is not valid for ticketed events.
Times: Open 28 Mar-Jun & Sep-Oct daily (closed Fri ex Good Fri)
10.30-5; Jul-Aug daily 10.30-5; Property closes in very bad weather.
Telephone on day of visit to check. **Fee:** £3.80 (ch £1.90). Family ticket
£8.50. **Facilities:** P (0.5m) 🍽 ⅋ (ramp & audio tours) toilets for
disabled ⅋ 🍴

THE NEEDLES PARK
PO39 0JD
➲ (signposted, on B3322)
☎ 0870 458 0022   🖹 01983 755260
e-mail: info@theneedles.co.uk

Overlooking the Needles on the western edge of the Island,
the park has attractions for all the family: included in the
wide range of facilities is the spectacular chair lift to the
beach to view the famous coloured sandcliffs, Needles Rocks

continued

and lighthouse. Other popular attractions include Alum Bay Glass and the Isle of Wight Sweet Manufactory.

Times: Open 23 Mar-30 Oct, daily 10-5. Hours extended in high season & on special event days **Fee:** ✱ No admission charged for entrance to Park. All day car park charge £3. Pay as you go attractions or Supersaver Attraction discount ticket £7.50 (ch £5.50).

Facilities: 🅿 (charged) 🍽 ✗ licensed ♿ designated parking toilets for disabled shop 🛍

ARRETON   Map 04 SZ58

ROBIN HILL COUNTRY PARK
Downend PO30 2NU

⊃ (0.5m from Allerton village next door to the Hare and Hounds pub)

☎ 01983 527352   🖷 01983 527347

Set in 88 acres of downland and woods, Robin Hill offers a Tree Top Trail, Mazes, Snake Slides, Troll Island, Toboggan Run Ride, Squirrel Tower, Forest Sculptures and a Countryside Centre and the 3 largest rides on the island.

Times: ✱ Open 25 Mar-3 Nov, daily 10-5 (last admission 4).

Facilities: 🅿 🍽 ✗ ♿ (most areas are accessible. ramps access) toilets for disabled shop

BEMBRIDGE   Map 04 SZ68

BEMBRIDGE WINDMILL
PO35 5SQ

⊃ (0.5m S of Bembridge on B3395)

☎ 01983 873945   **2 for 1**

The only windmill on the island to survive, Bembridge mill was built about 1700 and was in use until 1913. The stone-built tower, with its wooden cap and machinery, has been restored for visitors to explore along with breathtaking views of glorious unspoilt countryside. The 2-for-1 voucher is not valid for ticketed events.

Times: Open 29 Mar-29 Oct, Sun-Fri, 10-5 (Closed Sat ex Etr Sat); Jul-Aug, daily 10-5. **Fee:** £2 (ch £1). **Facilities:** 🅿 (200yds) shop ✗ (ex guide dogs) 🥾 🛍

> If an attraction name appears in *italics*, details have not been confirmed for 2005.

BLACKGANG   Map 04 SZ47

BLACKGANG CHINE FANTASY PARK
PO38 2HN

⊃ (follow signs from Ventnor for Whitnell & Niton. From the village of Niton follow signs for Blackgang)

☎ 01983 730330   🖷 01983 731267

e-mail: info@blackgangchine.com

Opened as scenic gardens in 1843 covering some 40 acres, the park has imaginative play areas, water gardens, maze and coastal gardens. Set on the steep wooded slopes of the chine are the themed areas Smugglerland, Nurseryland, Dinosaurland, Fantasyland and Frontierland. St Catherine's Quay has a maritime exhibition showing the history of local and maritime affairs.

Times: Open 22 Mar-Oct daily, 10-5. 18 Jul-4 Sep open until 10.

Fee: ✱ Combined ticket to chine, sawmill & quay £7.50. Saver ticket (4 people) £27. **Facilities:** 🅿 (charged) 🍽 ♿ (some paths steep) toilets for disabled shop 🛍

BRADING   Map 04 SZ68

ISLE OF WIGHT WAX WORKS
46 High St PO36 0DQ

⊃ (on A3055, in Brading High St)

☎ 0870 4584477   🖷 01983 402112

e-mail: waxworks@

bradingisleofwight.fsnet.co.uk

Set in 3/4 acre in the historic 'Kynge's Towne' of Brading, the Rectory mansion is filled with famous and infamous characters from the past, the chamber of horrors, Great British Legends Gallery, world of nature, Professor Copperthwaithe's extraordinary collection of oddities, and demonstrations on the art of candle-carving.

Times: Open all year, Summer 10-5, Winter 10.30-4.30 (last admission 1hr before closing) **Fee:** £5.50 (ch 5-14, £3.75, under 5 free, pen £4.50). Family £17 (2 ad+2 ch), Family £20 (2 ad+3 ch). Party 20+.

Facilities: 🅿 🍽 ♿ (Disabled route planner) toilets for disabled shop 🛍

LILLIPUT ANTIQUE DOLL & TOY MUSEUM
High St PO36 0DJ

⊃ (A3055 Ryde/Sandown road, in Brading High Street)

☎ 01983 407231   🖷 01983 404663

e-mail: lilliput.museum@btconnect.com

This private museum contains one of the finest collections of antique dolls and toys in Britain. There are over 2000 exhibits, ranging in age from 2000BC to 1945 with examples of almost every seriously collectable doll, many with royal connections. Also dolls' houses, teddy bears and rare and unusual toys.

Times: Open all year, daily, 10-5. **Fee:** £1.95 (ch & pen £1.15, ch under 5 free). Party on request. **Facilities:** 🅿 (200 yds) ♿ (ramps provided on request) shop 🛍

MORTON MANOR
PO36 0EP

⊃ (off A3055 in Brading, well signposted) **2 for 1**

☎ 01983 406168

The manor dates back to 1249, but was rebuilt in 1680 with further changes during the Georgian period. The house contains furniture of both the 18th and 19th centuries, but its main attraction lies in the gardens and vineyard. The garden is landscaped into terraces, with ornamental ponds, a

continued

sunken garden and a traditional Elizabethan turf maze. There is also an established vineyard and winery.
Times: Open Apr-Oct, daily 10-5.30 (Closed Sat) Last admissions 4.30.
Fee: ✱ £4.50 (ch £2, pen £4). Party 15+ £3.50 each.
Facilities: 🅿 ♨ ✗ licensed ♿ shop garden centre

NUNWELL HOUSE & GARDENS
Coach Ln PO36 0JQ
➲ (Off Ryde-Sandown Rd, A3055)
☎ 01983 407240   **2 for 1**
Set in beautiful gardens, Nunwell is an impressive, lived-in and much loved house where King Charles I spent his last night of freedom. It has fine furniture and interesting collections of family militaria. In summer, concerts are occasionally held in the music room.
Times: Open House & Gardens: 29 & 30 May then 4 Jul-7 Sep, 1-5. Tours of the house at 1.30, 2.30 and 3.30. **Fee:** £4 inc guide book. (concessions £3.50, under 10's £1) **Facilities:** 🅿 shop ✘ (ex guide dogs)

BRIGHSTONE   Map 04 SZ48
BRIGHSTONE SHOP AND MUSEUM NEW
North St PO30 4AX
➲ (North St, next to post office, Brightstone just off B3399)
☎ 01983 740689   **FREE**
Within a row of pretty, thatched cottages you will find this museum which contains an evocative tableau and an interesting exhibition on village life in the 19th century.
Times: Open: 2 Jan-27 Mar, Mon-Sat 10-1; 29 Mar-22 May, Mon-Sat 10-4; 23 May-24 Oct, Mon-Sat 10-5, Sun 12-5; 25 Oct-31 Dec, Mon-Sat 10-4. **Facilities:** 🅿 ♿ shop ✘ (ex guide dogs)

CARISBROOKE   Map 04 SZ48
CARISBROOKE CASTLE
PO30 1XY
➲ (1.25m SW of Newport, off B3401)
☎ 01983 522107   🖻 01983 528632
A royal fortress and prison to King Charles I, Carisbrooke is set on a sweeping ridge at the heart of the Isle of Wight. Don't miss the donkeys that can be seen working a 16th-century wheel to draw water from the well.
Times: Open all year, Apr-Sep, daily 10-6; Oct-Mar, daily 10-4. (Closed 24-26 Dec & 1 Jan). **Fee:** ✱ £5 (ch £2.50, concessions £3.80). Family £12.50. Prices & opening times relate to 2004, for further details phone or log onto www.english-heritage.org.uk/visits **Facilities:** 🅿 ♨ ♿ shop ⚏

FRESHWATER   Map 04 SZ38
DIMBOLA LODGE
Terrace Ln, Freshwater Bay PO40 9QE
➲ (off A3054)
☎ 01983 756814   🖻 01983 755578
e-mail: administrator@dimbola.co.uk
Home of Julia Margaret Cameron, the pioneer Victorian portrait photographer. The house has the largest permanent collection of Cameron prints on display in the UK, as well as galleries exhibiting work by young, up and coming, and acclaimed modern photographers; and a large display of cameras and accessories.
Times: ✱ Open all year 10-5 (Closed 5 days at Xmas).
Facilities: 🅿 ✗ ♿ chairlifts toilets for disabled shop ✘ (ex guide dogs) 🍴

MOTTISTONE   Map 04 SZ48
MOTTISTONE MANOR GARDEN
PO30 4ED
➲ (2m W of Brighstone on B3399)
☎ 01983 741302

The garden of this 16th and 17th-century manor house, which is tenanted, is noted for its colourful herbaceous border, grassy terraces planted with fruit trees and lovely sea views. There are also some delightful walks between the Downs and the coast.
Times: Open 30 Mar-Oct, Tue & Wed 11-5.30, Sun & BH Mons 2-5.30
Fee: £3 (ch £1.50) Family £7.50 **Facilities:** 🅿 ♨ ♿ (limited access) toilets for disabled shop garden centre ⚏

NEWTOWN   Map 04 SZ49
OLD TOWN HALL   **2 for 1**
Town Ln PO30 4PA
➲ (1m N of A3054 between Yarmouth & Newport)
☎ 01983 531785

The small, now tranquil, village of Newtown once sent two members to parliament and the Town Hall was the setting for, often, turbulent elections. Full of local history, mysterious benefactors and set in a wonderful nature reserve, the Town Hall is well worth a visit. The 2-for-1 voucher is not valid for ticketed events.
Times: Open 29 Mar-30 Jun & Sep-20 Oct, Mon, Wed & Sun, 2-5 (also open Good Fri & Etr Sat); Jul & Aug Sun-Thu, 2-5. **Fee:** £1.80 (ch 90p). Family £4.50 **Facilities:** 🅿 ♿ toilets for disabled ✘ (ex guide dogs) ⚏

OSBORNE HOUSE Map 04 SZ59
OSBORNE HOUSE
PO32 6JY
➲ (1m SE of East Cowes)
☎ 01983 200022 📠 01983 281380

The beloved seaside retreat of Queen Victoria offers a glimpse into the private life of Britain's longest reigning monarch. The royal apartments are full of treasured mementos. The Dunbar Room evokes the atmosphere of India as experienced by Queen Victoria. Visit the gardens and the charming Swiss Cottage.
Times: Open House: Apr-Sep, daily 10-6; Oct-Mar, Sun-Thu guided tours only. Closed 24-26 Dec & 1 Jan. **Fee:** ✱ House & Gardens: £8.50 (ch £4.30, concessions £6.40). Garden only: £5 (ch £2.50, concessions £3.80). Family £21.30 (2 adults+3 children). Prices & opening times relate to 2004, for further details phone or log onto www.english-heritage.org.uk/visits **Facilities:** 🅿 💷 ♿ shop ✈ ♯

PORCHFIELD Map 04 SZ49
COLEMANS ANIMAL FARM
Colemans Ln PO30 4LX
➲ (from A3054 Newport-Yarmouth Rd, follow brown tourist signs)
☎ 01983 522831 📠 01983 537534
e-mail: info@colemansfarm.net

Ideal for young children, this extensive petting farm has donkeys, goats, rabbits, guinea pigs, pigs, Highland cattle, Shetland ponies, chickens, ducks and geese. There is also a fun barn with slides and swings, an adventure playground, a Tractor Fun Park, and an Old Barn Café for adults who need to relax. Visitors can cuddle, stroke and feed the animals at special times throughout the day. Other daily events run all day.
Times: Open 20 Mar-7 Nov, Tue-Sun 10-5. (Closed Mon, ex during school and BH's) **Fee:** £4.95 (ch & concessions £3.95)
Facilities: 🅿 💷 ♿ toilets for disabled shop 🍴

SHANKLIN Map 04 SZ58
SHANKLIN CHINE
12 Pomona Rd PO37 6PF
➲ (turn off A3055 into Chine Hollow, Shanklin Old Village, between Crab Inn & Pencil Cottage to Upper entrance or turn off A3055 at lights, left into Hope Rd & continue onto Esplanade for entrance)
☎ 01983 866432 📠 01983 866145
e-mail: jill@shanklinchine.co.uk

Part of Britain's national heritage, this scenic gorge at Shanklin is a magical world of unique beauty and a haven for rare plants and wildlife. A path winds through the ravine with overhanging trees, ferns and other flora covering the steep sides. 'The Island-Then and Now' is an exhibition detailing the history of the Isle of Wight, including its military importance in WWII.
Times: Open daily, Apr-Oct (late May-late Sep illuminated after dusk) **Fee:** £3.50 (ch under 16 £2, pen & students £2.50). Family ticket £9 (2 ad & 2 ch), £11 (2 ad & 3 ch). Group rates available.
Facilities: 🅿 (450yds) 💷 (access via lower entry only) shop 🍴

VENTNOR Map 04 SZ57
SMUGGLING MUSEUM
Botanic Gardens PO38 1UL
➲ (on A3055, 1m W of Ventnor)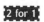
☎ 01983 853677

Situated underground in extensive vaults, this unique museum shows methods of smuggling used over a 700-year period right up to the present day.
Times: Open Apr-Sep, daily 10-5. **Fee:** £3 (ch, pen & stu £1.50). Parties by arrangement. **Facilities:** 🅿 (charged) shop

VENTNOR BOTANIC GARDEN
Undercliff Dr PO38 1UL
➲ (on A3055 coastal road, 1.5m W of Ventnor)
☎ 01983 855397 📠 01983 856756
e-mail: alison.ellsbury@iow.gov.uk

Due to the unique microclimate of the 'Undercliff', plants that can only survive in a Mediterranean climate thrive on the Isle of Wight. Built on the site of a Victorian hospital for TB sufferers, the garden was founded in 1970 by Sir Harold Hillier, and opened in 1972 by Earl Mountbatten. The garden has plants from Australasia, Africa, America, the Mediterranean, and the Far East, and is a great day out for anyone remotely interested in exotic flora.
Times: Gardens: open all year; Visitor Centre & Green House: Mar-Oct, daily 10-5 & Nov-Feb, wknds only 10-4 **Fee:** Free admission to Gardens & Visitor Centre; Green House £1 **Facilities:** 🅿 (charged) 💷 ♿ lifts in garden, wheelchairs toilets for disabled shop garden centre 🍴 (ex guide dogs) 🍴

WROXALL Map 04 SZ57
APPULDURCOMBE HOUSE
PO38 3EW
➲ (off B3327, 0.5 miles W)
☎ 01983 852484

The shell of Appuldurcombe, once the grandest house on the Isle of Wight, stands in its own grounds, designed by 'Capability' Brown. An exhibition of prints and photographs depicts the house and its history.
Times: Open 14 Feb-Apr, daily 10-4; May-Sep, daily 10-5; Oct-15 Dec, daily 10-4 (last admission to property 1hr before closing). Closed 16 Dec-13 Feb. **Fee:** ✱ £2.50 (ch £1.50 & concessions £2.25). Family ticket £7. Prices & opening times relate to 2004, for further details phone or log onto www.english-heritage.org.uk/visits
Facilities: 🅿 ♿ shop ✈ (ex dogs on leads) ♯

YARMOUTH Map 04 SZ38
YARMOUTH CASTLE
Quay St PO4 1OP
➲ (adjacent to car ferry terminal)
☎ 01983 760678

The last addition to Henry VIII's coastal defences completed in 1547, the Tudor castle is set in a beautiful old seaside town. See the Isle of Wight paintings and memorable photographs of Old Yarmouth.
Times: Open Apr-Sep, Sat, Sun & BH Mons 10-5 **Fee:** ✱ £2.50 (ch £1.30, concessions £1.90). Prices & opening times relate to 2004, for further details phone or log onto www.english-heritage.org.uk/visits
Facilities: 🅿 (200yds) ♿ shop ♯

WILTSHIRE

EVENTS & FESTIVALS

April
30th Downton Cuckoo Fair, medieval fair in
village centre

May
1st-14th Swindon Festival of Literature,
(various venues)
27th-30th Chippenham Folk Festival
27th-12th Jun Salisbury Festival
(various venues)

June
18th-25th Corsham Festival
30th-3rd Jul Calne Country Music Festival,
Lower Beversbrook Showground, Calne

July
8th-10th Marlborough International Jazz
Festival, various venues
tbc Larmer Tree Festival, Larmer Tree Victorian
Pleasure Gardens, Cranbourne Chase
(festival of world music)

August
tbc Wiltshire Festival (music), Lydiard Park,
Lydiard Tregoze, West Swindon

October
1st-9th Calne Music & Arts Festival
(provisional)
tbc Cricklade Festival

Above: Castle Combe, By Brook

AVEBURY · Map 04 SU06

ALEXANDER KEILLER MUSEUM

High St SN8 1RF
➲ (6m W of Marlborough. 1m N of the Bath Road
(A4) on A4361 and B4003)
☎ 01672 539250 ▤ 01672 539388
e-mail: avebury@nationaltrust.org.uk
This is one of the most important megalithic monuments in
Europe, and was built before Stonehenge. The museum,
including an exhibition in the 17th-century threshing barn,
presents the full archaeological story of the stones using
finds from the site, along with inter-active and audio-visual
displays.
Times: Open Apr-Oct, daily 10-6 or dusk if earlier; Nov-Mar 10-4
(closed 24-26 Dec) **Fee:** ✱ £4.20, ch £2.10, family £10. (2 ad + 3 ch),
family £7 (1 ad + 3 ch). **Facilities:** ▣ (charged) ▦ ✗ licensed
& (Braille guide, large print guide, drop off point) toilets for disabled
shop ✖ (ex guide dogs) ▦ ✖ ▤

AVEBURY MANOR

SN8 1RF
➲ (from A4 take A4361/B4003)
☎ 01672 539250 ▤ 01672 538038
e-mail: avebury@nationaltrust.org.uk
Avebury Manor has a monastic origin, and has been much
altered since then. The present buildings date from the early
16th century, with notable Queen Anne alterations and
Edwardian renovation. The flower gardens contain medieval
walls, and there are examples of topiary.
Times: Open: House 4 Apr-Oct, Mon, Tue, Sun 2-4.40 Mon 2-5.30 &
BH Mon 2-5.30 (last admission 4.40). Garden 2 Apr-Oct daily except
Wed, Thur 11-5.30 (last admission 5 or dusk if earlier). Garden only
open Good Fri. **Fee:** ✱ Manor & Garden £3.80 (ch £1.90). Garden
£2.90 (ch £1.40). **Facilities:** ▣ (charged) ▦ ✗ & (Audio visual,
Braille/large print guide, induction loop) toilets for disabled shop ✖
✖ ▤

BRADFORD-ON-AVON · Map 03 ST86

BRADFORD-ON-AVON TITHE BARN

➲ (0.25m S of town centre, off B3109)
This impressive tithe barn, over 160ft long by 30ft wide, once
belonged to Shaftesbury Abbey. The roof is of stone slates,
supported outside by buttresses and inside by massive
beams and a network of rafters.
Times: Open all year, daily 10.30-4. (Closed 25 Dec).
Facilities: ▣ (charged) & ✖ ▦

GREAT CHALFIELD MANOR

SN12 8NJ
➲ (3m SW of Melksham off B3107 via Broughton
Gifford Common)
☎ 01225 782239 ▤ 01225 783379
Built during the Wars of the Roses, the manor is a beautiful,
mellow, moated house restored in the 1920s. There is a
small 13th-century church next to the house.
Times: Open 22 Mar-30 Oct, Tue-Thu & Sun, guided tours only at
12.15, 2.15, 3, 3.45, 4.30. **Fee:** £4.60 (ch £2.30). Family ticket £11.80
Facilities: ▣ Access with assistance ✖ ✖

THE PETO GARDEN AT IFORD MANOR NEW
Iford Manor BA15 2BA
☎ 01225 863146   ▤ 01225 862364
An award-winning garden in the romantic setting of the
Frome Valley. Designed by Harold Peto between 1899 and
1933, this Italian style garden features terraces, statues and
ponds. Recitals and operas take place in the garden
throughout the summer season as part of the Iford Arts
programme
Times: May-Sept - closed Mon & Fri except BH Mons. Oct - open Sun
only 2pm-5pm **Fee:** ✱ £4 (concessions £3.50) **Facilities:** ▣ ▆

CALNE   Map 03 ST97

BOWOOD HOUSE & GARDENS
SN11 0LZ
➲ (off A4 Chippenham to Calne road, in Derry Hill
village)
☎ 01249 812102   ▤ 01249 821757   `2 for 1`
e-mail: houseandgardens@bowood.org
Built in 1624, the house was finished by the first Earl of
Shelburne, who employed celebrated architects, notably
Robert Adam, to complete the work. Adam's library is
particularly admired, and also in the house is the laboratory
where Dr Joseph Priestley discovered the existence of oxygen
in 1774. The house overlooks terraced gardens towards the
40-acre lake and some beautiful parkland. The gardens were
laid out by 'Capability' Brown in the 1760s, and are carpeted
with daffodils, narcissi and bluebells in spring. There is also
an adventure playground and new soft play area.
Times: Open Apr-Oct, daily 11-6, including BH. Rhododendron
Gardens (separate entrance off A342) open 6 weeks during mid
Apr-early Jun, 11-6. **Fee:** ✱ House & Gardens £6.40 (ch 2-4 £3.25;
5-15 £4.10; pen £5.30). Rhododendrons only £3.60 or £2.60 if
combined with a vist to Bowood House & Gardens on the same day.
Children free. **Facilities:** ▣ ▆ ✕ licensed ♿ (parking by
arrangement) toilets for disabled shop ✖ (ex guide & hearing
dogs) ▆

CORSHAM   Map 03 ST87

CORSHAM COURT
SN13 0BZ
➲ (4m W of Chippenham off the A4)
☎ 01249 701610   ▤ 01249 701610

The Elizabethan manor was built in 1582, and then bought
by the Methuen family in the 18th century to house their
collections of paintings and statues. 'Capability' Brown made
additions to the house and laid out the park, and later John
continued

CORSHAM COURT
HOME OF THE METHUEN FAMILY
Corsham Court is one of England's finest Stately
Homes. It was a Royal Manor in the days of the
Saxon Kings, and the present building is based upon
an Elizabethan Manor dating from 1582. Magnificent
Georgian State Rooms were added in 1760. It
houses one of the oldest and most distinguished
collections of Old Masters and Furniture in the
country, and with its 'Capability' Brown gardens
and arboretum, and architecture by John Nash and
Thomas Bellamy, Corsham Court provides the visitor
with a wonderful opportunity to enjoy the many
delights of the historic and beautiful Stately Home.

Tel/Fax: 01249 701610
For opening times see gazetteer entry

Nash made further changes. There is furniture by
Chippendale, Adam, Cobb and Johnson inside, as well as the
Methuen collection of Old Master paintings. The garden has
flowering shrubs, herbaceous borders, a Georgian bath
house and peacocks.
Times: Open Summer: 20 Mar-Sep daily ex Mon Fri, but incl BHs
2-5.30. Winter: Oct-19 Mar open wknds only 2-4.30pm. Last admission
30 minutes before closing. (Closed Dec). Open throughout year by
appointment for groups 15+. **Facilities:** ▣ ▆ ♿ shop
See advertisement on this page

HOLT   Map 03 ST86

THE COURTS
BA14 6RR
➲ (3m SW of Melksham, 2.5m E of Bradford on
Avon, on south side of B3107 follow signs to Holt)
☎ 01225 782875   ▤ 01225 782340
e-mail: courtgarden@nationaltrust.org.uk
Weavers came to The Courts to have their disputes settled
until the end of the 18th century. The house is not open, but
it makes an attractive backdrop to the gardens - a network
of stone paths, yew hedges, pools and borders with a
strange, almost magical atmosphere.
Times: Open 27 Mar-17 Oct, daily (ex Wed) 11-5.30; out of season by
appointment only. **Fee:** ✱ £4.50 (ch £2.25).Family ticket £11.50.
Groups £4 (ch £2) **Facilities:** ▣ ♿ toilets for disabled shop
✖ (ex guide dogs) ▲

LACOCK Map 03 ST96

LACKHAM COUNTRY PARK
Wiltshire College, Lackham SN15 2NY
➲ (3m S of Chippenham, on A350. 6m S of M4 Junct 17)
☎ 01249 466800 📠 01249 444474
e-mail: daviaj@wiltscoll.ac.uk
2 for 1

Various visitor attractions are situated within the 210-hectare estate of Wiltshire College - Lackham. Thatched and refurbished farm buildings accommodate the farm museum and the grounds feature a walled garden, glasshouses, and a farm park. Also grown in this garden was the largest citron (large lemon) which earned a place in the Guinness Book of Records. There is also a self-guided picturesque woodland walk available.
Times: Open Etr-Aug, Sun & BH Mon, Tue-Thu in Aug 10-5. Last admission 4pm. **Fee:** ✱ £2 (concessions £1.50, up to 2 ch under 16 free). **Facilities:** 🅿 💻 ⚹ (wheelchair available) parking for disabled toilets for disabled shop garden centre

LACOCK ABBEY, FOX TALBOT MUSEUM & VILLAGE
SN15 2LG
➲ (3m S of Chippenham, E of A350, signposted to car park)
☎ 01249 730227 (abbey) 01249 730459
📠 01249 730501
e-mail: courtsgarden@nationaltrust.org.uk
Magnificent late Victorian country house with extensive servants quarters, gardens and wooded estate.
Times: Museum, Cloisters & Grounds, Mar-Oct, daily 11-5.30. Closed Good Fri. Abbey, 27 Mar- Oct daily, ex Tue, 1-5.30. Closed Good Fri.
Fee: ✱ Museum, Abbey, Grounds & Cloisters £7 (ch £3.50) Family ticket £17.90 (2 ad & 2 ch). Cloisters & Museum only £4.40 (ch £2.20) Family ticket £11.20. Abbey Cloisters & garden only £5.60 (ch £2.80) Family ticket £14.30. Museum (Winter) £3 (ch £1.50). Family £7.70.
Facilities: 🅿 ⚹ (Manual wheelchairs, Braille/large print & audio guides) toilets for disabled shop ✗ ♨

LONGLEAT Map 03 ST84

LONGLEAT
The Estate Office BA12 7NW
➲ (Turn off A36 Bath-Salisbury onto A362 Warminster-Frome).
☎ 01985 844400 📠 01985 844885
e-mail: enquiries@longleat.co.uk
Nestling within magnificent 'Capability' Brown landscaped grounds in the heart of Wiltshire, Longleat House is widely regarded as one of the most beautiful stately homes open to the public. Longleat House was built by Sir John Thynne and completed in 1580. It has remained the home of the same family ever since. Many treasures are contained within the house: paintings by Tintoretto and Wooton, exquisite Flemish tapestries, fine French furniture and elaborate ceilings by John Dibblee Crace. The murals in the family apartments in the West Wing were painted by Alexander Thynne, the present Marquess, and are fascinating and remarkable additions to the collection. Apart from the ancestral home, Longleat is also renowned for its safari park, the first of its kind in the UK. Here, visitors have the rare opportunity to see hundreds of animals in natural woodland and parkland settings. Among the most magnificent sights are the famous pride of lions, white tiger, wolves, rhesus monkeys and zebra. Other attractions which ensure a fun family day out include
continued

the 'World's Longleat Hedge Maze', the 'Adventure Castle', 'Longleat Railway', 'Pets' Corner' and the 'Safari Boats'.

Times: Open 12 Feb-6 Nov. Telephone for opening times
Fee: ✱ Longleat passport: £16 (ch 3-14 yrs & pen £13)
Facilities: 🅿 💻 ✗ licensed ⚹ (Informative leaflet available or see website) toilets for disabled shop (on leads, kennels for Safari) 🍴

LUDGERSHALL Map 04 SU25

LUDGERSHALL CASTLE AND CROSS
SP11 9QR
➲ (7m NW of Andover on A342)
Ruins of an early 12th-century royal hunting palace and medieval cross. The visitor can see large earthworks of the Norman motte-and-bailey castle and the flint walls of the later hunting palace. The stump of a medieval cross stands in the village street.
Times: Open all reasonable times. **Facilities:** 🅿 ⚹ ♨

LYDIARD PARK Map 04 SU18

LYDIARD PARK
Lydiard Tregoze SN5 9PA
➲ (from M4 junct 16. Follow brown Tourist Information signs)
☎ 01793 770401 📠 01793 877909
Set in country parkland, Lydiard Park belonged to the St John family (the Bolingbrokes) for 500 years up until 1943 when the Swindon Corporation purchased it. Since then the house has been restored and many of the original furnishings returned, together with a family portrait collection dating from Elizabethan to Victorian times. Exceptional plasterwork, early wallpaper, a rare painted glass window, and a room devoted to the talented 18th-century amateur artist, Lady Diana Spencer (Beauclerk), can also be seen.
Times: ✱ Open all year, House: Mon-Sat 10-5, Sun 2-5. Winter closing 4pm (Nov-Feb). Park: all year, daily closing at dusk each day.
Facilities: 🅿 💻 ⚹ (telephone 01793 770401 for access information sheet) toilets for disabled shop ✗ (ex guide dogs in house)

An asterisk * indicates that opening times and prices are for 2004. Please contact the attraction for up-to-date information.

MARLBOROUGH   Map 04 SU16
CROFTON BEAM ENGINES
Crofton Pumping Station, Crofton SN8 3DW

➲ (signposted from A338/A346/B3087 at Burbage and from A4 at Froxfield, A338 Hungerford to Salisbury follow signs to Great Bedwyn, then the brown signs)

☎ 01672 870300

e-mail: enquiries@croftonbeamengines.org

The oldest working beam engine in the world still in its original building and still doing its original job, the Boulton and Watt 1812, can be found in this rural spot. Its companion is a Harvey's of Hayle of 1845. Both are steam driven, from a hand-stoked, coal-fired boiler, and pump water into the summit level of the Kennet and Avon Canal with a lift of 40ft.

Times: Open daily 9 Apr-26 Sep, 10.30-5 (last entry 4.30). 'In Steam' Etr, BH wknds & last wknd of Jun, Jul & Sep **Fee:** ✱ In Steam wknd: £4.50 (ch £1, under 5 free & pen £3.50). Family ticket £10. Non-In Steam days £3 (ch £1, pen £2.50) Family £7 **Facilities:** 🅿 (charged) 💻 & (phone warden in advance, sighted guides provided) shop

MIDDLE WOODFORD   Map 04 SU13
HEALE GARDENS, PLANT CENTRE & SHOP
SP4 6NT

➲ (4m N of Salisbury, between A360 & A345)

☎ 01722 782504 📠 01722 782504

Heale House and its eight acres of beautiful garden lie beside the River Avon at Middle Woodford. Much of the house is unchanged since King Charles II sheltered here after the Battle of Worcester in 1651. The garden provides a wonderfully varied collection of plants, shrubs, and musk and other roses, growing in the formal setting of clipped hedges and mellow stonework.

Times: Plant centre open daily 10-5. Gardens open daily (closed Mon ex BH's) **Fee:** ✱ £3.75 (ch 5-15 £1.50 under 5's free). **Facilities:** 🅿 💻 & Most part accessible shop garden centre ✈ (ex guide dogs) 🍴

SALISBURY   Map 04 SU12
THE MEDIEVAL HALL (SECRETS OF SALISBURY)
Cathedral Close SP1 2EY

➲ (look for signs within Salisbury Cathedral Close)

☎ 01722 412472 & 324731 📠 01722 339983

e-mail: medieval.hall@ntworld.com

Visit the historic 13th century Medieval Hall and watch the fascinating 40 minute sound and picture guide to the city and region. A witty and informative soundtrack, (sometimes available in other languages) specially composed music and some startling effects accompany hundreds of images to provide an insight into Salisbury's extraordinary past, the colourful city of today, and many of the attractions in the area. Enjoy refreshments 'while you watch'. Contact the Hall for full details of special events.

Times: Open Apr-Sep, from 11-5. Also open throughout year for pre-booked groups. Occasionally closed for special events. **Fee:** ✱ £2.25 (ch under 18 £1.75, ch under 6 free). Family tickets available **Facilities:** 🅿 (charged) 💻 & (ramp access) shop

MOMPESSON HOUSE
The Close SP1 2EL

➲ (on N side of Choristers Green in the Cathedral Close, near High Street Gate)

☎ 01722 335659 📠 01722 321559

e-mail: mompessonhouse@nationaltrust.org.uk

With its high wrought-iron railings and perfect proportions, this Queen Anne house makes an impressive addition to the elegant Cathedral Close in Salisbury. Inside are stucco ceilings, a carved oak staircase and period furniture plus an important collection of 18th-century glasses, china and some outstanding paintings.

Times: Open 9 Apr-Oct, daily (ex Thu & Fri) 11-5. **Fee:** ✱ £4 (ch £2). Group rate £3.50. Garden only 80p. **Facilities:** 🅿 (260 yds) (limited disabled parking available) 💻 & (ramps, Braille guide) toilets for disabled shop ✈ 🍴

OLD SARUM
Castle Rd SP1 3SD

➲ (2m N on A345)

☎ 01722 335398 📠 01722 416037

The site of the original city of Salisbury. The 56-acre ruins of this once bustling town are rich in history and woodland. Founded in the Iron Age and occupied until the 16th-century. Romans, Saxons and Normans have all left their mark.

Times: Open all year, Apr-Jun & Sep, daily 10-5; Jul-Aug, daily 9-6; Oct & Mar, daily 10-4; Nov-Feb daily 11-3. (Closed 24-26 Dec & 1 Jan). **Fee:** ✱ £2.80 (ch £1.40, concessions £2.10. Prices & opening times relate to 2004, for further details phone or log onto www.english-heritage.org.uk/visits **Facilities:** 🅿 & (assess to outer bailey and grounds only) shop 🍴

SALISBURY CATHEDRAL
33 The Close SP1 2EJ

➲ (South of the city centre & Market Sq)

☎ 01722 555120 📠 01722 555116

e-mail: visitors@salcath.co.uk

Built in one phase between 1220 and 1258, the Cathedral is probably Britain's finest piece of medieval architecture. The spire is 123 metres tall, making it the tallest in England. The Chapter House displays a frieze depicting scenes from Genesis and Exodus, also the finest surviving Magna Carta. The Choir continues a tradition that began around 800 years ago, with performances at daily services. They are accompanied by Europe's finest romantic church organ. The

continued

surrounding Cathedral Close contains two museums, two small stately homes and acres of lawn.
Times: Open all year, daily 7.15-6.15; Jun-Aug, Mon-Sat 7.15-7.15. **Fee:** ✱ Suggested Voluntary Donations: £3.80 (ch 5-17 £2, pen & students £3.30). Family £8.50. **Facilities:** P (100yds) 💺 ✗ licensed ᶜ (loop system, interpretative model for blind, wheelchairs) toilets for disabled shop (closed 25 Dec) 🍴

SALISBURY & SOUTH WILTSHIRE MUSEUM
The King's House, 65 The Close SP1 2EN
➲ (in Cathedral Close)
☎ 01722 332151 🖷 01722 325611   **2 for 1**
e-mail: museum@salisburymuseum.org.uk

One of the most outstanding of the beautiful buildings in Cathedral Close houses this local museum. Galleries feature Stonehenge, History of Salisbury, the Pitt Rivers collection, ceramics and pictures and the Wedgwood room, a reconstruction of a pre-NHS surgery, and a costume, lace and embroidery gallery.
Times: ✱ Open all year Mon-Sat 10-5; also Suns Jul & Aug, 2-5. (Closed Xmas). **Fee:** £4 (ch £1.50, concessions £3). Family ticket £9.50 **Facilities:** P (100 metres) (nearby parking charge) ✗ ᶜ (parking by prior arrangement,induction loop in lecture hall) toilets for disabled shop ✗ (ex guide dogs) 🍴

STONEHENGE   Map 04 SU14
STONEHENGE
SP4 7DE
➲ (2m W of Amesbury on junct A303 and A344/A360)
☎ 01980 624715

Britain's greatest prehistoric monument and a World Heritage Site. What visitors see today are the substantial remains of the last in a series of monuments erected between c3000 and 1600BC.
Times: Open all year, 16 Mar-May, daily 9.30-6; Jun-Aug, daily 9-7; Sep-15 Oct, daily 9.30-6. 16 Oct-15 Mar, daily 9.30-4. (Closed 24-26 Dec & 1 Jan). **Fee:** ✱ £5.20 (ch £2.60, concessions £3.90). Prices & opening times relate to 2004, for further details phone or log onto www.english-heritage.org.uk/visits. **Facilities:** P 💺 ᶜ shop ✗ (ex guide & hearing dogs) ⌘

STOURHEAD   Map 03 ST73
STOURHEAD GARDEN & HOUSE
Stourhead Estate Office BA12 6QD
➲ (At Stourton off B3092, 3m NW Mere A303, follow brown tourist signs)
☎ 01747 841152 🖷 01747 842005   **2 for 1**
e-mail: stourhead@nationaltrust.org.uk

An outstanding example of the English landscape style, this splendid garden was designed by Henry Moore II and laid out between 1741 and 1780. Classical temples, including the Parthenon and Temple of Apollo, are set around the central lake at the end of a series of vistas, which change as the visitor moves around the paths and through the mature woodland with its extensive collection of exotic trees.
Times: Garden open all year 9-7 (or dusk if earlier). House open 19 Mar-Oct ,11-5 (closed Wed & Thu); King Alfred tower open 19 Mar-Oct, daily 12-5. **Fee:** ✱ Garden & House £9.40, ch £4.50, Garden or House £5.40, ch £3, Garden only (Nov- end Feb) £4.10, ch £2, King Alfred Tower £2, ch £1. **Facilities:** P 💺 ✗ licensed ᶜ (wheelchairs, electric buggy, telephone in advance) toilets for disabled shop garden centre ✗ (ex in gardens Nov-Feb only) ☃ 🍴

STOURTON   Map 03 ST73
STOURTON HOUSE FLOWER GARDEN
Stourton House BA12 6QF
➲ (3m NW of Mere, on A303)
☎ 01747 840417

Set in the attractive village of Stourton, the house has more than four acres of beautifully maintained flower gardens. Many grass paths lead through varied and colourful shrubs and trees. Stourton House also specialises in unusual plants and dried flowers, many of which are for sale. It also has collections of daffodils, delphiniums and hydrangeas.
Times: ✱ Open Apr-end Nov, Wed, Thu, Sun & BH Mon 11-6 (or dusk if earlier). Also open Dec-Mar, wkdays for plant/dried flower sales. **Facilities:** P 💺 ᶜ (wheelchairs available) toilets for disabled shop (plants for sale) garden centre ✗ (ex by arrangement)

SWINDON   Map 04 SU18
STEAM - MUSEUM OF THE GREAT WESTERN RAILWAY
Kemble Dr SN2 2TA
➲ (from M4 junct 16 & A420 follow brown signs to 'Outlet Centre' and Museum)
☎ 01793 466646 🖷 01793 466615   **2 for 1**
e-mail: steampostbox@swindon.gov.uk

Nominated for European Museum of the Year, this fascinating day out tells the story of the men and women who built, operated and travelled on the Great Western Railway. Hands-on displays, world-famous locomotives, archive film footage and the testimonies of ex-railway workers bring the story to life. A reconstructed station platform, posters and holiday memorabilia recreate the glamour and excitement of the golden age of steam. Located next door to the McArthurGlen Designer Outlet Great Western, Steam offers a great day out for all. Good value group packages, special events and exhibitions, shop and café.
Times: Open daily 10-5, (Closed 25-26 Dec & 1 Jan) **Fee:** ✱ £5.95 (ch £3.80, pen £3.90) Family ticket £14.70 (2 ad+2 ch) **Facilities:** P (charged) 💺 ᶜ wheelchair or scooter can be pre-booked toilets for disabled shop ✗ (ex guide dogs) 🍴

Directions are provided by the attractions.

TEFFONT MAGNA — Map 03 ST93
FARMER GILES FARMSTEAD
SP3 5QY
➲ (11m W of Stonehenge, off A303 to the village of Teffont. Follow brown signs)
☎ 01722 716338 🖹 01722 716993
e-mail: tdeane6995@aol.com

Forty acres of Wiltshire downland with farm animals to feed, ponds, inside and outside play areas, exhibitions, tractor rides, and giftshop.
Times: Open 18 Mar-5 Nov, daily 10-6, wknds in winters, 10-dusk. Party bookings all year. **Fee:** ✱ £3.95 (ch £2.85, under 2's free & pen £3.50) Family ticket £13. **Facilities:** 🅿 ✗ licensed & (complete access for disabled/wheelchairs available for use) toilets for disabled shop 🍴

TISBURY — Map 03 ST92
OLD WARDOUR CASTLE
SP3 6RR
➲ (2m SW)
☎ 01747 870487
This 14th-century castle stands in a romantic lakeside setting. Landscaped grounds and elaborate rockwork grotto surround the unusual hexagonal ruins. Scenes from *Robin Hood, Price of Thieves*, starring Kevin Costner were filmed here.
Times: Open all year, Apr-Jun & Sep, daily 10-5; Jul-Aug, daily 10-6; Oct, daily 10-4; Nov-Mar, Sat-Sun 10-4. (Closed 24-26 Dec & 1 Jan). **Fee:** ✱ £2.80 (ch £1.40, concessions £2.10). Prices & opening times relate to 2004, for further details phone or log onto www.english-heritage.org.uk/visits **Facilities:** 🅿 & ♯

TOLLARD ROYAL — Map 03 ST91
LARMER TREE GARDENS NEW
SP5 5PT
➲ (Just off the A354 Blandford to Salisbury road, follow brown signs with a flower on)
☎ 01725 516228 🖹 01725 516321 **2 for 1**
e-mail: events@larmertreegardens.co.uk
Created by General Pitt Rivers in 1880 as a pleasure ground for 'public enlightenment and entertainment' the gardens are an extraordinary example of Victorian extravagance and vision. The garden contains a wonderful collection of ornate buildings, majestic trees and intimate arbours, retained in an
continued

enchanted and tranquil atmosphere. The 2-for-1 vouchers are not valid for special event days.
Times: Garden open: Feb-Nov, Mon-Thu 11-5 (Sun from Etr-Oct). Tea Pavilion Sun & BHs Etr-Sep 11-5 **Fee:** £3.75 (ch over 5's £2.50, concessions/groups 15+ £3) Family £12.50 **Facilities:** 🅿 💻 ✗ licensed & toilets for disabled shop 🍴 (ex guide dogs) 🍴

WESTBURY — Map 03 ST85
BROKERSWOOD COUNTRY PARK
Brokerswood BA13 4EH
➲ (turn off A36 at Bell Inn, Standerwick. Follow brown signs)
☎ 01373 822238 & 823880 🖹 01373 858474
e-mail: woodland.park@virgin.net
Brokerswood Country Park's nature walk leads through 80 acres of woodlands, with a lake and wildfowl. Facilities include a woodland visitor centre (covering wildlife and forestry), two children's adventure playgrounds (Etr-Oct school holidays & wknds only), guided walks and the woodland railway, over a third of a mile long.
Times: Open all year; Park open daily 10-5. (Closed 25 & 26 Dec & 1 Jan). Ring for museum opening hours. **Fee:** ✱ £3 (ch 3-16yrs £2, pen £2.50) **Facilities:** 🅿 💻 & (ramp access to cafe) toilets for disabled shop 🍴

WESTWOOD — Map 03 ST85
WESTWOOD MANOR
BA15 2AF
➲ (1.5m SW of Bradford on Avon, off B3109)
☎ 01225 863374 🖹 01225 867316
This late 15th-century stone manor house was altered in the early 17th century and has late Gothic and Jacobean windows and fine plasterwork. There is a modern topiary garden.
Times: Open 3 Apr-28 Sep, Tue, Wed & Sun, 2-5. **Fee:** £4.60 (ch £2.30). Family ticket £11.70. **Facilities:** 🅿 & 🍴 🚗 ✗

WILTON (NEAR SALISBURY) — Map 04 SU03
WILTON HOUSE
SP2 0BJ
➲ (3m W of Salisbury, on the A30, 10m from Stonehenge & A303)
☎ 01722 746720 & 746729(24 hr line) **2 for 1**
🖹 01722 744447
e-mail: tourism@wiltonhouse.com
This fabulous Palladian mansion amazes visitors with its treasures, including magnificent art, fine furniture and interiors by Inigo Jones. The traditional and modern gardens, some designed by the 17th Earl, are fabulous throughout the season and continue to delight visitors, whilst the adventure playground is a firm favourite with children.
Times: Open 2 Apr-Oct daily 10.30-5.30. Last admission 4.30. House closed Mon, ex BHs. **Fee:** ✱ £9.75 (ch 5-15 £5.50, students & pen £8). Family ticket £24. **Facilities:** 🅿 💻 & (induction loop) toilets for disabled shop garden centre 🍴 (ex service dogs) 🍴

WOODHENGE — Map 04 SU14
WOODHENGE
➲ (1.5m N of Amesbury, off A345 just S of Durrington)
A Neolithic ceremonial monument dating from about 2300 BC, consisting of six concentric rings of timber posts, now marked by concrete piles. The long axis of the rings, which are oval, points to the rising sun on Midsummer Day.
Times: Open all reasonable times. **Facilities:** 🅿 & ♯

WORCESTERSHIRE

EVENTS & FESTIVALS

May
13th-15th Spring Garden Show, Three
    Counties Showground, Malvern
tbc Upton Folk Festival (various venues),
    Upton-upon-Severn

June
17th-19th Three Counties Show, Three
    Counties Showground, Malvern
24th-26th Upton Jazz Festival, Upton-upon-
    Severn, various venues

July
15th-17th Upton Blues Festival, Upton-upon-
    Severn (provisional)
tbc Worcester Carnival

August
6th-12th Three Choirs Festival, Worcester
    Cathedral, choirs of Hereford, Gloucester
    and Worcester cathedrals

September
24th-25th The Malvern Autumn Show, Three
    Counties Showground, Malvern

December
tbc Victorian Christmas Fayre, Worcester

Above: Queen Victoria Commemorative Beacon (1897)

BEWDLEY   Map 07 SO77

SEVERN VALLEY RAILWAY
Comberton Hill DY10 1QN
☎ 01299 403816   🖷 01299 400839
(For full entry see Kidderminster)

WEST MIDLAND SAFARI & LEISURE PARK
Spring Grove DY12 1LF
➲ (on A456 between Kidderminster & Bewdley)
☎ 01299 402114   🖷 01299 404519
e-mail: info@wmsp.co.uk
Located in the heart of rural Worcestershire, this 200-acre
site is the home to a drive-through safari and Kingdom of the
White Lions. There are a variety of rides, amusements and
live shows suitable for all members of the family. Other
features include Discovery Trail, Hippo Lakes, Goat Walk,
Seal Aquarium Creepy Crawlies exhibit, animal and reptile
encounters and Sealion Theatre.
Times: Open Apr-Oct, daily from 10 including BHs. **Fee:** ✷ £7.25
(ch 4 free). Multi ride wristband £8.50. Junior restricted £7 (restricted
rides only). Ride tickets £3 for two tickets from machines (various no of
tickets per ride). **Facilities:** 🅿 🖵 ✕ licensed ⅙ (most area
accessible slopes/tarmac paths) shop ✖ (ex guide dogs) 🍴

BROADWAY   Map 04 SP03

BROADWAY TOWER & ANIMAL PARK
WR12 7LB
➲ (off A44, 1m SE of village)
☎ 01386 852390   🖷 01386 858038   **2 for 1**
e-mail: info@broadwaytower.co.uk
The 65ft tower was designed by James Wyatt for the 6th Earl
of Coventry, and built in 1799. The unique building now
houses exhibitions depicting its colourful past and various
uses such as holiday retreat to artist and designer William
Morris. The viewing platform is equipped with a telescope,
giving wonderful views over 13 counties.
Times: Open Apr-Oct, daily 10.30-5. Nov-Mar (tower only) wknds
weather permitting 11-3 or by prior booking. **Fee:** Tower, £3.50
(ch 4-14 £2 & concessions £3) Family (2ad & 3ch) £10
Facilities: 🅿 🖵 ✕ licensed shop 🍴

BROMSGROVE   Map 07 SO97

AVONCROFT MUSEUM OF HISTORIC BUILDINGS
Stoke Heath B60 4JR
➲ (2m S, off A38)
☎ 01527 831886   🖷 01527 876934
e-mail: avoncroft1@compuserve.com
A visit to Avoncroft takes you through nearly 700 years of
history. Here you can see 25 buildings rescued from
destruction and authentically restored on a 15 acre rural site.
There are 15th and 16th-century timber framed buildings,
18th-century agricultural buildings and a cockpit. There are
industrial buildings and a working windmill from the 19th
century, and from the 20th a fully furnished pre-fab.
Times: ✷ Open Jul-Aug daily 10.30-5; Apr-Jun & Sep-Oct 10.30-4.30
(wknds 5.30), (Closed Mon); Mar & Nov 10.30-4, (Closed Mon & Fri).
Open BHs. **Facilities:** 🅿 🖵 ⅙ (ramps, wheelchair available) toilets
for disabled shop 🍴

EVESHAM   Map 04 SP04

THE ALMONRY HERITAGE CENTRE

Abbey Gate WR11 4EJ

➲ (on A4184, opposite Merstow Green, main North/South route through Evesham)

☎ 01386 446944   🖨 01386 442348

e-mail: almonry@eveshamtc.ndirect.co.uk

The 14th-century stone and timber building was the home of the Almoner of the Benedictine Abbey in Evesham. It now houses exhibitions relating to the history of Evesham Abbey, the Battle of Evesham, and the culture and trade of Evesham. Evesham Tourist Information Centre is also located here.

Times: Open all year, Mon-Sat & BHs (ex Xmas & Sun in Nov-Feb) 10-5, Sun 2-5. **Fee:** ✱ £2.50 (ch 16 free, pen & students £1.50)

Facilities: 🅿 (110yds) shop ✗

GREAT WITLEY   Map 03 SO76

WITLEY COURT

WR6 6JT

➲ (on A433)

☎ 01299 896636

Discover the spectacular ruins of this once-great house destroyed by fire in 1937. Explore the magnificent landscaped gardens which feature the stunning Perseus and Andromeda fountains and contemporary sculpture. Step back in time with the audio tour.

Times: Open all year, Mar-May, daily, 10-5; Jun-Aug, daily, 10-6; Sep-Oct, daily, 10-5; Nov-Feb, Thu-Mon, 10-4. (Closed 24-26 Dec & 1 Jan). **Fee:** ✱ £4.90 (ch £2.50, concessions £3.70, family £12.30). Prices & opening times relate to 2004, for further details phone or log onto www.english-heritage.org.uk/visits **Facilities:** 🅿 💷 ⑊ shop ✗ ✿

HANBURY   Map 03 SO96

HANBURY HALL

School Rd WR9 7EA

➲ (4.5m E of Droitwich, 1m N of B4090 and 1.5m W of B4091)

☎ 01527 821214   🖨 01527 821251   **2 for 1**

e-mail: hanburyhall@nationaltrust.org.uk

This William and Mary style red-brick house, completed in 1701, was built by a prosperous local family. The house contains outstanding painted ceilings and staircase by Thornhill, and the Watney collection of porcelain. The 18th-century garden has recently been restored with many features including parterre, bowling green and working orangery.

Times: Open Mar-Oct, Sat-Wed 11-5.30. Last entry 4.30

Fee: ✱ House & Garden £5.40. Family ticket £13. Garden only £3.50.

Facilities: 🅿 💷 ⑊ (Braille guide, 2x wheelchairs) toilets for disabled shop ✗ (ex in park) ⛶ 🍴

KIDDERMINSTER   Map 07 SO87

SEVERN VALLEY RAILWAY

Comberton Hill DY10 1QN

➲ (on A448, clearly signposted)

☎ 01299 403816   🖨 01299 400839

The leading standard gauge steam railway, with one of the largest collections of locomotives and rolling stock in the country. Services operate from Kidderminster and Bewdley to Bridgnorth through 16 miles of picturesque scenery along the River Severn. Special steam galas and "Day out with Thomas" weekends take place during the year along with Santa Specials.   *continued*

Times: Trains operate wknds throughout year, daily early May to late Sep, plus school holidays & half terms, Santa Specials, phone for details. **Fee:** ✱ Subject to Review. (Train fares vary according to journey. Main through ticket £10.80 return, Family ticket £29)

Facilities: 🅿 (charged) 💷 ⑊ (some specially adapted trains, call for details) toilets for disabled shop (at Kidderminster/Bridgnorth) 🍴

See advertisement on this page

WORCESTERSHIRE COUNTY MUSEUM

Hartlebury Castle, Hartlebury DY11 7XZ

➲ (4m S of Kidderminster clearly signed from A449)

☎ 01299 250416   🖨 01299 251890

e-mail: museum@worcestershire.gov.uk

Housed in the north wing of Hartlebury Castle, the County Museum contains a delightful display of crafts and industries. There are unique collections of toys, costume, domestic life,   *continued* room settings and horse-drawn vehicles as well as a reconstructed forge, schoolroom, wheelwright's and tailor's shop. **Times:** Open Feb-Nov, Mon-Thu 10-5, BHs 11-5, Fri & Sun 2-5. (Closed Sat & Good Fri). **Facilities:** 🅿 💻 ⅙ (car parking spaces, close to main building) toilets for disabled shop ✖ (ex guide dogs & in grounds) ➡

REDDITCH — Map 03 SP06

FORGE MILL NEEDLE MUSEUM & BORDESLEY ABBEY VISITOR CENTRE

Forge Mill, Needle Mill Ln, Riverside B98 8HY
➲ (N side of Redditch, off A441. M42 junct 2)
☎ 01527 62509
e-mail: museum@redditchbc.gov.uk
The Needle Museum tells the fascinating and sometimes gruesome story of how needles are made. Working, water-powered machinery can be seen in an original needle-scouring mill. The Visitor Centre is an archaeological museum showing finds from excavations at the nearby Bordesley Abbey.
Times: ✱ Open Etr-Sep, Mon-Fri 11-4.30, Sat-Sun 2-5; Feb-Etr & Oct-Nov, Mon-Thu 11-4 & Sun 2-5. Parties by arrangement.
Facilities: 🅿 ⅙ (wheelchair available, audio tour of museum) toilets for disabled shop ✖ (ex guide dogs) ➡

SPETCHLEY — Map 03 SO85

SPETCHLEY PARK GARDENS

Spetchley Park WR5 1RS
➲ (3m E of Worcester)
☎ 01905 345213 or 345224 ▤ 01453 511915
e-mail: hb@spetchleygardens.co.uk
The 110-acre deer park and the 30-acre gardens surround an early 19th-century mansion (not open), with sweeping lawns and herbaceous borders, a rose lawn and enclosed gardens with low box and yew hedges. There is a large collection of trees (including 17th-century Cedars of Lebanon), shrubs and plants, many of which are rare or unusual.
Times: Open Apr-Sep, Tue-Fri 11-6, Sun 2-6; BH Mons 11-6, (last admission 4). Other days by appointment. **Fee:** ✱ £4 (ch £2). Party 25+ £3.80.
Facilities: 🅿 💻 ⅙ (most of garden accessible) ✖ (ex guide dogs)

STONE — Map 07 SO87

STONE HOUSE COTTAGE GARDENS

DY10 4BG
➲ (2m SE of Kidderminster, on A448)
☎ 01562 69902 ▤ 01562 69960
e-mail: louisa@shcn.co.uk
A beautiful walled garden with towers provides a sheltered area of about one acre for rare shrubs, climbers and interesting herbaceous plants. Adjacent to the garden is a nursery with a large selection of unusual plants.
Times: Open Mar-mid Sept, Wed-Sat, 10-5.30 **Fee:** £3 (ch free).
Facilities: 🅿 ⅙ garden centre ✖

WORCESTER — Map 03 SO85

CITY MUSEUM & ART GALLERY

Foregate St WR1 1DT
➲ (Located in City Centre, 150m from Foregate St Train Station)
☎ 01905 25371 ▤ 01905 616979 [FREE]
e-mail: artgalleryandmuseum@cityofworcester.gov.uk
The gallery has temporary art exhibitions from both local and national sources. Museum exhibits cover geology, local and natural history. Of particular interest is a complete 19th-century chemist's shop. There are collections relating to the

continued

Worcestershire Regiment and the Worcestershire Yeomanry Cavalry.
Times: Open all year, Mon-Fri 9.30-5.30, Sat 9.30-5. (Closed Sun, 25-26 Dec, 1 Jan & Good Fri) **Facilities:** 🅿 (city centre) 💻 ⅙ (lift, induction loop) toilets for disabled shop ✖ ➡

ELGAR'S BIRTHPLACE MUSEUM

Crown East Ln, Lower Broadheath WR2 6RH
➲ (3m W of Worcester, signposted off A44 to Leominster).
☎ 01905 333224 ▤ 01905 333426 [2 for 1]
e-mail: birthplace@elgarmuseum.org
In 2000, the Elgar Centre was opened, to complement the historic Birthplace Cottage and to provide additional exhibition space for more treasures from this unique collection, telling the story of Elgar's musical development and inspirations. Listen to his music as the audio tour guides you round the easily accessible displays.
Times: Open daily 11-5, last admission 4.15. (Closed 23 Dec-end Jan).
Fee: ✱ £4.50 (ch £2 & pen £4). Family ticket £11. Party rates available.
Facilities: 🅿 ⅙ (large print guides, audio facilities, wheelchair) toilets for disabled shop ✖ (ex guide dogs) ➡

HAWFORD DOVECOTE

➲ (3 miles N of Worcester, half mile E of A449).
▤ 01527 821251
e-mail: hanburyhall@nationaltrust.org
An unusual square, half-timbered 16th-century dovecote. Access on foot only via the entrance drive to the adjoining house.
Times: Open Apr-Oct, daily 9-6 or sunset. (Closed Good Fri). Other times by prior appointment only. **Fee:** ✱ £1 **Facilities:** 🅿 (on street parking) ✖ ⅙

MUSEUM OF WORCESTER PORCELAIN

Severn St WR1 2NE
➲ (M5 Junct 7, follow signs to city centre, at 7th set of lights take 1st left into Edger Street & bear left with road into Severn St. At T Junct bear right & after 700yds take 1st left. Museum on left)
☎ 01905 746000 ▤ 01905 617807
e-mail: museum@royal-worcester.co.uk
The Victorian buildings lead into the heart of a world famous porcelain industry and was founded in 1751. The guided tours and the Museum of Worcester Porcelain take visitors on a design journey through time. Exhibits include room settings, dining scenes and shop fronts in the Georgian, Victorian and 20th century galleries.
Times: Open all year, Mon-Sat 9-5.30, Sun 11-5. closed 25, 25 Dec & Etr Sun. **Facilities:** 🅿 (charged) ⅙ (ex factory) toilets for disabled shop ✖ ➡

WORCESTER CATHEDRAL

WR1 2LH
➲ (Worcester city centre, signed from M5 junct 7)
☎ 01905 28854 & 21004 ▤ 01905 611139
e-mail: info@worcestercathedral.org.uk
Worcester Cathedral is one of England's loveliest cathedrals, with Royal Tombs, medieval cloisters, an ancient crypt and Chapter House and magnificent Victorian stained glass. The tower is open in the summer. There are a number of different celebrations each year, including the Heart of England Food Fair and many concerts.
Times: Open all year, daily 7.30-6. **Fee:** Donations. (Suggested £3 per adult.) **Facilities:** 🅿 (500yds) 💻 ⅙ (Access from College Green) toilets for disabled shop ✖ (ex guide dogs) ➡

EAST RIDING OF YORKSHIRE

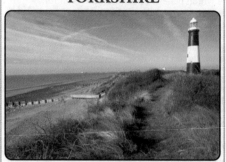

EVENTS & FESTIVALS

May
16th-31st Bridlington Arts Festival, various venues (provisional)
26th-30th Beverley & East Riding Early Music Festival, Beverley Minster and various East Riding churches (provisional)

June
16th-19th Beverley & East Riding Folk Festival, various venues in Beverley
30th-2nd Jul Hornsea Music Festival

July
tbc Driffield Agricultural Show, Driffield Showground

September
2nd-3rd Sea Fever 2005, international sea shanty festival, Hull Marina, Hull
10th Hull Show, East Park, Hull
tbc Beverley & East Riding Chamber Music Festival

October
7th-15th Hull Fair, Walton Street Fairground, Hull

November
tbc Hull Literature Festival (various venues)

Above: Spurn Head lighthouse at the mouth of the River Humber

BEMPTON   Map 08 TA17
RSPB NATURE RESERVE
YO15 1JD
➲ (take cliff road from B1229, Bempton Village and follow brown tourist signs)
☎ 01262 851179 ▤ 01262 851533   **2 for 1**
Part of the spectacular chalk cliffs that stretch from Flamborough Head to Speeton. This is one of the best sites in England to see thousands of nesting seabirds including gannets and puffins at close quarters. Viewpoints overlook the cliffs, which are best visited from April to July. Over 2 miles of chalk cliffs rising to 400ft with numerus cracks and ledges. Enormous numbers of seabirds nest on these cliffs including guillemots, razorbills, kittiwakes, fulmars, herring gulls and several pairs of shag. This is the only gannetry in England and is growing annually. Many migrants pass offshore including terns, skuas and shearwaters. Wheatears, ring ouzels and merlins frequent the clifftop on migration. Grey seal and porpoise are sometimes seen offshore.
Times: Visitor centre open daily, Mar-Nov 10-5. Dec-Feb 9.30-4.
Fee: £3.50 per car, £6 per minibus, £10 per coach.
Facilities: 🅿 (charged) 🍽 & toilets for disabled shop 🚩

BEVERLEY   Map 08 TA03
THE GUILDHALL
Register Sq HU17 9AU
➲ (in Register Sq, next to the post office. Register Sq is adjacent to the main pedestrian thoroughfare in town centre, next to County Hall)
☎ 01482 392776 ▤ 01482 392779
e-mail: stefan.ramsden@eastriding.gov.uk
A Guildhall has been on this site since 1500, although parts of the building date back to a private dwelling of 1320. Largely remodelled in the Palladian style in the 1760s, the Courtroom features a magnificent stucco work ceiling, and the Magistrate's Room houses rare 17th-century Civic furniture.
Times: Open every Fri, 10-4. Please phone for guide tours at other times. **Fee:** ✱ Free on Fri. Charge for guided tours at other times.
Facilities: & disabled parking 100yds 🐾 (ex guide dogs)

BURTON AGNES   Map 08 TA16
BURTON AGNES HALL
Estate Office YO25 0ND
➲ (on A614)
☎ 01262 490324 ▤ 01262 490513
e-mail: burton.agnes@farmline.com

Built in 1598, this is a magnificent Elizabethan house, with furniture, pictures and china amassed by the family owners
continued

over four centuries. There is a walled garden with maze, potager, herbaceous borders, clematis, campanula and geranium collections, and jungle garden, as well as woodland walks.
Times: Open Apr-Oct, daily 11-5. **Fee:** ✱ Hall & grounds £5.20 (ch £2.60, pen £4.70). Grounds only £2.60 (ch £1.15, pen £2.35). Party 30+. **Facilities:** 🅿 ⬛ ♿ (scented garden for the blind) toilets for disabled shop garden centre ⛟

BURTON AGNES MANOR HOUSE
➲ (in Burton Agnes, 5m SW of Bridlington on A166)
A rare and well-preserved example of a Norman house. Some interesting Norman architectural features can still be seen, but the building was encased in brick during the 17th and 18th-centuries. The house is near Burton Agnes Hall and the gardens are privately owned and not managed by English Heritage.
Times: Open Apr-Oct, 11-5. ⌗

GOOLE   Map 08 SE72
THE WATERWAYS MUSEUM NEW
Dutch River Side DN14 5TB
➲ (M62 junct 36, enter Goole & turn right at the next 3 sets of traffic lights onto Dutch River Side. 0.75m down Dutch River Side, follow brown signs)
☎ 01405 768730 🖷 01405 769868
e-mail: waterwaysmuseum@btinternet.com
Discover the story of the Aire & Calder Navigation and the growth of the 'company town' of Goole and its busy port. Find out how to sail and, in the interactive gallery, see how wooden boats were built. Enjoy the unique 'Tom Pudding' story, brought to life through the vessels on the canal and the boat hoist in South Dock. Rediscover the Humber keels and sloops, and Goole's shipbuilding history through the objects, photos and memories of Goole people.
Times: Open: Mon-Fri 9-4 (Sun Apr-Sep, 12-5) **Fee:** ✱ £2.50 (concessions £1.50) Boat Trip £3. **Facilities:** 🅿 ⬛ ♿ disabled access on boats, nature trail toilets for disabled shop ✖ (ex guide dogs)

HORNSEA   Map 08 TA14
HORNSEA MUSEUM
11 Newbegin HU18 1AB
➲ (turn off A165 onto B1244)
☎ 01964 533443   ▐2 for 1▌
A former farmhouse whose outbuildings now illustrate local life and history. There are 19th-century period rooms and a dairy, plus craft tools and farming implements. Photographs, local personalities and industries are also featured along with a large display of Hornsea pottery.
Times: Open Etr-Sep & Oct half-term hols, Tue-Sat 11-5, Sun 2-5 (last admission 4). **Fee:** ✱ £2 (concessions £1.50). Family ticket £6 **Facilities:** 🅿 (50yds) ♿ (audio interpretation for blind/partially sighted) toilets for disabled shop ✖ (ex guide dogs)

KINGSTON UPON HULL   Map 08 TA02
MAISTER HOUSE
160 High St HU1 1NL
➲ (city centre)
☎ 01482 324114 🖷 01482 227003
The house is a mid-18th-century rebuilding, notable for its splendid stone and wrought-iron staircase, ornate stucco work and finely carved doors. Only the staircase and entrance hall are open.
Times: ✱ Open all year, Mon-Fri 10-4 (Closed BH). **Facilities:** 🅿 ✖ 🚌 ♨

MARITIME MUSEUM
Queen Victoria Square HU1 3DX
➲ (from M62 follow A63 to town centre, museum is within pedestrian area of town centre)
☎ 01482 613902 🖷 01482 613710
e-mail: museums@hullcc.gov.uk
Hull's maritime history is illustrated here, with displays on whales and whaling, ships and shipping, and other aspects of this Humber port. There is also a Victorian court room which is used for temporary exhibitions. The restored dock area, with its fine Victorian and Georgian buildings, is well worth exploring too.
Times: ✱ Open all year, Mon-Sat 10-5 & Sun 1.30-4.30. (Closed 25-2 Jan & Good Fri). **Facilities:** 🅿 (100yds) ♿ shop ✖ (ex guide dogs)

'STREETLIFE' - HULL MUSEUM OF TRANSPORT
High St HU1 1PS
➲ (A63 from M62, follow signs for Old Town)
☎ 01482 613902 🖷 01482 613710
e-mail: museums@hullcc.gov.uk
This purpose built museum uses a 'hands-on' approach to trace 200 years of transport history. With a vehicle collection of national importance, state-of- the-art animatronic displays and authentic scenarios, you can see Hull's Old Town brought vividly to life. The mail coach ride uses the very latest in computer technology to recreate a Victorian journey by four-in-hand.
Times: ✱ Open all year, Mon-Sat 10-5, Sun 1.30-4.30. (Closed 24-25 Dec & Good Fri). **Facilities:** 🅿 (500mtrs) ♿ toilets for disabled shop ✖ (ex guide dogs)

THE DEEP
HU1 4DP
➲ (follow signs from Hull City Centre)
☎ 01482 381000 🖷 01482 381010
e-mail: info@thedeep.co.uk
"The World's Only Submarium" tells the story of the oceans, from the Big Bang to the present day and into the future using stunning aquaria and the latest hands-on interactives. Highlights of Europe's deepest aquarium centre include a massive fossil wall, Europe's first pair of green sawfish and a lift ride through the waters of the tanks, bringing you face to face with sharks, eels and hundreds of other marine creatures.

Times: Open daily 10-6. (Closed 24-25 Dec) **Fee:** £6.75 (ch under 16 £4.75, pen £5.25). Family ticket (2 ad & 2 ch) £21, (2 ad & 3 ch) £24 **Facilities:** 🅿 (charged) ⬛ ♿ (signing for the deaf if booked in advance, Braille) toilets for disabled shop ✖ (ex guide dogs) ⛟
See advertisement on opposite page

WILBERFORCE HOUSE
23-25 High St HU1 1NE
⮑ (A63 from M62 or A1079 from York, follow signs for Old Town)
☎ 01482 613902 📠 01482 613710
e-mail: museums@hullcc.gov.uk

The early 17th-century Merchant's house was the birthplace of William Wilberforce, who became a leading campaigner against slavery. There are Jacobean and Georgian rooms and displays on Wilberforce and the anti-slavery campaign. The house also has secluded gardens. There are special exhibitions throughout the year.
Times: ✱ Open all year, Mon-Sat 10-5 & Sun 1.30-4.30. (Closed 25-26 Dec, 1 Jan & Good Fri). **Facilities:** P (500mtrs) (meters on street) ঌ (large print, video area & audio guides) shop ✖ (ex guide dogs)

POCKLINGTON   Map 08 SE84
BURNBY HALL GARDEN & STEWART COLLECTION
The Balk YO42 2QF
⮑ (off A1079 at turning for Pocklington off B1247)
☎ 01759 302068
e-mail: burnbyhallgardens@hotmail.com

The two lakes in this garden have an outstanding collection of 80 varieties of hardy water lilies, designated a National Collection. The lakes stand within nine acres of beautiful gardens including heather beds, a rock garden, a spring and summer bedding area, woodland walk and Victorian garden. The museum contains sporting trophies and ethnic material gathered on world-wide travels.
Times: Open 26 Mar-2 Oct, daily 10-6 (last admission 5pm).
Fee: ✱ £3 (ch 5-15 £1.50, pen £2.50). Party 20+.£2 each
Facilities: P 🅿 ঌ (free wheelchair hire, viewing platform for wheelchairs) toilets for disabled shop ✖ (ex guide dogs) ▄

SEWERBY   Map 08 TA16
SEWERBY HALL & GARDENS
YO15 1EA
⮑ (2m NE of Bridlington on B1255 towards Flamborough)
☎ 01262 673769 📠 01262 673090
e-mail: sewerby.hall@eastring.gov.uk

Sewerby Hall and Gardens, set in 50 acres of parkland overlooking Bridlington Bay, dates back to 1715. The Georgian House, with its 19th century Orangery, contains art galleries, archaeological displays and an Amy Johnson Room with a collection of her trophies and mementoes. The grounds include magnificent walled Old English and Rose gardens and host many events throughout the year. Activities for all the family include a Children's Zoo and play areas, golf, putting, bowls, plus woodland and clifftop walks. Phone for details of special events.
Times: Estate open all year, dawn-dusk. Hall open Etr-end Oct. Please contact for further details. **Fee:** ✱ £3.10 (ch 5-15 £1.20, pen £2.30). Family ticket £7.50. Group 10+ **Facilities:** P 🅿 ঌ toilets for disabled shop ▄

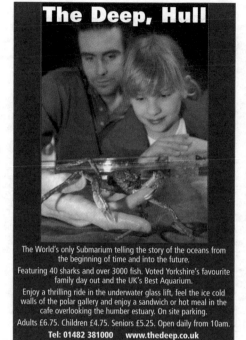

The Deep, Hull

The World's only Submarium telling the story of the oceans from the beginning of time and into the future.

Featuring 40 sharks and over 3000 fish. Voted Yorkshire's favourite family day out and the UK's Best Aquarium.

Enjoy a thrilling ride in the underwater glass lift, feel the ice cold walls of the polar gallery and enjoy a sandwich or hot meal in the cafe overlooking the humber estuary. On site parking.

Adults £6.75. Children £4.75. Seniors £5.25. Open daily from 10am.
Tel: 01482 381000   www.thedeep.co.uk

SPROATLEY   Map 08 TA13
BURTON CONSTABLE HALL
HU11 4LN
⮑ (1.5m N of Sproatley. 14m from Beverley, follow A165 Bridlington road. From Hull take A165, then follow brown historic house signs)
☎ 01964 562400 📠 01964 563229   `2 for 1`
e-mail: enquiries@burtonconstable.com

This superb Elizabethan house was built in 1570, but much of the interior was remodelled in the 18th century. There are magnificent reception rooms and a Tudor long gallery with a pendant roof: the contents range from pictures and furniture to a unique collection of 18th-century scientific instruments. Outside are 200 acres of parkland landscaped by 'Capability' Brown, with oaks and chestnuts, and a lake with an island.
Times: Open, Hall & Grounds Etr Sat-end Oct. Grounds 12.30-5, Hall 1-5. Last admission 4. Closed Fri. **Fee:** ✱ House £5 (ch £2, pen £4.50). Family ticket £11. **Facilities:** P 🅿 ঌ (stair lift to first floor, wheelchairs) toilets for disabled shop

NORTH YORKSHIRE

EVENTS & FESTIVALS

April
28th-8th May Harrogate Spring Flower Show,
   Great Yorkshire Show Ground, Harrogate
29th-1st May Moor & Coast Festival, Whitby,
   music, song, dance and arts
30th-2nd May Ripon Spring Festival

June
19th North Yorkshire County Show,
   Otterington Hall, South Otterington
tbc Grassington Festival, Town Hall,
   Grassington

July
8th-16th York Early Music Festival
12th-14th Great Yorkshire Show, Great
   Yorkshire Showground, Harrogate
15th-16th Masham Steam Engine
   & Fair Organ Rally
21st-5th Aug Harrogate International Festival
   (various venues)

August
13th Ripley Show, Ripley Castle Park, Ripley
tbc Feva 2005, Knaresborough Festival of
   entertainment and visual arts

September
16th-18th Harrogate Autumn Flower Show,
   Great Yorkshire Show Ground, Harrogate
19th Nidderdale Show, Bewerley Park,
   Pately Bridge
tbc Ripon International Festival
   of Music & the Arts

Above: Richmond Castle

ALDBOROUGH   Map 08 SE46

ALDBOROUGH ROMAN SITE
YO5 9ES
➲ (0.75m SE of Boroughbridge, on minor road off
B6265 within 1m of junction of A1 & A6055)
☎ 01423 322768
View two spectacular mosaic pavements and discover the
remains of the once principal Roman town.
Times: Open Apr-Jun, Thu-Mon, 10-5; Aug, daily, 10-6; Sep, Thu-Mon,
10-5. **Fee:** ✱ £2 (ch £1, concessions £1.50). Prices & opening times
relate to 2004, for further details phone or log onto
www.english-heritage.org.uk/visits **Facilities:** shop ✿

AYSGARTH   Map 07 SE08

NATIONAL PARK CENTRE
DL8 3TH
➲ (off A684, Leyburn to Hawes road at Falls junct,
Palmer Flatt Hotel & continue down hill over river,
centre 500yds on left)
☎ 01969 663424   📠 01969 663105   **FREE**
e-mail: aysgarth@ytbtic.co.uk
A visitor centre for the Yorkshire Dales National Park, with
maps, guides, walks and local information. Interactive
displays explain the history and natural history of the area.
Plan the day ahead with a light lunch in the coffee shop.
Various guided walks begin here throughout the year.
Times: Open Apr-Oct, daily 10-5; Winter open Fri-Sun, 10-4.
Facilities: 🅿 (charged) 💺 ♿ (viewing platform at Falls) toilets for
disabled shop ✖ (ex guide dogs) 🍴

BEDALE   Map 08 SE28

BEDALE MUSEUM
DL8 1AA
➲ (on A684, 1.5m W of A1 at Leeming Bar.
Opposite church, at N end of town)
☎ 01677 423797   📠 01677 425393
Situated in a building dating back to the 17th-century, the
Bedale is a fascinating museum. The central attraction is the
Bedale fire engine, which dates back to 1742. Other artefacts
include documents, toys, craft tools and household utensils,
which all help to give an absorbing picture of the lifestyle of
the times.
Times: Open Tue & Fri 10-12.30 & 2-4, Wed 2-4, Thu-Sat 10-12
Facilities: 🅿 ♿ ✖ (ex guide dogs)

BENINGBROUGH   Map 08 SE55

BENINGBROUGH HALL
YO6 1DD
➲ (off A19, 8m NW of York. Entrance at Newton
Lodge)
☎ 01904 470666   📠 01904 470002
e-mail: ybbrgb@smtp.ntrust.org.uk
Beningbrough was built around 1716. It houses 100 pictures
from the National Portrait Gallery in London. Ornately carved
wood panelling is a feature of several of the rooms. The
other side of country house life can be seen in the restored
Victorian laundry.
Times: ✱ Open 23 Mar-3 Nov daily (ex Thu/Fri) open Good Friday,
Jul/Aug daily ex Thu 12-5. Grounds 11-5.30. **Facilities:** 🅿 ✖ licensed
♿ (access to Victorian laundry, shop & restaurant) toilets for disabled
shop ✖ 🐾

BRIMHAM — Map 08 SE26

BRIMHAM ROCKS
Summerbridge HG3 4DW
➲ (10m NW of Harrogate, off B6265)
☎ 01423 780688 ▤ 01423 781020
e-mail: brimhamrocks@nationaltrust.org.uk
The rocks stand on National Trust open moorland at a height of 950ft, enjoying spectacular views over the surrounding countryside. The area is filled with strange and fascinating rock formations and is rich in wildlife. An old shooting lodge in the area is now an information point and shop.
Times: Open 8-dusk, (facilities may close in bad weather): shop with exhibition room, kiosk 20 Mar-23 May & Oct, Sat & Sun 11-5, 29 May-Sep daily 11-5, 7 Nov-19 Dec Sun 11-5. Also open daily; local school hols, BHs, 26 Dec & 1 Jan (weather permitting). **Fee:** Cars (up to 4hrs £3, over 4hrs £4). Minibuses £7. Coaches £12. Motorcycles free. **Facilities:** ▣ (charged) ⬛ ✕ ⬥ specially adapted path(steep in places), Braille guide toilets for disabled shop ⬥ ⬛

CASTLE BOLTON — Map 07 SE09

BOLTON CASTLE
DL8 4ET
➲ (off A684, 6m W of Leyburn)
☎ 01969 623981 ▤ 01969 623332
e-mail: harry@boltoncastle.co.uk
Medieval castle completed in 1399, overlooking Wensleydale. Stronghold of the Scrope family. Mary Queen of Scots was imprisoned here for 6 months. The castle was besieged and taken by Parliamentary forces in 1645. Tapestries, tableaux, arms and armour can be seen. Medieval gardens including maze.
Times: Open Apr-Oct, 10-5; Nov-Mar, 10-4/dusk. **Fee:** ✱ £5 (ch, pen & students £3.50). Family ticket £12. **Facilities:** ▣ ⬛ shop ✕ (ex guide dogs) ⬛

CASTLE HOWARD

See **Malton**

CLAPHAM — Map 07 SD76

CLAPHAM NATIONAL PARK CENTRE
LA2 8ED
➲ (signposted off A65 at Clapham)
☎ 015242 51419
A comprehensive information centre with displays on the local countryside and limestone scenery. A wide range of maps, guides, information leaflets, gifts and souvenirs are stocked and knowledgeable staff are on duty to answer questions.
Times: ✱ Open Apr-Oct, daily 10-5. Limited opening Nov-Mar.
Facilities: ▣ (charged) (Radar key scheme) shop ⬛

COXWOLD — Map 08 SE57

BYLAND ABBEY
YO6 4BD
➲ (2m S of A170 between Thirsk & Helmsley, near Coxwold village)
☎ 01347 868614
A hauntingly beautiful monastic ruin set in peaceful meadows in the shadow of the Hambleton Hills. Marvel at the collection of medieval floor tiles still in their original setting.
Times: Open Apr-Jul, Thu-Mon, 10-5; Aug, daily, 10-6; Sep, Thur-Mon, 10-5. **Fee:** ✱ £2.50 (ch £1.30, concessions £1.90). Prices & opening times relate to 2004, for further details phone or log onto www.english-heritage.org.uk/visits **Facilities:** ▣ ⬥ (garden/grounds partly accessible) toilets for disabled ⬛ ⬛

DANBY — Map 08 NZ70

MOORS CENTRE
Lodge Ln YO21 2NB
➲ (turn S off A171 signed the Moors Centre Danby. Turn left at cross road in Danby village and follow road for 2m, The Moors Centre is at a bend on the right)
☎ 01287 660654 ▤ 01287 660308 `FREE`
e-mail: moorscentre@ytbtic.co.uk
The ideal place to start exploring the North York Moors National Park. There is an exhibition about the area as well as events, video, a shop and local walks. The Moorsbus service also operates from this site - phone for details.
Times: Open all year, Apr-Oct, daily 10-5. Nov, Dec & Mar daily 11-4. Jan & Feb wknds only 11-4. **Facilities:** ▣ (charged) ⬛ ⬥ (woodland & garden trails, motorised & manual wheelchairs) toilets for disabled shop ✕ (ex guide dogs & in grounds) ⬛

EASBY — Map 08 NZ10

EASBY ABBEY
➲ (1m SE of Richmond off B6271)
Set beside the River Swale, this Premonstratensian Abbey was founded in 1155 and dedicated to St Agatha. Extensive remains of the monks' domestic buildings can be seen.
Times: Open Apr-Sep, daily, 10-6; Oct, daily, 10-5; Nov-Mar, daily, 10-4. (Closed 24-25 Dec). **Facilities:** ▣ ⌗

ELVINGTON — Map 08 SE74

YORKSHIRE AIR MUSEUM & ALLIED AIR FORCES MEMORIAL `2 for 1`
Halifax Way YO41 4AU
➲ (from York take A1079 then immediate right onto B1228, museum is signposted on right)
☎ 01904 608595 ▤ 01904 608246
e-mail: museum@yorkshireairmuseum.co.uk

This award-winning museum and memorial is based around the largest authentic former WWII Bomber Command Station open to the public. There is a restored tower, an air gunners museum, archives, an Airborne Forces display, Squadron memorial rooms, and much more. Among the exhibits are replicas of the pioneering Cayley Glider and Wright Flyer, along with the Halifax Bomber and modern jets like the Harrier GR3.
Times: Open daily, 10-5 (summer), 10-3.30 (winter). Closed 25 & 26 Dec. **Fee:** £5 (ch £3 & pen £4). **Facilities:** ▣ ⬛ ✕ licensed ⬥ toilets for disabled shop ⬛

See advertisement on page 277

FAIRBURN   Map 08 SE42
RSPB NATURE RESERVE
Fairburn Ings, The Visitor Centre, Newton Ln WF10 2BH
➲ (W of A1, N of Ferrybridge. Signed from Allerton
Bywater off A656. Signed Fairburn Village off A1)
☎ 01977 603796
e-mail: chris.drake@rspb.org.uk
One-third of the 700-acre RSPB reserve is open water, and
over 270 species of birds have been recorded. A visitor
centre provides information, and there is an elevated
boardwalk, suitable for disabled visitors.
Times: ✱ Access to the reserve via car park, open 9-dusk. Centre open
10-5 weekends and 11-4 weekdays (closed 25-26 Dec).
Facilities: 🅿 ♿ (raised boardwalk for wheelchair) toilets for disabled
shop ✖ (ex guide dogs)

GRASSINGTON   Map 07 SE06
NATIONAL PARK CENTRE
Hebden Rd BD23 5LB
➲ (situated on B6265 in the main Grassington car
park)
☎ 01756 752774   🖷 01756 753358   **FREE**
e-mail: grassington@ytbtic.co.uk
The centre is a useful introduction to the Yorkshire Dales
National Park. It has a video and a display on 'Wharfedale -
Gateway to the Park', and maps, guides and local
information are available. There is also a 24-hr public access
information service through computer screens and a full
tourist information service.
Times: Open Apr-Oct daily, 10-5; Nov-Mar Wed, Fri, & Sat-Sun, 10-4
(also daily in school hols). **Facilities:** 🅿 (charged) ♿ toilets for
disabled shop

GUISBOROUGH   Map 08 NZ61
GISBOROUGH PRIORY
TS14 6HG
➲ (next to parish church)
☎ 01287 633801
The remains of the east end of the 14th-century church
make a dramatic sight here. The priory was founded in the
12th century for Augustinian canons.
Times: Open all year, Apr-Sep, Tue-Sun 9-5; Oct-Mar, Wed-Sun 9-5.
(Closed 24 Dec-1 Jan). **Fee:** ✱ £1.10 (ch 55p, concessions 75p). Prices
& opening times relate to 2004, for further details phone or log onto
www.english-heritage.org.uk/visits **Facilities:** 🅿 🍽 ♿

HARROGATE   Map 08 SE35
RHS GARDEN HARLOW CARR
Crag Ln, Otley Rd HG3 1QB
➲ (off B6162 Otley Rd, 1.5 miles from Harrogate
centre)
☎ 01423 565418   🖷 01423 530663
e-mail: admin-harlowcarr@rhs.org.uk
Established in1950, RHS Garden Harlow Carr provides a
beautiful garden setting to assess the suitability of plants for
growing in the North. The 58 acres includes a breathtaking
streamside garden, peaceful woodland and arboretum,
scented, herb and foliage gardens and National Collections.
There is also a Museum of Gardening and a library on site.
Times: Open all year, daily 9.30-6, (or 4 Nov-Mar.) Last admission 1hr
before closing. **Fee:** ✱ £5 (ch under 6 free, 6-16 £1, pen £4.50)
Facilities: 🅿 🍽 ♿ (electric and push wheelchairs available, scented
garden) toilets for disabled shop garden centre ✖ (ex guide dogs) 🍴

THE ROYAL PUMP ROOM MUSEUM
Crown Place HG1 2RY
➲ (Take A61 into Harrogate town centre and
follow brown heritage signs to museum)
☎ 01423 556188   🖷 01423 556130
e-mail: lg23@harrogate.gov.uk
Housed in delightful early Victorian pump room Over the
town's sulphur wells, the museum tells the story of
Harrogate's heyday as England's European spa. Visitors
discover some of the amazing spa treatments; taste the
sulphur water; and explore stories of Russian royalty,
communal ox-roasts and early bicycles, among many others.
Changing exhibitions complement permanent displays
Times: Open all year, Apr-Oct, Mon-Sat 10-5, Sun 2-5, (Nov-Mar close
at 4). (Closed 24-26 Dec & 1 Jan). **Fee:** ✱ £2.50 (ch £1.25, concession
£1.50). Family rate £6.50 (2 ad & 2 ch). Party. Combined seasonal
tickets available for The Royal Pump Room Museum & Knaresborough
Castle & Museum. **Facilities:** 🅿 (100yds) (restricted to 3hrs, need
parking disc) ♿ toilets for disabled shop ✖ (guide dogs only) 🍴

HAWES   Map 07 SD88
DALES COUNTRYSIDE MUSEUM CENTRE & TIC
Station Yard DL8 3NT
➲ (Off A684 in the Old Station Yard).
☎ 01969 667450 & 667494   🖷 01969 667165
e-mail: hawes@ytbtic.co.uk
Fascinating museum telling the story of the people and
landscape of the Yorkshire Dales. Static steam loco and
carriages with video and displays. Added features include
hands-on interactive displays for children, audio points,
temporary exhibitions & events.
Times: Open all year 10-5. **Fee:** Museum: £3 (ch free, concessions
£2) . National park centre free. **Facilities:** 🅿 (charged) ♿ (lifts, ramps
and parking) toilets for disabled shop ✖ (ex guide dogs) 🍴

HELMSLEY   Map 08 SE68
DUNCOMBE PARK
YO62 5EB
➲ (Duncombe Park is located within the North
York Moors National Park, 25m N of York, off the
A170 Thirsk-Scarborough road, 1m from Helmsley
market place).
☎ 01439 770213   🖷 01439 771114   **2 for 1**
e-mail: liz@duncombepark.com
Duncombe Park stands at the heart of a spectacular 30-acre
early 18th-century landscape garden which is set in 300
acres of dramatic parkland around the River Rye. The house,
originally built in 1713, was gutted by fire in 1879 and rebuilt
in 1895. Its principal rooms are a fine example of the type of
grand interior popular at the turn of the century. Home of the
Duncombes for 300 years, for much of this century the house
was a girls' school. In 1985 the present Lord and Lady
Feversham decided to make it a family home again and after
major restoration, opened the house to the public in 1990.
Part of the garden and parkland were designated a 250-acre
National Nature Reserve in 1994. Special events include a
Country Fair (May), an Antiques Fair (June), Steam Fair (July),
Antiques Fair (November). Please telephone for details.
Times: Open: 13 Apr-24 Oct Sun-Thu; Gardens, Parkland Centre tea
room & shop & Parkland walks 11-5.30. House by guided tour only
every hour from 12.30-3.30. **Fee:** House & Gardens £6.50
(ch 10-16, £3, concessions £5) Gardens & Parkland £3.50 (ch £1.50,
concessions £3) Parkland only £2 (ch £1). **Facilities:** 🅿 ✖ licensed
♿ portable ramp, lift, wheelchair for loan) toilets for disabled shop
✖ (ex park & guide dogs) 🍴

HELMSLEY CASTLE
YO6 5AB
☎ 01439 770442
An atmospheric ruin with formidable double earthworks. Also, an exhibition of the history of the castle.
Times: Open all year, Apr-Sep, daily 10-6; Oct-Mar,Thu-Mon, 10-4. (Closed 24-26 Dec & 1 Jan). **Fee:** ✱ £4 (ch £2, concessions £3, family £10). Prices & opening times relate to 2004, for further details phone or log onto www.english-heritage.org.uk/visits **Facilities:** ▣ (charged) shop ✿

KIRKHAM   Map 08 SE76
KIRKHAM PRIORY
Whitwell-on-the-Hill YO6 7JS
➲ (5m SW of Malton on minor road off A64)
☎ 01653 618768
Discover the ruins of this Augustinian priory, which includes a magnificent carved gatehouse, set in a peaceful and secluded valley by the River Derwent.
Times: Open Apr-Sep, daily 10-6; Oct, daily 10-5. **Fee:** ✱ £2.50 (ch £1.30, concessions £1.90). Prices & opening times relate to 2004, for further details phone or log onto www.english-heritage.org.uk/visits
Facilities: ▣ & ✿

KNARESBOROUGH   Map 08 SE35
KNARESBOROUGH CASTLE & MUSEUM
Castle Yard HG5 8AS
➲ (turn off the High St towards the Market Square. Continue past the Market Square then turn right at the police station into the Castleyard.)
☎ 01423 556188 ▤ 01423 556130
e-mail: lg23@harrogate.gov.uk
High above the town of Knaresborough, the ruins of this 14th-century castle look down over the gorge of the River Nidd. This imposing fortress was once the hiding place of Thomas Becket's murderers and served as a prison for Richard II. Remains include the keep, the sally-port, parts of the curtain wall and the Old Court of Knaresborough. It now houses a local museum, and entrance is part of the combined ticket price.
Times: Open Good Fri-end Sep, daily 10.30-5. Guided tours regulary available. **Fee:** ✱ £2.50 (ch £1.25, concessions £1.50). Family ticket (2 adults & 2 ch) £6.50. Party 10+. Joint & season tickets available for Knaresborough Castle & Museum & The Royal Pump Room Museum. **Facilities:** ▣ (charged) & toilets for disabled shop ✖ (ex guide dogs)

LAWKLAND   Map 07 SD76
YORKSHIRE DALES FALCONRY & WILDLIFE CONSERVATION CENTRE NEW
Crows Nest LA2 8AS
➲ (on A65 follow brown signs)
☎ 01729 822832 ▤ 01729 825160   `2 for 1`
The first privately owned falconry centre in the north of England. The main aim of the centre is to educate and promote awareness that many of the world's birds of prey are threatened with extinction. Successful captive breeding and educational programmes will help to safeguard these creatures. Regular free flying demonstrations throughout the day with strong encouragement for audience participation.
Times: Open all year summer 10-6; winter 10-4. Closed 25 Dec
Fee: ✱ £5.25 (ch & pen £3.25) Family ticket £14.95. Group 15+ £3.50 (ch£2.50) **Facilities:** ▣ ▱ & Ramp for w/chair into Tea Room toilets for disabled shop ✖ (ex guide dogs) 🖾

MALHAM   Map 07 SD96
MALHAM NATIONAL PARK CENTRE
BD23 4DA
➲ (Turn off A65 at Gargrave opp. petrol stn. Malham 7m).
☎ 01729 830363 ▤ 01729 830673   `FREE`
e-mail: malham@ytbtic.co.uk
The national park centre has maps, guides and local information together with displays on the remarkable natural history of the area, local community and work of conservation bodies. Audio-visuals are provided for groups and a 24-hour teletext information service is available.
Times: Open Apr-Oct, daily 10-5. Winter, Fri-Sun, 10-4.
Facilities: ▣ (charged) & (Radar key scheme for toilet) toilets for disabled shop 🖾

MALTON   Map 08 SE77
CASTLE HOWARD
YO60 7DA
➲ (15m NE of York, off A64, follow the brown heritage signs to Castle Howard)
☎ 01653 648333 ▤ 01653 648529
e-mail: house@castlehoward.co.uk

Castle Howard is one of Britain's finest historic houses, with magnificent 18th-century architecture set in a dramatic landscape featuring temples, lakes, statues and fountains. Historical character guides are located inside the house, and visitors can join outdoor tours. Additional attractions include the Women of Castle Howard exhibition, a children's adventure playground, boat trips and a summer events programme.
Times: Open March-Oct. Grounds open 11-6.30/dusk, last admission 4pm. Stable courtyard open 10-5 all yr **Fee:** ✱ £10 (ch £7, pen £9). Grounds only £7 (ch £5, pen £6.50). **Facilities:** ▣ ▱ ✖ licensed & (wheelchair lift, free adapted transport to house) toilets for disabled shop garden centre ✖ (ex guide dogs) 🖾

EDEN CAMP MODERN HISTORY THEME MUSEUM
Eden Camp YO17 6RT
➲ (junct of A64 & A169, between York & Scarborough)
☎ 01653 697777 ▤ 01653 698243   `2 for 1`
e-mail: admin@edencamp.co.uk
The story of the people's war unfolds in this museum devoted to civilian life in World War II. The displays, covering the blackout, rationing, the Blitz, the Home Guard and

continued

others, are housed in a former prisoner-of-war camp built in 1942 for German and Italian soldiers. Hut 13, part of a Millennium project, covers the conflicts that Britain has been involved with from 1945 to present day. Huts 24-29 cover the military and political events of the war, whilst Hut 11 is dedicated to telling the story of World War I.

Times: Open 2nd Mon in Jan-23 Dec, daily 10-5. Last admission 4pm. **Fee:** £4.50 (ch & pen £3.50) Party 10+.£3.50 (ch & pen £2.50) **Facilities:** 🅿 💷 ♿ (taped tours, Braille guides) toilets for disabled shop

MALTON MUSEUM
Old Town Hall, Market Place YO17 7LP
➲ (leave A64, follow signs for Malton town centre)
☎ 01653 695136

The extensive Roman settlements in the area are represented and illustrated in this museum, including collections from the Roman fort of Derventio. There are also displays of local prehistoric and medieval finds plus changing exhibitions of local interest.

Times: Open Etr Sat-Oct, Mon-Sat 10-4. **Fee:** ✱ £1.50 (ch, pen & students £1) Family ticket £4 (2 adults & 2 ch) **Facilities:** 🅿 (adjacent) (pay & display-2hrs) ♿ shop ✈ (ex guide dogs)

MASHAM   Map 08 SE28

THEAKSTON WORKING BREWERY & VISITOR CENTRE
The Brewery HG4 4YD
➲ (on A6108)
☎ 01765 680000 🖷 01765 684330
e-mail: bookings@theakstons.co.uk

Visit the Theakston Brewery in Masham, home of the legendary 'Old Peculier' and witness the creation of real taste first-hand. Discover how traditional brewing techniques are still being applied to create today's award winning pint. As these tours are thirsty work, you'll be invited, to round off your visit in the bar with a glass of real British beer at its best.

Times: ✱ Open 1 Apr-5 Nov, daily 10.30-4.30; 6 Nov-12 Dec, Wed, Sat, Sun 10.30-4.30. **Facilities:** 🅿 (400yds) ♿ (ex brewery tours) toilets for disabled shop ✈ (ex guide dogs) 🍺

MIDDLEHAM   Map 07 SE18

MIDDLEHAM CASTLE
DL8 4RJ
➲ (2m S of Leyburn on A6108)
☎ 01969 623899

Explore the maze of rooms and passageways at this impressive castle, once the boyhood home of the ill-fated Richard III. Oak viewing Gallery of the magnificent views of the 12th-century keep and exhibition.

Times: Open all year, Apr-Sep, daily 10-6; Oct-Mar,Thu-Mo, 10-4. (Closed 24-26 Dec & 1Jan) **Fee:** ✱ £3 (ch £1.50, concessions £2.30). Prices & opening times relate to 2004, for further details phone or log onto www.english-heritage.org.uk/visits **Facilities:** 🅿 ♿ (ex tower) shop ♯

MIDDLESBROUGH   Map 08 NZ42

CAPTAIN COOK BIRTHPLACE MUSEUM
Stewart Park, Marton TS7 6AS
➲ (3m S on A172)
☎ 01642 311211 🖷 01642 515659
e-mail: captaincookmuseum@
middlesbrough.gov.uk

Opened to mark the 250th anniversary of the birth of the voyager in 1728, this museum illustrates the early life of James Cook and his discoveries with permanent and temporary exhibitions. Located in spacious and rolling parkland, the site also offers outside attractions for the visitor. Recently refurbished, the museum has a special resource centre which has fresh approaches to presentation with computers, films, special effects, interactives and educational aids.

Times: ✱ Open all year: Tue-Sun, Mar-Oct 10am-5.30pm. Winter hrs 9am-3.30pm. Last entry 45 mins before closure. (Closed Mon except BH, 24-28 Dec & 31 Dec-7 Jan). **Fee:** ✱ £2.40 (con £1.20) Family £6 **Facilities:** 🅿 💷 ♿ (lift to all floors, car parking) toilets for disabled shop ✈ (ex guide dogs) 🍺

NEWBY HALL & GARDENS   Map 08 SE36

NEWBY HALL & GARDENS
HG4 5AE
➲ (4m SE of Ripon & 2m W of A1M, off B6265, between Boroughbridge and Ripon)
☎ 01423 322583 🖷 01423 324452
e-mail: info@newbyhall.com

A late 17th-century house with beautifully restored Robert Adam interiors containing an important collection of classical sculpture, Chippendale furniture and Gobelin

continued

tapestries. 25 acres of award-winning gardens include a miniature railway, an adventure garden for children and a woodland discovery walk with contemporary sculpture park (Jun-Sep).
Times: Open Apr-Sep, Tue-Sun & BHs, also Mon in school hols; Gardens 11-5.30; House 12-5. Last admission 5pm (Gardens), 4.30pm (House), **Fee:** ✱ House & Garden £7.20, (ch £4.70, pen £6.20). Gardens only £5.70 (ch £4.20, pen £4.70). Party rates and family tickets on application. **Facilities:** 🄿 💻 ✗ licensed ♿ (wheelchairs available, maps of wheelchair routes) toilets for disabled shop garden centre ✈ (ex guide dogs) ⌑

NORTH STAINLEY   Map 08 SE27
LIGHTWATER VALLEY THEME PARK
HG4 3HT
➲ (3m N of Ripon on the A6108)
☎ 0870 458 0060 & 458 0040
▤ 01765 635359
e-mail: leisure@lightwatervalley.co.uk
The family sized theme park with thrills of all sizes, from Europe's longest rollercoaster 'The Ultimate' and 'The Grizzly Bear' log flume, to family favourites such as the 'ladybird' rollercoaster and Grand Prix Go Karting along with spinning teacups, vintage cars and much more for younger children. You just pay once and enjoy the fun all day long!
Times: ✱ Open 23 Mar-7 Apr, weekends only; 13 Apr-26 May inc BH Mon; daily from Jun-2 Sep, weekends only 7 Sep-13 Oct. daily 19 Oct- 27 Oct. **Facilities:** 🄿 💻 ✗ licensed ♿ (even pathways) toilets for disabled shop ✈ (ex guide dogs) ⌑

NUNNINGTON   Map 08 SE67
NUNNINGTON HALL
YO6 5UY
➲ (4.5m SE of Helmsley)
☎ 01439 748283   ▤ 01439 748284
e-mail: yorknu@smtp.ntrust.org.uk
This large 16th to 17th-century house has panelled rooms and a magnificent staircase. The Carlisle collection of miniature rooms is on display.
Times: ✱ Open 23 Mar-3 Nov, Mar-May & Sep-Nov, daily (ex Mon/Tue) open BH Mons 1.30-4.30 (last admission 5pm May & Sep); Jun-Aug; daily ex Mon (open BH Mon) 1.30-5. **Facilities:** 🄿 💻 ♿ (w/chairs, Braille guide, scented garden) toilets for disabled shop ✖

ORMESBY   Map 08 NZ51
ORMESBY HALL
TS7 9AS
➲ (3m SE of Middlesborough, W of A19 take the A174 to the A172 . Follow signs for Ormesby Hall. Car entrance on Ladgate Lane)
☎ 01642 324188   ▤ 01642 300937
e-mail: ormesbyhall@ntrust.org.uk
An 18th-century mansion, Ormesby Hall has stables attributed to John Carr of York. Plasterwork, furniture and 18th-century pictures are on view.
Times: ✱ Open 24 Mar-2 Nov: daily ex Mon, Fri & Sat (open Good Fri & BH Mons) 1.30-4.30. **Facilities:** 🄿 💻 ♿ (parking, Braille guide, special tours) toilets for disabled shop ✖ ✖

OSMOTHERLEY   Map 08 SE49
MOUNT GRACE PRIORY
DL6 3JG
➲ (1m NW)
☎ 01609 883494   ▤ 01609 883361
The best preserved Carthusian monastery in the country, set in breathtakingly beautiful woodland surroundings and gardens, including fully reconstructed Monks cells and herb garden, illustrating the solitary life of the monk.
Times: Open Apr-Sep, daily, 10-6; Oct-Mar, Thu-Mon, 10-4. (Closed 24-26 Dec & 1 Jan). **Fee:** ✱ £3.50 (ch £1.80, concessions £2.60, family £8.80). National Trust members free. Prices & opening times relate to 2004, for further details phone or log onto www.english-heritage.org.uk/visits **Facilities:** 🄿 shop ✈ ✿ ✖

PARCEVALL HALL   Map 07 SEO6
GARDENS
PARCEVALL HALL GARDENS
BD23 6DE
➲ (Off B6265 between Grassington and Pateley Bridge)
☎ 01756 720311   ▤ 01756 720441
e-mail: info@parcevallhallgardens.co.uk
Enjoying a hillside setting east of the main Wharfedale Valley, these beautiful gardens surround a Grade II listed house which is used as the Bradford Diocesan Retreat House (not open to the public).
Times: Open Apr-Oct, daily 10-6. Winter visitors by appointment.
Fee: £3.50 (ch up to 16, 50p). **Facilities:** 🄿 💻 shop

PATELEY BRIDGE   Map 07 SE16
STUMP CROSS CAVERNS
Greenhow HG3 5JL
➲ (situated on the B6265 between Pateley Bridge and Grassington)
☎ 01756 752780   ▤ 01756 752780
Discovered by the brothers Mark and William Newbould in 1860, Stump Cross Caverns have been an attraction for visitors since 1863 when one shilling was charged for entrance. Among the few limestone show caves in Britain, these require no special clothing, experience or equipment, as walkways are gravel and concrete and floodlighting is provided. Stalagmites, stalagtites and calcite precipitation make this an eerie day out.
Times: ✱ Open daily, mid Mar-2 Nov, then wknds (winter months) 10-5. **Facilities:** 🄿 💻 shop ✈ (ex guide dogs) ⌑

PICKERING   Map 08 SE78
NORTH YORKSHIRE MOORS RAILWAY
Pickering Station YO18 7AJ
➲ (from A169 take roads towards Kirkbymoorside at traffic lights turn right, Stn 400 yds on left)
☎ 01751 472508   ▤ 01751 476970
e-mail: admin@nymr.pickering.fsnet.co.uk
Operating through the heart of the North York Moors National Park between Pickering and Grosmont, steam trains cover a distance of 18 miles. The locohhhhmotive sheds at Grosmont are open to the public. Events throughout the year include Day Out with Thomas, Steam Gala, Santa Specials.
Times: Open 29 Mar-Oct, daily; Dec, Santa specials and Christmas to New Year running. Further information available from Pickering Station.
Fee: Return: £12 (ch £6, pen £10.50). Family ticket £27 (2ad+3ch), others on request). Party 20+. **Facilities:** 🄿 (charged) 💻 ✗ licensed ♿ (ramp for trains) toilets for disabled shop (at Pickering, Goathland & Grosmont) ⌑

PICKERING CASTLE
YO6 5AB
☎ 01751 474989
Splendid 12th-century castle, on the edge of the Yorkshire Moors, originally built by William the Conqueror. Visit the exhibition on the castle's history and take in the views from the keep.
Times: Open Apr-Sep, daily, 10-6; Oct, Thu-Mon, 10-4. **Fee:** ✱ £3 (ch £1.50, concessions £2.30, family £7.50). Prices & opening times relate to 2004, for further details phone or log onto www.english-heritage.org.uk/visits **Facilities:** 🅿 ⅃ (ex motte) shop ⊞

REDCAR   Map 08 NZ62

RNLI ZETLAND MUSEUM
5 King St TS10 3AH
➲ (on corner of King St and The Promenade)
☎ 01642 485370 & 471813
The museum portrays the lifeboat, maritime, fishing and local history of the area, including its main exhibit 'The Zetland' - the oldest lifeboat in the world, dating from 1802. There is also a replica of a fisherman's cottage c1900 and almost 2000 other exhibits. The museum is housed in an early lifeboat station, now a listed building.
Times: ✱ Open May-Sep, Mon-Fri 1-4, Sat & Sun 12-4. Also Etr. Other times by appointment. **Facilities:** 🅿 (20m) (50p per hour) ⅃ (ground floor accessible only) shop

RICHMOND   Map 07 NZ10

GREEN HOWARDS MUSEUM
Trinity Church Square, Market Place DL10 4QN
➲ (Take any turning on the A1, between Catterick & South Corner, signposted to Richmond. Located in centre cobbled market square, in Holy Trinity Church).
☎ 01748 826561 📠 01748 821924
e-mail: green.howardsmus@aol.com
This award-winning museum traces the military history of the Green Howards from the late 17th century onwards. The exhibits include uniforms, weapons, medals and a special Victoria Cross exhibition. Regimental and civic plate is displayed, and there is CD ROM and touch screen video of the First World War Western Front and the Green Howards in the Second World War. Audio guide available.
Times: Open Feb, Mon-Fri 9-4.30; Mar, Mon-Fri 9-4.30; mid Apr-Oct, Mon-Sat 9-4.30 & Sun 2-4.30; Nov, Mon-Sat 9-4.30. **Fee:** ✱ £2.50 (unaccompanied ch £1.50, pen £2). Family ticket £5. Richmondshire residents and accompanied children free. **Facilities:** 🅿 (in Market place) (disk parking, 2hr max) ⅃ (stairlift for access to all floors, lightweight wheelchair) shop ✱ (ex guide dogs)

RICHMOND CASTLE
DL10 4QW
☎ 01748 822493
Overlooking the River Swale and market town of Richmond, the views from the keep are stunning. Built by William the Conqueror to subdue the rebellious North, the castle now houses an exciting interactive exhibition.
Times: Open all year, Apr-Sep, daily, 10-6; Oct-Mar, Thu-Mon, 10-4. (Closed 24-26 Dec & 1 Jan). **Fee:** ✱ £3.50 (ch £1.80, concessions £2.60, family £8.80). Prices & opening times relate to 2004, for further details phone or log onto www.english-heritage.org.uk/visits
Facilities: 🅿 (800 yds) ⅃ toilets for disabled shop ⊞

RIEVAULX   Map 08 SE58

RIEVAULX ABBEY
➲ (2.25m W of Helmsley on minor road off B1257)
☎ 01439 798228
Explore the magnificent romantic ruin set in a tranquil wooded valley of the River Rye. Find out about monastic life with the help of our audio tour and exhibition.
Times: Open Apr-Sep, daily, 10-6; Oct-Mar, Thu-Mon, 10-4. (Closed 24-26 Dec & 1 Jan) **Fee:** ✱ £4 (ch £2, concessions £3). Prices & opening times relate to 2004, for further details phone or log onto www.english-heritage.org.uk/visits **Facilities:** 🅿 ⅃ shop 🚐 ⊞

RIEVAULX TERRACE & TEMPLES
YO62 5LJ
➲ (2m NW of Helmsley on B1257)
☎ 01439 798340 📠 01439 748284
This curved terrace, half a mile long, overlooks the abbey, with views of Ryedale and the Hambleton Hills. It has two mock-Greek temples, one built for hunting parties, the other for quiet contemplation. There are also remarkable frescoes by Borgnis, and an exhibition on English landscape design.
Times: ✱ Open 23 Mar-3 Nov: daily 10.30-6 (5pm Oct & Nov). Last admission 1hr before closing. **Facilities:** 🅿 ⅃ (w/chair/runaround vehicle/Braille guide/ramp) shop 🌿

RIPLEY   Map 08 SE26

RIPLEY CASTLE
HG3 3AY
➲ (off A61, Harrogate to Ripon road)
☎ 01423 770152 📠 01423 771745
e-mail: enquiries@ripleycastle.co.uk   **2 for 1**

Ripley Castle has been home to the Ingilby family since 1320, and stands at the heart of an estate with deer park, lake and Victorian walled gardens. The Castle has a rich history and a fine collection of Royalist armour housed in the 1555 tower. There are also walled gardens, tropical hot houses, woodland walks, pleasure grounds and the National Hyacinth collection in spring.
Times: Open Sep-Jun, Tue, Thu, Sat & Sun 10.30-3, Jul-Aug daily 10.30-3, also BH and school holidays. Groups all year by prior arrangement. Gardens open daily 9-5.30. **Fee:** Castle & Gardens £6 (ch £3.50, pen £5). Gardens only £3.50 (ch £2, pen £3). Party £3.
Facilities: 🅿 ⬛ ✕ licensed ⅃ (mobility buggy for hire, audio loop) toilets for disabled shop garden centre ✱ (ex guide dogs) 🏴

RIPON   Map 08 SE37

FOUNTAINS ABBEY & STUDLEY ROYAL
HG4 3DY
➲ (4m W of Ripon off B6265)
☎ 01765 601002 ▤ 01765 601002

Founded by Cistercian monks in 1132, Fountains Abbey is the largest monastic ruin in Britain. It was acquired by William Aislabie in 1768, and became the focal point of his landscaped gardens at Studley. Other interesting features include Fountains Hall, built between 1598 and 1611 using the stone from the abbey ruins.
Times: Open all year, daily (except Fri in Nov, Dec & Jan); Apr-Sep, 10-6; Oct-Mar 10-4 or dusk if earlier. **Fee:** ✹ £5.50 (ch £3). Family ticket £15 **Facilities:** ⊞ ➤ ✗ licensed & (W/chairs, Braille/large print guides) toilets for disabled shop ♨ ◀

NORTON CONYERS HALL
HG4 5EQ
➲ (from Ripon take A61 to Thirsk. At top of hill just outside Ripon, turn sharp left onto Wath Road)
☎ 01765 640337 ▤ 01765 692772

This late medieval house with Stuart and Georgian additions has belonged to the Grahams since 1624. It was visited by Charles I and James II. Another visitor was Charlotte Brontë: a family legend of a mad woman confined in the attics is said to have given her the idea for the mad Mrs Rochester in *Jane Eyre*. Family costumes are on display. Please note that ladies are requested not to wear stiletto-heeled shoes.
Times: ✹ Open - House & Garden, Etr Sun & Mon, BH Sun & Mon; 25 Apr-27 Jun & 4 Jul-29 Aug Sun only; 28 Jun-3 Jul daily, House 2-5, Garden 12-5. Gardens open Thu 12-4, throughought year.
Facilities: ⊞ & (ramp at entrance) toilets for disabled shop ➤ (ex guide dogs)

SALTBURN-BY-THE-SEA   Map 08 NZ62

SALTBURN SMUGGLERS HERITAGE CENTRE
Old Saltburn TS12 1HF
➲ (adjoining Ship Inn, on A174)
☎ 01287 625252 ▤ 01287 625252

Set in old fisherman's cottages, this centre skillfully blends costumed characters with authentic sounds and smells. Follow the story of John Andrew "King of Smugglers", who was at the heart of illicit local trade 200 years ago.
Times: Open Apr-Sep, daily 10-6: Winter open by arrangement only telephone 01642 470836. **Fee:** ✹ £1.95 (ch £1.45). Family ticket £5.80. Party. **Facilities:** ⊞ (200 mtrs) (charged) shop ➤

SCARBOROUGH   Map 08 TA08

SCARBOROUGH CASTLE
Castle Rd YO11 1HY
➲ (E of town centre)
☎ 01723 372451

This 12th-century fortress housed many important figures in history. Enjoy the spectacular coastal view and see the remains of the great keep still standing over three storeys high. Discover the castle's exciting history through the free audio tour.
Times: Open all year, Apr-Sep, daily 10-6; Oct-Mar, Thu-Mon, 10-4. (Closed 24-26 Dec & 1 Jan). **Fee:** ✹ £3.20 (ch £1.60, concessions £2.40, family £8). Prices & opening times relate to 2004, for further details phone or log onto www.english-heritage.org.uk/visits
Facilities: ⊞ (100 yds) & (ex in keep) ✜

SEA LIFE & MARINE SANCTUARY
Scalby Mills Rd, North Bay YO12 6RP
➲ (follow brown and white tourist signs after entering Scarborough. Centre is in 'North Bay Leisure Parks' area of town)
☎ 01723 376125 ▤ 01723 376285 *2 for 1*

Made up of three large white pyramids, this impressive marine sanctuary overlooks the white sandy beaches of the North Bay, Scarborough's Castle, and Peasholm Park. The sanctuary features Jurassic seas, jellyfish, Otter River, penguins, and sea turtles.
Times: Open daily ex 25 Dec. **Fee:** ✹ Prices to be confirmed.
Facilities: ⊞ (charged) ➤ & (lift to cafe) toilets for disabled shop ➤ (except guide dogs) ◀

SKINNINGROVE   Map 08 NZ71

CLEVELAND IRONSTONE MINING MUSEUM
Deepdale TS13 4AP
➲ (Located in Skinningrove Valley, just off A174 near coast between Middlesbrough and Whitby)
☎ 01287 642877 ▤ 01287 642970 *2 for 1*
e-mail: visits@ironstonemuseum.co.uk

On the site of the old Loftus Mine, this museum offers visitors a glimpse into the underground world of Cleveland's ironstone mining past. Discover the special skills and customs of the miners who helped make Cleveland the most important ironstone mining district in Victorian and Edwardian England.
Times: Open Apr-Oct, daily from 1 (last admission 4pm). Nov-Mar, pre-booked parties can be arranged at any time **Fee:** ✹ £4 (ch £2). Family ticket (2ad+2ch) £10. **Facilities:** ⊞ & (Please telephone to discuss) toilets for disabled shop ➤ (ex guide dogs)

Above: Robin Hood's Bay

SKIPTON   Map 07 SD95
SKIPTON CASTLE
BD23 1AQ
➲ (in town centre at the head of the High Street)
☎ 01756 792442 📠 01756 796100
e-mail: info@skiptoncastle.co.uk

Skipton is one of the most complete and well-preserved medieval castles in England. Some of the castle dates from the 1650s when it was rebuilt after being partially damaged following the Civil War. However, the original castle was erected in Norman times and became the home of the Clifford family in 1310 and remained so until 1676. Illustrated tour sheets are available in a number of languages.
Times: Open daily from 10 (Sun noon). Last admission 6 (4 Oct-Feb). (Closed 25 Dec). **Fee:** ✱ £5 (inc illustrated tour sheet) (ch under 18 £2.50, under 5 free, concessions £4.40). Family ticket £13.90. Party 15+.
Facilities: 🅿 (200m) 🏪 shop garden centre 🍴

SUTTON-ON-THE-FOREST   Map 08 SE56
SUTTON PARK
YO61 1DP
➲ (off A1237 onto B1363 York to Helmsley Road. 8m North of York City Centre)
☎ 01347 810249 & 811239
📠 01347 811251   2 for 1
e-mail: suttonpark@fsbdial.co.uk
The early Georgian house contains fine furniture, paintings and porcelain. The grounds have superb, award-winning terraced gardens, a lily pond and a Georgian ice house. There are also delightful woodland walks as well as spaces for caravans.
Times: Gardens 2 Apr-end Sep, daily 11-5. House open 2 Apr-27 Sep, Wed & Sun, also Good Fri, Etr Mon and all BH Mons. **Fee:** Prices not confirmed for 2005 **Facilities:** 🅿 🏪 & wheelchair and lift in house, ramps in garden toilets for disabled shop ✖ (ex guide dogs in garden)

WHITBY   Map 08 NZ81
WHITBY ABBEY
YO22 4JT
➲ (on clifftop E of Whitby town centre)
☎ 01947 603568 📠 01947 825561
Uncover the full story of these atmospheric ruins in their impressive clifftop location above the picturesque fishing town with associations ranging from Victorian jewellery and whaling, to Count Dracula.
Times: Open all year, Apr-Sep, daily, 10-6; Oct-Mar, Thu-Mon, 10-4. (Closed 24-26 Dec & 1 Jan). **Fee:** ✱ £4 (ch £2, concession £3, family £10). Prices & opening times relate to 2004, for further details phone or log onto www.english-heritage.org.uk/visits **Facilities:** 🅿 (charged) 🏪 (parking available) shop ♯

WINTRINGHAM   Map 08 SE87
WOLDS WAY LAVENDER
Deer Farm Park, Sandy Ln, Wintringham YO17 8HW
➲ (Off A64 between Malton & Scarborough, follow brown signs.)
☎ 01944 758641   FREE
e-mail: admin@deerparkfarm.com
The medicinal and therapeutic benefits of lavender are extolled at this 12-acre site close to the Yorkshire Wolds. Four acres are currently planted with lavender, and a wood-burning still for the extraction of lavender oil will soon be in place (2005). Visitors can be calmed by the Sensory Areas, enjoy a cuppa at Lavender Lil's Tearoom, and purchase all manner of lavender items at the farm shop.
Times: Open daily, week before 21 Mar-Oct, 10-4 (Jun, Jul & Aug 10-5)
Facilities: 🅿 🏪 & Sensory garden, raised flower beds garden centre Lavender & herb plants ✖ (ex guide dogs) 🍴

YORK   Map 08 SE65
THE ARC
St Saviourgate YO1 8NN
➲ (Follow A19 or A64 to york City centre, follow pedestrian signposts for Archaeological Resource Centre)
☎ 01904 543403 📠 01904 627097   2 for 1
e-mail: enquiries@vikingjorvik.com
The ARC is the perfect place to visit to experience an unusual way to discover York's Viking history. Visitors have the opportunity to become an archaeologist and handle genuine 1000 year-old objects that once belonged to the Vikings themselves. With the help of a special detective guidebook, it is possible to deduce what life was really like at that time.
Times: Open: School term time Mon-Fri 10-3.30. School holidays Mon-Sat 11-3 **Fee:** ✱ £4.50. (ch, students & pen £4) Family £15. Group rates available on request. **Facilities:** 🅿 (50yds) & (induction loop, sensory garden, hearing posts) toilets for disabled shop ✖ (ex guide dogs) 🍴

CLIFFORD'S TOWER
Tower St YO1 1SA
☎ 01904 646940
Visit this proud symbol of the might of England's medieval kings - and enjoy magnificent views over York. The original wooden tower was built to help William the Conqueror subdue the North. It was burned down during the persecution of the Jewish community in 1190 and rebuilt in a rare design of interlocking circles by Henry III in the 13th-century.
Times: Open Apr-Sep, daily 10-6; Oct, daily 10-5; Nov-Mar, daily 10-4. (Closed 24-26 Dec & 1 Jan). **Fee:** ✱ £2.50 (ch £1.30, concessions £1.90, family £6.30). Prices & opening times relate to 2004, for further details phone or log onto www.english-heritage.org.uk/visits
Facilities: 🅿 shop ✖ 🚌 ♿

FAIRFAX HOUSE
Castlegate YO1 9RN
➲ (city centre, close to Jorvik Centre and Cliffords Tower)
☎ 01904 655543 📠 01904 652262   **2 for 1**
e-mail: peterbrown@fairfaxhouse.co.uk
An outstanding mid 18th-century house with a richly decorated interior, Fairfax House was acquired by the York Civic Trust in 1983 and restored. The house contains fine examples of Georgian furniture, porcelain, paintings and clocks which were donated by Mr Noel Terry, the great grandson of the founder of the York-based confectionery business. There is a special display of a recreated meal dating from 1763 in the dining room and kitchen.
Times: Open 7 Feb-5 Jan, Mon-Sat 11-5, (Fri guided tours only at 11& 2). Sun 1.30-5. Last admission 4.30 **Fee:** ✱ £4.50 (ch £1.50, pen & student £3.75) **Facilities:** 🅿 (50yds) (3hr short stay) ♿ (with assistance, phone before visit) shop ✖ (ex guide dogs) 🍴

GUILDHALL
Coney St YO1 9QN
➲ (5mins walk from the rail station)
☎ 01904 613161 📠 01904 551052
The present Hall dates from 1446 but in 1942 an air raid virtually destroyed the building. The present Guildhall was carefully restored as an exact replica and was re-opened in 1960. There is an interesting arch-braced roof decorated with colourful bosses and supported by 12 solid oak pillars. There are also some beautiful stained-glass windows.
Times: ✱ Open all year, May-Oct, Mon-Fri 9-5, Sat 10-5, Sun 2-5; Nov-Apr, Mon-Fri 9-5.(Closed Good Fri, Spring BH, 25-26 Dec & 1 Jan). **Facilities:** 🅿 (15-20 mins walk) ♿ (electric chair lift & ramps) toilets for disabled ✖ (ex guide dogs) 🚌

JORVIK
Coppergate YO1 9WT
➲ (Follow the A19 or A64 to York, situated in the coppergate shopping area in the city centre, follow the signs to Jorvik)
☎ 01904 543403 📠 01904 627097
e-mail: enquiries@vikingjorvik.com
Explore York's Viking history on the very site where archaeologists discovered remains of the city of Jorvik. Encounter Viking residents, learn what life was like here 1000 years ago, and journey through a reconstruction of actual Viking streets. The 'Fearsome Craftsmen' exhibit reveals the skills and artistry of the Vikings, while 'Unearthed' tells how the people of ancient York lived and
continued

died, as revealed by real bone material. Special events throughout the year.

Times: Open all year, Apr-Oct daily 10-5; and Viking festival Nov-Mar daily 10-4 (Closed 25 Dec). Opening times subject to change, please telephone for up to date details. **Fee:** ✱ £7.20 (ch 5-15 £5.10, under 5 free, student & pen £6.10) Family of 4 £21.95 & family of 5 £26.50. Telephone bookings on 01904 543403 (£1 booking fee per person at peak times). **Facilities:** 🅿 (400 yds) (limited to 3 hours) 🚌 ♿ (lift & time car designed to take wheelchair, hearing loop) toilets for disabled shop ✖ (ex guide dogs) 🍴

MERCHANT ADVENTURERS' HALL
Fossgate YO1 9XD
➲ (located in town centre, between Piccadilly and Fossgate)
☎ 01904 654818 📠 01904 616150
e-mail: enquiries@theyorkcompany.co.uk
The medieval guild hall of the powerful Merchant Adventurers' Company was built 1357-1361 and is one of the finest in Europe. The Hall contains early furniture, one piece dating from the 13th century, paintings, silver, and weights and measures.
Times: Open 4 Jan-20 Mar & 3 Oct-23 Dec, Mon-Sat 9-3.30 (closed Sun); 21 Mar-2 Oct, Mon-Thu 9-5, Fri-Sat 9-3.30, Sun 12-4. (Closed over Xmas) **Fee:** ✱ £2 (ch under 7 free, ch 7-17yrs 70p, pen & students £1.70). **Facilities:** 🅿 (500yds) ♿ (access from Fossgate, lift) toilets for disabled ✖ (ex guide dogs)

NATIONAL RAILWAY MUSEUM
Leeman Rd YO26 4XJ
➲ (NRM is situated behind the railway station. Signposted from all major approach roads)
☎ 01904 621261 📠 01904 611112   **FREE**
e-mail: nrm@nmsi.ac.uk
York boasts the world's largest railway museum, and families can spend all day exploring the three giant halls that house this impressive collection. Among the exhibits are the huge Chinese Locomotive, built in 1935 and weighing in at 193 tons with tender; the Mallard, which still holds the world speed record for steam traction on rail (126mph in 1938); the legendary Stephenson's Rocket; and various rail-related items like winding engines, bridges and a horse-drawn ambulance for injured horses.
Times: Open all year, Mon-Sun 10-6. (Closed 24-26 Dec).
Facilities: 🅿 (charged) 🚌 ✖ licensed ♿ ("Please Touch" evenings) usually in June toilets for disabled shop ✖ (ex guide/hearing dogs) 🍴

St Williams College

5 College St YO1 7JF

➲ (adjacent to York Minster at east end)

☎ 01904 557233   📠 01904 557234

e-mail: info@yorkminster.org

St Williams College, a 15th-century timber-framed building, housed chantry priests until 1549. It now contains York Minster's Conference & Banquet Centre, shop, restaurant and the medieval rooms are open to view when not being used for functions; an ideal venue for wedding receptions and medieval banquets. Craft Fairs most weekends.

Times: Open all year 10-5 for viewing of medieval rooms subject to private bookings - phone for details. Closed 24-26 Dec & Good Fri.

Fee: Medieval Rooms £1 (ch 50p) subject to functions.

Facilities: P ⬤ ✗ licensed shop ✗

Treasurer's House

Chapter House St YO1 7JL

➲ (in Minster Yard, on N side of Minster

☎ 01904 624247   📠 01904 647372

e-mail: yorkth@smtp.ntrust.org.uk

Named after the Treasurer of York Minster and built over a Roman Road, the house is not all it seems. Come & discover why! Nestled behind the Minster, the size, splendour and contents of the house are a constant surprise to visitors - as are the famous ghost stories. Children's trails and access to the tea room free.

Times: ✱ Open Apr-Oct, daily except Fri, 11-5. **Facilities:** P (800 mtrs) ⬤ ✗ ⅙ (Braille guide/tactile pictures/induction loop/scented path) ✗ (ex guide dogs) 🐾

The York Brewery Co Ltd

12 Toft Green YO1 6JT

➲ (within City Walks)

☎ 01904 621162   📠 01904 621216   **2 for 1**

e-mail: tony@yorkbrew.co.uk

One of the North's finest independent breweries now offers a tour of its premises inside the city walls. Visitors can observe all the processes that go into producing beers like Centurion's Ghost, Full Bloom, Guzzler, and Silly Mid Off. Those made intolerably thirsty by the sight of all this brewing expertise will be glad to know that the adult ticket price includes one pint of beer.

Times: Open daily tours at 12.30, 2, 3.30 and 5 Mon-Sat (Sun May-Sep) **Fee:** ✱ £4.50 (£4 pen & ch 14-17yrs £3).

Facilities: P 50yds shop ✗ (ex guide dogs) 🍺

York Castle Museum

The Eye of York YO1 IRY

➲ (city centre, next to Clifford's Tower)

☎ 01904 653611   📠 01904 671078

Fascinating exhibits that bring memories to life, imaginatively displayed through reconstructions of period rooms and two indoor streets, complete with cobbles, a Hansom cab and a park. The museum is housed in the city's former prison and is based on an extensive collection of 'bygones' acquired at the beginning of the twentieth century.

continued

It was one of the first folk museums to display a huge range of everyday objects in an authentic scene. The Victorian street includes a pawnbroker, a tallow candle factory and a haberdasher's. There is even a reconstruction of the original sweet shop of the York chocolate manufacturer, Joseph Terry. An extensive collection of many other items ranging from musical instruments to costumes and a gallery of domestic gadgets from Victorian times to the 1960s (entitled 'Every home should have one') are further attractions to this remarkable museum. The museum also has one of Britain's finest collections of Militaria; this includes a superb example of an Anglo-Saxon helmet - one of only three known. A special exhibition called 'Seeing it Through' explores the life of York citizens during the Second World War. The museum includes the cell where highwayman Dick Turpin was held. Please contact the museum for deatils of exhibition and events.

Times: ✱ Open all year, Apr-Oct Mon-Sat 9.30-5.30, Sun 10-5.30; Nov-Mar, Mon-Sat 9.30-4, Sun 10-4. (Closed 25-26 Dec & 1 Jan).

Facilities: ⬤ ⅙ toilets for disabled shop ✗ 🍺

York City Art Gallery

Exhibition Square YO1 7EW

➲ (3min walk from the minster in the centre of York).

☎ 01904 551861   📠 01904 551866

e-mail: art.gallery@york.gov.uk

The gallery is remarkable for the range and quality of its collections that provide a survey of most developments in Western European painting over the past six centuries, something that most regional galleries cannot claim to do. Works by Parmigianino, Bellotto, Lely, Reynolds, Frith, Boudin, Lowry and Nash and nudes by Etty are on permanent display. There are also fine collections of watercolours and pottery.

Times: ✱ Open all year, daily 10-5. (Closed 25 & 26 Dec & 1 Jan).

Facilities: P (500mtrs) ⅙ (chair lift) toilets for disabled shop ✗ (ex guide dogs) 🍺

The York Dungeon

12 Clifford St YO1 9RD

➲ (A64/A19/A59 - head for city centre)

☎ 01904 632599   📠 01904 612602

e-mail: yorkdungeons@merlinentertainments.biz

Deep in the heart of historic York, buried beneath its very paving stones, lies the York Dungeon bringing more than 2,000 years of gruesomely authentic history vividly back to life...and death. As you delve into the darkest chapters of our grim and bloody past, recreated in all its dreadful detail remember - everything you experience really happened... A warning - in the dungeon's dark catacombs it always pays to keep your wits about you. The 'exhibits' have an unnerving habit of coming back to life... The journey includes features of Dick Turpin, Guy Fawkes, Witch Trials, Clifford's Tower, Pit of Despair and Gorvik - the real Viking experience.

Times: ✱ Open all year, daily 10.30-5 (closes 4.30 Oct-Mar). Closed 25 Dec. **Facilities:** P (500yds) ⅙ (wheelchair ramps, stairlifts, award winning access) toilets for disabled shop 🍺

YORK MINSTER

Deangate YO1 7EW
➲ (easy access via A19, A1 or A64)
☎ 01904 557216 ▤ 01904 557218
e-mail: visitors@yorkminster.org

Enjoy the peaceful atmosphere of the largest Gothic
cathedral in Northern Europe, a place of worship for over
1,000 years, and a treasure house of stained glass. Take an
audio tour of the Undercroft to find out more about the
Minster's fascinating history and climb the Tower for an
amazing view.
Times: Open from 7 for services. Visitors Mon-Sat 9-4.45 (9.30 in
winter), Sun noon-3.45. Phone for 2005 details. **Fee:** ✱ £4.50
(ch16 free, concessions £3). Small charge also for the Undercroft and
Tower). **Facilities:** P (440yds) & (tactile model, Braille & large print
guide) toilets for disabled shop ✖ (ex guide dogs) ▄

YORKSHIRE AIR MUSEUM & ALLIED AIR FORCES MEMORIAL

See advert on this page, see full entry under ELVINGTON.

YORKSHIRE MUSEUM

Museum Gardens YO1 7FR
➲ (park & ride service from 4 sites near
A64/A19/A1079 & A166, also 3 car parks within
short walk)
☎ 01904 551800 ▤ 01904 551802
e-mail: yorkshire.museum@york.gov.uk
The Yorkshire Museum is set in 10 acres of botanical
gardens in the heart of the historic City of York, and displays
some of the finest Roman, Anglo-Saxon, Viking and
Medieval treasures ever discovered in Britain. The
Middleham jewel, a fine example of English Gothic jewellery,
is on display, and in the Roman Gallery, visitors can see a
marble head of Constantine the Great. The Anglo-Saxon
Gallery houses the delicate silver-gilt Ormside bowl and the
Gilling sword.
Times: ✱ Open all year, daily 10-5. **Facilities:** P (5 mins walk)
& (ramps & lift) toilets for disabled shop ✖ ▄

This symbol **2-for-1**
indicates
attractions
which have chosen to
participate in our 2-for-1
voucher scheme

SOUTH YORKSHIRE

EVENTS & FESTIVALS

January
6th The Ancient Haxey Hood Game,
Doncaster

May
29th-30th Sheffield Mayfest, Hillsborough
Park, folk festival with live music & dance
(provisional)
tbc Highland Fling Country Fair,
Graves Park, Sheffield
tbc South Yorkshire Festival of Music &
Dance, Wath-upon-Dearne

June
tbc Firth Park Festival, Firth Park, Sheffield
tbc Grenoside Gala, Grenoside Park, Sheffield
tbc Sheffield Children's Festival
tbc Sheffield Festival of Transport
tbc Sheffield Motor Show,
Hillsborough Park, Sheffield

July
tbc Abbeyfield Park Multicultural Festival
tbc City Centre Carnival, Sheffield
tbc Hillsborough Gala,
Hillsborough Park, Sheffield
tbc Sharrow Festival,
family festival with music and art

August
tbc 3DOM Festival, free urban festival, Devon
Green, Sheffield

September
tbc Ecclesfield Gala, Ecclesford Park, Sheffield
tbc Sheffield Fayre, Norfolk Park

November
tbc Sheffield International Documentary
Festival

Above: Conisbrough Castle, Conisbrough

BARNSLEY   Map 08 SE30

MONK BRETTON PRIORY
S71 5QD
➲ (1m E of Barnsley town centre, off A633)
The priory was an important Cluniac house, founded in 1153.
The considerable remains of the gatehouse, church and
other buildings can be seen.
Times: Open all year, Apr-Sep, daily 10-6; Oct, daily 10-5; Nov-Mar,
daily 10-4. (Closed 24-26 Dec & 1 Jan). **Facilities:** 🅿 ♿

CONISBROUGH   Map 08 SK59

CONISBROUGH CASTLE
DN12 3HH
➲ (NE of town centre off A630)
☎ 01709 863329
The white, circular keep of this 12th-century castle is a
spectacular structure. Made of magnesian limestone, it is the
oldest of its kind in England. Recently restored, with two
new floors and a roof, it is a fine example of medieval
architecture and was the inspiration for Sir Walter Scott's
classic novel *Ivanhoe*.
Fee: Prices not confirmed for 2005 **Facilities:** 🅿 ♿ & (wheelchair
access limited) shop ✱ ♿

CUSWORTH   Map 08 SE50

THE MUSEUM OF SOUTH YORKSHIRE LIFE
CUSWORTH HALL
Cusworth Ln DN5 7TU
➲ (3m NW of Doncaster)
☎ 01302 782342 📠 01302 782342
e-mail: museum@doncaster.gov.uk
The Museum of South Yorkshire is located in Cusworth Hall,
an 18th-century country house set in a landscaped park. It
has displays which illustrate the way local people here lived,
worked and entertained themselves over the last 200 years.
Times: ✱ Open Mon-Fri 10-5, Sat 11-5 & Sun 1-5. (4pm Dec & Jan).
Closed Good Fri, Xmas & 1 Jan. Hall & Park undergoing restoration and
at times some areas may not be open to the public. Telephone for
details. **Facilities:** 🅿 ♿ & (wheelchair available) toilets for disabled
shop ✱ (ex guide dogs)

DONCASTER   Map 08 SE50

BRODSWORTH HALL & GARDENS
Brodsworth DN5 7XJ
➲ (between A635 & A638)
☎ 01302 722598 📠 01302 337165
This Victorian country house has survived largely intact.
Imagine how the serving classes fared below stairs, then
experience, in contrast, the opulent 'upstairs' apartments.
Outside, visitors can enjoy a leisurely stroll around the
extensive newly restored gardens.
Times: House: open Apr-26 Sep, Tue-Sun & Bank Hols, 1-5; Oct,
Sat-Sun, 12-4. Gardens; open Apr-Sep, Tue-Sun & Bank Hols, 12-5.30,
Mon, 11-4; Oct, Sat-Sun, 11-4.30. **Fee:** ✱ House & Gardens; £6 (ch £3,
concessions £4.50). Gardens only; £4 (ch £2, concessions £3). Prices &
opening times relate to 2004, for further details phone or log onto
www.english-heritage.org.uk/visits **Facilities:** 🅿 ♿ & toilets for
disabled shop (12-6) ✱ ♿ ▄

DONCASTER MUSEUM & ART GALLERY
Chequer Rd DN1 2AE
➲ (off inner ring road)
☎ 01302 734293   🖷 01302 735409
e-mail: museum@doncaster.gov.uk
The wide-ranging collections include fine and decorative art and sculpture. Also ceramics, glass, silver, and displays on history, archaeology and natural history. The historical collection of the Kings Own Yorkshire Light Infantry is housed here. Temporary exhibitions are held.
Times: Open all year, Mon-Sat 10-5, Sun 2-5. (Closed Good Fri, 25-26 Dec & 1 Jan). **Facilities:** 🅿 ♿ (lift, hearing loop in lecture room) toilets for disabled shop ✖ (ex guide dogs)

EARTH CENTRE
Denaby Main DN12 4EA
➲ (follow brown signs from A1M. From junct 36 follow brown Earth Centre signs along A630, then A6023 towards Mexborough. Earth Centre next right after Coniston Train Stn)
☎ 01709 513933   🖷 01709 512010
e-mail: info@earthcentre.org.uk
Earth Centre is a park for active leisure and learning with outdoor activities such as climbing, archery and canoeing. Shipwreck Island, an adventure golf course, Blue Beard's Galleon and Amazon Adventure are some of the activities to be enjoyed. Visitors can also take a guided tour on Hope's Express, the bright red road train.
Times: Open all year, daily (ex Xmas day) 10-5 (peak), 10-4 (off peak), 10-7 (school holidays). **Facilities:** 🅿 (charged) 🍴 ✖ licensed ♿ (prebooked wheelchairs/electric cars for hire) toilets for disabled shop ✖ (ex guide dogs) 🍴

MALTBY   Map 08 SK59
ROCHE ABBEY
S66 8NW
➲ (1.5m S off A634)
☎ 01709 812739
Visit the enchanting valley designed by 'Capability' Brown and discover the fascinating ruins of Roche Abbey, founded in 1147 by the Cistercians.
Times: Open Apr-Jul, Thu-Mon, 10-5; Aug, daily, 10-6; Sep, Thu-Mon, 10-5. **Fee:** ✱ £2.50 (ch £1.30, concessions £1.90). Prices & opening times relate to 2004, for further details phone or log onto www.english-heritage.org.uk/visits **Facilities:** 🅿 ♿ shop ✤

ROTHERHAM   Map 08 SK49
MAGNA SCIENCE ADVENTURE CENTRE
Sheffield Rd, Templeborough S60 1DX
➲ (M1 junct 34 , follow Templeborough sign off rdbt, then follow brown heritage signs)
☎ 01709 720002   🖷 01709 820092
e-mail: jeyre@magnatrust.co.uk
Magna is the UK's first Science Adventure Centre, an exciting exploration of Earth, Air, Fire, Water and Power. A chance for visitors to create their own adventure through hands-on interactive challenges. Visit the five Adventure Pavilions, two shows and the outdoor adventure park and have fun unearthing the mysteries of our world.
Times: Please phone for 2005 details **Facilities:** 🅿 🍴 ✖ licensed ♿ (lifts, portable seating, wheelchair hire) toilets for disabled shop ✖ (ex guide dogs) 🍴

SHEFFIELD   Map 08 SK38
BISHOPS HOUSE
Meersbrook Park, Norton Lees Ln S8 9BE
➲ (2m S of Sheffield, on A61 Chesterfield road)
☎ 0114 278 2600
e-mail: info@sheffieldgalleries.org.uk
This 15th and 16th-century yeoman's house has been restored and opened as a museum of local and social history. Several rooms have been furnished and there are displays of life in Tudor and Stuart times. Special educational facilities can be arranged for schools and colleges. Please ring for details.
Times: ✱ Open Sat 10-4.30. Sun 11-4.30 **Facilities:** 🅿 (roadside parking on nearby streets) ♿ shop ✖ (ex guide dogs)

KELHAM ISLAND MUSEUM
Alma St S3 8RY
➲ (0.5m NW of city centre, take A61 N to West Bar, follow signposts)
☎ 0114 272 2106   🖷 0114 275 7847
e-mail: postmaster@simt.co.uk
The story of Sheffield, its industry and life, with the most powerful working steam engine in Europe, reconstructed workshops, and craftspeople demonstrating traditional 'made in Sheffield' skills - this is a 'living' museum. During the year Kelham Island stages events, displays and temporary exhibitions culminating in the annual Christmas Victorian Market.
Times: ✱ Open Mon-Thu 10-4, Sun 11-4.45.Closed Fri and Sat. Check opening days/times at Christmas & New Year before travelling.
Facilities: 🅿 🍴 ♿ (wheelchair on request) toilets for disabled shop ✖

MILLENNIUM GALLERIES
Arundel Gate S1 2PP
☎ 0114 278 2600   🖷 0114 278 2604
e-mail: info@sheffieldgalleries.org.uk
With four different galleries under one roof, the Millennium Galleries has something for everyone. Enjoy new blockbuster exhibitions drawn from the collections of Britain's national galleries and museums, including the Victoria & Albert Museum and Tate Gallery. See the best of contemporary craft and design in a range of exhibitions by established and up-and-coming makers. Be dazzled by Sheffield's magnificent and internationally important collection of decorative and domestic metalwork and silverware. Discover the Ruskin Gallery with its wonderful array of treasures by Victorian artist and writer John Ruskin.
Times: ✱ Open daily Mon-Sat 10-5, Sun 11-5. **Facilities:** 🅿 🍴 ✖ licensed ♿ (hearing loop) toilets for disabled shop ✖ (ex guide dogs) 🍴

Are there any excellent Days Out that we've missed? Use the Readers' Report form at the back of the book to tell us about them.

WEST YORKSHIRE

EVENTS & FESTIVALS

March
25th Bradford Film Festival, National Museum of Photography, Film & Television
28th World Coal Carrying Championship, Royal Oak Pub, Owl Lane, Ossett

April
tbc Complementary Medicine Festival, Kings Hall Winter Gardens, Ilkley

May
14th-21st Wharfedale Music Festival, various venues in Ilkley (competitive festival of music, dance, poetry, speech and drama)
tbc Todmorden Gang Show, Todmorden

June
18th Todmorden Agricultural Show, Central Vale Park, Burnley Road, Todmorden
18th Wetherby Agricultural Show, Grange Park, Wetherby

July
1st-3rd Cleckheaton Folk Festival, various venues (provisional)
17th Arthington Show, Old Showfield, Pool Bank, Bramhope
tbc Bradford Festival & Mela, Peel Park

October/November
tbc Leeds International Film Festival, Town Hall, Leeds (provisional)

November
18th-27th Huddersfield Contemporary Music Festival
tbc Complementary Medicine Festival, Kings Hall Winter Gardens, Ilkley

Above: West Bretton's Yorkshire Sculpture Park

BRADFORD   Map 07 SE13

BOLLING HALL
Bowling Hall Rd BD4 7LP
➲ (1m from city centre off A650)
☎ 01274 723057 ▤ 01274 726220   FREE
A classic West Yorkshire manor house, complete with galleried 'housebody' (hall), Bolling Hall dates mainly from the 17th century but has medieval and 18th-century sections. It has panelled rooms, plasterwork in original colours, heraldic glass and a rare Chippendale bed.
Times: Open all year, Wed-Fri 11-4, Sat 10-5, Sun 12-5. (Closed Mon ex BH, Good Fri, 25 & 26 Dec). **Facilities:** ₽ ₺ shop ✖ (ex guide dogs)

BRADFORD INDUSTRIAL MUSEUM AND HORSES AT WORK
Moorside Mills, Moorside Rd, Eccleshill BD2 3HP
➲ (off A658)   FREE
☎ 01274 435900 ▤ 01274 636362
Moorside Mills is an original spinning mill, now part of a museum that brings vividly to life the story of Bradford's woollen industry. There is the machinery that once converted raw wool into cloth, and the mill yard rings with the sound of iron on stone as shire horses pull trams, haul buses and give rides. Daily demonstrations and changing exhibitions.
Times: Open all year, Tue-Sat 10-5, Sun 12-5. (Closed Mon ex BH, Good Fri, 25/26 Dec) **Facilities:** ₽ ⬛ ₺ (induction loop in lecture theatre, lift) toilets for disabled shop ✖ (ex guide dogs)

CARTWRIGHT HALL ART GALLERY
Lister Park BD9 4NS
➲ (1m from city centre on A650)
☎ 01274 431212 ▤ 01274 481045   FREE
e-mail: cartwright.hall@bradford.gov.uk
Built in dramatic Baroque style in 1904, the gallery has permanent collections of 19th and 20th-century British art, contemporary prints, and older works by British and European masters.
Times: Open all year, Tue-Sat 10-5, Sun 1-5. (Closed Mon ex BH, Good Fri, 25 & 26 Dec). **Facilities:** ₽ ⬛ ₺ (wheelchair available, lift) toilets for disabled shop ✖ (ex guide dogs)

COLOUR MUSEUM
Perkin House, 1 Providence St BD1 2PW
➲ (from city centre follow signs B6144 (Haworth), then follow brown heritage signs)
☎ 01274 390955 ▤ 01274 392888   2 for 1
e-mail: museum@sdc.org.uk
Europe's only Museum of Colour comprises two galleries packed with visitor-operated exhibits demonstrating the effects of light and colour, including optical illusions, and the story of dyeing and textile printing. There is a programme of special exhibitions and events. Please telephone for details.
Times: Open 2 Jan-18 Dec, Tue-Sat, 10-4. **Fee:** ✱ £2 (concessions £1.50). Family ticket £4 **Facilities:** ₽ (300 yds) ₺ (lifts, ramps at door) toilets for disabled shop ✖ (ex guide dogs) ▣

NATIONAL MUSEUM OF PHOTOGRAPHY, FILM & TELEVISION

BD1 1NQ

⮑ (2m from end of M606, follow signs for city centre)

☎ 0870 7010200 ▤ 01274 394540

e-mail: talk.nmpft@nmsi.ac.uk

Experience the past, present and future of photography, film and television with amazing interactive displays and spectacular 3D IMAX cinema.

Times: Open all year, Tue-Sun, BHs & main school hols 10-6. (Closed Mon). **Fee:** ✱ Admission to permanent galleries free, IMAX Cinema £5.95 (concessions £4.20). Groups 20% discount.

Facilities: ℙ (adjacent) 💻 ✗ licensed & (tailored tours,Braille signs,induction loop,cinema seating) toilets for disabled shop ✖ (ex guide dogs) ➡

BRAMHAM   Map 08 SE44

BRAMHAM PARK

LS23 6ND

⮑ (on A1, 4m S of Wetherby, take Bramham/Thorner slip road and follow signs)

☎ 01937 846000 ▤ 01937 846007   `2 for 1`

e-mail: enquiries@bramhampark.co.uk

This fine Queen Anne house was built by Robert Benson and is the home of his descendants. The garden has ornamental ponds, cascades, temples and avenues.

Times: Open Apr-Sep, daily 11.30-4.30. (Closed 7-14 Jun & 16 Aug-4 Sep) **Fee:** ✱ Gardens only £4 (ch under 16 & pen £2, under 5's free). House open by appointment only for groups of 10+

Facilities: ℙ & toilets for disabled

GOMERSAL   Map 08 SE22

RED HOUSE

Oxford Rd BD19 4JP

⮑ (M62 Junct 26, take A58 towards Leeds then right onto A651 towards Gomersal. Red House is on the right hand side)

☎ 01274 335100 ▤ 01274 335105

Delightful redbrick house displayed as the 1830s home of a Yorkshire wool clothier and merchant. The house and family was frequently visited by Charlotte Brontë in the 1830s and featured in her novel *Shirley*. The gardens have been reconstructed in the style of the period and there are exhibitions on the Brontë connection and local history in restored Barn and Cartsheds.

Times: ✱ Open all year, Mon-Fri 11-5, Sat-Sun 12-5. Telephone for Xmas opening. (Closed Good Fri & 1 Jan). **Facilities:** ℙ & (Braille & T-setting hearing aid available) toilets for disabled shop ✖ (ex guide dogs) ➡

HALIFAX   Map 07 SE02

BANKFIELD MUSEUM

Boothtown Rd, Akroyd Park HX3 6HG

⮑ (museum is on A647 Bradford via Queensbury road, 0.5m from Halifax town centre)

☎ 01422 354823 & 352334 ▤ 01422 349020

e-mail: bankfield-museum@calderdale.gov.uk

Built by Edward Akroyd in the 1860s, this Renaissance-style building is set in parkland on a hill overlooking the town. It has an outstanding collection of costumes and textiles from many periods and parts of the world, including a new gallery featuring East European textiles. There is also a section on toys, and the museum of the Duke of Wellington's Regiment
continued

---

is housed here. Temporary exhibitions are held and there is a lively programme of events, workshops and activities. Please ring for details.

Times: ✱ Open all year, Tue-Sat 10-5, Sun 2-5, BH Mon 10-5.(extended closing times at Xmas and New Year, phone for details) **Facilities:** ℙ & (audio guide & tactile objects) toilets for disabled shop ✖ (ex guide dogs) ➡

EUREKA! THE MUSEUM FOR CHILDREN

Discovery Rd HX1 2NE

⮑ (M62 junct 24 follow brown heritage signs to Halifax centre (A629))

☎ 01422 330069 ▤ 01422 330275

e-mail: info@eureka.org.uk

With over 400 'must touch' exhibits, interactive activities and challenges, visitors are invited to embark upon a journey of discovery through four main gallery spaces: Me and My Body, Living and Working Together, Our Global Garden and SoundSpace, an amazing new music gallery inviting children to explore the science behind sound, rhythm and technology. They can find out how their bodies and senses work, discover the realities of daily life, travel from the familiar 'backyard' to amazing and faraway places and explore the world of communications.

Times: Open all year, daily 10-5 (except 24-26 Dec) **Fee:** ✱ £5.95. (under 3's free) Family Saver ticket £27.50 **Facilities:** ℙ (charged) 💻 & (lift, staff trained in basic sign language, large print) toilets for disabled shop ✖ (ex guide dogs) ➡

PIECE HALL

HX1 1RE

⮑ (follow brown tourist signs, close to Halifax railway station)

☎ 01422 358087 ▤ 01422 349310

e-mail: karen.belshaw@calderdale.gov.uk

The merchants of Halifax built the elegant and unique hall in 1779, and it has over 300 merchant's rooms around a courtyard, now housing an industrial museum, art galleries and shops selling antiques, books etc. There is an open market on Friday and Saturday, and a flea market on Thursday. There is a lively programme of exhibitions, workshops, activities and events throughout the year, and a festival in the summer, please ring for details.

Times: ✱ Open all year daily (Closed 25-26 Dec). Art Gallery. Tue-Sun & BH Mons 10-5. **Facilities:** ℙ (50 yds) 💻 & (lifts, shopmobility on site & audio guide available) toilets for disabled shop ➡

SHIBDEN HALL

Lister's Rd HX3 6XG

⮑ (2km E of Halifax on A58)

☎ 01422 352246 & 321455 ▤ 01422 348440

e-mail: shibden.hall@calderdale.gov.uk

The house dates back to the early 15th century, and its rooms have been laid out to illustrate life in different periods of its history. Craft weekends, featuring over 30 craftworkers demonstrating historic skills, are held, and there's a lively programme of craft events, workshops and family activities. Please apply for details.

Times: Open Mar-Nov, Mon-Sat 10-5, Sun 12-5. Dec-Feb, Mon-Sat 10-4, Sun 12-4. **Facilities:** ℙ 💻 & (garden only partially accessible) toilets for disabled shop ✖ (ex guide dogs) ➡

HAREWOOD Map 08 SE34

HAREWOOD HOUSE & BIRD GARDEN
LS17 9LQ
➲ (junc A61/A659 Leeds/Harrogate road)
☎ 0113 218 1010 🖷 0113 218 1002
e-mail: business@harewood.org
Designed in 1759 by John Carr, Harewood House is the home of the Queen's cousin, the Earl of Harewood. His mother, HRH Princess Mary, Princess Royal lived at Harewood for 35 years and much of her memorabilia is still displayed. The House, renowned for its stunning architecture and exquisite Adam interiors, contains a rich collection of Chippendale furniture, fine porcelain and outstanding art collections from Italian Renaissance masterpieces and Turner watercolours to contemporary works. The old kitchen contains the best collection of noble household copperware in the country giving visitors a glimpse into below stairs life. The grounds include a restored parterre terrace, oriental rock garden, walled garden, lakeside and woodland walks, a bird garden and for youngsters, an adventure playground.
Times: Open 4 Feb-mid Nov, (grounds until mid Dec), Grounds (inc Bird Gardens) daily from 10, House from 11. **Fee:** ✱ 'Freedom ticket' (house, grounds, bird garden, terrace gallery) Mon-Sat £10 (ch £5.50, pen £8.25) Family £30.50. Sun & BH £11 (ch £6, pen £9.25) Family £33.50. Bird Garden & Grounds: £7.25 (ch £4.25 pen £6.25) Family £23. Sun & BH £8.25 (ch £5, pen £7.25) Family £26. **Facilities:** 🅿 ⬛ ✘ licensed ⅙ (electric ramp, lift, free audio tour) toilets for disabled shop ✘ (ex guide dogs or in gardens) ◼

HAWORTH Map 07 SE03

BRONTË PARSONAGE MUSEUM
BD22 8DR
➲ (A629 & A6033 follow signs for Haworth, take Rawdon Rd, pass 2 car parks, next left, then right)
☎ 01535 642323 🖷 01535 647131 `2 for 1`
e-mail: bronte@bronte.org.uk
Haworth Parsonage was the lifelong family home of the Brontës. An intensely close-knit family, the Brontës saw the parsonage as the heart of their world and the moorland setting provided them with inspiration for their writing. The house contains much personal memorabilia, including the furniture Charlotte bought with the proceeds of her literary success, Branwell's portraits of local worthies, Emily's writing desk and Anne's books and drawings.
Times: Open Apr-Sep, daily 10-5.30; Oct-Mar daily 11-5 (final admission 30 min before closing). Closed 24-27 Dec & 2-31 Jan.
Fee: ✱ £4.80 (ch 5-16 £1.50, concessions £3.50). Family ticket £10.50.
Facilities: 🅿 (charged) ⅙ (Information in large type & Braille) shop ✘ (ex guide dogs) ◼

KEIGHLEY & WORTH VALLEY RAILWAY & MUSEUM
Keighley BD22 8NJ
➲ (1m from Keighley on A629 Halifax road, look out for 'Brown Sign').
☎ 01535 645214 & 677777 🖷 01535 647317
The line was built mainly to serve the valley's mills, and goes through the heart of Brontë country. Beginning at Keighley (shared with Railtrack), it climbs up to Haworth, and terminates at Oxenhope, which has a storage and restoration building. At Haworth there are locomotive workshops and at Ingrow West, an award-winning museum.
Times: ✱ All year weekend service, but daily all BH wks & 19 Jun-1 Sep. **Facilities:** 🅿 (charged) ⬛ ⅙ (wheelchairs can be accommodated in brake car). toilets for disabled shop ◼

HUDDERSFIELD Map 07 SE11

TOLSON MEMORIAL MUSEUM
Ravensknowle Park, Wakefield Rd HD5 8DJ
➲ (on A629), 1m from town centre.
☎ 01484 223830 🖷 01484 223843
Displays on the development of the cloth industry and a collection of horse-drawn vehicles, together with natural history, archaeology, toys and folk exhibits. There is a full programme of events and temporary exhibitions.
Times: Open all year. Mon-Fri 11-5, Sat & Sun noon-5. (Closed Xmas).
Facilities: 🅿 ⅙ mini-com, partial stairlift, induction loop, parking toilets for disabled shop ✘ (ex registered guide dogs) ◼

ILKLEY Map 07 SE14

MANOR HOUSE GALLERY & MUSEUM
Castle Yard, Church St LS29 9DT
➲ (behind Ilkley Parish Church, on A65) `FREE`
☎ 01943 600066 🖷 01943 817079
This Elizabethan manor house, one of Ilkley's few buildings to pre-date the 19th century, was built on the site of a Roman fort. Part of the Roman wall can be seen, together with Roman relics and displays on archaeology. There is a collection of 17th and 18th-century farmhouse parlour and kitchen furniture, and the art gallery exhibits works by contemporary artists and craftsmen.
Times: Open all year, Tue-Sat 1-5, Sun 1-4. (Closed Good Fri, 25-28 Dec).(open BH Mons) **Facilities:** 🅿 5mins ⅙ shop ✘ (ex guide dogs)

KEIGHLEY Map 07 SE04

CLIFFE CASTLE MUSEUM & GALLERY
Spring Gardens Ln BD20 6LH
➲ (NW of town off A629)
☎ 01535 618231 🖷 01535 610536 `FREE`
French furniture from the Victoria and Albert Museum is displayed, together with collections of local and natural history, ceramics, dolls, geological items and minerals. The grounds of this 19th-century mansion have a play area and an aviary.
Times: Open all year, Tue-Sat 10-5, Sun 12-5. Open BH Mon. (Closed Good Fri & 25-28 Dec). **Facilities:** 🅿 ⬛ ⅙ toilets for disabled shop garden centre ✘ (ex guide dogs)

EAST RIDDLESDEN HALL
Bradford Rd BD20 4EA
➲ (1m NE of Keighley on south side of Bradford Rd)
☎ 01535 607075 🖷 01535 691462
e-mail: yorker@smtp.ntrust.org.uk
This charming 17th-century Yorkshire manor house is typical of its kind, although the plasterwork and oak panelling are contemporary. A small secluded garden is found in the grounds, which also feature one of the largest medieval tithe barns in the north of England.
Times: ✱ Open 23 Mar-3 Nov daily (ex Mon/Thu/Fri) open Good Fri, BH Mons and Mons in Jul/Aug 12-5 (Sat 1-5) **Facilities:** 🅿 ⬛ ⅙ shop ✘ 🐾

LEEDS   Map 08 SE33

ABBEY HOUSE MUSEUM
Abbey Walk, Abbey Rd, Kirkstall LS5 3EH
➲ (3m W of Leeds city centre on A65)
☎ 0113 230 5492   🖷 0113 230 5499
e-mail: abbeyhouse.museum@virgin.net
Displays at this museum include an interactive childhood
gallery, a look at Kirkstall Abbey, and an exploration of life in
Victorian Leeds. Three reconstructed streets allow the visitor
to immerse themselves in the sights and sounds of the late
19th century, from the glamourous art furnishers shop to the
impoverished widow washerwoman.
Times: ✱ Open all year Tue-Fri 10-5, Sat noon-5, Sun 10-5. Closed
Mon ex BH Mon (open 10-5) **Facilities:** 🅿 💷 ✕ licensed ♿ (Braille
plaques on wall, tactile tours by request) toilets for disabled shop
✖ (ex guide dogs) ◀

CITY ART GALLERY   `FREE`
The Headrow LS1 3AA
➲ (city centre, next to town hall and library)
☎ 0113 247 8248   🖷 0113 244 9689
Home to one of the best collections of 20th-century British
art outside London, as well as Victorian and late 19th-
century pictures, an outstanding collection of English
watercolours, a display of modern sculpture and temporary
exhibitions focusing on the contemporary.
Times: Open all year, Mon-Sat 10-5, Wed until 8, Sun 1-5.Closed BHs.
Facilities: 🅿 💷 ✕ licensed ♿ (restricted access to upper floor)
toilets for disabled shop ✖ (ex guide dogs)

KIRKSTALL ABBEY
Abbey Rd, Kirkstall LS5 3EH
➲ (off A65, W of city centre).
☎ 0113 230 5492   `FREE`
e-mail: abbey.house@leeds.gov.uk
The most complete 12th-century Cistercian Abbey in the
country stands on the banks of the River Aire. Many of the
original buildings can still be seen, including the cloister,
church and refectory. Regular tours take visitors to areas not
normally accessible to the public. During the summer the
Abbey hosts plays, fairs and musical events.
Times: Open all year. Abbey site open dawn-dusk.
Facilities: 🅿 ♿ toilets for disabled shop

LEEDS INDUSTRIAL MUSEUM AT ARMLEY MILLS
Canal Rd, Armley LS12 2QF
➲ (2m W of city centre, off A65)   `2 for 1`
☎ 0113 263 7861
Once the world's largest woollen mill, Armley Mills evokes
memories of the 18th-century woollen industry, showing the
progress of wool from the sheep to knitted clothing. The
museum has its own 1930s cinema illustrating the history of
cinema projection, including the first moving pictures taken
in Leeds. There are demonstrations of static engines and
steam locomotives, a printing gallery and a journey through
the working world of textiles and fashion.
Times: Open all year, Tue-Sat 10-5, Sun 1-5. Last entry 1 hr before
closing. (Closed Mon ex BHs). **Fee:** ✱ £2 (ch 50p pen, students &
UB40's £1) Friends & Family ticket £5 (2 adults & 3 ch)
Facilities: 🅿 ♿ (chair-lifts between floors) toilets for disabled shop
✖ ◀

MIDDLETON RAILWAY
Moor Rd, Hunslet LS10 2JQ
➲ (M621 junct 5 or follow signs from A61)
☎ 0113 271 0320 (ansaphone)
🖷 01977 620585
e-mail: info@middletonrailway.org.uk
This was the first railway authorised by an Act of Parliament
(in 1758) and the first to succeed with steam locomotives (in
1812). Steam trains run each weekend in season from
Tunstall Road roundabout to Middleton Park. There is a
programme of special events.
Times: ✱ Moor Road Station open for viewing every wknd. Trains run
Sat, Sun & BH, Apr-Dec. **Facilities:** 🅿 💷 ♿ (ramped access to all
areas) toilets for disabled shop ◀

ROYAL ARMOURIES MUSEUM
Armouries Dr LS10 1LT
➲ (off A61 close to Leeds centre, follow brown
heritage signs)
☎ 0113 220 1999 & 0990 106 666
🖷 0113 220 1934
e-mail: enquiries@armouries.org.uk
The museum is an impressive contemporary home for the
renowned national collection of arms and armour. The
collection is divided between five galleries: War,
Tournament, Self-Defence, Hunting and Oriental. The Hall of
Steel features a 100ft-high mass of 3000 pieces of arms and
armour. Extensive interactive displays, dramatisations of
jousting tournaments etc. and the chance to see leather
workers and armourers at work all make for an exciting day
out.
Times: ✱ Open daily, from 10-5. (Closed 24-25 Dec)
Facilities: 🅿 (charged) 💷 ✕ licensed ♿ (induction loops,
wheelchairs, signers, low level counter) toilets for disabled shop ✖ (ex
guide/hearing dogs) ◀

TEMPLE NEWSAM HOUSE & PARK
LS15 0AE   `2 for 1`
➲ (off A63)
☎ 0113 264 7321 (House) & 264 5535 (Park)
🖷 0113 260 2285
This Tudor and Jacobean mansion boasts extensive
collections of decorative arts in their original room settings,
including an incomparable Chippendale collection. Set in
1500 acres of parkland (landscaped by 'Capability' Brown),
there is a Rare Breeds Centre, and the gardens have a
magnificent display of rhododendrons. Free audio guides
tour you around the house and tell you more about the
people who lived there. On special days, visitors can join in
with the laundry maids washing at the dolly tub, watch the
blacksmith hammer out shoes and see logs cut at the sawmill.
Times: Open all year. House: Tue-Sat 10-5, Sun 1-5; Nov-28 Dec &
Mar, Tue-Sat 10-4, Sun 12-5. Open Bank Hols. Home Farm: Tue-Sun,
10-4 (3 in winter); Gardens: 10-dusk. Estate: daily, dawn-dusk.
Closed Jan-Feb re-opens 28 Feb. **Fee:** ✱ Joint ticket £5 (ch £3). Family
tickets £13 (2 ad+2 ch). **Facilities:** 🅿 (charged) 💷 ♿ ramps for full
access to parkland, wheelchairs(electric) toilets for disabled shop
✖ (ex guide dogs) ◀

THACKRAY MUSEUM

Beckett St LS9 7LN

⮑ (M1 junct 43, onto M621 junct 4. Follow signs for Harrogate & St James Hospital, follow brown tourist signs)

☎ 0113 244 4343 📠 0113 247 0219 `2 for 1`

e-mail: info@thackraymuseum.org

Housed in a large Victorian building, next to the famous St James's Hospital, the Thackray Museum offers a unique hands-on experience. A cow from Gloucester, green mould and smelly toilets - all these things have helped transform our lives. Find out how by walking back in time and exploring the sights, sounds and smells of Victorian slum life.

Times: Open all year, daily 10-5. Closed 24-26 & 31 Dec & 1 Jan

Fee: ✱ £4.90 (ch 4-16 £3.50, pen, students & unemployed £3.90). Family ticket (2 adults & 3 ch) £16. Group rates available.

Facilities: 🅿 (charged) 💺 ♿ (wheelchairs, induction loop, texts) toilets for disabled shop ✖ (ex guide dogs) ▄

TROPICAL WORLD

Canal Gardens, Roundhay Park LS8 2ER

⮑ (3m N of city centre off A58 at Oakwood)

☎ 0113 266 1850 📠 0113 237 0077 `2 for 1`

The atmosphere of the tropics is recreated here as visitors walk on the beach among exotic trees. A waterfall cascades into a rock-pool and other pools contain terrapins and carp. There are reptiles, insects and more than 30 species of butterfly. Feel the dry heat of the desert and the darkness of the nocturnal zone, and watch out for the piranhas and other exotic fish in the depths of the aquarium.

Times: Open Winter (GMT), daily 10-4 (last admission 3.30pm); Summer (BST), 10-6 (last admission 5.30pm). **Fee:** ✱ £3 (ch 8-15 £2, under 8's & Leeds card holders free). **Facilities:** 🅿 💺 ♿ toilets for disabled shop ✖ (ex guide dogs) ▄

LOTHERTON HALL   Map 08 SE43

LOTHERTON HALL   `2 for 1`

Aberford LS25 3EB

⮑ (off the A1, 0.75m E of junct with B1217)

☎ 0113 281 3259

Built in Edwardian times, the museum contains furniture, pictures, silver and ceramics from the Gascoigne collection, and works of art on loan from Leeds galleries. Outside, the Edwardian garden, bird garden and deer park are delightful places in which to stroll.

Times: Open Tue-Sat 10-5. Sun 1-5. Bank Hols. Nov-Dec & Mar Tue-Sat 10-4, Sun 12-4. **Fee:** ✱ Hall, £2 (ch, pen & students £1, unaccompanied ch 50p). Family & Friends ticket £5 (2 adults & 3 ch). Party 15+. Free admission to Bird Garden, Gardens & Parkland. Free admission to house for driver. **Facilities:** 🅿 (charged) 💺 ✖ licensed ♿ shop ✖ (ex in park) ▄

MIDDLESTOWN   Map 08 SE21

NATIONAL COAL MINING MUSEUM FOR ENGLAND

Caphouse Colliery, New Rd WF4 4RH

⮑ (on A642 between Wakefield & Huddersfield)

☎ 01924 848806 📠 01924 844567 `FREE`

e-mail: info@ncm.org.uk

A unique opportunity to go 140 metres underground down one of Britain's oldest working mines. Take a step back in time with one of the museum's experienced local miners who will guide parties around the underground workings, where models and machinery depict methods and conditions of mining from the early 1800s to present day. Other attractions include the pithead baths, Victorian steam winder, nature trail and adventure playground and meet the last ever working pit ponies. You are strongly advised to wear sensible footwear and warm clothing.

Times: Open all year, daily 10-5. (Closed 24-26 Dec & 1 Jan).

Facilities: 🅿 💺 ✖ licensed ♿ (nature trail not accessible) toilets for disabled shop ✖ (ex guide dogs) ▄

NOSTELL PRIORY   Map 08 SE41

NOSTELL PRIORY

Doncaster Rd WF4 1QE

⮑ (5m SE of Wakefield towards Doncaster, on A638)

☎ 01924 863892 📠 01924 865282

e-mail: yorknp@smtp.ntrust.org.uk

Built by Paine in the middle of the 18th century, the priory has an additional wing built by Adam in 1766. It contains a notable saloon and tapestry room, and displays pictures and Chippendale furniture. There is a lake in the grounds. Events held include the Royal British Legion Rally and a Country Fair.

Times: ✱ Open 2-17 Mar, Sat & Sun only, grounds, shop & tearoom 11-4. House closed 23 Mar-3 Nov, daily ex Mon/Tue (open Good Fri & BH Mon) 1-5.30. grounds open 11-6, shop & tearoom 11.30-5.30. 9 Nov-15 Dec: Sat/Suns only 12-4. Grounds, shop & tea room 11-4.30

Facilities: 🅿 💺 ♿ (lift, Braille guide/tactile books, w/hchair) toilets for disabled shop 🐾

OAKWELL HALL   Map 08 SE22

OAKWELL HALL

Nutter Ln, Birstall WF17 9LG

⮑ (6m SE of Bradford, off M62 junct 26/27, follow brown heritage signs, turn off A652 onto Nutter Lane)

☎ 01924 326240 📠 01924 326249

e-mail: oakwell.hall@kirklees.gov.uk

A moated Elizabethan manor house, furnished as it might have looked in the 1690s. Extensive 110-acre country park with visitor information centre, period gardens, nature trails, arboretum and children's adventure playground.

Times: Open all year, daily Mon-Fri 11-5; Sat & Sun 12-5. (ex Good Fri, 24 Dec-1 Jan). **Fee:** ✱ Hall £1.40 (ch & wheelchair users 50p). Family ticket £3. Charges Mar-Oct. Free admission Nov-Feb. Vistor centre and park free all year. **Facilities:** 🅿 💺 ♿ (herb garden for the blind, large print & Braille guide) toilets for disabled shop ✖ (park only ex guide dogs) ▄

WAKEFIELD   Map 08 SE32

WAKEFIELD ART GALLERY
Wentworth Ter WF1 3QW
➲ (N of city centre by Wakefield College and Clayton Hospital)
☎ 01924 305796 ▤ 01924 305770   **FREE**
e-mail: museumsandarts@wakefield.gov.uk

Wakefield was home to two of Britain's greatest modern sculptors - Barbara Hepworth and Henry Moore. The art gallery, which has an important collection of 20th-century paintings and sculptures, has a special room devoted to these two local artists. There are frequent temporary exhibitions of both modern and earlier works.
Times: Open all year, Tue-Sat 10.30-4.30, Sun 2-4.30.
Facilities: P (on street) (on street parking restricted to 2hrs) & shop ✖ (ex guide dogs)

WEST BRETTON   Map 08 SE21

YORKSHIRE SCULPTURE PARK
WF4 4LG
➲ (From M1 J38, follow Brown Heritage signs to the A637. Turn left at the rdbt signposted to Yorkshire Sculpture Park)
☎ 01924 832631 ▤ 01924 832600   **FREE**
e-mail: info@ysp.co.uk

Set in the beautiful grounds and gardens of a 500 acre, 18th century country estate, Yorkshire Sculpture Park is one of the
continued

world's leading open-air galleries and presents a changing programme of international sculpture exhibitions. The landscape provides a variety of magnificent scenic vistas of the valley, lakes and 18th century estate buildings and bridges. By organising a number of temporary exhibitions each year, the park ensures that there is always something new to see. The new Visitor's Centre provides all-weather facilities including a large restaurant, shop, coffee bar, audio-visual auditorium and meeting rooms.
Times: Open all year 10-6 (summer) 10-4 (winter). (please phone for details of Xmas closures) **Facilities:** P (charged) ☕ ✖ licensed & (free scooters, parking, trail accessible for wheelchairs) toilets for disabled shop ✖ (ex assist dogs)

KIRBY MISPERTON   Map 08 SE77

FLAMINGO LAND THEME PARK & ZOO
The Rectory YO17 6UX
➲ (turn off A64 onto A169, Pickering to Whitley road)
☎ 01653 668287 ▤ 01653 668280
e-mail: info@flamingoland.co.uk

Set in 375 acres of North Yorkshire countryside with over 100 rides and attractions there's something for everyone at Flamingo Land. Enjoy the thrills and spills of 12 white knuckle rides or enjoy a stroll through the extensive zoo where you'll find tigers, giraffes, hippos and rhinos. The theme park also boasts 6 great family shows.
Times: ✱ Open end Mar-2 Nov from 10. Closing times vary depending upon season. **Facilities:** P ☕ ✖ licensed & (parking, wheelchair hire) toilets for disabled shop 🍴

Above: Hebden Bridge

GUERNSEY

EVENTS & FESTIVALS

February
tbc Guernsey Eisteddfod Festival

May
8th Guernsey Classic Vehicle Show,
  Saumarez Park
9th Liberation Day Celebrations,
  St Peter Port (60th anniversary)

June
4th-12th Floral Guernsey Festival Week,
  featuring Floral Guernsey Show
  (provisional)
19th Healthspan Half Marathon,
  Pleinmont to Bulwer Avenue
tbc Little Russell Regatta

July
4th Le Viaer Marchi (the Old Market),
  traditional arts, crafts, dance and music,
  Saumarez Park
30th-6th Aug St Peter Port Town Carnival
tbc North Regatta, St Sampsons Harbour

August
17th-18th West Show, agricultural show
  (provisional)
24th-25th North Show, agricultural show &
  Battle of Flowers (provisional)

September
30th-1st Sep Guernsey Jazz Festival, Duke of
  Richmond Hotel, St Peter Port (provisional)
tbc Guernsey International Air Rally
  (provisional)

October
tbc Guernsey Lily International Amateur Film
  Festival & Video Festival,
  La Villette Hotel, St Martins

Above: Rocks at Jerbourg Point

FOREST   Map 16

GERMAN OCCUPATION MUSEUM
GY8 0BG
➲ (Behind Forest Church near the airport)
☎ 01481 238205
The museum has the Channel Islands' largest collection of
Occupation items, with tableaux of a kitchen, bunker rooms
and a street during the Occupation. Liberation Day 9th May
will be celebrated with special events and exhibitions.
Times: Open Apr-Oct 10-5, Nov-Mar 10-1 (Closed Mon).
Facilities: 🅿 💻 ♿ (ramps & handrails)

ROCQUAINE BAY   Map 16

FORT GREY AND SHIPWRECK MUSEUM
GY7 9BY
➲ (on coast road at Rocquaine Bay)
☎ 01481 265036   🖹 01481 263279   **2 for 1**
e-mail: admin@museums.gov.gg
The fort is a Martello tower, built in 1804, as part of the
Channel Islands' extensive defences. It is nicknamed the 'cup
and saucer' because of its appearance, and houses a
museum devoted to ships wrecked on the treacherous
Hanois reefs nearby.
Times: Open Apr-Sep, 10-5 **Fee:** ✱ Fort Grey, £2.50 (pen £1.25), 3
Venue Ticket £9 (pen £5) **Facilities:** 🅿 (opposite fort) shop
✘ (ex guide dogs) 🍴

ST ANDREW   Map 16

**GERMAN MILITARY UNDERGROUND HOSPITAL
& AMMUNITION STORE**
La Vassalerie GY6 8XR
➲ (St Andrews Parish, centre of island)
☎ 01481 239100
The largest structure created during the German Occupation
of the Channel Islands, a concrete maze of about 75,000 sq.
ft, which took slave workers three-and-a-half years to
complete, at the cost of many lives. Most of the equipment
has been removed, but the central heating plant, hospital
beds and cooking facilities can still be seen.
Times: Open Jul-Aug, daily 10-noon & 2-4.30; May-Jun & Sep, daily
10-noon & 2-4; Apr & Oct, daily 2-4; Mar & Nov, Sun & Thu 2-3.
Fee: ✱ £3 (ch £1). **Facilities:** 🅿 ♿ shop

We endeavour to be as
accurate as possible, but
changes to times and other
information can occur after
the guide has gone to
press.

An asterisk * indicates
that opening times and
prices are for 2004. Please
contact the attraction for
up-to-date information.

ST MARTIN Map 16

SAUSMAREZ MANOR
Sausmarez Rd GY4 6SG
➲ (Halfway between airport & St Peter Port)
☎ 01481 235571 ▤ 01481 235572
e-mail: sausmarezmanor@cwgsy **2 for 1**

The Manor has been owned and lived in by the same family
for centuries. The style of each room is different, with
collections of Oriental, French and English furniture and
paintings. Outside the Formal Garden has herbaceous
borders, and the Woodland Garden, set around two small
lakes and a stream, is planted with colourful shrubs, bulbs
and wild flowers from the subtropics. Also on view, a
sculpture park, which is now the most comprehensive in
Britain.
Times: Open Etr-Oct 10.30 & 11.30, Mon-Thu; Jun-Aug 10.30, 11.30 & 2
Mon-Thu; or by appointment. **Fee:** ✱ House £5.90 (ch £2, pen
£4.50). Woodland Garden £4 (accompanied ch & pen £3, disabled
free). Dolls House Collection £2.50 (ch £1.50, stu & pen £2). Family
ticket £7. Sculpture Park £4 (accompanied ch & pen £3, disabled free).
Facilities: ℗ �<u>▬</u> ⬤ (free admission, partial access to garden,
wheelchair loan) shop (Specialises in dolls houses etc) ✖ (ex dogs for
blind and deaf)

ST PETER PORT Map 16

CASTLE CORNET
GY1 UG
➲ (0.5m from town centre)
☎ 01481 721657 ▤ 01481 715177
e-mail: admin@museums.gov.gg **2 for 1**

The history of this magnificent castle spans eight centuries
and its buildings now house several museums, the Refectory
Cafe and a shop. Soldiers fire the noonday gun in a daily
ceremony. Look for the Maritime Museum that charts
Guernsey's nautical history, the 'Story of Castle Cornet' with
its mystery skeleton, and special exhibitions in the Royal
Guernsey Militia Museum and the 201 squadron RAF
Museum.
Times: Open Apr-Sep, daily 10-5. **Fee:** ✱ £6 (pen £4). 3 venue ticket
£9 (pen £5) **Facilities:** ℗ (100 yds) ▬ shop ✖ (ex guide dogs) ▰

GUERNSEY MUSEUM & ART GALLERY
Candie Gardens GY1 1UG
➲ (On the outskirts of St Peter Port set in the
Victorian 'Candie gardens')
☎ 01481 726518 ▤ 01481 715177
e-mail: admin@museums.gov.gg

The museum tells the story of Guernsey and its people.
There is an audio-visual theatre and an art gallery, and
special exhibitions are arranged throughout the year. It is
surrounded by beautiful gardens with superb views over St
Peter Port harbour.
Times: Open Feb-Dec daily 10-5 (Winter 10-4) **Fee:** ✱ £3.50
(pen £2.50). 3 venue ticket £9 (pen £5) **Facilities:** ℗ (outside
museum) (2hr & 5hr) ▬ ⬤ toilets for disabled shop
✖ (ex guide dogs) ▰

VALE Map 16

ROUSSE TOWER
Rousse Tower Headland
➲ (On Island's W coast, signposted)
☎ 01481 726518 & 726965 ▤ 01481 715177
e-mail: peter@museum.guernsey.net

One of the original fifteen towers built in 1778-9 in prime
defensive positions around the coast of Guernsey. They were
designed primarily to prevent the landing of troops on nearby
beaches. Musket fire could be directed on invading forces through
the loopholes. An interpretation centre displays replica guns.
Times: ✱ Open Apr-Oct 9-dusk, Nov-Mar Wed, Sat & Sun 9-4.
Facilities: ℗ ✖ (ex guide dogs)

Above: Grandes Rocques Beach

JERSEY

EVENTS & FESTIVALS

April
2nd-3rd Spring Flower Show, Royal Jersey
   Horticultural Society
2nd-10th Spring Garden Festival, guided walks
   and open gardens
16th-24th Island Flavours – a Taste of Jersey in
   Springtime, various venues

May
9th Liberation Day (60th anniversary), various
   activities and events
14th-21st Spring Walking Week, escorted
   history and heritage walks
28th-30th Country Fayre – Royal Jersey
   Showground, La Route de la Trinite, Trinity

June
11th-12th Early Summer Flower Show, Royal
   Jersey Showground, La Route de la Trinite,
   Trinity
18th-19th Early Summer Rose & Flower
   Festival, Samarès Manor

July
17th-24th Jersey in Bloom, open gardens,
   guided walks and demonstrations

August
2nd-7th Jersey International Football
   Tournament
11th-12th Jersey Battle of Flowers

September
10th-18th Seafood & Cider – a Taste of Jersey
   in Autumn, various venues
15th International Air Display
17th-25th Autumn Walking Week,
   countryside, coastal and history walks

October
7th-9th Autumn Fruit & Flower Festival, Royal
   Jersey Showground, Trinity

November
26th-4th Dec Fête dé Noué (Christmas
   festival), various activities and events

Above: Seagulls off the Jersey coast

GOREY   Map 16

MONT ORGUEIL CASTLE
JE3 6ET
➲ (A3 or coast road to Gorey)
☎ 01534 853292   ▤ 01534 854303
e-mail: marketing@jerseyheritagetrust.org
Standing on a rocky headland, on a site which has been
fortified since the Iron Age, this is one of the best-preserved
examples in Europe of a medieval concentric castle, and
dates from the 12th and 13th centuries.
Times: Open daily throughout the year 10-6; Last admission 5pm.
Times in winter change (Fri-Mon 10-dusk) **Fee:** ✱ £5.10 (ch 10-16, pen
& students £4.30, ch under 6 free). Family and discount tickets
Facilities: ⓟ (200 yds) shop ✹ (ex guide dogs) ◪

LA GREVE DE LECQ   Map 16

GREVE DE LECQ BARRACKS
JE3 3EN
➲ (on right hand side of valley, overlooking the
beach)
☎ 01534 483193 & 482238   〔FREE〕
▤ 01534 485873
e-mail: enquiries@nationaltrustjersey.org.je
Originally serving as an outpost of the British Empire, these
barracks, built in 1810, were used for civilian housing from
the end of WWI to 1972, when they were bought by the
National Trust and made into a museum that depicts the life
of soldiers who were stationed here in the 19th century. Also
includes a collection of old horse-drawn carriages.
Times: Open 4 May-26 Sep, Tue-Sat 11-5 & Sun 2-5. (Closed Mon).
Facilities: ⓟ ᕕ (wheelchair ramps) toilets for disabled shop
✹ (ex guide dogs) ▥

GROUVILLE   Map 16

LA HOUGUE BIE
JE2 7UA
➲ (A6 or A7 to Five Oaks at mini-rdbt take B28 to
site)
☎ 01534 853823   ▤ 01534 856472
e-mail: marketing@jerseyheritagetrust.org
This Neolithic burial mound stands 40ft high, and covers a stone-
built passage grave that is still intact and may be entered. The
passage is 50ft long, and built of huge stones, the mound is made
from earth, rubble and limpet shells. On top of the mound are
two medieval chapels, one of which has a replica of the Holy
Sepulchre in Jerusalem below. Also on the site is an underground
bunker built by the Germans as a communications centre.
Contact the Jersey Museum for information on special events.
Times: Open 29 Mar-end Oct, daily 10-5. **Fee:** ✱ £5.10 (student &
concession £4.30, ch under 6 free). Discount & family tickets.
Facilities: ⓟ ᕕ shop ✹ (ex guide dogs) ◪

ST BRELADE   Map 16

JERSEY LAVENDER FARM
Rue du Pont Marquet JE3 8DS
➲ (on the B25 from St Aubin's Bay to Redhouses)
☎ 01534 742933   ▤ 01534 745613
e-mail: admin@jerseylavender.co.uk
Jersey Lavenders grows nine acres of lavender, distils out the
essential oil and create a range of fine toiletry products.
Visitors are able to see the whole process from cultivating,
through to harvesting, distillation and the production of the
final product. There is a national collection of lavenders,
extensive gardens, herb beds and walks among the lavender
continued

fields. There are also other herbs that are grown and distilled, namely eucalyptus, rosemary and tea tree.
Times: Open 10 May-18 Sep, Mon-Sat 10-5. **Fee:** £3.30 (ch under 14 free). **Facilities:** P ⬛ ♿ (Free wheelchair loan) toilets for disabled shop garden centre ⬛

ST CLEMENT   Map 16

SAMARÈS MANOR
JE2 6QW
➲ (2m E of St Helier on St Clements Inner Road)
☎ 01534 870551 ▤ 01534 768949   **2 for 1**
e-mail: barbara@samaresmanor.com
The manor stands in 14 acres of beautiful gardens. The Japanese Garden occupies an artificial hill, and has a series of waterfalls cascading over Cumberland limestone. There are a craft centre, farm animals and a children's play area. Tours of the manor house, family Scavenger Hunt and medieval music.
Times: Open 3 Apr-16 Oct. **Fee:** £4.95 (ch under 16 £1.95, pen £4.50). Sat prices: £3.95 (ch under 16 £1.75, pen £3.50)
Facilities: P ⬛ ✖ licensed ♿ toilets for disabled shop garden centre ✖ (ex guide dogs) ⬛

ST HELIER   Map 16

ELIZABETH CASTLE
JE2 3WU
➲ (access by causeway or amphibious vehicle)
☎ 01534 723971 ▤ 01534 610338
e-mail: marketing@jerseyheritagetrust.org
The original Elizabethan fortress was extended in the 17th and 18th centuries, and then refortified by the Germans during the Occupation. Please telephone for details of events.
Times: Open 29 Mar-Oct, daily 10-6. Last admission 5. **Fee:** ✱ £5.10 (concessions & students £4.30, ch under 6 free). Discounts and family tickets **Facilities:** P ⬛ ♿ toilets for disabled shop ✖ (ex guide dogs) ⬛

JERSEY MUSEUM
The Weighbridge JE2 3NF
➲ (near bus station on weighbridge)
☎ 01534 633300 ▤ 01534 633301
e-mail: marketing@jerseyheritagetrust.org
Home to 'The Story of Jersey', Jersey's art gallery, an exhibition gallery which features a changing programme, a lecture theatre, and an audio-visual theatre. Special exhibitions take place throughout the year.
Times: Open all year, daily 10-5. Winter daily 10-4. (Closed 24-26 Dec & 1 Jan). **Fee:** ✱ £5.10 (ch under 6 free, students & concessions £4.30). Discount and family tickets **Facilities:** P (100yds) (paycard at most public parking) ✖ licensed ♿ (audio loop, car park) toilets for disabled shop ✖ (ex guide dogs) ⬛

See entry on page 290

MARITIME MUSEUM & OCCUPATION TAPESTRY GALLERY
New North Quay JE2 3ND
➲ (alongside Marina, opposite Liberation Square)
☎ 01534 811043 ▤ 01534 874099
e-mail: marketing@jerseyheritagetrust
This converted 19th-century warehouse houses the tapestry consisting of 12 two-metre panels that tells the story of the occupation of Jersey during World War II. Each of the 12 parishes took responsibility for stitching a panel, making it the largest community arts project ever undertaken on the island. The Maritime Museum celebrates the relationship of islanders and the sea, including an award winning hands-on experience, especially enjoyed by children.
Times: Open all year, daily 10-5 (winter closing at 4pm).
Fee: ✱ £5.95 (pen/student £5.10).Under 6's free. Discount and family tickets **Facilities:** P (paycards in public car parks) ♿ (Braille books, audio guide etc) toilets for disabled shop ✖ (ex guide dogs) ⬛

ST LAWRENCE   Map 16

GERMAN UNDERGROUND HOSPITAL
Les Charrieres Malorey JE3 1FU
➲ (bus route 8A from St Helier)
☎ 01534 860808 ▤ 01534 860886
e-mail: info@jerseywartunnels.com
On 1 July 1940 the Channel Islands were occupied by German forces, and this vast complex dug deep into a hillside is the most evocative reminder of that Occupation. A video presentation, along with a large collection of memorabilia, illustrates the lives of the islanders at war and a further exhibition records their impressions during 1945, the year of liberation.
Times: Open 14 Feb-19 Dec, daily 9.30-5.30 Last admission 4pm.
Fee: ✱ £8 (ch £4, students & serving armed forces £6 & pens £7).
Facilities: P ⬛ ✖ licensed ♿ (ramp to restaurant & lift in Visitor Centre to restaurant) toilets for disabled shop ✖ (ex guide dogs) ⬛

HAMPTONNE COUNTRY LIFE MUSEUM
La Rue de la Patente JE3 1HS
➲ (5m from St Helier on A1, A10 & follow signs)
☎ 01534 863955   🖹 01534 863935
e-mail: marketing@jerseyheritagetrust.org
Here visitors will find a medieval 17th-century home, furnished in authentic style and surrounded by 19th-century farm buildings. Guided tours every weekday. Perpetual living history interpretation and daily demonstrations.
Times: Open 29 Mar-end of Oct, daily 10-5. **Fee:** ✱ £5.10 (student & concessions £4.30, ch under 6 free). Discount and family tickets.
Facilities: 🅿 🍴 ♿ (Sensory Garden) toilets for disabled shop ✱ (ex guide dogs) 🍴

ST OUEN   Map 16
THE CHANNEL ISLANDS MILITARY MUSEUM
Five Mile Rd
➲ (Northern end of the 5 Mile Road, at the rear of the Jersey Woollen Mill & across the rd from Jersey Pearl).
☎ 01534 723136
e-mail: damienhorn@jerseymail.co.uk
The museum is housed in a German coastal defence bunker, which formed part of Hitler's Atlantic Wall. It has been restored, as far as possible, to give the visitor an idea of how it looked. The visitor can also see German uniforms, motorcycles, weapons, documents, photographs and other items from the 1940-45 occupation.
Times: Open week before Etr-Oct **Fee:** ✱ £4 (ch £2) Groups by arrangement. **Facilities:** 🅿 🍴 ♿ (All parts accessible ex 1 small room) toilets for disabled shop ✱ (ex guide dogs)

KEMPT TOWER VISITOR CENTRE
Five Mile Rd
☎ 01534 483651 & 483140   【FREE】
🖹 01534 485289
e-mail: marketing@jerseyheritagetrust.org
The centre has displays on history and the wildlife of St Ouen's Bay, including Les Mielles, which is Jersey's miniature national park. Nature walks are held every Thursday (May to September). Check local press for details.
Times: Open BH's & Apr & Oct, Thu & Sun only 2-5; May-Sep, daily (ex Mon) 2-5. **Facilities:** 🅿 shop ✱

ST PETER   Map 16
THE LIVING LEGEND
Rue de Petit Aleval JE3 7ET
➲ (From main town of St Helier. Go along main esplanade-turn right to Bel Royal. Turn left and follow road to The Living Legend signposted from the German Underground Hospital)
☎ 01534 485496   🖹 01534 485855
e-mail: info@jerseyslivinglegend.co.je
Pass through the granite archways into the landscaped gardens and the world of the Jersey Experience where Jersey's exciting past is recreated in a three dimensional spectacle. Learn of the heroes and villains, the folklore and the story of the island's links with the UK and her struggles with Europe. Other attractions include an adventure playground, street entertainment, the Jersey Craft and Shopping Village, a range of shops and the Jersey Kitchen Restaurant. Two 18 hole adventure golf courses suitable for all ages.
Times: Open daily, Mar-Nov 9.30-5, Sat-Sun 10-5 **Fee:** ✱ £7.10 (ch 7-13 £4.85, pen £6.80, student £5.50, disabled £5.60).
Facilities: 🅿 🍴 ✱ licensed ♿ (wheelchair available) toilets for disabled shop ✱ (ex guide dogs) 🍴

LE MOULIN DE QUETIVEL
St Peters Valley, Le Mont Fallu JE3 3EN
➲ (Travel out of St Helier via first tower (A1) heading W. Take the A11 through St Peter's Valley. The mill is located on the left, with the junct of Le Mont Fallu B58)
☎ 01534 483193 & 01534 745408
🖹 01534 485873
e-mail: enquiries@nationaltrustjersey.org.je
There has been a water mill on this site since 1309. The present granite-built mill was worked until the end of the 19th century, when it fell into disrepair; during the German Occupation it was reactivated for grinding locally grown corn, but after 1945 a fire destroyed the remaining machinery, roof and internal woodwork. In 1971 the National Trust for Jersey began restoration, and the mill is now producing stoneground flour again.
Times: Open 18 May-23 Sep, Tue-Thu 10-4. **Fee:** ✱ £2 (pen & students £1.50, ch under 16 free). Free entry UK National Trust card.
Facilities: 🅿 ♿ shop ✱ (ex guide dogs) 🍴

TRINITY   Map 16
DURRELL WILDLIFE CONSERVATION TRUST
Les Augres Manor, La Profunde Rue JE3 5BP
☎ 01534 860000   🖹 01534 860001
e-mail: info@durrell.org

Gerald Durrell's unique sanctuary and breeding centre for many of the world's rarest animals. Visitors can see these remarkable creatures, some so rare that they can only be found here, in modern, spacious enclosures in the gardens of the 16th-century manor house. Major attractions are the magical Aye-Ayes from Madagascar and the world-famous family of Lowland gorillas. There is a comprehensive programme of keeper talks, animal displays and activities.
Times: Open all year, daily 9.30-6 (summer)9.30-5 (winter). (Closed 25 Dec). **Fee:** ✱ £9.95 (ch 4-16 £7.25, pen £8.35). **Facilities:** 🅿 🍴 ✱ ♿ toilets for disabled shop ✱ 🍴

See advertisement on page 289

ISLE OF MAN

EVENTS & FESTIVALS

March
26th Manx Mountain Marathon, from Ramsey to Port Erin over 12 peaks

April
tbc Shennaghys Jiu (tradition today), Ramsay, dance and music festival for young people

May
28th-10th Jun Isle of Man TT Motorcycle Festival, various venues

June
tbc Mananan International Summer Festival of Music & the Arts, various venues

July
5th Tynwald Day, Tynwald Hill & Fair Field, St John's
tbc Manx International Car Rally, rallying on closed roads throughout the island
tbc Yn Chruinnaght Inter-Celtic Festival, various venues, Ramsey

August
12th-13th Royal Manx Agricultural Show, Sulby
tbc Manx Traditional Boat Festival, Peel

September
tbc Mananan International Opera Festival, Erin Arts Centre, Port Erin (provisional)

December
tbc Mananan International Winter Festival of Music & the Arts, various venues

Above: Cass-ny-Hawin Head

BALLASALLA   Map 06 SC27
RUSHEN ABBEY
IM9 3DB
➲ (In Ballasalla turn right at the Whitestone Inn, left at next rdbt, then 1st right over the bridge, car park on left)
☎ 01624 648000 📄 01624 648001
e-mail: enquiries@mnh.gov.im
The most substantial and important medieval religious site in the Isle of Man. Remains of medieval buildings, exhibitions and displays, set in beautifully landscaped gardens.
Times: ✱ Open Apr-late Oct, daily 10-5. **Facilities:** 🅿 & toilets for disabled shop ✖ (ex guide dogs) 🍴

BALLAUGH   Map 06 SC39
CURRAGHS WILD LIFE PARK
IM7 5EA
➲ (on main road halfway between Kirk Michael & Ramsey)
☎ 01624 897323 📄 01624 897327
e-mail: curraghswlp@gov.im
This park has been developed adjacent to the reserve area of the Ballaugh Curraghs and a large variety of animals and birds can be seen. A walk-through enclosure lets visitors explore the world of wildlife, including local habitats along the Curraghs nature trail. The miniature railway runs on Sundays.
Times: Open all year Etr-Oct, daily 10-6. Last admission 5pm. Oct-Etr, Sat & Sun 10-4. **Fee:** ✱ £4.50 (ch £2.50, under 5's free, pen £3). Party.
Facilities: 🅿 🖵 & (loan of wheelchair & electric wheelchair) toilets for disabled shop ✖ (ex guide dogs by arrangement)

CASTLETOWN   Map 06 SC26
CASTLE RUSHEN
The Quay IM9 1LD
➲ (centre of Castletown)
☎ 01624 648000 📄 01624 648001
e-mail: enquiries@mnh.gov.im
One of Britain's most complete medieval castles, Castle Rushen is a limestone fortress rising out of the heart of the old capital of the island, Castletown. Once the fortress of the Kings and Lords of Mann, Castle Rushen is bought alive with rich decorations, and the sounds and smells of a bygone era. In summer battles are re-enacted and the lifestyle of the period recreated by enthusiasts.
Times: ✱ Open daily, 10-5, Apr-late Oct. **Facilities:** 🅿 (100 yds) Disc Zone Parking & shop ✖ (ex guide dogs) 🍴

NAUTICAL MUSEUM
➲ (From Castletown Centre, cross the footbridge over the harbour. Museum is on the right)
☎ 01624 648000 📄 01624 648001
e-mail: enquiries@mnh.gov.im
Set at the mouth of Castletown harbour this museum is home to an 18th-century armed yacht, *The Peggy*, built by a Manxman in 1791. A replica sailmaker's loft, ship model and photographs bring alive Manx maritime life and trade in the days of sail.
Times: ✱ Open daily 10-5, Apr-late Oct. **Facilities:** 🅿 & shop ✖ (ex guide dogs) 🍴

OLD GRAMMAR SCHOOL

IM9 1LE

➲ (centre of Castletown, opposite the castle)

☎ 01624 648000 🖷 01624 648001

e-mail: enquiries@mnh.gov.im

Built around 1200AD, the former capital's first church, St Mary's, has had a significant role in Manx education. It was a school from 1570 to 1930 and evokes memories of Victorian school life.

Times: ✱ Open daily 10-5, Apr-late Oct. **Facilities:** 🅿 shop ✈ (ex guide dogs)

THE OLD HOUSE OF KEYS

IM9 1LA

➲ (opposite Castletown Rushen in centre of Castletown)

☎ 01624 648000 🖷 01624 648001

e-mail: enquiries@mnh.gov.im

The Old House of Keys is a portrayal of the long and often turbulent history of Manx politics. It has been restored to its appearance in 1866 and visitors are invited to participate in a lively debate with interactive Members of Tynwald, the Manx parliament.

Times: ✱ Open Apr-late Oct, daily 10-5. **Facilities:** 🅿 30yds disc zone parking ☂ ✈ (ex guide dogs)

CREGNEISH   Map 06 SC16

CREGNEASH VILLAGE FOLK MUSEUM

➲ (2m from Port Erin/Port St Mary, signposted)

☎ 01624 648000 🖷 01624 648001

e-mail: enquiries@mnh.gov.im

The Cregneash story begins in Cummal Beg - the village information centre where you can experience what life was really like in a Manx crofting village during the early 19th century. As you stroll around this attractive village, set in beautiful countryside, call into Harry Kelly's cottage, a Turner's shed, a Weaver's house, and the Smithy. The Manx Four-horned Loghtan Sheep can be seen grazing along with other animals from the village farm.

Times: ✱ Open Apr-late Oct, daily 10-5. **Facilities:** 🅿 ☕ shop ✈ (ex guide dogs) ◣

DOUGLAS   Map 06 SC37

MANX MUSEUM

IM1 3LY

➲ (Signposted in Douglas)

☎ 01624 648000 🖷 01624 648001

e-mail: enquiries@mnh.gov.im

The Island's treasure house provides an exciting introduction to the "Story of Mann" where a specially produced film portrayal of Manx history complements the award winning displays. Galleries depict natural history, archaeology and the social development of the Island. There are also examples of famous Manx artists in the National Art Gallery together with the Island's National archive and reference library

Times: ✱ Open daily all year, Mon-Sat 10-5. (Closed 25/26 Dec & 1 Jan). **Facilities:** 🅿 ✗ licensed ☂ (Lift) toilets for disabled shop ✈ (ex guide dogs) ◣

SNAEFELL MOUNTAIN RAILWAY

Banks Circus IM1 5PT

➲ (Manx Electric Railway from Douglas and change at Laxey)

☎ 01624 663366 🖷 01624 663637

e-mail: info@busandrail.dtl.gov.im

Snaefell is the Isle of Man's highest mountain. Running up it is Britain's oldest working mountain railway, which was laid in 1895. From the top of Snaefell, on a clear day, England, Ireland, Scotland and Wales are all visible.

Times: Open 25 Apr-25 Sep **Fee:** Various fares charged.

Facilities: 🅿 ☕ shop ◣

LAXEY   Map 06 SC48

GREAT LAXEY WHEEL & MINES TRAIL

➲ (signposted in Laxey village)

☎ 01624 648000 🖷 01624 648001

e-mail: enquiries@mnh.gov.im

Built in 1854, the Great Laxey Wheel, 22 metres in diameter, is the largest working water wheel in the world. It was designed to pump water from the lead and zinc mines and is an acknowledged masterpiece of Victorian engineering. The wheel was christened by Lady Isabella, the wife of the Lieutenant Governor of the Isle of Man.

Times: ✱ Open Apr-late Oct, daily 10-5. **Facilities:** 🅿 ☂ shop ✈ (ex guide dogs) ◣

PEEL   Map 06 SC28

HOUSE OF MANANNAN

Mill Rd IM5 1TA

➲ (In Peel follow signs to the house)

☎ 01624 648000 🖷 01624 648001

e-mail: enquiries@mnh.gov.im

This £6 million centre is an unforgettable experience. Reconstructions, interactive displays, audio visual presentations and original material explore the Celtic, Viking and maritime traditions of the Isle of Man. A visit will leave you in awe of the diversity of Manx heritage and eager to learn more.

Times: ✱ Open daily, 10-5. (Closed 25-26 Dec & 1 Jan).

Facilities: 🅿 ☂ toilets for disabled shop ✈ (ex guide dogs) ◣

PEEL CASTLE

IM5 1TB

➲ (on St Patrick's Isle, facing Peel Bay, signposted in Peel)

☎ 01624 648000 🖷 01624 648001

e-mail: enquiries@mnh.gov.im

One of the Island's principle historic centres, this great natural fortress with its imposing curtain wall set majestically at the mouth of Peel Harbour is steeped in Viking heritage. The sandstone walls of Peel Castle enclose an 11th century church and Round Tower, the 13th century St German's Cathedral and the later apartments of the Lords of Mann.

Times: ✱ Open Apr-late Oct, daily 10-5. **Facilities:** 🅿 shop ✈ (ex guide dogs)

PORT ST MARY   Map 06 SC26

SOUND VISITOR CENTRE NEW
The Sound IM1 3LY
➲ (towards Castletown, follow coastal road towards Port Erin/Port St Mary. Past Cregneash village towards most southern point of Island)
☎ 01624 648000 & 01624 838123   FREE
📠 01624 648001
e-mail: enquiries@mnh.gov.im

The Sound Visitor Centre is set in one of the Island's most scenic areas overlooking the natural wonders of the Sound and the Calf of Man. Along with information and audio presentations about the area, a new car park and high quality refreshments are provided for the enjoyment and convenience of visitors.

Times: Open daily 10-5 incl BHs. For Winter schedule contact Manx Museum 01624 648000. **Facilities:** 🅿 💺 ♿ toilets for disabled

RAMSEY   Map 06 SC49

'THE GROVE' RURAL LIFE MUSEUM
IM8 3UA
➲ (on W side of Andreas Road. Signposted in Ramsey)
☎ 01624 648000   📠 01624 648001
e-mail: enquiries@mnh.gov.im

This Victorian time capsule was a country house built as a summer retreat for a Liverpool shipping merchant. Rooms are filled with period furnishings together with a costume exhibition. In the adjacent farmyard are buildings containing displays on farming and 19th century vehicles. Around the grounds you may see Loghtan sheep, ducks and perhaps a Manx cat.

Times: ✱ Open Apr-late Oct, daily 10-5. **Facilities:** 🅿 💺 ♿ shop 🐕 (ex guide dogs) 🍴

Above: A tram from the Manx Electric Railway

SCOTLAND

EVENTS & FESTIVALS

January
31st Dec-1st Stonehaven Fireballing Festival, Stonehaven, various venues
1st Men's & Boy's 'Ba', mass football game, Kirkwall, Orkney Isles
12th-30th Celtic Connections Festival (International Celtic music festival), various venues, Glasgow
25th Up Helly Aa, Lerwick, Shetland Islands

February
tbc Glasgow Festival of Love

March
10th-26th Glagow International Comedy Festival
17th-20th StAnza Poetry Festival, St Andrews
25th-28th Edinburgh Easter Festival, free events in Princes Street Gardens and Easter Sunday parade
tbc Reivers Festival, Hawick

April
2nd-12th Edinburgh International Science Festival, various venues
15th-16th Scottish Grand National, Ayr Racecourse (provisional)
28th-1st May Shetland Folk Festival
30th Beltane Fire Festival, Carlton Hill, Edinburgh

May
19th-30th Perth Festival of the Arts
tbc Big in Falkirk, Scotland's National Street Arts Festival
tbc Scottish International Children's Festival

June
10th-26th West End Festival, Glasgow, theatre, music, exhibitions, film, markets and Midsummer Carnival
23rd-26th Royal Highland Show, Ingliston, Edinburgh
24th-25th Scottish Traditional Boat Festival, Portsoy, Banff

tbc Glasgow International Jazz Festival
tbc Highland Festival, Inverness, music, theatre, art, comedy and street events
tbc St Magnus Festival, Orkney, music, drama, dance and visual art

July
29th-7th Aug Edinburgh International Jazz & Blues Festival (provisional)
tbc Glasgow's River Festival
tbc T in the Park, Balado Airfield

August
3rd-13th Aberdeen International Youth Festival, various venues throughout the NE
7th-29th Edinburgh Festival Fringe
tbc Edinburgh International Festival
tbc Edinburgh International Film Festival
tbc Edinburgh Military Tattoo
tbc Largs Viking Festival, Largs, Lanarkshire

September
3rd Braemar Gathering, Princess Royal & Duke of Fife Memorial Park
3rd-4th Edinburgh Mela, Pilrig Park
10th RAF Leuchars Airshow, Leuchars, Fife
12th-23rd Techfest, Aberdeen, various venues
15th-17th Ayr Gold Cup, Ayr Racecourse
tbc Merchant City Festival, multi-arts festival, Glasgow

October
tbc Scottish International Storytelling Festival, Edinburgh

November
tbc Glasgay, multi-arts festival, Glasgow

December
tbc Edinburgh's Hogmanay Festival

Top: Abbey cloisters on Iona
Above: Boats at Corpach on Lochs Linnhe and Eil

ABERDEEN CITY

ABERDEEN   Map 15 NJ90

ABERDEEN ART GALLERY
Schoolhill AB10 1FQ
➲ (located in city centre)
☎ 01224 523700 ▪ 01224 632133
e-mail: info@aagm.co.uk
One of the city's most popular tourist attractions Aberdeen's splendid art gallery houses an important fine art collection with many 19th and 20th century works.
Times: ✱ Open all year Mon-Sat 10-5, Sun 2-5. Closed Xmas & New Year **Facilities:** P (500yds) ▪ & (ramp, lift) toilets for disabled shop ✖ (ex guide dogs)

ABERDEEN MARITIME MUSEUM
Shiprow AB11 5BY
➲ (located in city centre)
☎ 01224 337700 ▪ 01224 213066
e-mail: info@aagm.co.uk
The museum is in Provost Ross's House, Aberdeen's oldest building (1593). It highlights the city's maritime history, its oil industry, and its shipbuilding.
Times: ✱ Open all year Mon-Sat 10-5, Sun 12-3. Closed Xmas & New Year. **Facilities:** P (250yds) ▪ ✖ licensed & (ramps, lifts) toilets for disabled shop ✖ ▬

CRUICKSHANK BOTANIC GARDEN
University of Aberdeen, St Machar Dr AB24 3UU
➲ (enter by gate in Chanonry, in Old Aberdeen)
☎ 01224 272704 ▪ 01224 272703   FREE
e-mail: pss@abdn.ac.uk
Developed at the end of the 19th century, the 11 acres include rock and water gardens, a rose garden, a fine herbaceous border, an arboretum and a patio garden. There are collections of spring bulbs, gentians and alpine plants, and a fine array of trees and shrubs.
Times: Open all year, Mon-Fri 9-4.30; also Sat & Sun, May-Sep 2-5.
Facilities: P (200metres) & ✖

THE GORDON HIGHLANDERS MUSEUM
St Lukes, Viewfield Rd AB15 7XH
☎ 01224 311200 ▪ 01224 319323
e-mail: museum@gordonhighlanders.com
Presenting a large collection of artefacts, paintings, films and reconstructions, the Gordon Highlanders Museum is the perfect day out for anyone interested in British military history. The grounds also contain a tea-room, shop, the home and paintings of Scottish artist, Sir George Reid, and gardens.
Times: Open Apr-Oct Tue-Sat 10.30-4.30, Sun 1.30-4.30. (Closed Mon). Open by appointment only at other times. **Fee:** Prices not confirmed for 2005 **Facilities:** P ▪ & (low level cases, hearing loop) toilets for disabled shop ✖ (ex guide dogs) ▬

PROVOST SKENE'S HOUSE
Guestrow AB10 1AS
➲ (off Broad St)
☎ 01224 641086
e-mail: info@aagm.co.uk
Experience the epitome of style and elegance in this 16th-century townhouse, furnished and decorated in the styles of earlier times. See changing fashions in the Costume Gallery
continued

and view an important cycle of religious paintings in the gallery.
Times: ✱ Open all year Mon-Sat 10-5, Sun 1-4. closed Xmas & New Year. Telephone for details. **Facilities:** P (200yds) ▪ ✖ (ex guide dogs)

SATROSPHERE ("HANDS-ON" SCIENCE & TECHNOLOGY CENTRE)
179 Constitution St AB24 5TU
➲ (located very close to Aberdeen Beach Esplanade. Follow signs to fun beach, then Satrosphere)
☎ 01224 640340 ▪ 01224 622211   2 for 1
e-mail: info@satrosphere.net
Satrosphere, the Discovery Place, is different from many museums or exhibition centres. It is an Interactive Centre where everything is 'hands-on'. Displays aren't locked in glass cases and there are certainly no "Do Not Touch" signs. The emphasis is on doing and finding out, not just looking and standing back. Over 100 exhibits, interactive shows, workshops and special weekend events.
Times: Open all year, Mon-Sat 10-5, Sun 11.30-5. (Closed 25-26 Dec & 1-2 Jan). **Fee:** ✱ £5.25 (under 3's free, ch & concessions £3.75).
Facilities: P ▪ & toilets for disabled shop ✖ (ex guide dogs) ▬

PETERCULTER   Map 15 NJ80

DRUM CASTLE
AB31 5EY
➲ (3m W, off A93)
☎ 01330 811204 ▪ 01330 811962
e-mail: drum@nts.org.uk
The great 13th-century Square Tower is one of the three oldest tower houses in Scotland and has associations with Robert the Bruce. The handsome mansion, added in 1619, houses a collection of family memorabilia. The grounds contain the 100-acre Old Wood of Drum, a natural oak wood and an old rose garden.
Times: Open Apr-May & Sep, daily 12.30-5.30, Jun-Aug, daily 10-5.30. Grounds all year, daily 9.30-sunset. Times may change for 2005 please telephone or check on www.nts.org.uk **Fee:** ✱ £7 (concession £5.25) Family ticket £19. Groups adult £5.60 (child/school £1). Please book groups in advance. Garden & grounds only £2.50 (concession £1.90) Groups adult £2 (child/school £1). Admission free to NTS members. For other details please phone 0131 243 9387 or check website.
Facilities: P ▪ & (wheelchair available) shop ✖ (ex guide dogs) ♟

ABERDEENSHIRE

ALFORD   Map 15 NJ51

ALFORD VALLEY RAILWAY
AB33 8AD
➲ (A944 Alford Village)
☎ 019755 62326 & 62811 ▪ 019755 63182
Narrow-gauge passenger railway between Alford and Haughton Park, approx one mile. Steam on peak weekends. Diesel traction. Exhibitions.
Times: Open Apr, May & Sep wknds 1-5, Jun-Aug daily from 1pm (30 min service). Party bookings also available at other times.
Fee: Prices not confirmed for 2005 **Facilities:** P & (ramps at station platforms) toilets for disabled shop

CRAIGIEVAR CASTLE
AB33 8JF
➲ (On A980, 6m S of Alford)
☎ 013398 83635

A fairytale like castle, the Great Tower completed in 1626. The collection includes family portraits and 17th and 18th century furniture.
Times: Open Apr-Sep, Fri-Tue 12-5.30. Guided tours only. Grounds all year, daily 9.30-sunset. Times may change for 2005 please telephone or check on www.nts.org.uk **Fee: ✱** £9 (concession £6.50). Family ticket £23. Admission free to NTS members. For other details phone 0131 243 9387 or check website. **Facilities:** **P**

BALMORAL   Map 15 NO29

BALMORAL CASTLE GROUNDS & EXHIBITION
AB35 5TB
➲ (on A93 between Ballater & Braemar)
☎ 013397 42534 ▤ 013397 42034
e-mail: info@balmoralcastle.com

Queen Victoria and Prince Albert first rented Balmoral Castle in 1848, and Prince Albert bought the property four years later. He commissioned William Smith to build a new castle, which was completed by 1856 and is still the Royal Family's Highland residence. Country walks and pony trekking can be enjoyed, and an exhibition of paintings and other works of art can be seen in the castle ballroom, together with a Travel and Carriage exhibition and a wildlife exhibition.
Times: Open Apr-Jul, daily 10-5. **Facilities:** **P** (100yds) **▭**
& (wheelchairs & battricars available, reserved parking) toilets for disabled shop ✖ (ex guide dogs/in grounds) ◀

BANCHORY   Map 15 NO69

BANCHORY MUSEUM
Bridge St AB31 5SX
➲ (located in Bridge St beside tourist information centre, 100 yards from main car park and 25 yards from High St through Scott Skinner Square)
☎ 01771 622906 ▤ 01771 622884
e-mail: heritage@aberdeenshire.gov.uk

The museum has displays on Scott Skinner (The 'Strathspey King'), natural history, royal commemorative china, local silver artefacts and a variety of local history displays.
Times: ✱ Open May, Jun & Sep, Mon-Sat 11-1 & 2-4.30; Jul-Aug, Mon-Sat 11-1, 2-4.30 & Sun 2-4.30. Tel. for Apr & Oct opening times.
Facilities: **P** (100yds) (limited) & toilets for disabled shop ✖ (ex guide dogs)

BANFF   Map 15 NJ66

BANFF MUSEUM
High St AB45 1AE
☎ 01771 622906 ▤ 01771 622884
e-mail: heritage@aberdeenshire.gov.uk

Displays of geology, natural history, local history, Banff silver, arms and armour, and displays relating to James Ferguson (18th-century astronomer) and Thomas Edward (19th-century Banff naturalist).
Times: ✱ Open Jun-Sep, Mon-Sat 2-4.30. **Facilities:** **P** (200yds) & shop ✖ (ex guide dogs)

DUFF HOUSE
AB45 3SX
➲ (0.5m S, access south of town)
☎ 01261 818181

The house was designed by William Adam for William Duff, later Earl of Fife. The main block was roofed in 1739, but the planned wings were never built. Although it is incomplete, the house is still considered one of Britain's finest Georgian baroque buildings. Duff House is a Country House Gallery of the National Galleries of Scotland.
Times: ✱ Telephone for details of opening dates and times.
Facilities: **P** ✖ & toilets for disabled shop ✖ ◀

CORGARFF   Map 15 NJ20

CORGARFF CASTLE
AB36 8YL
➲ (8m W of Strathdon village)
☎ 01975 651460

The 16th-century tower was besieged in 1571 and is associated with the Jacobite risings of 1715 and 1745. It later became a military barracks. Its last military use was to control the smuggling of whisky between 1827 and 1831.
Times: Open all year, Apr-Sep, daily 9.30-6.30; Oct-Mar, wknds only. (Closed 25-26 Dec & 1-2 Jan). Groups 11+ 10% discount. Prices valid until 2 Jan 2005. Please telephone for further details. **Facilities:** **P** shop ◀

CRATHES   Map 15 NO79

CRATHES CASTLE & GARDEN
AB31 5QJ
➲ (On A93, 3m E of Banchory)
☎ 01330 844525 ▤ 01330 844797
e-mail: crathes@nts.org.uk

This impressive 16th-century castle with magnificent interiors has royal associations dating from 1323. There is a large walled garden and a notable collection of unusual plants, including yew hedges dating from 1702. The grounds contain six nature trails, one suitable for disabled visitors, and an adventure playground.
Times: Open: Castle & Visitor Centre: Apr-Sep, daily 10-5.30, Oct daily 10-4.30. To enjoy your visit & for safety reasons, admission to the castle is by timed ticket (limited numbers: entry may be delayed). Garden & grounds all year, daily 9-sunset. Times may change for 2005 please telephone or check on www.nts.org.uk **Fee: ✱** £9 (concessions £6.50) Admission free to NTS members. For other details please phone 0131 243 9387 or check website. **Facilities:** **P** ✖ licensed & (tape for visually impaired) toilets for disabled shop ✖ (ex guide dogs) ♨

FETTERCAIRN   Map 15 NO67

FASQUE
AB30 1DN
➲ (0.5m N on B974)
☎ 01561 340569 & 340202
▤ 01561 340325 & 340569

Fasque has been the home of the Gladstone family since 1829, and W E Gladstone, four times Prime Minister, lived here from 1830 to 1851. There are impressive state rooms and a handsome, sweeping staircase, as well as extensive servants' quarters. The spacious park has red deer and Soay sheep.
Times: ✱ Open Jul-Aug, daily 11-5. (Closed 5.30). Groups at all other times by arrangement at any other time all year round.
Facilities: **P** **▭** & (wheelchairs available) shop ✖

HUNTLY Map 15 NJ53

BRANDER MUSEUM
The Square AB54 8AE
⮕ (In centre of Huntly, sharing building with library, museum on ground floor)
☎ 01771 622906 🖷 01771 622884
e-mail: heritage@aberdeenshire.gov.uk
The museum has displays of local and church history, plus the 19th-century Anderson Bey and the Sudanese campaigns. Exhibits connected with George MacDonald, author and playwright, can also be seen.
Times: ✱ Open all year, Tue-Sat 2-4.30. **Facilities:** P (25yds) 🚻 (access difficult due to 3 large steps at entrance) shop 🦮 (ex guide dogs)

HUNTLY CASTLE
AB54 4SH
☎ 01466 793191
The original medieval castle was rebuilt a number of times and destroyed, once by Mary, Queen of Scots. It was rebuilt for the last time in 1602, in palatial style, and is now an impressive ruin, noted for its ornate heraldic decorations. It stands in wooded parkland.
Times: Open all year, Apr-Sep, daily 9.30-6.30; Oct-Mar, daily 9.30-4.30. (Closed Thu & Fri in winter, 25-26 Dec & 1-2 Jan).
Fee: ✱ £3.30 (ch £1, concessions £2.50). Groups 11+ 10% discount. Prices valid until 2 Jan 2005. Please phone for details.
Facilities: P shop 🦮

INVERURIE Map 15 NJ72

CARNEGIE MUSEUM
Town House, The Square AB51 3SN
⮕ (In centre of Inverurie, on left side of townhouse building, above library)
☎ 01771 622906 🖷 01771 622884
e-mail: heritage@aberdeenshire.gov.uk
This fine museum contains displays on local history and archaeology, including Pictish stones, Bronze Age material and the Great North of Scotland Railway.
Times: ✱ Open all year, Mon & Wed-Fri 2-4.30, Sat 10-1 & 2-4. (Closed Tue & public holidays) **Facilities:** P (50yds) shop 🦮 (ex guide dogs)

KEMNAY Map 15 NJ71

CASTLE FRASER
AB51 7LD
⮕ (off A944, 4m N of Dunecht)
☎ 01330 833463
e-mail: castlefraser@nts.org.uk
The massive Z-plan castle was built between 1575 and 1636 and is one of the grandest of the Castles of Mar. The interior was remodelled in 1838 and decoration and furnishings of that period survive in some of the rooms. A formal garden inside the old walled garden, estate trails, a children's play area and a programme of concerts are among the attractions.
Times: Open Apr-Jun & Sep, Fri-Tue 12-5.30, Jul-Aug, daily 11-5.30. Times may change for 2005 please telephone or check on www.nts.org.uk **Fee:** ✱ £7 (concessions £5.25) Groups adult £5.60, child £1, please book groups in advance. Admission free to NTS members. For other details please phone 0131 243 9387
Facilities: P 🍴 🚻 shop garden centre 🦮 (ex guide dogs, certain areas) 🦬

KILDRUMMY Map 15 NJ41

KILDRUMMY CASTLE
AB54 7XT
⮕ (10m SW of Alford)
☎ 01975 571331
An important part of Scottish history, at least until it was dismantled in 1717, this fortress was the seat of the Earls of Mar. Now it is a ruined, but splendid, example of a 13th-century castle, with four round towers, hall and chapel all discernible. Some parts of the building, including the Great Gatehouse, are from the 15th and 16th centuries.
Times: Open Apr-Sep, daily 9.30-6.30. **Fee:** ✱ £2.20 (ch 75p, concessions £1.60). Groups 11+ 10% discount. Rates valid until 2 Jan 2005. Please phone for further details. **Facilities:** P 🚻 toilets for disabled shop 🦮

KILDRUMMY CASTLE GARDENS
AB33 8RA
⮕ (on A97 off A944. 10 miles west of Alford)
☎ 019755 71277 & 71203 🖷 019755 71277
e-mail: information@
kildrummy-castle-gardens.co.uk
With the picturesque ruin as a backdrop, these beautiful gardens include an alpine garden in an ancient quarry and a water garden. There's a small museum and a children's play area.
Times: Open Apr-Oct, daily 10-5. **Fee:** ✱ £2.50 (ch free)
Facilities: P 🍴 🚻 toilets for disabled shop garden centre

MACDUFF Map 15 NJ76

MACDUFF MARINE AQUARIUM
11 High Shore AB44 1SL
⮕ (off A947 to Macduff, aquarium signposted)
☎ 01261 833369 🖷 01261 831052 `2 for 1`
e-mail: macduff.aquarium@
aberdeenshire.gov.uk
Exciting displays feature local sealife. The central exhibit, unique in Britain, holds a living kelp reef. Divers feed the fish in this tank. Other displays include an estuary exhibit, splash tank, rock pools, deep reef tank and ray pool. Young visitors especially enjoy the touch pools. There are talks, video presentations and feeding shows throughout the week.
Times: Open 10-5 daily (last admission 4.15). (Closed 25-26 Dec & 31 Dec-2 Jan) **Fee:** ✱ £4.50 (ch £2, concessions £2.50). Family ticket (2 adults & 2 ch) £11.50. Groups 10+ **Facilities:** P 🚻 (audio tour for visually impaired) toilets for disabled shop 🦮 (ex guide dogs) 🍴

MARYCULTER Map 15 NO89

STORYBOOK GLEN
AB12 5FT
⮕ (5m W of Aberdeen on B9077)
☎ 01224 732941 🖷 01224 732941
This is a child's fantasy land, where favourite nursery rhyme and fairytale characters are brought to life. Grown-ups can enjoy the nostalgia and also the 20 acres of Deeside country, full of flowers, plants, trees and waterfalls.
Times: Open Mar-Oct, daily 10-6; Nov-Feb, daily 10-4. **Fee:** ✱ £4.15 (ch £3.10, pen £3.25). **Facilities:** P 🍴 ✗ licensed 🚻 toilets for disabled shop garden centre 🦮 (ex guide dogs) 🍴

METHLICK   Map 15 NJ83

HADDO HOUSE

AB41 7EQ
➲ (off B999, 4m N of Pitmedden)
☎ 01651 851440 🖳 01651 851888
e-mail: haddo@nts.org.uk

Haddo House is renowned for its association with the Haddo Choral Society and is the venue for international concerts. It is a splendid Palladian-style mansion built in the 1730s to designs by William Adam. Home to the Earls of Aberdeen, the house was refurbished in the 1880s in the 'Adam Revival' style. The adjoining country park offers beautiful woodland walks.

Times: Open, House: Jun, Fri-Mon 11-4.30; Jul-Aug, daily 11-4.30. Guided tours only, departing set times. Garden open all year, daily 9.30-6. Times may change for 2005 please telephone or check on www.nts.org.uk **Fee:** ✱ £7 (concessions £5.25). Family ticket £19. Groups adult £5.60, child/school £1. Admission free to NTS members. For other details please phone 0131 243 9387 or check website.

Facilities: 🅿 ✗ ♿ (lift to first floor of house & wheelchair) toilets for disabled shop 🐕 (ex in grounds & guide dogs) ♨

MINTLAW   Map 15 NJ94

ABERDEENSHIRE FARMING MUSEUM

Aden Country Park AB42 5FQ
➲ (1m W of Mintlaw on A950)
☎ 01771 622906 🖳 01771 622884   FREE
e-mail: heritage@aberdeenshire.gov.uk

Housed in 19th-century farm buildings, once part of the estate which now makes up the Aden Country Park. Two centuries of farming history and innovation are illustrated, and the story of the estate is also told. The reconstructed farm of Hareshowe shows how a family in the north-east farmed during the 1950s - access by guided tour only.

Times: Open May-Sep, daily 11-4.30; Apr & Oct, wknds only noon-4.30. Last admission 30 mins before closing. Park open all year, Apr-Sep 7-10, winter 7-7. **Facilities:** 🅿 (charged) 🍴 ♿ (sensory garden) toilets for disabled shop 🐕 (ex guide dogs)

OLD DEER   Map 15 NJ94

DEER ABBEY

➲ (2m W of Mintlaw on A950)   FREE
☎ 01466 793191

The remains of the Cistercian Abbey, founded in 1218, include the infirmary, Abbot's House and the southern claustral range. The University Library at Cambridge now houses the famous Book of Deer.

Times: Open at all reasonable times. **Facilities:** 🅿 🐕 ▌

OYNE   Map 15 NJ62

ARCHAEOLINK

Berryhill AB52 6QP
➲ (1m off A96 on B9002)
☎ 01464 851500 🖳 01464 851544   2 for 1
e-mail: info@archaeolink.co.uk

A stunning audio-visual show, a Myths and Legends Gallery and a whole range of interpretation techniques help visitors to explore what it was like to live 6000 years ago. In addition there are landscaped walkways, and outdoor activity areas including an Iron Age farm, Roman marching camp and Stone Age settlement in the 40-acre park. Enjoy daily hands-on activities for all ages, guided tours with costumed guides

continued

or relax in the coffee shop. Special weekend events held regularly.

Times: Open all year, daily 11-5. **Fee:** ✱ £4.75 (ch 3-16 £3.25, concessions £4.25) Family from £11.25 **Facilities:** 🅿 🍴 ✗ licensed ♿ (induction loop in theatre, wheelchair) toilets for disabled shop 🐕 (ex guide dogs) 🍴

PETERHEAD   Map 15 NK14

ARBUTHNOT MUSEUM & ART GALLERY

St Peter St AB42 1QD
➲ (in centre of Peterhead, at St.Peter Street & Queen Street x-roads, above library)
☎ 01771 622906 🖳 01771 622884
e-mail: heritage@aberdeenshire.gov.uk

Specialising in local exhibits, particularly those relating to the fishing industry, this museum also displays Arctic and whaling specimens and a British coin collection. The regular programme of exhibitions changes approximately every six weeks.

Times: ✱ Open all year, Mon, Tue & Thu-Sat 11-1 & 2-4.30, Wed 11-1. (Closed Sun and BHs). **Facilities:** 🅿 (150 yds) shop 🐕 (ex guide dogs)

PITMEDDEN   Map 15 NJ82

PITMEDDEN GARDEN

AB41 7PD
➲ (1m W of Pitmedden on A920)
☎ 01651 842352 🖳 01651 843188
e-mail: aclipson@nts.scot.demon.co.uk

The fine 17th-century walled garden, with sundials, pavilions and fountains dotted among the parterres, has been authentically restored, and there is a Museum of Farming Life and a woodland walk.

Times: Open - May-Sep, daily 10-5.30. Grounds: all year, daily. Times may change for 2005 please telephone or check on www.nts.org.uk **Fee:** ✱ £5 (concession £3.75) Family ticket £13.50. Groups adult £4, child/school £1. Please book groups in advance. Admission free to NTS members. For other details please phone 0131 243 9387 or check website. **Facilities:** 🅿 🍴 ♿ (2 wheelchairs available) toilets for disabled shop ♨

TOLQUHON CASTLE

AB41 7LP
➲ (2m NE off B999)
☎ 01651 851286

Now roofless, this late 16th-century quadrangular mansion encloses an early 15th-century tower. There is a fine gatehouse and a splendid courtyard.

Times: Open all year, Apr-Sep, daily 9.30-6.30; Oct-Mar, wknds only. (Closed 25-26 Dec & 1-2 Jan). **Fee:** ✱ £2.20 (ch 75p, concessions £1.60). Groups 11+ 10% discount. Prices valid until 2 Jan 2005. Please phone for further details. **Facilities:** 🅿 ♿ toilets for disabled shop 🐕 ▌

RHYNIE   Map 15 NJ42

LEITH HALL & GARDEN

Kennethmont AB54 4NQ
➲ (on B9002, 1m W of Kennethmont)
☎ 01464 831216 🖳 01464 831594
e-mail: leithhall@nts.org.uk

Home of the Leith family for over 300 years, the house dates back to 1650, and has a number of Jacobite relics and fine

continued

examples of needlework. It is surrounded by charming gardens and extensive grounds.
Times: Open - House: Good Fri-Etr Mon, daily 12-5; May-Sep, Fri-Tue 12-5. Garden & grounds all year, daily 9.30-sunset. Times may change for 2005 please telephone or check on www.nts.org.uk **Fee:** ✱ £7 (concession £5.25) Family ticket £19. Garden & grounds only £2.50 (concession £1.90) Admission free to NTS members. For other details please phone 0131 243 9387 **Facilities:** 🅿 💺 ♿ (parking next to hall, scented garden for the blind) toilets for disabled ✖ (ex guide dogs) ♨

STONEHAVEN   Map 15 NO88
DUNNOTTAR CASTLE
AB39 2TL
➲ (2m S of Stonehaven on A92)
☎ 01569 762173
This once-impregnable fortress, now a spectacular ruin, was the site of the successful protection of the Scottish Crown Jewels from the might of Cromwell. A must for anyone who takes Scottish history seriously.
Times: Open all year, summer Mon-Sat 9-6, Sun 2-5; winter open Fri-Mon only. Last entry 30mins before closing. (Closed 25-26 Dec & New Year). **Fee:** ✱ £4 (ch 5-15 £1) **Facilities:** 🅿

TOLBOOTH MUSEUM
Old Pier AB39 2JU
➲ (On harbour front)
☎ 01771 622906   🖹 01771 622884
e-mail: heritage@aberdeenshire.gov.uk
Built in the late 16th century as a storehouse for the Earls Marischal at Dunnottar Castle, the building was the Kincardineshire County Tollbooth from 1600-1767. Displays feature local history and fishing.
Times: ✱ Open May-Oct, Wed-Mon, 1.30-4.30. (Closed Tue). **Facilities:** 🅿 (20yds) ♿ shop ✖ (ex guide dogs)

TURRIFF   Map 15 NJ75
FYVIE CASTLE
Fyvie AB53 8JS
➲ (8m SE of Turriff on A947)
☎ 01651 891266   🖹 01651 891107
e-mail: aclipson@nts.scot.demon.co.uk
This superb castle, founded in the 13th century, has five towers, each built in a different century, and is one of the grandest examples of Scottish Baronial. It contains the finest wheel stair in Scotland, and a 17th-century morning room, lavishly furnished in Edwarian style. The collection of portraits is exceptional, and there are also displays of arms and armour and tapestries.
Times: Open Apr-Jun & Sep, Fri-Tue 12-5; Jul-Aug, daily 11-5. Grounds all year, daily, 9.30-sunset. Times may change for 2005 please telephone or check on www.nts.org.uk **Fee:** ✱ £7 (concession £5.25) Family ticket £19. Groups adult £5.60, child/school £1. Please book groups in advance. Admission free to NTS members. For other details please phone 0131 243 9387 **Facilities:** 🅿 💺 ♿ (small lift, Braille sheets) toilets for disabled shop ✖ (ex guide dogs) ♨

ARBROATH   Map 12 NO64
ARBROATH ABBEY
DD11 1EG
☎ 01241 878756
The 'Declaration of Arbroath' - declaring Robert the Bruce as king - was signed at the 12th-century abbey on 6 April 1320. The abbot's house is well preserved, and the church remains are also interesting.
Times: Open all year, Apr-Sep, daily 9.30-6.30; Oct-Mar, daily 9.30-4.30. (Closed 25-26 Dec & 1-2 Jan). **Fee:** ✱ £3.30 (ch £1, concessions £2.50). Groups 11+ 10% discount. Prices valid until 2 Jan 2005. Please phone for further details. **Facilities:** 🅿 ♿ ✖ ♨

ARBROATH MUSEUM
Signal Tower, Ladyloan DD11 1PU
➲ (on A92 adjacent to harbour. 16m NE of Dundee)
☎ 01241 875598   🖹 01241 439263   FREE
e-mail: signal.tower@angus.gov.uk
Fish and Arbroath Smokies, textiles and engineering feature at this local history museum housed in the 1813 shore station of Stevenson's Bell Rock lighthouse.
Times: Open all year, Mon-Sat 10-5; Jul-Aug, Sun 2-5. (Closed 25-26 Dec & 1-2 Jan). **Facilities:** 🅿 ♿ (induction loop) shop ✖ (ex guide dogs)

BRECHIN   Map 15 NO66
BRECHIN TOWN HOUSE MUSEUM NEW
28 High St DD9 7AA
➲ (Turn off A90 at sign for Brechin, 2m into town centre)
☎ 01356 625536   FREE
e-mail: brechin.museum@angus.gov.uk
Within a former courtroom, debtor's prison and seat of local government, this museum covers the history of the little City of Brechin from the earliest settlement, through the market town to the industrialisation in the form of flax, jute mills, distilling, weaving and engineering. Brechin's fascinating history of development is portrayed in vivid displays.
Times: Mon & Tues, Thu-Sat 10-5, Wed 10-1 **Facilities:** 🅿 (150yds 2hrs max in free car park) ♿ toilets for disabled shop ✖ (ex guide dogs)

PICTAVIA VISITOR CENTRE
DD9 6RL
➲ (off A90)
☎ 01356 626813   🖹 01356 626814
e-mail: renniedg@angus.gov.uk
Find about more about the ancient pagan nation of the Picts, who lived in Scotland nearly 2000 years ago. Visitors can learn about Pictish culture, art and religion through film, interactive displays and music. There are also nature and farm trails, a pets' corner, and an adventure playground.
Times: Open daily; Apr-Sep, Mon-Sat 9.30-5.30, Sun 10.30-5.30; Oct-Mar, Mon-Sat 9.30-5, Sun 10-5. (Closed 25-26 Dec & 1 Jan)
Fee: £3.25 (ch & concessions £2.25) **Facilities:** 🅿 💺 ✖ licensed ♿ toilets for disabled shop garden centre ◼

CARNOUSTIE Map 12 NO53

BARRY WATER MILL
Barry DD7 7RJ
➲ (N of Barry village between A92 & A930, 2m W of Carnoustie)
☎ 01241 856761
This restored 18th-century mill works on a demonstration basis. Records show that the site has been used for milling since the 16th century. Displays highlight the important place the mill held in the community. There is a waymarked walk and picnic area.
Times: Open Apr-Oct, Fri-Tue, 12-5. Times may change for 2005 please telephone or check on www.nts.org.uk **Fee:** ✱ £5 (concessions £3.75) Adult group £4, child/school group £1. Family ticket £13.50. Admission free to NTS members. For other details please phone 0131 243 9387 or check website **Facilities:** ⓟ ₯ (ramp from car park to mill) toilets for disabled (grounds only) ㅱ

EDZELL Map 15 NO56

EDZELL CASTLE
DD9 7UE
➲ (on B966)
☎ 01356 648631
The 16th-century castle has a remarkable walled garden built in 1604 by Sir David Lindsay. Flower-filled recesses in the walls are alternated with heraldic and symbolic sculptures of a sort not seen elsewhere in Scotland. There are ornamental and border gardens and a garden house.
Times: Open all year, Apr-Sep, daily 9.30-6.30; Oct-Mar, daily 9.30-4.30. (Closed Thu & Fri in winter, 25-26 Dec & 1-2 Jan).
Fee: ✱ £3 (ch £1, concessions £2.30). Groups 11+ 10% discount. Prices valid until 2 Jan 2005. Please phone for further details.
Facilities: ⓟ ₯ shop ▮

FORFAR Map 15 NO45

THE MEFFAN ART GALLERY & MUSEUM
20 West High St DD8 1BB
➲ (turn off A90, 13m N of Dundee. The Meffan is in the town centre)
☎ 01307 464123 & 467017   FREE
🖹 01307 468451
e-mail: the.meffan@angus.gov.uk
This lively, ever-changing contemporary art gallery and museum are full of surprises. Walk down a cobbled street full of shops, ending up at a witch-burning scene! Carved Pictish stones and a diorama of an archaeological dig complete the vibrant displays.
Times: Open all year. (Closed 25-26 Dec & 1-2 Jan).
Facilities: ⓟ (150yds 30 mins limit on street) ₯ (handrails, wide door, portable ramp) toilets for disabled shop (ex guide dogs) ▰

GLAMIS Map 15 NO34

ANGUS FOLK MUSEUM
Kirkwynd Cottages DD8 1RT
➲ (off A94, in Glamis)
☎ 01307 840288 🖹 01307 840233
A row of stone-roofed, late 18th-century cottages now houses the splendid Angus Folk Collection of domestic
continued

equipment and cottage furniture. Across the wynd, an Angus stone steading houses 'The Life on the Land' exhibition.
Times: Open Apr-Jun & Sep, Fri-Tue 12-5; Jul & Aug 12-5. Times may change for 2005 please telephone or check on www.nts.org.uk **Fee:** ✱ £5 (concession £3.75) Groups adult £4, child/school group £1, groups please book in advance. Family ticket £13.50. Admission free to NTS members. For other details please phone 0131 243 9387 or check web **Facilities:** ⓟ ₯ toilets for disabled (ex guide dogs) ㅱ

GLAMIS CASTLE
DD8 1RJ
➲ (5m W of Forfar on A94)
☎ 01307 840393 🖹 01307 840733
e-mail: enquires@glamis-castle.co.uk
Glamis Castle is the family home of the Earls of Strathmore and Kinghorne and has been a royal residence since 1372. It is the childhood home of the late The Queen Mother, the birthplace of her daughter the late Princess Margaret and the setting for Shakespeare's play *Macbeth*. Though the Castle is open to visitors it remains the home of the Strathmore family.
Times: Open Mar-Oct, 10-6. Last admission 4.30. **Fee:** ✱ Castle & grounds £6.80 (ch £3.70, pen & students £5.50). Family ticket £19. Grounds only £3.50 (ch, pen & students £2.50). Group 20+
Facilities: ⓟ ✗ licensed ₯ (Castle tour not suitable as no of stairs) toilets for disabled shop (ex in grounds, guide dogs) ▰

KIRRIEMUIR Map 15 NO35

J M BARRIE'S BIRTHPLACE
9 Brechin Rd DD8 4BX
➲ (on A90/A926 6m NW of Forfar)
☎ 01575 572646
e-mail: aclipson@nts.scot.demon.co.uk
The creator of Peter Pan, Sir James Barrie, was born in Kirriemuir in 1860. The upper floors of No 9 Brechin Road are furnished as they may have been when Barrie lived there, and the adjacent house, No 11, houses an exhibition about him. The wash-house outside was his first 'theatre' and gave him the idea for Wendy's house in *Peter Pan*.
Times: Open Apr-Jun & Sep, Fri-Tue 12-5; Jul-Aug, daily 12-5. Times may change for 2005 please telephone or check on www.nts.org.uk **Fee:** ✱ £5 (concessions £3.75) Groups adult £4, child/school group £1, please book groups in advance. Family ticket £13.50. Admission free to NTS members. For other details please phone 0131 243 9387 or check web site **Facilities:** ⓟ (100yds) ▰ ₯ (stairlift, audio programmes) shop (ex guide dogs) ㅱ

KIRRIEMUIR GATEWAY TO GLENS MUSEUM NEW
The Town House, 32 High St DD8 4BB
➲ (In town centre, right in the square. 30mins from Dundee, N on A90, follow signs to Kirriemuir)
☎ 01575 575479   FREE
e-mail: kirrie.gateway@angus.gov.uk
Housed in the town house dating from 1604, this museum covers the history of Kirriemuir and the Angus Glens from prehistoric times. A realistic model of Kirriemuir on market day in 1604 can be seen and local voices can be heard telling their part in the area's history from sweet making to linen weaving. Animals and birds can be seen at close range in the Wildlife diorama.
Times: Open Mon-Wed, Fri & Sat 10-5, Thu 2-5 **Facilities:** ⓟ (200yds free car park) ₯ toilets for disabled shop (ex guide dogs)

MONTROSE   Map 15 NO75
HOUSE OF DUN
DD10 9LQ
➲ (on A935, 3m W of Montrose)
☎ 01674 810264   🖨 01674 810722
e-mail: houseofdun@nts.org.uk
This Georgian house, overlooking the Montrose Basin, was built for Lord Dun in 1730 and is noted for the exuberant plasterwork of the interior. Family portraits, fine furniture and porcelain are on display, and royal mementos connected with a daughter of King William IV and the actress Mrs Jordan, who lived here in the 19th century. There is a walled garden and woodland walks.
Times: Open - House: Apr-Jun, & Sep, Fri-Tue 12-5, Jul-Aug, daily 12-5. Garden & grounds all year daily 9.30-sunset. Times may change for 2005 please telephone or check on www.nts.org.uk **Fee:** ✱ £7 (concession £5.25) Family ticket £19. Groups adult £5.60, child/school £1. Please book groups in advance. Admission free to NTS members. For other details please phone 0131 243 9387 or check web site **Facilities:** 🅿 ✖ ⚬ (Braille sheets, house wheelchair & stair lift) toilets for disabled shop ✖ (ex guide dogs) ☒

MONTROSE MUSEUM & ART GALLERY
Panmure Place DD10 8HE
➲ (opposite Montrose Academy in town centre, approach via A92 from Aberdeen or Dundee)
☎ 01674 673232   FREE
e-mail: montrose.museum@angus.gov.uk
Extensive local collections cover the history of Montrose from prehistoric times, the maritime history of the port, the natural history of Angus, and local art.
Times: Open all year, Mon-Sat 10-5. (Closed 25-26 Dec & 1-2 Jan). **Facilities:** 🅿 ⚬ shop ✖ (ex guide dogs)

ARGYLL & BUTE

ARDUAINE   Map 10 NM71
ARDUAINE GARDEN
PA34 4XQ
➲ (20m S of Oban, on A816)
☎ 01852 200366   🖨 01852 200233
An outstanding 18-acre garden on a promontory bounded by Loch Melfort and the Sound of Jura, climatically favoured by the North Atlantic Drift. It is famous for its rhododendrons and azalea species and other rare trees and shrubs.
Times: Open all year, daily 9.30-sunset. Reception Apr-Sep 9.30-4.30. Times may change for 2005 please telephone or check on www.nts.org.uk **Fee:** ✱ £3.50 (concessions £2.60) Groups adult £2.80, child/school £1, please book in advance. Family ticket £9.50. Admission free to NTS members. For other details please phone 0131 243 9387 or check web site. **Facilities:** 🅿 ⚬ toilets for disabled ✖ (ex guide dogs) ☒

ARROCHAR   Map 10 NN20
ARGYLL FOREST PARK
Forest Enterprise, Ardgartan Visitor Centre G83 7AR
➲ (on A83 at the foot of "The Rest and Be Thankful")
☎ 01301 702597   🖨 01301 702597   FREE
e-mail: robin.kennedy@forestry.gsl.gov.uk
This park extends over a large area of hill ground and forest, noted for its rugged beauty. Numerous forest walks and picnic sites allow exploration; the Arboretum walks and the
continued

route between Younger Botanic Gardens and Puck's Glen are particularly lovely.
Times: Open all year. **Facilities:** 🅿 shop 🍴

AUCHINDRAIN   Map 10 NN00
AUCHINDRAIN TOWNSHIP-OPEN AIR MUSEUM
PA32 8XN
➲ (6m SW of Inverarary on A83)
☎ 01499 500235
Auchindrain is an original West Highland township of great antiquity, and the only communal tenancy township to have survived on its centuries-old site. The buildings are furnished and equipped to present a fascinating glimpse of Highland life in the last century.
Times: Open Apr-Sep, daily 10-5. **Fee:** £4.50 (ch £2.20, pen £3.50). Family ticket £12. **Facilities:** 🅿 Access possible, but difficult shop

BARCALDINE   Map 10 NM94
SCOTTISH SEA LIFE SANCTUARY
PA37 1SE
➲ (10m N of Oban on A828, towards Fort William)
☎ 01631 720386   🖨 01631 720529   2 for 1
e-mail: obansealife@merlinentertainments.biz
Set in one of Scotland's most picturesque locations, the Scottish Sea Life Sanctuary provides dramatic views of native undersea life including stingrays, seals, octopus and catfish. There are daily talks and feeding demonstrations and during the summer young seals can be viewed prior to their release back into the wild. Recent additions include Otter Creer - a large naturally landscaped enclosure with deep diving pool with underwater viewing and cascading streams through other pools 'into the deep', a themed interactive area displaying living creatures from the deep. There is a restaurant, gift shop, children's play park and a nature trail.
Times: Open all year, mid Feb-Nov, daily 10-5. Dec & Jan, Sat, Sun & school holidays only. **Fee:** £7.95 (ch £5.50, pen £6.50). Group 15+. **Facilities:** 🅿 🖥 ✖ ⚬ (assistance available for wheelchairs) toilets for disabled shop ✖ (ex guide dogs) 🍴

BENMORE   Map 10 NS18
BENMORE BOTANIC GARDEN
PA23 8QU
➲ (7m N of Dunoon on A815)
☎ 01369 706261   🖨 01369 706369
e-mail: benmore@rbge.org.uk
From the formal gardens, through the hillside woodlands, follow the paths to a stunning viewpoint with a spectacular outlook across the garden and the Holy Loch to the Firth of Clyde and beyond. Amongst many highlights are the stately conifers, the magnificent avenue of Giant Redwoods, and an extensive magnolia and rhododendron collection.
Times: Open Mar-Oct, daily, 10; Mar & Oct, close 5. Apr-Sep, close 6. **Fee:** ✱ £3.50 (ch £1, concessions £3). Family £8. Party rates. **Facilities:** 🅿 🖥 ✖ licensed ⚬ Assistance dogs welcome toilets for disabled shop garden centre ✖ (on short lead) 🍴

CARNASSERIE CASTLE   Map 10 NM80
CARNASSERIE CASTLE
PA31 8RQ
➲ (2m N of Kilmartin off A816)
A handsome combined tower house and hall, home of John Carswell, first Protestant Bishop of the Isles and translator of the first book printed in Gaelic. Very fine architectural details of the late 16th century.
Times: Open at all reasonable times. **Facilities:** ✖ ▌

GIGHA ISLAND Map 10 NR64

ACHAMORE GARDENS
PA41 7AD

☎ 01583 505267 & 505254 ▤ 01583 505244
e-mail: william@isle-of-gigha.co.uk

Wonderful woodland gardens of rhododendrons and azaleas, created by Sir James Horlick, who bought the little island of Gigha in 1944. Many of the plants were brought in laundry baskets from his former home in Berkshire. Sub-tropical plants flourish in the rich soil and virtually frost-free climate, and there is a walled garden for some of the finer specimens.

Times: ✽ Open all year, daily. **Facilities:** ▣ &

HELENSBURGH Map 10 NS28

THE HILL HOUSE
Upper Colquhoun St G84 9AJ
➲ (off B832, between A82 & A814)
☎ 01436 673900 ▤ 01436 674685

The Hill House is a handsome example of Charles Rennie Mackintosh's work, modern but part-inspired by Scottish tower houses. It was commissioned by the publisher Walter Blackie. The gardens are being restored to Blackie's design, with features reflecting the suggestions of Mackintosh. There is also a special display about Mackintosh.

Times: Open Apr-Oct, daily 1.30-5.30. Morning visits available for pre-booked groups. Times may change for 2005 please telephone or check on www.nts.org.uk **Fee:** ✽ £7 (concessions £5.25). Family ticket £19. For other details phone 0131 243 9387 or check web site **Facilities:** ▣ ▣ shop ✖ ♨

INVERARAY Map 10 NN00

BELL TOWER OF ALL SAINTS' CHURCH
The Avenue PA32 8YX
➲ (through the arches on Front St, into Avenue car park)
☎ 01546 602315 ▤ 01546 602519
e-mail: dean.sedati@virgin.net

The tower was built in the 1920s and stands at 126ft. It has the world's second heaviest ring of ten bells, installed as a Campbell War Memorial in 1931. An exhibition on campanology is mounted inside and visiting bell ringers give recitals, usually once a month. A splendid view rewards those who climb to the roof.

Times: Open Etr-Sep, daily 10-1 & 2-5. **Facilities:** ▣ (adjacent to tower) & ✖ (ex guide dogs)

INVERARAY CASTLE
PA32 8XE
➲ (on A83 Glasgow to Campbeltown road)
☎ 01499 302203 ▤ 01499 302421
e-mail: enquiries@inveraray-castle.com

The third Duke of Argyll engaged Roger Morris to build the present castle in 1743; in the process the old Burgh of Inveraray was demolished and a new town built nearby. The 5th Duke commissioned the beautiful interior decoration. The great armoury hall and staterooms are of particular note.

Times: Open 1st Sat in Apr-last Sun in Oct. Apr-May, Oct, Mon-Thu & Sat 10-1 & 2-5.45. Sun 1-5.45; Jun-Sep, Mon-Sat 10-5.45, Sun 1-5.45. Last admission 12.30 & 5. **Fee:** ✽ £5.90 (ch under £3.90, concessions £4.90) Family ticket £16. School parties. Groups 20+. **Facilities:** ▣ ▣ & toilets for disabled shop ✖ (ex guide dogs) ▦

INVERARAY JAIL
Church Square PA32 8TX
➲ (on A82/A83 main Campbeltown road)
☎ 01499 302381 ▤ 01499 302195
e-mail: inverarayjail@btclick.com

Enter Inveraray Jail and step back in time. See furnished cells and experience prison sounds and smells. Ask the 'prisoner' how to pick oakum. Turn the heavy handle of an original crank machine, take 40 winks in a hammock or listen to Matron's tales of day-to-day prison life. Visit the magnificent 1820 courtroom and hear trials in progress. Imaginative exhibitions including 'Torture, Death and Damnation' and 'In Prison Today'. New at Inveraray Jail, a fully preserved "Black Maria", built in 1891.

Times: Open all year, Nov-Mar, daily 10-5 (last admisssion 4); Apr-Oct, daily 9.30-6 (last admission 5). (Closed 25 Dec & 1 Jan). **Fee:** £5.75 (ch £2.80, pen £3.75). Family ticket £15.70. **Facilities:** ▣ (100 yds) & (wheelchair ramp at rear, induction loop in courtroom) toilets for disabled shop ▦

KILMARTIN Map 10 NR89

DUNADD FORT
➲ (2m S of Kilmartin on A816)

Dunadd was one of the ancient capitals of Dalriada from which the Celtic kingdom of Scotland was formed. Near to this prehistoric hill fort (now little more than an isolated hillock) are carvings of a boar and a footprint; these probably marked the spot where early kings were invested with their royal power.

Times: Open at all reasonable times. **Facilities:** ✖ ▥

KILMARTIN HOUSE MUSEUM
PA31 8RQ
➲ (in centre of village, adjacent to church)
☎ 01546 510278 ▤ 01546 510330
e-mail: museum@kilmartin.org

Kilmartin may seem to be a quiet Scottish village, but at least 150 prehistoric sites lie within six miles of it. There are mysterious carved rocks, enigmatic standing stones, fascinating burial cairns and the fortress of the earliest Scottish Kings. Thousands of years of history are traced in a museum that explores ancient peoples' struggles for survival, their attempts to understand the world around them, early agriculture, and social strife in the shape of aggression and conflict. There is also an audio-visual extravaganza that uses 12 projectors to project 600 slides in 16 minutes. The presentation deals with the history and beauty of the landscape of Mid Argyll.

Times: Open daily 10-5.30. (Closed 25 Dec & 1 Jan) **Facilities:** ▣ ▣ & toilets for disabled shop ✖ (ex guide dogs) ▦ ▦

LOCHAWE Map 10 NN12

CRUACHAN POWER STATION
Dalmally PA33 1AN
➲ (A85 18m E of Oban) **2 for 1**
☎ 01866 822618 ▤ 01866 822509
e-mail: visit.cruachan@scottishpower.com

A vast cavern hidden 1km inside Ben Cruachan, which contains a 400,000-kilowatt hydro-electric power station, driven by water drawn from a high-level reservoir up the mountain. A guided tour takes you inside the mountain and reveals the generators in their underground cavern.

Times: Open Etr-Nov, daily 9.30-5 (last tour 4.15). Aug 9.30-6 (last tour 5.15) **Fee:** £4 (ch 6-16 £1.50, concessions £3) **Facilities:** ▣ ▣ & toilets for disabled shop ✖ (ex guide dogs) ▦

MINARD — Map 10 NR99

CRARAE GARDENS
PA32 8YA
➲ (10m S of Inveraray on A83)
☎ 01546 886614 📠 01546 886614
Set beside Loch Fyne, these gardens are among Scotland's loveliest, noted for their rhododendrons, azaleas, conifers and ornamental shrubs, which include a number of rare species.
Times: Open all year, daily, 9-sunset. Visitor centre, Etr-Oct, daily 10-5. Times may change for 2005 please telephone or check on www.nts.org.uk **Fee:** ✱ £3.50 (concession £2.60). Family ticket £9.50. Groups adult £2.80, child/school £1. Please book groups in advance. Admission free to NTS members. For other details phone 0131 243 9387 or check web site. **Facilities:** 🅿 ♨ ⚹ toilets for disabled shop garden centre ⬛

OBAN — Map 10 NM83

DUNSTAFFNAGE CASTLE
PA37 1PZ
➲ (3m N on peninsula)
☎ 01631 562465
Now ruined, this four-sided stronghold has a gatehouse, two round towers and walls 10ft thick. It was once the prison of Flora MacDonald.
Times: Open all year, Apr-Sep, daily 9.30-6.30; Oct-Mar, daily 9.30-4.30. (Closed Thu & Fri in winter, 25-26 Dec & 1-2 Jan).
Fee: ✱ £2.50 (ch 75p, concessions £1.90). Groups 11+ 10% discount. Prices valid until 2 Jan 2005. Please phone for further details.
Facilities: 🅿 shop ▮

TAYNUILT — Map 10 NN03

BONAWE IRON FURNACE
PA35 1JQ
➲ (0.75m NE off B845)
☎ 01866 822432
The furnace is a restored charcoal blast-furnace for iron-smelting and making cast-iron. It was established in 1753 and worked until 1876. The works exploited the Forest of Lorne to provide charcoal for fuel.
Times: Open Apr-Sep, daily 9.30-6.30. **Fee:** ✱ £3 (ch £1, concessions £2.30). Groups 11+ 10% discount. Rates valid until 2 Jan 2005. Please telephone for further details. **Facilities:** 🅿 ♨ toilets for disabled shop ▮

The Hotel Guide 2005 — Britain's best-selling hotel guide for all your leisure needs. *Just AAsk.*
www.theAA.com

BALERNO — Map 11 NT16

MALLENY GARDEN
EH14 7AF
➲ (off Lanark Rd (A70))
☎ 0131 449 2283
The delightful gardens are set round a 17th-century house (not open to the public). Shrub roses, a woodland garden, and a group of four clipped yews, survivors of a group planted in 1603, are among its notable features. The National Bonsai Collection for Scotland is also at Malleny.
Times: Garden: all year daily 10-6 or dusk if earlier. House not open. Times may change for 2005 please telephone or check on www.nts.org.uk **Fee:** ✱ £2 (concession £1). Admission free to NTS Members. For other details please phone 0131 243 9387 or check web site. **Facilities:** 🅿 ♨ ⚹ (ex guide dogs) ⚐

EDINBURGH — Map 11 NT27

BRASS RUBBING CENTRE
Trinity Apse, Chalmers Close, High St EH1 1SS
➲ (located on the Royal Mile)
☎ 0131 556 4364 📠 0131 557 3364
Housed in the 15th-century remnant of Trinity Apse, the Centre offers the chance to make your own rubbing from a wide range of replica monumental brasses and Pictish stones. Tuition is available.
Times: Open Apr-Sep, Mon-Sat 10-5 (during Edinburgh Festival Sun 12-5). **Facilities:** 🅿 (250mtrs) (parking meters, few spaces) shop ⚹ (ex guide dogs)

CAMERA OBSCURA & WORLD OF ILLUSIONS
Castlehill, Royal Mile EH1 2ND
➲ (next to Edinburgh Castle)
☎ 0131 226 3709 📠 0131 225 4239
e-mail: info@camera-obscura.co.uk
A unique view of Edinburgh - as the lights go down, a brilliant moving image of the surrounding city appears. The scene changes as a guide operates the camera's system of revolving lenses and mirrors.
Times: ✱ Open all year, daily, Apr-Oct 9.30-6; Nov-Mar 10-5. (Closed 25 Dec). Open later Jul-Aug, phone for details.
Facilities: 🅿 (300mtrs) shop ⚹ (ex guide dogs) ⬛

CITY ART CENTRE
2 Market St EH1 1DE
➲ (opposite rear of Waverley Stn)
☎ 0131 529 3993 📠 0131 529 3986
e-mail: enquiries@city-art-centre.demon.uk
The City Art Centre houses the city's permanent fine art collection and stages a constantly changing programme of temporary exhibitions from all parts of the world. It has six floors of display galleries (linked by an escalator).
Times: Open Mon-Sat 10-5 (& Sun 12-5 Jul-Aug).
Facilities: 🅿 (500yds) (single yellow lines) ♨ ♨ (induction loop, lifts, Braille signage, escalator) toilets for disabled shop ⚹ (ex guide dogs) ⬛

CRAIGMILLAR CASTLE
EH16 4SY
➲ (2.5m SE, off A68)
☎ 0131 661 4445
Mary, Queen of Scots retreated to this 14th-century stronghold after the murder of Rizzio. The plot to murder Darnley, her second husband, was also hatched here. There are 16th and 17th century apartments.
Times: Open all year, Apr-Sep, daily 9.30-6.30; Oct-Mar, daily 9.30-4.30. (Closed Thu & Fri in winter, 25-26 Dec & 1-2 Jan).
Fee: ✱ £2.50 (ch 75p, concessions £1.90). Groups 11+ 10% discount. Prices valid until 2 Jan 2005. Please phone for further details.
Facilities: 🅿 & toilets for disabled shop ▯

DEAN GALLERY
73 Belford Rd EH4 3DS
➲ (20 min walk from Edinburgh Haymarket stn & Princes St)
☎ 0131 624 6200 🖷 0131 343 3250
e-mail: enquiries@nationalgalleries.org
Opened in March 1999, the Dean Gallery provides a home for the Eduardo Paolozzi gift of sculpture and graphic art, the Gallery of Modern Art's renowned Dada and Surrealist collections, a major library and archive centre, along with temporary exhibition space for modern and contemporary art.
Times: ✱ Open all year, Mon-Sat 10-5, Sun 12-5. Extended opening during Edinburgh Festival. (Closed 25-26 Dec). **Facilities:** 🅿 🅿 & (ramps & lift) toilets for disabled shop ✖ (ex guide dogs) ◀

DYNAMIC EARTH
Holyrood Rd EH8 8AS
➲ (on edge of Holyrood Park, opposite Palace of Holyrood House)
☎ 0131 550 7800 🖷 0131 550 7801   **2 for 1**
e-mail: enquiries@dynamicearth.co.uk
Dynamic Earth explores the extremes of planet Earth. Travel back in time to witness the Big Bang and feel the earth shake by an erupting volcano. Fly over glaciers, feel the chill of polar ice and get caught in a tropical rainstorm.
Times: Open Apr-Oct daily & Nov-Mar Wed-Sat 10-5, (last entry 3.50); Jul-Aug daily, 10-6, (last entry 4.50). (Closed 24-26 Dec). **Fee:** £8.95 (ch £5.45). Family ticket (2ad & 2ch) £24.50. **Facilities:** 🅿 (charged) 🅿 ✖ licensed & (audio guides, large print gallery guides) toilets for disabled shop ✖ (ex guide dogs) ◀

EDINBURGH CASTLE
EH1 2NG
☎ 0131 225 9846
This historic stronghold stands on the precipitous crag of Castle Rock. One of the oldest parts is the 11th-century chapel of the saintly Queen Margaret, but most of the present castle evolved later, during its stormy history of sieges and wars, and was altered again in Victorian times. The Scottish crown and other royal regalia are displayed in the Crown Room. Also notable is the Scottish National War Memorial.
Times: Open all year, Apr-Sep daily 9.30-6.30; Oct-Mar 9.30-4.30. (Closed 25-26 Dec & 1-2 Jan). **Fee:** ✱ £9.50 (ch £2, concessions £7). Prices valid until 2 Jan 2005. Please phone for further details.
Facilities: 🅿 (charged) 🅿 ✖ licensed & (free transport to top of Castle Hill lift) toilets for disabled shop ✖ ▯

THE EDINBURGH DUNGEON
31 Market St EH1 1QB
➲ (Close to Waverly Train Station)
☎ 0131 240 1000 & 240 1002
🖷 0131 240 1002   **2 for 1**
e-mail: edinburghdungeon@ merlinentertainments.biz
From the same team at The London Dungeon, there comes a Scottish "feast of fun with history's horrible bits". A mixture of live actors, rides, shows and special effects take the brave visitor back into a dark past that includes such delights as the 18th-century Judgement of Sinners, the 17th-century Plague, and the new attraction, Clan Wars, which attempts to recreate the horror of the Glencoe Massacre of 1692.
Times: Open all year (ex 25 Dec). Nov-Feb 11-4, wknds 10.30-4.30, Mar 10.30-4.30, Apr-Jun 10-5, Jul-Aug 10-7, Sep-Oct 10-5.
Fee: ✱ £9.95(ch 4-9 £4.95, ch 10-14 £6.95) **Facilities:** 🅿 (100mtrs) (Metered bays limited to 1-2hrs) & toilets for disabled shop ✖ (ex guide dogs) ◀

EDINBURGH ZOO
Murrayfield EH12 6TS
➲ (3m W of City Centre on A8 towards Glasgow)
☎ 0131 334 9171 🖷 0131 314 0382
e-mail: marketing@rzss.org.uk
Scotland's largest wildlife attraction, set in 80 acres of leafy hillside parkland, just ten minutes from the city centre. With over 1,000 animals ranging from the tiny poison arrow frog to massive white rhinos, including many threatened species. See the world's largest penguin pool with underwater viewing, and the Darwin Maze, based on the theme of evolution.
Times: Open all year, Apr-Sep, daily 9-6; Oct & Mar, daily 9-5; Nov-Feb, daily 9-4.30. **Fee:** £8.50 (ch 3-14 & disabled £5.50, student £6.50, pen £6). **Facilities:** 🅿 (charged) 🅿 ✖ licensed & (wheelchair loan free, 1 helper free - phone in advance) toilets for disabled shop ✖ (ex guide dogs) ◀

GEORGIAN HOUSE
7 Charlotte Square EH2 4DR
➲ (2 mins walk W end of Princes Street)
☎ 0131 226 3318 🖷 0131 226 3318
e-mail: thegeorgianhouse@nts.org.uk
The house is part of Robert Adam's splendid north side of Charlotte Square, the epitome of Edinburgh New Town architecture. The lower floors of No 7 have been restored in the style of the early 1800s, when the house was new. There also videos of life in the New Town, and this house in particular.
Times: Open Apr-Oct, daily 10-5; Mar & Nov-24 Dec daily 11-3. Times may change for 2005 please telephone or check on www.nts.org.uk **Fee:** ✱ £5 (concessions £3.75) Family ticket £13.50. Groups adult £4, (child/school £1). Please book groups in advance. Admission free for NTS members. For other details please phone 0131 243 9387 or check web site. **Facilities:** 🅿 (100 yds) (meters. disabled directly outside) & (induction loop, Braille guide) shop ✖ (ex guide dogs) ❦

GLADSTONE'S LAND
477b Lawnmarket EH1 2NT
➲ (5 mins walk from Princes Street via Mound)
☎ 0131 226 5856 🖷 0131 226 4851
Built in 1620, this six-storey tenement, once a merchant's house, still has its arcaded front - a rare feature now. Visitors can also see unusual tempera paintings on the walls and ceilings. It is furnished as a typical 17th-century merchant's

continued

home, complete with ground-floor shop front and goods of the period.

Times: Open Apr-Oct, Mon-Sat, 10-5, Sun 2-5. Times may change for 2005 please telephone or check on www.nts.org.uk **Fee:** ✱ £3.50 (concession £2.60) Family ticket £9.50. Groups adult £2.80, child/school £1. Please book groups in advance. Admission free to NTS members. For other details please phone 0131 243 9387 or check web site. **Facilities:** P (440yds) (outside for disabled) ♿ (tours for the blind can be arranged) shop ✕ (ex guide dogs) 🐾

JOHN KNOX HOUSE

The Netherbow, 43-45 High St EH1 1SR
➲ (between The Castle and Holyrood House)
☎ 0131 556 9579 📠 0131 557 5224

John Knox the Reformer is said to have died in the house, which was built by the goldsmith to Mary, Queen of Scots. Renovation work has revealed the original floor in the Oak Room, and a magnificent painted ceiling.

Times: ✱ Open all year, Mon-Sat 10-5 & Sun in Jul -Aug 12-5. (Closed Xmas). Phone for details. **Facilities:** P (5 min walk) (paying car park) ♿ (transcript of tapes for deaf, tours for blind, with notice) toilets for disabled shop ✕ (ex guide dogs) 🍴

LAURISTON CASTLE

Cramond Rd South, Davidson's Mains EH4 5QD
➲ (NW outskirts of Edinburgh, 1m E of Cramond overlooking the Forth at Silverknowles)
☎ 0131 336 2060 📠 0131 312 7165

The castle is a late 16th-century tower house with 19th-century additions but is most notable as a classic example of the Edwardian age. It has a beautifully preserved Edwardian interior and the feel of a country house, and the spacious grounds are very pleasant.

Times: Open all year by guided tour only; Apr-Oct, 11-1 & 2-5; Nov-Mar, wknds 2-4. (Closed Fri). **Facilities:** P ♿ toilets for disabled shop ✕ (ex guide dogs)

MUSEUM OF CHILDHOOD

42 High Street, Royal Mile, EH1 1TG
➲ (On the Royal Mile)
☎ 0131 529 4142 📠 0131 558 3103

One of the first museums of its kind, it was reopened after major expansion. It has a wonderful collection of toys, games and other belongings of children through the ages, to delight visitors both old and young. Ring for details of special events.

Times: Open all year, Mon-Sat, Jun-Sep 10-6; Oct-May 10-5; (also Sun 12-5 in Jul-Aug). **Facilities:** P ♿ (3 floors only) toilets for disabled shop ✕ (ex guide dogs)

MUSEUM OF EDINBURGH

142 Canongate, Royal Mile EH8 8DD
➲ (located on the Royal Mile)
☎ 0131 529 4143 📠 0131 557 3346

Housed in one of the best-preserved 16th-century buildings in the Old Town. It was built in 1570 and later became the headquarters of the Incorporation of Hammermen. Now a museum of local history, it has collections of silver, glassware, pottery, and other items such as street signs.

Times: Open all year, Mon-Sat 10-5. (During Festival period only, Sun 2-5). **Facilities:** P (200yds) (parking meters, limited spaces) ♿ shop ✕ (ex guide dogs)

MUSEUM OF SCOTLAND

Chambers St EH1 1JF
☎ 0131 247 4219 📠 0131 220 4819
e-mail: info@nms.ac.uk

The museum is a striking new landmark in Edinburgh's historic Old Town. It houses more than 10,000 of the nation's most precious artefacts, as well as everyday objects which throw light on life in Scotland through the ages. Admission to the Royal Museum which is adjacent to the Museum of Scotland is also free. Telephone for details of special events.

Times: Open all year, Mon, Wed-Sat 10-5, Tue 10-8 & Sun 12-5. **Facilities:** P 🍽 ✕ licensed ♿ toilets for disabled shop ✕ (ex assist dogs) 🍴

NATIONAL GALLERY OF SCOTLAND

The Mound EH2 2EL
➲ (off Princes Street)
☎ 0131 624 6200 📠 0131 343 3250
e-mail: enquiries@nationalgalleries.org

Occupying a handsome neo-classical building designed by William Playfair, the gallery is home to Scotland's greatest collection of European paintings and sculpture from the Renaissance to Post-Impressionism. It contains notable collections of works by Old Masters, Impressionists and Scottish artists.

Times: ✱ Open all year, Mon-Sat 10-5, Sun 12-5. Extended opening hours during the Edinburgh Festival period. (Closed 25-26 Dec). **Facilities:** P (150yds) ♿ (ramps & lift, room A1 not accessible) toilets for disabled shop ✕ (ex guide dogs) 🍴

NATIONAL WAR MUSEUM OF SCOTLAND

Edinburgh Castle EH1 2NG
☎ 0131 225 7534 📠 0131 225 3848
e-mail: info@nms.ac.uk

Explore the Scottish experience of war and military service over the last 400 years.

Times: Open all year, daily, Apr-Oct, 9.45-5.45; Nov-Mar, daily, 9.45-4.45 **Facilities:** P ♿ toilets for disabled shop ✕ (ex assist dogs)

NELSON MONUMENT

Calton Hill EH7 5AA Calton Hill
➲ (Overlooking end of city)
☎ 0131 556 2716 📠 0131 557 3346

Designed in 1807 the monument dominates the east end of Princes Street. The views are superb, and every day except Sunday the time ball drops at 1pm as the gun at the castle goes off.

Times: Open all year, Apr-Sep, Mon 1-6 & Tue-Sat 10-6; Oct-Mar Mon-Sat 10-3. **Facilities:** P shop ✕ (ex guide dogs)

PALACE OF HOLYROODHOUSE

EH8 8DX
➲ (at east end of Royal Mile)
☎ 0131 556 5100 📠 020 7930 9625
e-mail: holyrood@royalcollection.org.uk

The Palace grew from the guest house of the Abbey of the Holyrood, said to have been founded by David I after a miraculous apparition. Mary, Queen of Scots had her court here from 1561 to 1567, and 'Bonnie' Prince Charlie held levees at the Palace during his occupation of Edinburgh. The Palace is still used by the Royal Family, but can be visited when they are not in residence. The picture gallery is notable for its series of Scottish Monarchs.

Times: ✱ Open daily, Apr-Oct 9.30-6 (last admission 5.15); Nov-Mar 9.30-4.30 (last admission 3.45). Closed 25-26 Dec and when The Queen is in residence. **Fee:** ✱ £8 (ch 17 £4, pen & students £6.50). Family ticket (2ad+3ch) £20. Under 5's free **Facilities:** 🅿 (charged) 🅿 ♿ (first floor by lift, wheelchair available) toilets for disabled shop 🐕 (ex guide dogs) ◀

PARLIAMENT HOUSE

Supreme Courts, 2-11 Parliament Square EH1 1RQ
➲ (behind St Giles Cathedral)
☎ 0131 225 2595 📠 0131 240 6755

Scotland's independent parliament last sat in 1707, in this 17th-century building hidden behind an 1829 façade, now the seat of the Supreme Law Courts of Scotland. A large stained glass window depicts the inauguration of the Court of Session in 1540.

Times: ✱ Open all year, Mon-Fri 10-4. **Facilities:** 🅿 (400 mtrs) metered parking in high street 🅿 ✗ ♿ toilets for disabled 🐕 (ex guide dogs)

THE PEOPLE'S STORY

Canongate Tolbooth, 163 Canongate, Royal Mile
EH8 8BN
➲ (On the Royal Mile)
☎ 0131 529 4057 📠 0131 556 3439

The museum, housed in the 16th-century tolbooth, tells the story of the ordinary people of Edinburgh from the late 18th century to the present day. Reconstructions include a prison cell, 1930s pub and 1940s kitchen supported by photographs, displays, sounds and smells.

Times: Open, Mon-Sat 10-5. Also, open Sun Sun during Edinburgh Festival 2-5. **Facilities:** 🅿 (100yds) (parking meters) ♿ (lift, induction loop in video room, touch facilities) toilets for disabled shop 🐕 (ex guide dogs)

The End of World War II.

2005 sees the 60th anniversary of both VE (Victory in Europe) and VJ (Victory over Japan) Days. Local celebrations are planned, as are a number of national events.

THE REAL MARY KING'S CLOSE

2 Warriston's Close, High St EH1 1PG
➲ (off High Street, opposite St. Giles Cathedral)
☎ 08702 430160 📠 0131 225 0671
e-mail: info@realmarykingsclose.co.uk

Step back in time to walk through a warren of hidden streets, deep beneath The Royal Mile. Meet some of the real characters who used to inhabit these closes and hear tales of extraordinary apparitions as you are guided through dramatic episodes from Edinburgh's hidden past.

Times: Open all year daily, tours run every 20mins from 10am. Last tour Apr-Oct 9pm, Nov-Mar 4pm Sun-Fri & 9pm Sat (Closed 25 Dec) **Fee:** ✱ £7 (ch £5, pen & student £6). Family ticket (2 adults + 2 ch) £21 **Facilities:** 🅿 ♿ toilets for disabled shop 🐕 (ex guide dogs) ◀

ROYAL BOTANIC GARDEN EDINBURGH

20A Inverleith Row EH3 5LR
➲ (1m N of city centre, off A902)
☎ 0131 552 7171 📠 0131 248 2901 `FREE`
e-mail: info@rbge.org.uk

Established in 1670, on an area the size of a tennis court, the Garden is now over 70 acres of beautifully landscaped grounds. Spectacular features include the Rock Garden and the Chinese Hillside. The amazing glasshouses feature Britain's tallest palm house and the magnificent woodland gardens and arboretum.

Times: Open all year, daily; Apr-Sep, 10-7; Mar & Oct, 10-6; Nov-Feb, 10-4. (Closed 25 Dec & 1 Jan). Facilities close 30 mins before the Garden. **Facilities:** 🅿 (restricted at certain times) 🅿 ✗ licensed ♿ (wheelchairs available at east/west gates) toilets for disabled shop garden centre 🐕 (ex guide dogs) ◀

ROYAL MUSEUM

Chambers St EH1 1JF
➲ (5min from Edinburgh Castle and the Royal Mile in city centre)
☎ 0131 247 4219 (info) 📠 0131 220 4819
e-mail: info@nms.ac.uk

This magnificent museum houses extensive international collections covering the Decorative Arts, Natural History, Science, Technology and Working Life, and Geology. Temporary exhibitions, films, lectures and concerts take place throughout the year.

Times: Open all year, Mon-Sat 10-5, Sun 12-5 (Tue late opening till 8). (Closed 25 Dec. Phone for times on 26 Dec/1 Jan). **Facilities:** 🅿 🅿 ✗ licensed ♿ (induction loops) toilets for disabled shop 🐕 (ex assist dogs) ◀

THE ROYAL YACHT BRITANNIA
Ocean Terminal, Leith EH6 6JJ
⮑ (Follow signs to North Edinburgh & Leith.
Situated within Ocean Terminal)
☎ 0131 555 5566 📄 0131 555 8835
e-mail: enquiries@tryb.co.uk

Visit the Royal Yacht Britannia, now in Edinburgh's historic port of Leith. The experience starts in the Visitor Centre where you can discover Britannia's fascinating story. Then step aboard for a self-led audio tour which takes you around five decks giving you a unique insight into what life was like for the Royal Family, Officers and Yachtsmen. Highlights include the State Apartments, Admirals Cabin, Engine Room, Laundry, Sick Bay and Royal Marine Barracks.
Times: Open Jan-Mar & Oct-Dec: 10-3.30 (close 5). Apr-Sep 9.30-4.30 (close 6). Closed 25 Dec & 1 Jan **Fee:** ✱ £8 (ch under 5 free, 5-17 £4, pen £6). Family ticket (2 ad & 3 ch) £20. **Facilities:** 🅿 ♿ (lift to ship, all areas ramped, written scripts) toilets for disabled shop ✖ (ex guide dogs) 🍴

SCOTCH WHISKY HERITAGE CENTRE
354 Castlehill, The Royal Mile EH1 2NE
☎ 0131 220 0441 📄 0131 220 6288
e-mail: enquiry@whisky-heritage.co.uk
This fascinating heritage centre reveals the history of the Scottish Whisky industry. The tour has four main areas: The Making of Scotch Whisky, The Distillery, The Blender's Ghost, and Whisky Barrel Ride. The Whisky Bond Bar has over 280 different whiskies available.
Times: Open daily, 10-5.30 (extended in summer). (Closed 25 Dec).
Fee: £7.95 (ch 5-17 £4.25, concessions £5.95). Family ticket £18 **Facilities:** 🅿 (100m) metered parking & NCP 🍴♿ (Braille script) toilets for disabled shop ✖ (ex guide dogs) 🍴

SCOTTISH NATIONAL GALLERY OF MODERN ART
Belford Rd EH4 3DR
⮑ (in West End, 20min walk from Haymarket station)
☎ 0131 624 6200 📄 0131 343 3250
e-mail: enquiries@nationalgalleries.org
An outstanding collection of 20th-century painting, sculpture and graphic art. Includes major works by Matisse, Picasso, Bacon, Moore and Lichtenstein and an exceptional group of Scottish paintings. Set in leafy grounds with a sculpture garden.
Times: ✱ Open all year, Mon-Sat 10-5 & Sun 12-5. Extended opening hours during the Edinburgh Festival. (Closed 25-26 Dec).
Facilities: 🅿 🍴♿ (ramps & lift) toilets for disabled shop ✖ (ex guide dogs) 🍴

SCOTTISH NATIONAL PORTRAIT GALLERY
1 Queen St EH2 1JD
⮑ (parallel to Princes Street, just behind St Andrew Square)
☎ 0131 624 6200 📄 0131 558 3691
e-mail: enquiries@nationalgalleries.org
The collection provides a visual history of Scotland from the 16th century to the present day, told through the portraits of the people who shaped it. Among the most famous are Mary, Queen of Scots, Ramsay's portrait of David Hume and Raeburn's Sir Walter Scott. The building also houses the National Collection of Photography.
Times: ✱ Open all year, daily, Mon-Sat 10-5, Sun 12-5. Extended opening hours during the Edinburgh Festival. (Closed 25-26 Dec).
Facilities: 🅿 (200yds) 🍴♿ (ramps & lift) toilets for disabled shop ✖ (ex guide dogs) 🍴

THE WRITERS' MUSEUM
Lady Stair's House, Lady Stair's Close, Lawnmarket EH1 2PA
⮑ (off the Royal Mile)
☎ 0131 529 4901 📄 0131 220 5057
e-mail: enquiries@writersmuseum.demon.co.uk
Situated in the historic Lady Stair's House which dates from 1622, the museum houses various objects associated with Robert Burns, Sir Walter Scott and Robert Louis Stevenson. Temporary exhibitions are planned throughout the year.
Times: Open all year, Mon-Sat 10-5. (During Festival period only, Sun 2-5). **Facilities:** 🅿 (500mtrs) (parking meters) shop ✖ (ex guide dogs)

GOGAR   Map 11 NT17
SUNTRAP GARDEN
43 Gogarbank EH12 9BY
⮑ (between A8 & A71 W of city bypass)
☎ 0131 339 7283 📄 0131 339 2891 **2 for 1**
e-mail: suntrap@btopenworld.com
The three-acre garden comprises of many gardens within a single garden, including Italian, Rock, Peat and Woodland.
Times: Open all year: Oct-Apr, 10-4; May-Sep, 10-6 **Fee:** ✱ £1 (accompanied ch and NT members free). **Facilities:** 🅿 ♿ (limited access wknds to toilet facilities toilets for disabled) garden centre (open Mon-Fri)

SOUTH QUEENSFERRY   Map 11 NT17
DALMENY HOUSE
EH30 9TQ
☎ 0131 331 1888 📄 0131 331 1788
e-mail: events@dalmeny.co.uk
This is the home of the Earl and the Countess of Rosebery, whose family have lived here for over 300 years. The house, however, dates from 1815 when it was built in Tudor Gothic style. There is fine French furniture, tapestries and porcelain from the Rothschild Mentmore collection. Early Scottish furniture is also shown, with 18th-century portraits, Rosebery racing mementoes, a display of pictures and one of the world's most important Napoleonic collections.
Times: Open Jul-Aug, Sun, Mon & Tue 2-5.30. Last admission 4.30. Open other times by arrangement for groups. **Fee:** ✱ £5 (ch 10-16 £3, pen & students £4). Party 20+. **Facilities:** 🅿 🍴♿ toilets for disabled ✖ (ex guide dogs or in grounds)

HOPETOUN HOUSE
EH30 9SL
➲ (2m W of Forth Road Bridge, off A904)
☎ 0131 331 2451   📋 0131 319 1885
e-mail: marketing@hopetounhouse.com

Hopetoun House at South Queensferry is just a short drive from Edinburgh and has all the ingredients for a great family day out. Whether it is a leisurely stroll, afternoon tea or a touch of nostalgia you crave, Hopetoun will fit the bill. Built some 300 years ago, it is a delight to wander the corridors and historical rooms of one of the most splendid examples of the work of Scottish architects Sir William Bruce and William Adam. It shows some of the finest examples in Scotland of carving, wainscoting and ceiling painting. With 100 acres of parkland including a deep park, the gardens are a colourful carpet of seasonal flowers. After a gentle walk, indulge yourself with a traditional tea and a browse through our shop.
Times: Open daily Etr-Sep **Fee:** ✱ £6.50 (ch £3.50). Grounds £3.50 (ch £2). **Facilities:** 🅿 💷 ৬ (ramps) toilets for disabled shop 🝙

INCHCOLM ABBEY
Inchcolm Island
➲ (1.5m S of Aberdour. Access by ferry Apr-Sep)
☎ 01383 823332

Situated on a green island on the Firth of Forth, the Augustinian abbey was founded in about 1192 by Alexander I. The well-preserved remains include a fine 13th-century octagonal chapter house and a 13th-century wall painting.
Times: Open Apr-Sep, daily 9.30-6.30. **Fee:** ✱ £3 (ch £1, concessions £2.30). Additional charge for ferry trip. Groups 11+ 10% discount. Rates valid until 2 Jan 2005. Please phone for further details.
Facilities: ৬ toilets for disabled shop 🝙 🖈

QUEENSFERRY MUSEUM
53 High St EH30 9HP
➲ (A90 from Edinburgh)
☎ 0131 331 5545   📋 0131 557 3346   `FREE`

The museum commands magnificent views of the two great bridges spanning the Forth and traces the history of the people of Queensferry and Dalmeny, the historic passage to Fife, the construction of the rail and road bridges and the wildlife of the Forth estuary. An ancient annual custom, in August, is Burry Man, who is clad from head to toe in burrs, and parades through the town. See the full size model of the Burry Man in the museum.
Times: Open all year, Mon & Thu-Sat 10-1, 2.15-5 (Sun noon-5). Last admission 1/2 hour before closing. Closed 25 & 26 Dec, 1& 2 Jan
Facilities: 🅿 (0.25m) ৬ (Induction loop at reception) shop 🝙 (ex guide dogs)

CITY OF GLASGOW

GLASGOW   Map 11 NS56
BURRELL COLLECTION
2060 Pollokshaws Rd G43 1AT
➲ (3.5m S of city centre)
☎ 0141 287 2550   📋 0141 287 2597   `FREE`
e-mail: museums@cls.glasgow.gov.uk

Set in Pollok Country Park, this award-winning building makes the priceless works of art on display seem almost part of the woodland setting. Shipping magnate Sir William Burrell's main interests were medieval Europe, Oriental art and European paintings. Colourful paintings and stained glass show the details of medieval life. Furniture, paintings, sculpture, armour and weapons help to complete the picture.

continued

Rugs, ceramics and metalwork represent the art of Islam. There is also a strong collection of Chinese and other Oriental ceramics. Paintings on display include works by Bellini, Rembrandt and the French Impressionists.
Times: Open all year, Mon-Thu & Sat 10-5, Fri & Sun 11-5. (closed 24-25 & 31 [pm] Dec, 1-2 Jan) **Facilities:** 🅿 (charged) 💷 ✘ licensed ৬ (wheelchairs available, tape guides, lifts) toilets for disabled shop 🝙

CLYDEBUILT
Braehead Shopping Centre, King Inch Rd G51 4BN
➲ (M8 junct 25A, 26, follow signs for Braehead Shopping Centre, then the Green car park)
☎ 0141 886 1013   📋 0141 886 1015
e-mail: clydebuilt@tinyworld.co.uk

On the banks of the River Clyde, home of the Scottish shipbuilding industry, visitors can discover how Glasgow's famous ships were built, from the design stages through to the launch. There are also displays on the textile and cotton industries, iron and steel, and tobacco. Hands-on activities allow you to operate a real ship's engine, become a ship's riveter, and steer a virtual ship up the Clyde.
Times: Open Mon-Thu & Sat 10-5.30; Sun 11-5. (Closed Fri, open on local hols) **Fee:** £3.50 (ch & concessions £1.75). Family ticket £8
Facilities: 🅿 ৬ (lift/ramps/wheelchairs from shopping centre) toilets for disabled shop 🝙 (ex guide dogs)

GALLERY OF MODERN ART
Royal Exchange Square G1 3AH
➲ (centre of Glasgow, just off Buchanan St & close to Central Station & Queen Street Stn)
☎ 0141 229 1996   📋 0141 204 5316   `FREE`
e-mail: museums@cls.glasgow.gov.uk

GoMA offers a thought-provoking programme of temporary exhibitions and workshops. It displays work by local and international artists, as well as addressing contemporary social issues through its major bi-annual projects.
Times: Open all year, Mon-Tue & Sat 10-5, Thu 10-8, Fri & Sun 11-5.
Facilities: 🅿 (200yds) 💷 ৬ toilets for disabled shop 🝙 (ex guide dogs)

GLASGOW CATHEDRAL
Castle St G4 0QZ
➲ (M8 junct 15, in centre of Glasgow)
☎ 0141 552 6891   `FREE`

The only Scottish mainland medieval cathedral to have survived the Reformation complete (apart from its western towers). Built during the 13th to 15th centuries over the supposed site of the tomb of St Kentigern. Notable features in this splendid building are the elaborately vaulted crypt, which included an introductory display and collection of carved stones, the stone screen of the early 15th century and the unfinished Blackadder Aisle.
Times: Open all year, Apr-Sep daily 9.30-6.30; Oct-Mar daily 9.30-4.30. (Closed 25-26 Dec & 1-2 Jan). **Facilities:** ৬ (telephone for disabled access details) shop 🝙 🖈

GLASGOW MUSEUMS RESOURCE CENTRE
200 Woodhead Rd, South Nitshill Ind Estate G53 7NN
➲ (on S side of Glasgow. Close to Rail Stn)   `FREE`
☎ 0141 276 9300   📋 0141 276 9305

GMRC is the first publicly-accessible store for the city's museum service, offering a behind-the-scenes look at 200,000 treasures held in storage. Please note that access to the stores is by guided tour only. Viewings of a specific

continued

object can be arranged, with two weeks prior notice. Activities, tours and talks are held throughout the year - see website or phone for details. **Times:** Open all year Mon-Thu & Sat 10-5, Fri-Sun 11-5. Guided tours for public at 2.30 **Facilities:** 🅿 ♿ toilets for disabled 🐾 (ex guide dogs)

GLASGOW SCIENCE CENTRE
50 Pacific Quay G51 1EA
➲ (follow brown signs from M8 junct 24 or M77 junct 21, across the Clyde from SECC) **2 for 1**
☎ 0141 420 5000 📠 0141 420 5011
e-mail: admin@glasgowsciencecentre.org
The centre is home to many entertaining and exciting attractions and contains hundreds of interactive exhibits. Highlights include the Scottish Power Space Theatre, Scotland's only IMAX cinema and the 127m Glasgow Tower, a remarkable free-standing structure that gives breathtaking views of the city (check availability before visiting). GSC presents the world of science and technology in new and exciting ways.
Times: Open daily 10-6. **Fee:** ✱ Science Mall* or Imax: £6.95 (ch & concessions £4.95).Science Mall & Imax: £9.95 (ch & concessions £7.95). 10% off for groups 4+. * Scottish Power Space Theatre extra £2. **Facilities:** 🅿 🔊 ♿ (induction loops) toilets for disabled shop 🐾 (ex guide/hearing dogs) ◀

GREENBANK GARDEN
Flenders Rd, Clarkston G76 8RB
➲ (off A726 on southern outskirts of the city)
☎ 0141 639 3281
The spacious, walled woodland gardens are attractively laid out in the grounds of an elegant Georgian house, and best seen between April and October. A wide range of flowers and shrubs are grown, with the idea of helping private gardeners to look at possibilities for their own gardens. A greenhouse and garden designed for the disabled gardener also displays specialised tools.
Times: Open daily 9.30-sunset. Times may change for 2005 please telephone or check on www.nts.org.uk **Fee:** ✱ £3.50 (concession £2.60) Family ticket £9.50. Groups adult £2.80, child/school £1. Please book groups in advance. Admission free to NTS members. For other details please phone 0131 243 9387 or check web site.
Facilities: 🅿 🔊 ♿ (wheelchairs available) toilets for disabled shop 🐾 (ex guide dogs) 🌾

HOLMWOOD HOUSE
61-63 Netherlee House, Cathcart G44 3YG
➲ (Off Clarkston Rd)
☎ 0141 637 2129 📠 0141 571 0184
Built in the mid 19th century, the architectural style of the house is an adaptation of classical Greek. Many rooms are richly ornamented in wood, plaster and marble.
Times: Open - Apr-Oct, daily 12-5. Morning visits available for pre-booked groups. Times may change for 2005 please telephone or check on www.nts.org.uk **Fee:** ✱ £3.50 (concession £2.60). Family ticket £9.50. Groups adult £2.80, child/school £1. Please book groups in advance. For other details please phone 0131 243 9387

Directions are provided by the attractions.

HOUSE FOR AN ART LOVER
10 Dumbreck Rd, Bellahouston Park G41 5BW
➲ (Exit M8 W junct 23 signed B768, left at top of slip road onto Dumbreck Rd. Bellahouston Park on right)
☎ 0141 353 4770 📠 0141 353 4771
e-mail: info@houseforanartlover.co.uk
Originally designed by Glasgow's most celebrated architect, Charles Rennie Mackintosh, in 1901, this unusual cultural, corporate and academic resource began construction in 1989 and was completed in 1996. Contains art galleries and rooms to hire for conferences, private parties and weddings.
Times: Open Apr-Sep, Mon-Wed 10-4 & Thu-Sun 10-1; Oct-Mar, Sat-Sun 10-1, telephone for wkday opening details. **Fee:** Prices not confirmed for 2005 **Facilities:** 🅿 🔊 ✗ licensed ♿ (lift to 2nd floor) toilets for disabled shop 🐾 (ex guide dogs) ◀

HUNTERIAN ART GALLERY
82 Hillhead St, The University of Glasgow G12 8QQ
➲ (On University of Glasgow Campus in Hillhead District, 2m W of City Centre)
☎ 0141 330 5431 📠 0141 330 3618 **FREE**
e-mail: hunter@museum.gla.ac.uk
The founding collection is made up of paintings bequeathed in the 18th century by Dr William Hunter, including works by Rembrandt and Stubbs. The Gallery now has works by James McNeill Whistler, major displays of paintings by the Scottish Colourists, and a graphics collection holding some 300,000 prints. A popular feature is the re-construction of the interiors of The Mackintosh House.
Times: Open Mon-Sat 9.30-5. Telephone for BH closures.
Facilities: 🅿 (500 yds) (pay & display) 🔊 ♿ (lift, wheelchair available) toilets for disabled shop 🐾 (ex guide dogs) ◀

HUNTERIAN MUSEUM
Gilbert Scott Building, The University of Glasgow G12 8QQ
➲ (on University of Glasgow campus in the Hillhead District, 2m W of city centre)
☎ 0141 330 4221 📠 0141 330 3617 **FREE**
e-mail: hunter@museum.gla.ac.uk
Named after the 18th-century physician, Dr William Hunter, who bequeathed his large and important collections of coins, medals, fossils, geological specimens and archaeological and ethnographic items to the university. The exhibits are shown in the main building of the university, and temporary exhibitions are held.
Times: Open all year, Mon-Sat 9.30-5. (Closed certain BH's phone for details). **Facilities:** 🅿 (100yds) pay & display ♿ (lift) toilets for disabled shop 🐾 (ex guide dogs) ◀

HUTCHESONS' HALL
158 Ingram St G1 1EJ
➲ (near SE corner of George Square)
☎ 0141 552 8391 📠 0141 552 7031 **FREE**
e-mail: hutchesonshall@nts.org.uk
This handsome early 19th-century building was designed by David Hamilton and houses a visitor centre and shop. There is a video about Glasgow's merchant city, and the Hall can be booked for functions. Telephone for details of concerts, recitals, etc.
Times: Gallery: open Mon-Sat, 10-5. Closed 24 Dec-mid Jan. Hall: open subject to functions. Times may change for 2005 please telephone or check on www.nts.org.uk **Facilities:** 🅿 (on street) (meters)(outside for disabled) ♿ toilets for disabled shop 🐾 🌾

McLellan Galleries

270 Sauchiehall St G2 3EH
➲ (N side of Sauchiehall St, close to the Glasgow School of Art)
☎ 0141 565 4137 ▤ 0141 565 4111 **FREE**
e-mail: museums@cls.glasgow.gov.uk

The McLellan Galleries first opened in 1854 and featured the personal collection of Glasgow industrialist and coachbuilder Archibald McLellan. With over 1,200 sq metres of top gallery space, the McLellan Galleries provide Glasgow Museums with the opportunity to hold major exhibitions and establish Glasgow as Britain's second art city. With Kelvingrove Art Gallery closed for refurbishment until Spring 2006, the McLellan Galleries are showing 200 of Kelvingrove's famous paintings and objects in the exhibition 'Art Treasures of Kelvingrove' (closes Nov 2005).
Times: Open all year, Mon-Thu & Sat 10-5, Fri & Sun 11-5. (Closed 24-25 & 31 Dec [pm], 1-2 Jan) **Facilities:** P (500mtrs) ▇ & (assistance available, lift) toilets for disabled shop ✗

Museum of Transport

1 Bunhouse Rd G3 8DP
➲ (1.5m W of city centre)
☎ 0141 287 2720 ▤ 0141 287 2692 **FREE**
e-mail: museums@cls.glasgow.gov.uk

Visit the Museum of Transport and the first impression is of gleaming metalwork and bright paint. All around you there are cars, caravans, carriages and carts, fire engines, buses, steam locomotives, prams and trams. The museum uses its collections of vehicles and models to tell the story of transport by land and sea, with a unique Glasgow flavour. Visitors can even go window shopping along the recreated Kelvin Street of 1938. Upstairs 250 ship models tell the story of the great days of Clyde shipbuilding. The Museum of Transport has something for everyone.
Times: Open all year, Mon-Thu & Sat 10-5, Fri & Sun 11-5.
Facilities: P (charged) ▇ & (assistance available) toilets for disabled shop ✗ (ex guide dogs)

People's Palace and Winter Gardens

Glasgow Green G40 1AT
➲ (1m SE of city centre)
☎ 0141 271 2951 ▤ 0141 271 2960 **FREE**
e-mail: museums@cls.glasgow.gov.uk

Glasgow grew from a medieval town located by the Cathedral to the Second City of the British Empire. Trade with the Americas, and later industry, made the city rich. But not everyone shared in Glasgow's wealth. The People's Palace on historic Glasgow Green shows how ordinary Glaswegians worked, lived and played. Visitors can discover how a family lived in a typical one-room Glasgow 'single end' tenement flat, see Billy Connolly's amazing banana boots, learn to speak Glesga, take a trip 'doon the watter' and visit the Winter Gardens.
Times: Open all year, Mon-Thu & Sat 10-5, Fri & Sun 11-5. (Closed 24-25 & 31 Dec [pm], 1-2 Jan) **Facilities:** P (50yds) ▇ & (lifts) toilets for disabled shop garden centre ✗

Pollok House

Pollok Country Park, 2060 Pollokshaws Rd G43 1AT
➲ (3.5m S of city centre, off M77 junct 2, follow signs for Burrell Collection)
☎ 0141 616 6410 ▤ 0141 616 6521
e-mail: pollokhouse@nts.org.uk

The house is one of Glasgow's most elegant, and was built by the Maxwell family in the 18th century and expanded between
continued

1890 and 1901, including extensive servants' quarters. The rooms are decorated with 18th-century plasterwork, fine furniture and the Stirling Maxwell art collection, including works by El Greco, Goya and William Blake.
Times: House: open daily 10-5, closed 25 & 26 Dec & 1 & 2 Jan.
Fee: ✱ Apr-Oct £6 (concession £4) Family ticket £15. Groups adult £4, child/school £1. Please book groups in advance. Admission free to NTS members. For other details please phone 0131 243 9387
Facilities: P ✗ licensed & (lifts) toilets for disabled shop ✗

Provand's Lordship

3 Castle St G4 0RB
➲ (1m E of city centre)
☎ 0141 552 8819 ▤ 0141 552 4744 **FREE**
e-mail: museums@cls.glsgow.gov.uk

Provand's Lordship is the only house to survive from Medieval Glasgow. For over 500 years it has watched the changing fortunes of the city and the nearby Cathedral. Bishop Andrew Muirhead built the house as part of St Nicholas' Hospital in 1971. The prebendary of Barlanark later bought it for use as a manse. Inside, the displays recreate home life in the middle ages. Behind the house is the St Nicholas Garden, built in 1997. It is a medical herb garden, in keeping with the original purpose of the house.
Times: Open all year, Mon-Thu & Sat 10-5, Fri & Sun 11-5.
Facilities: P (50 yds) ▇ & (please contact for details) shop ✗ (ex guide dogs)

St Mungo Museum of Religious Life & Art

2 Castle St G4 0RH
➲ (1m NE of city centre)
☎ 0141 553 2557 ▤ 0141 552 4744 **FREE**
e-mail: museums@cls.glasgow.gov.uk

The award-winning St Mungo Museum explores the importance of religion in peoples' everyday lives and art. It aims to promote understanding and respect between people of different faiths and of none. Highlights of the collection include the Salvador Dali painting *Christ of St John of the Cross*. The museum also features stained glass, objects, statues and video footage. Within the grounds is Britain's first Japanese Zen garden.
Times: Open all year, Mon-Thu & Sat 10-5, Fri & Sun 11-5.
Facilities: P (50yds) ▇ & (taped information & lift) toilets for disabled shop ✗ (ex guide dogs)

The Scottish Football Museum

The National Stadium, Hampden Park G42 9BA
➲ (3m S of city centre, follow brown tourist signs)
☎ 0141 616 6139 ▤ 0141 616 6101 **2 for 1**
e-mail: info@scottishfootballmuseum.org.uk

Using 2500 pieces of footballing memorabilia, the Scottish Football Museum covers such themes as football's origins, women's football, fan culture, other games influenced by football, and even some social history. The exhibits include the world's oldest football, trophy and ticket, a reconstructed 1903 changing room and press box, and items of specific import, such as Kenny Dalglish's silver cap, Jimmy McGrory's boots, and the ball from Scotland's 5-1 win over England in 1928.
Times: Open Mon-Sat 10-5, Sun 11-5. (Closed match days, special events and Xmas/New Year, please telephone in advance for confirmation) **Fee:** Museum or stadium tour £5 (concessions & ch under 16 £2.50). Combined ticket £7.50 (concessions & ch under 16 £3.75) **Facilities:** P ▇ & (ramps throughout) toilets for disabled shop ✗ (ex guide dogs) ▇

THE TALL SHIP AT GLASGOW HARBOUR
100 Stobcross Rd G3 8QQ
➲ (from M8 junct 19 onto A814 follow signs for 'The Tall Ship')
☎ 0141 222 2513 📠 0141 222 2536 **2 for 1**
e-mail: info@thetallship.com
Visit The Tall Ship at Glasgow Harbour and step back in time to the days of sail. Experience Glasgow's maritime history at first hand and explore the UK's only remaining Clydebuilt sailing ship, the Glenlee. Exhibitions on board and in the visitor centre on the quayside tell the story of the ship and the Glasgow Harbour area. If you have ever wondered what it would have been like to be a sailor on a tall ship, this is your chance to find out! Children can have fun by joining in the hunt for Jock, the ship's cat. An unmissable experience, The Tall Ship offers guided tours, changing exhibitions, children's activities, a nautical gift shop and café.
Times: Open daily Mar-Oct 10-5, Nov-Feb 10-4. Fee: £4.50 (concessions £3.25, 1 ch free with paying adult/concession, additional ch £2.50). Facilities: 🅿 💺 ✕ licensed & toilets for disabled shop 🍴

TENEMENT HOUSE
145 Buccleuch St, Garnethill G3 6QN
➲ (N of Charing Cross)
☎ 0141 333 0183
e-mail: tenementhouse@nts.org.uk
This shows an unsung but once-typical side of Glasgow life: it is a first-floor flat, built in 1892, with a parlour, bedroom, kitchen and bathroom, furnished with the original recess beds, kitchen range, sink, and coal bunker, among other articles. The home of Agnes Toward from 1911 to 1965, the flat was bought by an actress who preserved it as a 'time capsule'. The contents vividly portray the life of one section of Glasgow society.
Times: Open Mar-Oct, daily 2-5. Weekday morning visits available for pre-booked educational & other groups. Times may change for 2005 please telephone or check on www.nts.org.uk Fee: ✱ £3.50 (concessions £2.60) Family ticket £9.50. Groups adult £2.80, child/school £1. Admission free to NTS members. For other details please phone 0131 243 9387 Facilities: 🅿 (100yds) (restricted, recommend parking in town) (Braille guide) 🐕 (ex guide dogs) 🌿

TRADES HALL NEW
85 Glassford St G1 1UH
☎ 0141 552 2418 📠 0141 552 5053
e-mail: info@tradeshallglasgow.co.uk
The Trades Hall is the historic home of Glasgow's 14 Incorporated Crafts and the Trades House which dates back to 1605. Established to regulate trade, they played a vital role in shaping and making the city Glasgow the city it is today.
Times: Open Apr-Oct, Mon-Fri 10-5, Sat 10-2, Sun 12-5; Nov-Mar Sun 12-5 Fee: ✱ £3.50 (ch£2, pen £2.50, ch under 5 free). Groups 10+ £3 each. Facilities: 🅿 (100yds) 💺 & shop

UNIVERSITY OF GLASGOW VISITOR CENTRE
University Av G12 8QQ
➲ (M8 junct 19 (E) or junct 18(W))
☎ 0141 330 5511 📠 0141 330 5225
e-mail: visitorcentre@gla.ac.uk
The Visitor Centre is spacious and pleasant, with leaflets, publications and video displays explaining how the university works and its history, plus what courses are available and which university events are open to the public. Historic attractions, include the Memorial Chapel, Professors'
continued

Square and Lion and Unicorn Staircase. Hunterian Museum is not part of the tour but visitors are welcome to view the museum on their own.
Times: Open all year, Mon-Sat 9.30-5. Also May-Sep, Sun 2-5.
Fee: Prices not confirmed for 2005 Facilities: 🅿 (880yds) (few spaces available) 💺 & (designated seating) toilets for disabled shop 🐕 (ex guide dogs) 🍴

CLACKMANNANSHIRE

ALLOA   Map 11 NS89
ALLOA TOWER
Alloa Park FK10 1PP
➲ (on A907)
☎ 01259 211701 📠 01259 218744
Beautifully restored, the tower, completed in 1467, is the only remaining part of the ancestral home of the Earls of Mar. The structure retains rare medieval features, notably the complete timber roof structure and groin vaulting. A superb loan collection of portraits and chattels of the Erskine family includes paintings by Raeburn.
Times: Open Apr-Oct, daily 1-5. Weekday morning visits available for pre-booked groups. Times may change for 2005 please telephone or check on www.nts.org.uk Fee: ✱ £3.50 (concessions £2.60) Groups adult £2.80, child/school group £1. Family ticket £9.50. Admission free to NTS members. For other details please phone (0131) 243 9387 Facilities: 🅿 & toilets for disabled 🐕 🌿

ALVA   Map 11 NS89
MILL TRAIL VISITOR CENTRE
Glentana Mill, West Stirling St FK12 5EN
➲ (situated on A91 approx 8m E of Stirling) **FREE**
☎ 01259 769696 📠 01259 763100
In the heart of Scotland's woollen mill country, the Centre recounts the history of Scotland's woollen and tweed traditions, and features machines from spinning wheels to large motorised looms of the type in use today. Hear 12 year-old Mary describe her working day as a mill girl 150 years ago, and then contrast her story with our modern working woollen mill. Factory bargains and local crafts, tourist information centre, café.
Times: Open all year, Jan-Jun 10-5; Jul-Aug 9-5; Sep-Dec 10-5.
Facilities: 🅿 💺 & toilets for disabled shop 🐕 (ex guide dogs) 🍴

DOLLAR   Map 11 NS99
CASTLE CAMPBELL
FK14 7PP
➲ (10m E of Stirling on A91)
☎ 01259 742408
Traditionally known as the 'Castle of Gloom', the 15th to 17th-century tower stands in the picturesque Ochil Hills, gives wonderful views, and can be reached by a walk through the magnificent Dollar Glen. Care must be taken in or after rain when the path may be dangerous.
Times: Open all year, Apr-Sep, daily 9.30-6.30; Oct-Mar, Mon-Wed & Sat-Sun 9.30-4.30. (Closed Thu & Fri in winter, 25-26 Dec & 1-2 Jan).
Fee: ✱ £3 (ch £1, concessions £2.30). Groups 11+ 10% discount. Prices valid until 2 Jan 2005. Please phone for further details.
Facilities: 🅿 ✕ shop 🔔 🌿

DUMFRIES & GALLOWAY

ARDWELL   Map 10 NX14
ARDWELL HOUSE GARDENS
DG9 9LY
➲ (10m S of Stranraer, on A716)
☎ 01776 860227   ▤ 01776 860288
Country house gardens and grounds with flowering shrubs and woodland walks. Plants for sale. House not open to the public.
Times: Open Mar-Oct, 10-5. Walled garden & greenhouses close at 5.
Fee: £2 (ch & pen £1). **Facilities:** 🅿 garden centre

CAERLAVEROCK   Map 11 NY06
CAERLAVEROCK CASTLE
Glencaple DG1 4RU
➲ (8m SE of Dumfries, on B725)
☎ 01387 770244
This ancient seat of the Maxwell family is a splendid medieval stronghold dating back to the 13th century. It has high walls and round towers, with machicolations added in the 15th century.
Times: ✷ Open all year, Apr-Sep, daily 9.30-6.30; Oct-Mar, daily 9.30-4.30. (Closed 25-26 Dec & 1-2 Jan). **Fee:** ✷ £4 (ch £1, concessions £3). Groups 11+ 10% discount. Prices valid until 2 Jan 2005. Please phone for further details. **Facilities:** 🅿 ✗ ♿ toilets for disabled shop ▮

WWT CAERLAVEROCK
Eastpark Farm DG1 4RS
➲ (9m SE of Dumfries, signed from A75)
☎ 01387 770200   ▤ 01387 770539   **2 for 1**
e-mail: caerlaverock@wwt.org.uk
This internationally important wetland is the winter habitat of the entire Svalbard population of Barnacle Geese which spends the winter on the Solway Firth. Observation facilities include 20 hides, 3 towers and a heated observatory. A wide variety of other wildlife can be seen, notably the rare Natterjack Toad and a family of Barn Owls which can be observed via a CCTV system.
Times: Open daily 10-5. (Closed 25 Dec). **Fee:** ✷ £4 (ch £2.50 & concessions £3.25). Family ticket £10.50 **Facilities:** 🅿 💷 ♿ toilets for disabled shop ✖ (ex guide dogs)

CARDONESS CASTLE   Map 11 NX55
CARDONESS CASTLE
DG7 2EH
➲ (1m SW of Gatehouse of Fleet, off A75)
☎ 01557 814427
A 15th-century stronghold overlooking the Water of Fleet. It was once the home of the McCullochs of Galloway. The architectural details inside the tower are of very high quality.
Times: Open Apr-Sep, daily 9.30-6.30; Oct-Mar, wknds only. (Closed 25-26 Dec & 1-2 Jan). **Fee:** ✷ £2.50 (ch 75p, concessions £1.90). Groups 11+ 10% discount. Prices valid until 2 Jan 2005. Please phone for further details. **Facilities:** 🅿 shop ▮

> Directions are provided
> by the attractions.

CASTLE DOUGLAS   Map 11 NX76
THREAVE CASTLE
DG7 1RX
➲ (3m W on A75)
☎ 0411 223101
Archibald the Grim built this lonely castle in the late 14th century. It stands on an islet in the River Dee, and is four storeys high with round towers guarding the outer wall. The island is reached by boat.
Times: Open Apr-Sep, daily 9.30-6.30. **Fee:** ✷ £2.50 (ch 75p, concessions £1.90). Charge includes ferry trip. Groups 11+ 10% discount. Prices valid until 2 Jan 2005. Please phone for further details.
Facilities: 🅿 ✖ ▮

THREAVE GARDEN & ESTATE
DG7 1RX
➲ (1m W of Castle Douglas, off A75)
☎ 01556 502575   ▤ 01556 502683
e-mail: threave@nts.org.uk
The best time to visit is in spring when there is a dazzling display of daffodils. The garden is a delight in all seasons, however, and is home to the National Trust for Scotland's School of Practical Gardening.
Times: Estate & Garden: all year, daily 9.30-sunset. Walled Garden & Glasshouse daily 9.30-5. Visitor Centre, Countryside Centre & exhibition Feb-Mar & Nov-23 Dec, daily 10-4; Apr-Oct, daily 9.30-5.30. House Mar-Oct, Wed-Fri & Sun, 11-4 (guided tours only, admission by timed ticket).Times may change for 2005 please telephone or check on www.nts.org.uk **Fee:** ✷ £9 (concessions £6.50) Family ticket £23. Garden only £5 (concessions £3.75) Admission free for NTS members. For other details please phone 0131 243 9387 .
Facilities: 🅿 ✖ licensed ♿ (wheelchairs available incl. electric wheelchair) toilets for disabled shop garden centre ✖ (ex guide dogs) ♨

CREETOWN   Map 11 NX45
CREETOWN GEM ROCK MUSEUM
Chain Rd DG8 7HJ
➲ (follow signs from A75 at Creetown bypass)
☎ 01671 820357 & 820554   **2 for 1**
▤ 01671 820554
e-mail: gem.rock@btinternet.com
The Gem Rock is the leading independent museum of its kind in the UK, and is renowned worldwide. Crystals, gemstones, minerals, jewellery and fossils, the Gem Rock displays some of the most breathtaking examples of nature's wonders. See the audio-visual 'Fire in the Stones', explore the Crystal Cave, and relax in the Prospector's Study.
Times: Open Etr-Sep, daily 9.30-5.30; Oct-Nov & Mar-Etr, daily 10-4; Dec-Feb, wknds 10-4 or by appointment wkdays. (Closed 23 Dec-Jan).
Fee: ✷ £3.50 (ch £2 under 5 free, concessions £3). Family ticket £9 (2ad+3ch). **Facilities:** 🅿 💷 ♿ (Ideal attraction for wheelchair users) toilets for disabled shop ✖ (ex guide dogs) ◀

DRUMCOLTRAN TOWER   Map 11 NX86
DRUMCOLTRAN TOWER
➲ (7m NE of Dalbeattie, in farm buildings off A711)
A well-preserved tower of mid 16th-century date simply planned and built, sitting within a busy modern farmyard.
Times: Open at any reasonable time. **Facilities:** 🅿 ✖ ▮

DUMFRIES Map 11 NX97

BURNS MAUSOLEUM
St Michael's Churchyard
➲ (at junction of Brooms Rd [ATS] and St
Michael's St (B725))
☎ 01387 255297 🖹 01387 265081 FREE
e-mail: dumfriesmuseum@dumgal.gov.uk
The mausoleum is in the form of a Greek temple, and
contains the tombs of Robert Burns, his wife Jean Armour,
and their five sons. A sculptured group shows the Muse of
Poetry flinging her cloak over Burns at the plough.
Times: Unrestricted access. **Facilities:** P (50yds) ♿ (visitors with
mobility difficulties tel 01387 255297)

DUMFRIES MUSEUM & CAMERA OBSCURA
The Observatory, Rotchell Rd DG2 7SW
➲ (A75 from S Carlisle or SW from Castle
Douglas, museum in Maxwellton area of
Dumfries)
☎ 01387 253374 🖹 01387 265081 2 for 1
e-mail: dumfriesmuseum@dumgal.gov.uk
Situated in and around the 18th-century windmill tower, the
museum's collections were started over 150 years ago and
exhibitions trace the history of the people and landscape of
Dumfries & Galloway. The Camera Obscura is to be found on
the top floor of the windmill tower.
Times: Open all year, Apr-Sep Mon-Sat 10-5, Sun, 2-5; Oct-Mar,
Tue-Sat 10-1 & 2-5. **Fee:** Free except Camera Obscura £1.55
(concessions 80p) **Facilities:** P ♿ (camera obscura, parking
available) toilets for disabled shop

OLD BRIDGE HOUSE MUSEUM
Mill Rd DG2 7BE
➲ (at western end of Devorgilla's Bridge)
☎ 01387 256904 🖹 01387 265081 FREE
e-mail: dumfriesmuseum@dumgal.gov.uk
The Old Bridge House was built in 1660, and is the oldest
house in Dumfries. A museum of everyday life in the town, it
has an early 20th-century dentist's surgery, a Victorian
nursery and kitchens of the 1850s and 1900s.
Times: Open Apr-Sep, Mon-Sat 10-5 & Sun 2-5. **Facilities:** P ♿ shop

ROBERT BURNS CENTRE
Mill Rd DG2 7BE
➲ (on Westbank of River Nith)
☎ 01387 264808 🖹 01387 265081 2 for 1
e-mail: dumfriesmuseum@dumgal.gov.uk
This award-winning centre explores the connections
between Robert Burns and the town of Dumfries. Situated in
the town's 18th-century watermill, the centre tells the story
of Burns' last years spent in the busy streets and lively
atmosphere of Dumfries in the 1790s. In the evening the
centre shows feature films in the Film Theatre.
Times: Open all year, Apr-Sep, daily 10-8 (Sun 2-5); Oct-Mar, Tue-Sat
10-1 & 2-5. **Fee:** Free admission. Audio visual theatre £1.55
(concessions 80p). **Facilities:** P 🅿 ✗ ♿ (induction loop hearing
system in auditorium, chairlift) toilets for disabled shop 📷

ROBERT BURNS HOUSE
Burns St DG1 2PS
➲ (signed from Brooms Rd [ATS] car park)
☎ 01387 255297 🖹 01387 265081 FREE
e-mail: dumfriesmuseum@dumgal.gov.uk
It was in this house that Robert Burns spent the last three
continued

years of his short life; he died here in 1796. It retains much
of its 18th-century character and contains many fascinating
items connected with the poet. There is the chair in which he
wrote his last poems, many original letters and manuscripts,
and the famous Kilmarnock and Edinburgh editions of his
work.
Times: Open all year, Apr-Sep, Mon-Sat 10-5, Sun 2-5; Oct-Mar Tue-Sat
10-1 & 2-5. **Facilities:** P (opposite) Please phone for details shop

DUNDRENNAN Map 11 NX74

DUNDRENNAN ABBEY
DG6 4QH
➲ (6.5m SE of Kirkcudbright, on A711)
☎ 01557 500262
The now ruined abbey was founded for the Cistercians. The
east end of the church and the chapter house are of
exceptional architectural quality. Mary, Queen of Scots is
thought to have spent her last night in Scotland here on 15
May 1568, before seeking shelter in England, where she was
imprisoned and eventually executed.
Times: Open, Apr-Sep, daily 9.30-6.30; Oct-Mar wknds only. (Closed
25-26 Dec & 1-2 Jan). **Fee:** Prices not confirmed for 2005
Facilities: P ♿ ✗ ⃒

GLENLUCE Map 10 NX15

GLENLUCE ABBEY
DG8 0AF
➲ (2m NW, off A75)
☎ 01581 300541
The abbey was founded for the Cistercians in 1192 by
Roland, Earl of Galloway. The ruins include a vaulted chapter
house, and stand in a beautiful setting.
Times: Open all year, Apr-Sep, daily 9.30-6.30; Oct-Mar, wknds only.
(Closed 25-26 Dec & 1-2 Jan). **Fee:** ✱ £2 (ch 75p, concessions £1.50).
Groups 11+ 10% discount. Prices valid until 2 Jan 2005. Please phone
for further details. **Facilities:** P 🅿 ♿ ✗ ⃒

KIRKCUDBRIGHT Map 11 NX65

BROUGHTON HOUSE & GARDEN
12 High St DG6 4JX
➲ (off A711/A755)
☎ 01557 330437
e-mail: aclipson@nts.scot.demon.co.uk
An 18th-century house where Edward A Hornel, one of the
'Glasgow Boys' group of artists, lived and worked from 1901-
1933. It features a collection of his work, an extensive library
of local history, including rare editions of Burns' works, and
a Japanese-style garden that he created.
Times: House may be closed part of 2004. Garden Feb-Mar & 1-20
Oct, Mon-Fri 11-4; Apr-Sep, Mon-Sat 11-5, Sun 1-5. Times may change
for 2005 please telephone or check on www.nts.org.uk **Fee:** ✱ £2
(concession £1). Admission free for NTS members. For other price
details please phone 0131 243 9387 **Facilities:** P (on street) (limited
space) ✗ (ex guide dogs) 🦮

MACLELLAN'S CASTLE
➲ (in Kirkcudbright on A711)
☎ 01557 331856
This handsome structure has been a ruin since the mid 18th-
century. It was once an imposing castellated mansion,
elaborately planned with fine architectural detail. Something
of its 16th-century grandeur still remains.
Times: Open Apr-Sep, daily 9.30-6.30. **Fee:** ✱ £2.20 (ch 75p,
concessions £1.60). Groups 11+ 10% discount. Rates valid until 2 Jan
2005. Please phone for further details. **Facilities:** P shop ✗ 🚌 ⃒

STEWARTRY MUSEUM

St Mary St DG6 4AQ

➲ (from A711 through town, pass parish church, museum approx 200mtrs on right)

☎ 01557 331643   ▤ 01557 331643   **FREE**

e-mail: david@dumgal.gov.uk

A large and varied collection of archaeological, social history and natural history exhibits relating to the Stewartry district.

Times: Open May, Jun & Sep Mon-Sat 11-5 Sun 2-5, Jul Aug Mon-Sat 10-5 Sun 2-5 Oct Mon-Sat 11-4 Sun 2-5 Nov-Apr Mon-Sat 11-4

Facilities: P (outside) & shop ✖ (ex guide dogs)

TOLBOOTH ART CENTRE

High St DG6 4JL

➲ (From A711, through town pass parish church & Stewartry Museum, take 1st right into High St)

☎ 01557 331556   ▤ 01557 331643   **FREE**

e-mail: DavidD@dumgal.gov.uk

Dating from 1629, the Tolbooth was converted into an art centre and provides an interpretive introduction to the Kirkcudbright artists's colony, which flourished in the town from the 1880s. It also provides studio and exhibition space for contemporary local and visiting artists. There is a programme of exhibitions from March to October.

Times: Open May, Jun & Sep, Mon-Sat 11-5 Sun 2-5; Jul & Aug Mon-Sat 10-6 Sun 2-5; Oct Mon-Sat 11-4 Sun 2-5; Nov-Apr Mon-Sat 11-4 **Facilities:** P (on street parking) ▅ & (lift for access to upper floors) toilets for disabled shop ✖ (ex guide dogs)

NEW ABBEY   Map 11 NX96

NEW ABBEY CORN MILL

DG2 8BX

➲ (7m S of Dumfries on A710)

☎ 01387 850260

Built in the late 18th century, this water-driven corn mill is still in working order, and regular demonstrations are held.

Times: Open all year, Apr-Sep, daily 9.30-6.30; Oct-Mar, daily 9.30-4.30. (Closed Thu & Fri in winter, 25-26 Dec & 1-2 Jan).

Fee: ✱ £3 (ch £1, concessions £2.30). Groups 11+ 10% discount. Rates valid until 2 Jan 2005. Please phone for details.

Facilities: P (100yds) shop ✖ ▊

SHAMBELLIE HOUSE MUSEUM OF COSTUME

DG2 8HQ

➲ (7m S of Dumfries, on A710)

☎ 01387 850375   ▤ 01387 850461

e-mail: info@nms.ac.uk

Shambellie House is a beautiful Victorian country house set in attractive wooded grounds. You are invited to step back in time and experience Victorian and Edwardian grace and refinement. See period costume from the 1850s to the 1950s displayed in appropriate room settings with accessories, furniture and decorative art. Telephone for details of special events.

Times: Open Apr (or Good Fri if earlier)-Oct, 11-5. **Facilities:** P ▅ & (house inaccessible for wheelchair users) shop ✖ (ex guide/hearing dogs) ▆

SWEETHEART ABBEY

DG2 8BU

➲ (on A710)

☎ 01387 850397

Lady Devorgilla of Galloway founded Balliol College, Oxford in memory of her husband John Balliol; she also founded this *continued*

abbey in his memory in 1273. When she died in 1289 she was buried in front of the high altar with the heart of her husband resting on her bosom; hence the name 'Sweetheart Abbey'. The abbey features an unusual precinct wall of enormous boulders.

Times: Open all year, Apr-Sep, daily 9.30-6.30; Oct-Mar, daily 9.30-4.30. (Closed Thu & Fri in winter, 25-26 Dec & 1-2 Jan).

Fee: ✱ £2 (ch 75p, concessions £1.50). Groups 11+ 10% discount. Prices valid until 2 Jan 2005. Please phone for further details.

Facilities: P & (with assistance) ✖ ▊

PALNACKIE   Map 11 NX85

ORCHARDTON TOWER

➲ (6m SE of Castle Douglas on A711)

A charming little tower house of mid 15th-century date. It is, uniquely, circular in plan.

Times: Open all reasonable times. (Closed 25-26 Dec).

Facilities: P ✖ ▊

PORT LOGAN   Map 10 NX04

LOGAN BOTANIC GARDEN

DG9 9ND

➲ (on B7065, 14m S of Stranraer)

☎ 01776 860231   ▤ 01776 860333

e-mail: logan@rbge.org.uk

Logan's exceptionally mild climate allows a colourful array of tender plants to thrive out-of-doors. Amongst the many highlights are tree ferns, cabbage palms, unusual shrubs, climbers and tender perennials found within the setting of the walled, water, terrace and woodland gardens.

Times: Open Mar-Oct, Mar & Oct daily 10-5. Apr-Sep 10-6

Fee: ✱ £3.50 (ch £1, concessions £3). Family £8

Facilities: P ✖ licensed & (access limited, wheelchairs available for loan) toilets for disabled shop garden centre ✖ (ex guide dogs) ▆

RUTHWELL   Map 11 NY16

RUTHWELL CROSS

➲ (sited within the parish church on B724)

Now in a specially built apse in the parish church, the carved cross dates from the 7th or 8th centuries. Two faces show scenes from the Life of Christ; the others show scroll work, and parts of an ancient poem in Runic characters. It was broken up in the 18th century, but pieced together by a 19th-century minister.

Times: Open all reasonable times. Contact Key Keeper for access on 01387 870249. **Facilities:** P ✖ ▊

SAVINGS BANKS MUSEUM

DG1 4NN

➲ (off B724, 10m E of Dumfries & 6m W of Annan)

☎ 01387 870640

e-mail: tsbmuseum@btinternet.com

Housed in the building where Savings Banks first began, the museum traces their growth and development from 1810 up to the present day. The museum also traces the life of Dr Henry Duncan, father of savings banks, and restorer of the Ruthwell Cross. Multi-lingual leaflets available.

Times: Open all year, daily (ex Sun & Mon Oct-Etr), 10-1 & 2-5.

Facilities: P & (touch facilities for blind, guide available) ✖ (ex guide dogs)

SANQUHAR   Map 11 NS70

SANQUHAR TOLBOOTH MUSEUM
High St DG4 6BN
➲ (on A76 Dumfries-Kilmarnock road)
☎ 01659 250186 ▤ 01387 265081 FREE
e-mail: dumfriesmuseum@dumgal.gov.uk
Housed in the town's fine 18th-century tolbooth, the
museum tells the story of the mines and miners of the area,
its earliest inhabitants, native and Roman, the history and
customs of the Royal Burgh of Sanquhar and local traditions.
Times: Open Apr-Sep, Tue-Sat 10-1 & 2-5, Sun 2-5.
Facilities: ▱ & (Museum up steps phone for info) shop

STRANRAER   Map 10 NX06

CASTLE KENNEDY GARDENS
Stair Estates, Rephad DG9 8BX
➲ (5m E of Stranraer on A75, signed at Castle
Kennedy Village)
☎ 01776 702024 ▤ 01776 706248 **2 for 1**
e-mail: info@castlekennedygardens.co.uk
Situated on a peninsula between two lochs, the gardens
around the Old Castle were first laid out in the early 18th
century. Noted for their rhododendrons and azaleas (at their
best May and early Jun) and walled kitchen garden with fine
herbaceous borders (best in Aug and Sep). The gardens
contain many avenues and walks amid beautiful scenery.
Times: Etr-Sep daily 10-5 **Fee:** ✱ £4 (ch £1, pen £3). Party 20+ 10%
discount. **Facilities:** ▱ ◍ & (Tearoom to enable access) toilets for
disabled shop garden centre ▰

GLENWHAN GARDENS
Dunragit DG9 8PH
➲ (7m E of Stranraer, signed)
☎ 01581 400222 ▤ 01581 400222
e-mail: tess@glenwhan.freeserve.co.uk
Enjoying spectacular views over the Mull of Galloway and
Luce Bay, Glenwhan is a beautiful 12-acre garden set on a
hillside. There are two lakes filled with rare species, alpines,
scree plants, heathers, conifers, roses, woodland walks and
fascinating garden sculpture.
Times: Open Apr-Sep daily 10-5 **Fee:** ✱ £3.50 (ch £1.50, concessions
£3) **Facilities:** ▱ ◍ ✗ licensed & (wheelchairs provided) toilets for
disabled shop garden centre

THORNHILL   Map 11 NX89

DRUMLANRIG CASTLE
DG3 4AQ
➲ (4m N of Thornhill off A76)
☎ 01848 331555 ▤ 01848 331682 **2 for 1**
e-mail: bre@drumlanrigcastle.org.uk
This unusual pink sandstone castle was built in the late 17th
century in Renaissance style. It contains a outstanding
collection of fine art. There is also French furniture, as well
as silver and relics of 'Bonnie' Prince Charlie. The old stable
block has a craft centre with resident craft workers, and the
grounds offer extensive garden plant centre, working forge,
continued

DRUMLANRIG CASTLE

Dumfriesshire home of the
Duke of Buccleuch and Queensberry KT.
17th century house, with extensive gardens
and Country Park. Renowned art collection.
French furniture.
Bonnie Prince Charlie relics.

Castle shop with quality goods
Tearoom – Working Forge
Craft Workshops – Plant Centre
Adventure Playground – Visitor Centre

18 miles north of Dumfries on A76
16 miles from Elvanfoot off M74

Tel: 01848-331555

mountain bike hire and woodland walks. For details of
special events phone 01848 331555.

Times: Open early May-late Aug, Castle open seven days a week.
Guided tours and restricted route may operate at various times, please
verify before visiting. **Fee:** ✱ £6 (ch £2 & pen £4). Grounds only £3.
Party 20+ £4 each. **Facilities:** ▱ ✗ licensed & (lift for wheelchair
users) toilets for disabled shop ✖ (ex in park on lead) ▰
See advertisement on this page

WANLOCKHEAD   Map 11 NS81

MUSEUM OF LEAD MINING
ML12 6UT
➲ (Signed from M74 and A76)
☎ 01659 74387 ▤ 01659 74481
e-mail: ggodfrey@goldpan.co.uk

Wanlockhead is Scotland's highest village, set in the beautiful Lowther Hills. Visitors can see miners' cottages, the miners' library as well as the 18th-century lead mine. Visitors can also pan for gold.
Times: ✱ Open Apr-2 Nov, daily 10.30-4.30; Jul & Aug 10-5.
Facilities: 🅿 ♨ ✗ licensed ᕕ (induction loops) toilets for disabled shop ⊀ (ex guide dogs) ▦

WHITHORN   Map 10 NX44

WHITHORN-CRADLE OF CHRISTIANITY
45-47 George St DG8 8NS
➲ (Follow directions S from junct at Newton Stewart & Glenluce A75. Centre on main street in centre of Whithorn)
☎ 01988 500508
e-mail: enquiries@whithorn.com
The Whithorn Dig is the site of the first Christian settlement in Scotland - the Candida Casa of St Ninian. Friendly guides explain the excavation, and there's a museum of Early Christian stones.
Times: ✱ Open daily, Apr-Oct 10.30-5. **Facilities:** 🅿 ♨ ᕕ (one short staircase with 'stairmatic') toilets for disabled shop ▦

WHITHORN PRIORY
DG8 8PY
➲ (on A746)
☎ 01988 500508
The first Christian church in Scotland was founded here by St Ninian in 397AD, but the present ruins date from the 12th century. These ruins are sparse but there is a notable Norman door, the Latinus stone of the 5th century and other early Christian monuments.
Times: ✱ Open Apr-Sep daily 10-5 **Facilities:** 🅿 ᕕ ⊀ ▮

> Directions are provided
> by the attractions.

DUNDEE CITY

DUNDEE   Map 11 NO43

BROUGHTY CASTLE MUSEUM
Broughty Ferry DD5 2TF
➲ (Turn S off A930 at traffic lights by Eastern Primary School in Broughty Ferry)
☎ 01382 436916 ▤ 01382 436951   **FREE**
e-mail: broughty@dundeecity.gov.uk
The 15th-century castle was rebuilt to defend the Tay estuary in the 19th century. It now houses fascinating displays on Dundee's whaling history, arms and armour, local history and seashore life. There are superb views across the Tay estuary from the observation room.
Times: Open all year Apr-Sep, Mon-Sat 10-4, Sun 12.30-4; Oct-Mar, Tue-Sat 10-4, Sun 12.30-4. (Closed Mons, 25-26 Dec & 1-3 Jan).
Facilities: 🅿 ♨ (unsuitable for wheelchairs) shop
⊀ (ex guide dogs)

CAMPERDOWN COUNTRY PARK
DD2 4TF
➲ (A90 to Dundee then onto A923 (Coupar Angus road), turn left at 1st rdbt to Camperdown Country Park)
☎ 01382 431818 ▤ 01382 431810
e-mail: camperdown@dundeecity.gov.uk
The 19th-century mansion of Camperdown House was built for the son of Admiral Lord Duncan, who defeated the Dutch at the Battle of Camperdown in 1797. The house is set in nearly 400 acres of fine parkland, which includes a wildlife centre, an adventure play area and an extensive network of footpaths and forest trails to follow.
Times: ✱ Open all year - park. Wildlife Centre - daily, Apr-Sep 10-3.45, Oct-Mar 10-2.45. **Facilities:** 🅿 ᕕ (ramps) toilets for disabled shop
⊀ (ex guide dogs)

DISCOVERY POINT & RRS DISCOVERY
Discovery Quay DD1 4XA
➲ (in Dundee follow the brown heritage signs for Historic Ships)
☎ 01382 201245 ▤ 01382 225891
e-mail: info@dundeeheritage.sol.co.uk

Discovery Point is the home of *RRS Discovery*, Captain Scott's famous Antarctic ship. Spectacular lighting, graphics and special effects re-create key moments in the *Discovery* story. The restored bridge gives a captain's view over the ship and the River Tay. Learn what happened to the ship after the

continued

expedition, during the First World War and the Russian Revolution, and find out about her involvement in the first survey of whales' migratory patterns.

Times: ✱ Open Apr-Oct, Mon-Sat 10-6. Sun 11-6; Nov-Mar, Mon-Sat 10-5. Sun 11-5. **Facilities:** 🅿 (charged) 💺 ♿ (in-house wheelchairs & lifts, parking, ramps onto ship) toilets for disabled shop ✖ (ex guide & hearing dogs) 🖃

HM FRIGATE UNICORN

Victory Dock DD1 3JA

➲ (From W follow A85 from A90 at Invergowrie. From E follow A92. Located near N end of Tay Road Bridge)

☎ 01382 200900 & 200893

📠 01382 200923

2 for 1

e-mail: frigateunicorn@hotmail.com

The *Unicorn* is the oldest British-built warship afloat, and Scotland's only example of a wooden warship. Today she houses a museum of life in the Royal Navy during the days of sail, with guns, models and displays.

Times: Open all year Apr-Oct daily 10-5; Nov-Mar, Wed-Fri 12-4, Sat & Sun 10-4 (closed Mon/Tue & 2 weeks at Xmas & New Year).

Fee: £3.50 (concessions £2.50). Family ticket £7.50-£9.50. Groups 10+ £2 each. **Facilities:** 🅿 💺 ♿ (audio visual presentations, introductory video) shop ✖ 🖃

McMANUS GALLERIES

Albert Square DD1 1DA

➲ (Turn off A90 & follow signs for Dundee city centre, located in city centre)

☎ 01382 432350 📠 01382 432369   **FREE**

e-mail: mcmanus.galleries@dundeecity.gov.uk

A remarkable Gothic building housing one of Scotland's most impressive collections of fine and decorative art. There are also displays on local archaeology, civic and social history, trades and industries and wildlife and the environment. Touring exhibitions are a regular feature.

Times: Open all year. Mon-Sat 10.30-5, Thu 10.30-7, Sun 12.30-4. (closed 25-26 Dec & 1-3 Jan) Closed for refurbishment in Sept 2005, please check for details. **Facilities:** 🅿 (100 yds) 💺 ♿ (wheelchair available, lift, high arm chairs & audio loop) toilets for disabled shop ✖ (ex guide dogs) 🖃

MILLS OBSERVATORY

Balgay Park, Glamis Rd DD2 2UB

➲ (1m W of Dundee city centre, in Balgay Park, on Balgay Hill. Vehicle entrance at Glamis Rd gate to Balgay Park)

☎ 01382 435967 📠 01382 435962

e-mail: mills.observatory@dundeecity.gov.uk

The observatory was built in 1935, and has a Victorian 10in Cooke refracting telescope among its instruments. The gallery has displays on astronomy and space exploration; visitors can view a safe projection of the sun on bright days. There is a small planetarium for booked groups only. Open nights during the winter months, children's activities during the summer holidays.

Times: Open all year, Apr-Sep, Tue-Fri 11-5, Sat & Sun 12.30-4; Oct-Mar, Mon-Fri 4-10, Sat & Sun 12.30-4. (Closed 25-26 Dec & 1-3 Jan). **Fee:** Free except for planetarium shows extra, £1 (ch 50p) Groups £10. **Facilities:** 🅿 ♿ (portable telescopes available, images on screen) toilets for disabled shop ✖ (ex guide dogs)

VERDANT WORKS

West Henderson's Wynd DD2 5BT

➲ (in Dundee follow brown tourist signs)

☎ 01382 225282 📠 01382 221612

e-mail: info@dundeeheritage.sol.co.uk

Dating from 1830, this old Jute Mill covers 50,000 sq ft and has been restored as a living museum of Dundee and Tayside's textile history and award-winning European Industrial Museum. Phase I explains what jute is, where it comes from and why Dundee became the centre of its production. Working machinery illustrates the production process from raw jute to woven cloth. Phase II deals with the uses of jute and its effects on Dundee's social history.

Times: Open Apr-Oct, Mon-Sat 10-5, Sun 11-5. Nov-Mar, Mon-Sat 10-4, Sun 11-4. Venue closes 1hr after last entry. Please check for winter opening times. (Closed 25-26 Dec & 1-2 Jan). **Facilities:** 🅿 (charged) ♿ (wheelchairs, induction loops) toilets for disabled shop ✖ (ex guide & hearing dogs) 🖃

EAST AYRSHIRE

GALSTON   Map 11 NS53

LOUDOUN CASTLE THEME PARK

KA4 8PE

➲ (signed from A74(M), from A77 and from A71)

☎ 01563 822296 📠 01563 822408

e-mail: loudouncastle@btinternet.com

Loudoun Castle Theme Park is a great day out for the whole family. Theme park rides, live entertainment and Mcdougles Farm are just a taste of what's on offer.

Times: Open Apr-Aug & following days in Sep 3, 9-10, 16-17, 22-25, 29-30. Also 1-2, 7-8, 14-22 Oct. **Fee:** ✱ Height: over 1.25m £10, over 0.90m £9, under 0.90m free (pen £5). Family ticket £25 (2 adults & 2 ch). **Facilities:** 🅿 💺 ✖ licensed ♿ toilets for disabled shop ✖ (ex guide dogs) 🖃

KILMARNOCK   Map 10 NS43

DICK INSTITUTE MUSEUM & ART GALLERIES

Elmbank Ave KA1 3BU

➲ (Follow brown tourist signs from A77, S of Glasgow, into Kilmarnock town centre)

☎ 01563 554343 📠 01563 554344

Temporary and permanent exhibitions spread over two floors of this grand Victorian building. Fine art, social and natural history feature upstairs, whilst the downstairs galleries house temporary exhibitions of art and craft.

Times: Open all year, Gallery & Museum: Mon-Tue, Thu-Fri 10-8, Wed & Sat 10-5. (Closed Sun & PH's). **Facilities:** 🅿 ♿ (wheelchair available) toilets for disabled shop ✖ (ex guide dogs)

EAST DUNBARTONSHIRE

BEARSDEN   Map 11 NS57
ANTONINE WALL: BEARSDEN BATH-HOUSE
Roman Rd G61 2SG
➲ (signed from Bearsden Cross on A810)
Considered to be the best surviving visible Roman building in
Scotland, the bath-house was discovered in 1973 during
excavations for a construction site. It was originally built for
use by the Roman garrison at Bearsden Fort, which is part of
the Antonine Wall defences. This building dates from the 2nd
century AD. Visitors should wear sensible footwear.
Times: Open all reasonable times. Facilities: ⅄ ✕ �

MILNGAVIE   Map 11 NS57
MUGDOCK COUNTRY PARK
Craigallian Rd G62 8EL
➲ (N of Glasgow on A81, signed)
☎ 0141 956 6100 956 6586   FREE
🖹 0141 956 5624
e-mail: lain@mcp.ndo.co.uk
This country park incorporates the remains of Mugdock and
Craigend castles, set in beautiful landscapes as well as an
exhibition centre, craft shops, orienteering course and many
walks.
Times: Open all year, daily. Facilities: ▣ ⬛ ⅄ toilets for disabled
shop garden centre ◥

EAST LOTHIAN

ABERLADY   Map 12 NT47
MYRETON MOTOR MUSEUM
EH32 0PZ
➲ (1.5m from A198, 2m from A1)
☎ 01875 870288 & 07947 066666   2 for 1
🖹 01368 860199
The museum has on show a large collection, from 1899, of
cars, bicycles, motor cycles and commercials. There is also a
large collection of period advertising, posters and enamel
signs etc.
Times: Open, Apr-Oct daily 11-4, Nov-Mar weekends only 11-3
Fee: £5 (ch £2). Facilities: ▣ ⅄ ✕ (ex guide dogs)

DIRLETON   Map 12 NT58
DIRLETON CASTLE
EH39 5ER
➲ (on A198)
☎ 01620 850330
The oldest part of this romantic castle dates from the 13th
century. It was besieged by Edward I in 1298, rebuilt and
expanded, and then destroyed in 1650. Now the sandstone
ruins have a beautiful mellow quality. Within the castle
grounds is a garden established in the 16th century, with
ancient yews and hedges around a bowling green.
Times: Open all year, Apr-Sep daily 9.30-6.30; Oct-Mar daily 9.30-4.30.
(Closed 25-26 Dec & 1-2 Jan). Fee: ✱ £3 (ch £1, concessions £2.30).
Groups 11+ 10% discount. Prices valid until 2 Jan 2005. Please phone
for further details. Facilities: ▣ shop ♦

EAST FORTUNE   Map 12 NT57
MUSEUM OF FLIGHT
East Fortune Airfield EH39 5LF
➲ (Signed from A1 near Haddington. Turn onto
B1347, past Athelstaneford)
☎ 01620 880308 🖹 01620 880355
e-mail: info@nms.ac.uk

Situated on 63 acres of one of Britain's best preserved
wartime airfields, the museum has three hangars, with more
than 50 aeroplanes, plus engines, rockets and memorabilia.
Items on display include two Spitfires, a Vulcan bomber and
Britain's oldest surviving aeroplane, built in 1896; recent
exhibits include a phantom jet fighter and harrier jump-jet.
Times: Open daily, 10.30-5, Apr-Oct; 11-4, wknds only Nov-Mar
Facilities: ▣ ⬛ ⅄ toilets for disabled shop ✕ (ex assist dogs) ◥

EAST LINTON   Map 12 NT57
HAILES CASTLE
➲ (1.5m SW of East Linton on A1)
A beautiful sited ruin incorporating a fortified manor of 13th-
century date, extended in the 14th and 15th centuries. There
are two vaulted pit-prisons.
Times: Open at all reasonable times. Facilities: ▣ ✕ ♦

PRESTON MILL & PHANTASSIE DOOCOT
EH40 3DS
➲ (signed from A1)
☎ 01620 860426
This attractive mill, with conical, pantiled roof, is the oldest
working water-driven meal mill to survive in Scotland, and
was last used commercially in 1957. Nearby is the charming
Phantassie Doocot (dovecote), built for 500 birds.
Times: Open Apr-Sep, Thu-Mon 12-5, Sun 1-5. Times may change for
2005 please telephone or check on www.nts.org.uk Fee: ✱ £3.50
(concession £2.60) Family ticket £9.50. Groups adult £2.80,
child/school £1). Admission free to NTS members. For other details
please phone 0131 243 9387 Facilities: ▣ ⅄ toilets for disabled shop
✕ (ex guide dogs) ☙

INVERESK   Map 11 NT37
INVERESK LODGE GARDEN
EH21 7TE
➲ (A6124, S of Musselburgh)
☎ 01721 722502
This charming terraced garden, set in the historic village of Inveresk, specialises in plants, shrubs and roses suitable for growing on small plots. The 17th-century house makes an elegant backdrop.
Times: Open all year daily 10-6 or dusk if earlier. Times may change for 2005 please telephone or check on www.nts.org.uk **Fee:** ✱ £2 (concession £1). Admission free to NTS members. For other details please phone 0131 243 9387 **Facilities:** 🅿 ᴔ ✖ (ex guide dogs) ♨

NORTH BERWICK   Map 12 NT58
SCOTTISH SEABIRD CENTRE
The Harbour EH39 4SS
➲ (follow A1 from Edinburgh, take A198 to North Berwick. Brown heritage signs clearly marked from A1)
☎ 01620 890202   📠 01620 890222   ⌗2 for 1⌗
e-mail: info@seabird.org
Get close to nature with a visit to this award-winning centre. With panoramic views over the islands of the Firth of Forth and sand-fringed bays of North Berwick, the area is a haven for wildlife. Use state-of-the-art 'Big Brother' cameras to see wide variety of wildlife action live - including gannet colony, hundreds of puffins seals and sometimes bottlenose dolphins. Wildlife boat safari with landings on the islands and passenger ferry to Fife (summer).
Times: Open all year, Apr-Oct 10-6 (every day), Nov-Jan 10-6 (Mon-Fri) 10-5.30 (Sat & Sun), Feb-Mar 10-5 (Mon-Fri) 10-5.30 (Sat & Sun). (Closed Xmas) **Fee:** £5.95 (ch & concessions £3.95). Family ticket (4 persons) £16.50. **Facilities:** 🅿 ⬛ ᴔ (1 w/chair, parking on site, walking frame available) toilets for disabled shop ✖ (ex guide dogs)

TANTALLON CASTLE
EH39 5PN
➲ (3m E, off A198)
☎ 01620 892727
A famous 14th-century stronghold of the Douglases facing towards the lonely Bass Rock from the rocky Firth of Forth shore. Nearby 16th and 17th-century earthworks.
Times: Open all year, Apr-Sep, daily 9.30-6.30; Oct-Mar, daily 9.30-4.30. (Closed Thu & Fri in winter, 25-26 Dec & 1-2 Jan).
Fee: ✱ £3 (ch £1, concessions £2.30). Groups 11+ 10% discount. Prices valid until 2 Jan 2005. Please phone for further details.
Facilities: 🅿 shop ✖ ᴨ

PRESTONPANS   Map 11 NT37
PRESTONGRANGE MUSEUM
Prestongrange
➲ (on B1348)
☎ 0131 653 2904   📠 01620 828201
e-mail: elms@eastlothian.gov.uk
The oldest documented coal mining site in Scotland, with 800 years of history, this museum shows a Cornish Beam Engine and on-site evidence of associated industries such as brickmaking and pottery. It is located next to a 16th-century customs port. Special Events - weekend events for families and children in July/August.
Times: ✱ Open end Mar-mid Oct, daily 11-4. Last tour 3pm.
Fee: Prices not confirmed for 2005 **Facilities:** 🅿 ⬛ ᴔ (grounds partly accessible) toilets for disabled shop ✖ (ex guide dogs or outside)

BIRKHILL   Map 11 NS97
THE BIRKHILL FIRECLAY MINE
EH51 9AQ
➲ (A706 from Linlithgow, A904 from Grangemouth, follow brown signs to Steam Railway & Fireclay Mine)
☎ 01506 825855   📠 01506 828766
e-mail: mine@srps.org.uk
Tour guides will meet you at Birkhill Station and lead you down into the ancient woodland of the beautiful Avon Gorge, and then into the caverns of the Birkhill Fireclay mine. See how the clay was worked, what it was used for and find the 300-million-year-old fossils in the roof of the mine.
Times: Open 3 Apr-Oct wknds only; Jul-Aug Tue-Sun.
Facilities: 🅿 ☕

BO'NESS   Map 11 NT08
BO'NESS & KINNEIL RAILWAY
Bo'ness Station, Union St EH51 9AQ
➲ (A904 from all directions, signed)
☎ 01506 822298   📠 01506 828233
e-mail: railway@srps.org.uk
Historic railway buildings, including the station and train shed, have been relocated from sites all over Scotland. The Scottish Railway Exhibition tells the story of the development of railways and their impact on the people of Scotland. Take a seven mile return trip by steam train to the tranquil country station at Birkhill. Special events take place throughout the year.
Times: Open Apr-Jun & Sep-Oct, Sat-Sun; Jul-Aug, Tue-Sun. Steam trains daily, depart 11, 12.15, 1.45 & 3, diesel departs at 4.15. Ring for details of special events. **Facilities:** 🅿 ⬛ ✖ ᴔ (ramps to station & adapted carriage) toilets for disabled shop ☕

KINNEIL MUSEUM & ROMAN FORTLET
Duchess Anne Cottages, Kinneil Estate EH51 0PR
➲ (Follow tourist signs from Heritage Railway, off M9. Establishment is at the E end of town accessed via Dean Rd)
☎ 01506 778530
The museum is in a converted stable block of Kinneil House. The ground floor has displays on the industrial history of Bo'ness, while the upper floor looks at the history and environment of the Kinneil Estate. The remains of the Roman fortlet can be seen nearby. An audio visual presentation shows 2000 years of history.
Times: ✱ Open all year, Mon-Sat 12.30-4. **Facilities:** 🅿 ᴔ shop ✖ (ex guide dogs)

FALKIRK   Map 11 NS88
ROUGH CASTLE
➲ (1m E of Bonnybridge, signed from B816)
The impressive earthworks of a large Roman fort on the Antonine Wall can be seen here. The buildings have disappeared, but the mounds and terraces are the sites of barracks, and granary and bath buildings. Running between them is the military road, which once linked all the forts on the wall and is still well defined.
Times: Open any reasonable time. **Facilities:** 🅿 ✖ ᴨ

FIFE

ABERDOUR Map 11 NT18

ABERDOUR CASTLE
KY3 0SL
➲ (In Aberdour, 5m E of Forth Bridges on A921)
☎ 01383 860519
The earliest surviving part of the castle is the 14th-century keep. There are also later buildings, and the remains of a terraced garden, a bowling green and a fine 16th-century doocot (dovecote).
Times: Open all year, Apr-Sep, daily 9.30-6.30; Oct-Mar, daily 9.30-4.30. (Closed Thu & Fri in winter, 25-26 Dec & 1-2 Jan).
Fee: ✱ £2.50 (ch 75p, concessions £1.90) Groups 11+ 10% discount. Prices valid until 2 Jan 2005. Please telephone for further details.
Facilities: ⓟ ✕ ♿ (wheelchairs) toilets for disabled shop ◪

ANSTRUTHER Map 12 NO50

SCOTTISH FISHERIES MUSEUM
St Ayles, Harbour Head KY10 3AB
➲ (from Edinburgh A90 take A92 to Kirkcaldy & then A915 to Upper Largo, A917 then B942 through Colinsburgh to Pittenweem, then A917 to Anstruther)
☎ 01333 310628 ▤ 01333 310628 **2 for 1**
e-mail: info@scottish-fisheries-museum.org

This award-winning national museum tells the story of Scottish fishing and its people from the earliest times to the present. With 10 galleries, 2 large boatyards and a restored fisherman's cottage, which contain many fine paintings and photographs, boat models and actual boats, clothing and items of daily life to see, a visit to the museum makes for an exceptional day out.
Times: Open all year, Apr-Sep, Mon-Sat 10-5.30, Sun 11-5; Oct-Mar, Mon-Sat 10-4.30, Sun 12-4.30. (Closed 25-26 Dec & 1-2 Jan). Last admission 1 hr before closing. **Fee:** £4.50 (concessions £3.50). Party 12+ £3 (concessions £2, primary ch £1) Accompanied ch free.
Facilities: ⓟ (20yds) (charge in summer) 💺 ♿ (ramps throughout to provide full access) toilets for disabled shop ✈ (ex guide dogs) ◪
See advertisement on page 323

Directions are provided by the attractions.

BURNTISLAND Map 11 NT28

BURNTISLAND EDWARDIAN FAIR MUSEUM
102 High St KY3 9AS
➲ (in the centre of Burntisland)
☎ 01592 412860 ▤ 01592 412870 **FREE**
Burntisland Museum has recreated a walk through the sights and sounds of the town's fair in 1910, based on a painting of the scene by local artist Andrew Young. See reconstructed rides, stalls and side shows of the time.
Times: Open all year, Mon, Wed, Fri & Sat 10-1 & 2-5; Tue & Thu 10-1 & 2-7. (Closed public holidays) **Facilities:** ⓟ 20m (on street parking) ✈ (except guide dogs)

CULROSS Map 11 NS98

CULROSS PALACE, TOWN HOUSE & THE STUDY
West Green House KY12 8JH
➲ (off A985, 3m E of Kincardine Bridge)
☎ 01383 880359 ▤ 01383 882675
A royal burgh, Culross dates from the 16th and 17th centuries and has remained virtually unchanged since. It prospered from the coal and salt trades, and when these declined in the 1700s, Culross stayed as it was. It owes its present appearance to the National Trust for Scotland, which has been gradually restoring it. In the Town House is a visitor centre and exhibition; in the building called The Study can be seen a drawing room with a Norwegian painted ceiling, and The Palace has painted rooms and terraced gardens.
Times: Open - Palace, Study & Town House: Good Fri-Sep, daily 12-5. Garden all year 10-6 or sunset if earlier. Times may change for 2005 please telephone or check on www.nts.org.uk **Fee:** ✱ £5 (concessions £3.75). Family ticket £13.50. Groups adult £4, child/school £1. Please book groups in advance. Admission free to NTS members. For other details phone 0131 243 9387 **Facilities:** ⓟ 💺 ♿ toilets for disabled shop ✈ (ex guide dogs) ◪

CUPAR Map 11 NO31

HILL OF TARVIT MANSIONHOUSE & GARDEN
KY15 5PB
➲ (2.5m S of Cupar, off A916)
☎ 01334 653127 ▤ 01334 653127
Built in the first decade of the 20th century, the Mansionhouse is home to a notable collection of paintings, tapestries, furniture and Chinese porcelain. The grounds include formal gardens, and there is a regular programme of concerts and art exhibitions.
Times: Open Apr-Sep, daily 1-5; Oct wknds 1-5. Garden & grounds all year, daily 9.30-sunset. Times may change for 2005 please telephone or check on www.nts.org.uk **Fee:** ✱ £5 (concessions £3.75). Family ticket £13.50. Groups adult £4 (child/school £1). Please book groups in advance. Garden & grounds £2. Admission free to NTS members. For other details please phone 0131 243 9387 **Facilities:** ⓟ 💺 ♿ toilets for disabled shop ✈ (ex guide dogs) ◪

THE SCOTTISH DEER CENTRE
Bow-of-Fife KY15 4NQ
➲ (3m W of Cupar on A91)
☎ 01337 810391 ▤ 01337 810477 **2 for 1**
Guided tours take about 30 minutes and allow you to meet and stroke deer. There are indoor and outdoor adventure play areas. Other features include regular falconry displays, viewing platform and a tree top walkway.
Times: Open daily, Etr-Oct 10-6, Nov-Etr 10-5. **Fee:** ✱ £4.95 (ch 3-15 £3.45) **Facilities:** ⓟ 💺 ♿ (special parking bay, loan of wheelchairs) toilets for disabled shop ✈ (ex guide dogs) ◪

DUNFERMLINE   Map 11 NT08
ABBOT HOUSE HERITAGE CENTRE
Abbot House, Maygate KY12 7NE
➲ (city centre)
☎ 01383 733266 ▤ 01383 624908
e-mail: dht@abbothouse.fsnet.co.uk
For the better part of a millennium, pilgrims have beaten a path to Dumfermline's door. Today visitors can still share the rich royal heritage of the capital of Fife's Magic Kingdom. The volunteer-run Abbot House Heritage Centre - dubbed 'The People's Tardis' - propels the traveller through time from the days of the Picts - a time warp peopled by a veritable Who's Who of characters from Dumfermline's past: Scotland's royal saint, Braveheart's Wallace and Bruce, Scotland's Chaucer, steel magnate Andrew Carnegie and a whole panoply of kings, ending with the birth of ill-starred Charles I.
Times: Open daily 10-5. Last entry to upper exhibitions 4.15. (Closed 25 Dec & 1 Jan). **Fee:** ✱ £3 (accompanied ch under 16 free & concessions £2). Party 20+ **Facilities:** P (150yds) (disabled parking at establishment) ▣ & (parking on site, videos of inaccessible areas) toilets for disabled shop ✖ (ex guide dogs) ⬛

ANDREW CARNEGIE BIRTHPLACE MUSEUM
Moodie St KY12 7PL
➲ (400yds S from Dunfermline Abbey)
☎ 01383 724302 ▤ 01383 721862
e-mail: carnegiebirthplace@hotmail.com
The museum tells the story of the handloom weaver's son, born here in 1835, who created the biggest steel works in the USA and then became a philanthropist on a huge scale. The present-day work of the philanthropic Carnegie Trust is also explained.
Times: Open Apr-Oct, Mon-Sat 11-5, Sun 2-5. **Fee:** £2 (ch under 16 free, concessions £1). **Facilities:** P & (Photo Album) toilets for disabled shop ✖ (ex guide dogs)

DUNFERMLINE ABBEY
Pittencrieff Park
☎ 01383 739026
The monastery was a powerful Benedictine house, founded by Queen Margaret in the 11th century. A modern brass in the choir marks the grave of King Robert the Bruce. The monastery guest house became a royal palace, and was the birthplace of Charles I.
Times: Open all year, Apr-Sep, daily 9.30-6.30; Oct-Mar, daily 9.30-4.30. (Closed Thu & Fri in winter, 25-26 Dec & 1-2 Jan).
Fee: ✱ £2.50 (ch 75p, concessions £1.90). Groups 11+ 10% discount. Rates valid until 2 Jan 2005. Please phone for further details.
Facilities: P shop ✖♦

PITTENCRIEFF HOUSE MUSEUM
Pittencrieff Park KY12 8QH
➲ (turn off A994 on to Coal Rd, turn left into Pittencriefff Park Car Park. Attraction on W edge of town)
☎ 01383 722935 & 313838   FREE
▤ 01383 313837
A fine 17th-century house standing in the beautiful park gifted to the town by Andrew Carnegie. Accessible displays tell the story of the park's animals and plants, with plenty of photographs of people enjoying the park over the last 100 years.
Times: Open daily Apr-Sep, 11-5 **Facilities:** P (800yds) & (ramp) toilets for disabled shop ✖ (ex guide dogs)

FALKLAND   Map 11 NO20
FALKLAND PALACE & GARDEN
KY15 7BU
➲ (off A912, 11m N of Kirkaldy)
☎ 01337 857397 ▤ 01337 857980
The hunting palace of the Stuart monarchs, this fine building, with a French-Renaissance style south wing, stands in the shelter of the Lomond Hills. The beautiful Chapel Royal and King's Bedchamber are its most notable features, and it is also home to the oldest royal tennis court in Britain (1539). The garden has a spectacular delphinium border. Recorded sacred music is played hourly in the Chapel. Please telephone for details of concerts, recitals etc.
Times: Open Mar-Oct, Mon-Sat 10-6, Sun 1-5. Times may change for 2005 please telephone or check on www.nts.org.uk **Fee:** ✱ £7 (concessions £5.25). Family ticket £19. Groups adult £5.60 (child/school £1). Garden only £3.50 (concessions £2.60). Family ticket £9.50. Groups adult £2.80 (child/school £1). Admission free to NTS members. For other details please phone 0131 243 9387 **Facilities:** P & shop ✖ (ex guide dogs) ♥

KELLIE CASTLE &   Map 12 NO50
GARDENS
KELLIE CASTLE & GARDENS
KY10 2RF
➲ (3m NW of Pittenweem on B9171)
☎ 01333 720271 ▤ 01333 720326
e-mail: aclipson@nts-scot.demon.co.uk
The oldest part dates from about 1360, but it is for its 16th and 17th-century domestic architecture that Kellie is renowned. It has notable plasterwork and painted panelling, and there are also interesting Victorian gardens.
Times: ✱ Open - Good Fri-Etr Mon & Jun-Sep, daily 1-5. Garden & grounds all year, daily 9.30-sunset. **Facilities:** P ▣ & (Induction loop for the hard of hearing) shop ✖ (ex guide dogs) ♥

KIRKCALDY   Map 11 NT29
KIRKCALDY MUSEUM & ART GALLERY
War Memorial Gardens KY1 1YG
➲ (next to Kirkcaldy train station)
☎ 01592 412860 ▤ 01592 412870   FREE
e-mail: kirkcaldy.museum@fife.gov.uk
Set in the town's lovely memorial gardens, the museum houses a collection of fine and decorative art, including 18th to 21st-century Scottish paintings among them the works of William McTaggart and S J Peploe. An award-winning display 'Changing Places' tells the story of the social, industrial and natural heritage of the area.
Times: Open all year, Mon-Sat 10.30-5, Sun 2-5. (Closed local hols).
Facilities: P ▣ & (ramp to main entrance & lift to 1st floor galleries) toilets for disabled shop ✖ (ex guide dogs)

NORTH QUEENSFERRY   Map 11 NT17
DEEP SEA WORLD
KY11 1JR
➲ (from N, M90 take exit for Inverkeithing. From S follow signs to Forth Rd Bridge, 1st exit left)
☎ 01383 411880 ▤ 01383 410514
e-mail: info@deepseaworld.co.uk
The world's longest underwater tunnel gives you a diver's eye view of an underwater world. Come face to face with Sand Tiger sharks, and watch divers hand feed a wide array of sea life. Visit the Amazon experience with ferocious piranhas and electric eels and the amazing amphibian

continued

display featuring the world's most poisonous frog. The really brave will enjoy the dangerous animals tank.
Times: Open all year daily from 10, Nov-Mar 10-5, Apr-Oct 10-6 wknds & school hols 10-6 **Fee:** ✱ £7.50 (ch 3-5 £5.50, concessions £6). Family ticket & group discounts available. **Facilities:** 🅿 🅴 ᵺ (ramps & disabled parking) toilets for disabled shop ✖ (ex guide dogs) 🖃

ST ANDREWS   Map 12 NO51

BRITISH GOLF MUSEUM
Bruce Embankment KY16 9AB
➲ (opposite Royal & Ancient Golf Club)
☎ 01334 460046 460053
📱 01334 460064   **2 for 1**
e-mail: alisonwood@randa.org
Where better to find out about golf than in St Andrews, the home of golf. Using diverse and exciting interactive displays, this museum explores the history of British golf from its origins to the personalities of today. The 18th Hole is fun for all the family, with dressing up, a mini-putting green and loads to do!
Times: Open all year, Etr-mid Oct daily 9.30-5.30; mid Oct-Etr Thu-Mon 11-3. (closed Tue & Wed). **Fee:** ✱ £4 (ch 15 £2, pen & students £3). Family ticket £10. Group 10+ **Facilities:** 🅿 (charged) ᵺ toilets for disabled shop ✖ (ex guide dogs) 🖃

CASTLE & VISITOR CENTRE
KY16 9AR
☎ 01334 477196
This 13th-century stronghold castle was the scene of the murder of Cardinal Beaton in 1546. The new visitor centre incorporates an exciting multi-media exhibition describing the history of the castle and nearby cathedral.
Times: Open all year, Apr-Sep, daily 9.30-6.30; Oct-Mar, daily 9.30-4.30. (Closed 25-26 Dec & 1-2 Jan). **Fee:** ✱ £3 (ch £1, concessions £2.30). Joint ticket with St Andrews Cathedral available £4 (ch £1.25, concessions £3. Groups 11+ 10% discount. Rates valid until 2 Jan 2005. Please phone for further details. **Facilities:** 🅿 ᵺ toilets for disabled shop ✖ ▮

CATHEDRAL (& MUSEUM)
KY16 9QU
☎ 01334 472563
The cathedral was the largest in Scotland, and is now an extensive ruin. The remains date mainly from the 12th and 13th centuries, and large parts of the precinct walls have survived intact. Close by is St Rule's church, which the cathedral was built to replace. St Rule's probably dates from before the Norman Conquest, and is considered the most interesting Romanesque church in Scotland.
Times: Open all year, Apr-Sep, daily 9.30-6.30; Oct-Mar, daily 9.30-4.30. (Closed 25-26 Dec & 1-2 Jan). **Fee:** ✱ £2.50 (ch 75p, concessions £1.90). Joint ticket for St Andrews Castle available £4 (ch £1.25, concessions £3). Groups 11+ 10% discount. Rates valid until 2 Jan 2005. Please phone for further details. **Facilities:** 🅿 shop ✖ ▮

> If an attraction name appears in *italics*, details have not been confirmed for 2005.

ST ANDREWS AQUARIUM
The Scores KY16 9AS
➲ (Signed in town centre)
☎ 01334 474786 📱 01334 475985
This continually expanding aquarium is home to shrimps, sharks, eels, octopi, seals and much much more. Special features include the Seahorse Parade, and the Sea Mammal Research Unit, which is committed to the care of sea mammals and their environment.
Times: ✱ Open daily from 10. Please phone for winter opening **Facilities:** 🅿 (charged) 🅴 ✖ licensed ᵺ toilets for disabled shop ✖ (ex guide dogs) 🖃

SCOTTISH FISHERIES MUSEUM
See advert on opposite page, see full entry under ANSTRUTHER.

HIGHLAND

AVIEMORE   Map 14 NH81
STRATHSPEY STEAM RAILWAY
Aviemore Station, Dalfaber Rd PH22 1PY
➲ (From A9 take B970 for Coylumbridge, on B9152, left after crossing railway bridge, car park 0.25m on left. Other stations: Boat of Garten in village; Broomhill, off A95, 3.5m S of Grantown-on-Spey)
☎ 01479 810725
e-mail: information@strathspeyrailway.co.uk
This steam railway covers the ten miles from Aviemore via Boat of Garten to Broomhill. The journey takes about 40 minutes, but allow around two hours for the round trip. Shorter trips are possible and timetables are available from the station and the tourist information centre. Special events include visits from Thomas the Tank Engine, telephone for details of dates.
Times: Open daily Etr, 23-29 Mar, 29 May-30 Sep, Apr, Wed & Sun; May & Oct, Wed, Thu, Sat, Sun & BH Mon, 9.30-4.30 **Fee:** £9 basic roundtrip (ch £4.50); £21 Family roundtrip. Day Rover £12 (ch £6) Family £30 **Facilities:** 🅿 🅴 ✖ ᵺ (ramps) toilets for disabled shop 🖃

BALMACARA   Map 14 NG82
BALMACARA ESTATE & LOCHALSH WOODLAND GARDEN
IV40 8DN
➲ (3m E of Kyle of Lochalsh, off A87)
☎ 01599 566325 📱 01599 566359
e-mail: balmacara@nts.org.uk
The Balmacara Estate comprises some 5,600 acres and seven crofting villages, including Plockton, a conservation area. There are excellent views of Skye, Kintail and Applecross. The main attraction is the Lochalsh Woodland Garden, but the whole area is excellent for walking.
Times: Open - Estate: all year. Woodland garden daily 9-sunset. Balmacara Square Visitor Centre, Apr-Sep, daily, 9-5 (Fri 9-4). Times may change for 2005 please telephone or check on www.nts.org.uk **Fee:** ✱ Garden £2 (concessions £1). Visitor Centre £1 (honesty box). Admission free to NTS members. For other details please phone 0131 243 9387 **Facilities:** 🅿 ☙

BETTYHILL   Map 14 NC76
STRATHNAVER MUSEUM
KW14 7SS
☎ 01641 521418
e-mail: strathnavermus@ukonline.co.uk
The museum has displays on the Clearances, with a fine
collection of Strathnaver Clearances furnishings, domestic
and farm implements, and local books. There is also a Clan
Mackay room. The museum's setting is a former church, a
handsome stone building with a magnificent canopied pulpit
dated 1774. The churchyard contains a carved stone known
as the Farr Stone, which dates back to the 9th century and is
a fine example of Pictish art.
Times: Open Apr-Oct, Mon-Sat 10-1 & 2-5; Nov-Mar restricted
opening. **Fee:** ✱ £1.90 (pen £1.20 ch 50p). **Facilities:** 🅿 ⴖ shop
✘ (ex guide dogs)

BOAT OF GARTEN   Map 14 NH91
LOCH GARTEN OSPREY CENTRE
RSPB Reserve Abernethy Forest, Forest Lodge,
Nethybridge PH25 3EF
⮑ (Signed from B970 & A9 at Aviemore, follow
'RSPB Ospreys' signs)
☎ 01479 831476 📠 01479 821069
Home of the Loch Garten Osprey site, this reserve holds one
of most important remnants of Scots Pine forest in the
Highlands. Within its 30,760 acres are forest bogs, moorland,
mountain top, lochs and crofting land. In addition to the
regular pair of nesting ospreys, there are breeding Scottish
crossbills, capercaillies, black grouse and many others. The
ospreys can be viewed through telescopes and there is a live
TV link to the nest.
Times: Osprey Centre open daily, Apr-Aug 10-6. **Fee:** ✱ £2.50
(ch 50p, concessions £1.50). **Facilities:** 🅿 ⴖ (low level viewing slots
& optics) toilets for disabled shop ✘ (ex guide dogs in centre) ⬛

CARRBRIDGE   Map 14 NH92
LANDMARK FOREST THEME PARK
PH23 3AJ
⮑ (off A9 between Aviemore & Inverness)
☎ 01479 841613 & 0800 731 3446
📠 01479 841384
e-mail: landmarkcentre@btconnect.com
This innovative centre is designed to provide a fun and
educational visit for all ages. Microworld takes a close-up
look at the incredible microscopic world around us. There is
a 65ft forest viewing tower and a treetop trail. There are
demonstrations of timber sawing, on a steam-powered
sawmill and log hauling by a Clydesdale horse throughout
the day. Attractions include a 3-track Watercoaster, a maze
and a large covered adventure play area, mini electric cars
and remote controlled truck arena.
Times: ✱ Open all year, daily, Apr-mid Jul 10-6; mid Jul-mid Aug 10-7;
Sep-Oct 10-5.30; Nov-Mar 10-5. **Facilities:** 🅿 ⬛ ✘ licensed
ⴖ (ramps to shop/restaurants) toilets for disabled shop ⬛

THE SCOTTISH FISHERIES MUSEUM
St Ayles, Harbour Head, Anstruther, KY10 3AB
Situated in Anstruther, in the heart of the Fife fishing community,
the Museum tells and researches the story of the Scottish fishing
industry and its people from the earliest times to the present. The
comprehensive Collection includes ships, models, paintings,
photographs, equipment and the written word.

E-mail: info@scottish-fisheries-museum.org
Website: www.scottish-fisheries-museum.org

Apr–Sept 10–5.30 (11–5 Sun)
Oct–Mar 10–4 (12–4.30 Sun)

Tel: 01333 310628
Fax: 01333 310628 ⬧

See entry on page 320

CAWDOR   Map 14 NH85
CAWDOR CASTLE
IV12 5RD
⮑ (on B9090, off A96)
☎ 01667 404401 📠 01667 404674
e-mail: info@cawdorcastle.com
Home of the Thanes of Cawdor since the 14th century, this
lovely castle has a drawbridge, an ancient tower built round
a tree, and a freshwater well inside the house. Gardens
Weekend takes place in June - guided tours of gardens and
Bluebell Walk in Cawdor Big Wood.
Times: Open May-9 Oct, daily 10-5.30. (Last admission 5).
Fee: ✱ £6.50 (ch 5-15 £3.70, pen £5.50). Family ticket £19. Party 20+
£5.70 each. Gardens, grounds & nature trails only £3.50.
Facilities: 🅿 ⬛ ✘ licensed ⴖ (ramps to restaurants, shops and
gardens) toilets for disabled shop ✘ (ex guide dogs) ⬛

CLAVA CAIRNS   Map 14 NH74
CLAVA CAIRNS
⮑ (6m E of Inverness, signed from B9091)   ▐FREE▌
☎ 01667 460232
A well-preserved Bronze Age cemetery complex of passage
graves, ring cairns, kerb cairn and standing stones in a
beautiful setting. In addition, the remains of a chapel of
unknown date can be seen at this site.
Times: Open at all reasonable times. **Facilities:** 🅿 ✘ ▌

CROMARTY Map 14 NH76

HUGH MILLER'S COTTAGE
Church St IV11 8XA
➲ (on A382)
☎ 01381 600245

The cottage houses an exhibition on the life and work of Hugh Miller, a stonemason born here in 1802 who became an eminent geologist and writer. It was built by his great-grandfather around 1698, and now has a charming cottage garden.
Times: Open Good Fri-Sep, daily 12-5; Oct, Sun-Wed 12-5. Times may change for 2005 please telephone or check on www.nts.org.uk
Fee: ✹ £2.50 (concessions £1.90) Family ticket £7. Groups adult £2, child/school £1. Admission free to NTS members. For other details please phone 0131 243 9387 **Facilities:** 🅿 (5mins) (disabled is directly outside) ♿ ✈ (ex guide dogs) ♨

CULLODEN MOOR Map 14 NH74

CULLODEN BATTLEFIELD
IV2 5EU
➲ (B9006, 5m E of Inverness)
☎ 01463 790607 ⓑ 01463 794294
e-mail: culloden@nts.org.uk

A cairn recalls this last battle fought on mainland Britain, on 16 April 1746, when the Duke of Cumberland's forces routed 'Bonnie' Prince Charles Edward Stuart's army. The battlefield has been restored to its state on the day of the battle, and in summer there are 'living history' enactments. This is a most atmospheric evocation of tragic events. Telephone for details of guided tours.
Times: Open - site daily, all year. Visitor Centre: Feb-Mar & Nov-Dec, daily 11-4; Apr-Jun & Sep-Oct, daily 9-6; Jul-Aug, daily 9-7. Times may change for 2005 please telephone or check on www.nts.org.uk
Fee: ✹ £5 (concessions £3.75) Family ticket £13.50. Group adult £4 (child/school £1). Please book groups in advance. Admission free to NTS members. For other details please phone 0131 243 9387
Facilities: 🅿 ✕ ♿ (wheelchair, induction loop, raised map) toilets for disabled shop ✈ (ex guide dogs) ♨

DRUMNADROCHIT Map 14 NH52

OFFICIAL LOCH NESS MONSTER EXHIBITION CENTRE
IV3 6TU
➲ (on A82, 12m S Inverness)
☎ 01456 450573 & 450218 ⓑ 01456 450770
e-mail: brem@loch-ness-scotland.com

A fascinating and popular multi-media presentation lasting 30 minutes. Seven themed areas cover the story from the pre-history of Scotland, through the cultural roots of the legend in Highland folklore, and into the 50-year controversy which surrounds it. Using latest technology in computer animation, lasers and multi-media projection systems.
Times: ✹ Open all year; Etr-May 9.30-5.30; Jun-Sep 9.30-6 (9-8.30 Jul & Aug); Winter 10-4. Last admission 30mins before closing.
Facilities: 🅿 💷 ✕ licensed ♿ (parking) toilets for disabled shop ✈ (ex in grounds/guide dogs) 🍴

URQUHART CASTLE
IV63 6XJ
➲ (on A82)
☎ 01456 450551

The castle was once Scotland's biggest and overlooks Loch Ness. It dates mainly from the 14th century, when it was
continued

built on the site of an earlier fort, and was destroyed before the 1715 Jacobite rebellion.
Times: Open all year, Apr-Sep, daily 9.30-6.30; Oct-Mar, daily 9.30-4.30. (Closed 25-26 Dec & 1-2 Jan). **Fee:** ✹ £6 (ch £1.20, concessions £4.50). Groups 11+ 10% discount. Prices valid until 2 Jan 2005. Please phone for further details. **Facilities:** 🅿 shop ✈ ♥

DUNBEATH Map 15 ND12

LAIDHAY CROFT MUSEUM
KW6 6EH
➲ (1m N of Dunbeath on A9)
☎ 01593 731244

The museum gives visitors a glimpse of a long-vanished way of life. The main building is a thatched Caithness longhouse, with the dwelling quarters, byre and stable all under one roof. It dates back some 200 years, and is furnished as it might have been 100 years ago. A collection of early farm tools and machinery is also shown. Near the house is a thatched winnowing barn with its roof supported on three 'Highland couples', or crucks.
Times: Open Etr-Oct, daily 10-6. **Fee:** £2 (ch 50p) **Facilities:** 🅿 💷 ♿ toilets for disabled

ELPHIN Map 14 NC21

HIGHLAND & RARE BREEDS FARM
IV27 4HH
➲ (on A835 in Elphin)
☎ 01854 666204 ⓑ 01854 666204 **2 for 1**

There are highland cattle, traditional 4-horned sheep with coloured fleeces, traditional Scottish ewes and lambs, rare breeds of pigs and goats. Many types of poultry, duck ponds, and a farm walk among the animals. Also on display are farm tools, crofting history, wool crafts and hand-spinning.
Times: Open Jul & Aug only **Fee:** ✹ £3.95 (ch £2.95, students & pen £3.50) **Facilities:** 🅿 ♿ (assistance available) toilets for disabled shop ✈ ➡

FORT GEORGE Map 14 NH75

FORT GEORGE
IV1 2TD
➲ (11m NE of Inverness)
☎ 01667 462777

Built following the Battle of Culloden as a Highland fortress for the army of George II, this is one of the outstanding artillery fortifications in Europe and still an active army barracks.
Times: Open all year, Apr-Sep daily 9.30-6.30; Oct-Mar daily 9.30-4.30. (Closed 25-26 Dec & 1-2 Jan). **Fee:** ✹ £6 (ch £1.50, concessions £4.50). Groups 11+ 10% discount. Prices valid until 2 Jan 2005. Please phone for further details. **Facilities:** 🅿 ✕ ♿ toilets for disabled shop ✈ ♥

QUEEN'S OWN HIGHLANDERS REGIMENTAL MUSEUM COLLECTION
IV2 7TD
➲ (turn off A96 5m from Inverness)
☎ 01463 224380 ⓑ 01463 224380

Fort George has been a military barracks since it was built in 1748-69, and was the Depot of the Seaforth Highlanders until 1961. The museum of the Queen's Own Highlanders (Seaforth and Camerons) is sited in the former Lieutenant Governor's house, where uniforms, medals and pictures are displayed.
Times: Open Apr-Sep, daily 10-6; Oct-Mar, Mon-Fri 10-4. (Closed Xmas, New Year & BH). **Fee:** ✹ Free. (Admission charged by Historic Scotland for entry to Fort George). **Facilities:** 🅿 ♿ (stair lift to 1st floor, wheelchair on 1st floor) toilets for disabled shop ✈ (ex guide dogs)

FORT WILLIAM   Map 14 NN17

INVERLOCHY CASTLE
PH33 6SN
➲ (2m NE of Fort William, off A82)
A fine well-preserved 13th-century castle of the Comyn family; in the form of a square, with round towers at the corners. The largest tower was the donjon or keep. This is one of Scotland's earliest castles.
Times: Open at all reasonable times. Facilities: P ✗ ♠

WEST HIGHLAND MUSEUM
Cameron Square PH33 6AJ
➲ (follow signs to tourist office, museum is next door)
☎ 01397 702169 ▤ 01397 701927
e-mail: info@westhighlandmuseum.org.uk
The displays illustrate traditional Highland life and history, with numerous Jacobite relics. One of them is the 'secret portrait' of 'Bonnie' Prince Charlie, which looks like meaningless daubs of paint but reveals a portrait when reflected in a metal cylinder.
Times: Open all year Jun-Sep, Mon-Sat 10-5 (also Jul-Aug Sun 2-5); Oct-May, Mon-Sat 10-4. Fee: £3 (ch 50p, concessions £2)
Facilities: P (100yds) (charge May-Oct, max. 2hrs stay) ♿ toilets for disabled shop ✗ (ex guide dogs)

GAIRLOCH   Map 14 NG87

GAIRLOCH HERITAGE MUSEUM
Achtercairn IV21 2BP
➲ (On junct of A382 & B8021 near police station & public car park)
☎ 01445 712287
e-mail: info@gairlochheritagemuseum.org.uk
A converted farmstead now houses the award-winning museum, which shows the way of life in this typical West Highland parish from early times to the 20th century. There are hands-on activities for children and reconstructions of a croft house room, a school room, a shop, and a smugglers' cave. You can also view Gairloch through one of the largest lenses assembled by the Northern Lighthouse Board.
Times: Open Apr-Sep, Mon-Sat 10-5; Oct, Mon-Fri 10-1.30 last admission 4.30. Winter months by arrangement.
Facilities: P ♿ shop ✗ (ex guide dogs)

GLENCOE   Map 14 NN15

GLENCOE & NORTH LORN FOLK MUSEUM
PH49 4HS
➲ (Turn off A82 at Glencoe crossroads then immediately right again into Glencoe village)
☎ 01855 811664
Two heather-thatched cottages in the main street of Glencoe now house items connected with the Macdonalds and the Jacobite risings. A variety of local domestic and farming exhibits, dairying and slate-working equipment, costumes and embroidery are also shown.
Times: Open 20 May-Sep, Mon-Sat 10-5.30. Fee: ✱ £2 (ch free, concessions £1.50). Facilities: P ♿ shop

GLENCOE VISITOR CENTRE
PA39 4HX
➲ (on A82, 17m S of Fort William)
☎ 01855 811307 & 811729 ▤ 01855 811772
Glencoe has stunning scenery and some of the most challenging climbs and walks in the Highlands. Red deer,
continued

wildcats, eagles and ptarmigan are among the wildlife. It is also known as a place of treachery and infamy. The Macdonalds of Glencoe were hosts to a party of troops who, under government orders, fell upon the men, women and children, in a bloody massacre in 1692. The Visitor Centre tells the story.
Times: Open - Site all year, daily. Visitor Centre Apr-Aug, 9.30-5.30; Mar-Apr & Sep-Oct, daily 10-5; Nov-Feb, Fri-Mon 10-4. (last admission 30 mins before closing). Times may change for 2005 please telephone or check on www.nts.org.uk Fee: ✱ 50p (ch & pen 30p). Includes parking. For more details phone 0131 243 9387 Facilities: P ⬤
♿ (induction loop in video programme room) toilets for disabled shop ✗ (ex guide dogs) ☕

GLENFINNAN   Map 14 NM98

GLENFINNAN MONUMENT
PH37 4LT
➲ (on A830, 18.5m W of Fort William)
☎ 01397 722250
e-mail: glenfinnan@nts.org.uk
The monument commemorates the Highlanders who fought for 'Bonnie' Prince Charlie in 1745. It stands in an awe-inspiring setting at the head of Loch Shiel. There is a visitor centre with information (commentary in four languages) on the Prince's campaign.
Times: Site open all year, daily. Visitor centre: daily Apr-Jun & Sep-Oct 10-5; Jul-Aug 9.30-5.30. Times may change for 2005 please telephone or check on www.nts.org.uk Fee: ✱ £2.50 (concessions £1) Admission free to NTS members. For other details please phone (0131) 243 9387 or check website. Facilities: P ⬤ ♿ (information centre only) shop ☕

GOLSPIE   Map 14 NH89

DUNROBIN CASTLE
KW10 6SF
➲ (1m NE on A9, from Golspie)
☎ 01408 633177 & 633268 ▤ 01408 634081
e-mail: info@dunrobincastle.net
The ancient seat of the Earls and Dukes of Sutherland is a splendid, gleaming, turreted structure, thanks largely to 19th-century rebuilding, and has a beautiful setting overlooking the sea. Paintings, furniture and family heirlooms are on display, and the gardens are on a grand scale to match the house. There are also falconry displays in the gardens.
Times: Open Apr-15 Oct, Mon-Sat 10.30-5.30, Sun 12-5.30. Closes 1 hr earlier Apr, May & Oct. Last admission half hour before closing.
Facilities: P ⬤ (access by arrangement only) shop ✗ 🚂

HELMSDALE   Map 14 ND01

TIMESPAN
Dunrobin St KW8 6JX
➲ (off A9 in centre of village, by Telford Bridge)
☎ 01431 821327 ▤ 01431 821058   [2 for 1]
e-mail: admin@timespan.org.uk
Located in an historic fishing village, this museum relates to the social and natural history of the area, and the art gallery has changing exhibitions of contemporary art and works by local artists. The garden has over 100 varieties of herbs and plants. There is a gift shop, and a café with beautiful views of the Telford Bridge.
Times: Open Apr- Oct, Mon-Sat 10-5, Sun 12-5. Fee: £4 (ch £2 pen & student £3). Family ticket £10. Facilities: P (150 mtrs) ⬤ ♿ (lift) toilets for disabled shop garden centre ✗ (ex guide dogs) 🚂

KINCRAIG   Map 14 NH80
HIGHLAND WILDLIFE PARK
PH21 1NL
➲ (on B9152, 7m S of Aviemore)
☎ 01540 651270 📠 01540 651236
e-mail: info@highlandwildlifepark.org
As you drive through the main reserve, you can see awe-inspiring European bison grazing alongside wild horses, red deer and highland cattle plus a wide variety of other species. Then in the walk-round forest, woodland and moorland habitats prepare for close encounters with animals such as wolves, capercaillie, arctic foxes, wildcats, pine martens, otters and owls. Special events every weekend April to October.
Times: Open throughout the year, weather permitting. Apr-Oct, 10-6; Jun-Aug 10-7; Nov-Mar 10-4. last entry 2 hours before closing. **Fee:** £8 (child £5.50, pen £7). **Facilities:** 🅿 ᵈᵉ & toilets for disabled shop ✗ ➡

KINGUSSIE   Map 14 NH70
HIGHLAND FOLK MUSEUM
Duke St PH21 1JG
➲ (12m SW of Aviemore off A9 at Kingussie)
☎ 01540 661307 📠 01540 661631
e-mail: highland.folk@highland.gov.uk
First established in 1935, this was Britain's first open-air museum. For a glimpse of life in a Blackhouse or a look at farming implements and domestic objects and furniture, this museum offers an internationally renowned collection of items. The Museum Store, not accessible to visitors in previous years, now displays in excess of 1,500 objects.
Times: Open Apr-Aug, Mon-Sat 9.30-5.30; Sep & Oct Mon-Fri, 9.30-4.30 **Fee:** ✱ £2.50 (ch & pen £1.50). **Facilities:** 🅿 & (ramp, door, rails) toilets for disabled shop ✗ (ex guide dogs) ➡

RUTHVEN BARRACKS
➲ (1m SE from Kingussie, signed from A9 and A86)
☎ 01667 460232   `FREE`
An infantry barracks erected in 1719 following the Jacobite rising of 1715, with two ranges of quarters and a stable block. Captured and burnt by Prince Charles Edward Stuart's army in 1746.
Times: Open at any reasonable time. **Facilities:** 🅿 ✗ 🅁

KIRKHILL   Map 14 NH54
MONIACK CASTLE (HIGHLAND WINERY)
IV5 7PQ
➲ (7m from Inverness on A862, near village of Beauly, on S side of Beauly Firth)
☎ 01463 831283 📠 01463 831419   `2 for 1`
e-mail: jg@moniackcastle.co.uk
Commercial wine-making is not a typically Scottish industry, but nevertheless a wide range of country-style wines is produced, including elderflower and silver birch; mead and sloe gin are also made here. A selection of related products and tours of the production area are available at this unique attraction, situated in a 16th-century castle.
Times: Open all year, Apr-Oct Mon-Sat 10-5. Nov-Mar, Mon-Fri 11-4. **Fee:** ✱ £2. **Facilities:** 🅿 shop ✗ ➡

NEWTONMORE   Map 14 NN79
CLAN MACPHERSON HOUSE & MUSEUM
Main St PH20 1DE
➲ (off A9 at junct of Newtonmore and Kingussie, museum on left after entering village)
☎ 01540 673332 📠 01540 673332
Containing relics and memorials of the clan chiefs and other Macpherson families as well as those of Prince Charles Edward Stuart, this museum also displays the Prince's letters to the Clan Chief of 1745 and one to the Prince from his father, the Old Pretender, along with royal warrants and the green banner of the clan. Other interesting historic exhibits include James Macpherson's fiddle, swords, pictures, decorations and medals.
Times: Open Apr-Oct, Mon-Sat 10-5, Sun 2-5. Other times by appointment. **Fee:** ✱ Free. Donations welcome.
Facilities: 🅿 & (ramp entrance from car park) toilets for disabled shop ✗ (ex guide dogs) ➡

HIGHLAND FOLK MUSEUM
Aultlarie Croft PH20 1AY
➲ (on A86, follow signs off A9)
☎ 01540 661307 📠 01540 661631
e-mail: highland.folk@highland.gov.uk
An early 18th-century farming township with turf houses has been reconstructed at this award-winning museum. A 1930's school houses old world maps, little wooden desks and a Coates library. Other attractions include a working croft with rare breed animals and tailor's workshop. Vintage buses run throughout the site.
Times: Open Apr-Aug, Mon-Sun 10.30-5.30; Sep Mon-Sun, 11-4.30; Oct Mon-Fri, 11-4.30 **Fee:** ✱ £5 (ch & pen £3) **Facilities:** 🅿 ➡ & (vintage bus with full disabled access) toilets for disabled shop ✗ (ex guide dogs) ➡

POOLEWE   Map 14 NG88
INVEREWE GARDEN
IV22 2LG
➲ (6m NE of Gairloch, on A832)
☎ 01445 781200 📠 01445 781497
e-mail: inverewe@nts.org.uk
The influence of the North Atlantic Drift enables this remarkable garden to grow rare and sub-tropical plants. At its best in early June, but full of beauty from March to October, Inverewe has a backdrop of magnificent mountains and stands to the north of Loch Maree.
Times: Open - Garden all year, Apr-Oct, daily 9.30-9 (or sunset if earlier). Nov-Mar, 9.30-4. Visitor Centre Apr-Sep, daily 9.30-5; Oct, daily 9.30-4. Times may change for 2005 please telephone or check on www.nts.org.uk **Fee:** ✱ £7 (concessions £5.25) Family ticket £19. Groups adult £5.60 (child/school £1). Admission free to NTS members. For other details please phone 0131 243 9387
Facilities: 🅿 ✗ licensed & (some paths difficult) toilets for disabled shop ✗ (ex guide dogs) ☕

ROSEMARKIE   Map 14 NH75
GROAM HOUSE MUSEUM
High St IV10 8UF
➲ (Turn off A9 at Tore onto A832)
☎ 01381 620961 & 01381 621730   `FREE`
📠 01381 621730
e-mail: groamhouse@ecosse.net
Opened in 1980, this community-based museum explores the history, culture and crafts of the mysterious Picts, who faded from history over a thousand years ago. Visitors can

continued

see the Rosemarkie Stones, large slabs that show Pictish carvings; paintings, a replica Pictish harp, and a collection of photographs of Pictish stones all over the country and interactive computer programmes. Temporary exhibitions take place, often as loans from other major museums.
Times: Open Etr week, daily 2-4.30; May-Sep, Mon-Sat, 10-5, Sun 2-4.30; Oct-Apr, Sat-Sun 2-4.30. Other times by appointment. Closed 13 Dec-5 Mar. **Facilities:** 🅿 ﹠ shop ✗ (ex guide dogs) ☕

STRATHPEFFER   Map 14 NH45
HIGHLAND MUSEUM OF CHILDHOOD
The Old Station IV14 9DH
➲ (take A9 N of Inverness, then at Tore rdbt, follow signs to Dingwall. Strathpeffer 5m W of Dingwall on A834)
☎ 01997 421031 📠 01997 421031   **2 for 1**
e-mail: info@
highlandmuseumofchildhood.org.uk
Located in a renovated Victorian railway station of 1885, the museum tells the story of childhood in the Highlands amongst the crofters and townsfolk; a way of life recorded in oral testimony, displays and evocative photographs. An award-winning video, "A Century of Highland Childhood" is shown. There are also doll and toy collections.
Times: Open Apr-Oct, daily 10-5, (Sun 2-5) also Jul & Aug evenings open to 7pm. Other times by arrangement. **Fee:** £2 (ch, pen & students £1.50). Family ticket £5 (2ad+3ch). **Facilities:** 🅿 🅿 ﹠ (tape tour with induction loop for partially sighted) shop ✗ (ex guide dogs) ☕

TORRIDON   Map 14 NG85
TORRIDON COUNTRYSIDE CENTRE
The Mains IV22 2EZ
➲ (N of A896)
☎ 01445 791221 📠 01445 791378
e-mail: aclipson@nts.scot.demon.co.uk.
Set amid some of Scotland's finest mountain scenery, the centre offers audio-visual presentations on the local wildlife. At the Mains nearby there are live deer to be seen.
Times: Open - Countryside Centre Good Fri-Sep, daily 10-6. Estate and Deer Museum daily all year. **Fee:** ✱ £2 (concessions £1) Admission free to NTS members. For other details please phone (0131) 243 9387 or check website. **Facilities:** 🅿 ﹠ toilets for disabled ☕

WICK   Map 15 ND35
CASTLE OF OLD WICK
➲ (1m S of Wick on Shore Road)   **FREE**
☎ 01667 460232
The ruin of the best-preserved Norse castle in Scotland. Dating from the 12th-century this spectacular site is on a spine of rock protecting the sea, between two deep, narrow gullies. Visitors must take great care and wear sensible shoes.
Times: Open at all reasonable times. **Facilities:** ✗ ▮

WICK HERITAGE CENTRE
20 Bank Row KW1 5HS
➲ (close to the harbour)
☎ 01955 605393 📠 01955 605393
The heritage centre is near the harbour in a complex of eight houses, yards and outbuildings. The centre illustrates local history from Neolithic times to the herring fishing industry. In addition, there is a complete working 19th-century lighthouse, and the famous Johnston collection of photographs.
Times: ✱ Open Jun-Sep, Mon-Sat 10-5. (Closed Sun).
Facilities: 🅿 ﹠ toilets for disabled

GREENOCK   Map 10 NS27
McLEAN MUSEUM & ART GALLERY
15 Kelly St PA16 8JX
➲ (close to Greenock West Railway Station and Greenock Bus Station)
☎ 01475 715624 📠 01475 715626   **FREE**
e-mail: museum@inverclyde.gov.uk

James Watt was born in Greenock, and various exhibits connected with him are shown. The museum also has an art collection, and displays on shipping, local and natural history, Egyptology and ethnography.
Times: Open all year, Mon-Sat 10-5. (Closed local & national PH).
Facilities: 🅿 (200mtrs) ﹠ (induction loop) toilets for disabled shop ✗ (ex guide & service dogs)

PORT GLASGOW   Map 10 NS37
NEWARK CASTLE
PA14 5NH
➲ (In Port Glasgow on A8)
☎ 01475 741858
The one-time house of the Maxwells, dating from the 15th and 17th centuries. The courtyard and hall are preserved. Fine turrets and the remains of painted ceilings can be seen, and the hall carries an inscription of 1597.
Times: Open Apr-Sep, daily 9.30-6.30. **Fee:** ✱ £2.50 (ch 75p, concessions £1.90). Groups 11+ 10% discount. Rates valid until 2 Jan 2005. Please phone for further details. **Facilities:** 🅿 shop ▮

CRICHTON   Map 11 NT36
CRICHTON CASTLE
EH37 5QH
➲ (2.5m SW of Pathhead, off A68)
☎ 01875 320017
The castle dates back to the 14th century, but most of what remains today was built over the following 300 years. A notable feature is the 16th-century wing built by the Earl of Bothwell in Italian style, with an arcade below.
Times: Open Apr-Sep, daily 9.30-6.30. **Fee:** ✱ £2.20 (ch 75p, concessions £1.60). Groups 11+ 10% discount. Prices valid until 2 Jan 2005. Please phone for further details. **Facilities:** 🅿 ▮

DALKEITH Map 11 NT36
EDINBURGH BUTTERFLY & INSECT WORLD
Dobbies Garden World, Lasswade EH18 1AZ
➲ (0.5m S of Edinburgh city bypass at Gilmerton junct or Sherrifhall rdbt)
☎ 0131 663 4932 🖷 0131 654 2774   **2 for 1**
e-mail: info@edinburgh-butterfly-world.co.uk
Richly coloured butterflies from all over the world can be seen flying among exotic rainforest plants, trees and flowers. The tropical pools are filled with giant waterlilies and colourful fish, and are surrounded by lush vegetation. Also scorpions, leaf cutting ants, beetles, tarantulas and other remarkable creatures. There is a unique honeybee display and daily insect handling sessions.
Times: Open Summer daily 9.30-5.30; winter daily 10-5. (Closed 25-26 Dec & 1 Jan). **Fee:** ✱ £4.70 (ch, concessions & students £3.60). Family ticket £15 (2ad+2ch). Party 10+. **Facilities:** 🅿 💷 ♿ toilets for disabled shop garden centre ✖ (ex guide dogs) ◼

NEWTONGRANGE Map 11 NT36
SCOTTISH MINING MUSEUM
Lady Victoria Colliery EH22 4QN
➲ (10m S of Edinburgh City on A7, signed from Edinburgh City bypass)
☎ 0131 663 7519 🖷 0131 654 0952   **2 for 1**
e-mail: visitorservices@
scottishminingmuseum.com
Based at Scotland's National Coalmining Museum offering an outstanding visit to Britains' finest Victorian colliery. Guided tours with miners, magic helmets, exhibitions, theatres, interactive displays and a visit to the coal face. Home to Scotland's largest steam engine.
Times: Open all year, daily Mar-Nov, 10-5. Last entry 3.30. Dec-Feb daily 10-4. Last entry 2.30 **Fee:** ✱ £4.95 (ch & concessions £3.30). Family ticket £15. Party 20+. **Facilities:** 🅿 💷 ✖ ♿ (Tactile Opportunites, interactive, audio tours) toilets for disabled shop ✖ (ex guide dogs) ◼

PENICUIK Map 11 NT26
EDINBURGH CRYSTAL VISITOR CENTRE
Eastfield EH26 8HB
➲ (on A701, Edinburgh to Peebles road)
☎ 01968 675128 🖷 01968 674847
e-mail: visitorcentre@edinburgh-crystal.co.uk
Watch skilled craftsmen as they take molten crystal and turn it into intricately decorated glassware. Not only can you talk to the craftsmen themselves but there is also video footage, story boards, artefacts and audio listening posts to help you understand the 300-year-old history of glassmaking. The shop includes the largest selection of Edinburgh crystal plus seconds at bargain prices. Coffee shop.
Times: Open Mon-Sat 10-5, Sun 11-5. **Fee:** ✱ Tours £3.50 (concessions £2.50). Family ticket £9. Party 12+. **Facilities:** 🅿 💷 ✗ licensed ♿ (ramp to first floor) toilets for disabled shop ✖ (ex guide dogs) ◼

MORAY

BALLINDALLOCH Map 15 NJ13
THE GLENLIVET DISTILLERY
Glenlivet AB37 9DB
➲ (off B9008, 10m N of Tomintoul)
☎ 01340 821720 🖷 01340 821718   **FREE**
e-mail: betty.munro@chivas.com
The visitor centre includes a guided tour of the whisky production facilities and a chance to see inside the vast bonded warehouses where the spirit matures. The new multimedia exhibition and interactive presentations communicate the unique history, and traditions of Glenlivet Scotch Whisky.
Times: Open Apr-Oct, Mon-Sat 10-4, Sun 12.30-4. **Facilities:** 🅿 💷 ♿ (cafeteria, lift to exhibition) toilets for disabled shop ✖ (ex guide dogs) ◼

BRODIE CASTLE Map 14 NH95
BRODIE CASTLE
IV36 2TE
➲ (4.5m W of Forres, off A96)
☎ 01309 641371 🖷 01309 641600
e-mail: brodiecastle@nts.org.uk
The Brodie family lived here for hundreds of years before passing the castle to the NTS in 1980. It contains many treasures, including furniture, porcelain and paintings. The extensive grounds include a woodland walk and an adventure playground. Wheelchairs for disabled visitors are available. Please telephone for details of recitals, concerts, open-air theatre etc.
Times: Open Apr & Jul-Aug, daily 12-4; May-Jun & Sep, Sun-Thu 12-4. Grounds all year, daily, 9.30-sunset. Times may change for 2005 please telephone or check on www.nts.org.uk **Fee:** ✱ £5 (concession £3.75) Groups adults £4 (child/school £1), please book groups in advance. Family ticket £13.50. Garden, grounds & car parking £1. Admission free to NTS members. For other details please phone 0131 243 9387
Facilities: 🅿 💷 ♿ (audio tape & information sheet in Braille) toilets for disabled shop ✖ (ex guide dogs) ♨

BUCKIE Map 15 NJ46
BUCKIE DRIFTER MARITIME HERITAGE CENTRE
Freuchny Rd AB56 1TT
➲ (off A98 at March Rd Industrial Estate. Follow road N to rdbt, straight ahead and follow road to left. Buckie Drifter car park is on right at bottom of hill)
☎ 01542 834646 🖷 01542 835995
e-mail: buckie.drifter@moray.gov.uk
An exciting maritime heritage centre, where you can discover what life was like in the fishing communities of Moray District during the herring boom years of the 1890s and 1930s. Sign on as a crew member of a steam drifter and
continued

find out how to catch herring. Try your hand at packing fish in a barrel.

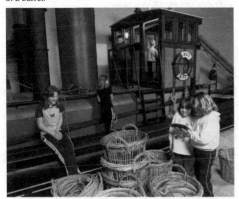

Times: ✱ Open end Mar-end Oct **Facilities:** 🅿 💷 ♿ (car parking, touch display on lower floor) toilets for disabled shop ✖ (ex assistance dogs) 🍴

CRAIGELLACHIE   Map 15 NJ24

SPEYSIDE COOPERAGE VISITOR CENTRE
Dufftown Rd AB38 9RS
➲ (1m S of Craigellachie on A941)
☎ 01340 871108 📠 01340 881437
e-mail: info@speyside-coopers.demon.co.uk
A working cooperage with unique visitor centre, where skilled coopers and their apprentices practise this ancient craft. Each year they repair around 100,000 oak casks which will be used to mature many different whiskies. The 'Acorn to Cask' exhibition traces the history and development of the coopering industry.
Times: Open all year, Mon-Fri 9.30-4. (Closed Xmas & New Year).
Fee: ✱ £3.10 (ch £1.80 & pen £2.50). Family ticket £8.50. Party 15+.
Facilities: 🅿 💷 ♿ (Special picnic table) toilets for disabled shop ✖ (ex guide dogs) 🍴

DUFFTOWN   Map 15 NJ34

BALVENIE CASTLE
AB55 4DH
➲ (In Dufftown on A941)
☎ 01340 820121
The ruined castle was the ancient stronghold of the Comyns, and became a stylish house in the 16th century.
Times: Open Apr-Sep, daily 9.30-6.30. **Fee:** ✱ £2.20 (ch 75p, concessions £1.60). Groups 11+ 10% discount. Prices valid until 2 Jan 2005. Please phone for further details. **Facilities:** 🅿 ♿ toilets for disabled ▮

GLENFIDDICH DISTILLERY
AB55 4DH
➲ (N of town, off A941)
☎ 01340 820373 📠 01340 822083
Set close to Balvenie Castle, the distillery was founded in 1887 by William Grant and has stayed in the hands of the family ever since. Visitors can see the whisky-making process in its various stages, including bottling, and then sample the finished product.
Times: ✱ Open all year Mon-Fri 9.30-4.30, also Etr-mid Oct Sat 9.30-4.30, Sun 12-4.30. (Closed Xmas & New Year).
Facilities: 🅿 ♿ (ramp access to production area & warehouse gallery) toilets for disabled shop ✖ (ex guide dogs)

DUFFUS   Map 15 NJ16

DUFFUS CASTLE
➲ (5m NW of Elgin on B9012 to Burghead) 🆓
☎ 01667 460232
One of the finest examples of a motte and bailey castle in Scotland with a later, very fine, stone hall house and curtain wall. The original seat of the Moray family.
Times: Open at all reasonable times. **Facilities:** 🅿 ✖ ▮

ELGIN   Map 15 NJ26

ELGIN CATHEDRAL
North College St IV30 1EL
☎ 01343 547171
Founded in 1224, the cathedral was known as the 'Lantern of the North' and the 'Glory of the Kingdom' because of its beauty. In 1390 it was burnt, along with most of the town. Although it was rebuilt, it fell into ruin after the Reformation. The ruins are quite substantial however, and there is still a good deal to admire, including the fine west towers and the octagonal chapter house.
Times: Open all year, Apr-Sep, daily 9.30-6.30; Oct-Mar, daily 9.30-4.30. (Closed Thu & Fri in winter, 25-26 Dec & 1-2 Jan).
Fee: ✱ £3 (ch £1, concessions £2.30). Groups 11+ 10% discount. Prices valid until 2 Jan 2005. Please phone for further details.
Facilities: 🅿 ♿ shop ▮

ELGIN MUSEUM
1 High St IV30 1EQ
➲ (East end of High Street, opp 'Safeway'. Follow brown heritage signs)
☎ 01343 543675 📠 01343 543675
e-mail: curator@elginmuseum.org.uk
This award-winning museum is internationally famous for its fossil fish and fossil reptiles, and for its Pictish stones. The displays relate to the natural and human history of Moray.
Times: Open Apr-Oct, Mon-Fri 10-5, Sat 11-4, Sun 2-5.
Facilities: 🅿 (50mtrs) ♿ (handrails, case displays at sitting level with large fonts) toilets for disabled shop ✖ (ex guide dogs)

PLUSCARDEN ABBEY
IV30 8UA
➲ (6m SW on unclass road)
☎ 01343 890257 📠 01343 890258   🆓
e-mail: monks@pluscardenabbey.org
The original monastery, founded by Alexander II in 1230, was burnt, probably by the Wolf of Badenoch who also destroyed Elgin Cathedral. It was restored in the 14th and 19th centuries, and reoccupied in 1948 by Benedictines from Prinknash. Once more a religious community, retreat facilities are available for men and women. All services (with Gregorian chant) are open to the public. Pluscarden Pentecost Lectures held annually on Tuesday, Wednesday and Thursday after Pentecost.
Times: Open all year, daily 4.45am-8.30pm
Facilities: 🅿 ♿ (induction loop, ramps to shop, garden partially accessible) toilets for disabled shop garden centre 🍴

FOCHABERS   Map 15 NJ35

BAXTERS HIGHLAND VILLAGE
IV32 7LD
➲ (1m W of Fochabers on A96)
☎ 01343 820393 📠 01343 821790   🆓
e-mail: highland.village@Baxters.co.uk
The Baxters food firm started here over 130 years ago and now sells its products in over 60 countries. Visitors can see
continued

the shop where the story began, watch an audio-visual display, and visit five shops. See the great hall, audio-visual theatre and cooking theatre. A food tasting area is open to visitors.
Times: Open all year, Jan-Mar 10-5; Apr-Dec 9-5.30.
Facilities: ⊞ ✗ licensed & (parking facilities) toilets for disabled shop ✗ (ex guide dogs) ◀

FORRES   Map 14 NJ05
DALLAS DHU DISTILLERY
IV36 2RR
➲ (1m S of Forres, off A940)
☎ 01309 676548
A perfectly preserved time capsule of the distiller's art. It was built in 1898 to supply malt whisky for Wright and Greig's 'Roderick Dhu' blend. Visitors are welcome to wander at will through this fine old Victorian distillery, or to take a guided tour, dram included.
Times: Open all year, Apr-Sep, daily 9.30-6.30; Oct-Mar, daily 9.30-4.30. (Closed Thu & Fri in winter, 25-26 Dec & 1-2 Jan).
Fee: ✱ £3.50 (ch £1, concessions £2.60). Groups 11+ 10% discount. Prices valid until 2 Jan 2005. Please phone for further details.
Facilities: ⊞ & toilets for disabled shop ✗ ▯

FALCONER MUSEUM
Tolbooth St IV36 1PH
➲ (11 miles W of Elgin, 26 miles E of Iverness)
☎ 01309 673701 ▤ 01309 673701   FREE
e-mail: museums@moray.gov.uk
Founded by bequests made by two brothers, Alexander and Hugh Falconer. Hugh was a distinguished scientist, friend of Darwin, recipient of many honours and Vice-President of the Royal Society. On display are fossil mammals collected by him, and items relating to his involvement in the study of anthropology. Other displays are on local wildlife, geology, archaeology and history. Also you can see the Forres Quincentennial Time Capsule.
Times: Open all year - Apr-Oct, Mon-Sat 10-5; Nov-Mar, Mon-Thu 11-12.30 & 1-3.30. (Closed Good Fri & May Day).
Facilities: ⊞ & (induction loop system) shop ✗ (ex guide dogs)

SUENO'S STONE
➲ (E end of Forres, off A96)
☎ 01667 460232   FREE
The most remarkable sculptured monument in Britain, probably a cenotaph, standing over 20 feet high and dating back to the end of the first millennium AD. Covered by a protective glass enclosure.
Times: Open at all reasonable times. **Facilities:** ⊞ ✗ ▯

KEITH   Map 15 NJ45
STRATHISLA DISTILLERY
Seafield Av AB55 5BS
➲ (follow A96 Aberdeen to Inverness road, Strathisla is signed midway through the town)
☎ 01542 783044 ▤ 01542 783039
e-mail: jeanett.grant@chivas.com
Tour the oldest distillery in the highlands, founded in 1786. Discover the art of the blender before sipping a dram in luxurious comfort.
Times: Open Apr-Oct, Mon-Sat 10-4, Sun 12.30-4 **Fee:** £5 per person (ch free, children under 8 not admitted to production areas, but welcome in the centre) **Facilities:** ⊞ & (access is very limited) toilets for disabled shop ✗ (ex guide dogs) ◀

MARYPARK   Map 15 NJ13
GLENFARCLAS DISTILLERY
AB37 9BD
➲ (4m W of Aberlour on A95 to Grantown-on-Spey)
☎ 01807 500245 & 500257 ▤ 01807 500234
e-mail: J&GGrant@glenfarclas.demon.co.uk
Established in 1836, Glenfarclas Distillery is proud of its independence. There is guided tour illustrating their whisky's history and production, followed by a dram in the splendour of the Ships Room or a chance to browse in the gift shop.
Times: ✱ Open Jan-Mar, Mon-Fri 10-4; Apr-Sep, Mon-Fri 10-5, Jul-Sep also open Sat 10-5; Oct-Dec, Mon-Fri 10-4. (Closed Sun).
Facilities: ⊞ & (only visitor centre is accessible) toilets for disabled shop ✗ (ex guide dogs in visitor centre) ◀

ROTHES   Map 15 NJ24
GLEN GRANT DISTILLERY
AB38 7BS
➲ (on A941, Elgin-Rothes road)
☎ 01340 832118 ▤ 01340 832104   FREE
e-mail: jennifer.robertson@chivas.com
Founded in 1840 in a sheltered glen by the two Grant brothers. Discover the secrets of the distillery, including the delightful Victorian garden originally created by Major Grant, and now restored to its former glory, where you can enjoy a dram.
Times: Open Apr-Oct, Mon-Sat 10-4, Sun 12.30-4.
Facilities: ⊞ & (reception centre & still house) toilets for disabled shop ✗ (ex guide dogs) ◀

SPEY BAY   Map 15 NJ36
THE MORAY FIRTH WILDLIFE CENTRE
IV32 7PJ
➲ (off A96 onto B9014 at Fochabers, follow road approx 5m to village of Spey Bay. Turn left at Spey Bay Hotel and follow road for 500mtrs)
☎ 01343 820339 ▤ 01343 829109   FREE
e-mail: enquiries@mfwc.co.uk
The centre, owned and operated by the Whale and Dolphin Conservation Society, lies at the mouth of the River Spey and is housed in a former salmon fishing station, built in 1768. There is a free exhibition about the Moray Firth dolphins and the wildlife of Spey Bay. Visitors can browse through a well-stocked gift shop and enjoy refreshments in the cosy tea room.
Times: Open Apr-Oct 10.30-5. Check for winter opening times
Facilities: ⊞ ▣ & toilets for disabled shop ✗ (ex guide dogs & outside) ◀

TOMINTOUL   Map 15 NJ11
TOMINTOUL MUSEUM
The Square AB37 9ET
➲ (on A939, 13m E of Grantown)
☎ 01309 673701 ▤ 01309 673701   FREE
e-mail: museums@moray.gov.uk
Situated in one of the highest villages in Britain, the museum features a reconstructed crofter's kitchen and smiddy, with other displays on the local wildlife, the story of Tomintoul, and the local skiing industry.
Times: Open 25 Mar-May, Mon-Fri 9.30-12 & 2-4; Jun-Aug, Mon-Sat, 9.30-12 & 2-4.30; Sep, Mon-Sat, 9.30-12 & 2-4; 30 Sep-25 Oct, Mon-Fri, 9.30-12 & 2-4. (Closed May Day & Good Fri.)
Facilities: ⊞ & (Induction loop and sound commentaries) shop ✗ (ex guide dogs)

NORTH AYRSHIRE

IRVINE Map 10 NS34
THE BIG IDEA
The Harbourside KA12 8XX
➲ (Turn off A78 Irvine & follow signs for Irvine Harbourside & The Big Idea. The Big Idea on right)
☎ 08708 404030 ▤ 08708 403130
e-mail: net@bigidea.org.uk
The Big Idea is a permanent Millennium exhibition on the Ardeer Peninsula linked to Irvine harbourside by a retractable pedestrian bridge. It features 100 years of Nobel Laureates, and 1,000 years of invention and creative genius. Visitors can explore the history of mankind's inventions, creations and innovations.
Times: Open Mon-Fri, 10-5, Sat & Sun 10-6. Please phone for winter opening hours (Nov-Feb). **Facilities:** 🅿 🏧 ⬥ (wheelchairs) toilets for disabled shop ✖ (ex guide dogs or outside) 🍴

SCOTTISH MARITIME MUSEUM
Harbourside KA12 8QE
➲ (Follow AA signs from Irvine)
☎ 01294 278283 ▤ 01294 313211 [2 for 1]
e-mail: smm@tildesley.fsbusiness.co.uk
The museum has displays that reflect all aspects of Scottish maritime history. Vessels can be seen afloat in the harbour and undercover. Experience life in a 1910 shipyard worker's tenement flat. Visit the Linthouse Engine Shop originally built in 1872, which is being developed and holds a substantial part of the museum's collection in open store.
Times: Open Apr-Oct 10-5 **Fee:** ✱ £2.50 (ch & pen £1.75). Family ticket £5. **Facilities:** 🅿 🏧 ⬥ (audio tapes for blind) toilets for disabled shop ✖ (ex guide dogs)

VENNEL GALLERY
10 Glasgow Vennel KA12 0BD
☎ 01294 275059 ▤ 01294 275059 [2 for 1]
e-mail: vennel@north-ayrshire.gov.uk
The Vennel Gallery has a reputation for exciting and varied exhibitions, ranging from international to local artists. Behind the museum is the Heckling Shop where Robert Burns, Scotland's most famous poet, spent part of his youth learning the trade of flax dressing. In addition to the audio-visual programme on Burns, there is a reconstruction of his lodgings at No.4 Glasgow Vennel, Irvine.
Times: Open all year Thu-Sun 10-1 & 2-5 **Facilities:** 🅿 (residential area) ⬥ shop ✖ (ex guide dogs)

LARGS Map 10 NS25
KELBURN CASTLE AND COUNTRY CENTRE
Fairlie KA29 0BE
➲ (on A78, 2m S of Largs)
☎ 01475 568685 ▤ 01475 568121 [2 for 1]
e-mail: admin@kelburncountrycentre.com
Historic home of the Earls of Glasgow, Kelburn is famous for its romantic Glen, family gardens, unique trees and spectacular views over the Firth of Clyde. Glen walks, riding and trekking centre, adventure course, activity workshop, Kelburn Story Cartoon Exhibition and a family museum. The "Secret Forest" at the centre, Scotland's most unusual attraction, is a chance to explore the Giant's Castle, maze of
continued

the Green Man and secret grotto. Also included is a new Falconry Centre.
Times: Open all year, Etr-end Oct, daily 10-6; Nov-Mar, 11-dusk, Grounds only. **Fee:** ✱ £5 (concessions £3.50). Family tickets £15.
Facilities: 🅿 🏧 ✖ licensed ⬥ (Ranger service to assist disabled) toilets for disabled shop 🍴

VIKINGAR!
Greenock Rd KA30 8QL
➲ (opposite RNLI lifeboat station on A78, 0.5m into Largs)
☎ 01475 689777 ▤ 01475 689444
e-mail: anyone@vikingar.co.uk
A multi-media experience that takes you from the first Viking raids in Scotland to their defeat at the Battle of Largs.
Times: ✱ Open daily, Apr-Sep, Mon-Fri & Sun 10.30-5.30, Sat 12.30-3.30; Oct-Mar, daily 10.30-5.30; Nov & Feb, wknds only, Sat 12.30-3.30, Sun 10.30-3.30. (Closed Dec & Jan). **Facilities:** 🅿 🏧 ⬥ toilets for disabled shop ✖ (ex guide dogs) 🍴

SALTCOATS Map 10 NS24
NORTH AYRSHIRE MUSEUM
Manse St, Kirkgate KA21 5AA
☎ 01294 464174 ▤ 01294 464174 [2 for 1]
e-mail: namuseum@north-ayrshire.gov.uk
This museum is housed in an 18th-century church, and features a rich variety of artefacts from the North Ayrshire area, including archaeological and social history material. There is a continuing programme of temporary exhibitions.
Times: Open all year, Mon-Sat (ex Sun & Wed) 10-1 & 2-5.
Facilities: 🅿 (100mtrs) ⬥ toilets for disabled shop ✖ (ex guide dogs)

NORTH LANARKSHIRE

COATBRIDGE Map 11 NS76
SUMMERLEE HERITAGE TRUST
Heritage Way, West Canal St ML5 1QD
➲ (Follow main routes towards town centre, adjacent to Coatbridge central station)
☎ 01236 431261 ▤ 01236 440429 [FREE]
e-mail: museums@northlan.gov.uk
A 20-acre museum of social and industrial history centering on the remains of the Summerlee Ironworks which were put into blast in the 1830s. The exhibition hall features displays of social and industrial history including working machinery and recreated workshop interiors. Outside, Summerlee operates the only working tram in Scotland, a coal mine and reconstructed miners' rows with interiors dating from 1840.
Times: Open daily 10-5. Nov-Mar 10-4. (Closed 25-26 Dec & 1-2 Jan).
Facilities: 🅿 🏧 ⬥ (wheelchair available & staff assistance) toilets for disabled shop ✖ (ex guide dogs)

MOTHERWELL Map 11 NS75
MOTHERWELL HERITAGE CENTRE
High Rd ML1 3HU
➲ (M74 junct 6, A723 for town centre. At top of hill turn left, after pedestrian crossing and just before railway bridge)
☎ 01698 251000 ▤ 01698 268867 [FREE]
e-mail: museums@northlan.gov.uk
This award-winning audio-visual experince, 'Technopolis', traces the history of the area from Roman times to the rise of
continued

19th-century industry and the post-industrial era. There is also a fine viewing tower, an exhibition gallery and family history research facilities. A mixed programme of community events and touring exhibitions occur throughout the year. **Times:** Open Wed-Sat 10-5 (Thu 10-7), Sun 12-5. (Closed Mon & Tue, except for BH's). **Facilities:** 🅿 ㅤ& (lifts, audio info & Braille buttons) toilets for disabled shop 🖈 (ex guide dogs)

PERTH & KINROSS

ABERFELDY　　　　　　Map 14 NN84

DEWAR'S WORLD OF WHISKY
Aberfeldy Distillery PH15 2EB
➲ (from A9 take A827 for Aberfeldy at Ballinluig)
☎ 01887 822010 ▤ 01887 822012 　2 for 1
e-mail: worldofwhisky@dewars.com
Tradition and the latest technology are combined here to tell the story of Dewar's White Label Whisky. Visitors are able to sample the product in the Nosing and Tasting Bar, and have a guided tour of the Aberfeldy distillery, where they can see traditional techniques being employed by skilled craftsmen. **Times:** Open Apr-Oct, Mon-Sat 10-6, Sun noon-4; Nov-Mar, Mon-Sat 10-4. (Closed Xmas & New Year). **Fee:** Prices not confirmed for 2005 **Facilities:** 🅿 🍺 & (visitor centre only accessible) toilets for disabled shop 🖈 (ex guide dogs) 🍴

BLAIR ATHOLL　　　　　　Map 14 NN86

BLAIR CASTLE
PH18 5TL
➲ (7m NW of Pitlochry, off A9 at Blair Atholl & follow signs to Blair Castle)
☎ 01796 481207 ▤ 01796 481487
e-mail: office@blair-castle.co.uk

Ancient seat of the Dukes of Atholl and the Atholl Highlanders, the Duke's unique private army. The castle dates back to the 13th century but was altered in the 18th, and later given a castellated exterior. The oldest part is Cumming's Tower, built in about 1270. There are paintings, furniture, porcelain, historic artefacts, Jacobite relics, lace, tapestries, and Masonic regalia. The extensive grounds include a deer park, and a restored 18th-century walled garden. Events are held throughout the year, including the annual parade of the Duke's Private Army (ring for details). **Times:** Open 2 Nov-15 Mar, Tue-Sat 9.30-12.30 (last admission); 19 Mar-28 Oct, daily 9.30-4.30 (last admission). **Fee:** Prices not confirmed for 2005 **Facilities:** 🅿 🍺 ✗ licensed & (scooter, parking) shop 🖈 (ex guide dogs) 🍴

CRIEFF　　　　　　Map 11 NN82

INNERPEFFRAY LIBRARY
PH7 3RF
➲ (4.5m SE on B8062)
☎ 01764 652819
e-mail: library@innerpeff.fsnet.co.uk
This is Scotland's oldest free lending library. It was founded in 1680 and is still open every day except Thursdays. It is housed in a late 18th-century building, and contains a notable collection of bibles and rare books. Adjacent is St Mary's Chapel, the original site for the library and the Drummond family burial place. **Times:** Open all year, Mon-Wed & Fri-Sat 10-12.45 & 2-4.45, Sun 2-4. (Closed Thu). Nov-Feb appointment only. **Fee:** £2.50 (ch under 15 50p) **Facilities:** 🅿 🍺 🖈 (ex guide dogs)

THE FAMOUS GROUSE EXPERIENCE
The Hosh PH7 4HA
➲ (1.5m NW off A85)
☎ 01764 656565 ▤ 01764 654366
e-mail: enquiries@famousgrouse.com
A trip to Crieff is incomplete without a visit to The Famous Grouse Experience, set in Scotland's oldest, most visited and award-winning distillery. Opened in July 2002, this attraction is a fun and interesting day out which combines the traditional distillery visit with a unique exciting sensory experience. Spend a relaxing few hours absorbing the history of the brand. Test your senses and see if you have what it takes to become a 'Whisky Nose'. Have lunch, a snack or even a barbecue at the family restaurant. Visit the well-stocked shop or enjoy a peaceful woodland walk over The Brig O' Dram. **Times:** Open daily 9-6 (last tour 4.30). (Closed 25 & 26 Dec.) **Facilities:** 🅿 🍺 ✗ licensed & Lifts in all areas toilets for disabled shop 🖈 (ex guide dogs) 🍴

DUNKELD　　　　　　Map 11 NO04

THE ELL SHOP & LITTLE HOUSES
The Cross PH8 0AN
➲ (off A9, 15m N of Perth)
☎ 01350 727460 　　FREE
e-mail: dunkeld@nts.org.uk
The National Trust owns two rows of 20 houses in Dunkeld, and has preserved their 17th/18th-century character. They are not open to the public, but there is a display and audio-visual show in the Information Centre. **Times:** Open Ell Shop mid Mar-Sep, Mon-Sat, 10-5.30, Sun 12.30-5.30. Oct-mid Dec, Mon-Sat 10-4.30, Sun 12.30-4.30. **Facilities:** 🅿 (300yds) & toilets for disabled shop 🖈 🍴

KILLIECRANKIE　　　　　　Map 14 NN96

KILLIECRANKIE VISITOR CENTRE
NTS Visitor Centre PH16 5LG
➲ (3m N of Pitlochry on B8079)
☎ 01796 473233 ▤ 01796 473233 　FREE
e-mail: killiecrankie@nts.org.uk
The visitor centre features an exhibition on the battle of 1689, when the Jacobite army routed the English, although the Jacobite leader, 'Bonnie Dundee', was mortally wounded in the attack. The wooded gorge is a notable beauty spot, admired by Queen Victoria, and there are some splendid walks. **Times:** Visitor Centre: Apr-Jun & Sep-Oct, daily 10-5.30, Jul & Aug, daily 9.30-6. Site: open all year daily. Times may change for 2005 please telephone or check on www.nts.org.uk **Facilities:** 🅿 🍺 & (visitor centre only) toilets for disabled shop 🍴

KINROSS
Map 11 NO10

KINROSS HOUSE GARDENS
KY13 8ET
➲ (M90 (Edinburgh to Perth), junct 6 to Kinross, and signed in village)
☎ 01577 862900   ▤ 01577 863372
e-mail: jm@kinrosshouse.com
Yew hedges, roses and herbaceous borders are the elegant attractions of these formal gardens. The 17th-century house was built by Sir William Bruce, but is not generally open to the public.
Times: ✱ Gardens only open Apr-Sep, daily 10-7.
Facilities: ▯ & ✖ (ex guide dogs)

LOCH LEVEN CASTLE
Castle Island KY13 7AR
➲ (on an island in Loch Leven accessible by boat from Kinross)
☎ 01786 450000
Mary, Queen of Scots was imprisoned here in this five-storey castle in 1567 - she escaped 11 months later and so gave the 14th-century castle its special place in history.
Times: Open Apr-Sep, daily 9.30-6.30. **Fee:** ✱ £3.50 (ch £1.20, concessions £2.50). Charge includes ferry trip. Groups 11+ 10% discount. Rates valid until 2 Jan 2005. Please phone for further details.
Facilities: ▯ shop ✖ ▮

RSPB NATURE RESERVE VANE FARM
By Loch Leven KY13 9LX
➲ (on S shore of Loch Leven, entered off B9097 to Glenrothes, 2m E M90 junct 5)
☎ 01577 862355   ▤ 01577 862013   **2 for 1**
e-mail: vane.farm@rspb.org.uk
Well placed beside Loch Leven, with a nature trail and hides overlooking the Loch and a woodland trail with stunning panoramic views. Noted for its pink-footed geese. The area also attracts whooper swans, greylag geese and great spotted woodpeckers amongst others. Details of special events are available from the Visitors' Centre.
Times: Open daily, 10-5. Closed 25-26 Dec, 1-2 Jan. **Fee:** £3 (ch 50p, concessions £2). Family £6. **Facilities:** ▯ ▮ & (wheelchair extensions, ramps, telescopes) toilets for disabled shop ✖ (ex guide dogs) ▅

MILNATHORT
Map 11 NO10

BURLEIGH CASTLE
KY13 7XZ
➲ (0.5m E of Milnathort on A911)
The roofless but otherwise complete ruin of a tower house of about 1500, with a section of defensive barmkin wall and a remarkable corner tower with a square cap-house corbelled out. This castle was often visited by James IV.
Times: Open summer only. Keys available locally, telephone 01786 45000. **Facilities:** ✖ ▮

MUTHILL
Map 11 NN81

DRUMMOND GARDENS
PH7 4HZ   **2 for 1**
➲ (2m S of Crieff on A822)
☎ 01764 681257 & 681433   ▤ 01764 681550
e-mail: thegardens@drummondcastle.sol.co.uk
The gardens of Drummond Castle were originally laid out in 1630 by John Drummond, 2nd Earl of Perth. In 1830, the

parterre was changed to an Italian style. The multi-faceted sundial was designed by John Mylne, Master Mason to Charles I. These are Scotland's largest formal gardens and amongst the finest in Europe.
Times: Open Gardens May-Oct, daily 1-6 (Last admission 5). Also Etr for 4 days. **Fee:** Prices not confirmed for 2005 **Facilities:** ▯ & toilets for disabled shop

PERTH
Map 11 NO12

BLACK WATCH REGIMENTAL MUSEUM
Balhousie Castle, Hay St PH1 5HR
➲ (Follow signs to Perth & Black Watch Museum, approach via Dunkeld Road)
☎ 0131 310 8530   ▤ 01738 643245
e-mail: rhq@theblackwatch.co.uk
The museum of Scotland's oldest highland regiment, which portrays the history of the Black Watch from 1725 to the present day. A memorial room remembers the soldiers of WWI with a lifelike figure in a trench, video footage and many artefacts from the period. Silver, uniforms, weapons and pictures are on display to enable visitors to feel what it was like to be in the regiment.
Times: Open all year. May-Sep, Mon-Sat 10-4.30 (Closed last Sat in Jun); Oct-Apr, Mon-Fri, 10-3.30 (Closed 23 Dec-6 Jan). Other times & Parties 16+ by appointment. **Fee:** Donations. **Facilities:** ▯ & (1 bay parking for disabled) toilets for disabled shop ✖ (ex guide dogs) ▅

BRANKLYN GARDEN
116 Dundee Rd PH2 7BB
➲ (on A85)
☎ 01738 625535
e-mail: aclipson@nts.scot.demon.co.uk
The gardens cover two acres and are noted for their collections of rhododendrons, shrubs and alpines. Garden tours and botanical painting courses are held.
Times: Apr & Jul-Sep, Fri-Tue 10-5; May-Jun, daily, 10-5. Times may change for 2005 please telephone or check on www.nts.org.uk
Fee: ✱ £5 (concessions £3.75) Group adult £4 (child/school £1), groups please book in advance. Family ticket £13.50. Admission free to NTS members. For other details please phone 0131 243 9387
Facilities: ▯ ✖ (ex guide dogs) ▯

> We endeavour to be as accurate as possible, but changes to times and other information can occur after the guide has gone to press.

> This symbol indicates attractions which have chosen to participate in our 2-for-1 voucher scheme
> **2-for-1**

HUNTINGTOWER CASTLE
PH1 3JL
➲ (2m W)
☎ 01738 627231
Formerly known as Ruthven Castle and famous as the scene of the so-called 'Raid of Ruthven' in 1582, this structure was built in the 15th and 16th centuries and features a painted ceiling.
Times: Open all year, Apr-Sep, daily 9.30-6.30; Oct-Mar, daily 9.30-4.30. (Closed Thu & Fri in winter, 25-26 Dec & 1-2 Jan).
Fee: ✱ £2.50 (ch 75p, concessions £1.90). Groups 11+ 10% discount. Rates valid until 2 Jan 2005. Please phone for further details.
Facilities: 🅿 shop ✖ ♫

PERTH MUSEUM & ART GALLERY
78 George St PH1 5LB
➲ (in town centre)
☎ 01738 632488 ▤ 01738 443505
e-mail: museum@pkc.gov.uk
Visit Perth Museum and Art Gallery for a fascinating look into Perthshire throughout the ages. Collections cover silver, glass, art, natural history, archaeology and human history.
Times: ✱ Open all year, Mon-Sat 10-5. (Closed Xmas-New Year).
Facilities: 🅿 (adjacent) ♿ toilets for disabled shop ✖ (ex guide dogs)

PITLOCHRY   Map 14 NN95

EDRADOUR DISTILLERY
PH16 5JP
➲ (2.5m E of Pitlochry on A924)
☎ 01796 472095 ▤ 01796 472002   FREE
It was in 1825 that a group of local farmers founded Edradour, naming it after the bubbling burn that runs through it. It is Scotland's smallest distillery and is virtually unchanged since Victorian times. Have a dram of whisky while watching an audio-visual in the malt barn and then take a guided tour through the distillery itself.
Times: Open Jan-Feb, Mon-Sat 10-5, Sun 12.4; Mar-Oct Mon-Sat 9.30-6, Sun 11.30-6; Nov-Dec, Mon-Sat 9.30-5, Sun 12-5. (Last tour 1hr before close, private tours arranged for a fee). **Facilities:** 🅿 ♿ toilets for disabled shop ✖ (ex guide & hearing dogs)

SCOTTISH & SOUTHERN ENERGY VISITOR CENTRE, DAM & FISH PASS
PH16 5ND
➲ (Turn off A9, 24m N of Perth)
☎ 01796 473152 ▤ 01882 634 709
The visitor centre features an exhibition showing how electricity is brought from the power station to the customer, and there is access to the turbine viewing gallery. The salmon ladder viewing chamber allows you to see the fish as they travel upstream to their spawning ground.
Times: Open Apr-Sep, Mon-Fri 10-5.30. (Wknd opening Jul, Aug & BH's) **Fee:** Prices not confirmed for 2005 **Facilities:** 🅿 ♿ (monitor viewing of salmon fish pass) toilets for disabled shop ✖ (ex guide dogs) ◄

QUEEN'S VIEW   Map 14 NN85

QUEEN'S VIEW VISITOR CENTRE
PH16 5NR
➲ (7m W of Pitlochry on B8019)
☎ 01350 727284 ▤ 01350 728635
e-mail: peter.fullarton@forestry.gsi.gov.uk
Queen Victoria admired the view on a visit here in 1866; it is possibly one of the most famous views in Scotland. The
continued

area, in the heart of the Tay Forest Park, has a variety of woodlands that visitors can walk or cycle in. A new exhibition and audio-visual display 'The Cradle of Scottish Forestry' tells the history of the people and the forests of highland Perthshire.
Times: Open Apr-Oct, daily 10-6. **Fee:** Prices not confirmed for 2005
Facilities: 🅿 (charged) ▆ ♿ toilets for disabled shop ◄

SCONE   Map 11 NO12

SCONE PALACE
PH2 6BD
➲ (2m NE of Perth on A93)
☎ 01738 552300 ▤ 01738 552588   2 for 1
e-mail: visits@scone-palace.co.uk
Scottish kings were crowned at Scone until 1651 and it was the site of the famous coronation Stone of Destiny from the 9th century until the English seized the Stone in 1296. The castellated edifice of the present palace dates from 1803 but incorporates the 16th-century and earlier buildings. The interior houses objets d'art, including French & Scottish furniture, an extensive porcelain collection and paintings. The grounds include a Pinetum, the original Douglas Fir, the unique Murray Star Maze, woodland walks and herbaceous plantings. Also David Douglas Trail.
Times: Open Apr-Oct. **Fee:** Prices not confirmed for 2005
Facilities: 🅿 ▆ ✖ licensed ♿ (stairlift which gives access to all state rooms) toilets for disabled shop ◄

WEEM   Map 14 NN84

CASTLE MENZIES
PH15 2JD
➲ (Follow signs from main roads)
☎ 01887 820982 ▤ 01887 820982
e-mail: menziesclan@tesco.net
Restored seat of the Chiefs of Clan Menzies, and a fine example of a 16th-century Z-plan fortified tower house. Prince Charles Edward Stuart stayed here briefly on his way to Culloden in 1746. The whole of the 16th-century building can be explored, and there's a small clan museum.
Times: Open Apr-13 Oct, Mon-Sat 10.30-5, Sun 2-5. **Fee:** £3.50 (ch £2, concessions £3). **Facilities:** 🅿 ♿ toilets for disabled shop ✖ (ex guide dogs)

KILBARCHAN   Map 10 NS46

WEAVER'S COTTAGE
The Cross PA10 2JG
➲ (off A737, 12m SW of Glasgow)
☎ 01505 705588
e-mail: aclipson@nts.scot.demon.co.uk
The weaving craft is regularly demonstrated at this delightful 18th-century cottage museum, and there is a collection of weaving equipment and other domestic utensils.
Times: Open Apr-Sep, Fri-Tue, 1-5; morning visits available for pre-booked groups. Times may change for 2005 please telephone or check on www.nts.org.uk **Fee:** ✱ £3.50 (concessions £2.60) Family ticket £9.50. Groups adult £2.80 (child/school £1). Please book groups in advance. Admission free to NTS members. For other details please phone 0131 243 9387 **Facilities:** 🅿 ✖ (ex guide dogs) ♒

LANGBANK   Map 10 NS37

FINLAYSTONE COUNTRY ESTATE
PA14 6TJ
➲ (on A8 W of Langbank, 10m W of Glasgow
Airport, follow Thistle signs)
☎ 01475 540505 📋 01475 540285   `2 for 1`
e-mail: info@finlaystone.co.uk
A beautiful country estate, historic formal gardens which are
renowned for thier natural beauty, woodland walks and play
areas. The 'Dolly Mixture', an international collection of
dolls, can be seen in the Visitor Centre.
Times: Open all year. Woodland & Gardens daily, 10-5.
Fee: ✱ Garden & Woods £3 (ch & pen £2). 'The Dolly Mixture' Doll
Museum free. **Facilities:** 🅿 💷 ♿ (lift to second floor pathways for
wheelchairs) toilets for disabled shop ▰

LOCHWINNOCH   Map 10 NS35

RSPB LOCHWINNOCH NATURE RESERVE
Largs Rd PA12 4JF
➲ (on A760, Largs road, opposite Lochwinnoch
station, 16m SW of Glasgow)
☎ 01505 842663 📋 01505 843026   `2 for 1`
e-mail: Lochwinnoch@rspb.org.uk
The reserve, part of Clyde Muirshiel Regional Park and a Site
of Special Scientific Interest, comprises two shallow lochs
fringed by marsh which in turn is fringed by scrub and
woodland. There are two trails leading to three hides and a
visitor centre with a viewing.
Times: Open all year, daily 10-5. (Closed 1-2 Jan & 25-26 Dec).
Fee: Prices not confirmed for 2005 **Facilities:** 🅿 ♿ (hides are all
wheelchair accessible) toilets for disabled shop ✖ ▰

PAISLEY   Map 11 NS46

COATS OBSERVATORY
49 Oakshaw St West PA1 2DE
➲ (M8 junct 27, follow signs to town centre until
on Gordon St (A761). Turn left onto Causeyside St,
left onto New St then left onto High St.)
☎ 0141 889 2013 📋 0141 889 9240   `FREE`
e-mail: museums.els@renfrewshire.gov.uk
The Observatory, funded by Thomas Coats and designed by
John Honeyman, was opened in 1883. It houses a 5 inch
telescope under the dome at the top. Weather recording
activities have been carried out here continuously since
1884. There is also earthquake-measuring equipment and
the Renfrewshire Astronomical Society holds regular
meetings here.
Times: Open all year, Tue-Sat 10-5, Sun 2-5. Last entry 15 minutes
before closing. **Facilities:** 🅿 150yds (meters/limited street parking)
shop ✖ (ex guide dogs)

PAISLEY MUSEUM & ART GALLERIES
High St PA1 2BA M8 J27
➲ (A741), rdbt 2nd exit (A761-town centre). At
traffic lights take left lane towards Kilbride. Onto
Gordon St, right onto Causeyside St, left onto New
St, left onto High St.)
☎ 0141 889 3151 📋 0141 889 9240   `FREE`
e-mail: museums.els@renfrewshire
Pride of place here is given to a world-famous collection of
Paisley shawls. Other collections illustrate local industrial
and natural history, while the emphasis of the art gallery is
continued

on 19th-century Scottish artists and an important studio
ceramics collection.
Times: Open all year, Tue-Sat 10-5, Sun 2-5. BH 10-5.
Facilities: 🅿 (330yds) ♿ (parking on site) toilets for disabled shop
✖ (ex guide dogs)

COLDSTREAM   Map 12 NT84

HIRSEL
Douglas & Angus Estates, Estate Office, The Hirsel
TD12 4LP
➲ (0.5m W on A697, on northern outskirts of
Coldstream)
☎ 01890 882834 & 882965 📋 01890 882834
e-mail: rogerdodd@btconnect.com
The seat of the Home family, the grounds of which are open
all year. The focal point is the Homestead Museum, craft
centre and workshops. From there, nature trails lead around
the lake, along the Leet Valley and into woodland noted for
its rhododendrons and azaleas.
Times: Garden & Grounds open all year, daylight hours. Museum 10-5.
Craft Centre Mon-Fri, 10-5, wknds noon-5. **Fee:** ✱ £2 per car
Facilities: 🅿 (charged) 💷 ✖ ♿ toilets for disabled shop

DRYBURGH   Map 12 NT53

DRYBURGH ABBEY
TD6 0RQ
➲ (5m SE of Melrose on B6404)
☎ 01835 822381
The abbey was one of the Border monasteries founded by
David I, and stands in a lovely setting on the River Tweed.
The ruins are equally beautiful, and the church has the
graves of Sir Walter Scott and Earl Haig.
Times: Open all year, Apr-Sep daily 9.30-6.30; Oct-Mar daily 9.30-6.30.
(Closed 25-26 Dec & 1-2 Jan). **Fee:** ✱ £3 (ch £1, concessions £2.30).
Groups 11+ 10% discount. Prices valid until 2 Jan 2005. Please phone
for further details. **Facilities:** 🅿 ♿ shop ✖ 🏵

DUNS   Map 12 NT75

MANDERSTON
TD11 3PP   `2 for 1`
➲ (2m E of Duns on A6105)
☎ 01361 883450 882636 📋 01361 882010
e-mail: palmer@manderston.co.uk
This grandest of grand houses gives a fascinating picture of
Edwardian life above and below stairs. Completely
remodelled for the millionaire racehorse owner Sir James
Miller, the architect was told to spare no expense, and so the
house boasts the world's only silver staircase. The
staterooms are magnificent, and there are fine formal
gardens, with a woodland garden and lakeside walks.
Manderston has been the setting for a number of films, most
recently *The Edwardian Country House*.
Times: Open mid May-end Sep, Thu & Sun 2-5 (also late May & Aug
English BH Mons). Gardens are open until dusk. **Fee:** ✱ House &
Gardens £6.50 (ch £3) gardens only: £3.50 (ch £1.50).
Facilities: 🅿 💷 ♿ shop ✖ (ex guide dogs & in gardens)

EYEMOUTH Map 12 NT96

EYEMOUTH MUSEUM
Auld Kirk, Manse Rd TD14 5JE
➲ (Turn off A1 onto A1107, follow signs to town centre. Museum in town centre)
☎ 018907 50678
The museum was opened in 1981 as a memorial to the 129 local fishermen lost in the Great Fishing Disaster of 1881. Its main feature is the 15ft Eyemouth tapestry, which was made for the centenary. There are also displays on local history.
Times: ✱ Open Apr-Jun & Sep, Mon-Sat 10-5, Sun 1-4; Jul-Aug, Mon-Sat 10-5; Sun 1-5; Oct, Mon-Sat 10-4, (closed Sun).
Facilities: P (250yds) (45min on street outside) & shop

GALASHIELS Map 12 NT43

LOCHCARRON OF SCOTLAND VISITOR CENTRE
Waverley Mill, Huddersfield St TD1 3BA
➲ (32m S of Edinburgh on A7, follow signs to mill)
☎ 01896 752091 & 751100   **2 for 1**
▤ 01896 758833
e-mail: quality@lochcarron.com
The museum brings the town's past to life and the focal point is a display on the woollen industry. Guided tours of the mill take about 40 minutes.
Times: Open all year, Mon-Sat 9-5, Sun (Jun-Sep) 12-5. Mill tours Mon-Thu at 10.30, 11.30, 1.30 & 2.30, Fri am only. **Fee:** Museum free. Mill tour £2.50 (ch 14 free). **Facilities:** P & toilets for disabled shop ◀

GORDON Map 12 NT64

MELLERSTAIN HOUSE
TD3 6LG
➲ (signed on A6089 (Kelso-Gordon road), 1m W)
☎ 01573 410225 ▤ 01573 410636   **2 for 1**
e-mail: enquiries@mellerstain.com
One of Scotland's finest Georgian houses, begun by William Adam and completed by his son Robert in the 1770s. It has beautiful plasterwork, period furniture and pictures, terraced gardens and a lake.
Times: Open Etr & May-Sep, Sun, Mon & Wed-Fri 12.30-5 (last admission 4.30) & wknds in Oct **Fee:** ✱ £5.50 (ch free) Party 20+ £5 (if normal opening times) Garden £3 **Facilities:** P ◀ & shop garden centre ✖ (ex guide dogs) ◀

HERMITAGE Map 12 NY59

HERMITAGE CASTLE
TD9 0LU
➲ (5.5m NE of Newcastleton, on B6399)
☎ 01387 376222
A vast, eerie ruin of the 14th and 15th centuries, associated with the de Soulis, the Douglases and Mary, Queen of Scots. Much restored in the 19th century.
Times: Open Apr-Sep, daily 9.30-6.30. **Fee:** ✱ £2.20 (ch 75p, concessions £1.60). Groups 11+ 10% discount. Rates valid until 2 Jan 2005. Please phone for further details. **Facilities:** P & ▯

Directions are provided by the attractions.

INNERLEITHEN Map 11 NT33

ROBERT SMAIL'S PRINTING WORKS
7/9 High St EH44 6HA
☎ 01896 830206
e-mail: smails@nts.org.uk
These buildings contain a Victorian office, a paper store with reconstructed waterwheel, a composing room and a press room. The machinery is in full working order and visitors may view the printer at work and experience typesetting in the composing room.
Times: Open Good Fri-Etr Mon & Jun-Sep,Thu-Mon 12-5, Sun 1-5. Times may change for 2005 please telephone or check on www.nts.org.uk **Fee:** ✱ £3.50 (concessions £2.60) Family ticket £9.50. Groups adult £2.80 (child/school £). Admission free for NTS members. For other details please phone 0131 243 9387 **Facilities:** P (300yds) & shop ✖ (ex guide dogs) ☙

JEDBURGH Map 12 NT62

JEDBURGH ABBEY
☎ 01835 863925
Standing as the most complete of the Border monasteries (although it has been sacked and rebuilt many times) Jedburgh Abbey has been described as 'the most perfect and beautiful example of the Saxon and early Gothic in Scotland'. David I founded it as a priory in the 12th century and remains of some of the domestic buildings have been uncovered during excavations.
Times: Open all year, Apr-Sep, daily 9.30-6.30; Oct-Mar, daily 9.30-4.30. (Closed 25-26 Dec & 1-2 Jan). **Fee:** ✱ £3.50 (ch £1.20, concessions £2.50). Groups 11+ 10% discount. Rates valid until 2 Jan 2005. Please phone for details. **Facilities:** P & (limited access) toilets for disabled shop ✖ ▯

JEDBURGH CASTLE JAIL & MUSEUM NEW
Castlegate TD8 6BD
➲ (turn off A68 towards town centre, follow signs to top of Castlegate)
☎ 01835 863254 ▤ 01835 864750
The social history of 19th-century Jedburgh, a town with a colourful past, is revealed in a museum at the Castle Jail. The jail itself is interesting as possibly the last surviving example of its kind. Built in the 1820s on the site of a medieval castle, it served as a county prison, and the three blocks were used to incarcerate different types of offenders.
Times: 26 Mar-Oct, Mon-Sat 10-4.30, Sun 1-4 **Fee:** £2 (ch free. concessions £1). **Facilities:** P & (special pathways, hearing loop) toilets for disabled shop ✖ (ex guide dogs)

KELSO Map 12 NT73

FLOORS CASTLE
Roxburghe Estates Office TD5 7SF
➲ (from town centre follow Roxburghe Street to main gates)
☎ 01573 223333 ▤ 01573 226056   **2 for 1**
e-mail: marketing@floorscastle.com
The home of the 10th Duke of Roxburghe, the Castle's lived-in atmosphere enhances the superb collection of French furniture, tapestries and paintings. The house was designed by William Adam in 1721 and enjoys a magnificent setting overlooking the River Tweed and the Cheviot Hills beyond.
Times: Open 25 Mar-30 Oct, daily 10-4.30. (last admission 4). **Fee:** £6 (ch £3.25, pen & students £5). **Facilities:** P ◀ ✖ licensed & (lift) toilets for disabled shop garden centre ◀

KELSO ABBEY
☎ 0131 668 8800   FREE

Founded by David I in 1128 and probably the greatest of the four famous Border abbeys, Kelso became extremely wealthy and acquired extensive lands. In 1545 it served as a fortress when the town was attacked by the Earl of Hertford, but now only fragments of the once-imposing abbey church give any clue to its long history.

Times: Open at any reasonable time. **Facilities:** 🅿 🎕

LAUDER   Map 12 NT54

THIRLESTANE CASTLE
TD2 6RU
⮑ (off A68, S of Lauder)
☎ 01578 722430 🖹 01578 722761
e-mail: admin@thirlestanecastle.co.uk

One of the seven "Great Houses of Scotland" this fairy-tale castle has been the home of the Maitland family, the Earls of Lauderdale, since the 12th century. Some of the most splendid plasterwork ceilings in Britain may be seen in the 17th-century state rooms. The family nurseries house a sizeable collection of antique toys and dolls. There is a vaulted dungeon display. The informal riverside grounds, with their views of the grouse moors, include a woodland walk, picnic tables and adventure playground.

Times: ✱ Open Apr-Oct **Facilities:** 🅿 💷 shop
✕ (ex guide dogs) 🍴

MELROSE   Map 12 NT53

ABBOTSFORD
TD6 9BQ
⮑ (2m W off A6091, on B6360)
☎ 01896 752043 🖹 01896 752916
e-mail: abbotsford@melrose.bordernet.co.uk

Set on the River Tweed, Sir Walter Scott's romantic mansion remains much the same as it was in his day. Inside there are many mementoes and relics of his remarkable life and also his historical collections, armouries and library, with some 9,000 volumes. Scott built the mansion between 1811 and 1822, and lived here until his death ten years after its completion.

Times: Open daily from 3rd Mon in Mar-Oct, Mon-Sat 9.30-5. Sun in Mar-May & Oct 2-5. Sun Jun-Sep 9.30-5. **Fee:** ✱ £4.50 (ch £2.25). Party £3.70 (ch £1.85). **Facilities:** 🅿 💷 🅿 (parking at private entrance, ramps at entrance) toilets for disabled shop
✕ (ex guide dogs & hearing dogs) 🍴

HARMONY GARDEN
St Mary's Rd TD6 9LJ
⮑ (Opposite Melrose Abbey)
☎ 01721 722502 🖹 01721 724700

Set around the early 19th century Harmony Hall (not open to visitors), this attractive walled garden has magnificent views of Melrose Abbey and the Eildon Hills. The garden comprises lawns, herbaceous and mixed borders, vegetable and fruit areas, and a rich display of spring bulbs.

Times: Open Good Fri-Etr Mon & Jun-Sep, Mon-Sat 10-5, Sun 1-5. Times may change for 2005 please telephone or check on www.nts.org.uk **Fee:** ✱ £2 (concessions £1). Admission free for NTS members. For other price details please phone 0131 243 9387
Facilities: 🅿 ♿ ✕ 🎕

MELROSE ABBEY & ABBEY MUSEUM
TD6 9LG
☎ 01896 822562

The ruin of this Cistercian abbey is probably one of Scotland's finest, and has been given added glamour by its connection with Sir Walter Scott. The abbey was repeatedly wrecked during the Scottish wars of independence, but parts survive from the 14th century. The heart of Robert the Bruce is buried somewhere within the church.

Times: Open all year, Apr-Sep, daily 9.30-6.30; Oct-Mar daily 9.30-4.30 (Closed 25-26 Dec & 1-2 Jan). **Fee:** ✱ £3.50 (ch £1.20, concessions £2.50). Groups 11+ 10% discount. Rates valid until 2 Jan 2005. Please phone for further details. **Facilities:** 🅿 ♿ shop ✕ 🎕

PRIORWOOD GARDEN & DRIED FLOWER SHOP
TD6 9PX
⮑ (off A6091, in Melrose, adjacent to the Abbey. On National Cycle Route 1)
☎ 01896 822493 🖹 01896 822965
e-mail: priorwooddriedflowers@nts.org.uk

This small garden specialises in flowers suitable for drying. It is formally designed with herbaceous and everlasting annual borders, and the attractive orchard has a display of 'apples through the ages'. Dried flowers are on sale in the shop.

Times: Open Good Fri-Etr Mon, May-Jun & Sep-24 Dec, Mon-Sat 12-5, Sun 1-5; Jul-Aug, Mon-Sat 10-5, Sun 1-5. Times may change for 2005 please telephone or check on www.nts.org.uk **Fee:** ✱ £2.50 (concessions £1.90. Family ticket £7. Groups adult £2 (child/school £1). Please book groups in advance. Admission free for NTS members. For other details please phone 0131 243 9387 **Facilities:** 🅿 ♿ (ramps, paths) shop 🍴

PEEBLES   Map 11 NT24

KAILZIE GARDENS
EH45 9HT
⮑ (2.5m SE on B7062)
☎ 01721 720007 🖹 01721 720007
e-mail: angela@buchan-hepburn.freeserve.co.uk

These extensive grounds, with their fine old trees, provide a burnside walk flanked by bulbs, rhododendrons and azaleas. A walled garden contains herbaceous, shrub rose borders, greenhouses and a formal rose garden. A garden for all seasons - don't miss the snowdrops. A large stocked trout pond and rod hire available, and an 18-hole putting green, plus an open bait pond, ornamental duck pond and osprey viewing centre.

Times: Open 25 Mar-Oct, daily 11-5.30. Grounds close 5.30pm. Garden open all year. **Fee:** mid Mar-Jun £2.50, Jun-Oct £3 (end Oct-mid Mar £2 honesty box) (ch 5-12 80p) **Facilities:** 🅿 💷 ✕ licensed ♿ (ramps in garden) toilets for disabled shop

NEIDPATH CASTLE
EH45 8NW
⮑ (0.5m of Peebles W on A72)
☎ 01721 720333   2 for 1
e-mail: estateoffice@wemyssandmarch.co.uk

Occupying a spectacular position on the Tweed, this 14th-century stronghold was adapted to 17th-century living; it contains a rock-hewn well, a pit prison, a small museum, and a tartan display. There are fine walks and a picnic area.

Times: Etr wknd, May-Sep (closed Mon & Tue except BH's) Wed-Sat 10.30-5 Sun 12.30-5 **Fee:** £3 (ch £1, concessions £2.50). Family ticket £7.50. Party 20+. **Facilities:** 🅿 shop

SELKIRK   Map 12 NT42

BOWHILL HOUSE AND COUNTRY PARK
TD7 5ET
➲ (3m W of Selkirk off A708)
☎ 01750 22204 ▯ 01750 22204   **2 for 1**
e-mail: bht@buccleuch.com
An outstanding collection of pictures, including works by
Van Dyck, Canaletto, Reynolds, Gainsborough and Claude
Lorraine are displayed here. Memorabilia and relics of
people such as Queen Victoria and Sir Walter Scott, and a
restored Victorian kitchen add further interest inside the
house. Outside, the wooded grounds are perfect for walking.
A small theatre provides a full programme of music and
drama. **Times:** Open, Park: Apr-Aug daily 12-5 (ex Fri). House & park: Jul, daily
1-4.30. Please phone for details as may vary. **Fee:** House & grounds £6
(ch under 5 & wheelchair users free, pen & groups £4). Grounds only
£2. **Facilities:** ▯ ◢ ✗ licensed ⅚ (guided tours for the blind by
appointment) toilets for disabled shop ✖ (ex in park on leads) ◢

HALLIWELLS HOUSE MUSEUM
Halliwells Close, Market Place TD7 4BC
➲ (off A7 in town centre)
☎ 01750 20096 ▯ 01750 23282
e-mail: museums@scotborders.gov.uk
A row of late 18th-century town cottages converted into a
museum. Displays recreate the building's former use as an
ironmonger's shop and home, and tell the story of the Royal
Burgh of Selkirk. The Robson Gallery hosts a programme of
contemporary art and craft exhibitions.
Times: ✱ Open Apr-Sep, Mon-Sat 10-5, Sun 10-12; Jul-Aug, Mon-Sat
10-5.30, Sun 10-12; Oct, Mon-Sat 10-4. **Facilities:** ▯ (charged) ⅚ (lift
to first floor, large print, interpretation) toilets for disabled shop
✖ (ex guide dogs) ◢

SIR WALTER SCOTT'S COURTROOM
Market Place TD7 4BT
➲ (on A7 in town centre)
☎ 01750 20096 ▯ 01750 23282
e-mail: museums@scotborders.gov.uk
Built in 1803-4 as a sheriff court and town hall this is where
the famous novelist, Sir Walter Scott dispensed justice when
he was Sheriff of Selkirkshire from 1804-1832. Displays tell
of Scott's time as Sheriff, and of his place as a novelist as
well as those of his contemporaries, writer, James Hogg and
the explorer, Mungo Park.
Times: ✱ Open Apr-Sep, Mon-Fri 10-4, Sat 10-2; May-Aug also Sun
10-2; Oct, Mon-Sat 1-4. **Facilities:** ▯ (100mtrs) (30min on street, car
park 50p for 2hrs) shop ✖ (ex guide dogs) ◢

SMAILHOLM   Map 12 NT63

SMAILHOLM TOWER
TD5 7RT
➲ (6m W of Kelso on B6937)
☎ 01573 460365
An outstanding example of a classic Border tower-house,
probably erected in the 15th century. It is 57ft high and well
preserved. The tower houses an exhibition of dolls and a
display based on Sir Walter Scott's book *Minstrels of the
Border.*
Times: Open Apr-Sep, daily 9.30-6.30; Oct-Mar, wknds only. (Closed
25-26 Dec & 1-2 Jan). **Fee:** ✱ £2.20 (ch 75p, concessions £1.60).
Groups 11+ 10% discount. Prices valid until 2 Jan 2005. Please phone
for further details. **Facilities:** ▯ shop ✖ ▯

STOBO   Map 11 NT13

DAWYCK BOTANIC GARDEN
EH45 9JU
➲ (8m SW of Peebles on B712)
☎ 01721 760254 ▯ 01721 760214
e-mail: dawyck@rbge.org.uk
From the landscaped walks of this historic arboretum an
impressive collection of mature specimen trees can be seen -
some over 40 metres tall and including the unique Dawyck
beech-stand. Notable features include the Swiss Bridge, a
fine estate chapel and stonework/terracing produced by
Italian craftsmen in the 1820s.
Times: Open daily 14 Feb-14 Nov. Feb & Nov 10-4. Mar-Oct 10-5.
Apr-Sep 10-6 **Fee:** ✱ £3.50 (ch £1, concessions £3). Family ticket £8
Facilities: ▯ ◢ ⅚ toilets for disabled shop garden centre
✖ (ex guide dogs) ◢

TRAQUAIR   Map 11 NT33

TRAQUAIR HOUSE
EH44 6PW
➲ (At Innerleithen take B709, house in 1m)
☎ 01896 830323 & 830785 ▯ 01896 830639
e-mail: enquiries@traquair.co.uk
Said to be Scotland's oldest inhabited house, dating back to
the 12th century, 27 Scottish monarchs have stayed at
Traquair House. William the Lion Heart held court here, and
the house has associations with Mary, Queen of Scots and
the Jacobite risings. The Bear Gates were closed in 1745, not
to be reopened until the Stuarts should once again ascend
the throne. There is croquet, a maze and woodland walks by
the River Tweed, craft workshops and a children's mini
adventure playground. Also a brewery museum and shop,
and antique shop.
Times: Open Etr-Oct **Fee:** Please telephone for admission costs.
Facilities: ▯ ◢ ✗ licensed ⅚ toilets for disabled shop ◢

SOUTH AYRSHIRE

ALLOWAY   Map 10 NS31

BURNS NATIONAL HERITAGE PARK
Murdoch's Lone KA7 4PQ
➲ (2m S of Ayr)
☎ 01292 443700 ▯ 01292 441750   **2 for 1**
e-mail: info@burnsheritagepark.com
The birthplace of Robert Burns, Scotland's National Poet. An
introduction to the life of Robert Burns, with an audio-visual
presentation - a multi-screen 3D experience describing the
Tale of Tam O'Shanter. This attraction consists of the
museum, Burn's Cottage, visitor centre, tranquil landscaped
gardens and historical monuments. Please telephone for
further details.
Times: Open all year, Apr-Sep 9.30-5.30, Tam O'Shanter experience 10
- 5.30, Oct-Mar 10-5. Closed 25-26 Dec & 1-2 Jan **Fee:** Adult passport
£5 (pen & ch passport £2.50). **Facilities:** ▯ ◢ ✗ licensed
⅚ (wheelchair available) toilets for disabled shop ✖ (ex guide &
hearing dogs) ◢

> **If an attraction name
> appears in *italics*, details
> have not been confirmed
> for 2005.**

BARGANY

See **Old Dailly**

CULZEAN CASTLE   Map 10 NS21

CULZEAN CASTLE & COUNTRY PARK
KA19 8LE
➲ (4m W of Maybole, off A77)
☎ 01655 884455   ▤ 01655 884503
e-mail: culzean@nts.org.uk

This 18th-century castle stands on a cliff in spacious grounds and was designed by Robert Adam for the Earl of Cassillis. It is noted for its oval staircase, circular drawing room and plasterwork. The Eisenhower Room explores the American general's links with Culzean. The 563-acre country park has a wide range of attractions - shoreline, woodland walks, parkland, an adventure playground and gardens.
Times: Open - Castle: Apr-Oct, daily 10.30-5 (last entry 4). Visitor centre: Apr-Oct, daily 9-5.30; Nov-Mar, wknds 11-4. Country Park: open all year 9.30-sunset. Times may change for 2005 please telephone or check on www.nts.org.uk **Fee:** ✱ £9 (concessions £6.50). Groups adult £9 (concessions £6.50) Family ticket £23. Country Park only Apr-Oct £5 (concessions £3.75). Family ticket £13.50. Group adult £4 (child/school £1) Admission free to NTS members. For other details please phone 0131 243 9387 **Facilities:** ▣ ▆ ✖ licensed க (wheelchairs, lift in castle, Braille guides) toilets for disabled shop garden centre ✈ (ex castle, ex guide dogs) ᴪ

KIRKOSWALD   Map 10 NS20

SOUTER JOHNNIE'S COTTAGE
Main Rd KA19 8HY
➲ (on A77, 4m SW of Maybole)
☎ 01655 760603
e-mail: aclipson@nts.scot.demon.co.uk

'Souter' means cobbler and the village cobbler who lived in this 18th-century cottage was the inspiration for Burns' character Souter Johnnie, in his ballad *Tam O'Shanter*. The cottage is now a Burns museum and life-size stone figures of the poet's characters can be seen in the restored ale-house in the cottage garden.
Times: Open - Apr-Sep, Fri-Tue 11.30-5. Times may change for 2005 please telephone or check on www.nts.org.uk **Fee:** ✱ £2.50 (concessions £1.90) Family ticket £7. Groups adult £2 (child/school £1). Please book in advance for groups. Admission free to NTS members. For other details please phone 0131 243 9387 **Facilities:** ▣ (75yds) க (only one small step into cottage) ✈ (ex guide dogs) ᴪ

MAYBOLE   Map 10 NS20

CROSSRAGUEL ABBEY
KA19 5HQ
➲ (2m S)
☎ 01655 883113

The extensive remains of this 13th-century Cluniac monastery are impressive and architecturally important. The monastery was founded by Duncan, Earl of Carrick and the church, claustral buildings, abbot's house and an imposing castellated gatehouse can be seen.
Times: Open Apr-Sep, daily 9.30-6.30. **Fee:** ✱ £2.20 (ch 75p, concessions £1.60). Groups 11+ 10% discount. Prices valid until 2 Jan 2005. Please phone for further details **Facilities:** ▣ ✈ ▮

OLD DAILLY   Map 10 NX29

BARGANY GARDENS
KA26 9PH
➲ (4m NE on B734 from Girvan)
☎ 01465 871249   ▤ 01465 871282

Woodland walks with a fine show of azaleas and rhododendrons. Plants on sale from the gardens.
Times: Open Gardens Sat, Sun & Mon, May wknds only 10-5.
Fee: ✱ £2 (ch under 12 free). **Facilities:** ▣ க (only rock garden not accessible)

TARBOLTON   Map 10 NS42

BACHELORS' CLUB
Sandgate St KA5 5RB
➲ (on B744, 7.5m NE of Ayr)
☎ 01292 541940

In this 17th-century thatched house, Robert Burns and his friends formed a debating club in 1780. Burns attended dancing lessons and was initiated into freemasonry here in 1781. The house is furnished in the style of the period.
Times: Open Apr-Sep, Fri-Tue 1-5. Morning visits available for pre-booked groups. Times may change for 2005 please telephone or check on www.nts.org.uk **Fee:** ✱ £2.50 (concessions £1.90) Groups adult £2 (child/school £1). Family ticket £7. Admission free for NTS members. For other details please phone 0131 243 9387 **Facilities:** ▣ (in village) க ✈ (ex guide dogs) ᴪ

SOUTH LANARKSHIRE

BIGGAR   Map 11 NT03

GLADSTONE COURT MUSEUM
ML12 6DT
➲ (On A702 40m from Glasgow, 30m from Edinburgh, entrance by 113 High St)   `2 for 1`
☎ 01899 221050   ▤ 01899 221050
e-mail: margaret@bmtrust.freeserve.co.uk

An old-fashioned village street is portrayed in this museum, which is set out in a century-old coach-house. On display are reconstructed shops, complete with old signs and advertisements - a bank, telephone exchange, photographer's booth and other interesting glimpses into the recent past.
Times: Open Etr-Oct, Mon-Sat 11-4.30, Sun 2-4.30. **Fee:** ✱ £2 (ch £1, pen £1.50). Family ticket £4. Party £1.25 each. **Facilities:** ▣ க shop ✈ (ex guide dogs)

GREENHILL COVENANTERS HOUSE

Burn Braes ML12 6DT
➲ (On A702, 30m from Edinburgh, 40m from Glasgow)   `2 for 1`
☎ 01899 221050   ▤ 01899 221050
e-mail: margaret@bmtrust.freeserve.co.uk

This 17th-century farmhouse was brought, stone by stone, ten miles from Wiston and reconstructed at Biggar. It has relics of the turbulent 'Covenanting' period, when men and women defended the right to worship in Presbyterian style. Audio presentations.
Times: Open mid May-Sep, wknds only 2-4.30. **Fee:** ✱ £1 (ch 50p, pen 70p). Family ticket £2.50. Party 70p each.
Facilities: ▣ க ✈ (ex guide dogs)

MOAT PARK HERITAGE CENTRE
ML12 6DT
➲ (On A702, 30m from Edinburgh, 40m from Glasgow)
☎ 01899 221050 ▤ 01899 221050 `2 for 1`
e-mail: margaret@bmtrust.co.uk
The centre illustrates the history, archaeology and geology of the Upper Clyde and Tweed valleys with interesting displays.
Times: Open all year, Apr-Oct, daily 11.30-4.30, Sun 2-4.30; Nov-Feb, wkdays during office hours. Other times by prior arrangement.
Fee: ✹ £2 (ch £1, pen £1.50). Family ticket £4. Party £1.25 each.
Facilities: 🅿 ♿ (upper floor with assistance on request) toilets for disabled shop ✖ (ex guide dogs)

BLANTYRE   Map 11 NS65

DAVID LIVINGSTONE CENTRE
165 Station Rd G72 9BT
➲ (M74 junct 5 onto A725, then A724, follow signs for Blantyre, right at lights. Centre is at foot of hill)
☎ 01698 823140 ▤ 01698 821424
Share the adventurous life of Scotland's greatest explorer, from his childhood in the Blantyre Mills to his explorations in the heart of Africa, dramatically illustrated in the historic tenement where he was born. Various events are planned throughout the season.
Times: Open Apr-24 Dec, Mon-Sat 10-5, Sun 12.30-5. Times may change for 2005 please telephone or check on www.nts.org.uk
Fee: ✹ £3.50 (concessions £2.60) Family ticket £9.50. Groups adult £2.80 (child/school £1). Please book groups in advance. Admission free to NTS members. For other details please phone 0131 243 9387
Facilities: 🅿 ▣ ♿ toilets for disabled shop ✖ (ex guide dogs/lead grounds) ❦ ◀

BOTHWELL   Map 11 NS75

BOTHWELL CASTLE
G71 8BL
➲ (approach from Uddingston off B7071)
☎ 01698 816894
Besieged, captured and 'knocked about' several times in the Scottish-English wars, the castle is a splendid ruin. Archibald the Grim built the curtain wall; later, in 1786, the Duke of Buccleuch carved graffiti - a coronet and initials - beside a basement well.
Times: Open all year, Apr-Sep, daily 9.30-6.30; Oct-Mar, daily 9.30-4.30, (Closed Thu & Fri in winter, 25-26 Dec & 1-2 Jan).
Fee: ✹ £2.50 (ch 75p, concessions £1.90). Groups 11+ 10% discount. Prices valid until 2 Jan 2005. Please telephone for futher details.
Facilities: 🅿 shop ▮

EAST KILBRIDE   Map 11 NS65

MUSEUM OF SCOTTISH COUNTRY LIFE
Wester Kittochside G76 9HR
➲ (From Glasgow take A749 to East Kilbride. From Edinburgh follow M8 to Glasgow, turn off junct 6 onto A725 to East Kilbride. Kittochside is signed before East Kilbride)
☎ 01355 224 181 ▤ 01355 571290
e-mail: info@nms.ac.uk
A fascinating museum built on a 170-acre farm and offering an insight into the working lives of people in rural Scotland. The museum runs a programme of events throughout the
continued

year, demonstrating its working collection and contrasting modern and traditional farming methods.

Times: Open daily 10-5 (Closed 25-26 Dec & 1-2 Jan)
Facilities: 🅿 ▣ ♿ (disabled parking, exhibition building is fully accessible) toilets for disabled shop ✖ (ex assist dogs) ◀

HAMILTON   Map 11 NS75

CHATELHERAULT COUNTRY PARK
Ferniegair ML3 7UE
➲ (2.5km SE of Hamilton on A72 Hamilton-Larkhall/Lanark Clyde Valley tourist route)
☎ 01698 426213 ▤ 01698 421532 `FREE`
Designed as a hunting lodge by William Adam in 1732, Chatelherault, built of unusual pink sandstone, has been described as a gem of Scottish architecture. Situated close to the motorway, there is a visitor's centre, shop and adventure playground. Also a herd of white Cadzow cattle.
Times: Open all year, Mon-Sat 10-5, Sun 12-5. House closed all day Fri & Sat. **Facilities:** 🅿 ▣ ♿ (ramps, parking, large print guide) toilets for disabled shop garden centre ✖ (ex in grounds & guide dogs) ◀

LOW PARKS MUSEUM
129 Muir St ML3 6BJ
➲ (By ASDA superstore, off M74 junct 6)
☎ 01698 328232 ▤ 01698 328412
The museum tells the story of Hamilton and the Clyde Valley, created by linking the former District Museum and The Cameronians (Scottish Rifles) Museum. Housed in the town's oldest building, dating from 1696, the museum features a restored 18th-century assembly room and exhibitions on Hamilton Palace and The Covenanters.
Times: ✹ Open late Mar-mid Oct; Sun-Thu 10.30-5, house 11-4 (Sep-Oct 11-3). Gardens & tearoom open during winter, please contact for opening times. **Facilities:** 🅿 ♿ shop ✖ (ex guide dogs) ◀

NEW LANARK   Map 11 NS84

NEW LANARK VISITOR CENTRE
New Lanark Visitor Centre, Mill 3, New Lanark Mills ML11 9DB
➲ (4m S of Lanark, less than an hour from Glasgow (M74/A72) and Edinburgh (A70). From the south, the village is 30 mins from A74 junct 13)
☎ 01555 661345 ▤ 01555 66538 `2 for 1`
e-mail: trust@newlanark.org
Founded in 1785, New Lanark became well known in the early 19th century as a model community managed by enlightened industrialist and educational reformer Robert
continued

Owen. Surrounded by woodland and situated close to the Falls of Clyde, this unusual heritage site explores the philosophies of Robert Owen, using theatre, interactive displays, and the 'New Millennium Experience', a magical chair ride through history. Accommodation is also available at the New Lanark Mill Hotel.

Times: Open daily 11-5 (ex Xmas Day & New Years Day) **Fee:** ✱ £5.95 (ch, concessions £3.95) family ticket (2ad+2ch) £16.95 family ticket (2ad + 4ch) £19.95 **Facilities:** 🅿 💷 ✗ licensed ♿ (ramps, disabled parking) toilets for disabled shop ✗ (ex guide dogs) ➡

STIRLING

BANNOCKBURN   Map 11 NS89

BANNOCKBURN HERITAGE CENTRE
Glasgow Rd FK7 0LJ
➲ (2m S of Stirling off M80/M9 junct 9)
☎ 01786 812664   🗐 01786 810892
The Heritage Centre stands close to what is traditionally believed to have been Robert the Bruce's command post before the 1314 Battle of Bannockburn, a famous victory for the Scots and a turning point in Scottish history.
Times: Open all year, daily. Heritage Centre Apr-Oct, daily 10-5.30; Feb-Mar & Nov-24 Dec, daily 10.30-4. Last audio-visual show half-an-hour before closing. **Facilities:** 🅿 💷 ♿ (Induction loop for the hard of hearing) toilets for disabled shop ✗ (ex site only) ❦

BLAIR DRUMMOND   Map 11 NS79

BLAIR DRUMMOND SAFARI & LEISURE PARK
FK9 4UR
➲ (M9 junct 10, 4m on A84 towards Callander)
☎ 01786 841456 & 841396   🗐 01786 841491
e-mail: enquiries@safari-park.co.uk
Drive through the wild animal reserves where zebras, North American bison, antelope, lions, tigers, white rhino and camels can be seen at close range. Other attractions include the sea lion show, a ride on the boat safari through the waterfowl sanctuary and around Chimpanzee Island, an adventure playground, giant astraglide, and pedal boats. There are also African elephants, giraffes and ostriches.
Times: ✱ Open Apr-1 Oct, daily 10-5.30. Last admission 4.30.
Facilities: 🅿 💷 ✗ licensed ♿ (special menus & waitress service if booked in advance) toilets for disabled shop ✗ (ex guide dogs)

CALLANDER   Map 11 NN60

ROB ROY AND TROSSACHS VISITOR CENTRE
Ancaster Square FK17 8ED
➲ (on A84)
☎ 01877 330342   🗐 01877 330784
e-mail: robroy&t@aillst.ossian.net
From Highland hero to Hollywood legend, follow the story of Scotland's most famous Highlander, Rob Roy. Hear his innermost thoughts and witness his exploits. Step back in time and explore a reconstructed 18th-century farmhouse, just as Rob Roy would have experienced it.
Times: Open Apr-May, daily 10-5; Jun-Sep, 10-6; Oct 10-5; Nov-Feb 11-4; Mar 10-5. (winter openings may vary, please contact) **Fee:** Prices not confirmed for 2005 **Facilities:** 🅿 ♿ toilets for disabled shop ✗ ➡

DOUNE   Map 11 NN70

DOUNE CASTLE
FK16 6EA
➲ (8m S of Callander on A84)
☎ 01786 841742
The 14th-century stronghold with its two fine towers has been restored. It stands on the banks of the River Teith, and is associated with 'Bonnie' Prince Charlie and Sir Walter Scott.
Times: Open all year, Apr-Sep, daily 9.30-6.30; Oct-Mar, daily 9.30-4.30. (Closed Thu & Fri in winter, 25-26 Dec & 1-2 Jan).
Fee: ✱ £3 (ch £1, concessions £2.30). Groups 11+ 10% discount. Prices valid until 2 Jan 2005. Please phone for further details.
Facilities: 🅿 shop ♠

KILLIN   Map 11 NN53

BREADALBANE FOLKLORE CENTRE
Falls of Dochart FK21 8XE
➲ (on A85)
☎ 01567 820254   🗐 01567 820764
e-mail: killin@aillst.ossian.net
Overlooking the beautiful Falls of Dochart, the centre gives a fascinating insight into the legends of Breadalbane - Scotland's 'high country'. Learn of the magical deeds of St Fillan and hear tales of mystical giants, ancient prophesies, traditional folklore and clan history. Housed in historic St Fillans Mill which features a restored waterwheel. Tourist Information and gift shop.
Times: Open Mar-May & Oct, daily 10-5; Jun & Sep, daily 10-6; Jul-Aug, daily 9.30-6.30. (Closed Nov-Feb). **Fee:** Prices not confirmed for 2005 **Facilities:** 🅿 (30mtrs) ♿ shop ✗ ➡

PORT OF MENTEITH   Map 11 NN50

INCHMAHOME PRIORY
FK8 3RA
➲ (4m E of Aberfoyle, off A81)
☎ 01877 385294
Walter Comyn founded this Augustinian house in 1238, and it became famous as the retreat of the infant Mary, Queen of Scots in 1547. The ruins of the church and cloisters are situated on an island in the Lake of Menteith.
Times: Open Apr-Sep, daily 9.30-6.30. **Fee:** ✱ £3.50 (ch £1.20, concessions £2.50). Admission charge includes ferry trip. Groups 11+ 10% discount. Rates valid until 2 Jan 2005. Please phone for further details. **Facilities:** 🅿 shop ♠

STIRLING   Map 11 NS79

MAR'S WARK
Broad St FK8 1EE
A remarkable Renaissance mansion built by the Earl of Mar, Regent for James VI in 1570 and later used as the town workhouse. It was never completed and now the façade can be seen.
Times: Open all reasonable times. **Facilities:** ✗ ♠

MUSEUM OF ARGYLL & SUTHERLAND HIGHLANDERS
The Castle FK8 1EH
➲ (museum in Stirling Castle)
☎ 01786 475165   🗐 01786 446038
e-mail: museum@argylls.co.uk
Situated in the King's Old Building in Stirling Castle, the museum tells the history of the Regiment from 1794 to the

continued

present day. Displays include uniforms, medals, silver, paintings, colours, pipe banners, and commentaries.
Times: Open Etr-Sep, daily 9.30-5; Sep-Etr, daily 10-4.15. **Fee:** Prices not confirmed for 2005 **Facilities:** 🅿 (castle esplanade) shop ✖

NATIONAL WALLACE MONUMENT
Abbey Craig, Causewayhead FK8 2AD
➲ (from A907 (Stirling to Alloa road) follow brown tourist signs)
☎ 01786 472140 📠 01786 461322
e-mail: nationalwallacemonument@
aillst.ossian.net
Meet Scotland's national hero, William Wallace, and join his epic struggle for a free Scotland. Step into Westminster Hall and witness his trial. Climb the 220 foot tower and experience one of the finest views in Scotland.
Times: Open all year Jan-Feb & Nov-Dec, daily 10.30-4; Mar-May & Oct, daily 10-5; Jun, daily 10-6; Jul-Aug, daily 9.30-6.30; Sep, daily 9.30-5. **Fee:** ✱ £6 (ch & pen £4, student £4.50). Family ticket £16.
Facilities: 🅿 📳 ⅃ (limited access) shop ✖ 🍴

OLD TOWN JAIL
Saint John St FK8 1EA
➲ (follow signs for castle up the hill, jail on left at top of Saint John's St)
☎ 01786 450050 📠 01786 471301
e-mail: otjva@aillst.ossian.net
Experience life in a Victorian prison, where real history performances bring the past to life. Come face to face with Stirling's notorious hangman and you may even witness an attempted jailbreak. Stunning rooftop panorama and gift shop. Multi-lingual audio tour.
Times: Open Apr-Sep, daily 9.30-5.30; Oct & Mar, daily 9.30-4.30; Nov-Feb, daily 9.30-3.30. **Fee:** ✱ £5.50 (ch & pen £3.65, student £4.25). Family ticket £14.65. **Facilities:** 🅿 ⅃ toilets for disabled shop ✖ 🍴

SMITH ART GALLERY & MUSEUM
Dumbarton Rd FK8 2RQ
➲ (M9 junct 10, follow Stirling Castle signs)
☎ 01786 471917 📠 01786 449523 [FREE]
e-mail: museum@smithartgallery.demon.co.uk
This award-winning museum and gallery presents a variety of exhibitions drawing on its own rich collections and works from elsewhere. A range of programmes and events take place, ring for details.
Times: Open all year, Tue-Sat 10.30-5, Sun 2-5 (Closed Mon, 25-26 Dec & 1 Jan). **Facilities:** 🅿 📳 ⅃ (wheelchair lift, induction loop in theatre) toilets for disabled shop

STIRLING CASTLE
Upper Castle Hill FK8 1EJ
☎ 01786 450000
Sitting on top of a 250ft rock, Stirling Castle has a strategic position on the Firth of Forth. As a result it has been the scene of many events in Scotland's history. James II was born at the castle in 1430. Mary, Queen of Scots spent some years there, and it was James IV's childhood home. Among its finest features are the splendid Renaissance palace built by James V, and the Chapel Royal, rebuilt by James VI.
Times: Open all year, Apr-Sep, daily 9.30-6; Oct-Mar, daily 9.30-4.30. (Closed 25-26 Dec & 1-2 Jan). **Fee:** ✱ £8 (ch £2, concessions £6). Groups 11+ 10% discount. Prices valid until 2 Jan 2005. Please phone for further details. **Facilities:** 🅿 (charged) ✖ licensed ⅃ toilets for disabled shop ✖ 🍴

DUMBARTON   Map 10 NS37
DUMBARTON CASTLE
G82 1JJ
☎ 01389 732167
The castle, set on the 240ft Dumbarton Rock above the River Clyde, dominates the town (the capital of the Celtic kingdom of Strathclyde) and commands spectacular views. Most of what can be seen today dates from the 18th and 19th centuries, but there are a few earlier remains.
Times: Open all year, Apr-Sep, daily 9-6.30. Oct-Mar, daily 9-4.30. (Closed Thu & Fri in winter, 25-26 Dec & 1-2 Jan). **Fee:** ✱ £2.50 (ch 75p, concessions £1.90). Groups 11+ 10% discount. Prices valid until 2 Jan 2005. Please phone for further details. **Facilities:** 🅿 shop ✖🍴

LINLITHGOW   Map 11 NS97
BLACKNESS CASTLE
EH49 7AL
➲ (4m NE)
☎ 01506 834807
This was once one of the most important fortresses in Scotland. Used as a state prison during covenanting time and in the late 19th-century as a powder magazine, it was one of four castles left fortified by the Articles of Union. Most impressive are the massive 17th-century artillery emplacements.
Times: Open all year, Apr-Sep, daily 9.30-6.30; Oct-Mar, daily 9.30-4.30. (Closed Thu & Fri in winter, 25-26 Dec & 1-2 Jan). **Fee:** ✱ £2.50 (ch 75p, concessions £1.90). Groups 11+ 10% discount. Rates valid until 2 Jan 2005. Please telephone for further details. **Facilities:** 🅿 shop 🍴

HOUSE OF THE BINNS
EH49 7NA
➲ (4m E of Linlithgow off A904)
☎ 01506 834255
e-mail: houseofthebinns@nts.org.uk
An example of changing architectural tastes from 1612 onwards, this house reflects the transition from fortified stronghold to spacious mansion. The original three-storey building, with small windows and twin turrets, evolved into a fine crenellated house with beautiful moulded plaster ceilings - the ancestral home of the Dalyell family. There is a magnificent display of snowdrops and daffodils in spring.
Times: House: Jun-Sep, Sat-Mon 2-5. Parkland: Apr-Oct, daily 10-7, Nov-Mar, daily 10-4. Times may change for 2005 please telephone or check on www.nts.org.uk **Fee:** ✱ £5 (concessions £3.75) Family ticket £13.50. Groups adult £4 (child/school £1). Admission free to NTS members. For other details please telephone 0131 243 9387 **Facilities:** 🅿 ⅃ (Braille sheets) ✖ (ex guide dogs) 🐾

LINLITHGOW PALACE
EH49 7AL
➲ (off M9)
☎ 01506 842896
The magnificent ruin of a great Royal Palace, set in its own park or 'peel'. All the Stewart kings lived here, and work commissioned by James I, III, IV, and VI can be seen. The

continued

great hall and the chapel are particularly fine. James V was born here in 1512 and Mary, Queen of Scots in 1542. **Times:** Open all year, Apr-Sep, daily 9.30-6.30; Oct-Mar, daily 9.30-4.30. (Closed 25-26 Dec & 1-2 Jan). **Fee:** ✱ £3 (ch £1, concessions £2.30). Groups 11+ 10% discount. Rates valid until 2 Jan 2005. Please phone for details. **Facilities:** 🅿 shop ✖️ 🏮

LIVINGSTON   Map 11 NT06
ALMOND VALLEY HERITAGE CENTRE
Millfield EH54 7AR
➲ (2m from M8 junct 3)
☎ 01506 414957   🖥 01506 497771
e-mail: info@almondvalley.co.uk
A combination of fun and educational potential ideal for children, Almond Valley has a petting zoo of farm animals, an interactive museum on the shale oil industry, a narrow gauge railway, and tractor rides. Special events throughout the year - ring for details.
Times: Open all year, daily 10-5. **Fee:** £3 (ch £2). Family (2+4) £10. **Facilities:** 🅿 🅿 ♿ toilets for disabled shop 🍴

SCOTTISH ISLANDS

ARRAN, ISLE OF

BRODICK   Map 10 NS03
BRODICK CASTLE, GARDEN & COUNTRY PARK
KA27 8HY
➲ (Ferry from Ardrossan-Brodick. Or ferry from Lochranza to Kintyre (frequent in Summer, limited in winter))
☎ 01770 302202 & 302462   🖥 01770 302312
e-mail: brodick@nts.org.uk
The site has been fortified since Viking times, but the present castle dating from the 13th century was a stronghold of the Dukes of Hamilton. Splendid silver, fine porcelain and paintings acquired by generations of owners can be seen, including many sporting pictures and trophies. There is a magnificent woodland garden, started by the Duchess of Montrose in 1923, world famous for its rhododendrons and azaleas.
Times: Open Apr-Oct, daily 11-4.30 (closes 3.30 in Oct). Country Park: open all year, daily 9.30-sunset. Times may change for 2005 please telephone or check on www.nts.org.uk **Fee:** ✱ £8 (concessions £6) Groups adult £6 (child/school £2), please book groups in advance. Family ticket £20. Country Park only Apr-Oct £4 (concessions £3) Groups adult £3 (child/school £2). Family ticket £12. £2. Admission free to NTS members. **Facilities:** 🅿 ✖️ ♿ (Braille, wheelchairs motorised buggy & stairlift) toilets for disabled shop 🍴 (ex guide dogs) 🍷

ISLE OF ARRAN HERITAGE MUSEUM
Rosaburn KA27 8DP
➲ (Right at Brodick Pier, approx 1m)
☎ 01770 302636
e-mail: tom.macleod@arranmuseum.co.uk
The setting is an 18th-century croft farm, including a cottage restored to its pre-1920 state and a 'smiddy' where a blacksmith worked until the late 1960s. There are also several demonstrations of horse-shoeing, sheep-shearing and weaving and spinning throughout the season - please ring for details. There is a large archaeology and geology section with archive, where help with research is available.
Times: Open Apr-Oct, daily 10.30-4.30. **Fee:** ✱ £2.25 (ch £1, pen £1.25) Family £6. **Facilities:** 🅿 🅿 ♿ toilets for disabled shop 🍴 (only in garden, ex guide dogs)

LOCHRANZA   Map 10 NR95
ISLE OF ARRAN DISTILLERY VISITOR CENTRE
KA27 8HJ
➲ (from Brodick Ferry Terminal take coast road N for 14m. Distillery on edge of village)
☎ 01770 830264   🖥 01770 830364
e-mail: visitorcentre@arranwhisky.com
Located amidst beautiful surroundings, the distillery was built to revive the dormant traditions of Arran single malt whisky production. After a guided tour of the distillery, visitors can now taste some of the first whiskies to be ready after production began in 1995.
Times: ✱ Open daily Mar-Oct; Nov-Dec, open 4 days a week. (Closed Jan). **Facilities:** 🅿 ✖️ licensed ♿ (ex working distillery, chair lift in visitor centre) toilets for disabled shop 🍴 (ex guide dogs) 🍴

BUTE, ISLE OF

ROTHESAY   Map 10 NS06
ARDENCRAIG
PA20 9HA
➲ (1m off A844, S of Rothesay)
☎ 01700 504225   🖥 01700 504225
e-mail: allan.macdonald@argyll-bute.co.uk
Particular attention has been paid to improving the layout of the garden and introducing rare plants. The greenhouse and walled garden produce plants for floral displays throughout the district. A variety of fish is kept in the ornamental ponds and the aviaries have some interesting birds.
Times: ✱ Open May-Sep. **Facilities:** 🅿 🅿 ♿ 🍴 (ex guide dogs)

BUTE MUSEUM
Stuart St PA20 0EP
➲ (on road behind castle)
☎ 01700 505067
e-mail: Ivor@butemuseum.fsnet.co.uk
Local and natural history displays, including birds, mammals and seashore items; varied collections of recent bygones, a collection of early Christian crosses, and flints and pots from various Mesolithic and Neolithic burial cairns.
Times: Open all year, Apr-Sep, Mon-Sat 10.30-4.30, Sun 2.30-4.30; Oct-Mar, Tue-Sat 2.30-4.30 (Closed Sun & Mon). **Facilities:** 🅿 (3 mins walk) ♿ (touch table for blind, ramps) shop

ROTHESAY CASTLE
PA20 0DA
☎ 01700 502691
The focal point of Rothesay is this 13th-century castle. It has lofty curtain walls defended by drum towers that enclose a circular courtyard.
Times: Open all year, Apr-Sep, daily 9.30-6.30; Oct-Mar, daily 9.30-4.30. (Closed Thu & Fri in winter, 25-26 Dec & 1-2 Jan). **Fee:** ✱ £2.50 (ch 75p, concessions £1.90). Groups 11+ 10% discount. Rates valid until 2 Jan 2005. Please phone for further details. **Facilities:** 🅿 shop 🏮

> If an attraction name appears in *italics*, details have not been confirmed for 2005.

GREAT CUMBRAE ISLAND

MILLPORT   Map 10 NS15
MUSEUM OF THE CUMBRAES
Garrison House KA28 0DG
➲ (Ferry to Millport, from Largs Cal-Mac Terminal.
Bus meets each ferry)
☎ 01475 531191 📠 01475 531191   **2 for 1**
e-mail: namuseum@north-
ayrshire.gov.uk
A small museum which displays the history and life of the
Cumbraes. There is also a fine collection of local
photographs.
Times: Open Apr-Sep, Thu-Mon 10-1, 2-5. **Facilities:** 🅿 🕭 shop
✖ (ex guide dogs)

LEWIS, ISLE OF

ARNOL   Map 13 NB34
BLACK HOUSE MUSEUM
PA86 9DB
➲ (11m NW of Stornoway on A858)
☎ 01851 710395
A traditional Hebridean dwelling, built without mortar and
roofed with thatch on a timber framework. It has a central
peat fire in the kitchen, no chimney and a byre under the
same roof.
Times: Open all year, Apr-Sep, Mon-Sat 9.30-6.30; Oct-Mar, Mon-Sat
9.30-4.30. (Closed 25-26 Dec & 1-2 Jan). **Fee:** ✱ £3 (ch £1,
concessions £2.30). Groups 11+ 10% discount. Prices valid until 2 Jan
2005. Please telephone for further details. **Facilities:** 🅿 🕭 toilets for
disabled shop ✖ ♥

CALLANISH   Map 13 NB23
CALLANISH STANDING STONES
PA86 9DY
➲ (12m W of Stornoway off A859)
☎ 01851 621422
An avenue of 19 monoliths leads north from a circle of 13
stones with rows of more stones fanning out to south, east
and west. Probably constructed between 3000 and 1500BC,
this is a unique cruciform of megaliths.
Times: ✱ Site accessible at all times. Visitor Centre open Apr-Sep,
Mon-Sat 10-7; Oct-Mar, Mon-Sat 10-4. **Facilities:** 🅿 ✖ 🕭 toilets for
disabled shop ♥

CARLOWAY   Map 13 NB24
DUN CARLOWAY BROCH
➲ (1.5m S of Carloway on A858)
Brochs are late-prehistoric circular stone towers, and their
origins are mysterious. One of the best examples can be
seen at Dun Carloway, where the tower still stands about
30ft high.
Times: Open at all reasonable times. **Facilities:** 🅿 ♥

Directions are provided
by the attractions.

MULL, ISLE OF

CRAIGNURE   Map 10 NM73
MULL & WEST HIGHLAND NARROW GAUGE
RAILWAY
Craignure (old pier) Station PA65 6AY
➲ (0.25 mile from Craignure Ferry Terminal, just
off road to Iona)
☎ 01680 812494 (in season) or 01680 300389
📠 01680 300595
e-mail: mullrail@dee-emm.co.uk
The first passenger railway on a Scottish island, opened in
1984. Both steam and diesel trains operate on the ten-and-a-
quarter inch gauge line, which runs from Craignure to
Torosay Castle. The 1.25 mile line offers dramatic woodland
and mountain views taking in Ben Nevis, Glencoe and the
Isle of Lismore.
Times: Open Etr-mid Oct **Facilities:** 🅿 🕭 (provision to carry person
seated in wheelchair on trains) shop 🛆

TOROSAY CASTLE & GARDENS
PA65 6AY
➲ (1.5m S of Ferry Terminal at Craignure)
☎ 01680 812421 📠 01680 812470   **2 for 1**
e-mail: torosay@aol.com
The Scottish baronial architecture of this Victorian castle is
complemented by the magnificent setting, and inside the
house there are displays of portraits and wildlife pictures,
family scrapbooks and a study of the Antarctic. The gardens
include a statue walk and water garden, an avenue of
Australian gum trees, and an Oriental garden. Within the
grounds there is a narrow gauge steam and diesel railway.
Times: Open end Mar-end Oct, daily 10.30-5. Gardens all year.
Fee: ✱ House & Gardens: £5 (ch £1.75, student & pen £4) Family £12.
Gardens only: £4 (ch £1.25, student & pen £3) Family £10.
Facilities: 🅿 ⬛ shop garden centre ✖ (ex guide/hearing dogs) 🛆

ORKNEY

BIRSAY   Map 16 HY22
EARL'S PALACE
KW15 1PD
➲ (on A966)
☎ 01856 721205 & 841815   **FREE**
The gaunt remains of the residence of the 16th-century Earl
of Orkney, constructed round a courtyard.
Times: Open at all reasonable times. **Facilities:** ✖ ♥

DOUNBY   Map 16 HY22
BROUGH OF BIRSAY
➲ (off A966)
☎ 01856 841815
This ruined Romanesque church stands next to the remains
of a Norse village. The nave, chancel and semicircular apse
can be seen, along with claustral buildings. Crossings must
be made on foot at low-water - there is no boat.
Times: Open mid Jun-Sep (tides permitting), daily 9.30-6.30.
Fee: ✱ £1.80 (ch 50p, concessions £1.30). Groups 11+ 10% discount.
Prices valid until 2 Jan 2005. Please phone for further details. ♥

CLICK MILL
➲ (2.5m from Dounby on B905)
☎ 01856 841815 [FREE]

The last surviving horizontal water mill in Orkney, of a type well represented in Shetland and Lewis. The mill is in working condition and visitors should wear sensible footwear.
Times: Open at all reasonable time. ▮

SKARA BRAE
KW16 3LR
➲ (19m W of Kirkwall on B9056)
☎ 01856 841815

Engulfed in drift sand, this remarkable group of well-preserved Stone Age dwellings is the most outstanding survivor of its kind in Britain. Stone furniture and a fireplace can be seen.
Times: Open all year, Apr-Sep, daily 9.30-6.30; Oct-Mar, daily 9.30-4.30. (Closed Sun am in winter, 25-26 Dec & 1-2 Jan). **Fee:** ✱ £5 (ch £1.30, concessions £3.75). Groups 11+ 10% discount. Prices valid until 2 Jan 2005. Please phone for details. **Facilities:** 🅿 ✗ ⅙ toilets for disabled shop ✖▮

FINSTOWN   Map 16 HY31
MAES HOWE CHAMBERED CAIRN
➲ (9m W of Kirkwall, on A965)
☎ 01856 761606

The masonry of Britain's finest megalithic tomb is in a remarkably good state of preservation. Dating from neolithic times, it contains Viking carvings and runes.
Times: Open all year, Apr-Sep, daily 9.30-6.30; Oct-Mar, daily 9.30-4.30. (Closed Sun am in winter, 25-26 Dec & 1-2 Jan). **Fee:** ✱ £3 (ch £1, concessions £2.30). Groups 11+ 10% discount. Rates valid until 2 Jan 2005. Please phone for further details. **Facilities:** 🅿 ✗ shop ✖▮

STONES OF STENNESS CIRCLE AND HENGE
➲ (5m NE of Stromness on B9055)
☎ 01856 841815 [FREE]

Dating back to the second millennium BC, the remains of this stone circle are near the Ring of Brogar - a splendid circle of upright stones surrounded by a ditch.
Times: Open at any reasonable time. **Facilities:** 🅿 ▮

HARRAY   Map 16 HY31
CORRIGALL FARM & KIRBUSTER MUSEUM
KW17 2JR
☎ 01856 771411 & 771268 🗎 01856 874615

The museum consists of two Orkney farmhouses with outbuildings. Kirbuster (Birsay) has the last surviving example of a 'Firehoose' with its central hearth; Corrigall (Harray) represents an improved farmhouse and steading of the late 1800s.
Times: ✱ Open Mar-Oct, Mon-Sat 10.30-1 & 2-5, Sun 2-7.
Facilities: 🅿 ⅙ shop ✖ (ex guide dogs) ◄

KIRKWALL   Map 16 HY41
BISHOP'S & EARL'S PALACES
KW15 1PD
➲ (In Kirkwall on A960)
☎ 01856 875461

The Bishop's Palace is a hall-house of the 12th century, later much altered, with a round tower built by Bishop Reid in 1541-48. A later addition was made by the notorious Patrick Stewart, Earl of Orkney, who built the adjacent Earl's Palace between 1600 and 1607 in a splendid Renaissance style.
Times: Open Apr-Sep, daily 9.30-6.30. **Fee:** Prices not confirmed for 2005 **Facilities:** shop ▮

SCAPA FLOW VISITOR CENTRE & MUSEUM
Hoy KW15 1DH
➲ (on A964 to Houton, ferry crossing takes 45 mins, visitors centre 2 mins from ferry terminal)
☎ 01856 791300 🗎 01856 871560
e-mail: museum@orkney.gov.uk

Also known as the Lyness Interpretation Centre, this fascinating museum is home to a large collection of military equipment used in the defence of the Orkneys during the First and Second World Wars. There are also guns salvaged from the German ships scuppered in WWII. Visitors arrive at the island after a short boat trip from the Orkney mainland.
Times: ✱ Open all year: Mon-Fri 9-4.30 (mid May-Oct also Sat, Sun 10.30-3.30) **Facilities:** 🅿 ▄ ⅙ toilets for disabled shop ✖ (ex guide dogs) ◄

THE ORKNEY MUSEUM
Broad St KW15 1DH
➲ (town centre)
☎ 01856 873191 🗎 01856 874616
e-mail: museum@orkney.gov.uk

One of the finest vernacular town houses in Scotland, this 16th-century building now contains a museum of Orkney history, including the islands' fascinating archaeology.
Times: ✱ Open, Oct-Mar Mon-Sat, 10.30-12.30 & 1.30-5, Apr-Sep, 10.30-5 Mon-Sat. **Facilities:** 🅿 (50yds) ⅙ shop ✖ (ex guide dogs) ◄

STROMNESS   Map 16 HY20
ORKNEY MARITIME & NATURAL HISTORY MUSEUM
52 Alfred St KW16 3DF
☎ 01856 850025

The museum focuses on Orkney's broad maritime connections, including fishing, whaling, the Hudson's Bay Company, the German Fleet in Scapa Flow, and the award-winning Pilot's House extension. The Natural History Gallery is fully restored, displaying a fine collection of curios and rare and interesting exhibits.
Times: ✱ Open Apr-Sep, Mon-Sun 10-5; Oct-Mar, Mon-Sat 11-3.30. (Closed Xmas, New Year & 3 wks Feb-Mar). **Facilities:** 🅿 (50yds) ⅙ toilets for disabled shop ✖ (ex guide dogs)

PIER ARTS CENTRE
KW16 3AA
☎ 01856 850209 🗎 01856 851462
e-mail: info@pierartscentre.com

The collection is housed in a warehouse standing on its own stone pier. There is a constantly changing programme of exhibitions.
Times: ✱ Open all year, Tue-Sat 10.30-12.30 & 1.30-5.
Facilities: 🅿 (100yds) ⅙ shop ✖ (ex guide dogs)

WESTRAY   Map 16 HY44
NOLTLAND CASTLE
➲ (1m W of Pierowall village)
☎ 01856 841815 [FREE]

A fine, ruined Z-plan tower, built between 1560 and 1573 but never completed. The tower is remarkable for its large number of gun loops and impressive staircase.
Times: Open 11 Jun-Sep, daily 9.30-6.30. **Facilities:** ✖▮

SHETLAND

LERWICK Map 16 HU44
CLICKIMIN
ZE1 0QX
⮑ (1m SW of Lerwick on A970)
☎ 01466 793191
The remains of a prehistoric settlement that was fortified at the beginning of the Iron Age with a stone-built fort. The site was occupied for over 1000 years. The remains include a partially demolished broch (round tower) which still stands to a height of 17ft.
Times: Open at all reasonable times. ▮

FORT CHARLOTTE
ZE1 0JN
⮑ (in centre of Lerwick)
☎ 01466 793191
A five-sided artillery fort with bastions projecting from each corner. The walls are high and massive. It was built in 1665 to protect the Sound of Bressay from the Dutch, but taken by them and burned in 1673. It was rebuilt in 1781.
Times: Open at all reasonable times. Key available locally. ▮

SHETLAND MUSEUM
Lower Hillhead ZE1 0EL
☎ 01595 695057 📇 01595 696729 FREE
e-mail: shetland.museum@sic.shetland.gov.uk
The massive brass propeller blade outside the building is from the 17,000-ton liner *Oceanic*, wrecked off Foula in 1914. The archaeology gallery covers Neolithic burials, axe-making, Bronze Age houses, Iron Age farming and domestic life. There are also agricultural and social history displays, including peat-working, corn harvest, local businesses, medals, bootmaking and Shetland weddings. Changing displays of local contemporary art. Please note the current Museum is due to close on 31st March 2005. It will re-open as the New Shetland Museum and Archives in early 2006.
Times: Up to 31 Mar, Wed-Sat 10-5. (Closed 31 Mar 2005 & new Museum opens early 2006) **Facilities:** 🅿 ⟨ (lift, wheelchair available) toilets for disabled shop ✖ (ex guide dogs) ◼

MOUSA ISLAND Map 16 HU42
MOUSA BROCH
⮑ (accessible by boat from Sandwick)
☎ 01466 793191 FREE
This broch is the best-preserved example of an Iron Age drystone tower. The tower is nearly complete and rises to a height of 40ft. The outer and inner walls both contain staircases that may be climbed to the parapet.
Times: Open at all reasonable time. ▮

SCALLOWAY Map 16 HU33
SCALLOWAY CASTLE
ZE1 0TP
⮑ (6m from Lerwick on A970)
☎ 01466 793191 FREE
The ruins of a castle designed on the medieval two-step plan. The castle was actually built in 1600 by Patrick Stewart, Earl of Orkney. When the Earl, who was renowned for his cruelty, was executed in 1615, the castle fell into disuse.
Times: Open at all reasonable time. **Facilities:** 🅿 ▮

SUMBURGH Map 16 HU30
JARLSHOF PREHISTORIC SITE
⮑ (At Sumburgh Head, approx 22m S of Lerwick)
☎ 01950 460112
One of the most remarkable archaeological sites in Europe. There are remains of Bronze Age, Iron Age and Viking settlements as well as a medieval farm. There is also a 16th-century Laird's House, once the home of the Earls Robert and Patrick Stewart, and the basis of 'Jarlshof' in Sir Walter Scott's novel *The Pirate*.
Times: Open Apr-Sep, daily 9.30-6.30. **Fee:** ✱ £3.30 (ch £1, concessions £2.50). Groups 11+ 10% discount. Rates valid until 2 Jan 2005. Please phone for further details. **Facilities:** 🅿 shop ▮

SKYE, ISLE OF

ARMADALE Map 13 NG60
ARMADALE CASTLE GARDENS & MUSEUM OF THE ISLES
IV45 8RS
⮑ (16m S of Broadford on A851. Follow Clan Donald Centre or Armadale Castle Gardens & Museum of the Isles signs. Easily reached by Skye Bridge or the Mallaig A830 to Armdale Ferry)
☎ 01471 844305 & 844227 📇 01471 844275
e-mail: office@cland.demon.co.uk
Armadale Castle and Gardens were built in 1815 as the home of Lord Macdonald. The warming effect of the Gulf Stream allows exotic trees and plants to flourish. Within the 40 acres of gardens is the Museum of the Isles, where visitors can discover the history of the Highlands.
Times: ✱ Open daily 9.30-5.30. Garden & Museum open Apr-Oct. **Facilities:** 🅿 ◼ ✖ licensed ⟨ (wheelchairs available) toilets for disabled shop ◼

DUNVEGAN Map 13 NG24
DUNVEGAN CASTLE
IV55 8WF
⮑ (Follow A87 over Skye Bridge. Turn onto A863 at Sligachan and continue to castle)
☎ 01470 521206 📇 01470 521205
e-mail: info@dunvegancastle.com
This fortress stronghold set on the sea loch of Dunvegan has been the home of the Chief of Macleod for 800 years. On view are books, pictures, arms and treasured relics of the clan. A pedigree Highland Cattle fold is also an attraction, as is the boat trip to the nearby Seal Colony.
Times: Open 24 Mar-Oct, daily 10-5.30 (last entry 5). Castle & Gardens, Nov-Mar, daily 11-4 (last entry 3.30). (Closed 25-26 Dec & 1-2 Jan) **Fee:** ✱ Castle & Gardens: £6.50 (ch 5-15 yrs £3.50, pen & students £5.50). Group (Min 10 adults) £5.50. Gardens only: £4.50 (ch 5-15 £2.50, pen & students £2.50). Seal Boats: £5.00 (ch 5-12 £2.50). **Facilities:** 🅿 ◼ ✖ licensed ⟨ (restaurant has ramps for wheelchair access) toilets for disabled shop garden centre ✖ (ex guide dogs & in grounds) ◼

Directions are provided by the attractions.

WALES

EVENTS & FESTIVALS

March
tbc Wrexham Science Festival, Wrexham

April
1st-17th International Festival of Musical
Theatre, Cardiff

February
tbc Y Grael, the Cauldron of Inspiration,
Caernarfon Castle

May
27th-5th Jun Hay Festival of Literature,
Haye-on-Wye
28th-5th Jun St David's Cathedral Festival,
St David's, Pembrokeshire
tbc Llantilio Crossenny
Festival of Music & Drama

June
tbc Llandudno Festival, week of events,
concerts, crafts, parades and street festival

July
1st-3rd North Wales Bluegrass Festival,
Bodlondeb Field, Llandudno, Conwy

1st-9th Llangollen Fringe Festival (provisional)
5th-10th Llangollen International Musical
Eisteddfod, International Pavilion, Abbey
Road, Llangollen
18th-21st Royal Welsh Show, Royal Welsh
Showground, Builth Wells
tbc Brecon County Show
tbc Cardiff International Street Festival
tbc Conwy River Festival, Harbour, Conwy
tbc Fishguard International Music Festival
(various venues), Fishguard, Pembrokeshire
tbc Royal National Eisteddfod of Wales,
Tredegar Park, Newport
tbc Welsh Proms, St David's Hall,
The Hayes, Cardiff

August
1st-9th Talgarth Festival of the Black
Mountains
29th World Bog Snorkelling Championship
(race through trench cut in peat bog with
snorkel and flippers)
tbc Anglesey County Show, Anglesey
Showground, Gwalchmai, Holyhead

September
tbc North Wales International Music Festival,
the Cathedral, St Asaph
tbc Tenby Arts Festival (various venues),
Tenby, Pembrokeshire

October
27th-9th Nov Dylan Thomas Festival, Dylan
Thomas Centre, Somerset Place Swansea

November
9th-19th Cardiff Screen Festival,
various venues
28th-29th Royal Welsh Agricultural Winter
Fair, Royal Welsh Showground, Builth Wells

Top: Portmerion   Above: Mawddach Estuary at low tide

BRIDGEND

BRIDGEND   Map 03 SS97

NEWCASTLE
☎ 01656 659515   FREE

The small castle dates back to the 12th century. It is ruined, but a rectangular tower, a richly carved Norman gateway and massive curtain walls enclosing a polygonal courtyard can still be seen.

Times: Open - accessible throughout the year. Key keeper arrangement. **Facilities:** 🅿 ✗ ☺

COITY   Map 03 SS98

COITY CASTLE
CF35 6BG

➲ (2m NE of Bridgend, off A4061)
☎ 01656 652021   FREE

A 12th to 16th-century stronghold, with a hall, chapel and the remains of a square keep.

Times: Open all year, at all times. Key keeper arrangement. **Facilities:** 🅿 ✗ ☺

CAERPHILLY

CAERPHILLY   Map 03 ST18

CAERPHILLY CASTLE
CF8 1JL

➲ (on A469)
☎ 029 2088 3143

The concentrically planned castle was begun in 1268 by Gilbert de Clare and completed in 1326. It is the largest in Wales, and has extensive land and water defences. A unique feature is the ruined tower - the victim of subsidence - which manages to out-lean even Pisa! The south dam platform, once a tournament-field, now displays replica medieval siege-engines.

Times: Open Apr-May & Oct, daily 9.30-5; Jun-Sep, daily 9.30-6; Nov-Mar, Mon-Sat 9.30-4, Sun 11-4. Telephone for Xmas opening times. **Fee:** £3 (ch 5-15, pen & students £2.50, disabled visitors and assisting companion free). Family ticket (2 ad & 3 ch) £8.50. Group rates available. Prices quoted apply until 31 Mar 2005. **Facilities:** 🅿 ♿ shop ✗ ☺ ➡

LLANCAIACH FAWR MANOR
Gelligaer Rd, Nelson CF46 6ER

➲ (M4 junct 32, A470 to Merthyr Tydfil. Towards Ystrad Mynach A472 follow brown heritage signs)
☎ 01443 412248   🖹 01443 412688   2 for 1
e-mail: allens@caerphilly.gov.uk

Step back in time to the Civil War period at this fascinating living history museum. The year is 1645 and visitors are invited into the Manor to meet the servants of 'Colonel' Edward Prichard - from the puritanical to the gossipy.

Times: Open Mon-Fri 10-3.30 (last admission), Sat & Sun 10-4.30. (Closed Mon, Nov-Feb & 24 Dec-2 Jan). **Fee:** £4.95 (ch & concessions £3.25). Family ticket £13. **Facilities:** 🅿 ➡ ✗ licensed ♿ (personal stereo, photo album & Braille map) toilets for disabled shop ✗ (ex guide dogs) ➡

CWMCARN   Map 03 ST29

CWMCARN FOREST DRIVE
Nantcarn Rd NP11 7FA

➲ (8m N of Newport on A467, M4 junct 28, follow brown tourist signs)
☎ 01495 272001   🖹 01495 271403
e-mail: cwmcarn-vc@caerphilly.gov.uk

A seven-mile scenic drive with spectacular views over the Bristol Channel and surrounding countryside. Facilities include barbecues, picnic and play areas, and forest and mountain walks. Special events are held throughout the year, please ring for details.

Times: ✱ Open Forest Drive: Mar & Oct 11-5; Apr-Aug 11-7 (11-9 wknds during Jul & Aug); Sep, 11-6; Nov 11-4 (wknds only). Visitor Centre: all year except between Xmas & New Year. **Facilities:** 🅿 ➡ ♿ toilets for disabled shop ➡

CARDIFF

CARDIFF   Map 03 ST17

CARDIFF CASTLE
Castle St CF10 3RB

➲ (From M4, A48 & A470. Follow signs to city centre)
☎ 029 2087 8100   🖹 029 2023 1417
e-mail: cardiffcastle@cardiff.gov.uk

Cardiff Castle is situated in the heart of the city. Contained within its mighty walls is a history spanning nearly 2000 years, dating from the coming of the Romans to the Norman Conquest. Discover spectacular interiors on your guided tour, and enjoy magnificent views of the city from the top of the 12th-century Norman keep.

Times: Open all year, daily (ex 25-26 Dec & 1 Jan) including guided tours, Mar-Oct, 9.30-6 (last tour 5); Nov-Feb, 9.30-5.30 (last tour 4). Royal Regiment of Wales Museum closed Tue. Queen's Dragoon Guards Museum closed Fri. **Fee:** Full conducted tour, military museums, green, Roman Wall & Norman Keep £6 (ch & pen £3.70). Family £17.60. Roman Wall, Norman Keep, & military museum £2.90 (ch & pen £1.80). **Facilities:** 🅿 (200 yds) ➡ ♿ (access to Castle Green & Museum) toilets for disabled shop ✗ (ex in grounds & guide dogs) ➡

DYFFRYN GARDENS
St Nicholas CF5 6SU M4 J33

➲ (onto A4232 to Barry, rdbt take 1st exit, exit at junct with A48/A4050. At Culverhouse Cross rdbt take 4th exit A48 signed Cowbridge. Turn left at lights in St Nicholas Village & Dyffryn is on right after 1.5m)
☎ 029 2059 3328   🖹 029 2059 1966
e-mail: jehopkins@valeofglamorgan.gov.uk

One of Wales' finest Edwardian gardens, the beautiful grounds offer an endless variety of colour and form with many small garden rooms now restored with the aid of a Heritage Lottery fund grant. Additional works are still ongoing and some areas may be subject to closure.

Times: Etr-Sep, 10-6; Oct 10-5. **Fee:** ✱ £3.50 (ch & pen £2.50, disabled £2, carers free). Family ticket £7. **Facilities:** 🅿 ➡ ♿ (wheelchairs for hire, parking, ramps) toilets for disabled shop garden centre ➡

LLANDAFF CATHEDRAL
Llandaff CF5 2LA
➲ (exit at M4 junct 29 to A48(M), then A48 and follow brown signs. From E M4 exit at junct 32 onto A470 towards Cardiff, leave A48 and follow brown signs)
☎ 029 2056 3897 ▤ 029 2056 4554 `FREE`
e-mail: office@llandaffcathedral.org.uk
A medieval cathedral begun in the 12th century on the site of an early Christian place of worship. The cathedral was severely damaged during the bombing raids on Cardiff during World War II. The interior is dominated by a modernistic post-war 'Christ in Majesty' sculpture by Epstein.
Times: Open all year, daily 8-7 (Sun 7-7 & Mon 8.30-7).
Facilities: P (100yds) Parking limited & (wheelchair available) toilets for disabled shop ✺ (ex guide dogs)

MILLENNIUM STADIUM TOURS
Millennium Stadium, Westgate St, Gate 3 CF10 1JA
➲ (M4 junct 32, take A470 to Cardiff City Centre. Westgate St is opposite Cardiff Castle far end)
☎ 029 2082 2228 ▤ 029 2082 2040 `2 for 1`
In the late 1990s this massive stadium was completed as part of an effort to revitalise Welsh fortunes. It replaced Cardiff Arms Park, and now hosts major music events, exhibitions, and international rugby and soccer matches. Its capacity of around 75,000 and its retractable roof make it unique in Europe. The current home of five controlling bodies; Welsh Rugby, Welsh Football, English Football ASS, Football league (English) & British Speedway.
Times: Open Mon Sat, 10-5; Sun 10-4 **Fee:** ✱ £5 (ch up to 16 £2.50, ch under 5 free, concessions £3). Party 20+ **Facilities:** P Opposite gate 3 ▣ & (lifts escalators disabled parking) toilets for disabled shop ✺ (ex guide dogs) ▰

NATIONAL MUSEUM & GALLERY CARDIFF
Cathays Park CF10 3NP
➲ (in Cardiff's Civic Centre, 5 mins walk from the city centre, 20 mins walk from Cardiff's bus and train station. M4 junct 32)
☎ 029 2039 7951 ▤ 029 2037 3219 `FREE`
e-mail: post@nmgw.ac.uk
This establishment is unique amongst British museums and galleries in its range of art and science displays. 'The Evolution of Wales' exhibition takes visitors on a spectacular 4600-million year journey, tracing the world from beginning of time and the development of Wales. There are displays of Bronze Age gold, early Christian monuments, Celtic treasures, silver, coins and medals, ceramics, fossils and minerals. A significant collection of French Impressionist paintings sits alongside the work of Welsh artists, past and present in the elegant art galleries.
Times: Open all year, Tue-Sun 10-5. Closed Mon (ex BHs) & 24-26 Dec. **Facilities:** ▣ (charged) ▣ ✗ licensed & (wheelchair available, Tel 029 2057 3509 for access guide) toilets for disabled shop ✺ (ex guide dogs) ▰

TECHNIQUEST
Stuart St CF10 5BW
➲ (M4 junct 33, follow A4232 to Cardiff Bay)
☎ 029 2047 5475 ▤ 029 2048 2517
e-mail: info@techniquest.org
Located in the heart of the Cardiff Bay, there's always something new to explore at this exciting science discovery

continued

centre. Journey into space in the planetarium, enjoy an interactive Science Theatre Show or experience one of the 150 hands-on exhibits.

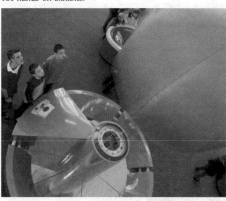

Times: Open all year (ex Xmas), Mon-Fri 9.30-4.30; Sat-Sun & BH's 10.30-5, school holidays 9.30-5. **Fee:** ✱ £6.75 (ch 5-16 & con £4.65). Family ticket £18.50 (2ad+3ch). Friend season ticket £48. Groups 10+
Facilities: ▣ (50mtrs) Limited parking for disabled visitors ▣ & (lift, hearing loop) toilets for disabled shop ✺ (ex guide dogs) ▰

ST FAGANS   Map 03 ST17
MUSEUM OF WELSH LIFE
CF5 6XB
➲ (4m W of Cardiff, 3m from M4 junct 33, on A4232)
☎ 029 2057 3500 ▤ 029 2057 3490 `FREE`
e-mail: post@nmgw.ac.uk
A stroll around the indoor galleries and 100 acres of beautiful grounds will give you a fascinating insight into how people in Wales have lived, worked and spent their leisure hours since Celtic times. You can see people practising the traditional means of earning a living, the animals they kept and at certain times of year, the ways in which they celebrated the seasons.
Times: Open all year daily, 10-5. Closed 24-26 Dec.
Facilities: ▣ (charged) ▣ ✗ licensed & (wheelchairs available on a 'first come-first served' basis) toilets for disabled shop ✺ (ex in grounds if on lead) ▰

TONGWYNLAIS   Map 03 ST18
CASTELL COCH
CF4 7YS
➲ (A470 to Tongwynlais junct, then B4262 to castle on top of hill)
☎ 029 2081 0101
Castell Coch is Welsh for red castle, an appropriate name for this fairy-tale building with its red sandstone walls and conical towers. The castle was originally built in the 13th century but fell into ruins, and the present castle is a late-19th-century creation. Inside, the castle is decorated in fantasy style.
Times: Open Apr-May & Oct, daily 9.30-5; Jun-Sep, daily 9.30-6; Nov-Mar, Mon-Sat 9.30-4, Sun 11-4. Telephone for Xmas opening times. **Fee:** £3 (ch 5-15, pen & students £2.50, disabled visitors and assisting companion free). Family ticket (2 ad & 3 ch) £8.50. Group rates available. Prices quoted apply until 31 Mar 2005.
Facilities: ▣ shop ✺ ⊕ ▰

CARMARTHENSHIRE

ABERGWILI   Map 02 SN42
CARMARTHENSHIRE COUNTY MUSEUM
SA31 2JG
➲ (2m E of Carmarthen, just off A40, at Abergwili rdbt)
☎ 01267 228696 ▤ 01267 223830   **FREE**
e-mail: cdelaney@carmarthenshire.gov.uk
Housed in the old palace of the Bishop of St David's and set in seven acres of grounds, the museum offers a wide range of local subjects to explore, from geology and prehistory to butter making, Welsh furniture and folk art. Temporary exhibitions are held.
Times: Open all year, Mon-Sat 10-4.30. (Closed Xmas-New Year).
Facilities: ⓟ 📖 ♿ (lift) toilets for disabled shop ✖ (ex guide dogs)

CARREG CENNEN CASTLE   Map 03 SN61
CARREG CENNEN CASTLE
SA19 6UA
➲ (unclassified road from A483 to Trapp village)
☎ 01558 822291
A steep path leads up to the castle, which is spectacularly sited on a limestone crag. It was first built as a stronghold of the native Welsh and then rebuilt in the late 13th century. Most remarkable among the impressive remains is a mysterious passage, cut into the side of the cliff and lit by loopholes. The farm at the site has a rare breeds centre.
Times: Open all year, Apr-Oct, daily 9.30-6.30; Nov-Mar, daily, 9.30-dusk. Telephone for Xmas opening times. **Fee:** £3 (ch 5-15, pen & students £2.50, disabled visitors & assisting companion free). Family ticket (2 ad & 3 ch) £8.50. Group rates available. Prices quoted apply until 31 Mar 2005. **Facilities:** ⓟ 📖 shop ✖ ⊙ 📧

DRE-FACH FELINDRE   Map 02 SN33
NATIONAL WOOLLEN MUSEUM
SA44 5UP
➲ (16m W of Carmarthen off A484, 4m E of Newcastle Emlyn)
☎ 01559 370929   **FREE**
The museum is housed in the former Cambrian Mills and has a comprehensive display tracing the evolution of the industry from its beginnings to the present day. Demonstrations of the fleece to fabric process are given on 19th-century textile machinery.
Times: Apr-Sep, daily 10-5; Oct-Mar, Tue-Sat 10-5. **Facilities:** ⓟ 📖 ♿ (wheelchair access to ground floor & ample seating) toilets for disabled shop ✖ (ex guide dogs) 📧

DRYSLWYN   Map 02 SN52
DRYSLWYN CASTLE
➲ (on B4279)
☎ 029 2050 0200   **FREE**
The ruined 13th-century castle was a stronghold of the native Welsh. It stands on a lofty mound, and was important in the struggles between English and Welsh. It is gradually being uncovered by excavation.
Times: Open - entrance by arrangement with Dryslwyn Farm.
Facilities: ⓟ ✖ ⊙

KIDWELLY   Map 02 SN40
KIDWELLY CASTLE
SA17 5BQ
➲ (via A484)
☎ 01554 890104
This is an outstanding example of late 13th-century castle design, with its 'walls within walls' defensive system. There were later additions made to the building, the chapel dating from about 1400. Of particular interest are two vast circular ovens.
Times: Open Apr-May & Oct, daily 9.30-5; Jun-Sep, daily 9.30-6; Nov-Mar, Mon-Sat 9.30-4, Sun 11-4. Telephone for Xmas opening times. **Fee:** £2.50 (ch 5-15, pen & students £2, disabled visitors & assisting companion free). Family ticket (2 ad & 3 ch) £7. Group rates available. Prices quoted apply until 31 Mar 2005.
Facilities: ⓟ ♿ toilets for disabled shop ✖ ⊙ 📧

KIDWELLY INDUSTRIAL MUSEUM
Broadford SA17 4LW
➲ (signed from Kidwelly by-pass & Kidwelly Town, stack clearly visible from by-pass)   **FREE**
☎ 01554 891078
Two of the great industries of Wales are represented in this museum: tinplate and coal mining. The original buildings and machinery of the Kidwelly tinplate works, where tinplate was hand made, are now on display to the public. There is also an exhibition of coal mining with pit-head gear and a winding engine, while the more general history of the area is shown in a separate exhibition.
Times: Open Etr, Jun-Sep, BH wknds, Mon-Fri 10-5, Sat-Sun 12-5. Last admission 4. Other times by arrangement for parties only.
Facilities: ⓟ 📖 ♿ (ramps on entrances) toilets for disabled shop

LAUGHARNE   Map 02 SN31
DYLAN THOMAS' BOAT HOUSE
Dylans Walk SA33 4SD
➲ (14m SW of Carmarthen)
☎ 01994 427420 ▤ 01554 747501   **2 for 1**
e-mail: dylanthomas@carmarthenshire.gov.uk

The home of Dylan Thomas and his family during the last four turbulent and creative years of his life. The house and its surrounding estuary, town and countryside feature considerably in the poet's work, including his famous '*Under Milk Wood*'. The house contains interpretive display, original

continued

furniture, bookshop and tearoom. Evening events during the summer, phone for details.
Times: Open all year, May-Oct & Etr wknd, daily 10-5.30 (Last admission 5); Nov-Apr, daily 10.30-3.30 (Last admission 3). **Fee:** Prices not confirmed for 2005 **Facilities:** P (200yds) ☕ (not accessible for wheelchairs) shop ✖ (ex guide dogs) ◼

LAUGHARNE CASTLE
King St SA33 4SA
➲ (on A4066)
☎ 01994 427906
Newly opened to the public, picturesque Laugharne Castle stands on a low ridge overlooking the wide Taff Estuary. A medieval fortress converted into an Elizabethan mansion, it suffered a civil war siege and later became the backdrop for elaborate Victorian gardens, now recreated. Laugharne Castle has also inspired two modern writers - Richard Hughes and Dylan Thomas.
Times: Open Apr-Sep, daily 10-5. **Fee:** £2.75 (ch 5-15, pen & students £2.25, disabled visitors & assisting companions free). Family ticket (2 ad & 3 ch) £7.75. Group rates available. Prices quoted apply until 31 Mar 2005. **Facilities:** P (150 mtrs) ♿ toilets for disabled shop ✖ ⊕ ◼

LLANARTHNE   Map 02 SN52
MIDDLETON, THE NATIONAL BOTANIC GARDEN OF WALES
Middleton Hall SA32 8HG
➲ (8m E of Carmarthen on A48 (M4), dedicated intersection - signed)
☎ 01558 668768   🖷 01558 668933
e-mail: info@gardenofwales.org.uk
Set amongst 568 acres of Parkland in the beautiful Towy Valley in West Wales, just 7 miles from Carmarthen. The Gardens centrepiece is the Great Glasshouse, an amazing tilted glass dome with a six-metre ravine. The Mediterranean landscape enables the visitor to experience the aftermath of an Australian bush fire, pause in an olive grove or wander through Fuchsia collections from Chile. A 220mtr herbaceous board walk forms the spine of the garden and leads to the children's play area and our 360-surround screen cinema to the Old Stables Courtyard. Here the visitor can view art exhibitions, wander in the gift shop or enjoy a meal in the restaurant. Land train tours will take the visitor around the necklace of lakes, which surround the central garden.
Times: ✱ Open 30 Mar-25 Oct 10-6, 26 Oct-27 Mar 10-4.30
Facilities: P ☕ ✖ licensed ♿ (braile interpretation wheelchairs/scooters shuttle service) toilets for disabled shop garden centre ✖ (ex guide dogs) ◼

LLANDEILO   Map 03 SN62
DINEFWR PARK
SA19 6RT
➲ (off A40 Carmarthenshire, on the western outskirts of Llandeilo)
☎ 01558 823902   🖷 01558 822036   2 for 1
e-mail: dinefwr@nationaltrust.org.uk
At the heart of Welsh history for a thousand years, the Park as we know it today took shape in the years after 1775 when the medieval castle, house, gardens, woods and deer park were integrated into one vast and breathtaking landscape. Access to Church Woods and Dinefwr Castle is through the landscaped park.
Times: Open Mar-Oct, daily (ex Tue & Wed) 11-4.30. Last admission 30 mins before closing. **Fee:** Prices not confirmed for 2005
Facilities: P (charged) ☕ ♿ toilets for disabled ✖ (ex outer park on lead) ☕ ◼

LLANELLI   Map 02 SN50
NATIONAL WETLAND CENTRE WALES
Penclacwydd, Llwynhendy SA14 9SH
➲ (3m E of Llanelli, off A484)
☎ 01554 741087   🖷 01554 741087   2 for 1
e-mail: wwtllanelli@aol.com
A wide variety of wild birds, including oystercatchers, redshanks, curlews, little egrets and occasionally ospreys, can be seen here during the right season. The grounds are beautifully landscaped, and include CCTV transmitting pictures of wild birds on the reserve, a wetland craft area and a flock of colourful Caribbean Flamingos. There is also a Discovery Centre and outdoor activities for visitors to take part in. Facilities for the disabled include easy access on level paths, special viewing areas and wheelchair loan.
Times: Open summer 9.30-5; winter 9.30-4.30. (Closed 24-25 Dec).
Fee: ✱ £5.50 (ch £3.50, pen £4.50). Family £14.50. **Facilities:** P ☕ ✖ ♿ toilets for disabled shop ✖ (ex guide/hearing dogs) ◼

LLANGATHEN   Map 02 SN52
ABERGLASNEY GARDENS
SA32 8QH
➲ (4m W of Llandeilo, follow signs from A40)
☎ 01558 668998   🖷 01558 668998
e-mail: info@aberglasney.org.uk

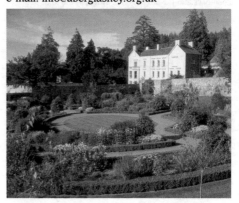

With a history stretching back to the 15th century, Aberglasney was reworked by the 17th-century Bishop of St David's, the 18th-century poet, John Dyer and the 19th-century surgeon John Walters Phillips. Falling into disrepair through the 20th century, the house and its gardens were eventually rescued in 1995, and are now largely restored to their original Jacobean splendour. A mysterious and beautiful day out.
Times: Open all year, Apr-Oct, daily 10-6 (last entry 5); Nov-Mar, daily 10.30-4. (Closed 25 Dec) **Fee:** £6 (ch £3, pen £5). Party 10+ £5.50 (ch £3, pen £4.50). **Facilities:** P ✖ licensed ♿ (most areas accessible, wheelchairs available) toilets for disabled shop garden centre ✖ (ex guide dogs) ◼

LLANSTEFFAN   Map 02 SN31
LLANSTEFFAN CASTLE
➲ (off B4312)
☎ 01267 241756   FREE
The ruins of this 11th to 13th-century stronghold stand majestically on the west side of the Towy estuary.
Times: Open - access throughout the year. **Facilities:** ✖ ⊕

PUMSAINT   Map 03 SN64

DOLAUCOTHI GOLD MINES
SA19 8RR
➜ (on A482, signed both directions)
☎ 01558 650177 📠 01588 650707 **2 for 1**
e-mail: dolaucothi@nationaltrust.org.uk
Here is an opportunity to spend a day exploring the gold
mines and to wear a miner's helmet and lamp while touring
the underground workings. The information centre and a
walk along the Miners' Way disclose the secrets of 2,000
years of gold mining. This is the only place in Britain where
the Romans mined gold.
Times: Open end Mar-end Oct, daily 10-5. **Fee:** Prices not confirmed
for 2005 **Facilities:** 🅿 🖭 ♿ toilets for disabled shop ⛟ ☕

CEREDIGION

ABERAERON   Map 02 SN46

LLANERCHAERON
SA48 8DG
➜ (2.5m E of Aberaeron off A482)
☎ 01545 570200 📠 01545 571759 **2 for 1**
e-mail: llanerchaeron@nationaltrust.org.uk
A rare survivor of a once typical late 18th-century Welsh
country estate. The property was owned by the same family
for ten generations, spread over three centuries, and the
famous architect John Nash was commissioned to design a
new villa for the estate in the 1790s. It is now a perfect
example of a self-sufficient country property of its time. Today
it is a working organic farm and produce is available for
purchase at the Visitor Building. Phone for current events list.
Times: Open early Apr-late Oct, Wed-Sun & BH Mons 11-5. Last
admission 1hr before closing. Park open all year dawn to dusk.
Fee: ✱ £5 (ch £2.50). Family ticket £12 (2ad & 2 ch). Special group
rates available **Facilities:** 🅿 🖭 ♿ (Ramp for access to ground floor
of villa) toilets for disabled ✖ (except guide dogs) ⛟

ABERYSTWYTH   Map 06 SN58

NATIONAL LIBRARY OF WALES
Penglais SY23 3BU
➜ (Off Penglais Hill, A487 in northern area of
Aberystwyth)
☎ 01970 632800 📠 01970 632882
e-mail: holi@llgc.org.uk
This huge library is one of Britain's six copyright libraries,
and specialises in Welsh and Celtic literature. It has maps,
manuscripts, prints and drawings. There is a programme of
travelling exhibitions. Please telephone for details.
Times: Open on selected BH's. Please check for details by telephone
or on website before travelling. **Fee:** ✱ Free. Admission to reading
rooms available by readers ticket, proof of identity required. Free
admission to all exhibitions. **Facilities:** 🅿 ✖ ♿ toilets for disabled
shop ✖ (ex guide dogs)

CAPEL BANGOR   Map 06 SN68

**RHEIDOL HYDRO ELECTRIC POWER STATION &
VISITOR CENTRE**
Cwm Rheidol SY23 3NF
➜ (off A44 at Capel Bangor)
☎ 01970 880667 📠 01970 880670
A guided tour of the power station and fish farm can be
taken. There is a visitor centre, nature trail and scenic drive.
Times: ✱ Open Apr-Oct, daily 10-4 for free tours of the Power Station,
fish farm & visitor centre. **Facilities:** 🅿 🖭 ♿ toilets for disabled

CENARTH   Map 02 SN24

THE NATIONAL CORACLE CENTRE
Cenarth Falls SA38 9JL
➜ (on A484 between Carmarthen and Cardigan,
centre of Cenarth village, beside bridge and river)
☎ 01239 710980
e-mail: martinfowler.coraclecentre@virgin.net
Situated by the beautiful Cenarth Falls, this fascinating
museum has a unique collection from all over the world,
including Tibet, India, Iraq, Vietnam, and North America.
Cenarth has long been a centre for coracle fishing, coracle
rides are often available in village during summer holiday.
Look out for the salmon leap by the flour mill.
Times: ✱ Open Etr-Oct, Sun-Fri 10.30-5.30. All other times by
appointment. **Facilities:** 🅿 🖭 ♿ shop ☕

EGLWYSFACH   Map 06 SN69

RSPB NATURE RESERVE
Cae'r Berllan SY20 8TA
➜ (6m S of Machynlleth on A487 in Eglwys-Fach.
Signed from main road)
☎ 01654 700222 📠 01654 700333
e-mail: ynyshir@rspb.org.uk
The mixture of different habitats is home to an abundance of
birds and wildlife. The saltmarshes in winter support the
only regular wintering flock of Greenland white-fronted
geese in England and Wales in addition to peregrines, hen
harriers and merlins. The sessile oak woodland is home to
pied flycatchers, wood warblers, redstarts in the summer but
woodpeckers, nut hatches, red kites, sparrow hawks and
buzzards are here all year round. Otters, polecats, 30
butterfly and 15 dragonfly species are also present.
Times: Open daily, 9am-9pm (or sunset if earlier). Visitor Centre:
Apr-Oct 9-5 daily; Nov-Mar 10-4 (Wed - Sun) **Fee:** ✱ £3.50 (ch £1,
concessions £2.50) Family £7 RSPB members free.
Facilities: 🅿 ♿ (Can take car to viewpoint) ✖ (ex guide dogs) ☕

FELINWYNT   Map 02 SN25

FELINWYNT RAINFOREST & BUTTERFLY CENTRE
Rhosmaen SA43 1RT
➜ (from A487 Blaenannerch Airfield turning, turn
onto B4333. Signed 6m N of Cardigan)
☎ 01239 810882 & 810250 **2 for 1**
📠 01239 810465
e-mail: dandjdevereux@btinternet.com
A chance to wander amongst free-flying exotic butterflies
accompanied by the recorded wildlife sounds of the Peruvian
Amazon. A waterfall, ponds and streams contribute to a
humid tropical atmosphere and provide a habitat for fish and
native amphibians. See the exhibition of rainforests of Peru
and around the world. Free paper and crayons to borrow for
children.
Times: daily from Etr-Oct. **Fee:** ✱ £3.90 (ch 4-14 £1.50, pen £3.50)
Facilities: 🅿 🖭 ♿ toilets for disabled shop ✖ (ex guide dogs) ☕

STRATA FLORIDA   Map 03 SN76

STRATA FLORIDA ABBEY
SY25 6BT
➜ (unclassified road from Pontrhydfendigaid,
accessed from B4340)
☎ 01974 831261
Little remains of the Cistercian abbey founded in 1164,
except the ruined church and cloister. Strata Florida was an
important centre of learning in the Middle Ages, and it is

continued

believed that the 14th-century poet Dafyd ap Gwilym was buried here.

Times: Open Apr-Sep, Wed-Sun & BH Mon 10-5. Monument will be opened and unstaffed with no admission charge at all other times between 10-4. **Fee:** £2.25 (ch 5-15, pen & students £1.75, disabled visitors & assisting companion free). Family ticket (2 ad & 3 ch) £6.25. Group discounts available. Prices quoted apply until 31 Mar 2005. **Facilities:** 🅿 ♿ shop ✕ ✛ ☕

CONWY

BETWS-Y-COED   Map 06 SH75
CONWY VALLEY RAILWAY MUSEUM
Old Goods Yard LL24 0AL
➲ (signed from A5 into Old Church Rd, adjacent to train station)
☎ 01690 710568   🖳 01690 710132
The two large museum buildings have displays on both the narrow and standard-gauge railways of North Wales, including railway stock and other memorabilia. There are working model railway layouts, a steam-hauled miniature railway in the grounds, which cover over four acres, and a 15inch-gauge tramway to the woods. The latest addition is the quarter-size steam 'Britannia' loco that is now on display. For children there are mini-dodgems, Postman Pat, school bus and Toby Tram.
Times: Open daily, 10-5.30 (ex Xmas) **Fee:** ✱ £1 (ch & pen 50p). Family ticket £2.50. Steam train ride £1. Tram ride 80p.
Facilities: 🅿 ⬛ ♿ (ramps & clearances for wheelchairs) toilets for disabled shop ☕

CERRIGYDRUDION   Map 06 SH94
LLYN BRENIG VISITOR CENTRE
LL21 9TT
➲ (on B4501 between Denbigh & Cerrigydrudion)
☎ 01490 420463   🖳 01490 420694   **FREE**
e-mail: llyn.brenig@dwrcymru.com
The 1800-acre estate has a unique archaeological trail and round-the-lake walk of 10 miles. A hide is available and disabled anglers are catered for with a specially adapted fishing boat and an annual open day. The centre has an exhibition on archaeology, history and conservation and an audio-visual programme.
Times: Open mid Mar-Oct, daily 9-5. **Facilities:** 🅿 (charged) ⬛ ♿ (boats for disabled & fishing open days) toilets for disabled shop ✕ (ex guide dogs)

COLWYN BAY   Map 06 SH87
WELSH MOUNTAIN ZOO
Old Highway LL28 5UY
➲ (A55 junct 20 signed Rhos-on-Sea)
☎ 01492 532938   🖳 01492 530498
e-mail: welshmountainzoo@enterprise.net
The zoo and gardens are set in a 37-acre estate overlooking Colwyn Bay, with magnificent panoramic views of the coast and mountains. The animals are housed in natural settings, interspersed with gardens and woodland. The traditional range of zoo animals can be seen, from lions and elephants to penguins and parrots, and the zoo also attracts a variety of local wildlife. There are falconry displays during the summer months, and Californian sealions can be seen performing tricks at feeding time. Visit the Chimpanzee World complex, featuring the unique Chimp Encounter, and a South American small monkey breeding centre. There is

continued

also a Jungle Adventureland and Tarzan Trail activity area, and a Children's Farm.
Times: Open all year, Mar-Oct, daily 9.30-6; Nov-Feb, daily 9.30-5. (Closed 25 Dec) **Facilities:** 🅿 ✕ ♿ toilets for disabled shop ✕ ☕

CONWY   Map 06 SH77
ABERCONWY HOUSE
LL32 8AY
➲ (At junct of Castle St & High St)
☎ 01492 592246   🖳 01492 564818   **2 for 1**
This house dates from the 14th century; it is the only medieval merchant's house in Conwy to have survived the centuries of turbulence, fire and pillage in this frontier town. Furnished rooms and an audio-visual presentation show daily life in the house at different periods in its history.
Times: Open 19 Mar-6 Nov, Wed-Mon 11-5. Last admission 30 mins before closing. **Fee:** ✱ £2.40 Joint £3 Party adult £2 & ch £1 (ch £1.20). Family ticket £6. Party. **Facilities:** 🅿 (100yds & 0.5 mile) Limited to 40mins on street shop ✕ (ex guide dogs) ♨

CONWY CASTLE
LL32 8AY
➲ (by A55 or B5106)
☎ 01492 592358
The castle is a magnificent fortress, built 1283-7 by Edward I. There is an exhibition on castle chapels on the ground floor of the Chapel Tower. The castle forms part of the same defensive system as the extensive town walls, which are among the most complete in Europe.
Times: Open Apr-May & Oct, daily 9.30-5; Jun-Sep, daily 9.30-6; Nov-Mar, Mon-Sat 9.30-4, Sun 11-4. Telephone for Xmas opening times. **Fee:** £3.75 (ch 5-15, pen & students £3.25, disabled visitors & assisting companion free). Family ticket £10.75. Joint ticket for both monuments £6.50 (concessions £5.50, disabled visitors & assisting companion free) Family ticket £18.50. Group rates available. Prices quoted apply until 31 Mar 2005. **Facilities:** 🅿 ♿ toilets for disabled shop ✕ ✛ ☕

CONWY SUSPENSION BRIDGE
LL32 8LD
➲ (adjacent to Conwy Castle)
☎ 01492 573282   **2 for 1**
Designed by Thomas Telford, one of the greatest engineers of the late 18th and early 19th century, this was the first bridge to span the river at Conwy. The bridge has been restored and the toll house furnished as it would have been a century ago.
Times: Open daily 26 Mar-Oct 10 - 5 **Fee:** ✱ £1.20 (ch 60p) Joint £3.
Facilities: 🅿 ♿ ✕ ♨

PLAS MAWR
High St LL32 8DE
☎ 01492 580167
Plas Mawr is an excellent example of an Elizabethan townhouse. Built by Robert Wynn between 1576 and 1585, the interior remains almost unaltered and displays decorated plaster ceilings and wooden screens.
Times: Open Apr-May & Sep, Tue-Sun 9.30-5; Jun-Aug, Tue-Sun 9.30-6; Oct, Tue-Sun 9.30-4. Open Mon on BH wknds. **Fee:** £4.50 (ch 5-15, pen & students £3.50, disabled visitors & assisting companion free). Family (2 ad & 3 ch) £12.50. Joint ticket for both monuments available £6.50 (ch 5-15, pen & students £5.50, disabled visitors & assisting companion free). Family (2 ad & 3 ch) £18.50. **Facilities:** shop ✛ ☕

SMALLEST HOUSE

The Quay LL32 8BB

➲ (leave A55 at Conwy sign, through town, at bottom of High St for the quay, turn left)

☎ 01492 593484 📠 01492 593484   **2 for 1**

The *Guinness Book of Records* lists this as the smallest house in Britain. Just 6ft wide by 10ft high, it is furnished in the style of a mid-Victorian Welsh cottage.

Times: Open Apr-May & Oct 10-5; Jun & Sep, 10-6, first half Jul 10-6 rest of Jul & Aug 10-9 **Fee:** ✱ 75p (ch under 16 50p, under 5 free). **Facilities:** P (100yds) ♿ shop

DOLWYDDELAN   Map 06 SH75

DOLWYDDELAN CASTLE

LL25 0EJ

➲ (on A470 Blaenau Ffestiniog to Betws-y-Coed)

☎ 01690 750366

The castle is reputed to be the birthplace of Llywelyn the Great. It was captured in 1283 by Edward I, who immediately began strengthening it for his own purposes. A restored keep of around 1200, and a 13th-century curtain wall can be seen. An exhibition on the castles of the Welsh Princes is located in the keep.

Times: Open all year, Apr-Sep, Mon-Sat 9.30-6.30 & Sun 11-4; Oct-Mar, Mon-Sat 9.30-4, Sun 11-4. Telephone for Xmas opening times. **Fee:** £2 (ch 5-15, pen & students £1.50, disabled visitors & assisting companion free). Family ticket (2 ad & 3 ch) £5.50. Group rates available. Prices quoted apply until 31 Mar 2005. **Facilities:** P ✖ ☺ ➡

LLANDUDNO JUNCTION   Map 06 SH77

RSPB NATURE RESERVE

LL31 9XZ

➲ (off A55, signed)

☎ 01492 584091

e-mail: alan.davies@rspb.org.uk   **2 for 1**

The visitor centre has a viewing area which overlooks the estuary and Conwy Castle, and there's a nature trail and four hides for viewing lapwings and shelduck amongst many others. Phone for details of events.

Times: Open all year, daily, 10-5 (Closed 25 Dec) **Fee:** £2.50 (ch £1, concessions £1.50) **Facilities:** P ♿ (Use of wheelchair & audio trail) toilets for disabled shop ✖ (ex guide dogs) ➡

LLANRWST   Map 06 SH86

GWYDYR UCHAF CHAPEL

➲ (0.5m SW off B5106)

☎ 01492 640578   **FREE**

Built in the 17th century by Sir John Wynn of Gwydir Castle, the chapel is noted for its painted ceiling and wonderfully varied woodwork.

Times: Open any reasonable time. **Facilities:** P ✖ 🚐 ☺

PENMACHNO   Map 06 SH75

TY MAWR WYBRNANT

LL25 0HJ

➲ (From A5 3m S of Betws-y-Coed take B4406 to Penmachno. House is 2.5m NW of Penmachno by forest road)

☎ 01690 760213

Situated in the beautiful, secluded Wybrnant Valley, Ty Mawr was the birthplace of Bishop William Morgan (1545-1604), the first translator of the entire Bible into Welsh. The house has been restored to its probable 16th-17th century

continued

appearance. The Wybrnant Nature Trail, a short walk, covers approximately one mile.

Times: Open 30 Mar-Sep, Thu-Sun & BH Mons 12-5; Oct, Thu, Fri & Sun 12-4. Last admission 30 mins before closing. **Fee:** ✱ £2 (ch £1). Family ticket £5. Party 15+. **Facilities:** P ✖ (ex in grounds) 🚐 33 seats (minibus access only) ♨

TAL-Y-CAFN   Map 06 SH77

BODNANT GARDEN

LL28 5RE

➲ (8m S of Llandudno & Colwyn Bay off A470. Also signed from A55 junct 19)

☎ 01492 650460 📠 01492 650448

e-mail: office@bodnantgarden.co.uk

Set above the River Conwy with beautiful views over Snowdonia, these gardens are a delight. Five Italian style terraces were constructed below the house - on the lowest terrace is a canal pool with an open-air yew hedge stage and a reconstructed Pin Mill. The garden is renowned for its collections of magnolias, camellias, rhododendrons and azaleas and the famous Laburnum Arch. Contact for details of open-air theatre.

Times: Open mid Mar-12 Nov, daily 10-5 (last admission half hour before closing) **Fee:** ✱ £5.50 (ch £2.75) Party of 20+ £5 **Facilities:** P 🍴 ♿ (ramps to gardens, wheelchairs & Braille guides) toilets for disabled shop garden centre ✖ (ex guide dogs) ♨ ➡

TREFRIW   Map 06 SH76

TREFRIW WOOLLEN MILLS

LL27 0NQ

➲ (on B5106 in centre of Trefriw, 5m N of Betws-y-Coed)

☎ 01492 640462 📠 01492 641821 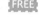

e-mail: info@t-w-m.co.uk

Established in 1859, the mill is situated beside the fast-flowing Afon Crafnant, which drives two hydro-electric turbines to power the looms. All the machinery of woollen manufacture can be seen here: blending, carding, spinning, dyeing, warping and weaving. In the Weaver's Garden, there are plants traditionally used in the textile industry, mainly for dyeing. Hand-spinning demonstrations.

Times: Mill open Etr-Oct, Mon-Fri 10-1 & 2-5. Weaving demonstrations & turbine house: open all year, Mon-Fri 10-1 & 2-5. Handspinning & weaver's garden Jun-Sep Tue-Thu Jul-Aug Mon-Fri 10-5 **Facilities:** P (35yds) 🍴 ♿ (access to shop, cafe, weaving & turbine house) shop ✖ (ex in grounds on lead) ➡

DENBIGHSHIRE

BODELWYDDAN   Map 06 SJ07

BODELWYDDAN CASTLE

LL18 5YA

➲ (just off A55, near St Asaph, follow brown signs)

☎ 01745 584060 📠 01745 584563

e-mail: enquiries@bodelwyddan-castle.co.uk

Bodelwyddan Castle houses over 100 portraits from the National Portrait Gallery's 19th-century collection. The portraits hang in beautifully refurbished rooms and are complemented by sculpture and period furnishings. Interactive displays show how portraits were produced and used in the Victorian era. The Castle Gallery hosts a

continued

programme of temporary exhibitions and events. The castle is set within 200 acres of woodland.

Times: ✱ Open Apr-Sep, daily 10.30-5. Oct-Apr, 10.30-4. Closed Mon & Fri **Facilities:** 🅿 🚭 ♿ (lift to first floor, Braille & audio guides) toilets for disabled shop ✖ (ex guide dogs) 🍴

CORWEN · Map 06 SJ04

EWE-PHORIA SHEEPDOG CENTRE
Glanrafon, Llangwm LL21 0PE
➲ (Turn off A5 to Llangwm, follow signs)
☎ 01490 460369
e-mail: info@ewe-phoria.co.uk

Ewe-Phoria is an Agri-Theatre and Sheepdog Centre that details the life and work of the shepherd on a traditional Welsh farm. The Agri-Theatre has unusual living displays of sheep with accompanying lectures on their history and breed, while outside sheepdog handlers put their dogs through their paces.
Times: ✱ Open Etr-end Oct, Tue-Fri & Sun. Closed Sat & Mon ex BH's
Facilities: 🅿 🚭 ✖ licensed ♿ toilets for disabled shop ✖ (ex guide dogs) 🍴

PEN-Y-BRYN FARM PARK
LL21 9PP
➲ (off A5 onto B5105. 5m from Cerrigydrudion)
☎ 01490 420244   🖳 01490 420244

Proudly catering to all ages, Pen-y-Bryn Park has a petting zoo, falconry, and 'Solo', its very own llama.
Times: ✱ Open Etr-Oct, Tue-Sun & BH's, 10-5 **Facilities:** 🅿 🚭 ♿ toilets for disabled shop garden centre

RUG CHAPEL
Rug LL21 9BT
☎ 01490 412025

Rug Chapel was built in 1637 for Colonel William Salusbury, famous Civil War defender of Denbigh Castle. A rare little altered example of a 17th-century private chapel, it reflects the Colonel's High Church religious views. Prettily set in a wooded landscape, the chapel's modest exterior gives little hint of the interior where local artists and carvers were given a free reign, with some spectacular results.
Times: Open Apr-Sep, daily 10-5. Access to Llangar is arranged daily at 2pm through Custodian at Rug Chapel, telephone 01490 412025 for details. Both monuments closed Mon & Tue (ex BH wknds).
Fee: £2.50 (ch 5-15, pen & students £2, disabled visitors & assisting companion free). Family ticket (2 ad & 3 ch) £7. Group rates available. Prices quoted apply until 31 Mar 2005. **Facilities:** 🅿 ♿ toilets for disabled shop ✖ ☺ 🍴

DENBIGH · Map 06 SJ06

DENBIGH CASTLE
➲ (via A525, A543 & B5382)
☎ 01745 813385

The castle was begun by Henry de Lacy in 1282 and has an inspiring and impressive gatehouse, with a trio of towers and a superb archway, which is surmounted by a figure believed to be that of Edward I.
Times: Open Apr-Sep, Mon-Fri 10-5.30, Sat & Sun 9.30-5.30. (The monument will be open and unstaffed with no admission charge at all other times). Telephone for Xmas opening hours. **Fee:** £2.50 (ch 5-15, pen & students £2, disabled visitors & assisting companion free). Family ticket (2 ad & 3 ch) £7. Group rates available. Prices quoted apply until 31 Mar 2005. **Facilities:** 🅿 ♿ shop ✖ ☺ 🍴

LLANGOLLEN · Map 07 SJ24

HORSE DRAWN BOATS CENTRE
The Wharf, Wharf Hill LL20 8TA
➲ (From A5 turn onto Llangollen High St, across river bridge to T-junction. The wharf is opposite)
☎ 01978 860702 & 01691 690322
🖳 01978 860799
e-mail: sue@horsedrawnboats.co.uk

Take a horsedrawn boat trip along the beautiful Vale of Llangollen. Visit the canal museum, inside the motor museum, approx 1m along the towpath from the wharf, which illustrates the heyday of canals in Britain. The displays include working and static models, photographs, murals and slides. There is also a narrowboat trip that crosses Pontcysyllte Aqueduct, the largest navigable aqueduct in the world. Full bar on board, commentary throughout.
Times: Open Etr-end Oct, daily 10-5. May be closed weekdays in Oct except school hols **Fee:** Prices not confirmed for 2005
Facilities: 🅿 (400yds) 🚭 ♿ (alighting/pick-up point available) toilets for disabled shop 🍴

LLANGOLLEN RAILWAY
Abbey Rd LL20 8SN
➲ (Llangollen Station - off A5 at Llangollen traffic lights onto A539, cross river bridge. Station on left at T-junct. Carrog Station - from A5 at Llidiart-y-Parc take B5437, station on right downhill after crossing railway bridge)
☎ 01978 860979 & 860951(timetable)
🖳 01978 869247
e-mail: office@llangollen-railway.co.uk

Heritage Railway featuring steam and classic diesel services along the picturesque Dee Valley. The journey consists of a 15-mile roundtrip between Llangollen and Carrog. A special coach for the disabled is available on some services. Please contact for more information.
Times: Open - station wknds, reduced services off peak, daily services Apr-Oct. Principally steam hauled, diesel trains please refer to timetable for off peak services. **Fee:** ✱ 2nd class return fare for full journey £8 (ch 3-16 £4, pen £6) Family ticket £18 (2 adult & 2 ch).
Facilities: 🅿 (400yds) free parking at Carrog Station 🚭 ♿ (special coach for disabled on some trains, notice required) toilets for disabled shop (at Llangollen only) 🍴

PLAS NEWYDD

Hill St LL20 8AW

➲ (Follow brown heritage signs from A5, close to Grapes public house in Llangollen)

☎ 01978 861314   📠 01824 708258

e-mail: rose.mcmahon@denbighshire.gov.uk

The 'Ladies of Llangollen', Lady Eleanor Butler and Sarah Ponsonby, lived here from 1780 to 1831. The original stained-glass windows, carved panels, and domestic miscellany of two lives are exhibited along with prints, pictures and letters.

Times: ✱ Open Apr-Oct, daily, 10-5. **Facilities:** 🅿 ♿ toilets for disabled ✖ (ex guide dogs or in grounds)

VALLE CRUCIS ABBEY

LL29 8DD

➲ (on B5103, off A5 W of Llangollen)

☎ 01978 860326

Set in a deep, narrow valley, the abbey was founded for the Cistercians in 1201 by Madog ap Gruffydd. Substantial remains of the church can be seen, and some beautifully carved grave slabs have been found. There is a small exhibition on the Cistercian monks and the abbey.

Times: Open Apr-Sep, daily 10-5. Monument open and unstaffed with no admission charge at all other times between 10-4. Telephone for Xmas opening times. **Fee:** £2 (ch 5-15, pen & students £1.50, disabled visitors & assisting companion free). Family ticket (2 ad & 3 ch) £5.50. Group rates available. Prices quoted apply until 31 Mar 2005. **Facilities:** 🅿 ♿ shop ✖ ☺ 🍴

RHUDDLAN   Map 06 SJ07

RHUDDLAN CASTLE

LL18 5AD

☎ 01745 590777

The castle was begun by Edward I in 1277, on a simple 'diamond' plan with round towers linked by sections of 9ft thick curtain wall. The moat was linked to a deep-water canal, allowing Edward's ships to sail from the sea right up to the castle.

Times: Open Apr-Sep, daily 10-5. **Fee:** £2.75 (ch 5-15, pen & students £2.25, disabled visitors & assisting companion free). Family ticket (2 ad & 3 ch) £7.75. Group discounts available. Prices quoted apply until 31 Mar 2005. **Facilities:** 🅿 ♿ shop ✖ ☺ 🍴

FLINTSHIRE

EWLOE   Map 07 SJ36

EWLOE CASTLE

➲ (1m NW of village on B5125)

Standing in Ewloe Wood are the remains of Ewloe Castle. It was a native Welsh castle, and Henry II was defeated nearby in 1157. Part of the Welsh Tower in the upper ward still stands to its original height, and there is a well in the lower ward. Remnants of walls and another tower can also be seen.

Times: Open at all times. **Facilities:** ✖ ☺

FLINT   Map 07 SJ27

FLINT CASTLE

CH6 5PH

➲ (NE side of Flint)

☎ 01352 733078   FREE

The castle was started by Edward I in 1277 and overlooks the River Dee. It is exceptional for its great tower, or Donjon,

continued

which is separated by a moat. Other buildings would have stood in the inner bailey, of which parts of the walls and corner towers remain.

Times: Open at all times. **Facilities:** 🅿 ✖ ☺

HOLYWELL   Map 07 SJ17

BASINGWERK ABBEY

Greenfield Valley Heritage Pk, Greenfield CH8 7GH

➲ (just S of A458)

☎ 01352 714172   FREE

The abbey was founded around 1131 by Ranulf de Gernon, Earl of Chester. The first stone church dates from the beginning of the 13th century. The last abbot surrendered the house to the crown in 1536. The Abbey is close to the Heritage Park Visitor Centre and access to the Museum and Farm Complex at Greenfield Valley.

Times: Open all year, daily 9-6. **Facilities:** 🅿 ✖ ♿ (disabled facilities in Heritage Park) toilets for disabled shop ✖ ☺

GREENFIELD VALLEY HERITAGE PARK

Greenfield Rd CH8 7GH

☎ 01352 714172   📠 01352 714791

e-mail: info@greenfieldvalley.com

This fascinating park covers one and a half miles of woodlands, reservoirs, ancient monuments and industrial history. Among the multitude of sights is a footpath that was once a railway line, the remnants of a number of mills relating to the copper industry, an environment centre, the shrine of St Winefride's Well, and Basingwerk Abbey.

Times: ✱ Park open all year. Museum & farm Apr-Oct, 10-4.30. **Facilities:** 🅿 🅿 ♿ (ramps to enter buildings) toilets for disabled shop

GWYNEDD

BANGOR   Map 06 SH57

PENRHYN CASTLE

LL57 4HN

➲ (1m E at Bangor, at Llandegai on A5122, just off A55)

☎ 01248 353084   📠 01248 371281   **2 for 1**

e-mail: penrhyncastle@nationaltrust.org.uk

A massive 19th-century castle built on the profits of Jamaican sugar and Welsh slate, crammed with fascinating artefacts such as a one-ton slate bed made for Queen Victoria and a grand staircase that took ten years to build. Also houses a doll museum, two railway museums and one of the finest collections of Old Master paintings in Wales. Regular programme of events throughout the season.

Times: Open 23 Mar-Oct, daily (ex Tue) Castle 12-5pm. Grounds and stableblock exhibitions 11-5 (Jul & Aug 10-5.30). Last admission 4.30pm. Last audio tour 4pm. **Fee:** All inclusive ticket: £7 (ch £3.50). Family ticket £17.50. Party 15+ £5.50 p.p. Grounds & stableblock only £5 (ch £2.50). **Facilities:** 🅿 ✖ licensed ♿ (wheelchairs & golf buggies pre bookable) toilets for disabled shop ☙

BEDDGELERT   Map 06 SH54

THE RED DRAGON HERITAGE CENTRE NEW

LL55 4NE

➲ (1m E of Beddgelert on A498. Turn off A5 from Llangollen left at Capel Curig onto A498)

☎ 01766 510100 & 510101

📠 01766 890595   **2 for 1**

e-mail: info@syguncoppermine.co.uk

Discover the very site where the Red Dragon of Wales conquered the White Dragon of England. Enter the ancient

continued

holy city of Dinas Emrys in the heart of Snowdonia, and uncover the mysteries and secrets of the legendary Merlin in this authentic Celtic village. Also learn about the history of the Celts, find out how they lived, see the blacksmith's forge, the potter's kiln, try the weaving loom, and search for metal.
Times: daily, 10-5 **Fee:** £7.95 (ch £5.95, pen £6.95)
Facilities: 🅿 💺 ♿ toilets for disabled shop 🍴

SYGUN COPPER MINE
LL55 4NE
➲ (1m E of Beddgelert on A498)
☎ 01766 510100 & 01766 510101
📠 01766 890595
e-mail: sygunmine@aol.com

`2 for 1`

Spectacular audio-visual underground experience where visitors can explore the workings of this 19th-century coppermine and see the magnificent stalactite and stalagmite formations. Other activities include archery, panning for gold, metal detecting and coin making. Marvel at the fantastic coin collection from Julius Caesar to Queen Elizabeth II, and visit the Time-Line Museum with Bronze Age and Roman artefacts.
Times: Open all year, 10-5 **Fee:** £7.95 (ch £5.95, pen £6.95).
Facilities: 🅿 💺 ♿ (wide access) toilets for disabled shop 🍴

BLAENAU FFESTINIOG   Map 06 SH74
HYDRO CENTRE FFESTINIOG
Ffestiniog Hydro Centre, First Hydro Company, Tan-Y-Grisiau LL41 3TP
➲ (off A496)
☎ 01766 830465 📠 01766 833472
e-mail: hydrocentre@edisonmission.com
The scheme was the first hydroelectric pumped storage scheme, and was opened by Her Majesty the Queen in 1963. Water is released from an upper dam, through turbines, to generate electricity when needed, and then pumped back up when demand is low. Guided tours are available, and the Hydro Centre has a café, gift shop and picnic area.
Times: ✱ Open Etr-Oct 10-4.30. **Facilities:** 🅿 💺 shop 🐕 (ex guide dogs)

LLECHWEDD SLATE CAVERNS
LL41 3NB
➲ (Beside A470, 1m outside Blaenau Ffestiniog.)
☎ 01766 830306 📠 01766 831260
e-mail: quarrytours@aol.com
The Miners' Underground Tramway carries visitors into areas where early conditions have been recreated, while the
continued

Deep Mine is reached by an incline railway and has an unusual audio-visual presentation. Free surface attractions include several exhibitions and museums, slate mill and the Victorian village which has Victorian shops, bank, Miners Arms pub, lock-up and working smithy.
Times: Open all year, daily from 10am. Last tour 5.15 (Oct-Feb 4.15). (Closed 25-26 Dec & 1 Jan). **Fee:** ✱ Single Tour £8.25 (ch £6.25, pen £7). Reductions for both tours **Facilities:** 🅿 💺 ✗ licensed ♿ toilets for disabled shop (also Victorian shops in the Village) 🐕 (ex on surface) 🍴

CAERNARFON   Map 06 SH46
CAERNARFON CASTLE
LL55 2AY
☎ 01286 677617
Edward I began building the castle and extensive town walls in 1283 after defeating the last independent ruler of Wales. Completed in 1328, it has unusual polygonal towers, notably the 10-sided Eagle Tower. There is a theory that these features were copied from the walls of Constantinople, to reflect a tradition that Constantine was born nearby. Edward I's son and heir was born and presented to the Welsh people here, setting a precedent that was followed in 1969, when Prince Charles was invested as Prince of Wales.
Times: Open Apr-May & Oct, daily 9.30-5; Jun-Sep, daily 9.30-6; Nov-Mar, Mon-Sat 9.30-4, Sun 11-4. Telephone for Xmas opening times. **Fee:** £4.50 (ch 5-15, pen & students £3.50, disabled visitors & assisting compainion free). Family ticket (2 ad & 3 ch) £12.50. Group rates available. Prices quoted apply until 31 Mar 2005.
Facilities: 🅿 shop 🐕 ✚ 🍴

SEGONTIUM ROMAN MUSEUM
Beddgelert Rd LL55 2LN
➲ (on A4085 to Beddgelert approx 1m from Caernarfon)
☎ 01286 675625 📠 01286 678416
e-mail: info@segontium.org.uk

`FREE`

Segontium Roman Museum tells the story of the conquest and occupation of Wales by the Romans and displays the finds from the auxiliary fort of Segontium, one of the most famous in Britain. You can combine a visit to the museum with exploration of the site of the Roman Fort, which is in the care of Cadw: Welsh Historic Monuments. The exciting discoveries displayed at the museum vividly portray the daily life of the soldiers stationed in this remote outpost of the Roman Empire.
Times: Open Tue-Sun 12.30-4. Closed Mon except BH
Facilities: 🅿 🐕 (ex guide dogs) 🍴

WELSH HIGHLAND RAILWAY NEW
St. Helen's Rd LL55 2YD
➲ (SW of Caernarfon Castle beside the harbour. Follow brown signs)
☎ 01286 677018 & 01766 516000
📠 01286 677018
e-mail: info@festrail.co.uk
A Millennium funded project to restore the old railway line from Caernarfon to Porthmadog. Experience the stunning scenery of Snowdonia National Park as the narrow gauge, steam and diesel trains travel between Caernarfon and Rhyd Ddu at the foot of Snowdon.
Times: Runs daily May-Oct, Etr & limited service in Winter, Feb half-term, 26 Dec-1 Jan. **Fee:** ✱ £14 adult return
Facilities: 🅿 (charged) ♿ (prior booking advisable) toilets for disabled 🍴

CRICCIETH — Map 06 SH43

CRICCIETH CASTLE
LL52 0DP
➲ (off A497)
☎ 01766 522227

The castle dates from the 13th century and was taken and destroyed by Owain Glyndwr in 1404. Evidence of a fierce fire can still be seen. The gatehouse leading to the inner ward remains impressive, and parts of the walls are well preserved.

Times: Open Apr-May & Oct, daily 10-5; Jun-Sep, daily 10-6. (The monument will be open and unstaffed with no admission charge at all other times). Telephone for Xmas opening times. **Fee:** £2.75 (ch 5-15, pen & students £2.25, disabled visitors & assisting companion free). Family ticket (2 ad & 3 ch) £7.75. Group rates available. Prices quoted apply until 31 Mar 2005. **Facilities:** 🅿 shop ✖ ☺ 🍴

CYMER ABBEY — Map 06 SH71

CYMER ABBEY
➲ (2m NW of Dolgellau on A494)
☎ 01341 422854

The abbey was built for the Cistercians in the 13th century. It was never very large, and does not seem to have been finished. The church is the best-preserved building, with ranges of windows and arcades still to be seen. The other buildings have been plundered for stone, but low outlines remain.

Times: ✱ Open all year, early Apr-Oct, daily 9.30-6; Nov-Mar, daily 9.30-4. (Closed 24-26 Dec & 1 Jan) **Facilities:** 🅿 ♿ ✖ ☺ 🍴

FAIRBOURNE — Map 06 SH61

FAIRBOURNE RAILWAY
Beach Rd LL38 2PZ
➲ (on A493 follow signs for Fairbourne, main terminus is just past level crossing on left)
☎ 01341 250362 📠 01341 250240
e-mail: enquiries@fairbourne-railway.co.uk

One of the most unusual of Wales's 'little trains'; built in 1890 as a horse-drawn railway to carry building materials it was later converted to steam, and now covers two-and-a-half miles. Its route passes one of the loveliest beaches in Wales, with views of the beautiful Mawddach Estuary.

Times: ✱ Open early/mid Apr-mid/late Sep, times vary according to season and events. Trains will run during Oct half term holiday and Santa Specials at Xmas. **Facilities:** 🅿 ☕ shop 🍴

GROESLON — Map 06 SH45

INIGO JONES SLATEWORKS
LL54 7UE
➲ (on A487, 6m S of Caernarfon towards Porthmadog)
☎ 01286 830242 📠 01286 831247
e-mail: slate@inigojones.co.uk
2 for 1

Inigo Jones was established in 1861 primarily to make school writing slates. Today the company uses the same material to make architectural, monumental and craft products. A self-guided audio/video tour takes visitors round the slate workshops, and displays the various processes used in the extraction and working of Welsh slate.

Times: Open all year, daily 9-5. (Closed 25-26 Dec & 1 Jan). **Fee:** £4 (ch & pen £3.50). **Facilities:** 🅿 ☕ ♿ toilets for disabled shop ✖ (ex guide dogs) 🍴

HARLECH — Map 06 SH53

HARLECH CASTLE
LL46 2YH
➲ (from A496)
☎ 01766 780552

Harlech Castle was built in 1283-81 by Edward I, with a sheer drop to the sea on one side. Owain Glyndwr starved the castle into submission in 1404 and made it his court and campaigning base. Later, the defence of the castle in the Wars of the Roses inspired the song *Men of Harlech*. Today the sea has slipped away, and the castle's great walls and round towers stand above the dunes.

Times: Open Apr-May & Oct, daily 9.30-5; Jun-Sep, daily 9.30-6; Nov-Mar, Mon-Sat 9.30-4, Sun 11-4. Telephone for Xmas opening times. **Fee:** £3 (ch 5-15, pen & students £2.50, disabled visitors & assisting companion free). Family ticket (2 ad & 3 ch) £8.50. Group rates available. Prices quoted apply until 31 Mar 2005. **Facilities:** 🅿 (disabled spaces in car park) shop ✖ ☺ 🍴

LLANBERIS — Map 06 SH56

DOLBADARN CASTLE
LL55 4UD
➲ (A4086)

Built by Llywelyn the Great in the early 13th century, this Welsh castle overlooks Llyn Padarn in the Llanberis Pass.
Times: ✱ Open any reasonable time. **Facilities:** 🅿 ✖ ☺ 🍴

LLANBERIS LAKE RAILWAY
Padam Country Park LL55 4TY
➲ (off A4086 at Llanberis)
☎ 01286 870549 📠 01286 870549
e-mail: info@lake-railway.co.uk

Steam locomotives dating from 1889 to 1948 carry passengers on a five-mile return journey along the shore of Padarn Lake. The terminal station is adjacent to the Welsh Slate Museum, in the Padarn Country Park. The railway was formerly used to carry slate. A new extension to Llanberis village opened in 2003.

Times: Open Etr-late Oct. Trains run frequently Sun-Fri (Sat in Jul & Aug), 11-4.30 in peak season. Send for free timetable. **Fee:** ✱ £6 (ch £4). Family ticket available. Reduced rates for groups.

Facilities: 🅿 (charged) ☕ ♿ (disabled carriage available) toilets for disabled shop (on trains, not in Cafe) 🍴

SNOWDON MOUNTAIN RAILWAY
LL55 4TY
➲ (on A4086, Caernarfon to Capel Curig road. 7.5m from Caernarfon)
☎ 0870 4580033 📠 01286 872518
e-mail: info@snowdonrailway.co.uk
The journey of just over four-and-a-half miles takes passengers more than 3,000ft up to the summit of Snowdon; breathtaking views include, on a clear day, the Isle of Man and the Wicklow Mountains in Ireland. The round trip to the summit and back takes two and a half hours including a half hour at the summit.
Times: Open 15 Mar-5 Nov, daily from 9am (weather permitting).
Fee: Return £20 (ch £14). Early bird discount on 9am train, (not for Jul & Aug) **Facilities:** 🅿 (charged) 🍴 ♿ (some carriages suitable for wheelchairs - must notify) toilets for disabled shop ✖ (ex guide dogs) 🍴

WELSH SLATE MUSEUM
Gilfach Ddu, Padarn Country Park LL55 4TY
➲ (0.25m off A4086. Museum within Padarn Country Park)
☎ 01286 870630 📠 01286 871906   FREE
e-mail: slate@nmgw.ac.uk
Set among the towering quarries at Llanberis, the Welsh Slate Museum is a living, working site located in the original workshops of Dinorwig Quarry, which once employed 15,000 men and boys. You can see the foundry, smithy, workshops and mess room which make up the old quarry, and view original machinery, much of which is still in working order.
Times: Open Etr-Oct, daily 10-5; Nov-Etr, Sun-Fri 10-4.
Facilities: 🅿 (charged) 🍴 ♿ (all parts accessible except patten loft) toilets for disabled shop ✖ (ex guide dogs) 🍴

LLANFIHANGEL-Y-PENNANT   Map 06 SH60

CASTELL-Y-BERE
➲ (off B4405)   FREE
☎ 029 2050 0200
The castle was begun around 1221 by Prince Llewelyn ap Iorwerth of Gwynedd to guard the southern flank of his principality. It is typically Welsh in design with its D-shaped towers. Although a little off the beaten track, the castle lies in a spectacular setting, overshadowed by the Cader Idris range.
Times: Open all reasonable times. **Facilities:** ✖ ⊕

LLANGYBI   Map 06 SH44

ST CYBI'S WELL
➲ (off B4354)   FREE
☎ 01766 810047
Cybi was a sixth-century Cornish saint, known as a healer of the sick, and St Cybi's Well (or Ffynnon Gybi) has been famous for its curative properties through the centuries. The corbelled beehive vaulting inside the roofless stone structure is Irish in style and unique in Wales.
Times: Open at all times. **Facilities:** ♿ ✖ ⊕

LLANUWCHLLYN   Map 06 SH83

BALA LAKE RAILWAY
The Station LL23 7DD
➲ (off A494 Bala to Dolgellau road)
☎ 01678 540666 📠 01678 540535
Steam locomotives which once worked in the slate quarries of North Wales now haul passenger coaches for four-and-a-half miles from Llanuwchllyn Station along the lake to Bala. The railway has one of the few remaining double-twist lever-locking framed GWR signal boxes, installed in 1896. Some of the coaches are open and some closed, so passengers can enjoy the beautiful views of the lake and mountains in all weathers.
Times: Open Etr-last wknd in Sep, daily. (Closed certain Mon & Fri, telephone for details). **Fee:** ✱ £6.70 return (pen £6.20). Family ticket £16 (2 ad & 2 ch). **Facilities:** 🅿 🍴 ♿ (wheelchairs can be taken on train) shop

LLANYSTUMDWY   Map 06 SH43

LLOYD GEORGE MUSEUM & HIGHGATE VICTORIAN COTTAGE
LL52 0SH
➲ (on A497 between Pwllheli & Criccieth)
☎ 01766 522071 📠 01766 522071
e-mail: amgueddfeydd-museums@gwynedd.gov.uk
Explore the life and times of David Lloyd George in this museum. His boyhood home is recreated as it would have been when he lived there between 1864 and 1880, along with his Uncle Lloyd's shoemaking workshop.
Times: Open Etr, daily 10-5; May-Jun, Mon-Fri 10.30-5 (open Sat in Jun); Jul-Sep daily 10.30-5; Oct, Mon-Fri, 11-4. Other times by appointment, telephone 01286 679098 for details.
Facilities: 🅿 ♿ (induction loop in audio visual theatre, shop & cottage) toilets for disabled shop ✖ (ex guide dogs) 🍴

PENARTH FAWR   Map 06 SH43

PENARTH FAWR
➲ (3.5m NE of Pwllheli off A497)   FREE
☎ 01766 810880
The hall, buttery and screen are preserved in this house which was probably built in the 15th century.
Times: Open at all times. **Facilities:** ♿ ✖ ⊕

PLAS-YN-RHIW   Map 06 SH22

PLAS-YN-RHIW
LL53 8AB
➲ (12m from Pwllheli signed from B4413 to Aberdaron)
☎ 01758 780219
This is a small manor house, part medieval, with Tudor and Georgian additions. The ornamental gardens have flowering trees and shrubs including sub-tropical specimens, divided by box hedges and grass paths. There is a stream and waterfall, which descends from the snowdrop wood behind.
Times: ✱ Open Mar-14 May, Thu-Mon noon-5; mid May-Oct, Wed-Mon noon-5. **Facilities:** 🅿 ♿ (Braille guides/scented plants) toilets for disabled shop ✖ 🚌 ♨

PORTHMADOG   Map 06 SH53

FFESTINIOG RAILWAY
Harbour Station LL49 9NF
➲ (SE end of town, on A487)
☎ 01766 516000 ▤ 01766 516006
e-mail: info@festrail.co.uk
A narrow gauge steam railway running for 13.5 miles through Snowdonia National Park, with breathtaking views and superb scenery. Buffet service on all trains including licensed bar (in corridor carriages). Please telephone for details of special events. The company also runs the Welsh Highland Railway Caernarfon, which will eventually link up with the Ffestiniog Railway.
Times: Open daily late Mar to end Oct. Limited Winter service mid week trains Nov & early Dec. Santa specials in Dec. Open Feb half term. **Fee:** ✱ Full distance return £13.80 (1 ch free with each ad, pen £11.10). Other fares available. **Facilities:** P (charged) ⬛ ✗ licensed ♿ (Wheelchair ramps) Trains mostly accessible toilets for disabled shop (closed 24/25 Dec) ◼

PORTMEIRION   Map 06 SH53

PORTMEIRION
LL48 6ET
➲ (Off A487 at Minffordd)
☎ 01766 770000 ▤ 01766 771331   **2 for 1**
e-mail: info@portmeirion-village.com
Welsh architect Sir Clough Williams Ellis built his fairy-tale, Italianate village on a rocky, tree-clad peninsula on the shores of Cardigan Bay. A bell-tower, castle and lighthouse mingle with a watch-tower, grottoes and cobbled squares among pastel-shaded picturesque cottages let as holiday accommodation. The 60-acre Gwyllt Gardens include miles of dense woodland paths and are famous for their fine displays of rhododendrons, azaleas, hydrangeas and sub-tropical flora. There is a mile of sandy beach and a playground for children. The village is probably best known as the major location for 1960's cult TV show, *The Prisoner*.
Times: Open all year, daily 9.30-5.30. **Fee:** £6 (ch £3, pen £5). Party 15+. **Facilities:** P ⬛ ✗ licensed ♿ toilets for disabled shop garden centre ✗ (ex guide dogs) ◼

TYWYN   Map 06 SH50

TALYLLYN RAILWAY
Wharf Station LL36 9EY
➲ (A493 Machynlleth to Dolgellau for Tywyn station, B4405 for Abergynolwyn)
☎ 01654 710472 ▤ 01654 711755
e-mail: enquiries@talyllyn.co.uk
The oldest 27in-gauge railway in the world, built in 1865 to run from Tywyn on Cardigan Bay to Abergynolwyn slate mine some seven miles inland. The railway climbs the steep sides of the Fathew Valley and with stops on the way at Dolgoch Falls and the Nant Gwernol forest. The return trip takes 2.5 hours. All scheduled passenger trains are steam hauled.
Times: Open Sun mid Feb-Mar, daily; Apr-early Nov & 26 Dec-2 Jan. Ring for timetable. **Fee:** ✱ £10 Day Rover (ch accompanied £2). Intermediate fares available. **Facilities:** P (charged) ⬛ ♿ (prior notice useful) toilets for disabled shop ◼

Y FELINHELI   Map 06 SH56

GREENWOOD FOREST PARK
LL56 4QN
➲ (leave A55 at junct 11, follow Llanberis signs onto A4244, signed from next rdbt)
☎ 01248 670076 ▤ 01248 670069
e-mail: info@greenwood-centre.co.uk
This forest park provides a wide range of exciting activities for the whole family. Try the Great Green Run - the longest slide in Wales, shoot a real longbow, build dens in the woods and saw a log. Ride the Green Dragon, the world's first people-powered family rollercoaster. Try the Jungle Boat Adventure and explore the rainforest. There are large interactive exhibitions in the oak-framed great hall and the Forest Theatre stages events and shows during school holiday periods. The Toddlers Village is ideal for young children.
Times: Open daily mid Mar-end Oct 10-5.30 (Sep/Oct 10-5).
Fee: ✱ Varies with time of year. £4.95-£6.95 (ch £3.95-£5.95, pen £4.50-£6.30, disabled 20% discount). Family ticket (2ad & 2ch) £15.65-£22.70; (2ad & 3 ch) £19.10-£27.95; (2ad & 4ch) £22.60-£33.15.
Facilities: P ⬛ ♿ (grounds partly accessible, parking) toilets for disabled shop ◼

ISLE OF ANGLESEY

BEAUMARIS   Map 06 SH67

BEAUMARIS CASTLE
LL58 8AP
☎ 01248 810361
Beaumaris was built by Edward I and took from 1295 to 1312 to complete. In later centuries it was plundered for its lead, timber and stone. Despite this it remains one of the most impressive and complete castles built by Edward I. It has a perfectly symmetrical, concentric plan, with a square inner bailey and curtain walls, round corner towers and D-shaped towers in between. There are also two great gatehouses, but these were never finished.
Times: Open Apr-May & Oct, daily 9.30-5; Jun-Sep, daily, 9.30-6; Nov-Mar, Mon-Sat 9.30-4, Sun 11-4. Telephone for Xmas opening times. **Fee:** £3 (ch 5-15, pen & students £2.50, disabled visitors and assisting companion free). Family ticket (2 ad & 3 ch) £8.50. Group rates available. Prices quoted apply until 31 Mar 2005.
Facilities: P ♿ shop ✗ ⊕ ◼

BEAUMARIS GAOL & COURTHOUSE
Steeple Ln LL58 8EW
☎ 01248 810921 & 724444 ▤ 01248 750282
With its treadmill and grim cells, the gaol is a vivid reminder of the tough penalties exacted by 19th-century law. The courthouse, built in 1614 and renovated early in the 19th century, is a unique example of an early Welsh court.
Times: ✱ Open Etr-Sep, daily 10.30-5. Other times by arrangement only. **Facilities:** P (500yds) ♿ (narrow gates may restrict some wheelchairs) shop ✗ (ex guide dogs)

MUSEUM OF CHILDHOOD
1 Castle St LL58 8AP
➲ (on A545. Opposite Beaumaris Castle)
☎ 01248 712498 ▤ 01248 716869   **2 for 1**
The museum illustrates the life and interests of children and families over 150 years. There are around 2,000 items in the museum's collection including money boxes, dolls,

continued

educational toys and games, early clockwork trains, cars and aeroplanes, push toys and cycles.
Times: Open daily 10.30-5.30, Sun 12-5. Last admission 4.30, Sun 4. (Closed Nov-2nd wk Mar). **Fee:** ✱ £3.50 (ch £2, pen & students £3). Family ticket £9.50. Free entry for wheelchairs. **Facilities:** P (50yds) ♿ shop ✖ (ex guide dogs)

BRYNCELLI DDU Map 06 SH57
BRYN CELLI DDU BURIAL CHAMBER
➲ (3m W of Menai Bridge off A4080) FREE
☎ 029 2050 0200
Excavated in 1865, and then again in 1925-9, this is a prehistoric circular cairn covering a passage grave with a polygonal chamber.
Times: Open at all times. **Facilities:** P ✖ ☺

BRYNSIENCYN Map 06 SH46
ANGLESEY SEA ZOO
LL61 6TQ
➲ (take 1st turning off Britannia Bridge onto Anglesey then follow Lobster signs along A4080 to zoo)
☎ 01248 430411 ▤ 01248 430213 2 for 1
e-mail: info@angleseyseazoo.co.uk
Nestling by the Menai Straits, this all-weather undercover attraction contains a shipwreck bristling with conger eels, a lobster hatchery, a seahorse nursery, crashing waves and the enchanting fish forest.
Times: Open 12 Feb-30 Oct. 10-6. Last admission 1hr before site closes. **Fee:** ✱ £5.95 (ch & student £4.95, pen & UB40 £5.50). Family ticket £14.95-£21.95. Party 10+. Please telephone to confirm 2005 prices. **Facilities:** P 💷 ✖ licensed ♿ (2 wheelchairs available, Braile tour notes) toilets for disabled shop ✖ (ex guide dogs) 🍴

FOEL FARM PARK
Foel Farm LL61 6TQ
➲ (Turn left off Britannia Bridge A55 onto A5/A4080 to Llanfairpwllgwyngyll & left on A4080 to Brynsiencyn. Follow signs from Brynsiencyn)
☎ 01248 430646 ▤ 01248 430066
e-mail: foelfarm@btinternet.com
Children will love this friendly farm experience, where they can meet animals big and small, and take tractor and trailer rides. The park also contains a luxury handmade chocolate business, a bistro and bar, as well as a tea room and gift shop.
Times: Open daily Mar-Oct 10.30-5.30; Also wknds Nov-Feb 10.30-4.30. Also open half term Feb. **Facilities:** P 💷 ✖ licensed ♿ toilets for disabled shop ✖ (ex guide dogs) 🍴

HOLYHEAD Map 06 SH28
RSBP NATURE RESERVE SOUTH STACK CLIFFS
Plas Nico, South Stack LL65 1YH
➲ (A5 or A55 to Holyhead then follow brown heritage signs). FREE
☎ 01407 764973 ▤ 01407 764973
High cliffs with caves and offshore stacks, backed by the maritime heathland of Holyhead Mountain, make this an ideal reserve to watch seabirds. Live video pictures of breeding seabirds are shown in the cliff-top information centre during the summer. Choughs, guillemots, razorbills, fulmars and puffins may be seen.
Times: Open: Information Centre daily, Etr-Sep, 11-5. Reserve open daily at all times. **Facilities:** P

LLANALLGO Map 06 SH58
DIN LLUGWY ANCIENT VILLAGE
➲ (0.75m NW off A5025)
The remains of a 4th-century village can be seen here. There are two circular and seven rectangular buildings, still standing up to head height and encircled by a pentagonal stone wall some 4 to 5ft thick.
Times: Open at all times. **Facilities:** ✖ ☺

PLAS NEWYDD Map 06 SH56
PLAS NEWYDD
LL61 6DQ
➲ (2m S of Llanfairpwll, on A4080) 2 for 1
☎ 01248 714795 ▤ 01248 713673
e-mail: plasnewydd@nationaltrust.org.uk
Set amidst breathtakingly beautiful scenery and with spectacular views of Snowdonia, this elegant 18th-century house was built by James Wyatt and is an interesting mixture of Classical and Gothic. The comfortable interior, restyled in the 1930s, is famous for its association with Rex Whistler, whose largest painting is here. There is also an exhibition about his work. A military museum contains campaign relics of the 1st Marquess of Anglesea, who commanded the cavalry at the Battle of Waterloo. There is a fine spring garden and Australasian arboretum with an understorey of shrubs and wild flowers, as well as a summer terrace and, later, massed hydrangeas and autumn colour. A woodland walk gives access to a marine walk on the Menai Strait.
Times: Open Apr-Oct, Sat-Wed. House 12-5; Garden 11-5.30. Last admission 4.30 **Fee:** ✱ £5 (ch £2.50). Family £12 (2ad+3ch). Parties 15+ £4.50 **Facilities:** P ✖ licensed ♿ (Close parking, wheelchairs, garden shuttle, Braille guide) toilets for disabled shop ✖ (ex assistance dogs) 🐾

MERTHYR TYDFIL

MERTHYR TYDFIL Map 03 SO00
BRECON MOUNTAIN RAILWAY
Pant Station Dowlais CF48 2UP
➲ (Follow Mountain Railway signs from A470 or A465 N of Merthyr Tydfil)
☎ 01685 722988 ▤ 01685 384854
Opened in 1980, this narrow-gauge railway follows part of an old British Rail route which closed in 1964 when the iron industry in South Wales fell into decline. The present route starts at Pant Station and continues for 3.5 miles through the beautiful scenery of the Brecon Beacons National Park, as far as Taf Fechan reservoir. The train is pulled by a vintage steam locomotive and is one of the most popular railways in Wales.
Times: Opening times on application to The Brecon Mountain Railway, Pant Station, Merthyr Tydfil. **Fee:** ✱ Fares are under review, please ring for details. **Facilities:** P 💷 ✖ licensed ♿ (adapted carriage) toilets for disabled shop 🍴

CYFARTHFA CASTLE MUSEUM & ART GALLERY
Cyfarthfa Park CF47 8RE
➲ (off A470, N towards Brecon, follow brown heritage signs) FREE
☎ 01685 723112 ▤ 01685 723112
e-mail: museum@cyfarthfapark.freeserve.co.uk
Set in wooded parkland beside a beautiful lake, this imposing Gothic mansion now houses a superb museum and art gallery. Providing a fascinating glimpse into 3,000 years of history, the museum displays wonderful collections of fine
continued

art, social history and objects from around the world in a Regency setting.
Times: Open Apr-Sep: Mon-Sun 10-5.30; Oct-Mar, Tue-Fri 10-4, Sat-Sun 12-4. (Closed between Xmas & New Year) **Facilities:** P ⬛ & (stair lift & wheelchair available) toilets for disabled shop ✖ (ex guide dogs)

MONMOUTHSHIRE

CAERWENT
Map 03 ST49

CAERWENT ROMAN TOWN
↺ (just off A48)
☎ 029 2050 0200 FREE
A complete circuit of the town wall of 'Venta Silurum', together with excavated areas of houses, shops and a temple.
Times: Open - access throughout the year. **Facilities:** ✖ ☺

CALDICOT
Map 03 ST48

CALDICOT CASTLE, MUSEUM & COUNTRYSIDE PARK
Church Rd NP26 4HU
↺ (M4 junct 23A onto B4245. From M48 junct 2 & follow A48 & B4245. Signed from B4245)
☎ 01291 420241 📠 01291 435094
e-mail: caldicotcastle@monmouthshire.gov.uk
Caldicot Castle's well-preserved fortifications were founded by the Normans and fully developed by the late 14th century. Restored as a family home by a wealthy Victorian, the castle offers the chance to explore medieval walls and towers in a setting of tranquil gardens and wooded country parkland, plus the opportunity to play giant chess or draughts.
Times: ✳ Open Mar-Oct, daily 11-5. **Facilities:** P ⬛ & (taped tour, level trails, induction loop, access guide) toilets for disabled shop (must be no lead) 🍴

CHEPSTOW
Map 03 ST59

CHEPSTOW CASTLE
NP6 5EZ
☎ 01291 624065
Built by William FitzOsbern, Chepstow is the first recorded Norman stone castle. It stands in a strategic spot above the Wye. The castle was strengthened in the following centuries, but was not besieged (as far as is known) until the Civil War, when it was twice lost to the Parliamentarians. The remains of the domestic rooms and the massive gatehouse with its portcullis grooves and ancient gates are still impressive, as are the walls and towers.
Times: Open Apr-May & Oct, daily 9.30-5; Jun-Sep, daily 9.30-6; Nov-Mar, Mon-Sat 9.30-4, Sun 11-4. Telephone for Xmas opening times. **Fee:** £3 (ch 5-15, pen & students £2.50, disabled visitors and assisting companion free). Family ticket (2 ad & 3 ch) £8.50. Group rates available. Prices quoted apply until 31 Mar 2005.
Facilities: P & shop ✖ ☺ 🍴

GROSMONT
Map 03 SO42

GROSMONT CASTLE
↺ (on B4347)
☎ 01981 240301 FREE
Grosmont is one of the 'trilateral' castles of Hubert de Burgh (see also Skenfrith and White Castle). It stands on a mound with a dry moat, and the considerable remains of its 13th-century great hall can be seen. Three towers once guarded the curtain wall, and the western one is well preserved.
Times: Open - access throughout the year. **Facilities:** & ✖ ☺

LLANTHONY
Map 03 SO22

LLANTHONY PRIORY
☎ 029 2050 0200 FREE
William de Lacey discovered the remains of a hermitage dedicated to St David. By 1108 a church had been consecrated on the site and just over a decade later the priory was complete. After the priory was brought to a state of siege in an uprising, Hugh de Lacey provided the funds for a new church, and it is this that makes the picturesque ruin seen today. Visitors can still make out the west towers, north nave arcade and south transept.
Times: Open - access throughout the year. **Facilities:** P & toilets for disabled ✖ ☺

LLANTILIO CROSSENNY
Map 03 SO31

HEN GWRT
↺ (off B4233)
☎ 029 2050 0200 FREE
The rectangular enclosure of the former medieval house, still surrounded by a moat.
Times: Open - access throughout the year. **Facilities:** ✖ 🚐 ☺

MONMOUTH
Map 03 SO51

NELSON MUSEUM & LOCAL HISTORY CENTRE
New Market Hall, Priory St NP25 3XA
↺ (Town centre)
☎ 01600 710630 FREE
e-mail: nelsonmuseum@monmouthshire.gov.uk

Commemorative glass, china, silver, medals, books, models, prints and Admiral Nelson's fighting sword feature here. The local history displays deal with Monmouth's past as a fortress market town, and include a section on the co-founder of the Rolls Royce company, Charles Stewart Rolls, who was also a pioneer balloonist, aviator and, of course, motorist.
Times: Open all year, Mon-Sat 10-1 & 2-5; Sun 2-5. (Closed Xmas & New Year). **Facilities:** P (200yds) (small daily charge) & toilets for disabled shop ✖ (ex guide dogs) 🍴

If an attraction name appears in *italics*, details have not been confirmed for 2005.

RAGLAN　　　　　　　Map 03 SO40

RAGLAN CASTLE
NP5 2BT
➲ (signed off A40)
☎ 01291 690228
This magnificent 15th-century castle is noted for its 'Yellow Tower of Gwent'. It was built by Sir William ap Thomas and destroyed during the Civil War, after a long siege. The ruins are still impressive however, and the castle's history is illustrated in an exhibition situated in the closet tower and two rooms of the gate passage.
Times: Open Apr-May & Oct, daily 9.30-5; Jun-Sep, daily 9.30-6; Nov-Mar, Mon-Sat 9.30-4, Sun 11-4. Telephone for Xmas opening times. **Fee:** £2.75 (ch 5-15, pen & students £2.25, disabled visitors & assisting companions free). Family ticket (2 ad & 3 ch) £7.75. Group discounts available. Prices quoted apply until 31 Mar 2005.
Facilities: 🅿 ᴧ shop ✻ ✛ 🍴

SKENFRITH　　　　　Map 03 SO42

SKENFRITH CASTLE
➲ (on B4521)
☎ 029 2050 0200　　　　　　　　FREE
This 13th-century castle has a round keep set inside an imposing towered curtain wall. Hubert de Burgh built it as one of three 'trilateral' castles to defend the Welsh Marches.
Times: Open - access throughout the year. Key keeper arrangement.
Facilities: 🅿 ✻ ✛ ✱

TINTERN PARVA　　　Map 03 SO50

TINTERN ABBEY
NP6 6SE
➲ (via A466)
☎ 01291 689251
The ruins of this Cistercian monastery church are still surprisingly intact. The monastery was established in 1131 and became increasingly wealthy well into the 15th century. During the Dissolution, the monastery was closed and most of the buildings were completely destroyed. During the 18th century many poets and artists came to see the ruins and recorded their impressions.
Times: Open Apr-May & Oct, daily 9.30-5; Jun-Sep, daily 9.30-6; Nov-Mar, Mon-Sat 9.30-4, Sun 11-4. Telephone for Xmas opening.
Fee: ✱ £3 (ch 5-15, pen & students £2.50, disabled visitors & assisting companions free). Family ticket (2 ad & 3 ch) £8.50. Group rates available. Prices quoted apply until 31 Mar 2005
Facilities: 🅿 ᴧ toilets for disabled shop ✻ ✛ 🍴

WHITE CASTLE　　　　Map 03 SO31

WHITE CASTLE
NP7 8UD
➲ (7m NE of Abergavenny, unclass road N of B4233)
☎ 01600 780380
The impressive 12th to 13th-century moated stronghold was built by Hubert de Burgh to defend the Welsh Marches. Substantial remains of walls, towers and a gatehouse can be seen. This is the finest of a trio of castles, the others being at Skenfrith and Grosmont.
Times: Open Apr-Sep, Wed-Sun & BH Mon 10-5. Monument open and unstaffed on Mon & Tue between Apr-Sep. The monument will be open and unstaffed with no admission charge at all other times between 10-4. Telephone for Xmas opening times. **Fee:** £2 (ch 5-15, pen & students £1.50, disabled visitors & assisting companion free). Family ticket (2 ad & 3 ch) £5.50. Group rates available. Prices quoted apply until 31 Mar 2005. **Facilities:** 🅿 ᴧ ✻ ✛ 🍴

NEATH PORT TALBOT

ABERDULAIS　　　　　Map 03 SS79

ABERDULAIS FALLS
SA10 8EU
➲ (from M4 junct 43 take A465, signed Vale of Neath. Turn onto A4109, Aberdulais Falls are next to Dulais Rock Pub)
☎ 01639 636674　📧 01639 645069
e-mail: aberdulais@nationaltrust.org.uk
For over 300 years this famous waterfall has provided energy to drive the wheels of industry. The Turbine House allows visitors access to the top of the falls, with views of the power equipment, fish pass and displays. Please contact for details of special events.
Times: Open: March: Sat & Sun 11am-4pm only. Apr-Oct Mon-Fri 10am-5pm, Sat, Sun & Bank Hols 11am-6pm. **Fee:** ✱ £3.20 (ch £1.60) Family ticket £8. Parties 15+. £2.40 (ch £1.20) **Facilities:** 🅿 ◗ ᴧ (lifts for disabled to view falls) toilets for disabled shop ✱ 🍴

CRYNANT　　　　　　Map 03 SN70

CEFN COED COLLIERY MUSEUM
SA10 8SN
➲ (1m S of Crynant, on A4109)
☎ 01639 750556　📧 01639 750556
The museum is on the site of a former working colliery, and tells the story of mining in the Dulais Valley. A steam-winding engine has been kept and is now operated by electricity, and there is also a simulated underground mining gallery, boilerhouse, compressor house, and exhibition area. Outdoor exhibits include a stationary colliery locomotive. Exhibitions relating to the coal mining industry are held on a regular basis.
Times: ✱ Open daily, Apr-Oct 10.30-5; Nov-Mar, groups welcome by prior arrangement. **Facilities:** 🅿 ᴧ toilets for disabled shop

CYNONVILLE　　　　　Map 03 SS89

SOUTH WALES MINERS MUSEUM
Afan Argoed Country Park SA13 3HG
➲ (on A4107 6m NE of Port Talbot, leave M4 at junct 40)
☎ 01639 850564　📧 01639 850446
e-mail: boastam@sagainternet.co.uk
The picturesquely placed museum gives a vivid picture of mining life, with coal faces, pit gear and miners' equipment. Guided tours of the museum on request. The country park has forest walks and picnic areas, and a visitor centre.
Times: Open all year daily, Apr-Sep 10.30-5 (Sat & Sun 10.30-6); Oct-Feb 10.30-4 (Sat & Sun 10.30-5). Closed Xmas week. **Fee:** ✱ £1.20 (ch & pen 60p). Concessionary rate for advance bookings.
Facilities: 🅿 (charged) ◗ ✻ ᴧ (mechanical & manual wheel chairs on request) toilets for disabled shop ✻ (ex guide dogs) 🍴

NEATH　　　　　　　Map 03 SS79

GNOLL ESTATE COUNTRY PARK
SA11 3BS
➲ (follow brown heritage signs from Neath town centre)
☎ 01639 635808　📧 01639 635694　FREE
The extensively landscaped Gnoll Estate offers tranquil woodland walks, picnic areas, stunning views, children's play areas, adventure playground, 9-hole golf course, and
continued

coarse fishing. Varied programme of events and school holiday activities.
Times: Open all year - Vistor centre, daily from 10am. (Closed 24 Dec-2 Jan). **Facilities:** P ⬛ & (wheelchair & scooter for hire, designated parking) toilets for disabled shop ✖ (ex guide dogs)

NEATH ABBEY
SA10 7DW
➲ (1m W off A465)
☎ 01639 812387   FREE
These ruins were originally a Cistercian abbey founded in 1130 by Richard de Grainville.
Times: Open at all times. Key keeper arrangement.
Facilities: P & ✖ ⊕

NEWPORT

CAERLEON ROMAN BATHS
NP6 1AE
➲ (on B4236)
☎ 01663 422518
Caerleon was an important Roman military base, with accommodation for thousands of men. The foundations of barrack lines and parts of the ramparts can be seen, with remains of the cookhouse, latrines and baths. The amphitheatre nearby is one of the best examples in Britain.
Times: Open Apr-Oct, daily 9.30-5; Nov-Mar, Mon-Sat, 9.30-5, Sun noon-5. Telephone for Xmas opening times. **Fee:** £2.50 (ch 5-15, pen & students £2, disabled visitors & assisting companion free). Family ticket (2 ad & 3 ch) £7. Group rates available. Prices quoted apply until 31 Mar 2005. **Facilities:** P & shop ✖ ⊕ ⬛

ROMAN LEGIONARY MUSEUM
High St NP18 1AE
➲ (close to Newport, 20 min from M4, follow signs from Cardiff & Bristol)
☎ 01633 423134   01633 422869   FREE
e-mail: roman@nmgw.ac.uk
The museum illustrates the history of Roman Caerleon and the daily life of its garrison. On display are arms, armour and equipment, with a collection of engraved gemstones, a labyrinth mosaic and finds from the legionary base at Usk. Please telephone for details of children's holiday activities - 01633 423134.
Times: Open all year: Mon-Sat 10-5, Sun 2-5. **Facilities:** P (100yds) & toilets for disabled shop ✖ (ex guide dogs) ⬛

TREDEGAR HOUSE & PARK
NP10 8YW
➲ (2m W of Newport, signed from A48 and M4 junct 28)
☎ 01633 815880   01633 815895
e-mail: tredegar.house@newport.gov.uk
Home to one of the greatest of Welsh families, the Morgans, later Lords Tredegar, for over five centuries. A tour of the interior gives a fascinating insight into life above and below stairs. The house and gardens are set in a 90-acre landscaped park, where carriage rides, formal gardens, self-guided trails, craft workshops, boating, and an adventure playground provide plenty to do and see.
Times: Open Etr-Sep. **Facilities:** P ⬛ & (wheelchairs for loan) toilets for disabled shop ⬛

PEMBROKESHIRE

COLBY WOODLAND GARDEN
SA67 8PP
➲ (1.5m inland from Amroth beside Carmarthen Bay, follow brown signs from A477)
☎ 01834 811885   01834 811885   2 for 1
From early spring to the end of June the garden is a blaze of colour, from the masses of daffodils to the rich hues of rhododendrons, azaleas and bluebells. Followed by hydrangeas in shaded walks through summer to glorious shades of autumn
Times: Open 25 Mar-30 Oct, daily 10-5. **Fee:** ✱ £3.40 (ch £1.70). Family ticket £7.50. Group £2.70 (ch £1.30) NT members free.
Facilities: P ⬛ & (Limited due to terrain) toilets for disabled shop on leads ⬝ ⬛

CAREW CASTLE & TIDAL MILL
SA70 8SL
➲ (on A4075, just off A477 Pembroke to Kilgetty road)
☎ 01646 651782   01646 651782
e-mail: enquiries@carewcastle.com
This magnificent Norman castle has royal links with Henry Tudor and was the setting for the Great Tournament of 1507. Nearby is the Carew Cross (Cadw), an impressive 13ft Celtic cross dating from the 11th century. Carew Mill is one of only four restored tidal mills in Britain, with records dating back to 1558.
Times: Open 25 Mar-5 Nov **Fee:** Prices not confirmed for 2005
Facilities: P & toilets for disabled shop ⬛

CILGERRAN CASTLE
SA43 2SF
➲ (off A484 & A478)
☎ 01239 615007
Set above a gorge of the River Teifi - famed for its coracle fishermen - Cilgerran Castle dates from the 11th to 13th centuries. It decayed gradually after the Civil War, but its great round towers and high walls give a vivid impression of its former strength.
Times: Open Apr-Oct, daily 9.30-6.30; Nov-Mar, daily 9.30-dusk. Telephone for Xmas opening times. **Fee:** £2.50 (ch 5-15, pen & students £2, disabled visitors & assisting companion free). Family ticket (2 ad & 3 ch) £7. Group rates available. Prices quoted aply until 31 Mar 2005. **Facilities:** & shop ✖ ⊕ ⬛

CASTELL HENLLYS FORT
Pant-Glas, Meline SA41 3UT
➲ (Off A487 between Cardigan and Newport)
☎ 01239 891319   01239 891319
e-mail: celts@castellhenllys.com
This Iron Age hill fort is set in the beautiful Pembrokeshire Coast National Park. Excavations began in 1981 and three roundhouses have been reconstructed, another roundhouse has been completed and is the largest on the site. Celtic roundhouses have been constructed in the original way using hazel wattle walls, oak rafters and thatched conical roofs. A forge, smithy and looms can be seen, with other

continued

attractions such as trails and a herb garden. Please telephone for details of special events.
Times: Open Apr-early Nov, daily 10-5. Last entry 4.30 **Fee:** Prices not confirmed for 2005 **Facilities:** 🅿 ⅊ (ramp access to shop, hearing loop in shop) toilets for disabled shop 🍴

FISHGUARD   Map 02 SM93

OCEANLAB
The Parrog, Goodwick SA64 0DE
➲ (Take A40 to Fishguard, turn at by-pass, follow signs for Stenaline ferry terminal, pass 2 garages, turn right at rdbt & follow signs to Ocean Lab)
☎ 01348 874737 🖹 01348 872528
e-mail: fishguardharbour-tic@
pembrokeshire.gov.uk
Overlooking the Pembrokeshire coastline, OceanLab is a multifunctional centre which aims to provide a fun-filled experience for the family. There is an Ice Age exhibition with a replica woolly mammoth, 'Oscar'. There is also a hands on ocean quest exhibition, a soft play area and a cybercafe where visitors can surf the internet.
Times: Open Apr-Oct 10-6, Nov-Mar 10-4. **Fee:** Telephone for details **Facilities:** 🅿 ⅊ ⅊ (lift, flat even ground) toilets for disabled shop 🐾 (ex guide dogs) 🍴

LAMPHEY   Map 02 SN00

LAMPHEY BISHOP'S PALACE
SA71 5NT
➲ (off A4139)
☎ 01646 672224
This ruined 13th-century palace once belonged to the Bishops of St David's.
Times: Open Apr-Mar, daily 10-5 **Fee:** £2.50 (ch 5-15, pen & students £2, disabled visitors & assisting companion free). Family ticket (2 ad & 3 ch) £7. Group discounts available. Price quoted apply until 31 Mar 2005. **Facilities:** 🅿 ⅊ toilets for disabled shop 🐾 ⊕ 🍴

LLANYCEFN   Map 02 SN02

PENRHOS COTTAGE
SA66 7XT
➲ (Near Maenclochog & Llanycefn, N of Haverfordwest)
☎ 01437 760460 🖹 01437 760460
Local tradition has it that cottages built overnight on common land could be claimed by the builders, together with the ground a stone's throw away from the door. This thatched cottage is an example, built with help from friends and family; and it gives an insight into traditional Welsh country life.
Times: ✱ Open mid May-Sep Mon-Fri, by appointment only. Tel: 01437 731328. **Facilities:** 🅿 (roadside) ⅊ shop 🐾 (ex in grounds or guide dogs)

LLAWHADEN   Map 02 SN01

LLAWHADEN CASTLE
➲ (off A40, 3m NW of Narberth)   **FREE**
☎ 01437 541201
The castle was first built in the 12th century to protect the possessions of the Bishops of St David's. The 13th and 14th-century remains of the bishops' hall, kitchen, bakehouse and other buildings can be seen, all surrounded by a deep moat.
Times: Open at all times. Key keeper arrangement. **Facilities:** ⅊ 🐾 ⊕

NARBERTH   Map 02 SN11

OAKWOOD PARK
Canaston Bridge SA67 8DE
➲ (M4 W junct 49, take A48 to Carmarthen, signed)
☎ 01834 861889 🖹 01834 891380
e-mail: park@oakwood-leisure.com
Wales' premier theme park, featuring the world's No. 1 wooden roller coaster Megafobia, the 50m-high sky coaster Vertigo, shot n' drop tower coaster The Bounce, and Snake River Falls. For young children there is KidzWorld featuring The Wacky Factory, The Lost Kingdom, Techniquest and Playtown. In summer there are firework displays and light shows at night.
Times: Open daily 3 Apr-3 Oct, from 10am. (closing times vary) **Fee:** ✱ £13.75 (under 2's free, ch 3-9 £12.95, pen & disabled £9.50). Family ticket £49, Party 20+ tickets available £11.75 **Facilities:** 🅿 ⅊ ✗ ⅊ (wheelchair hire, special access to some rides) toilets for disabled shop 🐾 (ex guide dogs) 🍴

NEWPORT   Map 02 SN03

PENTRE IFAN BURIAL CHAMBER
➲ (3m SE from B4329 or A487)   **FREE**
☎ 029 2050 0200
Found to be part of a vanished long barrow when excavated in 1936-37, the remains of this chamber include the capstone, three uprights and a circular forecourt.
Times: Open - access throughout the year. **Facilities:** 🐾 ⊕

PEMBROKE   Map 02 SM90

PEMBROKE CASTLE
SA71 4LA
➲ (W end of main street)
☎ 01646 681510 & 684585 🖹 01646 622260
e-mail: pembroke.castle@talk21.com

This magnificent castle commands stunning views over the Milford estuary. Discover its rich medieval history, and that of Henry VII, the first Tudor king, through a variety of exhibitions. There are lively guided tours and events each Sunday in July and August. Before leaving, pop into the Brass Rubbing Centre and make your own special souvenir. To complete the day, wander round the tranquil millpond and medieval town walls which surround other architectural gems from Tudor and Georgian times.
Times: Open all year, daily, Apr-Sep 9.30-6; Mar & Oct 10-5; Nov-Feb, 10-4; (Closed 24-26 Dec & 1 Jan). **Fee:** £3 (ch under 16 & pen £2, ch under 5 & wheelchairs users free). Family ticket £8.
Facilities: 🅿 (100yds) ⅊ ⅊ (induction loop, handrails, portable ramp) toilets for disabled shop 🍴

ST DAVID'S Map 02 SM72
St David's Bishop's Palace
SA62 6PE
➲ (on A487)
☎ 01437 720517

These extensive and impressive ruins are all that remain of the principal residence of the Bishops of St David's. The palace shares a quiet valley with the cathedral, which was almost certainly built on the site of a monastery founded in the 6th century by St David. The Bishop's Palace houses an exhibition: 'Lords of the Palace'.
Times: Open Apr-May & Oct daily 9.30-5; Jun-Sep, daily 9.30-6; Nov-Mar, Mon-Sat 9.30-4, Sun 11-4. Telephone for Xmas opening times. **Fee:** £2.50 (ch 5-15, pen & students £2, disabled visitors & assisting companions free). Family ticket (2 ad & 3 ch) £7. Group discounts available. Prices quoted apply until 31 Mar 2005.
Facilities: P & toilets for disabled shop ✗ ☺ ➡

St Davids Cathedral
The Close SA62 6PE
➲ (from Haverfordwest A487 into St Davids, pass Cross Sq, turn left into car park)
☎ 01437 720202 🖷 01437 721885
e-mail: **adminstrator@stdavidscathedral.org.uk**

Begun 1181 on the reputed site of St David's 6th century monastic settlement. The present building was altered during the 12th to the 14th centuries and again in the 16th. The ceilings of oak, painted wood and stone vaulting are of considerable interest.
Times: Open all year 8.30-6. **Facilities:** P (300yds) (no coach parking) ➡ & (hearing loop) toilets for disabled shop ✗ (ex guide dogs) ➡

ST FLORENCE Map 02 SN00
Manor House Wildlife & Leisure Park
Ivy Tower SA70 8RJ
➲ (on B4318 between Tenby & St Florence)
☎ 01646 651201 🖷 01646 651201

The park is set in 35 acres of delightful wooded grounds and award-winning gardens. The wildlife includes exotic birds, reptiles and fish. Also here are a pets' corner, a children's playground with free rides on an astraglide slide, and roundabouts. Other attractions include a natural history museum, a go-kart track, model railway exhibition. Daily

continued

falconry displays. Telephone for details of displays and animal feeding times.
Times: ✱ Open Etr-end Sep, daily 10-6. Please telephone for late opening Jul & Aug. **Facilities:** P ➡ & toilets for disabled shop ✗ ➡

SCOLTON Map 02 SM92
Scolton Visitor Centre
SA62 5QL **2 for 1**
➲ (5m N of Haverfordwest, on B4329)
☎ 01437 731328 (Mus) & 731457 (Park)
🖷 01437 731743

Scolton Manor Museum is situated in Scolton Country Park. The early Victorian mansion, refurbished stables and the exhibition hall illustrate the history and natural history of Pembrokeshire. There are new displays in the house and stables, plus a 'Pembrokeshire Railways' exhibition. The 60-acre grounds, partly a nature reserve, have fine specimen trees and shrubs. Environmentally friendly Visitor Centre, alternative energy and woodland displays, guided walks and children's play areas.
Times: Open; Museum Apr-Oct, Tue-Sun & BH's 10.30-1 & 1.30-5.30; Country Park all year ex 25 & 26 Dec, Etr-Sep 10-7, Oct-Etr 10-6.
Fee: Prices not confirmed for 2005 **Facilities:** P (charged) ➡ & (disabled parking area near house) toilets for disabled shop ✗ (ex guide dogs & in grounds)

TENBY Map 02 SN10
Tenby Museum & Art Gallery
Castle Hill SA70 7BP
➲ (Near town centre above Harbour)
☎ 01834 842809 🖷 01834 842809
e-mail: **tenbymuseum@hotmail.com**

The museum is situated on Castle Hill. It covers the local heritage from prehistory to the present in galleries devoted to archaeology, geology, maritime history, natural history, militaria and bygones. The art galleries concentrate on local associations with an important collection of works by Augustus John, Gwen John and others.
Times: ✱ Open all year, Etr-7 Dec, daily 10-5; 8 Dec-Etr, Mon-Fri 10-5. Last admission 4.30. **Facilities:** P (10 mins walk) & (lifts, levelled floors, ramps) toilets for disabled shop ✗ (ex guide dogs)

Tudor Merchant's House
Quay Hill SA70 7BX
➲ (turn left off lower end of High St, past Lifeboat PH and Caldey Shop) **2 for 1**
☎ 01834 842279 🖷 01834 842279

Recalling Tenby's history as a thriving and prosperous port, the Tudor Merchant's house is a fine example of gabled 15th-century architecture. There is a good Flemish chimney and on three walls the remains of frescoes can be seen. A small herb garden has been created.
Times: Open Apr-Sep, daily 10-5 (last admission 4.30); Oct daily 10-3 (last admission 2.30) **Fee:** ✱ £2 (ch £1). Family £5. Group 15+ £1.60 (ch 80p) **Facilities:** P (500yds) (no coaches nearby, no parking in town) & (garden could be accessed, Braille guide) shop ✗ (ex guide dogs) ♨

ABERCRAF   Map 03 SN81

DAN-YR-OGOF THE NATIONAL SHOWCAVES CENTRE FOR WALES
SA9 1GJ
➲ (M4 junct 45, midway between Swansea & Brecon on A4067, follow brown tourist signs)
☎ 01639 730284 & 730801 🖹 01639 730293
e-mail: info@showcaves.co.uk
This award-winning attraction includes three separate caves, dinosaur park, Iron Age Farm, museum, shire horse centre and covered children's play area.
Times: Open Apr-Oct, daily from 10 (last admission 3pm).
Facilities: 🅿 💷 shop ◾

BERRIEW   Map 07 SJ10

GLANSEVERN HALL GARDENS
Glansevern SY21 8AH
➲ (signed on A483 between Welshpool and Newtown)
☎ 01686 640200 🖹 01686 640829
Built in the Greek Revival style for Arthur Davies Owen, who chose a romantically positioned site on the banks of the River Severn. The current owners have developed the gardens, respecting the plantings and features of the past, and added a vast collection of new and interesting species. There are many fine and unusual trees, a lakeside walk, walled garden, water gardens and a rock garden with lamp-lit grotto.
Times: Open May-Sep, BH Mon, Fri-Sat 12-6. Parties other dates by arrangement. **Fee:** ✱ £3.50 (pen £3, ch under 15 free).
Facilities: 🅿 💷 ♿ (most areas accessible) toilets for disabled shop (must be on lead)

BRECON   Map 03 SO02

BRECKNOCK MUSEUM & ART GALLERY
Captain's Walk LD3 7DS
➲ (Near centre of town at junct of The Watton & Glamorgan St)
☎ 01874 624121 🖹 01874 624121   `2 for 1`
e-mail: brecknock.museum@powys.gov.uk
A wealth of local history is explored at the museum, which has archaeological and historical exhibits, with sections on folk life, decorative arts and natural history. Victorian Assize Court is interpreted with life-size figures, sound and light and there is one of the finest collections of Welsh Lovespoons. The museum also runs a lively programme of Welsh contemporary art exhibitions.
Times: Open all year, Mon-Fri 10-5, Sat 10-1 & 2-5; also open Sun 12-5 Apr-Sep. (Closed Good Fri, 25-26 Dec & New Year's Day). **Fee:** £1 (concessions 50p. ch free). Residents free. **Facilities:** 🅿 ♿ (limited parking, must be accompanied by able-bodied) toilets for disabled shop ✖ (ex guide dogs) ◾

THE SOUTH WALES BORDERERS (24TH REGIMENT) MUSEUM
The Barracks, The Watton LD3 7EB
➲ (close to town centre, well signed)
☎ 01874 613310 🖹 01874 613275
e-mail: swb@rrw.org.uk
The museum of the South Wales Borderers and Monmouthshire Regiment, which was raised in 1689 and has been awarded 23 Victoria Crosses. Amongst the collections

continued

is the Zulu War Room, devoted to the war and in particular to the events at Rorke's Drift, 1879, when 121 men fought 4,500 Zulus.
Times: Open wkdays 9-5 throughout the year, wknds & BH's 10-4 Apr-Sep **Fee:** ✱ £3 (ch up to 16 free) **Facilities:** 🅿 (town centre) ♿ toilets for disabled shop ✖ (ex guide dogs) ◾

LLANFAIR CAEREINION   Map 06 SJ10

WELSHPOOL & LLANFAIR LIGHT RAILWAY
SY21 0SF
➲ (beside A458, Shrewsbury-Dolgellau road)
☎ 01938 810441 🖹 01938 810861   `2 for 1`
e-mail: info@wllr.org.uk
The Llanfair Railway is one of the Great Little Trains of Wales. It offers a 16-mile round trip through glorious scenery by narrrow-gauge steam train. The line is home to a collection of engines and coaches from all round the world. Please ring for details of special events.
Times: Open weekends Etr-end Oct, daily during holiday periods phone for timetable enquiries. **Fee:** ✱ £9.50 return (ch £1, pen £8.50). **Facilities:** 🅿 💷 ♿ (three coachs adapted for wheelchairs) toilets for disabled shop ◾

MACHYNLLETH   Map 06 SH70

CELTICA
Y Plas, Aberystwyth Rd SY20 8ER
➲ (well signed to south of town)
☎ 01654 702702 🖹 01654 703604
e-mail: celtica@celticawales.com
Located in a restored mansion house, Celtica is an exciting heritage centre introducing the history and culture of the Celtic people. The sights and sounds of Celtic life are brought alive as you go on a journey portraying the Celtic spirit of the past, present and future. There's an interpretive centre dedicated to Welsh and Celtic history, a children's indoor play area, and conference rooms. Education resources are available and groups are welcome. Storytelling, lectures, music and craft events take place.
Times: ✱ Open daily 10-6. Closed Xmas, New Year & some dates in Jan. **Facilities:** 🅿 💷 ✖ licensed ♿ (Lift & ramps to public areas; Induction loop) toilets for disabled shop ✖ (ex guide dogs) ◾

CENTRE FOR ALTERNATIVE TECHNOLOGY
SY20 9AZ
➲ (3m N of Machynlleth, on A487)
☎ 01654 705950
e-mail: info@cat.org.uk
The Centre for Alternative Technology promotes practical ideas and information on sustainable technologies. The exhibition includes displays of wind, water and solar power, organic gardens, low-energy dwellings, and a unique water-powered railway which ascends a 200ft cliff from the car park. The Wave Tank and the underground 'Mole-Hole' are particularly popular with children.
Times: Open 7 Apr-31 Oct, daily 10-5; 1 Nov-6 Apr, daily 10-4.
Facilities: 🅿 💷 (wheelchair available) shop ✖ (ex guide dogs) ◾

KING ARTHUR'S LABYRINTH
King Arthur's Labyrinth, Corris SY20 9RF
➲ (on A487 between Machynlleth and Dolgellau)
☎ 01654 761584 🖹 01654 761575
e-mail: king.arthurs.labyrinth@corris-wales.co.uk
A subterranean storybook, a boat ride through the great waterfall and into the Labyrinth of tunnels and caverns carved into the ancient rocks of Wales. Tales of King Arthur

continued

and other legends are re-told as you walk through this underground setting.
Times: Open 19 Mar-6 Nov, daily 10-5. **Fee:** ✱ £5 (ch £3.50, pen £4.45). **Facilities:** 🅿 💺 ♿ toilets for disabled shop 🐾 (ex guide dogs) 🍴

MONTGOMERY   Map 07 SO29

MONTGOMERY CASTLE
☎ 029 2050 0200   FREE
Initially an earth and timber structure guarding an important ford in the River Severn, Montgomery was considered a 'suitable spot for the erection of an impregnable castle' in the 1220s. Building and modifications continued until 1251-53, but the final conquest of Wales by Edward I meant the castle lost much of its role.
Times: Open all year, any reasonable time. **Facilities:** ♿ 🐾 ☺

PRESTEIGNE   Map 03 SO36

THE JUDGE'S LODGING
Broad St LD8 2AD
➲ (In centre of town, off B4362, signed from A44 & A49)
☎ 01544 260650 📠 01544 260652   **2 for 1**
e-mail: info@judgeslodging.org.uk
A restored Victorian town house with integral courtroom, cells and service areas - step back into the 1860s, accompanied by an 'evesdropping' audiotour of voices from the past. Explore the fascinating world of the Victorian judges, their servents & felonious guests at this award-winning, 'hands on', historic house.
Times: Open daily, Mar-Oct 10-6; Nov-Dec Wed-Sun 10-4. Closed Jan-Feb. **Fee:** £4.50 (ch £3.50, concessions £3.95). Family ticket £13.50. Party rates available. **Facilities:** 🅿 (200mtrs) ♿ (lift, disabled pack for inaccesible items) shop 🐾 (ex guide dogs)

RHAYADER   Map 06 SN96

GILFACH NATURE DISCOVERY CENTRE AND RESERVE NEW
St Harmon LD6 5LF
➲ (Off A470, 3M N of Rhayader)
☎ 01597 870301 & 823298 📠 01597 823274
e-mail: radnorshirewt@cix.co.uk
Situated in the Cambrian Mountains, Gilfach is locally unique due to its wide variety of habitats; high moorland to enclosed meadow, oak woodland to rocky upland river. The reserve therefore supports a tremendous abundance of plants and animals within a relatively small area. This richness of wildlife has adapted to living in the various habitats created over the centuries through the practice of traditional farming. Visitors can take a number of planned walks including the Nature Trail, the Monks Trod Trail, and the Oakwood Path.
Times: Reserve open all year. Centre Apr-Jun, Sep-Oct-Fri-Mon 10-4.30; Jul-Aug all wk 10-4.30 **Fee:** ✱ Donations **Facilities:** 🅿 (charged) 💺 ♿ toilets for disabled shop

TRETOWER   Map 03 SO12

TRETOWER COURT & CASTLE
NP8 2RF
➲ (3m NW of Crickhowell, off A479)
☎ 01874 730279
The castle is a substantial ruin of an 11th-century motte and bailey, with a three-storey tower and 9ft-thick walls. Nearby is the Court, a 14th-century fortified manor house which has been altered and extended over the years. The two buildings

continued

show the shift from medieval castle to more domestic accommodation over the centuries.
Times: Open 22-31 Mar & Oct, daily 10-4; Apr-Sep, daily 10-5 **Fee:** £2.50 (ch 5-15, pen & students £2, disabled visitors & assisting companion free). Family ticket (2 ad & 3 ch) £7. Group rates available. Prices quoted apply until 31 Mar 2005. **Facilities:** 🅿 ♿ toilets for disabled shop 🐾 ☺ 🍴

WELSHPOOL   Map 07 SJ20

POWIS CASTLE
SY21 8RF
➲ (1m S of Welshpool, signed off A483)
☎ 01938 551920 📠 01938 554336
e-mail: ppcmsn@smtp.ntrust.org.uk
Laid out in the Italian and French styles, the Garden retains its original lead statues, an Orangery and an aviary on the terraces. The medieval castle contains one of the finest collections of paintings and furniture in Wales and a beautiful collection of treasures from India.
Times: ✱ Castle & museum open: Apr-Jun and Sep-Oct, Wed-Sun 1-5; Jul-Aug Tue-Sun 1-5; Open all Bank Hol's in season. Garden is open same days as castle and museum 11-6. Last admission to all parts is 30 mins before closing. **Facilities:** 🅿 ✗ licensed (photos of interior available from tearoom) shop garden centre 🐾 (ex guide dogs) 🐄 🍴

RHONDDA CYNON TAFF

TREHAFOD   Map 03 ST09

RHONDDA HERITAGE PARK
Lewis Merthyr Colliery, Coed Cae Rd CF37 7NP
➲ (between Pontypridd & Porth, off A470, follow brown heritage signs from M4 junct 32)   **2 for 1**
☎ 01443 682036 📠 01443 687420
e-mail: reception@rhonddaheritagepark.com
Based at the Lewis Merthyr Colliery, the Heritage Park is a fascinating 'living history' attraction. You can take the Cage Ride to 'Pit Bottom' and explore the underground workings of a 1950's pit, guided by men who were miners themselves. There are children's activities, an art gallery and a museum illustrating living conditions in the Rhondda Valley. Special events throughout the year, phone for details.
Times: Open all year, daily 10-6. (Closed Mon from Oct-Etr). Last admission 4.30. (Closed 25 Dec-3 Jan). **Fee:** ✱ £5.60 (ch £4.30, pen £4.95). Family ticket £16.50. **Facilities:** 🅿 💺 ✗ licensed ♿ (wheelchair available, accessible parking, lifts) toilets for disabled shop 🐾 (ex guide dogs) 🍴

SWANSEA

LLANRHIDIAN   Map 02 SS49

WEOBLEY CASTLE
SA3 1HB
➲ (from B4271 or B4295)
☎ 01792 390012
A 12th-to 14th-century fortified manor house with an exhibition on the history of Weobley and other historic sites on the Gower peninsula.
Times: Open all year, Apr-Oct, daily 9.30-6; Nov-Mar, daily 9.30-5. Telephone for Xmas opening times. **Fee:** £2 (ch 5-15, pen & students £1.50, disabled visitors & assisting companion free). Family ticket (2 ad & 3 ch) £5.50. Group rates available. Prices quoted apply until 31 Mar 2005. **Facilities:** 🅿 ♿ shop 🐾 ☺ 🍴

OXWICH   Map 02 SS48

OXWICH CASTLE
SA3 1NG
➲ (A4118 from Swansea)
☎ 01792 390359
Situated on the Gower peninsula, this Tudor mansion is a striking testament in stone to the pride and ambitions of the Mansel dynasty of Welsh gentry. The E-shaped wing houses an exhibition on historical Gower and 'Chieftains and Princes of Wales'.
Times: Open Apr-Sep, daily 10-5. **Fee:** £2 (ch 5-15, pen & students £1.50, disabled visitors & assisting companion free). Family ticket (2 ad & 3 ch) £5.50. Group rates available. Prices quoted apply until 31 Mar 2005. **Facilities:** P & (Radar key toilet) toilets for disabled ✕ ۞ ◀

PARKMILL   Map 02 SS58

GOWER HERITAGE CENTRE
Y Felin Ddwr SA3 2EH
➲ (Follow signs for South Gower on A4118 W from Swansea. W side of Parkmill village)
☎ 01792 371206 ▤ 01792 371471   2 for 1
e-mail: info@gowerheritagecentre.co.uk

Based around a 12th-century water-powered cornmill, the site also contains a number of craft workshops, two play areas, animals, a museum and a miller's cottage, all set in attractive countryside in an Area of Outstanding Natural Beauty.
Times: Open daily, Mar-Oct 10-5.30; Nov-Feb 10-4.30. (Closed 25 Dec). **Fee:** ✱ £3.70 (ch under 5 free, concessions £2.60). Family ticket £12 **Facilities:** P ➜ ✕ & (ramp entrance access) toilets for disabled shop ◀

SWANSEA   Map 03 SS69

GLYNN VIVAIN ART GALLERY
Alexandra Rd SA1 5DZ
➲ (Turn off M4 junct 42 along Fabian Way A483 up Wind St. Turn left at train station opposite library)
☎ 01792 516900 ▤ 01792 516903
e-mail: glynn.vivian.gallery@swansea.gov.uk
A broad spectrum of visual arts form the original bequest of Richard Glynn Vivian, including old masters and an international collection of porcelain and Swansea china. The 20th century is also well represented with modern painting and sculpture by British and foreign artists, with the emphasis on Welsh artists.
Times: ✱ Open all year, Tue-Sun & BH Mon 10-5. (Closed 25, 26 Dec & 1 Jan). **Facilities:** P (200 yds) & toilets for disabled shop ✕ (ex guide dogs & hearing dogs) ◀

PLANTASIA **NEW**
Parc Tawe SA1 2AL
➲ (M4 J42 follow A483 into Swansea, follow car park signs for Plantasia)
☎ 01792 474555 ▤ 01792 652588   2 for 1
e-mail: swansea.plantasia@swansea.gov.uk
A unique, giant hot house garden located in the city centre, Plantasia houses a huge variety of unusual and exotic plants of great interest including several species that are extinct in the wild. Also visit the Butterfly House and see a variety of species fly freely and observe various stages of butterfly development.
Times: Tue-Sun 10-5 (BH Mons, all Mons Jun-Aug **Fee:** ✱ £3 (concessions £2.10) **Facilities:** P ➜ & toilets for disabled shop ✕ guide dogs ◀

SWANSEA MUSEUM
Victoria Rd, Maritime Quarter SA1 1SN
➲ (M4 junct 42, on main road into city centre)
☎ 01792 653763 ▤ 01792 652585   FREE
e-mail: swansea.museum@swansea.gov.uk
This is the oldest museum in Wales, showing the history of Swansea from the earliest times until today. The museum has a Tramshed and floating boats to explore (summer only). There is a continuous programme of temporary exhibitions and events all year around.
Times: Open all year, Tue-Sun 10-5.(last admission 4.45pm). Closed Mon except BH Mon, 25-26 Dec & 1 Jan. **Facilities:** P (50yds) (charged) & toilets for disabled shop ✕ (ex guide dogs) ◀

TORFAEN

BLAENAVON   Map 03 SO20

BIG PIT NATIONAL MINING MUSEUM OF WALES
NP4 9XP
➲ (M4 junct 26 or 25, follow signs on A4042 & A4043 to Pontypool & Blaenavon. Signed off A465)
☎ 01495 790311 ▤ 01495 792618
e-mail: bigpit@nmgw.ac.uk
The Real Underground Experience! Big Pit is the UK's leading mining museum. It is a real colliery and was the place of work for hundreds of men, woman and children for over 200 years. A daily struggle to extract the precious mineral that stoked furnaces and lit household fires across the world.
Times: ✱ Open Mid Feb-End Nov, daily 9.30-5, telephone to confirm **Facilities:** P ➜ & (underground tours by prior arrangement) toilets for disabled shop (not on underground tours)

BLAENAVON IRONWORKS
North St
☎ 01495 792615
The Blaenavon Ironworks were a milestone in the history of the Industrial Revolution. Constructed in 1788-99, they were the first purpose-built, multi-furnace ironworks in Wales. By 1796, Blaenavon was the second largest ironworks in Wales, eventually closing down in 1904.
Times: Open 5 Apr-Oct, Mon-Fri 9.30-4.30, Sat 10-5, Sun 10-4.30. For details of opening outside this period, telephone Torfaen County Borough Council on 01633 648081. **Fee:** £2 (ch 5-16, pen & students £1.50, disabled visitors & assisting companion free). Family ticket (2 ad & 3 ch) £5.50. Group discounts available. Prices quoted apply until 31 Mar 2005. **Facilities:** P ✕ ۞ ◀

CWMBRAN   Map 03 ST29

GREENMEADOW COMMUNITY FARM

Greenforge Way NP44 5AJ
➲ (Follow signs for Cwmbran then brown heritage signs [with sheep on] to farm)
☎ 01633 862202 🖷 01633 489332   **2 for 1**
e-mail: greenmeadow_community_farm@
compuserve.com

This is one of Wales' leading tourist attractions - a community farm that was built during the 1980s on land threatened by developers. There are milking demonstrations, tractor and trailer rides, a dragon adventure play area, a farm trail, a nature trail and lots more. Phone for details of lambing weekends, shearing, country fair and agricultural shows, Halloween and Christmas events.
Times: Open Summer 10-6, Winter 10-4. (Closed 25 Dec).
Fee: ✱ Adult £4 (ch £3) Family (2ad+3ch) £14 **Facilities:** 🅿 💺 ♿ (tractor & trailer rides for wheelchair users) toilets for disabled shop 🍽

VALE OF GLAMORGAN

BARRY   Map 03 ST16

WELSH HAWKING CENTRE

Weycock Rd CF62 3AA
➲ (on A4226)
☎ 01446 734687 🖷 01446 739620
There are over 200 birds of prey here, including eagles, hawks, owls, buzzards and falcons. They can be seen and photographed in the mews and some of the breeding aviaries. There are flying demonstrations at regular intervals during the day. A variety of tame, friendly animals, such as pigs, lambs and rabbits will delight younger visitors.
Times: ✱ Open end Mar-end Sep, daily 10.30-5, 1hr before dusk in winter. **Facilities:** 🅿 💺 ♿ toilets for disabled shop 🍽 🍴

OGMORE   Map 03 SS87

OGMORE CASTLE

➲ (2.5m SW of Bridgend, on B4524)   **FREE**
☎ 01656 653435
Standing on the River Ogmore, the west wall of this castle is 40ft high. A hooded fireplace is preserved in the 12th-century, three-storey keep and a dry moat surrounds the inner ward.
Times: Open - access throughout the year. Key keeper arrangement.
Facilities: 🅿 ♿ 🍴 ☺

PENARTH   Map 03 ST17

COSMESTON LAKES COUNTRY PARK & MEDIEVAL VILLAGE

Lavernock Rd CF64 5UY
➲ (on B4267, close to M4 junct 33)
☎ 029 2070 1678 🖷 029 2070 8686   **2 for 1**
e-mail: NColes@valeofglamorgan.gov.uk
Deserted during the plagues and famines of the 14th century, the original village was rediscovered through archaeological excavations. The buildings have been faithfully reconstructed on the excavated remains, creating a living museum of medieval village life. Special events throughout the year include re-enactments and Living History.
Times: Open all year, daily 11-5 in Summer, 11-4 in Winter. (Closed 25 Dec). Country park open at all times. **Fee:** ✱ Entry to Village £3.50, (concessions £2) Family ticket £8. Entry to Country Park is free.
Facilities: 🅿 💺 ✕ ♿ (access ramps & wheelchair hire) toilets for disabled shop

ST HILARY   Map 03 ST07

OLD BEAUPRE CASTLE

➲ (1m SW, off A48)   **FREE**
☎ 01446 773034
This ruined manor house was rebuilt during the 16th century. Its most notable features are an Italianate gatehouse and porch. The porch is an unusual three-storeyed structure.
Times: Open - access throughout the year. Key keeper arrangement.
Facilities: 🅿 🍴 ☺

WREXHAM

CHIRK   Map 07 SJ23

CHIRK CASTLE

LL14 5AF
➲ (8m S of Wrexham, signed off A483)
☎ 01691 777701 🖷 01691 774706
e-mail: pcwmsn@smtp.ntrust.org.uk
Chirk Castle is one of a chain of late 13th-century Marcher castles. Its high walls and drum towers have hardly changed, but the inside shows the varied tastes of 700 years of occupation. One of the least altered parts is Adam's Tower. Many of the medieval-looking decorations were by Pugin in the 19th century. Varied furnishings include fine tapestries.
Times: ✱ Open 29 Mar-Sep, Wed-Sun & BH Mon 12-5 (castle), 11-6 (gardens); Oct, Wed-Sun 12-4 (castle), 11-5 (gardens). Last admission 30 mins before closing. **Facilities:** 🅿 ✕ licensed ♿ (stairclimber) toilets for disabled shop 🍴 (ex guide dogs) 🐾

WREXHAM   Map 07 SJ35

ERDDIG

LL13 0YT
➲ (off A525, 2m S of Wrexham & A483/A5152)
☎ 01978 355314 🖷 01978 313333
Built in 1680, the house was enlarged and improved by a wealthy London lawyer with a passion for gilt and silver furniture. Original furnishings remain, including a magnificent state bed in Chinese silk. The house is notable for the view it gives of both 'upstairs' and 'downstairs' life. The gardens, unusually, have been changed very little since the 18th century.
Times: ✱ Open 25 Mar-1 Nov, Sat-Wed (open Good Fri), house 12-5, garden 11-6 (Jul-Aug gardens 10-6); Oct-1 Nov, Sat-Wed, house 12-4, garden 11-5. **Facilities:** 🅿 ✕ licensed ♿ toilets for disabled shop garden centre 🍴 (ex guidance dogs) 🐾 🍽

NORTHERN IRELAND

EVENTS & FESTIVALS

February
7th-12th All-Ireland Dancing Championships, Waterfront Hall, Belfast

March
17th St Patrick's Day Parade, Armagh

May
28th Lord Mayor's Show, Belfast
tbc Balmoral Show, Balmoral Showgrounds, Belfast

June
24th-26th Hookers Regatta, Portaferry, Co Down (traditional Irish sailing boats)
tbc Fleadh Amhrán agus Rince, Castlewellan, Co Down (traditional music and dancing)

July
13th The Sham Fight, Scarva, Co Down, joust between William of Orange and James II

August
7th-15th Maiden of the Mournes Festival, Warrenpoint, Co Down (folk, country & western)
29th-30th Oul' Lammas Fair, Ballycastle, Co Antrim (traditional fair from 1606)

September
tbc Hillsborough Oyster Festival, Hillsborough, Co Down

October
21st-6th Nov Belfast Festival at Queens, Belfast (drama, comedy, ballet, music, film and art)
31st Halloween Celebrations, Belfast

November/December
tbc Cinemagic International Film Festival for Young People, Belfast

Above: Slieve Gullion Forest Park

BELFAST

BELFAST   Map 01 D5

BELFAST ZOOLOGICAL GARDENS
Antrim Rd BT36 7PN
⮞ (from M2 junct 4 signed to Glengormley. Follow
signs off rdbt to Belfast Zoo)
☎ 028 9077 6277 📠 028 9037 0578
e-mail: blackrhonda@belfastcity.gov.uk
The 50-acre zoo has a dramatic setting on the face of Cave
Hill, enjoying spectacular views. Attractions include the
award-winning primate house (gorillas and chimpanzees),
penguin enclosure, free-flight aviary, African enclosure, and
underwater viewing of sealions and penguins. There are also
red pandas, free-ranging lemurs and a group of very rare
spectacled bears.
Times: Open all year (ex 25 Dec), daily Apr-Sep 10-5; Oct-Mar 10-2.30.
Fee: ✱ Summer: £6.70 (ch £3.40), Winter: £5.40 (£2.70). Under 4's,
pen and Disabled persons free of charge. **Facilities:** 🅿 💷 ✗
& (free admission & reserved parking) toilets for disabled shop
✖ (ex guide dogs) 🍴

BOTANIC GARDENS
3 College Park BT7 1LP
⮞ (from City Hall, Bedford Street then Dublin road
for Botanic Avenue)
☎ 028 9032 4902 📠 028 9032 4902
e-mail: maxwellr@belfastcity.gov.uk
One highlight of the park is the beautiful glass-domed
Victorian Palm House, built between 1839-52. This palm
house pre-dates the one in Kew Gardens and is one of the
earliest curved glass and iron structures in the world.
Another feature is the Tropical Ravine - stand on a balcony
to get a wonderful view through a steamy ravine full of
exotic plants.
Times: Palm House Tropical Ravine: Apr-Sep 10-12, 1-5; Oct-Mar 10-12,
1-4. Sat & Sun & BH's 1-5 (Summer), 1-4 (Winter).
Facilities: 🅿 (street) &

GIANT'S RING
⮞ (0.75m S of Shaws Bridge)
☎ 028 9023 5000 📠 028 9031 0288
Circular, Bronze-age enclosure nearly 200ft in diameter
similar in style to Stonehenge, with a stone chambered grave
in the centre and bordered by banks 20ft wide and 12ft high.
Very little is known for certain about this site, except that it
was used for ritual burial.
Times: ✱ Open all times. **Facilities:** 🅿

ULSTER MUSEUM
Botanic Gardens BT9 5AB
⮞ (M1/M2 to Balmoral exit)
☎ 028 9038 3000 📠 028 9038 3003   FREE
Both a national museum and an art gallery, the collections
are Irish and international in origin and cover archaeology
and ethnography, art, botany and zoology, geology and local
history (including industrial archaeology). An annual
programme of changing temporary exhibitions and events
takes place.
Times: Open all year, Mon-Fri 10-5, Sat 1-5, Sun 2-5. Tel for details of
Xmas closures. **Facilities:** 🅿 (100yds on street) (Clearway 8-9.30 &
4.30-6) 💷 & (all galleries except one. Loop system, wheelchair lifts)
toilets for disabled shop ✖ (ex guide dogs) 🍴

W5 AT ODYSSEY
2 Queens Quay BT3 9QQ
☎ 028 9046 7700 📠 028 9046 7707
W5 investigates Who? What? Where? When? Why?... and
that pretty much sums up the intent behind Ireland's first
purpose built discovery centre. Visitors of any age will want
to get their hands on interactive science and technology
displays that include the laser harp, the fog knife,
microscopes, robots and computers. W5 is part of a massive
Millennium Landmark Project in the heart of Belfast.
Times: ✱ Open all year ex 25-26 Dec & 12 Jul. Mon-Sat 10-6, Sun
12-6. **Facilities:** 🅿 (charged) ✗ licensed & (hearing loop) toilets for
disabled shop ✖ (ex guide dogs) 🍴

CO ANTRIM

ANTRIM   Map 01 D5

ANTRIM ROUND TOWER
BT41 1BJ
⮞ (N of town)
☎ 028 9023 5000 📠 028 9031 0288
Antrim round tower stands among lawns and trees but it
was once surrounded by monastic buildings. Antrim was an
important early monastery, probably a 6th-century
foundation, closely linked with Bangor.
Times: ✱ Open all year. **Facilities:** 🅿 &

BALLYCASTLE   Map 01 D6

BONAMARGY FRIARY
⮞ (E of town, at golf course)
☎ 028 9023 5000 📠 028 9031 0288
Founded by Rory MacQuillan around 1500 and later passed
on to the MacDonnells, Earls of Antrim, there are still
remains of the friary gatehouse, church and cloister for
visitors to see.
Times: ✱ Open all year. **Facilities:** 🅿 & 🚐

BALLYLUMFORD   Map 01 D5

BALLYLUMFORD DOLMEN
⮞ (on B90 on NW tip of Island Magee)
☎ 028 9023 5000 📠 028 9031 0288
Incorporated in the front garden of a house in Ballylumford
Road are the remains of this huge 4-5,000-year-old single-
chamber Neolithic tomb, also known as the Druid's Altar.
Times: ✱ Open all year. **Facilities:** &

BALLYMENA   Map 01 D5

ECOS MILLENNIUM ENVIRONMENTAL CENTRE
Ecos Centre, Kernohams Ln, Broughshane Rd BT43 7QA
⮞ (follow signs from M2 bypass at Ballymena)
☎ 028 2566 4400 📠 028 2563 8984   2 for 1
e-mail: info@ecoscentre.com
Ecos is an "alternative environmental centre", which allows
visitors to explore alternative means of energy production,
including electricity generated using wood, wind and sun,
recycling, and alternative technologies such as willow
coppicing. Plenty of hands-on fun and educational potential.
Times: Open all year ex 24 Dec-1 Jan. Please phone for opening dates
Fee: £4 (ch & concessions £3). Family ticket £12.50 **Facilities:** 🅿 💷
& toilets for disabled shop ✖ (ex guide dogs) 🍴

HARRYVILLE MOTTE
➪ (N bank of River Braid)
☎ 028 9023 5000 ▤ 028 9031 0288
On a ridge to the south of the town, this Norman fort, with its 40ft-high motte and rectangular bailey, is one of the finest examples of Norman earthworks left in Northern Ireland.
Times: ✱ Open all year. **Facilities:** 🅿 ⅏ 🚌

LESLIE HILL OPEN FARM
Leslie Hill BT53 6QL
➪ (1m NW of Ballymoney on MacFin Rd)
☎ 028 2766 6803 ▤ 028 2766 6803
An 18th-century estate with a Georgian house, magnificent period farm buildings, and fine grounds with paths, lakes and trees. Attractions include an extensive collection of rare breeds, poultry, horsedrawn machinery and carriages, exhibition rooms, a museum, working forge, deer park, walled garden and an adventure playground.
Times: Open Jul-Aug Mon-Sat 11-6, Sun 2-6; Jun Sat-Sun & BHs 2-6; Etr-May, Sun & BHs 2-6, open all Etr wk 11-6. **Fee:** ✱ £3.20 (ch £2.20). Family ticket £9. **Facilities:** 🅿 ⅏ ⅏ (ramps) toilets for disabled shop garden centre

OLD BUSHMILLS DISTILLERY
BT57 8XH
➪ (on the Castlecatt Rd, in Bushmills Village)
☎ 028 2073 1521 ▤ 028 2073 1339
e-mail: scroskery@idl.ie
Old Bushmills was granted its licence in 1608 and is the oldest licenced whiskey distillery in the world. There's a guided tour, and afterwards you can take part in a comparative tasting session and become a whiskey expert.
Times: Open Apr-Oct, Mon-Sat 9.30-5.30, Sun 12-5.30, last tour 4; Nov-Mar, Mon-Fri 5 tours daily, 10.30, 11.30, 1.30, 2.30 & 3.30. Sat & Sun 3 tours, 1.30, 2.30, 3.30. (Closed 12 July , Xmas & New Year) **Fee:** £5 (pen & student £4, accompanied ch £2.50) Family ticket (2 ad + 2 ch)£13. **Facilities:** 🅿 ✕ licensed ⅏ (audio visual theatre, shops & restaurant) toilets for disabled shop ✕ (ex guide dogs) ⊟

CARRICK-A-REDE ROPE BRIDGE AND LARRYBANE VISITORS CENTRE
BTS4 6LS
➪ (E of Ballintoy on B15, 119A Whitepark Rd, Ballintoy)
☎ 028 2076 9839 & 2073 1582 (office)
▤ 028 2073 2963
e-mail: carrickarede@nationaltrust.org.uk
On the North Antrim Coastal Path is one of Northern Ireland's best-loved attractions: Carrick-a-Rede Rope Bridge and the disused limestone quarry of Larrybane. The island of Carrick is known as 'the rock in the road', as it is an obstacle on the path of migrating salmon, and fishermen have taken advantage of this to net the fish here for over 300 years.
Times: Bridge open daily, (weather permitting), 12 Mar-12 June, 10-6; 13-30 Jun 10-7, Jul & Aug 10-7; Sep 10-6. (last admission 45mins before closing). Coastal path open all year. **Fee:** £2.20, (ch £1.20) Family £5.60, Groups £1.70 each **Facilities:** 🅿 ⅏ ⅏ (information centre, telescope at wheelchair height) toilets for disabled ⅏

CARRICKFERGUS CASTLE
BT38 7BG
➪ (on N shore of Belfast Lough)
☎ 028 9335 1273 ▤ 028 9336 5190
Imposingly placed on a rocky headland overlooking Belfast Lough, this is the best preserved and probably the most fought-over Norman castle in Ireland. Built by John de Courcy, Earl of Ulster, after 1180, it served a military purpose for more than eight centuries. Exhibits include a giant model of the castle, a short film, and a banqueting suite. The castle is often used as a venue for medieval banquets and fairs. There is a visitors' centre, shop and refreshment point.
Times: ✱ Open all year, Apr-Sep, weekday 10-6, Sun 2-6; Oct-Mar closes at 4. **Facilities:** 🅿 ⅏ ⅏ toilets for disabled shop ✕

TOWN WALLS
☎ 028 9023 5000 ▤ 028 9031 0288
Lord Deputy Sir Arthur Chichester enclosed Carrickfergus with stone walls from 1611 onwards and more than half the circuit is still visible, often to its full height of 4 metres to the wall walk.
Times: ✱ Visible at all times. **Facilities:** 🅿 ⅏

CRANFIELD CHURCH
➪ (3.75m SW of Randalstown)
☎ 028 9023 5000 ▤ 028 9031 0288
This small medieval church is situated on the shores of Lough Neagh. Beside it is a famous holy well.
Times: ✱ Open all year. **Facilities:** 🅿 ⅏ 🚌

GIANT'S CAUSEWAY CENTRE
44 Causeway Rd BT57 8SU
➪ (2m N of Bushmills on B146)
☎ 028 2073 1855 ▤ 028 2073 2537
e-mail: causewaytic@hotmail.com
This dramatic rock formation is undoubtedly one of the wonders of the natural world. The Centre provides an exhibition and audio-visual show, and Ulsterbus provides a minibus service to the stones and there are guided walks, and special facilities for the disabled.
Times: ✱ Open all year, daily from 10am (closes 7pm Jul & Aug) Closed 1 wk Xmas **Fee:** Audio-visual presentation £1 (ch 50p) Family ticket £2.50 (2ad+2ch under 15). Group rate 80p (ch 40p). Car park charge £5 per car; £7.50 minibus. **Facilities:** 🅿 (charged) ⅏ ✕ ⅏ (mini bus transport with wheelchair hoist, reserved parking) toilets for disabled shop ✕ (ex guide dogs) ⊟

OLDERFLEET CASTLE
☎ 028 9023 5000 ▤ 028 9031 0288
A 16th-century tower house, the last surviving of three which defended Larne.
Times: Open at all times.

DUNEIGHT MOTTE AND BAILEY
➪ (2.3m S beside Ravernet River)
☎ 028 9023 5000 ▤ 028 9031 0288
Impressive Anglo-Norman earthwork castle with high mound-embanked enclosure, making use of the defences of an earlier pre-Norman fort.
Times: Open all year.

Irish Linen Centre & Lisburn Museum
Market Square BT28 1AG
➩ (signed both in and outside town centre) FREE
☎ 028 9266 3377   ▤ 028 9267 2624
e-mail: irishlinencentre@lisburn.gov.uk

The centre tells the story of the Irish linen industry past and present. The recreation of individual factory scenes brings the past to life and a series of imaginative hands-on activities describe the linen manufacturing processes. The Museum has a range of temporary exhibitions of local interest.
Times: Open all year, Mon-Sat, 9.30-5. **Facilities:** P (200mtrs) (limited for disabled and coaches) ▆ ᶦᵉ (lift, induction loop, staff trained in sign language) toilets for disabled shop ✖ (ex guide dogs) ◀

PORTBALLINTRAE   Map 01 C6

Dunluce Castle
➩ (off A2)
☎ 028 2073 1938   ▤ 028 2031 8288

Extensive and picturesque ruins of a 16th-century castle perched on a rocky crag high above the sea. Stronghold of the MacQuillans and MacDonnells, who significantly altered the original stonebuilt fortress. Randal MacDonnell built a house in the centre of the castle, of which parts of the Great Hall remain, as do the towers and early 17th-century gatehouse. The castle has new displays and there is an audio-visual show. The cave below the ruins provided a secret way into and out of the castle from the sea.
Times: ✱ Open all year, Apr-Sep, weekdays 10-7, Sun 2-7; Oct-Mar, Tue-Sat 10-4, Sun 2-4. **Facilities:** P ᶦᵉ toilets for disabled shop

TEMPLEPATRICK   Map 01 D5

Pattersons Spade Mill
751 Antrim Rd BT39 0AP
➩ (2m SE of Templepatrick on A6)
☎ 028 9443 3619   ▤ 028 9443 3619

This is the last surviving water-driven spade mill in Ireland. It has been completely restored by the National Trust and is now back in production.
Times: ✱ Open, Mar, Sun 2-6; Apr-May, wknds, BHs, 2-6 ; Jun-Aug, daily 2-6; Sep, wknds & BH's 2-6. **Facilities:** P ᶦᵉ (ramps, wheelchair available) toilets for disabled ♨

Templetown Mausoleum
BT39
➩ (in Castle Upton graveyard on A6, Belfast-Antrim road)

Situated in the graveyard of Castle Upton, this family mausoleum is in the shape of a triumphal arch and was designed by Robert Adam.
Times: Open daily during daylight hours. **Facilities:** P ▆ ♨

CO ARMAGH

ARMAGH   Map 01 C5

Armagh County Museum
The Mall East BT61 9BE
➩ (in city centre)
☎ 028 3752 3070   ▤ 028 3752 2631 FREE
e-mail: acm.um@nics.gov.uk

Housed in a 19th-century schoolhouse, this museum contains an art gallery and library, as well as a collection of
continued

local folkcrafts and natural history. Special events are planned thoughout the year.
Times: Open all year, Mon-Fri 10-5, Sat 10-1 & 2-5.
Facilities: P ᶦᵉ (entrance, ramp & lift for disabled) toilets for disabled shop ✖ (ex guide dogs) ◀

Armagh Friary
➩ (SE edge of town)
☎ 028 9023 5000   ▤ 028 9031 0288

Situated just inside the gates of the former Archbishop's Palace are the remains of the longest friary church in Ireland (163ft). The friary was established in 1263 by Archbishop O'Scanail and destroyed by Shane O'Neill in the middle of the 16th century to prevent it being garrisoned by Elizabethan soldiers.
Times: Open all year. **Facilities:** P ᶦᵉ

Armagh Planetarium
College Hill BT61 9DB
➩ (on main Armagh-Belfast road close to mall, city centre)
☎ 028 3752 3689 & 3752 4725
▤ 028 3752 6187
e-mail: kate@armaghplanet.com

The Planetarium is home to The Star Theatre, a multi-media environment equipped with the latest technology including a virtual reality digital system. Also featured are The Hall of Astronomy, the new Eartharium Building and surrounding the Planetarium is the Astropark, a 25-acre 'hands on' park.
Times: ✱ Open, Mon-Fri 2-4.45. Presentations Mon-Fri 3pm. Closed Sat, Sun & BHs. **Facilities:** P ᶦᵉ (Loop system in theatre) toilets for disabled shop ✖ (ex guide dogs) ◀

Palace Stables Heritage Centre
The Palace Demesne BT60 4EL
➩ (off Friary Road beside council offices)
☎ 028 3752 9629   ▤ 028 3752 9630   2 for 1
e-mail: stables@armagh.gov.uk

This picturesque Georgian building, set around a cobbled courtyard, has been lovingly restored and now houses a heritage centre. A daily Georgian interpretation is provided by authentic costumed characters.
Times: Open all year, Jul-Aug, Mon-Sat 10-5.30, Sun 1-5.30; Sep-Apr, Mon-Sat 10-5, Sun 2-5. Last tour 1hr before closing. **Fee:** ✱ Telephone for admission prices. **Facilities:** P ✖ licensed ᶦᵉ (ramps & Lift in stables) toilets for disabled shop ◀

Saint Patrick's Trian Visitor Complex
40 English St BT61 7BA
➩ (city centre)
☎ 028 3752 1801   ▤ 028 3751 0180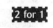
e-mail: info@saintpatrickstrain.com

This award-winning attraction incorporates three different exhibitions. 'The Armagh Story' traces the city's history; 'Patrick's Testament' examines Armagh's association with Ireland's patron saint; and 'The Land of Lilliput' where a giant tells the story of Gulliver's Travels.
Times: Open all year, Mon-Sat 10-5, Sun 2-5; Jul-Aug, Mon-Sat 10-5.30, Sun 2-5. Last tour 1hr before closing. **Fee:** ✱ £4 (ch £2.25, pen & student £2.75). Family ticket £10 **Facilities:** P (charged) ✖ licensed ᶦᵉ (specially designed for disabled) toilets for disabled shop ✖ (ex guide dogs) ◀

CAMLOUGH — Map 01 D5

KILLEVY CHURCHES

➩ (3m S lower eastern slopes of Slieve Gullion)

☎ 028 9023 5000 ▤ 028 9031 0288

The ruins of the two churches (10th and 13th-century) stand back to back, at the foot of Slieve Gullion sharing a common wall, but with no way through from one to the other. The churches stand on the site of an important nunnery founded by St Monenna in the 5th century. A huge granite slab in the graveyard supposedly marks the founder's grave. A holy well can be reached by climbing the path north of the graveyard. The nunnery was in use until the Dissolution in 1542.
Times: ✱ Open all year. **Facilities:** ᚼ

JONESBOROUGH — Map 01 D5

KILNASAGGART INSCRIBED STONE

➩ (1.25m S)

☎ 028 9023 5000 ▤ 028 9031 0288

A granite pillar stone dating back to 8th century, with numerous crosses and a long Irish inscription carved on it.
Times: Open all year. **Facilities:** P

MOY — Map 01 C5

ARGORY

Derrycaw Rd BT71 6NA

➩ (3m NE)

☎ 028 8778 4753 ▤ 028 8778 9598 `2 for 1`
e-mail: argory@nationaltrust.org.uk

Originally the home of the McGeough family, this Regency house is situated on a hillside overlooking the Blackwater River. The house is full of period furniture and bric-a-brac. Of particular interest is the very unusual acetylene lighting, installed by the family in 1906.
Times: Grounds: Open Oct-Apr, daily 10-4; May-Sep, daily 10-7. House: Open 17 Mar 1-6; 19 Mar-May & Sep, wknds & BH/PH, 1-6; Jun-Aug, daily 1-6; Sep wknds 1-6; 1-9 Oct, wknds 1-5. **Fee:** Grounds £2.50 per car. Grounds & House £4.50 (ch £2.40). Family £11.40. Group £4.10 (outside normal hours £5). **Facilities:** P (charged) ▨ ᚼ (special parking facilities, wheelchair available, Braille) toilets for disabled shop ✖ (ex guide dogs) ᨆ ▆

NEWRY — Map 01 D5

MOYRY CASTLE

➩ (7.5m S)

☎ 028 9023 5000 ▤ 028 9031 0288

This tall, three-storey keep was built by Lord Mountjoy, Queen Elizabeth's deputy, in 1601, its purpose to secure the Gap of the North which was the main route into Ulster.
Times: Open all year

OXFORD ISLAND — Map 01 D5

LOUGH NEAGH DISCOVERY CENTRE

Oxford Island National Nature, Reserve BT66 6NJ

➩ (signed from M1, junct 10)

☎ 028 3832 2205 ▤ 028 3834 7438
e-mail: oxford.island@craigavon.gov.uk

Learn about the history and wildlife of the Lough through a series of exciting audio-visual shows, interactive games and an exhibition, then experience the Island for yourself. In a spectacular setting on the water's edge, discover natural history, wildlife, family walks and much more.
Times: Open Apr-Sep, Mon-Sat 10-6; Sun 10-7, Oct-Mar, Wed-Sun 10-5. **Fee:** Telephone for admission prices. **Facilities:** P ▨ ᚼ (grounds accessible in part, bird watching hides) toilets for disabled shop ✖ (ex guide dogs) ▆

PORTADOWN — Map 01 D5

ARDRESS HOUSE

64 Ardress Rd, Annaghmore BT62 1SQ

➩ (On B28, 5m from Moy, 5m from Portadown, 3m from M1 junct 13)

☎ 028 3885 1236 ▤ 028 3885 1236 `2 for 1`
e-mail: ardress@ntrust.org.uk

A plain 17th-century house, transformed around 1770 by its visionary architect-owner George Ensor, who added elegant wings and superb Adamesque plasterwork. The house has a fine picture gallery on loan from the Earl of Castlestewart. The grounds are beautifully unspoilt and there is a farmyard with livestock and a display of farm implements.
Times: Open, 17 Mar, 2-6; 19 Mar-25 Sep, wknds, BHs & PHs 2-6; **Fee:** £3.30 (ch £1.70). Family £8.30. Group £3 (Group outside normal hours £5). **Facilities:** P ᚼ toilets for disabled shop ✖ (ex guide dogs) ᨆ

TYNAN — Map 01 C5

VILLAGE CROSS

☎ 028 9023 5000 ▤ 028 9031 0288

A carved High Cross, 11ft tall, which lay broken in two pieces for many years, but was skilfully mended in 1844.
Times: Open all year **Facilities:** P ᚼ

CO DOWN

ARDGLASS — Map 01 D5

JORDAN'S CASTLE

☎ 028 9054 6552

Although Ardglass is an important fishing port today, it was once the busiest seaport in Northern Ireland. Between the 14th and 15th centuries a ring of tower houses and fortified warehouses was built to protect the port. Jordan's Castle, a late 15th-century, four-storey tower house situated in the centre of town, is one of these. Besieged in the early 1600s and held for three years, the castle was bought, repaired and filled with bygones by a Belfast solicitor in the early part of the 20th century.
Times: Open Jul-Aug; Tue, Fri & Sat 10-1, Wed-Thu, 2-6. Other times on request. **Facilities:** ✖

BALLYWALTER — Map 01 D5

GREY ABBEY

➩ (on east edge of village)

☎ 028 9054 6552

Founded in 1193 by Affreca, daughter of the King of the Isle of Man, these extensive ruins of a Cistercian abbey, sitting in lovely sheltered parkland, are among the best preserved in Northern Ireland. The chancel, with its tall lancet windows, magnificent west doorway and an effigy tomb - believed to be Affreca's - in the north wall, are particularly interesting. The abbey was burned down in 1572, and then re-used as a parish church. There are many 17th and 18th-century memorials to be seen in the church ruins, which occupy a pleasant garden setting. The abbey now has a beautiful medieval herb garden, with over 50 varieties of plants, and a visitors' centre.
Times: ✱ Open Apr-Sep; Tue-Sat 10-7, Sun 2-7; Oct-Mar, wknds, Sat 10-4, Sun 2-4. **Facilities:** P ᚼ toilets for disabled

DRUMENA CASHEL
➲ (2.25m SW)
☎ 028 9023 5000   ▤ 028 9031 0288
There are many stone ring forts in Northern Ireland, but few so well preserved as Drumena. Dating back to early Christian times, the fort is 30m in diameter and has an 11m accessible underground stone-built passage, probably used as a refuge and for storage.
Times: Open all times   **Facilities:** P

WWT CASTLE ESPIE
Ballydrain Rd BT23 6EA
➲ (12m SE of Belfast. Take A22 from Comber towards Killyleagh, 1st left into Ballydrain Rd)
☎ 028 9187 4146   ▤ 028 9187 3857
e-mail: castleespie@wwt.org.uk
Home to the largest collection of wildfowl in Ireland. Comfortable hides enable you to watch the splendour of migratory waders and wildfowl. Beautiful landscaped gardens, a taxidermy collection and fine paintings by wildlife artists can also be seen. Thousands of birds migrate to the reserve in winter and birdwatch mornings are held on the last Thursday of every month. The Centre's effluent is treated in a reed bed filtration system which can be seen on one walk.
Times: ✱ Open all year Mar-Oct, Mon-Sat 10.30-5, Sun 11.30-5.30; Nov-Feb Mon-Fri 11-4 Sat & Sun 11-4.30. **Facilities:** P ▣ & (hides have wheelchair platforms) toilets for disabled shop

DOWN COUNTY MUSEUM
The Mall BT30 6AH
➲ (on entry to town follow brown signs to museum)
☎ 028 4461 5218   ▤ 028 4461 5590   FREE
e-mail: museum@downdc.gov.uk
The museum is located in the restored buildings of the 18th-century county gaol. In addition to restored cells that tell the stories of some of the prisoners, there are exhibitions on the history of County Down. Plus temporary exhibits, events, tea-room and shop.
Times: Open all year, Mon-Fri 10-5, wknds 1-5 **Facilities:** P (100yds) ▣ & (wheelchair available, handling boxes on application) toilets for disabled shop ✖ (ex guide dogs) ◼

INCH ABBEY
➲ (0.75m NW off A7)
☎ 028 9023 5000   ▤ 028 9031 0288
Beautiful riverside ruins of a Cistercian abbey founded by John de Courcy around 1180. Of particular note is the tall, pointed, triple east window.
Times: Open Apr-Sep 10-7, Sun 2-7. Oct-Mar free access.
Facilities: P &

LOUGHINISLAND CHURCHES
➲ (4m W)
☎ 028 9023 5000   ▤ 028 9031 0288
This remarkable group of three ancient churches stands on an island in the lough, accessible by a causeway. The middle church is the oldest, probably dating back to the 13th century, with a draw-bar hole to secure the door. The large North church was built in the 15th century, possibly to
continued

replace the middle church and continued in use until 1720. The smallest and most recent church is the South (MacCartan's) church.
Times: Open all times   **Facilities:** P & ◼

MOUND OF DOWN
➲ (on Quoile Marshes, from Mount Crescent)
☎ 028 9023 5000   ▤ 028 9031 0288
A hill fort from the Early Christian period, conquered by Anglo-Norman troops in 1177, who then built an earthwork castle on top. This mound in the marshes, beside the River Quoile, was the first town before the present Downpatrick.
Times: Open all times   **Facilities:** P

THE ST PATRICK CENTRE
St Patrick Visitor Centre, Market St BT30 6LZ
➲ (A7 from Belfast, follow brown heritage signs.)
☎ 028 4461 9000   ▤ 028 4461 9111
e-mail: director@saintpatrickcentre.com
This 21st-century multimedia, interactive, audio-visual feast is dedicated to the fascinating story of Ireland's Patron Saint, St. Patrick, who brought Christianity to Ireland in the 5th century. The Centre is located beside the saint's grave, in the heart of St. Patrick's country, forty minutes from Belfast and two hours from Dublin.
Times: Open all year Oct-Mar, Mon-Sat, 10-5 & St Patricks Day 9.30-7; Apr-May & Sep, Mon-Sat 9.30-5.30, Sun 1-5.30 (morning opening on request), Jun-Aug Mon-Sat 9.30-6, Sun 10-6. (Last admission 1.5 hrs before closing). **Fee:** ✱ £4.75 (ch £2.35, concessions £3.15) family ticket (2ad+2ch) £11.55. Groups 25+, £2.15 (ch £2.10, concessions £2.10) **Facilities:** P ▣ ✖ & (lifts+w/chairs available) toilets for disabled shop garden centre ✖ (ex guide dogs) ◼

STRUELL WELLS
➲ (1.5m E)
☎ 028 9023 5000   ▤ 028 9031 0288
Pilgrims come to collect the healing waters from these holy drinking and eye wells which are fed by a swift underground stream. Nearby are the ruins of an 18th-century church, and, even more interesting, single-sex bath-houses. The men's bath-house is roofed, has an anteroom and a sunken bath, while the ladies' is smaller and roofless.
Times: Open all times   **Facilities:** P ◼

LEGANANNY DOLMEN
➲ (4m S)
☎ 028 9023 5000   ▤ 028 9031 0288
Theatrically situated on the slopes of Slieve Croob, this tripod dolmen with its three tall uprights and huge capstone is the most graceful of Northern Ireland's Stone Age monuments. There are views to the Mourne Mountains.
Times: Open at all times   **Facilities:** & ◼

HILLSBOROUGH FORT
☎ 028 9268 3285   ▤ 028 9031 0288
On a site that dates back to early Christian times, the existing fort was built in 1650 by Colonel Arthur Hill to command a view of the road from Dublin to Carrickfergus. The building was ornamented in the 18th century. It is set in a forest park with a lake and pleasant walks.
Times: ✱ Open all year; Apr-Sep, Tue-Sat 10-7, Sun 2-7; Oct-Mar, Tue-Fri 10-4, Sat 10-4, Sun 2-4., **Facilities:** P &

GREENCASTLE

➲ (4m SW)

☎ 028 9023 5000 ▤ 028 9031 0288

Looking very much like an English Norman castle with its massive keep, gatehouse and curtain wall, this 13th-century royal fortress stands on the shores of Carlingford Lough, with fine views of the Mourne Mountains. Greencastle has an eventful military history, it was beseiged and taken by Edward Bruce in 1316, attacked and spoiled by the Irish at least twice later in the 14th century, and maintained as a garrison for Elizabeth in the 1590s.

Times: ✳ Open Jul-Aug, Tue-Sat 10-7, Sun 2-7. Facilities: ▣ &

SKETRICK CASTLE

➲ (3m E on W tip of Sketrick Islands)

☎ 028 9023 5000 ▤ 028 9031 0288

A badly ruined tall tower house, probably 15th century. The ground floor rooms include a boat bay and prison. An underground passage leads from the north-east of the bawn to a freshwater spring.

Times: Open at all times. Facilities: ▣ &

DUNDRUM CASTLE

➲ (4m N)

☎ 028 9054 6518

This medieval castle, one of the finest in Ireland, was built in 1777 by John De Courcy in a strategic position overlooking Dundrum Bay, a position which offers visitors fine views over the sea and to the Mourne Mountains. The castle was captured by King John in 1210 and was badly damaged by Cromwellian troops in 1652. Still an impressive ruin, it shows a massive round keep with walls 16m high and 2m thick, surrounded by a curtain wall, and a gatehouse which dates from the 13th century.

Times: ✳ Open Apr-Sep, Tue-Sat 10-7, Sun 2-7; Oct-Mar, wknds, Sat 10-4, Sun 2-4. Facilities: ▣ & toilets for disabled

MAGHERA CHURCH

➲ (2m NNW)

☎ 028 9023 5000 ▤ 028 9031 0288

The stump of a round tower, blown down in a storm in the early 18th century, survives from the early monastery, with a ruined 13th-century church nearby.

Times: Open all year. Facilities: ▣ &

MOUNT STEWART HOUSE, GARDEN & TEMPLE OF THE WINDS

Greyabbey BT22 2AD

➲ (5m SE off A20)

☎ 028 4278 8387 ▤ 028 4278 8569 `2 for 1`

e-mail: mountstewart@nationaltrust.org.uk

On the east shore of Strangford Lough, is a fascinating house which has survived for three centuries, famous for its many illustrious owners and guests and well renowned for its magnificent gardens created by Edith Lady Londonderry, wife of the 7th Marquess. In the inspired gardens, which are now a nominated world heritage site, many rare and subtropical trees thrive. Located by the shore is the Temple of the Winds,

continued

built by James 'Athenian' Stuart in 1782 for the first Marquess.

Times: Lakeside Gardens & Walks: Daily all year, 10-sunset;. Formal Gardens: Mar wknds & BHs 10-4; Apr & Oct, daily 10-6; May-Sep 10-8 (closed Nov-Feb). House: 12 Mar-end Apr wknds (including Etr) 12-6.; May, Jun & Sep, wknds 12-6, weekdays (ex Tue) 1-6; Oct, wknds 12-6 (Nov-Feb closed). Temple of Winds Apr-Oct, Sun & BH, 2-5.

Fee: House tour, gardens & Temple of Winds: £5.45, (ch £2.70). Family £13.60, Group 15+, £4.80 (group outside normal hours £6). Gardens: £4.20 (ch £2.20) Family £9.30. Group £3.90. Lakeside Walks Nov-Feb, £3 (ch £1.50) Family £7, Groups £2.75 Facilities: ▣ ▆ ✗ licensed & (4 wheelchairs (2 electric) available) toilets for disabled shop ⅋ ▬

SCRABO TOWER

Scrabo Country Park, 203A Scrabo Rd BT23 4SJ

➲ (1m W)

☎ 028 9181 1491 ▤ 028 9182 0695

The 135ft high Scrabo Tower, one of Northern Ireland's best-known landmarks, dominates the landscape of North Down and is also the centre of a country park around the slopes of Scrabo Hill. The Tower provides a fascinating series of interpretative displays about the surrounding countryside and the viewing platform boasts spectacular views over Strangford Lough and Co. Down. The park provides walks through fine beech and hazel woodlands and the unique sandstone quarries display evidence of volcanic activity as well as being breeding sites for peregrine falcons.

Times: ✳ Open end Mar-mid Sep, Sat-Thu 10.30-6.

Facilities: ▣ shop ✖

EXPLORIS AQUARIUM

The Rope Walk, Castle St BT22 1NZ

➲ (A20 or A2 or A25 to Strangford Ferry Service)

☎ 028 4272 8062 ▤ 028 4272 8396

e-mail: info@ards-council.gov.uk

Exploris Aquarium is Northern Ireland's only public aquarium and now includes a seal sanctuary. Situated in Portaferry on the shores of Strangford Lough it houses some of Europe's finest displays. The Open Sea Tank holds 250 tonnes of sea water, and the Shoaling Ring, where visitors are surrounded by hundreds of fish, is a tank 6m in diameter. The complex includes a park with duck pond, picnic area, children's playground, caravan site, woodland and bowling green.

Times: ✳ Open all year, Mon-Fri 10-6, Sat 11-6, Sun 1-6. (Sep-Feb closing 1 hr earlier). Facilities: ▣ ▆ & (2 lifts within complex) toilets for disabled shop ✖ (ex guide dogs) ▬

ROWALLANE GARDEN

BT24 7LH

➲ (1m S of Saintfield on A7)

☎ 028 9751 0131 ▤ 028 9751 1242

e-mail: rowallane@nationaltrust.org.uk

Beautiful and exotic 52-acre gardens, started by the Rev John Moore in 1860, containing exquisite plants from all over the world. They are particularly noted for their rhododendrons and azaleas and for the wonderful floral displays in spring and summer.

Times: ✳ Open Oct-Apr, 10-4; May-Sep, 10-8. Closed Dec 24-1 Jan.

Facilities: ▣ ▆ & (parking facilities, manual wheelchairs, scented plants) toilets for disabled ✖ ⅋

STRANGFORD   Map 01 D5

AUDLEY'S CASTLE
➲ (1.5m W by shore of Strangford Lough)
☎ 028 9023 0560   ▤ 028 9031 0288
Fifteenth-century tower house on Strangford Lough which offers lovely views from its top floor. The internal fittings are complete.
Times: ✱ Open Apr-Sep, daily 10-7. **Facilities:** ▣ ✸

CASTLE WARD
BT30 7LS
➲ (0.5m W of Strangford on A25)
☎ 028 4488 1204   ▤ 028 4488 1729
e-mail: castleward@nationaltrust.org.uk
The curious diversity of styles in this house is due to the fact that its owner and his wife could never agree; so classical themes and a more elaborate Gothic look were both incorporated. The servants' living quarters are reached by an underground passage. Gardens, complete with a small lake and classical summerhouse, are richly planted and especially beautiful in spring.
Times: ✱ Ground daily 10-4 (8 May-Sep). House & Wildlife Centre; 15 Mar-Apr wknds, BH/PH 12-6; May wknds 12-6, Mon, Wed & Fri 1-6; Jun-Aug, daily noon-6 (Jun wkdays from 1); Sep-Oct wknds 12-6
Facilities: ▣ (charged) ▰ ঙ (wheelchair available, may be driven to house, Braille) toilets for disabled shop ৬ ≡

STRANGFORD CASTLE
☎ 028 9023 5000   ▤ 028 9031 0288
A three-storey tower house built in the 16th century, overlooking the small double harbour of Strangford.
Times: ✱ Open all reasonable times. **Facilities:** ✸

CO FERMANAGH

BELLEEK   Map 01 B5

BELLEEK POTTERY
3 Main St BT93 3FY
➲ (Take A46 from Ennisuilla to Belleek. Pottery at entrance to village)
☎ 028 6865 9300   ▤ 028 6865 8625
e-mail: visitorcentre@belleek.ie
Known worldwide for its fine Parian china, Ireland's oldest pottery was started in 1857 by the Caldwell family. Meet the craftspeople at work whilst touring the Pottery and visit the museum, which has exhibits dating back over 140 years.
Times: Open all year, Apr-Sep Mon-Fri 9-6, Sat 10-6 & Sun 2-6; Jul & Aug Sun 11-6; Oct Mon-Fri 9-5.30. (Closed wknds except Oct, Sat 10-5.30 & Sun 2-6,) Jan, 17 Mar & Xmas) **Fee:** Prices not confirmed for 2005 **Facilities:** ▣ ✗ ঙ (2 wheelchairs) toilets for disabled shop ✸ (ex guide dogs) ≡

CASTLE ARCHDALE BAY   Map 01 C5

WHITE ISLAND CHURCH
➲ (in Castle Archdale Bay; ferry from marina)
☎ 028 9023 5000   ▤ 028 9031 0288
Lined up on the far wall of a small, roofless 12th-century church are eight uncanny carved-stone figures. Part Christian and part pagan in appearance, their significance has been the subject of great debate. The church ruins sit on an early monastic site.
Times: ✱ Open Jul-Aug, Tue-Sat 10-7, Sun 2-7. **Facilities:** ▣ ✸ ⛟

DERRYGONNELLY   Map 01 C5

TULLY CASTLE
➲ (3m N, on W shore of Lower Lough Erne)
☎ 028 9054 6552
Extensive ruins of a Scottish-style stronghouse with enclosing bawn overlooking Lough Erne. Built by Sir John Hume in the early 1600s, the castle was destroyed, and most of the occupants slaughtered, by the Maguires in the 1641 Rising. There is a replica of a 17th-century garden in the bawn.
Times: ✱ Open Jul & Aug, Wed-Sun, 10-6. **Facilities:** ▣ ঙ ✸

ENNISKILLEN   Map 01 C5

CASTLE COOLE
BT74 6JY
➲ (On A4, 1.5m from Enniskillen, towards Belfast)
☎ 028 6632 2690   ▤ 028 6632 5665
e-mail: castlecoole@nationaltrust.org.uk
No expense was spared in the building of this mansion. James Wyatt was the architect, the lovely plasterwork ceilings were by Joseph Rose, and the chimneypieces the work of Richard Westmacott. Vast amounts of Portland stone were specially imported, together with an Italian expert in stonework. The house is filled with beautiful Regency furniture.
Times: Grounds, Oct-Mar, daily 10-4; Apr-Sep, daily 10-8. House: 12 Mar-May, wknds & PHs/BHs 12-6; Jun, Wed-Mon 1-6; Jul-Aug daily 12-6; Sep wknds 12-6; 1-9 Oct wknds 12-5 **Fee:** Grounds Free. House Tour £4.20 (ch £2.10). Family ticket £10.50. Group £3.50 (group outside normal hours £4.50). **Facilities:** ▣ ▰ ঙ (may be driven to house, large print guide) toilets for disabled shop ✸ (ex in park & guide dogs) ৬ ≡

ENNISKILLEN CASTLE
BT74 7HL
☎ 028 6632 2711
Overlooking Lough Erne, this castle, a three-storey keep surrounded by massive stone-built barracks and with a turreted fairytale 17th-century water gate, now houses two museums and a heritage centre. In the castle keep is a small museum displaying Royal Enniskillen Fusiliers regimental exhibits, while the other rooms contain the Fermanagh County Museum's collection of local antiquities.
Times: ✱ Open all year Mon 2-5, Tue-Fri 10-5 (closed 1-2, Oct-Apr), Sat 2-5 May-Aug, Sun 2-5 Jul-Aug, all day BHs. **Facilities:** ▣ ঙ shop ✸

FLORENCE COURT
BT92 1DB
➲ (8 miles SW of Enniskillen via A4 and then A32 to Swanlibar, well signposted)
☎ 028 6634 8249   ▤ 028 6634 8873
e-mail: florencecourt@nationaltrust.org.uk
An 18th-century mansion overlooking wild and beautiful scenery towards the Mountains of Cuilcagh. The interior of the house, particularly noted for its flamboyant rococo plasterwork, was gutted by fire in 1955, but has been restored. There are pleasure grounds with an Ice House, Summer House, Water Powered Sawmill and also a walled garden.
Times: Grounds daily. Grounds, Oct-Mar 10-4; Apr-Sep 10-8. House: 12 Mar-May, wknds & BHs 12-6. Jun, Mon-Fri (ex Tue) 1-6, wknds 12-6; Jul-Aug, Daily 12-6. Sep, wknds 12-6; 1-9 Oct, wknds 1-5
Fee: Grounds: Car £3, Minibus £15, Coach £20, motorbike £1.50. House Tour: £4 (ch £2) Family £10. Groups £3.50 (outside hours £4.50 each) **Facilities:** ▣ (charged) ▰ ✗ ঙ (electric wheelchair available & wheelchair path, Braille) toilets for disabled shop ৬ ≡

MARBLE ARCH CAVES
Marlbank Scenic Loop BT92 1EW
➲ (off A4 Enniskillen-Sligo road)
☎ 028 6634 8855 📠 028 6634 8928
e-mail: mac@fermanagh.gov.uk
One of Europe's finest cave systems, under the Mountains of Cuilcagh. Visitors are given a tour of a wonderland of stalagmites, stalactites and underground rivers and lakes, starting with a boat trip on the lower lake. The streams, which feed the caves, flow down into the mountain then emerge at Marble Arch, a 30ft detached limestone bridge. The geological, historical and economic benefits of Marble Arch Caves and Cuilcagh Mountain Park were recognised on an international scale when they were jointly awarded the title of European Geopark.
Times: Open late Mar-Sep. From 10am daily. **Fee:** £6 (ch £3, student oap £4). Family ticket £14. **Facilities:** 🅿 💷 ♿ toilets for disabled shop ✖ (ex guide dogs) ➡

MONEA CASTLE
➲ (6m NW)
☎ 028 9023 5000 📠 028 9031 0288
A fine example of a plantation castle still with much of its enclosing bawn wall intact, built around 1618. Of particular interest is the castle's stone corbelling - the Scottish method of giving additional support to turrets.
Times: Open at any reasonable time. **Facilities:** 🅿 ♿

THE SHEELIN IRISH LACE MUSEUM
Ballanaleck BT92 2BA
➲ (from Enniskillen take A4 onto A509. Thatched Sheelin restaurant on left after 3m, museum in restaurant car park)
☎ 028 6634 8052 📠 028 6634 8200
e-mail: infoirishlacemuseum.com
The Irish Lace Museum has the largest and most comprehensive display of antique lace anywhere in Ireland. There are around 400 exhibits, representing the five main types of Irish lace: Inishmacsaint Needlelace, Crochet, Limerick, Carrickmacross, and Youghal Needlelace. The history of the Irish lace-making industry is described, and antique items can be bought in the museum shop.
Times: Open Mon-Sat 10-6. **Fee:** ✱ £2.50 (ch under 14 £1). Party 15+ £1.50 each **Facilities:** 🅿 ✖ licensed ♿ (toilets for disabled in restaurant) shop ✖ (ex guide dogs) ➡

LISNASKEA Map 01 C5
CASTLE BALFOUR
☎ 028 9023 5000 📠 028 9031 0288
Dating from 1618 and refortified in 1652, this is a T-plan house with vaulted rooms. Badly burnt in the early 1800s, this house has remained in ruins.
Times: Open at all times. **Facilities:** 🅿 ♿

NEWTOWNBUTLER Map 01 C5
CROM ESTATE
BT92 8AP
➲ (3m from A34, well signed from Newtownbutler)
☎ 028 6773 8118 6773 8174
📠 028 6773 8118
e-mail: crom@nationaltrust.org.uk
Featuring 2,000 acres of woodland, parkland and wetland, the Crom Estate is one of Northern Ireland's most important conservation areas. Nature trails are signposted through
continued

woodlands to the ruins of the old castle, and past the old boat house and picturesque summer house. Day tickets for pike fishing and boat hire are available from the Visitor Centre.
Times: Grounds: 12 Mar-Jun, daily 10-6; Jul-Aug, daily 10-8; Sep, daily 10-6; Oct, wknds 12-6. Visitor centre: 15 Mar-24 Apr, wknds & BH 10-6; May-Sep, daily 10-6; 1-9 Oct, wknds 1-5. **Fee:** car £4.70, boat £4.70, minibus £13, coach £16.70, motorbike £2 **Facilities:** 🅿 (charged) 💷 ♿ (adapted picnic bench & holiday cottage) toilets for disabled shop ✖ ➡

CO LONDONDERRY

COLERAINE Map 01 C6
HEZLETT HOUSE
107 Sea Rd, Castlerock BT51 4TW
➲ (5m W on Coleraine/Downhill coast road 1m from Castlerock)
☎ 028 7084 8728 📠 028 7084 8728 **2 for 1**
e-mail: hezletthouse@nationaltrust.org.uk
A low, thatched cottage built around 1690 with an interesting cruck truss roof, constructed by using pairs of curved timbers to form arches and infilling around this frame with clay, rubble and other locally available materials.
Times: Open Jun-Aug, please contact for opening times 028 7084 8728 **Fee:** £3.70 (ch £2.20). Family ticket £9.60. Group £3.10 each (ouside normal hours £4.50 each). Please contact office for more details. **Facilities:** 🅿 ♿ (parking) toilets for disabled ✖ (ex in gardens on lead) ➡

MOUNT SANDEL
➲ (1.25m SSE)
☎ 028 9023 0560 📠 028 9031 0288
This 200ft oval mound overlooking the River Bann is believed to have been fortified in the Iron Age. Nearby is the earliest known inhabited place in Ireland, where post holes and hearths of wooden dwellings, and flint implements dating back to 6650BC have been found. The fort was a stronghold of de Courcy in the late 12th century and was refortified for artillery in the 17th century.
Times: Open at all times. **Facilities:** 🅿 ♿

DOWNHILL Map 01 C6
MUSSENDEN TEMPLE BISHOP'S GATE AND BLACK GLEN **FREE**
Mussenden Rd BT51 4RP
➲ (1m W of Castlerock off A2, 6m from Coleraine)
☎ 028 7084 8728 📠 028 7084 8728
e-mail: downhillcastle@nationaltrust.org.uk
Spectacularly placed on a cliff edge overlooking the Atlantic, this perfect 18th-century rotunda was modelled on the Temple of Vesta at Tivoli. Visitors entering by the Bishop's Gate can enjoy a beautiful glen walk up to the headland where the temple stands. If you enjoy open windswept walks with views that stretch over the whole of the north coast of Ireland, then you must visit Downhill.
Times: Grounds Open, all year, dawn-dusk. Temple, 12 Mar-May wknds & BH 11-6; Jun, daily, 11-6; Jul-Aug, daily, 11-7.30; Sep wknds 11-6; Oct, wknds, 11-5. **Facilities:** 🅿 (charged) ♿ toilets for disabled ➡

DUNGIVEN   Map 01 C5

BANAGHER CHURCH
➲ (2m SW)
☎ 028 9023 5000   ▤ 028 9031 0288
This church was founded by St Muiredach O'Heney in 1100 and altered in later centuries. Today impressive ruins remain. The nave is the oldest part and the square-headed lintelled west door is particularly impressive. Just outside, the perfect miniature stone house, complete with pitched roof and the sculpted figures of a saint at the doorway, is believed to be the tomb of St Muiredach. The saint was said to have endowed his large family with the power of bringing good luck. All they had to do was to sprinkle whoever or whatever needed luck with sand taken from the base of the saint's tomb.
Times: Open at all times. **Facilities:** �P &

DUNGIVEN PRIORY
➲ (SE of town overlooking River Roe)
☎ 028 9023 5000   ▤ 028 9031 0288
Up until the 17th century Dungiven was the stronghold of the O'Cahan chiefs, and the Augustinian priory, of which extensive ruins remain, was founded by the O'Cahans around 1150. The church, which was altered many times in later centuries, contains one of Northern Ireland's finest medieval tombs. It is the tomb of Cooey na Gall O'Cahan who died in 1385. His sculpted effigy, dressed in Irish armour, lies under a stonework canopy. Below are six kilted warriors.
Times: Open - Church at all times, chancel only when caretaker available. Check at house at end of lane. **Facilities:** �P &

LIMAVADY   Map 01 C6

ROUGH FORT
➲ (1m W off A2)
☎ 028 7084 8728   ▤ 028 7084 8728
e-mail: **downhillcastle@nationaltrust.org.uk**
Early Christian rath picturesquely surrounded by pine and beech trees, making it a significant landscape feature. The Rough Fort is one of the best examples of an earthwork ring fort in Ireland.
Times: Open at all times. **Facilities:** 🚌 ❦

LONDONDERRY   Map 01 C5

CITY WALLS
☎ 028 9023 5000   ▤ 028 9031 0288
The finest and most complete city walls to be found in Ireland. The walls, 20-25ft high, are mounted with ancient cannon, and date back to the 17th century. The walled city is a conservation area with many fine buildings. Visitors can walk round the city ramparts - a circuit of one mile.
Times: Open all times. **Facilities:** �P (charged) &

FOYLE VALLEY RAILWAY MUSEUM
Foyle Rd BT48 6SQ
☎ 028 7126 5234   ▤ 028 7137 7633
A collection of relics from the four railway companies which served Londonderry are displayed at the Foyle Valley Railway Heritage Centre. Steam locomotives, diesel railcars and all the paraphernalia of a station can be seen and the Railway Gallery tells the story of the railways. Travel in the historic County Donegal railcars for a trip to the historic mill.
Times: ✱ Open all year, Apr-Sep Mon-Sat 10-5, Sun 2-5; Oct-Mar Mon-Sat 10-4. **Facilities:** �P & toilets for disabled shop garden centre ✖

TOWER MUSEUM
Union Hall Place BT48 6LU
➲ (directly behind city wall, facing guildhall)
☎ 028 7137 2411   ▤ 028 7137 7633
e-mail: **towermuseum@dnet.co.uk**
This exhibition recounts the history of Londonderry from pre-historic times to the present day using real artefacts, theatrical displays and eleven audio-visual programmes showing the spread of Irish monasticism, the famous Siege of Derry and the road to the partition of Ireland.
Times: ✱ Open all year, Sep-Jun Tue-Sat 10-5. Jul-Aug Mon-Sat 10-5, Sun 2-5. Also open all BH Mons. **Facilities:** �P (300 yds) & toilets for disabled shop ✖ (ex guide dogs) ■

MAGHERA   Map 01 C5

MAGHERA CHURCH
➲ (E approach to the town)
☎ 028 9023 5000   ▤ 028 9031 0288
Important 6th-century monastery founded by St Lurach, later a bishop's see and finally a parish church. This much-altered church has a magnificently decorated 12th-century west door. A cross-carved stone to the west of the church is supposed to be the grave of the founder.
Times: Key from Leisure Centre. **Facilities:** ▢ &

MONEYMORE   Map 01 C5

SPRINGHILL
BT45 7NQ
➲ (1m from Moneymore on B18 to Coagh)
☎ 028 8674 8210 & 8674 7927
▤ 028 8674 8210
e-mail: **springhill@nationaltrust.org.uk**
This pleasingly symmetrical manor house dates back to the 17th century. Today much of the family furniture, books and bric-a-brac have been retained. Outside, the laundry, stables, brewhouse, and old dovecote make interesting viewing, as does the excellent costume museum.
Times: ✱ Open 15 Mar-Jun, wknds & BH 2-6; Jul-Aug, daily 2-6; Sep, wknds only 2-6. **Facilities:** ▢ ▣ & (photograph album of 1st floor, wheelchair, scented plants) toilets for disabled shop ❦

CO TYRONE

ARDBOE   Map 01 C5

ARDBOE CROSS
➲ (off B73)
☎ 028 9023 5000   ▤ 028 9031 0288
Situated at Ardboe Point, on the western shore of Lough Neagh, is the best example of a high cross to be found in Northern Ireland. Marking the site of an ancient monastery, the cross has 22 sculpted panels, many recognisably biblical, including Adam and Eve and the Last Judgment. It stands over 18ft high and dates back to the 10th century. It is still the rallying place of the annual Lammas, but praying at the cross and washing in the lake has been replaced by traditional music-making, singing and selling of local produce. The tradition of 'cross reading' or interpreting the pictures on the cross, is an honour passed from generation to generation among the men of the village.
Times: Open at all times. **Facilities:** ▢ &

BALLYGAWLEY
Map 01 C5

U S GRANT ANCESTRAL HOMESTEAD & VISITOR CENTRE
Dergenagh Rd BT70 1TW
➲ (off A4, 2m on Dergenagh road, signed)
☎ 028 8555 7133 📖 028 8555 7133
e-mail: killymaddy@dstbc.org
Ancestral homestead of Ulysses S Grant, 18th President of the United States of America. The homestead and farmyard have been restored to the style and appearance of a mid-19th-century Irish smallholding. There are many amenities including a children's play area, purpose built barbecue and picnic tables and butterfly garden.
Times: Open by appointment only **Fee:** £1.50 (ch & concessions 0.75p). **Facilities:** 🅿 ⛐ (wide doorway to audio-visual area/entrances/exits) ✖ (ex guide dogs)

BEAGHMORE
Map 01 C5

BEAGHMORE STONE CIRCLES AND ALIGNMENTS
☎ 028 9023 5000 📖 028 9031 0288
Discovered in the 1930s, these impressive, ritualistic stones have been dated back to the early Bronze, and maybe even Neolithic Ages. There are three pairs of stone circles, one single circle, stone rows or alignments and cairns, which range in height from one to four feet. This is an area littered with historic monuments, many discovered by people cutting turf.
Times: Open at all times. **Facilities:** 🅿 ⛐

BENBURB
Map 01 C5

BENBURB CASTLE
☎ 028 9023 5000 📖 028 9031 0288
The castle ruins - three towers and massive walls - are dramatically placed on a cliff-edge 120ft above the River Blackwater. The northwest tower is now restored and has dizzy cliff-edge views. The castle, built by Sir Richard Wingfield around 1615, is actually situated in the grounds of the Servite Priory. There are attractive walks down to the river.
Times: Castle grounds open at all times. Special arrangements, made in advance, necessary for access to flanker tower. **Facilities:** 🅿 ⛐ ✖

CASTLECAULFIELD
Map 01 C5

CASTLE CAULFIELD
☎ 028 9023 5000 📖 028 9031 0288
Sir Toby Caulfield, an Oxfordshire knight and ancestor of the Earls of Charlemont, built this manor house in 1619 on the site of an ancient fort. It was badly burnt in 1641, repaired and lived in by the Caulfield/Charlemont family until 1670. It boasts the rare distinction of having had Saint Oliver Plunkett and John Wesley preach in its grounds. Some fragments of the castle are re-used in the fine, large 17th-century parish church.
Times: Open at all times. **Facilities:** 🅿 ⛐

If an attraction name appears in *italics*, details have not been confirmed for 2005.

COOKSTOWN
Map 01 C5

TULLAGHOGE FORT
➲ (2m S)
☎ 028 9023 5000 📖 028 9031 0288
This large hilltop earthwork, planted with trees, was once the headquarters of the O'Hagans, Chief Justices of the old kingdom of Tyrone. Between the 12th and 16th centuries the O'Neill Chiefs of Ulster were also crowned here - the King Elect was seated on a stone inauguration chair, new sandals were placed on his feet and he was then anointed and crowned. The last such ceremony was held here in the 1590s; in 1600 the stone throne was destroyed by order of Lord Mountjoy.
Times: Open at all times. **Facilities:** 🅿

WELLBROOK BEETLING MILL
20 Wellbrook Rd, Corkhill BT80 9RY
➲ (4m W, 0.5m off A505)
☎ 028 8674 8210 & 8675 1735
e-mail: wellbrook@nationaltrust.org.uk
This 18th-century water-powered linen mill was used for bleaching and, until 1961, for finishing Irish linen. Beetling was the name given to the final process in linen making, when the material was beaten by 30 or so hammers (beetles) to achieve a smooth and slightly shiny finish.
Times: ✱ Open 15 Mar-Jun wknds & BHs, daily 12-6; Jul-Aug daily 12-6; Sep, wknds only 12-6. **Fee:** Prices not confirmed for 2005 **Facilities:** 🅿 ⛐ toilets for disabled shop ⛐

DUNGANNON
Map 01 C5

TYRONE CRYSTAL VISITOR CENTRE
Tyrone Crystal, Killybrackey BT71 6TT
➲ (M1 junct 14/A45 to T-junct, turn left towards Dungannon, Tyrone Crystal 2.5m on left. Signed)
☎ 028 8772 5335 📖 028 8772 6260 **2 for 1**
e-mail: info@tyronecrystal.com
Crystal making in Tyrone is a comparatively modern enterprise, dating its beginnings from the days of Benjamin Edwards in the 1770s. Tyrone Crystal is hand-cut, and visitors can see this craft in action on guided tours of the factory. The spacious visitor centre and facilities contribute to a fascinating insight into the history and heritage of this industry.
Times: Visitor Centre Mon-Sat 9-5, Sun 1-5 (seasonal); Tour times Mon-Fri 11, 12, 2, 3. Sat tours prior booking only **Fee:** Prices not confirmed for 2005 **Facilities:** 🅿 ✖ ⛐ (Disabled parking spaces) toilets for disabled shop ✖ (ex guide dogs) ◼

NEWTOWNSTEWART
Map 01 C5

HARRY AVERY'S CASTLE
➲ (0.75m SW)
☎ 028 9023 5000 📖 028 9031 0288
The hilltop ruins of a Gaelic stone castle, built around the 14th century by one of the O'Neill chiefs, are the remains of the oldest surviving Irish-built castle in the north. Only the great twin towers of the gatehouse are left. A stairway enables the public to gain access to one of these.
Times: Open at all times. **Facilities:** ✖ 🚌

ULSTER AMERICAN FOLK PARK
BT78 5QY
➲ (5m NW Omagh on the NW passage route)
☎ 028 8224 3292   🖹 028 8224 2241   **2 for 1**
e-mail: info@uafp.co.uk
An outdoor museum that traces the history of Ulster's links with America and the emigration of Ulster residents to the US during the 18th and 19th centuries. The 70-acre site is divided into two parts - Old World and New World. There are demonstrations of Old and New World crafts, and a visitor centre, with exhibitions and audio-visual presentations. The Centre for Emigration Studies is based here, with a research library and emigration database - please ring for details.
Times: Open Etr-Sep, daily 10.30-6, Sun & BH 11-6.30; Oct-Etr Mon-Fri 10.30-5. Last admission 1hr 30mins before closing. Fee: £4 (ch & pen £2.50). Family ticket £10. Children under 5yrs free. Facilities: 🅿 💺 ✘ ♿ toilets for disabled shop 🐕 (ex guide dogs) 📷

ULSTER HISTORY PARK
Cullion BT79 7SU
➲ (7m on B48)
☎ 028 8164 8188   🖹 028 8164 8011
e-mail: uhp@omagh.gov.uk
The story of settlement in Ireland, told with the aid of full-scale models of the houses and monuments built through the ages. Exhibitions and audio-visual presentations expand the theme.
Times: ✱ Open all year, Jul-Aug daily 10-6.30; Apr-Jun & Sep, daily 10-5.30; Oct-Mar, Mon-Fri 10-5. Facilities: 🅿 💺 ♿ toilets for disabled shop 🐕 (ex guide dogs) 📷

MOUNTJOY CASTLE
Magheralamfield
➲ (3m SE, off B161)
☎ 028 9023 5000   🖹 028 9031 0288
Ruins of an early 17th-century brick and stone fort, with four rectangular towers, overlooking Lough Neagh. The fort was built for Lord Deputy Mountjoy during his campaign against Hugh O'Neill, Earl of Tyrone. It was captured and re-captured by the Irish and English during the 17th century and was also used by the armies of James II and William III.
Times: Open at all times. Facilities: 🅿

GRAY'S PRINTING PRESS
49 Main St BT82 8AU
➲ (in centre of Strabane)
☎ 028 7188 4094
Strabane was once an important printing and book-publishing centre, the only relic of this is a small shop in Main Street which now houses a museum illustrating the history of Strabane. The Print Museum, in a separate building, contains three 19th-century presses and shows the development of printing techniques over 150 years.
Times: ✱ Open Apr-Sep, Tue-Sat 2-5. Facilities: 🅿 (100yds) ♿ toilets for disabled 🐕 (ex guide dogs) 🐾

Above: Inch Abbey, Downpatrick, Co. Down

REPUBLIC OF IRELAND

EVENTS & FESTIVALS

January
1st Lord Mayor's New Year's
Day Parade, Dublin

March
16th-21st St Patrick's Festival, Dublin
tbc Feis Ceoil (competitive classical music
festival), Dublin

April
13th-18th Pan Celtic International Festival,
Kilkenny Castle
20th-22nd Fresh Film Festival, Limerick,
young people's films and workshops
28th-1st May Cork International Choral
Festival, various venues, Co Cork
tbc Dublin Film Festival, various venues

May
23rd-30th Fleadh Nua, Ennis, Co Clare
tbc Listowel Writers Week, Listowel, St John's
Arts & Heritage Centre, Listowel, Co Kerry

June
2nd-6th The Cat Laughs, international
comedy festival, various venues, Kilkenny
16th Bloomsday (James Joyce Festival), Dublin
tbc Enniscorthy Strawberry Festival,
Enniscorthy, Co Wexford

July
11th-24th Galway International Arts Festival,
various venues, Co Galway
29th-1st Aug Greystones Arts Festival, North
Wicklow

August
3rd-7th Dublin Horse Show,
Ballsbridge, Dublin
11th-14th Waterford Sings Festival
18th Connemara Pony Show, Showgrounds,
Clifden, Co Galway
tbc Fleadh Cheoil na hEireann, Enniscorthy
(biggest annual festival of Irish traditional
music in the world)
tbc Rose of Tralee Festival, Tralee

September
22nd-25th Galway International Oyster
Festival, Galway City, Co Galway
tbc Waterford International Festival of Light
Opera, Theatre Royal, Waterford, Co
Waterford

October
28th-31st Cork Jazz Festival, 75 venues
throughout the city
tbc Dublin Theatre Festival, various venues
(provisional)
tbc Wexford Festival Opera, Theatre Royal,
High Street, Wexford, Co Wexford

Top: Trinity College, Dublin   *Above: Custom House at dusk, Dublin*

CO CLARE

BALLYVAUGHAN Map 01 B3

AILLWEE CAVE
➲ (3m S of Ballyvaughan. Signed from Galway and Ennis)
☎ 065 7077036 ▯ 065 7077107
e-mail: fiona@aillweecave.ie
An underground network of caves beneath the world famous Burren. Guided tours take you through large caverns, over bridged chasms and alongside thunderous waterfalls. There is a craftshop, a dairy where cheese is made, a speciality food shop and a tearoom. Santa uses the cave as a workshop around Christmas time, while Easter sees a massive egg hunt in the woods. In addition, a garden centre has opened here in the last year.
Times: Open all year from 10am (mornings only in Dec). **Fee:** €9 (ch €5, pen €7). Family ticket €22-€26 **Facilities:** ▯ ▬ ✗ licensed ⅂ toilets for disabled shop garden centre ✈ (ex guide dogs) ⇥

BUNRATTY Map 01 B3

BUNRATTY CASTLE & FOLK PARK
➲ (8m from Limerick city on N18 towards Ennis)
☎ 061 360788 ▯ 061 361020
e-mail: reservations@shannondev.ie
Magnificent Bunratty Castle was built around 1425. The restored castle contains mainly 15th and 16th century furnishings and tapestries. Within its grounds is Bunratty Folk Park where 19th-century Irish life is tellingly recreated. Rural farmhouses, a village street and Bunratty House with its formal Regency gardens are recreated and furnished, as they would have appeared at the time.
Times: Open all year, daily 9-5.30, 9.30 Apr-May & Sep-Oct (last admission 4.15pm). Folk Park also open Jun-Aug 9-6 (last admission 5.15pm). Last admission to Castle 4pm all year. (Closed Good Fri & 24-26 Dec.) **Fee:** ✱ Castle € 10.50 (ch€5.95, pen €6.95 & student €8.50). **Facilities:** ▯ ▬ ✗ licensed ⅂ toilets for disabled shop ⇥

LISCANNOR Map 01 B3

CLIFFS OF MOHER VISITORS CENTRE
➲ (6m NW of Lahinch)
☎ 065 7081 565 ▯ 061 361020
e-mail: reservations@shannondev.ie
The Cliffs of Moher stand as a giant natural rampart against the aggressive might of the Atlantic Ocean, rising in places to 700ft, and stretch for almost 5 miles. O'Brien's Tower was built in the early 19th century as a viewing point for tourists on the highest point. There is a visitor centre with tourist information.
Times: Open Visitor Centre all year, 9.30-5.30; Jun-Aug 9-7. (Visitor centre closed 21-27 Dec.) O'Briens Tower open Mar-Oct 9.30-5.30 (weather permitting). **Fee:** ✱ O'Briens Tower € 1.50 (ch € 0.75). **Facilities:** ▯ (charged) ▬ ⅂ toilets for disabled shop ✈ (ex in grounds) ⇥

QUIN Map 01 B3

CRAGGAUNOWEN THE LIVING PAST EXPERIENCE
➲ (signed from N18 (Limerick to Galway road), off R462 from Cratloe and R469 from Ennis)
☎ 061 360788 ▯ 061 361020
e-mail: reservations@shannondev.ie
Contains a full-scale reconstruction of a crannog, a Bronze Age lake dwelling. The project includes a reconstructed ring fort and replicas of furniture, tools and utensils. Also on display is the *Brendan*, a replica of the leather boat used by St Brendan the Navigator in the 6th century. The boat was sailed across the Atlantic Ocean in 1976 and 1977.
Times: Open daily mid Apr-mid Oct, daily 10-6 (last admission 5pm).
Fee: ✱ €7 (ch € 4.20, pen & students € 5.60). **Facilities:** ▯ ▬ ⅂ toilets for disabled shop ⇥

CO CORK

BLARNEY Map 01 B2

BLARNEY CASTLE & ROCK CLOSE
➲ (5m from Cork on main road towards Limerick)
☎ 021 4385252 ▯ 021 4381518
e-mail: info@blarneyc.iol.ie
The site of the famous Blarney Stone, known the world over for the eloquence it is said to impart to those who kiss it. The stone is in the upper tower of the castle, and, held by your feet, you must lean backwards down the inside of the battlements in order to receive 'the gift of the gab'.
Times: Open - Blarney Castle & Rock Close, Jun-Aug Mon-Sat 9-7.30; May Mon-Sat 9-7; Sep Mon-Sat 9-6.30; Apr & Oct Mon-Sat 9-sunset; Summer Sun 9.30-5.30; Winter Sun 9.30-sunset. Blarney House & Gardens Jun-mid Sep Mon-Sat noon-6. **Fee:** ✱ Blarney Castle & Rock Close € 5.50 (ch € 2, pen & students € 4). Family ticket (2ad+2 ch) € 11.50 **Facilities:** ▯ ⅂ shop ✈ (ex guide dogs)

CARRIGTWOHILL (CARRIGTOHILL) Map 01 B2

FOTA ARBORETUM & GARDENS
Fota Estate
➲ (14km from Cork on Cobh road)
☎ 021 4812728 ▯ 021 4812728
Fota Arboretum contains an extensive collection of trees and shrubs extending over an area of approx 27 acres and includes features such as an ornamental pond and Italian walled gardens. The collection includes many tender plants that could not be grown at inland locations with many examples of exotic plants from the Southern Hemisphere.
Times: ✱ Open 1st wknd Apr-Oct, daily, Mon-Sat 9-6 & Sun 11-6; Nov-Mar, daily, Mon-Sat 9-5, Sun 11-5. (Closed Xmas).
Facilities: ▯ (charged) ⅂ toilets for disabled

FOTA WILDLIFE PARK
Fota Estate
➲ (10km E of Cork City. Take Cobh road from N25, Cork - Waterford road)
☎ 021 4812678 📠 021 4812744
e-mail: info@fotawildlife.ie

Established with the primary aim of conservation, Fota has more than 90 species of exotic wildlife in open, natural surroundings. Many of the animals wander freely around the park. Giraffes, zebras, ostriches, antelope, cheetahs and a wide array of waterfowl are among the species here.
Times: ✱ Open all year 17 Mar-Sep daily, 10-6 (Sun 11-6) Oct-17 Mar wknds only. Last admission 5. **Facilities:** 🅿 (charged) ✗ ♿ (Ramps where required) toilets for disabled shop ✘ 🍴

CLONAKILTY Map 01 B2

WEST CORK MODEL VILLAGE RAILWAY
Inchydoney Rd
➲ (From Cork N71 West Cork left at junct for Inchydoney Island, signed at road junction. Village is on bay side of Clonakilty)
☎ 023 33224
e-mail: modelvillage@eircom.net

This miniature world depicts Irish towns as they were in the 1940s, with models of the West Cork Railway and various animated scenes. The tea room is set in authentic railway carriages that overlook picturesque Clonakilty Bay.
Times: Open Feb-Oct daily 11-5, Jul-Aug, daily, extended hours 10-6.
Fee: ✱ €6 (concessions €4.50). Family ticket €19, Party 12+.
Facilities: 🅿 🍴 ♿ toilets for disabled shop ✘ (ex guide dogs) 🍴

COBH Map 01 B2

THE QUEENTOWN STORY
Cobh Railway Station
➲ (Off N25, follow signs for Cobh. Centre is located at Deepwater Quay, adjacent to Train Station)
☎ 021 4813591 📠 021 4813595
e-mail: info@cobhheritage.com
A dramatic exhibition of the origins, history and legends of Cobh. Between 1848 and 1950 over 3 million Irish people were deported from Cobh on convict ships. Visitors can explore the conditions onboard these vessels and learn about the harbour's connections with the *Lusitania* and the *Titanic*.
Times: May-Nov 10-6. Last admission 5pm. Nov-May 10-5. Last admission 4pm. **Fee:** ✱ €5 (ch12 €2.50, pen & students €4). Family ticket €15.50 **Facilities:** 🅿 🍴 ✗ ♿ (fully wheelchair accessible, wide access) toilets for disabled shop ✘ (ex guide dogs) 🍴

CORK Map 01 B2

CORK CITY GAOL
Convent Av, Sundays Well
➲ (2km NW from Patrick St. off Sundays Well Rd)
☎ 021 4305022 📠 021 4307230
e-mail: corkgaol@indigo.ie
A restored 19th-century prison building. Furnished cells, lifelike characters and sound effects combine to allow visitors to experience day-to-day life for prisoners and gaoler. There is an audio-visual presentation of the social history of Cork City. Individual sound tours are available in a number of languages. A new permanent exhibition, the Radio Museum Experience, is located in the restored 1920s broadcasting studio, home to Cork's first radio station, 6CK. Unfortunately the 1st and 2nd floors are not accessible to wheelchair users.
Times: Open Mar-Oct, daily 9.30-6; Nov-Feb, daily 10-5. Last admission 1hr before closing. (Closed 23-28 Dec.) **Fee:** ✱ €6 (ch €3.50, concessions €5) Family ticket €15 **Facilities:** 🅿 (charged) ♿ (customer care policy - individual attention) toilets for disabled shop ✘ (ex guide dogs)

CORK PUBLIC MUSEUM
Fitzgerald Park, Mardyke
➲ (N of University College)
☎ 021 4270679 📠 021 4270931
e-mail: museum@corkcity.ie
Displays illustrating the history of the city are housed in this museum. The collections cover the economic, social and municipal history from the Mesolithic period. There are fine collections of Cork Silver and Glass and Youghal Needlepoint Lace.
Times: ✱ Open all year, Jun-Aug Mon-Fri 11-1 & 2.15-6, Sun 3-5; Sep-May Mon-Fri 11-1 & 2.15-5, Sun 3-5. (Closed Sat, BH wknds & PH)
Facilities: 🅿 (100 yds) shop ✘ (ex guide dogs)

An asterisk * indicates that opening times and prices are for 2004. Please contact the attraction for up-to-date information.

GLENGARRIFF   Map 01 B2

GARINISH ISLAND
➲ (1.5km boat trip from Glengarriff)
☎ 027 63040 🖷 027 63149
Ilnacullin is a small island of 37 acres known to horticulturists and lovers of trees and shurbs all around the world as an island garden of rare beauty. The gardens of Ilnacullin owe their existence to the creative partnership, some 80 years ago, of Annan Bryce, then owner of the island and Harold Peto, architect and garden designer.
Times: ✱ Open Mar & Oct, Mon-Sat 10-4.30, Sun 1-5; Apr, Mon-Sat 10-6.30, Sun 1-6.30; May, Jun & Sep, Mon-Sat 10-6.30, Sun 11-6.30; Jul & Aug, Mon-Sat 9.30-6.30, Sun 11-6.30. Last landing 1hr before closing. Charge made by boat operators. **Facilities:** ▣ ♿ (limited access) toilets for disabled

KINSALE   Map 01 B2

CHARLES FORT
➲ (3km from Kinsale)
☎ 021 4772263 🖷 021 4774347
e-mail: charlesfort@duchas.ie
Built as part of the fortifications of the Irish coast in the late 17th century, Charles Fort was named after King Charles II. After the Battle of the Boyne in 1690, Williamite forces attacked and successfully besieged Charles Fort and the nearby James Fort, both of which held out for King James. The Fort also played a role in the Napoleonic Wars and was made a National Monument in 1973.
Times: ✱ Open all year, mid Mar-Oct, daily 10-6; Nov-mid Mar, Sat-Sun 10-5, wkdays by arrangement. (Last admission 1hr before closing) **Facilities:** ℙ ▣ ♿ (lift) toilets for disabled ✸ (ex guide dogs)

DESMOND CASTLE
Cork St
➲ (R600 from Cork City to Kinsdale. From post office, take 1st left then right, opposite Regional Museum then left and right again, castle on left)
☎ 021 4774855
e-mail: desmondcastle@duchas.ie
Built by the Earl of Desmond around the beginning of the 16th century, this tower was originally a custom house, but has also served as an ordnance office, prison, workhouse, stable and meeting place for the Local Defence Force during World War II. In 1938 it was declared a National Monument and restored. The Castle now houses the International Museum of Wine.
Times: Open mid Apr-Oct, daily 10-5.45. **Fee:** ✱ €2.75, (ch & students €1.25, pen €2) Family €7 **Facilities:** ℙ (200mtrs parking discs required in town) ✸ (ex guide dogs)

MIDLETON   Map 01 C2

OLD MIDLETON DISTILLERY
➲ (at E end of main street on left. Well signed)
☎ 021 4613594 🖷 021 4613642
e-mail: reservations@omd.ie

A tour of the Old Midleton Distillery consists of a 15-minute audio/visual presentation, then a 35-minute guided tour of the Old Distillery and then back to the Jameson Bar for a whiskey tasting - mineral water is available for children. The guided tour and audio-visual aids are available in seven languages.
Times: Open Nov-Feb daily, tours 11.30, 2.30 & 4. Mar-Oct daily 10-6 (last tour 5). (Closed Good Fri & Xmas) **Fee:** ✱ €7 (ch €3). Family (2ad+3ch) €18. **Facilities:** ℙ ▣ ✗ licensed ♿ toilets for disabled shop ✸ (ex certain areas/guide dogs) ⬛

CO DONEGAL

BALLYSHANNON   Map 01 B5

THE WATER WHEELS
Abbey Assaroe
➲ (cross Abbey River on Rossnowlagh Rd, next turning left & follow signs)
☎ 071 9851580   **FREE**
Abbey Assaroe was founded by Cistercian Monks from Boyle Abbey in the late 12th century, who excelled in water engineering and canalised the river to turn water wheels for mechanical power. Two restored 12th-century mills, one is used as coffee shop and restaurant; the other houses a small museum related to the history of the Cistercians. Interesting walks in the vicinity.
Times: Open May-Oct, daily 10.30-6.30 **Facilities:** ℙ ▣ ✗ licensed ♿ toilets for disabled shop garden centre

DONEGAL   Map 01 B5

DONEGAL CASTLE
☎ 074 9722405 🖷 074 9722436
This restored 15th-century castle and adjoining 17th-century ruined English manor house contain exhibitions of Irish historical events. Guided tours are available.
Times: ✱ Open mid Mar-mid Oct, daily 9.30-6.30 (last admission 5.45). **Facilities:** ℙ ✸ (ex guide dogs)

Directions are provided by the attractions.

If an attraction name appears in *italics*, details have not been confirmed for 2005.

GLEBE HOUSE & GALLERY
Churchill
➲ (signed from Letterkenny on R251)
☎ 074 9137071 📄 074 9137521
This Regency house, set in beautiful woodland gardens along the shore of Lough Gartan, was given to the nation by artist Derek Hill, along with his art collection. The interior of the house is decorated with original wallpapers and textiles by William Morris.
Times: ✱ Open Etr & mid-end Apr, daily 11-6.30; mid May-Sep, Sat-Thu 11-6.30. (Last tour of house 1hr before closing).
Facilities: 🅿 ⬛ ♿ ✼ (ex guide dogs)

GLENVEAGH NATIONAL PARK & CASTLE
Churchill
➲ (left off N56 onto L77)
☎ 074 9137090 & 9137262 📄 074 9137072
e-mail: talchorn@duchas.ie
Over 40,000 acres of mountains, glens, lakes and woods. A Scottish-style castle is surrounded by one of the finest gardens in Ireland, contrasting with the rugged surroundings.
Times: Open daily St. Patrick's Day 17 Mar-!st Sun in Nov
Fee: ✱ Park: free, Castle €2.75 (ch & students €1.25, pen €2). Family ticket €7, group 20+ €2. **Facilities:** 🅿 ⬛ ✗ ♿ (visitor centre, gardens have paths) toilets for disabled shop

CAVANACOR HISTORIC HOUSE & ART GALLERY
Ballindrait
➲ (1.5m from town off N14 Strabane/Letterkenny road)
☎ 074 9141143 📄 074 9141143
Built in the early 1600s and commanding a view of the Clonleigh Valley and the River Deele, Cavanacor House is the ancestral home of James Knox Polk, 11th President of the USA (1845-1849). King James II dined under the sycamore tree in front of the house in 1689. There are over 10 acres of landscaped gardens and an old-fashioned walled garden. The Art Gallery will feature exhibitions of new work by national and international artists. Please ring for details.
Times: ✱ Open Etr & Jul-Aug Tue-Sat 12-6, Sun 2-6. Art gallery open all year **Facilities:** 🅿 ⬛ ✗ ♿ shop ◼

CO DUBLIN

ARDGILLAN CASTLE
➲ (Pass Airport & Swords rdbt, take R127 & follow signs, or follow signs from M1 past Dublin Airport)
☎ 01 8492212 📄 01 8492786
A large and elegant country manor house built in 1738, set in 194 acres of parkland, overlooking the sea and coast as far as the Mourne Mountains. There is a permanent exhibition of the 17th century 'Down Survey' maps and various temporary exhibitions. Tours of the Gardens (June, July and August) begin at 3.30pm every Thursday. Guided tours of the house are conducted daily.
Times: Open Apr-Sep, Tue-Sun & BHs 11-6 (daily Jul-Aug); Oct-Mar, Wed-Sun & BHs 11-4.30. (Closed 23 Dec-1 Jan). **Fee:** ✱ €5 (pen & students €3). Family ticket €10. **Facilities:** 🅿 ⬛ ♿ toilets for disabled shop ✼ (ex guide dogs)

NEWBRIDGE HOUSE AND TRADITIONAL FARM
Newbridge Demesne
☎ 01 8436534 & 8462184 📄 01 8462537
Newbridge House was designed by George Semple and built in 1737 for Charles Cobbe, Archbishop of Dublin. The house contains many splendidly refurbished rooms featuring plasterwork, furniture and paintings. Special events throughout the year include demonstrations of sheep shearing, weaving, dying, pottery and harness making.
Times: ✱ Open Apr-Sep Tue-Sat 10-5, Sun & PH 2-6; Oct-Mar Sat-Sun & PH 2-5. Parties at other times by arrangement. **Facilities:** 🅿 ⬛ shop ✼

THE CASINO
off Malahide Rd, Marino, Dublin 3
➲ (3m N of Dublin City, turn left off Fairview Strand up Malahide Rd, through junction with Griffith Ave. Turn left at Nazareth House, gates are on left)
☎ 01 8331618 📄 01 8332636
e-mail: casinomarino@duchias.ie
Designed in 1757 by Sir William Chambers as a pleasure house for James Caulfield, 1st Earl of Charlemont, The Casino is possibly one of the finest 18th-century neo-Classical buildings in Europe. Its name means "small house", but The Casino surprisingly contains 16 finely-decorated rooms.
Times: Open Jun-Sep, daily 10-6; May & Oct, daily 10-5; Jan-Apr, Nov & Dec, Sat & Sun. 12-4 and for group bookings. Last admission 45 mins before closing. **Fee:** ✱ €2.75 (ch & students €1.25, pen €2). Family ticket €7 **Facilities:** 🅿 ♿ ✼ (ex guide dogs)

THE CHESTER BEATTY LIBRARY
The Clock Tower Building, Dublin Castle
➲ (10 mins walk from Trinity College, up Dame St towards Christ Church Cathedral)
☎ 01 4070750 📄 01 4070760
e-mail: info@cbl.ie
The contents of this fascinating gallery was bequeathed to Ireland by its first honorary citizen, American mining engineer and collector, Sir Alfred Chester Beatty (1875-1968). The collection includes manuscripts, prints, icons, miniatures, and objets d'art of great importance from 2700BC to the present day. See illuminated copies of the Qur'an and the Bible, Egyptian papyrus texts, and Buddhist paintings.
Times: ✱ Open all year, May-Sep, Mon-Fri 10-5; Oct-Apr, Tue-Fri 10-5, Sat 11-5, Sun 1-5. (Closed BH). **Facilities:** 🅿 (5mins walk) ⬛ ✗ ♿ toilets for disabled shop ✼ (ex guide dogs)

CHRIST CHURCH CATHEDRAL
Christchurch Place
➲ (at the top end of Dame St)
☎ 01 6778099 📄 01 6798991
e-mail: welcome@cccdub.ie
Founded in 1030, the present building dates from 1180 with a major restoration in the 1870s. The crypt is the second largest medieval crypt in Britain or Ireland. There are daily services and choral services on Sundays and during the week.
Times: Open all year (ex St Stephens Day 28 Dec), Mon-Fri 9.45-5, Sat & Sun 10-5 **Fee:** €5 (unwaged €2.50) **Facilities:** 🅿 (100yds) ♿ (for access to crypt advance notice required) shop ✼ (ex guide dogs) ◼

DRIMNAGH CASTLE
Long Mile Rd, Drimnagh DL12
⮑ (Dame St, left at Christchurch Cathedral into Patrick St, right into Cork St, through Dolphins Barn up to Crumlin Rd, past Halfway House. 500yds on right)
☎ 01 4502530 & 4508927 📠 01 4508927
e-mail: drimnaghcastle@eircom.net
The last surviving medieval castle in Ireland with a flooded moat, Drimnagh dates back to the 13th century and was inhabited until 1954. The Castle consists of a restored Great Hall and medieval undercroft, a tall battlement tower and lookout posts, and other separate buildings including stables, an old coach house and a folly. One of the most attractive features of Drimnagh is the garden, a formal 17th-century layout with box hedges, yews and mop heads.
Times: Open Apr-Oct. Wed & Sun 12-5; Nov-Mar, Sun 2-5. Last tour 4. Other times by appointment. Large groups advisable to book
Fee: ✱ €4 (ch €2, pen & students €3.50). Groups 20+ €3 each
Facilities: 🅿 ㄅ (limited access gravel courtyard and garden steps) ✖ (ex guide dogs)

DUBLIN CASTLE
Dame St
☎ 01 6777129 📠 01 6797831
With two towers and a partial wall, this is the city's most outstanding legacy of the Middle Ages. Of interest are the Record Tower, state apartments, Church of the Most Holy Trinity and Heraldic Museum. The inauguration of the President of Ireland and related ceremonies are held in St. Patrick's Hall, an elegant state apartment.
Times: ✱ Open all year, Mon-Fri 10-5, Sat-Sun & BH 2-5. (Closed 24-26 Dec & Good Fri). **Facilities:** 🅿 ✖ ㄅ toilets for disabled

DUBLINIA
St Michael's Hill, Christ Church
☎ 01 6794611 📠 01 6797116
e-mail: info@dublins.ie
The story of medieval Dublin. Housed in the former Synod Hall beside Christ Church Cathedral and developed by the Medieval Trust, Dublinia recreates the period from the arrival of Strongbow and the Anglo-Normans in 1170 to the closure of the monasteries by Henry VIII in 1540.
Times: Open Apr-Sep 10-5; Oct-Mar, Mon-Sat 11-4, Sun & BH 10-4.30. (Closed 24-26 Dec). **Fee:** ✱ €5.75 (ch €4.25 concessions €4.50). Family ticket (2ad + 3ch) €15 **Facilities:** 🅿 (100yds) 🍴 ㄅ (2 floors accessible, but bridge and tower are not) toilets for disabled shop ✖ (ex guide dogs) 🍴

DUBLIN WRITERS MUSEUM
18 Parnell Square
⮑ (on Parnell Sq, at North end of O'Connell St)
☎ 01 8722077 📠 01 8722231
e-mail: writers@dublintourism.ie
The Dublin Writers Museum is housed in a restored 18th-century building and a modern annexe with lecture rooms and exhibition spaces. Dublin's rich literary heritage can be followed, through displays, tracing the written tradition in Ireland from the Book of Kells in the 8th century to the present day.
Times: Open all year, Mon-Sat 10-5, Sun & BH 11-5; Jun-Aug, Mon-Fri 10-6. **Fee:** ✱ €6.25 (ch €3.75, concessions €5.25). Family ticket €17.50. Group discounts & combined ticket for related attractions available. **Facilities:** 🅿 (charged) 🍴 ✖ licensed shop ✖ (ex guide dogs) 🍴

DUBLIN ZOO
Phoenix Park
⮑ (10mins bus ride from city centre)
☎ 01 4748900 📠 01 6771660
e-mail: info@dublinzoo.ie
Dublin Zoo first opened to the public in 1830, making it one of the oldest zoos in the world and has consistently been Ireland's favourite attraction. The new 'African Plains' is the biggest single development undertaken by the zoo. This 30-acre development has doubled the size of the zoo and provides spacious new areas for African species. Dublin Zoo is a modern zoo with conservation, education & study as its mission. The majority of the animals here have been born and bred in zoos and are part of global breeding programmes to ensure their continued survival.
Times: ✱ Open Mar-Oct, Mon-Sat 9.30-6, Sun 10.30-6; Nov-Feb, daily 10.30-dusk. **Facilities:** 🅿 🍴 ✖ licensed ㄅ (Wheelchairs are available) toilets for disabled shop ✖ 🍴

GUINNESS STOREHOUSE
St James's Gate
⮑ (next to James' St)
☎ 01 4084800 & 4538364 📠 01 4084965
e-mail: guinness-storehouse@guinness.com
Established in 1876, the Storehouse remained crammed with hopsacks until 1957, then it was converted and is now a high-tech, 21st-century mix of an art centre, conference facility, restaurant and bar. Find out about the drink's history and then sample a glass.
Times: ✱ Open daily 9.30-5 (last admission 5). (Closed 24-26 Dec, 1 Jan & Good Fri.) **Facilities:** 🅿 ✖ ㄅ toilets for disabled shop ✖ 🍴

HOWTH CASTLE RHODODENDRON GARDENS
Howth
⮑ (9m NE of city centre, by coast road to Howth. Before Howth follow signs for Deer Park Hotel)
☎ 01 8322624 & 8322256 📠 01 8392405
e-mail: sales@deerpark.iol.ie
On the northern boundary of Dublin Bay, the castle is justly famous for its gardens and especially for its rhododendron walk. The walk is open all year, but is at its best in May and June. There are views north to the Mourne Mountains and to the west of Dublin Bay.
Times: ✱ Open all year, daily 8am-dusk. (Closed 25 Dec).
Facilities: 🅿 ㄅ (steep hills unsuitable, ramped entrance) toilets for disabled ✖ (ex guide dogs) 🍴

HUGH LANE MUNICIPAL GALLERY OF MODERN ART
Charlemont House, Parnell Square
☎ 01 8741903 📠 01 8722182
e-mail: info@hughlane.ie
Situated in Charlemont House, a fine Georgian building, the gallery's collection includes one of the most extensive collections of 20th-century Irish art. A superb range of international and Irish paintings, sculpture, works on paper and stained glass is also on show. There are public lectures every Sunday and regular concerts (at noon on Sundays) throughout the year.
Times: ✱ Open all year, Tue-Thu 9.30-6, Fri-Sat 9.30-5, Sun 11-5. Late night opening Thu until 8, Apr-Aug only. (Closed Mon, Good Fri & 24-25 Dec). **Facilities:** 🅿 (100 metres) (meter parking) 🍴 ㄅ (Ramp & reserved parking) toilets for disabled shop ✖ (ex guide dogs)

IRISH MUSEUM OF MODERN ART
Royal Hospital, Military Rd, Kilmainham
➲ (3.5km from city centre, just off N7 opposite Heuston Station)
☎ 01 6129900 ▤ 01 6129999
e-mail: info@imma.ie   **FREE**
Housed in the Royal Hospital Kilmainham, an impressive 17th-century building, the Irish Museum of Modern Art is Ireland's leading national institution for the collection and presentation of modern and contemporary art. It presents a wide variety of art and artists' ideas in a dynamic programme of exhibitions, which regularly includes bodies of work from the museum's own collection, its award-winning Education and Community Department and the Studio and National Programmes.
Times: Open all year Tue-Sat 10-5.30, Sun & BHs 12-5.30. (Closed Mon, 24-26 Dec) **Facilities:** ▣ ▣ & toilets for disabled shop ✖ (ex guide dogs)

JAMES JOYCE CENTRE
35 North Great George's St
➲ (near O'Connel Street and Parnell Square)
☎ 01 8788547 ▤ 01 8788488
e-mail: marketing@jamesjoyce.ie
Situated in a beautifully restored 18th-century Georgian town house, the Centre is dedicated to the promotion of a greater interest in, and understanding of, the life and works of James Joyce. After an introductory film visitors follow a self-guided tour through the house, that includes the door to No.7 Eccles Street, home of Leopold Bloom, the hero of *Ulysses*; furniture from Joyce's Paris flat, and an extensive reference library.
Times: Open all year, Mon-Sat 9.30-5, Sun & BH 12.30-5. (Closed Good Fri & 24-26 Dec). **Fee:** House Tour €5 (pen/students €4). Walking Tour €10 (pen/students €9) group rates 10+ available **Facilities:** ▣ & toilets for disabled shop ✖ (ex guide dogs) ▦

KILMAINHAM GAOL
Inchicore Rd
➲ (3.5km from city centre)
☎ 01 4535984 ▤ 01 4532037
One of the largest unoccupied gaols in Europe, covering some of the most heroic and tragic events in Ireland's emergence as a modern nation from the 1720s. Attractions include a major exhibition detailing the political and penal history of the prison and its restoration.
Times: ✱ Open Apr-Sep, daily 9.30-6 (last admission 4.45); Oct-Mar, Mon-Fri 9.30-5.30 (last admission 4), Sun 10-6 (last admission 4.45). Access by guided tour only. **Facilities:** ▣ (on street) ▣ & (tours available by prior appointment) toilets for disabled ✖

MARSH'S LIBRARY
St Patrick's Close
➲ (beside St Patrick Cathedral)
☎ 01 4543511 ▤ 01 4543511
e-mail: keeper@marshlibrary.ie
The first public library in Ireland, dating from 1701. Designed by William Robinson, the interior has been unchanged for 300 years. The collection is of approximately 25,000 volumes of 16th, 17th and early 18th century books.
Times: Open Mon & Wed-Fri, 10-1 & 2-5; Sat 10.30-1. **Fee:** €2.50 (students & pen €1.50, ch free). **Facilities:** ▣ (100 meters) ✖ (except guide dogs) ▦

NATIONAL BOTANIC GARDENS
Glasnevin
➲ (on Botanic Road, between N1 and N2)
☎ 01 8374388 & 8377596 ▤ 01 8360080
Ireland's premier Botanic Gardens, covers a total area of 19.5 hectares (48 acres), part of which is the natural flood plain of the River Tolka. The Gardens contain a large plant collection, which includes approximately 20,000 species and cultivated varieties. There are four ranges of glasshouses including the restored Curvilinear Range. Notable features include herbaceous borders, rose garden, rockery, alpine yard, arboretum, extensive shrub collections and wall plants.
Times: ✱ Open all year, Gardens: Summer Mon-Sat 9-6, Sun 11-6; Winter Mon-Sat 10-4.30, Sun 11-4.30. (Closed 25 Dec). Glasshouses: Summer Mon-Wed & Fri 9-5, Thu 9-3.15, Sat 9-5.45, Sun 2-5.45; Winter, Mon-Wed, Fri & Sat 10-4.15, Thu 10-3.15, Sun 2-4.15.
Facilities: ▣ (charged) ▣ & toilets for disabled ✖ (ex guide dogs)

NATIONAL GALLERY OF IRELAND
Merrion Square
➲ (5 mins walk from Pearse Station)
☎ 01 6615133 ▤ 01 6615372
e-mail: artgall@eircom.net
The gallery, founded in 1854 by an Act of Parliament, houses the national collections of Irish art and European Old Masters including Caravaggio, Poussin, El Greco, Roderic O'Conor and the Yeats'.
Times: ✱ Open all year, Mon-Sat 10-5.30 (Thu 10-8.30), Sun 2-5. (Closed 24-26 Dec & Good Fri). **Facilities:** ▣ (5 mins walk) (meter parking, 2hrs max) ✖ licensed & (Braille/audio tours, lifts, ramps, parking bay) toilets for disabled shop ✖

NATIONAL LIBRARY OF IRELAND
Kildare St
☎ 01 6030200 ▤ 01 6766690
Founded in 1877 and based on collections from The Royal Dublin Society. The National Library holds an estimated 5 million items. There are collections of printed books, manuscripts, prints and drawings, photos, maps, newspapers, mircofilms and ephemera. The library's research facilities are open to all those with genuine research needs. In addition to research facilities, services include a regular programme of exhibitions open to the public and Genealogy Service.
Times: ✱ Open all year, Mon-Wed 10-9, Thu-Fri 10-5 & Sat 10-1. (Closed Sun, BHs, Good Fri & 23 Dec-2 Jan). **Facilities:** & toilets for disabled shop ✖ (ex guide dogs) ▦

NATIONAL PHOTOGRAPHIC ARCHIVE
Meeting House Square, Temple Bar
➲ (opposite The Gallery of Photography)
☎ 01 6030200 ▤ 01 6777451
e-mail: photoarchive@nli.ie
The National Photographic Archive, which is part of the National Library of Ireland, was opened in 1998 in an award-winning building in the Temple Bar area of Dublin. The archive holds an unrivalled collection of photographic images relating to Irish history, topography and cultural and social life. The collection is especially rich in late 19th and early 20th-century topographical views and studio portraits, but also includes photographs taken during the Rebellion of 1916 and the subsequent War of Independence and Civil War, as well as other historic events.
Times: ✱ Open all year, Mon-Fri 10-5. (Closed BHs, Good Fri & 23 Dec-2 Jan). **Facilities:** & toilets for disabled shop ✖ (ex guide dogs) ▦

NATURAL HISTORY MUSEUM

Merrion St
➲ (in city centre)
☎ 01 6777444   🖷 01 6777828
e-mail: education.nmi@indigo.ie

The Natural History Museum, which is part of The National Museum of Ireland, is a zoological museum containing diverse collections of world wildlife. The Irish Room, on the ground floor, is devoted largely to Irish mammals, sea creatures and insects. It includes the extinct giant Irish deer and the skeleton of a basking shark. The World Collection, has as its centre piece, the skeleton of a 60ft whale suspended from the roof. Other displays include the Giant Panda and a Pygmy Hippopotamus.

Times: ✱ Open all year, Tue-Sat 10-5, Sun 2-5. (Closed Mon, Xmas day & Good Fri). **Facilities:** P (parking meters wkdays) ✖

NEWMAN HOUSE

University College Dublin, 86 St Stephens Green
➲ (South side of St Stephens Green)
☎ 01 7067422 & 4757255   🖷 01 7067211

Newman House consists of two superb Georgian town houses, containing some of Ireland's finest 18th-century plasterwork and decoration. As the founding home of University College Dublin in 1854, the house has been associated with many famous literary and historical figures, including John Henry Newman, Gerard Manley Hopkins and James Joyce.

Times: Open Jun-Aug, Tue-Fri 12-5, Sat 2-5. Tours, Tue-Fri; 12,2,3 & 4; Sat 2,3 & 4. At other times tours by prior arrangement only.
Fee: ✱ €5 (concessions €4). **Facilities:** P (100yds) ✖ licensed ✖ (ex guide dogs)

NUMBER TWENTY NINE

29 Lower Fitzwilliam St
➲ (on corner of Lower Fitzwilliam St & Upper Mount Sq)
☎ 01 7026165   🖷 01 7027796
e-mail: numbertwentynine@mail.esb.ie

Number Twenty-Nine is a lovingly restored middle class Dublin home from the late 18th and early 19th century, filled with a unique collection of original pieces, with excellent examples of Irish and international craftsmanship. Visitors are guided through the house from the basement kitchen to the attic nursery.

Times: Open all year, Tue-Sat 10-5, Sun 2-5. (Closed Mon & 2 wks prior to Xmas). **Fee:** ✱ €3.15 (ch under 16 free, other concessions €1.25). **Facilities:** P (on street/meter) 🕮 shop ✖ ▦

PHOENIX PARK VISITOR CENTRE

Phoenix Park
➲ (4km from Dublin)
☎ 01 677 0095   🖷 01 672 6454
e-mail: phoenixparkvisitorcentre@duchas.ie

Situated in Phoenix Park, the Visitor Centre provides an historical interpretation of the park from 3500BC, through a series of attractive displays. Part of the building is devoted to nature and there is a colourful film of Phoenix Park. The castle, probably dating from the early 17th century was restored to its former glory.

Times: ✱ Open all year, Jan-mid Mar, Sat & Sun 10-5; Mid-end Mar, daily 10-5.30; Apr-Sep, daily 10-6; Oct, daily 10-5.30; Nov & Dec, Sat & Sun 10-5. (Last admission 45 mins before closing) **Facilities:** P 🕮 ♿ toilets for disabled ✖ (ex guide dogs)

JAMES JOYCE TOWER

Joyce Tower, Sandycove
➲ (1m SE Dun Laoghaire by coast road to Sandycove Point or turn off main Dun Laoghaire-Dalkey road)
☎ 01 2809265 & 8722077   🖷 2809265
e-mail: joycetower@dublintourism.ie

Built by the British as a defence against a possible invasion by Napoleon, the tower has walls approximately 8ft thick and an original entrance door 13ft above the ground. The tower was once the temporary home of James Joyce, who depicted this setting in the opening scene of *Ulysses*. The structure is now a museum devoted to the author. Bloomsday, the day in 1904 on which all the action of *Ulysses* is set, is celebrated annually on 16th June. On this day, the museum is open from 8am-6pm for visits, readings from *Ulysses* and performances of various kinds, Edwardian costume is encouraged.

Times: Open Feb-Oct, Mon-Sat 10-1 & 2-5, Sun & BHs 2-6; Nov-Jan by arrangement. **Facilities:** P (100yds) ♿ shop ✖ (ex guide dogs) ▦

FRY MODEL RAILWAY

Malahide Castle, Demesne
➲ (in grounds of Malahide Castle, 8m N of Dublin city centre, follow signs for Malahide)
☎ 01 8463779 & 8462184   🖷 01 8463723
e-mail: fryrailway@dublintourism.ie

The Fry Model Railway is a rare collection of '0' gauge trains and trams, depicting the history of Irish rail transport from the first train that ran in 1834. Cyril Fry began to build his model collection in his attic, in the late 1920s. All the models are built to scale, and they are now housed in a purpose-built setting adjacent to Malahide Castle.

Times: Open Apr-Sep, Mon-Sat 10-5, Sun & PH 2-6; Parties at other times by arrangement. Closed 1-2 & on Fri. **Fee:** ✱ €6.25 (ch €3.75, concessions €5.25). Family ticket €17.50. Combined ticket for related attractions available. **Facilities:** P ♿ shop ✖ ▦

MALAHIDE CASTLE

➲ (From Dublin city centre follow signs for Malahide, then approaching the village, main entrance to castle is signed to right off main road)
☎ 01 8462184   🖷 01 8462537
e-mail: malahidecastle@dublintourism.ie

One of Ireland's oldest castles, this romantic and beautiful structure, set in 250 acres of grounds, has changed very little in 800 years. Tours offer views of Irish period furniture and historical portrait collections. Additional paintings from the National Gallery depict figures from Irish life over the last few centuries.

Times: Open all year, Apr-Oct, daily 10-5 (Sun & BHs 11-6); Nov-Mar, daily 10-5 (Sun & BHs 11-5). (Closed for tours 12.45-2). **Fee:** ✱ €6.25 (ch €3.75, concessions €5.25). Family ticket €17.50. Group rates available. Combined tickets for related attractions available. **Facilities:** P 🕮 ✖ shop ✖ ▦

TALBOT BOTANIC GARDENS

Malahide Castle
➲ (off R107 onto Back Rd, entrance 0.25m on left, well signed).
☎ 01 8462456   🖷 01 8463620

Bought by Dublin County Council in 1976, Malahide Castle has long been associated with ornamental gardening. Over seven hectares of shrubbery, and a Walled Garden of nearly

continued

two hectares are mainly the creation of Lord Milo Talbot de Malahide, whose family had lived at the estate for 800 years until his death in 1973. Lord Milo Talbot had travelled the world and brought home many exotic plants from Australia and Chile, among others. Visitors follow a path through the gardens, which gives them the best view of this impressive botanic garden.

Times: Open May-Sep 2-5. Groups by appointment only. Guided tour Wed at 2 for the general public. **Fee:** ✱ € 3.50 **Facilities:** 🅿 💺 ✗ ⅙ shop 🏋 (ex in parkland)

SKERRIES   Map 01 D4

SKERRIES MILLS
➲ (signed off M1) \
☎ 01 8495208 📠 01 8495213   FREE
e-mail: skerriesmills@indigo.ie
A collection of restored mills, including a watermill, a five-sail, and a four-sail windmill, all in working order. The site dates from the 16th century and was originally part of a monastic establishment. It came into private ownership in 1538, and a bakery has been there since 1840. Nature lovers will enjoy the millpond, and nearby wetlands.

Times: Open Apr-Sep, daily 10.30-5.30; 2 Jan-Mar & Oct-19 Dec, daily 10.30-4.30. (Closed Good Fri) **Facilities:** 🅿 💺 shop 🏋 🍴

CO GALWAY

GALWAY   Map 01 B3

ATLANTAQUARIA
Galway Atlantaquaria, Salthill
➲ (Follow signs for Salthill, over Wolfe Tone Bridge, along Fr Griffin Rd, White Sand Rd & along The Promenade. Next to Tourist Office at seafront rdbt)
☎ 091 585100 📠 091 584360
e-mail: atlantaquaria@eircom.net
Concentrating on the native Irish marine ecosystem, the Galway Atlantiquaria contains some 170 species of fish and sealife, and features both fresh and saltwater exhibits.

Times: Open Apr, May, Jun & Sep daily 10-5; Jul & Aug daily 10-6; Oct-Dec, Jan-Mar Wed-Sun 10-5. Closed Mon & Tue. **Facilities:** 🅿 💺 ✗ licensed ⅙ (reduced prices) toilets for disabled shop 🏋 (ex guide dogs) 🍴

GALWAY CITY MUSEUM
Spanish Arch
☎ 091 567641 📠 091 567641
Galway City Museum is devoted to the city's history, featuring examples of medieval stonework, stone axe heads and scrapers dating from 3500 BC, a peat fire, a large map of the city in 1651, photographs of 19th century traditional dress and memorabilia of Connaught Rangers Regiment.

Times: ✱ Open all year daily, Mar-Oct 10-5.15. Nov-Feb 2-4, times under review. **Facilities:** 🅿 (100yds) (parking discs required) ⅙ 🏋 (ex guide dogs)

NORA BARNACLE HOUSE MUSEUM
Bowling Green
➲ (close to St Nicholas Collegiate Church, in city centre)
☎ 091 564743
The smallest museum in Ireland, this tiny turn-of-century house was the home of Nora Barnacle, companion, wife and lifelong inspiration of James Joyce. It was here in 1909, sitting at the kitchen table that Joyce first met his darling's

mother. Letters, photographs and other exhibits of the lives of James Joyce and Nora Barnacle make a visit here a unique experience.

Times: Open Jun-Aug, days may change during week, opening times posted on window. **Fee:** € 2.50 (students € 2).
Facilities: 🅿 (100yds) (disc parking)

ROYAL TARA CHINA VISITOR CENTRE
Tara Hall, Mervue
➲ (N6 from Tourist Office. At rdbt take 2nd left & at lights turn right)
☎ 091 705602 📠 091 757574   FREE
e-mail: mkilroy@royal-tara.com
Royal Tara China visitor centre, located minutes from Galway City Centre, operates from a 17th-century house situated on five acres.

Times: Open all year, Mon-Sat 9-6, Sun 10-5 **Facilities:** 🅿 ⅙ (all facilities accessible for disabled) toilets for disabled shop 🏋 (ex guide dogs) 🍴

GORT   Map 01 B3

THOOR BALLYLEE
➲ (1km off N18, 1km off N66)
☎ 091 631436 & 537733 📠 091 631436
This tower house is the former home of the poet William Butler Yeats and is where he completed most of his literary works. The tower, restored to appear exactly as it was when he lived there, houses an Interpretative Centre with audio-visual presentations and displays of his work.

Times: Open 31 May-Sep 10-6 Mon-Sat **Fee:** € 6 (pen & students € 5.50). Family ticket € 12. Party. **Facilities:** 🅿 ⅙ (audio-visual presentation) toilets for disabled shop 🏋 (ex guide dogs) 🍴

KINVARRA   Map 01 B3

DUNGUAIRE CASTLE
➲ (Off N18 Ennis to Galway road, through Gort. Left at village of Ardrahan & continue to Kinvara)
☎ 061 360768 📠 061 361020
e-mail: reservations@shannondev.ie
The castle has stood for hundreds of years on the site of the 7th-century stronghold of Guaire, the King of Connaught. Today the restored castle gives an insight into the lifestyle of the people who lived there from 1520 to modern times.

Times: Open daily mid Apr-mid Oct, daily 9.30-5 (last admission 4.30). Medieval banquet, Apr-Oct 5.30 & 8.45 (reservations necessary).
Fee: ✱ € 4.50 (ch € 2.50, student € 2.95). **Facilities:** 🅿 ⅙ shop 🏋 (ex guide dogs) 🍴

PORTUMNA   Map 01 B3

PORTUMNA CASTLE & GARDENS
☎ 090 9741658 📠 090 9741889
e-mail: portumnacastle@duchas.ie
The great semi-fortified house at Portumna was built before 1618 by Richard Burke or de Burgo, 4th Earl of Clanricarde. This important Jacobean house, while influenced by Renaissance and English houses, remains distinctively Irish. It was the main seat of the de Burgo family for over 200 years, until it was gutted by fire in 1826. The ground floor of the house is now open to the public. To the north of the house is a formal, geometrically laid out garden, a feature often associated with large Jacobean mansions.

Times: ✱ Open Apr-Oct, daily 10-6. (Last admission 45mins before closing). **Facilities:** 🅿 ⅙ (access limited) 🏋 (ex guide dogs)

continued

ROUNDSTONE MUSIC, CRAFTS & FASHION
Craft Centre
➲ (Take N59 from Galway to Clifden. After approx 50m turn left at Roundstone sign, 7m to village. Roundstone Music at the top of Village)
☎ 095 35875 🖹 095 35980
e-mail: bodhran@iol.ie   **FREE**

The Roundstone Music Craft and Fashion shop is located within the walls of an old Franciscan Monastery. Here you can see Ireland's oldest craft: the Bodhran being made, and regular talks and demonstrations are given. The 1st RiverDance stage drums were made here and are still on display in the "Craftsman's Craftshop". There is an outdoor picnic area in a beautiful location alongside the bell tower by the water where the dolphins swim up to the wall in summer.

Times: Open Apr-Oct 9.30-6, Jul-Sep 9-7, Winter 6 days 9.30-6.
Facilities: 🅿 💵 ⚒ toilets for disabled shop 🐾 (ex guide dogs only)

CRAG CAVE
➲ (1m N, signed off N21)
☎ 066 7141244 🖹 066 7142352
e-mail: info@cragcave.com

Crag Cave is one of the longest surveyed cave systems in Ireland, with a total length of 3.81km. It is a spectacular world, where pale forests of stalagmites and stalactites, thousands of years old, throw eerie shadows around vast echoing caverns complemented by dramatic sound and lighting effects. Tours last about 30 minutes.

Times: Open daily, mid Mar-1 Nov 10-6 (Jul-Aug until 6.30). Last tour 30 minutes before closing time. **Fee:** Prices not confirmed for 2005
Facilities: 🅿 💵 ✗ licensed ⚒ (ramp to visitor centre) toilets for disabled shop 🐾 (ex guide dogs) 🍴

THE BLASKET CENTRE
➲ (10m W of Dingle town, on Slea Head Drive)
☎ 066 9156444 & 9156371 🖹 066 9156446
e-mail: mdemordha@eolga.ie

In the early part of this century a small group of writers from the remote Blasket Island, just off the coast of County Kerry, achieved world renown. They told their own story in their own language and the centre describes the lives of the Islanders before the sad abandonment of the island in 1953. Research and conference facilities also available.

Times: ✱ Open daily, Etr-late Oct 10-6 (7 Jul-Aug). Open on request all year for groups over 30. Last admission 45mins before closing.
Facilities: 🅿 💵 ✗ licensed ⚒ (reserved parking) toilets for disabled 🐾 (ex guide dogs)

KILLARNEY TRANSPORT MUSEUM
Scotts Hotel Gardens
➲ (centre of town, opposite railway station)
☎ 064 34677 🖹 064 36656

A unique collection of Irish veteran, vintage and classic cars, motorcycles, bicycles, carriages and fire engines. Exhibits include the 1907 Silver Stream, reputed to be the rarest car in the world, it was designed and built by an Irishman and he only made one!

Times: Open Apr, May, Sep & Oct 11-5; Jun, Jul & Aug 10-6 **Fee:** €5 (pen/students €3.50). Family ticket €12-€14 **Facilities:** 🅿 ⚒

MUCKROSS HOUSE, GARDENS & TRADITIONAL FARMS
Muckross
➲ (4m on Kenmare Road)
☎ 066 31440 & 35571 🖹 066 33926
e-mail: mucros@iol.ie

The 19th-century mansion house of the formerly private Muckross Estate. It now houses a museum of Kerry folklife. In the basement craft centre, a weaver, blacksmith and potter demonstrate their trades. The grounds include Alpine and bog gardens, rhododendrons, azaleas and a rock garden.

Times: ✱ Open Jul-Aug, daily 9-7; 17 Mar-Jun & Sep-Oct, 9-6; Nov-16 Mar 9-5.30. **Facilities:** 🅿 ✗ licensed ⚒ toilets for disabled shop 🐾 (ex guide dogs) 🍴

KERRY THE KINGDOM MUSEUM
Ashe Memorial Hall, Denny St
➲ (Town centre location, follow signs for museum & tourist information office)
☎ 066 7127777 🖹 066 7127444
e-mail: info@kerrymuseum.com

The museum tells the story of Kerry (and Ireland) from the Stone Age to the present day. Archaeological treasures are displayed in the Museum Gallery, while a stroll through the Medieval Experience reveals the streets of Tralee as they were in 1450, with all the sights, sounds and smells of a bustling community. Discover what people wore, what they ate and where they lived, and find out why the Earls of Desmond, who founded the town, also destroyed it.

Times: Open Jan-Mar, Tue-Fri 10-4.30; Apr-May, Tue-Sat 9.30-5.30; Jun-Aug, daily 9.30-5.30; Sep-Dec, Tue-Sat 9.30-5; BH wknds Sun & Mon 10-5. **Fee:** ✱ €8 (ch €5, pen/students €6.50). Family €22
Facilities: 🅿 (charged) 💵 ⚒ (special time car through Medieval Experience) toilets for disabled shop 🐾 (ex guide dogs) 🍴

THE SKELLIG EXPERIENCE
➲ (Ring of Kerry road, signed after Cahersiveen then Valentia bridge or ferry from Rena Rd Point)
☎ 066 9476306 🖹 066 9476351
e-mail: info@skelligexperience.com

The Skellig Rocks are renowned for their scenery, sea bird colonies, lighthouses, Early Christian monastic architecture and rich underwater life. The two islands - Skellig Michael and Small Skellig - stand like fairytale castles in the Atlantic

continued

Ocean, rising to 218 metres and their steep cliffs plunging 50 metres below the sea. The Heritage Centre, (on Valentia Island, reached from the mainland via a bridge), tells the story of the Skellig Islands in an exciting multimedia exhibition. Cruise around Valentia Habour.
Times: ✱ Open Mar-Jun 10-6; Jun-Aug 10-7; Sep-Oct 10-6.
Facilities: P ▣ ⟁ toilets for disabled shop ✖ (ex guide dogs) ▤
See advertisement on this page

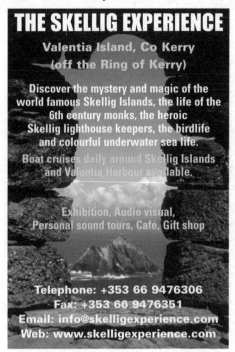

THE SKELLIG EXPERIENCE

Valentia Island, Co Kerry
(off the Ring of Kerry)

Discover the mystery and magic of the world famous Skellig Islands, the life of the 6th century monks, the heroic Skellig lighthouse keepers, the birdlife and colourful underwater sea life.

Boat cruises daily around Skellig Islands and Valentia Harbour available.

Exhibition, Audio visual, Personal sound tours, Café, Gift shop

Telephone: +353 66 9476306
Fax: +353 66 9476351
Email: info@skelligexperience.com
Web: www.skelligexperience.com

CO KILDARE

CELBRIDGE   Map 01 D4

CASTLETOWN
➲ (13m from Dublin, follow signs to Celbridge from N4)
☎ 01 628 8252 ▤ 01 627 1811
e-mail: castletown@duchas.ie
Ireland's largest and finest Palladian country house, begun c1722 for William Conolly, Speaker of the Irish House of Commons. The state rooms include the 'Pompeian' Long Gallery with its Venetian chandeliers, green silk drawing room and magnificent staircase hall with Lafranchini plasterwork. There is a fine collection of 18th-century Irish furniture and paintings.
Times: Open Apr-23 Sep, Mon-Fri 10-6, Sat-Sun & BH 1-6; Oct, Mon-Fri 10-5, Sun & BH 1-5; Nov, Sun 1-5 & pre-booked groups 20+ Mon-Fri. (Last admission 1hr before closing) **Fee:** ✱ €3.50 (ch & students €1.25, pen €2.50). Family ticket €8.25. Pre-booked groups 10+ €2.50. **Facilities:** P ▣ ⟁ (restricted access for disabled visitors) toilets for disabled ✖ (ex guide dogs)

KILDARE   Map 01 C3
IRISH NATIONAL STUD & JAPANESE GARDENS
Irish National Stud, Tully
➲ (off N7 (Tristor Way) junct 11 then R415 towards Nurney & Kildare. Stud & Gardens well signed from rdbt)
☎ 045 521617 ▤ 045 522964
e-mail: stud@irish-national-stud.ie
Situated in the grounds of the Irish National Stud, the gardens were established by Lord Wavertree between 1906 and 1910, and symbolise 'The Life of Man' in a Japanese-style landscape. You can also visit the Horse Museum which includes the skeleton of Arkle, an Irish racehorse that won a number of major races in the 1960s. The Commemorative Millennium Garden of St Fiachra seeks to capture the power of the Irish landscape in its rawest state, that of rock and water.
Times: Open 12 Feb-12 Nov, daily 9.30-6, last admission 5.
Fee: €8.50 (ch €4.50, pen/students €7). Family ticket €20
Facilities: P ✖ licensed ⟁ (all parts of stud accessible, only small part of gardens) toilets for disabled shop ✖ (ex on lead) ▤

We endeavour to be as accurate as possible, but changes to times and other information can occur after the guide has gone to press.

CO KILKENNY

KILKENNY   Map 01 C3
KILKENNY CASTLE
☎ 056 7721450 ▤ 056 7763488
Situated in a beautiful 50-acre park, the castle dates from 1172. The first stone castle was built 20 years later by William Marshall, Earl of Pembroke. It was home of the very powerful Butler family, Earls and Dukes of Ormonde from 1391 to 1935. Due to major restoration works, the central block now includes a library, drawing room, and bedrooms decorated in 1830's splendour, as well as the beautiful Long Gallery.
Times: ✱ Open all year, Apr-May, daily 10.30-5; Jun-Aug, daily 9.30-7; Sep, daily 10-6.30; Oct-Mar, daily 10.30-12.45 & 2-5. Last tour 45mins before closing. (Closed Xmas & Good Fri). **Facilities:** P (local authority restrictions) ▣ ⟁ (toilet close by) shop ✖ (ex guide dogs)

CO LIMERICK

FOYNES   Map 01 B3
FOYNES FLYING BOAT MUSEUM
➲ (on N69 in Foynes, 23m from Limerick)
☎ 069 65416 ▤ 069 65416
e-mail: famm@eircom.net
The museum recalls the era of the flying boats during the 1930s and early 1940s when Foynes was an important airport for air traffic between the United States and Europe. There is a comprehensive range of exhibits, graphic illustrations and a 1940's style cinema featuring a 17-minute film - all original footage from the 30s and 40s. Where Irish coffee was first invented by chef, Joe Sheridan, in 1942.
Times: Open Mar-Oct, daily 10-6. Last admissions 5.15 **Fee:** €5 (ch €3, student £€). Family ticket €12. **Facilities:** P ▣ ⟁ toilets for disabled shop ✖ (ex guide dogs) ▤

HOLYCROSS — Map 01 C3

LOUGH GUR STONE AGE CENTRE
Bruff Rd
➲ (17 km S of Limerick City, off R512 towards Kilmallock)
☎ 061 360788 ▤ 061 361020
e-mail: reservations@shannondev.ie
Lough Gur introduces visitors to the habitat of Neolithic Man on one of Ireland's most important archaeological sites. The visitor centre interprets the history of the area which dates back to 3000BC.
Times: Open daily May-Sep, daily 10-5.30 (last admission 5)
Fee: ✱ €4.50 (ch €2.50, students & pen €2.95).
Facilities: 🅿 & toilets for disabled shop ✖ (ex guide dogs) ▰

KILCORNAN — Map 01 B3

CELTIC PARK & GARDENS
➲ (N69 Limerick to Tralee road)
☎ 061 394243
Located on an original Celtic settlement in one of the most important Cromwellian plantations in the south-west of Ireland. As you walk through the park there's plenty to see, including a church built in 1250, a Mass rock, dolmen, a stone circle, lake dwellings, cooking site, Celtic tomb and a fine example of a ring fort. The gardens contain over 1,000 roses, flowering shrubs, a rockery, herbaceous borders, shrubbery, large pool and colonnades.
Times: Open mid Mar-Oct, daily 9.30-6. **Fee:** €5 (€4 pen/students, ch under 12 free accompanied by parent). **Facilities:** 🅿 ▰ shop

LIMERICK — Map 01 B3

KING JOHN'S CASTLE
Nicholas St
➲ (on historic Kings Island in the city)
☎ 061 360788 ▤ 061 361020
e-mail: reservations@shannondev.ie
The Castle was built between 1200 and 1210 and was repaired and extended many times in the following centuries. The interpretative centre at the Castle has been completely redesigned and now contains an imaginative historical exhibition. The courtyard and the Castle display some of the trades and traditions of the 16th century.
Times: Open all year Mar, Apr, & Oct daily 9.30-5 (last admission 4); May-Sep 9.30-5.30 (last admission 4.30); Nov-Feb 10-4.30 (last admission 3.30). Closed Good Fri & 24-26 Dec. **Fee:** ✱ €7.50 (ch €4.50, pen & students €5.95). **Facilities:** 🅿 (charged) & (lifts and ramps) toilets for disabled shop ✖ (ex guide dogs) ▰

THE HUNT MUSEUM
The Custom House, Rutland St
➲ (a short walk from Arthur's Quay)
☎ 061 312833 ▤ 061 312834
e-mail: info@huntmuseum.com
On show at the Hunt Museum is one of Ireland's finest private collections of art and antiquities. Reflecting Ireland's Celtic past as well as masterworks by da Vinci and Renoir. Set in an 18th-century customs house beside the broad majestic Shannon.
Times: Open daily Mon-Sat 10-5, Sun 2-5. **Fee:** ✱ €6.50 (ch €3.20, concessions €5.25). Family ticket €15. **Facilities:** 🅿 (50mtrs) (parking discs for street parking) ▰ ✖ licensed & toilets for disabled shop ✖ (ex guide dogs) ▰

CO LONGFORD

KEENAGH — Map 01 C4

CORLEA TRACKWAY VISITOR CENTRE
➲ (Off R397, 3km from village)
☎ 043 22386 ▤ 043 22442
The centre interprets an Iron Age bog road which was built in the year 148BC across the boglands close to the River Shannon. The oak road is the largest of its kind to have been uncovered in Europe and was excavated over the years by Professor Barry Raferty of University College Dublin. Inside the building, an 18-metre stretch of preserved road is on permanent display in a specially designed hall with humidifiers to prevent the ancient wood from cracking in the heat.
Times: ✱ Open Apr-Sep, daily 10-6. (Last admission 45 mins before closing). **Facilities:** 🅿 ▰ & toilets for disabled ✖ (ex guide dogs)

CO MAYO

BALLYCASTLE — Map 01 B5

CÉIDE FIELDS
➲ (5m W of Ballycastle on R314)
☎ 096 43325 ▤ 096 43261
e-mail: ceidefields@duchas.ie
Beneath the wild boglands of North Mayo lies Céide Fields, the most extensive Stone-age monument in the world; field systems, dwelling areas and megalithic tombs of 5,000 years ago. In addition, the wild flora of the bog is of international importance and is bounded by some of the most spectacular rock formations and cliffs in Ireland.
Times: ✱ Open mid Mar-May & Oct-Nov, daily 10-5; Jun-Sep, daily 10-6. Rest of year open to pre-booked groups. (Last admission 1hr before closing). **Facilities:** 🅿 ▰ & (parking) toilets for disabled ✖ (ex guide dogs)

CO MONAGHAN

INNISKEEN — Map 01 C4

PATRICK KAVANAGH RURAL & LITERARY RESOURCE CENTRE
Candlefort
➲ (From Dundalk take R178. Ignore sign on right for Inniskeen. Continue on to Conlon's Pub and turn right for Inniskeen)
☎ 042 78560 ▤ 042 78560
e-mail: infoatpkc@eircom.net
Birthplace of Patrick Kavanagh, one of Ireland's foremost 20th-century poets. The village grew around the ancient monastery of St Daig MacCairill, founded by 562, and its strong, 10th-century round tower still stands. The centre, housed in the former parish church, chronicles the ancient history of the region and its role in developing Kavanagh's work.
Times: Open all year, Tue-Fri 11-5, Sat 2-5. Jun-Sep Sun, 2-5 (Closed Oct-May, wknds & BHs Dec-16 Mar). **Fee:** ✱ €4 (ch 12 free, concessions €2). Kavanagh trail guide map available €0.65. Kavanagh Country Tours - a guided tour with live performances lasting 90 mins, advance booking essential €7.50 including admission to centre.
Facilities: 🅿 ▰ & toilets for disabled shop ▰

MONAGHAN — Map 01 C5

MONAGHAN COUNTY MUSEUM
1-2 Hill St
➲ (near town centre, opposite the market house exhibition galleries)
☎ 047 82928 ▤ 047 71189 **FREE**
e-mail: comuseum@monghancoco.ie
This is an award-winning museum of local archaeology, history, arts and crafts. Throughout the year various special exhibitions take place.
Times: Open Tue-Fri 10-1 & 2-5 Sat 11-1 & 2-5, (closed Sun & Mon)
Facilities: P (near town centre) (restricted on street parking) ⅙ ✕ (ex guide dogs)

CO OFFALY

BIRR — Map 01 C3

BIRR CASTLE DEMESNE
➲ (in town sq take exit beside Bank of Ireland and bear right. Turn left, entrance is on right, car park on left)
☎ 0509 20336 ▤ 0509 21583
e-mail: info@birrcastle.com
A large landscaped park with a lake, rivers and waterfalls, with important plant collections including magnolias, maples, limes and oaks. The Demesne is particularly colourful in the spring and autumn, and is noted for its formal gardens, containing the tallest box hedges in the world. It is also home to the Great Birr Telescope, built in 1844, and Ireland's Historic Science Centre, a series of galleries focusing on Ireland's scientific past.
Times: Open all year, Mar-Oct 9-6, Nov-Mar 10-5 **Fee:** ✱ €8.50 (ch €4.50, pen & students €6.50). Family ticket (2ad+2ch) €24.
Facilities: P ▣ ⅙ toilets for disabled shop garden centre ⌷

CO ROSCOMMON

BOYLE — Map 01 B4

KING HOUSE
➲ (in town centre, 1km from N4)
☎ 071 9663242 ▤ 071 9663243
e-mail: kinghouseboyle@hotmail.com
King House is a magnificently restored Georgian mansion built around 1730 by Sir Henry King, whose family were one of the most powerful and wealthy in Ireland. After its first life as a home, King House became a military barracks for the famous Connaught Rangers from 1788-1922. In more recent years it has also been a barracks for the National Irish Army. Today visitors can explore and delve into the dramatic episodes of its history with stories of tragic Irish romance, runaway lovers, a duel of honour, a murder trial and feats of bravery and hardship in war.
Times: Open Apr-Sep, daily 10-6 (last admission 5). Pre-booked groups welcome all year round, telephone for details. **Fee:** Prices not confirmed for 2005 **Facilities:** P ▣ ✕ ⅙ (lift to all areas, ramps, wide doors) toilets for disabled shop ✕ (ex guide dogs)

STROKESTOWN — Map 01 C4

STROKESTOWN PARK HOUSE GARDEN & FAMINE MUSEUM
Strokestown Park
➲ (23km from Longford on N5)
☎ 071 9633013 ▤ 071 9633712
e-mail: info@strokestownpark.ie
A fine example of an early 18th-century gentleman farmer's country estate. Built in Palladian style the house reflects perfectly the confidence of the newly emergent ruling class. The pleasure garden has also been restored, and the Famine Museum, located in the stable yard, commemorates the Great Irish Famine of the 1840s.
Times: Open 17 Mar-Oct, daily. **Fee:** € 13.50 (ch €5.70, concessions €11). Family ticket € 28. Group 20+ €9 each
Facilities: P ✕ licensed ⅙ toilets for disabled shop garden centre ✕ (ex guide dogs & in grounds) ⌷

CO TIPPERARY

CAHIR — Map 01 C3

SWISS COTTAGE
Kilcommon
➲ (1m from town on Ardfinnan road)
☎ 052 41144 ▤ 052 42324
A delightful thatched "cottage orné" built in the early 1800s on the estate of the Earls of Glengall to a design by the famous Regency architect John Nash.
Times: ✱ Open mid Mar-Apr & Oct-Nov, Tue-Sun 10-1 & 2-4.30; May-Sep, daily 10-6. Last admission 30mins before closing.
Facilities: P ✕ (ex guide dogs)

CASHEL — Map 01 C3

BRÚ BORÚ HERITAGE CENTRE
➲ (below Rock of Cashel in town)
☎ 062 61122 ▤ 062 62700
e-mail: bruboru@comhaltas.com
At the foot of the Rock of Cashel, a 4th-century stone fort, this Heritage Centre is dedicated to the study and celebration of native Irish music, song, dance, story telling, theatre and Celtic studies. There's a Folk Theatre where three performances are held daily in the summer, and in the evening, banquets evoke the Court of Brian Ború, 11th-century High King of Ireland with songs, poems and sagas. Promoted by Comhaltas Ceoltóirí Eireann. There is also a Subterranean, "Sounds of History", experience.
Times: ✱ Open Jan-May & Oct-Dec, Mon-Fri 9-5; Jun-Sep Tue-Sat 9-11, Sun-Mon 9-5. **Facilities:** P (charged) ▣ ✕ ⅙ (wheelchair bay in theatre) toilets for disabled shop ✕ (ex guide dogs) ⌷

CO WATERFORD

LISMORE Map 01 C2

LISMORE CASTLE GARDENS
⮱ (on N72 near town centre)
☎ 058 54424 📋 058 54896
e-mail: lismoreestates@eircom.net
Lismore Castle is the Irish home of the Duke of Devonshire. The beautifully situated walled and woodland gardens contain a fine collection of camellias, magnolias and other shrubs and a remarkable Yew Walk. Several pieces of contemporary sculpture have been installed in the garden.
Times: Open mid Apr-early Oct, daily 1.45-4.45. (Open at 11 during Jul & Aug). **Fee:** ✱ €5 (ch under 16: €2.50, party 20+ €2.25). Party 20+ €4.50. **Facilities:** 🅿 ♿ (some of grounds are accessible)

WATERFORD Map 01 C2

WATERFORD CRYSTAL VISITOR CENTRE
⮱ (on N25, 1m from city centre)
☎ 051 73311 📋 051 78539
There are factory tours to see mastercraftsmen mouth-blow and hand-cut this famous crystal. You can talk to the master engravers and see the crystal being sculpted. In the gallery there is the finest display of Waterford Crystal in the world.
Times: Tours of factory: Apr-Oct, daily 8.30-4, gallery daily 8.30-6; Nov-Feb, Mon-Fri 9-3.15, gallery 9-5. **Facilities:** 🅿 💷 ✗ ♿ (special tours on request) toilets for disabled shop 🎫 🍴

CO WEXFORD

FERRYCARRIG Map 01 D3

IRISH NATIONAL HERITAGE PARK
⮱ (3m from Wexford, on N11)
☎ 053 20733 📋 053 20911
e-mail: info@inhp.com
Fourteen historical sites set in a magnificent 35-acre mature forest explaining Ireland's history from the Stone and Bronze Ages, through the Celtic period and concluding with the Vikings and Normans. Among the exhibits are a reconstructed Mesolithic camp, a Viking boatyard with two full size ships and a Norman motte and bailey.
Times: Open daily 9.30-6.30 (last admission 5, times subject to seasonal variations) **Fee:** €7.50 (pen & students €6). Family (2 ad & upto 3 ch) €19. Group rates available on request. **Facilities:** 🅿 💷 ✗ licensed ♿ toilets for disabled shop 🎫 (ex guide dogs) 🍴

NEW ROSS Map 01 C3

DUNBRODY ABBEY VISITORS CENTRE
Dunbrody Abbey, Campile
⮱ (10m from New Ross at the base of the Hook Peninsular)
☎ 051 88603
e-mail: patrickbelfast@aol.com
The visitor centre is based around the Abbey itself and Dunbrody Castle. There is an intriguing yew hedge maze with 1,550 yew trees and a museum. In addition there is a golf pitch-and-putt course, a local craft centre and Dunbrody Abbey Cookery School.
Times: Open May-Sep 10-6. **Fee:** ✱ €2, Family ticket €5. Maze/Golf €4, (ch €2). Family €10. **Facilities:** 🅿 💷 ✗ ♿ shop garden centre

JOHN F KENNEDY ARBORETUM
⮱ (12km S of New Ross, off R733)
☎ 051 388171 📋 051 388172
The Arboretum covers 623 acres across the hill of Slievecoiltia which overlooks the Kennedy ancestral home at Dunganstown. There are 4,500 types of trees and shrubs representing the temperate regions of the world, and laid out in botanical sequence. There's a lake and a visitor centre.
Times: ✱ Open daily, May-Aug 10-8; Apr & Sep 10-6.30; Oct-Mar 10-5. Last admission 45 mins before closing. (Closed Good Fri & 25 Dec).
Facilities: 🅿 💷 ♿ toilets for disabled shop

WEXFORD Map 01 D3

THE IRISH AGRICULTURAL MUSEUM
Johnstown Castle Old Farmyard
⮱ (4m SW of Wexford town, signed off N25)
☎ 053 42888 📋 053 42213
e-mail: aosullivan@johnstown.teagasc.ie
This museum has displays on rural transport, farming and the activities of the farmyard and farmhouse; and includes a large exhibition on the history of the potato and the Great Famine (1845-49). Large scale replicas of different workshops, including a blacksmith, cooper and basket worker, and include displays on dairying, cycling, and sugar-beet harvesting and a collection of Irish country furniture. New permanent exhibitions on gardening and the Ferguson System.
Times: Open all year, Jun-Aug Mon-Fri 9-5 & Sat-Sun 11-5; Apr-May & Sep-14 Nov Mon-Fri 9-12.30 & 1.30-5, Sat-Sun 2-5; 15 Nov-Mar Mon-Fri 9-12.30 & 1.30-5 (Closed 25 Dec-2 Jan). **Fee:** ✱ €5 (ch & students €3). Family ticket €15. **Facilities:** 🅿 (charged May-Sep) 💷 ♿ toilets for disabled shop

JOHNSTOWN CASTLE GARDENS
Johnstown Castle
⮱ (4m SW of Wexford town, signed off N25)
☎ 053 42888 📋 053 42004
e-mail: aosullivan@johnstown.teagase.ie
The 19th-century mansion is closed to the public but visitors can explore the 50 acres of grounds containing over 200 different varieties of trees and shrubs, ornamental lakes with wildfowl, and walled gardens and hothouses. The ruins of Rathlannon Castle, a medieval tower house, can also be seen.
Times: Open all year, daily 9-5.30. (Closed 25 Dec).
Facilities: 🅿 💷 ♿ toilets for disabled

WEXFORD WILDFOWL RESERVE
North Slob
⮱ (8km NE from Wexford)
☎ 053 23129 📋 053 24785
The reserve is of international importance for Greenland white-fronted geese, Brent geese, Bewick's swans and wigeon. The reserve is a superb place for birdwatching and there are hides and a tower hide available as well as a visitor centre.
Times: ✱ Open all year, Etr-Sep, daily 9-6; Oct-Etr, daily 10-5. (Closed 25 Dec). Other hours by arrangement. **Facilities:** 🅿 ♿ toilets for disabled 🎫 (ex guide dogs)

CO WICKLOW

ENNISKERRY   Map 01 D4

POWERSCOURT GARDENS EXHIBITION
Powerscourt Estate
➲ (just off N11 S of Bray, next to Enniskerry)
☎ 01 2046000   📠 01 2046900
Begun by Richard Wingfield in the 1740s, the gardens are a blend of formal plantings, sweeping terraces, statuary and ornamental lakes together with secret hollows, rambling walks and walled gardens. The house itself incorporates an exhibition which traces the history of the estate, and tells the story of the disastrous fire of 1974 which gutted the house.
Times: Gardens & House Exhibition open daily 9.30-5.30 (Winter time may vary). Waterfall open daily 9.30-7 (Summer), 10.30-dusk (Winter).
Fee: ✱ Gardens & House Exhibition €8 (ch under 16 €4.50 ch under 5 free & students €7). Gardens only €6 (ch under 16 €3.50 ch under 5 free & students €5.50). House Exhibition only €2.50 (ch under 16 €1.60 ch under 5 free & students €2.20). Waterfall €4 (ch under 16 €3 ch under 5 free & students €3.50).
Facilities: 🅿 💺 ✗ licensed ♿ (Lift to first floor, Wheelchair available) toilets for disabled shop garden centre 🍴

KILQUADE   Map 01 D3

NATIONAL GARDEN EXHIBITIONS CENTRE
Calumet Nurseries
➲ (7m S of Bray - turn off N11 at Kilpedder)
☎ 01 2819890   📠 01 2810359
e-mail: calumet@clubi.ie
There are 20 different gardens designed by some of Ireland's leading landscapers and designers. There are lectures during the year and guided tours during summer. Ring for details and a calendar of events. The exhibitions are constantly changing and enjoy a high standard of maintenance. All plants clearly labelled.
Times: ✱ Open Feb-22 Dec, Mon-Sat 10-6, Sun 1-6.
Facilities: 🅿 💺 ♿ shop garden centre 🐾 (ex guide dogs) 🍴

RATHDRUM   Map 01 D3

AVONDALE HOUSE & FOREST PARK
➲ (S of Dublin on N11. At Rathnew on R752 to Glenealy and Rathdrum)
☎ 0404 46111   📠 0404 46333
e-mail: costelloe_j@coillte.ie
It was here in 1846 that one of the greatest political leaders of modern Irish history, Charles Stewart Parnell, was born. Parnell spent much of his time at Avondale until his death in October 1891. The house is set in a magnificent forest park with miles of forest trails, plus a children's play area and picnic areas.
Times: Open: House 17 Mar-Oct, 11-6. Closed Mon (Mar, Apr, Sep & Oct). Last admission 5. **Fee:** ✱ House €5 (pen €4.50). Family ticket (2 ad & 3 ch) €15. Parking; car €5, coach €25 (if pre-booked, no charge). **Facilities:** 🅿 (charged) ✗ licensed ♿ (special car park & one forest trail accessible) 🐾 (ex guide dogs) 🍴

Above: The Burren, northern Co. Clare

County Maps

The county map shown here will help you identify the counties within each country. You can look up each county in the guide using the county names at the top of each page. To find towns featured in the guide use the atlas and the index.

England

1 Bedfordshire
2 Berkshire
3 Bristol
4 Buckinghamshire
5 Cambridgeshire
6 Greater Manchester
7 Herefordshire
8 Hertfordshire
9 Leicestershire
10 Northamptonshire
11 Nottinghamshire
12 Rutland
13 Staffordshire
14 Warwickshire
15 West Midlands
16 Worcestershire

Scotland

17 City of Glasgow
18 Clackmannanshire
19 East Ayrshire
20 East Dunbartonshire
21 East Renfrewshire
22 Perth & Kinross
23 Renfrewshire
24 South Lanarkshire
25 West Dunbartonshire

Wales

26 Blaenau Gwent
27 Bridgend
28 Caerphilly
29 Denbighshire
30 Flintshire
31 Merthyr Tydfil
32 Monmouthshire
33 Neath Port Talbot
34 Newport
35 Rhondda Cynon Taff
36 Torfaen
37 Vale of Glamorgan
38 Wrexham

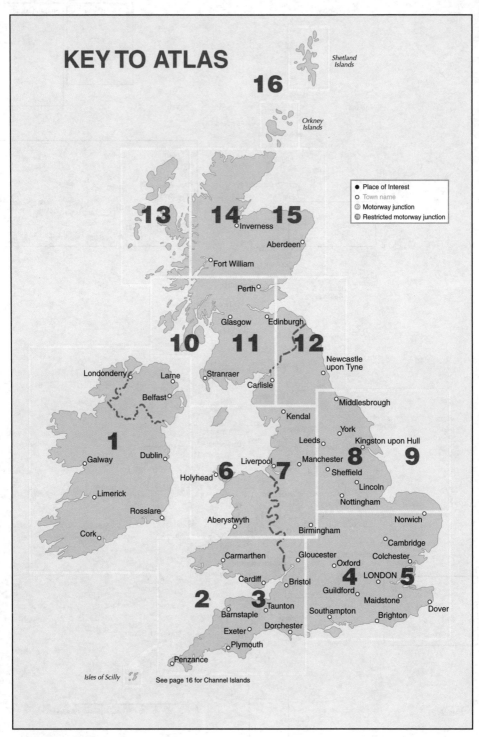

KEY TO ATLAS

16 Shetland Islands

Orkney Islands

●	Place of Interest
○	Town name
⬤	Motorway junction
⬤	Restricted motorway junction

13 **14** **15**

Inverness

Aberdeen

Fort William

Perth

Glasgow Edinburgh

10 **11** **12**

Newcastle upon Tyne

Londonderry Larne

Belfast Stranraer

Carlisle

Middlesbrough

Kendal

York

1 Leeds Kingston upon Hull

Galway Dublin Liverpool **7** Manchester **8** **9**

Holyhead **6** Sheffield

Limerick Lincoln

Rosslare Nottingham

Cork Aberystwyth Norwich

Birmingham

Cambridge

Carmarthen Gloucester Colchester

Cardiff Oxford

2 **3** Bristol **4** LONDON **5**

Barnstaple Taunton Guildford Maidstone

Southampton Brighton Dover

Exeter Dorchester

Plymouth

Penzance

Isles of Scilly See page 16 for Channel Islands

2

●	Place of Interest
○	Town name
BLAE G	Blaenau Gwent
BRDGND	Bridgend
CAERPH	Caerphilly
MYR TD	Merthyr Tydfil
NEWPT	Newport
RHONDD	Rhondda Cynon Taff
TORFN	Torfaen
V GLAM	Vale of Glamorgan

Aberaeron
CERE
Felinwynt
Cardigan
Cilgerran
Cenarth
Lampeter
Strumble Head
Newport
Fishguard
Dre-Fach
Felindre
Crymych
SN
CARMARTHE
St David's
PEMBROKESHIRE
Ramsey
Island
Scolton
Llanycefn
Abergwili
Llangath
Dryslwyn
St Brides Bay
Haverfordwest
Llawhaden
Carmarthen
Llanarthne
St Clears
Skomer Island
Narberth
Laugharne
Llansteffan
Skokholm
Island
Milford
Haven
Carew
St Florence
Amroth
Kidwelly
Llanelli
SWA
Pembroke
Lamphey
Tenby
Carmarthen
Bay
Llanrhidian
Caldey
Island
Oxwich
Parkm

SM

SW
Goonhavern
St Austell
A3058
Probus
Truro
A390
Pentewan
Zennor
St Ives
Redruth
A393 A39
A3078
Gorran
Chysauster Ancient Village
Pool
Trelissick Garden
Godolphin
Cross
Wendron
St Mawes
Pendeen
Marazion
Falmouth
Sancreed
Penzance
Mawnan Smith
Land's End
Helston
Gweek
Mount's
Bay
A3083
Lizard
Point
Lizard

SS
Ilfracombe
Comb
Marti
Lundy
Arlington
A361
Barnstaple
Hartland Point
Clovelly
Bideford
A39
Great
Torrington
A388
A386
A312
Bude
A3072
Okehampton
A30
SW
Land's End
Tintagel
Launceston
A30
A395
Lydford
Isles of Scilly
St Mary's
Camelford
A39
Trevose Head
Padstow
CORNWALL
Bodmin
Moor
Da
Tredinnick
Wadebridge
Morwellham
Tavistock
A388
Bodmin
A390
Calstock
Yelvertor
Newquay
Lanhydrock
A38
Dobwalls
Liskeard
Buckland
Abbey
Trerice
A392
A30
Restormel
PLYMOUTH
Plympton
A391
A387
Torpoint
Looe
Fowey
A30
A390
A3075
A30
SEE INSET
SX
A39
Dodman Point

Point of Ayre

Ravenglass

Ballaugh
Isle of Man
A10
A3
Ramsey
Maughold Head
Peel
A4
ISLE
OF
MAN
A1
A2
Laxey
A5
DOUGLAS
A3
A5
Cregneish
Ballasalla
Castletown
Port
St Mary
Dreswick Point

(SC)

Irish
Sea

ME

Carmel Head

Great
Ormes
Head

Llanallgo
A5025
Colwyn
Bay
Rhuddl

Holyhead
Anglesey
Llandudno
Junction
A55

Holy Island
Beaumaris
Conwy
Bodelwyd

Bryncelli
Ddu
Bangor
A55
Llandudno
Junction
Denbi

Brynsiencyn
Plas Newydd
Y Felinheli
Tal-y-Cafn
A525

ISLE OF
ANGLESEY
Caernarfon
A470
Trefriw
Llanrwst
A543

Llanberis
A5
CONWY
Ruthi

Caernarfon
Bay
A4086
Dolwyddelan
Betws-y-Coed
DENBIG

Groeslon
SH
Penmachno
A5
A49

Beddgelert
A498
A470
Cerrigydrudion

Llangybi
A499
A487
Blaenau
Ffestiniog
Corwen

Llanystumdwy
Porthmadog
A4212
Bala

Penarth
Fawr
Criccieth
Portmeirion
A494

Lleyn Peninsula
Harlech
A470
Llanuwchllyn

Plas-yn- Rhiw
GWYNEDD

Bardsey
Island
Cymer Abbey
A470

Fairbourne
Dolgellau
A458

A496

Llanfihangel-y-pennant
A487
A470
Llanfai
Caereinio

Tywyn
A493
Machynlleth
POWYS
Newtown

Cardigan Bay
Eglwysfach
A44

SN
Aberystwyth
A487
A483
A470

Capel
Bangor
CEREDIGION
Rhayader
A485

Legend:
- ● Place of Interest
- ○ Town name
- FLINTS Flintshire

0   10   20 miles
0   10   20   30 kilometres

9

5 6 7 8 9 0 1 2 3 4 5 6 7 8 9 0

4
3
2
1
0
9
8
7
6
5
4
3
2
1
0
9
8
7
6

Spurn Head

A1031

A57

A52

A158

Skegness

A52

TF

The

Wash

Hunstanton
Heacham
Titchwell
Great
Bircham
North
Creake
Holkham
Wells-next-the-Sea
Little Walsingham
A149
Sheringham
Weybourne
West Runton
Cromer
Felbrigg
Baconsthorpe
Thursford
Green
A148
Saxthorpe
Erpingham

TG

0   10   20 miles
0   10   20   30 kilometres

● Place of Interest
○ Town name

Sandringham
Castle Rising
Houghton
A148
Fakenham
Blickling
A140
Horsey

KING'S LYNN
A17
A47
Castle Acre
A1065
Gressenhall
A47
N O R F O L K
Lenwade
A1067
Horsham St Faith
A1151
A149
South Walsham
The Broads
Filby
Caister-on-Sea

Fens
A1101
Wisbech
A10
5
A47
○ Swaffham
NORWICH
A47
GREAT YARMOUTH

5 6 7 8 9 0 1 2 3 4 5 6 7 8 9 0

HY

ND

Place of Interest
Town name

0   10   20 miles
0   10   20   30 kilometres

Westray
Westray
Sanday
Rousay
Eday
Stronsay
Birsay
Mainland
Dounby
Harray
Shapinsay
Finstown
Stromness
Kirkwall
Hoy
South Ronaldsay

Orkney Islands

HP

HU

0   10   20 miles
0   10   20   30 kilometres

Unst
Yell
Fetlar
Whalsay
Mainland
Lerwick
Scalloway
Bressay
Mousa Island
Sumburgh

Shetland Islands

Jersey

0   1   2   3 miles
0   1   2   3   4 kilometres

La Greve de Lecq
St John
L'Etacq
Trinity
St Ouen
St Peter
St Lawrence
Gorey
St Brelade
St Aubin
St Helier
Grouville
St Clement

Vale
St Sampson

St Peter Port
St Andrew
Rocquaine Bay
St Martin
Forest

Alderney
Herm
Sark
Guernsey
Jersey

Guernsey

0   1   2   3 miles
0   1   2   3   4 kilometres

Index

Index

Index

Index

Index

Index

The Automobile Association would like to thank the following agencies for the assistance in the preparation of this book.
Sampson Lloyd/St Paul's Cathedral 3t

The remaining images for this book are held in the Association's own library (AA WORLD TRAVEL LIBRARY) with contributions from the following:

Martyn Adelman 197t; Pat Aithie 9; Adrian Baker 115; Peter Baker 266; Vic Bates 291, 293; Jeff Beazley 54t, 182; Andrew Besley 36t; M Birkitt 14, 30b, 180t, 186t, 197b; E A Bowness 54b; Michael Busselle 120, 224; Chris Coe 140; Ian Dawson 371, 382b; Steve Day 20, 88, 96, 100, 136b, 166, 191, 244b, 254, 278, 239b, 383b; Michael Diggin 382t, 397; Robert Elliott 294b; Derek Forss 16, 136t, 180b, 220; Stephen Gibson 11; Van Graves 132, 239t; Mike Hayward 198; A J Hopkins 45, 61, 210, 214, 238; Caroline Jones 22, 116, 119, 260; Max Jourdan 1, 3, 5, 144, 161; Cameron Lees 186b, 236; Simon McBride 383t; Tom Mackie 13, 46, 170, 215; S & O Mathews 250; Andrew Midgely 4; John Miller 84, 223, 230b; Roger Moss 36b, 202; Rich Newton 209, 244t; Michael Short 113; Tony Souter 2, 171, 235; Richard Surman 36c; Tom D Timms 347t; Rupert Tenison 8; Peter Trenchard 287, 288; Andy Tryner 30t; Wyn Voysey 74, 165, 273, 286, 347b; Jonathon Welsh 249; Stephen Whitehorne 294t; Linda Whitwam 80, 285; Harry Williams 219, 230t; Peter Wilson 263, 280; Jon Wyand 73

Please send this form to:
Lifestyle Guides,
The Automobile Association
15th Floor
Fanum House
Basingstoke RG21 4EA

or fax: 01256 491647
or e-mail: lifestyleguides@theAA.com

Readers' Report form

Please use this form to recommend any visitor attraction you have been to, whether it is in the guide or not currently listed. Feedback from readers helps us to keep our guide accurate and up to date. Please note, however, that if you have a complaint to make during a visit, we strongly recommend that you discuss the matter with the establishment management there and then so that they have a chance to put things right before your visit is spoilt. The AA does not undertake to arbitrate between you and the attraction's management, or to obtain compensation or engage in correspondence.

Date:

Your name (block capitals)

Your address (block capitals)

....

....

....

e-mail address: ....

(Please *only* give us your e-mail address if you wish to hear from us about other products and services from the AA and partners by e-mail)

Comments (please include the name & address of the attraction)

....

....

....

....

....

....

....

....

(please attach a separate sheet if necessary)

PTO

Readers' Report Form

Have you bought this guide before?   YES   NO

Have you bought any other Days Out guides recently? If yes, which ones?

....

....

Why did you buy this guide? (circle all that apply)

family holiday   short break   school holidays   special occasion

other..

How often do you have a Day Out? (circle one choice)

more than once a month   once a month   once in 2-3 months

once in six months   once a year   less than once a year

Please answer these questions to help us make improvements to the guide:

Which of these factors are most important when choosing a Day Out?

Price   Location   Previous experience   Recommendation   Type of attraction

Other (please state):..

Do you read the editorial features in the guide?   YES   NO

Do you use the location atlas?   YES   NO

Which elements of the guide do you find the most useful when choosing somewhere to visit?

              Description   Photo   Advertisement

Can you suggest any improvements to the guide?

....

....

....

....

....

The information we hold about you will be used to provide the products and services requested and for identification, account administration, analysis, and fraud/loss prevention purposes. More details about how that information is used is in our privacy statement, which you'll find under the heading "Personal Information" in our terms and conditions and on our web-site: **www.theAA.com**. Copies are available from us by post, by contacting the Data Protection Manager at AA, Southwood East, Apollo Rise, Farnborough, Hampshire, GU14 0JW

We may want to contact you about other products and services provided by us, or our partners (by mail, or e-mail) but please tick the box if you DO NOT wish to hear from us about such products and services by mail or e-mail.

☐

2 for 1

Terms: This voucher is valid at any venue specified as accepting vouchers within the AA 'The Days Out Guide 2005'. This voucher admits one adult or child free when presented at the time of purchase of one fully priced adult ticket. Valid until 31 Oct 2005. Subject to availability at the venue when presented. Photocopies will not be accepted.

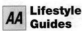 **Lifestyle Guides**

---

2 for 1

Terms: This voucher is valid at any venue specified as accepting vouchers within the AA 'The Days Out Guide 2005'. This voucher admits one adult or child free when presented at the time of purchase of one fully priced adult ticket. Valid until 31 Oct 2005. Subject to availability at the venue when presented. Photocopies will not be accepted.

AA Lifestyle Guides

---

2 for 1

Terms: This voucher is valid at any venue specified as accepting vouchers within the AA 'The Days Out Guide 2005'. This voucher admits one adult or child free when presented at the time of purchase of one fully priced adult ticket. Valid until 31 Oct 2005. Subject to availability at the venue when presented. Photocopies will not be accepted.

AA Lifestyle Guides

---

2 for 1

Terms: This voucher is valid at any venue specified as accepting vouchers within the AA 'The Days Out Guide 2005'. This voucher admits one adult or child free when presented at the time of purchase of one fully priced adult ticket. Valid until 31 Oct 2005. Subject to availability at the venue when presented. Photocopies will not be accepted.

AA Lifestyle Guides

---

2 for 1

Terms: This voucher is valid at any venue specified as accepting vouchers within the AA 'The Days Out Guide 2005'. This voucher admits one adult or child free when presented at the time of purchase of one fully priced adult ticket. Valid until 31 Oct 2005. Subject to availability at the venue when presented. Photocopies will not be accepted.

AA Lifestyle Guides

---

2 for 1

Terms: This voucher is valid at any venue specified as accepting vouchers within the AA 'The Days Out Guide 2005'. This voucher admits one adult or child free when presented at the time of purchase of one fully priced adult ticket. Valid until 31 Oct 2005. Subject to availability at the venue when presented. Photocopies will not be accepted.

AA Lifestyle Guides

---

2 for 1

Terms: This voucher is valid at any venue specified as accepting vouchers within the AA 'The Days Out Guide 2005'. This voucher admits one adult or child free when presented at the time of purchase of one fully priced adult ticket. Valid until 31 Oct 2005. Subject to availability at the venue when presented. Photocopies will not be accepted.

AA Lifestyle Guides

---

2 for 1

Terms: This voucher is valid at any venue specified as accepting vouchers within the AA 'The Days Out Guide 2005'. This voucher admits one adult or child free when presented at the time of purchase of one fully priced adult ticket. Valid until 31 Oct 2005. Subject to availability at the venue when presented. Photocopies will not be accepted.

AA Lifestyle Guides

---

2 for 1

Terms: This voucher is valid at any venue specified as accepting vouchers within the AA 'The Days Out Guide 2005'. This voucher admits one adult or child free when presented at the time of purchase of one fully priced adult ticket. Valid until 31 Oct 2005. Subject to availability at the venue when presented. Photocopies will not be accepted.

AA Lifestyle Guides

---

2 for 1

Terms: This voucher is valid at any venue specified as accepting vouchers within the AA 'The Days Out Guide 2005'. This voucher admits one adult or child free when presented at the time of purchase of one fully priced adult ticket. Valid until 31 Oct 2005. Subject to availability at the venue when presented. Photocopies will not be accepted.

AA Lifestyle Guides

AA Lifestyle Guides

Conditions: Only one voucher per person or party accepted. No change given. This voucher is valid during the published opening times for the establishments concerned, and will not be valid after 31 Oct 2005. This voucher cannot be used in conjunction with any other discount voucher or special offer. Redeemable cash value .01p. No cash alternative available.

AA Lifestyle Guides

Conditions: Only one voucher per person or party accepted. No change given. This voucher is valid during the published opening times for the establishments concerned, and will not be valid after 31 Oct 2005. This voucher cannot be used in conjunction with any other discount voucher or special offer. Redeemable cash value .01p. No cash alternative available.

AA Lifestyle Guides

Conditions: Only one voucher per person or party accepted. No change given. This voucher is valid during the published opening times for the establishments concerned, and will not be valid after 31 Oct 2005. This voucher cannot be used in conjunction with any other discount voucher or special offer. Redeemable cash value .01p. No cash alternative available.

AA Lifestyle Guides

Conditions: Only one voucher per person or party accepted. No change given. This voucher is valid during the published opening times for the establishments concerned, and will not be valid after 31 Oct 2005. This voucher cannot be used in conjunction with any other discount voucher or special offer. Redeemable cash value .01p. No cash alternative available.

AA Lifestyle Guides

Conditions: Only one voucher per person or party accepted. No change given. This voucher is valid during the published opening times for the establishments concerned, and will not be valid after 31 Oct 2005. This voucher cannot be used in conjunction with any other discount voucher or special offer. Redeemable cash value .01p. No cash alternative available.

AA Lifestyle Guides

Conditions: Only one voucher per person or party accepted. No change given. This voucher is valid during the published opening times for the establishments concerned, and will not be valid after 31 Oct 2005. This voucher cannot be used in conjunction with any other discount voucher or special offer. Redeemable cash value .01p. No cash alternative available.

AA Lifestyle Guides

Conditions: Only one voucher per person or party accepted. No change given. This voucher is valid during the published opening times for the establishments concerned, and will not be valid after 31 Oct 2005. This voucher cannot be used in conjunction with any other discount voucher or special offer. Redeemable cash value .01p. No cash alternative available.

AA Lifestyle Guides

Conditions: Only one voucher per person or party accepted. No change given. This voucher is valid during the published opening times for the establishments concerned, and will not be valid after 31 Oct 2005. This voucher cannot be used in conjunction with any other discount voucher or special offer. Redeemable cash value .01p. No cash alternative available.

AA Lifestyle Guides

Conditions: Only one voucher per person or party accepted. No change given. This voucher is valid during the published opening times for the establishments concerned, and will not be valid after 31 Oct 2005. This voucher cannot be used in conjunction with any other discount voucher or special offer. Redeemable cash value .01p. No cash alternative available.

AA Lifestyle Guides

Conditions: Only one voucher per person or party accepted. No change given. This voucher is valid during the published opening times for the establishments concerned, and will not be valid after 31 Oct 2005. This voucher cannot be used in conjunction with any other discount voucher or special offer. Redeemable cash value .01p. No cash alternative available.